Christian-Muslim Relations
A Bibliographical History

History of Christian-Muslim Relations

Editorial Board

David Thomas, University of Birmingham
Sandra Toenies Keating, Providence College
Tarif Khalidi, American University of Beirut
Suleiman Mourad, Smith College
Gabriel Said Reynolds, University of Notre Dame
Mark Swanson, Lutheran School of Theology at Chicago

Volume 22

Christians and Muslims have been involved in exchanges over matters of faith and morality since the founding of Islam. Attitudes between the faiths today are deeply coloured by the legacy of past encounters, and often preserve centuries-old negative views.

The History of Christian-Muslim Relations, Texts and Studies presents the surviving record of past encounters in authoritative, fully introduced text editions and annotated translations, and also monograph and collected studies. It illustrates the development in mutual perceptions as these are contained in surviving Christian and Muslim writings, and makes available the arguments and rhetorical strategies that, for good or for ill, have left their mark on attitudes today. The series casts light on a history marked by intellectual creativity and occasional breakthroughs in communication, although, on the whole beset by misunderstanding and misrepresentation. By making this history better known, the series seeks to contribute to improved recognition between Christians and Muslims in the future.

The titles published in this series are listed at *brill.com/hcmr*

Christian-Muslim Relations
A Bibliographical History

Volume 6. Western Europe (1500-1600)

Edited by
David Thomas and John Chesworth

with John Azumah, Stanisław Grodź,
Andrew Newman, Douglas Pratt

BRILL

LEIDEN • BOSTON
2014

Arts & Humanities Research Council

Cover illustration: This is the title page of an edition of Riccoldo da Monte di Croce's (d. 1320) *Improbatio alcorani* (also known as *Contra legem Saracenorum*), published in Seville on 20 March, 1500 (Houghton Library, Harvard University, Typ Inc 9543.5). The illustration shows Spanish Muslims listening under duress to a sermon from a Christian preacher, part of the requirements forced on them in the aftermath of the fall of Granada in 1492 (reproduced with permission from Houghton Library, Harvard University).

Library of Congress Cataloging-in-Publication Data

Christian Muslim relations : a bibliographical history / edited by David Thomas and John Chesworth; with John Azumah ... [et al.].
  p. cm. — (The history of Christian-Muslim relations, ISSN 1570-7350 ; v. 22)
  Includes index.
  ISBN 978-90-04-25073-4 (hardback : alk. paper) 1. Christianity and other religions—Islam. 2. Islam—Relations—Christianity. 3. Christianity and other religions—Islam—Bibliography. 4. Islam—Relations—Christianity—Bibliography. I. Thomas, David. II. Chesworth, John III. Azumah, John. IV. Title. V. Series.
  BP172.C4196 2009
  016.2612'7—dc22

2009029184

This publication has been typeset in the multilingual "Brill" typeface. With over 5,100 characters covering Latin, IPA, Greek, and Cyrillic, this typeface is especially suitable for use in the humanities. For more information, please see www.brill.com/brill-typeface.

ISSN 1570-7350
ISBN 978-90-04-25073-4 (hardback)
ISBN 978-90-04-28111-0 (e-book)

Copyright 2014 by Koninklijke Brill NV, Leiden, The Netherlands.
Koninklijke Brill NV incorporates the imprints Brill, Brill Nijhoff, Global Oriental and Hotei Publishing.

All rights reserved. No part of this publication may be reproduced, translated, stored in a retrieval system, or transmitted in any form or by any means, electronic, mechanical, photocopying, recording or otherwise, without prior written permission from the publisher.

Authorization to photocopy items for internal or personal use is granted by Koninklijke Brill NV provided that the appropriate fees are paid directly to The Copyright Clearance Center, 222 Rosewood Drive, Suite 910, Danvers, MA 01923, USA.
Fees are subject to change.

This book is printed on acid-free paper.

CONTENTS

Foreword	vii
Abbreviations	xi
Martha Frederiks, *Introduction: Christians, Muslims and empires in the 16th century*	1
Nabil Matar, *The Qur'an in English writings, 1543-1697*	11
Thomas E. Burman, *European Qur'an translations, 1500-1700*	25
Works on Christian-Muslim relations 1500-1600	39
Spain	41
Portugal	295
Italy and Malta	395
France and Northern Europe	603
Index of Names	867
Index of Titles	880

FOREWORD

David Thomas

Christian-Muslim relations. A bibliographical History 6 (*CMR* 6) continues the history of relations between Christians and Muslims as recorded in original sources in the period 1500-1600, following the same general approach as the earlier volumes in the series. *CMR* 6 focuses on works from the 16th century in the countries of Western Europe, and shows that, while many of the preoccupations that dominated the Middle Ages were still prominent, particularly issues of political and religious relations between Christianity and Islam, with further crusades a constant aspiration, and denunciations of Muḥammad and the Qur'an a staple of religious works, new concerns were beginning to emerge. Not least among these was the problem of what to do with the Muslims in Iberia following the overthrow of the emirate of Granada in 1492, and the issue of how to deal with the power of the Ottomans, who may have posed looming threats to eastern Europe, but were nevertheless potential allies in power balances within Europe and lucrative trade partners. Nascent imperial interests in the Indian Ocean were also raising problems of how to deal with Muslim subjects in new colonies and with neighbouring Muslim states, while travellers' tales were rousing curiosity about the lands of the East and the manners and customs of its people, not least on the Elizabethan stage, where plays about tyrants filled playhouses and eastern customs stirred the beginnings of Orientalist imaginings.

The intention of *CMR* is to include full accounts of all the known works written by Christians and Muslims about one another and against one another. These are intended to provide a basis for further investigation, paving the way for fuller knowledge of Christian-Muslim relations and deeper understanding of its importance in public and private life. This is more than a single person or group could accomplish and here, as in earlier volumes, the editors have drawn upon the expertise of the scholarly community and been assisted by leading authorities in the field, both young researchers with new studies of authors and works, and seasoned experts with knowledge of wide fields. The result is a succession of entries that reflect the latest scholarship, and in many instances take it forward and extend it beyond what was previously known.

After an introductory essay that surveys the political and religious situation in western Europe in the 16th century, this volume, like its predecessors, begins with some general essays. Following these come the entries that make up the bulk of the volume. The basic criterion has been to choose works written substantially about or against the other faith, or containing significant information or judgements that cast light on attitudes of one faith towards the other. Thus, by their very nature, apologetic and polemical works are included, while correspondence and works of literature, travel and history also frequently qualify. All the works that have been included contribute in a significant way towards building the picture of the one as seen by the other and of attitudes between them.

This principle criterion is easily applicable in many cases, but it proves difficult in a significant minority of instances. An inclusive approach has therefore been adopted, especially with respect to works that may contain only small though insightful details or only appear to touch obliquely on relations, and also to works that are no longer extant and whose contents can only be inferred from a title or a reference by a later author. Another criterion that should be explained is that inclusion of works within this volume was decided according to the date of their author's death, not according to the date when the works themselves appeared. A continuation of the practice in earlier volumes, the reason for this is that many works from this period give no clear indication of a date, though the adoption of this approach has led to evident anomalies at either end, where authors are mainly or almost entirely active in one century but have died at the beginning of the next. If this seems arbitrary, it is balanced by the consideration that any other criterion would also be likely to involve decisions that might just as easily be questioned.

Each entry is divided into two main parts. The first is concerned with the author, and it contains basic biographical details, an account of his (all authors appearing in this volume are male, although it is worth noting that in this period the first female author in the whole history makes her appearance, Queen Elizabeth I of England, who died in 1603 and is therefore included in a 17th century volume) main intellectual activities and writings, the major primary sources of information about him, and the latest scholarly works about him. Without aiming to be exhaustive, this section contains sufficient information for readers to pursue further details about the author and his general activities.

The second part of the entry is concerned with the works of the author that are specifically devoted to the other faith. Here completeness is the aim. A work is named and dated (where possible), and then in two important sections its contents are described and its significance in the history of Christian-Muslim relations is appraised. There follow sections listing the manuscript witnesses of the work where relevant (although if a recent edition or study provides an authoritative list of these, this work is cited instead of a complete list being given); editions and translations; and lastly studies. It is intended that these will be completely up to date at the time of going to press.

With this coverage, *CMR* 6 should provide sufficient information to enable a work to be identified, its importance appreciated, and editions and studies located. Each work is also placed as far as is possible together with other works from the same time written in the same area, though this grouping should be regarded more as a matter of convenience than anything else. Proximity between works in the bibliography is definitely not an indication of any necessary direct relationship between them, let alone influence (though this may sometimes be discernible). In this period, it is as likely that an author would be influenced by a work written hundreds of miles away or hundreds of years before as by another from his immediate locality or time.

The composition of *CMR* 6 has involved more than 100 contributors, who have readily and often enthusiastically accepted the invitations from the editors. Under the direction of David Thomas, the work for this volume was led by Clinton Bennett (British Isles and Scandinavia), Luis Bernabé Pons (Iberia), John Chesworth (Research Fellow), John-Paul Ghobrial (France), Stanisław Grodz (Europe), Emma Loghin (project secretary) and Davide Tacchini (Italy). These are members of a much larger team (or team of teams, since there are four teams altogether) that comprises about 25 specialists, covering all parts of the world (the results of the other members' work for the 16th century will be published in *CMR* 7). In addition, Carol Rowe copy edited the entire volume, Alex Mallett provided links with the staff editors at Brill, and Kate Landenberger translated entries from a range of languages. The *CMR* team are deeply indebted to everyone who has contributed in one way or another.

The project was funded by a grant made by the Arts and Humanities Research Council of Great Britain, and this is acknowledged with gratitude.

Strenuous efforts have been made to ensure that information is both accurate and complete, though it would be not only presumptuous but also entirely unrealistic to claim that these efforts have succeeded in every instance. Details (hopefully only minor) must have been overlooked, new works will have come to light, new editions, translations and studies will have appeared, and new datings and interpretations put forward. Corrections, additions and updates are therefore warmly invited. They will be incorporated into the online version of *CMR*, and into further editions. Please send details of these to David Thomas at d.r.thomas.1@bham.ac.uk.

ABBREVIATIONS

BL
: British Library

BNE
: Biblioteca Nacional de España

BNF
: Bibliothèque Nationale de France

BSOAS
: Bulletin of the School of Oriental and African Studies

DBI
: Dizionario biografico degli italiani, Rome, 1960-

DNB
: Dictionary of national biography, ed. L. Stephen and S. Lee, London, 1885-1901

EI2
: Encyclopaedia of Islam, 2nd edition

EI3
: Encyclopaedia of Islam Three

EIr
: Encyclopaedia Iranica, http://www.iranicaonline.org

ICMR
: Islam and Christian-Muslim Relations

JAOS
: Journal of the American Oriental Society

MW
: Muslim World

ODNB
: Oxford dictionary of national biography, from the earliest times to the year 2000, ed. H.C.G. Matthew and B. Harrison, Oxford, 2004

Q
: Qur'an

Steinschneider, *Polemische und apologetische Literatur*
: M. Steinschneider, *Polemische und apologetische Literatur in arabischer Sprache zwischen Muslimen, Christen und Juden*, Leipzig, 1877

Vat
: Biblioteca Apostolica Vaticana

Introduction: Christians, Muslims and empires in the 16th century

Martha Frederiks

Introduction

In the 16th century, the Ottoman Empire was at the peak of its power. It had usurped vast territories in central and eastern Europe, conquered large parts of the Middle East and North Africa and consolidated its power around the Black Sea, thus keeping the Persian Safavid dynasty at bay. At sea, due to their rapidly-increasing naval versatility, the Ottomans successfully contested Venice for its strongholds in the Aegean Sea during the Ottoman-Venetian wars and extended their control over the western Mediterranean, posing a threat to countries as far west as Spain and Morocco. The battle of Lepanto (1571) was the first occasion in the 16th century that the armies of the Holy League, consisting of the Papacy, Spain and Italian states such as Venice, Tuscany and Genoa, were able to reverse the stream of Ottoman successes and achieve victory over the 'Turks'.

Meanwhile, Roman Christendom was under siege, with Protestantism claiming large parts of northern and western Europe and Ottoman Muslim forces conquering central and eastern Europe. Only in southern Europe had Iberian Catholicism successfully secured its power. It had expelled the remaining ruler of the Naṣrid dynasty from Granada and purged Spain of its Muslim population and Islamic heritage, while simultaneously surveying the oceans for a New World that could safeguard the future of Christianity.

Despite these hostilities and military confrontations, the people of the Mediterranean – Christians and Muslims alike – shared deep cultural traditions. Places such as Sicily, Spain and Cyprus were as much contact-zones as battlefields. Moreover, merchants, travellers, scholars and diplomats had woven webs of trade and rapport across the borders of empires. It was in this world of fear, fascination and exploration of 'the other' that the study of the East began to proliferate and chairs in Arabic were being established in Europe.

This essay is intended as a short sketch of the historical background against which Christians in western Europe in the 16th century represented and reacted towards Muslims. Their views are mostly found in historical and theological works, but also in a surprising variety of other written forms, including letters, sermons, travelogues, plays and so on. The overview starts with a discussion of the aftermath of the Spanish *Reconquista*. This is followed by a sketch of political and religious changes in Europe, and the essay closes with a brief discussion of the rise of Oriental studies in early modern Europe.

Iberian (re)conquista

In the Iberian Peninsula, the 16th century was ushered in by the fall of Granada in 1492 and the surrender of Sultan Muḥammad XII of the Naṣrid dynasty (1248-1492) to *Los Reyos Catolicos*, Ferdinand II of Aragón and Isabella of Castile.[1] While the kingdom of Portugal had completed the *Reconquista* by the middle of the 13th century, it took another two and a half centuries before the sovereignties that later emerged as the Kingdom of Spain had 'reconquered' the remaining parts of the Peninsula.[2]

---

[1] The epitaph on their tomb summarises their quest: 'Destroyers of the Mohammedan sect and the annihilators of the heretical heresy (i.e. of the Jews)'; C. Lowney, *A vanished world. Muslims, Christians and Jews in medieval Spain*, Oxford, 2005, p. 254.

[2] For the story of the *Reconquista*, the Moriscos and Christian-Muslim relations on the Iberian Peninsula in the 15th and 16th centuries, see e.g. A.G. Chejne, *Islam and the West. The Moriscos. A cultural and social history*, Albany NY, 1993; A. Meyuhas Ginio (ed.), *Jews, Muslims and Christians in the Mediterranean world after 1492*, Abingdon, 1992; M. Halavais, *Like wheat to the miller. Community, convivencia, and the construction of Morisco identity in sixteenth-century Aragon*, New York, 2005; R. Fletcher, *Moorish Spain*, Berkeley CA, 2006², pp. 157-71; J.F. O'Callaghan, *Reconquest and crusade in medieval Spain*, Philadelphia PA, 2003; Lowney, *A vanished world*, pp. 227-70; M. Nash, *Sevilla, Cordoba and Granada. A cultural history*, Oxford, 2005; F. Soyer, *The persecution of the Jews and Muslims in Portugal. King Manuel I and the end of religious tolerance (1496-7)*, Leiden, 2007; M. Carr, *Blood and faith. The purging of Muslim Spain*, New York, 2009; R. Ingram (ed.), *The Conversos and Moriscos in late medieval Spain and beyond*, vol. 1. *Departures and change*, Leiden, 2009, pp. 211-311; R. Ingram (ed.), *The Conversos and Moriscos in late medieval Spain and beyond*, vol. 2, *The Morisco issue*, Leiden, 2012; R. Hitchcock, *Muslim Spain reconsidered. From 711-1502*, Edinburgh, 2014, pp. 183-94; G. Darby, *Spain in the seventeenth century*, Hoboken, 2014, pp. 1-36.

Ferdinand of Aragón and Isabella of Castile began a process of centralising power. The foundation of the monarchy of Spain was laid with the accession of their grandchild Charles I to the joint throne of Aragón, Léon and Castile in 1516, thus formally establishing the Kingdom of Spain. Charles I is best known as Charles V of Habsburg; he became Holy Roman Emperor in 1519.

As the *Reconquista* progressed, relations between the different religious communities became more strained and any harmonious coexistence gradually eroded. The growing intolerance towards the Jewish community from the 14th century onwards reached its lowest ebb with the expulsion of the Jews from the Iberian Peninsula between 1492 and 1497.[3] Initially, the rights of the Muslim community seemed better secured. The *Capitulations*, signed on 24 November 1491, respected religious freedom. According to the 17th-century historian Aḥmad al-Maqqarī,[4] there were 67 clauses in the *Capitulations* ensuring the rights of the Granada Muslim community, including the safeguarding of mosques, the use of Islamic law for Muslims, permission to meet for the *ṣalāt* and proclaim the *adhān*, and a prohibition against the imposition of distinctive clothing.[5]

Thus, at the outset, the fall of Granada did not seem significantly to alter the daily lives of the resident Muslim community. The German printer Hieronymus Münzer, who visited Granada in October 1494, a few years after its surrender, describes the large number of Muslims gathering at the mosque for Friday prayers, the splendour of the gardens and houses of the Muslim nobility, and the numerous mosques in the Albaicin quarter.[6] In 1501, nearly a decade after the surrender, the Flemish diplomat Antoine Lalaign, Count of Hoogstraten, made similar observations, albeit with less appreciation for Muslim presence and culture.[7]

Hernando de Talavera who was appointed as the first archbishop of Granada in 1493, is generally said to have maintained respectful relations with the Muslim community; he promoted an irenic approach with regard to the conversion of Muslims, advocating persuasion rather than force. To that end, he encouraged priests to learn Arabic, and ordered Pedro de Alcalá to compose a Castilian-Arabic grammar (published in 1515).[8]

---

[3] N. Roth, 'The Jews of Spain and the expulsion of 1492', *The Historian* 55 (1992) 17-30; N. Roth, *Jews, Visigoths and Muslims in medieval Spain. Cooperation and conflict*, Leiden, 1994, p. 135; F. Soyer, *The persecution of the Jews and Muslims in Portugal*, Leiden, 2007.

[4] For al-Maqqarī, see e.g. J.W. Meri, *Medieval Islamic civilization. An encyclopedia*, New York, 2006, p. 478.

[5] Cited in Hitchcock, *Muslim Spain reconsidered*, p. 187.

[6] A. Classen, 'Die iberische Halbinsel aus der Sicht eines humanistischen Nürnberger Gelehrten. Hieronymus Münzer, Itinerarium Hispanicum (1494-1495)', *Mitteilungen des Instituts für Österreichische Geschichtsforschung* 111 (2003) 317-40; see also Carr, *Blood and faith*, pp. 54-55.

[7] Carr, *Blood and faith*, p. 70.

[8] Hitchcock, *Muslim Spain reconsidered*, p. 189; Carr, *Blood and faith*, pp. 53-55.

From 1499 onwards, however, at the instigation of Cardinal Francisco Jiménez de Cisneros, Archbishop of Toledo, the situation in Granada began to deteriorate. De Cisneros, inspired by the example of El-Cid, advocated a hard-line approach towards the Granada Muslim community. In 1501, he ordered the burning of Islamic books (including Qur'ans), the transformation of mosques into churches, and the forced baptism of Muslims.[9] Protests against this violation of the *Capitulations*, such as the revolt of the Alpujarras (1499-1502), were brutally suppressed.[10] Due to the increasing tensions, Muslims began to emigrate, seeking refuge in North Africa, although stringent restrictions and taxations on those leaving prohibited mass emigration.[11] Most succumbed to the pressure and submitted to baptism; they became known by the pejorative term 'Moriscos'. The majority, it seems, practised some form of *taqiyya* (dissimulation) and remained Muslim under the guise of Christian observances.[12] A body of *Aljamiado* (Spanish in Arabic letters) literature testifies to the way in which the Moriscos persisted in their religion and transmitted their heritage.[13]

In 1525, harmonious relations began to wane further north in Aragón; after a bout of extreme violence against Muslims, Charles I of Spain (r. 1516-56), better known as Charles V, Holy Roman Emperor (r. 1519-56), banned all expressions of Morisco culture and compelled all Muslims in Aragón to convert or leave. Only after extensive negotiation and the payment of a vast amount of redemption money, was the edict suspended for 40 years. Later Morisco authors, such as the writer known as *El Mancebo de Arévalo* ('the young man from Arévalo') narrated the traumatic impact of this ruthless subjugation on the Muslim community.[14] His writings also witness to the considerable amount of Muslim literature retained by those who had converted, as well as what must have been

---

[9] Hitchcock, *Muslim Spain reconsidered*, pp. 187-92; Carr, *Blood and faith*, p. 71.

[10] Carr, *Blood and faith*, pp. 59-61. The violation of the *Capitulations* was also said to have provoked the Mamluks to retaliate against Coptic Christians and pilgrims in Egypt. Peter Martyr of Anghieri was dispatched as a special envoy to Egypt to mediate in the situation; Carr, *Blood and faith*, p. 67.

[11] Carr, *Blood and faith*, p. 71.

[12] For the 1504 *fatwā* by Abū l-'Abbās Aḥmad al-Maghrawī, *muftī* of Oran, on *taqiyya*, see D. Stewart, 'The identity of "The *Muftī* of Oran", Abū l-'Abbās Aḥmad b. Abī Jum'ah al-Maghrawī al-Wahrānī (d. 917/1511)', *Al-Qanṭara* 37 (2006) 265-301.

[13] Carr, *Blood and faith*, pp. 104-17; G. Wiegers, *Islamic literature in Spanish and Aljamiado. Yça of Segovia (fl. 1450), his antecedents and successors*, Leiden, 1994, pp. 209-14; A.R. Nykl, *A compendium of Aljamiado literature*, New York, 1929. The *Aljamiado* texts include traditional Islamic materials, such as extracts from the Qur'an, commentaries on the Qur'an, the Hadith, jurisprudence, etc., but there are also texts that consist of legends and myths from early Islamic history, travel accounts and anti-Christian polemics.

[14] L.P. Harvey, 'El Mancebo de Arévalo and his treatises on Islamic faith and practice', *Journal of Islamic Studies* 10 (1999) 249-76.

deliberate efforts to preserve by memory the beliefs and practices of earlier times.

Christian clergy in Spain were divided over the best way to approach the Moriscos, who were living alongside them and could not be ignored. Many, like de Cisneros, advocated compelling them to conform, through enforced attendance at church services. But there were others who, like de Talavera, realised that such strategies could never win hearts or minds, and favoured argument and persuasion in order to convince Muslims of the superior claims of Christianity. There are hints in the writings of some of those who held this view that they regarded Muslims as lost rather than recalcitrant, and that they thought the patient preaching of the Christian Gospel in the Muslims' own language, using terms that they would recognise (such as *miḥrāb* for altar, *ṣalāt* for the mass), would secure true conversions. Such attitudes contrast with the very different approach associated with the Inquisition and mass baptisms.

An interlude of relative calm for the Moriscos of Iberia occurred in the 1530s and 1540s, when Charles V was engaged in pressing issues elsewhere, fighting the Ottomans for supremacy in central Europe and the Mediterranean (in 1535 he led a large force against Tunis, which Hairaddin Barbarossa had taken the previous year), as well as combatting emergent Protestantism. He was also forced to react against the alliance between France and the Ottoman Empire that had been set up in 1536, an attempt by King Francis I (r. 1515-47) to outflank Charles, whose possessions in Spain, Italy and the Low Countries encircled France. Charles himself had earlier been in negotiations with to the Safavids in Persia, hoping to stir them against the Ottomans and so relieve the pressure the latter were constantly exerting on his possessions in eastern Europe.

Violence in Iberia flared up again with the accession of Philip II to the Spanish throne in 1556. Philip was resolved to uphold Catholic orthodoxy, yet faced growing support for Protestantism in his domains, as well as a Morisco community in his native Spain that seemed to persist in their adherence to Islam. Determined to exterminate all forms of heresy, Philip intensified religious instruction as well as the Inquisition, targeting Lutherans, Huguenots and Moriscos alike. Yet, to quote Matthew Carr: 'Even though Philip II presented himself as "the hammer of heretics", and the militant defender of Catholic religious orthodoxy, many leading European Christians continued to regard Spain as a suspect country, that had been fatally corrupted by the long centuries of Islamic domination.'[15]

---

[15] Carr, *Blood and faith*, p. 187. This included prominent figures such as Thomas More, Desiderius Erasmus, William of Orange and Martin Luther.

Representations of Spain as defiled and degraded because of its Islamic past became a popular trope in Protestant anti-Spanish propaganda.

Like his father, Philip II was engaged in a number of major confrontations with the Ottoman Empire. But, where Charles V had focussed on clashes in central Europe and the eastern Mediterranean, Philip II combatted Ottoman expansion in the western Mediterranean, fearing an Ottoman attack on Spain. The Ottoman navy had already expelled the Knights of Malta from Tripoli in 1551, seized the Spanish enclave at Bejaïa in Morocco in 1555, and raided the Balearic Islands in 1558. A Spanish-Moroccan counter-attack on Mostaganem (Algeria) in that same year ended in disaster, resulting in the mass capture of some 12,000 soldiers by the Ottomans.[16] This misfortune was followed by an even greater defeat in May 1560 during the battle of Djerba, where a Spanish-Italian coalition lost more than 60 ships and 20,000 men.[17] A small but very practical response to the captivity of vast numbers of European fighting men in North Africa was that officials, often Franciscan friars, were appointed to negotiate ransoms with the Ottoman captors and secure the release of those lucky enough to find friends ready to pay.

In addition to Ottoman expansionism, Barbary corsairs raided Spanish ships and coastal towns in search of booty and slaves.[18] By the middle of the 16th century, the corsair state of Algiers had become renowned as a den of pirates and slave-raiders who forced their captives to convert to Islam or face a life of slavery. Among the captives was Miguel de Cervantes Saavedra, author of *Don Quixote*, who was abducted from a ship in 1575 and spent five years in Algiers before he was ransomed. Cervantes later wrote a number of plays about his experiences in Algiers, such as *El trato de Argel* (1582) and *Los baños de Argel* (1615).[19]

Ottoman successes in the western Mediterranean and the audacious Barbary raids on the coast gave rise to allegations that the Morisco community was collaborating with Spain's enemies. On 7 November 1566,

---

[16] The Algerian corsair state was headed by the brothers Aruj and Khizr, more commonly known by their nick-name Barbarossa, who offered Algiers to the Ottoman sultan in 1517.

[17] Carr, *Blood and faith*, pp. 120-121.

[18] B. Fuchs and A.J. Ilika, 'Introduction', in M. de Cervantes, *'The bagnios of Algiers' and 'The great sultana'. Two plays of captivity*, ed. and trans. B. Fuchs and A.J. Ilika, Philadelphia PA, 2010, pp. xii-xvi. The elder of the Barbarossa brothers, Aruj, earned the honorific Baba Oraç (Father Aruj) for his assistance in helping Moriscos escape from Spain.

[19] M.-S. Omri, 'Representing the early modern Mediterranean in contemporary North Africa', in M. Fusaro, C. Heywood and M.-S. Omri (eds), *Trade and cultural exchange in the early modern Mediterranean. Braudel's maritime legacy*, London, 2010, p. 280; De Cervantes, *'The bagnios of Algiers' and 'The great sultana'*.

Philip II, in response to these allegations, issued a royal decree, the *Pragmatico*, to implement his father's 1526 edict prohibiting all expressions of Morisco culture in Granada. The harsh enforcement of the *Pragmatico* met with strong resistance among the Granada Moriscos and resulted in a protracted bloody revolt, known as the War of Alpujarras (1568-71), which left tens of thousands dead. In the aftermath, Philip II decreed that the Morisco community should be deported from the kingdom of Granada to Castile.[20] This deportation of the Granada Moriscos was the ominous beginning of what was to come later.

The repression reached its low point during the reign of Philip III (1578-1621), who advocated a hard-line approach to deal with 'the Morisco-problem'. Spearheaded by Juan de Ribera, Archbishop of Valencia, and Francisco Gómes de Sandoval y Rojas, Duke of Lerma, a number of horrific 'solutions' to 'the problem' were proposed, among them castration, enslavement, elimination and deportation. Voices in the late 16th century defending the Morisco cause were ignored, while creative attempts at negotiating space for the Moriscos in a Christian Spain, such as the 'discovery' of the (forged) *Lead books of Sacramonte* in Granada that evinced the Arab origins of Iberian Christianity, failed.[21] In September 1609, Phillip III ordered the deportation of all Moriscos from the Iberian Peninsula, beginning with Valencia. Between 1609 and 1614 an estimated 350,000 Moriscos were violently expelled to North Africa, many of them dying on the journey or shortly after arrival.[22]

Maritime expansion

The year 1492 is mainly associated with Christopher Columbus, who in May that same year embarked on his famous voyage to America. Though the Portuguese had been exploring the coast of West Africa since the mid-15th century, in popular imagination Columbus's voyage encapsulates the spirit of the era of Spanish and Portuguese exploration. It

---

[20] L.P. Harvey, *The Moors in Spain, 1500-1614*, Chicago IL, 2005, pp. 204-38; Carr, *Blood and faith*, pp. 131-66.

[21] M. Hagerty, *Los libros plúmbeos del Sacromonte*, Granada, 2007²; A.K. Harris, *From Muslim to Christian Spain. Inventing a city's past in pre-modern Spain*, Baltimore MD, 2007; E. Drayson, *The lead books of Granada*, New York, 2013; M. García-Arenal, *The Orient in Spain. Converted Muslims, the forged lead books of Granada, and the rise of Orientalism*, Leiden, 2013.

[22] Carr, *Blood and faith*, pp. 233-78; M.E. Perry, *The handless maiden. Moriscos and the politics of religion in early Modern Spain*, Princeton NJ, 2013, pp. 133-80.

is significant that in his diary, dedicated to his patrons Ferdinand and Isabella, Columbus framed his voyage as a continuation of the *Reconquista*, aimed at exploring the possibilities of evangelising 'the princes and peoples' of Asia, as well as at accumulating enough gold and spices to finance a crusade to 'conquer the Holy Sepulchre; for thus I urge your Highness to spend all the proceeds of this my enterprise on the conquest of Jerusalem' (entry for 26 December 1492).[23] Literature on the conquest of the Americas from this period frequently compares the 'barbarous pagan American Indians' to Muslims, thus emphasising the crusading nature of the venture.[24]

A kindred spirit of *Reconquista* drove the Portuguese in the 15th and 16th centuries. Wherever they went, Portuguese explorers, at the instigation of Prince Henry the Navigator (1394-1460), inquired after Prester John, a legendary, fabulously rich Christian ruler who had long been thought a potential ally in the struggle against Islam,[25] and they were driven as much by dreams of overcoming the Mamluks and Ottomans and of recovering the Holy Places of Christianity as by ambitions to tap new sources of wealth. John Blake aptly summarises these ventures in the words 'the quest for God and gold'.[26]

---

[23] *The diario of Christopher Columbus' first voyages to America 1492-1493. Abstracted by Fray Bartolomé de las Casas*, trans. O. Dunn and J.E. Kelly, Norman OK, 1989, pp. 16-21; Lowney, *A vanished world*, p. 249; C. Delaney, *Columbus and the quest for Jerusalem*, New York, 2011.

[24] R. Irwin, *For lust of knowing. The Orientalists and their enemies*, London, 2006, p. 64.

[25] For the Prester John narrative, see: C.F. Beckingham, *The achievements of Prester John*, London, 1966; F. Alvares, *The Prester John of the Indies. A true relation of the lands of Prester John, being the narrative of the Portuguese embassy to Ethiopia in 1520*, trans. Lord Stanley of Alderley, rev. and ed. with additional material by C.F. Beckingham and G.W.B. Huntingford, Nendeln, 1975; C.F. Beckingham, *Between Islam and Christendom. Travellers, facts and legends in the Middle Ages and the Renaissance*, Aldershot, 1983; L.N. Gumilev, *Searches for an imaginary kingdom. The legend of the kingdom of Prester John*, Cambridge, 1987; C.F. Beckingham and B. Hamilton, *Prester John, the Mongols and the ten lost tribes*, Aldershot, 1996; C.M. Newitt, *A history of Portuguese overseas expansion, 1400-1668*, London, 2008, pp. 101-2; C. Baldridge, *Prisoners of Prester John. The Portuguese mission to Ethiopia in search of the mythical king, 1520-1526*, Jefferson NC, 2012; P. Jackson, 'The Letter of Prester John', in *CMR* 4, pp. 118-23.

[26] J.W. Blake, *West Africa. The quest for God and gold 1454-1578. A survey of the first century of white enterprise in West Africa*, London, 1977². According to Bernard Lewis, Vasco da Gama seems to have explained the goal of his voyage as being 'in search of Christians and spice'; B. Lewis, *The Muslim discovery of Europe*, London, 1982, p. 33. See also S. Subrahmanyam, *The Portuguese empire in Asia 1500-1700. A political and economic history*, London, 1993 (2012²), pp. 49-50.

Old and new attitudes towards Islam

In other parts of Europe outside the Iberian Peninsula, Muslims would have been a rare sight. The coasts of Italy and southern France were plagued by corsairs, but otherwise for the great majority of the inhabitants of Western Europe, Islam, Muslims and the Turks were known only through stories, histories and a few travellers' accounts, and portrayals in the theatre.

In the early 16th century, the Qur'an was already available through translations, though very few people had obtained them or read them, and direct knowledge of Islamic sources was the preserve of no more than a handful of dedicated scholars. Many accounts of Islam continued to express the attitudes of previous centuries, and the influence of John of Damascus's scathing rejection of Muḥammad as a fraud in the mid-8th century was as potent in western Europe in the 16th century as it had been in the 12th or 15th. No good was found in Islam as a religion, for the obvious and well-rehearsed reasons that it denied the central truths of Christianity and claimed to supersede it as a more complete faith. Details of early Islamic history were known, though they were usually presented as parts of polemical proofs that showed that Islam possessed none of the irenic virtues of Christianity.

Some scholars made use of Byzantine sources, often *Apodeixeis historiōn* of Laonicus Chalcocondyles, a late 15th-century account of the rise of the Ottomans written by a diplomat who travelled between the Byzantine court and the Ottoman capital, and who may have spent time in Constantinople not long after its capture by Mehmed II. This and other more contemporary sources frequently remarked on virtues that were commended in Islam, and on such elements of Ottoman rule as the fairness of their legal system and their openness to the religious minorities within their empire. Such favourable comments contrasted with the general condemnation of the Turks as cruel, and given to physical excess and sodomy.

This contradictory mix of impressions provided fuel for stories about a people who were seen as fearsome yet also intriguing, and it also provided material for the London stage. Christopher Marlowe's Tamburlaine plays, about the 14th-century warlord, are the best-known of a whole sequence in the later 16th century in which Turkish characters feature. They frequently conformed to stereotype, but nevertheless they sometimes contained depths of character that made them more than merely two-dimensional tyrants.

The beginnings of Oriental studies

The 16th century also saw the beginning of academic interests in the Orient, with chairs in Arabic language being established in Paris (1539) and Leiden (1600). The study of Arabic and Islam was mainly conducted by learned 'amateurs' and autodidacts. Motives to study Arabic were many and various and included scholarly interests in gaining a better understanding of Hebrew, accessing Arabic scientific texts, and facilitating trade, diplomacy and mission, as well more theological reasons that aimed at gaining a better understanding 'the enemy' that posed such a threat to Christian Europe.[27]

A key figure in the early days of Orientalism was the somewhat eccentric Guillaume Postel (1510-81), who travelled extensively in the Middle East, collecting manuscripts. Though he is said to have studied Arabic mainly to improve his understanding of Hebrew, he is credited with producing the first ever grammar of classical Arabic in Europe, *Grammatica classica*, published posthumously in 1613. Others, such as Franciscus Raphelengius, Joseph Justis Scaliger and Johan Heinrich Hottinger, followed in Postel's footsteps.[28]

Theodor Bibliander, often remembered as a scholar of the Reformation, but essentially a Renaissance linguist, also studied Arabic. Interested in comparative linguistics, he argued that languages such as Hebrew, Arabic, Chaldean, Aramaic, Ge'ez, Latin and Greek, originated from a single common language, and tendered the hypothesis that they might indicate a single underlying faith. Thus Bibliander, in a time of great tensions between Muslims and Christians, emphasised commonalities between Christianity and Islam.[29] Bibliander is also known for commissioning a printed edition of the Latin translation of the Qur'an (Basel, Zürich, 1543, 1550) that had been made in 12th-century Toledo by Robert of Ketton. Through this initiative, the Qur'an was made available to a wider audience.[30]

---

[27] J. Loop, *Johan Heinrich Hottinger. Arabic and Islamic studies in the seventeenth century*, Oxford, 2013, p. 5. In the early 16th century, experiments were conducted to print Arabic texts, such as prayer books, psalters, bibles (1583) and the Qur'an (1537-8). These were mainly meant for missionary purposes, though is unclear whether they were aimed at Muslims or Orthodox Christians; Irwin, *For lust of knowing*, p. 75; H. Goddard, *A history of Christian-Muslim relations*, Edinburgh, 2000, p. 117.

[28] D. Vitkus, 'Early modern Orientalism. Representations of Islam in sixteenth and seventeenth-century Europe', in D.R. Blanks and R. Frassetto (eds), *Western views of Islam in medieval and early modern Europe. Perception of other*, New York 1999, pp. 207-30.

[29] R. Armour, *Islam, Christianity and the West. A troubled history*, Maryknoll NY, 2004, p. 112; Loop, *Johan Heinrich Hottinger*, pp. 26-30

[30] Irwin, *For lust of knowing*, p. 71.

The Qur'an in English Writings, 1543-1697

Nabil Matar

'The Renaissance inherited a confused and contradictory mass of grotesque notions concerning the Founder of Islam, and so long-lived are prejudices that, even when the scholarly and the curious had rendered accessible sources of information that at least approximated to the truth, these notions persisted almost unchallenged, were indeed fortified by new prejudices against the Ottoman conquerors of the Levant' (Samuel C. Chew, *The crescent and the rose*, New York, 1937, p. 387).

The history of knowledge about Islam in England can be approached from three perspectives. The first focuses on the image of the Prophet Muḥammad, perhaps the most demonised religious figure in English and European writings in the early modern period.[1] The second focuses on the representation of the Muslim Ottomans, who grew in the 16th and 17th centuries into a formidable military force, reaching the shores of Malta and the gates of Vienna. The fact that the initial English encounter with Islam coincided with the expansion of the Ottoman *devlet* (Ottomans never used the term 'empire') was instrumental in consolidating the image of Islam as militaristic and aggressive.[2] Twice a week during the Ottoman siege of Malta in 1556, at a time when the English still felt themselves part of the 'common corps of Christendom', worshippers offered 'earnest, hearty, and fervent prayer, to Almighty God for them [the Maltese], desiring him after the examples of Moses, Josaphat, Ezechias, and other godly men, in his great mercy to defend and deliver Christians'.[3]

These two perspectives so overlapped that it is rare for a 16th-century English text about Islam not to start with misrepresentations about the

---

[1] See the extensive study of the 'mythologies' about Muḥammad by M. Dimmock, *Mythologies of the Prophet Muhammad in Early Modern English culture*, Cambridge, 2013.

[2] The scholarship on the representation of the Ottomans in English drama and religious writings is extensive: see (in alphabetical order) the works of Bernadette Andrea, Emily Bartels, Richmond Barbour, Matthew Birchwood, Jonathan Burton, Jack d'Amico, Matthew Dimmock, Imtiaz Habib, Gerald MacLean, James Mather, Julia Schleck and Daniel Vitkus, as well as Chew and Matar.

[3] F.L. Baumer, 'England the Turk, and the common corps of Christendom', *American Historical Review* 50 (1944) 26-48; *Liturgies and occasional forms of prayer set forth in the reign of Queen Elizabeth*, ed. W.K. Clay, Cambridge, 1847.

Prophet's origins, birth, and life, and then move swiftly to the Ottoman armies and their conquest of Christian lands.[4] This 'popular' form of knowledge, to use the terms of Edward Muir,[5] was quite different from the 'elite' knowledge that developed largely, but not exclusively, in Latin and within the walls of the universities, more Oxford than Cambridge. This third perspective focuses on the Qur'an.[6] The publication of the 12th-century Latin translation of the Qur'an in 1543, followed by an Italian translation four years later, furnished European readers with 'liber legis diabolicae Saracenorum, qui Arabicae dicitur Alchoran', so diabolical a text that it required 500 pages of refutation.[7] The second section in the refutations was the 'Historia de Saracenorum sive Turcarum origine, moribus, nequitia, religione, rebus gestis', the lasting impact of which was the establishment of interchangeability between the terms 'Turk' and the 'religio' of Islam. Islam took the form of an Ottoman adversary moving from the European battlefields to an apocalyptic confrontation in the Christian soul.[8]

This essay will examine the 'elite' knowledge of Islam in England, and cover the period from the 1543 publication of Theodor Bibliander's edition of the Qur'an to 1697, when the bishop of Norwich, Humphrey Prideaux, published his influential biography of the 'imposter' Muḥammad. It will suggest the reasons why anti-Islamic 'notions persisted almost unchallenged, were indeed fortified by new prejudice'.

* * * * *

The first extensive account about the Ottomans in English appears in *The book of martyrs* by John Foxe (last edition during the author's lifetime

---

[4] As Ingram Anders has shown, the greatest number of publications about *Turcica* in England coincided with periods of Ottoman wars in western Europe: 'English literature on the Ottoman Turks in the sixteenth and seventeenth centuries' (Diss. Durham University, 2009), chart on p. 393.

[5] E. Muir, 'Introduction. Observing trifles', in *Microhistory and the lost peoples of Europe*, ed. E. Muir and G. Ruggiero, trans. E. Branch, Baltimore MD, 1991, vii-xxviii.

[6] For views on the Qur'an in England, see Chew, *The crescent and the rose*, pp. 434-51. For the Qur'an in medieval Europe, see T.E. Burman, *Reading the Qur'an in Latin Christendom, 1140-1560*, Philadelphia PA, 2007; for the Qur'an in the Enlightenment, see Z. Almasrafy, *The Enlightenment Qur'an*, Oxford, 2009.

[7] For an account of the Bibliander translation, see Almasrafy, *The Enlightenment Qur'an*, ch. 1.

[8] See R. Carr's collection of translations, *The Mahumetane or Turkish historie*, London, 1600; and even Consul Paul Rycaut's title, 'Turkish religion', in *The state of the Ottoman Empire*, London, 1668.

in 1570). Foxe (1517-87) merely mentioned the 'Beast' and his 'Alcoran' before launching into a chronological history of the Ottomans and their destruction of Christians. Islam was the 'Turke' because all the writers he consulted (and he included an incomplete list of his sources) were European, ranging from classical scholars to captives:[9] Foxe presented no information about Islam from within its own tradition or history. The influence of Foxe's depiction of Islam on English society was widespread (the book was placed next to the Bible in churches), as was the influence of Richard Hakluyt's *Navigations*, first published in 1589. Hakluyt (1552-1616) included travel accounts about the Islamic world, such as John of Mandeville's travelogue, which presented a derogatory image of the Prophet,[10] but like Foxe he had no primary sources in Arabic.

The establishment of the Medici Oriental Press in Rome in 1586 furnished readers on the Continent and in England with Arabic sources in Arabic print, sometimes accompanied by Latin translations.[11] But no Islamic texts from Hadith, biography/*sīra*, or jurisprudence were published in Arabic by this press. As a result, the catalogue of the Bodleian Library in 1605, for instance, listed few entries on Islam: an Arabic manuscript of the Qur'an (dated 1588), the Bibliander edition and translation, and *Confutatio alcorani*.[12] Meanwhile, Hakluyt's *Navigations*, which were read by politicians and playwrights, traders and sea captains, were followed by Samuel Purchas (1577-1626), who mentioned in his 1613 work, *Purchas his pilgrimage*, the Bibliander and Italian translations,[13] but relied heavily for his information about Islam on Continental travellers (Lodovico di Varthema and Pierre Bellonius), ambassadors (Bucsbeque and Guillaume Postel) and scholars (Joseph Scaliger) to describe the history of Islam. Purchas was honest enough to admit that he could not read Arabic, but that did not deter him from turning exegete and

---

[9] *The acts and monuments of John Foxe*, ed. G. Townsend et al. (repr. New York, 1965), iv, pp. 18-123, esp. p. 79.

[10] An earlier edition had been printed by Wynkyn de Worde. Hakluyt removed the Mandeville text in his 1599-1600 edition.

[11] Texts by Muslim authors in Arabic or/and in Latin print were scientific, not theological: see G. Roper, 'Early Arabic printing in Europe', in E. Hanebutt-Benz et al. (eds), *Middle Eastern languages and the print revolution*, Westhofen, 2002, 129-155, p. 135. The Medici Oriental Press closed down in 1595 because all the books were commercially unsuccessful (p. 147). The first Arabic book was on geography, and was printed in 1580: *Kitāb al-bustān fī 'ajā'ib al-arḍ wa-l-buldān* by the Mamluk author, Ibn Kundugdī. Later books included works by Avicenna, al-Idrīsī, Ibn al-Ḥājib, al-Zanjānī, and al-Ṭūsī (p. 138).

[12] *Catalogvs librorvm*, Oxford, 1605.

[13] *Purchas his pilgrimage*, 1613, p. 207; 1617, p. 285.

offering various interpretations of Qur'an passages, taken from Bibliander's refutations:

> Of Paradise he [Muḥammad] dreameth in this sort, Az. 65. He which feareth God shall receive the two Paradises full of all good, pleasant with streaming fountains. There they shall lie on silken and pure carpets, and shall be accompanied with many maidens, beautifull as the Hyacinth and pearles, neuer deflowered of men or Deuills, neuer menstruous, sitting in pleasant shades with their eyes fixed on their husbands: their eyes large, with the white of them exceeding white, and the blacke very blacke, lying on the shining greene. Fair yong men shall serue them with vials and other vessels of the most excellent liquor, which shall neither cause head-ach, nor drunkennesse and shall bring them the choicest fruits and flesh of fowles.[14]

Only after Purchas expanded his *Pilgrimage* did he mention English writers with direct access to Arabic sources. In his 1617 edition, he included references to Edward Brerewood and William Bedwell, whose publications had appeared in 1614 and 1615, respectively.

Bedwell (1563-1632) was the first scholar in England to offer an overview of Islam based on Arabic (and Latin) texts.[15] In 1615 (and again in 1624), he published the titles of the chapters of the Qur'an, *Index assuratarum Muhammedici Alkorani*, taken from 'Arabicke copies' of the Qur'an 'written in the East, or West amongst the Moores in Barbary'.[16] This Index was bound with *Mohammedis imposturae: That is, a discovery of the manifold forgeries, falshoods, and horrible impieties of the blasphemous seducer Mohammed... Delivered in a conference had betweene two Mahometans, in their returne from Mecha, and the Arabian Trvdgman*. Eager to refute Islam, Bedwell translated into English a 'conference' (*Muṣāḥaba rūḥāniyya*, usually attributed to the Jewish convert to Christianity, Giovanni Battista Eliano) that had been printed (in Arabic) in the 1570s for dissemination by Catholic missionaries in the East. Like many other writers about Islam, Bedwell was not always accurate about his information, whether with regard to historical facts (Muḥammad buried in Mecca, on which Purchas corrected him), or concerning translation from the Qur'an (*Sūrat al-an'ām* translated as 'Capitulum gratiarum', confusing the Arabic words for 'cattle' and 'grace'). In 1625, Purchas included a chapter about 'the Moslemen superstitions' in his *Hakluytus posthumus*, mistakenly claiming to derive it from 'divers Mahumetan authors in their

---

[14] *Purchas his pilgrims*, 1613, pp. 208-9.
[15] See the detailed study of Bedwell by A. Hamilton, *William Bedwell the Arabist, 1563-1632*, Leiden, 1985.
[16] Bedwell, index, O3v.

Arabicke bookes, by the said Maronites, Gabriel and John',[17] and ended by urging his readers to consult his 'learned friend Master Bedwell' who had published information 'out of the Alcoran'.[18]

The introduction of printed Arabic texts about Islamic history with facing Latin translations began on the Continent with the Gabriel Sionita-John Hesronita translation of the geographer al-Idrīsī in 1619, followed by the 1625 translation of the chronicle of Jirjis ibn al-'Amīd al-Makīn (d. 1273) by Thomas Erpenius (1684-1724). In 1642, John Selden (1584-1654) translated the history of Sa'īd ibn al-Baṭrīq (d. 940), which was the first Arabic printed text in England, and in 1650 and 1663 Edward Pococke (1604-91) translated the chronicle of Gregorius Abū l-Faraj (d. 1286). That all these Arab writers were Christians may have been the reason that they were introduced to European readers; no Muslim account about the rise of Islam would be published until the 18th century (the 1724 translation of Abū l-Fidā'). A French translation of the Qur'an appeared in 1647, which was turned into English two years later,[19] and in 1652 Joshua Notstock translated Juan Andrés' (Johannes Andreas) *Confusion of Muhameds sect*, in which the Muslim-turned-Christian author claimed first-hand information from Islamic sources.[20]

One of the unexpected effects of all these texts was the introduction of some favourable information about Islam: the Qur'an's deep respect for Jesus (notwithstanding rejection of his godhood), 'liberty of conscience' and thus toleration of Christians (unlike the persecution of Catholics and Dissenters in England), the non-representational ('anti-popish') nature of worship, and the strictness of religious piety. Such information could not but impress, or maybe shame, Christians,[21] and so English writers

---

[17] Gabriel Sionita and John Hesronita had translated al-Idrīsī's geography into Latin and published it in 1619 as *Geographia Nubiensis*. They added a long introduction of their own, which was hostile to the Prophet. It is from the introduction rather than the geographical text that Bedwell derived his information.

[18] *Hakluytus posthumus or Purchas his pilgrims*, Glasgow, 1905-7, ix, pp. 99-119.

[19] The French translation was frequently reprinted, unlike the English translation. Although the two printings of the 1649 Qur'an sold out, there was no other printing until 1688. See I. Binark and H. Eren, *World bibliography of translations of the meanings of the Holy Qur'an. Printed translations, 1515-1980*, ed. with introduction Ekmeleddin İhsanoğlu, Istanbul: Research Centre for Islamic History, Art, and Culture, 1986, pp. 178-206.

[20] But he did not know the difference between *sūra* (chapter of the Qur'an) and *ṣūra* (picture): *The confusion of Muhameds sect*, trans. I.N., London, 1652, p. civ. John Gregory, *The works*, 1665, a2v, described it as a mere 'disguise' of the Qur'an and 'not easily met with'. The English translation used the French translation (the text had originally been written in Spanish).

[21] See for instance, *A seasonable prospect for the view and consideration of Christians. Being a brief interpretation of the laws and conversations of infidels and heathens, as to*

adopted various strategies to confront any appeal Islam might have. First, they credited the Qur'an with views that did not belong to the text but to European polemic. Second, they relentlessly maintained the association between Islam and the Ottomans (even an Arabist such as Bedwell referred to the 'Turkish Alcoran').[22] And third, they buried the favourable information about Islam ('many excellent truths') among imprecations against the Prophet Muḥammad ('filthiness of life') and the incoherence of the Qur'an.[23] Whatever admiration a reader might develop for Islam and its intellectual legacy – and Erpenius in 1621, Matthew Pasore in 1627, and Thomas Greaves in 1639 all praised the Arabic tradition[24] – was undercut by references to Islam's 'Turkishness', its anti-Trinitarianism and theological falsifications, and its alleged cultural aberrations (harem, sodomy, forcible religious conversion, etc.). As a result, Robert Burton (1577-1640) believed that the luminaries of Islam, such as Averroes and Avicenna, would have rejected the religion had it not been 'for fear of the law';[25] the millenarian Nathaniel Homes (1599-1678) found the 'Alcoran' of the Turks to speak 'in substance according to the Scripture', though it was still a text of 'barbarians';[26] and Sir Thomas Browne (1605-82) wondered how the 'noble Geber, Avicenna, and Almanzor, should rest satisfied in the nature and causes of earthquakes, delivered from the doctrine of their Prophet; that is, from the motion of a great Bull, upon whose horns all the earth is poised', a view not found in the Qur'an.[27] Others pointed to customs that were more culturally and geographically Ottoman (or Moroccan or Persian) than theologically qur'anic: 'Mahometanism' thus came to be viewed as either perverse or outlandish. 'Their customs', wrote John Finch (1626-82) from Istanbul in February 1674 about the Ottoman communities, 'are everything quite different from or

---

religion and morality, in our age. Together with some reflections thereupon, in relation to us who profess Christianity. By a Gentleman, London, 1687.

[22] Title page of the Index.

[23] Lancelot Addison, *The life and death of Mahumed*, London, 1679, ch. 9 and title page.

[24] Even the mystic John Everard celebrated it: for him, the Arabic text of Hermes Trismegistus preceded Moses by 'some hundreds of years' (*Corpus Hermeticum*, London, 1650, 'To the reader').

[25] *The anatomy of melancholy*, ed. H. Jackson, London, 1977, 3, 4, 1, 3. It is not clear that Burton had read the Qur'an: see, *Anatomy*, 1, 2, 1, 2, where he mentions the 'Turks' Alcoran', though his note refers to 'Strozzius Cicogna, Omnifariae mag. Lib. 2, cap. 15'.

[26] Nathaniel Homes, *The resurrection revealed*, London, 1654, p. 419.

[27] Sir Thomas Browne, *Pseudodoxia epidemica*, ed. R. Robbins, Oxford, 1981, i, p. 28. As Robbins points out, Browne derived some of his information from the travelogue by Henry Blount, *Voyage into the Levant*, London, 1636. The 'Koran', he adds, was 'less often read than abused', ii, p. 663.

rather contrary to those of the Christians... Instead of Hatts they have Turbans.'[28]

English writings about Islam through its Arabic sources, especially the Qur'an, started in earnest after William Laud, Archbishop of Canterbury, began the collection of eastern manuscripts that bears his name at the Bodleian,[29] and after he appointed Edward Pococke as the first professor of Arabic at Oxford in 1636. By 1646, the Bodleian owned six manuscript copies of the Qur'an. The influence of these sources best appeared in John Gregory (d. 1646), a student of Pococke's at Christ Church. He used the manuscripts at 'our publick library' as well as material belonging to his friends and correspondents, especially John Selden,[30] emphasising that he had consulted the Arabic text of the Qur'an – and even mentioned the Bodleian shelf mark.[31] The preface to his posthumously published *Works* opened with the first admiring allusion to a qur'anic verse by an English writer:

> The Mahumetans say that the first thing that God created was a Pen: Indeed the whole Creation is but a Transcript, and God when he made the world did but write it out of that Copy which he had of it in his Divine understanding from all Eternity.[32]

This opening is striking because it refers to the first chronological verses of the Qur'an (from Q 96) and to the image of the *lawḥ maḥfūz*, 'the preserved tablet', as a kind of epigraph. The qur'anic words led Gregory to their interpretations by a Muslim author, 'Ibn Said Ali', and a Christian writer, the Catholic Gabriel Sionita. Gregory was preparing the reader for the amalgamation of Islamic with Christian Arabic sources and for situating the bi-religious Arabic corpus firmly within the tradition of the *prisca theologia*.[33] That is why, when later he mentioned the Qur'an as one of his sources, a text that he knew would evoke anxiety in his readers, he hastened to add that the word Qur'an 'signifieth but the Scripture, you need not be afraid of it' (p. a2r).

---

[28] MS BL Add 23215, fol. 84v.3.
[29] C. Wakefield, 'Arabic manuscripts in the Bodleian Library. The seventeenth-century collections', in G.A. Russell, *The 'Arabick' interest of the natural philosophers in seventeenth-century England*, Leiden, 1994, pp. 128-46.
[30] *The works of the reverend and learned Mr. John Gregory*, London, 1665, 2nd part, pp. 16, 76.
[31] 'Alcoran. Arab. MS. In Arch. Bodl', *The works of the reverend and learned Mr. John Gregory*, p. a2r.
[32] *The works of the reverend and learned Mr. John Gregory*, p. a1r.
[33] For the *prisca theologia*, see D.P. Walker, *The ancient theology*, London, 1972, ch. 1.

Gregory was the first English Arabist to challenge the predominantly negative views about the Qur'an and Islam. The starting point in the discussion of Islam, he urged, was that the Qur'an revealed a religion, which, like other religions, had a 'rational' component that was acquired through 'education'. Familiarity with the Qur'an showed Gregory that, while the Bible suffered from the division of its material between the 'canonical and apocryphal...here's no apocrypha in the Alcoran' (p. a3v). The Qur'an, he noted, had fewer problems about its formation than the Bible because it had fewer problems in the history of its transmission.[34] It would be impossible, wrote Gregory, to claim 'a miraculous conservation and incorruption of the text' of the Bible, but 'The Alcoran it self hath had much better luck' (p. b2v). Furthermore, the style of the Old Testament was 'unspeakably good, but not admirable' (p. b2v) and rather inferior to Islamic texts: 'Read Ben Syra and the Arabick Centuries of Proverbs: Read the Alcoran it self' (p. b3r).

Abraham Wheelock (1593-1653), professor of Arabic at Cambridge, was so incensed with the Qur'an that he wrote to his friend Samuel Hartlib in November 1647 that he desired to 'breath out my last breth in this cause...to write Notes against the aLCORAN in the Language of the aLCORAN, which is the Arabick'.[35] He never did. But, perhaps angered by Gregory's call to his countrymen to read the Qur'an, King Charles I's chaplain, Alexander Ross (1590-1654), translated it from French in order to show English readers how much it was a jumble of superstition and rant. In the 'needful caveat' that he appended to the translation, Ross poured out his venom on the Qur'an: 'A gallimaufry of errors' and 'misshapen issue of Mahomet's brain'.[36] So hostile was Ross in his views on the Qur'an that, when two Quakers were held prisoner on the Isle of Wight, their jailers thought fit to punish them by forcing them to read the 'Koran in English' so they would 'turn Turks'.[37]

Ross ignored the histories by the Christian Arab writers that had given a balanced account about the rise of Islam. Henry Stubbe (1632-76), however, consulted the Latin translations in the first full account about Muḥammad and the beginnings of Islam in English, *The originall & prog-*

---

[34] See the discussion in the first half of the 17th century about the canon of the Bible: N. Malcolm, 'Comenius, the conversion of the Turks, and the Muslim-Christian debate on the corruption of Scripture', *Church History and Religious Culture* 87 (2007) 477-508.

[35] Hartlib Papers, 'Ephemerides', 33/4/3A (12 November 1647), CD ROM.

[36] *The Alcoran of Mahomet* (1649), pp. A2v ff.

[37] CSPD Charles II, 1664-1665 (10 December 1664), iv, p. 109.

ress of Mahometanism.[38] Stubbe approached Islam as a corrective to the previous monotheisms, showing the importance of Muḥammad not only in laying the foundations for a powerful and tolerant polity, but also in transmitting the 'Coran', a text in the sequence of the previous 'Corans' of Moses and Jesus. No English writer before Stubbe said, or would say for generations, what he wrote about the Qur'an (from al-Ghazālī) in the last pages of his treatise:

> The Alcoran, a transcendent miracle, and which is more one that is permanent, from generation to generation. Nor is there any lasting miracle of the prophet, excepting that whereunto he appealed, challenging all the wits of Arabia (and Arabia did then abound with thousands whose chief study was eloquence and poetry) to make one chapter or more that might compare therewith and thereby demonstrated to the most incredulous, the truth of his prophesy. And God said concerning it, that if all men and angels should combine to write any thing like it, they should fail in their enterprise (p. 205).

It is interesting that Stubbe, ever meticulous in recording his sources, did not mention that the last sentence was the verse Q 17:88 (although he mentioned God as author).[39] Unless readers knew that this verse had been cited and discussed by the Swiss orientalist Johan Hottinger, whom Stubbe heavily consulted, they would have taken the qur'anic assertion as Stubbe's own.[40] But it was an assertion on which Stubbe elaborated: having read Pococke's translation of al-Ghazālī's *Tarjamat ʿaqīdat ahl al-sunna* ('Summary of the orthodox creed'),[41] Stubbe had no qualms about presenting that creed as his own overview: it is in the Qur'an that God is revealed, His oneness, omnipotence, and omniscience; the power of God over all the creation; the prophetic continuity in God's messengers to humankind including the importance of Jesus; reward and punishment; and the salvation of the damned (*apocatastasis*). No other early modern writer in England or on the Continent presented such a defence of Islam as did Stubbe.

In that same decade, and although he did not praise the Qur'an as highly as Stubbe did, George Fox (1624-91) equated it with the laws of Moses, Jesus and 'the great God'. Writing in 1680 to chastise the Algerian

---

[38] For an edition and study of this text, see N. Matar, *Henry Stubbe and the beginnings of Islam*, New York, 2013.
[39] 'Say: If men and jinn should combine together to bring the like of this Qur'an, they could not bring the like of it, though some of them were aiders of others.'
[40] *Historia orientalis*, 1650, p. 487.
[41] Pococke, *Specimen historiae Arabum*, Oxford, 1650, pp. 274-92.

'king' for the foul treatment of Quaker captives, Fox cited the Qur'an as a revelation of divine law, which the Muslim ruler was breaking. He therefore reminded the Muslim of the teachings of the Qur'an (in Ross's translation):

> Mahomet saith, chap. 3. pag. 34 That Jesus said, *Who shall sustain the Law of God in my absence? And the Apostles answered him, We will sustain the Law of God in thy absence, &c.* And therefore why do not you believe in the Law of God, according to Jesus and the Prophets; for Jesus' Apostles declared against such men as burned in their Lusts... and therefore you Turks that do such things, are Judged by the great God, and all his Holy Prophets, and Jesus Christ, and his Apostles, to Act contrary to God's pure, just, holy, righteous Law, and they are Witnesses against you, as is also your own Alcoran.[42]

The Qur'an, Fox asserted, did not condone violence towards captives and the Turk thus stood condemned not from a Christian perspective, but from God's qur'anic revelation. In similar vein, John Locke argued that men arrived at morality by 'comparing their actions to a rule', which invariably stemmed from 'divine law'. He continued: 'The Alcoran of the Mahumetans... being taken for a divine law it would have served men who made use of it and judged of their actions by it to have given them notions of morality or Moral Ideas.'[43] Because the Qur'an included notions of morality, Locke defended the toleration and indigenisation of Muslims in the Anglican polity.[44]

Meanwhile, other English writers continued in their attacks on the 'Turkish Alcoran' even though they realised, as Paul Rycaut (1629-1700) noted at the end of *The present state of the Ottoman Empire* (1668), that the Ottomans posed no military threat to England – and were much needed for trade. Rycaut's book was a landmark in the study of Islam and Ottoman society, as it was the first to be written by an Englishman who had lived in the Islamic East, from Aleppo to Izmir, and who had encountered the 'Turkish religion' first hand. Still, Rycaut felt no qualms about preparing a whole treatise without referring to Arabic, Ottoman

---

[42] Fox, *To the Great Turk and his King at Algiers*, London, 1680, p. 10; for Moses, p. 2.

[43] *The correspondence of John Locke*, ed. E.S. de Beer, Oxford, 1976-82, iv, p. 112 (4 August 1690). Locke was responding to James Tyrrell, who had criticised his *Essay concerning human understanding*.

[44] For an extended study of Islam and the Quakers, see J. Meggitt, *Early Quakers and Islam. Slavery, apocalyptic and Christian-Muslim encounters in the seventeenth century*, Uppsala, 2013. I am grateful to Dr Meggitt for sending me a pdf of his book before its publication.

or Persian sources; nor did he desist from describing the harem without ever having set foot in it.

In similar vein, and doing to the Moroccan 'empire' what Rycaut had done to the Ottoman, another chaplain, Lancelot Addison (1632-1703), wrote a history of 'Barbary' after spending some years there and learning about Muslim customs by talking with 'the Moors' and 'orientals'.[45] Although he was widely familiar with scholarship on Islam, often citing Pococke and al-Makīn, Johann Hottinger and Abū l-Faraj, his views remained deeply hostile. A few years later, Addison went on to write a full biography of Muḥammad, the first to appear in print in England, *The life and death of Mahumed, the author of the Turkish religion* (London, 1679).[46] In his dedication of the treatise to the secretary of state (the study of Islam was already part of political discourse), he explained that he wanted to correct errors ('free from many ridiculous but usual stories'). Later, he wrote that the Qur'an consisted of three books with 36 chapters, while the fourth book consisted of '175 chapters'![47]

Notwithstanding their emphasis on rationality, the Latitudinarians of the restored Anglican Church did not alter views on Islam. Isaac Barrow (1630-77), a shining star among them, denounced the *religio Turcica*[48] by associating it with paganism. Thomas Tenison, Archbishop of Canterbury (1636-1715), also included in his *Of idolatry: A discourse* a chapter entitled 'Of the idolatry of the Mahometans',[49] explaining that the oneness of God in the Qur'an was really more intended as an attack on the Trinity than as a celebration of divine unity. He then pointed to all the heroes and relics that Muslims venerated as proof of 'idolatry' similar to that of Catholics, who were much maligned in the late 1670s in England.[50] In 1683, an author writing under the initials R.B. stated in his *Strange and prodigious religions, customs, and manners, of sundry nations* that he was going to give 'a true account of the life of this infamous imposter' (rather than the inaccurate one he had presented a few

---

[45] *West Barbary, or, A short narrative of the revolutions of the kingdoms of Fez and Morocco with an account of the present customs, sacred, civil, and domestick*, Oxford, 1671, pp. 198-99.
[46] It was republished in London in 1687 as *The first state of Muhametism*.
[47] Addison, *The life and death of Muhamed*, ch. 9.
[48] 'Of the impiety and imposture of paganism and Mahometanism', in *The theological works of Isaac Barrow*, ed. A. Napier, Oxford, 1830, v, Sermon XIV; and 'Epitome fidei et religionis Turcicae, a Muhameto Kureischita, Arabum propheta', viii, pp. 145-68.
[49] *Of idolatry. A discourse*, London, 1678, ch. 7.
[50] *Of idolatry. A discourse*, pp. 412-15.

pages earlier), based on 'Alcoran, (pleasing to sensual minds)', a book in four volumes and 124 chapters.[51] Although he lifted numerous passages from Addison's *The first state of Mahumedism* (without crediting it), he was fascinated by Islamic views about the end of the world and the Day of Judgment, all of which 'frantic opinions and tenents', he asserted, were found in the 'Alcoran'. That none of the descriptions derived from the Qur'an (but from the travel writer 'Barthema'/ di Varthema) demonstrates that he had paid little attention to views so 'frequently mentioned in the Alcoran'.[52]

The most systematic attack on Muḥammad and the Qur'an appeared in the 1697 treatise against Deism by Humphrey Prideaux (1648-1724).[53] Although the bishop did not know Arabic, he had access to an extensive range of Latin and Greek sources, which he listed in a kind of annotated bibliography.[54] Sometimes, his examination of the life of 'Mahomet' consisted of citing chapter and verse from the Qur'an and then consulting Abū l-Faraj, al-Makīn and Sionita, along with Pococke, Hottinger, Philippe Guadagnol, Rodericus Toletanus, Andreas and others. Prideaux challenged some of the errors held about Islam, but concluded by confirming the 'folly, the confusedness and incoherency of the matter contained' in the Qur'an.[55] After reading Prideaux's book, a fellow anti-Deist, John Bradley, who had 'never read much' by Muslim writers, decided to read nothing 'except the Alcoran'.[56]

* * *

By the time Prideaux published his treatise, educated Englishmen had a wide range of sources about Islam. But with the exception of a handful, all writers embedded their information about the Qur'an or Islam among

---

[51] *Strange and prodigious religions, customs, and manners, of sundry nations*, London, 1683, pp. 50-51.
[52] *Strange and prodigious religions*, pp. 61-62, 56.
[53] See the study of Prideaux in S. Khairallah, 'Arabic studies in England in the late seventeenth and early eighteenth centuries' (Diss. University of London, 1972).
[54] *The true nature of imposture fully display'd in the life of Mahomet*, London, 1697, pp. 153-80. Two editions were published in the same year, and a French translation in 1698.
[55] *The true nature of imposture*, p. 36.
[56] *An impartial view of the truth of Christianity, with the history of the life and miracles of Apollonius Tyanaeus*, London, 1699, pp. 228-29.

negative 'notions' that 'persisted almost unchallenged'. Two reasons lay behind this persistence:

First, all English scholars of the Qur'an and Islam in the 16th and 17th centuries were ordained clergymen, chiefly Anglican but also Presbyterian/ Dissenter. They ranged from cathedral deans to chaplains, in England and in overseas factories, who could not but uphold an adversarial position: Richard Hakluyt, Samuel Purchas, William Bedwell, Abraham Wheelock, Sir Thomas Browne, Robert Burton, Edward Pococke, Alexander Ross, Richard Baxter, Isaac Barrow, Lancelot Addison, Paul Rycaut, Thomas Tenison and Humphrey Prideaux, among others. The sole exception was John Gregory (a chaplain). Four of these writers, Pococke, Rycaut, Barrow and Addison, had lived in Islamic lands, from the Ottoman Levant to the Moroccan West, and infused their writings with the anxieties and disaffections they had experienced among the 'Mahometans'. It is no coincidence that neither the only Englishman who presented a favourable description of Islam, Henry Stubbe, nor the only thinker who called for the naturalisation of Muslims in Britain, John Locke, was a man of the cloth.

Second, from Peter the Venerable (who had commissioned a Latin translation in the 12th century) to Martin Luther and others, there was continuous emphasis on the need to study the Qur'an in order to refute it.[57] In 1648, there was discussion in London about printing the 'Alcoran' so that English Levant merchants would 'insinuate' it among the Turks, with a 'Refutation...fairly written'.[58] A door was opened by Arabists, John Gregory being among the first in England, through which new and corrective information about Islam was introduced, not to refute but to engage it. But it was a door that required proficiency in Arabic, which very few writers on Islam in England had. Nor did writers hesitate to borrow from each other the same inaccurate information, without checking references, sometimes contradicting themselves on the same page, quoting unreliable or antagonistic sources, and confusing material from travellers' hearsay with Islamic teaching.

---

[57] A.S. Francisco, 'Luther's knowledge of and attitude towards Islam', in M. Siddiqui (ed.), *The Routledge reader in Christian-Muslim relations*, London, 2013, 129-53, pp. 132-34.

[58] Hartlib Papers, 'Ephemeredes,' 31/22/39B (June/July-December 1648), CD ROM.

At the beginning of the 18th century, the Dutch scholar Adrian Reeland (1676-1718) was still urging the study of Arabic.[59] Only in 1734 did the first English translation of the Qur'an from the original Arabic appear in print, preceded by an extensive 'Preliminary discourse'. It would remain the standard translation until the 19th century. The translator was the lawyer George Sale (1697-1736), an Arabist and not a clergyman.

---

[59] Adrian Reeland, *Of the Mahometan religion, two books. Done into English from the Latin*, London, 1712, p. 48.

European Qur'an translations, 1500-1700

Thomas E. Burman

A flawed forerunner[1]

In 1480-81, a Sicilian Jewish convert to Christianity named Flavius Mithridates (*alias* Guillelmus Raymundus de Montecathero) translated *sūras* 21 and 22 of the Qur'an into Latin for Federigo da Montefeltro, Duke of Urbino. They appear side by side with the Arabic text in two columns, accompanied by a commentary in a de luxe manuscript now preserved in the Vatican. We cannot help but see in the visually impressive presentation of Mithridates' edition and translation a nod to the values of humanist scholarship returning *ad fontes*, which is also to be found in other European – especially Latin – translations of the Qur'an in the early modern period. Indeed three different complete Latin Qur'an translations would appear during this period that presented the text along with elaborate, and remarkably learned, commentary, two of them offering their readers the Arabic and Latin versions side by side. Moreover, in Mithridates' version we find not a whiff of the typical polemic that shows up so often in conjunction with Qur'ans that circulated in the Latin West – there is no preface warning readers of the dangers of the text to follow, no marginal notes denouncing the mendacity of Muḥammad, no vicious jabs in the commentary at the bellicosity of Islam. Mithridates' translation may, by its utter lack of polemical apparatus, be seen to anticipate the fact that Qur'an translation in this period was not simply a matter of making Islam's holy book available for Christian fulmination and refutation. Widespread scholarly interest in Semitic languages and popular fascination with the exotic wonders of the East were also powerful incentives for translation, and such a fascination may indeed have given rise to Flavius Mithridates' version. For one thing, it is in fact an execrable

---

[1] The bibliography on the subject of Qur'an translations is substantial and growing apace. It is, therefore, impossible to include anything like a comprehensive listing of relevant works in an article of this length. Readers are urged to turn to the bibliography and notes of the works by Burman, Bobzin, Tommasino, and Hamilton and Richard discussed below where, collectively, a vast range of relevant scholarship is mentioned. See also H. Bobzin, art. 'Translations of the Qurʾān', in *Encyclopaedia of the Qurʾān*, Leiden, 2006, v, pp. 340-58.

translation, evidence that this apparently quite learned man was willing to play the charlatan when he thought no one was looking. On the second page of his edition, for example, he translates the common qur'anic verb *nūḥī* as the proper name *Nūḥ*, so that the text at Q 21:7 reads 'we sent before you Noah' (*missimus ante te noe*) where it should read 'we sent before you none but men whom we inspired'. Errors of this scale show up throughout his translation, and the apparently learned notes are often just as faulty, though this did not prevent the Latin text from being copied into other manuscripts, including another de luxe one. Owners of such a version of the Qur'an were clearly not interested in either real polemic and disputation (which requires at least a modicum of accuracy) or philological study. Produced at the cusp of the 16th century, therefore, Mithridates' version embodies much of the complexity of presentation and motive that characterises early modern European Qur'an translations, whether into Latin or into the vernacular.[2]

Like some of the other Qur'an translations of this period, moreover, Mithridates' version found only a small audience. Where wide readership is concerned, the period is dominated until the mid-17th century by the first Latin translation of the Qur'an, Robert of Ketton's 12th-century version, which not only continued to be copied in this period – an expensive Florentine manuscript of it, including a handsome author portrait of Muḥammad, appeared in 1516[3] – but was also printed (twice) in Theodore Bibliander's widely disseminated anthology of Latin works on Islam in 1543 and 1550,[4] and was translated into Italian in 1547. (This Italian version then became the basis for further vernacular translations into

---

[2] For the details of Mithridates' translation discussed here, see T.E. Burman, *Reading the Qurʾān in Latin Christendom, 1140-1560*, Philadelphia, 2007, pp. 14-15, 18-21, 24-6, 133-50. See also H. Bobzin, 'Guglielmo Raimondo Moncada e la sua traduzione della sura 21 ('dei profeti')', in M. Perani (ed.), *Guglielmo Raimondo Moncada alias Flavio Mitridate. Un ebreo converso siciliano. Atti del convegno internazionale Caltabellotta (Agrigento) 23-24 ottobre 2004*, Palermo, 2008, 173-83. On Mithridates' apparent authorship of a remarkably learned set of notes on portions of the Qur'an in Arabic, see Burman, *Reading the Qurʾān*, pp. 141-43, and B. Grévin, 'Un témoin majeur du rôle des communautés juives de Sicile dans la préservation et la diffusion en Italie d'un savoir sur l'arabe et l'Islam au XVe siècle. Les notes interlinéaires et marginales du 'Coran de Mithridate' (ms. Vat. Hebr. 357)', in B. Grévin et al. (eds), *Chrétiens, Juifs et Musulmans dans la Méditerranée médiévale. Études en hommage à Henri Bresc*, Paris, 2008, 45-55.

[3] See T.E. Burman and L. Giamalva, 'A sixteenth-century European author portrait of Muhammad and medieval Latin traditions of Qur'an reading', in C. Gruber and A. Shalem (eds), *The image of the Prophet between ideal and ideology. A scholarly investigation*, New York, 2014, 159-79.

[4] Theodore Bibliander, ed., *Machumetis Sarracenorum principis, eiusque successorum vita, ac doctrina, ipseque Alcoran . . .*, 3 vols, Basel, 1543, 1550.

German and Dutch.) Only in the mid-17th century, with the publication of André du Ryer's elegant, readable French translation, based directly on the Arabic original, did Robert's translation and its descendants begin to recede into obscurity, as du Ryer's was not only frequently reprinted, but became the basis for further translations into English, Dutch, German and Russian. The definitive end of Robert of Ketton's *long dureé* as the standard European version of the Qur'an came with the publication at the very end of this period of Ludovico Marracci's astounding *Alcorani textus universus*, a deeply learned edition, Latin translation, and refutation of the Qur'an that would serve as the basis of many vernacular versions.

Latin translations

Despite the continual growth of the European vernaculars as scholarly languages throughout this period, Latin remained a central learned language well into the 18th century, so it is not surprising that the Qur'an continued to circulate in, and be translated into, Latin right across these two centuries. Even Mark of Toledo's early-13th-century word-for-word translation, which, though made in Spain, circulated almost entirely in Italy and only on a limited scale, was recopied in the 16th century.[5] An abridged Qur'an – *Compendium Alchorani* based on a lengthy and detailed analytical table of contents written for Robert of Ketton's Latin Qur'an – circulated in a handful of manuscripts from 1537 on, and Johann Albrecht von Widmanstetter arranged for it to be printed in 1543.[6] In addition, various scholars tried their hand at making Latin versions of small portions of the qur'anic text. Guillaume Postel left a working draft of a translation of *sūras* 1-2:140, which he put to use in *De orbis terrae concordia*.[7] In 1617, the Orientalist Thomas Erpenius published a bilingual version of *sūra* 12 with the Arabic alongside his new Latin translation (comparing the latter with Robert of Ketton's medieval version). In the 1630s, a schoolmaster named Johannes Zechendorff published Latin

---

[5] As we find in MS Paris, BNF – lat. 3394, fols 1r-269r. For full descriptions of this manuscript, see T.E. Burman, *Religious polemic and the intellectual history of the Mozarabs, c. 1050-1200*, Leiden, 1994, pp. 217-23, and *Bibliothèque Nationale. Catalogue général des manuscrits latins*, Paris, 1966, v, pp. 393-41.

[6] Burman, *Reading the Qur'ān*, pp. 103-10.

[7] See Hartmut Bobzin's excellent discussion of this draft and Postel's work with the Qur'an in general in his *Der Koran im Zeitalter der Reformation. Studien zur Frühgeschichte der Arabistik und Islamkunde in Europa*, Beirut and Stuttgart, 1995, pp. 447-97.

versions of *sūras* 67, 78, 101 and 103; Christian Ravius published a bilingual version of *sūras* 1 and 2 in 1646.[8]

Still another partial version – and the most substantial of them – circulated in a handful of early-modern manuscripts, though it is of uncertain date and attribution. A note in Spanish in one of the copies reads *este Alcorano traduzido por l'obra del Reverendissimo Patriarca de Constantinopoli Cyrillo*, and for this reason the translation has been ascribed to the scholarly Greek patriarch, Cyril Lucaris (1572-1638), but it is much more likely that this note means that Lucaris commissioned a translator whose name is unknown.[9] Oscar de la Cruz, whose edition of this text is based on two closely related manuscripts, has argued that the text is an incomplete draft (containing *sūras* 1-3, then 5-30:8, and *sūras* 104-14) in which some substantial portions appear more than once. He also suggests that the text as we have it seems to be a mixture of the Qur'an proper and a commentary on it based, perhaps, on Arabic commentaries. As it happens, at least two further manuscripts of this translation have survived (MS Cambridge, Cambridge University Library – Mm. IV. 11 and MS Oxford, Bodleian Library – Arch. Selden B. 4 [and thus once the property of John Selden]), and these will doubtless shed light on this almost entirely unstudied work of qur'anic scholarship.[10]

Three complete, and completely new, Latin translations of the Qur'an also appeared in this period. While only the last, Marracci's *Alcorani textus universus*, found a wide readership, the other two are significant in various ways for what they tell us about European approaches to Islam's holy book. A generation after Mithridates' deeply flawed edition and translation of two *sūras*, a version that went a long way toward fulfilling its promise appeared in the form of an Arabic-Latin Qur'an edition commissioned by the Semitic scholar, Christian Kabbalist and prelate Cardinal Egidio da Viterbo (1469-1532). While travelling in Spain as papal legate in 1518, Egidio hired one Iohannes Gabriel Terrolensis,

---

[8] On Erpenius, Zechndorff, and Ravius see A. Hamilton and F. Richard, *André du Ryer and Oriental studies in seventeenth-century France*, Oxford, 2004, p. 92.

[9] The text is edited on the basis of two manuscripts in O. de la Cruz Palma, *La traducción del Corán atribuida al patriarca de Constantinopla Cirilo Lúcaris (1572-1638)*, Madrid, 2006.

[10] On this translation, see the introduction to the edition, de la Cruz Palma, *La traducción del Corán*, pp. xiv-xlvii passim, esp. pp. xviii, xxxvii-xxxviii, xl. On the two further manuscripts, see *A catalogue of the manuscripts preserved in the Library of the University of Cambridge*, Cambridge, 1861, iv, p. 220; and F. Madan and H.H.E. Craster, *A summary catalogue of Western manuscripts in the Bodleian Library at Oxford*, Oxford, 1922, ii/1, p. 605. The Cambridge manuscript in particular seems to include *sūras* that do not appear in de la Cruz Palma's edition – 95, 96, 97, and 99 among others (see fol. 128v).

almost certainly a convert from Islam, to make a new Latin translation of the Qur'an.[11] Though surviving in only two manuscripts, neither of which preserves its original scholarly apparatus in full, it is certain that Iohannes Gabriel's edition offered the Arabic original in the first of four parallel columns stretching across the verso and the recto of the folios open before the reader, with the transliteration of the Arabic into Roman script in the second column. The third column contained his new Latin translation, while in the fourth appeared a set of explanatory notes based directly on mainstream Muslim Qur'an commentators. The Latin version that survives in each manuscript is a reworking of the original text, which had also been corrected and supplemented by another Muslim convert, Leo Africanus. All this makes it nearly impossible to be certain of precisely how the original text read at many points, but there is no doubt that Iohannes Gabriel was consulting qur'anic commentaries as he worked. At Q 2:58, for example, believers are asked to remember when God told the followers of Moses, upon arriving at Jerusalem, to 'enter the gate in prostration, and say, *ḥiṭṭatun*!' On its own, this last puzzling term means either 'alleviation' or 'humiliation', though the preferred interpretation among Qur'an commentators was derived not from these meanings but from etymology. The root *ḥṭṭ* means, among other things, 'to take on a burden', and thus this exclamation could mean, al-Ṭabarī observed, 'God has taken over the burden from you of your sins.' Iohannes Gabriel inserted this interpretation directly into the text: *Et ingredimini per portam prostrate et dicite: 'Aufer nostras culpas'* ('And enter through the gate in prostration and say: "Take away our sins"').

The medieval Qur'an translators Robert of Ketton and Mark of Toledo had likewise turned to Muslim commentators as they worked (Flavius Mithridates quite clearly had not).[12] Neither, however, composed a commentary for their Latin Qur'ans like that in Egidio's edition. Surviving only partially in the 17th-century Milan manuscript, this commentary is overwhelmingly philological in its concerns. At Q 2:138, it tells us that the surprising term *ṣibgha*, 'colour' or 'dye', refers here to 'the baptism of the Christians', a view that conforms to what many commentators say, including *al-Zamakhsharī*, who is cited explicitly. But these notes do not just explain difficult terms or usages; they also frequently inform us

---

[11] K.K. Starczewska, 'Latin translation of the Qur'ān (1518/1621) commissioned by Egidio da Viterbo. Critical edition and introductory study', Barcelona, 2012 (PhD Diss., Universitat Autònoma de Barcelona).

[12] See Burman, *Reading the Qur'ān*, pp. 36-59.

about the occasion of revelation – the broader context in which Muslims believed that particular verses were revealed. Q 2:55-56, for example, discusses the people who told Moses that they would not believe him until they saw God plainly, at which point God struck them with a bolt of lightening and then raised them from the dead so that they might be grateful. In explanation of this story, commentators usually cited Islamic traditions relating that, after the Children of Israel had repented of their worship of the Calf, God had ordered Moses to come to him with a group of the Israelites who would apologize to him. So he chose 70 men. But after making their way to the place where they would apologize to God, they spoke the words of the verse – 'We will not believe you until we have seen God plainly.' They were then struck by lightening and died, but when Moses wept and besought God, He brought them back to life. Iohannes Gabriel's Latin note presents a concise version of just this event. It is true that there is almost no overt polemic in either this translation itself or the notes that accompany it. Nevertheless – or so I have argued – one cannot help but notice a preoccupation in the notes with the topics typically at issue in Christian attacks on Islam, such as the nature of jihad, the principle of qur'anic abrogation, the supposed biblical prophecies concerning Muḥammad, and the sex life of the Prophet.[13] Christian polemic is never far removed from European Qur'an reading throughout this period, as is clear in the two other complete Latin translations.

In the mid-17th century the Observant Franciscan, Dominicus Germanus of Silesia (d. 1670), produced a complete Latin translation of the Qur'an which, though lacking an edition of the Arabic text, did offer the reader a learned commentary, much as Egidio da Viterbo's Latin Qur'an had. Having travelled widely in the Middle East and learned Arabic, Persian and Turkish, Germanus spent the last 18 years of his life at the royal monastery of El Escorial outside Madrid, much of it working on this translation.[14] Dividing the qur'anic text into a long series of passages roughly equivalent in length, he presented these in Latin, each accompanied by a *scholium* that discussed a range of potential topics – rare words, exotic names, the occasion of revelation – intermixed with polemic and apologetic. As in many other cases, then, Germanus' enormous

---

[13] For the above details on Egidio da Viterbo's edition and translation, see Burman, *Reading the Qurʾān*, pp. 149-77.

[14] Germán de Silesia, *Interpretatio Alcorani litteralis. Parte I. La traducción latina; introducción y edición crítica*, Madrid, 2009.

philological efforts served, as he made quite clear in his preface, the goal of attacking Islam and defending Christianity. His translation itself often incorporates material from the qur'anic exegetical tradition, as when he gives us *amnis paradiseus* ('paradisial river') for the rare word *al-kawthar* in Q 108:1, a term that Qur'an commentators often explain as 'a river in paradise'. The *scholium* to this passage goes on to explain the occasion of revelation for this short *sūra*: 'They say that a male child had been born to Muḥammad, [and] he named him Ibrāhīm', but this child 'died while still an infant'. Muḥammad's enemies, Germanus observes, rejoiced at this, saying, 'Now our Muḥammad despairs, deceived of any hope of posterity, because he begets no male child after this.' This *sūra* with its gift of a 'paradisial river' was meant to console him. Like his interpolation of the phrase *amnis paradiseus*, this explanation of the occasion of revelation is based directly on traditions commonly cited in Qur'an commentaries, commentaries that Germanus, like Iohannes Gabriel Terrolensis, often cited by name. This remarkably learned work – like Egidio da Viterbo's Qur'an edition and translation – never made it into print, and the manuscripts in El Escorial and Montpellier that preserve various versions of it (Germanus continued to work on it up to to his death) were largely ignored until the late 19th century.[15]

When Germanus died in 1670, the greatest pre-modern European work of qur'anic scholarship, Ludovico Marracci's *Alcorani textus universus*, was already well under way.[16] Like Germanus, Marracci, an Italian priest of the order of the Chierici regolari della Madre di Dio who was also professor of Arabic at La Sapienza University as well as confessor to Pope Innocent XI, divided the text of the Qur'an into manageable sections which he presented to his readers first in carefully vocalized Arabic, and then in his new Latin translation, followed by a series of *notae* that address lexical, grammatical and interpretive problems. Like most other Latin Qur'an translators, Marracci often includes material drawn directly from Muslim commentators, usually placing these interpolations in italics or in italics and brackets, but his careful notes generally also supply far more explanatory material. At Q 2:104, for example, where Muslims are forbidden to use the phrase *rā'inā* ('watch over us!'), Marracci tells

---

[15] For details of this translation discussed here, see Burman, *Reading the Qur'ān*, pp. 53-6.

[16] Ludovico Marracci, *Alcorani textus universus ex correctioribus Arabum exemplaribus summa fide ac pulcherrimis characteribus descriptus. Eademque fide, ac pari diligentia ex Arabico idiomate in Latinum translatus...: His omnibus praemissus est prodromus in quo (Mahometis vita, ac res gestae... referuntur)*, 2 vols, Padua, 1698.

us that both *rā'inā* and *unzhurnā*, the term that they were to use instead, 'mean almost the same thing, that is: "watch over us" or "have regard for us".' He then quotes the commentator Jalāl al-Dīn al-Suyūṭī (first in Arabic and then in Latin), who makes clear that Jews were derisively greeting Muḥammad with the proscribed term, because in Hebrew it meant 'heckling' or 'flippancy', so God caused it to be forbidden.[17] By virtue of its extensive notes on the text throughout, Marracci's enormous edition provided his European readers with the Qur'an accompanied, as Alexander Bevilacqua has recently observed, by much of its 'traditional Sunnī interpretation'.[18]

As Roberto Tottoli demonstrates in a forthcoming article, moreover, an astonishing group of manuscripts, including working drafts of Marracci's translation and Arabic commentaries that he made use of, survives to this day in the library of his order. While this corpus of materials has only recently come to light, and merits extensive examination, it already seems likely that Marracci's claim that he translated the Qur'an four different times is correct, since among these materials are four separate versions of the translation as he worked on it. Furthermore, there is remarkable evidence here that Marracci initially used the commentary of the Andalusī Ibn Abī Zamānīn as the basis for his translation. Among his manuscripts is a copy in Maghribī script of this commentary, so widely influential in Iberia (only the fourth known manuscript, by the way). From this manuscript, Marracci made his own two-volume copy, setting out the first version of his Latin translation in the margins. This cache of manuscripts is by far the richest body of evidence from the pre-modern period of how a European scholar read and translated Islam's holy book – very likely one of the richest bodies of evidence relating to pre-modern translation of any kind – and it awaits comprehensive examination.[19]

Marracci's *Alcorani textus universus* is, without doubt, a monumental scholarly achievement, but just as polemical motives intermixed with philological concerns in the work of both Iohannes Gabriel Terrolensis and Germanus of Silesia, so Marracci's careful consultation of Qur'an commentaries was of a piece with defending Christianity and attacking

---

[17] For these details, see Burman, *Reading the Qur'ān*, pp. 163-4.
[18] A. Bevilacqua, 'The Qur'ān translations of Marracci and Sale,' *Journal of the Warburg and Courtauld Institutes* 76 (2013) 93-130, p. 110.
[19] R. Tottoli, 'New light on the translation of the Qur'ān of Ludovico Marracci from his manuscripts recently discovered at the Order of the Mother of God in Rome', in A. Rippin and R. Tottoli (eds), *Islamicae litterae /Books and written culture of Islamic world*, Leiden, 2014.

Islam. Not only is the first volume of this massive work an elaborate refutation of Islam, but after the *notae* that comment on each section of the Qur'an from a philological point of view, Marracci added an equally lengthy set of *refutationes* or *refutata* with the same purpose. The 'refutations' to Q 2:1-29, for example, begin by derisively observing that the three mysterious letters, *alif-lām-mīm*, 'are placed for no good reason at the beginning of this *sūra* if the understanding of them is reserved only for God'. Marracci goes on to attack, among other things, the Islamic belief that Jews and Christians corrupted their scriptures – nearly eight columns on this topic alone – that paradise contains carnal pleasures, and that God created the earth before the heavens, rather than the other way round.[20]

Vernacular translations

Marracci's edition and translation became influential almost immediately – a German version of the Qur'an based on his Latin translation appeared in 1703, just five years after the printing of *Alcorani textus universus* in Padua in 1698.[21] But by this point the Qur'an had already appeared in a number of European vernaculars. By far the earliest was a translation into Italian of Mark of Toledo's 13th-century Latin Qur'an made by Nicola Berti in 1461, fragments of which survive in a manuscript anthology of travel literature from the early 16th century.[22] Just as partial Latin translations appeared in this period, so also did partial vernacular ones, such as an unpublished mid-16th-century French translation of the first four *sūra*s of the same Latin Qur'an that survives in five gatherings added to the end of a 16th-century manuscript that contains all of Mark's translation.[23]

---

[20] Burman, *Reading the Qur'ān*, pp. 173-77.
[21] David Nerreter, *Neu eröffnete Mahometanische Moschea/worinn nach Anleitung der VI. Abtheilung von unterschiedlichen Gottes-Diensten der Welt/Alexander Rossens/Erstlich Der Mahometanischen Religion Anfang/Ausbreitung/Secten/Regierungen/mancherley Gebräuche/und vermuthlicher Untergang/Fürs andre/Der völlige Alkoran/Nach der besten Edition Ludovici Marraccii, verteutscht/und kürzlich widerlegt wird*, Nürnberg, 1703.
[22] See L. Formisano, 'La più antica (?) traduzione italiana del *Corano* e il *Liber Habentomi* di Ibn Tūmart in una compilazione di viaggi del primo Cinquecento', *Critica del testo* 7 (2004) 651-96 (partial edition of the translation, pp. 669-96).
[23] Formisano, 'La più antica (?) traduzione', p. 662. See the manuscript descriptions cited in n. 5 above.

The earliest vernacular version surviving in its entirety is *Alcorano di Macometto* published by Andrea Arrivabene in Venice in 1547.[24] Though the title page advertises that the volume contains the teaching, life, customs and laws of Muḥammad *tradotto nuouamente dall'Arabo in lingua Italiana*, Arabists such as Joseph Scaliger soon realised that what was on offer here was an Italian translation of Robert of Ketton's Latin version, which had been printed only four years previously. As was the case with many manuscripts of Robert's translation as well as that printed edition, Arrivabene presented his Italianized version together with most of the other works translated in the 12th century under Peter the Venerable's auspices. In his recent and richly detailed study of Arrivabene's Italian Qur'an and its historical and cultural context, Pier Mattia Tommasino has argued that this work, which appeared in three slightly different versions, was not only part of its publisher's well-known programme of publishing the works of heterodox thinkers, but also reflects Arrivabene's consistent interest in translating and publishing works of ancient and contemporary history. Moreover, Tommasino argues, 'it is not only a book of anti-Islamic polemic based on old medieval sources', but also 'a volume of historical, religious, political, and ethnographic information meant for a variety of readers', and, indeed, reflects an anti-Habsburg and philo-Ottoman agenda. He has, moreover, also advanced a detailed argument suggesting that the translator employed by Arrivabene – who clearly did not do this work himself – was one Giovanni Battista Castrodardo, a translator of historical works and commentator on Dante.[25] In 1616, the Nuremburg pastor Salomon Schwiegger (1551-1622) translated Arrivabene's Italian Qur'an into German.[26] This version was reprinted in expanded form in 1659 and 1664. The first Dutch version of the Qur'an, printed in 1641, is in turn based on Schwiegger's German translation.[27] Arrivabene's Italian Qur'an was even the basis for Hebrew and Spanish versions of the Qur'an that circulated among the Jews of Amsterdam in the 17th century.[28]

---

[24] A. Arrivabene (ed.), *L'Alcorano di Macometto, nel qual si contiene la doctrina, la vita, i costumi, e le leggi sue. Tradotto nuevamente dall 'Arabo in lengua italiana*, [Venice], 1547.

[25] P.M. Tommasino, *L'Alcorano di Macometto. Storia di un libro del Cinquecento europeo*, Bologna, 2013, pp. 19, 22, 66.

[26] Solomon Schweigger, *Alcoranus Mahometicus, Das ist: Der Türcken Alcoran/Religion und Aberglauben*, Nuremberg: Ludovicum Lochner, 1616.

[27] *De Arabische Alkoran, door de Zarazijnsche en de Turcksche propete Mahometh*, Hamburg, 1641.

[28] See H. Lazarus-Yafeh, 'A seventeenth-century Hebrew translation of the Qur'ān', *Scripta Mediterranea* 19-20 (1998-99) 199-211.

If the 16th-century Italian *Alcorano di Macometto* was thus the origin of further vernacular versions of the Qur'an that circulated in this period, another vernacular Qur'an, André du Ryer's *L'Alcoran de Mahomet*, published exactly 100 years later, became the source for several more.[29] Like Germanus of Silesia, du Ryer had lived and travelled widely in the Middle East and had mastered Arabic alongside Turkish and Persian, rather than – as was far more common among early-modern Orientalists – as an adjunct to the study of Hebrew. Despite introducing his French Qur'an as useful for Christian missionaries (Du Ryer, *L'Alcoran*, p. 18), it is clear, as Alexander Hamilton and Francis Richard have shown, that du Ryer was much more concerned to present Islam's holy book as an exotic work of eastern literature, rather like the Persian poetry that he likewise translated (Hamilton and Richard, *André du Ryer*, pp. 94, 101). For this reason he worked hard to achieve a readable, elegant French version that at points became a paraphrase. The Qur'an's final brief *sūra*, for example, reads 'Say: I seek refuge in the Lord of mankind, the King of mankind, the God of mankind, from the evil of the sneaking whisperer who whispers in the hearts of mankind, from among jinn and men.' In Du Ryer's French it becomes 'Dis leur, Ie me garderay des tentations du Diable et de la malice du people, par l'ayde du Seigneur du people, Roy du people' (Hamilton and Richard, *André du Ryer*, p. 103) Where the early-modern Latin versions of the Qur'an all follow the Arabic original closely, du Ryer's version, like Robert of Ketton's *Lex Mahumet* of the 12th century, departs from literal translation in order to offer its readers a Qur'an in a kind of elevated language that matches, at least to some extent, the high-register Arabic of the Qur'an itself.[30]

Since du Ryer was working directly from that Arabic original, however, and because he was an energetic collector of Arabic manuscripts, including many copies of Qur'an commentaries, we should not be surprised that, like most Latin translators, he was consulting such commentaries as he translated. His collection included the widely influential 15th-century *Tafsīr al-Jalālayn* by Jalāl al-Dīn al-Maḥallī and Jalāl al-Dīn al-Suyūṭī, the *Tafsīr al-kabīr* of al-Rāzī, and al-Bayḍāwī's *Anwār al-tanzīl wa-asrār al-ta'wīl*, among others, and his translation is shaped by his knowledge of them. At Q 4:157, where Jesus' crucifixion is described, and the commentators typically explain that the man who was crucified in his place actually looked like Jesus, du Ryer's French version helpfully includes

---

[29] André du Ryer, *L'Alcoran de Mahomet. Translaté d'arabe en françois*, Paris, 1647.
[30] Hamilton and Richard, *André du Ryer*, pp. 18, 94, 101, 103.

this extra-qur'anic information, saying of Jesus: 'Certainement ils ne l'ont pas tué, ny crucifié, ils ont crucifié un d'entr'eux qui luy ressembloit.' In this and many other cases, du Ryer provides his reader with no indication that his translation has been influenced by a qur'anic commentator, though he repeatedly suggests in marginal notes that such commentators be consulted. Near the beginning of the *sūra*, for example, we are urged to 'Voy l'explication de Gelaldin' (i.e. *Tafsīr al-Jalālayn*), a commentary he recommends repeatedly, though he also from time to time refers his readers to others, such as al-Bayḍāwī. While it is not clear how useful such references would be to the French readership that he had in mind – none of the commentaries existed in French (or even Latin) translation, and only a few European institutions and individuals (such as du Ryer) actually possessed copies of them – Hamilton and Francis are entirely right to observe that du Ryer's *L'Alcoran de Mahomet* was the first European work to make a broad, non-specialist audience aware of the huge Muslim tradition of commentary that surrounded the qur'anic text.[31]

As a well-informed, elegantly written, and frequently reprinted version of the Qur'an, it is not surprising that du Ryer's *L'Alcoran de Mahomet* was soon put into other languages – indeed almost immediately. In 1649, an anonymous English version, often, and wrongly, attributed to Alexander Ross, appeared. It follows the French closely, even maintaining du Ryer's marginal references to Qur'an commentaries ('See the explication of *Gelaldin*'), and found a sizeable readership. It was printed twice in 1649 and then again in 1688, and was included in the multi-volume work, *The compleat history of the Turks from their origin in the year 755 to the year 1718*, published in the latter year (Hamilton and Richard, *André du Ryer*, p. 113). Within nine years a professional translator named Jan Hendricksz Glazemaker, who had produced Dutch versions of a large number of Latin, French, German and Italian works, published *Mahomets Alkoran, door de Heer Du Ryer uit d'Arabische in de Fransche taal gestalt* which, like du Ryer's original, was written in elegant prose, and in later editions accompanied by handsome engravings, suggesting that it too was intended for a broad audience.[32] It too was reprinted many times, making it more successful than the anonymous English version. Glazemaker's Dutch version then became the source text for a German translation by

---

[31] Hamilton and Richard, *André du Ryer*, pp. 96-98, 99, 100.
[32] J.H. Glazemaker, *Mahomets Alkoran, door de Heer Du Ryer uit d'Arabische in de Fransche taal gestelt; beneffens een tweevoudige beschryving van Mahomets leven; en een verhaal van des zelfs reis ten hemel, gelijk ook zijn samenspraak met de Jood Abdias*, Amsterdam, 1658.

Johann Lange entitled *Vollständiges Türckishes Gesetz-Buch, Oder Des Ertz-betriegers Mahomets Alkoran*, published in 1688, which appeared not as an independent publication but as part of a large collection of cosmological and historical texts entitled *Thesaurus exoticorum*.[33]

Concluding observations

Translation of all kinds has been and remains a remarkably understudied aspect of the human experience, despite all the interest that the new discipline of Translation Studies has generated. Though scholars in the last two decades have produced some remarkable works focusing on the Qur'an translations under discussion here, these efforts have in many ways only scratched the surface of a densely rich soil of compelling evidence. I noted above that the newly discovered cache of manuscripts relating to Marracci's edition and translation awaits serious study, but the same is true of other codices at El Escorial connected to Germanus of Silesia's work. While an edition of that translation has appeared,[34] moreover, it does not include the *scholia* that follow each section of his Latin Qur'an. An edition of Egidio da Viterbo's edition and translation that is currently under way likewise does not include the notes which, as in Germanus' case, depend so heavily on Arabic Qur'an commentaries. A great deal of work needs to be done, therefore, in clarifying the approaches to Qur'an reading and the methods of translation and commentary that we find in these Latin translations, and much the same could be said for the vernacular versions. Recent scholarship has, however, provided excellent models for taking up such study. The works of Bobzin, Hamilton and Richard, and Tommasino offer sophisticated, thickly described, accounts of the place of Qur'an translation in the intellectual and cultural worlds of early modern Europe. One feature of all this work is that, while detailed analysis of translation method is hardly absent – and indeed is often essential to these works and of very high quality – the

---

[33] J. Lange, *Vollständiges Türckisches Gesetz-Buch / Oder Des Ertz-Betriegers Mahomets Alkoran. Welcher vorhin nimmer vollkommen herauszgegeben /noch im Druck außgefertiget worden. Auß der Arabischen in die Frantzösische Sprach übergesetzet Duch Herrn du Ryer. Aufl dieser aber in die Niederländische Durch H.J. Blasemacker* [sic]. *Und jetzo Zum allerersten mahl in die Hochteutsche Sprache versetzet*, in E.W. Happel (ed.), *Thesaurus Exoticorum, Oder eine mit Außländischen Raritäten und Geschichten Wohlversehene Schatz-Kammer Fürstellend Die Asiatische / Africanische und Americanische Nationes...*, Hamburg, 1688. On these further vernacular translations of du Ryer's version, see Hamilton and Richard, *André du Ryer*, pp. 110-19.

[34] See n. 14 above.

tired question of whether a particular version is a 'good' translation or not has largely been left behind in favour of far more useful and interesting analyses of why such translations were being undertaken in the first place, of how this activity fits with other cultural and intellectual currents, and of what other goals such translations serve besides making Islam's holy book available in new linguistic forms. A good starting point for all future scholarship is to bear in mind – as it too often is not – that communicating in language is the most sophisticated act in which humans engage, and that translating from one language to another is, therefore, not only a phenomenon that, quite literally, still eludes all systematic description or theorization, but an event of such complexity that it implicates every aspect of the human personality and the human community. It cannot, therefore, be usefully understood under a single frame of analysis or presumed to shed light on only a narrow dimension of the human character, especially when – as in the translations at issue here – it involves one of the most studied and revered texts in human history.

Works on Christian-Muslim relations
1500-1600

Spain

Disputa con los cristianos

Unknown author; possibly ʿAlī l-Gharīb

DATE OF BIRTH   Unknown; probably late 13th century or later
PLACE OF BIRTH Unknown; possibly Crown of Aragón
DATE OF DEATH   Unknown; probably mid-14th century or later
PLACE OF DEATH Unknown

BIOGRAPHY

The identity of ʿAlī l-Gharīb is uncertain. In addition to being mentioned in *Disputa con los cristianos*, the name is also found in the first folio of a Muslim anti-Jewish treatise entitled *Disputaçion con los judios* ('Controversy with the Jews') (MS BNE 4944, fols 1r-36r). In all probability, this is the Aljamiado (Spanish in Arabic letters) adaptation by ʿAlī l-Gharīb of an Arabic anti-Jewish polemic entitled *Taʾyīd al-milla* ('Fortification of the faith') (Wiegers, 'Biographical elements', pp. 505, 512). Al-Gharīb's Aljamiado adaptation of this work can also be found in MS Zaragoza, Fondo Documental Histórico de las Cortes de Aragón – 8 Calanda, and in MSS Madrid, Library of the CSIC – J8 and J9. Wiegers ('Biographical elements', p. 510 n. 36) notes that in MS J8 (17th century), al-Gharīb is called '*faqīh* steeped in the Qurʾan of the Muslims, and in the Torah and Gospels of the Jews and the Christians' (*alfaqí sabidor del al-Qurʾān de los Muçlimes i en la Tawra i en los Avanjelios de Judios i los Cristianos*). MS J9 (15th and 17th centuries) is an almost exact copy of J8 and has the same beginning.

Gharīb may be interpreted according to van Koningsveld and Wiegers as a synonym for 'Mudéjar' (someone living in the *ghurba*, or outside *Dār al-Islām*) (Wiegers, 'Biographical elements', pp. 510-11; van Koningsveld and Wiegers, 'Polemical works', p. 192 n. 104). Another possibility is that the gentilic name *al-Gharbī* ('from the Algarve') has been transformed by metathesis into *al-Gharīb*. This hypothesis is supported by the fact that among the Mudéjars living in 1409 in the alquería of Maurar (Valencia) is found a certain Ali Abualfaqui Algarbi ('Alī Abū l-Faqīh al-Gharbī) (Mateu Llopis, 'Nómina de los musulmanes', pp. 328-29).

Al-Gharīb may have been a contemporary of the 14th-century author Muḥammad al-Qaysī, and could have helped him in recording his anti-Christian polemic *Kitāb miftāḥ al-dīn* ('The key of religion') (van

Koningsveld and Wiegers, 'Polemical works', p. 179). According to BNE 4944 (fols 59r-v), al-Qaysī was a captive in Lerida, Catalonia. This information does not appear in *Kitāb miftāḥ al-dīn* (van Koningsveld and Wiegers, 'Polemical works', p. 190), and suggests that the contact between the two – if there was any – must have taken place during al-Qaysī's captivity. Moreover, al-Gharīb apparently had direct access to information about one of the sources of *Kitāb miftāḥ al-dīn*, 'Abdallāh al-Asīr. This information is not contained in the work of al-Qaysī, and al-Gharīb included it in his adaptation of *Kitāb miftāḥ al-dīn* (van Koningsveld and Wiegers, 'Polemical works', pp. 191-92). All this situates the person and work of al-Gharīb in the first half of the 14th century, if not at the very beginning. The copy of the adaptation of al-Gharīb in MS BNE 4944, *Disputa con los cristianos*, can probably be dated to the first half of the 16th century.

MAIN SOURCES OF INFORMATION

Primary
Nothing is known about 'Alī l-Gharīb other than the references to him in:
MS Madrid, BNE – 4944
MS Madrid, Library of the Consejo Superior de Investigaciones Cientificas – J8
MS Madrid, Library of the Consejo Superior de Investigaciones Cientificas – J9

Secondary
G. Wiegers, 'Biographical elements in Arabic and Spanish anti-Christian and anti-Jewish Mudejar writings', in A. Echevarría Arsuaga (ed.), *Biografías Mudéjares o la experiencia de ser minoría. Biografías islámicas en la España cristiana*, Madrid, 2008, 497-515
P.S. van Koningsveld and G. Wiegers, 'The polemical works of Muḥammad al-Qaysī (fl. 1309) and their circulation in Arabic and Aljamiado among the Mudejars in the fourteenth century', *Al-Qantara* 15 (1994) 163-99
A.G. Chejne, *Islam and the West. The Moriscos. A cultural and social history*, New York, 1983, pp. 85-92
D. Cardaillac, 'Algunos problemas evocados a partir de los mss. aljamiados 4944 de la BN de Madrid y V7 de la RAH de la Historia', in A. Galmés de Fuentes (ed.), *Actas del Coloquio Internacional de Literatura Aljamiada y Morisca*, Madrid, 1978, 413-24
L. Cardaillac, *Morisques et chrétiens: Un affrontement polémique (1492-1640)*, Paris, 1977, pp. 157-61
D. Cardaillac, 'La polémique anti-chrétienne du manuscript aljamiado N° 4944 de la Bibliothèque Nationale de Madrid', 2 vols, Montpellier, 1972 (Diss. University Paul Valéry)

F. Mateu Llopis, 'Nómina de los musulmanes de las montañas del Coll de Rates, del Reino de Valencia, en 1409. Según el Libro de la Colecta del morabatí del baile de Callosa precedida de unas notas sobre su toponímia', *Al-Ándalus* 7 (1942) 299-335

WORKS ON CHRISTIAN-MUSLIM RELATIONS

Disputa con los cristianos, 'Dispute with the Christians'
La disputa de los muçlimes con los cristianos sobre la unidad de Allah, 'The dispute of the Muslims with the Christians on the unity of God'

DATE   Most probably early 14th century (Aljamiado MS 16th century)
ORIGINAL LANGUAGE   Spanish in Arabic letters (Aljamiado)

DESCRIPTION
Disputa con los cristianos is an Aljamiado adaptation of the Arabic Muslim anti-Christian work of Muḥammad al-Qaysī, *Kitāb miftāḥ al-dīn wa-l-mujādala bayna l-Naṣārā wa-l-Muslimīn min qawl al-anbiyā' wa-l-mursalīn wa-l-'ulamā' al-rāshidīn alladhīna qara'ū-l-Anājīl* ('The key of religion or the disputation between the Christians and Muslims from the sayings of the prophets, the messengers and the rightly-guided scholars who have read the Gospels') (van Koningsveld and Wiegers, 'Polemical works', p. 184). The adaptation was written by 'Alī al-Gharīb, who most likely finished his work in the first half of the 14th century (van Koningsveld and Wiegers, 'Polemical works', p. 192). Al-Gharīb is also associated with the adaptation of several other Arabic polemics into Aljamiado. Wiegers notes that in some of these Aljamiado manuscripts 'Alī al-Gharīb (or Gharībo) tends to be introduced as the author (Wiegers, 'Biographical elements', p. 512). *Disputa con los cristianos* seems to have been very popular among the Mudéjars and the Moriscos, and it exists in four other Aljamiado manuscripts dated from the end of the 14th to the 16th century (Wiegers, 'Polemical works', pp. 186-7).

The most complete version of *Disputa con los cristianos* is that contained in MS BNE 4944, where it occupies about 45 folios (fols 36r-82v). The contents of *Disputa con los cristianos* largely correspond with those of *Kitāb miftāḥ al-dīn*, although the contents of the latter are reduced to their minimal expression (van Koningsveld and Wiegers, 'Polemical works', pp. 187, 191). The sections dealing with the description of the historical events of the expulsion of the Jews from France in 1306, the suppression of the Templars in 1312 and the attacks against the Muslims of Algeciras, Almería and Granada are not included in MS BNE 4944. The same is true of a poem commemorating these events and the personal feelings of al-Qaysī about them (van Koningsveld and Wiegers, 'Polemical works', p. 191). Two passages in *Disputa con los cristianos* in MS BNE 4944 do not appear in *Kitāb miftāḥ al-dīn*, MS Algiers, National Library – 1557 (fols 49-90; 1481). These are the passages on fols 50v.[11]-59r.[9] and fols 67v.[10]-73v (van Koningsveld and Wiegers, 'Polemical works', pp. 197-98), which contain the only Arabic quotations of qur'anic verses in the whole polemic. Folios 50v.[11]-59r.[9] are a refutation of the divinity of Jesus and refer to the Gospels of Matthew and John (Yuḥanna, fol. 51v; Yaḥyā, fol. 54r; *san Juan* 'Saint John', fols 51v and 54r). On fols 55r-56r we find the Muslim anti-Christian claim that the Paraclete (already mentioned on fols 50r-50v[10]) is no other than Muḥammad. The human nature of Jesus is discussed on fols 67v.[10]-73v, and explicit reference is made to the temptation of Christ by the devil in the desert (fols 70v-72v) and to the resurrection of Lazarus (73r-73v.[1]). Van Koningsveld and Wiegers do not commit themselves on whether these passages were authored by al-Gharīb, and further research is needed.

The text in BNE 4944 does not preserve the order of al-Qaysī's Arabic work, and the folios are mixed up in several places. This might explain the fact that, before comparison with *Kitāb miftāḥ al-dīn* was carried out, scholars believed that *Disputa con los cristianos* corresponded with the story that comes after the title of the work, the account of St Paul from Sayf ibn 'Umar al-Tamīmī's (8th century) *Kitāb al-ridda wa-l-futūḥ* ('The book of apostasy and conquest'), while the other parts of al-Gharīb's adaptation of al-Qaysī's work were seen as independent treatises. The fact that the other manuscripts containing *Disputa con los cristianos* are very short and fragmentary may have contributed to this confusion. As a result of this, the sections of al-Qaysī's single polemic have been referred to separately, viz. *Disputa de la unidad* 'Dispute on the unity'; *Polémica de al-Qaysī* 'Polemic of al-Qaysī' and *Desconcordamiento de los cristianos* 'Disunity of the Christians' (Cardaillac, 'Tratados', p. 168).

Only one version of al-Gharīb's adaptation of al-Qaysī's work has come down to us. This is not the case with respect to the adaptation of *Taʾyīd al-milla* in MS BNE 4944, which was most probably made by al-Gharīb (Wiegers, 'Biographical elements', pp. 505, 512). The copies of his adaptation included in MSS J8 and J9 (17th century) are not faithful renderings of MS BNE 4944. They present al-Gharīb as the author (see above) and include references to the Talmud. They also refer to the evil nature of the Jews, explained from the fact that they were driven from the planet Saturn, where they were engendered at the beginning of time (MS Library of the CSIC, Madrid – J8, fol. 404r, and MS Library of the CSIC, Madrid – J9, fol. 210v). The introduction of new elements points to the use of al-Gharīb's Aljamiado adaptations of Arabic polemical works by Mudéjars and Moriscos for an extended period of time and to the increasing impact of Christian polemical discourse contained in them.

SIGNIFICANCE

Disputa con los cristianos is a good example of a Mudéjar work that has long been seen as written by Moriscos. Al-Gharīb's adaptation was made almost directly after al-Qaysī's composition of *Kitāb miftāḥ al-dīn*, and this points to the involvement of Mudéjars at a very early stage in the transmission and adaptation of Muslim Arabic anti-Christian polemics into Aljamiado. The fact that al-Gharīb is the adaptor of the treatise against the Jews, *Taʾyīd al-milla*, which contains references to Christian anti-Jewish discourse, and that these two polemics are bound together in MS BNE 4944, suggests that Muslim anti-Christian and anti-Jewish polemics could have been closely related to each other. An example of this is the Aljamiado manuscript MS 8 Calanda, which contains a disputation against the Jews and the Christians that consists of a faithful summary of *Taʾyīd al-milla* to which four additional chapters of polemic against the Christians have been added. Unfortunately, we only have the titles of these chapters; the contents have been lost.

Disputa con los cristianos shows the impact of Christian missionary efforts upon the Muslims living in the Iberian Peninsula during the later Middle Ages, and Mudéjar efforts to acquire the knowledge necessary to engage successfully in disputes with Christians and Jews.

MANUSCRIPTS

MS Madrid, Royal Academy of History – XXXII (11/9416), 11 fols (fols 4r-4v probably belong to another work) (paper and letter from the 14th century)

MS Madrid, Royal Academy of History – XVII (11/9409), fols 36r-39r and 40r-41v (paper from the 14th to the 16th century)

MS Madrid, BNE – 4944, fols 36r-82v (first half of the 16th century)

MS Madrid, Royal Academy of History – XXXI (11/9416), fols 36r-40r[12] (second half of the 16th century)
MS Madrid, BNE – 5302, fols 79v[10] – end (16th century)

EDITIONS & TRANSLATIONS

Cardaillac, 'La polémique anti-chrétienne'

STUDIES

L. Cardaillac, 'Tratados de polémica religiosa', in A. Mateos Paramio (ed.), *Memoria de los Moriscos. Escritos y relatos de una diáspora cultural*, Madrid, 2010, 168-70
Wiegers, 'Biographical elements'
van Koningsveld and Wiegers, 'Polemical works'

Mònica Colominas Aparicio

Antonio García de Villalpando

DATE OF BIRTH   Before 1475
PLACE OF BIRTH Unknown; presumably Villalpando
DATE OF DEATH   10 August 1513
PLACE OF DEATH Toledo

BIOGRAPHY

Antonio García de Villalpando came from a family of Castilian lawyers and royal officials. Like his brother Francisco, who became chaplain to King Henry IV, Antonio followed an ecclesiastical career, though despite this he had several children. He was archdeacon of Ledesma from 1473 to 1476 and is described as a preacher and the 'humblest among the chaplains of the great [royal] chapels' (MS Madrid, fol. 1r). From 1489 to 1493, he served in the diocese of Osma, and by 1498 had been appointed onto the council of Francisco Jiménez de Cisneros, Archbishop of Toledo and regent after the death of Queen Isabella. Villalpando was made the archbishop's provisor and vicar general, his representative in the archdiocese, and he was evidently much valued: Cisneros refers to him as a 'special friend' (*Carta*, p. 45). Villalpando remained in this position of trust until his death.

Villalpando worked closely with Cisneros. In 1500, during the latter's mission to evangelise the Muslims of Granada, Villalpando wrote a catechism for the recently converted, entitled *Instrucción de la vida cristiana*. He also supported Cisneros in his crusading campaign against Islam, which resulted in the conquest of Orán in 1509, following which he took a lead in publishing the cardinal's letters about the victory.

In *Razonamiento de las reales armas*, which he wrote between 1480 and 1487, Villalpando expresses a range of harsh views about Muslims following the capture of Granada. In disagreement with the *ius gentium*, according to which Muslims could legally own land, he argues that, since the land had previously belonged to Christians and had only fallen into the hands of the infidels because of the sins of the Christians, this seizure by the Catholic Monarchs was holy and just. In order to support the war and free captive Christians, the monarchs could confiscate goods belonging to Jews and Muslims as well as the property of mosques. More than this, Muslims everywhere should be subdued because they prevent

Christians from reaching Jerusalem. Thus, Isabella and Ferdinand should conquer all territories occupied by the infidels, including the Holy Land and beyond (MS Madrid, fol. 201v). Jews and Mudéjar Muslims in the lands of the Castilian Crown should not only be segregated from the rest of the population, as the Catholic Monarchs decreed, but, because any communication between them and Christians is wrong, they should be expelled if they do not convert (MS Madrid, fol. 201r-v). Muslims and Jews are worse than Sodomites (MS Madrid, fol. 192r), and are like animals because their lack of understanding makes them incapable of comprehending the Christian faith (MS Madrid, fol. 51r-v).

MAIN SOURCES OF INFORMATION

Primary

MS Madrid, Biblioteca de la Fundación Lázaro Galdiano – 768 (Olim M 2-4-2, Inventario 15539) Antonio García de Villalpando, *Razonamiento de las reales armas de los católicos reyes don Fernando y doña Isabel* (after 1482 and before February 1492)

'Carta de D. Francisco Jiménez de Cisneros, al doctor Villalpando, capellán mayor y Vicario general de Toledo. Cartagena, 25 de mayo de 1509 y Carta del Maestro de Cazalla al Dr. Villalpando. Cartagena, 24 de mayo de 1509', in M.I. Hernández González (ed.), *El taller historiográfico. Cartas de relación de la conquista de Orán (1509) y textos afines*, London, 1997, nos 2 and 3

Secondary

A.I. Carrasco Manchado, 'Dos clérigos en una familia de oficiales reales. Notas sobre Francisco y Antonio García de Villalpando', *Anuario de Estudios Medievales* 35 (2005) 605-33

A.I. Carrasco Manchado, 'Antonio García de Villalpando. Contribución a la biografía del autor del Razonamiento de las Reales Armas de los Reyes Católicos', *Memorabilia. Boletín de Literatura Sapiencial* 7 (2003), http://parnaseo.uv.es./Memorabilia/Memorabilia7/Carrasco.htm

J. García Oro, *El Cardenal Cisneros. Vida y empresas*, Madrid, 1992

J. Meseguer Fernández, 'Relaciones del Cardenal Cisneros con su cabildo catedral', in *V Simposio Toledo Renacentista*, Toledo, 1980, i/i, 25-147

WORKS ON CHRISTIAN-MUSLIM RELATIONS

Instrucción de la vida Christiana, 'Instruction about the Christian life'

DATE   Before 25 February 1500

ORIGINAL LANGUAGE   Castilian

DESCRIPTION

No extant copies of the *Instrucción* are known, though there was certainly a copy in the library of Hernando Colón (1539). Until the 18th century it was thought to be a work of asceticism and contemplation, with no relation to Islam (Sáinz Rodríguez, *Introducción*, p. 224). But then Francisco Méndez published in his *Tipografía española* a note from Rafael Floranes (who may also have sent a copy of the book itself) that indicated its true intention: '*Instrucción de la vida cristiana*, composed for the newly converted Moriscos, by order of the Cardinal Archbishop Jiménez, by his visitor general and Canon of Toledo, Dr Antonio García del Villalpando, printed there by Pedro Hagenbach, German, 1500, on 25th February. Book in 4° of 57 pages.' Méndez must have read the work itself, because he noted that it was a book 'small in volume and great in substance, worthy of many re-prints' (Francisco Méndez, *Tipografía española*, Madrid, 1861², p. 148), and 'a piece, excellent of its type and one of the best of that time' (p. 308).

The *Instrucción* was written at a crucial time in the history of the Muslims in Castile. From the end of 1499, there were systematic and mass conversions in Granada, and tension and violence were stoked up by uprisings among the Muslim population in the Albaicín quarter of the town (1499), and in the Alpujarra mountains (1500). The policy of evangelisation and conversion had already begun with the Archbishop of Granada, Hernando de Talavera, but in 1499 the Archbishop of Toledo, Francisco Jiménez de Cisneros, became personally involved, with the aim of accelerating the religious and cultural transformation of the kingdom. At the beginning of 1500, Cisneros commissioned a group of clergy from Toledo Cathedral to undertake a mission of conversion in Granada. For this he ordered priestly vestments and other materials needed for pastoral work, and raised funds in order to make gifts to encourage baptisms. As part of this, Cisneros commissioned García de Villalpando to write a catechism, and he had it printed in order to have it circulated widely.

If the anti-Islamic attitudes of the *Razonamiento* are anything to go by, Villalpando's tone in the *Instrucción* was probably less didactic than authoritarian and adopted more of an apologetic than pastoral approach. At the time the *Instrucción* was printed, anti-Islamic polemic was still very much alive, fuelled by works such as the Castilian translation of Riccoldo da Monte di Croce's *Improbatio Alcorani* (see *CMR* 4, pp. 288-91), which was printed in Seville in 1500. In *Razonamiento* Villalpando consent of the Catholic Monarchs to pursue a policy of forced conversions. This intervention in the diocese of Granada, which was nominally under the Hieronymite Archbishop Hernando de Talavera, was a sign of a radical turn in the religious policy hitherto followed by the Catholic Monarchs, based on the toleration of Muslim practices in Granada and the adoption of peaceful evangelisation policies founded on dialogue and persuasion, as advocated by Talavera. Confronted with Cisneros, who had royal support and who based his principles on the doctrine of the Franciscan theologian Duns Scotus, the defenders of the peaceful way insisted that violence had never featured in the propagation of Christianity. This is the meaning and significance of Gómez's reflections on Islam.

In connection with this, the city of Seville, where the Monarchs were at the time, also saw the publication – promoted by a Hieronymite friar – of two editions of the *Improbatio Alcorani* by the Dominican Riccoldo da Monte di Croce (d. 1320), in 1500 (in Latin) and 1501 (in Spanish). Riccoldo's work was one of the pillars of Christian anti-Muslim apologetic literature during the late Middle Ages. It contains all the main elements of Gómez's arguments. For example, Gómez makes an incensed plea against the use of arms to defend Christianity because Christ's law is one of meekness and charity; furthermore, it must be propagated through persuasion and God's miracles, 'spiritual weapons' which must be used 'according to God's law and in order to honour him' against the 'carnal weapons' of those who pursue power, wealth and secular honour. In this regard, Gómez explicitly follows Aquinas' doctrine, which contradicts that of Scotus. In consequence, *Carro de dos vidas* belongs to the medieval theological current that favoured peaceful evangelisation of Muslims.

SIGNIFICANCE

The significance of *Carro de dos vidas* rests on its deployment and defence of classic arguments in favour of peaceful evangelisation of Muslims, precisely at the time when the religious policies followed by the Spanish crown veered towards the forced conversion of Muslims.

It is very significant that Gómez García's pioneering work made a connection between the explanation of Christian spirituality and the issue of the full conversion of the descendants of Jews and Muslims. This reflects the particular socio-religious structure of Spain in the first half of the 16th century, as is also shown in the work of the Franciscan Francisco de Osuna, the most successful spiritual author in Charles I's Spain.

ORIGINAL LANGUAGE   Castilian

DESCRIPTION

No extant copies of the *Instrucción* are known, though there was certainly a copy in the library of Hernando Colón (1539). Until the 18th century it was thought to be a work of asceticism and contemplation, with no relation to Islam (Sáinz Rodríguez, *Introducción*, p. 224). But then Francisco Méndez published in his *Tipografía española* a note from Rafael Floranes (who may also have sent a copy of the book itself) that indicated its true intention: '*Instrucción de la vida cristiana*, composed for the newly converted Moriscos, by order of the Cardinal Archbishop Jiménez, by his visitor general and Canon of Toledo, Dr Antonio García del Villalpando, printed there by Pedro Hagenbach, German, 1500, on 25th February. Book in 4° of 57 pages.' Méndez must have read the work itself, because he noted that it was a book 'small in volume and great in substance, worthy of many re-prints' (Francisco Méndez, *Tipografía española*, Madrid, 1861², p. 148), and 'a piece, excellent of its type and one of the best of that time' (p. 308).

The *Instrucción* was written at a crucial time in the history of the Muslims in Castile. From the end of 1499, there were systematic and mass conversions in Granada, and tension and violence were stoked up by uprisings among the Muslim population in the Albaicín quarter of the town (1499), and in the Alpujarra mountains (1500). The policy of evangelisation and conversion had already begun with the Archbishop of Granada, Hernando de Talavera, but in 1499 the Archbishop of Toledo, Francisco Jiménez de Cisneros, became personally involved, with the aim of accelerating the religious and cultural transformation of the kingdom. At the beginning of 1500, Cisneros commissioned a group of clergy from Toledo Cathedral to undertake a mission of conversion in Granada. For this he ordered priestly vestments and other materials needed for pastoral work, and raised funds in order to make gifts to encourage baptisms. As part of this, Cisneros commissioned García de Villalpando to write a catechism, and he had it printed in order to have it circulated widely.

If the anti-Islamic attitudes of the *Razonamiento* are anything to go by, Villalpando's tone in the *Instrucción* was probably less didactic than authoritarian and adopted more of an apologetic than pastoral approach. At the time the *Instrucción* was printed, anti-Islamic polemic was still very much alive, fuelled by works such as the Castilian translation of Riccoldo da Monte di Croce's *Improbatio Alcorani* (see *CMR* 4, pp. 288-91), which was printed in Seville in 1500. In *Razonamiento* Villalpando had defended the Catholic Monarchs' policy of segregating Muslims and Jews from Christians, and had gone further in vigorously advocating the expulsion of Muslims if they did not convert to Christianity.

Both the *Instrucción* and the *Razonamiento* come from a transitory period in which polemical and pastoral works were written to support the policy of erasing the medieval Mudéjar tradition. This culminated in Castile with the royal decrees of 1501, to expel free Muslims from Granada, and of 1502, to expel them from the whole of Spain.

SIGNIFICANCE

The catechism was to be a basic aid in the evangelisation of the recently and newly converted. However, it has to be asked whether this work was of any real use. Cisneros's predecessor in Granada, Archbishop Hernando de Talavera, had also ordered materials for evangelisation, such as those written and collected together by Pedro de Alcalá, including a bilingual vocabulary (*Vocabulista arauigo en letra castellana*), a book of grammar and a catechism in Arabic transliterated into roman characters (*Arte para ligeramente saber la lengua aráviga*). Hundreds of copies of these works were printed between 1501 and 1506. The amount known about this initiative contrasts with the little that is known about Villalpando's catechism and its circulation. Language was a problem when trying to teach the Moriscos, a factor that was quickly understood by Archbishop Hernando de Talavera, but evidently not by Villalpando, who in Toledo could not know that only a minority of Muslims in Granada would understand what he wrote. It is likely that his catechism was more use to clergy working to convert than to Muslims themselves.

EDITIONS & TRANSLATIONS

Instrucción de la vida cristiana, Toledo: Pedro Hagenbach, 25 February 1500 (no copies are known)

STUDIES

PhiloBiblon, *Bibliografía Española de Textos Antiguos (BETA)*: http://bancroft.berkeley.edu/philobiblon/searchperson_en.html

E. Ruiz and H. Carvajal, *La Casa de Protesilao. Reconstrucción arqueológica del fondo cisneriano de la biblioteca histórica 'Marqués de Valdecilla' (1496-1509)*, Madrid, 2011

A.L. Askins, 'Muestrario de incunables hispánicos extraviados de la Biblioteca colombina', in M.L. López-Vidriero and P.M. Cátedra (eds), *El libro antiguo español, I. Actas del primer coloquio internacional*, Salamanca, 1993, 37-54

Meseguer Fernández, 'Relaciones del Cardenal Cisneros con su cabildo catedral'
F. Vindel, *El arte tipográfico en España durante el siglo XV*, Madrid, 1945-54, vol. 6
P. Sáinz Rodríguez, *Introducción a la historia de la literatura mística en España*, Madrid, 1927
K. Haebler, *Bibliografía ibérica del siglo XV. Enumeración de todos los libros impresos en España y Portugal hasta el año de 1500*, The Hague, 1903

Ana Isabel Carrasco Manchado

Gómez García

DATE OF BIRTH   Before 1480
PLACE OF BIRTH Toledo
DATE OF DEATH   Early 16th century
PLACE OF DEATH Unknown

BIOGRAPHY

Very little is known about the life of Gómez García, and the few certain details that we do possess are contained in what he himself wrote. In his earliest and main work, *Carro de dos vidas*, which was first published in 1500, he refers to himself as a 'cleric in the city of Toledo', while on the cover and in the *Incipit* of his *Oratorio devotísimo*, published in about 1512, he is described as 'a father from Toledo'. Nothing is known about the date of his birth. According to M. Andrés Martín, his knowledge of Thomas Aquinas' *Summa theologica* could indicate that he studied at the University of Salamanca under Pedro Martínez de Osma, who died in 1480 (Andrés Martín, 'Introducción', pp. 10-11, 16), though the Thomistic elements in his work could be explained in other ways because Aquinas was well-known in Spain by 1500. If Andrés' hypothesis is accurate, Gómez' birth date could be set in the 1460s or even the 1450s.

It seems beyond doubt that Gómez had a close relationship with the de Silva family, counts of Cifuentes, one of the most powerful families in Toledo. This would explain his dedication of *Carro de dos vidas* to the nun Doña Leonor de Silva, sister of the third count. This relationship attests to the part that was played by Gómez in the dense networks of Christian spirituality that existed in the central regions of the Crown of Castile around the courts of major aristocratic families. These networks were promoted by reformist branches of the Franciscan and Dominican orders with the patronage of the de Silvas; indeed, some members of the family were lively participants in the movement (Pérez García, *Sociología y lectura*, pp. 157-70, 213-26; Andrés Martín, 'Introducción', pp. 13-15). Gómez' interest in the promotion of Christian spirituality in Spanish – a means of ensuring that it was available to everyone and a typical feature of Castilian Christian spirituality in this period – is shown in the publication of two short works, *Oratorio devotísimo* (c. 1512) and *Lamedor spiritual* (1516).

Gómez's active involvement in the theological debates of his time is revealed by his writings on another major issue: the conversion of Jews and Muslims to Christianity. The problem of converted Jews was particularly acute in Toledo, a city with a long Jewish tradition. Some of these Jews had been converting to Christianity from the late 14th century, while others did so only after 1492, when the Catholic Monarchs offered conversion as an alternative to expulsion. In the years that followed, however, the Inquisition punished many of these converts for carrying on Jewish traditions. During the reign of the Catholic Monarchs, the centre of the debate was Seville, so it may be no coincidence that *Carro de dos vidas*, with its copious references to the conversion of Jews and Muslims, was published there. This scant information locates Gómez between his home city of Toledo and Seville, perhaps with the patronage of Don Juan de Silva, who occupied the office of *Asistente* in Seville between 1482 and 1504. Nothing is known about the place and date of Gómez García's death.

MAIN SOURCES OF INFORMATION

Primary
Carro de dos vidas, Seville, 1500

Secondary
R.M. Pérez García, 'El problema del Islam en la Sevilla del Descubrimiento, 1492-1502. Polémica teológica y política religiosa', in F.T. Ceballos, J.R. Molina and M.J. Viguera Molins (eds), *VII Estudios de Frontera. Islam y Cristiandad. siglos XII-XVI*, Jaén, Spain, 2009, 659-80
R.M. Pérez García, *Sociología y lectura espiritual en la Castilla del Renacimiento, 1470-1560*, Madrid, 2005, pp. 157-70, 213-26
C. Griffin, *Los Cromberger. La historia de una imprenta del siglo XVI en Sevilla y Méjico*, Madrid, 1991, pp. 313, 317
M. Andrés Martín (ed.), 'Introducción', in *Gómez García, Carro de dos vidas*, Madrid, 1988, 9-31

WORKS ON CHRISTIAN-MUSLIM RELATIONS

Carro de dos vidas, 'The two ways'

DATE 1500
ORIGINAL LANGUAGE Spanish

DESCRIPTION

Carro de dos vidas was the first systematic treatise on Christian spirituality to be written in Spanish. It was printed in Seville in 1500, the year that saw the publication of García Jiménez de Cisneros's *Exercitatorio de la vida espiritual* in the Monastery of Montserrat in Catalonia. Together, these works opened a particularly brilliant period for Spanish religious literature, which was to reach its zenith throughout the 16th century with Francisco de Osuna, Teresa of Ávila and John of the Cross.

Carro de dos vidas comprises two parts, one dedicated to the contemplative and the other to the active life, classic topics in Christian literature. In Andrés' 1988 edition, which totals 691 pages, the section on Muslims takes up 11 pages. Although the work reveals an intense creative process and is expressed in the author's own style, the first part, which comprises 96 chapters, is basically a compilation of medieval texts in translation. Especially prominent among his sources are Richard of St Victor and the Carthusian Guigues II (author of *Scala paradisi*, erroneously attributed to St Augustine), and to a lesser degree St Augustine, Thomas Aquinas, Bonaventure, Gerhard of Zutphen and others. The second part, containing 173 chapters, is dedicated to the explanation of the active life, a catechism in which the articles of the Christian faith, the Virtues, the gifts of the Holy Spirit, the Gospel commandments, the Beatitudes and other elements of Christianity are examined.

The work's pastoral spirit is demonstrated by the long treatise (chs 21-32) on the divinity of Christ and his identification with the Messiah who is awaited by the Jews. Gómez thus inserts into the work an apologetic treatise that echoed the social and religious environment in Castile in his lifetime: the sincerity of some Jews in their conversion and the maintenance of crypto-Jewish practices. From Gómez García's perspective, however, this was not exclusively a Jewish problem, but also extended to the Muslims, because 'in our days, the Moors reject Christ's divinity, the Trinity and the sacrament of the altar' (ed. Andrés, ch. 21, p. 339).

This is also expressed in ch. 33 of the second part, an anti-Islamic diatribe (ed. Andrés, pp. 381-91). The title of the chapter presents the topic in a traditional way: 'Of the falsity of Muḥammad's law'. Gómez' argument is built on the contrast between the ways in which the Christian and Islamic religions were spread. Christianity came to replace the false pagan religions of Antiquity through the preaching of the Apostles among all the peoples of the world, a form of peaceful doctrine based not on the ability of preachers or their rhetorical strategies, but only on the grace of God and the confirmation of faith and doctrine through the performance of miracles and the delivery of signs to convince the unbelieving. By contrast, Muḥammad performed no miracles, because he was devoid of the grace of God. His 'sect' and his 'law' were based on falsehood, which he exercised to the limit in order to excite the avarice, ambition and lust of all people in order to attract them to his cause. As a 'teller of lies and son of perdition', Muḥammad created a 'beastly and entirely carnal law', promising a paradise of 'milk, honey and virginal girls', and allowing polygamy. By appealing to the innate human inclination to pleasure, he brought many to his side, in sharp contrast with Christianity, the main postulates of which (the fact that Christ was the Son of God, that he was born of a Virgin, and that he died only to then rise again) cannot be apprehended by human reason (as Gómez stresses by quoting St Augustine's *De civitate Dei*); in addition, these postulates were presented by the Apostles without any promises of temporal benefits or bodily pleasures. By contrast, Islam spread by force of arms, and this was the only thing keeping it alive in his own time.

In order to prove this last point, Gómez presents an abbreviated history of Islam from its origins to the conquest of Spain. This historical narrative (ed. Andrés, pp. 386-87), which is of enormous interest, is built upon the information provided by the Dominican Fray Tolomeo da Luca (d. 1327) in his *Historia ecclesiastica*, and by the Bishop of Burgos, Don Pablo de Santa María (d. 1435), in his 'commentary of Chapter XIV of the Book of Revelation'. According to this history, Muḥammad took advantage of the unrest among the subjects of the Byzantine Emperor Heraclius, and incited them to revolt against excessive taxation. Then, after leading them to victory, he created a new religion in order to consolidate his secular power as leader of the rebels. According to this reading, these were the circumstances in which Islam emerged and, with the help of the 'heretical monk' 'Sergio', it incorporated elements of Judaism and Christianity to make the ignorant believe that the new prophet was the guardian of both these religions.

This chapter is not only an apologetic text but also a public statement in defence of peaceful policies in support of the evangelisation of the Muslim community. The publication of *Carro de dos vidas* in Seville in July 1500 was not coincidental, and neither was the attention paid to the differences between Christianity and Islam: *Carro* appeared shortly after the beginning of the Mudéjar revolt in the Kingdom of Granada, triggered by the policies of the Franciscan Archbishop of Toledo, Francisco Jiménez de Cisneros. The Archbishop had arrived in Granada in the last months of 1499, invested with extraordinary inquisitorial powers and the consent of the Catholic Monarchs to pursue a policy of forced conversions. This intervention in the diocese of Granada, which was nominally under the Hieronymite Archbishop Hernando de Talavera, was a sign of a radical turn in the religious policy hitherto followed by the Catholic Monarchs, based on the toleration of Muslim practices in Granada and the adoption of peaceful evangelisation policies founded on dialogue and persuasion, as advocated by Talavera. Confronted with Cisneros, who had royal support and who based his principles on the doctrine of the Franciscan theologian Duns Scotus, the defenders of the peaceful way insisted that violence had never featured in the propagation of Christianity. This is the meaning and significance of Gómez's reflections on Islam.

In connection with this, the city of Seville, where the Monarchs were at the time, also saw the publication – promoted by a Hieronymite friar – of two editions of the *Improbatio Alcorani* by the Dominican Riccoldo da Monte di Croce (d. 1320), in 1500 (in Latin) and 1501 (in Spanish). Riccoldo's work was one of the pillars of Christian anti-Muslim apologetic literature during the late Middle Ages. It contains all the main elements of Gómez's arguments. For example, Gómez makes an incensed plea against the use of arms to defend Christianity because Christ's law is one of meekness and charity; furthermore, it must be propagated through persuasion and God's miracles, 'spiritual weapons' which must be used 'according to God's law and in order to honour him' against the 'carnal weapons' of those who pursue power, wealth and secular honour. In this regard, Gómez explicitly follows Aquinas' doctrine, which contradicts that of Scotus. In consequence, *Carro de dos vidas* belongs to the medieval theological current that favoured peaceful evangelisation of Muslims.

SIGNIFICANCE

The significance of *Carro de dos vidas* rests on its deployment and defence of classic arguments in favour of peaceful evangelisation of Muslims, precisely at the time when the religious policies followed by the Spanish crown veered towards the forced conversion of Muslims.

It is very significant that Gómez García's pioneering work made a connection between the explanation of Christian spirituality and the issue of the full conversion of the descendants of Jews and Muslims. This reflects the particular socio-religious structure of Spain in the first half of the 16th century, as is also shown in the work of the Franciscan Francisco de Osuna, the most successful spiritual author in Charles I's Spain.

EDITIONS & TRANSLATIONS

Gómez García, *Carro de dos vidas*, ed. M. Andrés Martín, Madrid, 1988

Carro de dos vidas, Seville: Johannes Pegnitzer de Nurenberg and Magno Herbst de Fils, 1500

STUDIES

R.M. Pérez García, 'El mundo editorial de la Sevilla de Diego López de Cortegana en el contexto de sus problemas culturales', in F.J. Escobar Borrego, S.D. Reboso and L.R. García (eds), *La 'metamorfosis' de un inquisidor. El humanista Diego López de Cortegana (1455-1524)*, Huelva, Spain, 2012, 61-88

R.M. Pérez García, 'Francisco de Osuna y las religiones. Judaísmo, Islam, filosofía y conversos en torno a la espiritualidad franciscana (c. 1492-1542)', in M. Peláez del Rosal (ed.), *El Franciscanismo en Andalucía. Perfiles y figuras del franciscanismo andaluz. XIV Curso de Verano*, Cordova, 2009, 347-64

Pérez García, 'El problema del Islam en la Sevilla del Descubrimiento'

Pérez García, *Sociología y lectura espiritual*, pp. 157-70, 213-26

P. Cátedra, 'Estudio preliminar', in Francisco de Ávila, *La vida y la muerte o Vergel de discretos (1508)*, Madrid, 2000, 111-12

C. Griffin, *Los Cromberger. La historia de una imprenta del siglo XVI en Sevilla y Méjico*, Madrid, 1991, pp. 313, 317

Andrés Martín, 'Introducción'

M. Andrés Martín, *La teología española en el siglo XVI*, Madrid, 1976, i, pp. 372-4

Repertorio de Historia de las ciencias eclesiásticas en España, Salamanca, 1967, i, pp. 329-30

A. García Boiza, 'Un incunable curioso (*Carro de dos vidas* de Gómez García, 1500)', *La Basílica Teresiana*, 3ª época 3 (1916) 1-5

Rafael Perez

Hernando de Talavera

DATE OF BIRTH Between 1428 and 1430
PLACE OF BIRTH Talavera de la Reina
DATE OF DEATH 14 May 1507
PLACE OF DEATH Granada

BIOGRAPHY

Hernando de Talavera was born in Talavera de la Reina between 1428 and 1430. Very little is known of his early years. He was probably the illegitimate son of one of the Álvarez de Toledo, lords of Oropesa, and his mother may have come from a family of converts. The Álvarez de Toledo family partially financed the studies of the young Talavera, who is first heard of in 1442, when he was in Barcelona studying calligraphy. Later he joined the University of Salamanca, where, in around 1444, he was studying a course in arts and later in theology.

In 1460, he was ordained priest, and between 1463 and 1466 he taught moral theology at Salamanca. In 1466, he entered the Order of St Jerome, and in 1470 became prior of the monastery of Nuestra Señora de Prado de Valladolid, where he drew up extensive reforms for the order. These were very productive years for him as a priest and pastor, as it was here that he developed and defined his cultural and religious function and his pastoral role amongst the upper classes as well as the lower classes. His writings and work among many at court resulted in the growth of his fame to the point where, at the beginning of the 1470s, he became confessor and counsellor to Isabella of Castile and, for a time, to Ferdinand of Aragón, which made him an active participant in the most important events affecting the crown.

Together with Pedro González de Mendoza and a new ruling class, which was predominantly university educated – many from the University of Salamanca – Talavera succeeded in laying the foundations for the development of Ferdinand and Isabella's monarchy as a new power, including at international level. This was an ambitious project that envisaged in Christianity an element that could fundamentally bring together and create a new era, the age of the future Catholic Monarchs. Pauline teachings had a profound effect on Talavera, particularly the messianic sense of the arrival of a new kingdom, from which in the fullness of time new laws, finally matured, would be given to humanity by the renewed and saving monarchy of Ferdinand and Isabella. His later formidable work in catechising and making converts should be considered in the light of this messianic vision, which resulted in his becoming one of the protagonists in the preaching campaign aimed at the newly converted Jews in Seville in 1478.

In order to defend these converts from the accusation of being crypto-Jews, he wrote *Católica impugnación*, a key work and a true Talavera manifesto on the methods for evangelising and acculturating converts. Talavera advocated strong collaboration between political and religious power. The ecclesiastical structure must catechise and have control over people, which would allow, should it be necessary, the anticipation and eradication of possible deviation. For him, the Inquisition was a pastoral instrument rather than a political one. He takes a politico-religious line that believes in a strong and active episcopacy not absent from their dioceses. Ideologically, Talavera was opposed to a discriminatory and exclusive doctrine of the Church because he perceived it as a denial of the evangelising mission of Christianity and as a disruptive element in the 're-conquering' and unifying mission of the renewed monarchy that he was trying to establish.

As Bishop of Ávila from 1486, he was head of an area with prominent Jewish and Mudéjar minorities. He was conscious of the complex social and cultural implications of the changes that could be brought about by conversion. His experience in Ávila certainly influenced his work after 1492 as the first archbishop of Granada and a man trusted by Isabella and Ferdinand, at least until the arrival in 1499 of Archbishop Francisco Jiménez de Cisneros in Granada, who brought with him his campaign of forced conversions.

Talavera's years in Granada were very intense and, although they ended with the destruction of the gradual Christianisation strategy he had implemented, the period was a valuable experience that greatly influenced Spanish religiosity. Granada was a 'laboratory' for new methods of Christianising the new faithful, and transforming and acculturating them into subjects within a population where Christians were in the minority. Talavera asked his priests to learn Arabic, and he translated short catechisms into Arabic so that the people could understand them. In 1506, he had to go before the Inquisition on accusations of Judaising, though papal intervention quashed the charges. His absolution arrived at the end of April 1507, shortly before he died on 14 May, probably unaware of the news that had been sent from Rome.

MAIN SOURCES OF INFORMATION

Primary

J. de Torres, *Vida del primer arzobispo de Granada, de santa memoria, abreviada, dirigida al papa bibiendo el mesmo arçobispo santo*, MSS Madrid, BNE – 2042 and 9545 (c. 1506)

J. de Madrid, abad de Santa Fe (attributed by some scholars to Juan Álvarez Gato), *Breve suma de la sancta vida del relixiosissimo Fray Hernando de Talavera, relixioso que fue de la horden del bienaventurado San Geronimo, y primer Arçobispo de Granada*, MS Madrid, BNE – 2042, fols 9-65; MSS 2049, 2878, 9545 (16th century)

A. Fernández de Madrid, *Vida de Fray Hernando de Talavera, primer Arzobispo de Granada*, between 1530 and 1536, Évora, 1557 with the title *Sumario de la vida del primer arzobispo de Granada don Fray Hernando de Talavera y de su gloriosa muerte*, ed. F. González Olmedo, Madrid, 1931; ed. with an introductory study by F.J. Martínez Medina, Granada, 1992

Fr P. de la Vega, *Crónica de los frayles de la orden del bienauenturado sant Iheronymo*, Alcalá de Henares, 1530

Fr J. de Sigüenza, *Historia de la Orden de San Jerónimo*, Madrid, 1605 (repr. Madrid, 1909, Valladolid, 2000)

Secondary

The most complete bibliography on Hernando de Talavera can be found in the works by M.A. Ladero Quesada and J. Fradejas Lebrero cited below.

F.J. Martínez Medina and M. Biersack, *Fray Hernando de Talavera, primer arzobispo de Granada. Hombre de iglesia, estado y letras*, Granada, 2011

I. Iannuzzi, *El poder de la palabra en el siglo XV. Fray Hernando de Talavera*, Salamanca, 2009

M.A. Ladero Quesada, 'Fray Hernando de Talavera en 1492. De la corte a la misión', *Chronica Nova* 34 (2008) 249-75

S. Pastore, *Il Vangelo e la spada. L'Inquisizione di Castiglia ed i suoi critici (1460-1498)*, Rome, 2003

J. Fradejas Lebrero, 'Bibliografía critica de fray Hernando de Talavera', in J.M. Soto Rábanos (ed.), *Pensamiento medieval hispano. Homenaje a Horacio Santiago-Otero*, Madrid, 1998, 1347-57

U. Tavares, art. 'Talavera, Hernando de', in F.W. Bautz (ed.), cont. by T. Bautz (ed.), *Biographisch-Bibliographisches Kirchenlexikon*, Herzberg, 1996, xi, 433-80

T. de Azcona, *Isabel la Católica. Estudio crítico de su vida y su reinado*, Madrid 1993 (revision of original 1964 edition)

L. Resines Llorente, *Hernando de Talavera, prior del Monasterio de Prado*, Valladolid, 1993

J. Suberbiola Martínez, *Real Patronato de Granada. El arzobispo Talavera, la Iglesia y el estado moderno (1486-1516). Estudios y documentos*, Granada, 1985

J. Meseguer Fernández, 'Fernando de Talavera, Cisneros y la Inquisición en Granada', in J. Pérez Villanueva (ed.), *La Inquisición española. Nueva visión, nuevos horizontes*, Madrid, 1980

Q. Aldea Vaquero, art. 'Talavera, Hernando de, OSH', in *Diccionario de historia eclésiastica de España*, Madrid, 1975, iv, 2517-21

F. Márquez Villanueva, 'Estudio preliminar', in F. Martín Hernández (ed.), *Hernando de Talavera, Católica impugnación de fray Hernando de Talavera*, Barcelona, 1961

T. de Azcona, *La elección y reforma del episcopado español en tiempos de los Reyes Católicos*, Madrid, 1960

F. Márquez Villanueva, *Investigaciones sobre Juan Álvarez Gato. Contribución al conocimiento de la literatura castellana del siglo XV*, Madrid, 1960 (repr. 1974 with corrections)

WORKS ON CHRISTIAN-MUSLIM RELATIONS

Instrucción del Arzobispo de Granada, 'Instruction from the Archbishop of Granada'

DATE About 1500
ORIGINAL LANGUAGE Castilian

DESCRIPTION

Instrucción del Arzobispo de Granada en respuesta a cierta petición que hicieron los vecinos del Albaicín sobre lo que debían hacer y las prácticas cristianas que debían observar was written around 1500, shortly after the Albaicín revolt of 1499 and the forced conversion of the Moriscos driven by Cisneros, Archbishop of Toledo. It is also known by the title *Memorial y tabla de ordenaciones dirigadas por Talavera para la comunidad morisca de Granada. Se les reglamenta taxativamente la vida religiosa que debían llevar y se les adelantan diversas exigencias para la buena convivencia con los cristianos*, a phrase found in the *incipit*. It is a very brief work, occupying a single folio. It brings together the provisions set out by Talavera, when he was archbishop of Granada, to manage the life of the newly converted Morisco community.

Instrucción is one of the catechetical works that Talavera wrote throughout his life, as instructions for the assimilation of newly converted

Jews and Muslims into Christianity. This work requires a priest to be prepared and able to evangelise, and to bring together newly converted and old Christians. Baptism alone did not suffice for this; rather, a strategy had to be set out that would enable the newly converted to fit into Christian society, and to live as far as possible like 'old' Christians (*Cristianos viejos*). The strategy had a dual purpose: on the one hand, it would make the former Muslims give up their old ways and integrate sooner into the new social fabric, and, on the other, it would help the 'old' Christians to accept the newly converted, facilitated by an attitude towards them as brothers rather than as foreign elements in society.

This was the original line of action taken by Talavera and which he had already expressed at length in his early writings about the problems of conversion, in particular in his *Católica impugnación*, written in 1479, about the presence of crypto-Jews among the newly converted in Seville. In this *Instrucción* the same attitude is present, though here he is even more adamantly eager for 'integration' in order to respond to the 'acceleration' that Cisneros had caused by the forced conversions of 1499. These had shattered the fragile equilibrium that Talavera's measures had established, and had provoked a revolt in the Albaicín area of the town.

In this *Instrucción*, Talavera shows the people of the Albaicín what they must do to live as good Christians. Significantly, he underlines the necessity of abandoning Morisco customs, particularly rites of passage. The Christian tradition must be followed through the outward signs of crossing oneself and going to church to pray and to attend services. The demonstration of faith is an important first step in assimilating new customs, at the same time ensuring that the wider community accepts the newly converted. It is so important that Talavera asks the Moriscos to participate in fraternities 'such as those the Christians have, to help you in life and death'.

The importance of education, and Talavera's call for the newly converted actively to cooperate and participate in furthering it, can be seen in his advice to those who can read, that they should 'have all the books in Arabic of the prayers and psalms that will be given you and also of this memorial'. The believer, in Talavera's religious instruction, is an active promoter of Christian teaching, rather than just a passive receiver.

Talavera attaches great importance to Christian symbols. He requires all Morisco families to have sacred images in their homes, 'of our Lord, or the Holy Cross or of our Lady the Virgin Mary or of a saint...'. Outward signs are necessary to register belonging to a group, both within the home and when socialising; thus, the Moriscos must have 'good and honest Christian conversation', and be Christian in their dress and eating habits.

It is striking to see that, at the end of the *Instrucción*, after acknowledging the existence and circulation of small books or primers of prayers in Arabic for the initial acculturation and teaching of these new Christians, Talavera asks that they should also 'forget' their language as soon as possible, above all when at home, in order to become Castilian. This is a particular catechising strategy, with a partial acceptance of the Morisco past, though its specific purpose is to carry out the Christianisation process in the best way possible, which in the second phase means cancelling out the interior and exterior manifestations of the Morisco past, and modifying the way of praying, walking, eating and above all talking.

SIGNIFICANCE

Instrucción offers insight into Talavera's particular conversion strategy following the revolt in the Albaicín in 1499 caused by Cisneros' violent evangelising campaign, though it is very much in line with Talavera's previous ideas. Talavera perceived the importance of the everyday as a normalising factor for both the newly converted and the host community. This is the great novelty of his approach. Only by carefully preparing the clergy in Christian teachings and in the culture of those who are to be converted is effective evangelisation possible. Thus, he was eager for his priests in Granada to learn Arabic, and before 1499 he set Pedro de la Vega of the Order of St Jerome to write an Arabic grammar, together with an abbreviated Christian catechism and an Arabic vocabulary. This work was completed in 1501.

In the cultural *milieu* of the University of Salamanca, Talavera had absorbed the ideas of Juan de Segovia and Nicolás de Cusa about the conversion of Muslims by addressing cultural differences as well as differences of belief. This explains why he possessed in his personal library two copies of the Qur'an, one in Latin and the other in the vernacular, and that it was probably thanks to him that in 1501 a Castilian version of Riccoldo de Monte di Croce's *Improbatio Alcorán* was printed.

Talavera recognised the importance of sanctions in this process, and his concluding words in the *Instrucción* are striking in this respect: 'For some to keep the things aforementioned some constraint would be necessary, and because the excommunication that we are able to set is very dangerous and not feared by them it is necessary that we and you and you and we beg the King and Queen our masters to order penalties against those who do not keep it and executors to execute it.' He is conscious that in this first phase only royal authority has any power, and that any sanctions used by the church will be ineffective. This is faith in realistic and practical implementation. He knew that conversion would be a lengthy process, and it could only be successful by educating and accustoming the newly converted to accept Christian values in the least traumatic way possible.

MANUSCRIPTS

MS Valladolid, Archivo General de Simancas – Diversos de Castilla, libro 8, fol. 114 (about 1500)

EDITIONS & TRANSLATIONS

M.A. Ladero Quesada, *Los mudejares de Castilla en tiempos de Isabel I*, Valladolid, 1969, doc. 127 (new edition in *Granada después de la conquista. Repobladores y mudéjares*, Granada, 1993, pp. 545-48

T. de Azcona, *Isabel la Católica. Estudio crítico de su vida y su reinado*, Madrid, 1964, Appendix, pp. 761-63

STUDIES

Martínez Medina and Biersack, *Fray Hernando de Talavera*, pp. 345-52
Iannuzzi, *El poder de la palabra en el siglo XV*, pp. 459-63
Ladero Quesada, 'Fray Hernando de Talavera en 1492', pp. 272-74
de Azcona, *Isabel la Católica*, pp. 686-90

Isabella Iannuzzi

The Mufti of Oran

Abū l-ʿAbbās Aḥmad ibn Abī Jumʿa l-Maghrāwī l-Wahrānī

DATE OF BIRTH   Unknown; probably mid-15th century
PLACE OF BIRTH   Probably Oran, Algeria
DATE OF DEATH   3 June 1511
PLACE OF DEATH   Fez, Morocco

BIOGRAPHY

In 1504, a *fatwā* was directed from North Africa to the Moriscos in Spain, allowing them to live under Christian rule, hide their beliefs and pretend to profess Christianity. It was written by a 'mufti of Oran' called (with variants) Abū l-ʿAbbās Aḥmad ibn Abī Jumʿa l-Maghrāwī l-Wahrānī, who is virtually unknown. From the information contained in the Aljamiado (Spanish in Arabic letters) copies of the text, it was originally believed that he was born in Almagro in Spain (so he would be acquainted with the situation of the Moriscos), but Harvey has insisted that he must have belonged to the Berber tribe of Maghrāwa.

The recent work of Stewart has revealed a number aspects of his life. His family was native to the region of Maghrāwa in north-western Algeria. He was born in Oran in the mid-15th century and later moved to Tlemcen, where he studied Islamic law with outstanding teachers and where he became a famous professor. There he composed *Jāmiʿ jawāmiʿ al-ikhtiṣār wa-l-tibyān fī mā yaʿruḍu li-l-muʿallimīn wa-ābāʾ al-ṣibyān* in 1493, on the elementary education of Muslim children, possibly to prove his credentials as a teacher. His son Muḥammad ibn Abī Jumʿa Shaqrūn, himself a prominent scholar whose biography in Maghribī sources is conflated with his father's, may have been born in Tlemcen.

Later Aḥmad ibn Abī Jumʿa moved to Fez, where he worked as professor of Islamic law. There, he wrote his famous *fatwā* to Moriscos in Spain on 8 December 1504, possibly, as Stewart has suggested, in opposition to the opinion of the mufti, the great Aḥmad al-Wansharīsī, and thereby gained a high reputation in Fez. Aḥmad died in the city on 3 June 1511.

MAIN SOURCES OF INFORMATION

Primary
MS Madrid, Biblioteca de la Real Academia de la Historia – Gayangos 1922/36, Abū l-ʿAbbās Aḥmad ibn Abī Jumʿa, *Fatwā*, fols 343r-346r

Secondary
J. Hendrickson, 'The Islamic obligation to emigrate. Al-Wansharīsī's 'Asnā al-matājir' reconsidered', Atlanta GA, 2009 (Diss. Emory University)
D. Stewart, 'The identity of the "muftī of Oran", Abū-l-ʿAbbās Aḥmad b. Abī Jumʿah al-Maghrāwī al-Wahrānī (d. 917/1511)', *Al-Qanṭara* 27 (2006) 265-301
L.P. Harvey, *Muslims in Spain 1500 to 1614*, Chicago IL, 2005, pp. 60-64
M.J. Rubiera Mata, 'Los moriscos como criptomusulmanes y la *taqiyya*', in *Actas del VIII simposio internacional de estudios Mudéjares. Mudéjares y Moriscos, cambios sociales y culturales*, Teruel, 2004, 537-47
H. Bouzineb, 'Respuestas de jurisconsultos magrebíes en torno a la inmigración de musulmanes hispánicos', *Hesperis Tamuda* 27-28 (1988-89) 53-66
L. Cardaillac, *Morisques et chrétiens. Un affrontement polémique (1492-1640)*, Paris, 1977 (Spanish trans. by M. García-Arenal, México, 1979)
L.P. Harvey, 'Crypto-Islam in sixteenth-century Spain', *Actas del Primer Congreso de Estudios Árabes e Islámicos (Córdoba, 1962)*, Madrid, 1964, 163-79
P. Longás, *Vida religiosa de los moriscos*, Madrid, 1915 (new edition, Granada, 1990)

WORKS ON CHRISTIAN-MUSLIM RELATIONS

Fatwa del muftí de Orán, 'Fatwa of the mufti of Orán'
Respuesta que hizo el mufti de Orán a ciertas preguntas que [le] hicieron desde la Andalucía, 'Answer written by the mufti of Oran to some questions raised to him from al-Andalus'

DATE 8 December 1504
ORIGINAL LANGUAGE Spanish in Arabic letters (Aljamiado)

DESCRIPTION
This is a short text of only about eight folios in almost all versions. Although one Aljamiado manuscript dates it to 1563, all the other versions agree on 1 Rajab 910 (8 December 1504) as the date of composition. All the extant versions are of Spanish origin, and no copy has been found in North Africa or elsewhere. The Aljamiado versions have some

differences between them, and these in turn have substantial differences from the version in Latin characters.

The text takes the form of an answer to a question posed to al-Maghrāwī by some Moriscos around 1504. Though neither the formulation of the original question nor any information about the people who asked it has survived, most scholars identify it as a *fatwā*, or legal opinion.

For some centuries there had been arguments among Muslims about the legality of Muslims living under Christian rule in the Iberian Peninsula. This *fatwā* shows that al-Maghrāwī assumes these Muslims were going to stay there, and it offers patterns of behaviour for an Islamic way of life among infidels. In this it adopts a view that is opposite to majority Mālikī opinion, which recommends Muslims to leave *dār al-kufr* (land of unbelief).

Al-Maghrāwī differs in his opinion from his contemporary, Aḥmad al-Wansharīsī, the mufti of Fez. While not exactly opposed, since its starting point is different, al-Maghrāwī's *fatwā* develops the idea of a concealed Islamic life in a situation of danger, which would have been difficult for al-Wansharīsī to accept.

The work instructs the believer about ways to hide his Muslim beliefs while observing Christian rites and customs. The basic requirement is always to remain strong in the faith, and then it is permissible to say Christian prayers, attack the Prophet Muḥammad, drink wine, marry Muslim women to Christians, and so on, as long as the right intention (*niyya*) precedes actions.

Since 1964, historians have stressed that, in setting out these instructions, al-Maghrāwī develops the concept of *taqiyya*, prudence in a hostile environment (although the term is never used in the document). Although this is usually associated with Shīʿī Islam, Stewart has shown how it has also been developed in Sunnī Mālikī thought.

SIGNIFICANCE

Al-Maghrāwī's *fatwā* has become a very well-known document, because it is the only text that clearly pronounces on how Muslims should follow their own way of life under Christian rule. It is a key document not only for understanding the religiosity of the Morisco community, but also for understanding – even today – Islamic thinking about Muslims living outside *Dār al-Islām*. Although it had no sequel, nor any echo in the 16th and 17th centuries outside Spain, in the 20th century its contents and their implications have made it known worldwide. It is still under discussion why al-Maghrāwī would have placed himself outside traditional Islamic thinking about Muslim immigrants. According to Stewart, he would have done it for the sake of notoriety in Fez and in opposition to al-Wansharīsī, although the *fatwā* was evidently not circulated outside Spain.

MANUSCRIPTS

MS Vat – Borgiano Arabo 171, fols 2-4 (after 1519; Arabic)
MS Madrid, Biblioteca de la Real Academia de la Historia – 280.13, fols 28r-32r (1563; Aljamiado)
MS Aix-en-Provence, Bibliothèque Méjanes – 1223, fols 130-138 (1609)
MS Madrid, Biblioteca de la Real Academia de la Historia – Gayangos 1922/36, fols 343r-346r (first half of the 17th century; Spanish in Latin characters)

EDITIONS & TRANSLATIONS

M. Rosa-Rodríguez, 'Simulation and dissimulation. Religious hybridity in a Morisco *fatwā*', *Medieval Encounters* 16 (2010) 143-80, pp. 165-80 (edition and English trans. of the text in Latin characters from MS Biblioteca de la Real Academia de la Historia – Gayangos 1922/36)

M. Rosa-Rodríguez, 'Religiosidades en tránsito. El simulacro aljamiado en el siglo XVI español', Atlanta GA, 2009 (Diss. Emory University), pp. 117-23 (facsimile of MS Biblioteca de la Real Academia de la Historia – Gayangos 1922/36), pp. 124-36 (critical edition)

Rubiera Mata, 'Los moriscos como criptomusulmanes y la *taqiyya*', pp. 541-44 (Spanish trans. of the Arabic text)

Harvey, *Muslims in Spain*, pp. 61-63 (English trans. of the Arabic text)

P. Dressendörfer, *Islam unter der Inquisition. Die Morisco-Prozesse in Toledo 1575-1610*, Wiesbaden, 1971, pp. 137-41 (German trans. of the Arabic text)

Harvey, 'Crypto-Islam in sixteenth-century Spain', pp. 163-83 (edition and English trans. of the Arabic text)

L.P. Harvey, 'The literary culture of the Moriscos. A study based on the extant mss. in Arabic and Aljamia', Oxford, 1958 (Diss. University of Oxford), ii, pp. 184-88

Muḥammad 'Abd Allāh 'Inān, 'Wathīqa 'arabiyya jadīda tulqī ḍaw'an 'alā tārīkh al-mūriskiyyīn', *Majallat al-Thaqāfa*, Cairo (1952) 8-9; (also in 'Inān, *Nihāyat al-Andalus wa-tārīkh al-'arab al-mutanaṣṣirīn*, Cairo, 1958², pp. 325-27, 1966³, pp. 342-44) (edition of the Arabic text)

J. Cantineau, 'Lettre du Moufti d'Oran aux Musulmans d'Andalousie', *Journal Asiatique* 210 (1927) 1-17 (edition and French trans. of the Aljamiado text in MS Méjanes 1223)

Longás, *Vida religiosa de los moriscos*, pp. 305-7 (repr. García-Arenal, *Los moriscos*, pp. 44-45) (abridgement of the Aljamiado text in MS Madrid, Biblioteca de la Real Academia de la Historia – 280.13)

STUDIES

D. Stewart, 'Dissimulation in Sunni Islam and Morisco *taqiyya*', *Al-Qanṭara* 34 (2013) 439-90

L.F. Bernabé Pons, '*Taqiyya, niyya* y el islam de los moriscos', *Al-Qanṭara* 34 (2013) 491-527

Rosa-Rodríguez, 'Simulation and dissimulation'

A. Cheddadi, 'Émigrer ou rester? Le dilemme des morisques entre les fatwas et les contraintes du vécu', *Cahiers de la Méditerranée* 79 (2009) 31-50

Hendrickson, 'The Islamic obligation to emigrate'

Stewart, 'The identity of the "muftī of Oran"'

Harvey, *Muslims in Spain*, pp. 61-64

Rubiera Mata, 'Los moriscos como criptomusulmanes y la *taqiyya*'

D. Stewart, 'Documents and dissimulation. Notes on the performance of *taqiyya*', in C. de la Puente (ed.), *Identidades marginales*, Madrid, 2003, 569-98

J.P. Molénat, 'Le problème de la permanence des Musulmans dans les territoires conquis par les Chrétiens, du point de vue de la loi islamique', *Arabica* 48 (2001) 394-400

K.A. Miller, 'Muslim minorities and the obligation to emigrate to Islamic territory. Two fatwā-s from fifteenth-century Granada', *Islamic Law and Society* 7 (2000) 256-88

P.S. van Koningsveld, and G. Wiegers, 'The Islamic statute of the Mudejars in the light of a new source', *Al-Qanṭara* 17 (1996) 19-58

P.S. van Koningsveld and G. Wiegers, 'Islam in Spain during the early sixteenth century. The views of the four chief judges in Cairo (introduction, translation and Arabic text)', in O. Zwartjes, G.J. van Gelder and E.C.M. de Moor (eds), *Poetry, politics and polemics. Cultural transfer between the Iberian Peninsula and North Africa*, Leiden, 1997, 133-52

L. Sabbagh, 'La religion des Moriscos entre deux fatwas', in *Les Morisques et leur temps*, Paris, 1983, 43-56

K. Abou El Fadl, 'Islamic law and Muslims minorities. The Juristic discourse on Muslim minorities from the second/eight to the eleven/seventeenth centuries', *Islamic Law and Society* 1 (1994) 141-86

L.P. Harvey, 'The political, social and cultural history of the Moriscos', in S.K. Jayyusi (ed.), *The legacy of Muslim Spain*, Leiden, 1994, 201-34

M. Fierro, 'La emigración en el Islam. Conceptos antiguos, nuevos problemas', *Awrāq* 12 (1991) 11-41

M. Razūq, *Al-Andalusiyyūn wa-hijratuhum ilā l-Maghrib khilāl al-qarnayn 16-17*, Casablanca, 1989, 10, 148-55

Bouzineb, 'Respuestas de jurisconsultos magrebíes en torno a la inmigración de musulmanes hispánicos'

M. de Epalza, 'L'identité onomastique et linguistique des Morisques', in A. Temimi (ed.), *Religion, identité et sources documentaires sur les Morisques Andalous*, Tunis, 1984, 269-79

L. Cardaillac, 'Un aspecto de las relaciones entre moriscos y cristianos. Polémica y *taqiyya*', in Á. Galmés de Fuentes (ed.), *Actas del Coloquio internacional sobre literatura Aljamiada y Morisca (Oviedo, 1972)*, Madrid, 1978, 107-22

J. Vernet, 'La exégesis musulmana tradicional en los coranes aljamiados', in *Actas del coloquio internacional sobre literatura aljamiada y morisca*, Madrid, 1978, 123-45

Cardaillac, *Morisques et Chrétiens* (Spanish trans. by García-Arenal, México City, 1979)

Dressendörfer, *Islam unter der Inquisition*

Harvey, 'Crypto-Islam in sixteenth-century Spain', pp. 163-79

Harvey, 'The literary culture of the Moriscos'

Cantineau, 'Lettre du Moufti d'Oran aux musulmans d'Andalousie'

Longás, *Vida religiosa de los moriscos*

Luis Bernabé Pons

Pedro de Alcalá

DATE OF BIRTH About 1455
PLACE OF BIRTH Unknown
DATE OF DEATH Unknown; after 1508
PLACE OF DEATH Unknown

BIOGRAPHY

Almost nothing is known about Pedro de Alcalá. Since at least four places bear the name Alcalá – Alcalá de Guadaira, Alcalá de Henares, Alcalá del Río and Alcalá la Real – his origins are uncertain. More details can be inferred from his grammar. He informs his readers that when he wrote it he was 'between the first and second third of the average male lifespan'. Since he finished it in 1501, this means that he would have been born around 1455 (Pezzi, *Vocabulario*, p. 12). When the publisher Juan de Varela moved to Toledo, he handed his stock over to Pedro de Alcalá, including his copies of Alcalá's *Arte* and *Vocabulista*. This was on 1 February, 1508, and the last documented date on which Alcalá was known to be still alive (Norton, *Descriptive catalogue*, pp. 127-28). Apart from these details, it is known that Alcalá was a priest of the Order of Jerome and that he dedicated the prologue of his grammar to another member of the same order, Hernando de Talavera, whose confessor he was, and who in his turn was the confessor to Queen Isabella of Castile. He also says that his command of Arabic was limited, since he was too busy with other issues to learn it properly.

It has been suggested that Alcalá was a New Christian from a Muslim background, but as Corriente points out this is not probable, since if he was an ex-Mudéjar he would have been more proficient in Arabic and he would not have needed the help of the *sabios alfaquis*. Corriente argues that it is more plausible to think of him as a New Christian from a Jewish background (*Léxico árabe andalusí*, p. ii), which is partly supported by references such as *dagueç, cameç* ('candilejos', 'cabañuelas de judíos'), although since these words appear in Antonio de Nebrija's dictionary of about 1495, this suggestion is not persuasive. In addition to his weakness in Arabic, Alcalá's knowledge of Castilian and grammar was not advanced.

MAIN SOURCES OF INFORMATION

Primary

Pedro de Alcalá, *Arte para ligeramente saber la lengua arauiga*, Salamanca, 1505
Pedro de Alcalá, *Vocabulista arauigo en letra castellana*, Salamanca, 1505

Secondary

O. Zwartjes, 'More on "Arabic linguistic terminology in Pedro de Alcalá"', *Historiographia Linguistica* 41 (2014) 247-97

O. Zwartjes, 'Algunas observacions sobre el *Vocabulista arauigo en letra castellana* (1505) de Pedro de Alcalá y el *Vocabulario español-latino* (c. 1495) de Antonio de Nebrija', in M.L. Calero Vaquera et al. (eds), *Actas del IX congreso internacional de la Sociedad Española de Historiografía Lingüística*, Münster, 2014 forthcoming

M. García Arenal, 'The religious identity of the Arabic language and the affair of the Lead Books of the Sacromonte of Granada', *Arabica* 56 (2009) 495-528, pp. 500-3

M.J. Framiñán de Miguel, 'Manuales para el adoctrinamiento de neoconversos en el siglo XVI', *Criticón* 93 (2005) 25-37, pp. 28-30

A. Lonnet, *Les textes de Pedro de Alcalá. Édition critique*, Paris, 2002, pp. 3-9

O. Zwartjes, 'El lenguaje en la catequización de los moriscos de Granada y los indígenas de Latinoamérica. Las obras de los gramáticos como vehículo entre instrucción religiosa y pensamiento lingüístico', in S. Dedenbach-Salazar Sáenz and L. Crickmay (eds), *La lengua de la cristianización en Latinoamérica. Catequización e instrucción en lenguas amerindias*, Schwaben, 1999, 17-40

Abdelouahab el-Imrani, 'Lexicografía hispano-árabe. Aproximación al análisis de cinco diccionarios elaborados por religiosos españoles', Madrid, 1998 (Diss., Universidad Complutense de Madrid), pp. 27-29

G. Drost, 'El Arte de Pedro de Alcalá y su vocabulista[.] de tolerancia a represión', in A. Temimi (ed.), *Las pácticas musulmanes de los moriscos andaluces (1492-1609)*, Zaghouan, 1989, 57-69

E. Pezzi, *El vocabulario de Pedro de Alcalá*, Almería, 1989

F. Corriente, *El léxico árabe andalusí según P. de Alcalá (Ordenado por raíces. Corregido, anotado y fonémicamente interpretado)*, Madrid, 1988, pp. i-vii

E. Pezzi, 'El problema de la confesión de moriscos en Pedro de Alcalá', in *Homenaje al profesor Darío Cabanelas Rodríguez, O.F.M., con motivo de su LXX aniversario*, Granada, 1987, 433-44

Á. Galmés de Fuentes, 1985. 'Los romancismos de Pedro de Alcalá como testimonio del mozárabe de Granada (Estudio fonético)', in A. Moll (ed.), *XVI Congrés internacional de lingüística i folologia Romàniques. Actes*, Palma de Mallorca, 1985, ii, 461-62

G. Drost, 'De Moriscos in de publicaties van Staat en Kerk (1492-1609). Een bijdrage tot het historisch discriminatieonderzoek', Leiden, 1984 (PhD Diss. University of Leiden), pp. 83-106

Y. Anssens-Lestienne, 'L'arabe andalou. Sources et bibliographie', in *Matériaux arabes et sudarabiques (MAS). Recherches en cours*, Paris, 1983, 20-23

F.J. Norton, *A descriptive catalogue of printing in Spain and Portugal, 1501-1520*, Cambridge, 1978, particularly pp. 124-26

J. Fück, *Die arabischen Studien in Europa bis in den Anfang des 20. Jahrhunderts*, Leipzig, 1955, pp. 29-34

A. Steiger, *Contribución a la fonética del hispano-árabe y de los arabismos en el ibero-románico y el siciliano*, Madrid, 1932

R. Ricard, 'Remarques sur l'*Arte* et le *Vocabulista* de Fr. Pedro de Alcalá', in Ricard, *Études et documents pour l'histoire missionnaire de l'Espagne et du Portugal*, Louvain, 1930

F.J. Simonet, 'Fuentes hispano-arábigas', in *Glosario de voces ibéricas y latinas usadas entre los mozárabes precedido de un estudio sobre el dialecto hispano-mozárabe*, Madrid, 1888, pp. clxv-clxix

WORKS ON CHRISTIAN-MUSLIM RELATIONS

Arte para ligeramente saber la lengua arauiga, 'The art of gently learning Arabic'

DATE 1505
ORIGINAL LANGUAGE Spanish

DESCRIPTION
This grammatical work contains 96 folios and describes colloquial Arabic as it was spoken in Granada, followed by religious texts, such as sermons, a catechism and other material. Most of these have the Spanish in the left-hand column and the Arabic translation on the right. Some sections, particularly the *articuli fidei* are bilingual (Latin and Arabic). There are two editions of the *Arte*. According to Norton (*A descriptive catalogue*), the first was printed in 1505 and the second possibly in 1506, though Fück (*Die arabischen Studien*, p. 31) holds that both were printed in 1505. There are very few differences between the two.

Alcalá does not mention any sources, but it is probable that he used Nebrija's Latin grammar (first edition 1481), and maybe also the bilingual edition that appeared in 1495, as well as some other sources (Zwartjes, 'Inflection and government', p. 215).

When the first mass conversions from Islam to Christianity took place in 1500, missionaries who gave instruction on Christianity needed help. The work was published on 5 February 1505, though since there were great changes in attitudes towards Muslims and new converts at about this time, it is difficult to see what use it then had. The former policy had been to reason with Muslims and to bring them to conversion by their own consent, but this was now abandoned in favour of forced baptism. The *Arte* was therefore composed just as the old policy was giving way to the new.

Alcalá's work is 'free from polemics' (Framiñán de Miguel, 'Manuales', p. 30), though with one small exception. In the Prologue he compares the 'real spiritual washing' of Christians with the Muslim ritual of washing the feet, using the term *Moros* and writing in the third person. He hints here that he regards Muslims as outsiders who do not speak 'our language' and who have a religion different from 'ours'. Apart from this, however, he goes out of his way to make new converts feel at home. In the religious texts the term *Allāh* is used for God, often with the accompanying adjective *azgueguel* or *azeguejél* (for Arabic *'azz wa-ẓall*) and the epitet *çubhánahu* (for *subḥānahu*), while *miḥrāb* is used for 'altar' and *ṣalāt* for 'mass'. These would be well-known to new converts from Islam, and their familiarity might ease the converts' acceptance of new ways.

SIGNIFICANCE

Hernando de Talavera (1428-1507), who became the first Archbishop of Granada in 1493, declared that priests should learn Arabic in order to reason with Muslims and lead them to voluntary conversion. This policy contrasted with that of Cardinal Francisco Jiménez de Cisneros (1436-1517), whose forced conversion policy culminated in a direct confrontation between the two religious groups. The *Arte*, with grammar and religious texts, followed by a Spanish-Arabic dictionary (*Vocabulista arauigo en letra castellana*) that had been compiled earlier, would have been written as part of Talavera's policy. Alcalá wrote his grammar for priests who were carrying out this policy to help them communicate Christianity more easily. It was a pioneering work, and incorporated the first system for transliterating Arabic into Roman characters.

EDITIONS & TRANSLATIONS

P. de Lagarde (ed.), *Petri Hispani de lingua arabica libri duo Pauli de Lagarde studio et sumptibus repetiti*, Gottingen, 1883, https://archive.org/details/petrihispanideloolagagoog

Arte para ligera mente saber la lengua arauiga emendada y añadida y Segundamente imprimida, Salamanca: Juan Varela, 1506 (facsimile edition, New York, 1928)

Arte para ligeramente saber la lengua arauiga, Salamanca: Juan Varela, before 5 February 1505

Vocabulista arauigo en letra castellana, Salamanca: Juan Varela, before 5 February, 1505, http://www.cervantesvirtual.com/obra-visor/vocabulista-arauigo-en-letra-castellana--3/html/

STUDIES

O. Zwartjes and M. Woidich, 'Damascus Arabic according to the *Compendio* of Lucas Caballero (1709)', in A. Schippers and L. Zack (eds), *Middle Arabic and mixed Arabic. Diachrony and synchrony*, Leiden, 2012, 295-333

F. Corriente, 'Missionary's Middle Arabic. The case of Late Andalusi', in J. Lentin and J. Grand'Henry (eds), *Moyen arabe et variétés mixtes de l'arabe à travers l'histoire. Actes du premier colloque international (Louvain-la-Neuve, 10-14 mai 2004)*, Louvain-la-Neuve, 2008, 87-98

F. Corriente, 'Ibero-Romance loanwords', in K. Versteegh (ed.), *Encyclopedia of Arabic language and linguistics*, Leiden, 2007, ii, pp. 287-90

O. Zwartjes, 'Agreement asymmetry in Arabic according to Spanish missionary grammarians from Damascus (18th century)', in O. Zwartjes, G. James and E. Ridruejo (eds), *Missionary linguistics III/ Lingüística misionera III. Morphology and syntax. Selected papers from the Third and Fourth International Conferences on Missionary Linguistics, Hong Kong/ Macau, 12-15 March 2005, Valladolid, 8-11 March 2006*, Amsterdam, 2007, 273-303

O. Zwartjes, 'Inflection and government in Arabic according to Spanish missionary grammarians from Damascus (XVIIIth century). Grammars at the crossroads of two systems', in H. Motzki and E. Ditters (eds), *Approaches to Arabic linguistics presented to Kees Versteegh on the occasion of his sixtieth birthday*, Leiden, 2007, 209-44

M.J. Framiñán de Miguel, 'Manuales para el adoctrinamiento de neoconversos en el siglo XVI', *Criticón* 93 (2005) 25-37

O. Zwartjes, 'El lenguaje en la catequización de los moriscos de Granada y los indígenas de Latinoamérica. Las obras de los gramáticos como vehículo entre instrucción religiosa y pensamiento lingüístico', in S. Dedenbach-Salazar Sáenz, and L. Crickmay (eds), *La lengua de la cristianización en Latinoamérica. Catequización e instrucción en lenguas amerindias/The language of Christianisation in Latin America. Catechisation and instruction in Amerindian languages*, Schwaben, 1999, 17-40

O. Zwartjes, 'Tradición e innovación en las gramáticas pioneras de Antonio de Nebrija y Pedro de Alcalá. La categoría gramatical del pronombre', in R. Escavy, J.M. Hernández Terrés and A. Roldán Pérez (eds), *Actas del Congreso Internacional de Historiografía Lingüística. Nebrija V Centenario*, Murcia, 1994, iii, 651-65

O. Zwartjes, 'El artículo en las gramáticas pioneras de Antonio de Nebrija y Pedro de Alcalá y las gramáticas de la tradición grecolatina', in M.P.A.M. Kerkhof, H. de Schepper and O. Zwartjes (eds), *Espana: ¿Ruptura 1492?*, Amsterdam, 1993, 261-86

F. Corriente, *Árabe andalusí y lenguas romances*, Madrid, 1992

G. Drost, 'El Arte de Pedro de Alcalá y su vocabulista. De tolerancia a represión', in A. Temimi (ed.), *Las pácticas musulmanes de los moriscos andaluces (1492-1609)*, Zaghouan, 1989, 57-69

J.R. Jones, 'Learning Arabic in Renaissance Europe (1505-1624)', London, 1988 (Diss. School of Oriental and African Studies)

E. Pezzi, 'El problema de la confesión de moriscos en Pedro de Alcalá', in D. Cabanelas (ed.), *Homenaje al profesor Darío Cabanelas Rodríguez, O.F.M.*, Granada, 1987, 433-44

G. Drost, 'De Moriscos in de publicaties van Staat en Kerk (1492-1609). Een bijdrage tot het historisch discriminatieonderzoek', Leiden, 1984 (Diss. University of Leiden)

Y. Anssens-Lestienne, 'L'arabe andalou. Sources et bibliographie', in *Matériaux arabes et sudarabiques (MAS). Recherches en cours*, Paris, 1983, 11-59

W. Cowan, 'Arabic grammatical terminology in Pedro de Alcalá', *Historiographia Linguistica* 8/2-3 (1981) 357-63

F. Corriente, 'Notas de lexicología hispano-árabe', *Awrāq* 4 (1981) 5-27

F.J. Simonet, 'Fuentes hispano-arábigas', in F.J. Simonet (ed.), *Glosario de voces ibéricas y latinas usadas entre los mozárabes precedido de un estudio sobre el dialecto hispano-mozárabe*, Madrid, 1888, clix-clxxi, https://archive.org/stream/glosariodevocesooespagoog#page/n0/mode/2up

W. Wright, 'Prologue', in Lagarde (ed.), *Petri Hispani de lingua arabica libri duo*, iii-vii

L. del Mármol Carvajal, *Historia del rebelión y castigo de los moriscos del Reino de Granada*, Málaga: Iuan Rene a costa del autor, 1600, 1852 (on-line edition: http://www.biblioteca.org.ar/libros/131280.pdf)

Otto Zwartjes

Juan Andrés

DATE OF BIRTH About 1450
PLACE OF BIRTH Játiva, Spain
DATE OF DEATH After 1515
PLACE OF DEATH Unknown

BIOGRAPHY

Born in eastern Spain, just inland from Valencia in Játiva, close to the middle of the 15th century, Juan Andrés, who was originally known as Ibn 'Abdallāh, was the son of the village's *faqīh* (jurisprudent). On his father's death, he inherited this office and worked as *faqīh* until he experienced a revelation in the Cathedral of Valencia during the service for the feast of the Assumption, led by the Dominican Juan Marqués in 1487. In this, '[they]removed and clarified the darkness of my understanding, and then the eyes of my soul opened', as he says in the prologue of his work *Confusión o confutación de la secta mahomética*. When he became a Christian, he took the name Juan Andrés.

According to Pérez Puchal, in 1418 Játiva and its surroundings had around 2,800 families, amounting to nearly 10,000 inhabitants (Pérez Puchal, *Geografía*, p. 14), while López Elum puts the number in 1493 at around 382 families (López Elum, 'La población', p. 162). Even taking into account different standards of measurement, this striking reduction in numbers suggests that a substantial percentage of the population either succumbed to illness or left the area during the course of the 15th century. Without doubt, Juan Andrés witnessed the emigration of many of those he grew up with and those whom he served in his legal work. Some emigrants would have gone to Valencia, others to the kingdom of Granada, or to North Africa.

As the son of the *faqīh*, Ibn 'Abdallāh would have studied in a centre such as Valencia or Granada (Bernabé Pons, 'Mudéjares valencianos', p. 153). His knowledge of Arabic is apparent from the skill with which he moves between the Qur'an and Sunna in his writing. One also senses his ease with the language in the way he talks about his travels after becoming a Christian through the newly conquered lands of the still Muslim Granada to preach in Arabic to the Muslim faithful. He must also have been fluent in Aragonese, into which he made a now lost translation of the Qur'an, and he had a cursory knowledge of Latin, was acquainted with elements of astrology (he mentions Ptolemy, ed. Ruiz García and García-Monge, p. 155), geography (p. 218), secular literature (he refers to Juan del Encina, p. 155), and current political events (the king's plan to conquer North Africa, p. 225), as well as the Bible.

Next to nothing is known about Juan's personal life apart from what he tells us in his work. On experiencing his vision in the cathedral of Valencia in August 1487, he asked to be baptised and to be given the names of the Apostles John and Andrew. He set out to convert his former co-religionists to Christianity, and in the prologue to *Confusión o confutación* he says that he converted many in Valencia: 'First I carried out conversions in the Kingdom of Valencia, and in the end I saved the souls of many Moorish infidels.' At some point after 1492, he was called by the rulers Isabel and Ferdinand to preach alongside Martín García and Hernando de Talavera to the Moors of Granada. By his own account, he was very successful and converted 'infinita morisma' (p. 90). Sometime later, certainly before 1504, his ecclesiastical career began in earnest as the Catholic monarchs made him a canon in Granada (p. 90). He does not mention holding other offices in the church, which might suggest that he did not advance further, unlike Martín García and Hernando de Talavera. In the summer of 1499, the Catholic Monarchs visited Granada and replaced Hernando de Talavera with Francisco Jiménez de Cisneros (1436-1517), who used a much heavier hand in his preaching. This change in approach to preaching, and the change in personnel, probably affected Juan's professional career.

Queen Isabel, who emerges as Juan Andrés's protector, arranged for him to return to Aragón to preach there, but she died in 1504 before he was able to begin. Since Ferdinand was much less keen than Isabel to force the Mudéjar population in Aragón to convert, Juan found a new patron in Granada, Martín García Puyazuelo (1441-1521), who had become bishop of Barcelona and then Inquisitor General of Aragón. For Martín García, Juan says that he translated the Qur'an with its glosses, and the books of the Sunna into Aragonese to aid in preaching to the Muslims in Aragón (p. 91). In late 1505, Fray Hernando de Talavera, Archbishop of Granada, with whom Juan had worked as a missionary in Granada, was accused of heresy by the Inquisition and imprisoned. The news spread throughout Spain and it must have affected Juan strongly.

Around 1515 when he was writing the prologue to *Confusión o confutación*, Juan says that he is in Valencia and is a priest (p. 90).

MAIN SOURCES OF INFORMATION

Primary

E. Ruiz García and M.I. García-Monge (eds), *Confusión o confutación de la secta mahomética y del Alcorán*, Mérida, 2003 (based on the original Spanish edition of 1515)

Nothing is known about Juan Andrés from contemporary sources, apart from what appears in *Confusión o confutación de la secta mahomética*.

Secondary

M.J. Framiñan de Miguel, 'Manuales para el adoctrinamiento de neoconversos en el siglo XVI', *Criticón* 93 (2005) 25-37

V. Pascual y Beltrán, 'Setabenses en la corte de los Reyes Católicos', *Cuadernos de la Historia Jerónimo Zurita* 19-20 (1997) 241-53

L.F. Bernabé Pons, 'Mudéjares valencianos viajan a Granada', *Sharq al-Andalus* 9 (1992) 151-55

M. De Epalza, *Los moriscos antes y después de la expulsion*, Madrid, 1992

R.G. Pérez de Tudela, 'Notas para un estudio de la Morería de Játiva (1519-1529)', in A. Temimi (ed.), *Religion, identité et sources documentaires sur les morisques andalous*, Tunis, 1984, 225-68

P. López Elum, 'La población de la morería de Játiva (1493)', in *Estudios de Historia de Valencia*, Valencia, 1978, 161-70

P. Pérez Puchal, *Geografía de la población valenciana*, Valencia, 1976

J. Vernet, 'Traducciones moriscas de El Coran', in *Der Orient in der Forschung. Festschrift für Otto Spies*, Wiesbaden, 1966, 686-705

F. Pons Boigues, 'Retazos moriscos', *El Archivo* 3 (1889) 131-34

WORKS ON CHRISTIAN-MUSLIM RELATIONS

Confusión o confutación de la secta mahomética, 'Confusion or confutation of the sect of Muḥammad'

DATE 1515
ORIGINAL LANGUAGE   Spanish

DESCRIPTION

Confusión o confutación de la secta Mahomética y del Alcorán was published in Valencia in 1515 in an edition 72 pages long. Juan Andrés intends that it will both cause Muslims to doubt their holy books, and refute in advance arguments that experts in Islam might put forward against Christianity.

The prologue recounts Muḥammad's birth and the emergence of Islam, and this leads into Juan's own former life as a Muslim, which he recalls in order to demonstrate his intimate knowledge of Islam and to argue that if he can convert then others would do well to follow him. His work is conceived and organised around the central purpose of laying out the inconsistencies and contradictions of Islam. There are 12 chapters.

Chapter 1 comments on the life and legacy of Muḥammad, while Chapters 2 and 3 address the principles of Islam found in the Qur'an and Sunna. Chapters 4 and 5 refute these works, with Juan denouncing the fallacies in them and adducing proofs to show that the Qur'an is not revelation. In the following chapters, he attacks the figure of the Prophet himself with little respect or tact, using such arguments as the disagreement among the first Muslims over Muḥammad's night journey, the redirecting of the *qibla* from Jerusalem to Mecca and the change in the season of fasting, both in order to distinguish Islam from Judaism. Juan appears to enjoy pointing out the Prophet's supposed errors, such as praising idols, or in falling prey to his own desire for one of his servant's wives, and he accuses Muḥammad of being a less than perfect example.

Juan devotes the whole of Chapter 7 to portraying Muḥammad as an adulterer with 11 wives, only two of them virgins, thus underlining the stark contrast between the Prophet and the virtuous Jesus Christ. Chapter 8 deals with Muḥammad's ascension on Alborak through the heavens until he finds Jesus in the seventh heaven. He questions how an animal could enter into paradise, given its bodily functions, and especially how Muḥammad could provide no witnesses for this miracle. In Chapter 9, he undermines Islamic arguments concerning the virgins and the gold and silver promised in paradise, in particular questioning the happiness of women in paradise when they realise their husbands are taking pleasure in other women's company. Chapter 10 deals with the contradictions in the Qur'an and some of Muḥammad's miracles, which he calls *burlas* ('jokes'). Chapter 11 is a defence of Christianity and Chapter 12 is a denial that the apparently miraculous expansion of the Islamic Empire is proof of its authenticity.

Juan's arguments are backed up with constant references from both Qur'an and Sunna, and on occasion he also cites the *Sīra*, the biography of the Prophet according to Ibn Hishām. He often quotes substantial passages from the Qur'an with translations, though his quotations from the Sunna are less frequent and more imprecise (ed. Ruiz García and

García-Monge, p. 44). He claims that Muḥammad used two *espaderos*, or Christian scribes, as principal sources for the Qur'an (ed. Ruiz García and García-Monge, p. 151), and he criticises Muḥammad's inability to work true miracles, which he says God used throughout sacred history to set apart true prophets.

Juan ends the work with a narrative of the extremely violent struggles for power among those who succeeded the Prophet. He points out the assassinations of the caliphs, one after another, implying how different the evolution of Islam was from that of Christianity.

SIGNIFICANCE

Juan's *Confusión o confutación* was published in Valencia by Juan Joffre. This *anti-alcorán* reflects a continuation of the medieval tradition of heavy-handed church propaganda against the minority Jewish and Muslim populations in Spain. At the same time, its language – Spanish vernacular with a popular tone – together with Juan's use of primary sources from the roots of Islam, shows that the spirit of Renaissance humanism had penetrated the minds of Morisco intellectuals from the small towns of eastern Spain. There is no known record of Juan Andrés after 1515, and his book quickly became scarce in Spain.

EDITIONS & TRANSLATIONS

Ruiz García and García-Monge, *Confusión o confutación de la secta mahomética y del Alcorán* (includes details of Italian editions from 1537, 1540, 1541, 1545, and 1597, and Latin editions from 1600 and 1656)

D. Capell, *Des für 200. Jahren bekelrten Doctoris, Professoris und Praedicatoris der Muhammedischen Lehre Johannis Andreae Mauri, Nachdenkliches Buch gegen den Mahomet und die Mahomedische falsche Lehere*, Hamburg: G. Wulff, 1685 (German trans.)

Joshua Notstock, *The confusion of Muhamed's sect, or a confutation of the Turkish Alcoran*, London: H. Blundell, 1652 (English trans.)

De verwoestinge van de Mahometische of Turxsche religie. dat is, een sonne-klaar ende onwederleggelijk bewijs, dat Mahomet een valsch, ende onse Saligmaker Jesus een waarachtig propheet is, Rotterdam, 1651 (Dutch trans.)

C. Celio and J. Lauterbach, *Confusio sectae Mahometanae*, Frankfurt, 1647 (Latin and German trans.)

C. Celio, *Confusio sectae mahometanae*, Lipsiae: N. Merlich, 1598 (German trans.)

Johannes Lauterbach and De Gisbertus Voetius, *Confusio sectae mahometanae*, Lipsiae: Abraham Lamberg, 1594 (Latin trans.)

De zeer wonderlijcke ende warachtighe historie van Mahomet. inde welcke beschreven ende verhaelt wordt zijn gheboorte, afcomste, leven ende valsche leeringhe, mette confutatie oft wederlegginge van den Alcoran ende quade secte des selfs Mahomet, trans. D.S., Antwerp, 1580 (Dutch trans.)

G. Le Fèvre de la Boderie, *Confusion de la secte de Muhamed*, Paris: M. Le Jeune, 1574 (French trans.)

Confusión o confutación de la secta mahomética y del Alcorán, 1543 (http://www.bibliotecadeextremadura.com/obras_bib_barca_4.htm)

Opera chiamata Confusione della setta machumetana, trans. Domenico de Gaztelu, Venice [?], 1537 (first Italian trans.)

Libro nueuamente imprimido que se llama confusion dela secta mahomatica y d'alcorā, Valencia, 1515

STUDIES

Framiñan de Miguel, 'Manuales para el adoctrinamiento de neoconversos en el siglo XVI', 25-37

Pascual y Beltrán, 'Setabenses en la corte de los Reyes Católicos'

Bernabé Pons, 'Mudéjares valencianos viajan a Granada'

De Epalza, *Los moriscos antes y después de la expulsion*

Pérez de Tudela, 'Notas para un estudio de la Morería de Játiva (1519-1529)'

López Elum, 'La población de la morería de Játiva (1493)'

Pérez Puchal, *Geografía de la población valenciana*

Vernet, 'Traducciones moriscas de El Coran'

Pons Boigues, 'Retazos moriscos'

Zachary Zuwiyya

Martín García

Martín García Puyazuelo

DATE OF BIRTH 1441
PLACE OF BIRTH Caspe, Zaragoza
DATE OF DEATH 1521
PLACE OF DEATH Caspe

BIOGRAPHY

In his early life Martín García was a simple shepherd in his native Caspe. He began his studies at La Seo de Zaragoza, and in 1476 he went on to the College of St Clemente of Bologna. He was made canon of La Seo de Zaragoza, and took part in the activities of the Inquisition. He also became concerned about Islam, and studied Arabic. In 1489, he was elected prior of San Vicente de Roda, and in 1494 Isabella and Ferdinand made him responsible for reforming the convents in the dioceses of Zaragoza, Huesca, Lérida and Tarazona.

In the early years of the 16th century, he was appointed by Queen Isabella, on the advice of Cardinal Francisco Jiménez de Cisneros, to give instruction to the Moors in Granada. He met Juan Andrés, a convert to Christianity, and with Juan's help he deepened his knowledge of Islam, and wrote a refutation, now lost, of the Qur'an and the Sunna, *Refutación del Corán*. His *Sermons* from these years also contain copious references to Islam.

In 1511, García was appointed Bishop of Barcelona, although he only took up his position some years later, because he served as ambassador in Rome and attended the Fifth Lateran Council. His advanced age prevented him from receiving the Emperor Charles V in Barcelona when a meeting of the Order of the Golden Fleece was held in Barcelona cathedral in 1519. He died in 1521 in Caspe, to where he had retired.

MAIN SOURCES OF INFORMATION

Primary
D. García, *Epítome de la santa vida y relación de la gloriosa muerte del venerable Pedro de Arbués*, Madrid, 1664
J.A. de Hebrera, *Vida prodigiosa del Ilmo. y V.D. Martín García, Obispo de Barcelona, hijo de la Fidelísima y Antigua Villa de Caspe*, Zaragoza, 1700

J.A. Sesma Muñoz, *El establecimiento de la Inquisición en Aragón (1484-1486), Documentos para su estudio*, Zaragoza, 1987

M. Combescure and M.A. Motis (eds), *El libro Verde de Aragón*, Zaragoza, 2003, pp. 204-9

Juan Andrés, *Confusion o confutación de la secta mahomética y del Alcorán*, ed. E. Ruiz García and M.I. García-Monge, Mérida, 2003, pp. 9-83

Martín García Puyazuelo, *La ética de Catón*, ed. and trans. J. Francisco Sánchez López, Zaragoza, 2009

Secondary

B. Ducharme, 'De Talavera a Ramírez de Haro. Actores y representaciones de la evangelización de los mudéjares y moriscos en Granada, Zaragoza y Valencia (1492-1545)', in E. Serrano Martín (ed.), *De la tierra al cielo. Líneas recientes de investigación en Historia Moderna*, Zaragoza, 2013, 39-52, www.hmoderna.cchs.csic.es/webfehm/

J. Baldó Alcoz, art. 'García Puyazuelo, Martín', in *Diccionario biográfico español*, Madrid, 2009, xx, 216-17

M. Gómez-Ferrer, 'El cardenal Guillem Ramón de Vich y las relaciones entre Roma y Valencia a comienzos del siglo XVI', in F. Lemerle, Y. Pauwels and G. Toscano (eds), *Cardinaux de la Renaissance et la modernité artistique*, Villeneuve d'Ascq, 2009, 197-216

J. Goñi, art. 'García, Martín', in *Diccionario de historia eclesiástica de España*, Madrid, 1987, Supplement i, 357-60

Á. Alcalá, *Los orígenes de la Inquisición en Aragón. San Pedro Arbués, mártir de la autonomía aragonesa*, Zaragoza, 1984

J. García Oro, *Cisneros y la reforma del clero español en tiempo de los Reyes Católicos*, Madrid, 1971

T. Azcona, *Isabel la Católica. Estudio crítico de su vida y de su reinado*, Madrid, 1964

L. Sancho Bonal, *Leyenda histórica sobre la vida del ilustre obispo de Barcelona don Martín García*, Zaragoza, 1905

WORKS ON CHRISTIAN-MUSLIM RELATIONS

Sermones eminentissimi Martini Garcie, 'Sermons of the most eminent Martín García'

DATE 1517
ORIGINAL LANGUAGE Latin

DESCRIPTION
A selection of Martín García's sermons, preached at different times of the year, was prepared for publication and translated into Latin from

the original Castilian (its title in full is *Sermones eminentissimi, totiusque Barchinonensis gregis tutatoris acerrimi, necnon immarcessibilis sacre theologie paludamento insigniti Martini Garcie*, 'Sermons of the most eminent Martín García, the most active guardian of the whole flock of Barcelona, adorned with the cloak of imperishable sacred theology'). The text comprises 155 sermons in 476 pages, with the structure of most following the typical pattern of the time: an *introduction*, which contains comments on a biblical text, and the *crux*, which applies it to the occasion being observed. It is in the latter that the arguments against Jews or Muslims are developed and the need to convert to Christianity emphasised. Most of the sermons are on themes related to the Virgin Mary, or on the occasions of the liturgical year. Martín García had a particular devotion to the Virgin and died at the foot of a statue of the Virgin of Monserrat.

The sermons that particularly focus on Jews and Muslims are: 5, 14-39, 68, 69, 86, 90, 106, 125, 127, 130 and 138. Here Martín cites the Qur'an, the Sunna and Muslim scholars more than 300 times, among them al-Bukhārī, Muslim ibn Ḥajjāj, al-Ghazālī and Ibn Sīnā, showing that he was making use of his own lost *Refutación del Corán*. In his comments about the Qur'an, he very often mixes the text itself with glosses from Muslim authors, a mistake which his great friend Juan Andrés, whose influence is evident throughout the sermons, never makes. Following Torquemada and Juan de Segovia, García was obsessed with proving the truth of the main Christian teachings, and engages in detailed analyses of them.

The sermons would have been addressed to congregations of both Muslims and old Christians, which meant that they had to contain clear justification for Christianity and also show the errors of Islam. Since Islam was for García a religion near to extinction, and conversion to the true faith was the obvious path to take, he tended to follow the traditional schemes of the treatises of earlier Christian polemics, even though he had at his disposal sources of information and instruments of critique and analysis of far higher quality than earlier authors.

SIGNIFICANCE

The difference between Martín García's sermons and many other contemporary Christian works is that he shows he thinks Islam is superfluous, closer to superstition than to religious belief, and he tends to treat it with some condescension. In order to prove his points he does not hesitate to make twisted and forced interpretations of the Qur'an and

Hadiths, or to attribute divinity to Muḥammad, and he makes the mistake of thinking that his listeners were ignorant people.

EDITIONS & TRANSLATIONS

Sermones eminentissimi, totiusque Barchinonensis gregis tutatoris acerrimi, necnon immarcessibilis sacre theologie paludamento insigniti Martini Garcie, Zaragoza, 1520

STUDIES

J.F. Sánchez López, 'Dialectismos aragoneses en las coplas a nuestro señor de Martín García Puyazuelo', *Anales. Anuario del Centro de la UNED de Catalayud* 17 (2009) 123-41

A. Echevarría, *The fortress of faith. The attitude towards Muslims in fifteenth-century Spain*, Leiden, 1999

J.M. Ribera Florit, 'La polémica cristiano-musulmana en los sermones del maestro inquisidor don Martín García', Barcelona, 1967 (Diss. University of Barcelona)

N. Daniel, *Islam and the West*, Edinburgh, 1962

S. Cirac Estepona, *Los sermones de Don Martín García, Obispo de Barcelona sobre los Reyes Católicos*, Zaragoza, 1956

S. Cirac Estepona, 'Don Martín García, canónigo de Zaragoza y obispo de Barcelona (s. XV-XVI), predicador máximo de la Virgen María', in C. Morcillo (ed.), *Estudios Mariológicos. Memoria del congreso Mariano nacional de Zaragoza*, Zaragoza, 1956, 663-712

Miguel Ángel de Bunes

Joan Martí Figuerola

DATE OF BIRTH About 1457
PLACE OF BIRTH Valencia
DATE OF DEATH After 23 July 1532
PLACE OF DEATH Unknown

BIOGRAPHY

Details about Joan Martí Figuerola's life are very sparse, and come mostly from his own works. He does not appear in traditional bibliographical lists, or (with the exception of Nicolás Antonio's *Bibliotheca Hispana nova*) is mistaken for another writer from the 14th century with the same name. He was a master in *sacra theologia* and a papal chaplain, and was attached to Valencia cathedral. He is known to have been in Italy in 1507, perhaps with the help of his uncle, Miguel Figuerola, bishop of Pati in Sicily. He knew Arabic, having been taught by the alfaqui of Teruel, who later converted to Christianity and took the name Joan Gabriel.

By order of King Ferdinand, he preached against Islam in Zaragoza in the years 1517-18. His belligerent attitude caused tension between Christians and Muslims, and he was ordered to stop by the Emperor Charles V. He retired to his home town, and must have died sometime after 23 July 1532, on which date his name appears on a document of exchange of benefice at the Church of San Martin in Valencia.

Joan Martí wrote only two works, in both of which he makes clear his disagreement with the religious policy of Charles V and the Consejo Real. *Disputas* ('Disputes') is an account of his preaching activities in Zaragoza, while *Lumbre de la fé contra la secta mahomética* ('Light of faith against the Muḥammadan sect') is a treatise demonstrating the superiority of the teachings of Christianity over the Qur'an.

MAIN SOURCES OF INFORMATION

Primary
MS Madrid, Biblioteca de la Real Academia de la Historia – Colección Gayangos 19-36: *Disputas*, fols 253ra-265rb; *Lumbre de la fé contra la secta mahomética*, fols Ora-vb, Cl-v, 1ra, 3vb, 91rb, 114rb, 207ra, 239rb, 267r

Secondary
K. Reinhardt and H. Santiago-Otero, *Biblioteca bíblica ibérica medieval*, Madrid, 1986, p. 264
M.M. Cárcel Ortí, 'La diócesis de Valencia y sus beneficiados (1501-1538)', Valencia, 1980 (Diss. University of Valencia), pp. 750, 1066
M. Andrés, *La teología española en el siglo XVI*, Madrid, 1976, i, p. 346
E. Llamas-Martínez, *Repertorio de historia de las ciencias eclesiásticas en España*, Salamanca, 1967, i, p. 104
J. Rodríguez, *Biblioteca valentina*, Valencia, 1747, p. 274
N. Antonio, *Bibliotheca Hispana nova*, Roma, 1672 (ed. facsimile, Madrid, 1996), iii, pp. 738 cols a-b, 739 col. a

WORKS ON CHRISTIAN-MUSLIM RELATIONS

Disputationes sive conferentias, 'Disputes'

DATE About 1519
ORIGINAL LANGUAGE Spanish

DESCRIPTION
This unpublished work survives in a single manuscript. Written in the first person, it gives an account of Joan's preaching activities in Zaragoza, and of the political repercussions that followed. He delivered his sermons in a mosque, causing the Muslim community to complain to Alfonso de Aragón, Archbishop of Zaragoza and illegitimate son of King Ferdinand. In his obstinacy, Joan sought an audience with Charles V, but this was refused, whereupon Joan retreated to his home town. In the work, he quotes Juan Andrés and Martin García, bishop of Barcelona, whose friend and pupil he considered himself. The amount of invective he poured into it caused it be included in the *Index et catalogus librorum prohibitorum*.

Joan says in the work that he was encouraged by his experiences to write a treatise against the Qur'an (fol. 265rb). Since he began this second work (which was to be the *Lumbre de la fé*) on 1 November 1519 (fol. 1r), he must have completed *Disputas* in the early months of 1519.

SIGNIFICANCE
The work gives insight into the attitude of the king and the Consejo Real towards their relationship with Muslim subjects. It makes clear that both the archbishop and the civil authorities of Zaragoza tried to follow a policy of appeasement and compromise with Muslims, and attempted to

curb Joan's aggressive impulses, though without success. The adoption of this new attitude marks an important change from to the measures taken at the end of the 15th century.

MANUSCRIPTS
    MS Madrid, Biblioteca de la Real Academia de la Historia – Colección Gayangos 19-36, fols 253ra-265rb

EDITIONS & TRANSLATIONS
    E. Ruiz García and others are currently preparing an edition.

Lumbre de la fé contra la secta machomética, 'Light of faith against the Muḥammadan sect'

DATE   Between 1 November 1519 and 19 June 1521
ORIGINAL LANGUAGE   Spanish

DESCRIPTION
This unpublished work is preserved only in the Madrid manuscript. It is the result of Joan's decision to use other means against Muslims, following the failure of his preaching in the mosque in Zaragoza. It is divided into four books, in which the structure and divisions of the version of the Qur'an he uses are followed accurately, with the text usually transliterated and translated into Spanish. He refutes each contrary teaching using arguments based on quotations from a range of sources. In addition to the Bible, these include about 60 authors, with Augustine of Hippo prominent among them. Joan does not insult his opponents, but relies on the strength of his arguments alone to show the superiority of his own position. He conveys the clear impression that he is fully confident of the correctness of what he argues.

SIGNIFICANCE
The work is important for the text of the Qur'an contained in it, as much as anything else. This sheds light on the versions of the text in circulation in Spain the first decades of the 16th century.

MANUSCRIPTS
    MS Madrid, Biblioteca de la Real Academia de la Historia – Colección Gayangos 19-36, fols 0ra-vb, Clr-v, 1ra-247rb + I-XIV (a quire with pen drawings intended to illustrate the edition)

EDITIONS & TRANSLATIONS
E. Ruiz García and others are currently preparing an edition.

Elisa Ruiz García

Pedro Ramírez de Alba

Pedro Ramiro de Alba, Pedro de Alba (or Alva)

DATE OF BIRTH Approximately 1480
PLACE OF BIRTH Alba de Tormes (Salamanca)
DATE OF DEATH 21 June 1528
PLACE OF DEATH Granada

BIOGRAPHY

It is thought that Pedro's parents knew Hernando de Talavera, Archbishop of Granada, and that they sent Pedro to live in his house. It is possible that he was a sacristan in the Church of Santa Fe, Granada, when Hernando de Talavera send him to study in Castilla (perhaps Salamanca), and that he was canon of Santa Fe. Later, he was a vicar in Loja, Granada. He made attempts to enter the Order of Jerome although he was at first refused because he was an adult (*edad de hombre*), and his health was not good. But he persisted and was accepted into the novitiate of the Hieronymite Monastery in Granada, where he made his profession. He was five times elected prior. In 1526, after Charles V heard him preaching in Granada, he was made archbishop.

As archbishop, he took responsibility for building the new cathedral and was also involved in establishing courses of study that were the foundation of the university. In 1527, Charles V charged him with the task of ensuring that Muslims in the town received instruction in Christianity, from which resulted his *Doctrina christiana*.

MAIN SOURCES OF INFORMATION

Primary
J. Sigüenza, *Historia de la Orden de San Jerónimo*, Madrid, 1909, ii, pp. 333-37

Secondary
R.M. López, 'Un memorial de 1528 al arzobispo de Granada, Gaspar de Ávalos, sobre las rentas y la administración del arzobispado', *Historia, Instituciones, Documentos* 23 (1996) 357-84
J.M. Sánchez, *Intento bibliográfico de la doctrina cristiana del P. Jerónimo de Ripalda*, Madrid, 1908, p. 20
J. de Echeverría, *Paseos por Granada y sus contornos*, Granada, 1814, ii, pp. 387-88

WORKS ON CHRISTIAN-MUSLIM RELATIONS

Doctrina christiana, 'Christian doctrine'

DATE 1527-28
ORIGINAL LANGUAGE Spanish

DESCRIPTION

Pedro must have worked on *Doctrina christiana* between 1527, when the Emperor Charles V issued the order to give instruction to Muslims, and his death in June 1528. There is no trace of the original composition, and the work is now known only through the edition published in Valencia in 1568.

Doctrina christiana is a work of 88 pages, divided into four chapters. It is written in expository style, and is not polemical in tone. Ch. 1 is about the importance of the Creed and what must be believed, and makes a comparison between Christian and Islamic teachings. Ch. 2 explains what must be done in services, giving instruction about making the sign of the cross, basic knowledge of the mass, the most common prayers, and the sacraments, with some references to Morisco practices. Ch. 3 briefly sets out the commandments of God, the teachings of the Church and 'some excellences of our Christian faith', making contrasts between Christian and Islamic beliefs, and showing knowledge of the Qur'an. It expresses an open desire for dialogue and reflection on each of the teachings it outlines.

Ch. 4, the most original, teaches what the new Christian Moriscos who have just been baptised must and must not believe, giving a long catalogue of Muslim beliefs that must be rejected because of their error.

There is no sign of contempt for Islam in the work, but only a faithful invitation to a change of attitude, conviction and practice. The work ends with a request to long-standing Christians (*Cristianos viejos*) sincerely to accept the newly converted, providing them with good examples and refraining from insults or signs of contempt that could cause enmity. Pedro's desire is to erase all signs of Islam from the Moriscos' lives and to replace them with Christian practices.

SIGNIFICANCE

Doctrina christiana is the expression of a desire to makes changes to the inner selves of the newly converted, as well as to their outer actions. When a gathering of those responsible for the conversion of Moriscos met in Valencia 40 years after Pedro's death, they remembered the work, and edited it for use in their area. This is an indication of the continuing value it had in the circumstances of 16th-century Spain.

EDITIONS & TRANSLATIONS

Doctrina christiana, Valencia: Joan Navarro, 1568 (in all likelihood, this follows the original edition probably published in 1528, with a few changes)

Luis Resines

Gonzalo Arredondo y Alvarado

DATE OF BIRTH First half of the 15th century
PLACE OF BIRTH Uncertain; possibly Arredondo, Santander, or Belorado, Burgos
DATE OF DEATH About 1520
PLACE OF DEATH San Pedro de Arlanza, Burgos

BIOGRAPHY

Nothing is known about Gonzalo Arredondo y Alvarado until the year 1504, when he was named abbot of the Benedictine monastery of San Pedro de Arlanza. The little information from after that time comes from his surviving works and from the records of the dispute amongst the Benedictines at the end of the 15th century and the beginning of the 16th century about bringing together all the monasteries into the Congregation of San Benito de Valladolid. After being expelled from the monastery by the monks who opposed this change, he was confirmed in his position by King Ferdinand the Catholic with the support of the papacy. In 1518, he resigned as abbot and withdrew to the Priory of San Andrés de Boada in Burgos. He is mentioned as the chronicler of the Catholic Monarchs, Ferdinand of Castile and Isabel of Aragón, although this has not been proved, and he occasionally exchanged correspondence with the Emperor Charles V. Some years later he returned to San Pedro de Arlanza, where he died in the 1520s.

MAIN SOURCES OF INFORMATION

Primary
Crónica Arlantina de los famosos y grandes hechos de los bienaventurados cavalleros sanctos conde Fernand González y Cid Rui Diez, Burgos, 1522
Castillo inexpugnable defensorio de la fee, Burgos: Juan de Junta, 1528

Secondary
M. Vivanco Gómez, art. 'Gonzalo Arredondo y Alvarado', in *Diccionario biográfico español*, Madrid, 2010, v, pp. 561-62
M. Vaquero, *Vida rimada de Fernán González*, Exeter, 1987
N. Toscano, 'Édición crítica de los versos inéditos de Arredondo sobre Fernán González', *Boletín de la Institución Fernán Gonzáles* 195 (1980) 273-326

A. Labandeira Fernández, 'Historicidad y estructura de la crónica Arlantina en verso', *Revista de archivos, bibliotecas y museos* 82 (1979) 225-44

M. Martínez Añibarro y Rives, *Intento de diccionario biográfico de autores de la provincia de Burgos*, Madrid, 1889 (repr. Salamanca, 1993), pp. 57-59

WORKS ON CHRISTIAN-MUSLIM RELATIONS

Castillo inexpugnable defensorio de la fee, 'The unassailably defended castle of faith'

DATE 23 June 1528
ORIGINAL LANGUAGE Spanish

DESCRIPTION

This work, whose full title is *Castillo inexpugnable defensorio de la fee y concionatorio para vencer a todos enemigos espirituales y corporales. Y verdadera relacion de las cosas maravillosas antiguas y modernas. Y exortación para yr contra el turco; y le vencer; y anichilar la seta de Mahoma. Y toda infelidad, y ganar la tierra sancta con famoso y bienaventurado triumph*, is addressed to the Emperor Charles V, with the approval of the emperor's personal secretary. It comprises 78 pages, divided into 77 chapters, with a complete index at the end. It was written in response to the defeat and death of Louis II of Hungary at the second battle of Mohács against the Turks. Gonzalo Arredondo y Alvarado must have finished writing it in 1527.

It takes the form of a dialogue between the widowed Queen Mary of Hungary (the sister of Charles V), a Benedictine monk, the prior of Bohada, and the abbot of San Pedro de Arlanza. The queen requests the help of all Christian princes and Pope Clement VII, encouraging them to join with the emperor to defeat the armies of Süleyman the Magnificent, to recover Constantinople and to expel the Muslims from the Holy Land. She supports calls for a new crusade against the Turks, which should be promulgated by the pope and ordered by the emperor. Her mother consoles her on her loss, and comments that 'all those killed by the Turks are martyrs'.

This is clearly a text inspired by Castilian outlooks, and it thus defines King Francis I of France as one of the key enemies who stand in the way of bringing about the union of Christian princes, given the open hostilities between him and the emperor. Thus, Francis is reminded in the dialogue that he could lose his title of 'most Christian monarch'. Several chapters are devoted to describing the figure of Muḥammad and discussing the main errors of Islam, and also to praising such doctrines as the Holy Trinity, the resurrection of Christ, and the courage and virtues of the Virgin Mary. The work also narrates in detail (with some mistakes) the siege and conquest of Rhodes by the Turks. It ends by highlighting the supernatural signs that have appeared in the sky to urge Christians to embark on this campaign, and by invoking the spirits of Count Fernán González (founder of the county and future kingdom of Castile) and the Cid (legendary Spanish hero of the Middle Ages). The last page includes a letter addressed to Charles V, asking him to make plans for the crusade.

SIGNIFICANCE

This is one of the first books printed in Spain on the dangers to the Christian world represented by the Ottoman Empire. It identifies the Ottomans, a group unknown to Spanish culture at the time, as an uncivilised, nomadic people, who had quickly been Islamised. It adds to the disparaging accounts of Islam and Muslims given by Peter the Venerable and Riccoldo da Monte di Croce, its own comments about the Turks' violence, love of warfare and cruelty.

It defends the authority of the emperor to lead a crusade to eradicate Islam and emphasises that the Spanish are brave enough to carry this out, although all Christians should unite to put an end to the threat that Islam represents. Süleyman the Magnificent's campaigns to expand Islam are as dangerous as the Arab invasions of the 7th and 8th centuries, so it is essential to react immediately to prevent further expansion.

Gonzalo makes use of the traditional theory that the Turks have been allowed by God to grow powerful because of the sins of the Christians and their leaders' disunity. But he often shows lack of detailed knowledge about the themes he touches on, and makes obvious historical mistakes, among them that Muḥammed died of poisoning.

EDITIONS & TRANSLATIONS

Castillo inexpugnable defensorio de la fee y concionatorio admirable para vencer a todos enemigos espirituales y corporales, Burgos, c. 1900

Castillo inexpugnable defensorio de la fee y concionatorio admirable para vencer a todos enemigos espirituales y corporales, Burgos, 1528

STUDIES

J. S. Geary, 'Arredondo's *Castillo inexpugnable de la fee*. Anti-Islamic propaganda in the age of Charles V', in J.V. Tolan (ed.), *Medieval Christian perceptions of Islam*, New York, 1996, 291-311

A. Mas, *Les Turcs dans la littérature espagnoles du Siècle d'Or*, París, 1967

Miguel Ángel de Bunes

Juan Gines de Sepulveda

DATE OF BIRTH 1490
PLACE OF BIRTH Pozoblanco
DATE OF DEATH 17 November 1573
PLACE OF DEATH Pozoblanco

BIOGRAPHY

Born into a family of humble origin in Pozoblanco, Juan Gines de Sepúlveda went to school in Cordova, where he learned Latin and Greek, and at the age of 20 to Alcala de Henares University for three years (1510-13) before studying theology for two years at Colegio de Sigüenza. In May 1515, he left for the prestigious Colegio de San Clemente in Bologna with the support of the Chapter of the Cathedral of Toledo and Cardinal Cisneros.

During his stay in Bologna (1515-22), Sepúlveda acquired a reputation as an outstanding Latin and Greek scholar: he was commissioned to write the life of Gil de Albornoz, founder of the Colegio, and began his translation into Latin of Aristotle's works. He kept company with powerful figures such as Cardinal Giulio di Giuliano de' Medici, who was to become Pope Clement VII in 1523 and was to be his most important protector. He also enjoyed the friendship of Alberto Pio, Prince of Carpi, whom he supported later in a controversy against Erasmus. Living in Rome under the protection of Clement VII from 1526, he witnessed the sack of the city by the troops of the Holy Roman Emperor in 1527.

He was invited by Cardinal Cayetano to Naples to contribute to a commentary on the New Testament, but Cardinal Francisco de Quiñones called him back to Rome to revise the Roman Breviary. It was in de Quiñones's retinue, where he stayed until 1534, that he went to Genoa in August 1529 to welcome Charles V, who was on his way to his coronation in Bologna in February 1530. On that occasion, Sepúlveda handed over to the emperor his *Oratio ad Carolum Quintum*, which he had just published in Bologna (1529), urging him to take up arms against the Turks. After meeting the emperor again between November 1532 and February 1533, he was appointed chronicler in 1536, an office he retained almost until his death. That year, he left Italy for Vienna and then Spain, and started to work on a Latin chronicle of the reign, *Historiarum rebus gestis Caroli V*. In 1542, he was appointed tutor to Prince Philip.

The emperor's favour and Sepúlveda's own reputation as a humanist did not protect him from difficulties: in 1535, he wrote *Democrates* to prove the compatibility of the use of arms with Christian life, but because of Dominican opposition he failed in his attempt to publish *Democrates secundus sive de iustis belli causis*, which he finished in 1544. In 1545, the Royal Council did not grant the right to publish, and then the universities of Alcala de Henares and Salamanca censured the book. In response, Sepúlveda wrote *Apologia pro libro de iustis belli causis*, published in Rome in 1550, which was immediately banned in Spain.

From 5 August to 30 September 1550, and again from mid-April to the beginning of May 1551, Sepúlveda was involved in a long series of debates in Valladolid with the Dominican Bartolomé de Las Casas, Bishop of Chiapas, over the legitimacy of war in the New World to subdue and convert the Indians. Sepúlveda maintained that the Spanish were entitled to use force in order to punish what he saw as the Indians' crimes against nature and to compel them to accept the true religion (an account of the arguments on both sides was written by Domingo de Soto). Sepúlveda was offended at the emperor's lack of support for him and withdrew to Pozoblanco. However, he visited Charles V in Yuste in 1557, and the following year was confirmed in his role as chronicler by Philip II, although allowed to reside away from court. He finished the chronicle of Charles V's reign, but did not try to publish it, along with *De regno*, a treatise on the art of government that would be published only in 1571 in Lerida. He also worked on a chronicle of Philip II's reign, which remained unfinished. He died in Pozoblanco on 17 November 1573 after giving up his responsibilities as chronicler on 1 July.

The polemic that was provoked by Sepúlveda's position in what became known as the Valladolid controversy certainly contributed to obscuring the part of his work that was imbued with civic humanism. He translated several of Aristotle's works into Latin (his translation of the *Politics* was published in Paris in 1548), he was historiographer of Charles V and Philip II, and he also wrote a treatise on ruling over men, *De regno*, published in 1571. Several of his texts are devoted to the justification of war: *Gonsalus seu de appetenda gloria dialogus* (1523), *Democrates sive de honestate disciplinae militari dialogus* (1535), *Democrates secundus sive de iustis belli causis* (unpublished), and *Apologia pro libro de iustis belli causis* (1550).

In addition to the short *Oratio* or *Cohortatio* (1529), several other works by Sepúlveda also deal with conflicts with Islam: his chronicles record activities against Muslims in North Africa (in particular Charles V's conquest of Tunis in 1535 and, more briefly, the failed attack on Algiers in 1541), and some episodes in the war against the Turks in Hungary and the defence of Vienna.

MAIN SOURCES OF INFORMATION

Primary
Juan Ginés de Sepúlveda, *Epistolarum libri septem*, Salamanca, 1557
A. Losada (ed.), *Epistolario de Juan Ginés de Sepúlveda*, Madrid, 1966
J.J. Valverde Abril (ed.), *Epistolario*, Munich, 2003
J. Solana Pujalte and I.J. Garcia Pinilla (ed. and trans.), *Obras completas de Juan Ginés de Sepúlveda*, Pozoblanco, 2007, ix, pt 1, *Epistolario, cartas 1-75 (1517-1548)*, and ix, pt 2, *Epistolario, cartas 76-139 (1549-1567)*

Secondary
F. Castilla Urbano, *El pensamiento de Juan Ginés de Sepúlveda. Vida activa, humanismo y guerra en el Renacimiento*, Madrid, 2013
S. Muñoz Machado, *Sepúlveda, cronista del emperador*, Edhasa, 2012
F. Castilla Urbano, 'Vida activa, virtud y gloria en la etapa italiana de Juan Ginés de Sepúlveda (1515-1536)', *Estudios Filosóficos* 58 (2009) 421-56
J.J. Valverde Abril, 'Juan Ginés de Sepúlveda. Filólogo, epigrafista, anticuario', in J.M. Maestre Maestre, J.P. Barea and L.C. Brea (eds), *Humanismo y pervivencia del mundo clásico*, Madrid, 2008, i, 2327-40
F. Castilla Urbano, *Juan Ginés de Sepúlveda*, Madrid, 2000
E. Rodriguez Peregrina, 'Juan Ginés de Sepúlveda. Un historiador al servicio de Carlos V', *Actas del Congreso Internacional V Centenario del Nacimiento del Dr. Juan Ginés de Sepúlveda*, Cordova, 1993, 106-27
A. Losada, *Juan Ginés de Sepúlveda a través de su Epistolario y nuevos documentos*, Madrid, 1949
A. Losada, 'Un cronista olvidado de la España imperial, Juan Ginés de Sepúlveda', *Hispania* 31 (1948) 234-307
A.F.G. Bell, *Juan Ginés de Sepúlveda*, Oxford, 1925
F. Cerdá y Rico et al., 'De vita et scriptis Io. Genesii Sepulvedae cordubensis commentarius', in *Ioannis Genesii Sepulvedae Cordubensis Opera, cum edita, tum inedita*, Madrid: Academia de la Historia, 1780, i, I-CXII

WORKS ON CHRISTIAN-MUSLIM RELATIONS

Cohortatio; *Oratio ad Carolum Quintum ut bellum suscipiat in Turcas*, 'Prayer to Charles V to wage war against the Turks'

DATE 1529
ORIGINAL LANGUAGE Latin

DESCRIPTION

The *Cohortatio* or *Oratio* (also known as *Ad Carolum V. Imperatorem invictissimum, ut facta cum omnibus Christianis pace, bellum suscipiat in Turcas, Io. Genesii Sepulvedae cohortatio*) is a short text consisting of no more than 21 paragraphs. In the 2003 edition (*Obras completas*, vii), it consists of 18 pages (16 in the edition *Opera cum edita tum edita*, Madrid, 1780). Its aim is to seek intimacy with the imperial court at a time when Charles V, after the Peace of Cambrai (also known as *la paix des Dames*), had sailed to Italy in order to be reconciled with the pope and to be crowned. As part of Cardinal Quiñones' retinue, Sepúlveda welcomed the emperor in Genoa in August 1529 and handed him the text, which he had just published in Bologna. It urged him to fight the Turks, who were considered then as an extreme peril: after their conquest of Belgrade (1521) and Rhodes, and the victory of Mohács (1526), where the Hungarian King Louis II, Charles V's brother-in-law, had died, Süleyman the Magnificent was well established in Hungary, thanks to John Zápolya, who was disputing the vacant throne with Ferdinand of Habsburg. At the same time, the Ottoman armies were besieging Vienna. The work emerges from this context of the Ottoman advance in Europe and the numerous calls for crusade, and is also an element in the debate on the legitimacy of war, even against the Turks.

Luther had stated that the Turkish invasion had to be borne because it was God's curse, and Erasmus, who was very influential at the emperor's court, had published several works hostile to war. He rejected the notion of a 'just war', and condemned the appetite for conquest that lay behind the crusade and the use of the Turkish threat by the princes to further exploit their subjects (*Dulce bellum inexpertis*, published for the first time in 1515; *Querela pacis*, 1516). Juan Luis Vivès, one of Erasmus's most faithful Spanish disciples, had been greatly affected by the Turkish threat, which led him to write *De conditione vitae Christianorum sub Turca* and *De Europae dissidiis et bello turcico* (Bruges, 1526). But he appealed less for a war against the Turks than for the end of dissension among Christians, which would only assist the Ottoman progress in Europe. In *De concordia et discordia in humano genere*, dedicated to Charles V in July 1529, he declared that one should not hate the Turks but try to convert them to Christianity instead of fighting them. In the *Cohortatio*, Sepúlveda responded to such Christian humanist arguments, having already published in 1523 his *Gonsalus*, in which he justified the desire for glory, especially when it was linked to wars with legitimate motives.

Sepúlveda first tries (paras 1-6) to depict the danger to the whole of Christendom, describing the yoke that the Turks had imposed on already vanquished nations – the Greek example is particularly used, and Sepúlveda refers to the *devşirme* – as well as upon their own subjects. Turkish domination is enslavement imposed by a barbaric, uneducated and lawless people, and is thus a form of tyranny over subjects who are really treated as slaves.

This depiction of the Ottoman peril brings Sepúlveda to exhort the emperor (paras 7-12) to take up arms and not to listen to those who refuse to fight – probably alluding here to Erasmus – and who have played into the hands of the Turks, maybe even accepting bribes from them. He then refutes arguments against war taken from the life of Jesus, and adduces examples, taken especially from the Old Testament, to legitimise a defensive war against the foes of Christendom. He argues that war against the Turks is a just war waged on numerous grounds because its purpose is to save the true religion and liberate Christians.

This principle once established, the last paragraphs (13-21) attempt to convince the emperor that victory over the Turks is possible: although they are greater in number, they come from Asia and are thus inferior to the emperor's soldiers, just as the Trojans (who according to certain writers were the ancestors of the Turks) and the Persians were inferior to the ancient Greeks; the victories of Alexander the Great, the Romans and Julius Caesar are also cited. Sepúlveda plays down the merits of the fearsome Janissaries, whose Christian origins were well known, and emphasises the superiority of the emperor's Italian, German and Spanish troops to encourage him to fend off the Turks and also to reclaim the Holy Land and other Turkish possessions, including Constantinople, the capital of the former Eastern Roman Empire. In conclusion, he catalogues the wealth of the Ottoman Empire and the considerable booty that the emperor will gain from this defence of Christian faith and Christendom.

SIGNIFICANCE

In this occasional text can be found the first steps towards the theories Sepúlveda would later develop in his works on the legitimacy of conquest, and hints at the natural superiority of certain peoples – such as the Spanish – over others. It is also a dialogue with humanist texts that were inspired by the *philosophia Christi*: the depiction of the wealth of Ottoman possessions recalls Scipio's speech in *De Europae dissidiis* by Vives (a speech followed by the more moderate answer by Tiresias, who asks Christians to turn to God rather than to fight). Erasmus was to reply to Sepúlveda's arguments in *Utilissima consultatio de bello Turcis inferendo et obiter enarratus psalmus XXVIII*, published in Freiburg in 1530.

The depiction of the Turks in this short work is very biased and less nuanced than in other contemporary writings that express fear mixed with admiration for the Ottomans: endurance, frugality, extraordinary bravery, and order among their armies are often noted. Sepúlveda never mentions his sources, and he is not particularly concerned with the accuracy of the information about the Turks then current in Europe. His succinct description of Ottoman power presented as tyrannical domination only mentions the elements relevant to the topic: lawlessness, absence of social hierarchy (nobility) and the transmission of statutes, and enslavement of subjects. The Turks themselves are quintessentially defined by cruelty and barbarism in order to set them up over and against civilisation.

The nature of the text explains its lack of nuance, and its sympathy for the enslaved Greeks contrasts sharply with the usual, rather contemptuous descriptions of them found in treatises and geographical works of the time, which present the fate of these schismatic Christians as well-deserved. The Ottoman Empire is frequently characterised as a tyranny in works written between the Battle of Mohács in 1526 and the two sieges of Vienna in 1529 and 1532.

EDITIONS & TRANSLATIONS

J.M. Rodríguez Peregrina and B. Cuart Moner, *Exhortación a Carlos V*, in *Obras completas de Juan Ginés de Sepúlveda*, Pozoblanco, 2003, vii, pp. 329-46 (Spanish trans.)

Á. Losada, *Exhortación a la guerra contra los turcos*, in *Tratados políticos de Juan Ginés de Sepúlveda*, Madrid, 1963, 1-27 (Spanish trans.)

Io. *Genesii Sepulvedae Cordubensis opera, cum edita, tum inedita*, IV, accurate Regia Historiae Academia, ex typographia Regia de la Gazeta, Matriti, 1780, in 4°, pp. 358-74

Ioannis Genesii Sepulvedae Cordubensis Sacrosanctae Theologiae Doctoris, Caroli V imperatoris historici Opera, quae reperiri potuerunt omnia, Coloniae Agrippinae in officina Birckmannica sumptibus Arnoldi Mylii, 1602, in 4°, pp. 446-60

Ad Carolum V. Imperatorem invictissimum ut, facta cum omnibus Christianis pace, bellum suscipiat in Turcas, Io. Genesii Sepulvedae cohortatio, Antverpiae, 1535, in 8°

Ad Carolum V. Imperatorem invictissimum, ut facta cum omnibus Christianis pace, bellum suscipiat in Turcas, Io. Genesii Sepulvedae cohortatio, Bononiae in aedibus Ioannis Baptistae Phaelli, 1529, in 4°

STUDIES

J.A. Fernández-Santamaría, *Juan Ginés de Sepúlveda. La guerra en el pensamiento político del Renacimiento*, Madrid, 2007

A. Merle, 'La guerre juste contre les Turcs et la monarchie catholique au XVIe siècle', in A. Molinié and A. Merle (eds), *L'Espagne et ses guerres*, Paris, 2004, 307-24

J.M. Rodríguez Peregrina, 'La *Cohortatio ad Carolum V*. Un episodio poco conocido de los desencuentros entre Sepúlveda y Erasmo', in B. Cuart Moner et al. (eds), *Obras completas de Juan Ginés de Sepúlveda*, Pozoblanco, 2003, vii, pp. CCCV-CCCVII (historical introduction to the critical edition of the text)

J.M. Rodríguez-Peregrina, 'Un manifiesto antipacifista. La *Cohortatio ad Carolum V ut bellum suscipiat in turcas* de Juan Ginés de Sepulveda', in J.M. Maestre Maestre, L.C. Brea and J.P. Barea (eds), *Humanismo y pervivencia del mundo clásico*, Madrid, 2002, v, pp. 2257-64

J.A. Fernández-Santamaría, 'Juan Ginés de Sepúlveda y la guerra', in J. Martínez Millán (ed.), *Carlos V y la quiebra del humanismo político en Europa (1530-1558)*, Madrid, 2001, i, pp. 37-92

J.A. Fernández-Santamaría, *The state, war and peace. Spanish political thought in the Renaissance, 1516-1559*, Cambridge, 1977

Alexandra Merle

Hernán López de Yanguas

DATE OF BIRTH About 1487
PLACE OF BIRTH Yanguas (Soria, Spain)
DATE OF DEATH In or after 1543
PLACE OF DEATH Unknown

BIOGRAPHY

Most of the available information about Hernán López de Yanguas appears in his own works. The *explicit* of the first edition of his *Triumphos de locura* ('The triumphs of madness'), from about 1521, states that this poem was written in September 1520, 'when its author was 33'. Since he was appointed executor of a will dated 1543, he must have died after this date.

Yanguas's parents' names are unknown, but some other relatives are mentioned in his works. He addresses the *Diálogo del mosquito* ('The dialogue of the mosquito') of 1520 to an uncle, Juan López, and the *Triumphos de locura* to his 'beloved sisters' (p. 5). Hernando and Espejo Surós consider that these 'sisters' may be nuns and, therefore, unrelated to him. Hernando ('El *Diálogo*') has suggested that he may be related to 'Petrus López de Yanguas', a scholar at the Spanish College of San Clemente in Bolonia in the 1520s. Although the relationship between Petrus and Hernán is strictly based on the coincidence in their name, the small size of the town of Yanguas makes it likely that they were related. This connection, if true, would be highly significant, given that Petrus left the Spanish College after failing to prove his *limpieza de sangre*, that is, the absence in his ancestry of Moorish or Jewish blood.

Espejo Surós has documented Yanguas's connection with the parishes of San Lorenzo and Santa María in Yanguas ('La obra dramática', pp. 99-101). It is probable, however, that his activity was not limited to this town. Several of his works are dedicated to members of the de la Cueva noble family, whose seat was in Cuellar, Valladolid: to Francisco de la Cueva, Duke of Alburquerque (*Farsa de la concordia*, 1529) and to his sons Diego (*Farsa turquesana*, c. 1530) and Gabriel de la Cueva (*Dichos de los siete sabios de Grecia*, 1543). The tone of the dedications indicates that Yanguas may have been employed as a tutor by Francisco de la Cueva.

Yanguas's works cover considerable thematic territory. A group of poems, probably written to satisfy the growing demand for material by the printing presses, adapts classic or Renaissance texts and themes: the *Dialogo del mosquito*, a Lucianesque dialogue on the theme of *contemptus mundi*; the *Triumphos de locura*, a verse version of Erasmus's *Moriae encomium*; the *Cincuenta vivas preguntas con otras tantas respuestas*, a collection of questions and answers on natural history in the tradition of the *quaestiones Salernitanae*; and the *Dichos de los siete sabios de Grecia*, a translation of some of the sayings contained in the *Disticha Catonis*.

Scholarship has paid particular attention to the *Dichos*. In 1567, Rodrigo del Rubio, a Christian of Islamic descent, from Albeta, Aragón, was brought to an inquisitorial court charged with owning an Aljamiado (Spanish written in Arabic script) manuscript copy of the *Dichos*, with the implication that owning this book might indicate his being a secret Muslim (Galmes de Fuentes, *Dichos*; Espejo Surós, 'La obra dramática', pp. 231-37).

More important in terms of literary history are his dramatic works, in which he develops the Iberian tradition of pastoral Christmas plays towards new thematic areas. Two of his plays, both titled *Egloga de la natividad* (1525 and later), reproduce the Christmas story: an angel appears to a group of shepherds, proclaims the birth of Christ and directs the shepherds to the manger, where they adore Jesus in Gospel-based speeches. The *Farsa del santísimo sacramento* (1520), preserved only in fragmentary form, moves this dramatic structure to the worship of the Eucharist. Again, an angel appears to three shepherds – who in this case are named after the Latin fathers Ambrose, Jerome and Augustine – and announces the feast of the body of Christ: as in the *Nativity*, their adoration takes the form of expressing the Catholic doctrine on the Eucharist. This play has been considered the first *auto sacramental* in Spanish literature, and Yanguas probably wrote it to be performed on the Feast of Corpus Christi (González Ollé, '*Farsa*'). The fourth play on a religious theme is the *Farsa del mundo y moral* (1524), liturgically connected to the feast of the Assumption of the Virgin Mary. The Annunciation of the angel is replaced by a meeting between the tempter named Mundo (World) and a shepherd, Apetito (Human desire). Opposing Mundo and enacting an inner debate, a hermit, who stands for the doctrine of the Church, persuades the shepherd to reject temptation and introduces him to Faith. Finally, Faith gives a lengthy account of the Virgin's Assumption to heaven.

Two other plays by Yanguas, the *Farsa de la concordia* and the *Farsa turquesana* use the same dramatic model to present secular events. The *Concordia* is a celebration of the Treaty of Cambrai between King Francis of France and the Emperor Charles V (1529). The allegorical-pastoral mix persists in this work, and in its construction it anticipates the *Turquesana*. Correo, a messenger travelling to Spain with news of the peace, meets a shepherd, Tiempo (Time), who celebrates this peace by dancing and singing the hymn *Gloria in excelsis*. The arrival of a second shepherd, Mundo (World), creates the dramatic space for a dialogue that presents the peace as an opportunity to unite the Christian kingdoms against the Turkish threat. A second scene shows a meeting of the messenger with Paz (Peace) and Justicia (Justice). When they see War, who runs away disguised as a pilgrim, they capture her, and Justice engages her in a debate about the opposing advantages of war and peace, translating some parts of Erasmus's *Querela pacis*. Peace and Justice defeat War and, when she cries for help, Time and World return to the stage and join Peace and Justice in the victory. Finally, Peace lets her go into exile in the Garamantas, the north coast of Africa, implying that this region will be the next target of the military effort of Christian Europe. As she escapes, War meets two more shepherds, Descanso (Rest) and Plazer (Pleasure), who go on to meet Peace and Justice, and celebrate the treaty in a speech of millenarian tone: the treaty is a sign of the arrival of the age of Charity and universal peace, which will make possible the recovery of Jerusalem.

MAIN SOURCES OF INFORMATION

Primary
Triumphos de locura [The triumphs of madness], Burgos, 1520, 1525
Diálogo del mosquito [The dialogue of the mosquito], Valencia, 1521
Farsa del santísimo sacramento [Farce of the holy sacrament], Valencia, 1521 [partially preserved in Cotarelo y Morí, 'El primer auto']
Égloga de la natividad [Nativity eclogue], (s.l.), (s.d.)
Farsa del mundo y moral [Allegory and farce of the world], (s.l.), 1524
Égloga de la natividad [Nativity eclogue], (s.l.), c. 1525
Farsa de la concordia [Farce of the treaty], (s.l.), c. 1529
Farsa turquesana [Turkish farce], (s.l.), c. 1530
Cincuenta vivas preguntas con otras tantas respuestas [Fifty compelling questions with their answers], Toledo, c. 1542
Los dichos o sentencias de los siete sabios de Grecia [The sayings or sentences of the seven wise men of Greece], Medina, 1543

Secondary

J. Espejo Surós, 'La obra dramática de Hernán López de Yanguas. Teatro y religión en la primera mitad del siglo XVI', Lleida, 2012 (Diss. University of Lleida)

J. Espejo Surós, 'El teatro religioso como artefacto mnemotécnico. Notas para una poética de la sacra memoria en el teatro de Hernán López de Yanguas', in L. González (ed.), *Miscelánea filológica dedicada a Alberto Porqueras Mayo*, Lleida, 2012, 73-82

J. Espejo Surós and J.F. Hernando (eds), *H. López de Yanguas, Triumphos de locura*, Madrid, 2012

R. Barroso Cabrera and J. Morín de Pablo, 'De nuevo sobre los yangüeses del Quijote', *Anales Cervantinos* 43 (2011) 145-61, p. 150

J. Espejo Surós and J. García Maestro, *Teatro religioso y corrientes de espiritualidad en tiempos de Hernán López de Yanguas*, Vigo, 2007

J. Espejo Surós, art. 'Hernán López de Yanguas (1487-ca. 1550)', in P. Jauralde, D. Gavela, P.C. Rojo and E. Varela (eds), *Diccionario filológico de literatura española. Siglos XVI y XVII. Textos y transmisión*, Madrid, 2007, 585-91

J. Espejo Surós, 'Una aproximación al espacio y el tiempo real e imaginario en el teatro conservado de Hernán López de Yanguas', in M.L. Lobato and F. Domínguez Matito (eds), *Memoria de la palabra. Actas del VI Congreso de la Asociación Internacional Siglo de Oro*, Madrid, 2004, 751-61

J.F. Hernando and J. Espejo Surós, 'La *Farsa turquesana* de Hernán López de Yanguas, estudio y edición', *Anexos LEMIR* (2002) 1-27

J.F. Hernando, 'Escritura y teatro en el s. XVI. Subtextualidad bíblica en la obra dramática de Hernán López de Yanguas (1487-?)', *Helmántica* 147 (1997) 453-65

M.A. Pallarés Jiménez, 'Una pieza incompleta de López de Yanguas conservada en el Archivo notarial de Zaragoza', *Epos* 13 (1997) 417-47

J.F. Hernando, 'Tiempo dramático, tiempo real y tiempo simbólico en las obras dramáticas de Hernán López de Yanguas', *Bulletin of the Comediantes* 49 (1996) 249-59

A. Hermenegildo, 'El teatro como instrumento de propaganda religiosa', in R. de la Fuente (ed.), *El teatro del siglo XVI*, Gijón, 1994, 89-123, pp. 94-96

J.F. Hernando, 'El *Diálogo de la Vida del sobervio y de la Muerte* (1550). Manuscrito nº 4247 de la Biblioteca Nacional de Madrid', Salamanca, 1992 (Diss. University of Salamanca), pp. 62-66

Á. Galmés de Fuentes (ed.), *Dichos de los siete sabios de grecia. Sentencias morales en verso*, Madrid, 1991

C. Martínez Fernández, 'Microuniversos semánticos en la formación del auto sacramental', in *Investigaciones semioticas, II: Lo teatral y lo cotidiano*, Oviedo, 1988, 251-64

M.A. Pérez Priego, 'Algunas consideraciones sobre el erasmismo y el teatro religioso en la primera mitad del siglo XVI', in *El erasmismo en España*, Santander, 1986, 509-23

F. González Ollé, 'Sobre el texto de la *Égloga de la Natividad*, de Fernán López de Yanguas', *Segismundo* 21-22 (1975) 61-63

R.A. Young, 'The *Farsa del mundo y moral* of Fernán López de Yanguas and the auto sacramental', *Segismundo* 19-20 (1974) 9-16

C. Merino Nuño, 'La adjetivación en cuatro obras dramáticas de Hernán López de Yanguas y su comparación con la de Juan de Mena en el *Laberinto de fortuna*', Deusto, 1973 (Diss. University of Deusto)

F. González Ollé, 'La *Farsa del santísimo sacramento* anónima y su significación en el desarrollo del auto sacramental', *Revista de Literatura* 71-72 (1969) 127-65

M. Bataillon, 'Un probleme d'influence d'Erasme in Espagne', in *Actes du Congres Erasme*, Rotterdam, 1969, 136-47

E. Asensio, 'Los estudios sobre Erasmo, de Marcel Bataillon', *Revista de Occidente* 63 (1968) 302-19

J.A. Pérez Rioja, 'Hernán López de Yanguas, humanista y autor dramático', *Celtiberia* 18 (1968) 163-82

F. González Ollé, 'El primer auto sacramental del teatro español', *Segismundo* 5-6 (1967) 179-84

F. González Ollé (ed.), *Fernán López de Yanguas. Obras dramáticas*, Madrid, 1966

A. García Morales (ed.), *Autos comedias y farsas de la Biblioteca Nacional de Madrid*, Madrid, 1962-64

A. Pérez Gómez (ed.), *Cuatro obras del bachiller Hernán López de Yanguas, siglo XVI*, Cieza, 1960

J.A. Gaya Nuño, 'Dos reliquias sorianas de arte y literatura en Cataluña', *Celtiberia* 3 (1952) 32-39

P. Bohigas (ed.), *H. López de Yanguas, Diálogo del mosquito*, Barcelona, 1951

A. Bonilla y San Martín, 'Fernán López de Yanguas y el bachiller de la Pradilla', *Revista Crítica Hispano-Americana* 1 (1915) 44-51

U. Cronan, *Teatro español del s. XVI*. Madrid, 1913

E. Kohler, *Sieben spanische dramatische Eklogen*, Dresden, 1911

M. Serrano y Sanz (ed.), '*Farsa sacramental* compuesta en el año 1521', *Revista de Archivos, Bibliotecas y Museos* 10 (1904) 67-71, 447-50

E. Cotarelo y Morí, 'El primer auto sacramental del teatro español y noticia de su autor, el Bachiller Hernán López de Yanguas', *Revista de Archivos, Bibliotecas y Museos* 7 (1902) 251-72

L. Rouanet, *Colección de autos, farsas y coloquios del s. XVI*, Barcelona, 1901

WORKS ON CHRISTIAN-MUSLIM RELATIONS

Farsa dicha Turquesana, contra el mundo muy galana, 'The most elegant Turkish farce, against the Turk'
Farsa turquesana, 'Turkish farce'

DATE About 1530
ORIGINAL LANGUAGE Spanish

DESCRIPTION

The *Farsa turquesana* is a short, semi-allegorical play in 968 verses that presents the Christian reaction to the European campaigns of the Ottoman Empire during the first half of the 16th century. Given that the only preserved print edition has no date, the only definite date *a quo* is 1523, the beginning of the pontificate of Pope Clement VII, one of the characters in the play. The gestures of mutual deference between Clement and Emperor Charles in the final scene coincide with those performed at Charles's coronation as emperor in 1530 and allow for the strong likelihood of a later date of writing; the text, however, fails to mention the 1529 siege of Vienna, which would be thematically congruent with its contents. The play shows how in Belgrade Sultan Süleyman resolves to conquer Rome and writes a letter to Pope Clement announcing his intention to do so. The sultan calls his messenger, Mahometo, asks him to read his letter aloud and sends him off to Rome. On the outskirts of Rome, Mahometo meets two shepherds, Pelayo and Silvano. Learning of the contents of his message, they attack him and he runs away. The shepherds talk about the Ottoman threat and lament the fact that the Christian princes are keener to make war on each other than to respond to this threat. The shepherds also express their hope that Fortune will turn against the Turk, and mention biblical and historical examples of rulers whose power was overthrown.

Mahometo arrives in Rome and meets Esfuerzo (Effort), the pope's standard-bearer, who takes him to Pope Clement. Clement reads the letter and gives it to Effort, who advises him to ask for the help of Emperor Charles. Clement takes this advice, writes a letter and calls Diligente (Diligent), his chief messenger. Clement reads the letter to Diligent, sends him off to Charles and sits down to write his response to the sultan. While he does so, Effort recites a short monologue of mildly anticlerical tone: the

HERNÁN LÓPEZ DE YANGUAS

pope should send against the Turk the young clerics and monks, whose vast number would suffice to conquer not one but a thousand empires, and the expedition could be financed by melting down the many sacred objects in Rome and Jerusalem.

Clement comes back to the stage and asks Effort to read his response to the Turk: in his letter the pope says that he gives no credence to the sultan's boasts, which are a sign of madness, and announces his intention to go to meet him with 'weapons, sails and oars' (633). Clement then calls for Mahometo and sends him back to Süleyman.

The scene changes to show the arrival of Diligent in the presence of the emperor. After reading the pope's letter, Charles tells Diligent to return to the pope with the news that, rather than wasting time writing a letter, Charles will assemble his army and take it immediately to Rome. On his way back, Diligent meets Mahometo and engages him in a debate on the respective merits of Islam and Christianity. After this, Diligent arrives in Rome and reports to Clement the results of his embassy. As he is doing so, Effort announces the arrival of Charles's army. Clement and Charles greet each other, and Clement expresses his hope that Portugal, England and France will follow Charles's example. Charles invites him to proceed against the sultan without delay, and Clement responds by making what amounts to a formal declaration of crusade by offering remission of sins to those that follow him against the Turk. The play ends with a *villancico* (folk song) expressing hope of victory over the Turks.

SIGNIFICANCE

The play portrays the well-documented state of anticipation of an Ottoman offensive against Italy in the early 1530s, as well as the late deployment of crusading ideology as a device to recover the medieval ideal of Christianity in the context of the emergence of nation states. The Ottoman threat, represented in apocalyptic terms, promotes a discourse about a European unity of purpose under the Holy Roman Empire and the authority of the pope.

The *Farsa* also reproduces the current repertoire of anti-Muslim arguments (also evidenced in e.g. Gonzalo de Arredondo's *Castillo inexpugnable*, 1528), presented in a dialogical framework that evokes late medieval public disputes. These arguments, however, are presented as ultimately futile. The articulation of the Muslim response to doctrinal dialogue is deliberately anti-rational, which implicitly supports the need to use military action as the only viable means to evangelise Muslims.

HERNÁN LÓPEZ DE YANGUAS

EDITIONS & TRANSLATIONS

Hernando and Espejo Surós, 'Farsa turquesana'
Farsa dicha turquesana (s.l.), c. 1530

STUDIES

Espejo Surós, 'Obra dramática'
Espejo Surós, 'Una aproximación'
Hernando and Espejo Surós, 'Farsa turquesana'
Hernando, 'Escritura y teatro'
Hernando, 'Tiempo dramático'
A. Mas, *Les turcs dans la littérature espagnole du Siècle d'Or. Recherches sur l'évolution d'un théme littéraire*, Paris, 1967

Julio Hernando

Antonio de Aranda

DATE OF BIRTH   Last quarter of the 15th century
PLACE OF BIRTH   Possibly Alcalá de Henares, Castile
DATE OF DEATH   After 1551
PLACE OF DEATH   Possibly Alcalá de Henares

BIOGRAPHY

Antonio de Aranda was a Franciscan friar. He studied in Alcalá de Henares and wrote a number of books, most notably *Verdadera información de la tierra sancta* (1533), the product of the time he spent in the Holy Land. By 1529 he had travelled from Alcalá de Henares to Jerusalem, where he lived in the Monastery of Mount Zion until 1531, one of 40 Franciscan friars who had the care of monasteries in the Holy Land in the years following the capture of Jerusalem by the Ottoman Turks under Süleyman. In 1531 he returned to Europe, it would appear with a secret mission from the head of the monastery to Emperor Charles V, whom he visited in Germany.

Aranda became the tenth Provincial of his order in Castile, elected in Escalona in 1538. He returned to govern the Franciscan province in 1546 and the following year he was elected for a second time as the thirteenth Provincial.

In addition to this work on the Holy Land, Aranda is attributed with two works of a spiritual nature: *Loores del dignissimo lugar de Calvario* (1551), *Loores de la Virgen nuestra Señora* (1552).

Primary
Coronica y historia de la fundación y progresso de la provincia de Castilla, de la Orden del bienaventurado padre San Francisco, Madrid: Impr. Real, 1612, vol. 2, fols 86-87
Diego Álvarez, *Memorial ilustre de los famosos hijos del... convento de Sta. María de Jesús, vulgo San Diego de Alcalá...*, Alcalá: Imprenta de Doña Maria Garcia Briones, 1753, pp. 73-79
Nicolás Antonio, 'F. Antonius de Aranda', in *Bibliotheca Hispana nova*, vol. 1, Matriti: J. de Ibarra, 1783[2], p. 96

Secondary
M. de Castro, 'Fr. Antonio de Aranda, O.F.M., confesor de doña Juana de Austria', *Archivo Íbero-Americano* 37 (1977) 101-23

WORKS ON CHRISTIAN-MUSLIM RELATIONS

Verdadera información de la Tierra Sancta según la disposición en que en este año de Mil y Quinientos y Treinta el autor la vio y passeo
'True information about the Holy Land'

DATE 1533
ORIGINAL LANGUAGE Spanish

DESCRIPTION
Verdadera información de la Tierra Santa (in full, *Verdadera información de la tierra sancta segun la disposición en que en este año de Mil y Quinientos y Treinta el autor la vio y passeo*, 'True information about the Holy Land according to the account in the year 1530 of the author's travels and journey') is a travelogue covering a rich variety of topics. It consists of two treatises, the first containing 38 chapters, and the second containing eight. Many of these are taken up with describing in detail the places where Jesus experienced his passion and death. Of particular interest are the sections containing references to the current situation. For example, Chapter 18 (fol. 46), 'Of the nations and differences of Christians in the church of the Holy Sepulchre and inhabitants of this Holy City of Jerusalem', carefully notes the characteristics of the Greeks, Georgians, Armenians, Jacobites, Abyssinians, Syrians, Maronites and Latins in the city. Aranda is clearly concerned with the form and language of worship: '[They employ] Arabic for the people to understand, as the common language of all Syria as well as Egypt is Arabic. Thus, in this land, the language in which the Greek converses with the Moor and all other nations, and in which other nations converse with nations that are not theirs, is Arabic or, to be better understood, Moorish.'

Aranda describes the Holy Places in detail, using as references biblical texts and the writings of Josephus and St Augustine, and he compares the geography of the Holy Land to similar places in Spain. He describes daily life and different social and religious groups, and the population of Jerusalem, which in 1530 was made up of around 1,000 Christians, 500 Jews and 2,500 Muslims. He refers to the tension between the Ottoman rulers and the Arab population, because Arabs were not considered trustworthy. He also mentions that various agreements were signed between the European powers and the Ottoman Empire to regulate and facilitate pilgrimages. In all this, the representation of the city of Jerusalem is idealised, and increasingly remote from its present condition.

SIGNIFICANCE

In *Verdadera información de la Tierra Santa*, Aranda helps to promote the tradition of considering Jerusalem as the centre of the world, although this is a Jerusalem that is idealised and, above all, preserved as in the time of Jesus Christ. The collective imagination of Christendom is focused by the description of the Holy Places and the idea of pilgrimage to them or, at least, that every Western kingdom should possess a relic, model, engraving, stone or simply pile of sand from the places in which the Redeemer was born, lived and died.

Agustín Redondo ('Devoción tradicional') was highly critical of this work, and raised the question of whether Aranda's parody of the real Jerusalem played a part in the creation of *Viaje de Turquía*: 'The minorite's text perhaps gave [the author] the very idea' for that work. He concludes that 'a certain part of the material of *Viaje de Turquía* is contained, more or less extensively, in *Verdadera información de Tierra Santa*.' Aranda's account, Redondo concludes, 'spurred on the author of *Viaje de Turquía*, as a good disciple of [Erasmus] the humanist of Rotterdam (of whose writings the work makes constant use, in particular the *Colloquies*), to oppose devotion to the ordinary with destructive irony, and to advocate instead a piety of the spirit, stripped of externalities, formalism and deceit.' In view of the playful way of opposing what happens *here* with what happens *there*, Redondo notes that 'unlike in the narrative of *Viaje de Turquía, here* designates the Holy Land, and *there* designates Spain'.

EDITIONS & TRANSLATIONS

> *Verdadera Informacion de la Tierra Sancta segun la disposicion en que en esta anno de MDXXX, el auctor la vio y passeo, Agora nueuamente en esta ultima impression muy corregida y emendada*, Alcalá: Francisco de Cormellas y Pedro de Robles, 1563; repr. Alcalá: Iuan de Villa nueua, 1568; repr. Alcalá: Hernan Ramerez [sic], 1584; repr. Madrid: Impr. Real. 1664
>
> *Verdadera Informacion de la Tierra Sancta segun la disposicion en que en esta anno de MDXXX, el auctor la vio y passeo*, Toledo, Juan de Ayala, 1537; repr. Alcalá de Henares: Juan de Brocar, 1539; repr. Sevilla: Juan Cromberger, 1539; repr. Toledo: Fernando de Sancta Catalina; repr. Toledo: Juan Ferrer, 1551

Verdadera informacion de la tierra sancta segun la disposición en que en este año de Mil y Quinientos y Treinta el autor la vio y passeo, Alcalá de Henares: Miguel de Eguya, 1533

STUDIES

L. Arciniega García, 'Evocaciones y ensueños hispanos del reino de Jerusalén', in I. Rodríguez Moya and V. Mínguez Cornelles (eds), *Arte en los confines del Imperio. Visiones hispánicas de otros mundos*, Castelló, 2011, 49-97, pp. 55, 65, 66, 82, 89

N. Baranda, 'Materia para el espíritu. Tierra Santa, Gran reliquia de las Peregrinaciones (siglo XVI)', *Via spiritus* 8 (2001) 7-29

N. Baranda, 'El camino espiritual a Jerusalén a principios del Renacimiento', in M.E. Schaffer and A. Cortijo Ocaña (eds), *Medieval and Renaissance Spain and Portugal. Studies in honor of Arthur L.-F. Askins*, Woodbridge, 2006, 23-41, pp. 23, 31

M. Ángel de Bunes Ibarra, *La imagen de los musulmanes y del Norte de África en la España de los siglos XVI y XVII. Los caracteres de una hostilidad*, Madrid, 1989, p. 341

P. Cátedra y Anastasio Rojo, *Bibliotecas y lecturas de mujeres. Siglo XVI*, Salamanca, 2004, pp. 148, 305, 379

J. Krejner and M. Wolman Krejner, *Tierra Santa y el Nuevo Mundo durante el imperio Otomano*, Buenos Aires: Fundación Internacional Raoul Wallenberg, Casa Argentina en Israel Tierra Santa, 2007, http://www.raoulwallenberg.net/es/articulos/tierra-santa-durante-imperio/

A. Redondo, 'Devoción tradicional y devoción erasmista en la Castilla de la primera mitad del siglo XVI. De la *Verdadera información de la Tierra Santa* de Antonio de Aranda al *Viaje de Turquía*', in L. López Grigera and A. Redondo (eds), *Homenaje a Eugenio Asensio*, Madrid: Gredos, 1988, 391-416, pp. 393, 405, 415 (repr. in *Revisitando las culturas del Siglo de Oro. Mentalidades, tradiciones culturales, creaciones paraliterarias y literarias*, Salamanca, 2007, 83-106, pp. 105-6)

A. Redondo, 'El mundo turco a través de las "relaciones de sucesos" de finales del siglo XVI y de las primeras décadas del siglo XVII. La percepción de la alteridad y su puesta en obra narrativa', in A. Paba and G. Andrés Renales (eds), *Encuentro de civilizaciones (1500-1750). Informar, celebrar, narrar*, Alcalá de Henares, 2003, 235-53

M. Serrano y Sanz, *Autobiografías y Memorias coleccionadas e ilustradas*, Madrid, 1905

Miguel Ángel Auladell

Bernardo Pérez de Chinchón

DATE OF BIRTH Before 1500
PLACE OF BIRTH Chinchón (Castilla)
DATE OF DEATH 1548
PLACE OF DEATH Gandía (Valencia)

BIOGRAPHY

Bernardo Pérez was born in Chinchón at the end of the 15th century. He possibly studied at the University of Alcalá de Henares, obtaining the degree of Master of Theology. A son and grandson of Jewish converts, his paternal grandfather was condemned by the Inquisition as a heretic and he contaminated all his descendants. But Bernardo Pérez was cleared by the Inquisitor General Alonso Manrique, which allowed him to hold certain positions. In 1523/5, for reasons that are not clear, he moved to Gandía in the Kingdom of Valencia, where he worked as teacher to the sons of the third Duke of Gandía, Juan de Borja. The duke was grateful for his work and appointed him first canon (1532) and afterwards precentor (1538) of the collegiate church of Gandía. In addition to this position, he enjoyed other ecclesiastical benefices, notably that of priest of Alcorcón.

Bernardo Pérez introduced Erasmianism to the ducal court of the Borjas. His sympathy for Erasmus was such that he ensured that Juan de Borja acquired numerous works by Erasmus for his library. Not satisfied with this, he translated several of Erasmus's works, becoming in this way his main translator into Castilian. He translated *Precatio dominica* (1528), the adage *Sileni Alcibiadis* (1529), *Lingua* (1531/33), *De praeparatione ad mortem* (1535) and perhaps *De immense Dei misericordia concio* (1528). He also translated *De bello Mediolanensi et rebus gestis...* (1536) by Galeazzo Flavio Capella, and *De subventione pauperum* by Juan Luis Vives, which he was not able to publish.

He was involved in the conversion of the Moriscos, participating in evangelising campaigns that were carried out in the Kingdom of Valencia, together with the Franciscan, Brother Bartolomé de los Angeles, and the Dominican, Brother Juan Micó. This commission to work as preacher to the Moriscos came his way after the publication of his two works *Libro llamado Antialcorano* (1532) and *Diálogos christianos contra la secta mahomética y contra la pertinacia de los judíos* (1534).

All his literary work was published between 1528 and 1536, which leads one to think that someone advised him or obliged him to keep silent after this, possibly because the historical circumstances of the time, after the death of Alfonso de Valdés and of Erasmus himself, were not favourable to Erasmianism. From 1536 until his death in 1548, he remained in Gandía without writing any other work, continuing in his position as precentor, and as tutor to Pedro Luis Galcerán de Borja, Grand Master of the Order of Montesa, and advisor to Duke Juan de Borja, and ensuring the future wellbeing of his family. On his death, his nephew, Diego Sánchez, who was very close to the new Duke, Francisco de Borja, inherited his position as precentor.

MAIN SOURCES OF INFORMATION

Primary
Erasmus, *Declaración del Pater Noster... Item el sermón de la grandeza y muchedumbre de las misericordias de Dios nuestro Señor*, trans. Bernardo Pérez?, Logroño: Miguel Eguía, 1528
Erasmus, *Silenos de Alcibíades*, trans. Bernardo Pérez, Valencia: Jorge Costilla, 1529
Bernardo Pérez, *Libro llamado Antialcorano, que quiere decir contra el Alcorán de Mahoma*, Valencia: Francisco Díaz Romano, 1532
Erasmus, *La Lengua de Erasmo nuevamente romanzada por muy elegante estilo*, trans. Bernardo Pérez, Sevilla: Juan Cromberger, 1533
Bernardo Pérez, *Diálogos christianos contra la secta mahomética y contra la pertinacia de los judíos*, Valencia: Francisco Díaz Romano, 1534
Erasmus, *Apercibimiento de la muerte y declaración sobre los diez mandamientos de la ley christiana*, trans. Bernardo Pérez, Valencia: Francisco Díaz Romano, 1535
Galeazzo Flavio Capella, *Historia de las cosas que han pasado en Italia*, trans. Bernardo Pérez, Valencia, 1536
Juan Luis Vives, *Tratado del Socorro de los pobres*, trans. Bernardo Pérez (MS Valencia, Biblioteca Serrano Morales, Sig. 6495) (before 1542)
Bernardo Pérez de Chinchón, *Antialcorano. Diálogos christianos. Conversión y evangelización de moriscos*, ed. F. Pons Fuster, Alicante: Universidad de Alicante, 2000

Secondary
F. Pons Fuster, 'Nuevas aportaciones biográficas sobre el maestro Bernardo Pérez de Chinchón', *Escritos del Vedat* 33 (2003) 332-67
F. Pons Fuster, *Erasmistas, mecenas y humanistas en la cultura valenciana de la primera mitad del siglo XVI*, Valencia, 2003

J. Parellada, 'Nuevos datos sobre la *raça* del maestro Bernardo Pérez de Chinchón', *Boletín de la Real Academia de las Buenas Letras de Barcelona* 46 (1998) 157-98

J. Parellada, 'Una traducción inédita de Bernardo Pérez de Chinchón. El *Tratado llamado Socorro de Pobres*, de Juan Luis Vives', *Voz y Letra* 9 (1998) 75-95

F. Pons Fuster, 'Bernat Pérez (de Chinchón). Un erasmista en la Cort dels Borja a Gandía', *Afers. Fulls de Recerca i Pensament* 11/23 (1996) 153-76

S. García Martínez, 'Las ediciones y los traductores valencianos de Erasmo (1528-1535)', *Erasme i l'Erasmisme*, Tarragona, 1986, pp. 171-93

M. Bataillon, *Erasmo y España. Estudios sobre la historia espiritual del siglo XVI*, México, 1979

L. Cardaillac, *Moriscos y cristianos. Un enfrentamiento polémico (1492-1640)*, Madrid, 1979

M. Bataillon, 'La *raça* del erasmista Bernardo Pérez de Chinchón', *Libro-homenaje a Antonio Pérez Gómez*, Cieza, Valencia, 1978, i, pp. 65-89

D. Severin, *La lengua de Erasmo romanzada por muy elegante estilo. Traducción espanola del siglo XVI por Bernardo Pérez de Chinchón* (Anejos del Boletín de la Real Academia Espanola 21), Madrid, 1975, pp. vii-xxxiv

WORKS ON CHRISTIAN-MUSLIM RELATIONS

Libro llamado Antialcorán, 'The book known as Against the Qur'an'

DATE 1532
ORIGINAL LANGUAGE Spanish

DESCRIPTION

Bernardo Pérez wrote *Antialcorano* as a response to a problem created by the forced baptisms of Valencian Muslims during the revolt of the Germanías (1519-22). For him the task of evangelisation of the new converts, the Moriscos, was arduous and complex since few clergy felt willing to preach to them and teach them Christian beliefs, but were content for them simply to attend Mass and fulfil the basic teachings of Christianity. The few priests who were in charge of Morisco parishes carried out minimal duties and did little beyond noting the reluctance of the Moriscos to give up their faith and customs. This was probably either because the priests' income was low, or due to the insecurity of their work or opposition from Valencian nobles. Armed with Christian zeal and personal commitment, Pérez set about writing *Antialcorano*, based on sermons by Martín García and also on *Confutación de la secta mahomética* by Juan Andrés, the former Muslim scholar of Xàtiva who had converted to Christianity. He also spoke to scholars in his circle, such as the judge (*alcadi*) Moscayre, Mangay and the scholar Zumilla (José Arávigo), with whom he mixed and even had friendly connections.

Antialcorano consists of 26 sermons, supposedly preached to a Morisco audience. Its style is direct and respectful to the listeners, and even though it is against the Qur'an and the principles of Islam, it is possible to find in it repeated calls for peace and agreement as necessary elements for eliminating discord between the Christian and Muslim communities. Pérez also appears to want to distinguish between Muslim teachings, which he thinks the Moricos do not know, and their own practices, which he sees mainly as localised customs.

Pérez covers the main themes of the Qur'an and Sunna, including paradise, circumcision, fasting, prayer, holy war, slaughter of animals, not drinking wine and not eating pork, and also their reluctance to talk about their beliefs, especially with Christians (he repeats this frequently). He discusses these themes simply and literally, and refutes them by comparing them with Christian law, which he considers as the truth.

The book contains stories from the life of Muḥammad, all of which it discredits, and it also refers to Muḥammad's dependence on Christianity for his teachings, about which Pérez comments that they were not accepted by some Muslim philosophers.

Finally, *Antialcorano* is full of everyday examples, which reinforces the impression that the sermons were really preached to the Moriscos of Valencia.

SIGNIFICANCE

The book did not have a wide circulation, despite the size of the Morisco population in Valencia. The Valencian clergy, to whom it was directed, did not use it in their evangelising work, and the second edition had as little success as the first. This second edition was brought out in Salamanca in 1595, paid for by the Bishop of Jaen, Francisco Sarmiento, for use by the priests of his diocese in their evangelisation work with the Moriscos who had been expelled from the kingdom of Granada after the uprising of 1568.

The work was, however, cited and responded to by Morisco authors who had been exiled to North Africa after the expulsion of 1609. This indicates that it aroused some interest among Muslim intellectuals.

EDITIONS & TRANSLATIONS

Antialcorano. Diálogos christianos. Conversión y evangelización de moriscos, ed. F. Pons Fuster, Alicante, 2000

Libro llamado antialcorano, Valencia, 1993 (microfiche of original edition)

Libro llamado Antialcorano, que quiere decir contra el Alcorán de Mahoma, Salamanca: Iuan y Andrés Renaut, 1595

Libro llamado Antialcorano, que quiere decir contra el Alcorán de Mahoma, Valencia: Francisco Díaz Romano, 1532

STUDIES

F. Pons Fuster, 'Bernardo Pérez de Chinchón y Juan Andrés. Dos escritores cristianos de polémica religiosa', *Valencianos en la Historia de la Iglesia* 4 (2013) 135-78

Pons Fuster, 'Nuevas aportaciones biográficas'

Pons Fuster, *Erasmistas, mecenas y humanistas*

Parellada, 'Nuevos datos sobre la *raça*'

Parellada, 'Una traducción inédita'

Pons Fuster, 'Bernat Pérez (de Chinchón)'

García Martínez, 'Las ediciones y los traductores valencianos'

Bataillon, *Erasmo y España*

Cardaillac, *Moriscos y cristianos*

Bataillon, 'La *raça* del erasmista'

Severin, *La lengua de Erasmo romanzada por muy elegante estilo*

Diálogos christianos contra la secta mahomética y contra la pertinacia de los judíos, 'Christian dialogue against the Muḥammadan sect and against the obstinacy of the Jews'

DATE 1535
ORIGINAL LANGUAGE Castilian

DESCRIPTION

In Pérez's own words, this work is a 'dispute made by way of dialogue'. It takes the form of a dialogue between two friends, Bernardo and José. Bernardo represents Pérez himself, and José represents José Arávigo (under the name Zumilla), Bernardo's master, the former alfaquí of Gandía, who is now a Christian convert. He plays the role of defender of the Islamic position. The work is dedicated to the absent Archbishop of Valencia, Ehrard de Lamarck, appealing to his responsibility as the highest ecclesiastical authority in the Kingdom of Valencia to engage in the evangelisation of the Moors. In this appeal, Pérez reminds him that he is not meant to start this task from scratch, because Pérez himself and others (he mentions Gaspar Rubio and the Vicar General John Gay) had already been engaged in it, and besides, the archbishop had ensured that the Moors had their own pastor to instruct them in Christian doctrine. All these efforts had been unsuccessful because the Moors raised all kinds of resistance to Christian beliefs, and were disinclined to give up their Islamic customs.

The setting of the dialogue is an orchard in Gandía, where the two friends walk together, talking throughout the conversation on friendly terms.

The work is divided into seven dialogues. In the first three, the conversation is lively and positive. In the fourth dialogue, the dialogue form breaks down and is replaced by a long doctrinal exposition from Bernardo. This becomes the fifth dialogue, which is interrupted, and the twelfth sermon from *Antialcorano* is inserted. Then, in the sixth and seventh dialogues (which are really monologues), Bernardo displays his learning by using scripture and St Augustine, as well as St Cyprian's two works against the Jews. At the end, José unsurprisingly acknowledges the superiority of the Christian law.

SIGNIFICANCE

The work went completely unnoticed at the time. No reference to it is found in any later Valencian author, nor in other Muslim or Christian authors. Many expressions found in it are reminiscent of those used earlier by Alfonso Valdes.

EDITIONS & TRANSLATIONS

Antialcorano. Diálogos christianos. Conversión y evangelización de moriscos, ed. F. Pons Fuster, Alicante, 2000

Diálogos christianos contra la secta mahomética y contra la pertinacia de los judíos, Valencia, Francisco Díaz Romano, 1535

Francisco Pons Fuster

Nicolaes Cleynaerts

Niklaas Cleynaerts (alias Beke, Bece, Beken, Beka, de Beka), Nicolas Clénard, Nicolau Clenardo, Nicolas Clenardus, Nicolaus Clenardus, Nicolaus Cleonardus, Nicolas Clenardus

DATE OF BIRTH 5/6 December 1493
PLACE OF BIRTH Diest, Belgium
DATE OF DEATH 5 November 1542
PLACE OF DEATH Granada

BIOGRAPHY

Nicolaes Cleynaerts was the eldest son of Peter Cleynaerts, known also as Beke. That second name is quite important since Nicolaes continued to use it into his thirties. In 1512, he enrolled at the University of Louvain as Nicolaus de Beka de Diest. After three years, he took his MA in the *artes liberales* and started his study of theology, which would take 12 years. During this period, he fully embraced humanist values.

In the course of the 1520s, the famous *Psalter of Nebbio*, containing the Psalms in five different languages, fell into his hands. Cleynaerts could read all the columns, except for one: that in Arabic script. He had to use all his creative powers to decipher the Arabic letters.

In 1527, Cleynaerts was awarded his degree in theology and started to teach Latin, Greek and Hebrew. For the benefit of his students he had some books printed: a Hebrew grammar (1529), edited by Dirk Martens, and *Six dialogues of Chrysostom*, a Greek text edition. His most important publication, *Institutiones in linguam Graecam* (April 1530), was a Greek grammar that was to make his name known throughout Europe. More than 500,000 copies of it were sold in the centuries after his death. In the spring of 1531, he published a small book, *Meditationes Graecanicae*, 'that will make professors of Greek redundant', which did indeed made it possible for amateurs to study Greek on their own.

Then, his life took a turn. At the beginning of October 1531, Cleynaerts met don Hernando Colón, the son of Christopher Columbus. Colón wanted to take a specialist with him to Spain to help him with his new library, the current *Biblioteca Colombina*. Within a few days, Cleynaerts was on his way to Seville. But in Salamanca, the local authorities were so pleased with his presence that they asked Colón to release Cleynaerts from his contract. Cleynaerts obtained an appointment at the old university and became a friend of Hernán Núñez, a professor who had studied Arabic in his youth. In 1533, Cleynaerts published another book, the text of Livy's *Ab urbe condita* Book 1.

In November 1534, João III of Portugal summoned Cleynaerts to Évora and made him the *preceptor* of Prince Henry, his younger brother. He held this post until 1538. In Braga, he published a Latin grammar (1538) and gave Latin lessons to all the inhabitants of the city by acting out little scenes, polishing his shoes, blowing his nose or playing the role of a fat cardinal, all using short Latin sentences repeated over and over (a conversational method still used today in tourist language guides, such as Assimil or Berlitz).

In November 1538, Cleynaerts decided to return home, but first he wanted to get hold of an Arabic master who was willing to follow him to Brabant, as a kind of 'living grammar'. His search took him from Coimbra, Évora and Seville to the Alhambra of Granada, where he met a Moorish slave, a certain Kharūf. With the help of this man, Cleynaerts perfected his knowledge of Arabic, starting to read the Qur'an, and immersing himself in the mysteries of Muslim theology. In these months, the dream of his life took shape: Cleynaerts wanted to engage in a 'peaceful crusade' against Islam and convert Muslims to Christianity *lingua et calamo* ('by tongue and pen'). But first, he went to Africa to get to know the Muslim milieu.

In April 1540, Cleynaerts crossed the Strait of Gibraltar and reached Fez, the spiritual centre of Islam in North Africa. After a favourable meeting with the sultan, he was housed in a sort of hotel called *Duana* (perhaps the Latin transcription of Diwān, a quarter in Fez), intended for foreign visitors and tradesmen. Cleynaerts tried to gain the confidence of the *Fassi* (the inhabitants of Fez), but got involved in a bitter conflict with the so-called 'monster', a person whom Cleynaerts never names but who was probably Sebastião de Vargas, the Portuguese delegate in Fez. He had to flee to the *Milla*, an enclosed part of the town, where the Jews enjoyed a certain degree of freedom. The situation worsened when the Portuguese court stopped its payments to Cleynaerts: apparently he had fallen into disgrace with Prince Henry. He had to leave Fez, penniless and disappointed.

Travelling via Asilah, Cleynaerts reached Cádiz and then Granada. There he wrote a letter to Charles V, asking for his support. It is not known whether the court replied to his request. In his last letter, addressed to his Portuguese friend Joannes Parvus, Cleynaerts announced that he would once again leave for Fez 'in a few days' time'. But this never happened: he died in the Alhambra on 5 November 1542.

MAIN SOURCES OF INFORMATION

Primary

A. Roersch, *Correspondance de Nicolas Clénard*, 3 vols, Brussels, 1940-1 (the standard edition of all Cleynaerts' known letters; vol. 1 consists of the Latin text of 64 letters, vol. 2 contains notes and comments, and vol. 3 gives a French translation of 42 letters; the bibliography, i, pp. xv-xvi, and ii, pp. 169-71, lists all important studies and articles published before 1940)

Secondary

G. Le Callatay, 'Apprendre l'arabe en autodidact est possible. Nicolaus Clenardus l'a fait au 16ème siecle et il nous explique comment', *Acta Orientalia Belgica* 25 (2012) 9-30

A.N.M. Correia, *Nicolau Clenardo (1493/1494-1542)*, Lisbon, 2011, www.arlindo-correia.com/240611.html

S. Weemans, 'Nicolaes Cleynaerts (1493-1542). "Een vergeten vreedzame kruistocht"', Louvain, 2005 (MA diss. University of Louvain)

G. Tournoy, 'Les relations entre Damião de Góis, Nicolas Clénard et l'université de Louvain', in *Actas do Congresso Internacional Damião de Góis na Europa do Renascimento* Braga, 2003, 719-29

J. Dewulf, 'As cartas do humanista Nicolau Clenardo sobre Portugal', in L.A. da Fonseca, L.C. Amaral and M.F. Ferreira Santos (eds), *Os Reinos Ibéricos na Idade Média*, Porto, 2003, i, 581-89

G. Tournoy et al., *Nicolaes Cleynaerts (1493-1542). The remarkable travel adventures of a 16th century humanist, Arabist and Islam-expert*, Louvain, 2002 (CD)

J.M. Ruiz Asencio, 'El equipo de trabajo de Hernando Colón en la organización de su biblioteca', in M.C. Hubert et al. (eds), *Actes du 12ème Colloque scientifique du Comité International de Paléographie latine*, Paris, 2000, 217-25

P.S. van Koningsveld, 'Mon Kharuf. Quelques remarques sur le maître tunisien du premier arabisant néerlandais, Nicolas Clénard (1493-1542)', in A. Temimi (ed.), *Nouvelles approches des relations islamo-chrétiens à l'époque de la Renaissance. Actes de la troisième rencontre scientifique*, Zaghouan, 2000, 123-41

R. Hoven, 'Les Institutiones grammaticae latinae de Nicolas Clénard', in R. Schnur et al. (eds), *Acta Conventus Neolatini Abulensis. Proceedings of the tenth international congress of Neo-Latin studies*, Tempe AZ, 2000, 353-60

J. Tulkens, A. van Dievoet and M.C. van Grunderbeek, 'Rouwdichten van Nicolaes Cleynaerts ter gelegenheid van Erasmus' overlijden', *Anderlechtensia. Driemaandelijks tijdschrift van de Geschied- en heemkundige kring van Anderlecht* 76 (1995) 3-13

J.C. Lavajo, 'Itinéraire islamo-arabisant de Clénard. Apport ibérique à un projet', in C. Vázquez de Benito and M.A. Manzano Rodríguez (eds), *Actas XVI Congresso de l'Union Européenne d'Arabisants et Islamisants*, Salamanca, 1995, 291-99

G. Tournoy, J. Tulkens and M. Ilegems, 'Nicolaes Cleynaerts (1493-1593). Van Diest tot Marokko', *De Brabantse Folklore en Geschiedenis* 278-9 (1993) (exhibition catalogue)

J. Tulkens, 'Een merkwaardige humanist, Nicolaes Cleynaerts (1493-1542)', *Hermeneus* 65 (1993) 173-79

J.R.C. Martin, 'Clenardo, Resende and Erasmus', *Euphrosyne. Revista de Filologia Clássica* n.s. 21 (1993) 375-88

J.C. Lavajo, 'L'humaniste Nicolas Clénard, un arabisant ami du Portugal et du Maroc', in *Actes du colloque Le Maroc et le Portugal. Dialogue des cultures*, Rabat, 1991, 11-15

P. Swiggers, 'Aspects linguistiques de la correspondence de Nicolas Clénard', in K. Dutz (ed.), *Speculum historiographiae linguisticae*, Münster, 1989, 395-403

S. Cornil, 'Humanistes belges au Portugal. Clénard et Vasaeus', in *Actes du 20ème Colloque international d'études humanistes*, Paris, 1984, 335-44

M.A. Rodrigues, 'Nicolau Clenardo hebraista', *Humanitas* 33-34 (1981-82) 49-80

L. Bakelants and R. Hoven, *Bibliographie des oeuvres de Nicolas Clénard 1529-1700*, Verviers, 1981

M. Breda-Simoes, 'Un pédagogiste du 16ème siècle. Nicolas Clénard', in *Pédagogues et juristes. Congrès du Centre d'Etudes Supérieures de la Renaissance de Tours*, Paris, 1963, 157-72

H. de Vocht, *History of the foundation and the rise of the Collegium Trilingue Lovaniense 1517-1550*, Louvain, 1951-55, ii, pp. 220-24 *et passim*; iii, pp. 164-70, 174-75, 185-88 *et passim*

L. Kukenheim, *Contributions à l'histoire de la grammaire grecque, latine et hébraïque à l'époque de la Renaissance*, Leyden, 1951, pp. 157-72

H. de Vocht et al., *Nicolaus Clenardus*, Antwerp, 1942

A. Lefranc, 'Nicolas Clénard, humaniste belge, et les commencements du Collège de France', *Humanisme et Renaissance* 7 (1940) 253-69

H. de Vocht, *Texts and studies about Louvain humanists in the first half of the 16th century*, Louvain, 1934, pp. 409-23

R. Le Tourneau, 'Notes sur les lettres latines de Nicolas Clénard relatant son séjour dans le royaume de Fès (1540-1541)', *Hespéris* 19 (1934) 45-63

J. Neve, 'Une lettre autographe inédite de Nicolas Clénard', *Revue Belge de Philologie et d'Histoire* 9 (1930) 887-96

M.G. Cerejeira, *O Renascimento em Portugal*, Coimbra, 1917-18 (1974-75²)
F. Watson, 'Clenard as an educational pioneer', *Classical Review* 29 (1915) 65-8, 97-100, 129-34 (article published in three consecutive issues of the journal)
C. Kampffmeyer, 'Nicolaus Clenardus', *Mitteilungen der Gesellschaft für deutsche Erziehungs- und Schulgeschichte* 18 (1908) 1-22
V. Chauvin and A. Roersch, *Etude sur la vie et les travaux de Nicolas Clénard*, Brussels, 1900

WORKS ON CHRISTIAN-MUSLIM RELATIONS

De professione Arabica militiaque constituenda adversus Machometum; De vreedzame kruistocht; La croisade pacifique; A cruzada pacífica, 'The peaceful crusade'

DATE 1539-42
ORIGINAL LANGUAGE Latin

DESCRIPTION

'The peaceful crusade' is an umbrella term given by modern scholars to Cleynaerts' peaceful approach towards Islam. The term is inspired by his *Epistola ad Christianos*, written in Fez, but never finished. At the top of this letter Cleynaerts wrote: *De professione Arabica militiaque constituenda adversus Machometum*. Modern scholars have borrowed the term *militia* (crusade) and extended it with the term 'peaceful' in order to emphasise Cleynaerts' intentions to fight the Muslims 'with tongue and pen'. However, the *Epistola ad Christianos* does not contain much information about Cleynaerts' project because the letter is a sort of biography that ends before Cleynaerts could say much about the birth of his peaceful plans in Granada. Most elements of his project are contained in the letters he wrote to his friends, especially those written between 1539 and 1542 (Roersch, *Correspondance*, i, nos 47-63; the page numbers that follow refer to this edition unless otherwise stated).

Cleynaerts' letters contain a lot of information about Morocco in the 16th century, about the *Fassi* and their customs. Concerning Muslim rites, Cleynaerts presents a remarkable insight into how a 16th-century Catholic theologian regarded the strange rituals of Islamic belief. Cleynaerts deals with the *ḥajj* (i, no. 47, ll. 196-241), Muslim marriage (i, no. 47, ll. 178-84), the wives of Muḥammad (i, no. 47, ll. 185-86), the Muslim paradise (i, no. 47, ll. 161-70) and the equanimity of Muslims in disasters (i, no. 54, ll. 286-92). He also refers to the rules for washing and urinating (i, no. 47, ll. 191-96), presents some traditional stories about Muḥammad (i, no. 63, ll. 116-27 and no. 54, ll. 216-47) and mentions the respect Muslims have for the Qur'an (i, no. 47, ll. 138-40 and no. 63, ll. 122-27). All this knowledge was to help him in the implementation of his peaceful crusade.

At first, Cleynaerts' interest in Arabic was mainly philological. As a humanist scholar he loved the study of languages and he was challenged by every text he could not read or understand at first sight. In 1539, though, his former colleague and friend in Salamanca, the theologian Francisco de Vitoria (c. 1480-1546), stimulated him to go further. Since a good part of Spain was – in his view – 'infected' by Islam, Cleynaerts had to prepare himself to write against Muḥammad. Later, his Latin book should be translated into Greek as well, because Greece was totally 'in the hands of Muḥammad' (i, no. 47, ll. 123-30).

In a letter addressed to his fellow townsman, Arnold Streyters (1496-1560), Cleynaerts explains how the dream of a peaceful crusade began to take shape: 'I have started to read the Qur'an in Arabic and gradually I have learned from my teacher what appalling errors the Muḥammadan people have ensconced themselves in. Whether I hit upon the idea coincidentally or whether God directed me, I decided to set aside all my other pursuits, leave the other languages as they stood and completely dedicate the years that God may grant me to the study of Arabic. I will not rest until I have mastered speaking and writing so that I can fight the followers of Muḥammad with tongue and pen' (i, no. 55, ll. 42-48).

In this plan, Cleynaerts' Moorish slave, the so-called *Charufius* (i, no. 58, l. 83), had to play an important role. According to P.S. van Koningsveld ('Mon Kharuf'), the man was called Muḥammad ibn Abī l-Faḍl ibn Kharūf al-Tūnisī, and he was a scholar from Tunisia who had been taken to Spain after the capture of Tunis in 1535. Arab biographers claim that there is a fragment of his autobiography (a *fihrist*) in a manuscript in the library of Rabat. However, the document cannot currently be found due to a careless signature. The loss is compensated for by a *fihrist* of one of Kharūf's pupils, Aḥmad al-Manjūr, who claims that his master, Kharūf al-Tūnisī, was assigned to a Spanish priest. Kharūf was said to have given Arabic lessons to the priest to help him read the Qur'an.

Obviously Kharūf had an excellent reputation in Fez. At the time when Cleynaerts first met the ruler of Fez, Aḥmad al-Waṭṭāsī, the Sultan asked him if Kharūf could come to Fez. Cleynaerts, who had hoped to take the man with him to Louvain, could not refuse without antagonising the sultan, so the learned Moor came to Fez, where he gave religious instruction until his death in 1559.

How did Cleynaerts picture his religious dialogue? As a theologian he shared the fundamental attitude of his contemporaries: the Christian faith was the only true faith, and other religious beliefs were deviations that every true believer had to fight against. This attitude is expressed not only in the letter addressed to Streyters, but also in other letters in which Cleynaerts ridicules the ethics and religious rites of the Muslims, or, at the very best, uses humour to put them into perspective. Examples of this kind of mockery are to be found in the letter of 12 July 1539, addressed to his former mentor, Jacobus Latomus (i, no. 47, ll. 138-234). Apart from that, the situation of the Muslims on the Iberian Peninsula did not make things any easier. As a Catholic theologian, Cleynaerts was required to support the intolerant actions of the ecclesiastical authorities, while as a humanist he, in essence, stood for a peaceful approach.

At first Cleynaerts followed the advice of Francisco de Vitoria: his plans were mainly directed at the conversion of Spanish and Greek Muslims. Later, he became more ambitious and intended to address all Muslims in their own language, orally as well as in writing. With this in mind, he asked members of the Spanish court to put surviving Arab manuscripts and books relating to Muslim theology at his disposal instead of consigning them to the flames (i, no. 47, ll. 109-18). In 1542, he directed the same request to Charles V (i, no. 61, ll. 172-74). Further, he wanted to translate the Qur'an into Latin and to ask European theologians to formulate their opinions on its contents. Universities also had to play their role (i, no. 52, ll. 50-52 and no. 53, ll. 21-24). Then, he would have the whole lot printed in Arabic and spread throughout Europe and Africa (i, no. 47, ll. 299-305).

On more than one occasion, Cleynaerts emphasises the importance of mastering languages. He pleaded strongly for the translation of the Talmud into Spanish, so that the Inquisitors could consult the books themselves. Moreover, those books contained many things that were worth reading (i, no. 53, ll. 55-68). And, of course, if one wished to approach Muslims, knowledge of Arabic was essential (i, no. 55, ll. 64-68). Ignorance, on the other hand, led to violence, lack of understanding, persecutions, death at the stake. Cleynaerts would rather take his example from the Apostles: they did not throw idolatrous statues into the fire; they did not chase anyone from his home. The Apostles started from the liberating power of God's word. When, in due course, the non-believers were convinced, they would burn their heretical books themselves (i, no. 53, ll. 38-39).

Now and then, Cleynaerts was so angry about the intolerance of the Spanish Inquisitors that he voiced strong and not completely harmless opinions: 'His Excellency the Marquis of Granada recently wrote to me that the *Colloquia* by Erasmus – along with lots of other books that lambasted the monks – have been consigned to the flames and that even Vives is in danger. What will happen to me, do you think, if they hear of my Qur'an? Well, let them rant on, let them give us the full blast of their wrath!' (i, no. 53, ll. 76-81).

When Cleynaerts' letters were published after his death, the Inquisition thought it necessary to censor certain passages (Tournoy et al., 'Van Diest tot Marokko', p. 282).

Cleynaerts believed that the Moorish heresy quite simply was based on a number of misunderstandings in their interpretation of the Old and New Testaments: 'I have started to read the Qur'an with my Moor, a book that means as much to Muḥammadans as the Pentateuch to Jews and the Gospel to Christians [...] Just as the appearance of the Gospel superseded the Law of Moses, so Muḥammad succeeded Christ, as they claim. That is the heart of the matter. The dialogue has to start here' (i, no. 47, ll. 138-45).

Muslims thus strongly believed that in the New Testament Muḥammad was appointed the successor to Christ. According to Cleynaerts, they based their claim on a passage from the Gospel of John (16:7) in which Jesus announces the coming of a *Paraclete*, so he sometimes speaks of Muḥammad as the 'false' or the 'Arab' *Paraclete* (i, no. 54, ll. 219-21, 317-18). It seems that Cleynaerts' attitude towards Muslims changed in the course of his stay in Fez. Thanks to his increasing knowledge of Islam and his positive character, his bold statements about the Moorish heresy softened. Now and then mockery gave way to esteem (i, no. 54, ll. 286-92). This inspired F.M. Olbrechts to a slightly romantic idealisation of Cleynaerts' demeanour and he claims that Cleynaerts' interest in the language, habits, science and education of 'the Mussulmen' was so passionate and so intense 'that he idolised them in his heart' (Olbrechts, 'Rond Cleynaerts' reis naar Marokko', p. 48).

Arab sources went even further. According to al-Manjūr, Moriscos in Andalusia believed that Cleynaerts was thinking about converting to Islam: 'That Christian [Cleynaerts] was one of their dignitaries. He was the son-in-law [*sic*] of the Marquis, Prince of Granada. It is said he was looking for the truth, that he was inclined towards Islam, that he wept when he read the Qur'an and that he died a Muslim. The Christians had suspected all this and so they had planned to burn him at the stake. But this did not come about, mainly because they wanted to hide [this shame] from the people and there were [also] political reasons because he was one of their priests. [This information] has been given to me by our teacher [Kharūf] who drew on news he had heard from others. Indeed, it was his custom to consult people who came from Andalusia to Fez. The priest got along well with our teacher, although he had acquired him for approximately 1,000 *uqiya*, probably because at that time Islam had not yet touched his heart' (Van Koningsveld, 'Mon Kharūf', pp. 128-29).

S. Weemans, however, considers that it is not realistic to assume that Cleynaerts 'was inclined towards Islam'. The expression 'that he wept, reading the Qur'an' is a set phrase that can be found in other, similar contexts (Weemans, 'Nicolaes Cleynaerts', p. 32, n. 121).

SIGNIFICANCE
During the Middle Ages, the sword was the most popular weapon in the battle against Islam. For a humanist such as Cleynaerts, this approach was fundamentally wrong. As a result, his efforts sharply contrasted with the intolerance of the Spanish and Portuguese authorities

However, his intentions were not unique. Cleynaerts shares a line of thinking that had survived among Christian intellectuals since the 13th century. The crusades had failed in their attempts to convert Muslims and so a number of scholars (e.g. Peter the Venerable, Roger Bacon, Ramon Martí, Ramon Llull, Riccoldo da Monte di Croce, Juan de Segovia, Nicholas of Cusa) favoured an alternative approach, sometimes interwoven with a more evangelical attitude. In his treatise on education (*De tradendis disciplinis*), Juan Luis Vives made an explicit plea for schools to be founded that would teach Arabic and other Islamic languages (Van Roey, 'Cleynaerts' Arabische studies', p. 144).

Cleynaerts himself wanted to establish a school in Louvain for the training of priests in Arabic, after which they would go to Africa to start a dialogue with Muslims and preach the Gospel. But, of course, those plans were rejected by the ecclesiastical and civil authorities. The Spanish royal court certainly agreed to support an Arabic school, but only if Cleynaerts would found it in Granada, where it could prepare Arabic-speaking priests for the Moriscos (i, no. 61, ll. 130-40).

Cleynaerts undoubtedly deserves some admiration for the way he sustained his pacifist attitude until the bitter end, for the risks he took to get hold of manuscripts in Fez, for the humour he showed despite the worst setbacks, for the courage with which he postponed his return to his beloved *dulce Lovanium* and for the single-mindedness with which he planned a second journey to Fez (i, no. 62, ll. 33-34). That the 'core of the heresy', to him, rested on a different interpretation of the word *Paraclete* is, of course, a naïve simplification. And his belief that imparting the correct – i.e. Christian – interpretation would lead to the conversion of Muslims was the product of a well-meant but unbridled enthusiasm.

In the centuries after his death, Cleynaerts' letters were translated and reprinted several times, but readers took more interest in what they said about the dangers of travelling and the customs of other people than in his peaceful crusade. Weemans, however, points to a project, developed by Jean Vendeville (1527-92), bishop of Tournai. Thirty years after Cleynaerts' death, Vendeville promoted the same ideas about the approach to other religions that Cleynaerts had recommended towards Islam: the establishment of ecclesiastical seminaries for the training of 'evangelical workers' who could establish themselves in non-believing communities. Within the Catholic Church, Vendeville's efforts contributed to establishing the Sacred Congregation for the Propagation of the Faith (*Propaganda Fidei* in Rome in 1622; renamed in 1967 Congregation for the Evangelisation of Peoples). But in the presentation of his project to various popes, Vendeville never used the name of Nicolaes Cleynaerts. At the end of the 16th century his peaceful crusade already seemed to have been forgotten (Weemans, 'Nicolaes Cleynaerts', pp. 77-78).

It is only during the last 30 years, characterised as they are by increasing migration, globalisation and confrontation with other religions and opinions, that Cleynaerts' message seems to have been heard again. Guido Vanheeswijck points to 'the rejected legacy' of the first generation of humanists of northern Europe (Desiderius Erasmus, Thomas More and his lesser-known colleagues, Nicolaes Cleynaerts and Pieter Gillis-Aegidius) (*Tolerantie en actief pluralisme*, Antwerp, 2008). Vanheeswijck considers them to be the first adepts of 'active pluralism'. Passive tolerance, Vanheeswijck claims, cannot solve the problems we are facing today. It is no longer possible to hide behind safe walls and to ignore the differences between cultures and religions.

MANUSCRIPTS

Two of Cleynaerts' autograph letters survive:

MS Olsztyn (Poland), Archive of Warmia Archdiocese (Archiwum Archidiecezji Warmińskiej) – AB D4 (Epistolae ad Joannem Dantiscum), fol. 116 (1531; no. 6 in Roersch's edition; a facsimile is reproduced in G. Tournoy, 'Van Diest tot Marokko', p. 239)

MS Vat – Lat. 6199, fols 70-71 (1536; no. 35 in Roersch's edition; addressed to Hieronymus Aleander [1480-1542])

Until recently, a third letter was preserved in MS Brussels, Collection J. Nève (1531; no. 10 in Roersch's edition, with a facsimile on pp. 9-10; addressed to Joannes Tartesius, originally bound in a book of P. Beroaldus, *Oratio Proverborum*, Bologna, 1499; the original MS is currently lost)

EDITIONS & TRANSLATIONS

J. Tulkens, *Perro cristão entre Muçulmanos*, Lisbon, 2007

J. Tulkens, *Christenhond tussen moslims*, Antwerp, 2006 (Dutch trans.)

Tournoy et al., *Nicolaes Cleynaerts (1493-1542)*

M. Gillain, *Nicolaes Cleynaerts, pastor de amor. Een muzikale vertelling over de dramatische lotgevallen van een Vlaming in het Spanje van de 16de eeuw*, Antwerp, 1999

Tulkens, van Dievoet and van Grunderbeek, 'Rouwdichten van Nicolaes Cleynaerts'

Tournoy, Tulkens and Ilegems, 'Van Diest tot Marokko', pp. 147-76 (Dutch trans. of ten letters of Cleynaerts by M. Ilegems)

J. Tulkens, *In de ban van Mohammed*, Antwerp, 1993

H. de Vocht et al., *Nicolaus Clenardus*, Antwerp, 1942, pp. 87-106 (Dutch trans. of excerpts from some letters by A. Deheegher)

A. Roersch, *Clénard, peint par lui-même*, Brussels, 1942

Roersch, *Correspondance de Nicolas Clénard* (vol. 3 contains a French trans. of 42 letters)

Cerejeira, *O Renascimento em Portugal*, i, pp. 235-386 (20 letters concerning Cleynaerts' stay in Portugal; extensive summary of the Latin text, alternated with large portions of a Portuguese trans.)

P. van der Aa, *Naauwkeurige voyagie van Nicolaas Clenard*, Leiden, 1706

A. van Nispen, *Verscheyde Voyagien ofte reisen*, Dordrecht, 1652, pp. 256-97

N. Clenardus, *Epistolarum libri duo*, Antwerp, 1556

N. Clenardus, *Peregrinationum ac de rebus Machometicis epistolae elegantissimae*, Louvain, 1555

STUDIES

This list is limited to studies that treat Cleynaerts' idea of peaceful crusade as a key issue:

G. Vanheeswijck, *Tolerantie en actief pluralisme. De afgewezen erfenis van Erasmus, More en Gillis*, Kampen-Kapellen, 2008, pp. 37, 47

Weemans, 'Nicolaes Cleynaerts'

J. Tulkens, 'Cleynaerts' peaceful crusade', topic 4 in Tournoy et al., *Nicolaes Cleynaerts (1493-1542). The remarkable travel adventures of a 16th century humanist, Arabist and Islam-expert*, Louvain, 2002 (CD)

Van Koningsveld, 'Mon Kharuf'

A. van Roey, 'Cleynaerts' Arabische studies en zijn vreedzame kruistocht tegen de islam', *De Brabantse Folklore en Geschiedenis*s 278-9 (1993) 133-46

Lavajo, 'Itinéraire islamo-arabisant de Clénard'

F.M. Olbrechts, 'Rond Niklaas Cleynaerts' reis naar Marokko en zijn verblijf in Fès', in H. de Vocht et al. (eds), *Nicolaus Clenardus*, Antwerp, 1942, 22-51

Roersch, *Correspondance de Nicolas Clénard*, ii, pp. 135-36

Cerejeira, *O Renascimento em Portugal*, ii, pp. 195-98

Chauvin and Roersch, *Étude sur la vie*, pp. 129-45

Joris Tulkens

Andrés Laguna

DATE OF BIRTH About 1511
PLACE OF BIRTH Segovia
DATE OF DEATH 1559
PLACE OF DEATH Possibly Guadalajara

BIOGRAPHY

Andrés Laguna was born in Segovia in about 1511 to parents who were converts from Islam. After his primary education in Salamanca, he travelled to Paris, where he completed his studies in the arts and medicine, and published his first works: a translation into Latin of the pseudo-Aristotle *De physiognomicis* (1535), his *Anatomica methodus seu de sectione humani corporis contemplatio* (1535) and a Latin version of the pseudo-Galen *De urinis* (1536).

Laguna returned to Spain at the end of 1535 or beginning of 1536, and held various jobs. It has been conjectured that he held some sort of medical position at court, which may have led to a minor chair at the University of Alcalá and that he gained a doctorate in Toledo, but there is no evidence for this. However, in 1538 he published in Alcalá a volume of three works: a translation of the pseudo-Aristotle *De mundo* and Latin versions of two dialogues attributed to Lucian, the *Tragopodagra* and the *Ocypus*.

At the beginning of 1539, he left Spain again and, after travelling through England, the Low Countries and Germany, he obtained a five-year contract as a municipal doctor in Metz. In the course of his work, he continued to write and publish: in 1542 in Strasbourg, he edited a short treatise on the plague and, after being given a permit for three months, he went to Cologne, where he published new works: the Latin version of an Italian tract about strange events that happened in Byzantium, which was accompanied by a brief description, not very original, on the origin and customs of the Turks, and a series of Latin translations of the pseudo-Galen *De philosophica historia*, the pseudo-Aristotle *De natura stirpium*, the last eight books of the *Geoponica* (together with some *Castigationes* to the earlier version by Jano Cornario) and the pseudo-Aristotle *De virtutibus*. He also edited his famous *Europa heautentimoroumene*, a discourse in favour of Charles V's imperial policy, but with an irenicist argument of Erasmian nature. Lastly, he also wrote, in the form of a letter, a short dietetics treatise on old age and care of the elderly.

His permit ended, Laguna returned to Metz, where two years remained of his contract as doctor. In this time, he made important gains after being put in charge of provisioning the imperial troops. In 1545, he set out for Rome and on the way acquired the title of Doctor at the University of Bologna. When he was in Rome, he was employed as doctor to Cardinal Mendoza and acquired some noble titles from the papal court. What are considered his *opera maiora* are from his Italian period: the *Epitomes* by Galen (Venice, 1548), a summary of all Galen's work based in the new Latin versions of the humanists, and the Spanish translation and commentaries of *De materia medica* by Dioscorides, alongside some works of textual erudition (*Annotationes in Galeni interpretes* [Venice, 1548] and *Annotationes in Dioscoridem* [Lyon, 1554]), as well as two medical monographs/papers (both in Rome, 1551).

In 1554, Laguna left Italy and returned to the Netherlands, where he published a Spanish version of Dioscorides's *De materia medica* (Antwerp, 1555), a Spanish translation of Cicero's Catiline orations (Antwerp, 1556) and an *Apologetica epistola* against Janus Cornarius (Cologne, 1557), whom he accused of plagiarising his annotations on Dioscorides. From there he returned to Spain in ill health, and died on 28 December 1559, possibly in Guadalajara, where he was part of the retinue that was making for Roncesvalles to welcome Isabel de Valois, the future wife of King Philip II.

Although Laguna did not strictly write any more about the Turks and their relations with Christians than in the volume described below, there are references to this topic in other of his works, particularly in *Europa heautentimorumene* and in some of his commentaries on Dioscorides. In *Europa*, in fact, he proposes peace between the Christian states, although not in order to wage war to recover lost territories from the Turks, but to achieve a balance of power and international peace. Also, his plan for a journey to the East should not be forgotten, which, according to his own words in *Discorides*, he was considering at the beginning of 1550. The Spanish ambassador in Venice, Francisco de Vargas, dissuaded him from this. Laguna's attitude on this matter, amongst other arguments, would fit the theory that led Bataillon to attribute *Viaje de Turquía* to him. This work, which remained unedited until the 20th century, exudes Erasmianism and irenicism and shows the Turks as an amalgam of moral rectitude in contrast to the degenerateness of the Christians.

MAIN SOURCES OF INFORMATION

Primary

D. de Colmenares, *Historia de la insigne ciudad de Segovia. Índice general de la historia y las vidas y escritos de los escritores segovianos*, Segovia, 1640, pp. 708-16

N. Antonio, *Bibliotheca hispana nova*, Madrid, 1788, i, pp. 75-78

A. Chinchilla Piqueras, *Historia de la medicina en España*, Valencia, 1841-46, i, pp. 357-69

A. Hernández Morejón, *Historia bibliográfica de la medicina española*, Madrid, 1842-52, ii, pp. 227-68

T. Baeza González, *Apuntes biográficos de escritores segovianos*, Segovia, 1877, pp. 48-83

J. Olmedilla y Puig, *Estudio histórico de la vida y escritos del sabio español Andrés Laguna, médico de Carlos I y Felipe II y célebre escritor botánico del siglo XVI*, Madrid, 1887

G.M. Vergara y Martín, *Ensayo de una colección bibliográfica-biográfica de noticias referentes a la provincia de Segovia*, Guadalajara, 1903, pp. 516-28

Secondary

M.Á. González Manjarrés, art. 'Andrés Laguna', in J.F. Domínguez Domínguez (ed.), *Diccionario biográfico y bibliográfico del humanismo español*, Madrid, 2012, 461-66

M.L. Alía Alberca, '¿La Materia médica de Dioscórides traducida por Andrés Laguna? Aportaciones de las nuevas teorías traductológicas', Madrid, 2010 (Diss. Complutense University of Madrid), http://eprints.ucm.es/11665/1/T32279.pdf

J. Pardo Tomás, 'Andrés Laguna y la medicina europea del renacimiento', in *Seminario 'Orotava' de Historia de la Ciencia. Los orígenes de la ciencia moderna*, Canarias, 2004, 45-67

J.L. García Hourcade and J.M. Moreno Yuste (eds), *Andrés Laguna. Humanismo, ciencia y política en la Europa renacentista*, Valladolid, 2001

M.Á. González Manjarrés, 'Introducción', in A. Laguna, *Europa heautentimorumene, es decir, que míseramente a sí misma se atormenta y lamenta su propia desgracia*, Valladolid, 2001, 27-115

M.Á. González Manjarrés, *Entre la imitación y el plagio. Fuentes e influencias en el Dioscórides de Andrés Laguna*, Segovia, 2000

M.Á. González Manjarrés, *Andrés Laguna y el humanismo médico. Estudio filológico*, Valladolid, 2000

M. Bataillon, *Lección Marañón. Política y literatura en el doctor Laguna*, Madrid, 1970

T. Hernando, 'Introducción', in A. Laguna, *Pedacio Dioscorides Anazarbeo. Acerca de la materia medicinal y de los venenos mortiferos*, Madrid, 1968, 16-168 (repr. in T. Hernando, *Dos estudios históricos. Vieja y nueva medicina*, Madrid, 1982)

M. Bataillon, 'Sur l'humanisme du docteur Laguna. Deux petits livres latins de 1543', *Romance Philology* 17 (1964) 268-99 (repr. in M. Bataillon, *Erasmo y el erasmismo*, Barcelona, 1997)

T. Hernando, 'Vida y labor médica del doctor Andrés Laguna', *Estudios Segovianos* 12/34-35 (1960) 71-185 (repr. in *Vida y obra del Dr. Andrés Laguna*, Salamanca, 1990)

C.E. Dubler, *La materia médica de Dioscórides. Transmisión medieval y renacentista*, Barcelona, 1953-9, iv, *Andrés Laguna y su época*

M. Bataillon, *Erasme et l'Espagne*, Paris, 1937; Spanish trans. 1979, pp. 669-92

F.J. Blanco Juste, *Laguna, traductor y comentarista de Dioscórides*, Segovia, 1935

M. Lemos, *André Laguna*, Porto, 1913

WORKS ON CHRISTIAN-MUSLIM RELATIONS

Rerum prodigiosarum quæ in urbe Constantinopolitana, et in aliis ei finitimis acciderunt anno a Christo nato MDXLII brevis atque succincta enarratio, 'A short and succinct account of the miracles that occurred in and around Constantinople in 1542'

DATE 1543
ORIGINAL LANGUAGE Latin

DESCRIPTION

At the request of Adolf Eichholz, Rector of the University of Cologne, Laguna translated into Latin an Italian tract that had been published in 1542 in Venice by the printer Niccolò Zoppino. As Laguna points out in the dedication to Heinrich von Stolberg, Dean of the church of Cologne (signed 11 December 1542), it was a brief document that, in the midst of the anxieties of war, should serve as an incentive and solace for Christians and strengthen them in their faith.

The Italian work, which was anonymous, was a fictitious letter written by an Italian in Gallipoli in the service of an envoy of Pope Paul III. It was written in Italian, so that people in Italy might learn of the awesome and miraculous events that occurred in Constantinople in June and July 1542, some of which the author says he has personally seen and others that have been related to him by men he trusts. Fourteen pages long in octavo, the work is structured in 13 chapters in which the following extraordinary events are narrated: the appearance of a plague of locusts, which destroy the crops in Constantinople; the presence of a comet seen for 40 consecutive days over the palace of the Turkish king; the appearance of a dragon that pulverised the treasure that the Turkish king was guarding in his palace of Castel Nuovo (Herceg Novi); a terrible storm that caused many fires, killing people and animals and devastating part of the royal palace of Byzantium; an earthquake of great strength, which destroyed a good part of Constantinople and other cities; the sound of an invisible army heard one night on the streets of Constantinople; strange lights; and a pack of 40 or 50 wolves. The Turkish king consulted 12 wise astrologers about these events, and – after puzzling out in Christian code, since later the astrologers declared themselves spiritually Christian – they saw in the events signs of the imminent ruin of Islam and all its power. They were sentenced to be burnt at the stake, but after an hour the fire went out and the scholars managed to reach Christian territory, where they formally converted. After the miracle, rumours took hold, and it was even said that the Turkish king himself was gravely ill.

This short fictional account would have been especially welcome in eastern parts of Europe, since the Turks were at the gates of Vienna in 1541. It is one of a number of such works that appeared from the 15th century, among them Giovanni Nanni da Viterbo's *Tractatus de futuris Christianorum triumphis in Turcos et Saracenos*, published in Genoa in 1481, and Antonio Arquato's *Prognosticon de eversione Europae*, probably written in 1480, with numerous editions throughout the 16th and 17th centuries (e.g. *Monstres prodigieux advenues en la Turquie*, Paris, 1624, and *Nuova rellatione o'vero copia d'una lettera venuta di Constantinopoli*, which appeared in Messina, Naples and Florence in 1630, with later reissues). The fictitious form of this letter could, in fact, go back to an anonymous work entitled *Declaratione delli horrendi segni apparsi in Constantinopoli*, published in Milan in 1535.

Laguna attached to this translation a work 11 pages long – more or less as an appendix – on the origins of the Turkish people, their way of life and warfare, *De prima truculentissimorum Turcarum origine, deque eorum tyrannico bellandi ritu, et gestis, brevis et compendiosa expositio* ('A brief and comprehensive account of the first origin of the extremely aggressive Turks, their tyrannical way of fighting and their customs'). It contains hardly anything original, and it should be placed in the context of works on the Turks from the 15th and 16th centuries that derived their information from earlier writings going back to the Byzantine historians. These include Niccola Sagundino's *De Turcarum origine* (1456), Johan Spiesshaymer's (Cuspinianus) *De Turcarum origine, religione, ac immanissima eorum in Christianos tyrannide* (Antwerp, 1541), and Paolo Giovio's popular *Commentario delle cose de' Turchi* (Rome 1532). Despite

Laguna's insistence that he has taken his information from first-hand sources ('from the Turks themselves and above all from the Venetian ambassadors'), almost all his material is in fact a compendium of Giovio and Cuspinianus.

De prima truculentissimorum Turcarum origine is divided into 11 chapters, including accounts of the Ottoman sultans from Osman I to Süleyman I (whom Laguna hopes will be the last in the line), Turkish customs and their methods of waging war. In conventional style, Laguna typifies the Turks as cruel, violent, lascivious and given to sodomy, inhuman and insensitive to any request, though in battle disciplined, valiant and reckless, particularly because they believe that their death is already predestined.

SIGNIFICANCE

Rerum prodigiosarum enarratio is a good example of anti-Turkish propaganda typical of the European Renaissance, which tended to stress that the defeat of the Turks was imminent and final by interpreting phenomena that affirmed God was with his people. Venice, where the Italian original of this tract was published, was a great centre for the spread of this literature. The ready reception of such works in northern Europe is attested by Laguna's Latin translation, which was intended for cultured people, published in both Cologne and Antwerp, and a German translation of the original Italian work, *Newe zeytung von Constantinopoli*, which would reach a much wider readership.

De prima truculentissimorum Turcarum origine was re-issued alone the following year in Antwerp, as part of an edition of Antonio Arquato's *Prognosticon de eversione Europae*.

EDITIONS & TRANSLATIONS

De origine rerum Turcarum compendiosa quaeda perioche per Andream a Lacuna Secobiensem collecta. De Turcarum cultu ac moribus enarratio quaedam breviuscula, in Antonio Arquato, *Prognosticon Antonii Torquati de eversione Europae*, Antuerpiae, apud Martinum Nuntium, 1544, fols 54v-62r

Rerum prodigiosarum quae in urbe Constantinopolitana et in aliis ei finitimis acciderunt anno a Christo nato MDXLII brevis atque succinta enarratio. De prima truculentissimorum Turcarum origine, deque eorum tyrannico bellandi ritu, et gestis, brevis et compendiosa expositio, Antuerpiae: Martinus Nuntius excudebat, 1543

Rerum prodigiosarum quae in urbe Constantinopolitana et in aliis ei finitimis acciderunt anno a Christo nato MDXLII brevis atque succinta enarratio. De prima truculentissimorum Turcarum origine, deque eorum tyrannico bellandi ritu, et gestis, brevis et compendiosa expositio, Coloniae: Ioannes Ruremundanus excudebat, 1543
Newe zeytung von Constantinopoli. Von einem Comet der bisz in die 40. tag am hymel ober des Türcken pallast gestanden ist, (s.l.), [1543] (German trans. of the Italian work)
Li particulari avisi delle cose occorse nuovamente nella città di Constantinopoli e li de intorno, Venezia, ad instantia del Zoppino, 1542 (original Italian work, possibly imitating the *Declaratione delli horrendi segni apparsi in Constantinopoli*, 1535)

STUDIES

M. Formica, *Lo specchio turco. Immagini del altro e riflessi del sé nella cultura italiana di età moderna*, Rome, 2012, pp. 72-77

A. Merle, *Le miroir otomanne. Une image politique des hommes dans la littérature géographique spagnole et française (XVI-XVII siècles)*, Paris, 2003

M.S. Ortolá, *Viaje de Turquía*, Madrid, 2000

González Manjarrés, *Andrés Laguna y el humanismo medico*, pp. 128-30

M. Donattini, 'Orizzonti geografici dell'editoria italiana (1493-1560)', in A. Prosperi and W. Reinhard (eds), *Il nuovo mondo nella coscienza italiana e tedesca del Cinquecento*, Bologna, 1992, 79-154, p. 110

K.M. Setton, *Western hostility to Islam and prophecies of Turkish doom*, Philadelphia PA, 1992, pp. 15-46

G. Lucchetta, 'L'Oriente mediterraneo nella cultura di Venezia tra il Quattro e il Cinquecento', in G. Arnaldi and M. Pastore Stocchi (eds), *Storia della cultura veneta. Dal primo Quattrocento al concilio di Trento*, Vicenza, 1980-81, ii, 375-432, pp. 396-97

P. Preto, *Venezia e i Turchi*, Florence, 1975, pp. 67-91

M. Bataillon, 'Mythe et conaissance de la Turquie en Occidente au milieu de XVI siècle', in A. Pertusi (ed.), *Venezia e l'Oriente fra tardo Medioevo e Rinascimento*, Firenze, 1966, 451-70, pp. 465-66

Bataillon, 'Sur l'humanisme du docteur Laguna', p. 290

Dubler, *Andrés Laguna y su época*, pp. 170-72

Miguel Ángel González Manjarrés

Juan Bautista Jerónimo Anyés

Juan Bautista Agnesio

DATE OF BIRTH 30 March 1480
PLACE OF BIRTH Valencia
DATE OF DEATH 6 August 1553
PLACE OF DEATH Valencia

BIOGRAPHY

Juan Bautista Jerónimo Anyés was one of the most important humanists of the Iberian Renaissance. Born in Valencia in 1480 into a family of Genoese origin, he studied at the University of Valencia where he received his doctorate in theology. During the course of his studies, he was particularly attracted to Greek and Latin as well as Aristotelian philosophy, which he got to know through original classical works. His interest was so strong that he decided to Latinise his last name from Anyés to Agnesio, justifying this decision on the basis of his father's supposed descent from the Roman martyr Saint Agnes. He explains this in a marginal note of his *Egloga in nativitate Christi* (see Alonso Asenjo, 'Optimates laetificare').

Very soon he occupied important positions in the Valencian curia. He was a *beneficiado* in the cathedral and became well known to aristocratic families. These connections enabled him to meet other intellectuals who were concerned with the problem of the Moriscos, such as Bernardo Pérez de Chinchón, whose *Antialcorano* (1532) and *Diálogos christianos contra la secta mahomética y contra la pertinacia de los judíos* (1535) influenced him. He also studied the works of Erasmus, though he was closer to other philosophers such as Juan Luis Vives.

Agnesio wrote a great number of works, though only the titles of most are now known. These reflect the range of his interests and the importance to him of the idea of religion as a community service. As pointed out by M. Andrés (*Historia de la teología española*, p. 521) and Llin Cháfer (*Juan Bautista Agnesio*, p. 45), Agnesio should be included among the minority of priests who were aware of the serious situation the Church was facing in his time with regard to large Morisco populations, and who worked to acquire knowledge of the humanities in order to renew faith among the people. He dedicated himself to preaching for over 40 years in areas such as Cofrentes, the valley of Ayora and Ribera (see Llin Cháfer, 'Juan Bautista Agnesio').

While he regarded the evangelisation of the Moriscos as urgent, he looked on them as innocent people who did not know the right way to the truth. So his methods were always peaceful, very similar to the work of Hernando de Talavera in Granada. He was against the forced baptisms that took place during the 16th century, recognising that this was not the way to obtain sincere conversions.

Agnesio was a friend of Joan de Joanes, one of the most important painters of the Iberian Renaissance (see Falomir Faus, 'Joanes y su entorno'). So close was their friendship that Joanes represented him in two paintings for Valencia Cathedral.

MAIN SOURCES OF INFORMATION

Primary
F. Diago, *Anales del Reyno de Valencia*, Valencia, 1613, pp. 50, 110
V. Ximeno, *Escritores del Reyno de Valencia*, Valencia, 1747, i, pp. 113-16

Secondary
B. Franco Llopis, 'Releyendo la obra de Joan de Joanes. Nuevas aportaciones en torno al *Bautismo de Cristo* de la Catedral de Valencia y la conversión morisca', *Espacio, Tiempo y Forma* 25 (2012) 67-82
M. Falomir Faus, 'Joanes y su entorno. Relaciones sociales y afinidades culturales', in L. Hernández Guardiola (ed.), *De pintura valenciana (1400-1600). Estudios y documentación*, Alicante, 2006, 271-87
P. Valsalobre, 'La poesia catalana del cinc-cents a la recerca d'una veu pròpia', *Revista de Catalunya* 210 (2005) 79-111
M. Durán, 'Un col·loqui satíric valencià de Joan B. Anyés (v. 1528)' in M. Gustà (ed.), *Homenatge Joaquim Molas (Barcelona 2001)*, (s.l.), 2003 (downloadable internet resource)
M. Durán, 'El conocimiento del griego por parte de Joan Baptista Anyés', in J.M. Maestre Maestre (ed.), *Humanismo y pervivencia del mundo clásico. Homenaje al profesor Antonio Fontán*, Madrid, 2002, v, 2449-56
E. Durán, 'Introducció', in J.B. Anyés, *Obra profana. Apologies, València 1545*, Barcelona, 2001, 1-26
D. Gorostidi, 'El *Apologeticon Panegyricon* de Joan Baptista Anyes. Erasmo y Jerónimo', in *X Congreso Español de Estudios Clásicos (Humanismo y Tradición Clásica)*, Madrid, 2001, 603-9
J. Alonso Asenjo, 'Optimates laetificare. La Egloga in Nativitate Christi de Joan Baptista Anyés o Agnesio', *Criticón* 66-67 (1996) 307-68

J.M. Escolà, 'Tradició clàssica a la poesia de Joan B. Anyes (14801553)', in M. Puig (ed.), *Tradició clàssica. Actes de l'XI^è Simposi de la Secció Catalana de la SEEC*, Andorra, 1996, 317-22

A. Llin Cháfer, 'Juan Bautista Agnesio y los nuevos conversos', *Anales Valentinos* 44 (1996) 409-15

J. Medina, *La poesia llatina dels països catalans. Segles XXX (Antologia)*, Bellaterra, Barcelona, 1996

D. Benito Goerlich, 'Lectura iconográfica de los Desposorios místicos del venerable Agnesio de Juan de Juanes', *Saitabi* 45 (1995) 53-67

J.F. Alcina, *Repertorio de la poesía latina del Renacimiento en España*, Salamanca, 1995, pp. 33-38

J-F. Maillard, J. Kecskeméti and M. Portalier (eds), *L'Europe des humanistes (XIV^è-XVII^è siècles)*, Paris, 1995, p. 23

J.F. Alcina, 'Entre latín y romance. Modelos neolatinos en la creación poética castellana', in J.M. Maestre Maestre and J. Pascual Barea (eds.), *Humanismo y pervivencia del mundo clásico. Actas del I Simposio sobre Humanismo y pervivencia del mundo clásico (Alcañiz, 8 al 11 de mayo de 1990)*, Cadiz, 1993, i, 3-28

J. Huguet, 'Una aristòcrata humanista de la València del XVI. Donya Mencia de Mendoza', *Revista de l'Alguer* 4 (1993) 77-92

A. Llin Cháfer, *Juan Bautista Agnesio. Apóstol de la Valencia renacentista*, Valencia, 1992

J.F. Alcina, 'La poesía latina del humanismo español: un esbozo', in *Los humanistas españoles y el humanismo europeo (IV Simposio de Filología Clásica)*, Murcia, 1990, 13-33

V.M. Rosselló, 'La *Laus Valentiae* a la literatura i la cartografia', in *Miscel·lània Joan Fuster. Estudis de llengua i literatura*, Barcelona, 1990, ii, 5-20

M. Cahner, 'Introducción', in J.B. Anyés, *Obra catalana*, Barcelona, 1987, 3-18

J. Murgades, *Teatre, prosa i poesia del segle XVI. Antologia*, Barcelona, 1986, pp. 136-45

M. Andrés, *Historia de la teología española. I. Desde sus orígenes hasta fines del siglo XVI*, Madrid, 1983, p. 521

E.J. Verger, *Antologia dels poetes valencians. I. Del segle XIV al XVIII*, Valencia, 1983

V. Cárcel Ortí, 'La archidiócesis de Valencia en tiempos de San Luís Bertrán', in *Corrientes espirituales en la Valencia del siglo XVI (1550-1600)*, Valencia, 1983, 37-52

S. García Martínez, 'Sobre la introducción del helenismo en la Universidad de Valencia durante la primera mitad del Quinientos', in *Actes du 1er colloque sur le pays valencien à l'époque moderne*, Pau, 1980, 363-97

J.F. Alcina, 'Tendances et caractéristiques de la poésie hispano-latine de la Renaissance', in A. Redondo (ed.), *L'humanisme dans les lettres espagnoles*, Paris, 1979, 133-50

J. Rubió Balaguer, 'Renaixement i humanisme', in *VIII Congreso de Historia de la Corona de Aragón*, III, Valencia, 1973, 30-33

E. Durán, 'Introducció', in J.B. Anyes, *La vida de Sant Julià*, Barcelona, 1971, 2-19

G. Hijarrubia Lodares, *El códice Panthalia del venerable Juan Bautista Agnesio*, Valencia, 1960

G. Hijarrubia Lodares, 'Los tiempos del pontificado de Sto. Tomás de Villanueva vistos por un poeta latino del siglo XVI', *Anales del Centro de Cultura Valenciana* 43 (1959) 36-52

F. Martí Grajales, *Ensayo de un diccionario biográfico y bibliográfico de los escritores que florecieron en el reino de Valencia hasta el año 1700*, Madrid, 1927, pp. 31-34

M. Guiló i Fuster, *Catálogo de obras en lengua catalana impresas desde 1474 hasta 1860*, Madrid, 1923

R. Vilanova, 'Un capítulo inédito de la biografía de Juanes. El Venerable Agnesio', *Almanaque de las Provincias para el año 1903* (1903) 257-64

J. Pastos Fuster, *Biblioteca valenciana de los escritores que florecieron hasta nuestros días con adiciones y enmiendas a la de D. Vicente Ximeno*, Valencia, 1817, pp. 94-95

WORKS ON CHRISTIAN-MUSLIM RELATIONS

Pro Agarenis neophytis, 'For newly converted Muslims'

DATE 1543
ORIGINAL LANGUAGE Latin

DESCRIPTION

Pro Agarenis neophytis is part of a compendium that Agnesio dedicated to the Marquis of Zenete and the Count of Oliva, nobles closely connected with control of the Moriscos. *Pro Agarenis* itself is dedicated to Jorge de Austria, a relative of the Emperor Charles V and archbishop of Valencia from 1538, who Agnesio believed would put new energy into the task of converting the Moors. It comprises five folios (48-52), and comes in the middle of the compendium. The title *Pro Agarenis neophytis* changes in the course of the work to *Pro Saracenis neophytis*.

The treatise is closely related to a letter that Agnesio had sent to his fellow priest, Juan Gays, on 15 January 1539, in which he says that he believes the conversion of the Moors, whom he calls 'my neophytes', is a worthwhile task, and laments the poor training of priests in Valencia. This letter is crucial to understanding the meaning of the treatise.

After an introduction, in which Agnesio explains his reasons for writing, the body of the letter comprises a poem of 87 verses that explain the situation faced by the Moriscos, using parables and references to pagan culture. The reason for this form is that the Count of Oliva had asked for an elegant 'poetic representation', effectively a theatrical play that would appeal to the people. However, the treatise is not quite a dramatic composition, and has been criticised as too difficult for Christians, let alone former Muslims, to follow. Rather than a dramatic piece for actual presentation, the treatise is probably better understood as a report of the state of the diocese, and a set of proposals for change.

The treatise covers the following topics: the necessity for cooperation between scholars, priests and nobles for the education of the Moriscos (mainly their children); the importance of converting the Moriscos because of their links with the Turkish Empire; and the necessity for the new archbishop, Jorge de Austria, to follow a strong policy on the matter. Agnesio describes his own approach as that of a physician treating infections, or of a farmer weeding the field in order to make the harvest strong and lasting. He stresses that the way to conversion is through education and comprehension, rather than force, seeing Moors as poor innocents, people who should be taught and helped towards the path of salvation. This attitude resembles that of Hernando de Talavera, and contrasts with that of earlier Valencian priests such as Jayme Bleda or Patriarch Ribera, who were much closer to the idea of expulsion than assimilation of the Moorish population.

SIGNIFICANCE
This treatise is important for an understanding of the attitude of the Spanish Church towards the evangelisation of Muslims. In Valencia, following the policy of forced baptisms in about 1525, a number of softer approaches were favoured. In *Pro Agarenis neophytis* Agnesio urges his fellow priests not to impose baptism, but rather let it follow naturally from teaching the faith. This approach was repeated some decades later by the Jesuits, who sometimes expressed sentiments similar to Agnesio's.

Agnesio regards Muslims as 'innocents', born in the wrong religion rather than personally sinful, and therefore in need of education. Approaches such as this led to the establishment of schools for the Moriscos, and even when they were expelled, their children were made to stay because it was thought they could be re-educated or 'healed'.

Agnesio's treatise was not influential. The Latin original was not translated into Spanish or republished, and there are virtually no references to it in other works. Maybe he did not employ the right style, and his work was too intellectual for preachers spreading the faith. It remains a model of the assimilationist outlook and an example of the great variety of thinking about the problem of the Moriscos in the Valencian curia in the 16th century.

EDITIONS & TRANSLATIONS

Apologia in defensionem virorum illustr. equestrium, bonorumq. ciuium Valentinorum, In ciuilem Valentini populi seditionem, quam... Germaniam... appellantur; Secunda Apologia, in laudem... Rhoderici Zeneti...; Apologia in venatores, pro auibus... Valentiae: Apud Sacram diui Thomae Apostoli aedem, per Ioannem Baldouinum, et Ioannem Mey, 1543, fols 48-52

Copies can be found in:

MS Valencia, University Library – BH Z-04/121

MS Valencia, San Miguel de los Reyes Library – XVI/581

MS Navarra, University Library – FA 134.118

MS Madrid, Complutense University – BH FLL 13818(2), http://books.google.com/books/ucm?vid=UCM5327257883&printsec=frontcover#v=onepage&f=false

STUDIES

Alonso Asenjo, 'Optimates laetificare'

Llin Cháfer, 'Juan Bautista Agnesio'

Llin Cháfer, *Juan Bautista Agnesio*

Borja Franco Llopis

Francisco López de Gómara

DATE OF BIRTH 1511
PLACE OF BIRTH Gómara (Soria)
DATE OF DEATH 1562
PLACE OF DEATH Gómara (Soria)

BIOGRAPHY

Francisco López de Gómara, a priest from Soria, is always associated with Hernán Cortés and the Spanish chronicles about the conquest of Mexico. However, he was also deeply involved in affairs within Spain and Europe. Before being ordained priest, he travelled to Italy in 1529 as a page of one of the noblemen in the entourage Charles V at his coronation as Holy Roman Emperor. When he returned to Spain, he was ordained priest and taught classes at the University of Alcalá de Henares. In 1531, he became chaplain at the College of San Clemente de Bologna (the Royal Spanish College), and lived there until 1539, when he travelled to Venice to enter the service of Diego Hurtado de Mendoza, the Spanish ambassador 'to their lordships' and one of the best humanists of his generation.

In 1541, Francisco was present during Charles V's attack on the city of Algiers, at which time it must have been agreed that he would go into the service of Hernán Cortés, whom he had known since the 1520s. In 1545 he wrote his biography of the Barbarossa brothers, and also his chronicle of Cortes's capture of New Spain, which was published in Zaragoza in 1551. In 1554, he travelled to Flanders with the intention of becoming official chronicler to Charles V, but he failed and returned to Valladolid. He died in Gómara in 1562.

MAIN SOURCES OF INFORMATION

Primary

F. López de Gómara, *Annals of the Emperor Charles V*, ed. and trans. R.B. Merriman, Oxford, 1912

F. López de Gómara, *Guerras de mar del Emperador Carlos V [Compendio de lo que trata Francisco López en el libro que hizo de las guerras de mar de sus tiempos]*, ed. and trans. M.A. Bunes and H. Jiménez, Madrid, 2002

Secondary

M.C. Martínez Martínez, 'Francisco López de Gómara y Hernán Cortés. Nuevos testimonios de la relación del cronista con los marqueses del Valle de Oaxaca', *Anuario de Estudios Americanos* 67 (2010) 267-302

J. Miralles Ostos, 'Gómara ¿Capellán de Cortés?', *Boletín de la Real Academia de la Historia* 206 (2009) 165-75

G. Carman, *Rhetorical conquests. Cortés, Gómara, and Renaissance imperialism*, West Lafayette IN, 2006

N.E. Jiménez, *Francisco López de Gómara*, Michoacán, Mexico, 2001

R.E. Lewis, 'El Testamento de Francisco López de Gómara y otros documentos tocantes a su vida', *Revista de Indias* 173 (1984) 61-79

R.E. Lewis, *The humanistic historiography of Francisco López de Gómara*, Austin TX, 1983

J. Pinilla, 'López de Gómara en el Archivo de Protocolos de Madrid', *Celtiberia. Revista del Centro de Estudios Sorianos* 1 (1951) 390-2

R. Iglesia, *Cronistas e historiadores de la conquista de México. El ciclo de Hernán Cortés*, Mexico City, 1942

M. Jiménez de la Espada, *De un curioso percance que tuvo en Anvers el presbítero López de Gómara*, Madrid, 1888

WORKS ON CHRISTIAN-MUSLIM RELATIONS

Crónica de los Barbarrojas, 'The chronicle of the Barbarossas'

DATE 1545
ORIGINAL LANGUAGE Spanish

DESCRIPTION

The *Crónica de los Barbarrojas* comprises no more than a few torn pages of a larger document entitled *Guerras de mar*, of which today only a compilation made by a copyist remains. It was written at the time when Hernán Cortés was making preparations for the conquest of Mexico. In his dedication of the work, which is to the Marquis of Astorga, Francisco admits that he had been advised not to write on this subject since it would not be possible to publish a document that extolled the deeds of an infidel. It includes an account of the origins of the Turkish people and a brief genealogy of the Ottoman sultans.

Francisco notes that the Barbarossa brothers were the sons of a Turkish father, who came from the *devşirme*, and of a Greek Christian mother. Oruç (Aruj) set sail with his father to trade and plunder, and was captured by the Knights of St John from Rhodes during a sea battle near Candia. After regaining his freedom, he mutinied aboard one of the sultan's ships and was forced to flee, along with two of his brothers, to North Africa. They were very successful in their first actions in the western Mediterranean, which earned them fame as good sailors and even better Muslims.

After taking the city of Algiers, Oruç was killed by Christian soldiers from Oran, which is why his brother Hayraddin Barbarossa's privateering activities were primarily aimed at the Spanish. Failed attempts to expel Hayraddin from Algiers and the victories he won against Charles V's armies, gradually turned him into one of the most famous warriors of his time. This explains why the Emperor went in person to fight against him in Tunisia. Before this, Ibrahim Pasha was named by Sultan Süleyman as commander of the Ottoman fleet. King Francis I of France, who was at odds with the Spanish, entered into an alliance with Süleyman, and the Turkish fleet helped the French in their wars against Charles V, with Barbarossa as a major ally of the Ottomans. Francisco records that the Spanish tried to avoid fighting against Barbarossa by attempting to win him over to their side, although the Sultan was fully aware of this.

SIGNIFICANCE

Like the *Viaje de Turquía*, the *Crónica* is a surprising work, which could only have been written during the reign of the Emperor Charles V. Francisco López de Gómara's approach, showing great admiration for the feats of the two Barbarossa brothers and emulating the style of Suetonius or Plutarch, meant that the work was not published in the 16th century. For him, the bravery and valour of these military leaders was more important than the fact that they were Muslims, and he thus transcends the conventional idea that their religion of Islam made them inferior and despicable beings.

Francisco's attempt to compare the Barbarossas' achievements with those of Hernán Cortés, whom he served during the years that he wrote this work, is also surprising. His chronicles about America were severely criticised in his time, and they were not reprinted in Spain after the 1550s – in fact, he himself was largely unknown until the end of the 20th century. In this work, at no time does he describe the way in which Islam might affect the character and personality of those who practise it, nor does he even criticise Muḥammad – in contrast to the common practice of his time – as he believed that such ideas arose from the narrow-minded subjective attitudes that were embedded in the harsh Spanish culture that then prevailed. He notes in the text that it was thanks to the Barbarossa brothers that the Ottoman Empire became a great power in the Mediterranean, and that it was they who put an end to the Emperor Charles V's ambitions in the region.

EDITIONS & TRANSLATIONS

Los corsarios Barbarroja, Madrid, 1989
Crónica de los Barbarrojas, Madrid, 1853

STUDIES

A.M. Cátedra, *Nobleza y lectura en tiempos de Felipe, II. La biblioteca de don Alonso Osorio, marqués de Astorga*, Valladolid, 2002

M.Á. Bunes Ibarra, 'Cortés y los hermanos Barbarrojas. Vidas ejemplares en los escritos de Francisco López de Gómara', *Revista de Indias* 182 (1987) 900-6

Miguel Ángel de Bunes

Vasco Diaz de Tanco de Fregenal

DATE OF BIRTH   Possibly 1490
PLACE OF BIRTH   Fregenal de la Sierra, Badajoz
DATE OF DEATH   Possibly 1573
PLACE OF DEATH   Possibly Orense, Galicia

BIOGRAPHY

Vasco Díaz Tanco was a humanist from Extremadura who pursued various professions, an actor and director, author of tragedies and a poet. By the year 1528 he had been ordained priest.

He wandered the roads of Spain and Portugal with a portable printing press that he himself had made, settling in at least three cities, Valencia, Porto and Orense. An indefatigable traveller, he probably spent some time in captivity in Turkish prisons. He travelled in France, Italy, Portugal and Greece, and acknowledged that in each place he was known and named differently: 'In Extremadura, which is my country, I am called Vasco Diaz, in Portugal and Galicia I have the name of Frexenal, in the Canaries I am the bachelor Tanco, in the kingdoms of Aragón and Catalonia I am the graduate Casero, in parts of France and Italy I am *el doctor del estanco*, in the provinces of Santmarcho I am Master Clauedan, and in the Greek kingdoms I am called the clergyman. And I am but one' (*Jardín del alma cristiana*, Valladolid, 1552, fol. 130r).

Of the 50 books Tanco mentions in *Jardín del alma cristiana*, only a few titles are extant. It appears that in 1530 he compiled his dramatic works into three volumes: *Terno dialogal autual* ('The dialogical suit'), *Terno comediario autual* ('The comedic suit') and *Terno farsario autual* ('The farcical suit'). In the same period he also wrote a poetic work, *Los veinte triunfos* ('The twenty triumphs'), which includes the romance *Vasco me llaman por nombre* . . . ('By name, they call me Vasco . . .'). He also wrote on religious themes, notably the *Jardín del alma xpriana* [sic] ('Garden of the Christian soul').

Acutely aware of the Turkish attacks on Italian territory, Tanco read extensively and formed his own opinions about Ottoman power and the actions that should be taken by the Christian kingdoms in view of their own weakness. During his stay in Italy, 1540-45, he read Paolo Giovio's *Commentario delle cose dei turchi*, and disapproved of its conciliatory tone. His reaction was to rewrite the work under the title

El libro llamado Palinodia, to correct the aspects he thought deficient. Its publication caused controversy, because it was dedicated to the future Philip II. Without attempting to conceal its anti-Turkish character, it calls on Christian rulers to put aside their quarrels and join together as allies in attacking the Turks: 'The time has come for the infidels to be put down, oppressed, overcome and subjected to the Christian faith, whose universal captain and advocate, chosen by God, is your [Philip's] father the Emperor Charles.'

The latest reference to Tanco is in a document of 1552, which alludes to a possible stay in Valladolid.

Primary

V. Barrantes y Moreno, 'La patria de Vasco Díaz', *El folklore frexnense*, Fregenal, 1882 (repub. 1989)

C. Alberto de La Barrera y Leirado, *Catálogo bibliográfico y biográfico del teatro antiguo español, desde sus orígenes hasta mediados del siglo XVIII*, Madrid, 1860, pp. 127-28

L. Fernández de Moratín, '*Vasco Díaz Tanco de Fregenal*', in *Orígenes del Teatro español*, in *Obras*, vol. 1, Madrid, 1830, pp. 150-51

M. Serrano y Sanz, 'Literatos españoles cautivos', *Revista de Archivos, Bibliotecas y Museos* 1 (1897) 500-1

Secondary

R. Ramos, 'Díaz Tanco, Vasco', in R. Gullón (ed.), *Diccionario de literatura española e hispanoamericana A-M*, Madrid, 1993, 450

J.J. García Arranz, 'Notas en torno a los grabados de la obra de Vasco Díaz Tanco "Los veinte triunphos"', *Norba. Revista de arte* 9 (1989) 29-44

M. Terrón Albarrán, 'Vasco Díaz Tanco', *Historia de la Baja Extremadura*, vol. 2, Badajoz, 1986

A. Hermenegildo, 'La tragedia española en el último tercio del siglo XVI', in F. López Estrada (ed.), *Historia y crítica de la literatura española*, vol. 2/1, 1980, 582-85, p. 583

M. Pecellín Lancharro, 'Vasco Díaz Tanco de Fregenal', *Literatura en Extremadura*, vol. 1, Badajoz, 1980

A. Rodríguez-Moñino, 'Vasco Díaz Tanco, témoin et chroniquer poétique du couronnement de Charles Quint', in *Fêtes et ceremonias au temps de Charles Quint*, Paris, 1960, 183-95

A. Rodríguez-Moñino, *Bibliografía de Vasco Díaz Tanco, clérigo, literato e impresor de tiempos de Carlos V*, Valencia, 1947

F.T., 'Aparato bibliográfico' Díaz Tanco de Frejenal, Vasco', *Bibliografía Hispánica* 6 (Madrid, 1946) 125

A. López, 'Los veinte triumphos hechos por Vasco Díaz de Frexenal', *Boletín de la Comisión de Monumentos de Orense* 10 (1935) 371-90

A. Rodríguez-Moñino, 'Los triunfos canarios de Vasco Díaz Tanco', El Museo Canario 2/4 (Las Palmas, 1935) 11-35

C. Rodríguez Cid, 'Testamento y codicilio de Vasco Díaz Tanco de Fregenal', Boletín de la Comisión de Monumentos de Orense 7 (1923) 89-105

J.E. Gillet, 'Apuntes sobre las obras dramáticas de Vasco Díaz Tanco de Fregenal', Revista de Archivos, Bibliotecas y Museos 44 (1923) 352-56

C. Moreno García, 'Migajas literarias: Vasco Díaz Hanco [sic]', Revista Castellana 2/7 (1916) 7-13

E. Carre Aldao, 'Vasco Díaz Tanco de Frexenal (1544-1547)', Boletín de la Real Academia Gallega 10 (La Coruña, 1915) 83-85

Palinodia de la nephanda y fiera nación de los turcos, 'Palinode on the unspeakable and fierce nation of the Turks'

DATE 1547
ORIGINAL LANGUAGE Castilian

DESCRIPTION

This work, dedicated to Prince Philip, is divided into chapters that successively deal with various characteristics of the Turks (its full title is *El libro llamado Palinodia que trata de las guerras de la nefanda nació turquesca y délos Capitanes: Príncipes: Reyes: y emperadores que entre ellos ha habido, y de los imperios Reynos: Principados: Comarcas: e Prouincias que señoreancon gran tiranía e crueldad. Y de la ordede sus batallas y gouernacio de su corte y casa real*, 'The book called *Palinode* which deals with wars and the nefarious Turkish nation and its rulers: princes, kings, and the emperors there have been among them, and the empires, kingdoms, principalities, regions, and provinces that were ruled with great tyranny and cruelty. And of their battles and the governorship of the court and royal household'). The chapters give accounts of the history of the Turkish nation and the various dignitaries of the court of the Grand Turk.

Chapter 1 describes the origins of the Turks, and Chapters 2-73 deal with the formation and rise of the Ottoman dynasty as far as Süleyman the Magnificent. In Chapters 74-83 Tanco describes the structure of Turkish society, the organisation of the military, the language used in court, and the Turkish attitude towards death. In Chapters 84-86 he gives practical advice to Christian leaders about how to overcome and defeat the disciplined, well-organised and trained Turkish army. The final two chapters refer to Pope Paul III, who acted as an intermediary between Emperor Charles V and the Senate of Venice and was instrumental in persuading powers to leave aside past disagreements and form the 'Holy League and Confederation' against the Ottoman Empire.

Tanco also displays an interest in the language. In Chapter 82 he draws a comparison between the Spanish and Turkish courts, and observes that just as in the Spanish court many languages are spoken in addition to Castilian, so in the Turkish court there are many languages in use: 'The main one is Turkish, spoken by his lordship, the second is Moorish, in which the law of the Qur'an is written, which they follow and write universally with Arabic letters, and the third is the language spoken at home among the Janissaries, the most profuse language of the world, according to their opinion. And the fourth language is Greek, used among the citizens and inhabitants of Constantinople and all of Greece.'

SIGNIFICANCE

Tanco displays here an anti-Turkish stance that was typical of Christian authors at the time. He emphasises the hatred he feels for the Ottoman Empire, as did other European chroniclers and historians of the humanist era, and uses derogatory and disparaging expressions, such as: 'the fierce Bayezid' and 'their false arts and tricks'; Selim is 'that bloody butcher', 'most ferocious butcher', 'cruel butcher'; Süleyman is 'that cursed prince Süleyman', 'heir to the vicious kingdom' which carries out 'terrible cruelty' and 'diabolical cruelty'. Turks are 'that damned nation', 'barbarous nation', 'nefarious nation.'

Tanco criticises the discord among the Christian countries and the inadequacy of their military strategy, and emphasises the discipline, modesty and absolute obedience of the Turkish soldiers. The very concept of the book as a palinode, a lament, illustrates its author's critical attitude.

EDITIONS & TRANSLATIONS

Palinodia de los Turcos. Reimpresión facsimilar de la rarísima edición de Orense, 1547, ed. A. Rodríguez Moñino, Badajoz, 1947 (facsimile reproduction of the 1547 edition)

Libro dell'origine et successione dell'Imperio Turchi... Nuovamente tradotto dalla lingua Spagnola nella Italiana par... A. di Ulloa, Venecia: G. Giolito de Ferrari, 1558 (Italian trans.)

Libro intitulado Palinodia, de la nephanda y fiera nación de los Turcos, y de su engañoso arte y cruel modo de guerrear. Y de los imperios, reynos, y prouincias que han subjectado, y posseen con inquieta ferocidad, Orense en la ympression del proprio actor, 1547

STUDIES

A. Redondo, 'El mundo turco a través de las "relaciones de sucesos" de finales del siglo XVI y de las primeras décadas del siglo XVII. La percepción de la alteridad y su puesta en obra narrativa', in A. Paba and G. Andrés Renales (eds), *Encuentro de civilizaciones (1500-1750). Informar, celebrar, narrar*, Alcalá, 2003, 235-53

L. Pavlovic-Samurovic, 'Los elementos renacentistas en la *Palinodia de los Turcos* (1547) de Vasco Díaz Tanco de Frejenal', in M. García Martín et al. (eds), *Actas del II Congreso Internacional de la AISO (1990)*, Salmanca, 1993, vol. 2, 753-59

A. Mas, *Les Turcs dans la littérature espagnole du Siècle d'Or*, 2 vols, Paris, 1967

M. Macías, 'Vasco Díaz Tanco de Frexenal. La Palinodia, Sinodades [sic] del Obispado de Orense. Su testamento', *Boletín de la Comisión de Monumentos de Orense* 7 (1923) 113-34

Miguel Ángel Auladell

The young man of Arévalo

Mancebo de Arévalo

DATE OF BIRTH   Uncertain; late 15th-early 16th century
PLACE OF BIRTH   Arévalo (Ávila)
DATE OF DEATH   Uncertain; possibly second half of the 16th century
PLACE OF DEATH   Uncertain; possibly Aragón

BIOGRAPHY

The *Mancebo de Arévalo* was a Morisco from Arévalo, a small town near Segovia in Old Castile, during the first years of the 16th century. His identity is uncertain, and all that is known about him comes from his own writings, especially the *Breve compendio de nuestra santa ley y sunna* and *Tafsira*, where he relates details of his travels through Spain collecting Islamic doctrines. At the same time, he seems to have worked as a trader or peddler (traders from Arévalo were especially famous in 16th-century Spain). We cannot be certain of the truthfulness of everything he says, but many of his meetings with elderly Moriscos in Granada, Valencia and Aragón were historically very likely.

It is possible that he was born towards the end of the 15th century, because he refers to King Ferdinand as not keeping his word to the Moriscos following the conquest of Granada in 1492, which implies that some of his journeys took place before Ferdinand's death in 1516.

He says that older women called him 'son' when they met him, implying that he really was young (*mancebo*). However, L.P. Harvey ('Castilian "Mancebo"') suggests that *mancebo* could be a reference to himself as *'abd* ('devotee') of God, a specifically Muslim designation.

He reports that he travelled widely throughout Spain, visiting notable Moriscos who had retained Muslim works after their conversion, in order to read them and make copies, quotations from some of which appear in his writings. At some point, he settled in Aragón, where Muslims could still freely express their faith up to 1525.

He wrote the *Breve compendio* together with the *faqīh* Ibrahim de Reminjo, and *Tafsira* eight years after the forced conversion of the Moriscos in Aragón, which took place in 1525-26, which would date them to around 1532-33.

He reports that his mother was still alive when he was collecting material and writing his works, and that she had been a Christian for 25 years, implying that she had converted (from Islam, or possibly from Judaism) before conversion was enforced. He visited the homes of a number of Jews, and indeed he repeatedly mentions Jewish scriptures, and even uses Hispanic Jewish terms. For this reason, Rubiera Mata ('El judeo-converso') has raised the possibility that the *Mancebo* came from a Jewish family that had converted to Christianity, and that he himself later converted to Islam. However, there are also grounds for thinking he came from a Christian background. In the *Breve compendio*, Ibrahim de Reminjo calls him *escolano* (one who has received a Christian schooling), while the *Mancebo* himself says that he has had conversations with Christian priests, and he also knows about Christian doctrine and Thomas à Kempis's *De imitatione Christi*. Whatever his background, he was evidently convinced that his Islamic faith was the only right one. The imminence of judgement day and the final triumph of Islam appear prominently in his writings.

What little is known about him has led to the suggestion that the *Mancebo* can be identified as Agustín de Ribera, *el mozo* ('the lad') (Tapia Sánchez, *La comunidad morisca*, p. 227; Harvey, *Muslims in Spain*, pp. 111-15). Before his arrest in Toledo in 1540, Agustin was 'held to be a prophet and the messenger of Muhammad' (Harvey, *Muslims in Spain*, p. 111). He was interrogated and eventually confessed in 1541, which presumably led to his execution (Harvey, *Muslims in Spain*, p. 112). The main difficulty with this identification is that in 1540 the *Mancebo* was in Aragón.

In addition to the *Breve compendio*, two other works are ascribed to the *Mancebo*, *Tafsira* and *Sumario de la relacíon y ejercicio spiritual*. He may have written in Roman script, but these works are preserved in Aljamiado (Castilian in Arabic script). What is clear is that he achieved fame as a scholar among the Morisco community in Aragón. Not only were his works copied at the end of the 16th century, but other Morisco authors also cited them at the beginning of the 17th century.

The *Mancebo*'s *Breve compendio* is closely related to his *Tafsira*. Both works mention a request from the Aragonese Moriscos that he write a Muslim treatise on doctrine, they both refer to dates about eight years after the conversion of the Aragonese Moriscos in 1525, and they have a lot of material in common, although presented with some variations and ordered differently. These extensive parallels do not fully extend to the third of his major works, the *Sumario de la relación y ejercicio spiritual*.

Although there are similar elements and characters in this, its focus is very different. It is difficult to decide the chronological relationship between these works: for some, the *Breve compendio* and *Tafsira* both derive from an earlier text that is now lost, while for others the *Breve compendio* is a revised version of *Tafsira*.

MAIN SOURCES OF INFORMATION

Primary

MS Cambridge, University Library – Dd.9.49, *Breve compendio de nuestra santa ley y sunna*

MS Madrid, Consejo Superior de Investigaciones Científicas – J LXII, *Tafsira*

MS Madrid, National Library – Res 245, 322 fols, *Sumario de la relación y ejercicio spiritual*

Secondary

L.F. Bernabé Pons, 'Una fama sin biografía. El Mancebo de Arévalo', in A. Echavarría Arsuaga (ed.), *Biografías mudéjares o la experiencia de ser minoría. Biografías islámicas en la España cristiana*, Madrid, 2008, 517-48

L.F. Bernabé Pons, 'Nota sobre una atribución al Mancebo de Arévalo', *Sharq al-Andalus* 18 (2003-7) 165-71

L.P. Harvey, *Muslims in Spain 1500-1614*, Chicago IL, 2005, pp. 170-93

M.T. Narváez Córdova, *Tratado [Tafsira]. Mancebo de Arévalo*, Madrid, 2003, pp. 18-31

M.J. Rubiera Mata, 'El judeo-converso y morisco "Mancebo de Arévalo", autor de las tres culturas hispánicas (s. XVI)', in M. Bernadini, *Europa e Islam tra i secoli XIV e XVI. Europe and Islam between 14th and 16th centuries*, Naples, 2002, ii, 839-56

L.F. Bernabé Pons, 'El calendario musulmán del Mancebo de Arévalo', *Sharq al-Andalus* 16-17 (1999-2002) 241-63

M.J. Rubiera Mata, 'El Islam cristianizado de los moriscos castellanos en época de Carlos V', in J. Martínez Millán (ed.), *Carlos V y la quiebra del humanismo político en Europa (1530-1558)*, Madrid, 2001, 469-85

L.P. Harvey, '*El Mancebo de Arévalo* and his treatises on Islamic faith and practice', *Journal of Islamic Studies* 10 (1999) 249-76

L.F. Bernabé Pons, 'Nueva hipótesis sobre Baray de Reminyo', *Sharq al-Andalus* 12 (1995) 299-314

S. de Tapia Sánchez, *La comunidad morisca de Ávila*, Ávila, 1991

L.P. Harvey, 'El alfaquí de Cadrete, Baray de Reminjo y *El breve compendio de nuestra santa ley y sunna*', *II Jornadas Internacionales de Cultura Islámica*, Madrid, 1990, 213-22

L.P. Harvey, 'In Granada under the Catholic Monarchs. A call from a doctor and another from a Curandera', in A. Deyermond and I. MacPherson (eds), *The age of the Catholic Monarchs. 1474-1516. Literary studies in memory of Keith Whinnom, Bulletin of Hispanic Studies* special issue (1989) 71-75

L.P. Harvey, 'El mancebo de Arévalo y la tradición cultural de los moriscos', in A. Galmés de Fuentes (ed.), *Actas del coloquio internacional de literatura Aljamiada y Morisca (Oviedo, 1972)*, Madrid, 1978, 36-38

L.P. Harvey, 'Castilian "Mancebo" as a calque of Arabic 'abd, or how el Mancebo de Arevalo got his name', *Modern Philology* 65 (1967) 130-32

L.P. Harvey, 'Un manuscrito aljamiado en la Biblioteca de la Universidad de Cambridge', *Al-Andalus* 23 (1958) 49-74

L.P. Harvey, 'The literary culture of the Moriscos, 1492-1609. A study based on the extant manuscripts in Arabic and Aljamia', Oxford, 1958 (Diss. University of Oxford)

L.P. Harvey, 'Yuse Banegas. Un moro noble en Granada bajo los Reyes Católicos', *Al-Andalus* 21 (1956) 297-302

P. de Gayangos, 'Language and literature of the Moriscos', *British and Foreign Review* 8 (January 1839) 63-95

WORKS ON CHRISTIAN-MUSLIM RELATIONS

Breve compendio de nuestra santa ley y sunna, 'Brief summary of our holy law and sunna'

DATE Possibly 1532-33
ORIGINAL LANGUAGE Spanish in Arabic letters (Aljamiado)

DESCRIPTION

The *Breve compendio de nuestra santa ley y sunna* is a lengthy Aljamiado manuscript of 430 folios, well preserved and copied with great care by a single hand. The work is presented as a collaboration between the *faqīh* Ibrāhīm de Reminjo and the *Mancebo de Arévalo*, referred to by the *faqīh* as a very wise man who is proficient in a number of languages. It is difficult to distinguish the parts written by each, although the last draft was by the *Mancebo*.

The main purpose of the *Breve compendio*, which is unique among 16th-century Spanish works, is to teach the Aragonese Moriscos the main elements of the doctrine of Islam, in order to help prevent the gradual loss of their Islamic background. But the book contains much more than this. In it the *Mancebo* recounts his travels through the Iberian Peninsula and his frequent interviews with elderly people still able to transmit Islamic doctrine. He quotes freely from Muslim, Christian and Jewish works, and also cites a surprisingly large number of Islamic authorities, although these quotations are largely spurious. Indeed, many of his doctrinal comments, including a reflection about a qur'anic *sūra*, seem to be his own work, unsupported by traditional Muslim authorities. No other Morisco author in Spain in the 16th century speaks about the matters mentioned here: rich Moorish landowners, Morisco spies, elderly women who possessed great knowledge of Islam in their memories, Christian priests with friendly relations to Moriscos, rites performed in Mecca, differences between Islamic groups, and so on.

One of the most striking elements of this and the *Mancebo*'s other works is that, although they clearly assert the superiority of Islam, his tone is never aggressively polemical against Jews or Christians. Though he points to their errors several times, he is prepared to quote their scriptures to support his own opinions. His language is very unusual in that he creates a number of neologisms, from Arabic and Spanish. These are unique and are not infrequently difficult to understand.

SIGNIFICANCE

The *Breve compendio* demonstrates that not all Morisco thought in the 16th century was limited to the mechanical repetition of earlier Islamic rituals and teachings. It shows a Muslim who moves throughout the country in search of what is secretly preserved, and offers surprisingly modern descriptions of Muslim experiences in a hostile environment. Rather than repeating earlier Muslim formulations of doctrine, he makes it contemporary with the society and spirituality of his own time.

This work was written and transmitted privately within a community that remained Muslim and did not want to see their beliefs eroded by lack of continuing contact with Muslim authorities. It helps show how Spanish Morisco society resisted Christian oppression.

MANUSCRIPTS

   MS Cambridge, University Library – Dd.9.49, 470 fols (approximately end of the 16th century)

EDITIONS & TRANSLATIONS

   An edition of the *Breve compendio* is currently in preparation by L.P. Harvey, M.T. Narváez and L.F. Bernabé Pons.
   L.F. Bernabé Pons, 'Interferencias entre el árabe y el romance en los textos coránicos aljamiados', in P. Bádenas et al. (eds), *Lenguas en contacto. El testimonio escrito*, Madrid, 2005, 109-26, pp. 125-26
   Harvey, *Muslims in Spain*, pp. 170-93

L.P. Harvey, 'Una referencia explícita a la legalidad de la práctica de la *taqîya* por los moriscos', *Sharq al-Andalus* 12 (1995) 561-64, pp. 563-64 (English versión in *Aljamía* 8 [1996], pp. 42-43)

Harvey, 'El alfaquí de Cadrete', pp. 220-22

L.P. Harvey, 'Límite de los intercambios culturales', *Actas de las I jornadas de cultura Islámica*, Madrid, 1989, 89-94, pp. 92-94

Harvey, 'In Granada under the Catholic Monarchs', pp. 71-75

L.P. Harvey, '"The thirteen articles of the faith" and "The twelve degrees in which the world is governed". Two passages in a sixteenth-century Morisco manuscript and their antecedents', in F.W. Hodcroft et al. (eds), *Medieval and Renaissance studies on Spain and Portugal in honour of P.E. Russell*, Oxford, 1981, 15-29, pp. 27-29

Harvey, 'El mancebo de Arévalo y la tradición cultural de los moriscos', pp. 36-38

J. Karp-Gendre, *El manuscrito aljamiado de la Biblioteca de la Universidad de Cambridge (folios 237v-249r). Introducción, texto y glosario*, Toulouse, 1978

L.P. Harvey, 'A morisco reader of Jean Lemaire des Belges?', *Al-Andalus* 28 (1963) 231-36, pp. 235-36

Harvey, 'Un manuscrito aljamiado', pp. 69-74

Harvey, *The literary culture of the Moriscos*, ii, appendix

Harvey, 'Yuse Banegas', pp. 299-302

STUDIES

Bernabé Pons, 'Una fama sin biografía'

Harvey, *Muslims in Spain*, pp. 111-15, 170-93

Harvey, '*El Mancebo de Arevalo* and his treatises on Islamic faith and practice'

Harvey, 'Una referencia explícita', pp. 561-64 (English in *Aljamía* 8 [1996], pp. 40-43)

Bernabé Pons, 'Nueva hipótesis'

Harvey, 'El alfaquí de Cadrete', 213-22

Harvey, 'El mancebo de Arévalo y la tradición cultural de los moriscos'

Harvey, 'Un manuscrito aljamiado'

Harvey, *The literary culture of the Moriscos*, ii, Appendix

Harvey, 'Yuse Banegas'

Tafsira, 'Commentary'

DATE Possibly 1532-33
ORIGINAL LANGUAGE Spanish in Arabic letters (Aljamiado)
DESCRIPTION

Although this work is entitled *Tafsira*, it is far from being a commentary on the Qur'an. Rather, it is an extensive commentary on various aspects of Islamic doctrine, particularly *uṣūl al-fiqh*, combined with autobiographical details. *Tafsira* has close parallels with the *Breve compendio*, though it also has original elements, and the relationship between the two works has yet to be determined. It is a carefully copied manuscript, though not as sumptuous as the *Breve compendio*, and is quite lengthy, amounting to 472 folios.

The work opens with a well-known passage in which the *Mancebo* is at prayer in Zaragoza with 20 other Muslims, as he was waiting to go on the *ḥajj*. At the end of the prayer, they all lament the oppression under which the Morisco community finds itself, and argue about what is most important to keep the faith strong. The *Mancebo* places this meeting eight years after the conversion of the Moriscos of Aragón, thus in about 1532-33.

As in the *Breve compendio*, the *Mancebo* relates his encounters with people who guide him in Islam, among them two elderly women, the Mora de Ubeda and Nozaita Kalderán, and records frequent contacts with Christians and Jews. He refers to works from the three religions, and gives long descriptions of various features of Islam. The sources and meaning of some parts have not yet been determined (e.g., the *annās* and *innās* as constituent parts of the human), though Narváez Córdova has discovered that one quotation about the chaotic world is a copy from the preface of *La celestina* by Fernando de Rojas (1492), which is a translation of Petrarch's *De remediis utriusque fortunae*.

The *Mancebo* speaks knowledgeably about his adventures in Spain: his meeting with Ali Sarmiento in Algecira del Conde (Algecira, near Castellote in Aragón), his purchase of sword blades in San Clemente (Cuenca), and encounters in Granada with people of the former Naṣrid Kingdom of Granada. However, when he refers to places outside Spain, such as the pilgrimage route to Mecca, his writing becomes more fanciful.

As in the *Breve compendio*, the *Mancebo* seems very familiar with Jews and Christians and their books, and adopts an apologetic and reasoned tone that avoids religious controversy. Although his belief that Islam is the true religion leads him to say that the religion of the Jews and Christians is wrong, he never gets into bitter arguments. For Narváez (*Tratado*, pp. 25-26), his familiarity with Jewish beliefs does not derive from any ancestral connections, but from solidarity between minority groups that are both being persecuted by Christian orthodoxy.

SIGNIFICANCE

As with the *Breve Compendio*, *Tafsira* is surprising among the writings from the Aragonese Morisco community from which it emerged. While the Moriscos generally used anonymous Spanish translations of Arabic works, in these two works the author is prepared to identify himself and to talk about faith in other than purely historical terms. The *Mancebo* bears witness to Islam and his readiness to stand up for it, recognising his duty as a Muslim to teach those who do not know about their own faith. He is unique in openly attesting to his faith.

Tafsira helps to make visible the survival of a deeper knowledge of Islam in Spain than was previously thought. Its possible date places it in the context of the forced conversion of Muslims in Aragón, 25 years after the conversion of Muslims in Granada.

MANUSCRIPTS

    MS Madrid, Consejo Superior de Investigaciones Científicas – J LXII (late 16th century)

EDITIONS & TRANSLATIONS

    M.T. Narváez Córdova (ed.), *Tratado [Tafsira]. Mancebo de Arévalo*, Madrid, 2003

    M.T. Narváez Córdova, 'Preceptos de la vida cotidiana. Ética, moral y buenas costumbres en un capítulo de la *Tafçira* del Mancebo de Arévalo', in *Homenaje a Alvaro Galmés de Fuentes*, Oviedo, 1985, ii, 628-30

    M.T. Narváez Córdova, 'Mitificación de Andalucía como "nueva Israel". El capítulo "Kaída del-Andaluzziyya" del manuscrito aljamiado la *Tafçira* del Mancebo de Arévalo', *Nueva Revista de Filología Hispánica* 30 (1981) 162-67

    J. Ribera and M. Asín Palacios, *Manuscritos árabes y aljamiados de la Biblioteca de la Junta*, Madrid, 1912, pp. 217-28

STUDIES

    Narváez Córdova, *Tratado [Tafsira]. Mancebo de Arévalo*

M.T. Narváez Córdova, 'El despertar y el sueño. Dos motives místicos en un texto aljamiado', in W. Mejías López (ed.), *Morada de la palabra. Homenaje a Luce y Mercedes López-Baralt*, Puerto Rico, 2002, ii, pp. 1213-21

M.T. Narváez Córdova, '¿Qué sabían los moriscos sobre misticismo y temas esotéricos?', in L. López-Baralt and L. Piera (eds), *El sol de medianoche. La experiencia mística. Tradición y actualidad*, Madrid, 1996, 163-80

M.T. Narváez Córdova, 'El mancebo de Arévalo, lector morisco de *La Celestina*', *Bulletin of Hispanic Studies* 72 (1995) 255-72

M.T. Narváez Córdova, 'Nozaita Kalderán. Partera y experta en el Corán', *La Torre* (Puerto Rico) 3-4 (1987) 501-17

M.T. Narváez Córdova, 'El Mancebo de Arévalo frente a Jesús y María. Tradición y novedad', in A. Temimi (ed.), *Actes de la première Table Ronde du C.I.E.M. sur la littérature aljamiado-morisque. Hybridisme linguistique et univers discursif*, Tunis, 1986, 109-15

Narváez Córdova, 'Preceptos de la vida cotidiana'

M.T. Narváez Córdova, 'Más sobre la *Tafçira* del Mancebo de Arévalo', in A. Temimi (ed.), *Religion, identité et sources documentaires sur les morisques andalous*, Tunis, 1984, 123-30

Narváez Córdova, 'Mitificación de Andalucía como "nueva Israel"'

Sumario de la relación y ejercicio espiritual, 'Summary of the description and spiritual exercise'

DATE Possibly just before 1550
ORIGINAL LANGUAGE Spanish in Arabic letters (Aljamiado)

DESCRIPTION

Sumario is different from the other two works of the *Mancebo de Arévalo*. Although it has the same elements, characters and authorities (travelling through Spain, encounters with wise Muslims, instructions on how to perform religious observances), it is more spiritual in purpose. It consists of long discourses that describe and emphasise the value of inner beliefs as opposed to outward actions, the validity of mental prayer, humility before God and the world.

Gregorio Fonseca Antuña has discovered that the work contains long passages from a Spanish translation of Thomas à Kempis's *De imitatione*

Christi. The *Mancebo* turned it into an Islamic work by carefully removing Christian references that would be unacceptable to a Muslim.

SIGNIFICANCE

While the *Mancebo*'s other works show considerable originality, *Sumario de la relación y ejercicio espiritual* expresses a unique attitude that comes close to the *devotio moderna* and is fully aligned with Christian spiritual trends of the first half of the 16th century. The second part of the title is obviously reminiscent of Ignatius of Loyola's *Spiritual exercises*, written in the first quarter of the 16th century. It has no parallel in the Morisco community of Aragón.

The extensive and deliberate use of Thomas à Kempis suggests that the *Mancebo* could have had a Christian education, a possibility that is strengthened by Ibrahim de Reminjo's comment at the beginning of the *Breve compendio* that the *Mancebo* was an *escolano*, from a Christian educational institution (Rubiera Mata, 'El judeo-converso y morisco', speaks of an *estudio particular* organised by Franciscans in Arévalo in the 16th century).

MANUSCRIPTS

MS Madrid, BNE – Res 245, 322 folios (late 16th century)

EDITIONS & TRANSLATIONS

G. Fonseca Antuña, *Sumario de la relación y ejercicio espiritual sacado y declarado por el Mancebo de Arevalo en nuestra lengua castellana*, Madrid, 2002

Harvey, 'Yuse Banegas'

STUDIES

Fonseca Antuña, *Sumario de la relación y ejercicio espiritual*

Rubiera Mata, 'El judeo-converso', 839-56

Rubiera Mata, 'El Islam cristianizado'

G. Fonseca Antuña, 'Algunos ejemplos de formación léxica en *El Sumario de la relación y ejercicio espiritual* del Mancebo de Arévalo', in *Homenaje a Álvaro Galmés de Fuentes*, Madrid, 1985, iii, 649-55

John Chesworth & Luis F. Bernabé Pons

Lope Obregón

Lope de Obregón, López Obregón,
Lupus de Obregón

DATE OF BIRTH   Probably between the last decade of the
    15th century and first third of the 16th century
PLACE OF BIRTH   Unknown, but possibly Cantabria
DATE OF DEATH   Second half of the 16th century
PLACE OF DEATH   Unknown, but possibly Ávila

BIOGRAPHY

Little is known of the life of Lope Obregón beyond the fact that he was a priest at the Basilica of San Vicente in Ávila around the middle of the 16th century. He worked under Bishop Diego de Álava y Esquivel, who, after returning from the first years of the Council of Trent in 1545-49, urged his clergy to preach to Moriscos and give them instruction (*Confutación*, p. 2r; El Kolli, 'Polémique', p. 122). We know from his work, which is directed to the bishop, that he was well versed in biblical and patristic sources in Latin, may have had a rudimentary knowledge of Arabic, and had a reasonable though distorted familiarity with the basic beliefs and history of Islam.

While the surname Obregón suggests a family hailing from the Cantabria region, nothing is known of his origins or youth. The general facts of his life must be gleaned from his attack on Islam, the *Confutación del alcorán y secta mahometana*.

MAIN SOURCES OF INFORMATION

Primary
Confutación del alcorán y secta mahometana, sacado de sus proprios libros, y de la vida del mesmo Mahoma, Granada, 1555, pp. 1v-3r

Secondary
M.J. Framiñán de Miguel, 'Manuales para el adoctrinamiento de neoconversos en el siglo XVI', *Criticón* 93 (2005) 25-37, pp. 32-33 (also published as 'Catequesis "tras" la frontera. Manuales para el adoctrinamiento de neoconversos en el siglo XVI', in J. San José Lera [ed.], *Praestans labore victor. Homenaje al profesor Víctor García de la Concha*, Salamanca, 2005, 129-40, pp. 135-36)

J. El Kolli, 'La polémique islamo-chrétienne en Espagne (1492-1640) à travers les réfutations de l'islam de Juan Andrés et Lope Obregón', Montpellier, 1983 (Diss. Paul-Valéry University – Montpellier III), pp. 122-31

E. Llamas Martínez, 'Orientaciones sobre la historia de la teología española en la primera mitad del siglo XVI (1500-1550)', in *Repertorio de historia de las ciencias eclesiásticas en España*, vol. 1, Salamanca, 1967, 94-174, p. 110

A. Hernández Sánchez, 'Catecismos para la instrucción de los moriscos', Salamanca, 1955 (Diss. Pontifical University of Salamanca), pp. 114-15

WORKS ON CHRISTIAN-MUSLIM RELATIONS

Confutación del alcorán y secta mahometana, sacado de sus propios libros, y de la vida del mesmo Mahoma; Confutación del alcorán y secta mahometana, 'Refutation of the Qur'an and the Muḥammadan sect'

DATE 1555
ORIGINAL LANGUAGE Spanish

DESCRIPTION

Confutación del alcorán y secta mahometana (1555) is one of a number of anti-Islamic treatises written by various authors in 16th-century Spain that also include *Confusión o confutación de la secta mahomética y del Alcorán* of Juan Andrés (1515), the *Sermones* of Martín García (1517), *Lumbre de la fé contra la secta mahometana* of Juan Martín de Figuerola, (1518-21), Cristóbol de San Antonio's *Triumphus crucis contra infideles* (1521), Bernardo Pérez de Chinchón's *Libro llamado antialcorano* (1532), and Juan Luis Vives's *De veritate fidei Christianae*, Book 4 (1543). Such works were directed at or discussed the Morisco population of Spain (those Muslims who remained in the Iberian Peninsula after the fall of Granada in 1492), most of whom were forcibly converted to Christianity in the early years of the 16th century under the direction of Cardinal Francisco Jiménez de Cisneros and other Spanish clergymen, but who, for the most part, continued to preserve their Muslim beliefs and customs in private. Along with a handful of catechetical guides written in the period, most of these works aimed to preach to the Morisco population in order more successfully to convert them to Christian belief and better integrate them into Spanish Catholic society.

Obregón's work follows in the tradition of these works but also stands apart from them in a number of ways. The work covers 143 pages (72 printed folios, including introductory material), and is made up of 15 chapters, the first ten of which are devoted to a critical biography of Muḥammad. It then deals with the history of the compilation of the Qur'an, followed by an overview of certain pro-Christian ideas in the Sunna and four chapters on the 'contradictions' (*contradiciones*), 'lies' (*mentiras*) and 'fables' (*fabulas, fabulosos dichos, fabulosas revelaciones*) found in the Qur'an. Obregón asserts that Muḥammad was possessed by the Devil, who used him to spread heresy in the world (pp. 20r, 47v).

Such arguments were typical in anti-Muslim writing in the Latin West, and Obregón seems to have been influenced in particular by Riccoldo da Monte di Croce, whose *Improbatio Alcorani* was published in Spain in Latin and in Castilian translation in the early years of the 16th century. Obregón specifically names a number of other Christian Latin authors and sources, including Gregory the Great (p. 6v), the 15th-century history *Fasciculus temporum* (p. 6v), the 'Archbishop of Florence' (Francesco Zabarella), Isidore of Seville and, most significantly, Denis (Dionysius) the Carthusian (in particular, Obregón seems to have used Denis's *Contra perfidiam Mahometi*, from c. 1462). He blends such references with content from the anti-Muslim works mentioned earlier, and he specifically mentions Juan Andrés, Pérez de Chinchón, and Martín García as his sources.

Like earlier anti-Muslim works, Obregón's attacks on Muslim belief and custom rest heavily on a specific attack on Muḥammad, including proofs that he performed no miracles, was a false prophet, and had an excessively carnal nature. He claims that Muḥammad faked his prophecy out of a desire for fame and power, basing his teaching on what he had learned of Christian tradition from two Christian sword makers, Jabr and Yasar (a claim based on *tafsīr* of Q 16:103-5). He also shows familiarity with the Baḥīrā legend, which alleges that Muḥammad was influenced by a schismatic Christian monk. Similarly, he mentions the legend of Muḥammad's debate with the Jew Abū l-Ḥārith 'Abdallāh ben Salām (called Abdias) (p. 50v *et passim*) and the legend of Muḥammad's alleged contact with and letter to Heraclius (pp. 42v-45r). Originally, the Western Christian legend of Abdias the Jew was based on the *Liber de doctrina Mahumet*, translated by Hermann of Carinthia as part of the *Collectio Toletana*, the cluster of translations ordered by Peter the Venerable of Cluny in the mid-12th century (Ferrero Hernández and De la Cruz,

'Hermann of Carinthia', pp. 501, 505). Although this work, along with the *Liber de generatione Mahumet* (another work in the *Collectio Toletana*), was published by Theodore Bibliander as part of his 1543 edition of Robert of Ketton's translation of the Qur'an, Bibliander's edition was probably not Obregón's source, since he does not follow Ketton's numbering of qur'anic books. Rather, Obregón very possibly drew his version of this material from Denis the Carthusian, whom he mentions as one of his sources (in particular, see Denis's *Contra perfidiam Mahometi* Book 3, articles XIII-XIV, for discussion of Abdias).

Obregón does not rely only on Christian sources, however, but quotes widely from Qur'an, the *Sīra* of Ibn Isḥāq, various books of Sunna (al-Bukhārī and Muslim), the *Kitāb al-shifā' bi-taʿrīf ḥuqūq al-muṣṭafā* of Qāḍī ʿIyāḍ of Ceuta (p. 9r), and a few works of *tafsīr* (al-Zamakhsharī and Ibn ʿAṭiyya), all drawn from Juan Andrés (for one example, see Szpiech, 'Preaching Paul', p. 337). He also names a few philosophers (Ibn Rushd, Ibn Sīnā, al-Ghazālī, p. 53r) but does not quote from them or show any knowledge of their work. He displays a patchy and idiosyncratic understanding of the *ḥajj* and other Muslim customs and traditions, and his knowledge seems to be drawn from earlier 16th-century Spanish authors.

Obregón's work is significant in following Juan Andrés in particular, because it makes reference to the division of the Qur'an into four books, a Maghribī practice first mentioned and used by Juan Andrés (and imitated by Martín García but not by Pérez de Chinchón). Obregón follows the same divisions used by Juan as well, starting the second group at Book 7, the third at Book 19, and the fourth at Book 38, although he takes some *sūra*s out of order and claims the fourth book contains 170 chapters (five fewer than Juan Andrés, who claims 175) (p. 47v). Also like Juan Andrés, Obregón regularly provides the Arabic of his citations in phonetic transliteration into Latin characters, a practice not found in any of the other 16th-century anti-Muslim sources named above except Juan Martín de Figuerola, who transliterates his qur'anic citations after providing them in Arabic characters. As no manuscripts of Juan Andrés's work or Lope Obregón's work survive, it is not known whether they too included Arabic characters in their texts, which were then left out in printing. It is worth noting in this context that Pérez de Chinchón's text refers to original citations and leaves space for them in the text, but does not include them in any form in the printed editions, thus suggesting that some kind of original-language citation was included in the manuscript. While Obregón's transliterations often match Juan's (for example,

Q 33:37 in Juan Andrés, *Confusión*, p. 48v, and Obregón, p. 21r), they also sometimes differ (for example, Q 3:3 in Andrés, p. 76r, and Obregón, p. 17r). Based on Obregón's many references to Christian sources, El Kolli believes that he did not know Arabic and could not read the sources he cites in the original ('La polémique', p. 125), and the presence of some garbled, shortened or mixed qur'anic citations (which are not as garbled in Juan Andrés's text) would seem to support this (for example, see Obregón's citations of Q 2:87 on p. 2v, or Q 5:44 on p. 11r). Then again, some changes to the text (for example, in this latter verse on fol. 11r, the transposition of *hudan wa-nūrun* as 'nuron guahunde', i.e. *nūrun wa-hudan*, a phrase found elsewhere in the Qur'an) suggest that either he or an Arabic-speaking collaborator produced some of his citations from memory rather than copying them from a written version.

As with Juan Andrés, this use of original Arabic sources is part of Obregón's missionising strategy towards the Moriscos. He specifically states his intention to speak directly to Muslims in order to convert them, and laments their stubborn resistance, saying, 'since it is prohibited to them to dispute [their law], most of the Muḥammadans do not take care to know or say more than "my father died a Muslim, so must I die a Muslim"' (*porque como les está vedado disputarla, todos los más de los mahometanos no se curan de saber ni dezir más sino moro murió mi padre, moro tengo de morir yo*, p. 5r). Thus he stresses that his work makes use of 'very authentic books of the Moors' (*libros muy autenticos entre los moros*, p. 9r) and argues only 'according to the very sayings of the Qur'an' (*por los propios dichos de su alcoran*, p. 2r). In this, he follows Juan Andrés, who similarly stresses the persuasive power of using the Qur'an itself as a source of proofs of Christian truth.

SIGNIFICANCE

Like its predecessors, this work draws heavily upon the work of Juan Andrés, combining this material with earlier sources. Unlike Juan's work, Obregón does not claim that his work is from the perspective of a convert from Islam, but instead inserts its missionising arguments into the historical context of the Council of Trent and the call to evangelise the Moriscos more effectively through better preaching. While the work is not particularly noteworthy for the originality of its arguments, it is significant for two reasons: first, because it represents one of the ways that older anti-Islamic ideas from the *Collectio Toletana* and Riccoldo da Monte di Croce were transmitted in 16th-century Spain in Spanish rather than Latin, and second, because it represents the last major missionary work of its kind before the second Alpujarras revolt (1568-71), when the Moriscos around Granada staged a failed rebellion against decrees of King Philip II that had enforced a ban on Morisco customs and prohibited the Arabic language and alphabet. In the disastrous wake of the rebellion, Spanish writing about Islam and the Moriscos began to take a more pessimistic tone, and the Moriscos were definitively expelled from Spain in 1609. As Bunes Ibarra has observed, Obregón's work already shows a more polemical tone than earlier missionising works ('El enfrentamiento', p. 52), perhaps hinting at the ensuing embitterment in Christian-Morisco relations in Spain in the second half of the 16th century.

Obregón's work was cited by various authors in the 16th and 17th centuries, including Antonio de Torquemada, *Jardín de flores curiosas* (1570), Juan de Pineda, *Tercera parte de la monarchia ecclesiástica o historia universal del mundo* (1606), and most significantly the Jesuit Tirso González de Santalla in his *Selectarum disputationum ex vniuersa theologia scholastica* (1680) and *Manuductio ad conversionem Mahumetanorum* (1687). Outside Spain, his work had only a moderate impact, being far overshadowed by the work of Juan Andrés, which was translated into numerous languages and very widely disseminated. It is known that a copy of Obregón's work was held in the library of Henry Percy, ninth Earl of Northumberland (and brother of William Percy, author of the early-modern English play 'Mahomet and his heaven' from 1601). His work was mentioned in the 18th century by philologist Georg Wilhelm Friedrich Freytag (*Analecta litteraria de libris rarioribus*, 1750) and was known to form part of the large library of the Dutch lawyer Samuel van Hulst, sold at auction (*Bibliotheca Hulsiana*, 1730).

EDITIONS & TRANSLATIONS

Confutación del alcorán y secta mahometana, sacado de sus proprios libros, y de la vida del mesmo Mahoma, Granada, 1555

(references to a second 1560 printing begin to appear sporadically in the early 18th century but no such copy is now known to exist, suggesting this is simply a cataloguing error)

STUDIES

R. Szpiech, 'Preaching Paul to the Moriscos', *La Corónica* 41 (2012) 317-43, p. 337

Ó. de la Cruz Palma and C. Ferrero Hernández, 'Hermann of Carinthia', in *Christian-Muslim relations. A bibliographical history. Volume 3 (1050-1200)*, ed. D. Thomas and A. Mallett, Leiden, 2011, 497-507

Y. El Alaoui, 'L'évangélisation des morisques ou comment effacer les frontières religieuses', *Cahiers de la Méditerranée* 79 (2009) 51-72, pp. 67-69

J.P.A. Torres, 'Bibliografía sobre las traducciones del Alcorán en el ámbito hispano', *TRANS. Revista de Traductología* 11 (2007) 261-72

Framiñán de Miguel, 'Manuales para el adoctrinamiento', pp. 32-33 ('Catequesis', pp. 135-36)

M.A. Bunes Ibarra, *La imagen de los musulmanes y del norte de África en la España de los siglos XVI y XVII. Los caracteres de una hostilidad*, Madrid, 1989, pp. 104, 203-16, 236, 260

M.A. Bunes Ibarra, 'El enfrentamiento con el islam en el Siglo de Oro. los antialcoranes', *Edad de Oro* 8 (1989) 41-58, pp. 52-53

G.W. Drost, 'Die Moriscos in de publicaties van Staat en Kerk (1492-1609)', Katwijk aan den Rijn, 1984 (Diss. University of Leiden), pp. 129-33, 377, 379

El Kolli, 'La polémique islamo-chrétienne', pp. 122-31, 146-59, 167-94, 202-367

B. Jiménez Duque, *La escuela sacerdotal de Ávila del siglo XVI*, Salamanca, 1981, pp. 74, 125-26

M. Andrés, *La teología española en el siglo XVI*, Madrid, 1976, i, pp. 345-46

Hernández Sánchez, 'Catecismos para la instrucción de los moriscos', pp. 114-42, 240-42

Ryan Szpiech

Vicente Rocca

DATE OF BIRTH   Unknown
PLACE OF BIRTH Valencia
DATE OF DEATH   Late 16th century
PLACE OF DEATH Unknown

BIOGRAPHY

The only information we have about Vicente Rocca comes from details he himself gives in his history. He was a knight from Valencia whose first language was Valencian, although he wrote in Castilian, a language he claimed not to have studied. He was obviously also familiar with Latin, French and Italian, since he uses sources in these languages. He was asked to write his book by Carlos de Borja, fifth Duke of Gandía and Marquis of Lombardy (1530-92), the son of St Francisco de Borja.

MAIN SOURCES OF INFORMATION

Primary
Hystoria en la qual se trata de la origen y guerras que han tenido los Turcos, desde su comienzo hasta nuestros tiempos, con muy notables sucesos que con diversas gentes y naciones les han acontecido: y de las costumbres y vida dellos. Dirigida al Illustrissimo señor don Carlos de Borja, Duque de Gandía y Marqués de Lombay. Recopiladas por Vicente Rocca, cavallero Valenciano, Valencia, 1556

Secondary
F. Pons Fuster, 'El mecenazgo cultural de los Borja de Gandía. Erasmismo e iluminismo', *Estudis. Revista de Historia Moderna* 18 (1992) 77-96
J.E. Serrano y Morales, *Reseña histórica en forma de Diccionario de las imprentas que han existido en Valencia*, Valencia, 1898-99, pp. 366-69

WORKS ON CHRISTIAN-MUSLIM RELATIONS

Hystoria en la qual se trata de la origen y guerras que han tenido los Turcos, 'History of the origin and wars waged by the Turks'

DATE   31 October 1555 or 1556
ORIGINAL LANGUAGE   Spanish

DESCRIPTION

This historical work, which was presumably completed not long before it was published (at the end the date 31 October 1555 is given, while it is generally thought to have been published in 1556), comprises three books. The first discusses the origin of the Turks, a people who, the author says, have not been described before. It deals briefly with various crusades, among them the crusades led by Frederick Barbarossa of Germany and Louis IX of France, and describes the conquests of the Ottoman sultans, ending with the disputes and battles that took place before Sultan Selim came to power. The second book focuses on the sultanates of Selim and Süleyman, with special emphasis on Süleyman's military campaigns. The rivalry that existed between the Emperor Charles V and Sultan Süleyman is the main focus, with the naval confrontation with Turgut Reis and Barbarossa given prominence. The third book describes the day-to-day life of the Turks, from the religion they practise to the manner in which the sultan's court in Istanbul is organised.

Rocca writes under the strong belief that the war being waged in the Mediterranean is between Christianity and Islam, represented by the king of Spain and the sultan of the Turks. Yet even though he acknowledges the clear religious, political, civil and cultural rivalries between the two sides, he does not fail to acknowledge that there are certain virtues in the ways Turkish society is organised and the sultans administer justice. There are evident indications of objectivity in the work.

SIGNIFICANCE

This work, the first written in Spanish about the Ottoman Turks, was one of the most popular in the 16th century; it circulated in many copies and was cited by many other authors. Rocca compiled the book by collecting most of the printed material available about the Ottomans in Europe in the 1550s, and he always cites the sources he uses, among them the Italians Menavio, Spanduino and Sansovino. He is mainly indebted to Giovanni Menavio's *I cinque libri della legge, religione et vita de' Turchi, et della corte* (Florence, 1551), which might suggest that he travelled to Italy to buy most of the printed material he used. Many of his statements and judgements were borrowed by later authors, particularly the anonymous author of *Viaje de Turquía* ('Voyage to Turkey').

EDITIONS & TRANSLATIONS

Hystoria en la qual se trata de la origen y guerras que han tenido los Turcos, Valencia, 1556 (Microfiche, Valencia, 1992)

STUDIES

F. Fernández Lanza, 'Los turcos y lo turco a través de los impresos y manuscritos hispanos del siglo XVI', in M. Casado Arboniés (ed.), *Escrituras silenciadas en la época de Cervantes*, Alcalá de Henares, Madrid, 2006, 75-96

M.A. de Bunes, *La imagen de los musulmanes y del Norte de África en el pensamiento español de los siglos XVI y XVII. Los caracteres de una hostilidad*, Madrid, 1989

A. Mas, *Les Turcs dans la littèrature espagnole du Siècle d'Or*, Paris, 1967

Miguel Ángel de Bunes

Viaje de Turquía

DATE OF BIRTH Unknown; presumably early 16th century
PLACE OF BIRTH Unknown
DATE OF DEATH Unknown; probably mid-late 16th century
PLACE OF DEATH Unknown

BIOGRAPHY

Viaje de Turquía ('Voyage to Turkey') is an anonymous work preserved in five manuscripts. M. Serrano y Sanz (pp. cx-cxiii), its first editor in 1905, thought it was autobiographical and suggested the humanist Cristóbal de Villalón (c. 1500-post 1558) as author, though on weak evidence. This identification has not been generally accepted.

The humanist Andrés Laguna (c. 1511-59) was championed by Marcel Bataillon from 1937 (*Erasme et l'Espagne*) onwards, on the basis of arguments such as his interest in the Turks, apparently autobiographical references in the text, marginal notes in MS BNE 3871, and similarities with his *Comentarios a Dioscórides*. This identification has proved popular, though it has not gone unchallenged. In 1955, W. Markrich suggested Juan de Ulloa Pereira, a Knight of the Order of St John who was active in the Middle East ('The *Viaje de Turquía*', pp. 36-37, 159-75), though this has attracted few supporters (mainly García Salinero).

The problem of authorship remains unresolved.

Secondary
Á. Delgado Gómez, 'La medicina y el *Viaje de Turquía*', *Boletín de la Biblioteca Menéndez Pelayo* 60 (1984) 115-84
F. García Salinero, 'El *Viaje de Turquía* y la Orden de Malta. Revisión de una interpretación de la obra y su autor', *Revista de Estudios Hispánicos* 14 (1980) 19-30
F. García Salinero, '*Viaje de Turquía*. Pros y contras de la tesis Laguna', *Boletín de la Real Academia Española* 59 (1979) 464-98
F. García Salinero, '*Spes et fortuna valete*. Puntualizaciones sobre la atribución al Dr. Laguna del *Viaje de Turquía*', *Estudios Segovianos* 79 (1975) 85-102
J.J. Kincaid, *Cristóbal de Villalón*, New York, 1973, pp. 58-78
M. Bataillon, 'Les manuscrits du *Viaje de Turquía*', in *Actele celui deal XII-lea, Congress International de Linguistica si Filologie Romanica*, Bucharest, 1971, i, pp. 37-41

M. Bataillon, 'Les livres prohibés dans la bibliothèque du Comte de Gondomar', in *Beiträge zur französischen Aufklärung und zur spanischen Literatur. Festgabe für Werner Krauss zum 70. Geburtstag*, Berlin, 1971, 493-502

M. Bataillon, 'Le docteur Laguna et son temps', *Extraits de l'Annuaire du Collège de France* 63 (1963) 481-85

M. Bataillon, 'Sur l'humanisme du Docteur Laguna. Deux petits livres latins de 1543', *Romance Philology* 17 (1963) 207-34

M. Bataillon, *Le docteur Laguna, auteur du Voyage en Turquie*, Paris, 1958

W. Markrich, 'The *Viaje de Turquía*. A study of its sources, authorship and historical background', Berkeley, 1955 (Diss. University of California, Berkeley)

M. Bataillon, 'Quelques notes sur le *Viaje de Turquía*', *Les Langues Néo-Latines* 128 (1954) 1-8

C.E. Dubler, *La materia médica de Dioscórides. Transmisión medieval y renacentista*, 6 vols, Barcelona, 1953-59

M. Bataillon, 'Études sur le *Viaje de Turquía* attribué à Andrés Laguna', *Annuaire du Collège de France* 52 (1952) 281-85

N. Alonso Cortés, 'Acervo biográfico. Cristóbal de Villalón', *Boletín de la Real Academia Española* 30 (1950) 221-24

M. Bataillon, 'À propos d'une épitaphe d'André de Laguna', *Humanisme et Renaissance* 7 (1940) 122-27

M. Bataillon, *Érasme et l'Espagne*, Paris, 1937 (for the evolution of Bataillon's thought on Laguna's authorship, see the posthumous edition of his *Érasme et l'Espagne*, ed. D. Devoto and C. Amiel, Geneva, 1991)

A. Farinelli, *Dos excéntricos: Cristóbal de Villalón, el Dr. Juan Huarte*, Madrid, 1936, pp. 9-51

M. Serrano y Sanz, art. 'Cristóbal de Villalón', in *Autobiografías y memorias*, Madrid, 1905, ii, pp. cx-cxxiii

WORKS ON CHRISTIAN-MUSLIM RELATIONS

Viaje de Turquía, 'Voyage to Turkey'

DATE Approximately 1556-58
ORIGINAL LANGUAGE Castilian

DESCRIPTION

The title *Viaje de Turquía* has been used since the Serrano y Sanz edition of 1905, although the two most important manuscripts only contain it on their flyleaves. Other earlier or more recent titles refer to the main character and his travels. The spine of MS Madrid, Real Academia Española – E-45-7112 has *Pedro de Urdimalas*, expanded to *Diálogo entre Pedro de Hurdimalas y Juan de Voto a Dios y Mátalas* within the manuscript itself. MS Madrid, Escorial – J-11-23 has *Juan de Boto a Dios, Mátalas Callando, Pedro de Ordimalas, interloquutores*, while MS Toledo, Biblioteca Pública – 259 has *Pedro de Vrdemalas. Tetrálogo entre Pedro de Urdemalas, Juan de Voto-Dios i Mátalas Callando. Discurriendo sobre las costumbres y ceremonias de los turcos y otras naciones, trabajos de los cautivos, descripción de Constantinopla y otras cosas curiosas y dignas de ver.*

MS BNE 3871, the earliest of the work, gives at the end of the dedication the date 1 March 1557, though this is crossed out. On fol. 138v, it gives the date 1558. Other manuscripts do not offer any more precise dating.

In the absence of a full critical edition, the edition by García Salinero (Madrid, 1980, revised 1985), is cited here (though it is not without defects).

Viaje de Turquía is in the form of a conversation over two days between the three former friends Pedro de Urdemalas, who has escaped from the Turks, and Juan de Voto a Dios and Mátalas Callando, who make a living by preying on pilgrims to Santiago. They meet on the outskirts of a Castilian city on the pilgrims' way, when Juan and Mátalas chance on Pedro, who is dressed like a pilgrim. On the first day, Pedro tells the others about his captivity and escape, and they in their turn tell him about events in Spain while he has been away. On the second day, Pedro describes the history, life and customs of the Ottomans. The overall purpose of the conversation is evidently to compare the Ottoman and Habsburg empires, and to use criticisms of the former in comments about the latter. At the same time, the questions from Juan and Mata to the very experienced Pedro help them improve their methods of tricking superstitious and gullible pilgrims on the way to Santiago. This framework gives dramatic liveliness to the exchanges, but it also means that every fact and detail carries an ironic twist (e.g., the comparison between the sultan's women in the seraglio and the cloistered nuns of Santa Clara, p. 440), which makes *Viaje de Turquía* a splendidly satirical work and one of the best literary entertainments created in the Castilian Renaissance. It also warns against too readily recognising any obvious autobiographical features it may contain.

As the Dedication says, the objective of the work is to 'paint vividly... the power, life, origin and customs [of the Turks]... and the lives the miserable captives are living' (pp. 88-89). These themes correspond to each of the two days of the conversation: captivity and flight in the afternoon and evening of the first day, and history and origin of Byzantines and Turks, life and customs of the Ottomans on the morning of the second.

The second day begins with the incomplete *Turcarum origo*, a surviving false appendix in MS BNE 3871, that must be restored to its lost position, because it greatly changes the interpretation of the literary and dialogical form in the overall text.

Pedro relates that he was in one of Andrea Doria's galleys at the Battle of Ponza in 1552 (pp. 121, 128-29). He is captured and decides to pass himself off as a doctor. He is given responsibility for the wounded, and by reading a medical text and experimenting on his fellow captives, in three months he knows the job: the satire on medicine is obvious, even though eastern and western medicine is a matter of great interest throughout the work (p. 369), is defended as experimental knowledge (pp. 321-23), is championed as superior to theology (pp. 323-24), and is dealt with from many different angles: deontology, studies, practices, superstitions and beliefs, and strict medical theory.

When the fleet arrives in Constantinople, Pedro continues to present himself as a doctor, and achieves success by healing leading members of Ottoman society. He is constantly requested to convert to Islam but he resists, and eventually he makes an escape, travelling through the Aegean Islands (pp. 292-329) and Italy (pp. 329-78).

Pedro's account of his captivity in Constantinople is detailed and animated, offering a striking picture of the lives of prisoners, Turkish customs and the places he passes through, though not adding to information that was currently available. When he describes Constantinople, he emphasises the refinement and industry of the people, and the magnificence of the monuments, in particular Santa Sofia (pp. 415, 430-32) and the imperial mosques (pp. 39, 176, 405, 489, 495), and he concludes that it outstrips even the greatest European cities (p. 498).

Medicine and religion appear as dominant concerns, though the comparison with Spain and the Habsburg empire is constant, from justice (p. 409), the army and warfare (pp. 418, 434), ambassadors and corsairs (p. 458), trades, food (pp. 158, 181, 183, 219, 273, 282, 324, 340, 467-84) and inns (p. 261), to weddings, women and clothing (pp. 437-39), and sexual practices (p. 443). The author makes criticisms of the Turks, particularly their beliefs, their cruelty and fondness for torture – such as their crucifixion of a Hungarian Christian (p. 240) – and their sexual behaviour, but he is close to Pierre Belon and Guillaume Postel in resisting the prejudice that sees the Turks as nothing more than barbarians or cruel monsters. He compares Ottoman and European cultures in terms of equality and perspective ('... they call us unbelieving pagans', p. 93), emphasising the good and bad of each (Delgado Gómez, 'Una visión comparada', pp. 39-40,

43). This leads to criticisms of the Habsburg Empire and Spain. He complains about the lack of education in Spain and throughout Europe ('... there are more people over there who can read and write than over here', p. 398), its general ignorance (pp. 116, 329, 358-59, 361-63), and specific ignorance of languages, theology and above all medicine (pp. 107-8, 121, 246-47, 321, 369), and the need for reforms to the curriculum in order to bring in study of Erasmus, Melanchthon and Donato (pp. 362-63).

Religion occupies a central place in this double criticism, particularly in the second part of the conversation. Christianity is superior, particularly when understood as a code of conduct (pp. 123, 150, 199-201, 212, 245-46, 328) – this is why Pedro refuses to convert during his captivity. But he does not flinch from criticising external shows of false piety among Christians (pp. 103-5, 110, 119-21, 124-26, 158, 230-31, 264-66, 293), or the ignorance and hypocrisy of the clergy, their failure to perform their duties, unchasteness (pp. 183, 249, 277, 284, 286, 339), perverse promoting of superstition (e.g. p. 349), confessors' openness to bribes and preachers' incompetence (pp. 165-68, 321-2). This all contrasts with the exemplary conduct of Greek priests (pp. 278, 285-87, 289) who, as St Paul taught, live on their income without burdening poor people. His denunciation stretches as far as the papal curia (pp. 344, 347, 396), who are only Christians in name (p. 471).

By contrast, apart from their practice of sodomy, the frequency of which he denounces, Pedro presents the Turks as more virtuous than Christians (pp. 54, 163, 203, 233, 406, 414, 432, 471): they are not gamblers, they are sober, devout, charitable, hard-working, go early to bed and rise early, and are not continually at parties, to the point where Juan comments: 'What a virtuous people they are, and how great is our confusion' (p. 456). 'Turkish justice', says Pedro, 'treats everyone as equals, Christians the same as Jews and Turks' (p. 409). For him, the only drawback among the Turks (or Jews) is their religion (pp. 213, 285, 386, 391, 440), yet their virtues obey 'the laws of nature'. One brief speech gives a key to the whole book: 'Wherever I have travelled – and that is a good third of the world – I have not seen more virtuous people ... apart from their belief in Mohammed, for which I know they are all going to hell; but I am speaking of the law of nature' (p. 457). Pedro reaches the surprising conclusion that the Turks are a tolerant people, virtuous, better organised than the West in economic, administrative and military spheres, while there are as many good Turks as there are bad Christians. His aside – 'I know that they are all going to hell, but I am speaking of the law of nature' – is said with enough flippancy to suggest he does not believe it and cannot believe that the Turks are damned according to the 'law of nature'.

Viaje de Turquía makes use of earlier and contemporary authorities such as (certainly) the diplomat Bartholomaeus Georgievitz (d. 1566), in the version by Domenichi, Pierre Belon (from whom it takes much of the material on Turkey, Asia Minor, Mount Athos and the Greek archipelago), serious compilers such as Münster and populariser of semi-fictitious facts such as Menavino (from whom he takes, among other things, the affirmation in the Dedication about how he has experienced all that he writes), writers such as Spandugino, Rocca, probably O.G. Busbecq whose 'Turkish letters' were in wide circulation, and others not yet fully known (Bataillon, *Erasme*, 1937, pp. 716-17, 725-35, and 'Peregrinaciones', pp. 121-37; Markrich, 'The *Viaje*', especially pp. 45-58, 72-75, 112-49; Corsi Prosperi, 'Sulle fonti', pp. 66-90). On this canvas of multiple influences – Mas calls it *supercherie documentaire* ('documentary fraud') (*Les Turcs*, i, p. 148) – the author weaves an ingenious fantasy and fictional dialogue to present in the most attractive form possible the new knowledge of the Turks that the West was wanting at this time. His most important contribution is the sense of detail and evocative accuracy of his depiction, generally allied closely to jokes and linguistic humour inspired by the classical satirist Lucian. He allows himself to be carried along by his linguistic capability, and his skill is rewarded because it removes his work from the normally cold, erudite treatises on Turkish subjects that were typical of the time. The thing of least importance is whether the information in it is second-hand or not. Its originality lies in its form, the ambiguity, paradox, double message, irony and ideology that its pages show. Spain at the beginning of 'hard times' produced an exceptional literary and satirical work that avoided ethnocentrism and offered a critical and self-critical picture of both worlds.

SIGNIFICANCE

At a time when stereotypes about the other were developing in both the Ottoman and Habsburg empires, and Western and Spanish dislike of Turks was spreading, the vision of Islam revealed in the *Viaje de Turquía*, along with its Erasmian or even more radical ideas about Christian excesses, made the book impossible to publish. It was not about harmless Moorish poetry from vanquished Granada, but about an effort of human sympathy and tolerance to understand a political adversary who was in the ascendant. This was only perceptible in humanists such as Belon or Postel in France, a country that forged alliances with Süleyman in order to weaken the Habsburg Empire; but was inadmissible in Spain, where the triumph of the true faith was prized above everything else, and where the earlier policy of integration and evangelisation of the Jews and Muslims was being re-examined. The period was one of anti-Turkish sentiment throughout Europe. And so the new way given in this book that opened up knowledge of Islam, combining it with a powerful political, religious and social self-criticism from within, was closed at the very time it was arising. Only a few privileged people would read the book, and only a few copies were made from the end of the 16th century.

MANUSCRIPTS

    MS Madrid, BNE – 3871 (1556-58; not the original autograph, but a rough copy in various hands, the earliest and best MS, of which the others are copies)

    MS Madrid, BNE – 6395 (late 16th or more probably early 17th century)

    MS Madrid, Real Academia Española – E-45-7112 (late 16th or early 17th century)

    MS Madrid, Real Biblioteca del Monasterio de San Lorenzo de El Escorial – J-11-23 (late 16th or early 17th century)

    MS Toledo, Biblioteca Pública – MS 259 (between 1556 and 1750)

    For digitalised texts of these five MSS, together with detailed descriptions by J.M. Valero-Moreno, see Biblioteca Digital de Diálogo Hispánico, University Complutense, Madrid, Dialogyca BDDH, http://www.ucm.es/info/dialogycabddh/ number BDDH 195.

EDITIONS & TRANSLATIONS

    Voyage de Turquie, trans. J. Ferreras and G. Zonana, Paris, 2006 (French trans. of the edition by M.S. Ortolá, without 'Table of contents' or 'Turcarum origo', following the chapterisation by G. Salinero)

    Viaje de Turquía. Diálogo entre Pedro Hurdimalas y Juan Voto a Dios y Mátalas Callando, que trata de las miserias de los cautivos de turcos y de las costumbres y secta de los mismos haciendo la descripción de Turquía, ed. M.S. Ortolá, Madrid, 2000 (critical edition from MS Madrid, BNE 3871; includes an edition of the 'Table of contents' and 'Turcarum origo', but placed in the appendix rather than their original place)

[Turcarum origo], 'Para la lectura completa del *Viaje de Turquía*. Edición de la *Tabla de materias* y de la *Turcarum origo*', ed. F. Sevilla and A. Vian, *Criticón* (Toulouse) 45 (1989) 5-70 (critical edition with apparatus of variants of the three MSS that retain the 'Turcarum origo')

C. de Villalón, *Törökországi utazás* [Journeys to Turkey], trans. Z. Tomcsányi, Budapest, 1984 (Hungarian trans. derived from the edition by Serrano y Sanz, with illustrations)

A. Laguna, *Aventure di un schiavo dei turchi*, ed. and intr. C. Acutis, Milan, 1983 (partial Italian trans. from the editions by Serrano y Sanz and probably García Salinero)

Viaje de Turquía (La odisea de Pedro de Urdemalas), ed. F. García Salinero, Madrid, 1980, 1985² (revised at some point, with various reprints, 1986, 1995; excludes the 'Table of contents' and 'Turcarum origo'), www.cervantesvirtual.com/obra-visor/viaje-de-turquia-la-odisea-de-pedro-de-urdemalasohtml/

Pedro'nun zorunlu İstanbul seyahati.16. yüzyıl'da Türkler'e esir düşen bir İspanyol'un anıları [The journey of Pedro, a forced labourer from the 16th century, to Istanbul. A memoir of a Spaniard captured by the Turks], ed. and trans. Fuad Carim, Istanbul, 1995 [1996], repr. 2002 (Turkish trans. of the part concerning Istanbul)

A. Portuondo Tamayo, '*Viaje de Turquía*, edition and study', Washington DC, 1975 (Diss. Catholic University of America)

C. de Villalón, *Viaje de Turquía*, intr. F.C. Sainz de Robles, Madrid, 1973 (incomplete, from the edition by García Solalinde, does not include 'Table of contents' or 'Turcarum origo')

Kanunî devrinde İstanbul. Dört asır yayınlanmadan köşede kalmış çok önemli bir eser ['Istanbul in the age of Kanuni. A most important work unpublished for four centuries'], ed. and trans. Fuad Carim, Istanbul, 1964 (Turkish trans. of the portion concerning Istanbul; it previously appeared in instalments in the Istanbul newspaper *Tercüman* – information courtesy of Gülisik Alkaç Morera)

C. de Villalón, *Viaje de Turquía*, adaptation of the original text by J.M. Velloso, illustrations by José Bort, Madrid, 1963 (adaptation of the text for use as an introduction for younger readers)

C. de Villalón, *Dal Viaggio in Turchia*, ed. A. Gasparetti, Milan, 1959 (selection of the Italian part of the journey, with an appendix of Italian curiosities)

C. de Villalón, *Viaje de Turquía*, ed. J. García Morales, Madrid, 1946. (incomplete edition from the text by García Solalinde; does not include the 'Table of contents' or the 'Turcarum origo')

C. de Villalón, *Viaje de Turquía*, ed. A. García Solalinde, 2 vols, Madrid-Barcelona, 1919, Madrid 1942², 1943, 1946, 1947, 1965, www.cervantes virtual.com/obra-visor/viaje-de-turquia--0/html/ (follows the edition by Serrano y Sanz and its system of chapterisation, and therefore includes neither the 'Table of contents' nor the 'Turcarum origo')

C. de Villalón, *Viaje de Turquía*, ed. M. Serrano y Sanz, in *Autobiografías y Memorias*, Madrid, 1905, 1-149 (transcription of MS Madrid, BNE 3871, completed with BNE 6395 and Toledo BP 259; an incomplete edition, lacking both the 'Table of Contents' and the 'Turcarum origo', and creating divisions of the text unconnected with the MS)

STUDIES

Bibliography on the *Viaje de Turquía* is very extensive. The list here is limited to works that have a bearing on Christian-Muslim relations. For an exhaustive version of the general bibliography, refer to the latest updating (2013) by J.M. Valero-Moreno and A. Vian-Herrero in *Dialogyca BDDH*; http://www.ucm.es/info/dialogycabddh/, BDDH 195

J. Pérez, 'El *Viaje de Turquía*. Un humanista adelantado a su tiempo', in *Humanismo en el Renacimiento español*, Madrid, 2013, 177-91

L. Balaborca Fattaccioli, '*Viaje de Turquía*. La representación de los turcos en el diálogo del siglo XVI', *Hispania Felix. Revista Hispano-Rumana de Cultura y Civilización de los Siglos de Oro* 2 (2011) 67-84

N. Ohana, 'Lecciones de allende la frontera. El *Viaje de Turquía* y su propuesta de apertura social', *Bulletin of Hispanic Studies* 88 (2011) 423-36

E. Sánchez García, 'El mundo femenino turco en la literatura castellana del siglo XVI', in J.A. González Alcantud and A. Stoll (eds), *El Mediterráneo plural en la Edad Moderna. Sujeto histórico y diversidad cultural*, Barcelona, 2011, 163-67

M.S. Ortolà, '*Viaje de Turquía*', in P. Jauralde Pou (ed.), *Diccionario filológico de literatura española. Siglo XVI*, Madrid, 2009, 978-86

M.A. Bunes Ibarra, 'El imaginario sobre los turcos en el mundo hispánico. El *Viaje de Turquía* y sus fuentes', in A. Servantie and R. Puig de la Bellacasa (eds), *L'Empire ottoman dans l'Europe de la Renaissance*, Leuven, 2005, 47-65

M. Polic Bobic, 'El *Viaje de Turquía* y una de sus posibles fuentes de información sobre *las cosas del Turco*', in C.M. Induráin and M. Zugasti (eds), *El Siglo de Oro en el nuevo milenio*, Pamplona, 2005, ii, 1415-26

M.S. Ortolà, 'Images des femmes dans le *Viaje de Turquía*', in P. Civil (ed.), *Siglos dorados. Homenaje a Augustin Redondo*, Madrid, 2004, ii, 1045-63

E. Sánchez García, 'Semblanza de una princesa turca. La hija de Solimán en el *Viaje de Turquía*', in Civil (ed.), *Siglos dorados*, ii, 1339-54

E. Sánchez García, 'Notas sobre la imagen de Persia en la prosa española del siglo XVI', in *Memoria de la palabra. Actas del VI Congreso de la Asociación Internacional Siglo de Oro*, Madrid, 2004, 1587-98, pp. 1588-89, 91, 93, 96

J. Lawrence, 'Europe and the Turks in Spanish literature of the Renaissance and early modern period', in N. Griffin, E. Southworth and C. Thompson (eds), *Culture and society in Habsburg Spain*, London, 2001, 17-33

E. Sánchez García, 'Pedro de Urdemalas o la heroicidad clásica en el Mediterráneo carolino', in C. Strosetzki (ed), *Aspectos históricos y culturales bajo Carlos V. Aspekte der Geschichte und Kultur unter Karl V*, Frankfurt, 2001, 309-24

J. Pérez, 'L'affrontement Turcs-Chrétiens vu de l'Espagne. Le *Voyage en Turquie*', in J. Pérez, *De l'humanisme aux lumières*, Madrid, 2000, 333-40

R. Fernández García, 'Visiones de Constantinopla y de la Grecia otomana en el *Viaje de Turquía*', Oviedo, 2000, http://uniovi .academia.edu/Rams%C3%A9sFern%C3%A1ndezGarc%C3% ADa/Papers/1246152/Alusiones_a_Grecia_y_a_Constantinopla_en_ El_viaje_de_Turquia_

L. Alcoba, 'Voces ajenas y voz propia en el *Viaje de Turquía*', in A. Redondo, P.M. Cátedra and M.L. López-Vidriero (eds), *El escrito en el Siglo de Oro. Prácticas y representaciones*, Salamanca, 1998, 13-19

S. Alcoba Rueda, 'La mirada y su réplica en el *Viaje de Turquía*', *Voz y Letra* 9 (1998) 37-46

E. Sánchez García, 'A comparison of the devotional systems in the *Viaje de Turquía*', in L.K. Twomey (ed.), *Faith and fanaticism. Religious fervour in early modern Spain*, Aldershot, 1997, 140-57

E. Sánchez García, '*Viaje de Turquía*. Las etapas de un viaje de ida y vuelta', in M. Criado de Val (ed.), *Caminería hispánica. Actas del II Congreso Internacional de Caminería hispánica*, Guadalajara, 1996, iii, 187-96

A. Vian-Herrero, 'La *Turcarum origo*, Una crónica ejemplar y burlesca en el *Viaje de Turquía*', in R.M. Aguilar, M. López Salvá and I. Rodríguez Alfageme (eds), *Homenaje a Luis Gil*, Madrid, 1994, 767-81

M.Á. Bunes Ibarra, 'La conquista de Bizancio según los cronistas europeos de los siglos XVI y XVII', *Erytheia* 13 (1992) 89-102

E. Sánchez García, 'Visiones del Mediterráneo en el siglo XVI. La *Suma de Geografía* y el *Viaje de Turquía*', in *Descubrir, describir, inventar el mundo. Actas del IV Simposio Internacional de la Asociación Española de Semiótica (Sevilla, 1990)*, Madrid, 1992, 1015-24

S. Yérasimos, *Les voyageurs dans l'Empire ottoman (XIVe-XVIe siècles). Bibliographie, itinéraires et inventaires des lieux habités*, Ankara, 1991

A. Vian-Herrero, 'La *Turcarum origo*. De falso apéndice a porción literaria integral del *Viaje de Turquía*', *Romanistisches Jahrbuch* 42 (1991) 267-89

F. Sevilla Arroyo, 'Sobre un apéndice del *Viaje de Turquía*. La *Turcarum origo*', in P. Jauralde, D. Noguera and A. Rey (eds), *La edición de textos. Actas del I Congreso Internacional de Hispanistas del Siglo de Oro*, London, 1990, 459-68

M.A. Bunes Ibarra, *La imagen de los musulmanes y del Norte de África en la España de los siglos XVI y XVII. Los caracteres de una hostilidad*, Madrid, 1989

M.Á. Bunes Ibarra, 'Constantinopla en la literatura española sobre los otomanos (ss. XVI-XVII)', *Erytheia* 7 (1989) 263-74

A. Vian-Herrero, 'Los manuscritos del *Viaje de Turquía*. Notas para una edición crítica del texto', *Boletín de la Real Academia Española* 68 (1988) 455-96

C. Allaigre, 'Mucho va de Pedro a Pedro. Aspects idéologiques et personnages exemplaires du *Viaje de Turquía*', *Bulletin Hispanique* 90 (1988) 91-118

G. Núñez Esteban, 'La Constantinopla del *Viaje de Turquía*', *Revista de Filología Clásica* 2 (1988) 333-52

A. Redondo, 'Devoción tradicional y devoción erasmista en la España de Carlos V. De la *Verdadera información a la Tierra Santa* de Fray Antonio de Aranda al *Viaje de Turquía*', in E. Asensio, L. López-Grigera and A. Redondo (eds), *Homenaje a Eugenio Asensio*, Madrid, 1988, 391-416

Á. Delgado Gómez, 'Una visión comparada de España y Turquía', *Cuadernos Hispanoamericanos* 444 (1987) 35-64

Á. Delgado Gómez, 'El viaje como medio de conocimiento. El *Viaje de Turquía*', in *Actas del VIII Congreso de la Asociación Internacional de Hispanistas*, Madrid, 1986, i, 483-90

Delgado Gómez, 'La medicina y el *Viaje de Turquía*'

S. Melón Fernández, 'Algunos aspectos cuantitativos del *Viaje de Turquía*', *Cuadernos del Norte* 22 (1983) 18-24

S. Melón Fernández, 'La gastronomía del *Viaje de Turquía*', *Cuadernos del Norte* 22 (1983) 25-29

M.S. Ortolà, *Un estudio del Viaje de Turquía. ¿Autobiografía o ficción?*, London, 1983

J. Goytisolo, 'El *Viaje de Turquía*', *Quimera* 6 (April 1981) 20-27

J. Aguadé, 'Inna Iladi ya'kulu wa-yasrabu takunu lahu l-haga. Ein Beitrag zur jüdish-christlichen Polemik gegen den Islam', in W. Röllig and W. von Soden (eds), *Die Welt des Orients. Wissenschaftliche Beiträge zur Kunde des Morgenlandes*, Göttingen, 1979, 61-72

A. Corsi Prosperi, 'Sulle fonti del *Viaje de Turquía*', *Critica Storica* 14 (1977) 66-90

F. Meregalli, 'L'Italia nel *Viaje de Turquía*', *Annali di Ca' Foscari* 13 (1974) 351-63

F. Meregalli, 'Partes inéditas y partes perdidas del *Viaje de Turquía*', *Boletín de la Real Academia Española* 54 (1974) 193-201

A. Mas, *Les Turcs dans la littérature espagnole du Siècle d'Or. Recherches sur l'évolution d'un thème littèraire*, Paris, 1967, i, 103-55

M. Bataillon, 'Mythe et connaissance de la Turquie en Occident au milieu du XVIe siècle', in A. Pertusi (ed.), *Venezia e l'Oriente fra tardo medio evo e Rinascimento*, Florence, 1966, 451-70

J. Gil and L. Gil, 'Ficción y realidad en el *Viaje de Turquía*. Glosas y comentarios al recorrido por Grecia', *Revista de Filología Española* 45 (1962) 89-160

M. Bataillon, 'Venise porte de l'Orient au XVIe siècle. Le *Viaje de Turquía*', in C. Pellegrini (ed.), *Venezia nelle letterature moderne*, Venice, 1961, 11-20

Markrich, 'The *Viaje*'

Ana Vian-Herrero

El Abencerraje

El Abencerraje y la hermosa Jarifa

DATE OF BIRTH Unknown
PLACE OF BIRTH Unknown
DATE OF DEATH Unknown
PLACE OF DEATH Unknown

BIOGRAPHY

Nothing is known about the author of this novella. The tale may have originated in a medieval chronicle that has since been lost. There are four extant versions, all of uncertain authorship. The second version, published in 1561, contains a dedication to Jerónimo Jiménez de Embún, Baron of Bárboles. The fourth version is incorporated at the end of Book 4 of the second edition of Jorge de Montemayor's pastoral romance *La Diana*, published posthumously in Valladolid in 1562. This version, which may or may not have been written by Montemayor before his death, is a revised version of the 1561 chapbook. The fourth version was included in Antonio de Villegas' anthology of his own verse, *El inventario*, first printed in 1565. Villegas presumably adapted this text from the 1561 chapbook; he also had access to the version published in Montemayor's *Diana*.

MAIN SOURCES OF INFORMATION

Secondary
E. Torres Corominas (ed.), *Literatura y facciones cortesanas en la España del siglo XVI. Estudio y edición del Inventario de Antonio de Villegas*, Madrid, 2008
F. López Estrada (ed.), *Historia del Abencerraje y de la hermosa Jarifa. Cuatro textos y su estudio*, Madrid, 1957

WORKS ON CHRISTIAN-MUSLIM RELATIONS

El Abencerraje y la hermosa Jarifa, 'The Abencerraje and the beautiful Jarifa'

DATE Between 1561 and 1565
ORIGINAL LANGUAGE Spanish

DESCRIPTION

El Abencerraje y la hermosa Jarifa, usually shortened to *El Abencerraje* ('The Abencerraje and the beautiful Jarifa' or just 'The Abencerraje') is an anonymous Spanish novella of the mid-16th century, extant in four versions, the longest of which is a mere 7,700 words. Brief as it is, it is considered the first Moorish novel, and thus the originator of the 'Maurophile' craze in late-16th-century Spain. This fad disseminated an idealised image of the Moors of Granada, which persisted through the Romantic period and beyond, up to the present day. Though its version of Islamic society is pure fantasy, it provides a depiction of harmony between Christians and Muslims that has proved irresistible.

Set along the 15th-century border between Christian and Muslim Spain, the tale begins with the capture of Abindarráez, descendant of the politically disgraced Abencerrajes of Granada, a semi-legendary clan said to have been falsely accused of treason against Boabdil, the last Naṣrid king of Granada. His captor is Rodrigo de Narváez, a Christian knight, captain of the guard at Álora. (Ostensibly set in the era of Ferdinand I of Aragón, who died in 1416, the tale anachronistically makes Álora a Christian town, though it was not conquered by the Catholic Monarchs until 1484.) Abindarráez fights valiantly, but once he has been taken captive his sighs prompt Narváez to ask what troubles him; he responds with the story of his love for Jarifa. Exiled at birth, Abindarráez was raised by Jarifa's father, captain of the fortress of Cártama, as his own son. Shortly after their discovery that they were not really siblings had opened the way to their sexual union, Abindarráez and Jarifa were separated due to her father's move to Coín, 14 km away. She sends word for him to join her secretly, but captivity spoils his plans. Hearing this tale, Narváez generously releases Abindarráez on condition that he returns in three days. Abindarráez resumes his journey, consummates his secret marriage with Jarifa and they both present themselves to Narváez as captives. At this point, however, he behaves less as their captor than as their host, even acting as marriage broker for the young couple. Jarifa's father is reluctant to have his daughter wed a member of the disgraced clan, but Narváez intercedes with the king of Granada, who authorises the marriage. Narváez again displays magnanimity in sending the newlyweds home without taking ransom. The narrator ends by stating that the three remained close friends for the rest of their lives, despite the difference in religion.

The tale may have originated in a medieval chronicle that has since been lost. The four extant versions, which have been edited in a single volume by Francisco López Estrada, are: *Historia del moro y Narváez* ('Tale of the Moor and Narváez') a simple, 1,000-word tale surviving in a single 16th-century manuscript transcription in the Biblioteca Nacional in Madrid (MS BNE 1752, fols 253-54). This version is believed to give an idea of how the story could have existed as part of a medieval chronicle, *Parte de la Corónica del ínclito infante don Fernando que ganó a Antequera* ('Part of the Chronicle of the renowned Prince don Fernando, who captured Antequera'), the earliest print version of *El Abencerraje* to have survived, a chapbook of which two copies are preserved, both from 1561. This chapbook is considered the source for the two later versions. Though anonymous, it contains a dedication to Jerónimo Jiménez de Embún, Baron of Bárboles and Oitura. A version of *El Abencerraje* incorporated at the end of Book 4 of the second edition of Jorge de Montemayor's pastoral romance *La Diana*, published posthumously in Valladolid in 1562. This version, which may or may not have been written by Montemayor before his death, is a revised version of the 1561 chapbook. *Historia del Abencerraje y la hermosa Jarifa*, as included in Antonio de Villegas' anthology of his own verse, *El inventario*, first printed in 1565. Villegas presumably adapted this text from the 1561 chapbook; he also had access to the version published in Montemayor's *Diana*.

While the truncated *Tale of the Moor and Narváez* gives some idea of how the fully-developed versions could have grown out of a medieval chronicle, no actual chronicle containing the story has ever surfaced. The documented chain of transmission begins with the anonymous *Corónica* version, which would already have been in wide circulation in the late 1550s, according to Torres Corominas' recent account (*Literatura y facciones cortesanas*, pp. 294-321). Jorge de Montemayor died in early 1561; whether he penned a refashioning of *La Corónica* himself is uncertain. What is clear is that when the Valladolid re-edition of Montemayor's *Diana* came out in 1562, *El Abencerraje* was already popular enough for the printer to choose to include it as a guarantee of commercial success. This short Moorish tale was included in subsequent editions of *La Diana*, helping to extend the life of Montemayor's work and making it one of the most popular books of the 16th century in and beyond Spain. This is the version most early modern readers would have read, among them Don Quixote, who knew *El Abencerraje* from a copy of *La Diana* in his library, as Cervantes' narrator explains in ch. 5 of Part One. In 1565, when Antonio de Villegas brought out the collection of his own poetry and prose titled *El inventario*, he probably had both the *Corónica* and *Diana* versions in front of him. True, he had already applied for a licence to publish *El inventario* in 1551, but in the absence of any indication of its intended contents, we cannot assume Villegas was already in possession of a version of *El Abencerraje* at that time. The most prudent assumption is that Villegas' editor, like Montemayor's, chose to incorporate the already popular tale as a way of stimulating sales of the book.

The primary theme of this little tale is the harmonious friendship between Christian and Muslim nobles, predicated on a shared heroic/chivalric code in which religion plays little part. The Christian knight, Narváez, is idealised as generous and noble, a man of the world who serves as a reliable guide for the younger, more naïve Abindarráez. The text avoids any explicit references to Islam; Abindarráez and Jarifa are represented more as 'pagans' than as 'infidels'. In an extended garden scene replete with pastoral elements, he expresses his feelings for her in terms of Greco-Roman myths of Venus, Salmacis and Hermaphrodite. The Moors of Granada are depicted as dashing, elegant and sensuous, but also disordered and even infantile, in need of the tutelage and guidance offered by the more mature, self-controlled Narváez. Thus, while the text is often interpreted as an affirmation of Renaissance humanist ideals of virtue and magnanimity, it is equally true that these ideals are presented within a clearly hierarchical framework which unequivocally establishes the superiority of the Christian knight over the Muslim one, and male over female. Submission to this hierarchical arrangement is a precondition for the much-vaunted tolerance of *El Abencerraje*. This is also the source of the nostalgia that pervades this text: the authors and their readers share a longing for the Naṣrid period, when Granada was separated by a political border, yet subordinate to Christian Spain in a tributary relationship. Moors were Moors and Christians Christians, unlike in the Morisco period when *El Abencerraje* was composed and circulated, when the descendants of the Moors of Granada, having received baptism, claimed equality of status and sought to abolish the distinction between themselves and other Christians.

SIGNIFICANCE

The positive view of Christian-Muslim relations within the framework of a shared code of honour has deep roots in medieval Iberian culture, as attested, for example, by Juan Manuel's *El Conde Lucanor*. In *El Abencerraje*, this understanding is presented through a deceptively simple story melding popular frontier ballads, along with pastoral elements, into a short chivalric tale of the type that had been popularised in early 16th-century chapbooks. Ariosto's *Orlando furioso* provides a crucial antecedent for developing the romantic Moorish tale as a separate genre.

The phenomenal success of this story, however, cannot be understood outside the historical circumstances of the last four decades of the 16th century. By the mid-1500s, tensions were on the rise between the dominant Christian majority and the ethno-religious minority of Moriscos, descended from the Moors. In 1568, just a few short years after *El Abencerraje* first appeared, the rebellion known as the War of the Alpujarras began, giving rise to the mass deportation in 1570 of Moriscos from Granada to other territories belonging to the Crown of Castile. The relationship between the Morisco question and the Maurophile fad spawned by *El Abencerraje* remains ambiguous. As Carrasco Urgoiti pointed out decades ago (*El problema morisco en Aragón*), the fact that *El Abencerraje* emerged initially from the court of Jiménez de Embún, Baron of Bárboles, in Aragón, is indicative of a feudal ideology in which Mudéjar (later, Morisco) subjects depended on the local aristocracy for protection and remained loyal to them, rather than to the central monarchy. Similar politico-economic circumstances in several outlying areas – the Ebro Valley, Valencia and, of course, Granada itself – provided a ready-made audience for such tales among the landed gentry. This aristocratic sensibility is perhaps reinforced by an attitude of tolerance among the ethno-religious minorities, associated by some scholars with the possible *converso* origin of several of those connected with the dissemination of this text, including Jiménez de Embún, Montemayor and Villegas. Yet these explanations do little to account for its popularity among all social classes, attested to by the wide circulation not only of this text itself, but especially of the many ballads inspired more or less directly by it. The intensity of this relatively short-lived fad may point, as Barbara Fuchs has argued, to a deep-seated Moorish *habitus* in early modern Castile. It is also likely that it reflects a desire, utopian though it may be, to imagine a more unified society – it must be added, however, that this unity is imagined only under Christian rule.

Many versions of the plot and characters of *El Abencerraje* appeared in verse form, first from the pens of Juan de Timoneda and Pedro de Padilla, and then in literally hundreds of Moorish ballads, written anonymously and published in *romancero* volumes during the late 1580s and early 1590s. Several of the young poets of the first generation of the Spanish Baroque started out composing versions of these ballads – most notably, Lope de Vega and Luis de Góngora. Lope also wrote a number of plays based on

El Abencerraje, chief among them *El remedio en la desdicha*. Curiously, a book-length narrative poem, *Historia de los amores del valeroso moro Abinderráez y de la hermosa xarifa*, was composed in Spanish by Francesco Baldi di Correggio and published in Milan in 1593 (a modern edition was published in Udine in 1993). Though the Moorish ballad had begun to wane by the mid-1590s, it received new life when Ginés Pérez de Hita, a shoemaker from Murcia, published his *Guerras civiles de Granada* (1595), a fictionalised account in prose and verse of the Abencerraje clan's role in the collapse of Naṣrid Granada and its conquest by Christian Spain. At the close of the century, Mateo Alemán, imitating the inclusion of *El Abencerraje* in editions of *La Diana*, incorporated a Moorish tale, *Ozmín and Daraja*, into his picaresque novel *Guzmán de Alfarache* (1599). In one form or another, the Moorish novel continued to be imitated, most famously by Miguel de Cervantes (in 'The captive's tale', in Part One of *Don Quixote*, 1605), Mme de Lafayette (*Zayde*, 1670), Chateaubriand (*Les aventures du dernier Abencerage*, 1827), and Washington Irving (*Tales of the Alhambra*, 1832). There were many stage adaptations of these tales. Filtered through the Romantic sensibility of the early 1800s, this idealisation of Moorish culture contributed to the Orientalist fantasies of such artists as Delacroix, Gérôme, Ingres, and eventually Matisse.

The critical reception of *El Abencerraje* is closely tied to interpretations of Maurophilia. Since the introduction of the term by Cirot in 1938, scholars have fallen into roughly two camps. On the one hand are those for whom the primary significance of *El Abencerraje* lies in its tolerance toward the Muslim other, and who thus see it as a thinly veiled defence of the Morisco cause against the prevailing trend in royal policy. Among these scholars are Carrasco Urgoiti, Márquez Villanueva and, more recently, Fuchs. Over against these are numerous critics who prefer to emphasise the evasive and nostalgic aspects of the tale, as well as its paternalistic, even patriarchal, tone. These include Guillén, Shipley, Burshatin and Bass. Burshatin's treatment is particularly noteworthy for applying Said's *Orientalism*. More recent research, such as that by García-Arenal and Rodríguez Mediano, and Childers, emphasises the role of Granada's autochthonous elite, who claimed descent from the Moors of legend, in promoting the Maurophile image, perhaps as a way of distancing themselves from the rest of the Morisco minority. The time may have come to acknowledge that Maurophile literature, as defined by its originating text, *El Abencerraje*, served to open a space for public debate, a forum within which to explore, in the absence of a public sphere in our sense, the thorny issue of the place of Moorishness (and thus of the Morisco minority) in the emergent Spanish nation.

Regardless of how we read it, *El Abencerraje* it is a precious bauble of the Spanish Renaissance. Its influence need not be pernicious; at a minimum, it promotes a sentiment of mutual acceptance which, though not by itself sufficient, can contribute to a broader, more intellectually-grounded tolerance of another's religion and culture.

MANUSCRIPTS

MS Madrid, BNE – 1752, fols 233r-234r (exact date unknown, late 16th century)

EDITIONS & TRANSLATIONS

The publishing history of *El Abencerraje* is complicated by the multiplicity of versions. López Estrada has edited the four main variants in one volume:

F. López Estrada (ed.), *Historia del Abencerraje y de la hermosa Jarifa. Cuatro textos y su estudio*, Madrid, 1957

Each of these four versions is presented in a separate section below.

Historia del moro y Narváez (MS Madrid, BNE – 1752, fols 233r-234r)

M.S. Carrasco Urgoiti (ed.), 'El relato "Historia del moro y Narváez" y *El Abencerraje*', *Revista Hispánica Moderna* 34 (1968) 242-55

López Estrada, *Historia del Abencerraje*, pp. 415-21

G. Irving Dale (ed.), 'An unpublished version of the *Historia de Abindarráez y Jarifa*', *Modern Language Notes* 39 (1924) 31-33

J. Conde, 'Anécdota curiosa', in *Historia de la dominación de los árabes en España*, Madrid, 1821, 262-65 (There are slight differences between this and later transcriptions.)

Parte de la Chrónica/Corónica del ínclito Infante don Fernando que ganó Antequera (1561)

Each of the two slightly different versions of this publication is preserved in a single extant copy:

1. *Chrónica*... Toledo: Miguel Ferrer, 1561. The only extant copy of this edition, preserved at the Real Academica de la Historia, Madrid (RAH 2/3471), is missing the preliminaries and first page. There are two modern editions based on this copy:

F. López Estrada, 'El *Abencerraje* de Toledo, 1561. Edición crítica y comentarios', *Anales de la Universidad Hispalense* 19 (1959) 1-60

A. Rumeau, 'L'Abencérage, un texte retrouvé', *Bulletin Hispanique* 59 (1957) 369-95

2. *Parte de la Corónica del ínclito Infante don Fernando que ganó a Antequera* (place and date of publication unknown). Also preserved in a single, incomplete copy, in the private library of Bartolomé March y Servera. Three 20th-century editions appeared:

López Estrada, *Historia del Abencerraje*, pp. 349-74

H. Mérimée, 'El *Abencerrage* d'après diverses versions publiées aux XVIme siècle,' *Bulletin Hispanique* 30 (1928) 147-82

G. Cirot, 'Une édition mal connue et incomplète de l'histoire de l'*Abencerraje*', *Bulletin Hispanique* 25 (1923) 172-3

La Diana
J. de Montemayor, *Los siete libros de la Diana*, 2nd, posthumous edition, Valladolid, 1562

The first edition of *La Diana* did not include *El Abencerraje*. Beginning in 1562, with the second edition, printed in Valladolid, the story is incorporated into the numerous 16th- and 17th-century printings of the work.

Modern editions of *La Diana* generally follow the *princeps*, but the version of *El Abencerraje* included in the 1562 Valladolid edition of *La Diana* appeared at least four times in 20th-century publications:

E. Fosalba Vela (ed.), *El Abencerraje pastoral. Estudio y edición*, Barcelona, 1990, pp. 1-35

López Estrada, *Historia del Abencerraje*, pp. 377-413

M. de Montolíu (ed.), *Novelas moriscas*, Barcelona, 1943, 37-60

Cuentos viejos de la vieja España, Madrid, 1941, pp. 463-90

M. Menéndez y Pelayo (ed.), *Orígenes de la novela*, Madrid, 1907, ii, pp. 306-14

El Abencerraje y la Hermosa Jarifa, text from Antonio de Villegas' *Inventario*, 1565

This text, acknowledged to be the finest from a literary standpoint, appears in the four complete editions of Antonio de Villegas' *Inventario* published to date:

E. Torres Corominas (ed.), *Literatura y facciones cortesanas en la España del siglo XVI. Estudio y edición del* Inventario *de Antonio de Villegas*, Madrid, 2008, pp. 640-61

F. López Estrada (ed.), *Inventario*, Madrid, 1955-56, ii, pp. 63-89

Inventario, Medina del Campo, 1565, fols cix-cxxxi

Inventario, Medina del Campo, 1577, fols 93v-112v

This version has been published on its own at least 18 times since the middle of the 19th century, with authorship at times erroneously attributed to Antonio de Villegas. There are at least five translations into English, and several editions for Spanish language learners, either bilingual Spanish-English or modernised/simplified versions.

- B. Fuchs, L. Brewer-García and A. Ilika (ed. and trans.), *'The Abencerraje' and 'Ozmín and Daraja'. Two sixteenth-century novellas from Spain*, Philadelphia PA, 2014
- J. Knauss (ed. and trans.), *El Abencerraje*, Tucson AZ, 2012 (bilingual Spanish-English edition)
- J. Pallarés Moreno and M. Ángeles Pérez Rubio (eds), *Historia del Abencerraje y la hermosa Jarifa*, Barcelona, 2011
- M. Groundland (ed.), *El Abencerraje*, Newark DE, 2006
- V. de Lama and E. Peral Vega (eds), *El Abencerraje y la hermosa Jarifa* (Castalia Didáctica), Madrid, 2000
- A. d'Agostino (ed. and trans.), *L'Abencerraje e la bella Sharifa*, Venice, 1997 (bilingual Spanish-Italian edition; follows López Estrada's 1993 edition)
- F. López Estrada (ed.), *El Abencerraje (Novela y romancero)*, Madrid, 1985, pp. 103-37 (9th edition, expanded, Madrid, 1993)
- P. León and D. Mosher (trans.), *The Abencerraje, or The story of Abindarráez and the beautiful Jarifa, by Antonio de Villegas*, Toronto, 1974 (English trans.)
- C. Guillén (ed.), *Lazarillo de Tormes* and *El Abencerraje*, New York, 1966 ('spelling and punctuation have been modernized')
- J.E. Keller (trans.) and F. López Estrada (ed.), *The Abencerraje and the beautiful Jarifa. Spanish text according to the* Inventario *of Antonio de Villegas and translation*, Chapel Hill NC, 1964 (bilingual Spanish-English edition)
- Á. Flores (ed.), *Great Spanish short stories*, New York, 1962 (also in *Masterpieces of the Spanish Golden Age*, New York, 1957)
- López Estrada, *Historia del Abencerraje*, pp. 307-45
- R.H. Olmstead (ed.), *El Abencerraje*, New York, 1948
- J. María Castro (ed.), *El Abencerraje por Antonio de Villegas*, Barcelona, 1946
- J. María Millás Vallicrosa (ed.), *Historia del Abencerraje y la hermosa Jarifa*, Barcelona, 1941
- Gil Benumeya (ed.), *Historia del Abencerraje y la hermosa Jarifa, y otros cuentos*, Madrid, 1928 (Gil Benumeya is also known as R. Gil Torres)

J.P. Wickersham Crawford (ed.), *Los Abencerrajes. Two old Spanish stories adapted for intermediate classes, edited with notes, direct-method exercises, and vocabulary*, New York, 1928, pp. 1-16

G. le Strange, *El Abencerraje. La historia de Abindarráez y la hermosa Jarifa*, Cambridge, 1924 ('presented in the original Spanish, with some modernisation of spelling and grammar')

H. Mérimée, 'El *Abencerraje* d'après l'*Inventario* et la *Diana*', *Bulletin Hispanique* 21 (1919) 143-66

C. Pérez Pastor, *La imprenta en Medina del Campo*, Madrid, 1895, pp. 209-18

Extravagantes opúsculos amenos y curiosos de ilustres autores, Barcelona, 1884, pp. 249-72

El Abencerraje, Facsimile edition of the corresponding pages from Villegas' 1565 *Inventario*, (s.l.), (s.d.) [c. 1880]

B. Carles Aribau (ed.), *Novelistas anteriores a Cervantes*, Madrid, 1876, pp. 507-12

E. de Ochoa (ed.), *Tesoro de novelistas españoles antiguos y modernos*, Paris, 1847, pp. 1-14

B. Maestre (ed.), *El Siglo pintoresco*, Madrid, 1845, vol. 1, pp. 8-16

STUDIES

J. Irigoyen-García, *The Spanish Arcadia. Sheep herding, pastoral discourse, and ethnicity in early modern Spain*, Toronto, 2013, pp. 152-61

M.B. Quinn, *The Moor and the novel. Narrating absence in Early Modern Spain*, New York, 2013, pp. 54-75

A. Rey Hazas, 'Sobre los romances moriscos de Padilla y "El Abencerraje". ¿Era Padilla morisco?', *Edad de Oro* 32 (2013) 327-50

E. Torres Corominas, '*El Abencerraje*: una lección de virtud en los albores del confesionalismo filipino', *Revista de Literatura* 75 (2013) 43-72

J. Carlos Terradas, 'El Abencerraje como problema heroico. Una lectura según modelos homéricos', *Revista de Literatura* 74 (2012) 65-92

E. Marsh, 'En clave femenina. Mujer e intertextualidad en la *Historia del Abencerraje y la hermosa Jarifa*', *Hispania* 94 (2011) 615-27

A. Peláez, 'La imagen de poder de los *Abencerrajes* a través de las fuentes nazaríes,' *Studia Aurea* 4 (2010) 93-115

D. Salas-Díaz, 'Escrito con la pluma de un ángel. Intercambio y economía simbólica en *El Abencerraje y la hermosa Jarifa*', *Hispanic Journal* 31 (2010) 9-22

M.S. Carrasco Urgoiti, 'Apuntes sobre el calificativo "morisco" y algunos textos que lo ilustran', in A. Stoll (ed.), *Averroes dialogado y otros momentos literarios y sociales de la interacción cristiano-musulmana en España e Italia*, Kassel, 1998, 187-209

M.S. Carrasco Urgoiti, 'Apuntes sobre el mito de los Abencerrajes y sus versiones literarios', *Miscelánea de Estudios Árabes y Hebraicos. Sección Árabe-Islam* 47 (1998) 65-88

A.M. Calvosa Vergara, 'The social and literary framework of the "Abencerraje" and "Ozmín y Daraja." A reception analysis of the interpolated Moorish novel', see *Dissertation Abstracts International, Section A: The Humanities and Social Sciences* 58 (1997) 453

R. Krauel, 'El esquema heroico de la historia de Abindarráez', *Romance Notes* 37 (1996) 39-47

M.S. Carrasco Urgoiti, 'Una huella de *El Abencerraje* en *Las Navidades de Madrid* de Mariana de Carvajal: "El esclavo de su esclavo" ', *Quaderns de filologia. Estudis literaris* 1 (1995) 221-8

E. Fosalba Vela, *Estudios sobre la difusión de la 'Diana' en los siglos XVI y XVII*, Barcelona, 1995

J.M. Ribera Llopis, 'La narrativa breve en las literaturas peninsulares. *Història de Jacob Xalabín* y *El abencerraje y la hermosa Jarifa*', in J. Paredes (ed.), *Medioevo y literatura, I-IV: Actas del V Congreso de la Asociación Hispánica de Literatura Medieval*, Granada, 1995, iv, 123-35

A. Stoll, 'Avatares de un cuento del Renacimiento. El Abencerraje, releído a la luz de su contexto literario cultural y discursivo', *Sharq al-Andalus* 12 (1995) 429-60

E. Fosalba Vela, *La Diana en Europa. Ediciones, traducciones e influencias*, Barcelona, 1994

A. Parodi de Geltman, 'El Abencerraje y la hermosa Jarifa. Un vivo retrato', *Filología* 26 (1993) 149-65

L. López-Baralt, 'Two sides of the coin. The Moor in Spanish Renaissance literature', in L. López-Baralt, *Islam in Spanish literature. From the Middle Ages to the present*, Leiden, 1992, 209-13

M.M. Gaylord, 'Spain's renaissance conquests and the retroping of identity', *Journal of Hispanic Philology* 16 (1992) 125-36

D.M. Wright, 'Temas moriscos. Del romancero a la novela morisca', in N. Toscano Liria (ed.), *Estudios alfonsinos y otros escritos en homenaje a John Esten Keller y a Anibal A. Biglieri*, New York, 1991, 254-61

E. Fosalba Vela, *El Abencerraje pastoril*, Barcelona, 1990

F. Sevilla Arroyo and A. Rey Hazas, 'Contexto y punto de vista en el Abencerraje', *Dicenda* 6 (1987) 419-28

E. Sánchez García, 'Una traducción italiana manierista de *El Abencerraje*', *Annali Istituto Universitario Orientale* 27 (1985) 491-537

I. Burshatin, 'Power, discourse, and metaphor in the *Abencerraje*', *Modern Language Notes* 99 (1984) 195-213

D.H. Darst, 'The literariness of *El Abencerraje*', in A. González et al. (eds), *Estudios sobre el Siglo de Oro en homenaje a Raymond R. MacCurdy*, Albuquerque, 1983, 265-73

L. Rubio González, 'El tema del "Abencerraje" en una versión épica del siglo XVI', *Castilla: Estudios de Literatura* 5 (1983) 109-31

C. Guillén, 'El "Abencerraje" y la novela morisca', in F. López Estrada (ed.), *Siglos de Oro. Renacimiento*, Barcelona, 1980, 307-13

W. Holzinger, 'The militia of love, war, and virtue in the *Abencerraje y la hermosa Jarifa*. A structural and sociological reassessment', *Revista Canadiense de Estudios Hispánicos* 2 (1978) 227-38

J. Navarro Gómez, 'El autor de la versión del "Abencerraje" contenida en la "Diana" ¿era Montemayor?', *Revista de Literatura* 39 (1978) 101-4

G.A. Shipley, 'La obra literaria como monumento historico. El caso de El Abencerraje', *Journal of Hispanic Philology* 2 (1978) 103-20

M.S. Carrasco-Urgoiti, *The Moorish novel. El Abencerraje and Pérez de Hita*, Boston MA, 1976, 53-72

E.R. Gonzalez, 'Metáfora y simetría en el prólogo de *El Abencerraje*', *Explicación de Textos Literarios* 5 (1976) 35-38

P.R. León, '"Cortesia". Clave del equilibrio estructural y tematico en *El Abencerraje*', *Romanische Forschungen* 86 (1974) 255-64

M.S. Carrasco Urgoiti, 'Las Cortes señoriales del Aragón mudéjar y *El Abencerraje*', in R. Pincus Sigele, G. Sobejano and M. Aub (eds), *Homenaje a Casalduero. Crítica y poesía*, Madrid, 1972, 115-28

J. Gimeno Casalduero, '*El Abencerraje y la hermosa Jarifa*. Composición y significado', *Nueva Revista de Filologia Hispanica* 21 (1972) 1-22

C. Guardiola, '*El Abencerraje y la hermosa Jarifa*. Estudio de su estructura', in A. Beltrán (ed.), *Homenaje a Francisco Ynduráin*, Zaragoza, 1972, 163-74

C. Guillén, 'Literature as historical contradiction. *El Abencerraje*, the Moorish novel, and the eclogue', in *Literature as system. Essays toward the theory of literary history*, Princeton NJ, 1971, 159-217

M.S. Carrasco Urgoiti, *El problema morisco en Aragón al comienzo del reinado de Felipe II. Estudio y apéndices documentales*, Chapel Hill NC, 1969

M.S. Carrasco Urgoiti, 'El relato "Historia del moro y Narváez" y *El Abencerraje*', *Revista Hispánica Moderna* 34 (1968) 242-55

A. Soons, 'Deux moments de la nouvelle mauresque. *El Abencerraje* (avant 1565) et *Ozmin y Daraja* (1599)', *Romanische Forschungen* 78 (1966) 567-69

R.F. Glenn, 'The moral implications of *El Abencerraje*', *Modern Language Notes* 80 (1965) 202-9

C. Guillén, 'Individuo y ejemplaridad en el *Abencerraje*', in M.P. Hornik (ed.), *Collected studies in honour of Americo Castro's eightieth year*, Oxford, 1965, 175-97

F. López Estrada, 'Tres notas al *Abencerraje*', *Revista Hispánica Moderna* 21 (1965) 264-72

F. López Estrada, 'El *Abencerraje* de Toledo, 1561', *Anales de la Universidad Hispalense* 19 (1959) 1-60

K. Whinnom, 'The relationship of three texts of *El Abencerraje*', *Modern Language Review* 54 (1959) 507-17

F. Márquez Villanueva, 'Investigaciones recientes. Un libro sobre *El Abencerraje*', *Archivo Hispalense* 28 (1958) 270-72

A. Rumeau, ' "L'Abencérage". Un texte retrouvé', *Bulletin Hispanique* 59 (1957) 369-95

F. López Estrada, *Historia del Abencerraje y de la hermosa Jarifa. Cuatro textos con su estudio*, Madrid, 1957

M.S. Carrasco Urgoiti, *El moro de Granada en la literatura (del siglo XV al XX)*, Madrid, 1956, pp. 55-63 (facsimile edition with intro. by J. Martínez Ruiz, Granada, 1989)

E. Moreno Báez, 'El tema del *Abencerraje* en la literatura española', *Archivum* 4 (1954) 310-29

M. Bataillon, '¿Melancolía renacentista o melancolía judía?', in *Estudios hispánicos. Homenaje a Archer M. Huntington*, Wellesley MA, 1952, 39-50

G. Cirot, 'La maurophilie littéraire en Espagne au XVIe siècle', *Bulletin Hispanique* 40-46 (1938-44); on *El Abencerraje*, 40 (1938) 433-47

M. Bataillon, 'Salmacis et Trocho dans l'*Abencérrage*', in *Hommages à Ernest Martinenche. Etudes hispaniques et américaines*, Paris [1938 ?], 355-63

B. Matulka, 'On the European diffusion of the "Last of the Abencerrajes" story in the sixteenth century', *Hispania* 16 (1933) 369-88

W.C. Salley, 'A possible influence of the *Abencerraje* story on Calderón's *El Príncipe Constante*', *Romanic Review* 23 (1932) 331-33

G.I. Dale, 'A second source of Lope's *El castigo del discreto*', *Modern Language Notes* 43 (1928) 310-12

H. Mérimée, '*El Abencerrage* d'après diverses versions publiées aux XVIme siècle', *Bulletin Hispanique* 30 (1928) 147-82

H.A. Deferrari, *The sentimental Moor in Spanish literature before 1600*, Philadelphia PA, 1927

H.A. Deferrari, 'Trocho in *El Abencerraje*', *Modern Language Notes* 42 (1927) 529-30

J.P. Wickersham Crawford, '*El Abencerraje* and Longfellow's *Galgano*. A parallel', *Hispania* 9 (1926) 165-69

G.I. Dale, 'An unpublished version of the *Historia de Abindarráez y Jarifa*', *Modern Language Notes* 39 (1924) 31-33

G. Cirot, 'Une édition mal connue et incomplète de l'histoire de l'*Abencerraje*', *Bulletin Hispanique* 25 (1923) 172-73 (includes facsimile edition of *Chrónica*)

H. Mérimée, '*El Abencerraje* d'après l'*Inventario* et la *Diana*', *Bulletin Hispanique* 21 (1919) 143-66

M. Menéndez y Pelayo, 'Introducción', *Orígenes de la novela*, Madrid, 1905, i, pp. ccclii-ccclx

William Childers

Martín Pérez de Ayala

DATE OF BIRTH 11 November 1503/1504
PLACE OF BIRTH Segura de la Sierra, Jaén, Spain
DATE OF DEATH 1 August 1566
PLACE OF DEATH Valencia

BIOGRAPHY

The main source of information about the theologian Archbishop Martín Pérez de Ayala is an autobiographical work, called today *Discurso de la vida*, that details the main events of his life in 23 chapters.

He was born in Segura de la Sierra, a village in the province of Jaén, which belonged to the Order of Santiago. He grew up in a poor family with little social status: his father experienced successive financial difficulties and eventually joined the army, leaving the family home when Martin was six. His mother moved to Yeste (Albacete), where the family lived with her father until his death, when Martin was 14. From early childhood he was forced to make his own way in life.

According to his own testimony, at the age of five Martin started studying Latin letters in his hometown, and at the age of ten he began a study of Nebrija's grammar, guided by a tutor in Yeste. At 14, he set off for the University of Alcalá to study arts at the College of San Eugenio, where he was a student of the scholar Encinas, among others. He completed his education with studies in logic and theology, obtaining his Bachelor of Arts in 1525.

Forced to find a means of earning his living, he sought the protection of knights of the Order of Santiago, who helped him enter the Monastery of Uclés (Cuenca) and receive the habit of the Order of Santiago. He had some problems with his superiors, but in 1528 the prior of the Order facilitated his access to the University of Salamanca, where he was taught by Francisco de Vitoria. A year later, he returned to the University of Alcalá, from where, after completing three courses, he obtained his degree in arts and then his Masters (on 16 October and 5 November 1532). In spite of his attempts, he did not graduate in theology.

That same year, the Archbishop of Granada, Don Gaspar de Avalos, offered a newly-created professorial chair in arts at the university. This allowed Pérez de Ayala to combine teaching with his studies in theology, a specialisation in which he finally received his doctoral degree in 1538. He spent two years teaching theology, during which he wrote his first work, printed in Granada in 1537, *Dilucidarum quaestionum super quinque universalia Porphirii juxta vias in scholis receptissimas*, a review of Thomist, Scotist and nominalist theories.

In Granada, Pérez de Ayala came into contact with the Bishop of Jaen, Francisco de Mendoza, who appointed him his confessor, giving him ecclesiastical benefits and entrusting him with the administration of his diocese for two years (1540-42) while he was away. In 1543, Pérez de Ayala accompanied his protector on a journey to Germany with Emperor Charles V, though he left the bishop for a stay in Leuven. He remained at Leuven University for several years, studying Greek and perfecting his Hebrew (which he had started learning in his homeland), at the same time benefitting from reading 'all the books of heretics of note. This University has permission from the pope for the doctors who live there to do this' (*Discurso*, ch. 7).

In 1545, Pérez de Ayala was sent by Charles V as a theologian to attend the Diet of Worms, convened to mediate in the dispute with the Lutherans. He was then appointed chaplain to the emperor, whom he accompanied to the Diet of Regensburg. Some years later, he was summoned to the Diet of Augsburg to assist in developing the *Interim Augustanum* or imperial decree on religious observance, which was enacted in May 1548 and became law in the empire. On that occasion, Pérez de Ayala was nominated by Charles V to be bishop of Guadix, Granada, where he remained for 12 years until 1560, when Philip II offered him the bishopric of Segovia. Four years later, the king made him archbishop of Valencia, his last pastoral role, where he remained until his death on 1 August 1566.

During his life, Pérez de Ayala combined the roles of prominent theologian and active pastor. He excelled in both areas and left a unique legacy, which is known today from his abundant written works.

His work as a theologian developed in parallel to the phases of the Council of Trent, in whose sessions he was actively involved, first as advisor to Bishop Francisco de Mendoza, then as a Council Father. He attended a variety of sessions. First, he participated in sessions between 1546 and 1547 (with a break from December to April, when he travelled to Rome, Venice, Milan, Bologna, Florence and other Italian cities, accompanying his protector, Mendoza). Second, as bishop of Guadix, he attended the second phase of the Council, between March 1551 and April

1552. Finally, in the reign of Philip II, as bishop of Segovia, he attended sessions held between March 1562 and April 1564. His *De divinis, apostolicis atque ecclesiasticis traditionibus*, on the place of church tradition in the shaping of doctrine, was influential throughout Europe.

Alongside his devotion to theology, Pérez de Ayala was very active pastorally, beginning in Guadix, a town with a large Moorish population. There he reorganised the diocesan structure, before retreating to some hamlets within the diocese, accompanied by two Jewish converts, to devote himself to the study of the Old Testament (*Discurso*, ch. 16). He repeated his activities in church reorganisation in the other dioceses where he served.

MAIN SOURCES OF INFORMATION

Primary

M. Serrano y Sanz, 'Discurso de la vida del Ilustrísimo y Reverendísimo Señor Don Martín Pérez de Ayala', in M. Serrano y Sanz, *Autobiografías y memorias*, Madrid, 1905, 211-38

P. González de Mendoza (ed.), *Discurso de la vida*, Buenos Aires, 1947, pp. 9-73

Secondary

Q. Aldea Vaquero, T. Marín Martínez and J. Vives Gatell (eds), *Diccionario de historia eclesiástica de España*, Madrid, 1973, iii, pp. 1963-65

Á. Gómez Moreno, *Biografía de Martín Pérez de Ayala* (web-based biography) www.mcnbiografias.com/app-bio/do/show?key=perez-de-ayala-martin

WORKS ON CHRISTIAN-MUSLIM RELATIONS

Catecismo para instrucción de los nuevamente convertidos de Moros, 'Catechism for the instruction of the newly converted among the Moors'

DATE Before 1566
ORIGINAL LANGUAGE Castilian

DESCRIPTION

The *Catecismo para instrucción de los nuevamente convertidos de Moros* was published in Valencia by Pedro Patricio Mey in 1599. Although it was substantially written by Pérez de Ayala, he left it incomplete when he died, and it appears that it was put in final order by Tomás de Espinosa, Bishop of Morocco, at the request of Pérez de Ayala's successor as archbishop of Valencia, Juan de Ribera. It is plausible that Pérez de Ayala wrote the bulk of it when he was bishop of Guadix in 1548-60 and came into close contact with Moors. The extent of Tomás de Espinosa's contribution remains an open question. It is divided into two Books, comprising 442 pages in all. The first is a short treatise on anti-Muslim apologetics, whilst the second is devoted to instruction of the Moriscos. It is written in dialogue form between a master and his disciple, though as the work proceeds the questions and responses tail off until they disappear completely.

Book 1 contains 25 dialogues, on God, human nature, sin, and the one way to find God. In dialogues 13-19, Pérez de Ayala writes about the inadequacy of Islam, the dissolute life of Muḥammad, and the mistakes and contradictions in the Qur'an. Then in the remaining dialogues he shows by contrast the completeness of Christianity, the dignity of the person of Christ and the truth of the Gospel.

The tone is set in the first two dialogues, where the master explains to the disciple the conditions necessary for the instruction that follows to be useful: 'First, you should entrust yourself to God with all your heart. [...] Second, you should endeavour to turn aside from your sin. [...] Third, you must shed and relinquish all the opinions and sects from your past and cast them aside and be as if you had never known them' (Book 1, dialogue 1, pp. 8-9). The disciple must listen hard to reason.

From here, he argues that there is only one way to the truth. This is not the way of the philosophers, and not the way of any religion other than Christianity. Thus, both Judaism and Islam are wrong. In his arguments against Islam, Pérez de Ayala does not make any new arguments, but relies on earlier authors.

He concludes Book 1 with a defence of Christianity, demonstrating that it is everything Islam is not.

Book 2 contains teachings about the Christian way of life in the form of an exposition of Christian basics in five parts: faith, hope, charity, the sacraments, and obedience, following traditional Christian teachings. There are no direct references to Islam, although there is a brief denial that the Bible has been corrupted, as Muslim teachings hold (Book 2, dialogue 6, pp. 266-67).

SIGNIFICANCE

The *Catecismo* exhibits both similarities with other works of the kind from the 16th century and its own distinct features. For example, the approach followed in Book 1, in the part on anti-Muslim apologetics, bears resemblances to Bernardo Pérez de Chinchón's *Libro llamado anti-Alcorano* of 1532, in which Chinchón also refutes the teachings of the Qur'an, using arguments based on natural reason, although the *Catecismo* is more tightly structured. Similarly, the rational arguments in Book 1, dialogues 4 and 5, are like those used by Juan Luis Vives in his *Refutación del Islam*, the fourth book of which, *De veritate fidei Christianae*, is also written in the form of a dialogue between an alfaqui and a Christian. However, the account of Muḥammad and his law in this section contains none of the insults that are usual in works of anti-Muslim apologetics, such as Lope de Obregón's *Confutación del Alcorán y secta Mahometana* of 1555, or Pedro Guerra de Lorca's *Catecheses mystagogicae por advenis ex secta Mahometana* of 1586.

In the same way, in Book 2 there are understandable parallels with the *Catecismos* of Astete and Ripalda (1591) as they expound the same catechetical details. But Pérez de Ayala adopts an unaffectedly popular tone that is unique to his work.

EDITIONS & TRANSLATIONS

Catecismo para instrucción de los nuevamente convertidos de Moros, Valencia: Casa de Pedro Patricio Mey, 1599

STUDIES

M. Jesús Framiñán de Miguel, 'Manuales para el adoctrinamiento de neoconversos en el siglo XVI', *Criticón* 93 (2005) 25-37

L. Resines, *Catecismo del Sacromonte y doctrina Christiana de Fr. Pedro de Feria. Conversión y evangelización de Moriscos e Indios*, Madrid, 2002, pp. 37-40

F.B. Medina, 'Apostolado Morisco', in C. O'Neill and J.M. Domínguez (eds), *Diccionario histórico de la Compañía de Jesús*, Madrid, 2001, iii, pp. 2748-49

R. García Cárcel, *Herejía y sociedad en el siglo xvi. La inquisición en Valencia, 1530–1690*, Barcelona, 1980, pp. 52-69, 118-24

R. García Cárcel, 'La Inquisición y los Moriscos Valencianos. Anatomía de una represión', in *Actas de las jornadas de cultura árabe e islámica*, Madrid, 1981, 401-17

A. Hernández Sánchez, 'Catecismos para la instrucción religiosa de los Moriscos', Salamanca, 1955 (Diss. Universidad Pontificia de Salamanca), pp. 187-226

Doctrina christiana en lengua arábiga y castellana para la instrucción de los nuevamente convertidos del Reino de Valencia, 'Christian doctrine in Arabic and Castilian for the instruction for the newly converted in the Kingdom of Valencia'

DATE 1566
ORIGINAL LANGUAGE Spanish

DESCRIPTION
Martín Pérez de Ayala wrote two complementary works for the instruction of Moriscos. One was a short bilingual Spanish-Arabic handbook written mainly for clergy in the style of a school primer, entitled *Doctrina Christiana en lengua arábiga y castellana [...] para la instrucción de los nuevamente convertidos de este Reino*, printed in Valencia by Ioannes Mey in 1566, in octavo. The second was a substantial manual of doctrine, a work that was not published during Pérez de Ayala's lifetime. It was assembled and sent to the press by his successor in the diocese, under the title *Catechismo para la instrucción de los nuevamente convertidos de Moros, impreso por orden del Patriarcha de Antioquía y Arçobispo de Valencia D. Juan Ribera*, published in Valencia by Pedro Patricio Mey in 1599, in quarto.

Pérez de Ayala indicates that these two works were part of the same project when he writes to the Moors in the preface to his *Doctrina Christiana*: 'And if you are still besieged with much doubt, convey it to your leaders, namely, your prelate, your rectors or your vicars, and to your catechists who we will assign. For this *we have made another catechism, or higher instruction*, to inform you of the faith at greater length, and to satisfy your doubts. And although it is written in Castilian, it will be delivered in Arabic by the catechists and preachers we will send, whom we have chosen because they know your language well, so that nothing will be missing in accomplishing your instruction' (fol. 4r).

This is supported by a letter that serves to introduce the *Catecismo*, written by its compiler, Bishop Juan de Ribera, who says that *Doctrina Christiana* was completed between 1564 and 1566.

Doctrina Christiana is 24 folios long, with the main text in Castillian and interlined with an Arabic translation in Latin letters. It comprises: 'the prayers that all Christians should know' and 'the prayers to be said in church and mass', with three brief appendices on bodily movements and posture during mass, the order in which the contents of the work are to be taught, and 'the rules for reading the Arabic terms of this *Doctrina*' (fols 22r-24r). At the end is a translation of the contents of the work into the Arabic dialect of Moriscos in Valencia in the 16th century.

SIGNIFICANCE

This short work of catechetical instruction follows the precedent set in the early 16th century by Pedro de Alcalá with his *Arte para ligeramente saber la lengua arábiga* (Granada, 1505). This was followed by two further catechisms written in and around Valencia, by Archbishop Jorge of Austria assisted by Antonio Ramírez de Haro, entitled *Les instructions e ordinacions per als novament convertits del regne de Valencia*, issued in the 1540s, and by Francisco de Navarra, Inquisitor and later Archbishop of Valencia, entitled *Cartilla y breu instructió de la doctrina Christiana*, printed in 1571.

The three Valencian works share the common aim of bringing about the cultural assimilation of Moriscos through conciliatory means, in response to the inquisitorial offensive against the Moriscos that was being conducted in Valencia in the period 1540-66. Pérez de Ayala's decision to use Arabic as the language of instruction appears the most progressive, although the method he uses, making a literal Arabic translation of the Spanish original, produced mechanical versions of prayers, and may not have brought successful results.

EDITIONS & TRANSLATIONS

Doctrina Christiana en lengua arábiga y castellana para instrucción de los moriscos del Ilustrísimo Sr. D. Martín de Ayala, Valencia, 1911 (repr, Valencia, 1980)

Doctrina Christiana en lengua Arábiga y Castellana, compuesta e impressa por mandado del Ilustrísimo y Reverendísimo Señor don Martín de Ayala, arzobispo de Valencia, para la instrucción de los nuevamente convertidos deste reyno, Valencia: Ioannes Mey, 1566

STUDIES

Framiñán de Miguel, 'Manuales para el adoctrinamiento de neoconversos'

Resines, *Catecismo del Sacromonte*

M. Bataillon, *Erasmo y España*, México, 1986, pp. 507-9, 554-55

P. Boronat y Barrachina, *Los Moriscos españoles y su expulsion. Estudio histórico-crítico*, Valencia, 1901 (repr. Granada, 1992, with introductory essay by R. García Cárcel)

E. Nieves Sanz, 'La Edición Crítica Bilingüe de la Obra "De divinis, apostolicis atque ecclesiasticis traditionibus...", de D. Martín Pérez de Ayala (1.504-66)' in Grupo de investigación, 'Humanismo giennense (siglos xv-xvii)' (web based research project, includes list of editions of Martín Pérez de Ayala's works), www.ujaen.es/investiga/hum669/perez_de_ayala_martin.htmwww.ujaen.es/investiga/hum669/Edicion_bilingue_Perez_de_Ayala.pdf

María Jesús Framiñán de Miguel

Pedro Barrantes Maldonado

DATE OF BIRTH January 1510
PLACE OF BIRTH Alcántara, Cáceres
DATE OF DEATH Between mid-October and the end of November 1579
PLACE OF DEATH Alcántara

BIOGRAPHY

When he was only 11 years old, Pedro Barrantes went to fight in the War of the Comunidades (1520-22) in support of Charles V. He later served as a page at the court of Francisco de Sotomayor, Duke of Béjar, accompanying the duke on the Hungarian campaign against the Turks in 1530. They travelled via Portugal, France, Flanders, Germany and Hungary, which gave him the opportunity to learn Latin, French, Italian and Portuguese. This expedition led him to write his *Itinerario de la jornada de Hungría* ('Itinerary of the Hungarian expedition') and other works, including a translation of Paulo Giovio's *Commentario delle cose de' Turchi*, written in 1532.

Barrantes lived in Alcántara until 1537, when he went to the court in Valladolid to defend the city's interests. In the same year, he married Mariana Ordoñez de Pareja, and also began work on *Ilustraciones de la Casa de Niebla* ('Illustrations of the House of Niebla') for the Duke of Medina Sidonia, who was also Count of Niebla. On 10 December 1540, he survived the attack on Gibraltar led by Caramani and other pirate friends of Barbarrossa, which inspired the *Dialogo entre Pedro Barrantes Maldonado y un cavallero estrangero* ('Dialogue between Pedro Barrantes Maldonado and a stranger').

At the end of 1541, he settled in Alburquerque, devoting himself to writing books and leisure pursuits. Then in 1549, his brother Alonso made him governor of Alcántara, where he then lived for the rest of his life. His house is still preserved.

In all, Barrantes wrote 40 works, the majority of them now lost. In those that are extant there is a continuing theme of opposition to the 'Moors' and 'Turks'.

MAIN SOURCES OF INFORMATION

Primary
MS Madrid, BNE – R/9420 (*Las trobas siguientes hizo Pedro Barrantes Maldonado estando en Alemaña en la guerra del turco en loor de los españoles con vn romance en que se recuenta la súpita y muy valerosa partida del Ilmo. Señor duque de Bejar a la mesma guerra*)
Diálogo entre Pedro Barrantes Maldonado y un cauallero estrangero, Alcala de Henares: en casa de Sebastian Martinez, 1566

Secondary
D.A. Martín Nieto, 'Pedro Barrantes Maldonado (1510-1579)', in D.A. Martín Nieto et al. (eds), *Noticias de Alcántara. Pedro Barrantes Maldonado y sus antigüedades de la villa de Alcántara*, Jaraiz de la Vera, Cáceres, 2011, 25-72
J.F. Maura, art. 'Barrantes Maldonado, Pedro', in *Diccionario biográfico español*, Madrid, 2010, vii, 87-8
J. Ruiz Jiménez, 'Power and musical exchange. The Dukes of Medina Sidonia in Renaissance Seville', *Early Music* 37 (2009) 401-15
D. Brenes, 'Lazarillo de Tormes. Roman à clef', *Hispania* 69 (1986) 234-43
V. Barrantes, *Católogo razonado y crítico de los libros, memorias y papeles, impresos y manuscritos, que tratan de las provincias de Extremadura, así tocante á su historia, religión y geografía, como á sus antigüedades, nobleza y hombres célebres*, Madrid, 1863, 4-10, https://archive.org/details/catlogorazonadooospagoog

WORKS ON CHRISTIAN-MUSLIM RELATIONS

Diálogo entre Pedro Barrantes Maldonado y un cauallero estrangero, 'Dialogue between Pedro Barrantes Maldonado and a stranger'

DATE 1566
ORIGINAL LANGUAGE Spanish

DESCRIPTION
This work of 96 pages was published in 1566 – its full title is *Diálogo entre Pedro Barrantes Maldonado y un cauallero estrangero en que se cuenta el saco que los turcos hizieron en Gibraltar y el vencimiento destruycion que la armada de España hizo en la de los turcos. Año de 1540* ('Dialogue between Pedro Barrantes Maldonado and a stranger, in which he recounts the raid on Gibraltar by the Turks and the vanquishing and destruction that the Spanish armada wrought on the Turkish armada. In the year 1540'). It

is in two parts, the first describing the Turkish attack on Gibraltar (1889 edition, pp. 1-127), and the second the history of Spanish reprisals against the Turks (1889 edition, pp. 129-61).

The first part contains an account of the attack on Gibraltar by the fleet that set sail from Algiers for Cádiz on 6 August 1540, but which ended up raiding Gibraltar on 10 September 1540 and was routed by the Spanish. Its main section (there are four in all) is in the form of a dialogue between Barrantes, who is on his way home after the victory, and a stranger, who is surprised to find so many armed men on the road. In addition to his description of the attack and the destruction of the North African fleet, Barrantes gives a short account of Turkish manners and customs. Since he does not understand them, he ridicules the customs that distinguish Turks from Spanish Christians, especially those concerning marriage and eating. As a result, the *Diálogo* is full of preconceived ideas about the presumed peculiarities of the enemy, which give a distorted view that bears little relation to the actual situation.

SIGNIFICANCE

Barrantes' triumphalist tone in the *Dialogo* does not represent historical reality, even though it is the same as that found in official chronicles. The actual outcome of the North African attack was the isolation and destruction of Gibraltar, which lacked effective protection at the time of the assault.

MANUSCRIPTS

Two MSS were preserved until the mid-19th century, one in the Cartuja de Jerez, and the other in BNE (referred to by Gayangos). Both are now lost.

EDITIONS & TRANSLATIONS

J. López Romero (ed), *Diálogo entre Pedro Barrantes Maldonado y un cauallero estrangero*, Seville, 2009, https://archive.org/details/coleccondelibro19almauoft

Tres relaciones históricas. Gibraltar, Los Xerves, Alcazarquivir, 1540, 1560, 1578, Madrid, 1889, pp. 1-127, 129-61

Diálogo entre Pedro Barrantes Maldonado y un cauallero estrangero, Alcalá de Henares, Madrid, 1566

STUDIES

A.M. Carabias Torres, 'Turcos contra católicos. Barrantes Maldonado y la deformación interesada de los hechos militares', *Tiempos Modernos. Revista Electrónica de Historia Moderna* 6 (2009), http://www.tiemposmodernos.org/tm3/index.php/tm/article/view/177/234

A. Castro Díaz, 'Barrantes Maldonado, Pedro, Diálogo entre Pedro Barrantes Maldonado y un cauallero estrangero que cuenta el saco que los turcos hizieronen Gibraltar en 1540', *Archivo Hispalense. Revista Histórica, Literaria y Artística* 92/279-81 (2009) 407-10

A.M. Carabias Torres, 'İspanya'da Türklere Karşı Yapılan Deniz Savaşlarıyla İlgili Dokümentasyonun İncelenmesi. Barrantes Maldonado Örneği', in Ö. Kumrular (ed.), *Türkler ve Deniz*, Istanbul, 2007, 247-64

Ana María Carabias Torres

Alonso de Orozco

DATE OF BIRTH 17 August 1500
PLACE OF BIRTH Oropesa (Toledo)
DATE OF DEATH 19 September 1591
PLACE OF DEATH Madrid

BIOGRAPHY

The son of Hernando de Orozco and María de Mena, Alonso spent his childhood in Oropesa, Talavera de la Reina and Toledo, where he was a page (*seise*) in the cathedral. His parents sent him and his older brother Francisco to study in Salamanca, with the intention that they should become priests. Francisco died before he could complete the novitiate, but Alonso made his religious profession in the Augustinian Order of Salamanca on 9 June 1523.

He intended to participate in the evangelisation of the New World, but after setting sail he was forced by illness to turn back from the Canary Islands and he went to the convent of Valladolid. He presided over the provincial chapter of the order in 1557, and as court preacher he went to Toledo and in 1561 to Madrid. He lived in the convent of St Philip, and attained a reputation of holiness for his charitable works.

Alonso founded the convent of Las Beatas de San Agustin in Talavera, where his sister Francisca made her profession, and also a monastery for men of his order. Later he founded the convent of the Magdalene in Madrid, for women, and some years afterwards the convent of St Elisabeth for women and the monastery of Doña María de Aragón for men (the present Spanish senate house).

He wrote many books and papers on theology and spirituality in Latin and Spanish before his death in 1591. He was beatified on 15 January 1882.

MAIN SOURCES OF INFORMATION

Primary

T. Aparicio, 'Beato Alonso de Orozco. Varón santo y hombre de doctrina insigne', in R. Lazcano (ed.), *Alonso de Orozco. Obras completas, I. Obras castellanas (1)*, Madrid, 2001, xiii-xxiv

Secondary

M.Á. Orcasitas, *San Alonso de Orozco, un toledano universal*, Toledo, 2003

J. Márquez, *Vida de San Alonso de Orozco agustino*, Madrid, 2002

R. Lazcano, 'Bibliografía orozquiana', in R. Lazcano (ed.), *Alonso de Orozco. Obras completas, I. Obras castellanas (1)*, Madrid, 2001, xcix-cxxiv

A. de Orozco, *Crónica de San Agustín y de los santos y beatos y doctores de su orden. Instrucción de religiosos: declaración de la regla de San Agustín*, ed. and intr. M.G. Velasco, Madrid, 2001

R. Lazcano, *Figura y obra de Alonso de Orozco, O.S.A., 1500-1591. Actas de las jornadas del IV centenario de su muerte*, Madrid, 1992

A. de Mier, 'Alonso de Orozco en el marco histórico general de su época', in R. Lazcano (ed.), *Figura y obra de Alonso de Orozco*, Madrid, 1992, 15-41

T. Aparicio López, *Fray Alonso de Orozco. Hombre, sabio y santo. 1591-1991*, Valladolid, 1991

P.L. Moráis Antón, *Alonso de Orozco, un santo en la corte de Felipe II*, Madrid, 1991

A. de Orozco, *The confessions of Blessed Alonso de Orozco*, trans. M.J. O'Connell, ed. J.E. Rotelle, Villanova PA, 1991

A.A. Giol, 'La relación entre De los nombres de Cristo de Fray Luis de León y De los nueve nombres de Cristo atribuido al beato Alonso de Orozco', Bryn Mawr PA, 1982, (Diss. Bryn Mawr College)

A.J. Bulovas, *El amor divino en la obra del beato Alonso de Orozco*, Madrid, 1975

E.J. Schuster, 'Alonso de Orozco and Fray Luis de León. De los nombres de Cristo', *Hispanic Review* 24 (1956), 261-70

J. van de Rakt, *P. Alfons d'Orozco*, Kontich, 1946

A. de Orozco, *Victoria de la muerte, por el heroico siervo d'Dios beato Alonso d'Orozco*, Madrid, 1921

T. Cámara, *Life of Blessed Alphonsus Orozco, O.S.A.*, trans. W.A. Jones, Philadelphia PA, 1895

V.G. Baquero, *Compendio de la vida del Beato Alonso de Orozco, extractado de la excelente obra escrita por el R. P. Fr. Tomás Cámara, y puesto en romance castellano por V.G.B.*, Barcelona, 1888

A. de Orozco, *Certamen bonum monachis potissime orthodoxisque omnibus perutile*, Guadalupe, 1887

T. Cámara, *Vida y escritos del Beato Alonso de Orozco del Orden de San Agustín, predicador de Felipe II*, Valladolid, 1882

WORKS ON CHRISTIAN-MUSLIM RELATIONS

Cathecismo prouechoso hecho por el Padre Fray Alonso de Orozco, predicador de su M. En el qual se declara solamente nuestra ley Christiana ser la verdadera. Y todas las otras sectas ser engaños del demonio, 'Useful Catechism written by Friar Alonso de Orozco, preacher of his majesty, in which is declared that only our Christian faith is true and all other sects are falsehood of the devil'

DATE 1568
ORIGINAL LANGUAGE Spanish

DESCRIPTION

This substantial catechism, comprising 100 pages in the 1736 edition, was written as an imaginary dialogue between an Augustinian friar and a certain Felipe, a Morisco who has just converted to Christianity. Felipe says that he wants a book that contains arguments to assist Muslims living in Aragón to make a conversion that is sincere and not just for convenience. The ensuing dialogue seeks to provide such a text by setting out the elements of the Christian faith as the truth that has been given by God. No questions are left open, and no doubts expressed. It states uncompromisingly that the Church is the embodiment of truth, and all that it teaches and offers is true and the only possible truth, while all that does not agree with its teachings is simple error, coming from the devil. The Church is the means that God has given for salvation, and thus any disagreements with its teachings automatically set divergent groups in the way of error. This is the work of the devil, as the determined enemy of humankind.

The book is intended primarily to convert Muslims, though it is also meant to strengthen Moriscos who have made a show of conversion. Thus, the great majority of its teachings are polemical in form, even its exposition of the Catholic faith. It loses no opportunity to expose the errors of Islam, rather than emphasising elements that Christianity and Islam hold in common, because truth and error cannot stand together: thus, for example, Chapter 2 is entitled 'How our faith condemns the sect of Muḥammad' (ed. Resines, pp. 731-36). Orozco evidently knows the Qur'an well, and he quotes it to show its incoherencies and false teachings. He does not hesitate to insult Islam and Muḥammad, whom he portrays as the archetype of one who instils error in his followers. He also uses the Qur'an to attack Jews, because they are not loyal to the call of God, and retain a pointless Messianic hope. This *Cathecismo* of Orozco bears a strong similarity to the *Catecismo del Sacromonte* that was written by an anonymous Jesuit at about the same time with the purpose of converting the Moriscos of Sacromonte in Granada. Both works express the attitude that there is no alternative for Moriscos or Muslims than to accept the salvation that is offered only by the Catholic Church.

SIGNIFICANCE

The fact that three editions of the *Cathecismo* were published in a brief period of time (1568, 1572 and 1575) is an indication of its popularity when it was written, especially in Aragón, though its form and hostile attitude almost certainly deterred Muslims from following its instructions. It was too uncompromising in condemning even non-Christians who could not have known the teachings of the Church.

In later years, Orozco's *Cathecismo* appears to have exerted little influence. The 1736 edition was simply published as part of his complete works, while the so-called synthesis by the Augustinian friar Jerónimo Colinas is actually a very different book. Colinas was using the book's title and Orozco's name to give his own work status.

EDITIONS & TRANSLATIONS

L. Resines, *Catecismo provechoso*, in R. Lazcano (ed.), *Alonso de Orozco. Obras completas, I. obras castellanas (1)*, Madrid, 2001, 695-843

Cathecismo Christiano escrito por el Vne. Padre Fray Alonso de Orozco, predicador de su Magestad, en el cual se declara solamente nuestra Ley ser la verdadera, y todas las otras sectas ser engaños del demonio. Va en diálogo entre un religioso y un recién convertido, in *Obras del Ven. Siervo de Dios Fr. Alonso de Orozco, del Orden de N.P.S. Agustín, Fundador del colegio de la Encarnación de Madrid (llamado Doña María de Aragón), cuyas virtudes en grado heroico están aprobadas por la Iglesia para el efecto de su Canonización, Tomo I. Dalas a luz la Provincia de Castilla del Orden de nuestro Padre San Agustín, en esta tercera impresión*, Madrid: Imp. Ven. Alonso de Orozco, 1736 (the title is changed from *Cathecismo provechoso* to *Cathecismo Christiano*)

Cathecismo provechoso, Salamanca: Domingo de Portonariis, 1575
Cathecismo provechoso, Zaragoza, 1572
(The *Cathecismo* is not included in the *Recopilación de todas las obras que ha escrito el P. Fray Alonso de Orozco*, Alcalá, 1570)
Cathecismo prouechoso. Hecho por el Padre Fray Alonso de Orozco, predicador de su M. En el qual se declara solamente nuestra ley Christiana ser la verdadera. Y todas las otras sectas ser engaños del demonio. Impresso con licencia del señor obispo de Vtica, visitador y vicario general, por el excelentissimo Señor don Hernando de Aragon, Arçobispo de Çaragoça. Y con licencia de los Señores Inquisidores. En çaragoça en casa de Iuan Millan, 1568 (134 fols)

STUDIES

Resines, *Catecismo provechoso*, pp. 697-734

L. Resines, 'El Catecismo de Alonso de Orozco entre los catecismos del siglo XVI', *Revista Agustiniana* 41 (2000) 843-70

L. Resines, 'Estudio sobre el Catecismo de Alonso de Orozco', in R. Lazcano (ed.), *Figura y obra de Alonso de Orozco* (Historia Viva 5), Madrid, 1992, 131-83

J.M. Sánchez, *Bibliografía Aragonesa (1501-1600)*, vol. 2, Madrid, 1914 (facsimile edition, Madrid, 1991)

Cathecismo de la Doctrina Christiana, compendiado por Fr. Gerónymo Colinas de el que con más extensión escribió el Bto. Alonso de Orozco. Síguese en él el méthodo y distribución del Cathecismo usado en Castilla la Vieja, y Montañas, llamado "Astete", Madrid, 1768 (despite the title, this really has almost no relation to what Orozco wrote)

Luis Resines

Diego Hurtado de Mendoza

Diego Hurtado de Mendoza y Pacheco,
Diego de Mendoza, Diego de Mendoç

DATE OF BIRTH 1503
PLACE OF BIRTH Granada
DATE OF DEATH 14 August 1575
PLACE OF DEATH Madrid

BIOGRAPHY

Born in the Alhambra Palace, Granada, Diego Hurtado de Mendoza y Pacheco was the youngest son of the second Count of Tendilla, captain general of the Kingdom of Granada. He began his studies in Granada, in an atmosphere and environment that was influenced on the one hand by the Moriscos and on the other by the Renaissance, as his tutor was Pietro Martire d'Anghiera, whom his father had brought with him from Italy. He continued his education at the University of Salamanca, receiving a substantial humanist education and learning to speak Arabic, Latin, Greek and Hebrew, after which he pursued a career in the army. He went as a soldier to Italy, where he became acquainted with Aristotelian philosophy, and considered pursuing studies in that field.

Family differences over his father's will resulted in his abandoning his army career, moving away from Granada and pursuing a career in diplomacy. In 1527, he travelled as Spanish ambassador to Venice, where he persuaded the state government to abandon negotiations with the Grand Turk, and also got to know about the secret negotiations between King Francis I of France and the sultan. In 1535, he participated in the expedition led by the Emperor Charles V to Tunis, where he encountered Garcilaso de la Vega. Under the protection of the emperor's secretary, Francisco de los Cobos, he was appointed in 1536 as ambassador to England, where he remained until 1538.

On 20 February 1545, Hurtado de Mendoza was appointed imperial ambassador to the Council of Trent, and on 3 December 1546 he went to Rome, being appointed ambassador to the city on 29 August 1547. His various roles provided him with the opportunity to travel around Italy, frequenting the intellectual schools of Rome, Venice and Padua. Returning to Spain in 1552, he was kept busy with minor tasks and did not appear at court until 23 July 1568. He was imprisoned by King Philip II for quarrelling loudly outside the bedroom of the king's dying heir, Don Carlos, and was not released until January 1569. He returned to Granada, and witnessed there the uprising of the Moriscos, which he recorded, on the basis of eyewitness accounts, in the *Guerra de Granada*.

Hurtado de Mendoza died in 1574, nominating as his heir King Philip II, who forbade publication of some of his writings because of the criticisms they contained. His history of the Morisco uprising was published in Lisbon only in 1627, publication in Spain finally being authorised in 1628.

MAIN SOURCES OF INFORMATION

Primary
The only direct sources on Hurtado de Mendoza's life are his letters and details he gives in *Guerra de Granada*.

Secondary
J. Castillo Fernández, 'La historiografía española del siglo XVI. Luis del Mármol Carvajal y su Historia del rebelión y castigo de los moriscos del reino de Granada. Análisis histórico y estudio critic', Granada, 2013 (Diss. University of Granada)

J. Varó Zafra, 'Carta de don Diego Hurtado de Mendoza al cardenal Espinosa sobre la guerra de Granada', *Manuscrits Cao* 12 (2012) 1-12

J. Varó Zafra, 'Diego Hurtado de Mendoza y las "cartas de los Bachilleres"', *Castilla. Estudios de Literatura* 1 (2010) 453-72

M. García Arenal and F. Rodríguez Mediano, *Un oriente español. Los moriscos y el Sacromonte en tiempos de Contrareforma*, Madrid, 2010, pp. 99-102

J. Varó Zafra, 'Notas sobre el pensamiento político en la correspondencia de Diego Hurtado de Mendoza', *Analecta Malacitana* 32 (2009) 7-35, 399-431

J. Castillo Fernández, 'La guerra de los moriscos granadinos en la historiografía de la época (1570-1627)', in M. Barrios Aguilera and Á. Galán Sánchez (eds), *La historia del Reino de Granada a debate. Viejos y nuevos temas. perspectivas de studio*, Málaga, 2005, 677-704

J. Castillo Fernández, 'Hurtado de Mendoza. Humanista, arabista e historiador', *El Fingidor. Revista de Cultura* 21 (2004) 25-27

M.A. de Bunes Ibarra, 'La embajada de Diego Hurtado de Mendoza en Venecia', in J. Martínez Millán (ed.), *Carlos V y la quiebra del humanismo político en Europa (1530-1558)*, Madrid, 2000, i, 591-618

B. Bassegoda, 'El *Libro de retratos* de Pacheco y la verdadera efigie de Diego Hurtado de Mendoza', *Locvs Amcenvs* 5 (2000-1) 205-16

A. Hobson, *Renaissance book collecting. Jean Grolier and Diego Hurtado de Mendoza, their books and bindings*, Cambridge, 1999

H. Nader, *Los Mendoza y el Renacimiento Español*, Guadalajara, 1985

D.H. Darst, 'El pensamiento histórico del granadino Diego Hurtado de Mendoza', *Hispania* 43 (1983) 281-94

E. Spivakovsky, 'Un episodio de la guerra contra los moriscos. La pérdida del gobierno de la Alhamra por el quinto conde de Tendilla (1569)', *Hispania* 118 (1971) 399-431

E. Spivakovsky, *Son of the Alhambra. Don Diego Hurtado de Mendoza 1504-1575*, Austin TX, 1970

E. Spivakovsky, 'El "Vicariato de Siena". Correspondiente de Felipe II, príncipe, con Diego Hurtado de Mendoza y Ferrange Gonzaga', *Hispania* 26 (1966) 585-96

P. González and C. Mele, *Vida y obras de Don Diego Hurtado de Mendoza*, Madrid, 1941-43

A. Vázquez and R. Selden (eds), *Algunas cartas de Don Diego Hurtado de Mendoza, escritas 1528-1552*, New Haven CT, 1935

R. Foulché-Delbosc, 'Un point contesté de la vie de Mendoza', *Revue Hispanique* 2 (1895) 208-303

R. Foulché-Delbosc, 'Étude sur la "Guerra de Granada" de don Diego Hurtado de Mendoza', *Revue Hispanique* 1 (1894) 101-65

WORKS ON CHRISTIAN-MUSLIM RELATIONS

Guerra de Granada, 'The war in Granada'

DATE About 1571
ORIGINAL LANGUAGE Spanish

DESCRIPTION

Hurtado de Mendoza wrote this work (its full title is *Guerra de Granada hecha por el rey de España don Phelipe contra los Moriscos de aquel reino, sus rebeldes*) around 1571, at the end of the Morisco uprising. He produced a number of manuscript copies with slight variations and titles, which were quickly circulated (three manuscripts of 171, 134 and 364 pages are extant). These versions continued to be copied into the 17th century (in some cases, with variations, which may well mean they are copies of other versions that are no longer extant). From this period, there are five manuscript copies of 112, 272, 212, 172 and 123 pages. Copies continued to be made even into the 18th century, of which one, with 128 folios, is extant.

In 1948, the Academy of History published the 1842 edition of the work by Juan Oliveres, thoroughly edited by Manuel Gómez-Moreno. This was re-edited by Bernardo Blanco-González in 1970 in a 464-page edition, which was reprinted in 1981 with some minor variations (468 pages). This edition is considered to be the most complete to date.

The work, one of Hurtado de Mendoza's later writings (he was previously best known as a poet), is written in the style that was in fashion in the 16th century, in which raw historical facts were reshaped into a literary narrative. The main part of the book focuses on the major battles that took place and the leaders on both sides. Hurtado de Mendoza does not hold back from expressing criticisms of the tactless mistakes made by the Christians in dealing with the Morisco minority before and after the uprising. He condemns the final culmination of these mistakes in the dramatic expulsion of the Moriscos that destroyed the delicate balance achieved in Granada since its fall in 1492.

SIGNIFICANCE

Hurtado de Mendoza exhibits an unusually subtle and nuanced attitude towards the Moriscos. Although as a devout Christian he regards Islam as inferior and entirely human in origin, he nevertheless sees the Moriscos as the rightful inhabitants of Granada, rejecting the myth of a pre-Islamic Christian origin of the town in favour of a more recent Muslim origin. The consequence is that he advocates a shared culture in the town, and he condemns Christian attitudes towards the Moriscos and the inhuman treatment of them, as well as the extreme positions taken by individuals on both sides.

MANUSCRIPTS

For a detailed list of manuscripts, see B. Blanco-González (ed.), *Guerra de Granada*, Madrid, 1970, pp. 71-74

EDITIONS & TRANSLATIONS

B. Blanco-González (ed.), *Guerra de Granada*, Madrid, 1970 (considered to be the most complete edition; see pp. 74-78 for a detailed list of other editions)

A. Hämel (trans.), *Don Diego Hurtado de Mendoza's Guerra de Granada contra los moriscos, mit Einleitung und Anmerkungen zum Schulgebrauch*, Leipzig, 1923 (German trans.)

M. Shuttleworth (trans.), *The war in Granada*, London, 1982 (English trans.)

O.C. Vallecchi (trans.), *La guerra di Granata fatta dal re Filippo II contro a'moreschi ribelli di quel reame*, Florence, 1873 (Italian trans.)

J.G. Magnabal (trans.), *Morceaux choisis de la Guerre de Grenade*, Paris, 1876 (repr. 1878), 1880[2], 1898[3], 2013[4] (French trans.)

STUDIES

Castillo Fernández, 'La historiografía española'

J. Varó Zafra, *Diego Hurtado de Mendoza y la Guerra de Granada en su contexto histórico*, Valladolid, 2012

Varó Zafra, 'Carta de don Diego Hurtado de Mendoza'

M. Agulló Cobo, 'A vueltas con el autor del Lazarillo. Un par de vueltas más', *Lemir* 15 (2011) 217-34

V. Iommi Echevarría, 'El movimiento de proyectiles en la *Mecánica* de Diego Hurtado de Mendoza y la nueva dinámica renacentista', *Asclepio* 63 (2011) 179-92

M. Agulló Cobo, *A vueltas con el autor del 'Lazarillo'*, Madrid, 2010

Varó Zafra, 'Diego Hurtado de Mendoza y las "cartas de los Bachilleres"'

García Arenal and Rodríguez Mediano, *Un oriente español*, pp. 99-102

Varó Zafra, 'Notas sobre el pensamiento político en la correspondencia de Diego Hurtado de Mendoza'

M.J. Bertoméu Masiá, *Cartas de un espía de Carlos V. La correspondencia de Jerónimo Bucchia con Antonio Perrenot de Granvela*, Valencia, 2005

Castillo Fernández, 'La guerra de los moriscos granadinos'

F. Vivar, 'Tucídides y la guerra de Granada de Hurtado de Mendoza', *Actas del VI congreso de la Asociación Internacional Siglo de Oro. Memoria de la palabra*, Madrid, 2004, ii, 1819-29

J. Martínez Millán, *Carlos V y la quiebra del humanismo político en Europa (1530-1558)*, Madrid, 2000, i, pp. 591-618

V. Sánchez Ramos, 'La guerra de las Alpujarras (1568-1570)', in M. Barrios Aguilera, (ed.), *Historia del Reino de Granada*, vol. 2. *La época morisca y la repoblación (1502-1630)*, Granada, 2000, 507-42

C. Davis, 'Tacitean elements in Diego Hurtado de Mendoza's *Guerra de Granada*', *Dispositio* 10 (1985) 85-96

G. Cirot, *La Guerra de Granada et l'Austriada*, Burdeos, 1920

R. Foulché-Delbosc, 'L'authenticité de "La Guerra de Granada"', *Revue Hispanique* 35 (1915) 194-96

L. de Torre and L. de Franco-Romero, 'Don Diego Hurtado de Mendoza no fue el autor de la *Guerra de Granada*', *Boletín de la Real Academia de la Historia* 65 (1914) 461-501

A. Morel-Fatio, 'Quelques remarques sur la *Guerre de Grénade* de D. Diego Hurtado de Mendoza', *Annuaire de l'École Pratique des Hautes Études, sec. historie*, París, 1914, 36-43

Foulché-Delbosc, 'Étude sur la "Guerra de Granada"'

Valeriano Sánchez-Ramos

Fernando de Herrera

'El Divino'

DATE OF BIRTH 1534
PLACE OF BIRTH Seville
DATE OF DEATH 1597
PLACE OF DEATH Seville

BIOGRAPHY

Fernando de Herrera was a poet, historian and literary critic, though hardly anything is known about him. He never left the city of Seville where he was born and where he must have studied at the school that Master Rodrigo de Santaella had set up at the University of Seville. As no title such as Master is associated with his name, he most probably did not finish his studies. He was admitted to Minor Orders but was not ordained priest, becoming instead a dean in the parish of San Andrés. In that capacity he received a modest salary on which he lived for the rest of his life.

De Herrera was a man of great culture, with knowledge of mathematics, medicine, geography, philosophy, Latin and Greek, and he wrote numerous literary works, most of which have been lost. He had a harsh character and was austere, cautious and very reserved, except within his circle of friends, who made up the so-called Academy of Seville that revolved around Juan Mal Lara. He is the main representative of the school of poetry of Seville in the 16th century.

MAIN SOURCES OF INFORMATION

Primary
F. Pacheco, *Libro de descripción de verdaderos retratos de illustres y memorables varones*, Seville, 1599
F. de Herrera, *Versos emendados i divididos por el en tres libros*, ed. F. Pacheco, Seville, 1619

Secondary
R. Herrera Montero, *La lírica de Horacio en Fernando de Herrera*, Seville, 1998
P. Ruiz Pérez, *Libros y lectura de un poeta humanista. Fernando de Herrera (1534-1597)*, Cordova, 1997

O. Macrí, *Fernando de Herrera*, Madrid, 1959, 1972²
F. Rodríguez Marín, *El divino Herrera y la condesa de Gelves*, Madrid, 1911
A. Coster, *Fernando de Herrera (El Divino) 1534-1597*, París, 1908
R.M. Beach, 'Was Fernando de Herrera a Greek scholar?', Philadelphia PA, 1908 (Diss. University of Pennsylvania)

WORKS ON CHRISTIAN-MUSLIM RELATIONS

Relación de la guerra de Chipre y suceso de la batalla naval de Lepanto, 'Account of the war of Cyprus and events of the naval battle of Lepanto'

DATE 1572
ORIGINAL LANGUAGE Spanish

DESCRIPTION
After the publication in 1572 of the *Relaciónde la guerra de Chipre*, one of many books published in Europe as a result of the Christian victory at Lepanto, Fernando de Herrera, who had a reputation as a poet, became known as a prose writer. The work, which is 92 pages long and divided into 28 chapters, ending with a 'song [poem] praising his Divine Majesty for the victory achieved by Don Juan of Austria', describes the events that led to the creation of the Holy League between the pope, Venice and Spain to confront the fleet of Sultan Selim II. The first part is devoted to the conquest of Cyprus and the negotiations that took place to unite the Christian naval force; it explains that the Christians were unable to assist the besieged population of the city of Famagusta, even though they had a sufficient number of galleys, with the result that the Venetians lost the island to the Turks. The second part focuses on the fleet commanded by Don Juan of Austria, the illegitimate son of Charles V, and the battle that took place near Lepanto. In addition to narrating specific incidents in the sea battle, the narrative gives a thorough account of the composition of the two fleets in order to explain why the Christians defeated the Ottomans.

SIGNIFICANCE
The *Relación* acknowledges the huge danger that the Ottoman Empire represented to the Christian West, not least because the Ottomans wanted to defeat Spain. However, the union of the Christian princes meant that the sultan had to confront an enemy of equal military strength, so that

the Turkish defeat was almost assured. From the beginning, even in the prologue, the book praises Spain, King Philip II and Don Juan of Austria for this great achievement, and stresses that the Spaniards were part of 'the divine plan' to restore the kingdom of Christ on earth, so that the battle of Lepanto could be considered to be a semi-prophetic affair.

EDITIONS & TRANSLATIONS

Colección de documentos inéditos para la historia de España (CODOIN), Madrid, 1852, xxi, pp. 261-382

Relación de la guerra de Chipre y suceso de la batalla naval de Lepanto, Seville, 1572

STUDIES

J. Montero Delgado, *Fernando de Herrera y el humanismo sevillano en tiempos de Felipe II. Antología de prosa herreriana en su contexto*, Seville, 1998

J. Montero Delgado, 'Poesía y prosa en torno a Lepanto. El ejemplo de Fernando de Herrera', in A.D. Ortiz (ed.), *Andalucía moderna III*, Cordova, 1995, 283-89

M. Gaylord Randel, *The historical prose of Fernando de Herrera*, London, 1970

J. López de Toro, *Los poetas de Lepanto*, Madrid, 1950

Miguel Ángel de Bunes

Diego de Simancas

Jacobus Simancas, Simancas

DATE OF BIRTH January 1513
PLACE OF BIRTH Cordova, Spain
DATE OF DEATH November 1583
PLACE OF DEATH Zamora, Spain

BIOGRAPHY

Diego de Simancas was one of the most important theorists of the Spanish Inquisition. A Castilian jurist of the 16th century, his career included appointments as university professor, judge in a royal appellate court, member of the Inquisition's governing council, special envoy to the papal court in Rome, and bishop. Throughout, Simancas persistently compiled and revised treatises on topics from inheritance law to the dignity of bishops; his principal writings were a collection of aphorisms about good government and a series of works on inquisitorial law. In the latter, he sought to provide a guide to inquisition procedures and to examine the more complex legal problems of Catholic inquisitions, while providing a set of justifications for them. He influenced not only the development of the Spanish Inquisition but also inquisitors in Italian tribunals and the growing body of inquisition legal theory; he was cited in other civil and ecclesiastical legal treatises as well. Simancas is well known to modern historians because he wrote an autobiography (*Vida*), which offers an inquisitor's account of his work.

Simancas's family was prominent in Cordova, connected to the cathedral and the Inquisition; he and his two brothers became secular clerics, and his three sisters married into the regional nobility. He began his studies at the prestigious University of Salamanca, but completed his doctorate in both laws (canon and civil) at the University of Valladolid, where he went on to gain a post in the legal faculty. He began his judicial career in Valladolid's Chancery, the preeminent royal appellate court; he moved from civil to inquisitorial law first as a consultant to the Inquisition in Valladolid. He was then appointed to the royal council of Inquisition (the *Suprema*) in 1559, at the height of a panic about Lutheran infiltration of the royal court and the ecclesiastical elite. The central focus of his inquisitorial career and his *Vida* was the 17-year trial

(1559-76) of Bartolomé de Carranza, Archbishop of Toledo. Carranza was accused of a variety of Lutheran heresies and was tried first by the Spanish Inquisition in Valladolid, then by Pope Pius V, and ultimately by Pope Gregory XIII, who concluded the case by sentencing Carranza to abjure 16 heretical propositions and then reconciling him to the Church. A prominent figure in each phase of the case, Simancas spent nine years in Rome representing the Spanish Inquisition. He was well connected among the elite courtiers of the Spanish monarchy and received a variety of temporary commissions, including a brief stint as interim viceroy of Naples during the papal election of 1572. At the same time, Simancas had an ecclesiastical career: made bishop of Ciudad Rodrigo in 1564, of Badajoz in 1569, and of Zamora in 1578, he held the first two appointments primarily without residing in his dioceses. Following his death in Zamora, he was buried in the chapel in Cordova Cathedral, which he and his two brothers had built, dedicated to the Holy Spirit.

Islam, Muslims, and even converts from Islam to Christianity played minimal roles in Simancas's writings. Moriscos (converts and their descendants) were never a primary focus of his judicial actions or his treatises, even though they increasingly became an object of the Spanish Inquisition's activities during his lifetime. Rather, he focused on what he deemed to be the threats posed by nascent Protestant heresies and by *judeoconversos*. In his vernacular Spanish autobiography, Islam made two brief appearances. The first was a rhetorical use of the Ottoman Turkish threat. Simancas recounted having advised King Philip II in 1573 that he was well within his rights to communicate with the pope about the on-going Carranza trial, given what others justified as the needs of state, namely that the king of France had made an alliance with 'the Turk', and that the Venetians were threatening that they would break the Catholic League (following the Battle of Lepanto) and make a Turkish alliance (*Vida*, p. 177). One of the last episodes narrated in the *Vida* concerns how, in June 1578, the king had entrusted to Simancas the voluntary conversion to Catholicism of Joán Alayde, a *moro de nación* who had arrived at the royal court. Simancas described taking the man into his household, arranging for his instruction in the faith and the language, personally baptising him, and eventually arranging for the new convert to become a soldier in Catalonia. He used the experience, moreover, to note that he had advised the king about the problem of *moros de Africa* who converted because of the prospect of material rewards. He implied that such converts tended to be bellicose and fortune-seeking, and that

Muslims in North Africa used riches to attract Christian apostates (*Vida*, pp. 201-2, 204).

MAIN SOURCES OF INFORMATION

Primary

J.I. Tellechea Idígoras, 'Cartas inéditas de un inquisidor por oficio. El Dr. Simancas y el proceso romano de Carranza', in A. Carreira, J.A. Cid, M. Gutiérrez Esteve, and R. Rubio (eds), *Homenaje a Julio Caro Baroja*, Madrid, 1978, 965-99

D. de Simancas, 'Vida y cosas notables del Señor Obispo de Zamora Don Diego de Simancas', in Manuel Serrano y Sanz (ed.), *Autobiografías y memorias*, Madrid, 1905, 151-210 (The only known manuscript copy to survive, of 1685, is 'La Vida y cosas notables del s[eñ]or obispo de Zamora D[o]n Diego de Simancas Cordubense, y colegial Vallesoletano, escripta desu mano, cuio trasumpto es este', MS Seville, Biblioteca Capitular – 84-6-29, Microfiche 58-5-23)

Secondary

K. Lynn, *Between court and confessional. The politics of Spanish inquisitors*, New York, 2013

M. Pérez Lozano and M. Moralejo Ortega, 'Don Diego de Simancas y la fundación de la capilla familiar en la Catedral-Mezquita de Córdoba', in M.D. Barral Rivadulla, E. Fernández Castiñeiras, B. Fernández Rodríguez, and J.M. Monterroso Montero (eds), *Mirando a Clío. El arte español espejo de su historia. Actas del XVIII Congreso del CEHA, Santiago de Compostela, 20-24 de septiembre de 2010*, Santiago de Compostela, 2012, 1501-13

M. Moralejo Ortega, 'El Obispo Diego de Simancas y su papel como virrey en Nápoles', *Librosdelacorte.es* 4 (2012) 141-53

S. Pastore, art. 'Simancas, Diego de', in *Dizionario storico dell'Inquisizione*, Pisa, 2010, iii, 1430-31

J.L. Bermejo Cabrero, 'Apuntamientos sobre la vida y escritos de Diego de Simancas', in S. de Dios, J. Infante, and E. Torijano (eds), *El derecho y los juristas en Salamanca (siglos XVI-XX). En memoria de Francisco Tomás y Valiente*, Salamanca, 2004, 567-87

S. Pastore, *Il Vangelo e la Spada. L'Inquisizione di Castiglia e i suoi critici (1460-1598)*, Rome, 2003, pp. 210-14, 242-53

T. Sánchez Rivilla, 'Inquisidores generales y consejeros de la Suprema. Documentación biográfica', in J. Pérez Villanueva and B. Escandell Bonet (eds), *Historia de la Inquisición en España y América*, Madrid, 2000, iii, p. 417

J. Caro Baroja, *El Señor Inquisidor y otras vidas por oficio*, Madrid, 1968

M. Alcocer and S. Rivera, *Historia de la Universidad de Valladolid: Bio-bibliografías de juristas notables*, Valladolid, 1924, p. 38

N. Antonio, *Bibliotheca hispana nova*, ed. M. Ruffini, Turin, 1963, i, 316-17

WORKS ON CHRISTIAN-MUSLIM RELATIONS

Institutiones Catholicae, 'Catholic Institutes'

DATE 1552, revised 1568-75
ORIGINAL LANGUAGE Latin

DESCRIPTION

Diego de Simancas's *Institutiones Catholicae* (in full, *Institutiones Catholicae quibus ordine ac brevitate diseritur quicquid ad praecavendas & extirpandas haereses necessarium est*) is a manual for inquisitors, designed for use in a Catholic legal institution that tried heresy as a crime. Simancas described how he composed his first draft after he began working as a legal consultant for the Spanish Inquisition in Valladolid in 1545 and found there to be an insufficient number of reference works of inquisitorial law (*Vida*, pp. 151-52). The first printed edition of the book, published in Valladolid in 1552, is 230 folios in length, organised into 64 alphabetically-ordered chapters. Each chapter considers an element of inquisitorial procedure or category of personnel, a possible jurisdiction of inquisition courts or category of heretical crime. Simancas adopts the form of a legal handbook, and assembles authorities and precedents through which to examine each point. He cites biblical texts, canon law, Church councils, Church fathers, and a range of ancient Greek and Roman writers, as well as more recent humanists and legal, theological and anti-heretical commentators. He occasionally mentions his own experience and observations. Among the longest and most complex chapters are those on the confiscation of heretics' goods (tit. 9, 32 folios), on witnesses (tit. 62, 9 folios), and on judicial torture (tit. 63, 9½ folios).

Christian-Muslim relations are a relatively minor part of the treatise. One of the many short chapters addresses Muslims ('De Mahumetanis', tit. 39, fols. 137r-138r). Divided into an introductory paragraph and three sub-points, roughly the first half of the chapter is dedicated to a pejorative and prejudicial definition of who Muslims are. Highly polemical in nature, it derides Muḥammad as an 'impostor' and a 'pseudoprophet', and the Qur'an as a 'collection of precepts' composed by him that contains many things contrary to the law of God. It portrays Muslims as the opposite of Christian ideals of the sacred, and heaps abuse on Islam and on Muḥammad. It uses stereotypical attacks, casting Muslim lands as marked by ignorance and superstition, lust and obscene crimes, and Islam as leading away from salvation, and producing no true holiness or miracles, contemplation of truth, or purity of heart. Simancas insists that truth compelled even Muḥammad to recognise Christ, and that Muslims recognise Mosaic law, even if they misunderstand its significance. In this chapter he cites fewer authorities than in others, referencing just the 15th-century tracts of Girolamo Savonarola and Denis the Carthusian to support his assault on Islam.

Beyond rehashing anti-Muslim polemics, Simancas primarily stresses that only those who have been baptised are subject to the jurisdiction of inquisitors. He explicitly describes Muslims and Jews as parallel cases, and praises the expulsion of both from Spanish lands. Thus he describes Spain as purged of infidels after 1502, guarded by a continuing diligent search for heretics, and he alleges that Spanish dominion over the people of the Indies is a reward by divine providence for this defence of the faith. He concludes the chapter with legal citations supporting inquisitorial jurisdiction over Christians who have converted to Islam (*sectam Saracenorum*) and their treatment as heretics and apostates, noting that royal statute allows the death penalty for the offence. He adds brief allusions to a series of controversial points in the writings of previous legal commentators: whether war against Muslims is justified when they are not living among Christians, in what circumstances the pope could try Muslims not under his rule, and whether Christians can use the aid of infidels in their own defence. Here Simancas refers his readers to, among others, the 14th-century canon law commentator Oldradus da Ponte, and the earlier 16th-century writings of the Spanish inquisitor and inquisitorial theorist Arnaldo Albertini.

Simancas makes a handful of other references to Islam and Muslims elsewhere in the book. The first sentence of the dedication to the future King Philip II (r. 1556-98) asserts Spain's exemplary Christian piety for having expelled not only Jews but also Muslims from its territory, a theme he repeats elsewhere (e.g. fol. 127r), and he seeks to show the monstrousness of Luther by describing him as even worse than Muḥammad (fol. 113 v). On the other hand, he reiterates another commentator's opinion that Jews are even worse than other infidels, and so creates a hierarchy of abusive claims, and notes that Oldradus had commented on the proposition that Jews who converted to Islam should not be punished (fol. 128r). He repeatedly notes that converts and their descendants might be suspected of heresy, describing them as more likely to do things that are unnatural because of the laws of their ancestors (he mentions circumcision, fol. 48r-v, cf. fol. 176r).

Simancas also notes varieties of suspicious behaviour that could be used as proof of heresy, such as Moriscos (those *ex genere Saracenorum*) who commit bigamy, thinking that Islamic law permits them to have more than one wife and so abusing the Catholic sacrament of marriage (fol. 138v), and converts who desire to die and be buried according to the rites of their ancestors and relatives. He contends that other open signs of heresy – and usable legal proofs – include 'adoring or celebrating the rites of Jews and Saracens', such as observing their fasts and ceremonies or saying their prayers, publicly stating heretical propositions, and worshipping the tomb of Muḥammad. He advocates the extremely harsh position that anyone who has abjured heresy (in a previous inquisitorial process) can be considered a relapsed heretic without hope of pardon if they associate with heretics, give them gifts, or show them favours (fols 184r, 186v).

When the first edition of the *Institutiones Catholicae* was published, Simancas was only an occasional legal consultant to a regional tribunal of the Spanish Inquisition. Over the course of his inquisitorial career, however, he continued to revise and augment his publications in accordance with his experience, his evolving thought, and the changing political and religious circumstances. As a royal councillor of the Spanish Inquisition and the judge in one of the most famous trials of his day, he used his inquisition manuals to lobby for his interpretations of inquisitorial law and good religious policy, and for the prestige and authority of the Spanish Inquisition. His busiest years of publication were those he spent in Rome during the Carranza case (1567-76). He published two new editions of his primary inquisition manual under the slightly revised title *De catholicis institutionibus* (in full, *De catholicis institutionibus liber ad praecavendas & extirpandas haereses admodum necessarius*); they were issued in Alcalá de Henares, Spain, in 1569, and in Rome in 1575. *De catholicis institutionibus* is a significant revision of the 1552 text, and there are additional smaller corrections and changes made for the final version. Both editions, which number 66 chapters, retain the alphabetical organisation of the 1552 volume, but add indices at the start of the volume and at the beginning of each chapter. The 1569 edition is 310 folios long, and the 1575 edition 522 pages. In general, Simancas clarifies his prose and makes his arguments more forceful.

In these revised editions, Simancas dedicates a similar amount of space to Islam and Muslims as he had in 1552, although he makes some notable revisions to the chapter *De Mahumetanis* (tit. 39, fols 177r-178v [1569]; pp. 291-93 [1575]). He retains the same general organization and emphases, broken into six indexed sub-points. There is evidence of attempts at clarification, as when he qualifies his statement that the conversion of a Catholic to Islam is a capital offence under royal law with the note that inquisitors instead use canon law (*iure pontificio*), under which such people are classified as apostates (and in that jurisdiction, it might be noted, not automatically subject to capital punishment if repentant). In his anti-Muslim polemic, he removes the mention of Muḥammad's recognition of Jesus, and adds his portrayal of Muslim beliefs about paradise and how it can be entered by killing or being killed in the service of Islam. He extends his condemnation of Muslim societies as purportedly dissolute and corrupt, adding references to Socrates and Aristotle to indict lascivious ways of life. He uses a typical image of Christian apologetics to describe Muḥammad as part of a throng who choose the wicked way (alongside Luther and other heretics), rather than Christ's narrow way which leads to salvation, and he lays even greater stress on Spain's evangelical role. He also drops the references to Oldradus, Albertini and Savonarola, and the mention of debated legal points, and he closes the chapter with citations of Nicholas of Cusa, Denis, Richard FitzRalph (Armacanus) and Juan Luis Vives. The 1569 and 1575 chapters are almost identical.

The coverage elsewhere in the new editions also retains similarities to the first edition. The 1569 edition contains the same dedication to Philip, although the 1575 dedication is to Gregory XIII, and makes no mention of Muslims. There are three index entries to Muslims, two to the principal chapter and the third directing readers to where Simancas had expanded his references to multiple marriage as a possible ingredient of apostasy to Islam (fol. 179v; pp. 295-96, respectively). He moderates his comments about relapsed heretics, removing the categorisation of some as without hope of pardon, but he retains his same general points about what ceremonies were signals of apostasy or heresy. He adds that a 'light' presumption of heresy could be made about Moriscos when they do not drink wine or eat pig's flesh or boar (e.g. fols 50r, 237r, 247r, 252r; pp. 84, 408, 416-17). He also adds the dictum that Christians should not have Jewish, Muslim or heretical servants, and should not themselves be servants to non-Christians (fol. 276v).

As he was revising the *Institutiones Catholicae*, Simancas also produced another format of inquisition law guide, his *Enchiridion Judicum violatae religionis*, explicitly labelled as a handbook of the theory and praxis of judging heresy. The *Enchiridion* is deliberately shaped as an abridged inquisitorial manual, geared to spread Simancas's views to the papal court and other Italian tribunals, as well as in the Spanish world. Printed in octavo format, four editions were issued, in Venice in 1568,

1569 and 1573, as well as in Antwerp in 1573. Unlike the *Institutiones Catholicae*, the chapters of the *Enchiridion* are ordered alphabetically, even though the 67 (Venice) or 68 (Antwerp) headings are similar to those in the longer treatise.

Unsurprisingly, the *Enchiridion* deals with Islam and Muslims even more briefly than the *Institutiones Catholicae*. The chapter *De Mahumetanis* (tit. 18) is arranged immediately to follow the chapter on Jews (*De Iudaeis*, tit. 17), underlining Simancas's view that they are parallel cases; he begins with the assertion that what he has written about the Jews and inquisitorial judgment applies also to Muslims (fol. 17r-v [1568]; fols 21v-22r [1573 Venice]). The chapter is very short, containing just two subpoints in which he first asserts the right of inquisitors to try any Christian convert to Islam as an apostate infidel (characterising Islam and Muslims in the most insulting terms, e.g. a 'bestial sect'), and secondly claims that Spain is an exemplary model to 'our unhappy world' for resisting heresy.

The *Institutiones Catholicae* and *Enchiridion* were reissued after Simancas's death. As part of Pope Gregory XIII's initiative to recompile and reissue the body of canon law, the *De catholicis institutionibus* was collected as one of 22 treatises in the volume dedicated to Inquisition law (*Tractatus illustrium in utraque tum Pontificii, tum Caesarei iuris facultate iurisconsultorum*, vol. 11, pt. 2 [Venice, 1584]), and the 1575 text was reprinted there in full, including the chapter *De Mahumetanis* (fol. 169r-v). A century later, the complete *De catholicis institutionibus* and *Enchiridion* (following the Rome and Venice editions, respectively) were reprinted in an annotated edition of Simancas's collected works (*Opera*, Ferrara, 1692; *De Mahumetanis*, pp. 264-65, 471-72). It appears that the manuals were not translated, nor were they reprinted after the end of the 17th century. Although recent scholarship has cited material from Simancas's inquisitorial manuals, they have received relatively little study.

SIGNIFICANCE

While Diego de Simancas's inquisition manuals devote relatively little space to Muslims and Islam, Simancas did not consider the topic unimportant, though it was one in which he added little to the existing debate, mainly recapitulating standard themes of Catholic polemic and showing by his demeaning and pejorative references his dismissive attitude towards Islam. He was primarily concerned to create a reference work for Catholic inquisition courts, and thus he presents Islam from the perspective of identifying and trying heretics in a nominally Catholic society. In inquisitorial law the matter was fairly clear-cut: apostasy from Christianity to Islam was a serious crime, but Muslims themselves were beyond the reach of inquisitorial jurisdiction.

There is some evidence that these points of law he makes were contested. Another Spanish inquisitor and inquisitorial theorist active in the 1560s and 1570s, Juan de Rojas, asserted that inquisitors could try Muslims and Jews who proselytised among the Christian population, performed Jewish or Islamic rites, or gave aid to heretics. Shaped by his experience as a judge in Valencia, where there was an especially substantial Morisco population, Rojas devoted more attention to such questions, and explicitly noted that he differed with Simancas on this (e.g. *Singularia iuris in favorem fidei*, Venice: Francesco Ziletti, 1583, fols 62v-63v).

Despite the minor place accorded to Islam in Simancas's manuals, he makes the importance of the theme clear. Muslims are explicitly likened to Jews, and Islam is sometimes mentioned in conjunction with Judaism and Protestantism, the most dangerous threat being Catholic conversion to any of these beliefs. Moreover, Islam plays a key role in Simancas's depiction of Spanish exceptionalism. He casts Spain as prominent in its defence of the Catholic faith for not tolerating infidels and expelling or mandating the conversion of its Muslim and Jewish minorities, and also for using the Spanish Inquisition to contain, prevent, and combat heretical threats (including apostasy to Islam among the Morisco population). For Simancas, the presence of a sizable population of Muslim descent made Spain even more admirable as a bastion of Catholicism in an era of intense politico-religious conflicts. And that population was, for him, yet one more argument for the legitimacy of the Spanish Inquisition's strategy of judicial management of religious orthodoxy. In sum, the primary significance of Simancas's *Institutiones Catholicae* and *Enchiridion* with regard to Christian-Muslim relations was their diffusion of circulating anti-Muslim stereotypes, and of the mandate for Catholic inquisition tribunals to try Christian apostasy to Islam as a serious crime.

EDITIONS & TRANSLATIONS

Opera Jacobi Simancae Episcopi Pacensis, et Postmodum Zamorensis Juriscons. Praestantiss. hoc est. De Catholicis Institutionibus Liber ad praecavendas, & extirpandas haereses admodum necessarius. Theorice, et Praxis Haereseos, Sive Enchiridion Judicum violatae Religionis. Annotationes in Zanchinum, Cum animadversionibus in Campegium, Et Liber Singularis de Patre Haeretico, Ferrara: Bernardino Pomatelli, 1692

De catholicis institutionibus liber ad praecavendas & extirpandas haereses admodum necessarius, in *Tractatus Illustrium in Utraque tum Pontificii, tum Caesarei Iuris facultate Iurisconsultorum, De Iudiciis Criminalibus S. Inquisitionios. Ex Multis in hoc Volumen Congesti,* fols 119r-208v. Volume 11, Part 2. Venice: Francesco Ziletti, 1584

De catholicis institutionibus liber ad praecavendas & extirpandas haereses admodum necessarius, Rome: in aedibus Populi Romani, 1575

Enchiridion Iudicum violatae religionis, ad extirpandas haeredes [sic], *theoricen & praxim... complectens... Cui accesserunt eiusdem auctoris opuscula duo: Unum, Annotationum in Zanchinum; Alterum de dignitate Episcopali*, Antwerp: Plantin, 1573

Theorice et praxis haereseos, sive Enchiridion Iudicum violatae religionis. Cui nunc primum accesserunt opuscula duo eiusdem argumenti, scilicet Annotationum, in Zanchinum, cum animadversionibus, in Campegium, liber singularis. De patre haeretico, liber singularis, eodem auctore... Venice: Giordano Ziletti, 1573

Enchiridion iudicum violatae religionis ad extirpandas haereses theoricen & praxim summa brevitate complectens...: cui accesserunt, eiusdem auctoris et argumenti, opuscula duo hactenus non impresa: unum annotationum in Zanchinum, alterum, de patre haeretico... Venice: Giordano Ziletti, 1569

De catholicis institutionibus liber, ad praecavendas & extirpandas haereses admodum necessarius, Alcalá de Henares: Andrea de Angulo, 1569

Praxis haereseos sive Enchiridion iudicum violatae religionis, Venice: Giordano Ziletti, 1568

Institutiones Catholicae quibus ordine ac brevitate diseritur quicquid ad praecavendas & extirpandas haereses necessarium est, Valladolid: Egidio de Colomies, 1552

STUDIES

K. Lynn, *Between court and confessional. The politics of Spanish inquisitors*, New York, 2013

J.L. Bermejo Cabrero, 'Apuntamientos sobre la vida y escritos de Diego de Simancas', in S. de Dios, J. Infante, and E. Torijano (eds), *El Derecho y los Juristas en Salamanca (Siglos XVI-XX). En Memoria de Francisco Tomás y Valiente*, Salamanca, 2004, 567-87

S. Pastore, *Il Vangelo e la Spada. L'Inquisizione di Castiglia e i suoi critici (1460-1598)*, Rome, 2003, pp. 210-14, 242-53

A. Errera, *'Processus in causa fidei'. L'evoluzione dei manuali inquisitoriali nei secoli XVI-XVIII e il manuale inedito di un inquisitore perugino*, Bologna, 2000

Kimberly Lynn

Fray Juan Bautista

Iuan Baptista, Giovanni Baptista

DATE OF BIRTH First half of the 16th century
PLACE OF BIRTH Unknown; Spain or Italy
DATE OF DEATH Second half of the 16th century
PLACE OF DEATH Unknown; possibly Morocco

BIOGRAPHY

Little is known about Fray Juan Bautista, a monk of the Order of Preachers or Dominicans, who wrote his *Chronica* while he was in the service of Muley 'Abd al-Malik (Abū Marwān 'Abd al-Malik I), probably after being taken captive. Although the *Chronica* is written in Spanish, it includes a sonnet in Italian at the end. Juan Bautista was thus probably Spanish, although an Italian origin cannot be discounted.

He must have entered 'Abd al-Malik's household during the latter's exile in Algiers (1557-75). Muley 'Abd al-Malik deployed significant diplomatic efforts in Istanbul to obtain from the Ottomans support for his claim to the Moroccan throne. He also engaged in a campaign to promote his claim in Spain through texts such as this panegyric, where he is portrayed as a learned and tolerant prince, and from which references to any any possible sources of conflict, including references to religion or to his alliance with the Ottomans, are omitted.

During his exile in Algiers, 'Abd al-Malik became acquainted with Andrea Gasparo Corso, an agent of Philip II of Spain (who was later commissioned to print the *Chronica* in Valencia, where his family was based, and who indeed paid for the edition). Fray Juan Bautista also became acquainted with Andrea Gasparo Corso, to whom he addressed a letter in reference to the panegyric, signed 'your servant and chaplain'. Both Fray Juan Bautista and Andrea Gasparo Corso participated in building up 'Abd al-Malik's image as a potential ally against the expansion of the Ottoman Empire, and as a man well acquainted with the culture and languages of the Christian kingdoms.

This is the only known work of Fray Juan Bautista, and it is unknown whether he ever returned to his homeland or remained in North Africa.

MAIN SOURCES OF INFORMATION

Primary
Chrónica de la vida y admirables hechos del muy alto y muy poderoso señor Muley Abdelmelech, Emperador de Marruecos y Rey de los reinos de Fez, Mequines y Sus, y del victoriosíssimo successo de la restauración de todos ellos, [Vallencia ?], 1577
M. García-Arenal, 'Textos españoles sobre Marruecos en el siglo XVI. Fr. Juan Bautista y su Chrónica de Muley Abdelmelech', *Al-Qanṭara* 2 (1981) 167-92

Secondary
M.A. Garcés, *Cervantes in Algiers. A captive tale*, Nashville, 2002, 51-54
B.E. Ogot, *General history of Africa*, vol. 5. *Africa from the sixteenth to the eighteenth century*, Berkeley CA, 1992, 200-33

WORKS ON CHRISTIAN-MUSLIM RELATIONS

Chronica de la vida y admirables hechos del muy alto y poderoso Señor Muley Abd el Melech, 'Chronicle of the life and remarkable deeds of the most high and powerful lord Prince Abdel Melech'
Chronica de Abdel Melech, 'Chronicle of Abdel Melech'

DATE 1577
ORIGINAL LANGUAGE Spanish

DESCRIPTION
The *Chronica de Abdel Melech* (in full *Chronica de la vida y admirables hechos del muy alto y poderoso Señor Muley Abd el Melech, emperador de Marruecos y Rey de los reinos de Fez, Mequines y Sus, y del victoriosíssimo successo de la restauración de todos ellos*) is a panegyric that was written by Fray Juan Bautista at the request of the Moroccan king Mulay 'Abd al-Malik, first ruler of the Saʿdī dynasty. It is a short work of 54 folios, including two opening and two closing sonnets (the last in Italian), 14 pages in prose dedicated to 'Abd al-Malik's life, from his exile to his conquest of Morocco and his triumphant entry into Marrakesh, and 30 pages in verse, reiterating the story of 'Abd al-Malik's conquest in a more epic manner.

The book was intended for a Spanish audience and the objective was to portray the Muslim ruler as heroic, learned and wise, with great affinity for, and interest in, the Christian powers of the day. This positive image, and particularly his openness towards Christianity, was aimed at facilitating diplomatic relations with Spain.

There is no mention in the work of any possible points of conflict between the Christian and Muslim faiths, and the few references to religion in the text follow the conventions of the period: thus, 'Abd al-Malik's victory is achieved by God, *Salieron todos [...] alabando a Dios que los había favorecido* ('They left, with thanks to God, who had favoured them...'); after the conquest, the realm is at peace thanks to God, who is entreated to make it longlasting: *con mucha paz y quietud, en que lo conserve Dios Nuestro Señor, el qual le augmente el poder y estado muchos años con perpetua victoria y triumpho* ('with peace and calmness, may they be preserved by God our Lord, and may he increase his ['Abd al-Malik's] power and state for many years with everlasting victory and triumph').

In the same way, the Ottoman Sultan Selim II, from whom 'Abd al-Malik requests justice against his brother, who has ordered him to be killed, is described as a 'great lord' who has the 'obligation to deliver justice'. Justice is also an attribute of 'Abd al-Malik, who, on entering Marrakesh, 'shows severity in punishing bad subjects as much as generosity in favouring good ones'.

The only explicit mentions of Islam are the brief description of 'Īd al-Kabīr (*la fiesta del cordero*), and of Friday as 'a festive day' (*día de fiesta*) dedicated to God through prayer (*la çala*).

SIGNIFICANCE

The overall tone of the work presents relations between Christian and Muslim kingdoms and their leaders as open and fluid, and religious differences are ignored in favour of recounting the virtues shared by great rulers. Islamic elements are relegated to the background, as diplomacy and political alliances or hostilities prevail over religious attitudes.

In this respect, the *Chronica* reflects some of the main preoccupations of the period. Where diplomacy or trade were involved, Christian-Muslim differences were set aside, and the main focus was political affairs. Most of the references by Christians to Islamic beliefs and practices were descriptive and devoid of criticism and confrontation, though it has to be noted that many of the traders and diplomats who travelled from Europe to Morocco did not have any extensive religious training that would enable them to engage in dispute or polemic, nor was this the purpose of their journeys.

MANUSCRIPTS
> MS London, BL – 1046-g-26 (1577)
> MS Paris, BNF – 03j51 (1577)

EDITIONS & TRANSLATIONS
> M. García-Arenal, M.A. de Bunes Ibarra, and V. Aguilar, *Repertorio bibliográfico de las relaciones entre la península Ibérica y el Norte de África (siglos XV-XVI). Fuentes y bibliografía*, Madrid, 1989
>
> B. Loupias, 'Crónica de la vida y admirables hechos del señor Abdelmelech [Valence?] 1577. Oeuvre en prose et en vers, de Fray Bautista', *Hespéris tamuda* 24 (1986) 53-212 (edition of the second part, French trans. and notes)
>
> P. Berthier and B. Loupias, 'Chrónica de la vida y admirables hechos del señor Muley Abdelmelech [Valence?] 1577. Oeuvre en prose et en vers, de Fray Bautista' [first part], *Hespéris tamuda* 23 (1985) 129-78 (new edition of the *Chronicle*, following that of M. García-Arenal, with French trans.)
>
> García-Arenal, 'Textos españoles' (partial edition)

STUDIES
> Berthier and Loupias, 'Chrónica de la vida'
> García-Arenal, 'Textos españoles'

Barbara Ruiz-Bejarano

Fray Luis Nieto

DATE OF BIRTH Unknown; 16th century
PLACE OF BIRTH Unknown; Spain
DATE OF DEATH Unknown; after 1579
PLACE OF DEATH Unknown

BIOGRAPHY

Nothing is known about the Dominican Fray Luis Nieto, apart from a reference to his *Relación de las guerras de Berbería* in R. Martínez Vigil, *La orden de Predicadores. Sus glorias en Santidad, Apostolado, Ciencias, Artes y Gobierno de los Pueblos. Seguidas de un Ensayo de una Biblioteca de Dominicos españoles*, Madrid, 1884.

At the beginning of the *Relación* he says that he wishes to dedicate to King Philip of Spain 'something from here', so he was possibly in charge of redeeming Christian prisoners in Morocco for a time before he wrote his short work.

MAIN SOURCES OF INFORMATION

Primary
'Relación de las guerras de Berbería y del suceso y muerte del Rey D. Sebastián', in F. Ramírez de Arellano, J. Sancho Rayón and F. Zabálburu (eds), *Colección de documentos inéditos para la historia de España*, Madrid, 1891, c, 419-58

WORKS ON CHRISTIAN-MUSLIM RELATIONS

Relación de las guerras de Berbería y del suceso y muerte del Rey D. Sebastián, 'Account of the wars of Barbary and the feats and death of King Sebastian'
Guerras de Berbería, 'Wars of Barbary'

DATE 1579
ORIGINAL LANGUAGE Spanish

DESCRIPTION

The *Relación de las guerras de Berbería* is an account of the Battle of Al-Ksar el-Kebir (*Alcazarquebir*), which took place on 4 August 1578 (for the date of the work, see De la Veronne, *Les sources inédites*, pp. 274-76). It is known as the Battle of the Three Kings because of the kings who died in the course of it. Dedicated to King Philip of Spain, the *Relación* is effectively a panegyric of King Sebastian of Portugal. In the 1891 edition, the text is just under 40 pages long. According to Hermann, it was first published outside Spain, in Paris, as 'in order to avoid implying that the Spanish king was promoting the printing of texts that portrayed King Sebastian and the Portuguese nobility in a negative way' ('El Ksar El-Kebir').

The *Relación* is divided into 14 chapters. It begins with a series of chapters on the rulers of Morocco, and the events that led up to the battle (chs 1-9). It then gives an account of the battle, the death of King Sebastian and the efforts to recover his body (chs 10-12), and it concludes with a reference to the Christians who were taken prisoner, and subsequent events in Morocco (chs 13-14). Fray Nieto's comment makes clear why he thinks so many Christians suffered: 'Our Lord sent such a painful punishment on the Christians, because of our many sins, that some two hundred men were enslaved, and some twelve thousand Christians were dead.'

SIGNIFICANCE

Fray Nieto depicts the fighting in North Africa in religious terms, as an opportunity to expand Christendom, and he presents King Sebastian as the model of a Christian ruler. But not everyone revered him as his followers did. His body disappeared at some point while it was awaiting return to Portugal, leading to the emergence of 'Sebastianism', a legend about this disappearance. It was celebrated by the Jews of Fes, who interpreted the Portuguese defeat and the extinction of the royal line (Sebastian had no descendants) as a divine punishment for the expulsion of the Jews from Portugal. The day of the battle was named 'Purim Sebastiano' or 'Purim of Christians', and it is still celebrated in Fes, Tetouan, Tangiers and elsewhere in the north of Morocco.

MANUSCRIPTS

MS Madrid, BNE – 2860 (*olim* I-161), 78 fols (16th century; includes a map of the battle, which does not appear in the printed edition)

EDITIONS & TRANSLATIONS

H. de Castries, *Les sources inédites de l'histoire du Maroc de 1530 à 1845*, Paris, 1905, i, pp. 437-505 (French trans.)

'Relación de las guerras de Berbería y del suceso y muerte del Rey D. Sebastián', in F. Ramírez de Arellano, J. Sancho Rayón and F. Zabálburu (eds) *Colección de documentos inéditos para la historia de España*, Madrid, 1891, c, pp. 419-58

STUDIES

J. Hermann. 'El Ksar El-Kebir. Narrativas e histórica sebástica na Batalha dos Três Reis. Marrocos, 1578', *História. Questôes e Debates* 45 (2006) 11-28

C. de la Veronne, *Les sources inédites de l'histoire du Maroc*, 1961, iii, pp. 474-76 ('Relation de la bataille del Ksar el-Kebir', account of the battle in French); 476-88 ('Respuesta a la carta de un abad de Vera', another account in Spanish); 489-528 ('Liste des gentilshommes portugais tués et faits prisonniers à la bataille d'El-Ksar el-Kebir', in French)

E.W. Bovill, *The Battle of Alcazar. An account of the defeat of Don Sebastian of Portugal at El-Ksar el-Kebir*, London, 1952

J. Oliver Asín. 'La hija de Agi Morato en la obra de Cervantes', *Boletín de la Real Academia Española* 27 (1947-8) 245-339

Barbara Ruiz-Bejarano

Pedro Guerra de Lorca

DATE OF BIRTH Early 16th century
PLACE OF BIRTH Granada
DATE OF DEATH 1597
PLACE OF DEATH Granada

BIOGRAPHY

In *Catecheses* (1586), the only one of his works that has been edited, Pedro Guerra de Lorca says that he is from Granada and a doctor of theology. At the end of the 'Vita Mahomedi' in this work, he says that he is from the Sanctillano valley of the 'Herrerae de Hibio' (fol. 7v), which was presumably near the town of Lorca on the frontier between Murcia and Granada. Lorca's learning is evident enough: his Latin is excellent, he cites the Complutense Bible in Greek (fol. 68v), and he possesses an impressive mastery of theological, polemical and legal works. In addition to *Catecheses mystagogicae*, he wrote two other works, both extant but neither edited.

More can be said about Lorca on the basis of these works. A.K. Harris identifies Lorca as one of the earliest authors of Granada's religious history, which sought to establish its ancient Christian identity. He was the son of an administrator in the Alhambra, held lucrative benefices, and was known as an excellent preacher for which he was appointed canon in the cathedral in 1588 (*From Muslim to Christian Granada*, p. 56; references below are to this work). He was the author of *La historia de la vida y martyrio de Sant Çecilio* (1584), and *Memorias eclesiásticas de la ciudad de Granada* (pp. 56-57). Among other themes, *Memorias* links the founding of Granada to Jews expelled by Nebuchadnezzar II, as in the Book of Daniel, and it includes discourses on the roots of the Castilian and Arabic languages, and on Christian martyrs during the second Alpujarras rebellion (pp. 57-58).

In *Un oriente español* (2010), M. García-Arenal and F. Rodríguez Mediano place Lorca at the heart of the Sacromonte affair. He served as emissary for Archbishop Pedro de Castro, who sent him to the scholar Arias Montano to evaluate the parchment of the Torre Turpiana. Despite strong criticisms (including from Montano himself), in *Memorias* Lorca defended its authenticity (pp. 54-56). Considering his close collaboration with Miguel de Luna, one of the fabricators of the false documents, García-Arenal and Rodríguez Mediano suggest Lorca may actually have indirectly participated in their fabrication (p. 180).

MAIN SOURCES OF INFORMATION

Primary
Pedro Guerra de Lorca, *Catecheses pro aduenis ex secta Mahometana. Ad parochos, & potestates*, Madrid: Apud Petrum Madrigal, 1586

Secondary
M. García-Arenal and F. Rodríguez Mediano, *Un oriente español. Los moriscos y el Sacromonte en tiempos de Contrarreforma*, Madrid, 2010
J. Busic, 'Saving the lost sheep. Mission and culture in Pedro Guerra de Lorca's *Catecheses pro aduenis ex secta Mahometana. Ad parochos, et potestates* (1586)', Columbus, 2009 (Diss. Ohio State University)
K.A. Harris, *From Muslim to Christian Granada. Inventing a city's past in early modern Spain*, Baltimore MD, 2007
J. Caro Baroja, *Los moriscos del reino de Granada. Ensayo de historia social*, Madrid, 2003 (repr. of 2000[5])
M. Barrios Aguilera, *Granada morisca, la convivencia negada. Historia y textos*, Granada, 2002
A.H. Sánchez, 'Catecismos para la instrucción de los moriscos', Salamanca, 1955 (Diss. Pontifical Ecclesiastical University of Salamanca)

WORKS ON CHRISTIAN-MUSLIM RELATIONS

Catecheses mystagogicae pro aduenis ex secta Mahometana. Ad parochos, & potestates, 'Catechisms of instruction for those coming from the Muḥammadan sect. To pastors and authorities' *Catecheses mystagogicae*, 'Catechisms of instruction'

DATE   1586
ORIGINAL LANGUAGE   Latin

DESCRIPTION
Pedro Guerra de Lorca published his *Catecheses mystagogicae* in 1586. There was only ever one edition, presumably because only 33 years after it appeared the final expulsions of Muslims from Spain began (1609), and

because the political context had changed after the Second Rebellion of the Alpujarras (1568-71). Lorca's aggressive evangelical-assimilationist approach was probably met with some scepticism by the secular and ecclesiastical authorities, due to the violence the rebellion had led to in Granada. Nonetheless, the work appears to have enjoyed modest success in distribution. Lorca wrote principally for ecclesiastical authorities in Castile who had received the Moriscos of Granada after King Philip II had ordered them to be moved during the rebellion in the Alpujarras in 1570. Lorca did not think these authorities were properly equipped to receive the Muslims.

Catecheses is 176 folios long. The introductory material includes an address to King Philip II, an exhortatory epistle to bishops and pastors, a polemical biography of the Prophet Muḥammad, a *scholia* on the same, an alphabetical list of the 'errors of the false Muḥammad', and 'On the errors of Muḥammad'. In his address to Philip II, Lorca encourages the king to join him in the continued evangelical mission to the Moriscos, while the exhortatory epistle reminds bishops and pastors of the grave responsibility they were given at their ordination. The remaining sections of the introduction describe Muḥammad, the Qur'an and Muslims according to the traditional Latin polemic against Islam, together with some references to Eulogius, the 9th-century priest who had written about the martyrs of Cordova, Lorca's source for the polemical biography.

The rest of the work consists of 16 catechisms related to the instruction and assimilation of the Moriscos. Their titles testify to the breadth and exhaustive nature of Lorca's project: 'On abjuring the sect of Muḥammad', 'On abandoning dress and language', 'On avoiding invocation to the devil', 'On abolishing circumcision', 'On fleeing fornication', 'On combatting other rites of the Muḥammadan sect', 'On avoiding superstition concerning food', 'On prohibiting communion with the Saracens', 'On making a proselyte from the Muḥammadan sect', 'On the instruction of children', 'On catechising the unlearned', 'On caring for the dead', 'On laws issued and to be issued', 'On punishing heretics', 'On the spiritual governance of proselytes', and 'On the temporal governance of proselytes'. As is evident from these titles, Lorca envisions a mission that involves both ecclesiastical and secular authorities, and that goes beyond doctrinal instruction. However, the polemical bent of the titles hides rich material about Granada's natives, such as descriptions of traditional Morisco dress, wedding celebrations, child-rearing, magic and dying.

Few catechisms for the Moriscos combine such a variety of source material as the *Catecheses*. With regard to polemic, Lorca uses traditional and non-traditional sources on Islam, though all are secondary. His 'Vita Mahomedi' is excerpted from Eulogius of Cordova's (d. 859) *Apologeticus martyrum* (16-20) and *Memoriale sanctorum* (1:20), which Eulogius wrote in defence of the Christian martyrs of the 850s in Cordova. Eulogius's works, together with his *Vita* (written by fellow apologist Alvarus of Cordova), had been published by Ambrosio de Morales in 1574. Of particular interest is Lorca's inclusion of historically inaccurate material, despite having access to more reliable sources. For example, the apocryphal biography of the Prophet that Eulogius encountered at the Monastery of Leire speaks of Muḥammad's hideous death, his claim that he would rise again after three days, and how his followers buried his remains after the stench had attracted dogs that made off with many parts of his corpse. Another example is his adoption of two contradictory polemical points in the 'Errors of Muḥammad': either Mary conceived by Joseph, or, if she did not, she would be Muḥammad's spouse in paradise (fol. 9r). The latter point comes from Eulogius's *Memoriale* (1:7), and Lorca makes no effort to resolve the contradiction.

Lorca draws on other texts as well. He cites the Qur'an at some length, but there is no evidence of his proficiency in Arabic, save colloquial expressions he probably learned in the streets of Granada. He cites it *in latinum sermonem verso* (fol. 77r), which is surely Robert of Ketton's translation from the 12th century; in 'De erroribus Mahomedi' he uses ch. 1 of Riccoldo da Monte di Croce's (d. 1320) *Confutatio alcorani*, and in the ninth catechism he uses ch. 6 of this work. He also cites Juan Luis Vives's 'Contra sectam Mahometi', the fourth book of *De veritate fidei Christianae*, published in 1543 (fols 29v, 86v). He was probably taking his references from Theodore Bibliander's (d. 1564) collection of polemic against Islam, published in 1543 and 1550.

While he does rely on secondary sources for his knowledge of Islam, his use of these sources is no mere repetition: he weaves them together in a way that both polemicises against Islam and advocates missionary efforts to the Moriscos. For example, through Eulogius's works and the martyr movement to which Eulogius gives voice, Lorca calls on the intercession of these 'saints' for successful mission among the Moriscos who are lost to the 'lies of Muḥammad' (fol. 7r-v). He thus makes evangelisation both a legacy and a responsibility. This is original use of polemic.

Catecheses also bring together a sizable body of canon and secular law, both ancient and more recent. From the Catholic Monarchs onwards, Lorca cites laws pertaining to the governance of the Moriscos and to those ministers who dealt directly with this minority group, such as judges and magistrates.

Lorca wrote after the Second Rebellion of the Alpujarras, which scholars have sometimes termed the 'point of no return'. Voices in favour of a general expulsion of Muslims were increasing, even among clergy (most notably Juan de Ribera, Archbishop of Valencia). Furthermore, while the forced distribution of the Moriscos of Granada throughout Castile was intended to encourage their assimilation, it often had the effect of increasing suspicion regarding the sincerity of the faith of even the assimilated native Moriscos of Castile. Indeed, the new arrivals brought with them 'Islamic' knowledge, not least of which was the use of Arabic, and they might teach Castilian Moriscos about their ancestral faith. However, recent scholarship following in the legacy of F.M. Villanueva's *El problema morisco* (1991) has shown that the three decades preceding the expulsion of 1609 were an intense time of debate, and that many authorities favoured continued evangelical efforts. Scholars such as Coleman, Ehlers, Fuchs, Fuster, García-Arenal, Harris, Latorre, Pedraza and Tueller, among others, have shown the complexity of Spain's treatment of this minority. The greatest significance of the *Catecheses* arises from its part within this debate.

Catecheses falls within the post-Tridentine environment of pastoral reform, of which Granada was a flagship under Archbishop Pedro Guerrero (r. 1546-76) – Lorca speaks fondly about him in his work. Lorca's position regarding the Moriscos is clearly that of persistent hope for their full incorporation into Christian society through evangelisation and assimilation, even the Moriscos of Granada who had recently rebelled against their king. He envisions a society where such division no longer exists, for example, in the thirteenth catechism, insisting that Moriscos who 'are found to be faithful imitators of Christ' (i.e. who assimilate in habits, dress and language) should be treated in exactly the same way as Christians who were not converts (fols 125v-126r). Indeed, he even suggests that children of convicted heretics should not be deprived of their material goods, if they prove to be good Christians (fol. 126r).

Notwithstanding these overtures, Lorca avoids any sense of a 'soft hand'; he has too much experience for that. Thus, the way children of heretics may prove their Christian faith is by testifying against their parents (fols 126r-127v). In 'De doctrina puerorum' (catechism 10), he explains how Morisco parents make their children wait in the streets in order to warn them if a priest is approaching (fol. 94r). Alleging in this catechism that some Moriscos avoid having all their children baptised by offering the same baby seven times, he provides instructions for priests and penalties for parents (fol. 92r-v). He advocates that a boy should be separated from his mother between the ages of five and 12, 'so that he be formed as a strenuous athlete of Christ, fighting manly against his fleshly and spiritual enemies' (fol. 93r). Along with the need for the catechist to promote a love for learning by kindness and reward, he must keep a record of his young charges and punish those who do not faithfully attend and participate in religious instruction (fol. 93v). Lorca's approach to catechesis for Morisco adults is similarly stringent (catechism 11).

Catholic Christianity for Lorca is both a religious and cultural issue: to be Christian means to assimilate into Old Christian society. The second catechism, 'De habitu, & lengua relegandis', is a treatise against Morisco dress and Arabic that addresses the argument of some 'who believe they know something concerning this matter', and argue that these practices are regional rather than religious (fol. 24v). Lorca begins the catechism with Ephesians 4:20-24 calling the Moriscos to 'put on Christ'. He takes liberty with the Paul's message, concluding that it points to the popular proverb, *Tal deue el hombre ser, como quiere parecer* ('a man is as he wishes to appear', fol. 24v). He addresses clothes, body art, jewellery and hairstyle, and shows how each is linked to the Islamic past. For example, shoes are easy to remove because Muslims cannot enter the mosque with them on; clothes are light and loose in order to lend flexibility for Muslim prayer; women wear enticing clothes and keep their hair short to indulge their carnal desires with their men. Indeed, as he says, in conversation with pious proselytes even the Moriscos themselves admit that it would have been best had the Catholic Monarchs imposed restrictions against these cultural practices early on (fol. 28r-v). Lorca's argument against Arabic is similar, since it is used in sacred texts as well as magic, and it serves as a reminder of the Moriscos' Islamic past.

Despite the wholesale condemnation of Morisco traditions in the fifth catechism, Lorca refuses to make blanket judgments about the Moriscos themselves and insists on proper discrimination. In the first catechism, 'De secta Mahomedi abiuranda', he divides these New Christians into four groups. In the first he includes those who have accepted baptism, but who maintain the dress, language, names, ceremonies and rites of the 'sect' of Muḥammad. In the second he categorises the New Christians who have renounced the external elements of their former life and adjusted 'to the Christians' (fol. 20v). In the third group, the most threatening, are those who trace their lineage from Arabia or Africa, and continue to observe their former practices. The final group is those born in mixed marriages. Concerning these, Lorca cites the Fourth Council of Toledo (633) regarding children born from a mixed union between Christian and Jew, one of the more marked examples of his archaic use of medieval canon law. More important, however, is his purpose in this categorisation: he wishes, 'in the manner of an expert physician', to prepare the appropriate medicine (fol. 20v). This explains the different approaches in the various catechisms, as well as why some argue that the Moriscos are no more than crypto-Muslims, while others proclaim them faithful Christians who should receive the appropriate legal rights.

Such discrimination requires knowledge, though the nature of that knowledge has been debated. L. Cardaillac characterises the *Catecheses* as a repetition of medieval Christian polemic against Islam and alleges Lorca's ignorance of Islam (*Moriscos*, pp. 319-20). Cantarino briefly addresses the work as notable for *el conocimiento que demuestra de costumbres moriscas* ('the knowledge that it shows of Morisco customs'), together with its exhaustive treatment of the Morisco problem ('Notas', pp. 140-41). Baroja (*Los moriscos*) and Longás (*La vida*) corroborate Cantarino's thesis. Longás cites the *Catecheses* as a source for Morisco wedding customs and burial practices (*Vida religiosa*, pp. 285, 288).

Lorca's reliance on secondary sources for Islamic doctrine does not translate into ignorance of Morisco cultural practices, even if his interpretation of their religious significance is erroneous. For example, the fifth catechism, 'De fornicatione fugienda', contains polemic against the alleged licentious nature of Islamic marriage and paradise. This discussion contextualises, however, a brilliant description of a Morisco wedding celebration. As he discusses the meals, he exclaims, 'If the food that they serve according to custom was not bound up with so much superstition, it should be served on the royal table' (fol. 56r).

We are a far cry from an author with 'no knowledge', as Cardaillac argues. While Lorca's prose is militant (his passages on Morisco weddings are exceptional in this respect), he bases much of it on observation. He discusses Morisco practices regarding dress, magic, rearing of the young, dying and burial, and so on in a polemical yet informed way. He often declares, as in the twelfth catechism, 'Since I have witnessed this, I commit it to writing' (fol. 111r). This knowledge he puts at the service of the two principles in which he believed: the greatness of Christian Spain, and the power of the evangelical message.

Lorca's wholehearted faith in Spain and the Gospel meant for him that lack of success in the mission to the Moriscos must be due to the failure of the Christian authorities, not the foundations of the undertaking itself. Lorca directs his most violent language against poorly motivated priests, lax secular authorities, and Christian lords. The threats of damnation in the 'Epistola exhortatoria' suggest at the outset Lorca's suspicion of some of his fellow clergy, and he blames lack of priestly attentiveness for allowing the Moriscos to avoid baptising all their young. In the twelfth catechism, 'De cura pro mortuis gerenda', he even portrays the New Christians as victims of corrupt priests who refuse to administer the final sacraments due to suspicion of the sincerity of the Moriscos' faith (fol. 118v). In the final catechism, 'De regimine temporali proselytorum', Lorca decries the common practice of dissimulation by secular authorities charged with imposing royal pragmatics against Morisco customs such as dress and use of the Arabic language (fols 150v-151v). His invective condemns these judges for their insubordination to the king and faithlessness to their responsibilities towards God. Lorca's words for Christian lords in Granada who wish for the natives to return are no kinder: they would sooner provide for their own comfort than the salvation of their Christian brethren (fol. 81v).

SIGNIFICANCE

Catecheses sheds light on the Morisco problem as authorities debated the fate of these New Christians in the final decades before their expulsion. As a text, it reveals the complexity both of the Moriscos and of the vision of a Christian leadership that sought the full incorporation of these New Christians into the Church and Spain's dominant culture, as well as the barriers they saw in the way of this goal. It also testifies to the deep sense of pastoral responsibility among Spanish clergy after the Council of Trent. Furthermore, Lorca's text shows how medieval polemic against Islam could be used in new contexts in innovative ways. While the major themes do not change, their employment in the early-modern context of Spain changes their meaning. Christian knowledge of Islam now has an immediate application, the evangelisation of the Moriscos, and may even serve, as in the case of Eulogius and the martyrs of Cordova, to legitimise the continuation of these evangelical efforts in troubled post-Alpujarras Spain. For all these reasons, Lorca's *Catecheses* richly increase understanding of the Christian encounter with Islam and the very concept of 'catechesis' in early modern Spain.

EDITIONS & TRANSLATIONS

J. Busic, 'Saving the lost sheep. Mission and culture in Pedro Guerra de Lorca's *Catecheses pro aduenis ex secta Mahometana: ad parochos, et potestates* (1586)', Columbus, 2009 (Diss. Ohio State University) (includes an appended translation that should be considered a draft in need of further revision)

A.H. Sánchez. 'Catecismos para la instrucción de los moriscos', Salamanca, 1955 (Diss. Pontifical Ecclesiatical University of Salamanca) (includes long citations in Latin throughout ch. 4, pp. 143-75)

P. Longás, *Vida religiosa de los moriscos*, Madrid, 1915 (contains Spanish trans. of sections from the first, fifth and twelfth catechisms)

P.G. de Lorca, *Catecheses pro aduenis ex secta Mahometana: ad parochos, & potestates*, Madrid: Apud Petrum Madrigal, 1586, http://www.cervantesvirtual.com/obra/catecheses-mystagogicae-pro-aduenis-ex-secta-mahometana-ad-parochos-potestates/

STUDIES

García-Arenal and Rodríguez Mediano, *Un oriente español*
Busic, 'Saving the lost sheep'
Harris, *From Muslim to Christian Granada*
Caro Baroja, *Los moriscos del reino de Granada*
Barrios Aguilera, *Granada morisca*
A. García Pedraza, *Actitudes ante la muerte en la Granada del siglo XVI. Los moriscos que quisieron salvarse*, 2 vols, Granada, 2002
V. Cantarino, 'Notas para la polémica contra el Islam en España', in *Spanien und der oriente im Frühen und Hohen Mittelalter. Kolloquium Berlin*, Mainz, 1991, 127-41
L. Cardaillac, *Moriscos y cristianos. Un enfrentamiento polémico, 1492-1640*, Madrid, 1979
L. Cardaillac, *Morisques et Chrétiens. Un affrontement polémique (1492-1640)*, Paris, 1977
Sánchez, 'Catecismos para la instrucción de los moriscos'
Longás, *Vida religiosa de los moriscos*

Jason Busic

Diego de Torres

DATE OF BIRTH 1526
PLACE OF BIRTH Amusco, Tierra de Campos, Palencia
DATE OF DEATH After 1579
PLACE OF DEATH Unknown

BIOGRAPHY

Little is known about the life of Diego de Torres, apart from what he recounts in *Relación del origen y sucesso de los Xarifes*, and especially in ch. 54. In August 1544, at the age of 18, he travelled to Seville in order to go abroad and find out about the world. In Seville he met Nicolás Núñez, who persuaded him to go to North Africa to join his son-in-law, Fernán Gómez de Almodóvar, who was working to rescue prisoners held by the Moors. Torres made his way to Marrakesh, arriving in June 1546, and was immediately presented to the Saʿdī Sultan, Muḥammad al-Shaykh.

Torres remained in the Saʿdī court for eight years as *alfaqueque*, rescuer of captives. First, he assisted Fernán Gómez, and he later carried on alone. He learnt Arabic, and became a friend and favourite of one of Muḥammed al-Shaykh's youngest sons, ʿAbd al-Muʾmin (ch. 77). As an eyewitness of the daily life of the Christians in the kingdom, merchants as well as prisoners, he relates many stories, including one about the secret church he set up in a house in Marrakesh (ch. 78).

In 1550, he was preparing to return to Spain, when a Jewish courtier who dealt with the finances of the Xarife, made him responsible for the debts that his predecessor, Fernán Gómez, had left. He was moved to Tarudante, and was held captive there for more than a year and a half until he was freed in 1553. He made his way to Fez, where he witnessed the taking of the city by Abū Ḥassun, ruler of Vélez, with the support of the Turks, and he devoted himself to rescuing the Xerife's prisoners, who had been abandoned in the city after its destruction. In 1554, he was allowed to go to Castile to raise money for this. He says that he was in Toledo in 1560 and in Seville in 1573, probably working on the history he had started in the Saʿdī court and which he finished before 1575.

In February 1577, as part of the preparations for the Alcazarquivir campaign, King Philip II sent Torres and Francisco de Aldana, disguised as Jewish merchants, to reconnoitre the country around Fez in order to help Philip decide whether to participate in the campaign planned by his nephew, Don Sebastian, King of Portugal. Torres arrived back in Lisbon in January 1578, and advised Don Sebastian to go to war, although this was against the general opinion.

In August 1578, Torres himself took part in the Alcazarquivir campaign, although not in the battle known as the Battle of the River Mejazén, or Battle of the Three Kings because of the three kings who died in it. He informed King Philip II about this catastrophe in a letter sent from Lisbon on 21 August 1578, also seeking permission to return to Africa to rescue the prisoners taken in battle. He was seen in Ceuta in December 1578, on his way to take ship for Gibraltar in the direction of Lisbon. The last news of him is that, at the beginning of 1579, he was on the way to Madrid to give an account of his work. The date of his death is unknown, though it cannot have been much after this.

MAIN SOURCES OF INFORMATION

Primary

Diego de Torres, *Relación del origen y sucesso de los Xarifes y del estado de los reinos de Marruecos, Fez, Tarudante y los demás que tienen usurpados*, Seville, 1586

Colección de documentos inéditos para la historia de España (CODOIN), Madrid, 1842-95, xxxix, pp. 113, 467, 476

Secondary

M. García-Arenal and M.A. de Bunes, *Los españoles y el norte de África. Siglos XV-XVIII*, Madrid, 1992

M.A. de Bunes, *La imagen de los musulmanes y del norte de África en la España de los siglos XVI y XVII. Los caracteres de una hostilidad*, Madrid, 1989

B. Bennassar, 'La vida de los renegados españoles y portugueses en Fez (hacia 1580-1615)', in M. García-Arenal and M.J. Viguera (eds), *Relaciones de la Península Ibérica con el Magreb (Siglos XIII-XVI)*, Madrid, 1988, 665-78

M. García-Arenal, 'Spanish literature on North Africa in the XVI century. Diego Torres', *Maghreb Review* 8 (1983) 53-59

J. Caro Baroja, *Una visión de Marruecos a mediados del siglo XVI, la del primer historiador de los Xarifes, Diego de Torres*, Madrid, 1956

F. Braudel, 'Les espagnols et l'Afrique du Nord, de 1492 a 1577', *Revue Africaine* 69 (1928) 184-233

WORKS ON CHRISTIAN-MUSLIM RELATIONS

Relación del origen y suceso de los Xarifes y del estado de los reinos de Marruecos, Fez y Tarudante y los demás que tienen usurpados, 'Account of the origin and succession of the Sharifs, and of the state of the kings of Morocco, Fez and Tarudante, and others who have been deposed'

DATE 1586
ORIGINAL LANGUAGE Spanish

DESCRIPTION

Relación del origen y suceso de los Xarifes is a history of the Moroccan kingdoms in the years 1502-74. It combines earlier sources with Torres's own personal experience and oral testimonies from people he met during his time in Morocco. The sources he uses most are Luis del Mármol's *Descripción general de África* (Granada, 1573) and Damião de Góis's *Chrónica del Rei Dom Emanuel* (Lisbon, 1566). According to García-Arenal, 'in a great many entire chapters, and passages from others, both texts – that of Torres and Mármol – are literally identical' (*Relación del origen*, p. 11). Some authors have said that it was Mármol who copied Torres, though García-Arenal points out that Torres must have copied Mármol because Mármol published the first part of his work before Torres finished his. He follows Damião de Góis and other works in the chapters referring to Portuguese places.

The work emphasises the Saʿdī dynasty, which governed part of present-day Morocco between 1509 and 1641. The name *Xarifes* refers to the fact that they considered themselves *sharīf*s, descendants of the Prophet Muḥammad, which gave them legitimacy. The work was not published until after Torres's death, when his widow arranged to have it published in Seville. This first edition, 288 pages long, was later translated into French, though no new edition of the Spanish appeared until that of Mercedes García-Arenal in 1980.

The work is divided into 112 chapters, which García-Arenal groups into three parts, according to whether Torres personally participated in the events related: chs 1-53, relating to events from 1502 to 1546, mainly derived from earlier sources; chs 54-101, describing Torres's time in Marrakesh (1546-50), Tarudante (1551-52) and Fez (1553-54) based on his personal experience, and the most original part of the work; chs 102-12, a brief account covering the longest period (1554-74), when Torres had already returned to Spain, including material from elsewhere.

Relación is part of the literature that was written by Spaniards and Portuguese about North Africa in order to give information to those who might wish to travel there, or to invade. It is considered an essential source for the study of Morocco in the first three-quarters of the 16th century, even though it is not well-known. It was written with a view to being sent to King Sebastian of Portugal (the original dedicatee), with the purpose of encouraging him to invade North Africa, and providing him with all the information that would be necessary, about the main towns, geography and economy. Since it was written with Portuguese interests mainly in mind, after the disaster of the Battle of Alcazarquivir, or of the Three Kings, in August 1578, it lost its relevance, because the time for expeditions to the Maghreb had passed.

While the work reflects conventional images of Islam current in the Iberian Peninsula in the 16th century, Torres also refers to the various beliefs of Christians living under the Saʿdīs. He describes the hardship endured by Christian prisoners and their attempts at escape, and their work in the dockyards of Fez and at the forges making weapons. He recounts incidents involving renegades and apostates, and mentions Christian merchants of all nationalities, many of whom lived in the House of Commerce in Marrakesh, where he himself set up a place of prayer. Equally, he talks about many confrontations between Muslims and Christians, and the reprisals taken by one side or the other. He also comments on typical themes of Christian-Muslim polemics: the status of Muḥammad and the stories and legends about him, discussions over the relative merits of Muḥammad and Jesus, polygamy, punishments, customs of Muslim women, festivals, the theme of the 'sleeping foetus', and funeral practices. He gives particular praise to the Islamic system of justice, and to the honesty of the court clerks.

SIGNIFICANCE

Relación is especially valuable for the author's own experiences as rescuer of Christian captives in the Muslim court at Marrakesh, and as an intermediary between followers of the two faiths. Torres does not distinguish between Spaniards, Portuguese and other nationalities, but speaks simply of Christians.

The history was later used by authors such as Gavy de Mendoça, *História do famoso cerco que o Xarife pos a fortaleza de Mazagão no año de*

1562 (Lisbon, 1607), José de Sigüenza, *Historia de lo Orden de San Jerónimo (1600-1605)*, Manuel de Faria y Sousa, *Africa Portuguesa* (Lisbon, 1681), the Jesuit Gabriel de Aranda, *Vida del siervo de Dios P. Fernando de Contreras* (Seville, 1692), and also by Lope de Vega, who quotes from it in one of his comedies. Likewise, Juan de Ferreras uses it in the volume on the 16th century in his *Synopsis histórico-chronológica de España*. It was also used by various French authors after it was translated into French in the 17th century, and it continued to be occasionally cited until the 19th century.

EDITIONS & TRANSLATIONS

Relacion del origen y sucesso de los Xarifes, y del citado de los reinos de Marruecos, Fez, Tarudáte, y los desmas q tienen usurpados, Orbigo, Santiago de Compostela, 2008

Muḥammad Akhḍar and Muḥammad Ḥajjī (trans.), *Tārīkh al-shurafā'*, Casablanca, 1980 (Arabic trans.)

M. García-Arenal, *Relación del origen y suceso de los xarifes y del estado de los reinos de Marruecos, Fez y Tarudante*, Madrid, 1980

L'Afrique de Marmol, de la traduction de Nicolas Perrot sieur d'Ablancourt, divisée en trois volumes, et enrichie des cartes géographiques de M. Sanson... avec l'Histoire des Chérifs, traduite de l'espagnol de Diego Torrès, par le duc d'Angoulesme le pere. Reveüe et retouchée par P. Richelet, Paris: Thomas Jolly, 1667 (French trans.)

Relation de l'origine et succez des Cherifs et de l'Estat des Royaumes de Maroc, Fez, et Tarudant faicte et escrite en espagnol par Diego de Torrés,... mise en françois par Charles de Valois, duc d'Angoulême, Paris, 1636 (French trans.)

Relación del origen y sucesso de los Xarifes y del Estado de los reinos de Marruecos, Fez y Tarudante y los demás que tienen usurpados, Seville: Impreso en casa de Francisco Pérez, 1586

STUDIES

García Arenal and de Bunes, *Los españoles y el norte de África*

M. García-Arenal, M.A. de Bunes, and V. Aguilar, *Repertorio bibliográfico de las relaciones entre la Península Ibérica y el norte de África (siglos XV-XVI). Fuentes y bibliografía*, Madrid, 1989

García-Arenal, 'Spanish literature on North Africa in the XVI century'

Caro Baroja, *Una visión de Marruecos a mediados del siglo XVI*

R. Ricard, 'Textes espagnols sur la Berbérie (XV, XVI et XVII siècles)', *Revue Africaine* (1945) 26-40

H. de Castries, *Les sources inédites de l'histoire du Maroc, première dynastie Saadienne, collection de lettres, documents et mémoires, Espagne*, Paris, 1921, vol. 1

Eva Lapiedra Gutiérrez

Catecismo del Sacromonte

Anonymous Jesuit priest

DATE OF BIRTH Early 16th century
PLACE OF BIRTH Unknown
DATE OF DEATH Unknown
PLACE OF DEATH Unknown

BIOGRAPHY

The *Catecismo* is part of a manuscript whose author is almost entirely unknown. He is called a *sacerdote* (priest), who is engaged in dialogue with a Morisco called *Novicio* (novice), though it is evident from a reference at one point to *nuestra compañía* ('our company') that he is a Jesuit. Names of possible authors include Juan de Albotodo, Father Isidoro, Juan de la Plaza and Juan B. Sánchez, who were in Granada at about the time the *Catecismo* was written.

MAIN SOURCES OF INFORMATION

Primary
MS in the Abbey of Sacromonte, Granada

Secondary
L. Resines, *El Catecismo del Sacromonte de Granada*, Madrid, 2002, pp. 11-153
F.B. Medina, art. 'Albotodo, Juan', in *Diccionario histórico de la Compañía de Jesús*, Rome, 2001, i, pp. 38-39
IHSJ, art. 'Albotodo, Juan', in *Diccionario de Historia Eclesiástica de España*, Madrid, 1975, 3

WORKS ON CHRISTIAN-MUSLIM RELATIONS

Catecismo del Sacromonte, 'Catechism of Sacromonte'

DATE 1588
ORIGINAL LANGUAGE Spanish

DESCRIPTION

The intention of the *Catecismo* is to present a basic form of Christianity for Moriscos who are already baptised but retain their original culture, language and habits, and also to induce Muslims to convert by demonstrating the emptiness of their faith. In the manuscript, it takes up 149 folios, and in Resines's edition it occupies pp. 161-321. Its full title is *Este es un catecismo util para todos los fieles Christianos, porque contiene una compendiosa y substancial declaracion de la doctrina Christiana, y especialmente muy provechoso para los Christianos nuevos de Moriscos, y para convertir a Moros porque el estilo es por via de disputa en defensa de nuestra santa fe catholica contra la secta de Mahoma. Va escripto en dialogo entre un sacerdote y un Christiano nuebo de morisco al que llama Novicio* ('This is a useful catechism for all Christian faithful, because it contains a condensed and substantial explanation of the Christian doctrine, and especially very profitable for new Christians [coming] from Moriscos, and for converting Moros [Muslims], because its form is by way of discussion in defence of our holy catholic faith against the sect of Muḥammad. It is written in the form of a dialogue between a priest and a new Christian [who comes] from Morisco, named Novice').

The text is directed at Moriscos, to establish them more strongly in Christianity. Since they retain their former way of life, they attract the suspicion that their conversion is not sincere, but under compulsion or simply out of self-interest (these suspicions increased with the armed revolt in the Alpujarras outside Granada in 1568). It shows that Islam is not from God, and emphasises that the Church is the only channel of salvation. All that is outside is error, and thus Muslims and baptised Moriscos who keep to their former ways are wrong.

The *Catecismo* argues that Muḥammad was a false prophet who was used as a channel of demonic error, and that the Qur'an is nothing more than his own composition. It also exposes the contradictions between Islamic and Christian doctrine, and argues that, even though there may be signs of similarity in the monotheistic doctrines of the two faiths, Christian monotheism is the highest form of religious expression which the Islamic form does not reach; since it is based on Judaism, it is defective and incomplete. It goes on to condemn Islamic religious rites because they do not mediate the same grace that is available in Christian rites, and to condemn practices such as polygamy. It accepts that there are sincere individuals within Islam, though these are always inferior to the saints of the Church. It contends that Morisco refusal to accept

Christianity results from blindness. It is not acceptable to say simply, 'My father was Moro; I also am Moro', a motto that it frequently repeats; to remain in this error is a clear sign of the absence of true faith.

Even though the *Catecismo* is presented as a dialogue between two speakers, there is actually no sign of an open dialogue within it. On the contrary, it is a closed dialogue between truth and error, light and darkness.

SIGNIFICANCE

The manuscript was never printed and was not widely circulated. If it had been published, its influence would quite probably have been largely detrimental because of its entirely negative attitude towards Islam.

MANUSCRIPTS

The MS containing this work is in the library of the Abbey of Sacromonte, Granada. It bears the overall title of *Catechismo*, and comprises 570 folios numbered only in recto (thus, 1140 pages). There is no author's name. It includes the following works:

1. *Catecismo* (fols 1r-149v)
2. *Libro de la sapiencia Cristiana* (fols 150r-423v)
3. *Tractado de la creación del mundo* (fols 428r-465v)
4. *Tractado de la creación del hombre y de su dignidad, y caída y reparación por nuestro Señor Jesucristo* (fols 468r-560v).

These works are unrelated apart from the last two, which have a certain connection. In the modern edition of the MS, the *Catecismo* is on pp. 161-321.

This manuscript is a unique exemplar. It may be a copy of another manuscript.

EDITIONS & TRANSLATIONS

L. Resines, *Catecismo del Sacromonte, y Doctrina Christiana de Pedro de Feria. Conversión y evangelización de moriscos e indios*, Madrid, 2002, pp. 157-321

STUDIES

Resines, *Catecismo del Sacromonte*, pp. 157-321 (a comparison of the Moriscos of Granada and a group of Indians from the Zapoteca region of Mexico, both of whom were objects of Christian preaching)

Luis Resines

Baltazar de Morales

DATE OF BIRTH   About 1520
PLACE OF BIRTH   La Rambla, near Cordova, Spain
DATE OF DEATH   After 1593
PLACE OF DEATH   Possibly Cordova

BIOGRAPHY

Although there is as yet no study of the life of Baltazar de Morales, it is possible to deduce some facts about him from his *Diálogo de las guerras de Orán*, because the character of Navarrete in this work is really a representation of Baltazar himself. At the beginning of the *Diálogo*, he says he is from La Rambla near Cordova, and that he was a captain in all the wars that were waged when the counts of Alcaudete were governors of Oran. The thoroughness and detail with which he describes the battles and other military exploits indicate clearly that he had been an eye-witness of the events.

Navarrete's account of himself starts in 1542, when he says he abandoned his studies and began his military career. Traces of Baltazar's own scholastic training can be seen in his preference for the dialogue form he uses, an imitation of the Renaissance style that was typical of the period, and also in his remark that he had read the Italian historian and biographer Paulo Jovio (*Diálogo de las guerras de Orán*, 1881, p. 257). Navarrete says that he took part in the defence of Perpignan, and afterwards joined the army of the Count of Alcaudete, Don Martín de Córdoba y Velasco, governor and captain general of Oran and Mazalquivir, who was recruiting men for the campaign against Tlemcen in 1542. He also took part in a series of campaigns against Mostaganem in 1543, 1547 and 1558, and as an infantry captain he was an eye-witness of the sieges conducted in 1556 and 1563 by the *beylerbeys* of Algiers with Ottoman support. In the 1563 siege, he was wounded, as is reported by the chronicler Luis de Córdoba (*Filipe II, rey de España*, fol. 312).

The *Diálogo* does not extend beyond the year 1564, so it gives no more information about Navarette/Baltazar, though Diego Suárez Montañés, who was serving in Oran in the last decades of the 16th century, says that in 1567 Baltazar was in charge of the defence of Canastel near Oran (*Historia del Maestre último que fue de Montesa...*, 2005, p. 228). Thus, he served for more than 20 years in various Spanish enclaves in North Africa.

MAIN SOURCES OF INFORMATION

Primary

F. de la Cueva, F.R. de Arellano Fuensanta del Valle, J.L.S. Rayón and B. de Morales, *Guerras de los españoles en África, 1542, 1543 y 1632*, in *Colección de libros raros y curiosos*, vol. 15, Madrid, 1881, pp. 239-379

D. Suárez Montañés, *Historia del Maestre último que fue de Montesa y de su hermano don Felipe de Borja. La manera como gobernaron las memorables plazas de Orán y Mazalquivir, reinos de Tremecén y Ténez, en África, siendo allí capitanes generales, uno en pos de otro, como aquí se narra*, MS Madrid, BNE – 7882 (17th century; ed. F. Guillén Robles, Madrid, 1889; M.Á. de Bunes Ibarra and B. Alonso Acero, Valencia, 2005, pp. 22, 228)

N. Antonio, *Bibliotheca hispana nova*, Madrid, 1788, vol. 1, p. 183

L. Cabrera de Córdoba, *Filipe II, rey de España*, Madrid, por Luis Sánchez, 1619, f. 312

B. de Morales, *Diálogo de las guerras de Orán compuesto por el capitán Baltazar de Morales, natural de la Rambla, que se halló en todas las que aquí se tratan del tiempo de los condes de Alcaudete tuvieron aquella tenencia*, Córdoba: en casa de Francisco de Cea, impresor de libros, 1593

Secondary

S. Malki, 'Orán, el espejo de la otra España bajo el mando de don Martín de Córdoba, conde de Alcaudete (1535-1558)', in I. Terki-Hassaine, E. Sola Castaño, A.R. Díez Torre and M. Casado Arboniés (eds), *Las Campanas de Orán, 1509-2009. Estudios en homenaje a Fatima Benhamamouche*, Madrid, 2012, 155-68

M. J. Rodríguez Salgado, ' "El león animoso entre las balas". Los dos cercos de Orán a mediados del siglo XVI', in M.Á. de Bunes Ibarra and B. Alonso Acero (eds), *Orán. Historia de la Corte Chica*, Madrid, 2011, 13-54

A. Madroñal, 'Orán en el teatro breve', in M.Á. de Bunes Ibarra and B. Alonso Acero (eds), *Orán. Historia de la Corte Chica*, Madrid, 2011, 243-62, p. 244

M. de Cervantes, *El gallardo español. La casa de los celos*, ed. F. Sevilla Arroyo and A. Rey Hazas, Madrid, 1997, p. xiii

G. Sánchez Doncel, *Presencia de España en Orán, 1509-1792*, Toledo, 1991

J. Canavaggio, *Cervantès dramaturgue. Un théâtre à naître*, Paris, 1977, pp. 53-55

C. de la Véronne, 'Relations entre le Maroc et la Turquie dans la seconde moitié du XVIe siècle et le début du XVIIe siècle (1554-1616)', *Revue de l'Occident Musulman et de la Méditerranée* 15 (1973) 391-401

A. Cotarelo y Valledor, *El teatro de Cervantes*, Madrid, 1915, pp. 259-60

P. Ruff, *La domination espagnole à Oran sous le gouvernement du Cte d'Alcaudette, 1534-1558, avec un appendice contenant six documents inédits, mémoire présenté à l'École des lettres d'Algers*, Paris, 1900 (new ed. 1998)

De la Cueva et al., *Guerras de los españoles en África*, pp. xv-xix

WORKS ON CHRISTIAN-MUSLIM RELATIONS

Diálogo de las guerras de Orán, 'Dialogue of the wars of Oran'

DATE 1593
ORIGINAL LANGUAGE Spanish

DESCRIPTION

The *Diálogo de las guerras de Orán* (in full, *Diálogo de las guerras de Orán compuesto por el capitán Baltazar de Morales, natural de la Rambla, que se halló en todas las que aquí se tratan del tiempo de los condes de Alcaudete tuvieron aquella tenencia*) was printed by Francisco de Cea in Cordova in 1593. It is dedicated to Martin Alonso de Montemayor, nephew of Don Martin de Córdoba y Velasco, first Count of Alcaudete. The first edition, of which a copy is still preserved in the Real Academia de la Historia, is in octavo form and has 64 pages. The first modern edition appeared in 1881, occupying pp. 239-379 of *Guerras de los Españoles en África. Colección de libros raros y curiosos* vol. 15.

The book is divided into three parts, each corresponding to a dialogue. Its main characters are Mendoza, Navarrete and Guzmán, who chance upon one another in the cathedral of Cordova and agree to go to Guzmán's garden so that Navarrete can tell the other two about events in the wars of Oran, from where he has just returned. Their three dialogues take place over two days.

The first dialogue focuses on the campaign against Tlemcen in February 1543, led by the governor of Oran, Don Martín de Córdoba y Velasco, first Count of Alcaudete. This campaign was a success, with the King of Tlemcen, Muley Baudila, submitting to King Charles V of Spain. In order to emphasise Alcaudete's prowess, Navarrete talks about his great military skills in the face of limited support from Charles V, scarcity of supplies and shortage of arms and ammunition, and he goes on to laud the Count's ancestry. This first part ends with lunch.

The second dialogue focuses on the unsuccessful campaign against Mostaganem in 1543, and a new attempt in 1547. The protagonists then have dinner and retire for the night. The next day, the third dialogue focuses on Turkish sieges of Oran in 1556 and 1563, and the devastation brought by plague in 1557, which forced the Spanish troops to leave the town. Navarrete continues with the third and last campaign to Mostaganem in 1558, the only time he accuses Alcaudete of making a mistake in letting some of his captains leave when things turned against them, which resulted in his death. The dialogue concludes with a detailed account of the siege of Oran in 1563, which highlights the fundamental contribution of Don Francisco de Mendoza, general of the Spanish galleys, to the lifting of the siege. With this, Guzmán, Mendoza and Navarrete finish their conversation and leave.

SIGNIFICANCE

In addition to its importance as the only known printed work from the 16th century on North African themes written in a dialogue form, Baltazar's text is a major source for the history of Spanish rule in North Africa in the mid-16th century. Written by a direct witness of the events in Oran and Mazalquivir between 1542 and 1567, it is of great importance for the understanding of frontier relations in North Africa in this period. Baltazar gives a reliable account of the kind of relationship that existed between the enclaves of Oran and Mazalquivir and the surrounding Muslim world. While it covers great military deeds, campaigns, conquests and sieges, it also faithfully describes the relationship between the Christians of Oran and neighbouring Muslims. These relationships oscillate between collaboration with and support for local Muslims against the rule of Algiers, and raids against hostile Moorish encampments.

Cotarelo y Valledor argued in 1915 that Miguel de Cervantes was inspired by this work to write his comedy *El gallardo español*, which takes as its central theme the siege of Oran in 1563. While this contention has been accepted by many, in 1977 Jean Canavaggio questioned it, arguing that many of the historical details that Cervantes includes in his work are not referred to in the *Dialogue*.

EDITIONS & TRANSLATIONS

    A. Rivas Morales, *Diálogos de las guerras de Orán. Los condes de Alcaudete en el norte de África*, Granada, 1993

R.F. Michel, 'Documents inédits sur l'histoire d'Oran sous la domination espagnole. [Dialogue sur les guerres d'Oran, de Baltazar de Morales]', *Bulletin de la Société de Géographie d'Orán* 9 (1889) 95-155 and 223-55 (French trans.)

F. de la Cueva, F.R. de Arellano Fuensanta del Valle, J.L.S. Rayón and B. de Morales, *Guerras de los españoles en África, 1542, 1543 y 1632*, in *Colección de libros raros y curiosos*, vol. 15, Madrid: Imprenta de Miguel de Ginesta, 1881, pp. 239-379

B. de Morales, *Diálogo de las guerras de Orán compuesto por el capitán Baltazar de Morales, natural de la Rambla, que se halló en todas las que aquí se tratan del tiempo de los condes de Alcaudete tuvieron aquella tenencia*, Córdoba: Francisco de Cea, 1593

STUDIES

S. Malki, 'Orán, el espejo de la otra España bajo el mando de don Martín de Córdoba, conde de Alcaudete (1535-1558)', in I. Terki-Hassaine, E. Sola Castaño, A.R. Díez Torre and M. Casado Arboniés (eds), *Las Campanas de Orán, 1509-2009. Estudios en homenaje a Fatima Benhamamouche*, Madrid, 2012, 155-68

M.J. Rodríguez Salgado, ' "El león animoso entre las balas". Los dos cercos de Orán a mediados del siglo XVI', in M.Á. de Bunes Ibarra and B. Alonso Acero (eds), *Orán. Historia de la Corte Chica*, Madrid, 2011, 13-54

Madroñal, 'Orán en el teatro breve', p. 244

M. de Cervantes, *El gallardo español. La casa de los celos*, ed. F. Sevilla Arroyo and A. Rey Hazas, Madrid, 1997, p. xiii

Sánchez Doncel, *Presencia de España en Orán, 1509-1792*

J. Canavaggio, *Cervantès dramaturge. Un théâtre à naître*, Paris, 1977, pp. 53-55

C. de La Véronne, 'Relations entre le Maroc et la Turquie dans la seconde moitié du XVIe siècle et le début du XVIIe siècle (1554-1616)', *Revue de l'Occident Musulman et de la Méditerranée* 15 (1973) 391-401

A. Cotarelo y Valledor, *El teatro de Cervantes*, Madrid, 1915, pp. 259-60

P. Ruff, *La domination espagnoleà Oran sous le gouvernement du Cte d'Alcaudette, 1534-1558, avec an appendice contenant six documents inédits. Mémoire présenté à l'Ecole des letters d'Algers*, Paris, 1900 (new ed. 1998)

De la Cueva et al., *Guerras de los españoles en África*, pp. xv-xix

Beatriz Alonso Acero

The lead books of Sacromonte

Los libros plúmbeos del Sacromonte

DATE Discovered 1588-99

ORIGINAL LANGUAGE Arabic

DESCRIPTION

On 18 March 1588, during the construction of the new cathedral of Granada, as the minaret of the old mosque was being demolished workers found a lead box coated with bitumen and containing a parchment scroll, a triangular canvas and a bone. The contents of the scroll bewildered its readers, as it contained a letter written by San Cecilio (the patron saint of Granada). It was written in Latin, Arabic and Castilian, despite appearing to be from the first century. It comprised a number of parts: A few lines in Arabic, an announcement of a prophecy of St John the Evangelist. An account, also in Arabic, by Cecilio, 'bishop of Granada', of his journey from Jerusalem to bring the relics. The prophecy of St John, written in Castilian by San Cecilio, who had translated it from a Greek version which St Dionysius had translated from Hebrew. The prophecy was arranged in a grid, divided into 1,392 squares (48 horizontal by 29 vertical) with a letter in each square. The prophecy was about persecutions of believers until the Day of Judgement. Six lines of Arabic text, a sort of commentary on the prophecy and the end of Cecilio's trip, plus an excerpt from the beginning of John's Gospel. Eight lines of Latin text (in a very Spanish form) containing an explanation of how the relics were brought there, signed by a priest named Patrick, a disciple of Cecilio, who purportedly had received them shortly before his martyrdom.

When the discovery was made, the papal nuncio in Spain immediately sought appropriate Arabic translators to interpret the texts. They were Luis Fajardo, a former professor of Arabic at the University of Salamanca, the Morisco Miguel de Luna, who was translator for King Philip II, and Francisco López Tamarid, a prebendary of Granada. An independent translation was also commissioned from Alonso del Castillo, another of Philip II's interpreters, who was also a Morisco.

As translations of the parchment were made, there arose a massive wave of opinion in favour of its authenticity, with very few dissenting voices, making the discovery one that placed the church in Granada on a par with other apostolic sites. Pope Sixtus V issued a papal *Breve* on 3 October 1588, giving responsibility for the continuing verification of the relics to the Archbishop of Granada. This was taken up by the newly appointed archbishop, Pedro de Castro y Quiñones.

On 21 February 1595, treasure hunters exploring a cave on Mount Valparaíso to the east of Granada found a lead sheet written in somewhat deformed Arabic characters. Once translated, it read that a certain Mesitón suffered martyrdom there during the reign of Nero, and was buried there. A second lead sheet, found five days later, gave the same information about a certain Hiscio, a disciple of Santiago (the Apostle St James), saying that the name of the hill where they were buried was *Sacro monte* (Holy mountain). On 30 March, some ashes and bones were found, and on 5 April a third plate was found, written by Tesifón (called Ibn 'Atar before his conversion), also a disciple of James, who said that he had written a book on lead plates entitled *Fundamentum ecclesiae*, which was in this hill. On 22 April, this book and some ashes appeared. It consisted of five thin circular sheets of lead, written in Arabic but with deformed characters that the book called 'Solomonic'. From then on, amid popular fervour in Granada, a series of wondrous books rapidly began to appear.

A total of 22 lead books were found in the caves of Valparaiso, initiating a process of authentication by the ecclesiastical authorities. They ordered numerous translations, including one by the Moriscos Castillo and Luna. The process caused a controversy, with one group led by Archbishop Castro y Quiñones defending their authenticity against strong opposition.

Criticisms of the texts, however, gradually grew in number and intensity, until the controversy surrounding them involved all Spanish intellectuals of the late 16th and early 17th centuries. Nevertheless, Archbishop Castro y Quiñones and the monks of the new Sacromonte Abbey remained strongly in favour of their authenticity, ignoring the requirements of Rome, which had early on requested that the books be sent for examination. After much discussion, they finally went to Rome, where they were condemned by Pope Innocent XI in 1682 as containing erroneous doctrine.

In 1999, during a reorganisation of the secret archives of the Vatican, the lead books reappeared and the then Cardinal Joseph Ratzinger, later Pope Benedict XVI, decided to return them to the archbishopric of Granada in 2000. Since then, some exemplars have been put on display in the museum of the Abbey of Sacromonte.

The texts have one feature in common: they provide information about Christianity and Christian doctrines, purportedly relayed from important figures in the early church, specifically the Virgin Mary and the Apostle James, and refer in ambiguous terms to fundamental tenets of faith. Although they contain different material, the books all emphasise the importance of Spain and of Granada in the development and spread of Christianity, supporting the tradition that St James came to Spain and brought with him a series of books, in particular one called *Book of the history of the truth of the Gospel*, which had been delivered to him by the Virgin Mary with the instruction to bury it on a mountain in Spain. They also claimed to contain a message that had remained hidden for centuries by the will of God.

To understand how these texts could penetrate Granadan society, it is essential to note that from the very beginning the lead books and their translations were accepted as authentic ancient Christian texts. Granada's Islamic past was still very present in this young diocese, and these texts appeared to offer a shining Christian past to the former capital of the Naṣrid emirs.

Critics have traditionally seen the lead books as presenting a syncretistic belief linking Christianity and Islam that sought to ameliorate the difficult situation of the Moriscos. More recently, however, the idea that the lead books were an Islamic polemical tool against Christianity has been gaining ground. The books speak of Christianity, Jesus and the Virgin in terms that, whilst being acceptable to Christians, are also perfectly recognisable to Muslims. So, according to this view, the Morisco authors tried to set out a testimony of faith and audaciously to circulate it amongst Christians and attempt to persuade them to agree with it. As part of a very calculated ambiguity, the lead books of Sacromonte offered a message that was acceptable to all.

Almost all scholars now agree that the authors of the texts were Moriscos of Granada. The names of Alonso del Castillo and Miguel de Luna, both doctors and translators involved in counterfeiting, have been frequently cited as the authors. Today it is thought that the elite of the Moriscos from Granada could have been behind the conception and production of the books.

SIGNIFICANCE

The lead books are the most sophisticated products of the Moriscos of Granada. Far from being a classical work of anti-Christian polemic, they presented to Christians 'true' Christianity, a faith that had not yet been altered and that was an 'Islamic' Christianity. Being deeply familiar with the Spanish society surrounding them, the authors of the books understood that they could veil an Islamic message in relics and the 'ancient' Arabic language of Spain. For instance, Jesus is consistently referred to as *rūḥ Allāh* ('spirit of God', as in Q 4:171) and never as Son of God. Similarly, in the *Book of the history of the truth of the Gospel*, Mary announces to James the 'truth of the Gospel' that has been brought down to her by the angel Gabriel from heaven amid shining light, in line with the model of prophetic revelation in Islam. She tells James that the mystery of the 'truth' will not be revealed in his time, but that it will lead to 'dissensions and heresy among nations about the Spirit of God, Jesus and the glorious Gospel'. It is not difficult to see behind her words a prophecy based on the Islamic doctrine of *taḥrīf*, the corruption of the text of scripture by Jews and Christians.

No further texts appeared in Granada linked to the Sacromonte texts. However, shortly afterwards, a gospel containing the life of Jesus told from the viewpoint of Islam was spoken of among exiled Moriscos in Tunisia. The *Gospel of Barnabas*, datable to the early 17th century, presents the life and message of Jesus according to the model of the Gospels, but written from an Islamic perspective. From this point of view, the lead books of Sacromonte can be seen as the ideal background against which the mysterious *Gospel of Barnabas* was created.

MANUSCRIPTS

The lead books are now deposited in the museum of the Abbey of Sacromonte, Granada.

There are a great number of later Spanish and Latin translations by many translators. Among them:

MS Granada, Archivo del Sacromonte – 1, 6, 13, 15, 19, 20, 22, 23, 25, 35, 36, 37, 39, 40, 41, 43, 45, 50, 53, 54, 56, 58, 59, 60, 75, 102, 109 and 115

MS Madrid, BNE – 205, 1603, 5732, 5785, 6437, 6637 and 12964

MS Madrid, Real Academia de la Historia de Madrid – 9-11-5, 9-11-6, 9-11-7 and 9-26-8

MS Milan, Biblioteca Ambrosiana – 259

MS London, BM – Harley 3507 (transcription plus Latin version by Bartolomeo de Pettorano)
MS London, BM – Harley 3500
MS London, BM – Egerton 1875

EDITIONS & TRANSLATIONS

There is as yet no complete edition of the lead books.
Partial editions:
P. Roisse, 'L'histoire du sceau de Salomon ou de la *coincidentia oppositorum* dans les "Livres de plomb"', *Al-Qanṭara* 24 (2003) 372-408
M.J. Hagerty, 'Transcripción, traducción y observaciones de dos de los "Libros plúmbeos del Sacromonte"', Granada, 1988 (Diss. University of Granada)
M.J. Hagerty, *Los libros plúmbeos del Sacromonte*, Madrid, 1980
L.P. Harvey, 'The literary culture of the Moriscos (1492-1609). A study based on the extant mss. in Arabic and Aljamía', Oxford, 1958 (Diss. University of Oxford), i, pp. 245-61; ii, pp. 161-83
A. Centurión y Córdoba, *Relación breve de las reliquias que se hallaron en la ciudad de Granada en una torre antiquíssima y en las cavernas del monte Illupitano de Valparayso*, Lyon, 1706

STUDIES

M. Barrios Aguilera, *La invención de los libros plúmbeos. Fraude, historia y mito*, Granada, 2011
M. García-Arenal and F. Rodríguez Mediano, *Un Oriente español. Los Moriscos y el Sacromonte en tiempos de Contrarreforma*, Madrid, 2010
M. Barrios Aguilera, 'Pedro de Castro y los libros plúmbeos en Sevilla', in J.A. González Alcantud and R.G. Peinado Santaella (eds), *Granada la andaluza*, Granada, 2008, 107-30
M. Barrios Aguilera and M. García-Arenal (eds), *¿La historia inventada? Los libros plúmbeos y el legado sacromontano*, Granada, 2008
M. Barrios Aguilera and M. García-Arenal (eds), *Los libros plúmbeos del Sacromonte. Invención y tesoro*, Valencia, 2006
Y. El Alaoui, *Jesuites, Morisques et Indiens. Étude comparative des méthodes d'évangélisation de la Compagnie de Jésus d'après les traités de José de Acosta (1588) et d'Ignacio de las Casas (1605-1607)*, Paris, 2006
M. Barrios Aguilera, 'Las invenciones del Sacromonte. Estado de las cuestiones y últimas propuestas', in I. Gómez de Liaño, *Los Juegos del Sacromonte*, Granada, 2005, vii-liii

L.P. Harvey, *Muslims in Spain. 1500-1614*, Chicago IL, 2005, pp. 264-90

M. Barrios Aguilera, 'El Sacromonte de Granada y la religiosidad contrarreformista', in J. Ruiz Fernández and V. Sánchez Ramos (eds), *La religiosidad popular y Almería*, Almería, Spain, 2004, 17-37

M. Barrios Aguilera, *Los falsos cronicones contra la Historia (o Granada, Corona martirial)*, Granada, 2004

M. García-Arenal, 'El entorno de los Plomos. Historiografía y linaje', *Al-Qanṭara* 24 (2003) 295-325 (extended version appears in Barrios Aguilera and García-Arenal, *Invención y tesoro*, 51-78)

P.S. van Koningsveld and G. Wiegers, 'The parchment of the "Torre Turpiana". The original document and its early interpreters', *Al-Qanṭara* 24 (2003) 327-58 (Spanish version in Barrios Aguilera and García-Arenal, *Invención y tesoro*, 113-40)

Roisse, 'L'Histoire du sceau de Salomon', 359-72 (extended Spanish version under the title 'La *Historia del Sello de Salomón*. Estudio, edición crítica y traducción comparada', in Barrios Aguilera and García-Arenal, *Invención y tesoro*, 141-72)

G. Magnier, 'Pedro de Valencia, Francisco de Gurmendi and the *Plomos* de Granada', *Al-Qanṭara* 24 (2003) 409-26 (Spanish version in Barrios Aguilera and García-Arenal, *Invención y tesoro*, 201-16)

B. Ehlers, 'Juan Bautista Pérez and the *Plomos de Granada*. Spanish humanism in the late sixteenth century', *Al-Qanṭara* 24 (2003) 427-47 (Spanish version in Barrios Aguilera and García-Arenal, *Invención y tesoro*, 253-70)

K.A. Woolard, 'Bernardo de Aldrete, humanist and *laminario*', *Al-Qanṭara* 24 (2003) 449-76 (Spanish version in Barrios Aguilera and García-Arenal, *Invención y tesoro*, 271-96)

M. Barrios Aguilera, 'El castigo de la disidencia en las invenciones plúmbeas. Sacrononte *versus* Ignacio de las Casas', *Al-Qanṭara* 24 (2003) 477-532 (extended version in Barrios Aguilera and García-Arenal, *Invención y tesoro*, 481-520)

G. Mora and J. Álvarez Barrientos, 'Las falsificaciones granadinas del siglo XVIII. Nacionalismo y arqueología', *Al-Qanṭara* 24 (2003) 533-46

J.A. González Alcantud, 'El mito fallido sacromontano y su perdurabilidad local a la luz del mozarabismo maurófobo de F.J. Simonet', *Al-Qanṭara* 24 (2003) 547-73 (also in Barrios Aguilera and García-Arenal, *Invención y tesoro*, 533-56)

M. Barrios Aguilera, 'Pedro de Castro y el Sacromonte de Granada. Sobre la realidad del mito sacromontano', in L. Lotti and R. Villari (eds), *Filippo II e il Mediterraneo*, Rome, 2003, 617-28

M. Barrios Aguilera, 'Nouvelles perspectives dans l'étude des Morisques du royaume de Grenade. Bilan historiographique et propositions', in J.A. González Alcantud and F. Zabbal (eds), *Histoire de l'Andalousie. Mémoire et enjeux*, Paris, 2003, 157-92

H.L. Ecker, '"Arab stones". Rodrigo Caro's translations of Arabic inscriptions in Seville (1634) revisited', *Al-Qanṭara* 23 (2002) 347-402 (extended version in Barrios Aguilera and García-Arenal, *Invención y tesoro*, 335-84)

R. Benítez Sánchez-Blanco, 'De Pablo a Saulo. Traducción, crítica y denuncia de los Libros plúmbeos por el P. Ignacio de las Casas, S.I.', *Al-Qanṭara* 23 (2002) 403-35 (extended version in Barrios Aguilera and García-Arenal, *Invención y tesoro*, 217-52)

F.J. Martínez Medina, 'Los hallazgos del Sacromonte a la luz de la historia de la Iglesia y de la teología católica', *Al-Qanṭara* 23 (2002) 437-76 (also in Barrios Aguilera and García-Arenal, *Invención y tesoro*, 79-112)

L.F. Bernabé Pons, 'Los mecanismos de una Resistencia. Los libros plúmbeos del Sacromonte y el *Evangelio de Bernabé*', *Al-Qanṭara* 23 (2002) 477-98 (also in Barrios Aguilera and García-Arenal, *Invención y tesoro*, 385-402)

F. Rodríguez Mediano and M. García-Arenal, 'Diego de Urrea y algún traductor más. En torno a las versiones de los "plomos"', *Al-Qanṭara* 23 (2002) 499-516 (extended version in Barrios Aguilera and García-Arenal, *Invención y tesoro*, 297-334)

A.K. Harris, 'The Sacromonte and the geography of the sacred in early modern Granada', *Al-Qanṭara* 23 (2002) 517-43 (Spanish version in Barrios Aguilera and García-Arenal, *Invención y tesoro*, 459-81)

M. Barrios Aguilera, 'Ignacio de las Casas y la polémica laminaria en la *Historia authéntica* de Viana y Laboraría. El texto', *Chronica Nova* 29 (2002) 343-405

R. Benítez Sánchez-Blanco, 'El discurso del licenciado Gonzalo de Valcárcel sobre las reliquias del Sacromonte', *Estudis* 28 (2002) 137-65 (extended version in Barrios Aguilera and García-Arenal, *Invención y tesoro*, 173-200)

L.F. Bernabé Pons, 'La nostalgia granadina de los moriscos', in J.A. González Alcantud and A. Malpica Cuello (eds), *Pensar la Alhambra*, Barcelona, 2001, 165-81

M. Barrios Aguilera, 'El bucle metahistórico. Los libros plúmbeos de Granada, realidad histórica y mito', *Fundamentos de Antropología* 10-11 (2001) 321-33

L.F. Bernabé Pons, 'Preliminary study', in M. de Luna, *Historia verdadera del rey don Rodrigo*, Granada, 2001, vii-lxx

M. Barrios Aguilera, 'Granada en escorzo. Luis Francisco de Viana y la historiografía del Sacromonte', *Demófilo* 35 (2000) 45-80

J. Godoy Alcántara, *Historia crítica de los falsos cronicones*, Madrid, 1868, (facsimile repr. Granada, 1999, with a preliminary study by O. Rey Castelao)

L.F. Bernabé Pons, *El texto morisco del Evangelio de San Bernabé*, Granada, 1998

M. Barrios Aguilera, 'Don Pedro de Castro y el Sacromonte de Granada en el *Místico Ramillete* de Heredia Barnuevo (1741)', in D.N. de Heredia Barnuevo, *Místico Ramillete. Vida de D. Pedro de Castro, fundador del Sacromonte*, Granada, 1998, vii-lxxiv

M. Barrios Aguilera, 'El Reino de Granada en la época de Felipe II a una nueva luz. De la cuestión morisca al paradigma contrarreformista', in J. Martínez Millán (ed.), *Felipe III (1598-1998). Europa y la Monarquía Católica*, vol. 3. *Inquisición, religión y confesionalismo*, Madrid, 1998, 63-88

G. Magnier, 'The dating of Pedro de Valencia's *Sobre el pergamino y láminas de Granada*', *Sharq al-Andalus. Estudios Mudéjares y Moriscos* 14-15 (1997-8) 353-73

G.A. Wiegers, 'The "Old" or "Turpiana" Tower in Granada and its relics according to Ahmad b. Qasim al-Hajarī', in R. Gyselen (ed.), *Sites et monuments disparus d'après les témoignages de voyageurs*, Leuven, 1996, 193-207

L.P. Harvey and G. Wiegers, 'The translation from Arabic of the Sacromonte Tables and the Archbishop of Granada. An illuminating correspondence', *Qurtuba. Estudios Andalusíes* 1 (1996) 59-78

L.F. Bernabé Pons, *El Evangelio de Bernabé. Un evangelio islámico español*, Alicante, 1995

J. Caro Baroja, *Las falsificaciones de la historia (en relación con la de España)*, Barcelona, 1991

M.J. Hagerty, 'La traducción interesada. El caso del Marqués de Estepa y los libros plúmbeos', in *Homenaje al prof. Jacinto Bosch Vilá*, Granada, 1991, ii, 1179-86

M. de Epalza, 'Etudes hispaniques actuelles sur l'Evangile islamisant de Barnabé', *Al-Masâq* 1 (1988) 33-38

M. de Epalza, 'Le milieu hispano-moresque de l'Evangile islamisant de Barnabé (XVIe-XVIIe siècle)', *Islamochristiana* 8 (1982) 159-76

D. Cabanelas, 'Intento de supervivencia en el ocaso de una cultura. Los libros plúmbeos de Granada', *Nueva Revista de Filología Hispánica* 30 (1981) 334-58

C. Alonso, *Los apócrifos del Sacromonte. Estudio histórico*, Valladolid, 1979

D. Cabanelas (ed.), *El Sacromonte, punto de confluencia doctrinal entre el Islam y la Cristiandad. La abadía del Sacromonte. Exposición artístico-documental. Estudios sobre su significación y orígenes*, Granada, 1974

L.P. Harvey, *The Moriscos and Don Quixote*, Inaugural lecture in the Chair of Spanish, University of London, King's College, 11 November, 1974

D. Cabanelas, 'Arias Montano y los libros plúmbeos de Granada', *Miscelánea de Estudios Árabes y Hebraicos* 18-19 (1969-70) 7-41

D. Cabanelas, *El morisco granadino Alonso del Castillo*, Granada, 1965, 1991[2] (preliminary study by J. Martínez Ruiz)

Z. Royo, *Reliquias martiriales y escudo del Sacro-Monte*, Granada, 1960

Luis Bernabé Pons

Luis del Mármol Carvajal

DATE OF BIRTH Between April and June 1524
PLACE OF BIRTH Granada, Spain
DATE OF DEATH Between 15 June and 13 November 1600
PLACE OF DEATH Unknown; probably Málaga, Spain

BIOGRAPHY

Luis del Mármol led an intense, itinerant life on both sides of the Mediterranean in a period of open confrontation between the Spanish and Ottoman empires. This enabled him to get to know Islamic culture at first hand. His historical works are a reflection of his personal experience in close contact with the inhabitants of North Africa and also with the descendants of the last Spanish Muslims. Until the middle of the 20th century, knowledge about him was reduced to brief autobiographical references in his books.

Mármol was born in Granada in 1524, 32 years after it was conquered by the Catholic Monarchs, and thus from his infancy he lived in a mixed society composed of Christians and converts to Christianity, Moriscos. He was the illegitimate son of Pedro del Mármol, who was from a converted Jewish family from Madrid and Toledo, and an official in the court of the Royal Chancellery. The identity of his mother is unknown, although some scholars have speculated (without firm evidence) that she may have been a Morisco.

At the age of just 11, Mármol joined the expedition of Emperor Charles V to conquer the city of Tunis in 1535. He must have remained in the Spanish garrisons in North Africa until around 1538, when he was taken prisoner by the Muslims. According to what he himself says, he spent seven years and eight months as a captive in various Islamic states (Morocco, Tarudant, Fez, Tremecen and Tunisia), although for the majority of this time he was in the hands of rulers of the Saʿdī dynasty, becoming one of the Christian servants at court. He took part in sub-Saharan and other expeditions, and learnt basic Arabic and Berber. He was released around 1546, but instead of returning to Christian territory he travelled around the Mediterranean, going as far as Egypt. At the beginning of the 1550s, he was in the Spanish garrison of Sicily, where he became friends with the exiled Tunisian sultan, Mulay Ḥasan, and from where he took part in the conquest of Mahdia. In Italy, he came across the work of Leo Africanus (also from Granada), *La descrittione dell'Africa*, which influenced him powerfully.

Mármol returned to Spain around 1557 and settled in Madrid, where he worked occasionally as a solicitor. In 1562, he married Doña María Ortiz in Toledo, probably a Jewish convert by origin, with whom he had at least two daughters.

When the uprising of the Moriscos in the Kingdom of Granada broke out (1568-71), Mármol returned to his native city to help against it. He carried out administrative and financial work in the armies of Juan de Austria and Luis de Requesens, and was temporarily jailed for apparent mismanagement. In 1573 in Granada, he published the first part of his *Descripción general de África*, a work in which he combines a history of Muslim and Christian confrontation, from the 7th century to the Battle of Lepanto in 1571, with a detailed geographical, economic and social description of North Africa. During his second stay in Granada, he lived in the Moorish district of Albaicín and established a friendship with the Moorish physician and translator Alonso del Castillo, who provided him with numerous translations of Arabic texts by local authors.

Mármol tried to get the Crown to recognise his services with some form of reward, requesting the post of royal chronicler. He did not have much success, but was finally given some confiscated properties of expelled Moriscos in Iznate, near Málaga, where he settled in 1574. Six years later he obtained the position of administrator of the royal estates in the Málaga region.

His reputation as an expert in Arab affairs kept him in contact with the court, which commissioned various translations from him, such as one about the captured Ottoman colours at the Battle of Lepanto (1572) and one of a letter from the new Moroccan sultan, Aḥmad al-Manṣūr (1578), both inadequate due to his limited knowledge of written Arabic. He also carried out an act of espionage in the Kingdom of Portugal in 1579, on the eve of the invasion by Philip II. These services almost led to his being made ambassador to Morocco, but this never happened. Similarly, he was one of the group of scholars who exposed the testimonies in Arabic lettering (parchment and lead books) by the so-called 'martyrs of Sacromonte' that appeared in Granada between 1588 and 1599, being one of the first to denounce them as fakes.

In the last two years of his life, he published the second part of his *Descripción general de África* (1599), and the *Historia del rebelión y castigo de los moriscos del reino de Granada* (1600), a detailed chronicle of the uprising in Granada.

MAIN SOURCES OF INFORMATION

Primary
Dedication and prologue of *Primera parte de la descripcion general de Africa*, Granada, 1573 (contains the main autobiographical details about Luis del Mármol)

Secondary
J. Castillo Fernández, 'Los Mármol, un linaje de origen converso al servicio de la monarquía española (siglos XV-XVIII)', *Historia y Genealogía. Revista de Estudios Históricos y Genealógicos* 4 (2014) 193-234, http://www.historia ygenealogia.com/numeros/hyg_4.pdf

J. Castillo Fernández, 'La historiografía española del siglo XVI. Luis del Mármol Carvajal y su *Historia del rebelión y castigo de los moriscos del reino de Granada*. Análisis histórico y estudio crítico', Granada, 2013 (Diss. University of Granada)

A.M. Puglisi, 'Escritura y ambición. La *Historia del rebelión y castigo de los moriscos* de Luis del Mármol Carvajal', *Investigaciones Históricas* 28 (2008) 141-56

F. Rodríguez Mediano, 'Luis de Mármol Carvajal. Veintidós años en África', in *Exploradores españoles olvidados de África*, Madrid, 2001, 49-80

A. Benjelloun, 'La figure de Luis del Mármol Carvajal et son voyage en Afrique du Nord, y compris en Libye et en Egypte', in *Mélanges Luce López-Baralt*, Tunisia, 2001, i, 101-19

V. Sánchez Ramos, 'Luis del Mármol y sus problemas de contabilidad militar', *Chronica Nova* 27 (2000) 305-14

V. Sánchez Ramos, 'El mejor cronista de la guerra de los moriscos. Luis del Mármol Carvajal', *Sharq al-Andalus* 13 (1996) 235-55, pp. 252-55

A. González de Amezua, 'Prólogo', in *Descripción General de África, (1573-1599)*, tomo I, Madrid, 1953, 9-38 (the first documented biography of Mármol)

R. Mauny, 'L'expédition marociane d'Ouadane (Mauritanie) vers 1543-1544', *Bulletin de l'Institut Français d'Afrique Noire* 11 (1949) 129-40

T. García Figueras, 'Españoles en África en el siglo XVI. I.- Los geógrafos e historiadores. Luis del Mármol Carvajal (1520-1599). Conferencia pronunciada en el Instituto de Estudios Africanos el 4 de abril de 1949', *Archivos del Instituto de Estudios Africanos* 10 (1949) 69-191

WORKS ON CHRISTIAN-MUSLIM RELATIONS

Descripción general de África, 'General description of Africa'

DATE 1573 and 1599
ORIGINAL LANGUAGE Spanish

DESCRIPTION

The *Descripción general de África* was conceived as a great historical and geographical work in 12 books, though they were finally left as 11 as the last, about the islands of Africa, was not included. It was published in two parts and three volumes. The first part was published in Granada in 1573, in two volumes, the first containing Books 1 and 2 (294 folios) and the second Books 3-6 (310 folios). The second part, including Books 7-11 (117 folios) appeared in Málaga in 1599. Books 1 and 2 contain a general description of the continent, and a history of the origins of Islam and Muslim wars against the Christians, and each of the others is devoted to one of the countries of North Africa, including Egypt and Ethiopia.

The fundamental objective of the work, as Mármol declares in the prologue, is to make North Africa known to Spaniards and Europeans in general in order to promote conquest and commercial exchange. These twin ideals are present throughout. There is a clear connection between this and the *Historia del rebelión y castigo de los moriscos del reino de Granada* (Málaga, 1600), in which the bloody uprising and suppression of the New Christians of Granada against the policies of acculturation by Philip II is described. In fact, Mármol had intended to publish the two together, but editorial problems and probably time constraints postponed the appearance of the *Historia*.

It is evident that, in structure as well as content, Mármol's work was inspired in good part by *La descrittione dell'Africa et delle cose notabli che ivi sono* (Venice, 1550), by the exiled Granadan Muslim, al-Ḥasan ibn Muḥammad al-Wazzān (c. 1494-c. 1554), better known as Leo Africanus, although analyses of both works highlight original contributions by Mármol, such as the use of other sources, including the chronicles of the Portuguese authors João de Barros (1496-1570) and Damião de Góis (1502-74). According to Rodríguez Mediano, 'It could be said on the structure that it was adapted from the work of Leo Africanus, and Mármol added texts that allowed him to tell of the Portuguese occupation of the Moroccan Atlantic coastline. In this way, in Mármol's text two writings meet, two almost contrary visions of Morocco that, more than being integrated into one unified discourse, are mixed' (Rodríguez Mediano, 'Luis de Mármol y el humanismo', pp. 386-87). The third source of information is the author's own personal experience, especially as regards the kingdoms of Morocco, where he spent the majority of his stay as a captive in the Saʿdī court.

Mármol also cites numerous classical authors, Greek, Latin and Byzantine, as well as Arabs and Europeans, although mostly it is a question of apocryphal quotes from texts by contemporary authors, especially Italian and Portuguese, in addition to the work by Leo Africanus. All this was because Mármol wanted to demonstrate greater learning than he really had. From the geographical aspect, his principal source is the 1548 review by the Italian cartographer, Giacomo Gastaldi, of the work of the 'great cosmographer', Claudius Ptolemy.

Book 2 contains a chronological account of Islamic expansion in the Middle East, Africa and Europe under the caliphs of Damascus and Baghdad until their decline (chs 1-29). From this point, the principal link feature is the successive 'African' or 'Moorish' dynasties of the Maghreb (chs 30-40). Throughout, Mármol pays special attention to confrontations between Islam and Christianity from the 7th century to the Battle of Lepanto in 1571.

In his cyclical conception of history, Mármol thought that Islamic civilisation was on the same level as others from Antiquity, such as the Chaldeans, Assyrians, Medes, Persians, Macedonians, Romans, Carthaginians and Byzantines. An emerging empire, driven by a charismatic leader in the person of Muḥammad, had expanded rapidly through the known world and had later entered into a period of decline due to internal dissension. Mármol hoped that dissent would confound the Ottomans, and the union of Christian states in the Holy League would then restore Jerusalem, Constantinople and Greece to Christianity in a new crusade.

The prevailing vision of politico-religious confrontation does not prevent the work from including positive elements about the North African regions. Mármol emphasises the high level of civilisation attained in cities such as Marrakesh and Fez, with magnificent monuments and colleges on a par with European universities. His intellectual attitude towards Islamic civilisation – present in both works – can be summed up in the following seemingly contradictory proposition: He was a profound admirer of Arab culture and a bitter enemy of the Islamic religion.

SIGNIFICANCE

The *Descripción general de África* had enormous influence, and is considered the initiator in Spain of what some authors have called the genre of the 'Berber chronicles', works by authors such as Diego de Torres, Suárez Montañés, Diego de Haedo and others, who relate their personal experiences and their knowledge of North Africa in order to promote a possible Spanish conquest, and who furthermore copied Mármol. According to de Bunes: 'For the Spaniards the accounts about Muslims and their territories can be divided into two periods, the last years of the 16th century being the dividing line, an age in which the work by the Granadan writer appears in print. That it should be the only comprehensive study on all the territory occupied by those practising Islam... and the author's own personality are the factors which make *Descripción general de África* a classic of European historiography on this subject' (M. Á de Bunes Ibarra, *La imagen de los musulmanes*, p. 3). However, its dissemination was even more advanced in scientific circles and among foreign intellectuals, especially after Nicolás Perrot's translation of the work into French (Paris, 1667). It was considered to be an almost unique authority and source on many aspects of the 17th-century Maghreb.

Despite the fact that we now know that, possibly because of his limited knowledge of Arabic, he consulted fewer Arabic texts than he admitted, his acknowledgement of the historiographical usefulness of Arabic sources constitutes a completely modern approach, and makes the *Descripción* a pioneering work in Spanish historiography and one unparalleled in what later would become known as Orientalism.

MANUSCRIPTS

MS Madrid, Biblioteca de la Real Academia de la Historia – 9-5088 (1572; the original autograph of Part 1, vol. 2, covering the kingdoms of Morocco, Fas, Tlemcen and Tunis)

EDITIONS & TRANSLATIONS

Muḥammad al-Qad and Muḥammad al-Jabrūnī (trans.), *Waṣf Ifrīqiyā*, Tangiers, 2013 (Arabic trans. of the whole work from the original Spanish edition)

J.P. Vittu and M. ben Miled (eds), *Histoire des derniers rois de Tunis du malheur des Hafçides, de la prise de Tunis par Charles Quint... de Kheyr-ed-Din Barberousse, Darghut... et autres valeureux raïs... d'après Marmol et Vermeyen*, Tunisia, 2007 (edition of the part on Tunis from the 1667 French edition)

Muḥammad Ḥajjī et al. (trans.), *Ifrīqiyā li-Marmūl Karfajāl, al-Faransiyya*, Rabat, 1984 (Arabic trans. from the abridged 1667 French trans.)

Descripción General de África (1573-1599), tomo I, Madrid, 1953 (partial facsimile edition, of the first volume of the 1573 Granada edition)

'A description of Africa, and all its Provinces', in J. Harris, *Navigantium atque Itinerantium Bibliotheca*, London, 1705, i, pp. 305-62 (trans. and adapted from Leo Africanus and Luis del Mármol Carvajal)

L'Afrique de Marmol, trans. N. Perrot, sieur d'Ablancourt, Paris, 1667 (inaccurate abridged French trans.)

Segvnda parte y libro septimo de la Descripcion General de Africa, donde se contiene las provincias de Numidia, Libia, la tierra de los Negros, la baxa y alta Etiopia, y Egipto, con todas las cosas memorables della..., Málaga, 1599

Libro tercero, y segvndo volvmen de la primera parte de la descripcion general de Affrica, con todos los sucessos de guerra, y cosas memorables..., Granada, 1573

Primera parte de la descripcion general de Affrica, con todos los succesos de guerras que a auido entre los infieles, y el pueblo Christiano, y entre ellos mesmos desde que Mahoma inue[n]to su secta, hasta el año del Señor mil y quinientos y setenta y vno, Granada, 1573

STUDIES

Castillo Fernández, 'La historiografía española del siglo XVI'

M. García-Arenal and F. Rodríguez Mediano, *Un Oriente español. Los moriscos y el Sacromonte en tiempos de Contrarreforma*, Madrid, 2010, pp. 363-66

F. Rodríguez Mediano, 'Luis de Mármol lecteur de Léon. Une appréhension espagnole de l'Afrique', in F. Pouillon et al. (eds), *Léon l'Africain*, Paris, 2009, 239-67

M. Martínez-Góngora, 'El discurso africanista del Renacimiento en *La primera parte de la Descripción General de África* de Luis del Mármol Carvajal', *Hispanic Review* 77 (2009) 171-95

A. Bouba Kidakou, 'África negra en los libros de viajes españoles de los siglos XVI y XVII', Madrid, 2006 (Diss. National University of Distance Education, Spain) (deals with Marmol's vision of the lands in the southern Sahara)

F. Rodríguez Mediano, 'Luis de Mármol y el humanismo. Comentarios sobre una fuente de la Historia del rebelión y castigo de los moriscos del reyno de Granada', *Bulletin Hispanique* 2 (2003) 371-404

P. Masonen, *The Negroland revisited. Discovery and invention of the sudanese middle ages*, Helsinki, 2003, pp. 215-33

M.D. Rodríguez Gómez, 'La influencia de León el Africano (ss. XV-XVI) en la obra de Luis del Mármol (s. XVI). Descripción de los núcleos de población del Rif', in C. del Moral (ed.), *En el epílogo del Islam andalusí. La Granada del siglo XV*, Granada, 2002, 359-96

A. Benjelloun, 'Luis de Mármol y Carvajal y su *Descripción general de Africa*', *Historia 16* 254 (1997) 116-23

A. Martín Casares, 'Escritura de concierto para la publicación de la Historia y descripción general del África, de Luis del Mármol Carvajal', *Revista del Centro de Estudios Históricos de Granada y su Reino*, 2ª época, 8 (1994) 273-77

O. Zihri, *L'Afrique au miroir de l'Europe. Fortunes de Jean Léon l'Africain à la Renaissance*, Geneva, 1991, pp. 165-73

M.Á. de Bunes Ibarra, *La imagen de los musulmanes y del norte de África en la España de los siglos XVI y XVII. Los caracteres de una hostilidad*, Madrid, 1989

L. Massignon, *Le Maroc dans les premières années du XVIe siècle. Tableau géographique d'après Léon l'Africain*, Algiers, 1906

Historia del rebelión y castigo de los moriscos del reino de Granada, 'History of the rebellion and punishment of the Moriscos in the Kingdom of Granada'

DATE 1600
ORIGINAL LANGUAGE Spanish

DESCRIPTION

Historia del rebelión y castigo de los moriscos is a chronology of the capture of Granada by Christian forces and of the events that followed over the next 90 years. It is divided into ten treatises or books, containing a total of 238 chapters in 245 printed folios. Book 1 gives a general description of the Emirate of Granada, covering its geography, origins, history and major monuments, and it continues with an account of the conquest by the Catholic Monarchs (1482-92), and the revolt of the Mudéjars (1499-1501) that culminated in their mass baptism. Books 2 and 3 deal with the principle events leading up to the outbreak of the revolt on Christmas Eve 1568, describing the growing religious suppression and forced acculturation of the converts, leading to the promulgation of the *Reales pragmáticas* (1566) in which the Moriscos' cultural practices were condemned, and the desperate efforts by moderates to negotiate on the eve of the rebellion. The main body of the work constitutes a detailed account of the uprising, with particular emphasis on the atrocities committed by the Moriscos in the Alpujarras (Book 4), the fighting that took place in and around Granada, and the final defeat of the Moriscos and their deportation to various parts of Castile (Books 5-10).

The work contains the fullest extant account of the fighting that took place during the conflict. Thanks to his considerable military experience, Mármol knew how to describe the strategies and tactics of both sides, and the activities of spies, renegades, collaborators and traitors, and he was also able to outline the limited support given to the rebels by North African states and the Ottoman Empire. In all, the work makes reference to almost 1,100 characters, a little more than 200 Muslims and Moriscos and almost 900 Christians.

In addition to his personal experience, Luis was able to draw for the *Historia* upon a great many recent official documents thanks to access via his father and brother to the registers of the Consejo Real and the Cámara de Castilla. His friend, the Morisco translator Alonso del Castillo, also made Arabic works accessible, both from the Morisco rebels and from earlier Granadan sources. These included the document of the surrender of Granada (1492), the *Memorial* against the *Reales pragmáticas* by the Morisco Francisco Núñez Muley, and translations of various Morisco prophecies of victory over the Christians.

A work that influenced the *Historia* extensively is the *Guerra de Granada* by the diplomat and humanist writer, Diego Hurtado de Mendoza (c. 1503-75), which was unpublished at the time Mármol was writing. As with the relationship between Leo Africanus's work and the *Descripción general de África*, Mendoza's work served mainly to inform the *Historia*. Mármol used it to make improvements to the first version of his own work, incorporating numerous comments, but also disagreeing with it on occasions, though without citing Mendoza at all. In no fewer than 74 (31%) of the 238 chapters in the *Historia*, traces 'borrowed' from *Guerra de Granada* can be identified, though it cannot be said that Mármol's work is a copy of Mendoza's because, amongst other things, it is longer and more complete than the earlier unfinished rough copy. *Guerra de*

Granada is the framework on which Mármol developed a more extensive, complete, ordered, grounded, contrasted and rigorous work.

Traditionally, it has been considered that the *Historia* was a reaction orchestrated by those in power to counteract the critical attitudes towards the conflict and the role of King Philip II that are evident in Mendoza's *Guerra de Granada*. The first to formulate this 'conspiracy theory' was the Swiss historiographer, Eduard Fueter, in his *Geschichte der neueren Historiographie* (Munich-Berlin, 1911). But it is now known that Mármol started his work in the autumn of 1571, a bare six months after the end of the war, and had already completed a first draft by March 1572, two years before Mendoza left his work unfinished in 1574. Furthermore, it was only published in 1600 and at Mármol's own expense, hardly what would be expected of a work that had been commissioned by the Crown as an apology for its actions.

SIGNIFICANCE

The most gruesome parts of the *Historia*, especially Book 4, which describes the crimes committed by the rebels against their Christian neighbours, were often used in later times by apologists for the expulsion of the Moriscos from Spain from the beginning of the 17th century, and by those promoting the cause of the so-called 'martyrs of the Alpujarras'. The work was also used and copied by well-known Spanish historians, among them Herrera y Tordesillas, Cabrera de Córdoba, Antolínez de Burgos, Bermúdez de Pedraza and Jaime Bleda (see Castillo Fernández, 'La guerra de los moriscos', pp. 694-700). The 1797 edition by Francisco Cerdá y Rico contributed greatly to its circulation in Spain and abroad. It was read in the 19th century by Washington Irving, William Prescott, Henry C. Lea, Albert de Circourt, Reinhart Dozy and Adolf Friedrich von Schack, and today the majority of scholars acknowledge its uniqueness, accuracy and supremacy as an indispensable reference for the history of Granada in the late 15th and 16th centuries.

The principal message the *Historia* tries to convey is the fatal destiny that awaits those who rise up against their natural masters. Its central argument is that a prosperous (although not free) people, the Moriscos of Granada, brought about their own destruction when they rebelled against their sovereign, Philip II. Nevertheless, the work is far from monochrome in attitude. It ranges from justification of Philip II's acculturation policy and condemnation of the Moriscos, to admiration for Arab culture and traditions. In this, Mármol's account often takes the opposite view from the majority of contemporary histories of Spanish towns, not only refusing to minimise or avoid the importance of Granada's Islamic past, but showing pride in its origins. Unlike other authors, who were defending a supposed Roman or early Christian origin, he defends its Muslim foundation. However, while he acknowledges that the policy of forced baptism was the spur to the Moriscos' uprising, he does not by any means exonerate them, because they were real heretics and were not prepared to abandon their former religion. At the same time, while he depicts them as base and cruel in their torture of the 'martyrs of the Alpujarras', he is clear about the untenable situation in which they found themselves, marginalised and oppressed because of their Muslim origins and unable to integrate into Christian society. His inclusion of the plea by the Morisco, Francisco Núñez Muley, and of the long documents that allowed the Christians entry into Granada in 1492, which were not honoured afterwards, illustrates this. In short, Mármol does not miss opportunities to point out that some intransigent sectors within Castilian society encouraged the Morisco revolt. His comment on the objective of the Council of Castile to finish off the Granadans is well-known: 'In truth it was a thing determined from above to eradicate the Moriscan nation from that land' (Book 2, ch. 11). While he does not seek to justify them, Mármol appears to understand the plight of the Moriscos involved in the rebellion. His honesty as a historian, despite his expressed opposition to the rebels, in many places makes him appear as the voice of the vanquished – as had been the case with certain classical Roman historians. Thus, he condemns the injustices and abuses of the Christians who were driven by greed and a desire to plunder and capture the Morisco peasants, whether they supported the rebels or not.

Mármol does not consider the Moriscos as a monolithic entity, but is aware of the social, cultural and geographical contrasts within the various Morisco communities of Granada, as well as how they evolved over time, as they were driven by the acculturation processes pursued by the Castilian authorities. He could speak with some feeling about the rebel side because his knowledge of Islamic societies was neither superficial nor indirect, unlike that of most of his contemporaries. His perception is the result of continuous and varied contact with different communities, ethnic groups and nationalities stamped with the Muslim mark, in Spain as well as in North Africa.

EDITIONS & TRANSLATIONS

Historia del rebelión y castigo de los moriscos del Reino de Granada, ed. J. Castillo Fernández, Granada (forthcoming)

Tārīkh thawrat wa-ʿiqāb andalusī mamlakat Gharnāṭa, trans. Jaʿfar ibn al-Ḥājj Sulamī, Tétouan, 1434 AH (2013) (Arabic trans. of Book 1)
Rebelion y castigo de los moriscos, Málaga, 1991 (facsimile of 1852 edition)
Historia del rebelión y castigo de los Moriscos del reino de Granada, ed. C. Rosell in, *Historiadores de sucesos particulares*, Madrid, 1852, i, pp. 123-365
Historia del rebelion y castigo de los Moriscos del reyno de Granada, 2 vols, Madrid, 1797
Historia del rebelion y castigo de los Moriscos del reyno de Granada, Málaga, 1600

STUDIES

J. Castillo Fernández, 'La historiografía española del siglo XVI'
J.A. González Alcantud, 'Lo que va de Luis del Mármol Carvajal a Pedro Soto de Rojas, o la clausura de la pluralidad en una ciudad mediterránea de la Edad Moderna', in J.A. González Alcantud and A. Stoll (eds.), *El Mediterráneo plural en la edad moderna. Sujeto histórico y diversidad cultural*, Barcelona, 2011, 85-111
Puglisi, 'Escritura y ambición'
J. Castillo Fernández, 'La guerra de los moriscos granadinos en la historiografía de la época (1570-1627)', in M. Barrios Aguilera and Á. Galán Sánchez (eds), *La historia del reino de Granada a debate. Viejos y nuevos temas. Perspectivas de estudio*, Málaga, 2004, 677-704
Rodríguez Mediano, 'Luis de Mármol y el humanismo'
Á. Galán Sánchez, *Rebelión y castigo de los moriscos*, Málaga, 1991, pp. 7-28
M.Á. de Bunes Ibarra, *Los moriscos en el pensamiento histórico. Historiografía de un grupo marginado*, Madrid, 1983, pp. 26-28
J. Caro Baroja, *Los moriscos del reino de Granada. Ensayo de historia social*, Madrid, 1957
E. Fueter, *Geschichte der neueren Historiographie*, Munich, 1911, pp. 240-42

Javier Castillo

Portugal

Carta de el-Rei D. Manuel

Anonymous; presumed to be King Manuel I
of Portugal

DATE OF BIRTH   31 May 1469
PLACE OF BIRTH   Alcochete, Portugal
DATE OF DEATH   13 December 1521
PLACE OF DEATH   Lisbon, Portugal

BIOGRAPHY
This letter has traditionally been attributed to Manuel I, King of Portugal, Lord of the Commerce, Conquest and Navigation of Arabia, Persia and India. However, scholars such as William Greenlee, Francis Rogers and Paulo Roberto Pereira find it improbable that it was sent from Lisbon to Castile because of the errors it contains, such as the mention of Pedro Álvares Cabral as leader of the royal fleet in 1502 rather than 1500, references to antiquated concepts such as Prester John, and the fact that it was addressed to the King of Castile rather than to the king of a unified Spain (though another letter of 1501 is addressed to 'El-Rei e à Raínha de Castela').

Known as 'the Fortunate' *(o Afortunado)* both for the events which brought him unexpectedly to the throne as well as the events that occurred during his reign, Manuel continued the voyages of discovery that had been started by his predecessors, leading to the discovery by Portugal of India, Brazil and the 'spice islands' of the Moluccas, and he started to organise imperial structures of administration. As a centralising king, he made Lisbon his permanent capital, strove to keep his nobles in check, and in 1521 promulgated an overhaul of the country's legal codes, which became known as the *Ordenações Manuelinas*. These were made known through the medium of print.

Manuel's reign saw the persecution of Jews and Muslims between 1496 and 1498, including the seizure of property, kidnapping and forcible conversion of Jewish children in March 1497, a massacre of Jews on the streets of Lisbon in 1506 (although suppressed by the King), and ultimately expulsion by a royal decree of 1507, leading to a major exodus of Moors and Marranos from Portugal. Then, as part of his marriage contract to Dona Maria of Aragón, Manuel agreed to the introduction of the Inquisition in Portugal in 1515. Some of this dramatic suppression may have been motivated by a desire to buy peace at home with Aragón and Castile, or else to ensure the papacy's approval of Portugal's territorial expansion. But more recent historians such as Luís Filipe Thomaz see Manuel's motivations as those of a messianist king who wanted to destroy Islam definitively, and establish an 'empire of universal peace'. To this end, Manuel responded to embassies by the Venetian Pisani in 1501 by sending a Portuguese squadron to help in the struggle against Islam in the eastern Mediterranean. While bent on the wholesale destruction of Islam, it might be pointed out, however, that he was open to a native African or Indian Christian priesthood, and promoted the appointment of Henry, the son of the king of Congo, to a bishopric in 1518.

Elsewhere, clerics and nobles were exempted from payment of the *dízima* tax, although Manuel's relationship with his nobles was far from conciliatory; bitter factionalism marked court politics and was even taken abroad to India. The prosperity brought to Portugal through the spice trade financed an artistic flowering that has become known as the 'Manueline' style, the construction of 26 monasteries and at least two cathedrals, including S. Jerónimos at Belém, and the completion of the convent at Tomar and the monastery of Santa Cruz in Coimbra.

MAIN SOURCES OF INFORMATION

Primary

'King Manuel's letter to the king and queen of Castile, July 1499', (repr. in E.G. Ravenstein [ed.], *Journal of the first voyage of Vasco da Gama, 1497-9*, Farnham, 2010, pp. 113-14)

'King Manuel to the Cardinal Protector, August 28, 1499', (repr. in Ravenstein, *Journal of the first voyage of Vasco da Gama*, pp. 114-16)

'Epistola de el-Rei D. Manoel ao Doge de Veneza (22 February 1501)', repr. Coimbra, 1907

'Letter of Dom Manuel to Catholic monarchs, dated August 28, 1501', copy from Venetian archives (repr. in C. Malheiro Dias, *História da colonização portuguesa do Brasil*, Porto, 1921-24, ii, pp. 165-67)

'The obedience of a king of Portugal', Venice, December 1501 (repr. Minneapolis: University of Minnesota Press, 1958)

'Epistola ad summum romanum pontificem' [Lisbon, 1505], ed. A. Anselmo, Lisbon, 1981

'Carta de D. Manuel a Fernando o Católico' [5 February 1506], in A. de la Torre and L. Suarez Fernandez (eds), *Documentos referentes a las relaciones com Portugal durante el reinado de los reyes Catolicos*, Valladolid, 1958-63, iii, pp. 145-47

'Epistola ad Julium Papam Secundum de victoria contra infidelis habita', Paris: Guillaume Eustace, 1507 (letter dated Abrantes, 25 September 1507)

'Epistola de provinciis i ciuitatibus: terris: & locis orientalis partis: sue ditioni fideique Christiane nouissime per eum subactis', Rome: Stephan Plannck, 1508 (letter signed Alcochete, 12 June 1508)

Martin Fernández de Figueroa of Salamanca, *Conquista de las indias de Persia & Arabia que fizo la armada del rey don Manuel de Portugal & de las muchas tierras: diuersas gentes: extrañas riquezas & grandes batallas que alla ouo*, Salamanca, 1512

Ordenações Manuelinas, ed. João Pedro Buonhomini, Lisbon: Valentim Fernandes, 1514

'Carta das Novas que vieram a el Rey nosso Senhor do descobrimento do preste Joham', Lisbon, 1521

João de Barros, *Da Ásia* (original 1553), ed. H. Cidade and M. Múrias, Lisbon, 1945 (second Decade, first Part)

Damião de Góis, *Chrónica do felicissimo rei D. Manuel*, Lisbon, 1567, ed. J.M. Teixeira de Carvalho and D. Lopes, Coimbra, 1926

Jerónimo Osório, *De rebus Emmanuelis*, Lisbon 1571 (trans. [Portuguese], *Da vida e feitos d'El Rei D. Manuel*, Lisbon, 1804; trans. [English] J. Gibbs, *The history of the Portuguese during the reign of Emmanuel*, London, 1752)

C. Radulet and L.F. Thomaz (eds), *Viagens portuguesas à Índia, 1497-1513. Fontes italianas para a sua história: o códice Riccardiano 1910 de Florença*, Lisbon, 2002

Secondary

F. Soyer, *The persecution of the Jews and Muslims of Portugal. King Manuel I and the end of religious tolerance*, Leiden, 2007

S. Subrahmanyam, 'The birth-pangs of Portuguese Asia. Revisiting the fateful "long decade" 1498-1509', *Journal of Global History* 2 (2007) 261-80

J.P. Oliveira e Costa, *Dom Manuel I, 1469-1521. Um princípe do Renascimento*, Lisbon, 2005

S. Subrahmanyam and L.F. Thomaz, 'Evolution of empire. The Portuguese in the Indian Ocean during the sixteenth century', in J. Tracy (ed.), *The political economy of merchant empires. State power and world trade, 1350-1750*, Cambridge, 1997, 298-331

L.F. Thomaz, 'L'idée impériale manuéline', in J. Aubin (ed.), *La découverte, le Portugal et l'Europe*, Paris, 1990, 35-103

F.M. Rogers, *The quest for Eastern Christians. Travels and rumour in the Age of Discovery*, Minneapolis, 1962

J.P. Oliveira Martins, *História de Portugal*, Lisbon, 1887[4], ii, pp. 5-30

WORKS ON CHRISTIAN-MUSLIM RELATIONS

Carta de el-Rei D. Manuel ao Rei Catholico narrando-ilhe as viagens portugezas a India desde 1500 ate 1505, 'Letter of King Dom Manuel to the Catholic king describing to him the Portuguese voyages to India from 1500 to 1505'

DATE 23 October 1505
ORIGINAL LANGUAGE Italian

DESCRIPTION
This 21-page work was published as a copy of a letter sent by the King of Portugal to the King of Castile, describing the progress made in discovering India up to 1505 (*successo de India*). However, it is actually a compilation of material from Manuel's letter of 1501, Vespucci's *Mundus novus* letter (1502/3), an anonymous Portuguese account of Pedro Álvares Cabral's voyage, and the account of the Priest Joseph (see Greenlee, *Voyage of Pedro Alvares Cabral*, pp. 97-113). It was probably compiled and printed on the orders of the members of the Portuguese embassy at Rome. Beginning with Cabral's expedition in 1500, it tells of voyages under João de Nova (1501), Vasco da Gama (1502), Afonso de Albuquerque (1503), Lopo Soares de Albergaria (1504) and D. Francisco de Almeida (1505). The gist of what is said follows on from Manuel's letter of July 1499, in which the idea of diverting the spice trade from the Moors 'to the natives and ships of our own kingdom' was underlined, with the greater plan of 'pushing with more ardour war against the Moors in the territories conquered by us'. Outright war on all fronts was not, however, a realistic proposition. Thus, while Calicut, an enemy from the time of Vasco da Gama's initial voyage of 1498, repeatedly figures as the object of Portuguese violence, in which laden ships were seized, others burned, fleets engaged and the city itself bombarded, friendly relations were entertained with Muslim port cities on the Swahili coast such as Quíloa (Kilwa) and Malindi, gifts were exchanged, treaties were signed and pilots granted to assist the Portuguese. The Portuguese considered Calicut particularly antagonistic for being stirred up by a group of 'Moors from Mecca' who were resident there.

Cochin, with its sizeable population of Mar Thoma Christians, who are described in this letter, became the port city on the Malabar coast with which the Portuguese resolved to do business. There are interesting ethnographic reports on polygamous marriage customs, with the criticism that it diminishes chastity, use of litters, and *sati* amongst the 'idolaters'. Inflammatory terminology for Muslims as *perros* or 'dogs', such as occurs in Álvaro Velho's account of Vasco da Gama's voyage of 1498, is avoided, and the Portuguese disgust at betel chewing, as expressed by Afonso de Albuquerque, is also absent. There are details regarding the spice trade and the types of coinage in use (*fanone, mitricale*), new types of combat craft (*tafforea*), and a brief description of 'neighbouring kingdoms', such as Ormuz, Julfar, Madagascar and Zanzibar, as well as some that are more difficult to identify (Canibar), and some that are incorrect (confusion, for example, between Sumatra and Sri Lanka). Speculation surrounding the movement of the Hottentots between the southern African Cape and the 'Antarctic pole' (probably meaning the newly discovered but little understood South American continent, as in Vespucci's *Mundus novus* letter) is also misplaced.

An interesting encounter with a victim of the expulsion of the Jews from Spain who had made her way from Seville to Calicut is reported: having been recaptured by her former inquisitors, she ends up throwing herself into the sea. Otherwise, it is perhaps surprising that there is no mention of the new fortresses being built in Angediva, Cannanore, Cochin, Sofala, and Santa Cruz do Cabo de Gué.

SIGNIFICANCE
The letter seems to have been written as a gauge by which it could be claimed that Manuel rivalled the Catholic Monarchs, following their conquest of Granada in 1492: it ends, 'so that we might see our navigation both peaceful and successful to the greater glory and increase of our Holy Faith'. Since Manuel's authorship has been widely doubted, scholars have often placed it along with the many fanciful accounts that were written in the 15th century. While this has compromised its importance among historians, it may nevertheless have circulated widely, as is attested by Ariosto's understanding of Ethiopian Christianity.

Many of the events it describes relating to the East were the subject of five further chapbooks published between 1506 and 1508, a number in Germany, after which a strange silence falls over the Portuguese enterprise between 1508 and 1513, despite important developments such as the capture of Goa in 1510. For these events, we are forced to look to the news published in Martin Fernández de Figueroa of Salamanca's *Conquista de las indias de Persia & Arabia que fizo la armada del rey don Manuel de Portugal & de las muchas tierras: diuersas gentes: extrañas riquezas & grandes batallas que alla ouo*, 1512.

Incidentally, next to Vespucci's *Mundus novus* letter of 1502/3, the letter is one of the first printed works to mention the discovery of Brazil.

MANUSCRIPTS

There are no known manuscripts of the letter. Peragallo reported in 1892 that only three copies of the original printed text apparently existed, one in the Biblioteca Marciana, Venice (as worked on by Francisco Adolfo de Varnhagen and A.C. Burnell), one in the Biblioteca Corsini, Florence (reported by H. Narducci), and one in the Biblioteca Columbina, Seville (discovered by Henry Harrisse). Since that time, further copies have been discovered in the Biblioteca Comunale Augusta in Perugia, the Biblioteca Civica Bertoliana in Vicenza, the British Library, and the James Ford Bell Collection, University of Minnesota.

EDITIONS & TRANSLATIONS

S.J. Pacifici, *Copy of a letter of the king of Portugal sent to the king of Castile, concerning the voyage and success of India*, Minneapolis MN, 1955

Carta de el-Rei D. Manuel ao Rei Catholico, narrando-lhe as viagens portuguezas á Inia desde 1500 até 1505, reimpressa sobre o prototypo romano de 1505, ed. P. Peragallo, Lisbon, 1892, pp. 9-66, http://archive.org

A.C. Burnell, *The Italian version of a letter from the king of Portugal (Dom Manuel) to the king of Castille (Ferdinand); written in 1505, giving an account of the voyages to and conquests in the East Indies from 1500 to 1505 A.D.; reprinted from the copy (printed by J. Besicken at Rome in 1505) in the Marciana Library at Venice, (one of the three now in existence), with notes, etc.*, London, 1881

Included in *Gesta proxime per Portugalenses in India. Ethiopia. [et] aliis orientalibus terries*, Rome: Johann Besicken, 1506 and 1507

Copia de vna littera del re de Portagallo ma[n]data al re de Castella del viaggio & successo de Jndia, Rome: Johann Besicken, 1505

Copia de una littera del re de Portagallo ma[n]data al re de Castella del uiaggio & sucesso de India, Milan: Pietro Martire di Mantegazzi, 1505

STUDIES

P.R. Pereira (ed.), *Os tres únicos testemunhos do descobrimento do Brasil*, Rio de Janeiro, 1999[2]

A. de la Torre and L. Suarez (eds), *Documentos referentes a las relaciones com Portugal durante el reinado de los Reyes Catolicos*, 3 vols, Valladolid, 1958-63

Rogers, *Quest for Eastern Christians*

G.C.A. Boehrer, (Review of Pacifici's edition), *The Americas* 13 (1957) 314-15

J.E. Gillet, (Review of Pacifici's edition), *Hispanic Review* 25 (1957) 132-33

G. Moser (Review of Pacifici's edition), *Books Abroad* 30 (1956) 228

W.B. Greenlee (ed.), *The voyage of Pedro Alvares Cabral to Brazil and India*, London, 1938, p. 42

Stefan Halikowski-Smith

Diário da viagem de Vasco da Gama

'Journal of the voyage of Vasco da Gama'

DATE Early 16th century
ORIGINAL LANGUAGE Portuguese

DESCRIPTION

The manuscript of *Diário da viagem de Vasco da Gama* was found at the Convent of the Holy Cross, Coimbra, by Alexandre Herculano in 1834. It is thought to be an early 16th-century copy of a now-lost original, with no title page or other autograph to identify the author. In Ames's translation, the text is 90 pages long.

There has been much speculation as to which one of da Gama's crew wrote the diary. Kopke, editor of the first edition (1838), listed 39 men known to have travelled on the voyage and, by a process of elimination, ended up with four possible candidates, two of whom are generally preferred: Álvaro Velho and João de Sá. Of these, many scholars favour Velho, reasoning that the standard of the language is poor and does not compare well with that of contemporary chronicles, and that the use of the phrase 'us others' signifies that the author identified himself as one of the crew rather than as an officer. The *Diário* finishes abruptly in Rio Grande, Guinea Bissau, leading some to argue that Velho was a *degredado* (convict exile) who chose not to return to Portugal. Valentim Fernandes states that Velho described to him in detail da Gama's voyage, as well as conditions in Guinea. Fernão Lopes de Castanheda's chronicle lends support to Velho's authorship by showing that João de Sá's reactions to events are at odds with those of the author of the manuscript. However, de Sá was the scribe (*escrivão*) on board da Gama's own boat, the São Rafael, and accompanied da Gama to several important meetings, so he would appear to be a strong candidate. It is also possible that neither of these two was the author, as only 39 of the 170 men who went on the voyage have been identified (Ames, *Em nome de Deus*, pp. 20-5; all quotations in this entry are taken from Ames's translation).

The *Diário* is not a complete account of the voyage; rather it relates various parts of the journey, notably interactions between Vasco da Gama and those he encountered in eastern Africa and India. Muslims, whom he encountered in eastern Africa, are described as being 'of the Mohammedan sect and speak like Moors' (p. 50), i.e. Muslims who spoke Arabic. Arab and Ottoman traders are called 'white Moors' to differentiate them from the black African Muslims.

The *Diário* relates several encounters between de Gama and Muslims in eastern Africa. In some cases, the encounter reveals distrust, with hostages being taken, as in Mozambique (pp. 49-57) and Mombasa (pp. 60-63), whereas in other cases, as in Malindi, the ruler made da Gama and his crew welcome (pp. 64-68).

The longest portion of the *Diário* concerns the time spent by de Gama and his men in Calicut (pp. 71-94). This refers to trade negotiations with the king, Zamorin and also records a meeting with Muslim traders from Tunis, who spoke Genoese and Castilian. One of them addressed de Gama with the words, 'May the devil take thee! What brought you hither?' (p. 71). The Portuguese were also asked why they had come, and they replied, 'In search of Christians and spices.'

The Muslim traders acted as intermediaries and translators, which led to misunderstandings and mutual distrust.

On several occasions, the *Diário* reports that the travellers have been told of Christians who were already present in the region. Sometimes this is a reference to Christians from the land of Prester John (Ethiopia) (p. 51), whilst on other occasions Indian Hindus are being referred to, Hindus being misidentified as Christians either by the author of the *Diário* or by his informants, whether Portuguese or Muslims. Misunderstandings of this kind occurred in eastern Africa, too, where informants regularly told da Gama of the presence of Christians, and in Calicut. The king of Calicut, Zamorin, was understood to be a Christian and the shore party were taken to pray in 'Christian churches', not realising that they were Hindu temples (pp. 75-76).

SIGNIFICANCE

Since the *Diário* was unknown until the 19th century, the text itself had little direct influence on travellers after de Gama's time, although it is clear that Fernão Lopes de Castanheda must have known it, since he used it as the basis of his account of da Gama's journey in *História do descobrimento e conquista da Índia* (1551). Luís Vaz Camões, in *Os Lusíadas*, turned the events described in the work into a poetic masterpiece.

The use of the term 'Moors' to describe Muslims is an indication that the Portuguese Christians identified Muslims in the terms with which they were most familiar.

The *Diário* has helped in the reinterpretation of events and the actions of the Portuguese in relation to the establishment of their rule in Goa and their attitudes to Muslims.

MANUSCRIPTS

MS Porto, Biblioteca Pública Municipal – 804 (early 16th century)

EDITIONS & TRANSLATIONS

G. Ames (trans.), *Em nome de Deus. The journal of the first voyage of Vasco da Gama to India, 1497-1499*, Leiden, 2009, pp. 33-112 (English trans. with introduction)

E. Axelson, *Vasco da Gama. The diary of his travels through African waters 1479-1499*, Somerset West, Cape Town, 1998, pp. 21-53 (includes full text of the diary in English, with introduction and extensive footnotes)

P. Teyssier, P. Valetin and J. Aubin (eds), *Voyages de Vasco da Gama. Relation des expédicions de 1497-1499 et 1502-1503*, Paris, 1995, pp. 85-167 (French trans.)

Vasco da Gama. De ontdekking van de zeeweg naar Indië. een ooggetuigenverslag 1479-1499, Baarn, 1991 (Dutch trans. of Giertz's German trans.)

L. de Albuquerque (ed.), *Grandes viagens maritimas*, Lisbon, 1989, pp. 7-51

G. Giertz (ed.), *Vasco da Gama. Die Entdeckung des Seewegs nach Indien. Ein Augenzeugenbericht 1497-1499*, Stuttgart, 1986, Darmstadt, 1990², pp. 35-143 (German trans.)

N. Águas (ed.), *Roteiro da primeira viagem de Vasco da Gama*, Lisbon, 1987, pp. 19-92

Á. Velho, 'Relação da primeira à Índia pela armada chefiada por Vasco da Gama', in J.M. Garcia (ed.), *As viagens dos descombrimentos*, Lisbon, 1983, 159-211

A. Cruz (ed.), *'Diário' da viagem de Vasco da Gama*, Porto, 1969 (facsimile)

J.P. Machado and V. Campos (eds), *Vasco da Gama e a sua viagem de descobrimento*, Lisbon, 1969, pp. 113-225

Á. Velho, 'Roteiro da viagem em que descobrimento da Índia pelo Cabo da Boa Esperança Fez Dom Vasco da Gama', in B. de Fonseca (ed.), *As grandes viagens Portuguesas*, Lisbon, 1964, 29-94

A. Baião and A. de Magalhães (eds), *Diário da viagem de Vasco da Gama*, 2 vols, Porto, 1945

A. Fontoura da Costa (ed.), *Roteiro da primeira viagem de Vasco da Gama (1447-1499) por Álvaro Velho*, Lisbon, 1940, 1960², 1969³, pp. 3-83

Á. Velho, 'Roteiro da viagem de Vasco da Gama', in A.B. Bragança Pereira (ed.), *Arquivo portugués oriental*, Goa, 1936, 10-70

E.G. Ravenstein (trans.), *Vasco da Gama's first voyage*, London, 1898 (first English trans.)

F. Hümmerich (ed.), *Vasco da Gama. Die Entdeckung des Seewegs nach Ostindien*, Munich, 1898, pp. 149-91 (first German trans.)

A. Morelet (trans.), *Journal du voyage de Vasco da Gama en MCCCCX-CVII*, trans. A. Morelet, Lyon, 1864, pp. 1-84 (French trans.)

A. Herculano (ed.), *Roteiro da viagem de Vasco da Gama em MCCCCX-CVII*, Lisbon, 1861

E-T. Charton (ed.), *Voyageurs anciens et modernes*, Paris, 1855, iii, pp. 219-64 (first French trans.)

D. Kopke and A. da Costa Paiva (eds), *Roteiro da viagem que em descombrieto da índia pelo Cabo da Boa Esperança fez Dom Vasco da Gama em 1497*, ed. Porto, 1838

STUDIES

N. Cliff, *The last crusade. The epic voyages of Vasco da Gama*, New York, 2011

Ames, *Em nome de Deus*, pp. 1-32

Axelson, *Vasco da Gama*, pp. 54-67

C.M. Radulet, 'Vasco da Gama and his successors', in G.D. Winius (ed.), *Portugal, the pathfinder. Journeys from the medieval toward the modern world*, Madison WI, 1995, 133-43, pp. 136-37

S. Subrahmanyam, *The career and legend of Vasco da Gama*, Cambridge, 1997, pp. 76-163

J.G. Garcia, art. 'Velho, Álvaro', in L. de Albuquerque and F.C. Domingues (eds), *Dicionário de história dos descobrimentos Portugueses*, Lisbon, 1994, ii, pp. 1064-5

S. Subrahmanyam, *The Portuguese Empire in Asia 1500-1700*, London, 1993, pp. 56-60

Ravenstein, *Vasco da Gama's first voyage*, pp. xi-xxxvi

John Chesworth

Navigatione de Lisbona a Callichut

'Voyage from Lisbon to Calicut'

DATE Early 16th century
ORIGINAL LANGUAGE Italian

DESCRIPTION

In 1500, Manuel I, King of Portugal, commissioned a fleet of 12 ships to be sent to India and East Africa. The expedition was to be led by Pedro Álvares Cabral and included some Franciscan friars and clergy, who were to remain in India. The king instructed Cabral to build a factory in Calicut, to establish relations with Christian kingdoms in India and to impede Muslim trade. The king sent letters to the kings of Kilwa, Malindi and Calicut, in Arabic and Portuguese, to consolidate the links made by Vasco da Gama.

Navigatione de Lisbona a Callichut was originally written in Portuguese, by a member of Cabral's fleet. The surviving manuscripts are in Italian and are translations from a lost Portuguese original; three of them date from very soon after the fleet's return to Portugal. The account is in the form of a diary of events, rather than a navigator's log or *Roteiro*. The Washington MS consists of 24 folio pages, and the Greenlee translation is 48 pages in length.

The identity of the author is uncertain, except that it is clear that he was on the voyage and accompanied Cabral on shore visits several times. Ravenstein (*Journal of the first voyage of Vasco da Gama*) notes that João de Sá travelled with both da Gama and Cabral and may have been the author of both accounts (Greenlee, *Voyage*, p. 55). However, the style of *Navigatione de Lisbona a Callichut* is more sophisticated than that of *Diário da Viagem de Vasco da Gama* and the author does not misidentify Hindus as Christians, as in the da Gama account.

The fleet was blown off course in a storm and 'discovered' Brazil (Greenlee, *Voyage*, pp. 58-60), before continuing their voyage to Zafalle (Sofala, Mozambique). Near Sofala, they found two Moorish ships. Their captain was questioned and stated that he was a cousin of the king of Malindi, whom Cabral considered a good friend of the Portuguese. The *Navigatione* reports that the Moorish captain asked if 'they had an enchanter who could recover gold lost overboard'. Cabral replied, 'We are Christians and that among us such things are not known' (Greenlee, *Voyage*, pp. 61-65). The fleet then visited Arab settlements in Mozambique and Kilwa. The narrative describes the rulers along the coast as Moors, and reports that the entire coast was inhabited by Moors, but that there were 'said to be Christians on the mainland, who wage many wars' (Greenlee, *Voyage*, p. 65).

In Malindi, they sent an Arabic-speaking translator to deliver a letter from Manuel to the king and to conduct negotiations, which appear to have been about trade. They were made welcome and treated with honour and were provided with a pilot to guide the fleet across to India (Greenlee, *Voyage*, pp. 65-68).

One chapter, 'Concerning the Red and Persian Seas', explains that the mouth of the Red Sea is where 'The House of Mecca and Saint Catherine of Mount Sinai are', and that the lands are ruled by kings who were either Moors or idolaters (Greenlee, *Voyage*, pp. 68-69).

Calicut had a Hindu ruler who was willing to trade with the Portuguese, but Arabic was the only language that could be used for negotiations, so Arabs were the intermediaries. A fight ensued between Arab traders and the Portuguese, which left many dead (Greenlee, *Voyage*, pp. 70-85).

The Portuguese did not build a factory in Calicut, but they were able to set one up in Cochin and did make contact with Indian Christians of the Mar Thoma Church. They were able to depart with trade goods and also took with them two Indian Christians who wanted to go to Jerusalem. These Christians were priests from the Mar Thoma Church; one is named as Priest Joseph (Greenlee, *Voyage*, pp. 85-89).

The account relates the voyage home by way of the East African coast and the Cape of Good Hope, and says that only six of the ships that set out returned to Lisbon in July 1501 (Greenlee, *Voyage*, pp. 88-91). This is followed by lists of spices and their value (Greenlee, *Voyage*, pp. 91-94).

SIGNIFICANCE

The narrative makes clear the presence of Moors along the East African coast, an indication that the Portuguese Christians identified Muslims using the terms they were familiar with from their own milieu.

Relations with Muslims were mixed: in some cases prospects for trade encouraged the development of good relations, as in Malindi, whereas where competition was seen as threatening, both parties resorted to violence.

In India, the Portuguese were able to learn more of the 'idolaters', that is, Hindus, thereby clearing up initial misunderstandings resulting from Vasco da Gama's reports (Greenlee, *Voyage*, p. 79).

Franciscan friars and priests were sent with the fleet, some to remain in India and East Africa in order to start missionary work. This adds support to the view that the Portuguese were not only interested in establishing trade, but were intent on spreading Christianity and so preventing the spread of Islam and its influence.

MANUSCRIPTS

MS Washington, Library of Congress – 94218598 Nauigatione de Colochut, fols 35v-58r (1503; in Venetian Italian, bound with the Letters of Angelo Trevisan di Bernadino)

MS Venice, Marciana National Library – Viaggi vi, 277, Contarini A and B (early 16th century; bound together; Italian translations of the original Portuguese text; Washington and Contarini B appear to be the earliest MSS, with Contarini A slightly later)

MS Venice, Marciana National Library – Ital., Cl. 6, No. 208, *Viaggiatori Antichi* (after 1523)

EDITIONS & TRANSLATIONS

'The anonymous narrative of the voyage of Pedro Alvares Cabral 1500', in G.S.P. Freeman-Grenville (ed.), *The East African coast. Select documents from the first to the earlier nineteenth century*, Oxford, 1960, London, 1975[2], 59-63 (extract from Greenlee's English trans. of the parts of the narrative concerning East Africa)

W.B. Greenlee (trans.), *The voyage of Pedro Álvares Cabral to Brazil and India*, London, 1937, pp. 56-94 (English trans.; contains an extensive Introduction by Greenlee, pp. i-lxix, 53-56, together with additional supporting contemporary documents about Cabral and the voyage)

T. de Aragão Morato (trans.), 'Navegaçao do Capitao Pedro Alvares Cabral escritta por hum piloto portuguez traduzida da lingoa portugueza para a italiana e novamen te do italiano para o portuguez', in *Collecçao de noticias para a Historia e Geografía das Naçoes Ultramarinas, que vivem nos dominios portuguezes, ou lhes sao visinhas*, Lisbon, 1812, ii/3 (Portuguese trans. from Italian MS)

J. Temporal, *Historiale description de l'Afrique*, Lyon, 1556, vol. 2 (French trans.)

G.B. Ramusio, *Delle navigationi et viaggi*, Venice, 1554, vol. 1

S. Grynaeus (ed.), *Die new Welt der Landschaften unnd Insulen. So bis hie her allen Altweltbeschrybern unbekant, Jungst aber von den Portugalesern vnnd Hispaniern im Nidergenglichen Meer herfunden...*, trans. M. Herr, Strassburg, 1534 (German trans. of *Novus orbis regionum*, includes *Navigatione de Lisbona a Callichut*)

S. Grynaeus (ed.), *Novus orbis regionum ac insularum veteribus incognitarum...*, Paris, 1532, Basle, 1537, 1555, pp. 1-153 (Latin trans.)

'Navigatione de Lisbona a Callichut, de lengua Portogallese in taliana', in *Paesi Noamente retrouati et Nouo Mondo da Alberico Vesputio intitulato*, Vicenza, 1507, vols 2 and 3, chs lxiii-lxxxiii (Italian trans. of the narrative, together with accounts of the voyages of Cadamosto and de Sintra, in a book which is regarded as one of the first collections of accounts of voyages)

STUDIES

N. Cliff, *The last crusade. The epic voyages of Vasco da Gama*, New York, 2011, pp. 282-88

C.M. Radulet, 'Vasco da Gama and his successors', in G.D. Winius (ed.), *Portugal, the pathfinder. Journeys from the medieval toward the modern world*, Madison WI, 1995, 133-44, pp. 138-39

S. Subrahmanyam, *The career and legend of Vasco da Gama*, Cambridge, 1997, pp. 174-84

Greenlee, *Voyage*, pp. i-lxix, 53-56

E.G. Ravenstein (ed. and trans.), *A journal of the first voyage of Vasco da Gama, 1497-1499*, London, 1898

John Chesworth

Martín Fernández de Figueroa

DATE OF BIRTH   Unknown
PLACE OF BIRTH   Possibly Salamanca
DATE OF DEATH   First half of the 16th century
PLACE OF DEATH   Possibly Salamanca

BIOGRAPHY

Little is known about the life of Martín Fernández de Figueroa, except that he was a member of the minor aristocracy in Salamanca and a relative of Pedro de Añaya (or Anaya), one of the Castilian captains who took part in the construction of a fort in Sofala for Manuel I of Portugal in 1505, and in the subsequent Portuguese exploration and conquest in the Indian Ocean. The *Conquista* is the story of his travels, but in its final version it depended on other hands. The editor of his *Conquista*, Juan Agüero (or Juan Remón) de Trasmiera, was a scholar from Cantabria who claimed to have family links with Figueroa. This relationship has often been accepted on the basis of their living near each other, but it can now be ascertained that Juan Remón de Trasmiera was the son of Juan de Trasmiera and Violante Remón de Figueroa, 'inhabitants' of Salamanca; he was, therefore, related to Martín Fernández de Figueroa through his Salamanca-born mother. Along with his parents, Juan Agüero left for Santo Domingo in the Caribbean on 5 October 1512, in the service of the bishop, Francisco García de Padilla (Archivo General de Indias, Contratación, 5536, L.1, fol. 184v). An uncorroborated report claims that Figueroa was *corregidor* (mayor) of Alcaraz (Albacete).

Juan Agüero had travelled before to Rome and wrote several works, including *Triunfo Raimundino* (1512), in which he praised the knightly families of Salamanca. Some of the heraldic descriptions contained in this work were commented and elaborated upon by Agüero. Some minor works are also known, such as the translation from the Italian of *Probadas flores Romanas* (Valencia, 1510), a collection of Latin verses composed to close *El libro del famoso y muy esforçado cavallero Palmerín de Oliva* (Salamanca, 1511) and a co-authored piece, *Repertorio de los tiempos. Con un tratado de la crescencia y decrescencia del dia y de la noche* (Salamanca, 1513).

Before 1514, he also wrote an anti-Jewish poem entitled 'Este es el pleyto de los Judios con el perro de Alba, y de la burla que les hizo. Nuevamente trobado por el Br. Juan de Trasmiera, residente en Salamanca, que hizo a ruego e pedimento de un Señor'. In this poem, the Jewish population of Alba is annoyed by a dog that is only friendly with 'old' Christians; the Jews try to punish the dog, but it finally gains the upper hand by getting rid of most of them. In later versions, the dog has a cat as a sidekick. This poem was highly popular, and was reprinted many times, as well as being frequently quoted in other works. In 1578, these poems were published once more by Pedro Malo's printing shop, in Barcelona, and the Jews were replaced by 'Moriscos', even though this was not Juan Agüero's original intention. It is of note that all Agüero's works were written before his departure for the American colonies in 1512, and were published in Salamanca before 1514.

MAIN SOURCES OF INFORMATION

Primary
MS Seville, Archivo General de Indias – Contratación, 5536, L.1, fol. 184v

Secondary
J. Martín Abad, *Post-incunables ibéricos*, Madrid, 2007, p. 263
L. Gil, (ed.), *Conquista de las Indias de Persia e Arabia que fizo la armada del rey don Manuel de Portugal e de las muchas tierras, diversas gentes, extrañas riquezas y grandes batallas que allá hubo. En sumario del bachiller Juan Agüero de Trasmiera*, Valladolid, 1999, pp. 18-21
L. Ruiz Fidalgo, *La imprenta en Salamanca. 1501-1600*, Madrid, 1994, pp. 227-28
J.B. McKenna (ed.), *A Spaniard in the Portuguese Indies. The narrative of Martín Fernández de Figueroa*, Cambridge MA, 1967, pp. 7-12
J.E. Gillet, 'Coplas del Perro de Alba', *Modern Philology* 23 (1926) 417-44; 26 (1928) 123-28

WORKS ON CHRISTIAN-MUSLIM RELATIONS

Conquista de la India de Persia & Arabia que fizo la armada del rey don Manuel de Portugal; Conquista de la India de Persia & Arabia, 'Conquest of India, Persia and Arabia by the fleet of King Manuel of Portugal'

DATE Between 1505 and 1512
ORIGINAL LANGUAGE Spanish

DESCRIPTION
Only one original printed copy of this work is preserved (its title in full is *Conquista de la India de Persia & Arabia que fizo la armada del rey don Manuel de Portugal & de las muchas tierras, diversas gentes, extrañas riquezas y grandes batallas que allá hubo. En sumario del bachiller Juan Agüero de Trasmiera*). An error by Nicolás Antonio resulted in its being attributed to Juan Agüero (or Remón) de Trasmiera, who was actually its editor, though it is impossible to ascertain to what degree it was composed by Martín Fernández de Figueroa, who is also the main character, and what help he could have been given by Juan Agüero. However, the events portrayed are authentic, as is demonstrated by later Portuguese works. The modern edition of the text (Gil, 1999) has 85 pages, containing 50 titles, some of them very brief. They narrate the very first exploration and establishment of the Portuguese around the rim of the Indian Ocean between 1505 and 1511.

The relationship between Christians and Muslims is a crucial theme throughout the *Conquista*, because the Muslims stand as the main obstacle to Portuguese expansion into the Indian Ocean. One of its most important features is the account it gives of the very first contact between Iberians and Muslims in eastern Africa (Mombasa, Malindi, Sofala) and India. In this regard, the description of Islamic customs among the partially Islamicised African groups is of enormous interest. The coastal area opposite Cape Verde, for instance, is populated by a people known as the 'Bezeguiche', who decorate themselves with trinkets, like the 'Moors'. In Sofala, King Yusuf receives Captain Pedro de Añaya and his men 'sitting on the ground, atop a green carpet', though his people worship the sun and the stars and cremate their dead. Equally, women in Sofala wear brass rings around their legs, but 'their heads are left uncovered'. Further south in Kilwa the inhabitants – 'rich Negroes' – are 'Moors', though they are not circumcised, and the inhabitants of Mozambique are 'Moor Negroes and rich merchants'. In Figueroa's Africa, the Muslim is generally regarded as an enemy, as is shown by the attacks launched against Brava in present-day Somalia and the island of Socotra. Conversely, whenever Muslims appear to be cooperating with the Portuguese expeditions, they are described as friendly.

As the expedition progresses past the Arabian Peninsula towards Ormuz, the antagonism towards Islam gains in force. This is shown, for instance, by Albuquerque's decision to take and burn the harbours found on the way, to which the expedition reacted 'happily and proud of previous heroic deeds, full of blood and eager to continue with a war that could not wait' (title XXVIII).

The sometimes extreme violence unleashed against Muslims is vividly portrayed. Similarly, the Christian nature of the enterprise is stressed by presenting the expedition as a war against the infidel. The ideals of crusade and martyrdom gain in prominence as Portuguese defeats recur and the difficulties in subduing the Indian Malabar coast multiply. The constant references to Christianity and the duty of the faithful, and to the valour and gallantry of the individuals involved, gives the story a value which goes well beyond the mere personal interest of the members of the expedition: they are known not only as 'Portuguese' or 'Spaniards', but also as 'Christians'. Even so, the violence with which the conquest is carried out is never disguised. The passages on the victory in Ormuz and the conquest of Brava are full of macabre descriptions: for example, the 3,000 enemy dead 'floating about in the harbour, and it was a pleasure to watch them dancing thus'; afterwards, the corpses were plundered for jewels or anything of value. The passages about the march to Diu and the assault on Calicut are no less lurid.

On reaching India, the mixture of religious beliefs – although most of the rulers that the Portuguese had to contend with were Muslims – led the Portuguese not to limit punishment to 'the Moors' but also 'to killing and beheading many people, Moors and gentiles alike'. Confronted with this confusion of 'Moors' and Hindus, Figueroa's response is sometimes to group them together under the general blanket of the struggle against the infidel. However, before the account of the assault and destruction of Calicut, the author gives a description of the religious mosaic of the Indian Ocean: 'they have the following sects: that of Muḥammad in Persia and Arabia, whereas in Goa, Khambhat, Çaúl and Dabhol they worship idols, and are darker in colour' (title XXXVIII). Figueroa therefore makes an effort to distinguish between the religious practices of different groups, and towards the end of the work he clarifies: 'Moors or infidels, which sometimes are called Moors, but which really are gentiles' (title XLVI). Indeed, on the Malabar coast Figueroa observes that, although the rulers are Muslims, other religions are practised by their subjects, pointing out that in Calicut and 'in many more Indian kingdoms the inhabitants are gentiles and worship idols and statues of animals'. He also indicates that this same people say they do not mix with inferior castes (title XL). Figueroa describes the inhabitants of Goa as gentiles, 'worshippers of the sun, the moon and animals', while deprecating their custom of immolating widows (title XLI).

Along with the Islamic kingdoms that the Portuguese encounter on their way, Figueroa/Trasmiera also mentions others: the Egyptian Mamluks, referred to frequently as *rumes*, as well as 'Turks', for example in the description of the battles of Diu and Goa. It is noteworthy that the term *Rūm*, which was used by Arab and Turkish Muslims for Christians and Byzantines (cf. Q 30:2), is used by the inhabitants of North India for the Turks and Egyptians themselves.

Figueroa is condescending towards Islamic rulers who cooperate, and he admires the large mosques the expedition encounters. In this regard, even though some mosques are burned, others, for example, in Ormuz – 'very big and as beautiful as can be' (title XXIX) – and in Khelve-Mahin, north of Mumbai, are praised. Figueroa also shows interest in the arts of divination he encountered in Ormuz; these were known in Spain as *jofores* and were practised by the Moriscos.

Other religions are only given marginal attention in the work. For example, Hinduism is dismissed as little more than idol-worship, though the inhabitants of Gujarat, whom they encounter in Malindi, are portrayed as 'very composed and enemies of chit-chat; many eat no mortal food, and with this I mean any living being with blood in it. They are also called Brahmans' (title XXIII). There is also a special mention of the Nestorian Christian community in Socotra (title XXIV), and their strange liturgy and customs – especially of the women – are remarked upon (title XXVI).

SIGNIFICANCE

This work gives a first-hand account of one of the earliest Portuguese expeditions to Africa, Arabia, India and Malacca, and is a very reliable source against which later works (it is one of the earliest in its genre) can be judged. Juan Agüero (or Remón) de Trasmiera's edition emphasises the struggle against the infidels, and presents the conquest as a faith-driven enterprise, a style that later authors also adhered to. The war against the infidel, who was predominantly Muslim but also 'gentile', and the subsequent expansion of the Christian faith, which play an all-important role in this text, also feature most prominently in later works, such as Afonso de Albuquerque's *Comentarios*, João de Barros's *Ásia*, Gaspar Correia's *Crónicas de D. Manuel e de D. João III até 1533* and Damião de Góis's *Bellum Cambaicum*.

EDITIONS & TRANSLATIONS

L. Gil (ed.), *Martín Fernández de Figueroa, Conquista de las Indias de Persia e Arabia que fizo la armada del rey don Manuel de Portugal e de las muchas tierras, diversas gentes, extrañas riquezas y grandes batallas que allá hubo. En sumario del bachiller Juan Agüero de Trasmiera*, Valladolid, 1999

J.B. McKenna (ed. and trans.), *A Spaniard in the Portuguese Indies. The narrative of Martín Fernández de Figueroa*, Cambridge MA, 1967 (English trans., includes facsimile of 1512 edition)

Conquista de la India de Persia & Arabia que fizo la armada del rey don Manuel de Portugal, Salamanca, 1512

STUDIES

Gil, *Martín Fernández de Figueroa*, pp. 18-21

McKenna, *A Spaniard in the Portuguese Indies*, pp. 7-12

Manuel Fernández Chaves and Rafael Perez García

Afonso de Albuquerque

DATE OF BIRTH   Between 1453 and 1462
PLACE OF BIRTH   Alhandra, Portugal
DATE OF DEATH   16 December 1515
PLACE OF DEATH   Aboard the ship Flor de Rosa, within sight of Goa

BIOGRAPHY

Afonso de Albuquerque was the second son of Gonçalo de Albuquerque, lord of Vila Verde dos Francos, near Lisbon. His family had connections to the high nobility, which opened doors to the court and royal employment, and he used the opportunity to further his education and gain military advancement. He acquired experience in North Africa, participated in the war against Castile in 1476, and in 1481 was part of the military expedition sent to assist Naples in the recovery of Otranto from the Ottomans.

Albuquerque started his career with Alfonso V, but it was under his successors that he achieved success and distinction. He became a member of the personal guard of João II (r. 1481-95), and was his close friend, being present at his deathbed. This did not endear him to Manuel I (r. 1495-1521), cousin of João II, who had begrudgingly named him as his successor. However, the discovery of the route to India in 1498 and the subsequent establishment of the Portuguese in Asia strengthened the trust between them when Albuquerque became a steadfast supporter and facilitator of the king's imperial strategy, modelling the organisation of the Portuguese state in India on the interests of the Portuguese crown.

Albuquerque began to play an active part in the king's projects in 1503, when he was nominated as captain of one of the fleets sailing to India that year. The captain of the second fleet was his cousin, Francisco de Albuquerque. Their role was crucial in the defeat of the Zamorim of Calicut, who had besieged Cochin, ultimately leading to the construction of a Portuguese fort in the port. Francisco was keen to name it Fort Albuquerque, after their family, while Afonso was determined to name it Fort Manuel, and Afonso prevailed.

In 1506, Albuquerque returned to India in the fleet led by Tristão da Cunha, under whose command he was ordered to sail until they reached the East African coast. There, they would exercise joint command to strengthen Portuguese influence in the coastal sultanates and to proceed with the construction of a fortress on the island of Socotra. This, the king believed, would prevent the access of Muslim spice vessels to the Red Sea. Albuquerque acted as captain general of the Portuguese fleet in the Arabian Sea in mid-1507, intending to launch a campaign around the coast of Oman and subdue the coveted port of Hormuz. His plan was aimed at the control of the commercial routes through the Arabian Gulf by building a Portuguese fortress in Hormuz. This strategy eventually came to nothing due to lack of support from other Portuguese captains, a frequent occurrence in Albuquerque's Asian career. His relationship with the first viceroy of India, Francisco de Almeida, was also tense, culminating in Almeida's refusal to hand over the government of the Portuguese state of India in 1508, which had been secretly ordered by the king three years before. After a period in jail, Albuquerque finally became governor in 1509.

As an advocate of King Manuel's ideology and imperial plans, Albuquerque was constantly involved in quarrels and disputes. Some leaders disagreed with the royal monopoly, which they thought hindered the spice trade. In their view, involvement in Asian politics only served to justify the royal monopoly and impeded the nobility from engaging in more lucrative activities such as privateering. Under Albuquerque's tenure, the Portuguese state in India gained control of the main commercial *entrepôts* in maritime Asia, Goa (1510), Malacca (1511) and Hormuz (1515). His failed attempt to capture the port of Aden in 1513, which would have secured control of the Red Sea, weakened his position at court, and his adversaries pressurised the king to have him removed from office in 1515. He died of an illness shortly after the news of his dismissal arrived in India.

MAIN SOURCES OF INFORMATION

Primary
W.G. Birch, *The commentaries of the great Afonso Dalboquerque, second viceroy of India*, London, 1875-84
R.A.B. Pato and H.L. de Mendonça, *Cartas de Affonso de Albuquerque seguidas de documentos que as elucidam*, Lisbon, 1884-1935
A.B.B. Pereira, *Arquivo português oriental*, 11 books in 3 vols, Bastora, 1936-40, vol. 1/2
A.S. Rego, *Documentação para a história das missões do padroado português do Oriente – Índia*, Lisbon, 1947-88, vol. 1

D. de Góis, *Crónica do felicíssimo rei D. Manuel*, Coimbra, 1949-55, vols 2-3
J. de Barros, *Da Ásia*, Lisbon, 1973, vols 3-4
G. Correia, *Lendas da Índia*, Oporto, 1975, vols 1-2
F.L. de Castanheda, *História do descobrimento e conquista da Índia pelos portugueses*, Oporto, 1979, vol. 1
L. de Albuquerque, *Crónica do descobrimento e primeiras conquistas da Índia pelos portugueses*, (s.l.), 1986

Secondary

A.R. Disney, 'Albuquerque', in *A history of Portugal and the Portuguese Empire*, vol. 2. *The Portuguese Empire*, Cambridge, 2009, 129-34
J.P. Oliveira e Costa and V.L. Gaspar Rodrigues, *Conquista de Malaca – 1511. Campanhas de Afonso de Albuquerque*, Lisbon, 2008
J.P. Oliveira e Costa and V.L. Gaspar Rodrigues, *Conquista de Goa – 1510-1512. Campanhas de Afonso de Albuquerque*, Lisbon, 2008
D. Couto and R.M. Loureiro, *Ormuz 1507 e 1622. Conquista e perda*, Lisbon, 2007
J. Aubin, *Le latin et l'astrolabe*, vol. 3. *Études inédites sur le règne de D. Manuel 1495-1521*, Paris, 2006
J.P. Oliveira e Costa, *D. Manuel I, 1469-1521. Um príncipe do renascimento*, (s.l.), 2005 (the fullest work about the king and his reign)
A. Pelúcia, 'A baronia do Alvito e a expansão manuelina no Oriente ou a reacção organizada à política imperialista', in J.P. Oliviera e Costa and V.L. Gaspar Rodrigues (eds), *A alta nobreza e a fundação do Estado da Índia*, Lisbon, 2004, 279-302
V.L. Gaspar Rodrigues, 'O reforço do poder naval português no Oriente com Afonso de Albuquerque (1510-1515). Suas implicações', *Anais de História de Além-mar* 3 (2002) 155-63
V.L. Gaspar Rodrigues, 'Da Goa de Albuquerque à Goa seiscentista. Aspectos da organização militar da capital do Estado da Índia', *Revista Militar* 51 (1999) 59-93
C.M. Santos, '*Goa é a chave de toda a Índia*'. *Perfil político da capital do Estado da Índia (1505-1570)*, Lisbon, 1999, pp. 93-149
J.C. Silva, 'Almeida e Albuquerque. Anatomia de um conflito', in *O fundador do 'Estado Português da Índia'. D. Francisco de Almeida. 1457 (?) – 1510*, (s.l.), 1996, 189-204
V.L. Gaspar Rodrigues, 'As companhias de ordenança no Estado Português da Índia, 1510-1580. Ensaios de criação, razões do insucesso', *Oceanos* 19/20 (1994) 212-18
M.C. Junqueiro, art. 'Albuquerque, Afonso de', in L. de Albuquerque and F.C. Domingues (eds), *Dicionário de história dos descobrimentos portugueses*, 1994, i, 34-9
I. Guerreiro and V.L. Gaspar Rodrigues, 'O "grupo de Cochim" e a oposição a Afonso de Albuquerque', *Stvdia* 51 (1992) 119-44

G. Bouchon, *Albuquerque, le lion des mers d'Asie*, Paris, 1992 (the best and most complete biography)

L.F.F.R. Thomaz, 'Factions, interests and messianism. The politics of Portuguese expansion in the east, 1500-1521', *Indian Economic and Social History Review* 28 (1991) 97-109

L.F.F.R. Thomaz, 'L'idée impériale manueline', in J. Aubin (ed.), *La découverte, le Portugal et l'Europe*, Paris, 1990, 35-103 (the most authoritative essay about the messianism associated with King Manuel I)

A.D. Farinha, 'A dupla conquista de Ormuz por Afonso de Albuquerque', *Stvdia* 48 (1989) 445-71

L.A. Noonan, *John of Empoli and his relations with Afonso de Albuquerque*, Lisbon, 1989

J. Aubin, 'L'apprentissage de l'Inde. Cochin 1503-1504', *Moyen-Orient et Océan Indien, XVIe-XIXe s.* 4 (1987) 1-96

M.C. Junqueiro, 'Afonso de Albuquerque à luz dos requisitos fundamentais da guerra justa', in L. de Albuquerque and I. Guerreiro (eds), *II Seminário internacional de história indo-portuguesa. Actas*, Lisbon, 1985, 187-99

J. Aubin, 'L'ambassade de Prêtre Jean à D. Manuel', *Mare Luso Indicum* 3 (1976) 1-56

J. Aubin, 'Cojeatar et Albuquerque', *Mare Luso Indicum* 1 (1971) 99-134

J. Aubin, 'Albuquerque et les négociations de Cambaye', *Mare Luso Indicum* 1 (1971) 3-63

E. Sanceau, *Indies adventure. The amazing career of Afonso de Albuquerque, captain-general and governor of India, 1509-1515*, London, 1936

E. Prestage, *Afonso de Albuquerque, governor of India. His life, conquests and administration*, Watford, 1929

WORKS ON CHRISTIAN-MUSLIM RELATIONS

Cartas de Afonso de Albuquerque, 'Letters of Afonso de Albuquerque'

DATE 1507-15
ORIGINAL LANGUAGE Portuguese

DESCRIPTION
This collection of letters comes from the period in which Afonso de Albuquerque was captain general of the Portuguese fleet in the Arabian Sea and later governor of the Portuguese State in India. The earliest is dated 6 February 1507 and the last 6 December 1515, only ten days before Albuquerque died. In all, there are 111 letters, as well as summaries of 12 others. The addressees include Francisco de Almeida, Viceroy of India,

members of the Portuguese court, including the queen, and Shah Ismail I, founder of the Safavid dynasty, although the majority are addressed to King Manuel I. How many of these survive is difficult to know, though Gaspar Correia, who worked as a clerk for Albuquerque, and was one of the main chroniclers of Portuguese exploits in Asia, states that Albuquerque routinely produced copious and detailed written reports for the king and for many others (Correia, *Lendas da Índia*, ii, p. 46).

When they made their first expeditions to India, the Portuguese were hoping to find 'Christians and spices'. Instead, in Calicut they found a strong and influential Islamic merchant community controlling the spice trade. They soon realised that these merchants dominated not only trade in Calicut, but also the regional and intercontinental trade system. The persistence of the newly arrived Europeans and the lack of mutual understanding between Christians and Muslins, further fuelled by ancient religious hostility, often turned their commercial rivalry into a military confrontation. On the Portuguese side, the antagonism was strengthened by memories of the formation of Portugal out of rebellion against the Islamic powers in the Iberian Peninsula, and of the crusade-like zeal of the 15th-century Portuguese expeditions in north-west Africa. In fact, many of the Portuguese nobility who went on to serve in Asia, including Albuquerque, had served as cavalrymen in North Africa, where they had got to know Islamic culture.

When he wrote his letters, Albuquerque was well aware of Manuel I's plans and of his expectations of his officials in Asia. At the core of Manuel's strategy was the economic objective to bypass and end the routes used for Islamic trade between India and Cairo, and to acquire the monopoly of the spice trade (Pato, *Cartas*, i, p. 35). Acknowledging the need to do this, Albuquerque states: 'In the places where one finds merchandise and Muslim merchants we cannot freely obtain gemstones or spices; if we forcibly want to have them it will have to be through warfare' (Pato, *Cartas*, i, p. 40). It is this realisation that lay behind Portuguese domination of sea routes in the Arabian Sea (Pato, *Cartas*, i, pp. 45-46, 222-33, 279-80), and also behind the seizure of the port cities of Goa, Malacca and Hormuz, previously dominated by Muslim merchants, and key centres in commercial links (Pato, *Cartas*, i, p. 378).

Albuquerque realistically acknowledges that the relationship between the Portuguese and Muslim traders is one of hostility: 'This is the situation between the Muslims and the Christians and it will be forever so' (Pato, *Cartas*, i, p. 35), and he regards Muslims as unprincipled and dissimulating in 'all their evilness, deceit and treachery', giving as examples the king of Hormuz, the sultan of Malacca and the sultan of Gujarat (Pato, *Cartas*, i, p. 37). However, he took the view that a Portuguese military advantage, combined with diplomatic efforts, would lead to peaceful though grudging coexistence. In this he was correct, reporting to the king in 1513 that the Portuguese in India enjoyed peaceful relations with all the territories and powers from the Straits of Hormuz to the Coromandel Coast (Pato, *Cartas*, i, p. 135), though he warned that even in times of peace it was necessary to remain watchful and to maintain a strong military presence as a deterrent (Pato, *Cartas*, i, p. 40).

Among the campaigns fought by the Portuguese, one held a particular significance for Albuquerque. This was the conquest of Goa on 25 November 1510, following the defeat of the army of Yusuf Adil Shah, Sultan of Bijapur. It was a determining factor in the establishment of the Portuguese State of India, providing a major point of defence against Bijapur, the kingdom of Calicut, a traditional ally of merchants from Arabia and Cairo, and the sultanate of Gujarat, and destroying the threat of the *Rumes*, mercenaries in the pay of the Egyptians and Ottomans who had come to fight in the battle of Diu in 1509 and had afterwards settled in Goa (Pato, *Cartas*, i, p. 182). Albuquerque also represents this conquest as a major symbolic act, since it showed the Indian powers that the Turkic people, who had ruled them for centuries, had been discredited and surpassed by the Portuguese (Pato, *Cartas*, i, p. 54).

The image of the Portuguese as a major military power led to respect for them in India, and even sometimes to alliances with Muslim rulers. But with regard to the Red Sea region, attitudes were very different. Both Albuquerque and Manuel I wanted the complete obliteration of the spice trade through the Red Sea to Egypt, which generated great wealth for the Mamluk sultanate. Their aim was not merely to seize the profits from this trade, but to continue the fight against Islam in the name of Christianity (Pato, *Cartas*, i, p. 18). While king and governor fought intensely for the commercial viability of the newly created Cape route, they ultimately aspired to the destruction of Islam.

Albuquerque's strategy towards this end was elaborate and ambitious (even fanciful). As a first step, he wanted to seize Aden and take control of the entrance to the Red Sea in order to strangle Mamluk shipping communications. On one occasion, he even suggested diverting the course of the Nile in order to cause a water shortage in Egypt (Pato, *Cartas*, i, p. 401). In 1513, he led a Portuguese fleet to the Red Sea but their attack on Aden did not succeed. Even so, Albuquerque thought it was a great achievement to have a Portuguese fleet in the area, and a 'great strike' against the 'house of Muḥammad, and to the discredit of the great sultan and merchants of Cairo' (Pato, *Cartas*, i, p. 250).

The second step was even more ambitious, and would have had significant political and religious consequences. The plan was to establish a strong alliance between the Portuguese State in India and the Christian kingdom of Prester John in Ethiopia. In Albuquerque's view, this could be achievable by the establishment of the Portuguese in Massawa on the African coast of the Red Sea; then the Portuguese and Ethiopians together could cross the Red Sea and take Jeddah, bringing them within reach of Mecca, just one day away (Pato, *Cartas*, i, pp. 170, 237, 280-83). Albuquerque wanted 'to burn it to ashes' in the name of Christ and the king of Portugal (Pato, *Cartas*, i, p. 282), and he urged Manuel to act on his plan, because it was 'a great service to our Lord to destroy their house of abomination and cause their destruction' (Pato, *Cartas*, i, p. 237).

The third and final stage of Albuquerque's ambitious programme encompassed a number of distinct objectives. Above all else, it was crucial to secure the presence of the Portuguese throughout the Red Sea and establish a military outpost in the Gulf of Suez. This would successfully provide a strong foothold from which to gain control over Alexandria at one end of the trading route from (Pato, *Cartas*, i, p. 280). The Mamluks were already alarmed at the failed attempt on Aden in 1513 and at the presence of the Portuguese in the Red Sea, and Albuquerque expected to disturb further the stability of a dynasty he knew was weak by penetrating into Lower Egypt. It seems clear that he intended to eradicate the Mamluks entirely (Pato, *Cartas*, i, pp. 236-39). If Manuel were to agree, Albuquerque envisioned 'the destruction of Mecca, the end and termination of Muḥammad's sect' (Pato, *Cartas*, i, p. 397). He deemed his plan possible, because he believed that his intended targets were insufficiently guarded and weakened by internal squabbles.

The Portuguese regarded the Egyptian sultanate as the champion of Sunnī Islam and the incarnation of 'Babylon', blocking the final emergence of Jerusalem as City of God. Therefore, at the beginning of the 16th century they made efforts to establish a rapport with Shīʿa Islam, embodied by Shah Ismail I in Persia (Pato, *Cartas*, i, pp. 397-98). The approach was timely, and it was soon reciprocated (Pato, *Cartas*, i, pp. 242-43). The mutual interests of the two powers in seeing the downfall of the Sunnī Mamluks explain why in 1515 Albuquerque sent Ismail I a proposal for a political and military alliance to mount a joint attack on

Mamluk territories. The Persians would follow the land route to Cairo, while at the same time the Portuguese army, led by King Manuel I himself, would appear from the sea and target Jerusalem (Pato, *Cartas*, i, pp. 388-89). In 1513, Albuquerque had already mentioned to Manuel his hopes of opening a pilgrimage route to the Holy City through the Red Sea (Pato, *Cartas*, i, p. 243). This was the means by which he was going to turn it into reality.

The letters raise a number of questions. What did Albuquerque envision would happen if the Luso-Safavid alliance came into being? How were the two powers to navigate their alliance in case of success? And, perhaps more interesting, what would happen to the future of Islam? While answers can only be speculative, it is nevertheless beyond argument that Albuquerque and the Portuguese passionately believed that their actions and victories were imbued with the spirit of divine providence (Pato, *Cartas*, i, p. 242). The particular context of the succession to the throne by Manuel, the arrival of the Portuguese in Asia and the foundation of the Portuguese State in India sparked and reinforced the king's messianic beliefs, a king who fervently trusted that the Portuguese were destined to great achievements on behalf of Christianity (Thomaz, 'L'idée impériale manueline').

Afonso de Albuquerque's faith manifested itself in two miraculous episodes in which the will of God had been revealed to him – so he recounts. As the Portuguese fleet was in sight of the kingdom of Prester John, he first saw a shining cross appear in the sky. Clouds gathered densely around it, but the cross would not break, and it finally shone ever more brightly, framed by the clouds around it (Pato, *Cartas*, i, p. 219). His second vision was of a sudden ray of fire projected from the land of Prester John into the sky, extending in a curve towards the region of Jeddah and Mecca, where it then landed (Pato, *Cartas*, i, p. 231).

SIGNIFICANCE

These letters provided detailed information for a restricted group of people, Manuel I and his closest confidants and retainers. They were scrutinised within the circle of Manuel's political advisers and, when there was propaganda advantage to be derived, they were sent to other courts in Europe or to the pope. Thus, in addition to providing information and analysis of events in India, they also served Manuel's ideological aspirations.

The letters reveal open antagonism towards Islam, in both African and Asian territories, and show how political developments in different regions were connected, as links can be discerned between these and similar collections of letters written by officials serving in the fortresses of North Africa. The chronicles, written under royal patronage between 1440 and 1510, share the same leitmotif when they describe the feats performed by leaders and fighting men in North Africa. The feature common to them all is the intention to undermine Islam and to further Christian expansion, both politically and religiously.

The uniqueness of the letters lies elsewhere. From the outset, they represent a first-hand account of the initial moments that shaped the character of the Portuguese presence in Asia and its relationship with the Islamic powers of the region. Furthermore, the privileged position of the writer makes possible a highly detailed reconstruction of the reasoning behind the decision-making that was going on at the political centre.

Afonso de Albuquerque's administration of Portuguese interests in Asia was the golden age of the imperialism of Manuel I, when Portuguese prosperity was frequently achieved to the detriment of Islamic commercial profits and territories. Keeping in mind religious rivalry, his letters exemplify a specific moment in Portuguese history, namely the charged expectations of a great and final crusade. The letters embody one of the last expressions of the medieval European idea of regaining control of the Holy Land and ultimately destroying Islam.

MANUSCRIPTS

The source materials, over 100 manuscripts, are held by the Portuguese National Archives-Torre do Tombo and by the Portuguese National Library both in Lisbon. Pato's edition provides complete references and locations for the sources it publishes.

EDITIONS & TRANSLATIONS

    R.B. Smith, *The letter of Afonso de Albuquerque in códice n.353 of the biblioteca nacional de Lisboa*, Lisbon, 1992

    T.F. Earle and J. Villiers, *Albuquerque, caesar of the East. Selected texts by Afonso de Albuquerque and his son*, Warminster, 1990 (partial edition and trans. of a few letters)

    M.C. Junqueiro and A.R. Guerra, 'Uma carta inédita de Afonso de Albuquerque', *Clio* 4 (1982) 61-9 (edition of a single letter)

    R.B. Smith, *Afonso de Albuquerque, being the Portuguese text of an unpublished letter of the Biblioteca Geral da Universidade de Coimbra relating the Portuguese conquest of Ormuz in 1507*, Bethesda, 1972

A. Baião, *Cartas para el-rei D. Manuel I*, Lisbon, 1942 (partial edition of letters sent by Afonso de Albuquerque to the king of Portugal)

R.A.B. Pato, *Cartas de Affonso de Albuquerque seguidas de documentos que as elucidam*, Lisbon, 1884-1935 (repr. Nendeln, 1976) (the most complete edition of Albuquerque's letters)

STUDIES

While the letters have served as source material in multiple studies, mainly related to the early history of the Portuguese in Asia, they have not so far been studied as a collection. However, the contents inspired Afonso's son, also named Afonso de Albuquerque, to form them into a chronicle:

Birch, *The commentaries of the great Afonso Dalboquerque*

Afonso de Albuquerque, the younger, *Commentarios de Afonso Dalboquerque capitão geral e gouernador da India colligidos por seu filho Afonso Dalboquerque das proprias cartas que elle escrevia ao muyto poderoso Rey dõ Manuel o primeiro deste nome em cujo tempo gouernou a India...*, Lisbon, 1557

Alexandra Pelúcia

Frei Diogo de Castilho

Diogo de Castilho

DATE OF BIRTH   Unknown
PLACE OF BIRTH Tomar, Portugal
DATE OF DEATH   Unknown; mid-16th century
PLACE OF DEATH Unknown

BIOGRAPHY

Frei Diogo de Castilho was a monk in the Cistercian monastery of Alcobaça. This information is found on the front page of his only known work, *Livro da origem dos turcos* (1538), a treatise on the genesis of the Ottoman dynasty. The 19th-century Portuguese poet António Feliciano de Castilho affirms that in the 18th century it was still possible to see Castilho's portrait in the monastery refectory.

Originally from Tomar, Castilho was the son of João de Castilho, widely considered the most important architect in Renaissance Portugal. Together with his master, Diogo de Arruda, João de Castilho spearheaded the renovation of the Convento de Cristo in Tomar, a monumental complex belonging to the Ordem de Cristo, the Portuguese continuation of the Templars, which Pope Clement V suppressed in 1312. He also participated in the development of the Hieronymite Monastery in Belém, an emblematic example of Portuguese late-gothic style.

MAIN SOURCES OF INFORMATION

Primary

D. Barbosa Machado, *Bibliotheca lusitana, historica, critica e chronologica*, Lisbon, 1741-59, i, p. 644

A. Feliciano de Castilho, *Camões. Estudo historico-poetico liberrimamente fundado sobre um drama francez dos senhores Victor Perrot e Armand du Mesnil*, Lisbon, 1863, iii, p. 28

I. Francisco da Silva, *Diccionario bibliographico portuguez*, Lisbon, 1869, ii, pp. 151-52

WORKS ON CHRISTIAN-MUSLIM RELATIONS

Livro da origem dos Turcos, 'On the origin of the Turks'

DATE 1538
ORIGINAL LANGUAGE Portuguese

DESCRIPTION

Diogo de Castilho's *Livro da origem dos Turcos* was printed by Rutger Rescius in Leuven in 1538. It consists of 179 pages, nine of which are a letter of dedication to the Portuguese *feitor* in Antwerp, Manuel Cirne, a nobleman and member of the king's entourage. In this letter, Castilho explains that the work was intended to spur the *feitor* to encourage King João III to take part in the crusade that Charles V was preparing against the Turks to retake Constantinople. Castilho thought that the Portuguese should not miss the opportunity to play a leading role, and a description of the origins, history and customs of the enemy would be helpful for any Portuguese who took part. Castilho also explains that the decision to write in Portuguese is due to the fact that Latin was not very well known in Portugal at that time.

From the very beginning, it is easy to recognise the main source and model of Castilho's book. Castilho himself declares that his aim is to accomplish what the Italian humanist Paolo Giovio had done a few years earlier in 1531 with the publication of his *Commentario delle cose de' Turchi*. Castilho faithfully respects the structure of Giovio's work, which is a sort of portrait gallery of the Turkish sultans in chronological order, and in some passages he translates Giovio's words literally.

In addition, Castilho also incorporates a vast set of Italian humanist sources from the 15th and 16th centuries, which he lists in his dedicatory letter: Raffaele Maffei's *Commentarii urbani* (1506), Marc'Antonio Sabellico's *Enneades sive rhapsodia historiarum* (1489-1504), Giovanni Battista Cipelli's *De Caesaribus libris tres* (1516) and the works of Aeneas Silvio Piccolomini (Pope Pius II), especially his *Historia rerum ubique gestarum locorumque descriptio* (1458, 1461). All these authors focus on the origins and genealogy of the Turks, as well as on the political history and geography of the Near East and Anatolia.

Castilho also makes use of selected letters written by Francesco Filefo in his *Epistolarum familiarum libri XXXVII* (1502), as well as two German sources, Johann Boemus's *Omnium gentium mores, leges, & ritus ex multis clarissimis rerum scriptoribus* (1520) and Johannes Carion's *Chronica* (1532, 1st ed. 1537, Latin). Boemus's work is more an anthropological description of the known world then a historical compilation, quite innovative in the early modern period, and Castilho uses it to provide more details about the traditions and customs of the Scythians, whom he regards as the ancestors of the Turks. Johannes Carion's *Chronica*, on the other hand, was in many ways a typical medieval historical description of European events, presented in chronological order and following the model of the biblical Book of Daniel in its description of the four empires that would be supplanted by God's eternal kingdom. After the success of the German edition, it was reviewed by Melachthon and other Lutheran humanists and published in Latin. Castilho makes use of the final part of Carion's *Chronica*, in which the German scholar presents various prophecies regarding the future battle between Christian Europe and the Islamic East, a battle that would serve as a prelude to the end of times and the advent of the kingdom of God.

SIGNIFICANCE

Castilho's *Livro da origem dos Turcos* is one of many such works that appeared all over Europe after the publication of Paolo Giovio's *Commentario*. It gains special significance, however, because of its Portuguese provenance and because it was written in Portuguese vernacular, a practically unique phenomenon in 16th-century Iberian literature. It is also important for the main topics it covers. Following Giovio, Castilho underscores the importance of Charles V's crusade to take Constantinople and the participation of the Portuguese in this effort. Perhaps the most significant aspects of Castilho's work, however, are those not found in Giovio. One is that he advances a theory of the Turks' Scythian origins, which Giovio does not mention but which had become popular since the historical works of Pius II. Another is that he develops Carion's prophecies, relating them to the Portuguese context of his time.

EDITIONS & TRANSLATIONS

Diogo de Castilho, *Livro da origem dos Turcos*, Leuven, 1538

STUDIES

C. Bettini, 'Reflexões à margem de uma investigação quinhentista', in *e-cadernos CES* 15 (2013) 98-117, http://www.ces.uc.pt/e-cadernos/pages/pt/numeros-publicados/2012/15--2012---debates-contemporaneos-jovens-cientistas-sociais-no-ces-vi-e-vii-ciclos-anuais.php

A.G. Cunha, 'Os eslavismos do 'Livro da origem dos turcos'. Estudo histórico etimológico', *Revista de Portugal série A, 'Língua Portuguesa'* 22 (1957) 277-83

Clelia Bettini

Damião de Góis

DATE OF BIRTH 2 February 1502
PLACE OF BIRTH Alenquer, Portugal
DATE OF DEATH 30 January 1574
PLACE OF DEATH Alenquer, Portugal

BIOGRAPHY

Damião de Góis (also Goes), one of the outstanding Portuguese figures of the 16th century, was a humanist and official of the Portuguese Crown. He was born to a noble family in the service of the kings of Portugal, and his grandfather, Gomes Dias de Góis, had been in the entourage of Prince Henry the Navigator. In 1511, at a young age, Góis entered the service of King Manuel I, first as page and later as *moço da câmara* (chamberlain), a position that his brother Fructo de Góis also held (Góis, *Fides, religio, moresqve Aethiopvm*, p. 12). In 1523, King João III sent him to Antwerp as secretary and treasurer of the Portuguese *feitoria* (commercial office). Between 1528 and 1531, he led a number of diplomatic missions to Poland, Lithuania, Denmark, Prussia, Sweden, France and Italy.

In 1533, Góis abandoned his job at the *feitoria* and became a student. Thereafter he met and befriended important figures, including André de Resende, João de Barros, Sebastian Münster, Erasmus, Ramusio, Melanchthon, Luther, Albrecht Dürer, Juan Luis Vives and Pietro Bembo. Between 1533 and 1539, he studied at the University of Padua. Then he lived for six years in Louvain until he went back to Portugal in 1545.

In Portugal, Góis faced two Inquisition charges, and was acquitted of both. In 1548, he was appointed *guarda-mor* (head) of the royal archives of Torre do Tombo, and in 1558 Cardinal Henrique gave him the task of writing the chronicle of Henrique's father, Manuel I. In 1571, a further inquisitorial trial was opened against him, and he was imprisoned in the monastery of Batalha. He died shortly afterwards in mysterious circumstance, at his home at Alenquer.

Góis produced a number of works, some of primary importance. Among them are two works on Christian Ethiopia, written in 1532 and 1540, a plea in favour of Lapland and the Sami people, the royal chronicle of Manuel I's reign, written in 1566-67, and a translation of Cicero's

Cato Maior. He also composed musical pieces and was the owner of a collection of paintings.

MAIN SOURCES OF INFORMATION

Primary

Damião de Góis, *Legatio magni Indorum imperatoris Presbyteri Ioannis, ad Emanuelem Lusitaniae Regem* ... Antwerp: Joan. Grapheus, 1532

Damião de Góis, *Fides, religio, moresqve Aethiopvmi: svb imperio Pretiosi Ioannis (quem vulgo Presbyterum Ioannem vocant) degentivm*, Lovanii: Rutgeri Resci, 1540

Damião de Góis, *Chronica do Felicissimo Rei Dom Emanuel composta per Damiam de Goes diuidida em quatro partes. ...* Lisboa: Francisco Correa, 1566-67

W.J.C. Henry, *Ineditos Goesianos, colligidos e annotados*, Lisbon, 1896-98

Damião de Góis, *Opúsculos históricos. Tradução do original latino*, trans. D. de Carvalho, Pôrto, 1945

A. Torres, *Noese e crise na epistolografia latina goisiana. I. As cartas latinas de Damião de Góis*, Paris, 1982

S. Uhlig and G. Bühring (trans.), *Damian de Góis' Schrift über Glaube und Sitten der Äthioper [1540]*, Wiesbaden, 1994

Secondary

A. Martínez d'Alòs-Moner, art. 'Góis, Damião de', in S. Uhlig and A. Bausi (eds), *Encyclopaedia aethiopica*, Wiesbaden, 2003-14, ii, 831-32

J.F. Tavares, *Damião de Góis. Um paradigma erasmiano no humanismo português*, Lisbon, 1999

J. Aubin, 'Damião de Góis dans une Europe évangelique', in J. Aubin (ed.), *Le latin et l'astrolabe. Recherches sur le Portugal de la Renaissance, son expansion en Asie et les relations internationales*, Lisbon, 1996, 211-35

J. Aubin, 'Como trabalha Damiao de Góis, narrador da segunda viagem de Vasco da Gama', in L. de S. Rebelo and H. Macedo (eds), *Studies in Portuguese literature and history in honour of Luís de Sousa Rebelo*, London, 1992, 103-13

I. de R. Pereira, 'O ecumenismo de Damião de Góis', in *O humanismo português. 1500-1600. Primeiro simpósio nacional (21-25 de outubro de 1985)*, Lisbon, 1988, 89-117

A. Torres, 'Damião de Góis e o erasmismo. Ambito conceptual e dados vivenciais', in *O humanismo português. 1500-1600. Primeiro simpósio nacional (21-25 de outubro de 1985)*, Lisbon, 1988, 69-87

J.A. Osório, 'Cícero traduzido para português no século XVI. Damião de Góis e o "Livro da velhice"', *Humanitas* 37-8 (1985-86) 191-266

E.B. Blackburn, 'John More's *The Christian empire of Prester John*', *Moreana* 4 (1967) 37-43

D. Goes and J. More, 'The legacy of "Prester John"', *Moreana* 4 (1967) 44-98

WORKS ON CHRISTIAN-MUSLIM RELATIONS

Legatio magni Indorum imperatoris Presbyteri Ioannis ad Emanuelem Lusitaniae regem, anno Domini M.D. XIII, 'The embassy of the Great emperor of the Indians, Prester John, to Manuel, king of Portugal, in the year 1513 AD'

DATE 1532
ORIGINAL LANGUAGE Latin

DESCRIPTION

Legatio magni Indorum imperatoris Presbyteri Ioannis is a Latin opuscule on Christian Ethiopia. It appears that it was published without Góis's permission in 1532 (for a ghost edition from 1531, see Blackburn, 'John More's *The Christian empire of Prester John*', pp. 37-38; see also the preface by Cornelius Grapheus in Góis, *Legatio*, and Góis, *Fides, religio, moresque Aethiopum*, 1540, p. 17). The work comprises 37 unnumbered pages, and includes a series of documents related to the diplomatic mission led by Christian Ethiopia's envoy Mateus to Portugal. The book opens with a text dedicated by Góis to his friend Johannes Magnum, Archbishop of Uppsala, in which he summarises the embassy from 1513-14 led by Mateus (real name Abraham) to the Portuguese King Manuel I on behalf of the *Nəguś* Ləbnä Dəngəl. Following this, it presents Góis's Latin translation of the 'Letter of the Prester John', actually written by the dowager queen of Ethiopia, Ǝleni (Góis, *Legatio*, fol. A4r and passim). Góis had received a Portuguese copy of the letter (originally written in Arabic and either Gəʿəz or Persian) when he was in northern Europe from his friend and *feitor* (overseer of a Portuguese commercial office) Rodrigo Fernandes, who in turn had received it from António Carneiro, secretary of Manuel I (Góis *Legatio*, fol. A3v; also Góis, *Chronica do Felicissimo Rei*, terceira parte, fol. 106v). There follows an *Indorum confessio illorum fidei*... with a list of 51 articles on Ethiopian Christianity, and a *Legatio de eorum patriarcha*... with 14 further articles on the Coptic metropolitan ruling over the Ethiopian Church (Góis, *Legatio*, unnumbered; see also Cortesão and Thomas, *Carta das novas*, pp. 66-67). Following this, a chapter entitled *De regno et statu imperatoris*... states that the kingdom of the Prester John has 60 'reigns' under his rule, including five that are Muslim (no. 12 of 27), and another chapter deals with the *ordine curiae*, on the court and monarchy (19 articles). After a summary of the Portuguese presence in

India and Mateus's journey, the *Legatio* concludes with a denunciation of the exploitation of the Sami people (*Pilapiis*, i.e. Laponians).

SIGNIFICANCE

Legatio was one of the works that gave Renaissance Europe its first information about Christian Ethiopia. It came after the *Carta das novas*, which was published in Lisbon in 1521, and before Góis's own *Fides* of 1540. Since only a few copies of the *Carta das novas* were printed, it is the *Legatio* that had a major impact. The text chiefly made known to a European readership the important letter of Ǝleni to Manuel I (a Portuguese version of the letter had already appeared in 1521 in the *Carta das novas*; see Cortesão and Thomas, *Carta das novas*, pp. 123-24). The letter was reproduced later by Góis himself in his *Fides* (pp. 13-16) and in his *Chronica do Felicissimo Rei Dom Emanuel* (terçeira parte, fols 106v-107v). In the letter, Ǝleni offers friendship to the Portuguese ruler and proposes matrimonial alliances between the two crowns. She informs Manuel about the preparation by the Mamluks of Egypt of an armada against the Portuguese in India and also offers men and logistical support to help the Portuguese reach Jeddah, to 'uproot the Moors from the face of the earth'. Therefore, the text can be taken as an important witness to the eschatological anti-Muslim agenda pursued by the Portuguese and Ethiopian crowns in the early modern period. Most of the major themes of the *Legatio* became the core of the more extensive and informative *Fides*, published eight years later.

EDITIONS & TRANSLATIONS

Goes and More, 'The legacy of "Prester John"' (repr. of text of More's 1553 English trans.)

Legatio David Aethiopiae Regis, ad Sanctissimum D. N. Clemetem Papam VII uná cum obedientia eidem sanctis. D. N. praestita, Paris: Antonio Augerello, 1533; Antwerp, 1534

The legacye or embassate of the great emperour of Inde prester Iohn..., trans. John More, London: W. Rastell, 1533

Legatio Magni Indorum Imperatoris Presbyteri Ioannis, ad Emanuelem Lusitaniae Regem... Antwerp: Joan. Grapheus, 1532 (repr. Dordrecht, Netherlands, 1618)

STUDIES

Blackburn, 'John More's *The Christian empire of Prester John*', pp. 37-43

A. Cortesão and H. Thomas (eds), *Carta das novas que vieram a el Rei nosso senhor do descobrimento do Preste João*, Lisbon, 1938

Fides, religio, moresqve Aethiopvm, 'The faith, religion and customs of the Ethiopians

DATE 1540
ORIGINAL LANGUAGE Latin

DESCRIPTION

Fides, religio, moresque Aethiopvm (its longer title is *Fides, religio, moresqve Aethiopvm svb Imperio Preciosi Ioannis (quem vulgo Presbyterum Ioannem vocant) degentium, vna cũ enarratione confoederationis ac amicitiae inter ipsos Aethiopum Imperatores, & Reges Lusitaniae initae*) was first published in Louvain in 1540. It can be regarded as the culmination of Góis's interest in Christian Ethiopia, which had begun with his earlier opuscule *Legatio Magni Indorum imperatoris*, published in 1532.

Fides has a composite character. It extends over 96 pages, and it includes the Latin version of a series of letters sent by Ethiopian rulers (Queen Dowager Ǝleni and *nəguś* Ləbnä Dəngəl) to European monarchs (Manuel I, João III and the pope), a long religious text by the Ethiopian cleric Ṣägga Zä'ab, and a *Deploratio Laapianae gentis* in defence of the Sami people. It opens with a dedication to Pope Paul III and an historical introduction that includes a summary of the Portuguese expansion in the Orient and its contacts with Christian Ethiopia. After this there are five letters, which include Ǝleni's letter and the four letters that Francisco Alvares had taken to Europe in 1527. Alvares had served as chaplain of a Portuguese embassy to Ethiopia led by Rodrigo da Lima and acted as official envoy of Ləbnä Dəngəl. The letters had been originally written in Gəʿəz (or Persian) and in Arabic, and afterwards translated into Portuguese; once in Italy, they were translated into Latin by the humanist Paolo Giovio (*Fides, religio, moresqve Aethiopvm*, 1540, pp. 19, 50-51). The documents convey the admiration of the Ethiopians for the Portuguese nation, who challenged Islamic and pagan states in the Red Sea region. They further emphasise the wish of the Ethiopian rulers, which had already been expressed in Ǝleni's 1509 letter, to combat the 'Moors' and expand Christianity in the Red Sea region (e.g. *Fides, religio, moresqve Aethiopvm*, pp. 21, 26, 28, 30, 34, 43-44).

The letters are followed by a treatise on the 'faith and religion of the Ethiopians' composed by Ṣägga Zä'ab (*Fides, religio, moresqve Aethiopvm*, pp. 53-94). In this piece, the Ethiopian cleric responds to a series of criticisms voiced at the Portuguese court against Ethiopian Christianity, which some Portuguese clergy considered too close to Islam and Judaism (e.g. *Fides, religio, moresqve Aethiopvm*, p. 82). Ṣägga Zä'ab urges upon his hosts the need to build a common front against Islam rather than scrutinising the correctness of each other's Christian faith (*Fides, religio, moresqve Aethiopvm*, pp. 82, 86). *Fides* concludes with a plea in favour of the Sami, which is an extended version of the piece that concludes the 1532 *Legatio*.

Góis reportedly started compiling and editing *Fides* in about 1533, when he was called back to Lisbon by Manuel I. There he met Ṣägga Zä'ab, whom he befriended (*Chronica do Felicissimo Rei*, terçeira parte, fol. 107r). He agreed to translate the Ethiopian's religious treatise into Latin, though he was only able to finish this a few years later in Padua, where he had moved to pursue his studies.

SIGNIFICANCE

Fides had a profound impact in 16th-century Europe, enjoying several early editions between 1540 and 1604 and a wide readership. Its chief documents, the Ethiopian royal letters taken to Europe by Alvares and the religious plea written by Ṣägga Zä'ab, provided further information on Ethiopian Christianity and the Solomonid state. Together with Francisco Alvares's *Verdadera informação das terras do Preste João das Indias* (Lisbon, 1540), it is the most important 16th-century European text about the Horn of Africa.

The work has characteristics of the ecumenical and eschatological drive that was being promoted by humanist sectors in Catholic Europe, a leitmotif of which was the union of the Christian churches to fight the Islamic, 'Moorish' and Arab states of the East (see Marcocci, *Consciência de um Império*, pp. 197-98).

Thanks to the ample space that *Fides* gives to Ṣägga Zä'ab's treatise, the book was banned from circulation in Portugal. Its later publication marked a turning point in the policy of the kingdom concerning Christian Ethiopia, which favoured the missions for conversion led by the Society of Jesus (Martínez, *Envoys of a human God*, ch. 1).

MANUSCRIPTS

There are no known MSS of *Fides*, nor of Ṣägga Zä'ab's treatise. Similarly, the original Ethiopian diplomatic letters to the European rulers appear to be lost.

EDITIONS & TRANSLATIONS

Uhlig and Bühring, *Damian de Góis' Schrift über Glaube und Sitten der Äthiopier* (German trans.)

J. Boemus, *The manners, lavves, and customes of all nations. Collected out of the best vvriters by Ioannes Boemus Aubanus, a Dutch-man. With many other things of the same argument, gathered out of the historie of Nicholas Damascen. The like also out of the history of America, or Brasill, written by Iohn Lerius. The faith, religion and manners of the Aethiopians, and the deploration of the people of Lappia, compiled by Damianus à Goes With a short disourse of the Aethiopians, taken out of Ioseph Scaliger his seuenth booke de Emendatione temporum. Written in Latin, and now newly translated into English. By Ed. Aston.*, London, 1610 (English trans. of Boemus. *Mores, leges, et ritus omnium gentium*, 1591, with selections from *Fides, religio & mores Aethiopum* in fols 503-88)

Fides, religio & mores Aethiopum, [Genf], 1604

Damiani a Goes,...Aliquot opuscula. Fides, religio, moresque Aethiopum. Epistolae aliquot Preciosi Joannis, Paulo Jovio et ipso Damiano interpretibus. Deploratio Lappianae gentis...Omnia ab ipso autore recognita. Item aliquot epistolae Sadoleti, Bembi et aliorum clarissimorum virorum...ad ipsum Damianum...ex officina R. Rescii, Louvain, 1544, Conimbricæ, 1791²

Fides, religio, moresque Aethiopum..., Parisiis: C. Wechelum, 1541

Fides, religio, moresqve Aethiopvmi. svb imperio Pretiosi Ioannis (quem vulgo Presbyterum Ioannem vocant) degentivm, Lovanii: Rutgeri Rescij, 1540

STUDIES

A. Martínez d'Alòs-Moner, *Envoys of a human God. The Jesuit mission to Christian Ethiopia, 1557-1632*, Leiden, 2015 (in press)

G. Marcocci, *Consciência de um Império (1)*, Coimbra, 2012

G. Marcocci, 'Gli umanisti italiani e l'impero portoghese. Una interpretazione della *Fides, religio, moresque Æthiopum* di Damião de Góis', *Rinascimento* 45 (2005) 307-36

Andreu Martinez

António Tenreiro

DATE OF BIRTH About 1500
PLACE OF BIRTH Portugal; possibly Coimbra
DATE OF DEATH Between 1560 and 1570
PLACE OF DEATH Coimbra

BIOGRAPHY

Most of the information about the life of António Tenreiro comes from his *Itinerário*. He is first known in 1523, when he was a soldier in Hormuz (Portuguese India). From there, he accompanied the embassy of Baltasar Pessoa, the city's *alcaide-mor*, to the court of Shah Ismail. He left the group after the death of Ismail, and started the journey to Jerusalem alone. He says he was imprisoned by the Turks in Diyarbakir (*Caraemita*) on a charge of spying, which is corroborated by a report from the Turkish *beylerber* of Diyarbakir, that a Portuguese renegade named Abdū al-'Allām, who had gone with the Portuguese ambassador to the shah, had remained after the departure of the embassy and converted to Islam. This all took place between 1524 and 1525 (Bacqué-Grammond, 'Un rapport ottoman'). He was taken to Cairo, where he met the Great Vizier Ibrāhīm Pasha, and he was eventually released. From Cairo he returned to Hormuz following a convoluted course through Alexandria, Cyprus, Syria, Aleppo, and down the Euphrates to the Persian Gulf.

From 1528 to 1529, he went on another journey, delivering messages to the king of Portugal. Passing along the Persian Gulf, he came to Basra, and then, crossing the desert to Aleppo, he made his way to Tripoli, from where he sailed to Cyprus, and from there to Europe. In May 1529, he arrived in Portugal, and in Lisbon he had an audience with King João III.

In 1539, the king made him a Knight of the Order of Christ and granted him a yearly pension. Settling in Coimbra, in 1560 he published his only work, the *Itinerário*, in which he declared that he was in the last stages of his life. He died sometime between 1560 and 1570.

Some present-day authors believe that Tenreiro worked as a spy in the pay of the Portuguese crown (Cunha, 'Relations with Persia').

MAIN SOURCES OF INFORMATION

Primary

F. de Andrade, *Crónica de D. João III*, M.L. de Almeida (ed.), Porto, 1976, p. 429

F. Lopes de Castanhede, *História do descobrimento e da conquista da Índia pelos portugueses*, ed. M.L. de Almeida, Porto, 1979, ii, pp. 489-91

J. de Barros, *Da Ásia, Terceira Década*, Lisbon, 1992, p. 300

D. do Couto, *Década Quarta da Ásia*, ed. M.A.L. Cruz et al., Lisbon, 1999, i, pp. 259-63

Secondary

J.T. e Cunha, art. 'Portugal, I. Relations with Persia in the Early Modern age (1500-1750)', in *EIr*

V. Resende, 'L'image de l'islam dans la littérature portugaise des voyages', *Anais de História de Além Mar* 7 (2006) 107-96

J.M. Herrero, *Libros de viajes de los siglos XVI y XVII en España y Portugal. Lecturas y lectores*, Madrid, 1999, 86-91

J.N. Carreira, 'Cronologia de viajantes. António Tenreiro e Fr. Pantaleão de Aveiro', *Anais da Academia Portuguesa de História* 37 (1998) 191-208

L. Albuquerque, *Navegadores, viajantes e aventureiros portugueses – sécs. XV e XVI*, Lisbon, 1987, ii, pp. 42-52

A.P. de Castro, 'Introduction', in *Peregrinação de Fernão Mendes Pinto e Itinerário de António Tenreiro, Tratado das cousas da China, Conquista do Reino de Pegu*, Porto, 1984, xlix-lxi

J.N. Carreira, 'A expansão portuguesa e a descoberta das civilizações orientais', *Arquipélago. Série Ciências Humanas* 6 (1984) 127-49

J.-L. Bacqué-Grammont, 'Un rapport ottoman sur António Tenreiro', *Mare Luso-Indicum* 3 (1976) 161-73

A. Gonçalves Losa, 'Comentário ao Itinerário de António Tenreiro', in D. Lopes (ed.), *Cultura islâmica e cultura árabe*, Lisbon, 1969, 21-44

A. Gonçalves Losa, 'O *itinerário* de António Tenreiro. O Islão visto por um português de quinhentos', in *Atti del terzo congresso di studi arabi e islamici*, Naples, 1967, 467-81

M. Saldanha, 'Viagens de Penetração e de Exploração no Continente Asiático. As Grandes Viagens de Alcance Geográfico incluindo a Penetração no Grão Mogol, no Grão Cataio e no Tibete', in A. Baião et al. (eds), *História da expansão Portuguesa no mundo*, vol. 2, Lisbon, 1940, 196-220, pp. 203-5

A. Baião, 'Prefácio' to *Itinerários da Índia a Portugal por terra*, Coimbra, 1923, v-xxxii

WORKS ON CHRISTIAN-MUSLIM RELATIONS

Itinerário, 'Itinerary'

DATE 1560
ORIGINAL LANGUAGE Portuguese

DESCRIPTION

Although the *Itinerário* (it has been given the fuller title *Itinerário de António Tenrreyro, que da India veyo per terra a este Reyno de Portugal*) has been published many times since the 16th century, there is still no critical edition, and there are variations between the manuscripts and the *princeps* edition of 1560 (Aubin, 'Pour une étude critique' [2000], pp. 527-28). In Castro's 1984 edition, which follows the *princeps* edition, the text is found on pages 679-773, and page numbers below follow this edition.

The entire work, describing António Tenreiro's journeys through Syria, Iraq, Iran, Armenia and Egypt on his first trip, and Iraq and Syria and on to Europe on his second, is about Muslims and their relationships with minority groups in the Islamic world. The only exceptions are three brief chapters on Cyprus (chs L-LII, pp. 747-49) and the three last chapters, which briefly mention two towns near Venice and the city of Ferrara (chs LXVII-LXIX, pp. 767-68).

Tenreiro's method of observation follows an unchanging pattern. He describes each city in terms of physical and human geography, and then adds details worthy of note, including physical features of the various races he encounters, and occasionally mentions his own experiences. The impression of Safavid Iran he creates is in keeping with the attitude that was shaping Portuguese policy at the time, according to which the *Sufi* (as the shah was called) was an ally against the Ottoman rivals. Tenreiro's depiction of the Persian population is always positive, not only because the people are 'white', but also because they are good-looking: the Persians from Hormuz (p. 686) and Shiraz (p. 695) are praised for their well-proportioned bodies, and their women for their beauty (pp. 686, 695); the Persians and Turkomans from Tabriz are 'light-skinned, handsome people' (p. 703). Similarly, when he compares the Turkish and Persian languages, he says that Persian is 'a sweeter and better tongue' (p. 695).

One of the very few chapters whose title is not linked to some geographical description is dedicated entirely to the rise of Shah Ismail (ch. V). Teneiro says that he received a Christian education, when in order to save his life he was taken as a boy by an astrologer to Christian monks in a monastery in Armenia (pp. 692-93).

Tenreiro distinguishes Shī'ī Islam, which he calls 'rafaui' (*rāfiḍī*) and says places 'Alī above Muḥammad ('Mafamede'), (p. 692), from Sunnī Islam, which is the Islam of the Grand Turk (p. 697), explaining that the Safavids publicly speak ill of the 'prophets' of the Turks, 'one whom they call *Otumão* and the other *Omar Bubaka*' (p. 723), thereby fusing the first and second caliphs, Abū Bakr and 'Umar into a single character. This lack of accuracy, which is apparently due to oral information from inexpert sources, is mirrored in other aspects of the work – in the chapter on the *ḥajj*, for example, preparations for which he witnessed when he was in Cairo (ch. XLIII). He omits the actual pilgrimage ritual but he mentions the well of Zamzam (though not by name) and the power of its waters to keep the pains of Purgatory from all who washed in them. He says that it and 'the House of Mecca' were the work of Abraham when he went there to sacrifice his son. He also mentions the *Medinat el Naby* (Madīnat al-Nabī) as the site of Muḥammad's tomb (pp. 739-40). Elsewhere, he names the city of *Mexeta de Ale* (Masjīd 'Alī), probably meaning Najaf, noting that 'many Moors make pilgrimage to the tomb of 'Alī' (p. 753).

The relationship between Muslims and Christians is a highlight of Teneiro's observations. He distinguishes between the various Christian communities, listing Armenians, Jacobites, Nestorians and Maronites, and he also refers to Jewish communities, mentioning especially the Spanish Jews he finds in Damascus, Cairo and Safed in Galilee. The Copts of Egypt, whom he calls simply Christians, receive special attention: they are 'very old' in the land, speak Arabic, and practise circumcision alongside baptism; they live in a quarter near the Nile outside the city, while the Jewish quarter is located inside (p. 741). In Tabriz, Armenians possess only small churches and oratories, where they celebrate 'after the fashion of the primitive church', though 'in fear' (p. 704), while the Christians of Ercis ('Argis') in Lower Armenia have 'more freedom than in other places, and have a good relationship with the Kurds (p. 716). The Armenian Christians of Bitlis ('Bytaliz') enjoy greater religious freedom than their Nestorian counterparts in Ahlat ('Aclata'), possessing churches 'more publicly' (p. 718). In Diyarbakir, he claims he saw Muslim men married to Christian women, each keeping their own religion, a privilege which he was told had been granted them by their prophet 'Mafamede'.

SIGNIFICANCE

The *Itinerário* was the first book of travel through the Middle East to be published in Portugal. Though many questions remain about the inconsistencies of Tenreiro's narrative, mainly concerning chronology (Aubin, 'Pour une étude critique'; Resende, 'L'image de l'islam'), his writings in both manuscript and printed form circulated widely in 16th-century Portugal and influenced a number of authors. The chronicler Fernão Lopes de Castanheda, in his *História do descobrimentos e conquista da Índia pelos Portugueses* ('History of discovery and conquest of India by the Portuguese'), describes the Portuguese embassy to the Safavid shah in 1523-24 and mentions details about Iran that he attributes to the *Itinerário* (Book VI), and in Book VII he devotes a whole chapter (LXX) to the story of Tenreiro's overland journey from Hormuz to Lisbon, though this does not correspond either to the known manuscripts or to the printed edition of the *Itinerário*. On the other hand, his description of Hormuz (Book II) corresponds almost entirely to the account in the *Itinerário* (Aubin, 'Pour une étude critique'). João de Barros also mentions the *Itinerário* in his *Década III da Ásia*, published in 1563, declaring that he used it in his unfinished *Geography*, which disappeared after his death (Aubin, 'Pour une étude critique'). Another traveller, Mestre Afonso, whose work was written about 1565 (though it remained unpublished until the 19th century), made extensive use of the *Itinerário*, especially in his description of the routes between Azerbaijan and Palestine (Resende, 'L'image de l'islam').

MANUSCRIPTS

MS Lisbon, Biblioteca da Ajuda – 50-V-22, fols 350-355v (1551-1600; partial)

MS Lisbon, Library of the Marquis of Fronteira – (16th century; partial)

EDITIONS & TRANSLATIONS

J. Pögl, *Als Briefkurier durch Persien. Auf dem Landweg von Indien nach Portugal; 1523-1529*, Stuttgart, 2002 (edition and German trans.)

A. Tenreiro, 'Itinerário', in N. Águas (ed.), *Viagens por terra da India a Portugal*, Sintra, Portugal, 1991, 19-120

A. Tenreiro, 'Itinerário', in de Castro, *Peregrinação de Fernão Mendes Pinto e Itinerário de António Tenreiro*, pp. 679-773

L. de Lemos, *Itinerário em que se contém como da India veio por terra a estes Reinos de Portugal*, Lisbon, 1971, 1980²

L. Ribeiro, 'A viagem da Índia a Portugal por terra, feita por António Tenreiro', *Studia* 3 (1959) 110-23 (edition of the partial MS in the Marquês da Fronteira Library)

F.G.P. Vidal, 'Uma nova lição da "Viagem por terra..." de António Tenreiro', in *I Congresso da história da expansão portuguesa no mundo, II secção: Portugueses no Oriente*, Lisbon, 1938, 106-28, pp. 119-28 (edition of the partial MS in Biblioteca da Ajuda)

A. Tenreiro, 'Itinerário', in A. Baião (ed.), *Itinerários da Índia a Portugal por terra*, Coimbra, 1923, 1-127

Itinerário de António Tenreiro cavaleiro da Ordem de Cristo em que se contem como da India veio por terra a estes Reinos de Portugal, Lisbon: Typ. Rollandiana, 1829 (vol. 4 of the *Peregrinação* of Fernão Mendes Pinto)

Pereginação de Fernão Mendes Pinto, e por ele escrita... e no fim della trata brevemente de algumas noticias, e da morte do Santo Padre Mestre Francisco Xavier... acrecentada com o itinerario de Antonio Tenreiro... e a conquista do Reyno de Pegu, Lisbon: João de Aquino Bulhões, 1762

Peregrinação de Fernão Mendes Pinto por elle escritta... accrescentada com o itinerario de Antonio Tenreiro... e a conquista do Reyno de Pegu, Lisbon: Offic. Ferreiriana, 1725

Itinerário de António Tenreiro cavaleiro da Ordem de Cristo em que se contem como na India veio por terra a estes Reinos de Portugal, Coimbra: João de Barreira, 1565

Itinerário de António Tenreiro cavaleiro da Ordem de Cristo em que se contem como na India veio por terra a estes Reinos de Portugal, Coimbra: António de Mariz, 1560

STUDIES

J.T. e Cunha, '"The eye of the beholder". The creation of a Portuguese discourse on Safavid Iran', in R. Matthee and J. Flores (eds), *Portugal, the Persian Gulf and Safavid Persia*, Louvain, 2011, 11-50

Cunha, art. 'Portugal, I. Relations with Persia in the Early Modern age (1500-1750)'

D.S. Couto, 'Méthodes en histoire du monde portugais', *Annuaire de l'École Pratique des Hautes Études (EPHE), Section des Sciences Historiques et Philologiques* 139 (2008), http://ashp.revues.org/488

D.S. Couto, 'Le Golfe en la cartographie portugaise de la première moitié du XVe siècle', in M. Taleghani, D.S. Couto and J.L. Braché-Grammont (eds), *Cartographie historique du Golfe persique*, Louvain, 2006, 79-114

Resende, 'L'image de l'islam'

L.F. Thomaz, 'La présence iranienne autour de l'océan Indien au XVIe siècle d'après les sources portugaises de l'époque', *Archipel* 68 (2004) 59-158

J.M. Herrero, *Libros de viajes de los siglos XVI y XVII en España y Portugal. Lecturas y lectores*, Madrid, 1999, pp. 86-91

De Castro, 'Introduction'

J.N. Carreira, 'Cronologia de viajantes. António Tenreiro e Fr. Pantaleão de Aveiro', *Anais da Academia Portuguesa de História* 37 (1998) 191-208

J.N. Carreira, *Outra face do Oriente. O Próximo Oriente em relatos de viagem*, Sintra: Mem Martins, 1997

J.N. Carreira, *Do Preste João às ruínas da Babilónia. Viajantes portugueses na rota das civilizações orientais*, Lisbon, 1990

Albuquerque, *Navegadores*, ii, pp. 42-52

J.N. Carreira, 'A expansão portuguesa'

Bacqué-Grammont, 'Un rapport ottoman'

R. Gulbenkian and H. Berbérian, 'La légende de David de Sassoun d'après deux voyageurs portugais du XVIe siècle', *Revue des Études Arméniennes* 8 (1971) 175-88 (repr. in R. Gulbenkian, *Estudos históricos*, Lisbon, 1995, vol. 1)

J. Aubin, 'Pour une étude critique de l'*Itinerário* d'António Tenreiro', *Arquivos do Centro Cultural Português* 3 (1971) 238-52 (repr. in *Le Latin et l'astrolabe*, Lisbon, 2000, ii, pp. 523-37)

J. Aubin, 'La survie de Shîlâu et la route du Khunj-ô-Fâl', *Iran. Journal of the British Institute of Persian Studies* 7 (1969) 21-37

Losa, 'Comentários sobre o Itinerário de António Tenreiro'

Losa, 'O *Itinerário* de António Tenreiro'

Saldanha, 'Viagens de Penetração e de Exploração no Continente Asiático'

F.G.P. Vidal, 'Uma nova lição da "Viagem por terra" de António Tenreiro', in *I congresso da história da expansão portuguesa no mundo, 2ª secção: Oriente*, Lisbon, 1938, 106-28

H. Murray, *Historical account of discoveries and travels in Asia from the earliest ages to the present time*, Edinburgh, 1820, pp. 367-81

Filomena Barros

Fernão Lopes de Castanheda

DATE OF BIRTH   Uncertain; possibly 1512
PLACE OF BIRTH Unknown
DATE OF DEATH   23 March 1559
PLACE OF DEATH Coimbra

BIOGRAPHY

Although Fernão Lopes de Castanheda gives the main outline of his life, his biography remains surrounded by some mystery. Born in or near 1512, he spent his early years in Santarém, where he studied at the Dominican Convent. Then, on 18 April 1528, he sailed with his father for Goa in the fleet of the new governor, Nuno da Cunha. He was to remain there for ten years.

In India, Castanheda may have met Duarte Barbosa, Gaspar Correia and Garcia da Orta, all authors of historical works on the Portuguese in the region. He returned to Portugal in 1538 and took a position at Coimbra University, where he remained in various posts for the rest of his life.

On 6 March 1551, the first book of his *História do descobrimento e conquista da Índia* was published, and from then on he was able to derive an income from the successive volumes that appeared. He died on 23 March 1559, and was buried in the church of S. Pedro de Coimbra.

MAIN SOURCES OF INFORMATION

Primary
Fernão Lopes de Castanheda, *História do descobrimento e conquista da Índia pelos Portugueses*, Coimbra, 1551

Secondary
A.P. Avelar, 'A "imagem" do Infante D. Henrique na cronística da Expansão. Gomes Eanes de Zurara, João de Barros e António Galvão', in A.T. de Matos and J.P. Oliveira e Costa, *A Herança do Infante*, Lisbon, 2011, 159-71
A. Martins de Carvalho, *Nuno da Cunha e os capitães da Índia (1529-1538)*, Lisbon, 2009
L.F. Barreto, *Damião de Goes. Os caminhos de um Humanista*, Lisbon, 2003
N. de Nazaré Castro Soares, 'A historiografia do renascimento em Portugal. Referentes estéticos e ideológicos humanistas', in L.F. Thomaz (ed.), *Aquém e Além da Taprobana. Estudos Luso-Orientais à memória de Jean Aubin e Denys Lombard*, Lisbon, 2002, 17-37

F.T. Fonseca et al. (eds), *Imprensa da Universidade de Coimbra. Uma história dentro da História*, Coimbra, 2001

A.P. Avelar, *Fernão Lopes de Castanheda. Historiador dos Portugueses na Índia ou Cronista do governo de Nuno da Cunha?*, Lisbon, 1997

F. de Figueiredo, *A épica Portuguesa no século XVI*, Lisbon, 1987

M.L. Carvalhão Buescu, *O estudo das línguas exóticas no século XVI*, Lisbon, 1983

WORKS ON CHRISTIAN-MUSLIM RELATIONS

História do descobrimento e conquista da Índia pelos Portugueses, 'History of the discovery and conquest of India by the Portuguese'

DATE 1551-61
ORIGINAL LANGUAGE Portuguese

DESCRIPTION

Castanheda's *História do descobrimento e conquista da Índia* is the first historical account of the Portuguese presence in Asia. He planned ten volumes, covering the period from Vasco da Gama's first voyage in 1467 to the 1550s. He started on the work while still in India, and continued at Coimbra. Book 1, which was printed on 6 March 1551 and offered to King João III when he visited the University of Coimbra, describes Portuguese expansion between 1497 and 1505. In its 267 pages, it includes details about fighting with local Muslim communities in India. Successive volumes then appeared at short intervals up to 1554, making seven in all during Castanheda's lifetime. They each followed the pattern of chronicling the periods of rule of the early governors, and detailing their relations with the rulers of Islamic states into whose lands the Portuguese were gradually expanding. It is a history of conflict. In 1554, a second edition of Book 1 appeared, with the main focus still on the conflicts between the Portuguese and neighbouring Islamic states.

After Castanheda's death, his sons had Book 8 published in 1561. Several later manuscript copies of 31 chapters of Book 9 are extant, covering the period up to 1545.

SIGNIFICANCE

Castanheda's *História* provides important information about the violent clashes between the Portuguese and local Islamic states in India. While it is structured as a chronicle, following the rule of each governor in sequence, it includes many digressions that provide either a context for the historical events it covers or an interpretation of these contexts.

From the time of its appearance, the *História* was recognised as an indispensable source for the history of the Portuguese presence in Asia. A translation of Book 1 into French appeared in 1553, into Spanish in 1554, Italian in (probably) 1556, German in 1565, and English in 1582.

EDITIONS & TRANSLATIONS

M. Lopes de Almeida (ed.), *História do descobrimento e conquista da Índia pelos Portugueses*, 2 vols, Porto, 1979

P. Augusto de S. Bartolomeu de Azevedo and P. Mateus Laranjo Coelho (eds), *Historia do descobrimento e conquista da India pelos portugueses*, 4 vols, Coimbra, 1924-33

Historia do descobrimento e conquista da India pelos portugueses, 7 vols, Lisbon, 1833

F. José dos Santos (ed.), *Historia do descobrimento, e conquista da India pelos portugueses*, 2 vols, Lisbon, 1797

D'Indiaensche historie der Portugeezen onder de regeeringe van vijf Portugeesche koningen, of anders, Het vervolg der historie van Don Emanuel, Koning van Portugael, sedert het jaer 1521 tot op het jaer 1610, Rotterdam, 1670 (Dutch trans.)

The first booke of the History of the discovery and Conquest of the East Indies. Enterprised by the Portingales, in their daungerous Navigations, in the time of King Don John, the second of that name, wich Historie conteineth much varietie of matter very profitable for all Navigatiors, and not unpleasaunt to readres. Set forth in the Portingale Language, by Hernan Lopes de Castanheda, and now translated into English by N. L., London: Thomas East, 1582, http://books.google.pt/books?id=YkoC-kx4TAgC&pg=1&redir_esc=y#v=onepage&f=false

Historia dell Indie Orientali, scoperte, & conquistate da portoghesi, di comissione dell' Inuittissimo Re Don Manuello, di gloriosa memoria: Nella quale, oltre alle strane usanze, maniere, riti e costumi di quele genti; si uienne anco in notitia di molte guerre fatte in quei paesi... Distinta in libri VII. Composti dal sig. Fernando Lopes di Castagneda; et nouamente di língua portoghese in italiana tradotti dal signor Alfonso Ulloa. I-II., Venice: Giordano Ziletti, 1577-78 (Italian trans.)

Le premier livre de l'histoire de l'Inde contenant comment l'Inde este decouverte par li commandement du Roy Emanuel et la guerre que les capitaines Portugalois ont menee contre Samosin Roy de Calecut,... Traduit de portugues en francois par Nicolas de Grouchy, Paris: J. Parant, 1576 (French trans.)

Warhafftige vnd volkomene Historia, Von erfindung Calecut vnd anderer Königreich, Landen vnd Jnseln, in Jndien, vnd dem Jndianischen Meer gelegen, So vormals von niemands mehr erkand, Daher biß auff den heutigen Tag allerley Gewürtz, Specerey vnd andere köstliche Wahr, Fast in die gantze Christenheit gebracht werden.... Auß Frantzösischer Sprach jetzt newlich ins Teutsch gebracht, (s.l.), 1565 (German trans.)

Ho octauo liuro da historia descobrimento & conquista da India pelos Portugueses, Coimbra: João de Barreira, 1561, http://purl.pt/15294/1/res-427-3-v/res-427-3-v_item1/index.html

Historia del descobrimento y conquista de la India por los portugueses compuesta por Hernan Lopes de Castaneda en linguaje português y traduzida nuevamente en romance castellano, Antuwerpen: Martin Nucio, 1554 (Spanish trans.)

Ho liuro primeiro dos dez da historia do descobrimento & conquista da India pelos Portugueses... Agora emme[n]dado e acrecentado, Coimbra: João de Barreira, 1554, http://purl.pt/15294/1/res-425-1-v/res-425-1-v_item1/index.html

Ho seitimo liuro da historia descobrimento & conquista da India pelos Portugueses [Coimbra: João de Barreira], 1554, http://purl.pt/15294/1/res-427-2-v/res-427-2-v_item1/index.html

Ho sexto liuro da historia descobrimento & conquista da India pelos Portugueses, Coimbra: João de Barreira, 1554, http://purl.pt/15294/1/res-427-1-v/res-427-1-v_item1/index.html

Le premier livre de l'histoire de l'Inde contenant comment l'Inde este decouverte par li commandement du Roy Emanuel et la guerre que les capitaines Portugalois ont menee contre Samosin Roy de Calecut,... Traduit de portugues en francois par Nicolas de Grouchy, Antwerpen: J. Steelsius, 1554 (French trans.)

Le premier livre de l'histoire de l'Inde contenant comment l'Inde este decouverte par li commandement du Roy Emanuel et la guerre que les capitaines Portugalois ont menee contre Samosin Roy de Calecut,... Traduit de portugues en francois par Nicolas de Grouchy, Paris: M. de Vascosan, 1553 (French trans.)

Os liuros quarto & qui[n]to da historia descobrimento & conquista da India pelos Portugueses, Coimbra: João de Barreira e João Alvares, 1553, http://purl.pt/15294/2/res-423-2-v/res-423-2-v_item2/index.html

Ho terceiro liuro da historia do descobrimento & conquista da India pelos Portugueses, Coimbra: João de Barreira e João Álvares, 1552, http://purl.pt/15294/2/res-423-1-v/res-423-1-v_item2/index.html

Historia do liuro segundo da historia descobrimento & conquista da India pelos Portugueses, Coimbra: João de Barreira e João Alvares, 1552, http://purl.pt/15294/2/res-425-2-v/res-425-2-v_item2/index.html

Historia do descobrimento & conquista da India pelos Portugueses, Coimbra: João de Barreira e João Alvares, 1551, http://archive.org/stream/historiadodescoboocast#page/n3/mode/2up

STUDIES

There are no studies of the appearance of Muslims in the *História*. For general studies, see the list of secondary sources to Castanheda's biography.

Ana Paula Avelar

Garcia da Orta

Garcia de Orta, Garcia d'Orta

DATE OF BIRTH About 1501
PLACE OF BIRTH Castelo de Vide, Portugal
DATE OF DEATH 1568
PLACE OF DEATH Goa, India

BIOGRAPHY

Garcia da Orta was born into a Converso family of Jewish origins around the beginning of the 16th century in the south of Portugal near the Spanish border. He attended the universities of Salamanca and Alcalá de Henares and returned to Portugal sometime around 1523, where he practised medicine for a while before lecturing in the University of Lisbon. In 1534, he left Portugal in the fleet commanded by Martim Afonso de Sousa to whose service he was attached and who would later become governor of the *Estado da Índia* (1542-45), and he stayed in the Subcontinent for the remainder of his life. Established mainly in Goa, he nevertheless had the opportunity to travel to other Indian locations, such as Gujarat, Deccan, Malabar and Ceylon, collecting material for what became the first systematic European survey of Asian plants, spices and medicinal drugs: the *Colóquios dos simples e drogas da Índia* (1563). Having obtained the title of 'physician to the King' (*physico d'el-Rey*) prior to his departure from Lisbon, his reputation as a skilled doctor expanded beyond the borders of the *Estado da Índia*, and he was sometimes called to attend to patients in the court of Burhān Shāh I, the second Niẓām of Aḥmadnagar, who befriended him.

MAIN SOURCES OF INFORMATION

Secondary
C.R. Boxer, *Two pioneers of tropical medicine. Garcia d'Orta and Nicolás Monardes*, London, 1963
C. de Ficalho, *Garcia da Orta e o seu tempo*, Lisbon, 1886, 1983[2]

WORKS ON CHRISTIAN-MUSLIM RELATIONS

Coloquios dos simples, e drogas he cousas mediçinais da India, 'Colloquies on the simples, drugs and *materia medica* of India'

DATE 1563
ORIGINAL LANGUAGE Portuguese

DESCRIPTION

Garcia da Orta's work (its full title is *Coloquios dos simples, e drogas he cousas mediçinais da India, e assi dalgũas frutas achadas nella onde se tratam algũas cousas tocantes a mediçina, pratica, e outras cousas boas, pera saber*, 'Colloquies on the simples, drugs and *materia medica* of India, and also some fruits found therein, and sundry matters concerning medicine, practice and other things good to know', and it totals 264 folios) is a treatise on oriental plants and drugs organised in the form of a dialogue between himself and an imaginary character called Ruano, a doctor just arrived from Portugal. Considered as the first European treatise on oriental botany and pharmacology, the *Colóquios* was soon translated to Latin, Spanish and Italian, and circulated among scientific experts of the time. Later re-editions saw Orta's book published together with other similar works, such as the *Tractado* of Cristóbal Acosta (Cristóvão da Costa), itself essentially a reworking of the *Colóquios*, and Nicolás Monardes' *Historia medicinal*. Nevertheless, it should be noted that these translations are restricted to the scientific aspects of the book; the original dialogue structure was removed and Orta's additional remarks on Indian civilisation completely omitted. Charles de l'Ecluse's influential translation, which became the source of subsequent European editions, seems to have set the standard in the matter.

Modern scholars have stressed the original character of the *Colóquios* inasmuch as it constitutes the result of thorough research combining elements of different traditions and backgrounds. Orta quotes the authoritative ancient authors (e.g., Dioscorides, Pliny) and some of his own contemporaries (e.g., Antonio Musa, Vesalius), but a good deal of the knowledge he displays derives from direct contact with Indian, Persian and Arab physicians, apothecaries, merchants, soldiers and officials. This intercultural approach is not uncommon in the Portuguese overseas writings of the 16th-17th centuries, but it looks more pioneering when set against current Western scientific practice. Another characteristic of

Orta's writings is the priority he gives to observation and experience over theory and established authority, a feature most famously illustrated by the following passage of the *Colóquios*: 'Do not frighten me with Dioscorides or Galen, I merely speak the truth and say what I know.'

SIGNIFICANCE

The importance of Orta's *Colóquios* for the study of Christian-Muslim relations resides less in the subject of the book itself than in the method and approach that permitted its author to carry out his research. In fact, other than dealing with the description of the various plants and their medicinal properties, Orta's text unveils many details about his own career as a botanist and physician in India, and through his own words he introduces a wide network of informants of various creeds, most of whom were Muslims. Furthermore, the *Coloquios* is filled with details concerning Islamic populations and their customs, the history and geography of India and the Middle East, and the etymological origins of certain terms. He translates and explains Oriental titles and epithets, distinguishes Turks from *Rumes* (the word the Portuguese employed to identify the Ottomans), and deduces a common ancestry for Mughals and Uzbeks.

Concerning religious matters, despite Orta's close contact with the Muslim world, his knowledge of Islam is not devoid of error; he states for instance that the Shīʿīs (whom he calls *Moalis*) are a sect hostile to Muḥammad, sharing the widespread misconception in the West that opposition to Sunnī Islam meant opposition to its founder. Like most Portuguese historians of the 16th century, he recounts a case of conversion to Islam albeit in an apologetic fashion; the story of a man called Sancho Pires, who, after serving in the ranks of the *Estado da Índia* as a gunner, escaped to Aḥmadnagar, turned Muslim, and rose to the post of general. He was now called Frang Khān and attended the sultan's council. Typically, Orta asserts that he remained secretly Christian for the rest of his life, notwithstanding his public embrace of his new creed.

What is most striking in the way Garcia da Orta deals with Islamic subjects is the spirit of tolerance and understanding his life seems to have embodied. Even if his knowledge of oriental languages was very limited, he managed to learn from Asian physicians the names of maladies and remedies, while teaching in return their Latin equivalents. Probably thanks to his own personal history, having been born to a New Christian family, he was ideally placed at the centre of a network of information where quest for knowledge was more important than any form of bigotry or sense of racial superiority. He encouraged the study of Arab authors against the opinion of his European counterparts, who considered them 'barbarian' compared with the Greeks. Free from religious constraints, Orta was able to develop his skills in botany and pharmacology, and in doing so contributed to a deeper knowledge of the Asian world in literate Europe.

EDITIONS & TRANSLATIONS

S. Messinger Ramos, A. Ramos and F. Marchand-Sauvagnargues (trans.), *Colloques des simples et drogues de l'Inde*, Arles, 2004 (French trans.)

C. Acosta, *Tratado das drogas e medicinas das Indias Orientais. No qual se verifica muito do que escreveu o doutor Garcia de Orta*, Lisbon, 1964 (intro. by J. Walter, the title acknowledging Garcia da Orta's contribution; Portuguese trans.)

C.R. Markham (trans.), *Colloquies on the simples & drugs of India*, London, 1913, Delhi, 1979 (English trans.)

C. de Ficalho (ed.), *Coloquios dos simples e drogas da India*, 2 vols, Lisbon, 1891-95 (repr. Lisbon, 1987, Charleston SC, 2013)

Colloquios dos simples e drogas e cousas medicinaes da India, e assi de algumas fructas achadas nella (varias cultivadas hoje no Brasil), Lisbon, 1872

J. de Bondt (trans.), *An account of the diseases, natural history, and medicines of the East Indies. Translated from the Latin of James Bontius, Physician to the Dutch Settlement at Batavls. To which are added annotations by a physician*, London, 1769

A. Colin (trans.), *Histoire des drogues, espiceries, et de certains medicamens simples, qui naissent és Indes, tant orientales que occidentales*, Lyon, 1602, 1619² (French trans. based upon l'Ecluse's abridged Latin edition)

C. Acosta, *Tractado de las drogas, y medicinas de las Indias orientales*, Burgos, 1578 (Spanish adaptation of Orta's work with minimal acknowledgement)

A. Briganti (trans.), *Due libri dell'historia de i semplici, aromati, e altre cose, che vengono portate dell'Indie Orientali, pertinenti al uso de la Medicina*, Venice, 1576, 1582, 1597, 1605, 1616 (Italian trans. based upon l'Ecluse's abridged Latin edition)

J. Fragoso, *Discvrsos de las cosas aromaticas, arboles y frutales, y de otras muchas medicinas simples. que se traen de la India Oriental, y siruen al vso de medicina*, Madrid, 1572 (said to be a Spanish trans. of Orta's work)

Charles de l'Ecluse (trans.), *Aromatum, et simplicium aliquot medicamentorum apud Indos nascentium Historia*, Antwerp, 1567 (facsimile Nieuwkoop, 1963, Lisbon, 1964; abridged Latin trans.)
Coloquios dos simples, e drogas he cousas mediçinais da India, e assi dalgũas frutas achadas nella onde se tratam algũas cousas tocantes a mediçina, pratica, e outras cousas boas, pera saber, Goa, 1563 (repr. Lisbon, 1963)

STUDIES

J. Pimentel and I. Soler, 'Painting naked truth. The *Colóquios* of Garcia da Orta (1563)', *Journal of Early Modern History* 18 (2014) 101-20

R.M. Loureiro, 'Information networks in the *Estado da Índia*, a case study. Was Garcia de Orta the organizer of the *Codex Casanatense* 1889?', *Anais de História de Além-Mar* 13 (2012) 41-72

P.F. da Costa and T.N. de Carvalho, 'Between East and West. Garcia de Orta's *Colloquies* and the circulation of medical knowledge in the sixteenth century', *Asclepio. Revista de Historia de la Medecina y de la Ciencia* 65 (2013) 1-13

T.N. de Carvalho, 'Invisible travellers and virtual tracks. Knowledge construction in *Coloquios dos simples e drogas de India*... of Garcia de Orta (Goa, 1563)', in A. Roca-Rosell (ed.), *The circulation of science and technology*, Barcelona, 2012, 288-93

R.M. Loureiro, 'Garcia de Orta e os *Colóquios dos simples*. Observações de um viajante sedentário', in G. Fragoso and A. Mendes (ed.), *Garcia de Orta e Alexander von Humboldt. Errâncias, investigações e diálogo entre culturas*, Lisbon, 2008, 135-45

I. Županov, 'Drugs, health, bodies and souls in the tropics. Medical experiments in sixteenth-century Portuguese India', *Indian Economic and Social History Review* 39 (2002) 1-43

L.F. Barreto, *Descobrimentos e Renascimento. Formas de ser e pensar nos séculos XV e XVI*, Lisbon, 1983, pp. 255-95

D.F. Lach, *Asia in the making of Europe*, 9 books in 3 vols, Chicago IL, 1965-93, vol. 1/2, pp. 192-95; vol. 2/3, pp. 433-37

A. da S. Rego, 'Garcia de Orta e a ideia de tolerância religiosa', *Garcia de Orta* 11 (1963) 663-76

Boxer, *Two pioneers of tropical medicine*

Ficalho, *Garcia da Orta*

Vasco Resende

Determinação de letrados

'Conclusions of the men of learning'

DATE 1569
ORIGINAL LANGUAGE Portuguese

DESCRIPTION

In January 1569, a committee of the *Mesa da Consciencia e Ordens* ('Board of Conscience and Orders'), comprising six scholars, met in Almeirim, Portugal, to come to a decision about an appropriate response to the murder of the Jesuit missionary Gonçalo da Silveira, who had been killed on the orders of the king of Monomotapa (in present day Zimbabwe), in 1561. The king had abandoned Christianity under Muslim influence and turned on Christians. The result of the committee meeting was *Determinação de letrados*. The manuscript is two folios long, while the text in da Silva Rego's edition is five pages long (pp. 162-71). The principal signatories are the Jesuit Martim Gonçalvez da Câmara (d. 1578) and Leão Henriquez Torres, with Duarte Carneiro Rangel, Paulo Afonso, Simão Gonçalvez Preto and Gonçalo Dias de Carvalho (d. 1598) also being named.

The document states that, after examining the records of the events, the committee regard it as proved that the people of Monomotapa killed innocent Portuguese traders and the priest Gonçalo da Silveira. They were influenced to do this by Muslims 'hostile to the faith of our Lord Jesus Christ' (p. 162), who had caused the king and his family to abandon 'the faith they had professed and the true way of salvation' (p. 65). It goes on to recall that it is the duty of the king of Portugal and his subjects to 'cause the Gospel to be proclaimed' in regions assigned to the Portuguese by papal authority, and to say that the king of Portugal may lawfully wage war against Monomotapa (pp. 166-67). Finally, it sets out what the king of Monomotapa should do with the 'Moors' under his protection, in order to avoid a reprisal (pp. 168-71).

SIGNIFICANCE

The *Determinação* provides an illustration of the belief of European rulers that it was their duty to introduce Christianity among the peoples whom their subjects encountered and to counteract the spread of Islam.

The immediate result of the document was the expedition led by Francisco Barretto to Monomotapa in 1571-73, which is recorded by the Jesuit Francisco Monclaro in his *Relaçao feita pelo Padre Francisco de Monclaro.*

MANUSCRIPTS

MS Lisbon, Biblioteca Nacional de Portugal – Manuscrits portugais, no. 8, fols 266-267v (1569)

EDITIONS & TRANSLATIONS

A. da Silva Rego, *Documentos sobre os portugueses em Moçambique e na África central, 1497-1840, Documents on the Portuguese in Mozambique and Central Africa, 1497-1840*, Lisbon, 1975, vii, pp. 162-71

G. Theal, *Records of south-eastern Africa collected in various libraries and archive departments in Europe*, London, 1899, iii, pp. 140-47

STUDIES

Theal, *Records of south-eastern Africa*, iii, pp. 148-49, 202-3

John Chesworth

João de Barros

DATE OF BIRTH   About 1496
PLACE OF BIRTH Viseu, Portugal
DATE OF DEATH   20 October 1570
PLACE OF DEATH Ribeira de Alitém, Pombal, Portugal

BIOGRAPHY

João de Barros, a great historian as well as a pioneer of the systematisation of Portuguese grammar, was born the illegitimate son of the *fidalgo* or nobleman Lopo de Barros. He was educated at the court of King Manuel I during the period of the golden age of Portuguese discoveries. At the young age of 20, he composed a novel of chivalry, the *Chronicle of Emperador Clarimundo*, dedicated to the prince Dom João, who, after ascending the throne as King João III in 1521, granted him the post of captain of the fortress of São Jorge da Mina in Guinea. De Barros held this post until 1525, and on his return to Portugal he was appointed treasurer of the India House, which he remained until 1528.

In order to escape from an outbreak of black plague, de Barros moved from Lisbon to Ribeira de Alitém near Pombal in 1530, where he composed a moral dialogue *Rhopicapneuma* at the request of his friend and relative Duarte de Resende. Called back by João III in 1532, he was appointed *feitor* or administrator of the House of India and Mina. While working there, he married Maria de Almeida. They had five sons and three daughters.

When João III began to divide the coast of Brazil into 13 captaincies, de Barros was granted the capitaincy of Maranhão. In 1539, he and two of his sons prepared a fleet of ten vessels to sail out to his new post, but the whole fleet was shipwrecked, which caused him serious financial loss.

After this disaster, João III asked de Barros to write a history of the Portuguese in India. While he was engaged in this work, the *Décadas da Ásia*, in 1539 he published a short Portuguese grammar called *Cartinha*, followed by the first systematic Portuguese grammar in 1540. The first volume of the *Décadas* appeared in 1552, the second in 1553, and the third in 1563, but the fourth and final volume was only published posthumously in 1615, completed by the Portuguese historian Diogo do Couto (c. 1542-1616). An edition of the whole work appeared in Lisbon in 1777-88.

Primary

J. de Barros and D. do Couto, *Da Ásia de João de Barros e Diogo do Couto, dos feitos que os portugueses fizeram no descobrimento dos mares e terras do Oriente*, Lisbon, 1777-78 (M. Severim de Faria, 'Vida de João de Barros', in vol. 9, pp. iii-lxiv)

Secondary

R.L. Panegassi, 'O pasto dos brutos. Contexto de João de Barros, \"horizonte histórico\" e política nas Décadas da Ásia', São Paulo, 2013 (Diss. University of São Paulo)

S.M.M. Casais de Almeida Rocha, *Dinâmicas de poder dos intérpretes. Língua Portugueses na Ásia de João de Barros*, Lisbon, 2011

J.M.N. Torrão, 'Os prólogos de João de Barros. Defesa de conceitos com tributo à antiguidade', *Ágora. Estudos Clássicos em Debate* 2 (2000) 137-44

A.B. Coelho, *João de Barros. Vida e obra*, Lisbon, 1997

A. da Costa Ramalho, 'João de Barros, humanista', *Oceanos* 27 (1996) 68-73

A.I. Buescu, 'João de Barros. Humanismo, mercancia e celebração imperial', *Oceanos* 27 (1996) 10-24

C.R. Boxer, *João de Barros. Portuguese humanist and historian of Asia*, New Delhi, 1981

A.A. Banha de Andrade, *João de Barros. Historiador do pensamento humanista português de quinhentos*, Lisbon, 1980

Décadas da Ásia, 'Decades of Asia'

DATE 1570
ORIGINAL LANGUAGE Portuguese

DESCRIPTION

The original four volumes of the work are as follows:

Primeira Década da Ásia dos Feitos, que os Portugueses fizeram no descobrimento, e conquista dos mares, e terras do Oriente, Lisbon: Germão Galhardo, 1552. In the 1777-78 edition, the two parts come to 478 and 447 pages.

Segunda Década da Ásia, Lisbon: Germão Galhardo, 1553. In the 1777-78 edition, its two parts come to 572 and 496 pages.

Terceira Década da Ásia, Lisbon: João Barreira, 1563. In the 1777-78 edition, its two parts come to 663 and 525 pages.

Quarta Década da Ásia, Madrid: Impressão Real, 1615, published posthumously, completed with notes and maps by João Baptista Lavanha. In the 1777-78 edition, the two parts come to 637 and 751 pages.

The title, *Décadas da Ásia* ('Decades of Asia'), was apparently derived from *Décadas*, the name by which Livy's Roman history, *Ab urbe condita*, was known. De Barros was evidently comparing his work to Livy's Roman history, and the Portuguese expansion and conquest of Asia to that of the Romans in Europe. (The title of the edition that was finally published in 24 volumes in 1777-78 is *Da Ásia de João de Barros e Diogo do Couto, dos feitos que os portugueses fizeram no descobrimento dos mares e terras do Oriente.*)

Each of these four original volumes has ten parts, and each part is made up of two to 16 chapters. The contents of each volume are as follows:

Vol. I, from the achievements of Prince Henry the Navigator to 1505

Vol. II, from the departure of Tristan da Cunha and Afonso de Albuquerque for the east coast of Africa and India in 1506 to the death of Albuquerque

Vol. III, from the dispatch of Governor Lopo Soares de Albergaria to India in 1515 to the death of Governor Henriquez de Menezes in 1526

Vol. IV, from the appointment of Lopo Vaz de Sampaio as governor in 1526 to the return of Governor Nuno da Cunha to Portugal in 1539 (he died on the way).

This last volume remained unfinished in de Barros's lifetime and was published in Madrid in 1615, long after his death, in a version edited by João Baptista Lavanha, who amplified the text with notes and maps. Prior to the publication of this fourth volume, Diogo do Couto's continuation of de Barros's work had been published in 1602. This is why there now exist two different fourth volumes of *Da Ásia*.

According to the description of the first chapter of *Da Ásia*, de Barros had apparently planned a comprehensive history of the Portuguese *Reconquista* and Portugal's overseas expansion. The structure was to have been the following: 1. Conquest – Europe, Africa (Morocco), Asia, Santa Cruz (Brazil); 2. Voyages; 3. Trade. The four volumes of *Da Ásia* as they now are roughly correspond to the part of the 'Conquest' of Asia he had first planned to write, and he also seems to have written much of the part on 'Africa'. The part on 'Voyages' was apparently supposed to consist of a description of navigation and world geography, and 'Trade' was to include a description of trade and goods around the world.

De Barros's *Décadas* covers the early history of the Portuguese in India and Asia. The first two volumes describe important sea battles and highlight the achievements of the Portuguese in sea trade. Prominent figures such as Vasco da Gama, Pedro Alvares Cabral, D. Francisco de Almeida and Fernão Peres de Andrade are introduced in their fight to give the country control over the Indian Ocean. The third volume refers to the Chinese empire, its laws, religious beliefs and administration system. While he was prejudiced against Muslims and Hindus, de Barros seems to have been fairly tolerant toward Chinese religious beliefs. He recognises the superiority of Chinese culture, and considers its achievements to be on the same level as that of science in ancient Greece and Rome.

Diogo do Couto's continuation deals with the history of Asia, especially in the Indian Ocean, from the beginning of the 16th century, including the rise and fall of the Bijapur and Gujarat Sultanates, as well as the Mughal and Ottoman Empires.

In *Décadas* de Barros presents the reader with a narrative that forges a causal link between the rise of Islam and the Portuguese presence in Asia. He opens the work as follows: 'The great Antichrist, Muḥammad, arisen in the land of Arabia (...) so forged the fury, like iron and fire, of his infernal sect that, through his captains and caliphs, he conquered all of Arabia in Asia and part of Syria and Persia and in Africa all of Egypt, both on this side of the Nile and beyond, within the span of a hundred years' (Book I.1). He goes on to explain how this conquest included the Iberian Peninsula, where the westward expansion was brought to a halt and where 'the brave Don Pelayo of Asturias' only three years later began the countermove of reconquering the peninsula, a 'victory' that was achieved only after a battle that lasted several hundred years and the sacrifice of many a brave man. He goes on to say that, having completed the expulsion of Muslims from the Iberian Peninsula, the Portuguese then proceeded to pursue this holy cause in Africa and Asia.

He thus frames the Portuguese discoveries and conquests in Africa and Asia as a continuation of the *Reconquista* and the crusades. According to his ideology, it was incumbent upon the Portuguese, and the royal family in particular ('their dowry and inheritance'), to safeguard the Christian faith and maintain 'this profile of war against infidels', high though the price may be: 'and that is why we can say that the Portuguese crown is founded on the blood of many martyrs and that those martyrs spread and enlarged it through all the universe...'.

SIGNIFICANCE

De Barros is usually quite factual in his remarks on Islam and Muslims. (In Book I.7, for example, he narrates that the shaykh of the island of Kamaran had Portuguese captives circumcised, but does so without comments of derision or anger.) There are, however, occasions when he lapses into what appears to be crusader ideology. Describing the fortifications of Jeddah in Book III.1, he remarks, 'It would not be very difficult for us to enter the Red Sea and thence to the city of Jeddah, a port very nearby, by which we could go to Mecca and thence to Medina to steal the body of their prophet and hold it in our possession in the same way as they hold Jerusalem, which is the home of our faith....'

This is one of the two oldest sources for the *Kilwa Chronicle*. In Book I.8, de Barros relates the *Cronica dos Reyes de Quiloa*, stating that descendants of Muḥammad's great-grandson Zayd migrated from Persia via the area of present-day Bahrain, where they were branded as *hereticos* and later settled in Kilwa, which gradually developed into an important medieval sultanate on the Swahili coast.

De Barros is also of interest because of his account of the rise of Shīʿī Islam among the Safavids. In Book II.10, he gives an extensive and fairly accurate exposition of the differences between Sunnī and Shīʿī Islam, and describes the rise of the Safavid dynasty and their adoption of Imāmī Shīʿism (including a reference to the practice of *taqiyya*).

In general, de Barros's *Décadas* is an instructive source for the spread and development of Islam in Asia as well as for the history of Muslim-Christian relations in the context of the rivalry and antagonism of the Indian Ocean trade. He describes the competition between Muslim Arab merchants and the Portuguese, depicting the Arab traders as treacherous and violent. The local Muslim leaders and communities in East Africa and Asia usually emerge more positively, as hospitable and courteous.

De Barros's text makes it plain that, despite the opening rhetoric of *Décadas*, trade interests prevailed over religious zeal in the Portuguese expansion into Asia.

EDITIONS & TRANSLATIONS

A. Lima Cruz, *Ásia de João de Barros. Dos feitos que os portugueses fizeram no descobrimento e conquista dos mares e terras do Oriente. Quarta década*, Lisbon, 2001 (repr. of the 1615 Madrid edition)

L. de Sousa Rebelo, D. Ramada Curto and T.F. Earle, *Cronística e historiografia do século XVI*, Lisbon, 2000 (anthology of the works of Gaspar Correia, Fernão Lopes de Castanheda and João de Barros)

Decadas da Asia de João de Barros, Lisbon, 1998 (integral edition, with indices of topographical and personal names)

E. Feust, *Die Asia*, Frankfurt am Main, 1995 (German trans. of vol. I.1-5)

I. Vilares Cepeda, *Ásia de João de Barros. Dos feitos que os portugueses fizeram no descobrimento e conquista dos mares e terras do Oriente. Terceida década*, Lisbon, 1992 (repr. of the Madrid, 1615 edition)

G. Pögl, *Heinrich der Seefahrer oder die Suche nach Indien. Eine Dokumentation mit Alvise da Cà da Mostos erstem Bericht über Westafrika und den Chroniken Zuraras und Barros' über den Infanten*, ed. and trans. G. Pögl and R. Kroboth, Darmstadt, 1989 (German trans.)

Ásia de João de Barros. Dos feitos que os portugueses fizeram no descobrimento e conquista dos mares e terras do Oriente. Secunda década, Lisbon, 1988 (repr. of the Madrid, 1615 edition)

H. Cidade and M. Múrias, *Ásia de João de Barros. Dos feitos que os portugueses fizeram no descobrimento e conquista dos mares e terras do Oriente*, 3 vols, Lisbon, 1988

Ikuta Shigeru and Ikegami Mineo Yaku, *Ajia shi. 2*, Tokyo, 1981 (Japanese trans. of *Década 2*)

Ikuta Shigeru and Ikegami Mineo Yaku, *Ajia shi. 1*, Tokyo, 1980 (Japanese trans. of *Década 1*)

J. de Barros and D. do Couto, *Da Asia de João de Barros e Diogo de Couto. Decada 1-12*, Lisbon, 1973-74, (repr. of the 1778-78 edition)

A. Baião and L.F.L. Cintra, *Asia de Joam de Barros. Dos feitos que os portugueses fizeram no descobrimento e conquista dos mares e terras do oriente. Segunda década*, Lisbon, 1974

M. Dion, 'Sumatra through Portuguese eyes. Excerpts from João de Barros' *Decadas da Asia*', *Indonesia* 9 (1970) 129-62

H. Cidade and M. Múrias, *Ásia de João de Barros. Dos feitos que os portugueses fizeram no descobrimento e conquista dos mares e terras do Oriente*, Lisbon, 1945

M. Gonçalves Viana, *Décadas da Ásia (excerptos das quatro décadas). Ensaio biográfico e histórico-crítico, selecção, notas e índices remissivos*, Porto, 1944

M.R. Lapa, *O descobrimento da India (Ásia, década I, livro IV)*, Lisbon, 1939, 1943², 1977³

J. Ferreira, *Década I, livro IV de João de Barros*, Porto, 1940

V. de Castro e Almeida, *Chronique de Damião de Goes, João de Barros, Casper Correa. Débuts du commerce et de la domination des mers en Orient*, Brussels, 1938 (French trans.)

A. Sérgio, *O descobrimento do caminho da India*, Lisbon, 1937 (*Década* I.4)

V. de Castro e Almeida, *Les grands navigateurs et colons Portugais du XVe et du XVIe siècles. Anthologie des écrits de l'époqie*, vol. 2. Chroniques de Ruy de Pina, Fra João Alvares, Damião de Goes, João de Barros, Garcia de Resende, Castanheda. Afrique du nord, Congo, Cap de Bonne-Espérance, Éthiopie, Paris, 1934 (French trans.)

V. de Castro e Almeida, *Chronique de Damião de Goes, João de Barros, Casper Correa, Garcia de Resende. La découverte de l'Inde par Vasco da Gama*, Brussels, 1934 (French trans.)

A. Baião, *Asia. Dos feitos que os Portugueses fizeram no descobrimento e conquista dos mares e terras do Oriente. 1. Década*, Coimbra, 1932

A. Baião (ed. and trans.), *Décadas. Selecção*, 4 vols, Lisbon, 1932, 1945-46², 1982-83³

A. de Campos, *Barros (Década 1)*, Lisbon, 1921

Asia. Selections (Década 1), Paris, 1920

A. Baião, *Documentos inéditos sôbre João de Barros. Sôbre o escritor seu homónimo contemporâneo, sôbre a família do historiador e sôbre os continuadores des suas 'Decadas'*, Coimbra, 1917

D. Ferguson, *The history of Ceylon, from the earliest times to 1600 A.D., as related by João de Barros and Diogo do Couto*, Colombo, 1909 (English trans.)

J. Ribeiro, *History of Ceilão, with a summary of de Barros, de Couto, Antonio Bocarro and the Documentos remettidos, with the Parangi Hatane and Kostantinu Hatane. Translated from the original Portuguese and Sinhalese*, trans. P.E. Pieris, Colombo, 1909 (English trans.)

D.W. Soltau, *Geschichte der entdeckungen und eroberungen der Portugiesen im Orient. Vom Jahr 1415 bis 1539*, 5 vols, Braunschweig, 1821 (German trans.)

D.W. Soltau, *Auf dem alten Seewege nach Indien. Beschreibung der Entdeckungs- und Eroberungsfahrten der Portugiesen in den Jahren 1415 bis 1503*, 4 vols, Cologne, 1821, 1910² (German trans.)

Da Asia da João de Barros e de Diogo de Couto, 24 vols, Lisbon, 1778-78

Decada primeira da Asia de João de Barros dos feitos, que os portuguezes fizeram no descobrimento, e conquista dos mares, e terras do Oriente, e novamente dada a luz, e offerecida ao Senhor João Bristow's, Lisbon, 1752

P. van der Aa, *Twee onderscheydene reys-togten d'eene ter zee en d'andere te land, in de West-Indien: beyde gedaan in het Jaar 1524, de erste door Gil Gonzales Davila... de tweede... door Ferdinand Cortes*, Leiden, 1707 (Dutch trans.)

P. van der Aa, *Aanzienelyke scheeps-togt door den grave Don Vasco da Gamma, als Ammiraal ter Zee en Onder-Konink van Indien, derwaarts gedaan in 't jaar 1524*, Leiden, 1707 (Dutch trans.)

P. van der Aa, *Roemwaardige scheeps-togten en dappere krygs-bedryven ter zee en te land, onder 't bestuur van Don Duarte de Menezes, als opperhoofd vande vloot en gouverneur van Oost-Indien*, Leiden, 1707 (Dutch trans.)

P. van der Aa, *Heldhaftige reys-togten, te land, door Ferdinand Cortes, in Nieuw-Spanje,... Mexico: in 't Jaar 1519*, Leiden, 1707 (Dutch trans.)

P. van der Aa, *Ongemeene scheeps-togten en manhafte krygs-bedryven te water en land, door Diego Lopez de Sequeira... in de Oost-Indien gedaan in 't Jaar 1518*, Leiden, 1707 (Dutch trans.)

P. van der Aa, *Uytvoerige reys-togten door Pedrarias Davila... naar de vaste kust van Darien in 't Jaar 1514*, Leiden, 1707 (Dutch trans.)

P. van der Aa, *Twee ongelukkige scheeps-togten na Oost-Indien, van Jorge de Mello in het jaar 1507. en Jorge d'Aguiar, in het jaar 1508*, Leiden, 1707 (Dutch trans.)

P. van der Aa, *Ongemeene scheeps-togten en manhafte krygs-bedryven te water en land, door Diego Lopez de Sequeira, als kapitein-generaal en gouverneur... met IX schepen derwaarts gedaan, in 't jaar 1518*, Leiden, 1706-7 (Dutch trans.)

P. van der Aa, *Staat-zugtige scheeps-togten en krygs-bedryven ter handhaving van der Portugyzen opper-bestuur in Oost-Indien, door Don Lopo Vaz deSampayo, gedaan in 'jaar 1526*, Leiden, 1706-7 (Dutch trans.)

P. van der Aa, *Vervolg der tien-jaarige scheeps-togten en manhaste krygs-bedryven door Nuno da Cunha, als gouverneur generaal gedaan in Oost-Indien, zederd het jaar 1536 tot aan zyn dood. Waar van de kort inhoud der verhaalen op de volgende blad-zyde worden aangeweezen*, Leiden, 1706 (Dutch trans.)

P. van der Aa, *Tien-jaarige scheeps-togten en heldhaftige krygs-bedryven te water en te land, door Nuno da Cunha, als gouverneur gedaan na en in Oost-Indien, in 't jaar 1528*, Leiden, 1706 (Dutch trans.)

P. van der Aa, *Scheeps-togt gedaan door Fernando Perez d'Andrade... uit last des konings Don Manuel van Portugaal, van Malacca afgezonden na de Golf van Bengale en de kusten van China in 't jaar 1516*, Leiden, 1706 (Dutch trans.)

P. van der Aa, *Scheeps-togten en manhaste krygs-bedryven te water en te land gedaan door Lopo Soares d'Albegeria uit last des Konings Don Manuel van Portugaal, als Kapitein Generaal en Gouverneur der Oost-Indien, met een vloot van XIII schepen derwaards gezonden in 't jaar 1515*, Leiden, 1706 (Dutch trans.)

P. van der Aa, *Twee bysondere scheeps-togten na Oost-Indien, van Gonsalo de Sequeira in het jaar 1510 en Garcia de Noronha in het jaar 1511*, Leiden, 1706 (Dutch trans.)

P. van der Aa, *Bloedige scheeps-togt van den Maarschalk Don Fernando Coutinho na Oost-Indien, met een vloot van 15 scheepen in 't jaar 1509*, Leiden, 1706 (Dutch trans.)

P. van der Aa, *Held-dadige scheeps-togt van Alfonso d'Albuquerque, na de Roode-Zee, in het jaar 1506. en vervolgens gedaan*, Leiden, 1706 (Dutch trans.)

P. van der Aa, *Scheeps-togt van Tristano d'Acunha na Oost-Indien, met een vloot van 14 scheepen, in het jaar 1506*, Leiden, 1706 (Dutch trans.)

P. van der Aa, *Roemrugte scheeps-togt van Francisco d'Almeida na Oost-Indien, eerste onder-koning dier landen, in 't jaar 1505*, Leiden, 1706 (Dutch trans.)

P. van der Aa, *Scheeps-togt van Pedro da Nhaya na Oost-Indien, met een vloot van 8 scheepen, in het jaar 1505*, Leiden, 1706 (Dutch trans.)

P. van der Aa, *Twee bysondere scheeps-togten na Oost-Indien, van Francisco D'Albuquerque, in het jaar 1503. en Lopo Soares in het jaar 1504*, Leiden, 1706 (Dutch trans.)

P. van der Aa, *Rampspoedige water-togt door Franciscus de Porras... van Jamaica naar Hispaniola in 't Jaar 1504*, Leiden, 1706 (Dutch trans.)

P. van der Aa, *Tweede scheeps-togt van Don Vasco da Gamma, zeevoogd van Arabien, Persien, Indien en het geheele Oosten, na Oost-Indien, met een vloot van 20 scheepen in het jaar 1502*, Leiden, 1706 (Dutch trans.)

J.L. Gottfried and P. van der Aa, *De doorlugtige scheeps-togten der Portugysen na Oost-Indiën, mitsgaders de voornaamste gedeeltens van Africa en de Roode-Zee*, Leiden, 1706 (Dutch trans.)

P. van der Aa, *Eerste scheeps-togt van Vasco da Gamma, tot ontdekking van de Indien, in het jaar 1497*, Leiden, 1706 (Dutch trans.)

P. van der Aa, *De alder-eerste scheeps-togten der Portugysen, ter ontdekking van vreemde landen uytgefonden, in het jaar 1419*, Leiden, 1706 (Dutch trans.)

M. Frz. de Villa Real, *Cinco livros da decada doze de Historia da India por Diogo do Couto*, 4 vols, Paris, 1645

J.B. Lavanha, *Asia. Dos feitos que os Portugueses fezerão no descobrimento & conquista dos mares & terras do Oriente. Decadas 1-4*, 4 vols, Lisbon, 1615-28

I. Rodriguez, *Decada primeira [-terceira] da Asia de Ioão de Barros, dos feitos qve os portvgveses fezerão no descobrimento & conquista dos mares & terras do Oriente*, 3 vols, Lisbon, 1628

Asia. Dos fectos que os Portugueses fizeram no descobrimento y conquista dos mares y terras do Oriente, Década IV, Madrid: Impresso Real, 1615 (published posthumously, completed with notes and maps by João Baptista Lavanha)

J. de Barros and D. do Couto, *Decada quarta da Asia, dos feitos que os Portuguezes fizeram na conquista e descobrimento das terras, & mares do Oriente: em quanto gouernaraõ a India Lopo Vaz de saõ Payo, & parte de Nuno da Cuna, etc.*, Lisbon: Pedro Crasbeeck, 1602 (continuation of de Barros's work)

E.M. Satow and C.R. Boxer, *Terceira decada da Asia de Ioam de Barros. Dos feytos que os Portugueses fizeram no descobrimento & conquista dos mares & terras do Oriente*, Lisbon, 1563

Asia. Dos fectos que os Portugueses fizeram no descobrimento y conquista dos mares y terras do Oriente, Década III, Lisbon: J. de Barreira, 1563

L'Asia. De' fatti de' Portoghesi nello scoprimento, & conquista de' mari & terre di Oriente, ed. A. de Ulloa, Venice: Appresso Vincenzo Valgrisio, 1562 (Italian trans.)

A. de Ulloa and V. Valgrisio, *L'Asia del S. Giovanni di Barros, consigliero del Christianissimo Re di Portogallo. De'fatti de' Portoghesi nello scoprimento, & conquista de'mari & terre di Oriente*, Venice: Appresso Vincenzo Valgrisio, 1561 (Italian trans.)

Asia. Dos fectos que os Portugueses fizeram no descobrimento y conquista dos mares y terras do Oriente, Década II, Lisbon: G. Galharde, 1553

Asia. Dos fectos que os Portugueses fizeram no descobrimento y conquista dos mares y terras do Oriente, Década I, Lisbon: G. Galharde, 1552

STUDIES

    Panegassi, 'O pasto dos brutos. Contexto de João de Barros'
    Casais de Almeida Rocha, *Dinâmicas de poder dos intérpretes*
    Torrão, 'Os prólogos de João de Barros'
    Coelho, *João de Barros. Vida e obra*
    Buescu, 'João de Barros'
    da Costa Ramalha, 'João de Barros, humanista'
    Boxer, *João de Barros*
    Banha de Andrade, *João de Barros*

Toru Maruyama

Gaspar da Cruz

DATE OF BIRTH   Probably 1520s
PLACE OF BIRTH Évora, Portugal
DATE OF DEATH   5 February 1570
PLACE OF DEATH Setúbal, Portugal

BIOGRAPHY

Gaspar da Cruz was born in Évora, Portugal, at an unknown date, perhaps in the early 1520s. He was admitted to the Dominican Convent of Azeitão near Setúbal, where he completed his religious education and was probably ordained. No details are known about this period of his life. In 1548, he sailed to India with that year's fleet from Portugal, with a group of Dominicans under the leadership of Fr Diogo Bermudez. They were travelling east in order to open up Dominican missionary stations in a number of parts of Asia that were then controlled by the Portuguese crown. We do not have much information about Gaspar's wanderings in Asia, but through his own writings (mainly the *Tractado*, published in Évora in 1570), and through Jesuit letters dispatched from India, it is possible to sketch his itinerary.

Gaspar spent the first six years on the west coast of India, in Goa, Chaul (now in ruins, 60 km south of Mumbai), and Kochi, which were then under Portuguese control and where the Dominicans had built their first convents. During this period, he briefly visited Ceylon. In 1554, he founded a Dominican house in Malacca, on the Malay Peninsula, where the Portuguese crown had for decades held a powerful fortress. In September 1555, he travelled to Cambodia with some Portuguese merchants, apparently at the request of the Cambodian King Ang Chan (r. 1516-66), and stayed for a year at Lovek, the capital city. Concluding that it would be extremely difficult to set up a Catholic mission there, in late 1556 he moved on, still in the company of merchants, and sailed to Langbaijiao, a small island off the coast of the Chinese province of Guangdong, where the merchants had been doing business for a few years. Between December 1556 and January 1557, he was in Guangzhou (Canton) but, disappointed by the lack of missionary opportunities, he sailed back to Malacca in early 1557, where Portuguese sources seem to lose track of him. Jesuit letters mention a Dominican friar who visited

Makassar between 1557 and 1559, and this was certainly Gaspar. In 1559, he travelled back to Goa, making a brief stopover at Mylapore, on the east coast of India.

Continuing his Asian itinerary, in early 1560 Gaspar sailed with a small group of Dominicans to Hormuz at the entrance of the Persian Gulf, which had been under the control of the Portuguese crown since the early years of the 16th century. He stayed there for three years, performing religious services for the Christian population, which included about 500 Portuguese soldiers and traders. He appears to have learned Persian, because he credits himself with the translation into Portuguese of a 14th-century *Cronica dos reys Dormuz* ('Chronicle of the kings of Hormuz'), which he later included in his *Tractado*.

In 1563, Gaspar sailed back to Goa, and the following year he began to travel back to Lisbon. His ship was forced to winter on the island of Mozambique, but in early 1565 he was back in Lisbon, after what appears to have been an official survey of Asian missionary fields on behalf of the Dominican Order. Catholic religious orders were then trying to define and control specific missionary areas within what was generally termed the Portuguese *Estado da Índia* ('State of India'). Gaspar probably settled in Évora, and he only reappears in 1569-70 in Lisbon and Setúbal, helping with the efforts against the plague epidemic that was then rampant. He himself died, a victor of the plague, on 5 February 1570.

On 20 February 1570, the Spanish printer André de Burgos completed the printing of the *Tractado em que se côtam muito por estêso as cousas da China cõ suas particularidades e assi do Reyno Dormuz*. This was the first European printed book entirely devoted to Chinese matters, and although its author had only spent one month in China, using his own experience and the oral and written accounts of other Portuguese travellers, he was able to produce a thorough and comprehensive monograph, encompassing all relevant aspects of the Chinese world. The *Tractado* stands out, not only for the richness of its content, the accuracy of the information it contains and the variety of sources used, but also for its attitude of open sympathy towards the Chinese world. Over many pages, Gaspar praises the effectiveness of Chinese forms of government, the impartiality of justice, the exemplary character of punishments, the respect for hierarchies, and much more. China is a true model society, worthy of the greatest admiration and interest, and only tainted by the fact that the Chinese live in 'ignorance of the truth' and totally alienated from the 'faith of Christ'. There is even a chapter on 'the Moors which

GASPAR DA CRUZ 371

there are in China', in which Gaspar tries to establish the Central Asian origin of Chinese Muslim communities. As an apparent afterthought, and with no obvious connection to the rest of the book, Gaspar appends his translation of the *Cronica dos reys Dormuz*.

MAIN SOURCES OF INFORMATION

Primary
Gaspar da Cruz, *Tractado em que se cõtam muito por estēso as cousas da China cõ suas particularidades e assi do Reyno Dormuz*, Évora, 1570
D.B. Machado, *Bibliotheca Lusitana*, 4 vols, Lisbon, 1741-59 (facsimile repr. Coimbra, 1965-67)
J. Wicki and J. Gomes (eds), *Documenta Indica*, 18 vols, Rome, 1948-88
L. de Sousa, *História de São Domingos*, ed. M. Lopes de Almeida, Porto, 1977
J. dos Santos, *Etiópia Oriental e vária história de cousas notáveis do Oriente*, ed. M. Lobato et al., Lisbon, 1999

Secondary
R.M. Loureiro, *Nas partes da China. Colectânea de estudos dispersos*, Lisbon, 2009, pp. 113-28
R.M. Loureiro, *Fidalgos, missionários e mandarins. Portugal e a China no século XVI*, Lisbon, 2000, pp. 617-45
D.F. Lach, *The century of discovery* (vol. ii of *Asia in the making of Europe*), Chicago IL, 1965, pp. 730-815
C.R. Boxer (ed.), *South China in the sixteenth century*, London, 1953, pp. lviii-lxvii

WORKS ON CHRISTIAN-MUSLIM RELATIONS

Relaçam da cronica dos reys Dormuz, 'Account of a chronicle of the kings of Hormuz'

DATE 1570
ORIGINAL LANGUAGE Portuguese

DESCRIPTION
The *Relaçam da cronica dos reys Dormuz* (in full, *Relaçam da cronica dos reys Dormuz, tirado dhũa Cronica q[ue] cõpos hũ rey do mesmo reyno, chamado Pachaturunxa, scripta em Arabigo, & sumariamente traduzida em lingoajem Portugues por hum religioso da ordem de Sam Domingos, q[eu] na ilha Dormuz fundou hũa casa de sua ordem*, 'Account of a chronicle of the kings of Hormuz, taken from a chronicle composed by one of the kings of the said kingdom, named Padeshah Turan Shah, written in

Arabic, and epitomised in the Portuguese language by a religious of the order of Saint Dominic that in the island of Hormuz founded a residence of his order') was first published as an appendix to the *Tractado em que se cõtam muito por estêso as cousas da China cõ suas particularidades e assi do Reyno Dormuz*. Although the frontispiece reads 1569, the colophon mentions that the printing was completed on 20 February 1570. The *Relaçam* runs to 12 pages. It is a digest of the original work, which was much longer, written by Padeshah Turan Shah I, ruler of Hormuz from 1346 to 1378. It has been suggested that the manuscript used by Gaspar was written in Persian in Arabic characters. There is no known extant copy of this work, which has tentatively been titled *Shahnameh* ('Book of kings').

The account begins with the decision of the ruler 'Mahometh' (Muḥammad Dirham-Kūb, who ruled part of Oman in the 11th century) to migrate with his people and found a new kingdom on the Persian coast. They eventually settled in the region of present-day Minab, and the new power attracted trade and merchants, and prospered immensely. It came into economic competition with the island of 'Cays' (Kish). During the reign of 'Cabadim' (Bahā' al-Dīn Ayāz, who ruled in the early years of the 14th century), under pressure from Persian enemies, the political and commercial centre of the kingdom was moved to the deserted island of 'Jarun', where the new city of Hormuz was built. In time, the island kingdom gained hegemony over the Straits of Hormuz, becoming a mercantile power with territorial dependencies on both sides of the Persian Gulf.

SIGNIFICANCE

The fact that a Catholic friar was able to learn Persian in Hormuz, and was able to acquire a Persian manuscript such as the *Shahnameh*, testifies to the cosmopolitan environment of the city in the 16th century, and the good relations between the Muslim inhabitants and the European Christian traders and missionaries who visited and settled there.

Gaspar da Cruz was not the first Portuguese author to use Persian sources on Hormuz. The historian João de Barros (1496-1570) used several works in his four *Décadas da Ásia* ('Decades of Asia') published in Lisbon between 1552 and 1563, and in Madrid in 1614. The second volume of this chronicle about the Portuguese in Asia in the first part of the 16th century, published in 1553, includes a chapter (Decade 2, Book 2, Chapter 2) on the history of Hormuz up to 1507, when Afonso de Albuquerque (c. 1453-1515) first made it a Portuguese protectorate.

Barros claimed that he used a chronicle of the kings of Hormuz that he had received from his informants in Asia, and which a Persian-speaking collaborator in Lisbon had translated for him. Although his and Gaspar's texts do not exactly coincide, this was certainly another version or copy of the *Shahnameh*.

In the final years of the 16th century, yet another version of the chronicle was translated into Spanish by Pedro Teixeira, a Portuguese physician of Jewish origin who in the 1590s lived in Hormuz and travelled widely in Persia. In his *Relaciones de Pedro Teixeira*, printed in Antwerp in 1610, one of the texts included was the *Breve relacion del principio del Reyno Harmuz y de sus reyes* ('Brief account of the origin of the Kingdom of Hormuz and its kings'), which, at 45 pages, was more comprehensive than Gaspar's 12-page summary. The two together preserve a Persian medieval chronicle that would have otherwise disappeared without a trace. It has been suggested that any original Persian versions were destroyed in 1622, when an Anglo-Persian attack ended Portuguese control of the island of Hormuz.

The *Relaçam* is an irreplaceable source for the early history of the kingdom of Hormuz. It was translated into English in the early 17th century by Samuel Purchas (1577-1626), and included in his monumental collection of travel accounts, *Purchas his pilgrimes*, as 'A relation of the kings of Ormuz, and of the foundation of the citie of Ormuz' (vol. 2, pp. 1785-805).

Although Gaspar evidently knew Muslims well and must have known about Islam, he leaves no trace of his attitude towards them. He merely translates the Persian original of this history without adding any hints of opinions he may have held. In the part of his *Tractado* on China, he does devote a few pages to the origins of the small Muslim communities that were scattered across the Chinese empire and makes a passing reference to 'this pestilential sect' (ch. 28). But he says no more, and it is difficult to draw any conclusions from this because the use of such adjectives in mentions of Muslims and Islam were commonplace at the time.

EDITIONS & TRANSLATIONS

R.M. Loureiro, *Tratado das coisas da China*, Lisbon, 2010

R.M. Loureiro, *Tratado das coisas da China*, Lisbon, 1997 (first Portuguese annotated edition of the *Relaçam*, pp. 267-79)

F. Calado and Fan Weixin, *Tratado em que se contam muito por extenso as cousas da China, com suas particularidades, e as do reyno de Ormuz*, Macau, 1996 (includes a Chinese trans. of the *Tratado*)

L. de Albuquerque, *Primeiros escritos Portugueses sobre a China*, Lisbon, 1989 (edition of the *Tratado*, pp. 51-181)

F. Mendes Pinto, *Peregrinação*, ed. M.L. de Almeida and A.P. de Castro, Porto, 1984 (edition of the *Tratado*, pp. 775-896)

João de Barros, *Ásia. Segunda década*, ed. A. Baião and L.F.L. Cintra, Lisbon, 1974 (includes information extracted from a Persian version of Turan Shah's *Shahnameh*, dec. 2, bk. 2, ch. 2)

Boxer, *South China in the sixteenth century* (the 'Relation of the Chronicle of the kings of Ormuz' is included, in a reprint of D. Ferguson's trans., with notes, pp. 228-39; Boxer adds some critical annotations of his own)

[Damião Peres], *Tractado em que se contam muito por extenso as cousas da China, com suas particularidades, e assi do Reyno de Ormuz*, Barcelos, 1937

Pedro Teixeira, *The travels of Pedro Teixeira with his Kings of Harmuz and extracts from his Kings of Persia*, ed. and trans. W.F. Sinclair and D. Ferguson, London, 1902 (English annotated trans., pp. 256-67)

F.M. Pinto, *Peregrinação*, Lisbon, 1829 (includes the 2nd edition of the *Tractado*, iv, pp. 5-195)

Samuel Purchas, *Purchas his pilgrimes*, London, 1624-25 (includes an English trans. of 'A relation of the kings of Ormuz, and of the foundation of the citie of Ormuz' by Gaspar da Cruz, vol. 2, pp. 1785-805)

Pedro Teixeira, *Relaciones de Pedro Teixeira d'el origen, descendência y succession de los Reyes de Persia, y de Harmuz, y de un viagem hecho por el mismo autor dendê la India Oriental hasta Italia por tierra*, Antwerp, 1610 (Spanish trans. by Teixeira of Turan Shah's *Shahnameh* is included, separate pagination, pp. 1-45)

'Relaçam da Cronica dos Reys Dormuz, tirado dhũa Cronica q[ue] cõpos hũ Rey do mesmo Reyno, chamado Pachaturunxa, scripta em Arabigo, & sumariamente traduzida em lingoajem Portugues por hum religioso da ordem de Sam Domingos, q[eu] na ilha dormuz fundou hũa casa de sua ordem', in *Tractado em que se cõtam muito por estẽso as cousas da China cõ suas particularidades e assi do Reyno Dormuz*, Évora, 1570, LVII-LVIII (first edition of the Portuguese translation of Turan Shah's *Shahnameh*)

STUDIES

M.B. Vosoughi, 'The kings of Hormuz. From the beginning until the arrival of the Portuguese', in L.G. Potter (ed.), *The Persian Gulf in history*, New York, 2009, 89-104

R.M. Loureiro, 'Drogas asiáticas e práticas médicas nas *Relaciones* de Pedro Teixeira (Antuérpia, 1610)', *Revista de Cultura / Review of Culture* 32 (2009) 24-41

Loureiro, *Nas partes da China*, pp. 113-28

W. Floor and F. Hakimzadeh, *The Hispano-Portuguese Empire and its contacts with Safavid Persia, the Kingdom of Hormuz and Yarubid Oman from 1489 to 1720. A bibliography of printed publications, 1508-2007*, Leuven, 2007

A. Pelúcia, 'A história de Ormuz segundo Pedro Teixeira. Uma perspectiva crítica', in L.F.F.R. Thomaz (ed.), *Aquém e Além da Taprobana. Estudos Luso-Orientais à memória de Jean Aubin e Denys Lombard*, Lisbon, 2002, 223-38

Loureiro, *Fidalgos, missionários e mandarins*, pp. 617-45

L.E. Pennington (ed.), *The Purchas handbook. Studies on the life, times and writings of Samuel Purchas, 1577-1626*, 2 vols, London, 1997

V.F. Piacentini, *Merchants, merchandise, and military power in the Persian Gulf. (Sūriyānj/Shahriyāj-Sīrāf)*, Rome, 1992

J. Aubin, 'Le royaume d'Ormuz au début du XVIe siècle', *Mare-Luso Indicum* 2 (1973) 77-179

Lach, *Century of discovery*, pp. 730-815

J. Aubin, 'Les princes d'Ormuz du XIII au XVe siècle', *Journal Asiatique* 241 (1953) 77-137

Boxer, *South China in the sixteenth century*

Pedro Teixeira, *The travels of Pedro Teixeira*

Rui Loureiro

Mestre Afonso

DATE OF BIRTH   Unknown; 16th century
PLACE OF BIRTH   Unknown, Portugal
DATE OF DEATH   Unknown; after 1566
PLACE OF DEATH   Unknown

BIOGRAPHY

Very little is known about Mestre Afonso's life other than what we can gather from his own travel account. He served as a physician in India during the governorships of Francisco Coutinho, count of Redondo (1561-4), and his interim successor João de Mendonça. Although he does not give any details about his professional career in the East, the title of his narrative describes his position as *solurgião-mor* ('master-surgeon'), which hints at close contact with the highest political ranks of the *Estado da Índia*. Furthermore, he himself adds that he owed a personal obligation to Mendonça. The arrival of the new Viceroy Antão de Noronha marked the end of Mestre Afonso's three-year service in Asia, and in early 1565 he set out to return to Portugal. But since the weather was unfavourable for travel round the Cape of Good Hope, he went to Hormuz and started a long overland journey through Persia, Armenia and Syria as a messenger, secretly carrying official letters to the Crown authorities in Portugal. He arrived in Lisbon 14 months later at the end of August 1566.

MAIN SOURCES OF INFORMATION

Primary
A. Baião (ed.), *Itinerários da Índia a Portugal por terra*, Coimbra, 1923, pp. 129-309

WORKS ON CHRISTIAN-MUSLIM RELATIONS

Ytinerario de Mestre Affonso, solurgiao mor que foi da India, 'Travels of Mestre Afonso, master-surgeon in India'

Itinerário de Mestre Afonso, 'Travels of Mestre Afonso'

DATE Between 1566 and 1571
ORIGINAL LANGUAGE Portuguese

DESCRIPTION

Mestre Afonso's travel account is divided into six chapters, each dealing with a different section of his journey across the Middle East and through the Mediterranean: ch. 1. Hormuz-Kāshān; ch. 2. Kāshān-Tabrīz; ch. 3. Tabrīz-Aleppo; ch. 4. Aleppo-Tripoli; ch. 5. Tripoli-Cyprus; ch. 6. Cyprus-Venice-Portugal. This structure, very unusual when compared with the travelogue standards of its time, accounts for the variation in the length of chapters, the first being extremely long and the later ones much shorter. With few references to written sources – although his descriptions of Azerbaijan and Syria are clearly extracted from António Tenreiro's *Itinerário* – Mestre Afonso's book is basically the product of his personal observations as a traveller, and includes a whole range of comments on almost everything from local folklore and religious traditions to famous historical people and events. Although he does not give a precise date for the writing of his narrative, a probable estimate would be sometime before 1571, for he mentions several times the siege of Malta (1565) but does not refer to the Battle of Lepanto.

The descriptions of Middle Eastern peoples and their physical appearance are particularly detailed, falling in general terms within the scope of the early modern literary canons of the genre. Mestre Afonso sets out an anthropological portrait of the various populations according to a uniform theoretical structure in which creed, ethnic identification and the main economic activity or means of subsistence take on overwhelming priority. Secondarily, race, language and clothing help fill out the portrait with additional details. These categories correspond to the reference framework of Portuguese overseas literature, and can also be found with slight differences in other sources.

Mestre Afonso describes numerous regions, mostly inhabited by Persians, Turks and Arabs, while also referring to important groups of Turkmen, Armenians and Kurds, especially in the vast frontier region that was constant prey to Ottoman and Safavid military campaigns in northwestern Iran and Upper Mesopotamia. It should be noted that he applies the term *mouro* ('Moor') to any follower of the Islamic creed, while the word *alarve* – meaning, etymologically, 'Arab' – more specifically identifies nomads living outside the urban setting, either in isolated tents or in temporary villages.

Mestre Afonso's narrative sheds light on the early history of the Safavid dynasty and its long-lasting conflict with the Ottoman empire, supplemented with frequent allusions to the state of utter destruction of Shah Ṭahmāsp's lands, a situation he explains as the result of both war and poor management. He also briefly mentions other historical figures such as the Āqquyūnlu ruler Uzūn Ḥasan and Maḥmūd of Ghazna, but some historical events are covered in a certain amount of detail, such as the exile of Prince Bayezid, Süleyman the Magnificent's son in the Persian court and his subsequent death in 1561.

SIGNIFICANCE

Mestre Afonso's portrait of the Muslim individuals he met during his journey falls within the norm of other contemporary travel accounts. Since most of the Portuguese enemies in the East were Muslim, it was expected from authors of travelogues to express open hostility towards any Islamic subject. However, the imperial ideology that supported the *Estado da Índia*'s political strategy was not uniformly followed, and the expression of anti-Muslim sentiment did vary significantly from one writer to another. It should be stressed that even if Mestre Afonso does not make any positive comment on Muslim people, he is equally critical and suspicious towards Jews and Eastern Christians, regardless of the fact that he relied heavily on the help provided by his fellow traveller – an experienced Armenian merchant named Simão Fernandes.

Not unlike other Portuguese sources of the 16th century dealing with Persia, Mestre Afonso reserves an important section of his narrative for the history of the country's new political dynasty and the spread of its idiosyncratic religion. Unsurprisingly, Safavid Shīʿa Islam is depicted as a rapidly expanding creed that was enforced on the Sunnī population after the accession of Shāh Ismail I to the throne and the foundation of the new dynasty in the early 16th century. In fact, the Portuguese writer often refers to the consequences of the war between Ottomans and Safavids and the religious antagonism that opposed the partisans of Shī'a to Sunnī Islam, a conflict further illustrated with anecdotes of militant proselytism and forced conversion. As was customary in Portuguese sources of this period, Mestre Afonso describes thoroughly the *tāj-i Ḥaidārī*, the red headgear that identified the Safavid followers (the *Qizilbāsh*), while laying bare the historical circumstances behind the foundation of the new dynasty. But differently from other authors, he does not mention the Christian element that was regarded as fundamental to the spiritual shaping of the newly established religion, and any reference to the planned rapprochement between the Persian ruler and the Roman Church is absent from Mestre Afonso's narrative.

MANUSCRIPTS

MS Lisbon, Arquivo Nacional da Torre do Tombo – Liv. 2262 (second half of the 16th century)

MS Lisbon, Biblioteca Nacional de Portugal – 11026 (second half of the 16th century; abridgement of an earlier version)

EDITIONS & TRANSLATIONS

N. Águas, *Viagens por terra da Índia a Portugal*, Sintra: Mem Martins, 1991

Baião, *Itinerários da Índia a Portugal*, 129-309

'Viagens por terra da India a Portugal em 1565', *Annaes maritimos e coloniaes* 4-5 (1845-46) pp. 214-32, 255-69, 315-18, 344-53, 408-18; 27-31, 78-92, 121-33, 165-79

STUDIES

V. Resende, 'Itinéraires et voyageurs portugais en Perse safavide', in R.M. Loureiro and V. Resende (eds), *Estudos sobre Don Garcia de Silva y Figueroa e os Comentarios da embaixada à Pérsia (1614-1624)*, Lisbon, 2011, 299-312

V. Resende, 'Viagens de um cirurgião português na Pérsia Safávida. O *Itinerário* de Mestre Afonso (1565-1566)', *Oriente* 19 (2008) 106-22

D. Couto, 'Arméniens et Portugais dans les réseaux d'information de l'océan Indien au 16e siècle', in S. Chaudhury and K. Kévonian (eds), *Les Arméniens dans le commerce asiatique au début de l'ère moderne*, Paris, 2008, 171-96

V. Resende, 'L'image de l'islam dans la littérature portugaise des voyages du XVIe siècle. Les itinéraires terrestres au Moyen Orient', *Anais de História de Além-Mar* 7 (2006) 107-96

S. Yérasimos, *Les voyageurs dans l'empire ottoman (XIVe-XVIe siècles). Bibliographies, itinéraires et inventaire des lieux habités*, Ankara, 1991, pp. 270-71

L. Graça, *A visão do Oriente na literatura portuguesa de viagens. Os viajantes portugueses e os itinerários terrestres (1560-1670)*, Lisbon, 1983

J.V. Serrão, *A historiografia portuguesa. Doutrina e crítica*, Lisbon, 1972-4, i, pp. 383-87

R. Gulbenkian and H. Berbérian, 'La légende de David de Sassoun d'après deux voyageurs portugais du XVIe siècle', *Revue des Études Arméniennes* 8 (1971) 175-88 (repr. in R. Gulbenkian, *Estudos históricos*, Lisbon, 1995, vol. 1)

L. de Matos, 'Alguns manuscritos ultramarinos da Biblioteca Nacional de Lisboa', *Boletim Internacional de Bibliografia Luso-Brasileira* 12 (1971) 509-54

S. Viterbo, *Viagens da Índia a Portugal por terra e vice-versa. Resenha histórica e documental*, Coimbra, 1898

Vasco Resende

Luís Vaz de Camões

Camões

DATE OF BIRTH Approximately 1524
PLACE OF BIRTH Probably Lisbon or Coimbra
DATE OF DEATH 10 June 1580
PLACE OF DEATH Lisbon

BIOGRAPHY

Luís Vaz de Camões is considered the greatest poet of the Lusophone countries because of the influence he had on the Portuguese language. His biography is richer in anecdotes than facts, and even the details of his birth are uncertain.

It is assumed that Camões was born in Lisbon or Coimbra in around 1525. According to one tradition, he attended courses in the humanities at the University of Coimbra, although without being registered. This may, in fact, be accurate, as from 1542 his uncle, the Augustinian Bento Camões, was chancellor of the university. After his return to Lisbon, he frequented court circles and encountered the new culture in which the classical tradition came into interaction with Italian and Castilian.

In about 1547, Camões first experienced Christian-Muslim confrontation when, in the course of a battle against the Moors at Ceuta in Morocco, he was injured and lost the vision in his right eye. Back in Lisbon, he was imprisoned from 16 June 1552 to 13 March 1553 for brawling. In 1553, he sailed to Goa and remained in the East for more than 15 years, working as a public official as well as taking part as a soldier in at least two military missions. During this time, he was again sent to prison twice, first in Macao then in Mozambique.

It was during this time in the East that Camões worked on *Os Lusíadas*, which he published in 1572, two years after his return to Lisbon. He died in Lisbon in 1580, aged 56.

MAIN SOURCES OF INFORMATION

Secondary
J.H. Saraiva, *Vida ignorada de Camões*, Lisbon, 1978
J. Nabuco, *The Lusiads as the epic of love*, Ithaca NY, 1909

WORKS ON CHRISTIAN-MUSLIM RELATIONS

Os Lusíadas, 'The Lusiads'

DATE 1572
ORIGINAL LANGUAGE Portuguese

DESCRIPTION

Os Lusíadas is an epic work, generally ranked among the masterpieces of world literature. Its title comes from *Lusíadas*, 'Portuguese', deriving from the Roman name for Portugal, Lusitania. It describes the explorations of the Portuguese and the voyage of Vasco da Gama on his discovery of the route to India, and it is also an account of the intense battle of Catholic Christendom against the advance of Islam, especially in its Sunnī form. Camões's verses reveal the hatred of the Christians for the Moors, whom they regard as heretics. He reiterates the typical classical Portuguese idea from the age of discoveries, that the ultimate goal of the activities in the Indies was the conquest of Egypt, the liberation of the Holy Land from Muslim rule, and the destruction of the holy sites in Mecca and Medina. In India, the Portuguese met a plethora of Islamic peoples, while at the same time they were confronting the Ottoman Empire and potentially seeking agreements with the Safavid rulers of Persia. During the 16th century, the earlier call for a *cruzada* ('crusade') became a rhetorical formula that was frequently employed but rarely led to large-scale military mobilisation against the Ottomans. Like many other early modern European men of letters, Camões demanded an all-out war against the 'Turk'.

The ideological axis of the poem focuses on the relationship of Portugal with the Islamic world, depicted as a just war waged against Islam. As Camões suggests, one cannot forget 'the great valour of that brave people the Portuguese', who 'have expelled the Muslim, for all his strength and numbers, from the entire region of the Tagus' (Canto I:42).

Os Lusíadas consists of ten cantos, which celebrate the defeat of Islam and the spread of Christianity through the southern hemisphere to South-East Asia. Each canto is composed in a variable number of *stanza*s (1,102 in total), which are based upon the decasyllabic *ottava rima* (rhyme scheme: ABABABCC). The narration, written in Homeric fashion, begins with the voyage of Vasco da Gama and ends with his return from India. Inserted into this narrative, it tells the history of Portugal (Canto III).

In the introduction, Camões, showing his classical background, pays homage to Virgil and Homer, and describes the ancient Greek gods.

Throughout, he creates a fusion of pagan, Christian and Islamic symbolism. Thus, in Canto II Vasco da Gama, who is in Mombasa, sends two convicts to assess the situation around the Portuguese group. An ambush has been set by the local Muslim king, but the goddess Venus and the Nereids intervene to help the Portuguese overcome the Moorish trick. Venus symbolises the higher purpose of the epic adventure, and also the redeeming essence of Christianity. In opposition to this, starting in Canto I, Bacchus represents the obstacle standing in the way of Christianity. He is the Lord of India, who fears having his power usurped by the Christian Portuguese, and also of the infidels, who must be redeemed.

Camões dedicated the poem to the young King Sebastian of Portugal, who was aged 24 at the time. A few days after the famous battle of Lepanto on 7 October 1571, in which European naval forces defeated the powerful Ottoman fleet, Camões invited King Sebastian to attack Morocco, using the mythological language of his own *Ecloga*, titled *Que grande variedade vão fazendo*. According to Vitor Aguiar e Silva, it is possible that King Sebastian was influenced in his crusade by these great poetic words. King Sebastian was killed on 4 August 1578 at al-Qaṣr al-Kabīr, in Morocco.

Camões's poem could be said to have contributed to the creation of 'Sebastianism', a popular national belief that the monarch was not really dead but had only disappeared, to one day return, reclaim the throne and fill the world with justice, a legend that shares commonalities with the Islamic belief in the Mahdī, who would appear to restore justice and righteous rule.

SIGNIFICANCE

Os Lusíadas shaped the Portuguese attitude towards Muslims. It portrays Islam, particularly as represented by the Turks, not only as heretical but also as the belief of the enemies of Catholic Portugal. Thus, Muslims must be defeated for Christianity finally to triumph in East and West.

This epic poem has exerted great influence in shaping Portuguese language and literature, with the consequence that the sentiments expressed in it towards Muslims and Islam have continued to influence the attitudes of Lusophones to the present day.

MANUSCRIPTS

The assessment of the manuscript tradition is still a matter of dispute among scholars.

EDITIONS & TRANSLATIONS

Os Lusíadas has appeared in many editions and translations. Below is a selected list reflecting its influence.

Z. Trzeszczkowska (trans.), *Luzjady. (Os Lusíadas). epos w dziesięciu pieśniach*, Sandomierz, Poland, 2013 (Polish trans.)

Os Lusíadas, ed. R. Arnold, trans. H.-J. Schaeffer, Darmstadt, 2010 (German trans.)

L.V. de Camões, *Obra completa*, ed. A. Salgado Jr, Rio de Janeiro, 2003

H. Barrilaro Ruas (ed.), *Os Lusíadas*, Lisbon, 2002

O. Gomes (trans.), *Lujhitāyaṇa*, Goa, 2003 (Konkani trans.)

R. Averini (trans.), *I Lusiadi*, Milan, 2001 (Italian trans. with parallel Portuguese text)

S. González (trans.), *Os Lusíadas*, Madrid, 1990 (Asturian trans.)

O. Ovcharenko (trans.), *Luziady; Sonety*, Moscow, 1988 (Russian trans. of *Os Lusíadas* and the Sonnets)

Os Lusiadas, Sao Paulo, 1982

Đ. Šaula (trans.), *Luzijadi*, Belgrade, 1981 (Serbian trans.)

Hideo Kobayashi (trans.), *Uzu rujiadasu: rushitania no hitobito*, Tokyo, 1978 (Japanese trans.)

A. Capuder (trans.), *Luzijada. Izbor*, Ljubljana, 1976 (selected excerpts in Slovenian)

F. Pierce (trans.), *Os Lusíadas*, Oxford, 1973 (English annotated trans.)

A. Covaci (trans.), *Lusiada*, Bucharest, 1965 (Romanian trans.)

G. Colom and M. Dolç (trans.), *Els lusíades*, Barcelona, 1964 (Catalan trans.)

K. Bednár (trans.), *Lusovci*, Prague, 1958 (Czech trans.)

R. Bismut (trans.), *Les luciades de Luis de Camões*, Lisbon, 1954 (French trans.)

W.C. Atkinson (trans.), *The Lusiads*, London, 1952 (English trans.)

Os Lusíadas, 3rd edition, Porto, 1933

J. Vrchlický (trans.), *Lusovci (Os Lusiadas). báseň o desíti zpěvech*, Prague, 1902 (abridged Czech trans.)

F. de Santo Agostinho Macedo (trans.), *A lusiada de Luiz de Camões. Traduzida en versos latinos*, Paris, 1890 (Latin trans.)

The Lusiad of Luis de Camoens, London, 1853 (English trans.)

J.J.C. Donner (trans.), *Die Lusiaden*, Stuttgart, 1833 (German trans.)

L. Stoppendaal (trans.), *De Lusiade. heldendicht in X zangen*, Antwerp, 1777 (Dutch trans.)

W.J. Mickle (trans.), *The Lusiad, or, The discovery of India. An epic poem*, Oxford, 1776 (English trans.)

N.N. Piemontese (trans.), *La Lusiadi. o sia la scoperta delle Indie Orientali*, Turin, 1772 (Italian trans.)

M. Duperron de Castera (trans.), *La lusiade de Camoens. Poeme heroique, sur la decouverte des Indes Orientales*, Amsterdam, 1735 (French trans.)

M. de Faria i Sousa (trans.), *Os Lusiadas*, Madrid, 1639 (Spanish trans.)

Os Lusiadas, Lisbon: Casa de Antonio Go[n]çaluez impressor, 1572

STUDIES

There are numerous scholarly works on the *Lusíadas*. Those that deal with Islam include:

V. Aguiar e Silva (ed.), *O Dicionário de Luís de Camões*, Alfragide, Portugal, 2011

C. Willis, *Camões, prince of poets*, Bristol, 2010

M.L. de Castro Soares, 'A aventura do amor e do espírito. A lírica e a epopéia de Camões', in M.L. de Castro Soares (ed.), *Tendências da literatura. Do Classicismo ao Maneirismo e ao Barroco e sua projecção na actualidade*, Vila Real, Portugal, 2009, 88-97

M.L. de Castro Soares, *Profetismo e espiritualidade de Camões a Pascoaes*, Coimbra, 2007, pp. 74-84

N. Bisaha, *Creating East and West. Renaissance humanists and the Ottoman Turks*, Philadelphia PA, 2004

F.F. Moreira, *Visão do amor e do homem. Uma análise lingüístico-estilística de oitavas rimas do Camões e de um soneto de Cruz e Souza*, Maceió, Brazil, 2005

M. Cavalcante, *Por mares muito antes navegados. A tradição de Camões na poesia colonial brasileira*, Bairro, Brazil, 2001, p. 73

M. de Lourdes Abreu de Oliveira, *Eros e tanatos no universo textual de Camões, Antero e Redol*, Pinheiros, Sao Paulo, 2000, pp. 20-31

R. Finlay, 'Portuguese and Chinese maritime imperialism. Camões's Lusiads and Loo Maodeng's Voyage of the San Bao eunuch', *Comparative Studies in Society and History* 34 (1992) 225-41

H.H. Hart, *Luis de Camoëns and the epic of the Lusiads*, Norman OK, 1962

Nicola Melis

Gaspar de Leão

DATE OF BIRTH   Unknown
PLACE OF BIRTH Lagos, Portugal
DATE OF DEATH   15 August 1576
PLACE OF DEATH Goa, India

BIOGRAPHY

Gaspar de Leão was born into a family of the minor nobility of the Algarve, in the south of Portugal. He studied at the University of Salamanca and graduated in ecclesiastical law in 1536. This means that he would have been studying in Salamanca at the same time as leading thinkers on natural law, such as Francisco Vitoria, Domingo de Soto and Azpilcueta Navarro, were developing their ideas, and when their theses on *ius gentium* (international law) were starting to be published and discussed. The influence of the thought of the Salamanca Law School is quite visible in some of Gaspar's writings.

After university, Gaspar began an ecclesiastical career. By 1538, he was preacher and chaplain to King John III's brother, Henry, who was then archbishop of Braga. In 1540, Henry was elected archbishop of Évora, where the royal court was established, and Gaspar accompanied him there. In 1551, he was made a canon of the cathedral, and in 1557 he was made archdeacon.

At this time, Évora was both the political and administrative centre of Portugal, and also the main cultural centre. Henry, who was elected cardinal in 1547, created conditions that attracted prominent intellectuals, such as Pedro Nunes, André de Resende and Nicholas Clenard, to the city. Gaspar may have been influenced by Clenard's plan to convert the Muslims of North Africa to Christianity by the peaceful means of preaching in their own language. Like Henry, Gaspar was attracted to mystical forms of Catholic religiosity, which also explains the presence of Luis de Granada in Évora during this period.

In 1558, Gaspar was elected to be the first archbishop of the recently created archdiocese of Goa. He was reluctant to take up the position, but, following a papal decree that instructed him to accept, he arrived in Goa as archbishop and Grand Inquisitor in 1560. By this time, he was thoroughly immersed in the ideas circulating in the court of Évora, which combined sometimes paradoxical trends, such as Renaissance and Counter-Reformation, mystical inner spirituality and Tridentinism, peaceful coexistence and imperialism.

Gaspar could not agree with the methods used by Jesuit missionaries in Goa to convert Indians to Christianity. He thought that conversion should be conducted by peaceful means, because the use of force would give the convert an antipathy towards the deeper dimensions of Christian devotion. News of this dispute went back to Lisbon and Rome, and Gaspar was forced to accept the practices that were being followed. Writing then became the way in which he could express his plans for Portuguese rule. Although his writings are expressly apologetic, against Judaism (*Tratado que fez mestre Hieronimo, medico do papa Benedicto 13, côtra os judeus: em que se prova o Messias da ley ser vindo*) and Islam (*Desengano de perdidos*), Gaspar nevertheless advocated a peaceful approach in matters of religious difference.

Gaspar finally succeeded in resigning from his position as archbishop in 1567. By this time, he had made arrangements for the foundation of a Franciscan house of strict observance, Madredeus convent in Daugim, Goa, where he could follow his true religious inclinations. However, he was compelled to resume office as archbishop in 1574, and at the time of his death in 1576 he was waiting to be replaced so that he could return to his convent.

MAIN SOURCES OF INFORMATION

Primary
Frei Jacinto de Deus, *Vergel de plantas e flores de Província de Madre de Deus dos Capuchos Reformados*, Lisbon, 1690
Diogo do Couto, *Décadas da Ásia*, Lisbon, 1736, iii (*Décadas* vii, viii, ix)
António Caetano de Sousa, *Agiológio Lusitano, dos santos e varões ilustres em virtude do Reino de Portugal, e suas conquistas*, Lisbon, 1744, iv, pp. 539-46
Frei Paulo da Trindade, *Conquista spiritual do Oriente*, ed. F. Félix Lopes, Lisbon, 1962
Francisco de Sousa SJ, *Oriente conquistado a Jesus Cristo*, 1710 (repr. Porto, 1978)

Secondary
R. Ventura, 'Arte e discurso da oração na obra de D. Gaspar de Leão, primeiro arcebispo de Goa', in *Via Spiritus. Revista de História da Espiritualidade e do Sentimento Religioso* 14 (2007) 21-30

R. Ventura, 'D. Gaspar de Leão e o *Desengano de perdidos*. Estudo histórico-cultural', Lisbon, 2005 (MA Diss., University of Lisbon)

R. Ventura, 'Estratégias de conversão ao tempo de D. Gaspar de Leão, 1º Arcebispo de Goa. Reconstituição histórica de uma controvérsia', in *A Companhia de Jesus na Península Ibérica nos séculos XVI e XVII. Espiritualidade e cultura*, Porto, 2005, 505-17

R. Ventura, 'Conversão e conversabilidade. Um esboço sobre a convivência, o diálogo e as disputas no Oriente, ao tempo de D. Gaspar de Leão', *Revista Internacional de Língua Portuguesa* 3 (2004) 249-67

V. d'Arienzo, 'La missione di un mistico. Dom Gaspar de Leão primo arcivescovo di Goa', *Studi e Ricerche sull'Oriente Cristiano* 10 (1987) 19-36, 113-35

WORKS ON CHRISTIAN-MUSLIM RELATIONS

Desengano de perdidos, 'Disillusion of the lost'

DATE 1573
ORIGINAL LANGUAGE Portuguese

DESCRIPTION

Desengano de perdidos (its full title is *Livro chamado desengano de perdidos, feito pera glória de Deus e consolação dos novamente convertidos e fracos na fé, e pera proveito dos que querem deixar os pecados e seguir as virtudes e o caminho da perfeição do amor divino*, 'Book entitled disillusion of the lost ones, made for the glory of God and the consolation of those newly converted and weak in their faith, and for the advantage of those who are willing to abandon sins and to seek virtues and the path of perfection and divine love') can be regarded as a book of doctrine and catechesis in dialogue form, addressed mainly to newly converted Christians. The *editio princeps* (1573) totals 189 folios, while Asensio's edition (1958) takes up 359 pages. The work is composed of three main parts, preceded by a dedication letter to King Sebastian and an introduction.

The three main parts consist of a dialogue between a Christian and a Turk, who are travelling on foot from Suez to Cairo. They are soldiers who have given up war because they have been crippled and are unable to fight. The confrontation between the two is verbal and doctrinal, though as they discuss various issues of everyday life, religion and politics, their talk becomes a dialogue of conversion, then catechetical instruction, and finally mystical practice. By the middle of the second part of the dialogue, the characters are no longer named 'Christian' and 'Turk', but 'Master' and 'Disciple'.

In many respects, *Desengano de perdidos* is a rhapsody on 16th-century culture in Portugal. Each part clearly focuses on a land-mark topic that occupied Christian intellectuals at the time. The dedication letter to King Sebastian presents anti-Machiavellian political theory in the manner of a *speculum principis*. The first part of the dialogue warns all Muslims about prophecies that foretold the end of the Islam, and discusses the concept of just war. The second presents a moral allegory based in the episode of Odysseus and the sirens from Book 12 of Homer's *Odyssey*. The third part consists of a mystical treatise about the marriage of the soul with God through divine love.

In 1570, Adil Shah, ruler of Bijapur, moved against Goa, and almost at the same time Nizam Shah, sultan of Ahmadnagar, besieged the fortress of Chaul, though both attacks were fought off. As Gaspar himself explains in the prologue, these attacks induced him to convert the catechetical book he was writing into a dialogue between a Christian and a Turk. Although he was in India, the Ottoman Empire would not have been absent from his mind. He may well have known about King Manuel I's alleged plan, supported by prophecies about the end of Islam, some of which had been circulating since the fall of Constantinople, to conquer the Holy Land by making alliances with Christian kings in the East, such as the mythical Prester John, and attack the Ottoman Empire from that direction. Like its antecedent, Diogo de Castilho's *Origem dos Turcos* ('The origin of the Turks'), published in 1538, *Desengano de perdidos* is one of the very few Portuguese works of this time that shows awareness of the Ottoman Empire in itself, rather than only of Ottoman allies in North Africa and elsewhere.

The action of the *Desengano* takes place between Suez and Cairo, far from Portuguese possessions. In a colloquial tone, the two main characters talk about their respective habits and customs, and they sometimes conclude that these are not as different as first appears. Each of them knows well the royal court of his ruler, and they are quite aware that their political interests are different.

Since Gaspar was writing a doctrinal and catechetical book for Christians, the opinion of the Christian is, of course, always more sound than the Turk's. The dialogue is directed towards the conversion of the Turk and is haunted from the beginning by the prediction of Islam's destruction, as found in the prophecies. As a church leader, Gaspar is very cautious about the prophetic sources he cites. He may have been aware of Joachim de Fiori, Ubertino da Casale and other dubious authors, but he only quotes from the Bible, mainly Isaiah and Revelation, identifying the Beast of Revelation 13 as Muḥammad.

Gaspar regards the allegedly miraculous victories of Chaul and Goa in 1570, and Lepanto in 1571, which he briefly describes in the first part of the *Desengano*, as clear signs that these prophecies were being fulfilled. The future King Sebastian of Portugal would play an important part in the unfolding of events: he was to marry Marguerite de Valois and influence the French not only to break their truces with the Turks, but also to join the Sacred League of Christian Princes that would be created to destroy the Ottoman Empire.

A main emphasis throughout the dialogue is that Christianity is founded on natural reason and Islam is not. This is expressed in the two main topics of war and paradise. On war, Gaspar argues that Turks do not observe rules, while Christians follow principles that are accessible through natural law. In making his arguments here, he applies the scholastic learning he had gained in Salamanca. On paradise in Islam, Gaspar argues that the Islamic conception is too physical and too much of a projection of human desires to be justifiable. In this he recalls ideas from the catechetical books written for the conversion of Mouriscos, such as João Soares' *Libro de la verdad de la fe* (1543) and Bernardo Pérez de Chinchón's *Antialcorano* (1532).

SIGNIFICANCE

In Gaspar's eyes, the arguments in his dialogue were maybe strong enough to make converts peacefully, though he was constructing them in a context of aggression and war. *Desengano de perdidos* emphasises the contradictions that were inherent in an era when men of peace favoured one approach, but political realities dictated a very different response to the enemy.

EDITIONS & TRANSLATIONS

E. Asensio (ed.), *Desengano de perdidos*, Coimbra, 1958

Livro chamado Desengano de perdidos, Goa: João Endem, 1573

STUDIES

Ventura, 'Arte e discurso da oração na obra de D. Gaspar de Leão'

Ventura, 'D. Gaspar de Leão e o *Desengano de perdidos*'

M. de Lourdes Sirgado Ganho, 'A obra *Desengano de perdidos* de D. Gaspar de Leão', in *África Oriental, Oriente e Brasil. Actas Congresso Internacional de História*, Braga, 1993, ii, 325-34

Ricardo Ventura

Francisco de Monclaro

DATE OF BIRTH 1531
PLACE OF BIRTH Benavente
DATE OF DEATH 1595
PLACE OF DEATH Goa

BIOGRAPHY

Francisco de Monclaro was born in Benavente, Portugal, in 1531, and became a member of the newly-founded Society of Jesus in 1554. He took part in the expedition led by Francisco Barreto, Portuguese governor of Mozambique, to Monomotapa in 1569 in retaliation for the killing of a Jesuit missionary. In the course of this expedition, he opposed some of Barreto's decisions as contrary to the instructions given by the king, and also to morality. From 1574, he served in India, where he died in Goa in December 1595.

In addition to valuable correspondence from Goa, he also wrote an account of the expedition to Monomotapa.

MAIN SOURCES OF INFORMATION

Primary
MS Paris BNF – Fonds portugais, no. 51 fols 241-65, *Relaçaõ do viagem que fizeraõ os Pes da Companhia de Jesus com Francisco Barreto*
Diogo do Couto, *Da Ásia, Décadas IV-XII*, Lisbon, 1974, vii, books ii-v; ix, chs xxi-xxiii (facsimile of 1777-78 edition)

Secondary
Silva, art. 'Francisco Monclaro', in *Enciclopédia verbo*, Lisbon, 2001, xx, col. 373
C. Sommervogel, *Bibliothèque de la Compagnie de Jésus*, Brussels, 1894, p. 1203

WORKS ON CHRISTIAN-MUSLIM RELATIONS

Relaçaõ do viagem que fizeraõ os Pes da Companhia de Jesus com Francisco Barreto na conquista do Monomotapa, 'An account of the expedition of the priests of the Society of Jesus with Francisco Barreto on the conquest of Monomotapa'

DATE About 1575
ORIGINAL LANGUAGE Portuguese

DESCRIPTION

Francisco Monclaro's account of Francisco Barreto's expedition to Monomotapa in present-day Zimbabwe is 24 folios long (its title in full is *Relaçaõ do viagem que fizeraõ os Pes da Companhia de Jesus com Francisco Barreto na conquista do Monomotapa, no anno de 1569 feita pelo Pe Monclaio [sic] da mesma Companhia*). It begins with an explanation of the reason for the expedition – the killing in 1561 of the Jesuit priest Gonçalo de Silveira in Monomotapa, whom the 'Moors' in those parts persuaded and bribed the local people to murder. In January 1569, King Sebastian of Portugal sent a force of fighting men to Monomotapa (Theal, 'Fr. Francisco Monclaro', pp. 202-3; references below are to this text).

The account goes on to relate the departure from Portugal in 1569, and the journey to East Africa (pp. 203-10), with descriptions of the various cities visited, including Kilwa, where reference is made to 'Saracens' trading (pp. 210-16). A marginal note on the manuscript, by Gaspar Alvarez de Lousada, states: 'All those of this coast are the white, hooded Moors, for there are three castes in India, those of one caste wear hoods, others wear small caps, and others turbans. Those who wear turbans are the most honourable' (p. 213). There is also a reference to the Imam of Malindi (Melinde) being the 'Moorish priest chief of all on the coast' (p. 215).

Travelling and trading on the coast continued until 1572, when Barreto finally started on his mission inland to Monomotapa (pp. 216-40). Monclaro comments that the local people 'think that to be a Christian has nothing to do with the next life, but simply means to be a friend of the Portuguese' (p. 225). An ambassador is sent to negotiate terms with the people of Monomotapa, setting three conditions: all 'Moors' are to be expelled, the Jesuits should be received and the ruler should follow the Christian faith, and a number of gold mines are to be given to the king of Portugal (pp. 246-48). Barreto himself then returned to the coast, where he died (pp. 250-51). The people of Monomotapa sent an embassy agreeing to expel the 'Moors' and to cede mines to Portugal, though they would wait to discuss Christianity when the Portuguese force arrived (pp. 251-53). But with the loss of so many men through war and sickness, the Portuguese abandoned the mission and returned to the coast.

Monclaro makes mention of animals and plants found on the group's journey, as well as referring regularly to Muslims and occasionally to Turks and 'Saracens' as traders. His attitude to the Muslims is varied: at times he reports that they are welcoming and friendly, and says that they live together with Christians in the same community; at other times he says they are untrustworthy, thieves and poisoners. Even though Monclaro is a Christian priest, he says nothing about attempts to proselytise either the 'Moors' or the 'Kaffirs'.

SIGNIFICANCE

The account gives details of the reactions of the Christian Portuguese to the influence of Muslims in their new territories. Its references to Muslims as 'Moors' illustrate the continued use of the name known in Portugal to identify the believers encountered in new territories.

The overall impression given by Monclaro is that Muslims are traders who are interfering with the trading opportunities of the Portuguese, rather than being people who can be evangelised.

MANUSCRIPTS

MS Paris BNF – Fonds portugais 51, fols 241-65 (about 1575)

EDITIONS & TRANSLATIONS

C. Sommervogel (ed.), *Monumenta Indica*, Rome, 1964-70, iii, pp. 673-739

F. Monclaro, SJ, 'Relacao da viagem que fizerao os padres da C.a de Jesus com Francisco Barreto na conquista do Monomotapa no ano de 1569', in *Documentos sobre os Portugueses em Moçambique e na África Central, 1497-1840*, Lisbon, 1962-68, iii, pp. 157-253

G. Theal (ed. and trans.), 'Fr. Francisco Monclaro, Account of the journey made by Fathers of the Company of Jesus with Francisco Barreto in the conquest of Monomotapa in the year 1569', in *Records of South-Eastern Africa. Collected in various libraries and archive departments in Europe*, London, 1899, iii, pp. 157-201 (Portuguese text), pp. 202-53 (English trans.)

STUDIES

M. Newitt, *A history of Mozambique*, London, 1995

J.P. Marques, art. 'Francisco Barreto', in Luís de Albuquerque (ed.), *Dicionário de história dos descobrimentos Portugueses*, Lisbon, 1994, pp. 123-24

J.M. Garcia, *Viagens dos descobrimentos*, Lisbon, 1983, pp. 153-224

E. de Eça, *Relação dos governadores da Índia (1571)*, ed. R.O.W. Goertz, Calgary, 1979, pp. 12-13

E.M. dos Santos, *Viagens de exploração terreste dos portugueses em África*, Lisbon, 1978, pp. 74-76

C.C. Montez, 'Apontamentos para o roteiro dos monumentos militares portugueses. Praça de Santiago Maior', *Monumenta* 6 (1970) 67-73

A. Silva, *Mentalidade missiológica dos jesuítas em Moçambique antes de 1579*, Lisbon, 1967

A. Zúquete, *Tratado de todos os vice-reis e governadores da Índia*, Lisbon, 1962

A.A. Andrade (ed.), *Relações de Moçambique setecentista*, Lisbon, 1955

D. Lopes (ed.), *Relação do reino do Congo e das terras circunvizinhas*, Lisbon, 1951, pp. 133-34

M. de F. Sousa, *Ásia Portuguesa*, trans. M. Burquets de Aguiar, Porto, 1945, iii/2, ch. 11; iv/1, chs 15-16

Verdadeira informação das terras do Preste João das Índias, Lisbon, 1889

D.B. Machado, *Memórias para a história d'El-Rey D. Sebastião*, Lisbon, 1751

Miguel Monteiro

Italy and Malta

Marsilio Ficino

DATE OF BIRTH   19 October 1433
PLACE OF BIRTH   Figline Valdarno, near Florence
DATE OF DEATH   1 October 1499
PLACE OF DEATH   Careggi, Florence

BIOGRAPHY

Marsilio Ficino is one of the most significant figures in 15th-century western European culture. He is best known for his translations from Greek into Latin of the works of Plato, Plotinus, Proclus and other Neoplatonists, as well as the *Hermetic corpus*, a collection of magical and philosophical writings attributed to the mythical Egyptian sage Hermes Trismegistus. Thanks to Ficino's translations and commentaries, European scholars gained access to Platonic texts that had only been partially or indirectly known in the Middle Ages. He was also the author of original works in Latin and in the vernacular, the latter written with the aim of reaching a broad public, including the emerging middle class of Florentine traders, which was involved in politics and cultural life. His translations, commentaries and original works have influenced Western culture in a number of fields, including philosophy, philology, religious studies and psychology. Scholars are still exploring the impact of Ficino's *oeuvre* on the early modern and modern world.

Ficino was the son of the physician Dietifeci d'Agnolo da Figline. He received an Aristotelian and medical education under the guidance of Niccolò Tignosi, among other prominent mentors of his time. Being close to the de' Medici family, Dietifeci introduced his son to the *milieu* of Cosimo de' Medici who, at the beginning of the 1460s, entrusted Ficino with the task of translating a Greek manuscript of the entire works of Plato. Lorenzo de' Medici, grandson of Cosimo, was later to become the most prominent patron of the arts and philosophical culture in Florence. From his influential position, he supported and promoted Ficino's work on Platonism until his death in 1492. Ficino's life coincided closely with the rebirth of Platonism and the associated ancient traditions; consequently, he was referred to as the 'second Plato' and became the central figure of the Platonic Academy of Careggi, a cultural circle established by Cosimo that became one of the most significant unofficial institutions of the Renaissance. Thanks to his prominent position, Ficino came into contact with many learned people, as well as cardinals and popes and prominent representatives of the middle class, as is shown by his extensive correspondence, partially published in a critical edition (ed. Gentile, *Lettere I* and *Lettere II*). His complete translation of Plato's works was published in 1484 and the complete series of commentaries in 1496, while his translation of Plotinus' *Enneads* was published in 1492 and a volume containing translations of other Neoplatonists in 1497.

Ficino remained committed to his life as the 'second Plato', although he also produced a vernacular translation of Dante Alighieri's *De monarchia* ('On monarchy') and several original works in various fields. In the 1460s, he wrote his commentary on Plato's *Symposium* in both Latin and the vernacular, which became one of the most influential treatises on love in following centuries.

In the 1470s, Ficino became canon of Florence Cathedral, Santa Maria del Fiore, accomplishing his ideal of being healer of both souls and bodies. During his years as canon, he produced his treatise *Della Cristiana religione* or *De Christiana religione* ('On the Christian religion'), published in both the vernacular and Latin. This treatise argued for the superiority of Christianity over other religions, while also advocating syncretism among different religions and philosophical traditions. The existence of a philosophical religion (*pia philosophia* and *docta religio*) that actually connected different traditions in a chain of ancient sages (*prisci theologi*) is the most significant idea consistently expressed in Ficino's writings. The work in which he elaborates and discusses most fully his concept of an inner harmony between Hermetism, Platonism, the Old Testament, Christianity and other religions and philosophies is *Theologia platonica de immortalitate animorum* ('Platonic theology on the immortality of souls'), written in the 1470s and published in 1482. In this work, considered the *summa* of his philosophy, Ficino argues that Plato and the other ancient sages demonstrated the immortality of the soul and prepared for the revelation of Christ. Ficino quotes his *Platonic theology* in *Della Cristiana religione*, which is evidence of the close association between the two treatises.

Ficino's most important published original work in the 1480s is the *De vita libri tres* ('Three books on life'), a medical, magical, astrological and philosophical treatise that confirms his commitment to being a healer of both souls and bodies. In the 1490s, he produced further original writings, such as a treatise titled *De sole* ('The book of the sun'), as well as completing the 12 books of his correspondence. He also became embroiled in an extended intellectual confrontation with the Dominican friar Girolamo Savonarola.

MAIN SOURCES OF INFORMATION

Primary
The primary sources on Ficino's life and works are too numerous to be listed. Here are given only the sources closely related to this entry:
Opera omnia, Basel: Heinrich Petri, 1576
P.O. Kristeller (ed.), *Supplementum Ficinianum*, Florence, 1938
The letters of Marsilio Ficino, trans. Language Dept. of School of Economic Science, London, 1975-2010
M. Ficino, *Lettere I. Epistolarum familiarum liber I*, ed. S. Gentile, Florence, 1990
M. Ficino, *Platonic theology*, ed. and trans. M.J.B. Allen and J. Hankins, 6 vols, Cambridge MA, 2001-6
M. Ficino, *Lettere II. Epistolarum familiarum liber II*, ed. S. Gentile, Florence, 2010

A complete list of editions and translations of Ficino's works is available in the following works:
P.O. Kristeller, *Marsilio Ficino and his work after five hundred years*, Florence, 1987
T. Katinis, 'Bibliografia ficiniana. Studi ed edizioni delle opere di Marsilio Ficino dal 1986', *Accademia* 2 (2000) 101-36, http://www.ficino.it/biblio.htm
T. Katinis and S. Toussaint, 'Bibliographie ficinienne – mise à jour', *Accademia* 3 (2001) 9-21 (updates available in later issues)

Secondary
There are hundreds of scholarly contributions on Ficino. Those closely related to this entry include:
C.S. Celenza, art. 'Marsilio Ficino', in E.N. Zalta (ed.), *The Stanford encyclopedia of philosophy* (Spring 2012 edition), http://plato.stanford.edu/archives/spr2012/entries/ficino/
C. Vasoli, art. 'Ficino, Marsilio (Marsilius Feghinensis)', in *Dizionario biografico degli italiani*, vol. 47, 378-95
A. Field, *The origins of the Platonic Academy of Florence*, Princeton NJ, 1988
G. Gentile, S. Niccoli and P. Viti (eds), *Marsilio Ficino e il ritorno di Platone. Mostra di manoscritti stampe e documenti 17 maggio-16 giugno 1984*, Florence, 1984, nos 63-8
R. Marcel, *Marsile Ficin, 1433-1499*, Paris, 1958

WORKS ON CHRISTIAN-MUSLIM RELATIONS

De Christiana religione et fidei pietate; De Christiana religione, 'On the Christian religion and spirituality of faith'

Della religione Cristiana; Della Cristiana religione, 'On the Christian religion'

DATE 1474 (first edition of the vernacular version), 1476 (first edition of the Latin version)
ORIGINAL LANGUAGE Latin and Italian

DESCRIPTION

Ficino himself oversaw the publication of both the vernacular and Latin versions of his treatise *De Christiana religione*, so one may be certain that they reflect his intentions as the author. As with his translation of Dante's *On monarchy* and the vernacular version of the commentary on Plato's *Symposium*, Ficino dedicated the vernacular version of the treatise to Bernardo del Nero, representative of the emerging Florentine bourgeoisie, for the reasons expounded in the *proemium* (copied in Kristeller, *Supplementum*, i, pp. 10-12). In the *proemium* of the Latin version, however, Ficino dedicates the treatise to Lorenzo de' Medici and sets forth the main purpose of his work, which is the reconciliation of philosophy and religion, considered inseparable by the ancient sages. Philosopher and priest should be two names for the same figure, the sage who guides souls on their path back to God through intellect as well as will and faith. In ch. 1, Ficino argues that religion is part of human existence, and that its truth can be demonstrated through reason and fact.

Several of the 37 chapters of the treatise contain direct or indirect references to Islam and some discuss extensively the relationship between Islam and Christianity. In ch. 4, Ficino claims that God permits the existence of different religions because variety could, perhaps, be a source of the great beauty of the universe. Nevertheless, it is necessary to recognise Christianity as the superior and only entirely true religion. Ch. 12 is entirely dedicated to Muslims, whom Ficino regards as heretical Christians, close to Arians and Manichaeans. In fact, the Qur'an recognises that Christ was God's spirit (Q 4:171) and performed miracles, and it affirms many other Christian truths. Muslims do not consider the Qur'an as contradictory to the Bible, but rather as its completion and full clarification.

Nevertheless, Muḥammad made two mistakes. First, like Arians, he considered Christ as not being consubstantial with the Father. Second, like Manichaeans, he believed that God took Christ to himself in an ascension to heaven before the Passion. In ch. 21, Ficino recalls that Muslims believe God sent Muḥammad as a powerful leader of warriors and Christ as a man able to perform miracles. In ch. 28, he argues that Muḥammad understood the Bible better than Jews with regard to Christ as the true Messiah. In ch. 30, he underlines the Qur'an's high consideration of both Christ and John the Baptist; the former as God's spirit and the latter as a great prophet. In ch. 34, he attacks Muḥammad, saying that he was not one of the prophets foretold in the Old Testament, but rather a tyrant who ruined the Jewish religion.

Ch. 36, the penultimate chapter, is completely devoted to a discussion of Islam. Ficino claims that Muḥammad supported the early Christians and considered the Gospels and the Apostles' writings as superior to the Old Testament. Nevertheless, Muslims are lying when they claim that Muḥammad was mentioned in the Gospels and references to him later removed in order to avoid admitting that Islam was the fulfilment of Christ's and God's will. In general, any Islamic accusation of manipulation of the Holy Scriptures must be unfounded. Furthermore, Muḥammad did not understand how the Father, Son and Holy Spirit can be one God, and accused Christians of worshipping three different gods. On the basis of Muḥammad's mistakes and overall attitude, Ficino calls him ignorant and arrogant. But despite all the negative aspects of Islam he identifies, he ends the chapter by emphasising that Muslims share with Christians belief in the last judgment and a part of the Lord's Prayer. Finally, in ch. 37, which briefly sets out the cause of the mistakes made by Jews, Muslims and pagans, Ficino recalls Muḥammad's violence. For an extended analysis of the treatise, see Vasoli, 'Ficino e il *De christiana religione*'.

De christiana religione and *Platonic theology* share an attempt to find common elements among different religious and philosophical traditions, and to demonstrate that Christ revealed the final truth. Islam, however, cannot be incorporated into the succession of preparations for the revelation of Christ, because Muḥammad lived after Christ and presented his own message as a revision and completion of Christianity. Thus, for Ficino, Islam is a heretical religion.

Ficino did not know Arabic and probably never left Tuscany, so his knowledge of Muslim culture and writings is indirect. There is evidence that he owned a Latin translation of the Qur'an, as well as the Dominican Riccoldo da Monte di Croce's (d. 1320) *Contra legem Saracenorum*

('Against the religion of the Saracens') and *Liber peregrinationis* ('The book of the pilgrimage') (Gentile, Niccoli and Viti, *Marsilio Ficino e il ritorno di Platone*, n. 60). Riccoldo is quoted only once in Ficino's treatise, in ch. 37, as the theologian Ricoldo Ebron, but Vasoli ('Per le fonti del *De Christiana religione*', pp. 210-19) has demonstrated that his *Contra legem Saracenorum* is the main source for all the sections on Islam contained in the work. So, it seems that Ficino's information and judgements are not original.

SIGNIFICANCE

Although Ficino's arguments are based on Riccoldo da Monte di Croce, the Italian version of his work, *Della religione Cristiana*, made the subject available to a broader public and, perhaps for the first time, the Italian middle classes were able to discover a fairly broad discourse on the relationship between Christianity and Islam. It is also remarkable that Ficino wrote and published his work after the Ottoman conquest of Constantinople in 1453. In fact, although the Ottoman Empire was threatening the whole of Europe, Ficino stresses the affinity between the Qur'an and the Gospels, emphasising the role of Christ in Islam. It is possible that he considered this to be the best way to confront Islam's incursion into Europe. Furthermore, Ficino uses Islam as a weapon to fight Judaism's misunderstanding of the Bible. Despite the lack of originality in his discourse on Islam, his treatise may have played a significant role in the history of Christian-Muslim relations, and this aspect of Ficino's legacy deserves further scholarly investigation.

MANUSCRIPTS

For a complete description of MSS of both the Latin and vernacular versions, see Gentile, Niccoli and Viti, *Marsilio Ficino*, nos 63-68, where there is also a complete bibliography of earlier studies. There is a further list of MSS in Kristeller, *Marsilio Ficino* (appendix III).

There are three extant MSS of the vernacular version. The first was copied in 1474, the year of the first vernacular edition, the second in 1476, the year of the first edition in Latin, and the third in 1519.

There are two MSS of the Latin version, copied between 1474 and 1476.

EDITIONS & TRANSLATIONS

For a complete description of the first vernacular and Latin editions, see Gentile, Niccoli, and Viti, *Marsilio Ficino*, nos 63-68, which discusses the relation between MSS and editions. Further details are in Kristeller

Marsilio Ficino, p. 113. For uncertain editions, see Kristeller, *Supplementum*, i, pp. lviii-lx.

There are too many editions of *De christiana religione* to list fully. The most important are:

La religione Cristiana, ed. R. Zanzarri, Rome, 2005 (Italian trans. of the Latin text and the only trans. available in a modern language)

Liber de religione christiana et fidei pietate opusculum, Bremae: typis Thomae Villeriani, 1617

De la religion chrestienne, traduit... par Guy Le Fèvre de la Boderie, Paris: chez Gilles Bays, 1578

Della religione cristiana, Fiorenza: Appresso i Giunti, 1568

Liber de religione christiana, Parisiis: apud Gulielmum Guillard..., 1559

De christiana religione, Venetiis:... per Caesarem Arrivabenum Venetum, 1518

Liber de religione christiana et fidei pietate opusculum, Impressum Parrhisiis:... Iacobi expe[n]sis m[a]g[ist]ri Bertholdi Re[m]bolt & Ioannis VVaterloes, 1510

Liber de religione christiana et fidei pietate opusculum, Argentinae: apud Joannem Knoblouch, 1507

De christiana religione, Venetiis: Impressit Ottinus Papiensis, 1500

Della cristiana religione, Pisa: Lorenzo e Agnolo Fiorentini, 1484 (expanded version)

De christiana religione, Firenze: Niccolò di Lorenzo, 1476

Della cristiana religione, Firenze: Niccolò Tedesco, 1474

STUDIES

G. Bartolucci, 'Il *De Christiana religione* di Marsilio Ficino e le "prime traduzioni" di Flavio Mitridate', *Rinascimento* 47 (2007) 345-55

G. Bartolucci, 'Per una fonte cabalistica del *De christiana religione*. Marsilio Ficino e il nome di Dio', *Accademia. Revue de la Société Marsile Ficin* 6 (2004) 35-46

C. Vasoli, 'Marsilio Ficino, il *De Christiana religione* e Sebastiano Salvini', *Studi Umanistici Piceni* 18 (1998) 177-86

G. Castellanelli, 'Il cristianesimo e le altre religioni nel *De pace fidei* di Nicolò Cusano e nel *De Christina religione* di Marsilio Ficino', in G. Canobbio et al. (eds), *Cristianesimo e religioni in dialogo*, Brescia, 1994, 45-77

C. Vasoli, 'Per le fonti del *De Christiana religione* di M. Ficino', *Rinascimento* 28 (1988) 135-233 (repr. in C. Vasoli, *Quasi sit Deus. Studi su Marsilio Ficino*, Lecce, 1999)

C. Vasoli, 'Ficino e il *De christiana religione*', in *Filosofia e religione nella cultura del Rinascimento*, Napoli, 1988, 19-73 (repr. in *Die Philosophie im 14. und 15. Jahrhundert. In memoriam Konstantiny Michalski (1879-1947)*, ed. O. Pluta, Amsterdam, 1988, 151-90)

Kristeller, *Marsilio Ficino*

Gentile, Niccoli and Viti (eds), *Marsilio Ficino e il ritorno di Platone*, nos 63-68

C.F. Bühler, 'The first edition of Ficino's *De Christiana religione*. A problem in bibliographical description', *Studies in Bibliography* 18 (1965) 248-52

Kristeller, *Supplementum Ficinianum*, i, pp. lviii-lix, lxxviii-lxxix, 7-15

Teodoro Katinis

Ludovico de Varthema

DATE OF BIRTH   About 1470
PLACE OF BIRTH Probably Bologna
DATE OF DEATH   Unknown; possibly 1517 or 1525
PLACE OF DEATH Rome

BIOGRAPHY

Little is known about Ludovico de Varthema prior to his journey to the Middle East. However, his knowledge of military techniques, which is evident from his travel description, leads to the assumption that he may have been a mercenary in the Italian wars of the late 15th century. Around 1501, he left Italy for unknown reasons. From Venice, he boarded a ship to Alexandria, possibly because he had heard that the Mamluks needed experts in artillery at the time and paid good salaries. From Egypt, it appears that he went to Syria, where he converted to Islam in order to enrol in the Mamluk elite forces. He would later describe this conversion as purely opportunistic and forced upon him by circumstances; in reality, he remained a Christian throughout.

In 1503, de Varthema was part of a Mamluk contingent that accompanied a *ḥajj* caravan. He is, therefore, one of the first Westerners to have been to Medina and Mecca. According to his own account, he then left the Mamluk troops and headed for Yemen. From the beginning of his stay in Yemen, his reports become few and unreliable. It is assumed that he travelled through several countries of the Middle East and South Asia, before finally joining a Portuguese fleet on the west coast of India in 1506. On the basis of his military experience and language skills, he found work with the Portuguese at their Indian base in Cannanore, Kerala. He finally returned to Europe in 1508, where his knighthood, which had already been conferred in India, was confirmed by King Manuel I of Portugal (r. 1495-1521). Thereafter, he seems to have spent his time lecturing about his experiences and publishing his travel memoirs. He died in Rome in the early 16th century, possibly in 1525.

An alternative interpretation of his whereabouts in the years between 1503 and 1506 would be that he never visited the countries he describes during this period. This suggestion is based on the fact that his travel report for these years becomes erroneous, fictional and unreliable, while evidence shows that until 1503, and after 1506, his accounts are totally reliable.

The assumption would then be that de Varthema remained in Mamluk military service throughout this period of time. He may have been one of the expert marine soldiers mentioned in Mamluk sources who, in 1505, built a new fleet to fight the Portuguese in the Indian Ocean. He would then presumably have been with the Mamluk fleet that was defeated at the battle of Cannanore, along with its local Indian allies. This would explain why di Varthema had such detailed knowledge of the battle and why his reports resumed their accuracy after his defection to the Portuguese in 1506. He may have assumed that the European public would find it difficult to accept that he had been a Mamluk soldier for five years, but during his time in the Mamluk domains, he would have gathered enough information on the Middle East to fool a 16th-century European audience with an account of travels in the region.

MAIN SOURCES OF INFORMATION

Primary

Ludouici patritii romani nouum itinerarium Aethiopiae, Aegipti utriusque Arabiae, Persidis, Siriae, ac Indiae, intra et extra Gangem, Milano: Giovanni Giacomo da Legnano & fratelli, 1511

G.P. Badger (ed. and trans.), *The travels of Ludovico di Varthema in Egypt, Syria, Arabia Deserta and Arabia Felix, in Persia, India, and Ethiopia, A.D. 1503 to 1508*, trans. J. Winter Jones, London: The Hakluyt Society, 1863 (English trans.; most recent repr. Farnham, 2010)

Secondary

C. Forti, 'Sull'itinerario di Ludovico di Varthema', in M. Donattini, G. Marcocci and S. Pastore (eds), *L'Europa divisa e i nuovi mondi. Per Adriano Prosperi*, Pisa, 2011, ii, pp. 21-31

P. Barozzi, *Ludovico de Varthema e il suo 'Itinerario'*, Rome, 1996

P. Barozzi, 'Un'ipotesi sull'itinerario di Ludovico de Varthema in Insulidia', *Bollettino della Società Geografica Italiana* 12 (1983) 349-68 http://www.societageografica.it/images/stories/1983.pdf

P. Barozzi, 'Ludovico de Varthema nelle "Indie Orientali" in età colombiana', in *Atti del II Convegno Internazionale di studi Colombiani*, Genoa, 1977, 415-27

F. Ragazzi, 'Un celebre viaggiatore Bolognese. Ludovico de Varthema', *La Mercanzia* (September 1956)

L. Luzio, 'La fortuna dell' "Itinerario" di Ludovico de Varthema bolognese nella letteratura e nella cartografia contemporanea', in *Atti del 14. Congresso geografico italiano*, Bologna, 1949, 511-14

E. Siracusa Cabrini, *Lodovico di Varthema alle isole della Sonda*, Turin, 1932
A. Bacchi Della Lega, 'Lodovico da Varthema viaggiatore bolognese del sec. XVI', *Atti e Memorie*, 4/7 (1917) 343-44

WORKS ON CHRISTIAN-MUSLIM RELATIONS

Itinerario de Ludouico de Varthema bolognese, 'Itinerary of Ludovico de Varthema of Bologna'

DATE 1510
ORIGINAL LANGUAGE Italian

DESCRIPTION

The first Italian version of de Varthema's travel account was published in Italy as early as 1510 (its title in full is *Itinerario de Ludouico de Varthema bolognese nello Egypto, nella Surria, nella Arabia deserta & felice, nella Persia, nella India, & nella Ethiopia. La fede, el uiuere, & costumi de tutte le prefate prouincie*). It proved so successful that the first German version was printed in Augsburg in 1515. By the middle of the 17th century, more than 30 editions had been released, showing the popularity that de Varthema's work had generated in contemporary Europe. This success could partly be attributed to the fact that it represented the first authentic description of the Muslim holy cities of Mecca and Medina, spiced up with a good serving of sex and crime. According to de Varthema, the Mamluks of Damascus had the right to force sexual relations on women in the streets. Because the women remained veiled during the act, the Mamluks would sometimes molest their own spouses without recognising them (Varthema, *Travels*, p. 14). In contrast, he is impressed that Muslim women and men have equal rights to divorce.

The descriptions he gives of Medina and Mecca are highly accurate and, for the first time, provided the European audience with authentic information. They also corrected contemporary misperceptions about the Muslim creed. De Varthema's observations were clearly aided by his complete fluency in Arabic; indeed, he transliterates Arabic conversations in which he took part, demonstrating his proficiency in the spoken language. He also provides a short description of the Prophet Muḥammad and his Companions.

SIGNIFICANCE

De Varthema took part in the annual pilgrimage (the *ḥajj*), providing the first detailed Western account of the rituals associated with it. His in-depth knowledge of Islam and Muslim practices provides clear evidence that de Varthema was a Muslim for quite some time. As a religious insider, he broadened knowledge of Islam in Europe and provided a basis for further dialogue.

EDITIONS & TRANSLATIONS

P. Teyssier (trans.), *Le voyage de Ludovico di Varthema en Arabie & aux Indes orientales (1503-1508)*, Paris, 2004 (French trans. with Introduction by G. Bouchon)

F. Reichert (trans.), *Reisen im Orient*, Sigmaringen, 1996 (German trans.)

'Abd al-Raḥmān 'Abd Allāh al-Shaykh (trans.), *Riḥlāt Vāritīmā (al-Ḥājj Yūnus al-Miṣrī)*, Cairo, 1994 (Arabic trans. from English 1863 edition)

V. Spinelli (trans.), *Itinerário*, Lisbon, 1949 (Portuguese trans.)

J. Balarin de Raconis (trans.), *Les voyages de Ludovico di Varthema, ou, Le viateur en la plus grande partie d'Orient*, Paris, 1888 (French trans.)

Itinerario de Ludouico de Varthema..., Bologna, 1885 (introduction by A. Bacchi della Lega)

Badger, *The travels of Ludovico di Varthema*

De Uytnemende en seer vvonderlijcke zee-en-landt reyse van de Heer Ludovvyck di Barthema, van Bononien, ridder &c. Gedaen inde Morgenlanden, Syrien, vrughtbaer en woest Arabien, Perssen, Indien, Egypten, Ethiopien, en andere, Utrecht, 1654 (Dutch trans. based on German edition of 1610)

H. Megiser (trans.), *Hodeporicon Indiae Orientalis, Das ist: Warhafftige Beschreibung Der ansehlich Lobwürdigen Reyß. Welche der Edel, gestreng... Ritter, H. Ludwig di Barthema...Jnn die Orientalische vnd Morgenländer, Syrien, beide Arabien, Persien vnd Indien, auch in Egypten vnd Ethyopien, zu Land vnd Wasser persönlich verrichtet; Neben eigentlicher Vermeldung Vielerley Wunderbahren Sachen, so er darinnen gesehen*, Leipzig, 1610 (German trans.)

R. Eden (trans.), *The Nauigation and vyages of Lewes Vertomannus... to the regions of Arabia, Egypte, Persia, Syria, Ethiopia, and East India, both within and without the ryuer of Ganges. &c. In the yeere of our Lorde. 1503. Conteynyng many notable and straunge thinges, both hystoricall and naturall*, London, 1577, Edinburgh, 1884 (English trans.)

C. de Arcos (trans.), *Itinerario del venerable varon micer Luis patricio romano. en el qual cuenta mucha parte de la Ethiopia, Egipto, y entrambas Arabias, Siria y la India*, Seville, 1520 (Castellan trans. from Latin)

Itinerario di Ludouico de Varthema bolognese nello Egypto, nella Surria, nella Arabia deserta & felice, nella Persia, nella India, & nella Ethiopia. La fede, el uiuere, & costumi de tutte le prefate Prouincie, Milan, 1519

Die ritterliche und lobwirdige Reyß des Ludowico Vartomans. welche sagt, von den Landen Egypto, Syria, von beiden Arabia, Persia, Jndia, und Ethiopia, Strassburg, 1516, Frankfurt, 1548 (German trans.)

Die Ritterlich und lobwirdig rayß des gestrengen und über all ander weyt erfarnen ritters und Lantfarers herren Ludowico vartomans von Bolonia..., Augsburg, 1515 (German trans.)

Itinerario de Ludouico de Varthema bolognese ne lo Egypto ne la Suria ne la Arabia Deserta & Felice ne la Persia. ne la India. & ne la Ethiopia. La fede el vinere & costumi de tutte le p fate, puicie, Venice, 1517

A. Madrignano (trans.), *Ludouici Patritii Romani nouum itinerarium Aethiopiae, Aegipti, utriusque Arabiae, Persidis, Siriae, ac Indiae, intra et extra Gangem*, Milan, 1511 (Latin trans.)

Itinerario de Ludouico de Varthema bolognese nello Egypto, nella Surria, nella Arabia deserta & felice, nella Persia, nella India, & nella Ethiopia. La fede, el uiuere, & costumi de tutte le prefate prouincie, Roma: Stephano Guillireti de Loreno, & Hercule de Nani bolognese ad instantia de maestro Lodouico de Henricis da Corneto vicentino, 1510

STUDIES

Forti, 'Sull'itinerario di Ludovico di Varthema'

Barozzi, *Ludovico de Varthema e il suo 'Itinerario'*

Barozzi, 'Un'ipotesi sull'itinerario di Ludovico de Varthema in Insulidia', http://www.societageografica.it/images/stories/1983.pdf

Barozzi, 'Ludovico de Varthema nelle "Indie Orientali" in età colombiana'

Siracusa Cabrini, *Lodovico di Varthema alle isole della Sonda*

Albrecht Fuess

Niccolò Machiavelli

DATE OF BIRTH 3 May 1469
PLACE OF BIRTH Florence
DATE OF DEATH 21 June 1527
PLACE OF DEATH Florence

BIOGRAPHY

The second son of a Florentine lawyer and his wife, both belonging to the Florentine nobility, Niccolò grew up with a strong humanist education. He entered the 'civil service' of the Florentine republic, as a member of its chancery in 1498, soon after the execution of the moralising Dominican monk Girolamo Savonarola, and in June of the same year he was confirmed as chancellor of the Second Chancery, where he dealt with Florentine domestic and foreign affairs, including war. In 1500, he was sent on a diplomatic mission to the king of France, Louis XII, where he had an exchange of views with the cardinal of Rouen, Georges d'Amboise, a powerful minister of France. Machiavelli refers to this in the third chapter of his *The prince*: 'When the Cardinal of Roano [Rouen] told me that Italians understood little about war, I replied to him that the French understood little about politics.'

He returned to France on other diplomatic expeditions in 1503, 1510 and 1511, and he spent a long time at the court of the Emperor Maximilian in 1507-8. In Italy he travelled to numerous courts, including a visit to Pope Julius II (1506), and met other prominent rulers, such as Cesare Borgia. When the Medici returned to power in Florence in November 1512, Machiavelli was sacked from his chancery job, and arrested in February 1513 because his name had been found on a list of supposed anti-Medici conspirators. He was eventually released and he retired to a small family estate near Florence, where he began writing *The prince*, as he explains in a letter of 10 December 1513. He also composed *The art of war*, *Discourses on Livy*, and *The history of Florence*, as well as some successful plays (the best known being *Mandragola* ['The mandrake']), short stories, some poetry and a *Dialogue on language*. Numerous letters of his have survived and vividly document his outspoken views and admirable linguistic verve. He never returned to a position of political influence in Florence or elsewhere, and died in 1527.

MAIN SOURCES OF INFORMATION

Primary
References in R. Ridolfi, *Vita di Niccolò Machiavelli*, Rome, 1954

Secondary
M. Viroli, *Machiavelli's God*, Princeton NJ, 2010
E. Brenner, *Machiavelli's ethics*, Princeton NJ, 2009
Q. Skinner, *Machiavelli. A very short introduction*, Oxford, 1981
P. Bondanella and M. Musa (eds and trans.), *The portable Machiavelli*, London, 1979
N. Machiavelli, *Tutte le opere*, ed. M. Martelli, Milan, 1971
S. Anglo, *Machiavelli. A dissection*, New York, 1969
J.R. Hale, *Machiavelli and Renaissance Italy*, London, 1961

WORKS ON CHRISTIAN-MUSLIM RELATIONS

Il principe, 'The prince'
De principatibus, 'On principalities'

DATE About 1513
ORIGINAL LANGUAGE Italian

DESCRIPTION
Muslim rulers are mentioned in only two chapters of Machiavelli's *Prince*, chs 4 and 19. In ch. 4 the Turkish emperor's state is presented as an example of a strong government ruled by one master and with devoted subjects, who are 'like slaves and have obligations to the leader', and therefore cannot be easily corrupted. It follows that if someone managed to conquer the Turkish state, which would be very difficult, it would then be relatively easier to hold on to it, provided the prince's family is extinguished, because of the total dedication of the administrators to one leader, unlike some Christian states such as France, where the barons, belonging to the old nobility, would cause problems to whoever was able to conquer the state. In ch. 19, which in the original manuscript bore the title in Latin *De contemptu et odio fugiendo* ('On avoiding being despised and hated') and in Italian *In che modo si abbia a fuggire lo essere sprezzato e odiato* ('How to avoid being despised and hated'), Machiavelli presents various examples of rulers who were defended by their subjects against enemies or conspiracies because they had been able to present themselves as 'princes', able to satisfy their citizens and not act against their 'honour or their property'. He then starts discussing the relationship

between armies and the prince, recognising that the problem was more serious for rulers in the distant past because they had standing armies and these were more important than civilians. In the 16th century, most armies were mercenary and therefore citizens were more important than soldiers, with the exception of 'the Turk and the sultan'.

In a modern Italian edition, such as that by Giogio Inglese, 1994, ch. 4 occupies pp. 24-29, and ch. 19 pp. 120-38, with the passage concerning Muslim armies on pp. 136-37.

Machiavelli claims that 'the Turk', namely Selim I (r. 1512-20) 'always maintains near him twelve thousand infantrymen and fifteen thousand cavalrymen, upon whom depend the safety and the strength of his kingdom, and it is necessary that, setting aside all other concerns, that ruler maintain them as his friends'.

He then moves on to talk of the sultan of Egypt, probably the last Tuman Bey, killed by the Turks in 1517: 'Likewise, the kingdom of the sultan being entirely in the hands of the soldiers, it is fitting that he, too, should maintain them as his friends without respect to the people. And you must note that this state of the sultan is unlike all the other principalities, since it is similar to a Christian pontificate, which cannot be called either a hereditary principality or a new principality; for it is not the sons of the old prince that are the heirs and that remain as lords, but instead the one who is elected to that rank by those who have the authority to do so.'

Machiavelli then returns to his main subject to prove that contempt or hatred has caused the ruin of many 'princes'.

SIGNIFICANCE

The remarks about Muslim rulers are little more than an *exemplum*, and yet they show the respect Machiavelli had for the organisation and importance of the state and the army in two important Muslim countries. The examples are also to be taken in the context of his discourse concerning Greek and Roman instances of relationship between a ruler and his soldiers, and it seems that the Muslim armies are more similar to the great instances of Antiquity.

MANUSCRIPTS

No autograph MS of *Il principe* has come down. The main MSS, which almost certainly belong to the period before Machiavelli's death (1527), are the following:

MS Carpentras, France, Carpentras Municipal Library – 303

MS Vat – Barberiniano Lat. 5093
MS Munich, Munich University Library – 4° 787
MS Florence, Laurenziana Library – 44 32
MS Paris, BNF – It. 709
MS Florence, Riccardiana Library – 2603

EDITIONS & TRANSLATIONS

There are hundreds of editions and translations of *Il principe*. A selection is given to show the influence of the work.

C. d'Istria (trans.), *Le Prince*, Paris, 2013 (French trans.)
J.F. Otten (trans.), *De vorst*, Haarlem, 2012 (Dutch trans.)
Il Principe de Maquiavel, Barcelona, 2010 (Spanish trans., first publication of 17th century trans.)
T. Parks (trans.), *The prince*, London, 2009 (English trans.)
J.M. Elexpuru Arregi (trans.), *Printzea*, Bilbao, 2008 (Basque trans.)
'Abd al-Qādir al-Jamūsī (trans.), *Al-amīr*, Beirut, 2008 (Arabic trans.)
Huan Dai (trans.), *Jun wang lun*, Hong Kong, 2007 (Chinese trans.)
Pong-nyong Sin (trans.), *Kunjuron*, Seoul, 2007 (Korean trans.)
H. Puigdomènech (trans.), *El príncipe*, Madrid, 2005 (Spanish trans.)
S.F. Udartsev (trans.), *Patsha. Il principe*, Almaty, Kazakhstan, 2003 (Kazakh trans.)
Gosudar', Moscow, 2002 (Russian trans.)
É. Lutter (trans.), *A fejedelem*, Budapest, 2001 (Hungarian trans.)
Politik kekuasaan, Jakarta, 1999 (Indonesian trans.)
E. Bini (trans.), *O príncipe*, Rio de Janeiro, 1998 (Portuguese trans.)
I. Frangeš (trans.), *Il principe = Vladar*, I. Frangeš trans., Zagreb, 1998 (Croatian trans.)
G. Inglese (ed.), *De principatibus*, Rome, 1994 (critical edition)
Principele. Eseu, Bucharest, 1994 (Romanian trans.)
M. Kasōtakē (trans.), *Ho hēgemonas*, Athens, 1993 (Greek trans.)
A. Gurćinova (trans.), *Vladelot*, Skopje, 1993 (Macedonian trans.)
G. Hoxha (trans.), *Sundimtari*, Priština, Kosovo, 1990 (Albanian trans.)
J. Stojanović (trans.), *Vladalac*, Belgrade, 1994 (Serbian trans.)
Muhammad Abu Bakar (trans.), *Penguasa. surat seorang negarawan kepada pemimpin republik*, Kuala Lumpur, 1989 (Malay trans.)
G. Shiloni (trans.), *Ha-nasikh*, Tel Aviv, 1988 (Hebrew trans.)
Dāryūsh Āshūrī (trans.), *Shahryār*, Tehran, 1987 (Persian trans. from English edition)
Bondanella and Musa, *The portable Machiavelli*

R. Zorn (trans.), *Der Fürst*, Stuttgart, 1978 (German trans.)

M. Ostroverkha (trans.), *Volodar*, New York, 1976 (Ukrainian trans.)

W. Rzymowski (trans.), *Książę*, Wrocław, 1969 (Polish trans.)

F. Kamoga and R. Tanner (trans.), *Mtawala*, Nairobi, 1968 (Swahili trans.)

E. Longfors and W. Pawl (trans.), *Fyrsten*, Copenhagen, 1962 (Danish trans.)

Vũ Mạnh Hồng and Nguyễn Hiền Chi (trans.), *Quân vương Thuật Trị Nước*, Saigon, 1960, Hanoi, 2005, 2007 (Vietnamese trans. from French edition)

K. Hybinette (trans.), *Fursten*, Stockholm, 1958 (Swedish trans.)

Makoto Ōiwa (trans.), *Kunshuron*, Tokyo, 1951 (Japanese trans.)

Tulaci (trans.), *Rāja tantiram*, Chennai, 1946 (Tamil trans.)

Fyrsten, Kristiania [Oslo], 1898 (Norwegian trans.)

G. Regis (trans.), *Der Fürst*, Stuttgart, 1842 (German trans.)

G. Cappel (trans.), *Le prince de Nicolas Machiauelle secretaire et citoien de Florence*, Paris, 1553 (French trans.)

Il principe, Rome: Antonio Blado, 1532 (first edition)

Project Gutenberg, *The prince by Niccolò Machiavelli*, http://www.gutenberg.org/ebooks/1232?msg=welcome_stranger

STUDIES

See the secondary sources for Machiavelli's biography. There is no specific study on attitudes towards Islam in the work.

Diego Zancani

Juan Gabriel

Juan Gabriel of Teruel

DATE OF BIRTH   Mid-15th century
PLACE OF BIRTH   Presumably Teruel
DATE OF DEATH   Early 16th century
PLACE OF DEATH   Unknown

BIOGRAPHY

Juan Gabriel of Teruel, the first translator of Egidio da Viterbo's Qur'an and the collaborator of Joan Martí de Figuerola, was most probably the former *alfaquí* of Teruel, known before his conversion as Alí Alayzar (Archivo Histórico Provincial de Teruel, *Consejo de Teruel*, Carpeta Azul, Documento 274, quoted in Utrillas Valero, 'Los mudéjares turolenses', pp. 820, 823).

The Catholic preacher, Fray Johan Martín de Figuerola, explains in his work *Lumbre de la fé contra el Alcorán* that he owed his knowledge of Arabic and of the Qur'an to the teaching of Maestre Johan Gabriel who had converted to Christianity (García-Arenal and Starczewska, ' "The law of Abraham the Catholic" '). Juan Gabriel was most probably forced to convert in 1502, together with other Moors of Aragón.

In addition to this, David Colville, the copyist of the Qur'an which originally belonged to the Cardinal Egidio da Viterbo (1469-1532), first claims that he knew from some characteristics of the translation that its author was 'either Hispanic or Hispano-Italian by birth', and later specifies that Juan Gabriel was Hispanic, from Zaragoza (Starczewska 'Latin translation of the Qurʾān', pp. xxi-xxii).

Very little is known about Juan Gabriel. It is not clear whether he worked with Egidio during the latter's time in Spain or whether he went back with him to Rome. It is, however, stated in the prologue to the Latin translation of the Qur'an (first version, 1518) that Ioannes Gabriel Terrolensis copied the Qur'an for the Cardinal in Arabic, transcribed it into the Roman alphabet, and then translated it into Latin, in addition to glossing the text in adjacent columns. Moreover, it is known from *Lumbre de la fé* that, by the time Figuerola was writing his work, Juan Gabriel was no longer near him and that he had taken some of his books with him (García-Arenal and Starczewska, ' "The law of Abraham the Catholic" ').

MAIN SOURCES OF INFORMATION

Primary
Joan Martín de Figuerola, *Lumbre de la fé contra el Alcorán*, MS Madrid, Biblioteca de la Real Academia de la Historia – Gayangos 1922/36
K.K. Starczewska, 'Latin translation of the Qur'ān (1518/1621) commissioned by Egidio da Viterbo. Critical edition and introductory study', Barcelona, 2012 (Diss. Universitat Autònoma de Barcelona)

Secondary
M. García-Arenal and K.K. Starczewska, ' "The law of Abraham the Catholic". Juan Gabriel as Qur'ān translator for Martín de Figuerola and Egidio da Viterbo', *Al-Qanṭara* 35 (2014) (forthcoming)
K.K. Starczewska, 'Critical edition of Egidio da Viterbo's Latin translation of the Qur'ān (1518). Some methodological problems', in A. Castro Correa et al. (eds), *Estudiar el pasado. Aspectos metodológicos de la investigación en Ciencias de la Antigüedad y de la Edad Media. Proceedings of the first postgraduate conference on studies of Antiquity and Middle Ages Universitat Autònoma de Barcelona, 26-28th October 2010*, Oxford, 2012, 353-59
T. Burman, *Reading the Qur'ān in Latin Christendom, 1140-1560*, Philadelphia PA, 2007
N.Z. Davis, *Trickster travels. A sixteenth-century Muslim between worlds*, New York, 2007
E. Ruiz García, 'Ante la próxima aparición de dos tratados antialcoránicos. Juan Andrés (1515) y Joan Martín de Figuerola (ms. Inédito de la RAH)', *Aljamía* 15 (2003) 89-92
E. Utrillas Valero, 'Los mudéjares turolenses. Los primeros cristianos nuevos de la Corona de Aragón', in *De mudéjares a moriscos. Una conversión forzada; Teruel, 15-17 de septiembre de 1999; actas*, Teruel, 2003, ii, 809-26
T. Burman, 'Cambridge University Library ms. Mm. v. 26 and the history of the study of the Qur'ān in medieval and Early-Modern Europe', in L. Shopkow, M. Meyerson, and T. Burman (eds.), *Religion, text, and society in medieval Spain and Northern Europe. Essays in honor of J.N. Hillgarth*, Toronto, 2002, 335-63
H. Bobzin, *Der Koran im Zeitalter der Reformation. Studien zur Frühgeschichte der Arabistik und Islamkunde im Europa*, Beirut, 1995

WORKS ON CHRISTIAN-MUSLIM RELATIONS

Latin translation of the Qur'an commissioned by Egidio da Viterbo

DATE 1518, 1525, 1621
ORIGINAL LANGUAGE Latin

DESCRIPTION

The original manuscript with the Latin translation of the Qur'an prepared for Cardinal Egidio da Viterbo (1469-1532) is now lost. However, two copies are preserved, one of them incomplete. What is known about the original translation is that it had four columns, the first with the Arabic text, the second with a transliteration into Roman characters, the third with a Latin translation, and the fourth with comments on the text. It is also known that the text was corrected for the first time in 1525 by Egidio's godson, Leo Africanus (d. 1534-35) in Viterbo, and then in 1621 it was systematically analysed and commented on by David Colville (d. 1629), who was the copyist of the Milan manuscript. In the meantime, corrections were made to a second manuscript, now preserved in Cambridge University Library. It is thanks to David Colville, who prefaced his copy with a three-folio prologue, that we know about the appearance of the original text and the people involved in making it. The translation can be regarded as an example of a humanist, philological study of the Qur'an.

According to what is stated in the prologue, this translation was made for Cardinal Egidio, who was at the time papal legate to the king of Portugal and Castile. Egidio left Rome for Spain on 15 April 1518, as Pope Leo X's legate to the Emperor Charles V in order to ask him to collaborate against the Turks; Egidio is known to have visited Barcelona in June 1518. During this period, he must have had an opportunity to meet Juan Gabriel of Teruel (also known as Iohannes Gabriel Terrolensis, or Joan Gabriel, formerly Alí Alayzar), a Muslim convert to Christianity, whom he employed to make a new translation of the Qur'an. According to some glosses left by the copyist David Colville, Juan Gabriel had only been the translator of the first volume, or the first book (Liber Primus, equal to the first half of the first volume) of the Qur'an. (Egidio da Viterbo's Qur'an follows almost exactly the Maghrebi division of the Qur'an into four parts.)

SIGNIFICANCE

Cardinal Egidio da Viterbo showed a great interest in philology throughout his life. Although he never retired from public office – he served as prior general of his order, papal legate and bishop of Viterbo – it seems that his real interest lay in theology and the scriptures. This Latin Qur'an, in which numerous layers of translations and corrections are gathered, reflects an attempt to understand the content of the text rather than to denigrate it. Comments such as those often found in Robert of Ketton's translation (1142-43), and then in Bibliander's edition (1543, 1550, 1556), are scarce in this text.

Together with the actual translation, some explanations of the qur'anic context have been preserved, often based on Arab authorities, sometimes quoting them by name, sometimes alluding to them in general. Although the use of Muslim commentaries in making translations of the Qur'an was already known (Burman, *'Tafsīr* and translation'), what makes this translation special is the strict division between the text and the gloss (Burman, *Reading the Qur'ān*, pp. 157-77). Egidio da Viterbo's translation, which as far as we know was never designed to be published, contained elements that would facilitate a philological study in its first version of 1518. However, these tools could also have been used for polemical purposes, should the need have arisen.

MANUSCRIPTS

MS Cambridge, University Library – Mm. v. 26 (Previously, this MS was thought to have been produced in the 1530s following the assumption that it was read by William Tyndale [c. 1494-1536]. However, it has recently been shown [Hamilton, 'The long apprenticeship', p. 306], that its second reader was Isaac Casaubon [1559-1614] and not Tyndale; therefore, its dating is still open to debate and should be based on its other characteristics.)

MS Milan, Biblioteca Ambrosiana – D 100 inf. (1621)

EDITIONS & TRANSLATIONS

Starczewska, 'Latin translation of the Qur'ān'

STUDIES

García-Arenal and Starczewska, ' "The law of Abraham the Catholic" '

K. Starczewska, 'Los primeros orientalistas frente al islam. La traducción latina del Corán del círculo del cardenal Egidio de Viterbo (1518)', in J.J. Caerols (ed.), *Religio in labyrintho. Encuentros y desencuentros de religiones en sociedades complejas*, Madrid, 2013, 145-55

Starczewska, 'Latin translation of the Qur'ān'

Starczewska, 'Critical edition'

A. Hamilton, 'The long apprenticeship. Casaubon and Arabic', in A. Grafton and J. Weinberg (eds), *'I have always loved the Holy Tongue'. Isaac Casaubon, the Jews, and a forgotten chapter in Renaissance scholarship*, Cambridge MS, 2011, 293-306

Davis, *Trickster travels*

Burman, *Reading the Qur'ān*

T. Burman, 'The Latin-Arabic Qur'ān edition of Egidio da Viterbo and the Latin Qur'āns of Robert of Ketton and Mark of Toledo', in M. Barceló Perelló and J. Martínez Gázquez (eds), *Musulmanes y cristianos en Hispania durante las conquistas de los siglos XII y XIII*, Bellaterra, 2005, 103–17

Burman, 'Cambridge University Library MS Mm. V. 26'

T. Burman, '*Tafsīr* and translation. Traditional Arabic Qur'ān exegesis and the Latin Qur'āns of Robert of Ketton and Mark of Toledo', *Speculum* 73 (1998) 703-32

T. Burman, 'Exclusion or concealment. Approaches to traditional Arabic exegesis in medieval Latin translations of the Qur'ān', *Scripta Mediterranea* 19-20 (1998-9) 181-97

Bobzin, *Der Koran im Zeitalter der Reformation*

Katarzyna Krystyna Starczewska

Teodoro Spandugino

Theodore Spandounes, Theodoro Spandugino Cantacuscino (Cantacuzeno)

DATE OF BIRTH   Unknown; mid-15th century
PLACE OF BIRTH Unknown; Italy
DATE OF DEATH   Unknown, but after 1538
PLACE OF DEATH Unknown

BIOGRAPHY

Teodoro Spandugino belonged to a Byzantine refugee family who had settled in Venice. What is known of his biography comes from his own work and from the studies by Sathas, Nicol and Villain-Gandossi.

On his mother's side, Spandugino was descended from the Byzantine imperial Cantacuzenus family that had produced emperors of Constantinople and princes in the Peleponnese. His mother had moved to Italy and married another Byzantine refugee, Matthew Spandounes or Spandugnino, who may have been one of the Greek cavalrymen in the service of Venice known as the *stradioti*, and he may have also been awarded the titles of Count and Knight of the Holy Roman Empire. Spandugino's great grandfather had served Constantine Palaeologus, Despot of the Peloponnese, the last Byzantine emperor.

The year of Spandugino's birth is unknown, though he says that he was a child (*in età puerile*) in 1465 when he saw Christian captives in Gallipoli (Nicol, *Theodore Spandounes*, p. 43). He probably grew up in Venice, but he had relatives in Thessalonica and in eastern Macedonia, and family connections in Serbia and Bosnia. Nicol (*Theodore Spandounes*, pp. vii-xvii) gives his genealogy, and says that, as a young boy, he was sent to Macedonia to his great-aunt Maria-Mara, a Serbian princess who had married the Ottoman Sultan Murad II and had been appointed favoured stepmother by his son and successor, Mehmed II. She maintained a privileged and protected Christian enclave in the Muslim world, and held court in Macedonia. It was here that Spandugino learnt some Turkish and acquired an interest in the history and customs of the Ottoman people and their rulers (Nicol, *Theodore Spandounes*, p. x). This, however, is not mentioned by Spandugino himself and, together with several other details of Spandugino's life and career, it cannot be proved (see Ganchou's fine and lucid review of Nicol's edition).

When the Turkish-Venetian war ended in 1503 after four years of conflict, he went to Constantinople to help his brother Alessandro, who had settled there, to regain his possessions, which had been lost to the Turks during the war. He found his brother dead and the family fortune lost for ever, and so, as he says in the prologue, he decided to write on Ottoman history and society. He returned to Venice in 1509, but shortly after this was forced into exile because of his friendship with the Byzantine humanist scholar Janus Lascaris, who as French ambassador in Venice was obliged to leave when the League of Cambrai was formed in 1508. Spandugino, suspected of being a Francophile, moved to France, which may well explain why the first printed version of his book was published in Paris in 1519.

Spandugino apparently finished his revised edition of the history in 1538, because, as he writes at the end of the first part, in that year he had to go to Rome, although the reasons for this are unknown. Spandugino did have important connections in Rome, serving as 'a confidant and adviser' to Popes Leo X, Clement VII and Paul III (Nicol, *Theodore Spandounes*, p. viii). He also served Pope Paul III's grandson, Alessandro Farnese (1520-89), who was made cardinal in 1534. This connection is documented by a letter from Spandugino to Farnese to which Bareggi has drawn attention (*Il mestiere di scrivere*, p. 117 n. 340).

Sathas believes that Spandugino wrote several reports about Turkish matters to Alessandro Farnese but, like many other statements in Sathas's study, this is a questionable claim. Sathas mentions in particular an anonymous work about the Turks written in 1533 by a Christian in Constantinople, and suggests that it is by Spandugino, calling it 'le mémoire anonyme de Spandounis' (Sathas, *Documents inédits*, p. xxvi). But it is hard to believe that this is by Spandugino because, while his treatise is characterised by a rather objective and informative approach, the tone here is far more aggressive and harsh towards the Turks, and furthermore even a quick reading shows that neither the vocabulary nor the spelling seem to match the language of Spandugino's history.

MAIN SOURCES OF INFORMATION

Primary
I diarii di Marino Sanuto (MCCCCXCVI-MDXXXIII) dall'autografo Marciano ital. cl. VII codd. CDXIX-CDLXXVII, Venezia: per cura di Rinaldo Fulin, Federico Stefani, Nicolò Barozzi, Guglielmo Berchet, Marco Allegri (Spandugino is mentioned a few times in Sanudo's diaries, vol. 21, quoted in Sathas, *Documents inédits*, pp. xxi-xxii, though the source is not a biography of Spandugino)

Secondary
T. Ganchou, review of D.M. Nicol, *Theodore Spandounes. On the origin of the Ottoman emperors*, Revue des Etudes Byzantines 56 (1998) 324-26
D.M. Nicol (ed. and trans.), *Theodore Spandounes. On the origin of the Ottoman emperors*, Cambridge, 1997, pp. vii-xxv
C. di Filippo Bareggi, *Il mestiere di scrivere. Lavoro intellettuale e mercato librario a Venezia nel Cinquecento*, Rome, 1988, p. 117, n. 340
C. Villain-Gandossi, 'La cronaca italiana di Teodoro Spandugino', Il Veltro. Rivista della Civiltà Italiana 2-4 (1979) 151-71, p. 152 n. 8
D.M. Nicol, *The Byzantine family of Kantakouzenos (Cantacuzenus) ca. 1100-1460*, Washington DC, 1968, pp. 130-33
G. Mazzatinti, A. Sorbelli, and L. Ferrari, *Inventari dei manoscritti delle biblioteche d'Italia*, vol. 77, Florence, 1950, p. 143
C.N. Sathas, *Documents inédits relatifs à l'histoire de la Grèce au moyen âge*, Paris, 1880-90, vol. 9, pp. iii-l

WORKS ON CHRISTIAN-MUSLIM RELATIONS

***Delle historie et origine de principi de Turchi*, 'On the history and origins of the leaders of the Turks'**
***De la origine deli imperatori Ottomani*, 'On the origin of the Ottoman emperors'**

DATE 1519 (first printed version)
ORIGINAL LANGUAGE: ITALIAN

DESCRIPTION
Spandugino's *De la origine deli imperatori Ottomani, ordini de la corte, forma del guerregiare loro, religione, rito, et costumi de la natione* is an account of the origins of the Turkish rulers and of their phenomenal rise to power. It is one of the earliest works of its kind, perhaps the first to be written in a vernacular and one of the first produced by an author of Byzantine Greek origin. It was indeed one of the most popular treatises on

the Ottoman Empire in the first half of the 16th century and was printed several times. Spandugino produced a number of versions of his treatise, revising, rewriting and adding new passages. The first version was written between 1513 and 1519 and, since Spandugino lived in exile from Venice in France from 1509, the first printed edition was a French translation of his manuscript, published in Paris in 1519: *La genealogie du Grant Turc a present regnant.*

According to C. Villain-Gandossi, who has transcribed the first part of the text ('La cronaca italiana', pp. 157-71), the first version of the Italian manuscript, which is found at the University of Montpellier, was dedicated to Pope Leo X (1513-21). According to D.M. Nicol, however, the first version of the manuscript was dedicated to King Louis XII of France (1498-1515) (Nicol, *Theodore Spandounes*, p. xvii; and repeated by Formica, *Lo specchio turco*, p. 44 n. 89). Nicol does not give such precise references as Villain-Gandossi, whose analysis appears more accurate and reliable, and he also gives slightly contradictory information about the different versions of the treatise (Nicol, *Theodore Spandounes*, pp. xii, xvii). The confusion must be due to the fact that there are at least three different versions of the Italian manuscript and several different translations into French of these first versions (Villain-Gandossi, 'La cronaca italiana', pp. 152-3). Spandugino himself dedicated them to different addressees, sending one to the pope, one to the French king, and another to papal secretary Giovanni Giberti (Villain-Gandossi, 'La cronaca italiana', p. 152).

The final – and amplified – version, finished in 1538, is dedicated to Henry of Valois, later King Henry II (1547-59). This version was first published in Lucca in 1550, then with many inaccuracies (according to Nicol, *Theodore Spandounes*, p. xviii) in Florence in 1551, and reproduced by Sansovino in his *Historia universale dell'origine et imperio de' Turchi* in 1565 (and many other editions to 1654). It is this version that the Greek scholar Sathas edited in 1890, and upon which the English translation by Nicol is based. Here, when treating the first two parts of Spandugino's treatise, the page numbers of Nicol's translation will be cited, and for the third part, which is not included in Nicol's edition, Sathas' edition will be cited.

The dedication expresses a plea to the pope and princes of Western Christendom to unite against the Turks who have inflicted 'ruin and total desolation' on the Christian world (p. 3). Spandugino wants to alert the Christians to the danger that threatens them from the east. His intention is to describe the origins and deeds of the Ottomans in order to show 'how such people had ascended to such heights and grandeur' (p. 3). Among his primary sources, he mentions two friends belonging to the Ottoman nobility, and he distinguishes himself from Western historians by his use of Turkish sources, *annali turchi*, though there is no evidence that he actually read any of them. He also distinguishes himself from Turkish historians by not only writing a short history of the deeds of the Ottomans, but by exploring further in order to present an 'understanding of the ritual of the court, the dignitaries, ministers and officials of the Turks in times of war and peace, with a general account of their manners, fashions and customs and a commentary on my findings' (p. 4). Nicol observes that the only contemporary 'Italian' chronicler to whose work Spandugino makes direct reference is Marinus Barletius, who wrote, among other things, an account of Mehmed II's siege of Skodra in Albania in 1474, and a biography of the celebrated Albanian leader George Kastriotes Skanderbeg (Nicol, *Theodore Spandounes*, p. xxii; Barletius was Albanian, though he may have been born to an Italian family). Spandugino may also have had knowledge of Sagundino's work on the Turks, *De origine et rebus gestis Turcarum*, written in 1456, or of Angiolello's account, *Historia Turchesca* (covering the years 1300-1514), even though they were only circulating in manuscript form at the time. He may also have known Giovio's treatise on the Ottomans, printed in 1531-32 (Nicol, *Theodore Spandounes*, pp. xxi-xxii).

In 1519, when the first version of Spandugino's treatise appeared, an intense debate about the problem of war against the Turks had been going on for some years, and authors such as Erasmus had written to Pope Leo X about the matter (cf. Michelacci, 'Enmity and otherness in Renaissance culture. Italian writings on Turks', forthcoming). The pope, who was known to be philhellenic, made plans for a crusade against Constantinople with a truce to be proclaimed throughout Christendom, but the project was not implemented.

The occasion of Spandugino's revised edition of the treatise might have been the peace treaty between Charles V and Francis I in Nice in July 1538. In the dedicatory epistle to Henry of Valois, Spandugino expresses the hope that the sacred proposals of these leaders will be put into effect, and that the French king will be the first to use his sword against the Turks and 'excel all other Christian princes in taking up arms, as did your blessed predecessors' (p. 5). Spandugino hopes that the pope, together with the Christian princes and the Persians – the latter being 'considered as powerful counterweights to and enemies of the Turks'

(p. 5) – will fight the Turks. The army of the Persians 'conforms in every respect to Christian standards, being quite different from the style and usages of warfare among the Turks' (p. 6).

The work is divided into four parts: The first deals with the origins and deeds of the Ottoman sultans; the second with the Ottoman court, military and government, and the Turks' way of life; the third is an account of the two Persian rulers Ismail I and his son Tahmasp, and the fourth is a short epilogue. The chapters do not bear titles.

Spandugino recounts the history of Christian-Ottoman relations from the 13th century up until 1538, when he interrupts his work because, as he says, he has to leave for Rome. The events between 1509 and 1538, corresponding to the last quarter of the first part, were added in the 1538 edition (Sathas, *Documents inédits*, p. xviii; Nicol, *Theodore Spandounes*, p. 103 n. 128). The third part, about the two Persian rulers, was also added in 1538.

The first and longest part deals with the origins and deeds of the Ottoman sultans. The first pages relate legends about the origins of the Ottomans, building, Spandugino claims, on mostly Turkish sources (oral and written). Instead of tracing the origins of the Turks back to the mythical Scythians, like many humanist scholars before him, Spandugino argues that the Turks stem from the Oguz tribe, who were shepherds from Tartary.

In his account, Spandugino follows a chronological order beginning with the Fourth Crusade (1204) and its consequences for the Byzantine Empire, going on to tell of the capture of Bursa by the first sultan Osman in 1326, civil wars in Byzantium, Mehmed II's conquests of Constantinople and Negroponte, his attacks on Belgrade, Rhodes, Dalmatia and Friuli, the war between Venice and Bayezid II (1499-1503), and so forth. He tells of Selim's war with the shah of Persia and the sultan of Cairo, about Süleyman's capture of Rhodes, Cairo and Hungary, his campaigns in Persia and – which is rarer in accounts of this kind – preparations for an invasion of Naples in 1537. Spandugino appears to focus on conflicts with the Greeks, Venetians and Persians, and does not recount Charles V's reconquest of Tunis in 1535, for instance, which plays a central role in many other Christian chronicles and narratives. This choice might be interpreted as a signal of his loyalty to the French king, to whom he dedicates one of the first editions.

Nicol refers to the lack of factual accuracy in Spandugino's text, and observes that he was not a trained or well-organised historian (*Theodore Spandounes*, pp. xxiv, 80-81, and see further K. Fleet's review of Nicol).

Spandugino often uses anecdotes about his illustrious relatives to document his points; he refers to statements by sultans or other prominent personalities, and to dialogues he has heard himself or that have been reported to him. He refers to dynastic relations, though often without mentioning any specific historical sources, and, in contrast to Menavino, he more often inserts autobiographical episodes in order to enliven and legitimise the narrative: 'I myself saw 73,000 men at work in Constantinople' (p. 63); the son of a Bosnian Duke 'stayed at our house for a few days' (p. 44) at the time of Mehmed's invasion of Bosnia; also, when writing of Christian prisoners taken by the Turks, he says: 'when I was a lad in Gallipoli I saw some of these who, up to that time, had not been ransomed' (p. 43). Not surprisingly, Spandugino also merges Byzantine history into the account more often than other contemporary Italian historians such as Menavino, Giovio or Cambini.

When comparing Christian rulers with the Ottomans, Spandugino often highlights the values of the latter: 'they did something generous and memorable – something which the Christian princes of the time could not bring themselves to do for the promotion of their faith' (p. 15). Among them, Selim was 'partial' to the Christians and he often took their part when he was judging in personal disputes between Christians and Turks, while 'all Christians who had denied Christ and become Muslims against their will were encouraged to revert to their Christian faith' (p. 64). By respecting and praising the Ottomans, Spandugino conveys how dangerous they were far better than he would have by simply describing them as violent beasts. This way of turning the Turks into heroes was not uncommon as a rhetorical device in Christian writings on the Ottomans, and had the effect of a mirror to Christian readers.

However, according to Spandugino, the dominant reason for the Turks' victories is the internal division among the Christians: the power of the Ottomans increased as a consequence of the Great Schism of 1054 between Greek and Latin Christians, and thus this division between Christians is described as a major sin for which God is now punishing the Christians by sending the Turks against them. Occupying Greek territories, Spandugino says, was easy because of the dissension and thus weakness among the Christian princes, and he seems quite critical of the Orthodox Church in particular: he calls the disobedient attitude of the patriarchs of Constantinople a 'plague' that became 'cancerous a few years before the Ottoman house came into being' (p. 12). In addition, internal fighting among the Greeks is also an explanation, beginning with the Byzantine Emperor Manuel, who did not manage to resolve the dissension between his seven sons, causing his own ruin and that of all Christendom (p. 25). The Ottomans always pray for division between the Christians, and in this respect their prayers appear to be sadly effective (p. 132).

The second part of the treatise has a different, more ethnographic character, and deals with the Ottoman court, their military and government, their way of life and 'the many ways in which they differ from the principalities of Christendom' (p. 109). Spandugino describes the Ottoman currency and the design of the coins, he describes the Seraglio and the many different kinds of servants of the sultan, explaining their numbers, functions and conditions. All of them, boys, eunuchs and women, are Christians or children of Christians brought as captives from Christian territories.

Spandugino describes the Ottoman government and its main officers. There are two heads of the Treasury, one in Europe and one in Asia, and 10,000 Janissaries in Constantinople, all sons of Christians recruited in the various provinces and brought up in the Turkish faith, customs and laws: 'Then they are toughened up by being made to carry stones and mortar on building projects', they learn the arts of war, and finally they are enrolled in the corps of the Janissaries (p. 117). Spandugino explains in great detail their pay, their way of life, their weapons and their clothes, especially their white caps 'similar to the headgear of the Jesuit friars' (p. 118).

He explains the function of the mufti, 'supreme doctor and expounder of (Islamic) law', and the *mütteferika*, the élite, consisting of 100 sons of noblemen, whose main duty is to follow the sultan when he goes to camp. He mentions the other functionaries: 'The total complement of the Sultan's court at present, on foot and on horse, is 35,000 salaried persons. The number of Christians: in the time of Bayezid it was found that they numbered 1,112,000 Christian vassals paying the *harac* or tribute' (p. 121). Spandugino is also very keen to give financial details about officials' pay, and devotes an entire chapter to 'the revenue of the sultan', including his taxes from 'the poor Christians' (pp. 121-22).

The last paragraphs of this second part deal with ethnographic aspects of the Ottomans' everyday life: their social customs and religious observances (pp. 127-31), their religion (pp. 131-39), and their way of approaching marriage and funerals (pp. 139-41). Spandugino does not often criticise what he describes, and he gives praise where he thinks it is due: speaking about the sultan's justice towards his subjects, he comments: 'A good and commendable form of justice is available to a poor man who has been wronged', and then he explains how an injured man can put a message with a request on the end of a stick and wait for the sultan to pass by in the street. The sultan will then call the man and hear his complaint. 'Süleyman, for all that he is a harsh persecutor of the Christians, follows something of the example of his forebears in this furtherance of justice; for he wants no one in his empire to be tyrannised or unjustly treated' (p. 122).

Describing the Turkish court and audience chamber (pp. 122-25), he praises the 'splendid sight' of 'their decorated turbans and colourful clothes' (p. 123), and he cannot refrain from observing that the success of the army is due to the energetic, tireless, vigilant and simple life of its soldiers.

Spandugino seems to admire the possibility of social advancement in the Ottoman Empire (p. 129) and the fact that 'these Turks pay respect to a man according to his rank, dignity and condition' (p. 129). He also underscores their charitable character, being 'constantly engaged in such pious and charitable works – far more so than we Christians' (p. 134). Furthermore, they treat their servants 'better than we do' (p. 135). When it comes to the situation of the Christians in Turkey, he is somewhat ambiguous, claiming that 'it is a wonder that they manage to survive' because they have to pay so many taxes and duties on food (p. 124), but that the Turks 'rate Christianity to be the next best and truest faith after their own' (p. 133). Spandugino is keen to show the similarities between Islam and Christendom: the Turks too believe that Mary was a virgin, he says, and they have many Christian prophets, but they do not believe that Jesus was the son of God; instead they believe that he was 'made by God' (p. 133).

Spandugino's attention towards the positive aspects of the Turkish way of governing can be considered a form of indirect criticism of the Christians. This is clear when he affirms that the Turks pray much more than Christians do and that they do not drink wine and never get drunk, which is one of his first observations regarding their social customs. He adds that Christians drink 'often more than they should' (p. 127), and thus bear the shame of their drunkenness. It had been a recurrent theme in 15th-century texts on the Turks to praise them in order to reinforce the attempt to rally the rulers of Christian states against the Ottomans. This strategy corresponds to a mirror play, in which the Other is useful as a *mise-en-scène* to show the limits and weaknesses of Christendom.

Spandugino also expresses a few negative judgments of the Ottomans. He claims that they are 'as much after money here as the Devil is after souls', and that you do not obtain anything without a present (p. 130), and he also claims that they are 'the most self-indulgent men in the world'. Finally, like Menavino, he observes an ambiguous attitude among them towards sodomy, which 'is openly practised even though it is forbidden'. But he does not speak of Islam as a sensual, lustful or demonic religion, and he does not oppose Christian civilisation and Muslim barbarity, as was the case in many writings of the 15th-century humanists. Rather, he tries to give reliable information (even though it is not always correct) based on empirical observations, personal experiences and acquaintances. Thanks to his family background and language skills, he had access to insider knowledge about the Ottomans.

Spandugino's way of discussing the subject of the Turks is first and foremost political, but at the same time he does not refrain from including medieval theological argument about the Turks as God's punishment for the Christians' sinful living: 'Almighty God allowed them to be humiliated because of our sins' (p. 12; and repeated for instance at p. 35). When he adds that Christian leaders have often invited the Turks themselves to help them fight other Christians, he introduces the theological argument again: 'The sins of the Christians blinded the eyes of their own leaders. Whenever they had a difference among themselves they called on one of the Ottomans for help against their rivals; and the poor wretches never saw that this was their own clear ruin. Thus have the Ottoman princes reached their dominating position in the present day, aided by the constant discord among the Christian princes' (p. 56). These statements must have been music to the ears of the leaders of the Church, who blamed the Christian princes for their sinful attitude and consequently made them pay financial tributes to the Church. However, the theological argument is only used to blame the Christians and not to judge the Turks. We do not find moral or religious judgments of the Turks in Spandugino's text, and thus it can be seen as an early example of the development of the discourse on the Turks at the beginning of the 16th century, when 'the comparisons with the Other are moving (...) from a cognitive and religious level to a political one' (L. Michelacci, 'Enmity and otherness'). M. Meserve (*Empires of Islam in Renaissance historical thought*, Cambridge MA, 2008, p. 9) has pointed out that Machiavelli was the first to treat the Turks from a strictly political perspective without moral or religious judgments in his *Discourses on Livy* (1531) and *Dell'arte della guerra* (1521), and Michelacci ('Enmity and otherness') has shown that he also does this in *The prince* (1532). Michelacci shows how Machiavelli establishes a connection between Roman and Turkish virtue, quoting from his *Discourses* (Book 1, ch. 30) in which he claims that: 'To avoid the necessity of having to spend his life suspecting people and displaying ingratitude, a prince should go in person on any expedition, as in beginning the Roman emperors did, as in our day the Turk does, and as courageous princes both have done and still do' (Michelacci, 'Emnity and otherness'). Spandugino, too, can be considered an example of the same tendency, since he does not judge the Ottomans from either a religious or a moral viewpoint in his treatise, which was published in its first version in 1519.

The third part of the treatise, added by Spandugino in 1538, is an account of the customs and warfare of two Persian kings, Shah Ismail I (r. 1501-24) and his son Shah Tahmasp (r. 1524-76). Nicol does not reproduce this text but summarises it very briefly, judging it a 'confused and confusing piece' (Nicol, *Theodore Spandounes*, p. 144). However, this part of Spandugino's text is interesting and does contain many correct or partially correct points of information on the empire of the Safavids and their founder Shah Ismail I. Spandugino's account of the Persians is apparently not well-known among modern scholars, who do not mention it when referring to Christian (or Italian) accounts of the Persian Empire (although they do refer to the accounts by Angiolello, Ramusio and Zeno), as is the case in the otherwise very thorough and detailed entry on Ismail (Savory and Karamustafa, 'Esmā'īl i Ṣafawī') in *EIr*. Spandugino's account confirms his (and thus his contemporaries') awareness of the potential political role of the Persian Empire in the conflicts between Ottoman and European powers: his intention is to make Christian leaders understand that the Persians are important allies against the Turks.

In his introductory dedication to Henry of Valois of this third part, Sandugino says that he is 'taking this work with me to Rome to show it to the pope' (p. 5). The existence of a letter, addressed not to the pope but to his grandson, Cardinal Alessandro Farnese (Biblioteca Nazionale Marciana, It. VI. 365 [5957], cf. Mazzatinti, Sorbelli, and Ferrari, *Inventari dei manoscritti*, p. 143), confirms that Spandugino presented his 'operetta' on the Persian kings at the papal court. He mentions a task with which he has been 'commissioned', and the text may initially have been the result of a request from Farnese (cf. Mazzatinti, Sorbelli, and Ferrari, *Inventari dei manoscritti*, p. 143).

Shah Ismail was the founder of the Safavid dynasty. He was crowned in 1501 at the age of 14, and Spandugino describes him in rather laudatory terms: honest, severe in matters of justice, and very generous: he did not accumulate treasures and riches, but preferred to spend and spill. He was adored by his people and praised as a prophet. Like his father and grandfather, Ismail headed the Safaviyya Sufi order. An invented genealogy claimed that Shaykh Safi (the founder of the order and Ismail's ancestor) was a lineal descendant of the Imam ʿAlī. When Spandugino explains the origin of the Shīʿa Muslims and some of the differences that distinguish them from the faith of the Ottomans, who are Sunnī Muslims, he follows this tradition and says that the Persians 'have ʿAlī more in reverence than Muḥammad' (Sathas, *Documents inédits*, p. 252, my translation, also in the following; hereafter, page numbers refer to this edition of Spandugino's text). Spandugino praises Ismail's son, Shah Tahmasp (Thomas) even more than his father for being 'beloved and revered', generous, righteous and religious (p. 258).

In recounting some of the stages in the expansion of Safavid power in Persia, Spandugino often compares Persians and Christians (directly and indirectly), opposing both to the Ottomans: as when he informs his readers that Ismail drank wine and ate pork, 'and in this and in other things [they] were different from the Turks' (p. 253). According to Spandugino, who apparently passes on information from one of Ismail's own domestics, Ismail bred pigs and even named them after the Ottoman sultans (p. 253).

The Persians are more similar to the Christians in their way of government and warfare: their ruler 'commands an army that conforms in every respect to Christian standards, being quite different from the style and usages of warfare among the Turks', and they get paid 'just like the Christians' (p. 258). When he compares the society and the government of the Persians and the Ottomans, he often underscores how different the former are from the latter: 'their government and costumes are different, he governs his people in another way', and 'in Turkey nobody has a feud' while 'in Persia there is an endless number of lords that have feuds, called the Turcomani' (p. 259).

The noble Persians stand above all the others, Spandugino explains, while in Turkey the lowest, if virtuous, can be judged more worthy than the most noble (p. 259). The Persians are more faithful and warlike than the Turks ('they fight and die more willingly for their religion than do the Turks', p. 259). He even claims that the Persians are more astute than the Turks in matters of war. Finally, although the Turkish ruler may be richer than the Persian, and own much more territory, the Persians are indeed 'gentlemen and noble' (p. 259); they are 'very much experts in war' and are more virtuous than the Turks.

The account concludes with a description of Süleyman's capture of Tabriz and Baghdad, and of the temporary Persian recovery of Tabriz. But at the moment of his writing (1538) the Persian Shah Thomas had established an alliance with the Tartars which, according to Spandugino, might mean that the Europeans would no longer have to fear the Turks.

After the battle of Chaldiran in 1514, in which Shah Ismail I lost territories to the invader Sultan Selim I, Ismail explored the possibility of alliance with European powers, with the object of attacking the Ottomans. He tried to establish contacts with both the king of Hungary and the king of Spain. Spandugino's account of the Persians seems to be part of a similar diplomatic strategy, reflecting his awareness of the same interest on behalf of the Papacy in the possibility of establishing a common alliance with Persia against the Ottomans. In an article on the knowledge of Iranian culture in Italy, Mario Casari observes that 'a new process of conscious political observation and of the cultural discovery of Persia emerged with the accession of Uzūn Ḥasan (r. 1457-78). The interest, particularly of the Republic of Venice and the Papacy, in the possibility of establishing a common alliance with Persia against the Ottomans, led to an active exchange of embassies' ('Italy', vii). The accession of Shah Ismail, the 'Sofi', was widely noticed in Italy, Casari observes, and he explains that this activity on the Italian side led to the publication of numerous accounts of Persia, mainly geopolitical in character: the travel diaries of Giosafat Barbaro (1413-94), Ambrogio Contarini (1429-99), Michele Membré (d. 1594) and Giovanni Maria Angiolello (1451-1525), whose chronicle, *Historia Turchesca*, which recounts the period between the rise of Uzūn Ḥasan and the death of Shah Ismail, might have influenced Spandugino in his short account of the Persian Empire.

In the fourth and concluding part of the treatise, which is a one-page chapter, Spandugino repeats that he has built on Turkish historians and that he has tried to give information that is as precise as possible – regarding the incomes of the Turks, for example.

Spandugino's treatise was meant to inform Christian princes and popes about Ottoman government, society, religion and customs, and to alert Christians to the danger that threatened them from the east. His Byzantine roots are visible in his narration, but 'to Spandounes the word Greece or Grecia meant Europe', in contrast to Sathas' patriotic reading, as is underscored by Nicol (*Theodore Spandounes*, p. xi). Spandugino was more interested in protecting Europe as a whole, including both the Roman and the Greek world, and not first and foremost the Greek. His religious persuasion may even have been closer to the Roman Church than to Byzantine Orthodoxy. He was a 'devout Christian' (Nicol, *Theodore Spandounes*, p. viii), he was delighted by Leo X's crusading efforts, and he expresses his disappointment in Pope Hadrian VI, who failed to support the Knights of St John in Rhodes. His loyalty towards the papal court is also reflected in his correspondence with Cardinal Alessandro Farnese and in his dedicatory prologues to the treatise.

SIGNIFICANCE

In spite of the claims expressed in the dedication about fighting the Turks, Spandugino's treatise cannot be considered as a part of the quantity of anti-Turkish propaganda writings that dominated humanist writings in the 15th century. Spandugino's portrait of the Turks is remarkable because he describes Constantinople and Ottoman society quite positively, as a well-functioning and complex reality in which Christians and Jews, for example, could have a successful career and work without fear. His treatise is characterised by objectivity and a profound knowledge of the Ottoman Empire, its customs, military, government etc., and it was thus an important contribution to the knowledge in western Europe of the Ottomans at the beginning of the 16th century. Spandugino inaugurates and represents (together with Machiavelli, Giovio and Menavino, among others) a tendency in early-16th-century Italian literature to treat the Ottomans in a more objective way.

Thanks to the objective value of Spandugino's book, historians have not been the only ones to use it as a source of knowledge about the Ottoman empire, but philologists have also cited it in order to trace the first appearance of Ottoman words in Italian and thus French (Villain-Gandossi refers to various works; 'La cronaca italiana', p. 157 n. 32). R. Merriman mentions Spandugino's book as 'one of the best of the earlier accounts' on the early history of the Ottoman Turks (*Suleiman the Magnificent*, p. 305).

Spandugino's treatise confirms that the image of the Turk as depicted in Italian Renaissance literature is highly complex, and that it develops through the period from the 14th to the 17th century. During the 15th century, many humanists had moved their focus from a religious to a more secular approach when treating the Turks, but they still maintained some of the stereotypes about savage barbarians as opposed to civilised Christians (cf. the studies of Hankins, Bisaha, Meserve). At the beginning of the 16th century, it is impossible to persist with the idea of the Turks as simply barbarians. Their military success is clear and Europeans begin to observe, analyse and, at times, admire the political system behind it. Spandugino represents this desire for a better understanding of the history of the rise and expansion of the Ottomans, and thus, through knowledge of the enemy, to find a way to combat him. Instead of the fanciful prophecies and anti-Islamic propaganda of earlier centuries, we find a more pragmatic and factual approach to the Turks and a sense of obligation to inform European leaders about Ottoman society, their military, and way of life.

As is the case with similar travel reports from the first half of the 16th century, however, while Spandugino's treatise is characterised on the one hand by its factual approach, on the other it is still embedded into the context of the idea of the Turkish menace, mostly indicated by the introductory remarks in the prologue. According to Höfert ('"Europe" and "religion"', p. 225), this contradiction seems to be a common trait of similar accounts from this period. However, he still sometimes uses the term *setta* ('sect').

Furthermore, even though Höfert does not mention Spandugino in her article, it seems that his treatise can very well be seen as a contribution to the very rise and development of the ethnographic genre she describes, a genre that emerges within travel reports on the Turks (and on America) in the first half of the 16th century.

Spandugino's work was contemporary with Menavino's, and we do find several similarities. Both men dedicated and presented a first draft of their treatises on the Ottomans to Pope Leo X in 1519. (Leo had imposed tithes for a war against the Turks in 1517, and planned a crusade.) Menavino's book on the Ottomans, *I cinque libri*, was written between 1514 and 1519, but only published in 1545 (in Venice by Valgrisi and Florence by Lorenzo Torrentino). Spandugino's treatise was already published in 1519, in France and in a French translation, and the success of the work in France might have inspired the Italian editors. One of the first Italian editions of Spandugino's work was published in Florence in

1551 by the same Lorenzo Torrentino who published Menavino's book. Spandugino treats the same arguments as Menavino, but in the reverse order: first the history of the Ottomans, then the different positions of retainers in the sultan's Seraglio, and finally a discussion of everyday life and Islam, which is less detailed than Menavino's. Spandugino has obtained his knowledge from contacts in the Seraglio and from Turkish historians. According to Dalzell, Spandugino's discussion of the boys in the Seraglio shows that a well-dispersed discussion of *icoglans* and other similar Christian slaves was circulating around Europe (before Menavino's publication), while there was only limited knowledge of the religious principles behind Islam (Dalzell, 'First line of contact', pp. 75-76).

Compared with Menavino, Spandugino's book was clearly more popular, since it was reprinted several times and soon translated into several languages. Menavino, though, had built on personal experience and firsthand contact with the sultan and life in the Seraglio, and he presents more accurate information about these matters, while Spandugino had never been inside the sultan's palace, the Topkapisaray, himself. Spandugino's text thus gives a less accurate picture and fewer details, but since his work was probably more widely read, it better represents how much Europeans would have known about the Ottomans.

MANUSCRIPTS

MS Montpellier, Library of the University of Montpellier (medicine section) – Italiani 389, *Theodoro Spandunino Cantacusino, Patritio Constantinopolitano del origine di Principi de Turchi, ordine de la corte loro et Costumi de la Natione* (early 16th century; dedicated to Pope Leo X [1513-21])

MS Chantilly, Bibliothèque du Musée Condé à Chantilly – XIV H 36, *Petit Traite de Theodore...Cantacuzin, Constantinopolitain, de l'origine des princes ou empereurs des Turcz, ordre de leur court et coustumes de la nation* (1512-15; French trans. – cf. Villain-Gandossi, 'La cronaca italiana', p. 153, n. 16)

MS Paris, BNF – fonds Francais N. 5588, 5640, 14681 (date unknown; three further MS versions of the French trans. by Raconis, dedicated to King Louis XII [r. 1498-1515] – see Villain-Gandossi, 'La cronaca italiana', p. 153, n. 17)

MS Paris, BNF – fonds italien, N.881 (c. 1538; A. Marsand, *I manoscritti italiani della Regia Biblioteca Parigina*, Paris, 1835, pp. 461-62, states that this MS could be the one presented to the Dauphin Henry in 1538, before his accession to the throne as Henry II)

EDITIONS & TRANSLATIONS

D.M. Nicol (ed. and trans.), *Theodore Spandounes, On the origin of the Ottoman emperors*, Cambridge, 1997 (partial English trans. based on the 1550 Lucca edition printed in Sathas, *Documents inédits*)

C. Villain-Gandossi, 'La cronaca italiana di Teodoro Spandugino', *Il Veltro. Rivista della Civiltà Italiana*, 2-4 (1979) 151-71 (edition of 38 folios of the first Italian version)

C.H.A. Schéfer (trans.), *Petit traicté de l'origine des Turcqz par Théodore Spandouyn Cantacasin*, Paris, 1896 (French trans.; cf. Villain-Gandossi, p. 154 n. 20 – a photographic reproduction of Schefer's book was published in Ankara in 1971)

C.N. Sathas, *Documents inédits relatifs à l'histoire de la Grèce au moyen âge*, Paris, 1890, ix, pp. 135-261 (after MS Paris, BNF – fonds Italien N. 881)

C. Hopf, *Chroniques gréco-romanes inédites ou peu connues*, Berlin, 1873, pp. 315-35 (an extract from the final redaction under the title, *Breve memoria de li discendenti de nostra casa Musachi*; cf. Sathas, *Documents inédits*, p. xix n. 2)

La généalogie du grand Turc et la dignité des offices et ordre de sa court, avec l'origine des princes et la manière de vivre et cérémonie des Turcz. Ensemble les vocables saluations, responces [sic], & leur maniere de compter. Plus vn briefue narration de la grande, execrable & inhumaine cruauté de Solten [sic] Solyman, grand Empereur des Turcz, contre Solten Mustapha, son filz aisné, traduict de Latin en Françoys, par F.I.P. de P., Lyon: Benoît Rigaud, 1591

Historia Universale dell'origine, guerre, et imperio de Turchi, Sansovino, Venezia: M. Francesco, 1554 (and many editions until 1654) (probably a reproduction of the 1551 edition)

I commentari di Theodoro Spandugino Cantacuscino gentilhuomo costantinopolitano, dell'origine de' principi turchi, et de' costumi di quella natione, Fiorenza: appresso Lorenzo Torrentino, del mese d'agosto 1551 (dedicated by Lodovico Domenichi to Camillo Vitelli; located in 26 libraries in Italy, cf. Edit16, http://edit16.iccu.sbn.it/web_iccu/imain.htm)

Theodoro Spandugnino della casa regale de Cantacusini patritio constantinopolitano, Delle historie, & origine de Principi de Turchi, ordine della corte, loro rito, & costume, Lucca: Vincentio Busdrago a di 17. di Settembre, 1550 (located in 11 libraries in Italy, cf. Edit 16, http://edit16.iccu.sbn.it/web_iccu/imain.htm)

Ensemble les vocables salutations, respon-ces, & leur maniere de compter. Plus vne briefue narration de la grande, execrable & unhumaine cruauté de Solten Solyman, || *grand Empereur des Turcz, contre Solten Mustapha, son filz aisné,* Lyon: Benoît Rigaud, 1590

La généalogie du grand Turc et la dignité des offices et ordre de sa court, avec l'origine des princes et la manière de vivre et cérémonie des Turcz, Lyon: François Durelle pour Benoît Rigaud, 1570 (three library copies [Universal Short Title Catalogue])

La généalogie du grand Turc et la dignité des offices et ordre de sa court, avec l'origine des princes et la manière de vivre et cérémonie des Turcz, Lyon: François Durelle pour Benoît Rigaud, 1569 (1 library copy)

La généalogie du grand Turq, Lyon: Benoît Rigaud et Jean Saugrain, 1557

Plus adiousté a la fin vne briefue naration [sic] de la grande execrable & inhumaine cruauté de Solten Solymã, grãd Empereur des Turcs, Contre Solten Mustapha, son filz aisné, Paris, 1556 (two library copies)

Genealogie du grant Turc a present regnant... Cy fini le present livre lequel fut achevé d'imprimer le VI. jour de novembre l'an mil cinq cent dix neuf pour Francois Regnault, Paris, 1519 (trans. Jean Balarin de Raconis; Villain-Gandossi ('La cronaca italiana', p. 153 n. 18), says there are two examples of this printed edition: one at the Bibliothèque Mazarine in Paris – 35488 according to Villain-Gandossi, or 35489 according to Universal Short Title Catalogue, and one at the Biblioteca del Museo Condé at Chantilly (IV E 23), though Universal Short Title Catalogue lists nine library copies, http://ustc.ac.uk/index.php/record/8367)

T. Spandugino, *Der Türcken heymligkeyt. Von der Türcken ursprung und gebreuchen in und ausser den zeitten des kriegs,* Bamberg, 1523 (German trans.; digital copy available via Bayerische Staatsbibliothek)

STUDIES

M. Formica, *Lo specchio turco. Immagini dell'Altro e riflessi del Sé nella cultura italiana d'età moderna,* Rome, 2012

L. Michelacci, 'Enmity and otherness in Renaissance culture. Italian writings on Turks', paper presented at an international conference on 'The role of Islamic culture in early modern European literature from the fall of Constantinople (1453) to the battle of Vienna (1683)', Copenhagen, 28-29 August, 2010

M. Meserve, *Empires of Islam in Renaissance historical thought*, Cambridge MA, 2008

A. Höfert, ' "Europe" and "religion" in the framework of sixteenth-century relations between Christian powers and the Ottoman Empire', in H-Å. Persson and B. Stråth (eds), *Reflections on Europe. Defining a political order in time and space*, Brussels, 2007, 211-30

A. Dalzell, 'The first line of contact. The young Christian made Ottoman slave in the sixteenth century', Philadelphia PA, 2007 (Senior Thesis, University of Pennsylvania), http://repository.upenn.edu/hist_honors/3

M. Casari, art. 'Italy, vii. Iranian studies, Islamic period', in *EIr*

N. Bisaha, *Creating East and West. Renaissance humanists and the Ottoman Turks*, Philadelphia PA, 2004

K. Fleet, review of D.M. Nicol (trans. and ed.), *Theodore Spandounes. On the origin of the Ottoman emperors*, International Journal of Middle East Studies 33 (2001) 295-97 (this review contains many important references to further literature on Spandugino)

R.M. Savory and A.T. Karamustafa, art. 'Esmā'īl i Ṣafawī', in *EIr*

Ganchou, review of Nicol

Nicol, 'Introduction', in Nicol, *Theodore Spandounes* (Nicol refers to two primary sources on the family background of Spandugino in addition to his biography, pp. xvi-xvii)

Di Filippo Bareggi, *Il mestiere di scrivere*, p. 117 n. 340

Villain-Gandossi, 'La cronaca italiana di Teodoro Spandugino'

Nicol, *The Byzantine family of Kantakouzenos*

Mazzatinti, Sorbelli, and Ferrari, *Inventari dei manoscritti delle biblioteche d'Italia*, p. 143

R.B. Merriman, *Suleiman the Magnificent 1520-1566*, Cambridge MA, 1944, p. 305

Sathas, *Documents inédits*, ix

Pia Schwarz Lausten

Leo Africanus

Al-Ḥasan ibn Muḥammad ibn Aḥmad al-Wazzān al-Fāsī;
Yuḥannā l-Asad al-Gharnāṭī l-Fāsī; Johannes Leo
Africanus; Johannes Leo Medici; Giovan Lioni Africano;
Joan Lione Granatino

DATE OF BIRTH 1486-88 or 1494
PLACE OF BIRTH Granada
DATE OF DEATH Possibly 1534-35
PLACE OF DEATH Possibly Tunis

BIOGRAPHY

Al-Ḥasan ibn Muḥammad was born in Granada in 1494, according to Rauchenberger (*Johannes Leo der Afrikaner*), or 1486-88, according to Davis (*Trickster travels*, pp. 17, 279-80), though his family moved to Fez either before or after the fall of Granada (1492). The first wave of Muslim migrants left Granada for Morocco in 1496, including possibly part of his father Muḥammad al-Wazzān's family, who were hosted and employed at the Fez court. Al-Ḥasan's uncle served as a diplomat for Sultan Muḥammad al-Shaykh, founder of the Waṭṭāsid dynasty. Al-Ḥasan began his education at a neighbourhood school, and then continued at a *madrasa* in Fez, where the curriculum included grammar, rhetoric, religious doctrine and *fiqh* according to the Mālikī school of law. Upon completing his studies (1506/7), he became a *faqīh*, a scholar trained in law.

Al-Ḥasan was accustomed to travelling from an early age: to the family vineyards in the Rif Mountains, to the family's rented castle above Fez, and to saints' tombs in the Middle Atlas. On an official mission, he visited Safi (1507) on the Atlantic coast, and he also claims to have visited Persia, Babylonia, Armenia and the central Asian lands of the Tartars, though 'there is little sign of it in his existing writing' (Davis, *Trickster travels*, p. 23).

He accompanied his uncle on embassies for Muḥammad al-Burtughālī to the ruler of Timbuktu (possibly in 1510/11) and to Gao, where he returned some years later. He also travelled in other parts of North Africa, went to Cairo (probably three times, in 1513, 1517 and 1518), to central Maghreb and Istanbul (1515-16) and then to Medina and possibly Mecca.

In 1518, he left Cairo and boarded a boat to return to Fez. On the journey, he was captured by a Spanish pirate, and handed to Pope Leo X. He was imprisoned in Castel Sant'Angelo, though he was allowed to borrow Arabic manuscripts from the Vatican Library soon after his arrival. He probably used the time of his imprisonment to improve whatever skills he had in Italian and Latin. His Latin teacher may have been the Dominican Zenobi Acciaiuoli, librarian of the Vatican.

Al-Ḥasan was baptised by Leo X at St Peter's on 6 January 1520, and was given the new name of Joannes Leo de Medicis, which linked him to the pope. After his baptism, he was free to leave Castel Sant'Angelo. He may have worked as a translator of documents from Arabic in the papal chancery and for papal secretaries, as well as helping in the Vatican Library. He also transcribed an Arabic translation of St Paul's Epistles for Alberto Pio, prince of Carpi. His other patron and student was Egidio da Viterbo, for whom he revised and corrected a Latin translation of the Qur'an in 1525.

In the early 1520s, Africanus was working with Jacob ben Samuel Mantino on an Arabic-Hebrew-Latin dictionary, completing it in 1524. In *La descrittione dell'Africa* he refers to other works he wrote at this time: *La brevita de le croniche mucamettani* ('The epitome of Muslim chronicles'), *Operino in la fede et lege di Mucametto secundo la religione di Malichi* ('The faith and law of Muḥammad according to the Mālikī school of law') and *Le vite de li philosophi arabi* ('The lives of Arab scholars'). His treatise on Arabic metrics, *De arte metrica liber*, was copied in 1527, together with *De viris quibusdam illustribus apud arabes*.

Most probably, Africanus left Rome after it was sacked by Charles V's troops in 1527. In 1532, Egidio da Viterbo informed Widmanstadt that Africanus had settled in Tunis (Davis, *Trickster travels*, p. 251).

Africanus's legacy consists of works that gave Europeans information about Muslim societies and their past, Arab scholars and Arabic poetry, and an Islam that differed from the stereotypes prevailing in Christian Europe (Davis, *Trickster travels*, p. 196). His annotations in Egidio da Viterbo's Qur'an are an important testimony to his collaboration in explaining the Muslim scripture to Christian clergy.

Africanus maintained his popularity as an author long after his departure from Rome. His major work, *La descrittione dell'Africa*, appeared in numerous editions, re-editions and translations from its first appearance, while his other works were also widely read.

MAIN SOURCES OF INFORMATION

Primary

MS Rome, Biblioteca Nazionale Centrale – V. E. 953 (*Libro de la cosmogrophia* [sic] *et geographia de Affrica*)

MS Madrid, Real Biblioteca de El Escorial – manuscritos árabes, 598 (Arabic-Hebrew-Latin dictionary)

MS Lawrence KS, University of Kansas, Spencer Research Library, Department of Special Collections – E53, vol. 2 (Paride Grassi, *Diarium An. 1513 ad 1521*)

Marino Sanuto, *I diari di Marino Sanuto*, Bologna, 1969, xxv, xxviii

Secondary

A. Donnini, 'La descrizione dell'Africa di Leone Africano. Studio e edizione del manoscritto di Roma', Geneva, 2013 (Diss., University of Geneva)

F. Romanini, 'Note sul testo della "Cosmographia et geographia de Affrica" di Giovanni Leone Africano', in G.F. Arcodia et al. (eds), *Tilelli. Scritti in onore di Vermondo Brugnatelli*, Rome, 2013, pp. 153-63

Oumelbanine Zhiri, 'Voyages d'Orient et d'Occident. Jean Léon l'Africain et Ahmad al-Hajari dans la littérature de voyage', *Arborescences. Revue d'Études Françaises* 2 (2012) 1-15, http://id.erudit.org/iderudit/1009272ar

T. Veneri, 'Leone l'Africano e l'immaginazione narrativa', *Studi Culturali* 2 (2010) 301-18

F. Pouillon et al. (eds), *Léon l'Africain*, Paris, 2009 (papers from the conference *Léon l'Africain*, École des Hautes Études en Sciences Sociales, Paris, 22-24 May 2003)

N.Z. Davis, *Trickster travels. A sixteenth-century Muslim between worlds*, New York, 2006

Oumelbanine Zhiri, 'Leo Africanus and the limits of translation', in C.G. di Biase (ed.), *Travel and translation in the Early Modern period*, Amsterdam, 2006, 175-86

Oumelbanine Zhiri, '"*Il compositore*", ou l'autobiographie éclatée de Jean Léon l'Africain', in Ali Benmakhlouf (ed.), *Le Voyage des théories*, Casablanca, 2000, 63-80 (repr. Al-Manahil, Rabat, 2012, in Arabic)

Editors, art. 'Leo Africanus', in *EI2*

D. Rauchenberger, *Johannes Leo der Afrikaner. Seine Beschreibung des Raumes zwischen Nil und Niger nach dem Urtext*, Wiesbaden, 1999

F. Secret, 'Postel et Jean Léon l'Africain', in F. Secret, *Postel revisité. Nouvelles recherches sur Guillaume Postel et son milieu*, Paris, 1998

Oumelbanine Zhiri, *Les sillages de Jean Léon l'Africain. XVIe au XXe siècle*, Casablanca, 1995

Oumelbanine Zhiri, *L'Afrique au miroir de l'Europe. Fortunes de Jean Léon l'Africain à la Renaissance*, Geneva, 1991

A. Maalouf, *Léon l'Africain*, Paris, 1986 (a novel)
F. Secret, 'Filippo Archinto, Girolamo Cardano et Guillaume Postel', *Studi Francesi* 13 (1969) 73-76
A. Codazzi, 'Il trattato dell'arte metrica di Giovanni Leone Africano', in R. Ciasca (ed.), *Studi orientalistici in onore di Giorgio Levi Della Vida*, Rome, 1956, i, 180-98
G. Levi della Vida, *Ricerche sulla formazione del più antico fondo dei manoscritti orientali della Biblioteca Vaticana*, Vatican City, 1939
Muḥammad al-Mahdī al-Hajwī, *Ḥayāt al-Wazzān al-Fāsī wa-atharuh*, Rabat, 1935

WORKS ON CHRISTIAN-MUSLIM RELATIONS

Libro de la cosmographia et geographia de Affrica,
'Cosmography and geography of Africa'
La descrittione dell'Africa, 'The description of Africa'

DATE 1526
ORIGINAL LANGUAGE Italian

DESCRIPTION
Libro de la cosmographia et geographia de Affrica is divided into nine parts: a general introduction on geography, weather, customs, economy and culture; seven separate parts devoted to: Morocco, the kingdom of Fes, the kingdom of Tlemcen, Bougie and Tunis, the southern parts of Algeria and Tunisia, Libya, and 'the land of the blacks' and Egypt; and a conclusion on rivers, minerals, plants, birds and animals. There are also autobiographical details, as well as mentions of Sufism, the four schools of Sunnī law, and Muslim sects. Africanus completed it in Rome on 10 March 1526. The sole surviving manuscript copy, in an early 16th-century Italian hand, is more than 900 pages long.

The first publisher of the work, under the title *La descrittione dell'Africa*, was the Venetian Giovanni Battista Ramusio (Venice, 1550). He changed the syntax, vocabulary and style to bring it into line with the standards of the time, and also altered the order of passages.

Rare among authors of the time, Africanus shows he is relatively impartial in his views of both Islam and Christianity. He is appreciative of Islam, and sees it as a force that united Africa, providing law and a framework for intellectual application. He regards Muslims as far above those tribes who had no religion at all.

He describes the recent battles between Christians and Muslims in the Maghreb as purely military-political encounters, as though his Christian audience might have objected to any religious commentaries accompanying his accounts. Nevertheless, his descriptions of the aftermath of the fighting are tinged with sorrow, 'whether during the Arab conquest of Christian Carthage, the Kharijite Berbers' revolts in the name of Islam against the caliphs, the struggles between declining Almohad sultans and upcoming Marinids, or the Portuguese seizure of Morocco's coastal towns. Ruins and depopulated towns, as [Leo Africanus] remembers them from his travels, evoke loss, nostalgia, and the memory of tears' (Davis, *Trickster travels*, pp. 182-83).

SIGNIFICANCE

Africanus moves back and forth between the various cultures and religions of Europe and Africa with a certain detachment from current Christian-Muslim relations, giving, for example, a relatively balanced account of the fighting between the Portuguese and Maghrebis. He must surely have been choosing his information and adopting the tone he did with the sensitivities of his Christian audience very much in mind. Davis (*Trickster travels*, p. 189) suggests that he may, in fact, have employed the Muslim practice of *taqiyya* (precautionary dissimulation), as his Christian references are reserved and limited; this may also account for the single reference to 'the pestilence of Mucametto', with its unusual form of the name Muḥammad. Even so, what is significant in the light of contemporary interactions between Christians and Muslims is Africanus's sorrowful and sceptical tone as he describes hostility and fighting.

Some of the Christian translators of the *Descrittione* found his impartiality disturbing, and added various anti-Islamic details in their versions of the work. This was certainly the case in the French translation of Jean Temporal and the Latin translation of John Florian.

Later editions and translations not only polished the style of the work, but also presented the author – now Giovanni Leone Africano – as a convinced Christian convert with anti-Islamic opinions, particularly in the French, Latin and English translations. Africanus called himself *compositore*, but in later editions his third-person references were changed into the first-person, as he was fitted into the mould of the Renaissance 'historian'.

The *Descrittione* circulated in manuscript form before its first edition, and the information it provided began to change perceptions of Africa, which had hitherto been influenced by Ptolemy. In its published form, it became widely read throughout Europe. Rauchenberger traces its reception in one of the appendices to *Johannes Leo der Afrikaner*.

MANUSCRIPTS

MS Rome, Biblioteca Nazionale Centrale – V.E. 953 (1526)

EDITIONS & TRANSLATIONS

Donnini, 'La descrizione dell'Africa di Leone Africano'

Rauchenberger, *Johannes Leo der Afrikaner*

S. Fanjul with N. Consolani (ed. and trans.), *Descripción general del África*, Barcelona, 1995

A. Épaulard (trans.), *Description de l'Afrique*, Paris, 1956, repr. 1980-81 (French trans. annotated by Alexis Épaulard, Théodore Monod, Henri Lhote and Raymond Mauny)

Muḥammad Ḥajjī (trans.), *Waṣf Ifrīqiyā*, Rabat, 1980 (Arabic trans.)

La descrizione dell'Africa di Giovan Lioni Africano, in G.B. Ramusio (ed.), *Navigazioni e viaggi*, ed. M. Milanesi, Turin, 1978, i, 19-460

C. Scheferm (ed.), *Description de l'Afrique tierce partie du monde escrite par Jean Léon African*, 3 vols, Paris, 1896-98

R. Brown (ed.), *The history and description of Africa and of the notable things therein contained, written by Al-Hassan Ibn-Mohammed Al-Wezaz Al-Fasi, a Moor, baptized as Giovanni Leone, but better known as Leo Africanus. Done into English in the year 1600 by John Pory*, 3 vols, London, 1896

G.W. Lorsbach (trans.), *Beschreibung von Africa*, Herborn, 1805 (for this German trans., Lorsbach returns, for the first time since 1556, to the Italian text of Ramusio)

J. Pory (trans.), *A Geographical Historie of Africa, Written in Arabicke and Italian by Iohn Leo a More, borne in Granada, and brought up in Barbarie*, London: George Bishop, 1600 (English trans.; its several editions of 1625, 1705 and 1738 reproduce this 1600 edition only imperfectly and incompletely)

Ioannis Leonis Africani, De Totius Africae Descriptione, Libri IX, trans. J. Florian (Johannes Blommaerts), Antwerp: Jan de Laet, 1556 (Latin trans., repr. 1558 and 1559. This version, with many errors, circulated widely outside the Mediterranean world; this trans., repr. 1632, was the basis for English [J. Pory, 1600] and Dutch [A. Leers, 1665] translations.)

J. Temporal (trans.), *Historiale Description de l'Afrique, tierce partie du monde... Escrite de nôtre tems* [sic] *par Iean Leon, African*, Lyon: Jean Temporal, 1556/7 (French trans.; repr. in the same year in Antwerp, then in 1564 in Lyon. In 1830, the 4th edition of Temporal's translation was published at the expense of the French government after the taking of Algiers. Charles Schefer re-edited Temporal's translation, *Recueil de Voyages et de documents pour servir a l'histoire de la geographie*, Paris, 1986)

La Descrittione dell'Africa, in G.B. Ramusio (ed.), *Primo volume, et Terza editione delle Navigationi et Viaggi*, 1r-95v, Venice, Giunti, 1563 (The Italian text was reprinted in 1588, 1606 and 1613. In 1837 the 7th edition of Ramusio's text was published in Venice.)

La Descrittione dell'Africa, in G.B. Ramusio (ed.), *Primo volume, et Seconda editione delle Navigationi et Viaggi*, 1r-103r, Venice: Giunti, 1554

STUDIES

Donnini, 'La descrizione dell'Africa di Leone Africano'

Romanini, 'Note sul testo della "Cosmographia et geographia de Affrica"'

Zhiri, 'Voyages d'Orient et d'Occident'

Veneri, 'Leone l'Africano e l'immaginazione narrativa'

D. Nordman, 'Le Maroc dans les premières années du XVIe siècle. Tableau géographique d'après Luis Massignon', in Pouillon et al. (eds), *Léon l'Africain*, 289-309

N.Z. Davis, 'Le conte de l'amphibie et les ruses d'al-Hasan al-Wazzân', in Pouillon et al. (eds), *Léon l'Africain*, 311-23

D. Rauchenberger, 'Note sur les *Trickster travels* de Natalie Davis', in Pouillon et al. (eds), *Léon l'Africain*, 325-31

A. Roussillon, 'Une lecture réformiste de Leo Africanus', in Pouillon et al. (eds), *Léon l'Africain*, 333-48

D. Rauchenberger, 'L'hypothèse du tableau', in Pouillon et al. (eds), *Léon l'Africain*, 365-71

D. Rauchenberger, 'Essai de chronologie critique', in Pouillon et al. (eds), *Léon l'Africain*, 373-83

'Cartes du Maroc et de la Méditerranée', in Pouillon et al. (eds), *Léon l'Africain*, 385-87

'Mémento sur les éditions du texte', in Pouillon et al. (eds), *Léon l'Africain*, 389-90

'Bibliographie des textes essentiels sur Léon l'Africain', in Pouillon et al. (eds), *Léon l'Africain*, 391-94

C. de Rouvray, 'Léon sur Internet', in Pouillon et al. (eds), *Leon l'Africain*, 349-61, also http://www.leoafricanus.com/index.html

Oumelbanine Zhiri, 'Sauvages et mahometans', in J. Dupèbe et al. (eds), *Esculape et Dionysos. Mélanges en l'honneur de Jean Céard*, Geneva, 2008, 1125-39

Davis, *Trickster travels*

Zhiri, 'Leo Africanus and the limits of translation'

I. Marchesani, H. Triki and A. Aouchar, *Fez dans la cosmographie d'Al-Hassan ben Mohammed al-Wazzan az-Zayyati, dit Léon l'Africain*, Mohammedia, Morocco, 2004

B. Andrea, 'The ghost of Leo Africanus from the English to the Irish Renaissance', in P.C. Ingham and M.R. Warren (eds), *Postcolonial moves. Medieval through modern*, New York, 2003, 195-215

C. Black, 'Leo Africanus's "Descrittione dell'Africa" and its sixteenth-century translations', *Journal of the Warburg and Courtauld Institutes* 65 (2002) 262-72

Oumelbanine Zhiri, 'Leo Africanus, translated and betrayed', in R. Blumenfeld-Kosinski, L. von Flotow and D. Russell (eds), *The politics of translation in the Middle Ages and the Renaissance*, Ottawa, 2001, 161-74

Zhiri, ' "*Il compositore*" ou l'autobiographie éclatée de Jean Léon l'Africain'

P. Masonen, *The Negroland revisited. Discovery and invention of the Sudanese Middle Ages*, Helsinki, 2000

F. Cresti, 'L'età preislamica del Maghreb nell la *Descrittione dell'Africa* di Giovanni Leone Africano', in M. Khanoussi, P. Ruggeri and C. Vismara (eds), *L'Africa romana. Atti del XIII convegno di studio*, Rome, 2000, 321-44

Rauchenberger, *Johannes Leo der Afrikaner*

Editors, art. 'Leo Africanus', *EI2*

J.O. Hunwick, *Timbuktu and the Songhay Empire. Al-Sa'di's Ta'rikh al-Sudan down to 1613 and other contemporary documents*, Leiden, 1999

F. Cresti, 'Il Maghreb centrale agli inizi del XVI secolo. Strutture politiche, economie urbane e territorio nella *Descrittione dell'Africa* di Giovanni Leone Africano', *Africa* [Rome] 53 (1998) 218-38

J. Burton, ' "A most wily bird". Leo Africanus, Othello and the trafficking in difference', in A. Loomba and M. Orkin (eds), *Post-colonial Shakespeares*, London, 1998, 43-63

Zhiri, *Les sillages de Jean Léon l'Africain*

K.F. Hall, *Things of darkness. Economies of race and gender in Early Modern England*, Ithaca NY, 1995

A. Siraj, 'Les villes antiques de l'Afrique du nord à partir de la "Description" de Jean-Léon l'Africain', in A. Mastino (ed.), *L'Africa romana*, 20, Sassari, Sardinia, 1992, 901-28

Zhiri, *L'Afrique au miroir de l'Europe*

Oumelbanine Zhiri, 'Jean-Léon l'Africain. Une œuvre et son lieu', *Nouvelle Revue du XVIe siècle* 7 (1989) 53-62

D.M. Hamani, *Au carrefour du Soudan et de la Berberie. Le sultanat touareg de l'Ayar*, Niamey, Niger, 1989

H.J. Fisher, 'Leo Africanus and the Songhay conquest of Hausaland', *International Journal of African Historical Studies* 11 (1978) 86-112

G. Camps, 'Une "société archéologique" à Fez au XVIe siècle. Le canesin de Jean-Léon l'Africain', *Revue de l'Occident Musulman et de la Méditerranée* 13-14 (1973) 211-16

R.S. O'Fahey and J.L. Spaulding, 'Comment. The geographic location of Gaoga', *Journal of African History* 14 (1973) 505-7

P. Kalck, 'Response', *Journal of African History* 14 (1973) 507-8

P. Kalck, 'Pour une localisation du royaume de Gaoga', *Journal of African History* 13 (1972) 520-40

J.-C. Garcin, 'Jean-Léon l'Africain et 'Aydhab', *Annales Islamologiques* [Cairo] 11 (1972) 189-209

R. Mauny, 'Note sur les "grands voyages" de Léon l'Africain', *Hespéris* 41 (1954) 379-94

A. Codazzi, 'Una "descrizione" del Cairo di Guglielmo Postel', in *Studi di paleografia, diplomatica, storia e araldica in onore di Cesare Manaresi*, Milan, 1953, 169-206

A. Codazzi, 'Dell'unico manoscritto conosciuto della *Cosmografia dell'Africa* di Giovanni Leone l'Africano', in *Comptes rendus du Congrès international de géographie. Lisbonne 1949*, Lisbon, 1952, iv, pp. 225-26

Levi Della Vita, *Ricerche sulla formazione*

R. Brunschvig, 'Léon l'Africain et l'embouchure du Chélif', *Revue Africaine* 79 (1936) 599-604

A. Codazzi, art. 'Leone Africano', in *Enciclopedia italiana*, Rome, 1933, xx, p. 899

G.S. Colin, 'La fausse "plaine des preux" des traducteurs de Jean-Léon l'Africain', *Hespéris* 10 (1930) 123-24

E. Lévi-Provençal, *Les historiens des chorfa. Essai sur la littérature historique et biographique au Maroc du XVIe au XXe siècle*, Paris, 1922 (repr. with a foreword by Bernard Rosenberger, Paris, 2001)

L. Massignon, *Le Maroc dans les premières années du 16e siècle. Tableau géographique d'après Léon l'Africain*, Algiers, 1906

De viris quibusdam illustribus apud arabes, 'On some illustrious men among the Arabs'

DATE Before 1527
ORIGINAL LANGUAGE Latin

DESCRIPTION

This work, which Africanus must have completed before 1527, the year in which a copy was made, is a collection of biographies of famous scholars of the Islamic world, 23 Muslims, three Christians and five Jews. The publication is 124 pages long, together with a 14 page addendum on Arabic poetical metre. Africanus calls himself *interpres*, and the title indicates that this is a translation from an Arabic work, which would be a work of *ṭabaqāt*, a biographical compendium (Davis, *Trickster travels*, p. 90).

The lives, arranged chronologically, cover geographical and family origins, occupations, publications, personal anecdotes and quotations, and they often include the names and opinions of previous biographers. Most of the individuals are physicians and philosophers, some distinguished in theology, astronomy, geography, law and poetry – they include the philosophers Abū Bakr al-Rāzī, al-Fārābī and Ibn Rushd, the theologians al-Ashʿarī, al-Bāqillānī, al-Ghazālī and Maimonides, the Nestorian physician Yuḥannā ibn Masawayh, and the geographer al-Idrīsī.

In this work, Africanus 'created vivid portraits of learned men, sometimes well substantiated by memory and whatever notes he had brought with him to Italy, sometimes improvised, approximate, or simply made up' (Davis, *Trickster travels*, p. 93).

SIGNIFICANCE

De viris contributed to contemporary European scholarship by adding information about persons who were known and introducing some who were not known. It contains no traces of religious polemic.

It appears that Egidio da Viterbo read a copy of the manuscript, and in 1658 the Dutch scholar Gerhard Voss (Vossius) quoted from it in *De philosophia et philosophorum sectis*. In 1664, Johann Heinrich Hottinger published it in *Bibliothecarius quadripartitus*, omitting some details about sexual matters, and in 1726 it was re-edited by Johann Albert Fabricius in *Bibliothecae graecae*. In 1805, Lorsbach quoted from it in his commentary on *Descrittione*.

MANUSCRIPTS

MS Florence, Biblioteca Medicea Laurenziana – Plut. 36.35, fols 31r-53v, 62r-69v (1527)

EDITIONS & TRANSLATIONS

J.H. Hottinger (ed.), *Bibliothecarius quadripartitus*, Zurich: Melchior Stauffacher, 1664, pp. 246-91

J.A. Fabricius, *Bibliothecae graecae*, Hamburg, 1726, xii, pp. 259-98

STUDIES

Oumelbanine Zhiri, 'Lecteur d'Ibn Khaldun. Le drame de la décadence', in Pouillon et al. (eds), *Léon l'Africain*, 211-36, pp. 211-13

Davis, 'Le conte de l'amphibie et les ruses d'al-Hasan al-Wazzân', pp. 311-13

Rauchenberger, 'Essai de chronologie critique', pp. 382-83

Davis, *Trickster travels*

A. Codazzi, 'Il trattato dell'arte metrica di Giovanni Leone Africano'

Katarzyna Krystyna Starczewska

Castiglione

Baldassar (Baldassare, Baldassarre) Castiglione

DATE OF BIRTH 6 December 1478
PLACE OF BIRTH Casatico, Mantua
DATE OF DEATH 8 February 1529
PLACE OF DEATH Toledo

BIOGRAPHY

Baldassar Castiglione was born in 1478 in Casatico near Mantua, to Cristoforo Castiglione, a man-at-arms of the Gonzagas, and Luigia (vel Aloisa) Gonzaga. He studied Greek and Latin in Milan under the guidance of the humanists Giorgio Merula and Demetrius Calcondila and attended the court of Ludovico il Moro. On returning to Mantua, he entered the service of the Marquis Francesco Gonzaga. In 1504, he established himself at the court of Urbino, where he remained until 1513, first employed by Guidobaldo da Montefeltro, and after Guidobaldo's death in 1508, in the service of his successor, Francesco Maria della Rovere. In Urbino, he met Pietro Bembo, Bernardo Dovizi da Bibbiena, Giuliano de' Medici, Bernardo Accolti (Unico Aretino), Ludovico da Canossa and the two brothers, Ottaviano and Federigo Fregoso, who would later become his interlocutors in *Il libro del cortegiano*.

During his time in Urbino, Castiglione carried out diplomatic assignments: in 1506, he visited Henry VII's court in England, and, in 1507, he was invited to Milan as an ambassador to the French King Louis XII; and he devoted himself to literature: in 1506, he composed *Tirsi*, an eclogue in the vernacular, and conceived *Il libro del cortegiano*, drafted shortly after the death of Guidobaldo da Montefeltro and completed in Rome and Mantua between 1513 and 1518.

From 1513 to 1516, Castiglione was in Rome as an ambassador of the Duke of Urbino, where he established a cordial friendship with Raphael. In 1516, he returned to Mantua to serve at the court of Francesco and later (1519) of Federico Gonzaga, where he was involved in various diplomatic missions. He married Ippolita Torelli from Mantua and, upon her death in 1520, began an ecclesiastical career. In 1523, he was appointed papal prothonotary, and travelled to Spain the following year as Clement VII's Nuncio to the court of Charles V. After the Sack of Rome (1527),

Castiglione was rebuked by the pope for not being able to foresee such a tragic event, but he justified himself in a letter and earned the pope's forgiveness. He died in Toledo of 'pestilential fever' a year after the release of the *Il cortegiano*.

MAIN SOURCES OF INFORMATION

Primary
Lettere del conte Baldessar Castiglione ora per la prima volta date in luce e con annotazioni storiche illustrate dall' abate Pier Antonio Serassi, ed. P. Serassi, Padua: Presso G. Camino, 1769
B. Castiglione, *Lettere*, ed. G. Gorni, Milan, 1969
B. Castiglione, *Le lettere*, ed. G. La Rocca, Milan, 1978 (a critical edition of the letters to March 1521)

Secondary
G. Rebecchini, 'The book collection and other possessions of Baldassarre Castiglione', *Journal of the Warburg and Courtauld Institutes* 61 (1998) 17-52
F.P. Di Teodoro, *Raffaello, Baldassar Castiglione e la Lettera a Leone X*, Bologna, 1994
B. Maier, art. 'Castiglione', in Vittore Branca (ed.), *Dizionario critico della letteratura italiana*, Turin, 1986, vol. 1, 550-54
R.W. Hanning and D. Rosand (eds), *Castiglione. The ideal and the real in Renaissance culture*, New Haven CT, 1983
V. Cian, *Un illustre nunzio pontificio del Rinascimento. Baldassar Castiglione*, Vatican, 1951
V. Cian, 'Nel mondo di Baldassarre Castiglione, documenti illustrati', *Archivo Storico Lombardo* 7/1-4 (1942) 3-97
J.M. Cartwright Ady, *Baldassare Castiglione, the perfect courtier. His life and letters, 1478-1529*, London, 1908

WORKS ON CHRISTIAN-MUSLIM RELATIONS

Il libro del cortegiano, 'The book of the courtier'
Il cortegiano, 'The courtier'

DATE Between 1508 and 1528
ORIGINAL LANGUAGE Italian

DESCRIPTION
Il cortegiano was written by Baldassare Castiglione between 1508 and 1516 and carefully revised until 1528, the year of its publication. It is considered one of the most representative pieces of literature of the Italian

Renaissance. It unfolds in four books the conversations that took place on four consecutive nights at the court of Urbino, and the interlocutors are some of the famous people of the time, including the Duchess Elisabetha, Princess Emilia Pio, Cardinal Bibbiena, Cesare Gonzaga, Bembo, Giuliano de' Medici, Ludovico di Canossa, Federico Fregoso and Unico Aretino. The dialogue builds on the proposal made by Fregoso to dedicate each evening to constructing in words the perfect courtier, and to describe the form of courtesy most suitable to a nobleman who lives at court. The first dialogue treats the issue of the upbringing and education of the nobleman, the second focuses on his social skills and behaviour in various circumstances, the third outlines the ideal of an accomplished lady, and the fourth analyses the relationship between the courtier and the prince, ending with a discourse on platonic love placed in the mouth of Bembo, the most influential theorist in this matter. The four books are divided into chapters, totalling 351 pages in Prezzolini's edition. In the final version, the issue of conquering the Muslims and converting them to Christianity takes up a passage in Book 4, ch. 38.

As Olga Zorzi Pugliese has demonstrated in her study of the manuscripts containing either autograph versions or revisions of *The courtier*, the importance Castiglione attributes to Christian-Muslim relations varies. In an early poem that he later discarded, he presents the 'Moors' as gentler than the French, Germans or Swiss (Zorzi Pugliese, 'French factor', p. 28). Zorzi Pugliese also stresses that Castiglione originally exhorted King Francis I of France, *re christianissimo*, to lead a religious crusade in order 'to remove from the world the Muslim sect that is so engrained and powerful' ('French factor', p. 33), following the example of the Hungarian king who had defeated the Turks in the mid-15th century. In this version of the text, Castiglione seems to be involved personally in the holy mission, saying that 'our' army is stronger than that of the infidels, and speaking of recovering Christ's burial place and repaying the injuries inflicted on the Christian religion by 'these treacherous dogs'. Castiglione later deleted these references.

'In the final version of the treatise, the question of the religious mission against the Muslim world stands much differently. After the revisions, the sole references remaining to the crusades in the vulgate are much muted, ultimately occupying a rather unimpressive brief passage in the section on politics in Book Four, where it is stated, in a pseudo-prophetic manner, that the crusade could succeed if Monsignore d'Angolem [Francis I] were to become king of France: "What more noble, glorious and profitable undertaking could there be than for Christians to direct their efforts to subjugating the infidels? Does it not seem to you that such a war, if it should meet with good success and where the means of turning so many thousands of men from the false sect of Mohammed to the light of Christian truth would be as pleasing to the defeated as to the victors?" (IV, 38: 321-22)' (Zorzi Pugliese, 'French factor', p. 33).

SIGNIFICANCE
Zorzi Pugliese gives a number of explanations for the final changes to the text, mentioning the views of Pierantonio Serassi (18th century) and others. It seems that the crusading ideal had diminished in urgency by the 1520s, as France had established friendly relations with the Turks (1519). Zorzi Pugliese also points out that 'by reducing the emphasis on crusades, Castiglione was also rejecting more medieval values. (...) Glory for Castiglione, as has been seen, is to be achieved not through crusades or feudal loyalty or other chivalric ideals, but through intellectual, worldly accomplishments. Letters, in as much as they commemorate events, provide true lasting glory, true salvation and eternity: "It is true glory", he writes, "that is entrusted to the sacred treasury of letters" (Book 1, ch. 43: 69). Moving beyond the medieval glorification of chivalry and the crusades, he transfers his focus and the concept of glory to cultural and artistic activities, thus attaining a system of thought that can safely be labelled as high Renaissance ideology, and eminently characteristic of Italy. As the early clarion call for a crusade is whittled down in the vulgate, there is also evidence of Castiglione's growing indifference to the topic of the orders of chivalry' (Zorzi Pugliese, 'French factor', pp. 33-34).

MANUSCRIPTS
For details of the four MSS of the work (including Castiglione's autograph), see O. Zorzi Pugliese et al., *Transcription of the early extant manuscripts of Baldassar Castiglione's 'Il libro del cortegiano'*, University of Toronto Library T-space, 2012, http://hdl.handle.net/1807/32401; and O. Zorzi Pugliese, *Castiglione's 'The book of the courtier' ('Il libro del cortegiano'). A classic in the making*, Naples, 2008.

EDITIONS & TRANSLATIONS
Translations were made from an early time, among them into Spanish by Boscán (1534), into French by Colin (1546) and English by Hoby (1561).

For the reception and translations of the work, see P. Burke, *The fortunes of the courtier. The European reception of Castiglione's Cortegiano*, Philadelphia, 1996.

Modern editions and translations include:

A. Pons, *Le livre du courtisan*, Paris, 1991, 2007² (French trans. based on Gabriel Chappuis 1580 edition and trans.)

F. Baumgart, *Das Buch vom Hofmann*, Munich, 1986 (German trans.)

G. Ghinassi, *La seconda redazione del Cortegiano*, Florence, 1968 (edition of the second redaction)

C.S. Singleton, *The book of the courtier*, Garden City NY, 1959 (English trans.)

V. Cian, *Il libro del cortegiano del conte Baldesar Castiglione*, Florence, 1947

Baldassar Castiglione Giovanni della Casa, *Opere. Il Cortegiano – Egloga Tirsi – Canzoni – Sonetti – Lettere*, ed. G. Prezzolini, Milan, 1937

STUDIES

O. Zorzi Pugliese, 'The development of dialogue in *Il libro del cortegiano*. From the manuscript drafts to the definitive version', in D. Heitsch and J.-F. Vallee (eds), *Printed voices. The Renaissance culture of dialogue*, Toronto, 2004, 79-94

O. Zorzi Pugliese, 'The French factor in Castiglione's *The book of the courtier (Il libro del cortegiano)*. From the manuscript drafts to the printed edition', *Renaissance and Reformation / Renaissance et Réforme* 27 (2003) 23-40

O. Zorzi Pugliese, 'Renaissance ideologies in *Il libro del cortegiano*. From the manuscript drafts to the printed edition', *Studi rinascimentali. Rivista internazionale di letteratura italiana* 1 (2003) 35-42

U. Motta, *Castiglione e il mito di Urbino. Studi sulla elaborazione del 'Cortegiano'*, Milan, 2003

O. Zorzi Pugliese, 'Time and space in the composition of *Il libro del cortegiano*', *Italian Studies in Southern Africa/Studi d'Italianistica nell'Africa Australe* 14 (2001) 17-32

O. Zorzi Pugliese, 'L'evoluzione della struttura dialogica nel Libro del cortegiano', in W. Geerts, A. Paternoster and F. Pignatti (eds), *Il sapere delle parole. Studi sul dialogo latino e italiano del Rinascimento*, Rome, 2001, 59-68

A. Quondam, *'Questo povero Cortegiano' Castiglione. Il libro, la storia*, Rome, 2000

Burke, *The fortunes of the courtier*

F. Massimo Bertolo, 'Nuovi documenti sull'edizione principe del *Cortegiano*', *Schifanoia* 13-14 (1992) 133-44

C.H. Clough, 'Francis I and the courtiers of Castiglione's *Courtier*', *European Studies Review* 8 (1978) 23-70

J. Guidi, 'Baldassar Castiglione et le pouvoir politique. Du gentilhomme de cour au nonce pontifical', in A. Rochon (ed.), *Les écrivains et le pouvoir en Italie à l'époque de la Renaissance*, Paris, 1973, i, pp. 243-78

P. Floriano, 'Idealismo politico del Cortegiano', *La Rassegna della Letteratura Italiana* 76 (1972) 43-52

P. Floriani, 'La genesi del *Cortegiano*. Prospettive per una ricerca', *Belfagor* 24 (1969) 373-85

G. Ghinassi, 'Fasi dell'elaborazione del *Cortegiano*', *Studi di Filologia Italiana* 26 (1967) 155-96

Katarzyna Krystyna Starczewska

Andrea Cambini

DATE OF BIRTH 24 August 1445
PLACE OF BIRTH Florence
DATE OF DEATH 5 March 1527
PLACE OF DEATH Florence

BIOGRAPHY

Andrea Cambini was an Italian historian, humanist and writer. He was a student of Cristoforo Landino, whose *Disputationes Camaldolenses* he translated into Italian, and he was an admirer of Marsilio Ficino, who put him in contact with the Accademia Platonica in Florence, and who inspired his translation of Cicero's philosophical dialogues, *De senectute*, dedicated to Lorenzo di Bernardo de' Medici, and *De amicitia*, dedicated to Antonio de' Medici.

Politically, Cambini was closely connected with the Medici family, in particular Lorenzo il Magnifico and Cardinal Giovanni Piccolomini. He worked as a diplomat for Il Magnifico and held administrative, political and military offices. Among other tasks, Lorenzo de' Medici sent him to the Este court in Ferrara in 1482-83. During his stay there, he was probably asked by the Este princes to translate Flavio Biondo's *Historiarum ab inclinatione Romanorum imperii decades* ('Decades of history from the decline of the Roman Empire') into Italian. This translation was probably completed in 1491 (for further details, see Guerrieri, 'Fra storia e letteratura', p. 394). Between 1485 and 1486, he was a prior in Florence, and afterwards he functioned as the official treasurer of Cardinal Giovanni de' Medici, son of Lorenzo. In 1488, he became the administrator of the Abbey of Montecassino, and in the following years he administered all the other abbeys of Giovanni de' Medici.

He was loyal to Cardinal Giovanni de' Medici and protected him even physically during the riots in Florence against the Medicis, though when they were forced into exile in 1494 he broke his relationship with them. In the first years of the Florentine Republic, he actively supported Girolamo Savonarola and Francesco Valori, but during the insurrection against the party of the *piagnoni* on 8 April 1498 he was involved in the downfall of Savonarola. He was fined and sentenced to ten years in exile. Between these events and 1528, the year of his death (perhaps of plague; see

Guerrieri, 'Fra storia e letteratura', p. 409), he did not participate much in the political life of Florence, though, as E. Guerrieri has documented, he was not completely absent from the political scene ('Fra storia e letteratura', pp. 407-8). Apparently, he dedicated himself to the study of the Ottoman Empire, and composed the uncompleted *Della origine de' Turchi et imperio delli Ottomanni*. This was published posthumously in 1529 (the only one of his works that saw publication), the year in which the Ottomans attempted to capture Vienna. Cambini's treatise became very successful and was reissued several times between 1529 and 1541. It was published together with Paolo Giovio's *Commentarii delle cose de' Turchi, con gli fatti e la vita di Scanderbeg* in 1541, and Francesco Sansovino included parts of the text in his *Dell'historia universale dell'origine et imperio de Turchi* (1560-61). Cambini also wrote another historical treatise, *Della progenie de' Re di Francia e della vita loro*.

MAIN SOURCES OF INFORMATION

Primary
N. Valori, *Vita del Magnifico Lorenzo Vecchio de' Medici*, Florence, 1568
M. Ficino, *Opera*, Basel, 1576, pp. 650, 671, 743, 898
M. Poccianti, *Catalogus scriptorum florentinorum omnis generis*, Florence, 1589, p. 10

Secondary
E. Guerrieri, 'Fra storia e letteratura. Andrea di Antonio Cambini', *Medioevo e Rinascimento* 22 (2008) 375-420 (an important article that corrects some of the statements in Giansante's article in *Dizionario biografico degli italiani*, and refers to further studies on Cambini's genealogy)
E. Cochrane, *Historians and historiography in the Italian Renaissance*, Chicago IL, 1981 (in n. 71, Cochrane incorrectly states that Cambini's book was not published in 1529 in Florence)
M. Giansante, art. 'Cambini Andrea', in *Dizionario biografico degli italiani*, vol. 17, 132-3
L. Forbes, *Early Western books, 1500-1599. The Ottoman Empire and the Mediterranean*, London, 1968, Leiden 1994[2]

WORKS ON CHRISTIAN-MUSLIM RELATIONS

Della origine de Turchi et imperio della casa ottomana, 'On the origin of the Turks and the rule of the Ottoman dynasty'

DATE 1529
ORIGINAL LANGUAGE   Italian

DESCRIPTION

Cambini's *Della origine de' Turchi* is a history of the Ottoman Empire consisting of four untitled 'books' (87 folios in the 1529 edition). The edition of 1529, which is quoted here, contains a dedicatory letter from the publisher Bernardo Giunta to Cambini's son, Girolamo, which is not included in any of the later editions. Giunta says that Cambini was an 'enemy of leisure', and that he left the work on the Turks unfinished at his death. He himself had encouraged Cambini to write this treatise, so that he could publish it for the 'common good', to make Christian leaders understand the Turkish threat and to stop their mutual squabbling and instead 'unite and take up just arms to fight the powerful enemy'. As Cambini did not dedicate his work to anybody, Giunta decided to dedicate it to Cambini's son. Cambini may have been spurred to write the work by the success of the Ottomans in Syria and Egypt (1516-17), though he may also have begun it as early as the end of the 15th century (see Guerrieri, 'Fra storia e letteratura', pp. 410-11, who refers to Gianluca Masi, 'Stefano il Grande e la Moldovia nei "Commentari" di Andrea Cambini e Theodoro Spandugino Cantacuzeno').

Cambini follows a chronological structure in his account of the history and deeds – rather than the origins – of the Ottoman sultans. The first book treats the Ottoman Empire from its foundation until Mehmed II's rise to power (c. 1300-1451), the second recounts the achievements of Mehmed II (1451-81), the third describes the events during the reign of Bayezid II (1481-1512), and the fourth deals with Selim I's reign (1512-20).

Cambini introduces the first book with the often debated question about the origin of the Turks. He rejects the thesis of their Trojan origin and claims instead that they are 'of a Barbarian and cruel nature, tracing their origin to the Scythian nation' (p. 2r). On the one hand, the Trojan origin of the Turks would explain their hatred of the Greeks (the Europeans), who had defeated the Trojans, but on the other it gave the Turks a noble origin, which Cambini could not accept. In line with most quattrocento humanists, such as Aeneas Silvio Piccolomini (later Pope Pius II), who 'spearheaded the campaign to eradicate the myth of the Turks' Trojan ancestry' (Bisaha, *Creating East and West*, p. 90), Cambini defended the Scythian thesis. This was also true of other 16th-century historians and humanists, such as Jean Lemaire de Belges and Erasmus, who denied the Trojan connection, favouring a 'barbaric' or 'nomadic' origin (Bisaha, *Creating East and West*, p. 90). Indeed, the majority of the quattrocento humanists argued that 'the Turks were savage Scythians, a people with an ancient and barbarous pedigree. But even so, this was a narrative of origins rooted not so much in classical ethnography as in misinterpretations of medieval chronicles and the wilder fringes of Christian apocalyptic' (Meserve, *Empires of Islam*, p. 244). According to Meserve, the moralising points earlier historians drew from this narrative of origins and the story of the Ottomans' conquests are not as frequently raised in authors such as Cambini (*Empires of Islam*, p. 241). However, he does judge the Ottomans negatively, and thus he belongs to the same anti-Turkish 'family' as the quattrocento humanists.

His sources are also to be found among them: Cambini may have been inspired by his own translation (finished in 1491) of Flavio Biondo's *Historiarum ab inclinatione Romanorum imperii decades* ('Decades of history from the decline of the Roman Empire', written from 1439 to 1453, published in 1483). Other humanists also referred to this treatise by Biondo in their treatment of the Ottomans' origin from Scythia. Furthermore, in his initial enumeration of all the territories conquered, plundered and ruined by the Ottomans, Cambini refers explicitly to Nicolò Sagundino as one of his sources, 'a learned man both in the Greek and the Latin languages' (p. 2v). Sagundino's treatise *De origine et rebus gestis Turcarum* had been written in 1454-56 for Pius II, who also used it himself as his most important source on the Ottomans in his work on Europe (*Asiae Europaeque elegantissima descriptio*). Cambini also uses Pius II's work as a source. K. Petkov has demonstrated that Cambini directly follows Pius on the subject of the Orthodox faith of the Serbians when he speaks of John Hunyadi's distrust of the Serbian despot George Brankovich in the 1440s (Petkov, 'England and the Balkan Slavs', p. 107 nn. 48 and 51): In Piccolomini's *Elegantissima descriptio*, it is said that the Brankovich 'did not keep either to the way of the Roman Church, or to the law of Mohamed' ('England and the Balkan Slavs', p. 107 n. 48). In Cambini, it is said that Hunyadi keeps parts of the conquered territories for himself because 'he could not trust the Despot since he was a man who did not account more for the Christian religion than for the Muslim one, and since he was located between the Hungarians and the Turks, turning his mind alternately towards the one and the other, having several times deceived both of them' (pp. 10v-11r). Finally, Cambini also refers to oral sources and mentions in particular the assistance he received from an interpreter named Giovanni Cerini (p. 85v).

Even if Cambini often highlights the cruelty and violence of the Turks and considers them barbarians, he describes the Ottoman sultans as virtuous leaders, as in the case of Osman I (1258-1324), who is presented as a man of 'great nobility and of modest wealth' and with 'a sagacious wit and a great mind' (pp. 2v-3r). However, Cambini also underscores that the victories of the Ottomans are due not only to their strength and virtue, but also to the lack of conscience and morality of the Christians. Thus, in his account of the Ottomans' military achievements and conquests, he continuously highlights the responsibility of the Greeks, and of the Christians in general, for the loss of Christian territories: Osman's raid on neighbouring Christian countries was facilitated by the Greeks' internal conflicts. This also applies to his successors, as for example Murad I (1359-89), whose conquest of Gallipoli is presented as a consequence of the internal strife between two of the Byzantine emperor's sons in Constantinople. Also during Bayezid I's reign (1389-1402), the Greeks did not defend themselves, Cambini claims, and had it not been for the intervention of the great Muslim leader and enemy of the Ottomans, Tamerlane (1336-1405), Constantinople would have been conquered by the Ottomans at that time. Tamerlane forced Bayezid to turn his attention towards other frontiers, and in the end killed him. Cambini inserts a long digression on Tamerlane and expresses huge admiration for him, commenting that, if there had been an author close to him to write about his achievements, 'beyond doubt he would have been counted among the first captains who are found among the ancient and the moderns' (p. 9r).

Mehmed I (1403-21), and his son and successor Murad II (1421-51, except for 1444-46), who married a Christian (the daughter of George the Despot of Serbia), were hard on the Christians, making them pay many taxes and, in Murad's case, fighting a long war against the Christian feudal lords of the Balkans. Here, he met resistance from another of Cambini's heroes, the Hungarian military leader John Hunyadi (1407-56). Cambini praises Hunyadi highly and claims that Turkish mothers use him to frighten their children: 'Hunyadi is coming', they say, to make them behave properly (p. 12r).

The account of the short peace treaty between Hungary and the Ottomans (p. 12v) again gives Cambini an occasion to launch an accusation against the Christians among whom, apart from Philip the Good, Duke of Burgundy (1396-1467), the pope could not find anyone to participate in a crusade to help the Greeks (p. 13r). In his account of the

Ottoman-Hungarian battles, Cambini emphasises that the final victory of the infidels was not due to their strength but to their number, and he often claims that there were more dead among the Turks than among the Christians (p. 15v).

The second book treats the period of Mehmed II's rule (1451-81). Mehmed was not satisfied with the great empire left by his father; he wanted to extend it and to conquer Constantinople. Again, Cambini inserts a long digression about the Greeks' vain cry for help to the other Christian kings and princes. They try to convince them of the manifest danger of the Byzantine Empire falling into the hands of 'such a brutal and cruel enemy nation, thirsty after Christian blood more than wine, or any other liquor' (p. 21v). But even if the Greeks make huge efforts 'to move the other Christians to feel commiseration', and even if they 'pour out fountains of tears, their efforts are vain' because the ears of the Christian princes are deaf and their eyes blind; they are occupied by their 'mutual hatred and private convenience' and they despise the universal and common good (p. 22r).

The fall of Constantinople is described at length and in much more detail than, for instance, in Teodoro Spandugino's contemporary treatise on the Ottomans. Also, Cambini's description is more dramatic, and focuses more on the cruelties of the Turks: 'The number of the victors was almost infinite and they did not have any other desire than to steal and lustfully to satisfy their bestial appetite, and being very dedicated to carnal voluptuousness and being cruel by nature, they did not spare anyone because of age or gender, but mixed up rapes with killings, and death with rapes' (p. 25v). He describes the destruction of the church of Santa Sophia with a similar sense of horror: '[it] is contaminated with all the dirtiness one can imagine, becoming a whores' brothel and a horses' stable', while the relics of the saints are thrown in the streets and trampled by men, dogs and pigs (p. 26r).

In his account of the conquests of Mehmed in Greece and the Balkans, Cambini presents another 'hero', the Albanian Christian and 'excellent captain' Scanderbeg, who has 'bravely defended Albania against the infidels, fighting only for religious zeal to maintain the belief of his nation in the faith of Christ's Gospel' (p. 30r). Only when Scanderbeg dies does Mehmed succeed in conquering the country.

Cambini's third book begins with the death of Mehmed and the accession to throne of Bayezid II (1481). He recounts the rivalry of Mehmed's two sons and how Bayezid succeeds with the help of the Janissaries, and his younger half-brother, Cem, is banished to Europe, first under the protection of the Knights of St John on the island of Rhodes and ultimately under that of the pope.

Cambini then describes the Ottomans' battles against the Mamluks in the Middle East and against the Venetians in Greece (especially during the war with Venice 1499-1502), and finally, he dwells on another succession battle between Bayezid's sons Selim I and Ahmet. He explains that, while Bayezid preferred Ahmet, the Janissaries preferred Selim, since he was 'by nature ambitious and only finds pleasure in using arms and riding horses', and because they were convinced that their situation would be much better under him than under Ahmet (p. 66v). After abdicating the throne in favour of Selim, Bayezid II leaves for Adrianople but falls ill and dies before getting there, 'or of grief or, rather, of poison, according to most people' (p. 68r).

The fourth book deals with Selim I's reign (1512-20), in particular with his campaigns in Syria and Egypt (1516-17). Cambini first recounts in detail that Selim I is obsessed with the idea of killing his brother Ahmet and how he succeeds and, after having removed these 'domestic obstacles', he turns his attention to the campaign in the Middle East against the Mamluks, after which the Ottoman Empire becomes the dominant power in the region and in the Islamic world. The final events of Cambini's account concern Selim's preparations for another sea attack, directed towards either Rhodes or Italy (p. 85r). However, at the moment when the army and all the soldiers were ready, the sultan called off the whole campaign without any visible reason. Cambini guesses that it might be because Selim had fallen ill (p. 85v), since during the winter he discovered a 'cancerous abscess' in the kidneys that caused 'a sore so big that a hand could enter it' (p. 85v). Finishing his account in 1520, shortly after Selim's death, Cambini describes Selim as a leader who has 'achieved many extraordinary things' (p. 86r).

This account by Cambini belongs to a new tendency in historical writings on the Turks to relate their history in a more objective way than was the case in earlier 14th- and 15th-century treatises. Many of the writings from the beginning of the 16th century, beginning with Machiavelli's analyses of the Ottoman Empire, thus focus on political and military aspects and to a lesser degree than previously on religious or moral judgments. Cambini can be compared to contemporary Italian authors such as Giovio, Spandugino and Menavino, and like them he inserts several moral judgments concerning the Christians. But he does not refrain from judging the Ottomans too, and he thus differs at some central points from the other authors. Unlike Menavino and Spandugino, he does not include many observations on the customs and society of the Turks. He had not travelled in the Ottoman Empire as they had, and to compile his historical work he had to rely on information from second-hand sources such as textual material or actual travellers (the majority of these introductions to the East came from the various Italian states, especially Venice). Cambini's account is more focused on military deeds, strategies and weapons, than on ethnographic characterisation. He describes the Ottoman sultans, their campaigns, and the composition of their armies, and again, unlike Spandugino and Menavino, he focuses on the sultans' cruelty, basing his account on a more unambiguous division between the Christians and their cruel, Ottoman enemies. His account is designed to increase the knowledge of Ottoman history among Christians, but at the same time it does contribute to the spreading of fear, and stirring up fervour for crusade.

In comparison with contemporary authors, Cambini's style too is a little more narrative and a little more 'sensational' – and thus popular. He focuses on actions and descriptions rather than analyses. He tells of the preparations for military campaigns, and gives details about battles, strategies, weapons and numbers of deaths. He recounts anecdotes and provides geographical explanations. He seems to consider his account a history both in the sense of historical writing and in the sense of story-telling. In fact, he frequently uses the same narrative device as is found in the chivalric romances of Boiardo and Ariosto, when the narrator returns to the narration after a long digression: *Ma tornando alla historia nostra* ('But returning to our history'), *Ma ritornando alla narratione delle cose turchesche* ('But returning to our narration about the Turkish matters'), or *Ma tornando alla narratione della historia nostra dove al principio la lasciamo* ('But returning to the narration of our history where we left it at the beginning'). This rhetorical device, stemming from the oral narrative tradition, serves to retain the audience's attention, while moving between different narrative episodes. Perhaps Cambini had been influenced by the very popular literary genre of the chivalric poem when he lived in Ferrara during the 1480s – a period in which Boiardo was also active at the court of Ferrara, performing and writing his *Orlando innamorato* for the Este princes. Or perhaps Cambini had read or listened to Ariosto's *Orlando furioso*, which had been printed in a first version in 1516.

Cambini's more polemical (and popular) tone regarding the Turks is also reflected in his use of a crusade rhetoric similar to that used by Pius II and other quattrocento humanists (and, again, the terminology of the chivalric poems dealing with medieval conflicts between Saracens and Christians): the Ottomans are frequently called by their medieval names of 'infidels', 'infidel occupiers of Greece' and 'enemies of the faith', and the war against them is considered a *gloriosa impresa*. Their religion is frequently referred to in medieval terms such as 'Muḥammad's bestial and foolish sect' – though the more neutral 'Muslim religion' can be found too.

Cambini's description of the fall of Constantinople is much longer than, for instance, in Spandugino's treatise, and he focuses to a much greater degree on the violence of the Ottomans as they repeat their meaningless rapes, killings and cruel slaughter of Christians. Lara Michelacci has emphasised that Cambini continuously 'stresses the distance between us and the other', describing the bloody praxis of the Ottoman succession to power, the savage treatment of Constantinople in 1453, and the portrait of Ottoman soldiers as preoccupied with 'primary needs', in contrast to the Christian army which prepares itself through religious devotion ('Il profilo del nemico', p. 158). Cambini does indeed repeat and dwell on the stereotypical picture of the Turks when he claims that 'the Turks are ambitious and avid to extend their domain' (p. 14v), and when he characterises them in terms of 'lust', 'bestial (...) appetite', 'carnal voluptuousness', and their 'cruel nature'. It is as though the tone of his writing gets closer to the chivalric poems when depicting the fall of Constantinople. For example, when he writes that the Turks 'mixed rape with murder, and death with rape', he might even have been inspired by Ariosto, who inserts a long historical digression on the Turks in song XVII of *Orlando furioso*, claiming among other things that: '(...) the Turks and Moors had overrun all their lands, committing rape and murder, pillage and outrage' (*Orlando furioso*, song XVII:6).

Thus, Cambini does not seem to have lost interest in the 'lurid details' of the alleged primordial barbarity of the Turks, as Meserve claims. He does count on more accurate information from travellers and ambassadors, but he does not represent a 'dispassionate empiricism', as contemporary authors might (Meserve, *Empires of Islam*, p. 241).

Cambini's negative judgment of the Ottomans and his focus on the brutality of their empire is also interesting in the light of his affiliation to Florence and to the Medicis, since Lorenzo de' Medici, who played an important role in Cambini's youth, was known as a Turcophile leader. At a mature age, Cambini thus contradicts Lorenzo's opinion, although there are other instances of humanists differing from their patrons' Turkish policies, such as Marsilio Ficino, who openly took pro-crusading positions despite Lorenzo de' Medici's known admiration for them. One could argue that Cambini had broken with the Medicis almost two decades before he began writing his treatise on the Turks. With his treatise he might instead seem to approaching the policy of the Holy See.

Nonetheless, Cambini's account of the Ottomans is not without admiration for them, and as in contemporary historical writings on the Turks, these elements of his account perform the function of a mirror for Christian readers: the professional character of the Ottoman army is highlighted – they were well paid, and thus made their lord happy by 'being in order both in terms of the bridling of their horses and their own clothing' (p. 49v); several times Cambini mentions the orderliness of the soldiers ('with his people ordered he conveyed to Cilicia' (pp. 50v, 58r and many other examples). Some of the sultans are characterised as very generous: after a battle, Bayezid returns to Constantinople, and re-orders his incomes 'without any sign of avarice or greed' (p. 49v), and the fourth and final book concludes with an anecdote about Selim, who is said to have returned some stolen goods to the Florentines at the end of his life: the story about the sultan's fairness and generosity is told to Cambini by a 'Persian of Muslim religion' in Florence, and translated by Cambini's interpreter, Giovanni Cerini. It is said that Selim's advisor, 'Perino Bascia', suggests to Selim to fetch some of the valuables he has stolen, and spend them before his death to build a hospital in order to leave a memorial to himself. Selim, however, answers that he does not want to 'honour himself with others' things' but instead wishes to return the valuables to those to whom they belong, 'and so he did' (p. 86v). Cambini explicitly uses this anecdote to moralise against the Christians: 'and this is said to confuse our Christian princes in whom in a case like that, I doubt, one would hardly see similar remorse of conscience' (p. 86v). The Ottomans thus function as a mirror to make the Christians reflect on their own lack of morality. Cambini does praise a few Christian heroes, such as George Scanderbeg and John Hunyadi, but he often blames the Christians for their internal strife and for their greed and selfishness.

Cambini's treatise is not subdivided into thematic parts that distinguish between chronological battle accounts and descriptions of Ottoman society and customs, as is the case with travellers such as Menavino and Spandugino. However, there are exceptions, and he does insert a few observations about Ottoman society and customs, as when he comments on Turkish polygamy: 'the nation of Turks have many lawful wives' (p. 10v), or when he makes linguistic observations and tells his readers the Turkish equivalent of certain expressions (p. 12v), or when he states that the Ottoman empire is 'a nation in which the children of private individuals are born happier than the children of the Lord and other Princes' (p. 18r), alluding to the practice of fratricide and patricide during the seizure of power.

Finally, when he explains the reactions to Selim's victories in the Middle East, Cambini inserts a long ethnographical digression on the Arabs, mainly in Africa, who remain sceptical about the Ottoman rule. He explains that these Arabs, 'whose frontiers since the beginning have been at the river Euphrates, and at present extend until the Ocean and who have populated the whole of Egypt and Africa, having continuously been at war with their neighbouring countries (…) they do not have either fixed or stationary homes, but like the Scythians they live on carts (…)' (p. 83v). These nomad Arabs, Cambini says, do not mix with other nations through marriage or in other ways, because they consider themselves the most noble and ancient generation of the world. He concludes his digression by praising the generosity of these peoples towards foreigners who happen to come to their countries, and claims that, if they did not cultivate so many old hostilities among one other, they could easily have subdued all their neighbouring countries. Perhaps Cambini, again is holding up a mirror to his Christian readers.

SIGNIFICANCE

Cambini's work enjoyed great success. The Venice 1541 edition, a compilation that comprised Paolo Giovio and Andrea Cambini's works on the Turks, as well as a life of Scanderbeg (probably written by Marino Barlezio), is a sign of their editorial success and of the enterprise of the Venetian printing house of Aldo Manuzio.

When Cambini's treatise was translated into English in 1562, it had a great influence on English writings on the Turks: according, to K. Petkov, his description of discord and rivalries among the Balkan rulers, both internal and external, contains details that were 'taken into English political, theological and sociological tracts to prove the disastrous consequences of civil dissension' ('England and the Balkan Slavs', pp. 86-117).

According to P. Preto, Cambini's work, together with other works of the same 'simple' and 'popular' style, was a widely read source of information on the Ottomans (*Venezia e i Turchi*, p. 14), while in his influential work on the fall of Constantinople, Steven Runciman claims that 'useful information can be obtained from the Florentine Andrea Cambini. For his work on Ottoman history, written towards the end of the 15th century, he seems to have consulted survivors from the siege' (*The fall of*

Constantinople, p. 197). This comment, though inaccurate about Cambini's sources, gives an idea of the influence of his work.

MANUSCRIPTS

MS Madrid, BNE – 17585 (16th century)

EDITIONS & TRANSLATIONS

Tvvo very notable commentaries, the one of the originall of the Turcks and Empire of the house of Ottomanno, written by Andrewe Cambine, and thother of the warres of the Turcke against George Scanderbeg, prince of Epiro, and of the great victories obteyned by the sayd George, as well against the Emperour of Turkie, as other princes, and of his other rare force and vertues, worthye of memorye, translated oute of Italian into Englishe by Iohn Shute, London: Rouland Hall for Humfrey, 1562

Commentarii delle cose de' Turchi, di Paulo Giouio, et Andrea Gambini, con gli fatti, et la vita di Scanderbeg, Venice: Eredi di Aldo Manuzio il vecchio, 1541 (38 library copies)

Commentario de Andrea Cambini fiorentino della origine de' Turchi et imperio della casa ottomanna, [Venice?], c. 1540 (10 library copies)

Commentario de Andrea Cambini fiorentino, della origine de' Turchi, et imperio della casa ottomanna, [Venice?], 1538 (18 library copies in Italy)

Commentario de Andrea Cambini della origine de Turchi, et imperio della casa ottoman, [Venice?], 1537 (four library copies in Italy)

Libro d'Andrea Cambini della origine de Turchi, et imperio deli Ottomani, Florence: Per Benedetto di Gionta, 1537 (20 library copies in Italy)

Libro d'Andrea Cambini fiorentino della origine de Turchi et imperio delli Ottomani, Firenze: Eredi di Filippo Giunta il vecchio, 1529 (25 library copies in Italy)

STUDIES

P. Preto, *Venezia e i Turchi*, Rome, 2013

L. Michelacci, 'Il profilo del nemico. L'immagine del turco tra Paolo Giovio, Andrea Cambini e Marino Barlezio', in L.S. Tarugi (ed.), *Oriente e Occidente nel Rinascimento. Atti del XIX Convegno Internazionale (Chianciano Terme-Pienza 16-19 luglio 2007)*, Florence, 2009, 151-63

Guerrieri, 'Fra storia e letteratura' (the most recent and most thorough study of Cambini's life and work)

M. Meserve, *Empires of Islam in Renaissance historical thought*, Cambridge MA, 2008

G. Masi, 'Stefano il Grande e la Moldavia nei 'Commentari' di Andrea Cambini e Theodoro Spandugino Cantacuzeno', *Annuario dell'Istituto Romeno di Cultura e Ricerca Umanistica* 6-7 (2004-5) 83-120

N. Bisaha, *Creating East and West. Renaissance humanists and the Ottoman Turks*, Philadelphia PA, 2004

K. Petkov, 'England and the Balkan Slavs 1354-1583. An outline of a late-medieval and Renaissance image', *Slavonic and East European Review* 75 (1997) 86-117

S. Runciman, *The fall of Constantinople 1453*, Cambridge, 1965

Pia Schwarz Lausten

Ludovico Ariosto

DATE OF BIRTH 8 September 1474
PLACE OF BIRTH Reggio Emilia
DATE OF DEATH 6 July 1533
PLACE OF DEATH Ferrara

BIOGRAPHY

One of the major poets of the Italian Renaissance, Ludovico Ariosto was born in 1474 in Reggio Emilia to Niccolò Ariosto (an employee of Ercole I d'Este) and Daria Malaguzzi Valeri. In 1484, the family moved to Ferrara, where, following the wishes of his father, Ludovico studied law at the local university from 1489 to 1494. Afterwards, unwilling to pursue a legal career, he applied himself to the study of Latin under the guidance of Gregorio da Spoleto, while participating in the vibrant cultural life of the ducal court. He established enduring friendships with prominent humanists and poets, such as Alberto Pio da Carpi, Ercole Strozzi and Pietro Bembo, and took his first steps as a poet, writing predominantly in Latin.

Niccolò Ariosto's death in 1500 left Ludovico in charge of his large family. In 1501, he accepted the position of commander of the citadel of Canossa, and in 1503 entered the service of Cardinal Ippolito d'Este, a brother of the ducal heir, Alfonso. Towards the end of that year, he took minor orders, which enabled him to receive ecclesiastical benefits. As the cardinal's courtier, he was expected to carry out a variety of tasks, ranging from administrative work to diplomatic missions to the Holy See during the War of the Holy League (1508-16). Having witnessed from close up the dramatic events that marked the first decades of the 16th century, he made numerous references to contemporary history in *Orlando furioso*, a poem designed to celebrate his patron and the Este dynasty.

Ariosto embarked on the composition of *Orlando furioso* in 1504-6. The first edition (a 40-canto version) was printed in 1516. Ariosto resented the cardinal's lack of appreciation of his masterpiece and their relationship soured beyond repair in 1517, when the poet refused to accompany Ippolito to Hungary. That year, Ariosto composed his first *Satira*, a satirical poem in tercets in which he gave vent to his frustration at the cardinal's behaviour. In the period between 1517 and 1525, he penned seven

Satire, each inspired by a specific event in his life. In 1518, he entered the service of Duke Alfonso I d'Este, which proved to be less burdensome than Ippolito's. However, his financial situation remained precarious and the interminable lawsuit with the ducal Camera over 'Le Arioste' (lands that had belonged to the Ariosto family) would be a source of constant anxiety for the rest of his days.

In 1518, Ariosto probably started to work on the *Cinque canti*, a continuation of *Orlando furioso*, which was left incomplete and published posthumously in 1545. In 1521, the second edition of *Orlando furioso* saw the light. Very similar to the *editio princeps*, it did not feature any new episodes. In 1522, Ariosto accepted the post of governor of Garfagnana, a remote province in the Apennines where banditry thrived. Upon returning to Ferrara in 1525, he devoted his time to revising and amplifying *Orlando furioso*. Moreover, in the period between 1528 and 1532, he was able to resume playwriting, his long-standing passion: he composed a new comedy, *La Lena*, and also revised the text of *Negromante* (1520) and produced versified versions of *Cassaria* (first performed in 1508) and *Suppositi* (first performed in 1509). In those years, he secretly married Alessandra Benucci, the widow of Tito Strozzi, with whom he had fallen in love in 1513. In 1531, Alfonso d'Avalos, the marquis of Vasto, granted him an annual pension of 100 gold ducats. In October 1532, the third edition of *Orlando furioso* (featuring six new cantos) was published, and in November the poet offered a copy to the Holy Roman Emperor Charles V, whom he met in Mantua. Ariosto was considering making further corrections and additions, but he fell ill at the end of December and died on 6 July 1533 in his house in Ferrara.

MAIN SOURCES OF INFORMATION

Primary

S. Fórnari, *La vita di M. Lodovico Ariosto*, in *La spositione di M. Simon Fórnari da Rheggio sopra l'Orlando furioso di M. Ludovico Ariosto*, Florence: Torrentino, 1549, 15-30

G.B. Pigna, *La vita di M. Lodovico Ariosto, tratta in compendio da i Romanzi del S. Giovan Battista Pigna*, in *Orlando furioso*, Venice: Valgrisi, 1556

F. Sansovino, *La vita di M. Ludovico Ariosto, tratta dall'opere sue medesime da M. Francesco Sansovino*, in *Orlando furioso*, Venice: Rampazetto, 1562

G. Garofalo, *Vita di M. Lodovico Ariosto scritta dal sig. Girolamo Garofalo ferrarese*, in *Orlando furioso*, Venice: De Franceschi, 1584

Secondary
Among the most important general studies on Ariosto are:
S. Jossa, *Ariosto*, Bologna, 2009
G. Ferroni, *Ariosto*, Rome, 2008
A. Casadei, 'Ludovico Ariosto', in G. Da Pozzo (ed.), *Storia letteraria d'Italia. Il cinqucento*, Padua, 2006, 777-822
D. Beeher et al. (eds), *Ariosto today. Contemporary perspectives*, Toronto, 2003
M. Santoro, *Ariosto e il Rinascimento*, Naples, 1989
C.P. Brand, *Ludovico Ariosto. A preface to the 'Orlando furioso'*, Edinburgh, 1974
N. Borsellino, *Ludovico Ariosto*, Bari, 1973
C. Segre, *Esperienze ariostesche*, Pisa, 1966
L. Caretti, 'Ariosto', in *Ariosto e Tasso*, Turin, 1961, 2001^3, 15-78
M. Catalano, *Vita di Ludovico Ariosto ricostruita su nuovi documenti*, 2 vols, Geneva, 1930-31

WORKS ON CHRISTIAN-MUSLIM RELATIONS

Orlando furioso, 'The frenzy of Orlando'; 'Mad Orlando'

DATE 1532 (final edition; the first edition was published in 1516)
ORIGINAL LANGUAGE Italian

DESCRIPTION

Orlando furioso, a chivalric romance in *ottava rima* (eight-line stanzas), is a sequel to Matteo Maria Boiardo's *Inamoramento de Orlando* ('Orlando in love', also known as *Orlando innamorato*). It comprises nearly 5,000 stanzas and totals 1,418 pages in L. Caretti's edition. Its 46 (40 in the 1516 edition) cantos describe the adventures of Christian and Saracen (Muslim) knights and damsels, which take place during or shortly after the war between Charlemagne and the African king Agramante. Picking up the narrative threads left hanging at Boiardo's death, Ariosto pays special attention to the stories of the titular character, the Christian paladin Orlando, and the Saracen knight Ruggiero, the main hero of Books II and III of the *Inamoramento de Orlando*. The former is driven mad by his unrequited love for the Saracen princess Angelica (his madness occurs in canto XXIII, halfway through the narrative), but he later regains his wits and contributes to the victory of the Christians by playing a leading role in the conquest of Biserta, the capital of Agramante's African kingdom (cantos XXXIX-XL), and killing Agramante in the duel on the island of Lipadusa or Lampedusa (XLII 7-9). Ruggiero converts to Christianity in canto XLVI and marries a Christian lady, Bradamante (canto XLVI), becoming the founder of the Este dynasty.

Orlando furioso also contains a plethora of other characters whose stories are intertwined with these principal plotlines. Apart from Angelica, Agramante and Ruggiero, the most prominent Saracens are: Atlante, Gradasso, Cloridano, Doralice, Ferraù, Fiordespina, Isabella, Lucina, Mandricardo, Marfisa, Marsilio, Martano, Medoro, Norandino, Orrigille, Rodomonte, Sacripante and Sobrino. While most of these characters were invented by Boiardo, the characters of Marsilio, Ferraù and Sobrino feature in both Boiardo's poem and the preceding chivalric tradition, and Cloridano, Medoro, Martano and Isabella are Ariosto's creations. The sheer number of Ariosto's infidels is testament to the fact that they are an important part of the universe of *Orlando furioso*. With the exception of the promiscuous Orrigille and the cowardly Martano (who betray Orrigille's Christian lover Grifone in canto XVII), none of the above-mentioned characters is depicted as evil, even if some of them occasionally violate the chivalric code.

Agramante is not as strong as his best champions, but is equal to them in courage. He is the son of King Troiano, one of the main heroes of the Italian versions of the 12th-century *Chanson d'Aspremont*. In the *Inamoramento de Orlando* Agramante wages war on Charlemagne in order to emulate Alexander the Great, his ancestor. By contrast, in *Orlando furioso* his main reason for sailing to France is to avenge the death of his father (I 1). Although he commits a number of unseemly acts (the greatest stain on his reputation is the fact that in canto XXXIX he breaks his oath and interrupts the one-to-one duel that was supposed to decide the outcome of the war), he believes in the chivalric code. Having suffered a crushing defeat, he refuses to convert to Christianity (the only realistic way to regain his lost kingdom) and chooses to fight with the invincible Orlando rather than lose his honour (XLI 36-45).

Marsilio (Marsile in French literature), king of Spain, appears in a large number of poems and prose narratives of the Carolingian cycle, including the *Chanson de Roland*. In both Boiardo's *Inamoramento de Orlando* and Ariosto's *Orlando furioso* he is Agramante's ally in the war against Charlemagne. Whereas Boiardo pokes fun at him, presenting him as a weak old man prone to fits of despair, in Ariosto he becomes a more dignified figure. Endowed with prudence, he is similar to Sobrino, the grey-haired king of Algocco who is the wisest man in the African army (Sobrino or Sobrin features in the 12th-century *Chanson d'Aspremont* and its Italian versions, where he faithfully serves King Agolante, Agramante's grandfather). However, if Sobrino is totally devoted to Agramante, Marsilio puts the interests of Spain above those of Africa (as is evident from the speech he delivers during the military encounter in XXXVIII 41-48). Fearing the wrath of the Saracen gods, Marsilio abandons his African ally when the latter breaks an oath sworn on the Qur'an (XXXIX 17, 66, 74). Sobrino follows Agramante to Africa after the Saracens' crushing defeat and fights by his side in the duel of Lipadusa. After Agramante's death he converts to Christianity (XLIII 192-94) and enters Charlemagne's service.

Gradasso, Ferraù, Mandricardo, Marfisa, Rodomonte, Ruggiero and Sacripante are portrayed as superb warriors and worthy opponents for the most celebrated Christian knights, such as Orlando and Rinaldo. These characters also distinguish themselves in various romance adventures. Gradasso, king of Sericana, has come to France to obtain Orlando's sword Durindana and Rinaldo's horse Baiardo. When he gets hold of both, he decides to return home, despite the fact that Agramante is in a desperate situation (XXXIII 94-95). Later, however, a storm drives his ship to an island, where he finds Agramante. He offers his services to his old friend (XL 46-52) and fights valiantly in the duel of Lipadusa (XL-XLI). He is slain by Orlando (XLII 9-11).

Like Gradasso, Mandricardo, emperor of Tartary, dreams of obtaining Durindana. His dream is fulfilled when Orlando goes mad and scatters his armour in the forest (XXIV 58-70). However, his happiness is short-lived, as he is killed soon after by Ruggiero with whom he fights over the right to the Trojan eagle (XXX 47-68). Mandricardo is both a fighter and a lover: in the latter capacity, he abducts Rodomonte's bride Doralice and then succeeds in winning her heart (XIV 39-64). Similarly, both Ferraù, Marsilio's nephew, and Sacripante, king of Circassia, are in love. The object of their affections is Angelica, whom they relentlessly pursue. However, Ferraù's amorous passion does not prevent him from embarking on another quest, that for Orlando's helmet (I 23-31). Both Ferraù and Sacripante remain alive at the end of *Orlando furioso*: the former presumably follows Marsilio back to Spain; the latter decides to return to the Orient, hoping to find his beloved.

Rodomonte and Ruggiero are the best African knights. One of the most interesting characters, Rodomonte, king of Sarza, performs miracles of prowess in the battle of Paris (XIV 108-34; XV 3-5; XVI 19-27; 85-89; XVII 6-16), dominating the main battle of the poem. However, while admiring his courage, Ariosto upbraids him for his recklessness, as his actions lead to the death of his soldiers. Rodomonte leaves the Saracen camp when

Doralice chooses Mandricardo over him and Agramante forces him to accept her decision (XXVII 102-11). Having withdrawn from the war, he intends to wait until his king is defeated and then help him to re-conquer his kingdom. In the final canto, he travels to Paris and accuses Ruggiero of betraying Agramante. Ruggiero kills him at the end of a dramatic duel and the poem ends with the image of his soul fleeing to the shores of Acheron (XLVI 140).

Ruggiero and his twin sister Marfisa are among the very few Saracen characters who convert to Christianity. Born to a Christian father and a Saracen mother, they were adopted by the Saracen magician Atlante after their mother's death. Still a child, Marfisa was stolen by an Arab tribe. She grew up into a formidable warrior. She takes part in the war against Charlemagne in order to increase her personal fame, but decides to change sides as soon as she learns that her father was a Christian and that Agramante's uncle and father were responsible for his death (XXXVI 59-78). Unlike his sister, Ruggiero continues to serve Agramante even after this revelation, as it was Agramante (his cousin) who dubbed him a knight. He is very attached to his Saracen identity and Agramante is extremely fond of him, not least because of the prophecy according to which Ruggiero will enable him to defeat Charlemagne. Ruggiero, however, is destined to convert to Christianity: he turns to Christ during a storm, fearing that otherwise he might perish in the tempestuous sea (XLI 19-22; 46-60). He will die seven years after his spiritual awakening (XLI 61). In the first half of the narration, his foster father Atlante tries to protect him from his destiny by luring him and other characters into various traps. As a result, Ruggiero participates in numerous romance adventures.

As far as the remaining Saracen characters are concerned, Cloridano and Medoro are two ordinary soldiers who are devoted to each other and to their lord Dardinello. They risk their lives trying to retrieve Dardinello's body from the battlefield (XVIII 165-92; XIX 1-16). While Cloridano dies during their nocturnal sally, the wounded Medoro is found by Angelica, who falls in love with him and becomes his wife (XIX 17-36), an event that triggers Orlando's madness. The fact that Angelica, an archetypal femme fatale, prefers an obscure Saracen soldier to the best Christian knight is all the more striking considering that in the chivalric tradition (though not in Boiardo) Saracen damsels tend to have a soft spot for Christian men, deeming them to be superior to Saracen men. In this respect, Fiordispina's and Isabella's stories are more conventional: both of them bestow their affections upon Christian knights. Marsilio's daughter Fiordispina has a secret affair with Bradamante's twin brother Ricciardetto (XXV 27-70). Isabella, the daughter of the king of Galizia, runs away in order to marry her Christian sweetheart Zerbino. She is captured by brigands, but Orlando rescues her (XII 91-94; XIII 1-44) and the two lovers are reunited (XXIII 54-69). However, their story has a tragic ending. Zerbino fights with Mandricardo and dies from his wounds (XXIV 58-85). Desperate to save her honour, Isabella tricks Rodomonte into beheading her so that he could not rape her (XXVIII 95-102; XXIX 8-27). Although Isabella is still a Saracen at the moment of her death (inasmuch as she has not been baptised), her sacrifice does not go unnoticed by the Christian God, who decrees that her name be given only to exceptional women (XXIX 28-30).

Like Isabella and Zerbino, Norandino, King of Damascus, and his wife Lucina, are bound together by love that can withstand anything. It is put to the test when a cannibalistic ogre captures Lucina. Although Norandino knows that the monster will not harm her, he refuses to abandon her. He devises an escape plan and when it goes wrong he hides in a flock of sheep in order to be close to her, placing his life in mortal peril. After four months, Lucina is rescued by Gradasso and Mandricardo (XVII 25-69). Norandino is not only a faithful lover, but he is also a noble and magnanimous ruler, even if Ariosto criticises him for his failure to let Grifone defend himself when the latter is slandered by Orrigille and Martano (XVIII 1-3). Damascus is described as a flourishing city lying in a fertile and picturesque plain (XVIII 18-22). Its inhabitants are courteous and hospitable, and magnificent jousts are held every four months. The Syrians wear armour after the European fashion because of Damascus' geographical proximity to Jerusalem, a Christian city (XVII 73). This historical anachronism (Jerusalem would be conquered by the Christians much later, during the First Crusade, and even then the Syrians would not adapt the Western style of armour) prompts Ariosto to deliver a passionate speech, urging Christian princes to stop fighting each other and launch a crusade against the Turks (XVII 73-79).

The tone of this authorial digression jars with the fairytale-like atmosphere of the cantos set in the Middle East (XV, XVII, XVIII). Ariosto describes Saracen cities without a shadow of hostility. It is in a neutral, matter-of-fact tone that he mentions the 15,000 former Christians (the Mamluks) who live in Cairo and serve the sultan (XV 64). However, there are tensions between the Ethiopians, who are ruled by the Christian emperor Senapo, the legendary Prester John ('Prete Ianni'), and their

Saracen neighbours (XXXIII 101). Miraculously cured of his blindness, Senapo helps Charlemagne's knights to conquer Biserta (XXXVIII 26-28; XL 16-19).

Like most medieval and Renaissance chivalric poems, *Orlando furioso* does not offer a realistic depiction of Islam and Islamic culture. In line with the chivalric tradition, Ariosto portrays Saracens as polytheists worshipping Macone and Trivigante (XII 59; XXXVIII 18). However, it seems that his Saracen characters also believe in a Supreme Being, an all-powerful God who controls everything in the universe (see, for example, XLI 44). Moreover, like real Muslims, they are not allowed to drink wine (XXIX 22). In addition, Ariosto mentions circumcision (XLII 5). These occasional references to Islamic culture suggest that the poet had at least some knowledge of it. It is intriguing that the novella of Giocondo, Astolfo and Fiammetta (a salacious story told by the innkeeper to Rodomonte in XXVIII 1-85) appears to mimic the frame story of *The thousand and one nights*. Although the first known European translation of the *Nights* was produced in the 18th century, it is possible that Ariosto knew the Arabic tale, probably through his friend Gian Francesco Valier (or Valerio), a famous Venetian diplomat and adventurer.

SIGNIFICANCE

There has been much debate surrounding the nature and meaning of *Orlando furioso*. While many scholars believe that it is a secular poem, others read it as a Christian epic (Andrew Fichter), or as a text that engages with various philosophical and theological doctrines (Peter Marinelli, Franco Picchio). For a number of influential critics (Francesco de Sanctis, Benedetto Croce) Ariosto's art is escapist. By contrast, more recent scholarship has suggested that, firmly anchored in contemporary reality, the poem possesses a political dimension and relevance.

Considering that *Orlando furioso* as a whole has given rise to a variety of interpretations, it is not surprising that studies focusing specifically on Ariosto's portrayal of Saracens and Islam have reached contradictory conclusions. It has been argued that the poem 'reveal[s] no prejudice based on a sense of the superiority of western culture over oriental civilization' (Donnelly, 'The Moslem enemy in Renaissance epic', p. 163) and that for Ariosto 'Virtue, heroic valor, wisdom, loyalty, God, are not exclusively Christian, just as bestiality, madness, betrayal, evil, or Satan are not exclusively Pagan' (Cuccaro, 'Cristianitade, pagania, cavalleria', p. 146). Angelo Pagliardini (who has recently published a series of articles on the Saracen Other in Pulci, Boiardo and Ariosto) maintains that the ideology underpinning *Orlando furioso* is the chivalric code, an ideology that knows no religious or racial boundaries. Gian Paolo Giudicetti (*Mandricardo e malinconia*; 'Mandricardo a cavallo'; 'I vinti dell'*Orlando furioso*') asserts that it is Mandricardo and Rodomonte – adventure seekers eager to explore what life has to offer – who embody the spirit of the poem, while Marco Dorigatti ('Sobrino') underscores the fact that Sobrino is one of the very few characters endowed with prudence, a rare and precious virtue in the folly-ridden universe of the poem.

Many other critics, however, claim that Ariosto sets up a binary opposition between Christians and Saracens. According to Roger Baillet ('L'occidentalisme'), the poet highlights the cultural differences between the East and the West, representing the Christian warriors as civilised and courteous and their Saracen opponents as bestial and treacherous. Similarly, in her recently published monograph on the non-Christian world in *Orlando innamorato* and *Orlando furioso* (*The world beyond Europe*), Jo Ann Cavallo argues that Ariosto's Saracens often violate the chivalric code. One of the principal contentions of Cavallo's study is that Ariosto is more conservative than his Ferrarese predecessor (who, Cavallo argues, breaks away from the preceding Carolingian tradition by showing a keen interest in non-Christian lands and portraying Saracens in a strikingly tolerant manner). Moreover, most critics who have analysed the figure of Rodomonte (a hero who has received the lion's share of attention) maintain that he is depicted as a bloodthirsty barbarian.

Not surprisingly, there is no unanimity of opinion as to whether Ariosto was influenced by contemporary perceptions of Muslims in general and the Turks in particular. Most scholars who believe that Ariosto does not distinguish between Christians and Saracens tend to avoid this question. By contrast, those who take the opposite view often attempt to read the poem in light of the Turkish menace. Thus, for Baillet ('L'occidentalisme') and Giovanni Ricci ('Cavalleria e crociata'), *Orlando furioso* reflects European antagonism towards the Turks (rekindled by the Fall of Constantinople in 1453), while Cavallo suggests that the defeat of the Saracens is 'a wish-fulfilment fantasy not simply of western Europe triumphing over Ottoman aggressors but of Italy over European invaders, and of Ferrara over neighbouring enemies on the peninsula' (*The world beyond Europe*, p. 207). Moreover, a number of studies devoted to Ariosto's treatment of the theme of war contend that the conflict between Agramante and Charlemagne could have been inspired by the contemporary wars between Christian states, with the Saracens standing for the foreign aggressors (the French and the Spanish) who had transformed Italy into a battleground.

The fact that modern scholarship is divided over the extent to which Ariosto's portrayal of the Saracen Other is positive and 'progressive' testifies to the complexity of the poem. While *Orlando furioso* ends with the victory of the Christians and hence the triumph of the Christian religion, it cannot be denied that Ariosto's voice is tinged with irony when he describes the favours that the Christian God showers on his faithful. Whereas it is true that many Saracen characters transgress the chivalric code at least once, it is equally true that many Christian characters fail to live up to the chivalric ideal.

It is also worth pointing out that early critics did not demonise Ariosto's Saracens. In the moral allegories appended to 16th-century editions of *Orlando furioso*, Saracen characters are often praised for their noble conduct. What is even more interesting is that some of Ariosto's early readers believed that the poem had the potential to become a bestseller in the Arab world and in the Ottoman Empire (see Pigna, *I romanzi*, p. 73). Late 16th-century critics mention an Arabic translation of *Orlando furioso* (see Camillo Pellegrini's *Il Caraffa, o vero della poesia epica*, 1584; *Degli Accademici della Crusca difesa dell'Orlando furioso dell'Ariosto*, 1585; Niccolò degli Oddi, *Dialogo in difesa di Camillo Pellegrini*, 1587). While it is highly unlikely that the poem was read outside Europe (by all appearances, it has yet to be translated into Arabic), the fact that Ariosto's Christian readers thought that *Orlando furioso* could appeal to Muslims means that they themselves did not consider it to be a piece of crusade propaganda.

Orlando furioso has proved to be an immensely influential work, a source of inspiration for many artists, musicians and writers. Its Saracen characters feature in paintings by Dosso Dossi, Simone Peterzano, Giovanni Lanfranco, Giovanni Battista Tiepolo, Jean-Auguste-Dominique Ingres and Odilon Redon, and operas by Francesca Caccini, Luigi Rossi, Antonio Vivaldi, George Frideric Handel, Jean-Baptiste Lully, Niccolò Piccinni and Joseph Haydn. Jorge Luis Borges expresses his fascination with Ariosto's Saracen Other in *Ariosto y los árabes* (a poem from *El hacedor*, a collection published in 1960), while Salman Rushdie makes numerous allusions to *Orlando furioso* in *The enchantress of Florence* (2008), a historical novel set in Renaissance Florence and the Mughal Empire, whose main heroine Qara Köz is modelled on Ariosto's Angelica.

EDITIONS & TRANSLATIONS

There have been numerous editions in Italian, of which the most recent and the earliest are:

    E. Bigi and C. Zampese (eds), *Orlando furioso*, Milan, 2012

    M. Dorigatti (ed.) with G. Stimato, *Orlando furioso secondo la princeps del 1516*, Florence, 2006 (edition of the 1516 version)

    E. Bigi (ed.), *Orlando furioso*, Milan, 1982

    L. Caretti (ed.), *Orlando furioso*, Turin, 1966, 2005³

    C. Segre (ed.), *Orlando furioso*, Milan, 1964

    S. Debenedetti and C. Segre (ed.), *Orlando furioso secondo l'edizione del 1532: con le varianti delle edizioni del 1516 e del 1521*, Bologna, 1960

    Orlando furioso, Lyons: Mathias Bonhomme, 1550

    Orlando furioso, con molte espositioni illustrato, Florence: Benedetto Giunta, 1544 (illustrated by P. Ulivi)

    Orlando furioso, Venetia: Gabriel Giolito, 1543

    Orlando furioso, Ferrara, 1532 (46 cantos)

    Orlando furioso, Ferrara, 1516, 1521² (40 cantos)

Translations of *Orlando furioso* have been made into many languages:

Editions in English include:

    D. Slavitt, *Orlando furioso. A new verse translation*, Cambridge MA, 2009 (repr. 2011)

    B. Reynolds, *The frenzy of Orlando. A romantic epic*, 2 vols, Harmondsworth, 1975

    G. Waldman, *Orlando furioso*, Oxford, 1974 (repr. 1983, 2008)

    A.H. Gilbert, *Orlando furioso. An English translation with introduction, notes, and index*, 2 vols, New York, 1954

    J. Harington, *Orlando furioso in English heroical verse*, London, 1591

Recent editions in other languages:

    French: M. Orcel, *Roland furieux*, Paris, 2000 (bilingual edition, with introduction by I. Calvino)

    A. Rochon, *Roland furieux*, Paris, 1998

    German: J.D. Gries (trans.), *Der rasende Roland*, ed. S. Eversmann, Munich, 1980

    Japanese: I. Waki, *Kurueru orurando*, Nagoya, 2001

    Polish: P. Kochanowski (trans.), *Orland szalony*, ed. R. Pollak, Wrocław, 1965 (includes portraits and facsimiles)

Russian: M.L. Gasparov (trans.), *Neistovyĭ Roland*, ed. M.L. Andreev et al., Moscow, 1993

Spanish: *Orlando furioso*, ed. C. Segre and M.N. Muñiz Muñiz, trans. J. de Urrea, Madrid, 2002 (bilingual edition)

STUDIES

There are countless studies of *Orlando furioso*. Most of the following scholarly works focus on or touch upon the representation of Saracens in the poem:

M. Pavlova, 'Rodomonte e Ruggiero. Una questione d'onore', *Rassegna Europea di Letteratura Italiana* 41 (2013 forthcoming)

J-A. Cavallo, *The world beyond Europe in the romance epics of Boiardo and Ariosto*, Toronto, 2013

J-A. Cavallo, 'Crocodiles and crusades. Egypt in Boiardo's *Orlando innamorato* and Ariosto's *Orlando furioso*', *Arthuriana* 21 (2011) 85-96

C. Montagnani, 'Lontano da sé. I cavalieri in Paganìa', *Rassegna Europea di Letteratura Italiana* 38 (2011) 61-71

E. Spiller, 'The conversion of the reader. Ariosto, Herberay, Munday, and Cervantes', in *Reading and the history of race in the Renaissance*, New York, 2011, 112-52

M. Dorigatti, 'Sobrino ariostesco e misconosciuto', *Belfagor* 65 (2010) 401-14

G.P. Giudicetti, *Mandricardo e malinconia. Discorsi diretti e sproloqui nell'"Orlando furioso"*, Brussels, 2010

G. Ricci, 'Cavalleria e crociata nella Ferrara del Rinascimento. Un piccolo stato davanti a un grande impero', in F. Meier (ed.), *Italien und das Osmanische Reich*, Herne, 2010, 75-86

G.P. Giudicetti, 'Mandricardo a cavallo di due poemi. Il suo ruolo nel terzo libro dell'*Inamoramento de Orlando* e nell'*Orlando furioso*', *Schifanoia* 36-37 (2009) 103-44

C. Anton, 'Un principe o un tiranno? Il capo saraceno nell'*Orlando furioso*', in Y. Catelly et al. (eds), *Limbă, cultură şi civilizaţie la începutul mileniului al treilea*, Bucharest, 2008, 26-32

E. Borelli, 'Le héros de l'Occident et la femme de l'Orient. Dans le laboratoire de la réécriture ariostesque', in G.P. Giudicetti (ed.), *L'Arioste. Discours des personnages, sources et influences*, Louvain-la-Neuve, 2008, 43-54

M. Dorigatti, 'Sobrino. Sagesse et éloquence d'un conseiller sarrasin', in G.P. Giudicetti, *L'Arioste*, 77-89

F. Strologo, 'Duels, discours et péripéties de l'ex-géant Ferraù dans l'*Orlando furioso*', *Lettres Romanes* (2008) 27-41

G.P. Giudicetti, 'I vinti dell'*Orlando furioso*. Rodomonte e Mandricardo nella struttura del poema', *Studi e Problemi di Critica Testuale* 76 (2008) 73-101

A. Pagliardini, 'Cristiani e pagani nell'epica cavalleresca italiana', *Carte di Viaggio* 1 (2008) 35-58

F. Picchio, *Ariosto e Bacco. Due Apocalisse e nuova religione nel 'Furioso'*, Cosenza, 2007

E. Ragni, 'Rodomonte e Gradasso. Storia incroiata di due "ruganti"', *Letteratura Italiana Antica* 8 (2007) 399-413

P. Casella, 'Il funzionamento dei personaggi secondari nell'*Orlando furioso*. Le vicissitudine di Sacripante', *Italianistica* 35 (2006) 11-26

A. Pagliardini and G. Fuchs, 'La rappresentazione del pagano/musulmano nell'epica cavalleresca rinascimentale (*Orlando innamorato, Morgante, Orlando furioso*)', in B. Van den Bossche et al. (eds), *Italia e Europa. Dalla cultura nazionale all'interculturalismo*, Rome, 2006, ii, 579-87

T. Gregory, 'Providence, irony and magic: Orlando furioso', in Gregory, *From many gods to one. Divine action in Renaissance epic*, Chicago, 2006, 102-139, pp. 126-33

A. Pagliardini and G. Fuchs, 'Raumkonzepte und Fremdbilder im Zusammenspiel. Zur Darstellungsweise des "Sarazenen" in Texten der italienischen Renaissance-Ritterepik', in B. Burtscher-Bechter et al. (eds), *Grenzen und Entgrenzungen*, Würzburg, 2006, 173-209

A. Pagliardini, 'Procedimenti di denominazione lessicale e onomastica del pagano/musulmano nell'epica cavalleresca del Rinascimento', in E. Cresti (ed.), *Prospettive nello studio del lessico italiano*, Florence, 2006, i, 229-33

R. Bruscagli, 'Medoro riconosciuto', in *Studi cavallereschi*, Florence, 2003, 75-101

J.-A. Cavallo, 'The pathways of knowledge in Boiardo and Ariosto. The case of Rodamonte', *Italica* 79 (2002) 303-20

L. Benedetti, 'I paradossi dell'amore. Atlante e Ruggiero dall'*Innamorato* al *Furioso*', *Quaderni d'Italianistica* 21 (2000) 113-26

F. Picchio, *Ariosto e Bacco. I codici del sacro nell'"Orlando furioso"*, Turin, 1999

M. Spampinato Beretta, 'La cornice delle Mille e una notte ed il canto XXVIII dell'*Orlando furioso*', in A. Pioletto et al. (eds), *Medioevo romanzo e orientale*, Soveria Mannelli, 1999, 229-49

G. Tocchini, 'Ancora sull'Ariosto e Alberti. Il naufragio di Ruggiero', *Studi Italiani* 19 (1998) 5-34

G.B. Pigna, *I romanzi*, ed. S. Ritrovato, Bologna, 1997

N. Lazzaro, 'Rodomonte e Ariosto nella battaglia di Parigi. Lettura dell'episodio', in D.J. Dutschke et al. (eds), *Forma e parola. Studi in memoria di Fredi Chiappelli*, Rome, 1992, 235-54

M. Santoro, *Ariosto e il Rinascimento*, Naples, 1989 (see 'L'Angelica del Furioso. Fuga della storia', 111-33; 'Rodomonte. La defezione della "ragione"', 263-74)

P. Marinelli, *Ariosto and Boiardo. The origins of Orlando furioso*, Columbia MO, 1987

P. DeSa Wiggins, 'Rodomonte', in *Figures in Ariosto's tapestry. Character and design in the 'Orlando Furioso'*, Baltimore MD, 1986, 41-66 (see also the chapters on Ruggiero, Angelica and Marfisa)

P. DeSa Wiggins, 'The *Furioso*'s third protagonist', *Modern Language Notes* 98 (1983) 30-54

D. Robinson Egoibe, 'The depiction of the Negro African in the *Orlando Furioso*', in 'The depiction of the Negro African in three old French chansons de geste and two Renaissance epico-chivalric poems', Bloomington IN, 1983 (Diss. Indiana University), 210-331

A. Fichter, 'Ariosto. The dynastic pair, Bradamante and Ruggiero', in A. Fichter, *Poets historical. Dynastic epic in the Renaissance*, New Haven CT, 1982, 70-111

P. Baldan, 'Marfisa. Nascita e carriera di una regina amazzone', *Giornale Storico della Letteratura Italiana* 158 (1981) 518-29

V. Cuccaro, 'Cristianitade, pagania, cavalleria', in V. Cuccaro, *The humanism of Ludovico Ariosto. From the 'Satire' to the 'Furioso'*, Ravenna, 1981, 145-58

R. Baillet, 'L'occidentalisme', in *Le monde poétique de l'Arioste*, Lyon, 1977, 385-424

J.P. Donnelly, 'The Moslem enemy in Renaissance epic. Ariosto, Tasso and Camoëns', *Yale Italian Studies* 1 (1977) 162-70

D. Delcorno Branca, *L"Orlando furioso' e il romanzo cavalleresco medievale*, Florence, 1973

F. Pool, 'Rodomonte', in *Interpretazione dell' 'Orlando furioso'*, Florence, 1968, 193-205

G. Reichenbach, 'L'eroe mal fortunato. Sacripante', *Memorie dell'Accademia Patavina di Scienze Lettere Arti* 75 (1962-3) 159-74

G. Levi della Vida, 'Fonti arabi dell'Isabella ariostesca', in *Anedotti e svaghi arabi e non arabi*, Milan, 1959, 170-90

E. Zanette, *Conversazioni sull' 'Orlando furioso'*, Pisa, 1959 (see 'Due Mori', 184-209; 'Cerco il vincitore', 332-48; 'Rodomonte', 349-95)

F. de Sanctis, 'L'*Orlando furioso*', in M. Petrini (ed.), *La poesia cavalleresca*, Bari, 1954, 88-169

G. Ravegnani, 'Vita, morte e miracolo di Rodomonte', in G. Ravegnani, *Dieci saggi dal Petrarca al Manzoni*, Genoa, 1937, 37-72

G. Fumagalli, 'La "bella istoria" di Rodomonte di Sarza', in G. Fumagalli, *Unità fantastica dell' 'Orlando Furioso'*, Messina, 1933, 68-117

E. Cerulli, 'Il volo di Astolfo sull' Etiopia nell'*Orlando furioso*', *Rendiconti della R. Accademia Nazionale dei Lincei* 8 (1932) 19-38

A. Momigliano, 'Rodomonte', in A. Momigliano, *Saggio su l'Orlando furioso*, Laterza, 1928, 279-307

B. Croce, *Ariosto, Shakespeare and Corneille*, London, 1920

Maria Pavlova

Paulo Giovio

Paulus Iovius, Paulo Jovio

DATE OF BIRTH 21 April 1483 or 1486
PLACE OF BIRTH Como, Italy
DATE OF DEATH 11 December 1552
PLACE OF DEATH Florence

BIOGRAPHY

Paolo Giovio was born in Como. There is uncertainty about the exact date of his birth, the date on his supposed grave being 21 April 1483, while he himself gives 1486. His family belonged to the local aristocracy; his father, Luigi, was a notary, and was married to Elisabetta Benzi. Paolo later changed his original surname, Zobio, to the Latin version, Iovius. His family's financial situation was precarious, especially after his father's death in about 1500.

Giovio probably began his studies in Milan in 1504, when he attended courses on Greek language and literature. The following year, he moved to Pavia with the aim of deepening his knowledge of philosophy and medical science. His interest in anatomy was strengthened by his stay at Pavia University. In 1511, Giovio obtained his degree in medical science and philosophy from the University of Pavia.

Soon after, Giovio embarked on a career as a doctor in Rome. In the Eternal City, his literary ambitions found rich soil, and he was appointed professor at the Roman University, which had recently been reformed by Pope Leo X. Giovio put extensive trust in the Medici pontiff, whom he considered the 'defender of Italian freedom' against the interference of foreign rulers.

During the papacy of Leo X, Giovio began writing *Historiae*, considered his most important work, in which he aims to analyse the reasons for the conflict that gripped the Peninsula after the fall of Charles VIII of Valois.

This monumental work had an international outlook that prompted the author towards a further study, one on society in the Islamic world, arising from the success of the Ottomans. Giovio was aware of the first indications of the threat that in the 16th century would become a major problem for the Christian world.

In 1517, Giovio entered the service of Giulio de' Medici, the future Clement VII, with whom he travelled to Florence for the first time. During this period, Giovio analysed the important transformations of his age: the rise of Charles V of Habsburg, the triumph of Süleyman the Magnificent, and the discovery of the New World.

Ottoman expansionism convinced Giovio that he should support the imperial efforts and he did in fact see Charles V as the protector of Christianity, in that he was the only person with the resources to protect Europe from the Turkish advance. His leaning towards the Habsburgs implied an opposition to French demands.

In 1527, Giovio was appointed bishop of Nocera dei Pagani as a reward for his loyalty to the pope.

His growing reputation as a respected member of the *literati* notwithstanding, Giovio left the Roman court in protest against the pope's conciliatory approach towards Francis I. He went to Ischia, where he was in contact with the literary circle of Vittoria Colonna. During the final years of Clement VII's papacy, he entered the entourage of Ippolito de' Medici, the pope's nephew. During this period, he was witness to Charles V's military campaign against the Ottomans in the Kingdom of Hungary.

After the death of Clement VII, Giovio found a new patron in Cardinal Alessandro Farnese, nephew of the new pope, Paul III, to whom he proposed a plan for peace in Europe: an alliance between the pope and the emperor against the French, a crusade against the Ottomans and a military campaign against the Protestants.

The resoluteness displayed by Paul III, and Charles V's triumph in Tunis in 1535 impelled Giovio to return to his draft of *Historiae*, which he had put aside after the Sack of Rome in 1527. Being in favour of reforms that would address the most evident abuses of the church, he initially supported Luther's requests, though he ultimately grew aware of the vast gulf between the Lutheran and Roman positions, which would make any kind of agreement impossible.

Giovio thought the purpose of the Council of Trent misguided because it appeared to consolidate schism, and he refused to attend. His relationships with the main supporters of imperial politics, in particular Ferrante Gonzaga, resulted in an irreparable breach in his relationship with Paul III.

During his final period in Rome, Giovio personally met Mulay Ḥasan, the overthrown Emir of Tunis, who was living in exile in the Italian Peninsula. This encounter was useful to Giovio, as their conversations enabled him to clarify several of his doubts about Maghreb culture.

In autumn 1550, Giovio moved to Florence where, surrounded by members of the Medici court, he finished his main work, *Sui temporis historiarum libri*, which was purposely dedicated to Cosimo I de' Medici. Printing was completed in September 1552. Giovio died in Florence in the night of 11-12 December 1552, and was buried in the church of San Lorenzo.

MAIN SOURCES OF INFORMATION

Primary
Works by Paolo Giovio with reference to Muslims:
Pauli Iovii Novocomensis Libellus de legatione Basilii Magni Principis Moschoviae, Roma: in aedibus F. Minitii Calvi, 1525
Legatio David Aethiopiae Regis, ad sanctissimum D. N. Clementem Papam VII una cum oboedientia eidem sanctissimo D. N. praestita. Eiusdem David Aethiopiae Regis legatio ad Emanuelem Portugalliae regem de regno Aethiopiae ac populo, deque moribus eiusque populi nonnula, Bononiae: apud Iacobum Kemolen Alostensem, 1533
Pauli Iovii Novocomensis Episcopi Nucerini Historiarum sui temporis tomus primus, Florentia: in officina Laurentii Torrentini, 1550
Pauli Iovii Novocomensis Episcopi Nucerini Historiarum sui temporis tomus secundus, Florentia: in officina Laurentii Torrentini, 1552

Secondary
There are a great many studies on Paolo Giovio. Among the most important are:
L. Michelacci, *Giovio in Parnaso. Tra collezione di forme e storia universale*, Bologna, 2004
F. Minonzio, *Studi gioviani*, Como, 2002-6
T.C.P. Zimmermann, art. 'Paolo Giovio', in *Dizionario biografico degli Italiani*, Rome, 2001, 430-40
L. Michelacci, 'Una forma della retorica di guerra. Le "cose turchesche" e Paolo Giovio', *Schede Umanistiche* 1 (2001) 49-72
Y.M. Bercé, *L'identification des héros de l'histoire selon Giovio*, in J. Balsamo (ed.), *Passer les monts. Français en Italie – l'Italie en France (1494-1525)*, Paris, 1998, 14-22
T.C.P. Zimmermann, *Paolo Giovio. The historian and the crisis of sixteenth-century Italy*, Princeton NJ, 1995
G. Le Thiec, 'L'entrée des Grands Turcs dans le "Museo" de Paolo Giovio', *Mélanges de l'École Française de Rome* 104 (1992) 781-830
L.S. Klinger and J. Raby, *Barbarossa and Sinan. A portrait of two Ottoman corsairs from the collection of Paolo Giovio*, in E.J. Grube (ed.), *Venezia e l'Oriente vicino*, Venice, 1989, 47-59

T.C.P. Zimmermann, 'La presunta data di nascita di Paolo Giovio', *Comense* 52 (1986-87) 187-92
P. Burke, 'European views of world history from Giovio to Voltaire', *History of European Ideas* 6 (1985) 237-51
Giovio. Il Rinascimento e la memoria, Como, 1985
K. Duncan-Jones, 'Two Elizabethan versions of Giovio's treatise on Imprese', *English Studies* 52 (1971) 18-123
F. Chabod, 'Paolo Giovio', *Periodico della Società Storica Comense* 38 (1954) 7-30

WORKS ON CHRISTIAN-MUSLIM RELATIONS

Commentario delle cose de' Turchi, 'Commentary on matters of the Turks'

DATE 1532
ORIGINAL LANGUAGE Italian

DESCRIPTION

The *Commentario delle cose de' Turchi* (*A shorte treatise upon the Turkes chronicles* in Peter Ashton's 1546 translation) is a brief discourse that Paolo Giovio began in the 1530s. He had just returned from Bologna, where Pope Clement VII had crowned Charles V of Habsburg Emperor of the Holy Roman Empire. At the same time, fear of the Turkish hordes was already widespread throughout Europe, following the unsuccessful siege of Vienna by the Ottomans in 1529. Therefore, rumours about a crusade against the Ottomans became increasingly persistent in the Old Continent. This work gave Giovio the opportunity to lay out clearly his own position in favour of a military campaign against the sultan.

Giovio dates his introduction as 22 January 1531, although he refers to the siege of Vienna as having taken place the previous year. The work is written in Italian without Tuscan 'ornaments', a straightforward style directly due to the need to present it as a type of *vademecum*, providing remedies and concrete solutions for victory against the Ottomans. It is addressed to Charles V, whom Giovio considered to be the only Christian prince capable of stopping the Turkish advance toward the west.

In the opening pages, Giovio defends the legitimacy of his work. He explains his method of collecting information about the Ottomans, which is to hold direct interviews with princes, diplomats and soldiers about the Ottoman Empire, as a substitute for travelling there in person.

The ultimate purpose of the work was to offer the emperor a study devoid of cliché, providing him with an understanding of the main reasons for Turkish power. Following his dedication, Giovio writes briefly about the origins of the Ottomans, who, in line with the consensus of European tradition, he says descended directly from the Scythians. He mentions in passing the early relationships between the Ottomans and Europeans that dated back to the crusade led by Godfrey of Bouillon to the Holy Land.

The main interest of the work is in Ottoman leaders, and they occupy the major part of the text. Sovereigns are represented as a gallery of images, which is typical of Giovio's narrative. Here the Turk, as sultan, embodies the symbol of Ottoman strength, against which the Christian monarch is unable to make an effective stand.

When describing the lives of the sultans, Giovio adopts an approach that differs from earlier and contemporary writers. Ottoman sultans of previous centuries had often been given legendary profiles, while Giovio refers to precise known events, drawn from his detailed studies of Turkish history.

At the same time, Giovio has varying views about the sultans of his time. The first contemporary sultan is Bayezid II, of whom Giovio has a relatively negative opinion. His authority is considered as deriving more from fortune that from any inherent skill: the untimely death of his brother Mustafa, Cem's escape to Europe, domestic infighting among his sons. Furthermore, Bayezid is remembered as being responsible for the greatest defeat ever experienced by the Ottomans: the campaign he ordered against the Mamluks.

Selim I embodies the precise attributes of a Muslim monarch according to the criteria most prevalent in 16th-century Europe. His accession to the throne resulted from the violent death of his father, which he appeared to instigate, and he is unjust, cruel and power-hungry. However, Giovio never denies Selim's military ability and courage, and refers to him as 'lion heart'.

The final biography is devoted to Süleyman the Magnificent, whom Giovio compares with Charles V, as they both succeeded in the same year. Comparison between the two monarchs is a sort of leitmotif involving the figure of Süleyman. First, Giovio mentions the misguided expectations of Christians concerning the young Süleyman, who, although the only son of Selim I, initially appeared to be completely different from his father, which resulted in his being compared to a lamb. However, his numerous triumphs forced Christian commentators quickly to transform their perception of him. In addition to the sultan's most important victories, Giovio also mentions his main collaborators, such as Ibrahim Pasha.

Finally, Giovio highlights Süleyman's financial resources, which were without compare among European rulers and made his army the most dreaded of his time. Giovio's assessment of Süleyman is well balanced, and the comparison between him and Charles V presents the sultan as one of the greatest of oriental rulers. Although Süleyman is not represented as exempt from the debauchery that was seen as typical of Muslims, the contrast between him and the emperor presents Süleyman as the ideal alter-ego of the most important of European princes.

The final part of the work focuses on the structure and constitution of the Ottoman army, the tool with which the Ottomans imposed their authority all the way into the heart of Europe. Giovio gives three main reasons for Ottoman military superiority over previous decades: the soldiers obey only the sultan, unlike in Christian Europe, where the aristocracy maintain prerogatives and privileges over the soldiers; Janissaries believe in a form of predestination, meaning that they do not fear battle; the food of the Ottoman ranks is more frugal, so members of the army are more resistant to the difficulties encountered in military campaigns. This final consideration highlights Giovio's medical background.

SIGNIFICANCE

In this work, Giovio looks for Charles V's victory against the sultan, while he is at the same time aware of European misconceptions about the Ottoman world. His aim, therefore, is to offer a reconstruction of Turkish history, free from the received stereotypes about the infidel enemy.

It is no coincidence that opinions of the book drew criticisms from contemporaries, to the point where the *conquistador* Gonzalo Jiménez de Queseda would accuse Giovio of being *aficionado a la nacion turquesca* ('an enthusiast of the Turkish nation').

Unlike his contemporaries, Giovio bases his analysis on the military aspects of the Ottoman Empire. Leaving aside the implicit bias of 16th-century works about Muslims, he highlights the enemy's good qualities rather than their shortcomings, since the basic aim of the book is to explain why the Ottomans appear unbeatable. Turkish religious and denominational matters are largely ignored; in fact, traditions and customs are only considered when they have consequences for the military organisation and strategies displayed by the Ottomans on the battlefield.

The work enjoyed immediate wide circulation throughout Europe. During the 16th century, it was reprinted several times in Italian, a Latin edition was published in Wittenberg by Francesco Negri, and it was published in French in Anvers and Paris. In the first German edition, the preface was written by Philipp Melanchthon, who had conducted an extended correspondence with Giovio's brother, Benedetto. In the Iberian Peninsula, Vasco Díaz Tanco referred to Giovio's book in his *Palinodia de los Turcos*.

In 1541, the book was included in a collected volume, *Commentarii delle cose de' Turchi*, along with *Gli fatti e la vita di Scanderbeg* by Marino Barlezio, and in 1560 it was included in Francesco Sansovino's edition of *Dell'historia universale dell'origine et imperio dei Turchi*.

Giovio's study is an essential source for any European humanist interested in understanding the reasons for Ottoman power during the Early Modern period.

EDITIONS & TRANSLATIONS

L. Michelacci (ed.), *Commentario de le cose de' Turchi*, Bologna, 2005 (most recent edition)

P. Modesti (trans.), *Türckische Kriegss Ordnung. Dariñ kurtz begriffen der türckischen Sultanen Macht, Bestellung der Kriegssämbter, Regiments Rechte vnd Gewohnheiten: wie auch die Vrsachen, warumb die Türcken den Christen bisshero vnd noch vberlegen. Vnd dann ein Bedencken vnd Rath, wie der Krieg wider diese Feinde anzugreiffen*, Frankfurt, 1595 (German trans.)

H. Pantaleon (trans.), *M. Pavli Iovii Von der Türckischen Keyseren härkommen, aufgang, vnnd Regiment mit sampt allen Historien [...] so sich von irem ersten Keyser Ottomanno, biss [...] zu disen unseren zeyten [...] zugetragen; demnach von der Statt Rom letsten eroberung [...] anno 1527 beschehen; und zu letst von der Moscouiteren art vnd eigenschafft [...]*, Basel, 1564 (German trans.)

A shorte treatise upon the Turkes chronicles, compyled by Paulus Jovius, byshop of Nucenie, and dedicated to Charles V, Emperour. Drawen out of the Italyen tong in to Latyne by Franciscus Niger Bassianates. And translated out of Latyne into Englysh by Peter Ashton, London: Edwarde Whitchurche, 1546 (first English trans.)

Commentario delas [sic] *cosas de los turcos*, Barcelona, 1543 (Spanish trans.)

Commentaire De Paulus Iovius Evesque De Nucere, Des Gestes Des Turcz. A Charles Cinquiesme, Empereur Auguste. Origine de Lempire des Turcz. Les vies de tous les Empereurs des Turcz. Ordre & discipline de la milice & cheualerie Turcique, Paris, 1540 (French trans.)

Vrsprung des turkischen Reichs, bis auff den itzigen Solyman, Wittenberg, 1538 (German trans. from Latin, published with Luther's Latin preface which first appeared in *Libellus de ritu et moribus Turcorum*, 1530 and an introduction by Philip Melancthon)

F. Negri (trans.), *Tvrcicarvm Rervm Commentarius Pauli Iouii Episcopi Nucerini ad Carolum. V. Imperatorem Augustum*, Antwerp, 1538 (Latin trans.)

Commentario de le cose de' Turchi, Roma: Blado, 1532 (available in the Biblioteca Reale, Turin – Sign. L. 10. 17, and the Biblioteca Centrale Nazionale, Rome – 68. 13. B. 28)

STUDIES

S. Schmuck, 'England's experience of Islam', in M. Hattaway (ed.), *A new companion to English Renaissance literature and culture*, Oxford, 2010, 543-56

C. Sodini, 'Il *Commentario delle cose de' Turchi* di Paolo Giovio', in S. Maffei, F. Minonzio and C. Sodini (eds), *Sperimentalismo e dimensione europea della cultura di Paolo Giovio*, Como, 2006, 127-40

Gennaro Varriale

Lodovico Dolce

DATE OF BIRTH 1508 or 1510
PLACE OF BIRTH Venice
DATE OF DEATH January 1568
PLACE OF DEATH Venice

BIOGRAPHY

Lodovico Dolce was one of the most active intellectuals in 16th-century Venice. A prolific humanist author, translator and editor, he is mainly known and remembered for his *Dialogo della pittura* ('Dialogue on painting', 1557). Not much is known about his life. He was born in 1508 or more likely 1510 into an old family that had once, but no longer, enjoyed access to the Great Council. His father died when he was two years old, and he was then entrusted to two patrician families: the Doge Leonardo Loredan (1436-1521), and the Cornaro family, who financed his studies in Padua. After his studies, he returned to Venice, where he worked first as a teacher for children, and then as an editor at the Giolito publishing house, where he remained until his death. He was buried in the Venetian church of S. Luca Evangelista.

Dolce was extremely productive as an editor, translator, commentator and author, probably partly because his poor circumstances forced him to work assiduously to support himself and his family.

In all, he was responsible for 358 works, including 96 works of his own, while, as an editor at the Giolito publishing house, he supervised editions of Dante, Petrarch, Boccaccio, Ariosto, Bembo and Castiglione. He also edited *Le sei giornate* by Sebastiano Erizzo (1567), in which are included three stories with 'Turkish' motifs, and in 1563 he edited a collection of fictional letters from Mehmed II to (primarily) European princes, *Lettere del Gran Mahumeto imperadore de' Turchi scritte a diversi re, prencipi, signori, e repubbliche con le risposte loro* ('Letters from the Great Mehmed, emperor of the Turks, written to various kings, princes, lords, and republics together with their answers'). This work had originally been composed in Latin by Laudivius Zacchia (1473), and was translated into Italian by Dolce. His immense influence on the transmission of literary texts is beyond doubt: to cite one example, his edition of Dante's *Comedia* (1555) was the first to describe it with the epithet 'divine'.

Among his own works there are comedies (*Ragazzo*, 1541), tragedies (*Marianna*, 1565), and prose dialogues such as *Dialogo della institution delle donne* (1545) and the better known *Dialogo della pittura intitolato l'Aretino* (1557). Even though it is commonly held that he was a 'mediocre versifier' (Romei, 'Lodovico Dolce', p. 10), he showed a lifelong devotion to the genre of chivalric romance, not only editing and commenting on Ariosto, but also publishing his own epic poems in *ottava rima* imitating Boiardo and Ariosto, among them *Sacripante* (1535) and *Le prime imprese del conte Orlando* (posthumous, 1572). His poem *Stanze composte per la vittoria Africana* (1535), written at the age of 25 or 27, is inspired by this particular tradition, even though it is not a courtly poem but belongs to popular culture. In his later *Vita di Carlo Quinto* (1561), Dolce treats the most popular historical figure of his time, the Emperor Charles V, presenting him as a Christian champion just as he had in *Stanze composte per la vittoria Africana*.

He was considered by some 18th-century scholars a simple 'taster' of literary genres (Tiraboschi, cited in Romei, 'Lodovico Dolce'), but for scholars nowadays he rather represents a new professional figure: the editor and the cultural mediator. He was very sensitive and open to changing literary trends (sometimes compared to Pietro Aretino), and to the taste of the reading public: as he said in his preface to Tasso's *Amadigi* (1560), it is necessary to 'adjust to the needs of the century in which one writes'.

MAIN SOURCES OF INFORMATION

Primary

For early sources on Dolce, see R.H. Terpening, *Lodovico Dolce. Renaissance man of letters*, Toronto, 1997, pp. 3-8

Secondary

Terpening, *Lodovico Dolce* (the most detailed study of Dolce, including a list of all his works, pp. 257-69)

G. Romei, art. 'Lodovico Dolce', in *Dizionario Biografico degli Italiani*, vol. 40

C. di Filippo Bareggi, *Il mestiere di scrivere. Lavoro intellettuale e mercato librario a Venezia nel Cinquecento*, Rome, 1988

E. Antonio Cicogna, 'Memoria intorno alla vita e gli scritti di Messer Lodovico Dolce letterato veneziano del secolo XVI', *Memorie dell'I.R. Istituto veneto di scienze, lettere e arti* 11 (1863-84) 93-200

WORKS ON CHRISTIAN-MUSLIM RELATIONS

Stanze composte nella vittoria Africana novamente avuta dal sacratissimo Imperatore Carlo Quinto, 'Stanzas composed on the African victory recently won by the most holy Emperor Charles V'
Stanze per la vittoria Africana, 'Stanzas for the African victory'

DATE 1535
ORIGINAL LANGUAGE Italian

DESCRIPTION

Lodovico Dolce's *Stanze composte nella vittoria Africana* consists of a prologue in prose and 147 unnumbered stanzas in *ottava rima*. There is no modern edition, though a facsimile copy of the first printed edition can be found in Beer and Ivaldi, *Guerre in ottava rima. IV. Guerre contro i Turchi (1453-1570)*, pp. 457-512.

The poem treats the Christian capture of Tunis from the Ottomans in 1535. It is dedicated to Don Lopes Soria, ambassador in Italy of the Habsburg Empire (1528-32). The prologue pays tribute to Charles V, called 'the true father of the universal homeland of the baptised', and it praises his triumphs, his piety and valour. Dolce modestly calls his text 'a little work', composed in only two days.

In the first seven introductory stanzas, Charles V is praised as the saviour of all Christians, a 'new Charles' who brings peace and protects against barbaric fury. Dolce asks his readers to listen to this 'real' account of Charles instead of giving attention to the 'fabulous old texts', by which he probably means earlier epic poems with their fictional wars and heroes. This appears to be a sign of Dolce's 'undoubted awareness' of a need among his contemporaries to reorient themselves towards reality and matters of contemporary history (Dionisotti, 'La guerra', p. 173).

The poem presents Charles V as if he were a crusader freeing the Holy Land from Saracens. The following stanzas (8-27) describe him and his army: he gathers his people together, and makes a speech inciting his soldiers to war and promising victory; not a war against Italy which is already 'tired and afflicted', but against the enemies of Christ who have attacked Vienna and who have caused much pain to the Christians. It is a 'just' war intended to punish the thief, Barbarossa.

Barbarossa's preparations are also described (28-33), and then the campaign begins. The Christians go ashore (34-56), construct strongholds, and engage in a series of battles with the Turks. A group of Greek slaves who have escaped from Barbarossa join the imperial army, and inform Charles about Barbarossa's preparations (57-75). Dolce takes this opportunity to give a long description of the Turkish army and Barbarossa (60-76), detailing the Turkish soldiers' appearance (they wear long shirts, look like women, are barefoot, unshaven and smell), and Barbarossa's army (most are badly dressed, with long hair, and carry only bows and poisoned arrows). Barbarossa himself is strong, intelligent and fast, with the cunning of Ulysses.

The attack on Tunis is then described in detail (76-110). When they capture the city, the Christians free the prisoners, and Barbarossa is forced to escape to Algeria (124-32). Finally, Charles's achievements here and elsewhere are praised.

The poem is one of Dolce's very first works, and he may have wished to obtain a position at court with it. It certainly contributes to Habsburg imperial propaganda and to the creation of the myth of Charles V as the saviour and leader of all Christians, a 'new Charles' who brings peace and protects against barbarians. In making him the successor to the Roman Empire, and the heir and direct scion of Charlemagne, Dolce employs a rhetorical combination of classical and Christian motifs that had been introduced by the Italian humanists in the 14th and 15th centuries, beginning with Petrarch. The same intertwinement is found in Charles's triumphal entries throughout the Empire, from 1529 up to his funeral procession in 1558, and 'crystallized in the Emperor's Triumphal Entry into Rome in 1536' after the conquest of Tunis (Pinson, 'Imperial ideology').

Throughout the poem, the Muslims are characterised as a proud, self-confident, cruel and uncivilised people in comparison with the more civilised Christians. This stereotypical presentation is reflected in the dishevelled appearances of the Turks, while the way in which they ride their horses bareback, together with their 'strange' language, contributes to creating the impression of primitiveness. The adjective repeatedly used of them is *strani* ('strange'), rhymed with *vani* ('futile'). Islam is presented as an unjust and foolish religion, with a God (wrongly called Muḥammad) who does not listen to its followers or understand them.

At the same time, however, the poem also expresses some admiration for the Turks when it describes the rich and beautiful clothes and helmets of some of the soldiers, and when it presents Barbarossa as comparable in quick-mindedness to Ulysses.

Poems in *ottava rima* became the most popular kind of publication in the first 50 years after the invention of printing. There were those inspired by such masters of literary narrative as Boccaccio and Ariosto, and those inspired by oral *cantari*. Early pamphlets in *ottava rima* dealing with various military battles, such as Dolce's *Stanze*, are closer to the popular, oral tradition than to the literary (cf. Wilhelm, *Italienische Flugschriften*, p. 123 n. 2), though Dolce also seems to be influenced by Ariosto's *Orlando furioso* (1532), which he edited and commented on in the 1530s.

These war accounts in *ottava rima* functioned as a kind of journalistic report, following the most important battles. They were written by both anonymous poets and named authors.

SIGNIFICANCE

According to Terpening, Dolce's *Stanze* may have influenced Tasso, whose lines at the start of *Gerusalemme liberata* are similar to those of Dolce (Terpening, *Lodovico Dolce*, pp. 30-31, referring to V. Vivaldi, *La Gerusalemme liberata studiata nelle sue fonti*, Trani, 1901). According to Vivaldi, Tasso was an admirer of Dolce's works, and Dolce's poem *Primaleone, figliuolo di Palmerino* (1562) could have been of significance for the duel of Tancredi and Clorinda.

EDITIONS & TRANSLATIONS

Stanze di M. Lodovico Dolce. Composte nella vittoria africana novamente havuta dal sacratissimo imperatore. Carolo Quinto, Paris, 2007 (CD-ROM)

Stanze di m. Lodovico Dolce composte nella vittoria africana nuovamente havuta dal sacratis. imperatore Carlo Quinto, Romae, 1535 (facsimile copy in M. Beer and C. Ivaldi, *Guerre in ottava rima*, Modena, 1989, iv, pp. 457-512)

Stanze di m. Lodovico Dolce composte nella vittoria africana nuovamente havuta dal sacratis. imperatore Carlo Quinto. Se vendeno a la botega de mestro Giovanne Antonio apresso a la Dugana, Genova: per Antonio Bellone, 1535

STUDIES

S. Giazzon, *Venezia in coturno. Lodovico Dolce tragediografo (1543-1557)*, Rome, 2011

A. Neuschäfer, *Lodovico Dolce als dramatischer Autor im Venedig des 16. Jahrhunderts*, Frankfurt am Main, 2004
Y. Pinson, 'Imperial ideology in the triumphal entry into Lille of Charles V and the Crown Prince (1549)', *Assaph. Studies in Art History* 6 (2001) 205-32, http://www2.tau.ac.il/InternetFiles/Segel/Art/UserFiles/file/09pinson.pdf
Terpening, *Lodovico Dolce* (contains useful bibliographical information on Dolce's original works, editions and translations)
R. Wilhelm, *Italienische Flugschriften des Cinquecento (1500-1550). Gattungsgeschichte und Sprachgeschichte*, Tübingen, 1996 (in particular the chapter 'Flugschriften in *ottava rima*: die *historia*', pp. 123-204, which contains information and many references important for this topic, in particular on the history and evolution of the genre and its linguistic and stylistic characteristics)
Romei, 'Lodovico Dolce'
di Filippo Bareggi, *Il mestiere di scrivere*
C. Dionisotti, 'La guerra d'Oriente nella letteratura veneziana del Cinquecento', in *Geografia e storia della letteratura italiana*, Turin, 1967, 163-82

Pia Schwarz Lausten

Michele Membré

DATE OF BIRTH 1509
PLACE OF BIRTH Cyprus
DATE OF DEATH 1595
PLACE OF DEATH Venice

BIOGRAPHY

Michele Membré was born in Cyprus to a non-patrician Venetian family, and was a small-time merchant who had been engaged by his relatives, the Benedetti merchant family, to travel to Turkey and Syria. Membré's abilities in Italian, Greek and especially Turkish led to his being recommended by the family to the governor of Cyprus to carry a letter from Venice ('the most illustrious signory') to the Safavid shah, where a dialect of Turkish was the court language, proposing closer ties in alliance against the Ottomans, their common enemy. Membré seems to have had some ability in Arabic and also acquired some facility in Persian on his travels.

He left Nicosia on 1 March 1539 and, using various disguises, travelled through Crete and Chios and reached the Ottoman mainland in April. However, he did not reach the Persian border until late summer 1539. There, he identified himself to local officials, and was then sent on to the shah himself. He spent some months in attendance, although his mission was thwarted when the shah heard that Venice was negotiating a treaty with the Porte, and in August 1540 the shah sent him from court. Membré reached Hormuz, on the Persian Gulf, in November and took passage to India. From there he travelled to Lisbon, where he arrived in August 1541. He reached Venice in May 1542, and presented the *Relazione* to the Collegio in July 1542. He continued to serve the Republic, being appointed Dragoman to Venice's Signoria in 1550. His retirement date from the post is not known.

MAIN SOURCES OF INFORMATION

Primary
M. Membré, *Mission to the Lord Sophy of Persia (1539-1542)*, trans. with an introduction and notes by A.H. Morton, London, 1993

Secondary

G. Rota, 'Safavid Persia and its diplomatic relations with Venice', in E. Herzig and W. Floor (eds), *Iran and the world in the Safavid age*, London, 2012, 149-60

M. Casari, art. 'Italy ii. Diplomatic and commercial relations', in *EIr*

B. Rahimi, 'From assorted to assimilated ethnography, transformation of ethnographic authority from Michele Membre to Jean Chardin, 1542-1677', in H. Schulz-Forberg (ed.), *Unravelling civilisation. European travel and travel writing*, Brussels, 2005, 107-27

A.H. Morton, 'Introduction', in Membré, *Mission to the Lord Sophy of Persia*, vii-xxviii

B. von Palombini, *Bündniswerben Abendländischer Mächte um Persien 1453-1600*, Wiesbaden, 1968

A. Bombaci, 'Une lettera turca in caratteri latini del dragomanno ottomano Ibrāhīm al veneziano Michele Membré (1567). Ancora sul trattato turco-veneto del 2 ottobre 1540', *Rocznik Orientalistyczny* 15 (1949) 129-44

A. Bombaci, 'Ancora sul trattato turco-veneto del 2 ottobre 1540', *Rivista delgi Studi Orientali* 20 (1943) 373-81

L. Bonelli, 'Il trattato turco-veneto del 1540', in *Centenario della nascita di Michele Amari*, Palermo, 1910, ii, 332-63

WORKS ON CHRISTIAN-MUSLIM RELATIONS

Relazione di Persia, 'Account of Persia', 'Mission to the Lord Sophy of Persia'

DATE 1542
ORIGINAL LANGUAGE Venetian Italian

DESCRIPTION

Relazione di Persia survives in a single manuscript, and was first cited only in 1910 by L. Bonelli ('Il trattato turco-veneto'). The text runs to 54 pages in Morton's English translation.

Membré offers comments on beliefs and practices of both Christians (especially Armenians) and Muslims with whom he comes into contact over the course of his trip. The latter include the Ottoman sultan (p. 9), the 'Turcoman' (sic) levies of the Safavid Shah Tahmasp (d. 1576), the shah himself and prominent figures at the court (pp. 18-19).

He notes the official cursing of the first three Rightly Guided Caliphs (p. 20), and also the use of the characteristically Shī'ī invocation "Alī is the wali of Allāh' (p. 24), that the shah (whom he sometimes calls the 'Sophy', i.e. Sufi) keeps a sister unmarried in preparation for the return of the Mahdī (i.e. the twelfth Imam) (p. 25); that the followers of the shah, whom he calls *sofiani*, wear a distinctive 12-sectioned hat (pp. 26-27), and that certain Sufi rites are practised (pp. 32, 42). He reports local curiosity about the fact that the symbol of Venice is a lion, as the Imām 'Alī was often represented as a lion (pp. 39-40); Membré claimed this as a sign of the Venetians' devotion to 'Alī. He also records ceremonies during the month of Muḥarram commemorating the death of Imām Ḥusayn (p. 43).

Although he mentions the Imāms 'Alī and Ḥusayn, Membré exhibits no awareness of Twelver Shī'ism, its doctrine or practices, or of how its features were 'translated' by the early Safavids. The identity of the 'Mahdī' as the twelfth Imām is not noted, for example, nor is the significance of the *tāj* (hat) having 12 sections noted as being in respect for the 12 Imāms.

SIGNIFICANCE

Relazione is notable for its details about Shī'ī Islam, although Membré does not show curiousity about these.

MANUSCRIPTS

MS Venice, Archivio di Stato – (details not given)

EDITIONS & TRANSLATIONS

Mission to the Lord Sophy of Persia, trans. Morton (English trans.)

F. Castro (ed.), *Relazione di Persia (1542)*, Naples, 1969

STUDIES

A. Morton (trans.), *Michele Membré, Mission to the Lord Sophy of Persia (1539-1542)*, London, 1993, pp. vii-xxviii

Andrew Newman

Luigi Bassano

Luigi Bassano da Zara

DATE OF BIRTH   About 1510
PLACE OF BIRTH Zadar, Dalmatia
DATE OF DEATH   Unknown; after 1552
PLACE OF DEATH Unknown

BIOGRAPHY

Little is known about Luigi Bassano, except from indications in the only book he published. He was from Zadar (in Venetian: Zara), the main city in Dalmatia, which had been under Venetian rule since 1409, and in the 16th century was under threat from the Ottomans. For unknown reasons, he was in Constantinople around 1537, perhaps from 1530 to 1540, returning apparently no later than 1541. In 1552, Charles V's ambassador to Venice, Hurtado de Mendoza, sent him on an otherwise unknown mission to Constantinople. Judging from his book, he must have had a fairly good knowledge of Latin. Hurtado de Mendoza calls him *hombre inteligente* ('capable man') in the note that is the source for our knowledge about his mission to Constantinople. Bassano's book is dedicated to Cardinal Rodolfo Pio di Carpi, his 'master and protector' (as he is called in the dedication; Bassano may have worked for the cardinal), and Bassano seems to have had personal knowledge not only about Venice but also about Rome.

MAIN SOURCES OF INFORMATION

Primary

I costumi et i modi particolari de la vita de Turchi, descritti da M. Luigi Bassano da Zara, Roma: Antonio Blado Asolano, 1545 (the number of copies was probably very limited, since this print is extremely rare)

Francesco Sansovino, *Dell'historia universale dell'origine et imperio de Turchi libri tre*, Venice, 1564, and later editions (Bassano's text is included in these publications)

Secondary

K. Pust, 'Luigi Bassano da Zara: "I costume et i modi particolari de' Turchi". Primer krscanskega opisovanja osmanov iz 16. stoletja', *Acta Histriae* 17/1-2 (2009) 59-82 (with an extensive summary in English and a short summary in Italian)

A. Höfert, *Den Feind beschreiben. 'Türkengefahr' und europäisches Wissen über das Osmanische Reich 1450-1600*, Frankfurt, 2003, esp. pp. 213-16, 266-74, 287-91

A. Höfert, 'Ist das Böse schmutzig? Das osmanische Reich in den Augen europäischer Reisender des 15. und 16. Jahrhunderts', *Historische Enthropologie* 11 (2003) 176-92

F. Babinger, art. 'Bassano, Luigi', in *Dizionario biografico degli Italiani*, vol. 7 (less extensive than the same author's introduction in his edition of Bassano's text)

F. Babinger (ed.), *Costumi et i modi particolari della vita de' Turchi*, Monaco di Baviera (Munich), 1963

WORKS ON CHRISTIAN-MUSLIM RELATIONS

I costumi et i modi particolari de la vita de Turchi, descritti da M. Luigi Bassano da Zara, 'Customs and particular habits of the Turks'

DATE 1545
ORIGINAL LANGUAGE Italian

DESCRIPTION

The introduction to this book expresses a wish to witness 'the destruction and ultimate extermination of those mad dogs', and the author foresees that his readers will want to shed tears at his accounts of the crimes (*sceleratezze*) and superstitions of these impious people and of the slavery of so many poor Christians. Yet the majority of the 54 chapters (63 pages) do in many respects provide a somewhat distanced, neutral depiction of mores and habits, and Bassano insists that the information he will provide is based on what he has seen with his own eyes 'and not without tears'. His book is not based on what he has heard or read elsewhere.

The very first thing he wants to relate is that the Turks get out of bed at sunrise when the 'priest' calls from a 'tower' and invites them to wake up in order to go to the 'temple'. They put on their clothes and go to the baths because the law commands that they must be clean in the temple in the presence of God. Taking this point of departure, Bassano immediately introduces a number of major themes: the religious regulation of everyday life, the 'law', the religious institution and the public baths. Several times he returns to the link between cleanliness and religion. The second chapter, the longest in the book, is then a detailed description of the public baths for men and what goes on there. Most are richly adorned. Interior and exterior are made of 'the finest marbles that are of inestimable value', as he writes, with a characteristic focus on values, in particular values beyond imagination. The interiors of the rooms and the various temperatures of the water are detailed and what he points out is all *finissimo, bellissimo* and *ben fatto*, well done. Also the customs for using the bath are spelled out – including the towel that men have to use in order to 'avoid showing any shameful (*dishonesta*) parts'; those who are 'without respect' are beaten and chased out of the baths. Here one more recurrent theme is introduced – the beating of those who do not follow rules. Among the services provided at the baths are also shaving and depilation, including of 'hair at the hidden parts', which it is considered a sin to leave. The subject of the next chapter is the women's baths and here the promised veracity is left behind. Like other authors who treat this subject, Bassano believes he knows what takes place there when women wash each other; it is an occasion of immoral, shameful behaviour.

The mosques are no less spectacular than the baths, in particular Hagia Sophia, where Bassano highlights the finest marble together with porphyry and the most exquisite (*superbissimi*) mosaics, as well as the most admirable (*mirabilissime*) columns. He mentions two other beautiful mosques in Constantinople, with 'many rooms, where their priests keep school for small children, and do many shameful things too'. This short subordinate clause is the only part of the chapter that deviates from the detailed admiring description. Similarly the description of the baths for women ends with a remark about meals taken by women in the baths, where Bassano adds that men do the same 'and I have done it with them myself, and I have seen Turks being drunk in the bath, go laughing out in the streets and behave in many shameful ways'. Although similar remarks add up to a distancing undertone, they are most often asides. In general, his book is descriptive.

One exception is his lashing out at the 'priests', another is the description of punishment by beating and an extremely detailed description of impalement, as well as an empathetic description of the slave market, where he points out that the high prices for boys compared with the prices for girls demonstrates that 'this nation is sullied [*machiata*] by the sin of sodomy'. Although there may be other reasons for the difference in prices, even one of the features Bassano finds most revolting is linked to detailed observation, i.e. of the prices.

Turning from daily life to the state, Bassano affirms that the more you take the manners of the Grand Turk into consideration, the more they deserve to be praised. The same goes in a sense for his army of 200,000-300,000 men, where any act of subordination is punished by beheading. If a similar order prevailed in the Christian armies, where all sorts of conflicts are generated by old enmities, factions, mendacity and care for honour, they would perhaps be more victorious.

SIGNIFICANCE

Bassano's book is one of the most detailed accounts from this period of various aspects of life in Constantinople. It focuses on everyday customs and behaviour in particular, but also describes other spheres of activity, such as law enforcement and punishment. What could be called ethnological description is predominant, whereas standard religious polemics and prejudices, which surface at various points, are secondary features.

Although the theological differences between Islam and Christianity are not Bassano's primary concern, he is very well informed on the subject, and on the relative toleration given to Jewish and Christian institutions and practice.

The book's approach is predominantly empirical, rather than conditioned by theological polemics or general rejection of 'Turkish' mores.

Despite the apparently limited original printing of Bassano's book, the text had a wide diffusion when from 1564 onwards it was inserted in numerous editions (including translations) of Francesco Sansovini's compilation, *Dell'historia universale dell'origine et imperio de Turchi libri tre* (first edition 1554, not including Bassano's text; the compilation had a variety of titles).

EDITIONS & TRANSLATIONS

Babinger, *Costumi et i modi particolari della vita de' Turchi*

Sansovino, *Dell'historia universale dell'origine et imperio de Turchi libri tre*, Venice, 1564, and later editions

I costumi et i modi particolari de la vita de' Turchi, descritti da M. Luigi Bassano da Zara, Roma: Antonio Blado Asolano, 1545

STUDIES

Pust, 'Luigi Bassano da Zara, "I costumi et i modi particolari de' Turchi"'
Höfert, *Den Feind beschreiben*
Höfert, 'Ist das Böse schmutzig?'
Babinger, 'Bassano, Luigi'
Babinger, *Costumi et i modi particolari della vita de' Turchi*, Introduction

Peter Madsen

Giovanni Battista Castrodardo

DATE OF BIRTH   About 1517
PLACE OF BIRTH Belluno, Italy
DATE OF DEATH   Between October 1587 and February 1588
PLACE OF DEATH Belluno, Italy

BIOGRAPHY

Giovanni Battista Castrodardo was born in Belluno in about 1517. His family was from Castel d'Ardo, a small village on the River Piave, in the diocese of Ceneda. His father, Alberto, studied law in Padua to be a *notarius* ('attorney'), a profession that Castrodardo's family members continued to follow until the beginning of the 19th century. His mother, Caterina Marenio Aleandro, was the daughter of Cristoforo Marenio (from Mareno di Piave) and Chiara Aleandro, the sister of the humanist Pietro Marenio Aleandro and second cousin of Cardinal Girolamo Aleandro. Alberto Castrodardo and Caterina had three children: Aleandro, Giovanni Battista and Andrea.

By 1534, Castrodardo, still a young man, was canon of San Martino Cathedral. On 20 October 1539, he was ordained priest by Filippo Donato, suffragan of the bishop of Belluno, Gasparo Contarini. Castrodardo continued to live in Belluno until about 1543, when he moved to Padua to study law. Here he was influenced by the intellectual legacy of Pietro Pomponazzi as well as by the Academy of the 'Infiammati' lead by Sperone Speroni and Alessandro Piccolomini. He lived between Padua and Venice until 1548, visiting the court of Pope Paul III in Rome, and working in Venice, and he started his career as translator of historical works and editor for the printer Michele Tramezino and the publisher and bookseller Andrea Arrivabene. Giorgio Piloni, a late 16th-century historian from Belluno, who knew Giovanni Battista personally, defined him as 'a man who studied law and literature for a long time' (*Historia della città di Belluno*, fol. 143v).

Castrodardo's very short and ambitious career as a scholar is concentrated between 1543 and 1548. In 1544, he worked for Michele Tramezino and translated a historical work in Latin by Niccolò Leonico Tomeo, *Devaria historia libri III*, into Italian as *Li tre libri di Niccolò Leonico de varie historie*. Castrodardo's second work was a commentary on Dante's

Divine comedy, which he wrote between 1544 and 1547; this is now unfortunately lost. His third work was the *Alcorano di Macometto* (Venice, 1547), the first printed translation of the Qur'an in a European vernacular language. It was published anonymously by Andrea Arrivabene, though the translation is certainly to be attributed to Castrodardo, as was demonstrated in 2008 (Tommasino, 'Giovanni Battista Castrodardo bellunese traduttore'). Arrivabene dedicated the book to Gabriel de Luetz, baron of Aramon, the fourth French ambassador to the Ottoman Empire (1547-53). He was charged by Francis I with negotiating an alliance between France and the Ottomans and with persuading Süleyman the Magnificent to launch a military campaign against the forces of the Holy Roman Empire in Hungary. The dedicatory letter is extremely important, because, in the middle of the Schmalkaldic war (1546-7), the French diplomat embodied the last anti-imperial and religious hopes of Italian heterodox groups.

Castrodardo's last work is a chronicle of the bishops of Belluno, which he wrote after returning to his home town in 1548. This work, frequently quoted by Giorgio Piloni, was considered lost, but a fragment of it was recently located in the Saxon State-Regional and University Library of Dresden. In this text, Castrodardo shows his strong antiquarian scholarship and his cultural withdrawal into local and ecclesiastical history after his return to Belluno.

Castrodardo abruptly interrupted his literary career in 1548 for no apparent reason. Once he returned to Belluno, he seems to have lived for 40 years without revealing his Venetian connections or his works as a translator, especially the translation of the Qur'an, which was finally proscribed by the *Index Tridentinus* in 1564. Although he had been the *canonicus antiquior* for more than 40 years, he never became dean of San Martino Chapter, and he died in Belluno between October 1587 and February 1588.

MAIN SOURCES OF INFORMATION

Primary
Archival sources
Belluno, Archivio Capitolare della Cattedrale – 14, Massaria capitolare, 1451-1572, fols 27v, 46r, 54v, 62v, 69r (presence of Castrodardo in Belluno)
Vittorio Veneto, Archivio Diocesano, Archivio Vecchio – Referato VI, rubrica VI, busta II, fasc. VII, pos. 14 (busta 119), fols 1v-2r; fasc. X, pos. 10 (busta 98) (Pietro Aleandro's will)

Manuscripts

MS Dresden, Sächsischen Landesbibliothek Staats-und Universitätsbibliothek di Dresden (SLUB) – F65ª, fols 88-96 (fragment of Castrodardo's chronicle of the bishops of Belluno)

MS Vat – Ottoboni 2419, fols 626v-628r (Aleandro's family tree)

MS Venice, Biblioteca Marciana – It. X, 73 (7097), fol. 198r (information about Castrodardo's commentary on Dante's *Divine Comedy*)

Printed works

N. Leonico Tomeo, *Li tre libri di Nicolo Leonico de varie historie, nuovamente tradotti in buona lingua volgare*, Venice: [Michele Tramezino], 1544

G. Piloni, *Historia della città di Belluno*, Venice, 1607 (repr. Bologna, 2002), fols 39r, 142v-143v, 180v, 517-518

Secondary

P.M. Tommasino, *L'Alcorano di Macometto. Storia di un libro del Cinquecento europeo*, Bologna, 2013, pp. 129-59

P.M. Tommasino, 'Piccolo prologo a Giovanni Battista Castrodardo (1517c.-1588c.) e al suo Alcorano di Macometto', *Archivio Storico di Belluno Feltre e Cadore* 84, 351 (January-April 2013) 37-60

P.M. Tommasino, 'Frammenti ritrovati di Giovanni Battista Castrodardo (c. 1517-c. 1588) storico dei vescovi di Belluno', *Studi Veneziani* 65 (2012) 87-132

P.M. Tommasino, 'Giovanni Battista Castrodardo bellunese traduttore dell'Alcorano di Macometto', *Oriente Moderno* 48:1 (2008) 15-40

N. Zemon Davis, *Trickster travels. A sixteenth-century Muslim between worlds*, New York, 2006, p. 305 n. 71

A. Da Rif, *Capitolo e Canonici della Chiesa Cattedrale di Belluno (853-2003)*, Belluno, 2003, p. 116

G. Tomasi, *La Diocesi di Ceneda. Chiese e uomini dalle origini al 1586*, Vittorio Veneto, 1998, i, pp. 139-40; ii, p. 147

WORKS ON CHRISTIAN-MUSLIM RELATIONS

L'Alcorano di Macometto, 'The Qur'an of Muḥammad'

DATE 1547
ORIGINAL LANGUAGE Italian

DESCRIPTION

The *Alcorano di Macometto* (in full *L'Alcorano di Macometto. Nel qual si contiene la dottrina, la vita, i costumi, et le leggi sue. Tradotto nuovamente dall'Arabo in lingua Italiana*) was published by Andrea Arrivabene in Venice in 1547. Arrivabene dedicated the book to Gabriel de Luetz, baron of Aramon, the fourth French ambassador to the Ottoman Empire (1547-53). Both the ambassador and the publisher were closely linked with Venetian evangelical circles and Italian reformers, who regarded Sultan Süleyman and France as allies during the Schmalkaldic war (1546-47). In spite of the fact that a promotional frontispiece claims that the work was newly translated from Arabic into the vernacular, it was actually translated from Robert of Ketton's Latin translation, published by Theodor Buchmann, known as Bibliander, and Johann Oporinus, in Basel in 1543. Nevertheless, the *Alcorano* is not merely a summarised and inaccurate translation of the medieval Latin Qur'an, neither is it an anti-Islamic polemic or a systematic textual refutation of contradictions in the Qur'an. It is a handy and useful historical companion to Islam more accessible to a large readership than Bibliander's Latin encyclopedia, which appeared in folio. Arrivabene wanted to present a new guide to Islam written in more comprehensible language and printed in a smaller and cheaper format (quarto). He wished to publish a volume aimed at furnishing Italian and Italophone readership – especially political and religious refugees in Istanbul, who were linked with the French embassies in both Venice and Istanbul – with information about Islamic history and about Islam as the dominant religion of the Ottoman Empire.

Three different versions of the same text were published by Arrivabene. The third and definitive version, dated 1547 but probably published a little after, consists of three books (100 folios) prefaced by a long introduction (50 folios), which is preceded by three preliminary texts: a dedicatory letter signed by Andrea Arrivabene, an anonymous dedicatory sonnet written by the poet Paolo Crivelli, who was a member of Aramon's delegation, and an anonymous letter to readers, which should be attributed to Giovanni Battista Castrodardo (six folios). The structure of the text is therefore very simple and clear. The introduction is based on contemporary *turcica*, polemical Morisco works and Venetian historiography; the first book is based on biographies of the Prophet Muḥammad and on historical tracts about early Islam collected in the *Corpus Islamolatinum*; the second and third books contain the Italian translation of the Qur'an, based on the medieval Latin translation by Robert of Ketton.

Although the *Alcorano* contains a considerable number of polemical marginalia, necessary to avoid Venetian censorship, its originality relies on the anti-Imperial and pro-Ottoman political propaganda in the text, especially in the introduction, as well as on Giovanni Battista Castrodardo's personal and very literal use of contemporary European sources on Islam, such as the polemical work attributed to Juan Andrés and the humanist Venetian histories of Bernardo Giustinian.

SIGNIFICANCE

The *Alcorano di Macometto* reflects the diplomatic context in which it was published: a military alliance between France and the Ottoman Empire. It is not a polemical text, but an encyclopedia of Islam that could have been used 'in war time as well as in peace time', as the publisher stresses in the dedicatory letter. Moreover, it contains a printed translation of the Qur'an into a language easily accessible to both European and Mediterranean audiences between 1547 and 1647. Thus, it was widely diffused through Europe and the Mediterranean and probably beyond. General readers, such as the prophet Scolio from Lucca and the miller Menocchio, studied by Carlo Ginzburg, owned a copy of this Islamic handbook. It is highly probable that it was here that Menocchio found the story of Abraham destroying the idols (Q 21) that he used as an argument to attack Catholic worship of saints. Moreover, European diplomats and travellers, Italian Reformers and Venetian book-sellers spread the *Alcorano* in Europe as a product of Italian Renaissance culture.

It is remarkable that its first readers in Britain were translators of Italian literature, such as William Thomas, Thomas Hoby (the translator of the *Cortegiano*), Henry Parker (the translator of Petrarch's *Trionfi*) and the exiled Italian Giacomo Castelvetro. In 17th-century England, both John Selden and Robert Ashley owned copies of it. Among French scholars, it was read by at least Guillaume Postel, Joseph Juste Scaliger, Antoine de Laval and Montesquieu, who owned a copy and probably used it for his *Persian letters*. Furthermore, around 1630 the French renegade Thomas/Osman d'Arcos wrote from Tunis to Nicolas-Claude Fabri de Pereisc to ask for a copy of 'the Latin, or of the Italian Koran'. In addition, at least two manuscript copies were taken from the printed text. So far, only one of these is known, kept in the Bancroft Library, Berkeley. A second, made in Russia in the 18th century, was sold in London in 1899. During the 17th century, Castrodardo's *Alcorano* was the basis for the German translation by Salomon Schweigger (1616), from which was taken a translation into Dutch (1641). Between the late 16th and 17th centuries, it was also translated into Hebrew and Spanish among Amsterdam's Sephardic Jews.

MANUSCRIPTS

MS Berkeley CA, University of California, The Bancroft Library – UCB 7 (17th century; MS version taken from the printed text)

MS Amsterdam, Ets Haim Bibliotheek – HS.EH.48.D.20 (17th century; Spanish trans.)

EDITIONS & TRANSLATIONS

L'ALCORANO | DI MACOMETTO. | LA VITA, LA DOT- | TRINA, I COSTVMI | ET LE SVE LEGGI | Nuouamente dal Arabo | tradotto in uolgare. | Con Gratie, e Priuilegi | M D XLVII | [4], xxxviii, 100; 4° | +⁴ a-i⁴ k² A-2B⁴ (first version)

L'ALCORANO | DI MACOMETTO, | NEL QVAL SI CONTIE | NE LA DOTTRINA, | LA VITA, I CO= | STVMI, ET LE | LEGGI SVE. | Tradotto nuouamente dall'Arabo | in lingua Italiana. Con Gratie, e Priuilegii. | M D XLVII | [5], xxxviii, 100 | πA⁴πB1 a-i⁴ k² A-2B⁴ (second version)

L'ALCORANO | DI MACOMETTO, | NEL QVAL SI CONTIE | NE LA DOTTRINA, | LA VITA, I CO= | STVMI, ET LE | LEGGI SVE. | Tradotto nuouamente dall'Arabo | in lingua Italiana. Con Gratie, e Priuilegii. | M D XLVII | [5], l, 100 | πA⁴πB1 a-i⁴ k² l-n⁴ A-2B⁴ (third version)

Alcoranus Mahometicus. Das is Der Türcken Alcoran Religion und Aberglauben [Nürnberg: Ludovicum Lochner, 1616] (German trans.)

De Arabische Alkoran, door de Zarazijnsche en de Turcksche prophete Mahometh, Hamburgh: for Barent Adriaensz, Berentsma, 1641 (Dutch trans.)

STUDIES

Tommasino, *L'Alcorano di Macometto*

A. Shalem (ed.), *Constructing the image of Muhammad in Europe*, Berlin, 2013

E.M. Dal Pozzolo, M.P. Pedani and R. Dorigo (eds), *Venezia e l'Egitto*, Milan, 2011

H. Bobzin and A. den Hollander (eds), *Early printed Korans. The dissemination of the Koran in the West*, Leiden, 2004

G. Vercellin, *Venezia e l'origine della stampa in caratteri arabi*, Padua, 2001

H. Bobzin, *Der Koran im Zeitalter der Reformation. Studien zur Frühgeschichte der Arabistik und Islamkunde in Europa*, Beirut, 1995

H. Lazarus-Yafeh, 'A seventeenth-century Hebrew translation of the Qurʾān', *Scripta Mediterranea* 19-20 (1998-99) 199-211

C. De Frede, *La prima traduzione italiana del Corano sullo sfondo dei rapporti tra Cristianità e Islam nel Cinquicento*, Naples, 1976

C. De Frede, *La prima traduzione italiana del Corano sullo sfondo dei rapporti tra Cristianità e Islam nel Cinquicento*, Naples, 1967

Pier Mattia Tommasino

Giovanni Antonio Menavino

DATE OF BIRTH   Approximately 1492
PLACE OF BIRTH   Voltri, near Genoa
DATE OF DEATH   Unknown; mid-16th century
PLACE OF DEATH   Unknown

BIOGRAPHY

Giovani Menavino is known for his work *I cinque libri della legge, religione, et vita de' Turchi*, also entitled *Trattato dei costumi dei Turchi*, published in 1548 in Venice and Florence, and based on a manuscript of 1519, *De rebus et moribus Turcarum*. All we know of Menavino's life comes from this account, and it does not reveal much about him. The date of his birth is not given, but since he informs his readers that he was 12 years old when he was captured by pirates in the Mediterranean Sea in 1504, the year of his birth must have been about 1492.

He was accompanying his father, a Genoese merchant, on a voyage from Genoa to Venice, when near Corsica three pirate galleys attacked their ship. Menavino was captured and, together with two other boys, he was presented as a gift to Sultan Bayezid II (1481-1512), whom he served as an *icoglan* (a personal page or attendant) from 1504 until 1512. After the death of Bayezid, Menavino served his son Selim I (1512-20) until he managed to flee during a battle (probably the battle of Chaldiran between the Ottomans and Safavids) and return to Italy. He tells his readers at the end that ten years had passed without seeing his family, so the date of his return must have been 1514.

Nothing certain is known about him after his return to Italy, but he must have gone to Rome around 1519, since there is a manuscript titled *De rebus et moribus Turcarum* at the Biblioteca Corsiniana, which contains in the dedication to Pope Leo X passages that confirm his presence in Rome, where he says he has been *transferito et presentato*. The manuscript consists of five books, and the contents are almost identical with Menavino's *I cinque libri delle legge, religion, et vita de' Turchi* published in 1548. Umberto Torretta, the only modern reader of Menavino who mentions this 1519 manuscript (apart from Paul Kristeller, who first located it), says it is in Latin, though despite its Latin title it is, in fact, in Italian. Torretta also erroneously claims that it was translated into Italian by Lodovico Domenichi. (It is not yet established that this manuscript was written by Menavino himself, and is not a copy.) Torretta suggests that Menavino may have gone to Rome to ask the pope for re-conversion and that he brought his account as a gift (Torretta, *Giovanni Antonio Menavino*, p. 17). He surmises that Menavino may have experienced some kind of expulsion or marginalisation in his native village and had to leave, not unlike others in similar circumstances (Torretta, *Giovanni Antonio Menavino*, p. 25). However, Menavino himself does not mention any of these circumstances either in his dedication to the pope or in his account.

In both the 1548 printed versions, the dedication is not to Pope Leo X but to the French king, to whom Menavino expresses his gratitude for being in his service. If this dedication is authentic, he must have worked at the French court for a certain period.

In 1548, more than 30 years after his return from Constantinople, Menavino's *Cinque libri* was published in both Venice and Florence, with the title *Trattato de costumi et vita de Turchi*. In Venice it was printed with two works by another former Christian slave at the Turkish court, the Croatian Bartolomeo Georgewic, whose *Prophetia de Mahometani, et la miseria de' prigioni, de' Christiani, che vivono sotto il Gran Turco, et altre cose turchesche, non piu vedute* was translated by Ludovico Domenichi. There is no indication that Menavino was still alive at this time: the publisher's preface to the Venice edition, dated 20 April 1548, states that the publisher, or rather his 'corrector' Apollonio Campano, author of the preface, has come across this book by chance and that he has not been in contact with its author. He expresses the hope that the author will be grateful to him for publishing it *ovunque si trovi* ('wherever he is').

MAIN SOURCES OF INFORMATION

Primary
Pauli Jovii historiarum sui temporis, s.l., 1549 [1550]
Nicolas de Nicolay, *Navigations et pérégrinations orientales*, Lyons, 1567

Secondary
U. Torretta, *Giovanni Antonio Menavino. Un genovese di Voltri schiavo dei turchi*, Lecce, Italy, 2013
A. Dalzell, 'The first line of contact. The young Christian made Ottoman slave in the sixteenth century', Philadelphia PA, 2007 (Senior Diss. University of Pennsylvania), http://repository.upenn.edu/hist_honors/3

S. Yérasimos, *Les voyageurs dans l'Empire ottoman (XIVe-XVIe siècles). Bibliographie, itinéraires et inventaire des lieux habités*, Ankara, 1991

C. di Filippo Bareggi, *Il mestiere di scrivere. Lavoro intellettuale e mercato librario a Venezia nel cinquecento*, Rome, 1988

WORKS ON CHRISTIAN-MUSLIM RELATIONS

I cinque libri delle legge, religione, et vita de' turchi: et della corte, et alcune guerre del Gran Turco, 'Five books about the laws, religion and life of the Turks, and the court and every war of the Grand Turk'
Trattato dei costumi dei Turchi, 'Treatise on the customs of the Turks'

DATE 1548
ORIGINAL LANGUAGE Italian

DESCRIPTION

While Menavino dedicated the first manuscript version of his account to Pope Leo X in 1519, he dedicated the printed edition of 1548 to the 'most Christian King of France', expressing his gratitude for the king's goodness and for being in his service. Menavino claims that the occasion is the king's decision 'that can never be praised enough', to declare war against 'our common enemy, the Turk'. Since Henry II was king of France from 1547 to 1559, it would appear that he was the addressee of Menavino's work. However, the dedication is undated, and it cannot be known whether Menavino had Francis I or Henry II in mind.

The dedication is unusual, since most writings on the Turks in this period were dedicated to the Emperor Charles V, who was far more involved than the French in battles against the Turks. Furthermore, Genoa, Menavino's home town, had established an alliance with Spain in 1528. Since the beginning of the 16th century France had made alliances with the Ottomans, and neither Francis I nor his son Henry II fought against the Turks. Francis I took the first steps to establish an alliance with the Ottomans in the 1520s, concluding an alliance in 1536 with Süleyman the Magnificent, 'the first non-ideological diplomatic alliance of its kind between a Christian and non-Christian empire' (R. Kann, *A history of the Habsburg Empire*, Berkeley CA, 1974, p. 62). His son, Henry II, made alliances with Sultan Sulieman in 1551. Why then dedicate a book like this to the French king?

The dedication could be an example of wishful thinking. Or maybe Menavino wrote it in one of the few short periods in which Christians could hope that Francis I would change his mind and cancel his alliance with the Turks, around 1524, for instance, when Francis, in his search for allies in central Europe to fight against Charles V, signed a Franco-Polish alliance with Sigismund I at a point when the Poles were being attacked by the Ottomans. (This alliance was cancelled the following year.) Or, more likely, Menavino could have written it between 1538 and 1542, when the French-Ottoman alliance was put on hold for a while because Francis I and Charles V had made peace through the Truce of Nice, and Francis officially changed alliances. In the truce, Charles and Francis made an agreement to ally against the Ottomans in order to expel them from Hungary. Open conflict between Charles and Francis, as well as Franco-Ottoman collaboration, would resume in 1542.

Furthermore, there seems to be an ambiguity between the message of the dedication on the one hand, and the contents of the rest of the work on the other: the dedication expresses the intention to support the anti-Ottoman battle, and praises the king's plan of a crusade against 'the tyrant', while the tone of the rest of the work is not particularly aggressive or condemnatory. Nevertheless, it is also important to note that Menavino does not refrain from sometimes expressing the superiority of Christianity and the need to combat the Ottomans.

The contrast between dedication and text, together with the question of the addressee, could be interpreted as signs that the dedication was not authentic. The possibilities are that it could have been written either by Menavino himself at an earlier time, as suggested above, or by the publisher.

If the new dedication was written by Menavino himself, it could also be a simple sign of pragmatism. In 1519, he had dedicated his work to the pope because he needed his protection and favours (maybe to witness his formal conversion), but in the 1520s or 1530s he might have needed to gain the favour of the French king. Formica suggests a more political interpretation: that Menavino might have had anti-imperialist opinions, and therefore indirectly wanted to criticise the Spanish Empire by dedicating his work to the French king and writing quite mildly about the Turks (*Lo specchio turco*, p. 56). She claims that it was no coincidence that the book was printed in Venice and Florence, since they were the most dynamic places and the most culturally open, even towards Reformation ideas (Formica, *Lo specchio turco*, p. 54). But her arguments are not strong enough, being based on questionable interpretations of brief passages in the work.

In his preface to the 1548 edition, A. Campano claims that he has found an old, lacerated almost unreadable book that he has corrected and made more presentable. He mentions the text as a book *dell'altrui stampe*, i.e. from another printing house, as if it was a *printed* book he had found. If so, it cannot be the manuscript dated 1519 and dedicated to the pope. The formulation is mysterious since the only other printed edition of Menavino's book is from the same year, printed in Florence, and it is difficult to imagine that it would have been reduced to such a worn condition in only a few months (that is, if it was printed before the Venice edition, which is not at all certain). Campano could have made up the whole story in order to legitimise the edition of a book that had already been published earlier in the same year by a Florentine publisher. Otherwise there is no explanation for this circumstance.

The five books of *I cinque libri* each contain an introduction followed by a number of chapters, ranging from 23 to 36, of uneven length, from a few lines to a couple of pages. The first book (23 chapters) is about Turkish everyday life and laws (*della vita, et legge turchesca*). The introduction is the longest part of the work and describes the capture of Menavino and his father, and his arrival at the sultan's palace. (Genoese merchants had purchased and liberated his father, who had returned to Constantinople to find his son.) At court, Bayezid II took an immediate liking to Menavino. He spoke to him in Italian, and praised Christians (in particular the Tuscans) for their wit and for the education they gave their children. He decided to keep him as an *icoglan*, and sent him to the Seraglio school together with four of his grandchildren. There he studied Islam and learned both written and spoken Turkish.

Menavino gives a detailed account of Islam and rarely compares Islam and Christianity, though when he does he highlights the similarities between the two religions rather than the differences. Generally speaking, he is more interested in cultural differences than in religious ones, although he does mention some paradoxes, such as the rule that forbids killing but permits an exception if the killing is 'either against the unfaithful or part of a just war in defence of the lords', or the rule against lust that is ignored because all Turks practise sodomy.

The second book (23 chapters) is about churches, hospitals, the religion of the Turks and their way of managing justice (*delle chiese, hospitali, et religione de Turchi et modo di ministrar giustitia*). Menavino describes the size and design of mosques, and explains how the sick – even the leprous – are taken care of in hospitals 'with great diligence (as if they were in their own homes)'. He presents the various kinds of religious functionaries (chs 3-13), and gives a description of the pilgrimage to Mecca (chs 14-16) that is very rare among European accounts of Islam. The description is so rich in detail that Menavino must have participated in the pilgrimage himself. He describes the significance of the wind directions, topographical features and the risk of bandits, and refers to the advice in the travel guides to take care around Cairo and Medina because of the risk of assault. Menavino also explains the Turks' view of Judgment Day, life after death, paradise and hell. Islam, he says, does not make any distinction between Christians, Jews and Muslims; what matters is only how one has behaved and whether one has been faithful or not.

The third book (26 chapters) is about life and rules in the sultan's Seraglio (*del vivere et ordini del Serraglio del Gran Turco*). The introduction is long and noteworthy because it contains a rare reference to clichés about Turks as uncivilised compared with Christians. Menavino compares Muslims to wild plants growing in distant stony desert places, and Christians to fruit trees tended in secure gardens. 'But if you remove these wild plants from uncultivated wastes and plant them elsewhere, that is if the Muslims converted and returned to the Christian faith, they would begin to bear sweet fruits as well.'

Menavino describes the food and drinking habits of the Turks, and he often spices up his account with anecdotes and proverbs. He describes their clothing in detail, and explains that the men do not have hair because Muḥammad declared that long hair deprives men of their strength. He describes women's hair with admiration, together with their shoes and veiled faces.

Menavino moves on to a detailed description of the Seraglio (chs 9-26), outlining its buildings and gardens, and the various slaves who attend on the sultan. He himself belonged to the group who were closest to the sultan and were responsible for looking after his private rooms and protecting him during the night. All slaves were sons of Christians except for the eunuchs, who were often Indian, and they were governed by strict rules until the age of 25, when they could expect to be given a responsibility somewhere in the empire. A Christian who had converted to Islam could advance to any important position, and even end as the vizier. When Menavino escaped at the age of 22 in 1513, he was close to the point of advancing.

The fourth book is about the soldiers in the pay of the sultan, their captains and the courtiers (*delle genti d'arme salariate dal Gran Turco & suoi capitani et gentil'huomini*). Menavino mentions the great numbers of Christian slaves taken by the Great Turk and converted to the Muslim 'superstition', and says he would like to see someone have the courage to destroy a society based on such wrong and punish the Ottomans for their cruelties. He describes the administrative positions at court, the Janissaries, the ambassadors and the Seraglio of the women with its 25 houses. The women of the Seraglio are always Christians who have been taken prisoner. There are usually 200 of them.

The fifth book describes the armies of Greece and Anatolia, and the fighting between the Turkish lords (*dell'essercito delle Grecia et Natolia, et delle battaglie fatte tra i signori della Turchia*). Instead of recounting general histories on the Turks, as many other European authors did, Menavino chooses to write only about events that took place while he lived at court. Among other things, he relates Selim's takeover of power from Bayezid, and the parricide committed by Selim, who bribed Bayazid's Jewish doctor to poison him: 'The Turks do not care whether they wash their hands in their own blood or in water if they strive for the realm as sultan Selim did.' In the last chapter of this book Menavino relates his escape and his return home.

SIGNIFICANCE

Menavino's account is unique: he represents a group of Christian captives who were very close to the Ottoman sultan. Only a few similar works are known, the earliest being Johannes Schiltberger's *Reisebuch*, published in 1476 but recounting experiences from the period 1396-1427, and then of a simple servant who was not given access to the inner parts of the palace. Menavino's account is much more intimate, being written from the perspective both of a Christian boy on his arrival and of a Muslim after what must have been a conversion during his ten-year stay in the Seraglio.

The book was widely read and had a great significance for future depictions of the Ottoman world. Paolo Giovio mentions his conversations with Menavino in his *Historiae* (1550, Book 14), and refers to Menavino's observation about the possible poisoning of Bayezid by his son Selim (Torretta, *Giovanni Antonio Menavino*, p. 16). Giovio also mentions that Menavino had dedicated his book to Pope Leo X.

Nicolas de Nicolay, the French traveller, soldier, artist and royal cartographer, also mentions Menavino's book and was inspired by it in his account of travels in Turkey, *Navigations et pérégrinations orientales* (published in 1567). The anonymous *Viaje de Turquìa* also seems to have been inspired by it (Formica, *Lo specchio turco*, p. 55 n. 129). Among modern scholars, Bisaha places Menavino (with Paulo Giovio and Andrea Cambini) within a growing tendency from the beginning of the 16th century to view the Turks 'from a less biased perspective' and to see 'beyond the barbarian stereotype to know their enemy' (*Creating East and West*, p. 178). Inalcik mentions Menavino as a source on the Seraglio (*The Ottoman Empire*, p. 79) although, as Dalzell sees it, he neglects Menavino's 'chief importance to any study of the Christian contacts with Islam'. Finally, Höfert uses Menavino as an example of a new epistemological pattern of ethnographic knowledge of the Turks after 1453: a tendency to treat the thing, 'la cosa', 'res', that is to use empirical observations and objectification (Höfert, 'The order of things', pp. 52-54).

It has been established that Menavino's book is the Italian source behind an English text from the 19th century that describes the lunatic asylum in Constantinople (Peloso, 'Hospital care of madness in Turkish sixteenth century'). In that period in Europe, the insane were mostly taken care of in their families or left to themselves.

Menavino excuses himself for being 'not much orderly and coarse', and says that he is not a 'learned writer' but a 'faithful interpreter or rather a true narrator of the things he has seen and learned'. His style is concrete and objective: he only tells what he has seen with his own eyes, he says, and he distinguishes himself by not inventing anything and instead showing knowledge from within – as Gölner remarks: 'Der geschichtliche Wert seines Werkes ist durch seinen sachlichen, von allen Phrasen freien Stil gekennzeichnet' (Gölner, *Turcica*, p. 413). However, even though his account is based on his personal experiences, he never gives prominence to himself and does not share his feelings or inner thoughts.

Unlike other depictions of Ottoman society, such as Spandugino's or Georgewic's, but similar to those of Giovio and Cambini, who try to depict less stereotypical aspects of the Ottoman Empire, Menavino's perspective is not purely European or critical towards Islam – he speaks of *Turchi* or *Maometthani* rather than heretics or barbarians. He has gained a deep knowledge of the Islamic religion and he often chooses to underscore the similarities with Christianity rather than the differences. He does not just repeat stereotypes about Islam as a corrupt or heretical religion, nor does he consider Muḥammad a false prophet, and instead of characterising Islam as violent or sensual, he depicts it as merciful. It is thus difficult to understand why Bareggi characterises the work as only 'a text of fashion in which the author in various ways shows the superiority of the westerners and assigns the Christian defeat to the divine wrath' (Bareggi, *Il mestiere di scrivere*, p. 71). At the end of his text Menavino does mention divine wrath in order to explain the Ottoman defeat at the battle of Chaldiran (wrongly perceived by Menavino as a lost battle), but in this context he does not include reflections on Christian-Turkish conflicts at all.

One could argue that he clearly rejects the Ottomans when he chooses to escape, even at great risk to his life and even though he may have had a good chance of making a career in the Ottoman administration or military. However, it must also be considered that Menavino belonged to Bayezid, whom he supported during the conflict with Selim, and whose violent death he witnessed. For this reason his life may very well have been in danger after these dramatic events, and under Selim his career opportunities may not have been the same as under Bayezid.

MANUSCRIPTS

MS Rome, Biblioteca Corsiniana (Accademia dei Lincei) – Fondo Niccolò Rossi 35 E 18 (Corsin. 389) (1519; Johannis Antonij Menavini de Vultri Genuensis, *Liber de rebus et moribus Turcarum* – except for minor linguistic corrections, this MS presents the same contents as the editions printed in 1548 and 1551)

EDITIONS & TRANSLATIONS

H. Mutluay (trans.), *Türklerin hayatı ve adetleri üzerine bir inceleme*, Istanbul, 2011 (Turkish trans.)

Menavino, Giovanni Antonio, *De Mahometanis Turcorum legibus, religione, vita. De Baiazethis filiorum cladibus*, Francofurti: excudebat Ioan. Wechelus, impensis Sigismundi Feyerabendii, 1584

Chronicorum Turcicorum, in quibus Turcorum Origo, Principes Imperatores, Bella, Prælia, Cædes, Victoriæ, reique militaris Ratio & cætera huic pertinentia... exponuntur, Francofurti: Phil. Lonicerus, 1584

De Mahometanis Turcorum legibus, religione, vita, tum etiam de aulae Turcicae apparatu... Quibus accedit narratio de Baiazethis filiorum cladibus, Italico Idiomate a Johanne Antonio Moenavino..., Francofurti ad Moenum: apud Joannem Feyrabend, 1578

Chronicorum Turcicorum Tomi 3, acc. Narratio de Bajazethis filionum Seditionibus [omnia collecta et expos. lat. a Ph. Lonicero], Francofurti: Philipp Lonicer, 1578

Türckische Chronica: warhaffte eigentliche und kurtze Beschreibung der Türcken Ankunfft, Regierung, Königen und Keysern, Kriegen Schlachten, Victorien und Sigen wider Christen und Heyden.../ [Von G. A. Menavino]; Vormals auss italianischer Sprach in unser Teutsche verdolmetscht durch Heinrich Müller..., Franckfurt am Mayn: Gedruckt bey Georg Raben in Verlegung Sigmund Feyrabendt, 1577 (German trans.)

Von der Türcken Religion und Gesatz, Frankfurt am Main, 1577 (German trans.)

Vasco Díaz Tanco, *Türckische Historien, Oder: Warhafftige Beschreibunge aller Türcken ankunfft, Regierung, Königen, vnd Keisern, Kriegen, Schlachten, Victorien, wider Christen vnd Heiden...*, trans. Heinrich Müller, Franckfurt am Mayn, 1572 (German trans.)

Giovanni Antonio Von dem Mahometischen Glauben, vol. 2, fols 1-88, Frankfurt am Main: [Paul Reffeler.], 1572 (German trans.)

Türckische Historien, von der Türcken Ankunfft, Regierung, Königen, vnd Keysern, Kriegen.... vnd Sigen, wider Christen vnd Heiden... item von der Türcken Religion vnnd Gesatz..., Frankfurt am Main, 1563 (VD16 D 1382) (German trans.)

I costumi, et la vita de Turchi, di Gio. Antonio Menavino Genovese da Vultri. Con una prophetia, & altre cose Turchesche, tradotte per M. Ludovico Domenichi, Florence: Lorenzo Torentino, 1551

I cinque libri delle legge, religione, et vita de' turchi: et della corte, et alcune guerre del Gran Turco: di Giovantonio Menavino Genovese da Vultri. Oltre ciò, una prophetia de' Mahomettani, et la miseria de' prigioni, de' Christiani, che vivono sotto il Gran Turco, et altre cose Turchesche, non piu vedute: tradotte da M. Lodovico Domenichi, Venice: Vincenzo Valgrisi, 1548 (with a preface by Appolonio Campano)

Trattato de costumi et vita de Turchi composto per Giouan Antonio Menauino Genouese da Vultri, Florence: Lorenzo Torrentino, 1548

STUDIES

Torretta, *Giovanni Antonio Menavino*

M. Formica, *Lo specchio turco*, Rome, 2012, pp. 54-56

Dalzell, 'The first line of contact', (http://repository.upenn.edu/hist_honors/3; this thesis is the only academic monograph on Menavino to date)

N. Bisaha, *Creating East and West. Renaissance humanists and Ottoman Turks*, Philadelphia PA, 2004, p. 178

A. Höfert, 'The order of things and the discourse of the Turkish threat. The conceptualisation of Islam in the rise of Occidental anthropology in the fifteenth and sixteenth centuries', in A. Höfert and A. Salvatore (eds), *Between Europe and Islam. Shaping modernity in a transcultural space*, Brussels, 2000, 39-64

P.F. Peloso, 'Hospital care of madness in the Turk sixteenth century according to the witness of G.A. Menavino from Genoa', *History of Psychiatry* 9/33 (1998) 35-38

H. Inalcik, *The Ottoman Empire. The classical age 1300-1600*, Cambridge 1997, p. 79

Yérasimos, *Les voyageurs dans l'Empire ottoman (XIVe-XVIe siècles)*

Di Filippo Bareggi, *Il mestiere di scrivere*

C. Gölner, *Turcica, die europäischen Türkendrucke des XVI. Jahrhunderts*, Berlin, 1961

Pia Schwarz Lausten

Jacob Mantino

Jacob Mantino ben Samuel

DATE OF BIRTH   Unknown
PLACE OF BIRTH Unknown
DATE OF DEATH   1549
PLACE OF DEATH Damascus

BIOGRAPHY

Coming from a Jewish home and remaining faithful to his Jewish faith throughout his life, Jacob Mantino worked for Christian patrons, taught in Christian institutions and translated philosophical and medical texts into Latin for the advancement of these subjects among his Christian, Latin-reading, audience. His key role was in providing clear and up-to-date translations of the works of Averroes and Avicenna, the principal Arabic/Islamic authorities on philosophy and medicine. He made these from Hebrew translations of the Arabic originals.

Mantino's parents originated from Tortosa in Spain, where he himself may have been born. He states that he studied medicine and possibly the arts at the University of Padua. He practised as a doctor in Bologna, and became an intimate of Pope Leo X, to whom he dedicated a translation of Averroes's Middle Commentary on Aristotle's *On animals* in 1521. In the same year, he dedicated his translation of the Compendium (Epitome) of Aristotle's *Metaphysics* to another patron, Ercole Gonzaga, Bishop of Mantua. This marks the beginning of a lifetime devoted to the translation of Averroes (both his philosophical commentaries and his medical work, the *Colliget*) and Avicenna.

At the time of the Fall of Rome (1527), Mantino moved to Verona, where he continued to be held in high esteem. The new pope, Clement VII, consulted him about Henry VIII's appeal to Rome concerning the legality of his marriage to Catherine, to which Mantino quoted the Hebrew Bible and the Talmud to claim that the divorce was wrong.

Mantino returned to Rome to be the personal physician to Pope Paul III (Alessandro Farnese; 1534-49). At the same time, he played an important role in the Jewish community there, and taught at La Sapienza University.

He was consulted by Jews on legal matters, and showed off his linguistic knowledge by deriving the pope's name from Etruscan, which he claimed was the same as Syriac, in which *pharnes* means 'shepherd'.

In 1544, Mantino left Rome to return to Venice. Several documents survive that renew the permission given to him to wear the black beret of the scholar rather than the yellow Jewish cap, although he continued to live in the Jewish ghetto there. Already when he was in Bologna he had shown an interest in learning Arabic. He obtained the collaboration of Leo Africanus to draw up an Arabic vocabulary, for which he started to find the equivalents in Hebrew and Latin. In 1549, he arranged to accompany the Venetian ambassador to Damascus as his doctor, in pursuit of Arabic texts, but died soon after his arrival there.

Primary
See the list in D. Kaufmann, 'Jacob Mantino. Une page de l'histoire de la Renaissance', *Revue des Etudes Juives* 26 (1893) 30-60, 207-38, pp. 220-38

Secondary
N.Z. Davis, *Trickster travels. A sixteenth-century Muslim between worlds*, New York, 2006, pp. 82-86 (Mantino and Leo Africanus)
D.S. Katz, *The Jews in the history of England 1485-1850*, Oxford, 1994, pp. 32-41 (Mantino and Henry VIII)
Kaufmann, 'Jacob Mantino. Une page de l'histoire de la Renaissance' (the most comprehensive study of Mantino)

Translations of Aristotle

DATE Before 1549
ORIGINAL LANGUAGE Latin

DESCRIPTION
In the preface to his translation of Averroes's Epitome on the *Physics*, Mantino promises Ercole Gozaga that, when he has finished translating a collection of medical works (first the *Colliget* of Averroes, and then the paraphrases of several works of Galen, made by Iohannitius – Ḥunayn ibn Isḥāq), he will 'obtain all those commentaries of Averroes which are in the Hebrew language and, with God's leadership, and your favour, translate them into the Latin idiom'. His motivation for doing this was that the earlier translations into Latin (usually directly from Arabic) were written in such a barbarous style that they were impossible to understand, and people blamed Averroes for doctrines that he did not hold. When the Giunta brothers undertook to publish 'all the works of Aristotle

with all the commentaries on those works that have come down to us' in Venice in 1550, they mentioned, on the title page itself in capital letters, that 'some of these [commentaries], having never been seen by the Latins before, have recently been translated by Jacob Mantino, while others have been more clearly and faithfully translated by him than ever before'. The fact that the editors could only include the first four books of the Middle Commentary on the *Topics* is an indication that that was as far as Mantino could reach before he died in Damascus.

Both Mantino and his admirers emphasise the clarity of his Latin translations, in spite of their having been written by a Jew. Sometimes, he only translated the most important and/or controversial parts of works, such as Book 3, chs 5 and 56, of Averroes's commentary on Aristotle's *On the soul*, which propose the unity of the possible intellect, and also the three parts ('fen') of Avicenna's *Canon of medicine* that were most studied in the schools of medicine. Mantino regarded Aristotle as indisputably the greatest philosopher, but that it was not possible to understand him without his commentator Averroes. Hence it was very necessary to present Averroes's words correctly. Similarly, Avicenna was 'first in renown among the Arabs in the art of medicine' (Mantino did not pay attention to Avicenna's philosophical works) and, again, had to be understood correctly. In turn, in a Jewish document from Rome, Mantino is called 'the prince of the physicians', and the editor of the 1562 printing of the Giunta edition of Aristotle-Averroes calls his translation 'golden' (*aurea translatio*, vol. 1, fol. 319r). In addition to translating works by Aristotle and Averroes, he translated an ethical work by Maimonides (*Eight chapters on ethics of Maimonidies dedicated to Guido Rangoni*) as well as the 'supercommentaries' on Averroes' Middle Commentaries on Aristotle's logic by Levi ben Gherson.

SIGNIFICANCE

Unlike other Jews of the Renaissance, Mantino, as far as we know, did not write works in Hebrew for his co-religionists. His significance is that he was consulted by Christian scholars as a repository of Jewish learning, and as someone who could reveal to Latin readers the works of Arabic/Islamic authorities in philosophy and medicine that had been preserved in Hebrew translations, as well as to improve, through these same Hebrew sources, the existing Latin translations of these Arabic texts. He was held in the greatest esteem by Christian scholars, particularly with regard to the study of Averroes. His translations held a key position in the interpretation of Averroes in the mid- to late-16th century, a time when Averroes's interpretation of Aristotle was most in vogue.

EDITIONS & TRANSLATIONS

Translations of Averroes (most of the following texts are included in *Aristotelis Stagiritae Omnia Quae extant opera... Averrois Cordubensis in ea opera omnes quii ad nos pervenere Commentarii... Quorum aliqui... nuper a Iacob Mantino sunt conversi...*, Venice, 1550-52):

    The Long Commentary to Aristotle's *Posterior analytics* (the first 150 Commenta of Book 1), Venice, 1562

    Middle Commentaries on the Peripatetic logical corpus: Porphyry's *Isagoge*, Aristotle's *Categories*, *On interpretation*, *Topics* (books 1-4 only), and *Poetics*, Venice, 1550/52

    Middle Commentary on Aristotle's *Physics* (first three books), Venice, 1550/52

    Paraphrase (Middle Commentary) on Plato's *Republic* (dedicated to Pope Paul III), Rome, 1539

    Proemium to the Long Commentary on Aristotle's *Physics*, Venice, 1550/52

    Middle Commentary on Aristotle's *De anima*, Venice, 1550/52

    Book 3, chs 5 and 56, of the Long Commentary on Aristotle's *De anima* (apparently translated from a Hebrew translation from Latin), Venice, 1550/52

    Proemium to Book 12 of Aristotle's *Metaphysics*, Venice, 1550/52

    Proemium to the Long Commentary on Aristotle's *Metaphysics*, Venice, 1550/52

    Colliget, Venice, 1550/52

    Supercommentaries of Levi ben Gherson on Averroes's Middle Commentaries on Aristotelian logic, Venice, 1550/52

    Compendium (Epitome) of the *Metaphysics*, Rome, 1521, Bologna, 1523, Venice, 1542, Venice, 1550/52

    Paraphrase (Middle Commentary) of Aristotle's *On the parts of animals* (4 books) and *On the generation of animals* (5 books), Rome, 1521 (dedicated to Pope Leo X)

Translation of Avicenna:

    Avicenna, *Canon of medicine*, Book 1, fen 1, and Book 4, fen 1 (possibly also Book 1, fen 4, and other parts of the *Canon*), Paris, 1538

Translation of Maimonides:
Eight Chapters on Ethics, Bologna, 1526

STUDIES

C. Burnett, 'Revisiting the 1552-1550 and 1562 Aristotle-Averroes editions', in *Renaissance Averroism and its aftermath. Arabic philosophy in Early Modern Europe*, ed. A. Akasoy and G. Giglioni, Dordrecht, 2013, 55-64 (Mantino's translations in the Giunta editions of Aristotle-Averroes)

R. Hissette, 'Guillaume de Luna – Jacob Anatoli – Jacob Mantinus. A propos du commentaire moyen d'Averroès sur le "De interpretatione"', *Bulletin de Philosophie Médiévale* 32 (1990) 142-58

M. Steinschneider, *Die hebraeischen Uebersetzungen des Mittelalters und die Juden als Dolmetscher*, Berlin 1893, pp. 685 (Avicenna), 976-77 (bibliography)

Charles Burnett

Giovanni Battista Ramusio

DATE OF BIRTH 20 June 1485
PLACE OF BIRTH Treviso
DATE OF DEATH 25 April 1557
PLACE OF DEATH Venice

BIOGRAPHY

Giovanni Battista Ramusio began his career with the Venetian state in 1505 as *straordinario di cancelleria* (secretary to the chancery). His career as a public official, which would last for 52 years until his death, saw him rise to the prestigious position of secretary of the Council of Ten, which he held for the last four years of his life. Alongside his career, he pursued and developed, without interruption, his interests in subjects that could broadly be defined as humanistic and scientific. For Ramusio, these two ambits of his life existed in constant dialogue with one another. The culture of humanism provided him with an important professional set of tools. His career, in turn, allowed him daily access to a wealth of information from a variety of countries. Venice was a prime point of convergence for this type of knowledge and the period was one in which the geographical understanding of the world was undergoing many transformations. In addition, his service abroad as secretary to various ambassadors provided him with an opportunity to acquire considerable linguistic skills (at least in French and Spanish), and also to familiarise himself with foreign countries (France in particular) and to create contacts and form relationships.

His relatively calm life of study and work (his only child, Paolo, was born in 1532 from his marriage, in 1524, to Franceschina Navagero, who died in 1536) was marked by a few important friendships with prominent members of the cultural scene: Pietro Bembo, for whom he often worked, assisting him in the administration of the Marciana library; Girolamo Fracastoro, a Veronese doctor, from whom Ramusio received seven letters between 1533 and 1550, and to whom he dedicated the three volumes of the *Navigationi*; Andrea Navagero (until Navagero's death in 1529), a poet and philologist, with whom Ramusio had distant ties of kinship. Through Navagero, the young Ramusio would come into contact with the printing office of Aldo Manuzio, who would dedicate his edition of Quintiliano's *Institutio oratoria* (1514) to him.

The first texts of geographical interest published by Ramusio are the three *Libri della historia delle Indie occidentali*. Published in 1534, they contain Italian translations of works by Pietro Martire d'Anghiera (Book 1), Oviedo (Book 2) and a text on the conquest of Peru (Book 3). In 1536, Ramusio published an Italian translation of the French edition (1525?) of *Viaggio fatto da gli Spagniuoli a torno a'l mondo*, written by Antonio Pigafetta, who had survived the expedition with Magellan. Though Ramusio's name does not appear in any of these books, scholars agree that he was responsible for editing them. During these years, he met figures such as Damião de Gois and Olaus Magnus, the Bishop of Uppsala, who helped him obtain material on world travel. Diego Hurtado de Mendoza, brother of the viceroy of New Spain and the Spanish ambassador to Venice, provided him with material and information on the Americas. Gonzalo Fernández de Oviedo, *cronista de las Indias*, was also in contact with Ramusio, though not just for matters of cultural exchange; in 1538 the two completed an agreement for the sale of leather and sugar from the Americas. Unfortunately we do not have any information about the outcome of the venture. Some years later, he was in contact with Sebastiano Caboto and the orientalist Guillaume Postel, who gave him a copy of Abū l-Fidā"s *Taqwīm al-buldān* ('A sketch of the countries').

Between 1544 and 1548, he started a school in his own house for the education of his son and other adolescents. Among his collaborators on the project was Giacomo Gastaldi, the most important Italian cartographer of the 16th century. Gastaldi's work was greatly enriched by his relationship with Ramusio, as can be seen in his maps of Africa and Asia and in the world map written in Turkish, created in Venice in 1568.

At the time of his death, in addition to the second volume of *Navigationi*, Ramusio was busy working on the Italian and Latin translation of Geoffroy de Villehardouin's chronicle of the Fourth Crusade (1204), a project that had been entrusted to him by the Council of Ten.

MAIN SOURCES OF INFORMATION

Primary

H. Fracastorii, *De sympathia et antipathia rerum*, Venice, 1546, fols 26v-28r ('De quibusdam dubiis a Rhamnusio scriptis')

MS Venice, Biblioteca Marciana – It.VII.138 (8749) and It.VII.139 (8324) (Ramusio's Italian trans. of G. de Villehardouin, *La conquête de Constantinople*) (16th century)

MS Venice, Archivio di Stato – *Notarile, Testamenti, Atti Marsilio* 1209 (454), 25 aprile 1557 (Ramusio's last will)

Lettere di XIII huomini illustri, Venice, 1576 (Navagero's and Fracastoro's letters to Ramusio, fols 326v-367r)

P. Manuzio, *Epistolarum libri XII*, Venice, 1584, pp. 149-52

MS Venice, Biblioteca Marciana – It.X.143 (6535) (letters to Ramusio by P. Bembo, G. Cortese and others)

MS Venice, Biblioteca Marciana – It.VII.325 (8839), *Cronaca Ramusia* (17th century)

E.A. Cicogna, *Delle inscrizioni veneziane*, Venice, 1827, ii, pp. 315-30

M. Sanudo, *I diarii*, ed. R. Fulin et al., Venice, 1879-1902 (references to Ramusio in vols 7, 16, 21, 23-31, 33, 37, 40-41, 43, 49, 51-52, 54, 56-58)

F. Tarducci, *Di Giovanni e Sebastiano Caboto. Memorie raccolte e documentate*, Venice, 1892

A. Gerbi, *La natura delle Indie Nove*, Milan, 1975, pp. 272-78 (contract between Ramusio and Oviedo)

M. Donattini, 'G.B. Ramusio e le sue "Navigationi". Appunti per una biografia', *Critica Storica* 17 (1980) 55-100

P. Bembo, *Lettere*, ed. E. Travi, 4 vols, Bologna, 1987-93

A. Del Ben, *G.B. Ramusio cancelliere e umanista. Con l'edizione di 45 lettere a P. Bembo*, Trieste, 2004

Secondary

M. Donattini, 'Ombre imperiali. Le *Navigationi et viaggi* di G.B. Ramusio e l'immagine di Venezia', in M. Donattini, G. Marcocci and S. Pastore (eds), *L'Europa divisa e i nuovi mondi. Per Adriano Prosperi*, Pisa, 2011, ii, 33-44

M. Donattini, 'Etica personale, promozione sociale e memorie di famiglia nella Venezia del Rinascimento. Note su Paolo Ramusio seniore (1443?-1506)', in G.P. Brizzi and G. Olmi (eds), *Dai cantieri della storia. Liber amicorum per Paolo Prodi*, Bologna, 2007, 317-29

B. Jestaz, 'Ramusio et le baume du Caire. Une curiosité à Venise au XVIe siècle', in O. Bonfait, V. Gerard Powell and P. Sénéchal (eds), *Curiosité. Études d'histoire de l'art en l'honneur d'Antoine Schnapper*, Paris, 1998, 269-75

M. Milanesi, 'G.B. Ramusio e i cosmografi portoghesi', in M.L. Cusati (ed.), *Il Portogallo e i mari. Un incontro tra culture. Atti del Convegno internazionale (Napoli, 15-17 dic. 1994)*, Naples, 1996, 231-48

A. Del Ben, 'La prima edizione della "Storia Veneta" del Bembo e una lettera inedita di G.B. Ramusio', *Atti e Memorie dell'Accademia Patavina di Scienze Lettere ed Arti. Classe di Scienze Morali* 107 (1994-5) 203-16

A. Holzheimer and D. Buisseret, *The 'Ramusio' map of 1534. A facsimile edition*, Chicago IL, 1992

M. Donattini, 'Una famiglia riminese nella società e cultura veneziane. I Ramusio', in D. Bolognesi (ed.), *Ravenna in età veneziana. Materiali presentati al convegno di studio, svoltosi nei giorni 9-11 dic. 1983*, Ravenna, 1986, 279-94

Donattini, 'G.B. Ramusio e le sue "Navigationi". Appunti per una biografia'

R. Almagià, 'A proposito del mappamondo in lingua turca della biblioteca Marciana', *Atti dell'Istituto Veneto di Scienze, Lettere ed Arti. Classe di Scienze Morali e Lettere* 118 (1959-60) 53-59

G.B. Parks, 'Ramusio's literary history', *Studies in Philology* 52 (1955) 127-48

G. Levi della Vida, *Ricerche sulla formazione del più antico fondo dei mss. orientali della Vaticana*, Vatican City, 1939, pp. 326, 336

S. Grande, 'Relazioni geografiche tra P. Bembo, G. Fracastoro, G.B. Ramusio e G. Gastaldi', *Memorie della Società Geografica Italiana* 12 (1905) 93-197

A. del Piero, 'Della vita e degli studi di G.B. Ramusio', *Nuovo Archivio Veneto* n.s. 2 (1902) 5-112

E.A. Cicogna, *Inscrizioni veneziane*, Venice, 1827, ii, 315-30

WORKS ON CHRISTIAN-MUSLIM RELATIONS

Delle navigationi et viaggi, 'Navigations and voyages'
Navigationi, 'Navigations'

DATE Between 1543 and 1559
ORIGINAL LANGUAGE Italian

DESCRIPTION

As far as is known, Ramusio's *Navigationi et viaggi* project began slowly and later in his life, when he was already more than 50 years old. The first record of it dates back to 1543, when a request to print one volume of the work was presented to the Venetian senate. The volume in question was different from those he would eventually publish. His correspondence with Fracastoro was essential for the mounting and final stages of the work.

The three volumes of *Navigationi* were published in Venice over the span of a decade. During Ramusio's lifetime, the first volume (1550, 405 folios; a second edition, expanded to include new texts followed in 1554, 436 folios) and the third volume (1556, 455 folios) were published. The second volume, published posthumously (1559, 191 folios), was introduced with a note to its readers signed by Tommaso Giunti. The note revealed the identity of the author, Ramusio, and attributed the late publication date to the loss in a fire of part of the material ready to print and the death of the author. The edition was indeed smaller than the others (the second edition, in 1574, 256 folios, was greatly expanded). The noticeable imbalances and differences between the three volumes testify to the extensive labour that must have been required to compile them. In the case of the first, the abundance of travel accounts (26 in all), coupled with 14 contributions by the editor, give a clear indication that he dedicated more time to this volume. Defined as 'discorsi' by Ramusio, these interventions are at times long and dense (for example, the one describing the flooding of the Nile, followed by a 'risposta' by Fracastoro; or his long text on the sale of spices). In this volume, contemporary accounts are often alternated with material from Antiquity, with the intent of demonstrating how much new knowledge of the world had been gained in comparison to the period of classical Antiquity. This aspect is much less present in the second volume (19 accounts and five discourses, in the edition of 1574) and in the third volume (25 accounts and seven discourses, which in general are very brief). Though this deficit in the third volume is related to the novelty of material on the subject, the Americas, the same cannot be said of the second volume, which remains the least finalised of the three. Together, the three volumes provided the contemporary reader with the best possible description of the continents outside Europe, by documenting the great discoveries that had revolutionised Europe's understanding of the world over the last half-century; with this very goal in mind, Ramusio embellished the first and the third volumes with geographical maps (three in the second edition of the first volume, drawn by Giacomo Gastaldi, on Africa, India and South East Asia; nine in the third).

Though Ramusio's layout of the material shows no explicit programme, it follows a clear geographical and political order that can easily be reconstructed. The first volume contains texts on Africa and South Asia, and also on the coastal regions of Brazil, the territories around which the Portuguese Empire was constructed. In the third volume, concentrated on the Americas, there is an evident distinction between materials related to the Spanish Empire (the majority) and those dedicated to the cold regions of the north-east, i.e. the French colonial efforts. In the second volume, dedicated to continental Asia, the material is divided into three unequal sections. Some accounts are about the expanses of Muscovy, under the growing power of the Tsar. Another two (Pietro Querini's text, and an account of the Zeno brothers' trip to Greenland in the second edition) take the reader towards more northern lands and seas. However, the texts that characterise the volume most, and which are contextualised and elaborated by Ramusio, deal with the regions extending from the Caucasus towards Persia and China, areas that were known and written about by generations of Venetian travellers. Besides that of Marco Polo, considered a civilising hero by Ramusio, the most important accounts are provided by a group of Venetian ambassadors (Barbaro, Contarini, Zeno) sent to Persia to negotiate an alliance with the Shiʿī ruler Uzūn Ḥasan (d. 1478), the scope of the alliance being anti-Ottoman in nature. In its entirety, the volume is a knowing exaltation of the great influence exerted by Venice on that part of the world during this period.

Two other important aspects characterise the layout of the work. First, Ramusio's investigation is focused on world geography and its recent transformations, but excludes any discussion of the anthropological problems brought about by European colonial expansion (a stark contrast with the perspective of Las Casas or Acosta). Second, the work is focused on the parts of the world that were still unknown, or at least little known. Therefore, regions such as the Near East or the Ottoman world, which were so present in Italian and Venetian writings of the time, are completely ignored.

SIGNIFICANCE

Navigationi et viaggi deals only indirectly with the relationship between Christianity and Islam, a question outside the direct interests of Ramusio, who ignores the relationship between civilisations or religious beliefs in his discourses. Ramusio's cultural openness (not uncommon for a humanist) is, however, worth underlining. A good Venetian, he is convinced of the civilising power of commerce, and of the capacity of European law to establish colonies in the most distant of lands, following the Roman model. At the same time, he evaluates his sources on the basis of their intrinsic value, without ethnic or religious prejudice. Thus, not only does he offer the reader accounts by travellers such as Niccolò de' Conti and Ludovico Varthema, both of whom converted in order to extend their travels in the Islamic world (this is a known fact in the case of Conti and can be hypothesised in the case of Varthema), but he also admiringly includes texts by Muslim authors such as Leo Africanus and Abū l-Fidā'. The former's *La descrittione dell'Africa* opens the first volume, and makes up a fourth of it. And according to Ramusio, the *Taqwīm al-buldān* by Abū l-Fidā', 'gran principe di Soria' (which Ramusio received from Postel, including a small section in the second volume, fol. 18r), was essential for understanding the itinerary of the first trip of the

Polo brothers, and for guaranteeing the credibility of the most important text of the second volume.

To conclude, for Ramusio, openness and exchange between cultures was an essential condition for understanding the *macchina del mondo* ('system of the world'), for mastering its structures and attributes, and for controlling it with reason – a necessary preparatory basis for any aspiration to political domination. Within this universal perspective, the knowledge supplied by the learned figures of the Islamic world carries just as much weight as that coming from their Christian counterparts.

In similar works that came after Ramusio's *Navigationi et viaggi*, this attitude gave way to another perspective. At the end of the 16th century, the culture of the Counter-Reformation gave life to a different reading of the world – exemplified by Giovanni Botero's *Relationi universali* – in which Christianity's spiritual conquest of the world becomes the central theme (Descendre, 'Dall'occhio della storia'). In the same period, but outside Italy, Richard Hakluyt, who knew Ramusio's volumes well and cited them at length, would diminish the universal scope of the original work by putting the knowledge collected by the Venetian secretary at the service of a national colonial project: indeed, his *Principal navigations* deals exclusively with 'the English nation'.

EDITIONS & TRANSLATIONS

Marco Polo, *Il Milione nell'edizione di G.B. Ramusio*, ed. F. Ursini, Rome, 2012

Léon l'Africain, *Description de l'Afrique*, trans. A. Époulard, Paris, 1980

M. Milanesi (ed.), *Navigazioni e viaggi*, 6 vols, Turin, 1978-88

R.A. Skelton (ed.), *Navigationi et viaggi. Venice, 1563-1606*, 3 vols, Amsterdam, 1967-70

Marco Polo, *Milión o záležitostech Tatarů ... ve zpracování G.B. Ramusia*, ed. M. Mattušová, Prague, 1961

Léon l'Africain, *Description de l'Afrique*, trans. A. Époulard, Paris, 1956

Marco Polo, *Delle cose de' Tartari e dell'Indie Orientali ... nella versione di G.B. Ramusio*, Venice, 1954

Marco Polo, *Il Milione nell'edizione di G.B. Ramusio*, ed. R. Giani, Rome, 1954

Marco Polo and G.B. Ramusio, *Á la découverte de l'Amérique du Nord...*, ed. L. Langlois and M.J. Simon, Paris, 1933

Léon l'Africain, *Description de l'Afrique*, ed. C. Schefer and H. Cordier, Paris, 1896-98

C. Zeno and G.B. Ramusio, *A narrative of Italian travels in Persia, with a preface by G.B. Ramusio*, ed. C. Grey, London, 1873

H.E.J. Stanley of Alderley (ed.), *Travels to Tana and Persia, by J. Barbaro and A. Contarini*, London, 1873

M.H. Michelant and A. Ramé (eds), *Voyage de J. Cartier au Canada en 1534 d'après l'edition de 1598 et d'après Ramusio*, Paris, 1865

'El conquistador anonimo. Relación de algunas cosas de la Nueva España y de la gran ciudad de Temixtitán Mexico escrita por un compañero de H. Cortés', in J. García Icazbalceta, *Colección de documentos ineditos para la historia de Mexico*, Mexico City, 1858, i, pp. 368-98 (edition of the text edited by Ramusio in *Navigationi*, vol. 3, in the Spanish trans. by J. García Icazbalceta)

G.B. Ramusio, *Il viaggio di Giovan Leone e le navigazioni di Alvise da Ca' da Mosto, di Pietro di Cintra, di Annone, di un piloto portoghese e di Vasco di Gama*...Venice, 1837

Léon l'Africain, *De l'Afrique*, Paris, 1830 (modern edition of the *Historiale description de l'Afrique*, Lyon, 1556)

'A relation of the discovery which...the fleet of...F. Cortéz made...Taken out of the third volume of J.B. Ramusio', in *Hakluyt's collection of the early voyages*, vol. 3, London, 1809

H. Fracastorii...*Carminum editio*, vol. 1, Padua, 1739 (contains Ramusio's *Discorso* on the Nile flood and Fracastoro's answer)

Navigationi et viaggi, vol. 1, Venice, 1613

Marco Polo, *Chorographia Tartariae, oder Warhafftige Beschreibung der überaus wunderbahrlichen Reise...sampt einem Discurs Herrn J.B. Rhamnusii*, Leipzig, 1611

Navigationi et viaggi, 3 vols, Venice, 1606

Navigationi et viaggi, vol. 1, Venice, 1588

Navigationi et viaggi, vol. 2, Venice, 1583

Navigationi et viaggi, vol. 2, Venice, 1574

Navigationi et viaggi, vol. 3, Venice, 1565

Navigationi et viaggi, vol. 1, Venice, 1563

Navigationi et viaggi, vol. 2, Venice, 1559

F. Alvares, *Historiale description de l'Ethiopie*, Antwerp, 1558 (pirated edition of the 2nd vol. of *Historiale description de l'Afrique* below)

Navigationi et viaggi, vol. 3, Venice, 1556

Léon l'Africain, Historiale description de l'Afrique, tiers partie du monde, Antwerp, 1556 (French trans. of the first volume of *Navigationi et viaggi*)

Léon l'Africain, Historiale description de l'Afrique, tiers partie du monde, Lyons, 1556 (French trans. of the first volume of *Navigationi et viaggi*)

Navigationi et viaggi, vol. 1, Venice, 1554

Navigationi et viaggi, vol. 1, Venice, 1550

STUDIES

T. Veneri, 'G.B. Ramusio, molto più di uno spettatore. Le quinte delle *Navigationi et viaggi*', *Italica* 89 (2012) 162-201

Giovanni Battista Ramusio 'editor' del 'Milione'. Trattamento del testo e manipolazione dei modelli. Atti del seminario di ricerca (Venezia, 9-10 settembre 2010), Rome, 2011

R. Descendre, 'Dall'occhio della storia all'occhio della politica. Sulla nascita della geografia politica nel Cinquecento (Ramusio e Botero)', in E. Mattioda (ed.), *Nascita della storiografia e organizzazione dei saperi*, Florence, 2010, 155-79

F. Romanini, *'Se fussero più ordinate, e meglio scritte…' G.B. Ramusio correttore ed editore delle* Navigationi et viaggi, Rome, 2007

J.M. Headley, 'The sixteenth-century Venetian celebration of the earth's total habitability. The issue of the fully habitable world for Renaissance Europe', *Journal of World History* 8 (1997) 1-27

M. Milanesi, 'G.B. Ramusio e le *Navigazioni e viaggi* (1550-1559)', in R. Zorzi (ed.), *L'epopea delle scoperte*, Florence, 1994, 75-101

L. Stegagno Picchio, 'Navigationi et viaggi', in A. Asor-Rosa (ed.), *Letteratura italiana. Le opere*, Turin, 1993, ii, pp. 479-515

M. Donattini, 'Orizzonti geografici dell'editoria italiana', in A. Prosperi and W. Reinhard (eds), *Il Nuovo Mondo nella coscienza italiana e tedesca del Cinquecento*, Bologna, 1992, 79-154

L. Binotti, 'Liburnio e Ramusio lettori delle *crónicas* delle conquiste spagnole', *Annali d'Italianistica* 10 (1992) 80-95

S. Albertan-Coppola and M.C. Gomez Géraud, 'La collection des *Navigationi et viaggi* (1550-1559) de G.B. Ramusio. Mécanismes et projets d'après les para-textes', *Revue des Etudes Italiennes*, n.s. 36 (1990) 59-70

M. Milanesi, 'Introduzione', in Milanesi, *Navigazioni e viaggi*, v, 1985, xi-xxiii

M. Milanesi, *Tolomeo sostituito. Studi di storia delle conoscenze geografiche nel XVI secolo*, Milan, 1984

L. Stegagno Picchio, *Portugal e Portugueses no Livro das "Navigationi" de G.B. Ramusio*, Lisbon, 1984
M. Milanesi, 'Introduzione', in Milanesi, *Navigazioni e viaggi*, i, 1978, xi-xxxvi
R.A. Skelton, 'Introduction', in Skelton, *Navigationi et viaggi. Venice*, vol. 1
D.F. Lach, *Asia in the making of Europe*, 1. *The century of discovery*, Chicago IL, 1965, pp. 204-8
M. Böhme, *Die grossen Reisesammlungen des 16. Jahrhunderts und ihre Bedeutung*, Amsterdam 1962^2, pp. 73-95
G.B. Parks, 'The contents and sources of Ramusio's *"Navigationi"* ', *Bulletin of the New York Public Library* 59 (1955) 279-313
S. Grande, *Le carte d'America di G. Gastaldi*, Turin, 1905

Massimo Donattini

Luca de Armenia

DATE OF BIRTH   About 1510
PLACE OF BIRTH Mdina, Malta
DATE OF DEATH   11 October 1579
PLACE OF DEATH Mdina, Malta

BIOGRAPHY

Luca de Armenia was a 16th-century Maltese notable who came from a family of corsairs who attacked Muslim Maghrebi shipping. He was the son of Antonio de Armenia, who served as Vice Portulano of the Maltese Islands in 1527. Antonio had two sons, Fra Leone, a Dominican preacher, and Luca.

De Armenia was probably born in the first decade of the 16th century, though his exact date of birth is unknown. He served as *jurat* of the Mdina Università (town council), and spent some time as Mdina representative in Sicily. When the Ottoman fleet appeared on 18 May 1565 off the north-west coast of Malta, only a few miles from the old town of Mdina, de Armenia was sent to Jean de Valette, Grand Master of the Knights Hospitaller, at Birgu. He presented the request of the townspeople that, if Mdina was to be abandoned, shelter must be provided for the people, and if the Old City was to be held, it should be garrisoned by professional soldiers and supplied with arms and ammunition.

The next day, the Grand Master sent troops and ammunition to defend Mdina. De Armenia was a leader of the troops, fought passionately, and was hailed as a hero of the siege.

Later in his life, on 15 March 1576, he was denounced to the Malta Inquisition for keeping his cap on and remaining seated rather than kneeling during the elevation of the Host at mass in the Mdina cathedral church. This was just over three years before his death in 1579. His poem of the siege is his only surviving work.

MAIN SOURCES OF INFORMATION

Primary
MS Mdina, National Archives – MCC Ced. Supp. Et Tax., vol. ii, 1565-66
MS Valletta, National Library of Malta – 1142 sec. ii, not. 595

MS Mdina, Cathedral Archives – Archives of the Inquisition of Malta, vol. 3B, fol. 726
I. Bosio, *Dell'istoria della sacra religione et ill.ma militia di S. Gio. Gerosolimitano*, Rome, 1602, iii, pp. 515-66

Secondary
G. Bonello, 'Maltese poets in the sixteenth century. Gregorio Xerri's poem for the Great Siege of 1565. Part 2', in *The Sunday Times of Malta* (30 March 2014)
G. Bonello, 'Gregorio Xerri's poem for the Great Siege of 1565', in *The Sunday Times of Malta* (23 March 2014)
G. Cassar 'The role of the Maltese inhabitants during the Great Siege', in G. Cassar (ed.), *Malta in 1565. Separating fact from fiction*, Malta, 2005, 89-98, pp. 93-94
D. Cutajar and C. Cassar, 'Malta and the sixteenth century struggle for the Mediterranean', in G. Cassar (ed.), *Malta in 1565. Separating fact from fiction*, Malta, 2005, 1-33, pp. 14-16
S. Fiorini, 'Mdina in 1565', in G. Cassar (ed.), *Malta in 1565. Separating fact from fiction*, Malta, 2005, 107-115, p. 114
C. Cassar, *Society, culture and identity in early modern Malta*, Malta, 2000
D. Cutajar and C. Cassar, 'Malta and the sixteenth century struggle for the Mediterranean', in *Mid-Med Bank Report and Accounts (1985)*, 22-59
C. Cassar, '"O Melita infelix". A poem on the Great Siege written in 1565', *Melita Historica* 8 (1981) 149-54, http://mhs.eu.pn/mh2/19816.html

WORKS ON CHRISTIAN-MUSLIM RELATIONS

Ad patriam, 'To the homeland'
O Melita infelix, 'O unhappy Malta'

DATE 18 May 1565
ORIGINAL LANGUAGE Latin

DESCRIPTION
The poem *Ad patriam* consists of a mere 12 lines written in simple Latin verse. At the end is a dedication in Italian which reads: *Al molto mag. Signor mio da fratello honorando* ('To my most great lord whom I honour as a brother'). The signature, however, is illegible and it is difficult to deduce to whom the poem was really dedicated.

Although the formal title of the poem is *Ad patriam*, de Armenia himself seems to prefer to call it *O Melita infelix* ('O unhappy Malta'), which constitutes the introductory phrase of the poem and recurs twice again at the end. The signature shows that de Armenia considers himself to be both a 'patrician' and a Maltese citizen.

Ad patriam was, until recently, the only poem known from a Maltese author of the 16th century on the siege of 1565. In 2014, Giovanni Bonello discovered *Inno alla Vittoria* ('Hymn to victory'), a poem in Italian by Gregorio Xerri, another notable of Mdina. However, the poem by de Armenia seems to have been written as soon as the Ottoman fleet reached Malta. The one by Xerri must have been written sometime after the siege.

The strength of de Armenia's feeling is evident in a few lines near the end:

Nunc furor aut ira est in te aut sententia celi
classe potens reditum sanguine et igne parat.
Heu patriamque fugimus solamque relinquimus urbem
dispersi veluti sors sua cuique datur.
('Now fury or anger is against you, or the judgement of heaven
Prepares a powerful return with fleet, blood and fire.
And we alas flee our native land, and leave the city alone,
Scattered as his destiny is given to each.')

Here de Armenia more than hints that God is sending the Ottomans as punishment against his people, and they could be forced to surrender, reduced to slavery and taken away, leaving the town empty. This had been the fate of the population of Gozo in 1551, when nearly the whole population was carried off.

SIGNIFICANCE

Although brief, *Ad patriam* is an invaluable contribution to the literature about the Ottoman siege of Malta of 1565, and is the only poem so far known to have been written during the siege itself. It is most valuable as a record of the fateful night of 18 May 1565, when the author, as the envoy of Mdina, was waiting for an answer from the Grand Master. The stress he was suffering must have compelled him to write pessimistically of the great danger his fellow townspeople faced.

MANUSCRIPTS

MS Mdina, National Archives – MCC Ced. Supp. Et Tax., vol. ii, 1565-66 (1565-66, the dates covered by vol. 2)
MS Valletta, National Library of Malta – 1142 sec. ii, not. 595 (s.d.)

MS Mdina, Cathedral Archives – Archives of the Inquisition of Malta, vol. 3B, fol. 726 (15 March 1576)

STUDIES

Cassar, ' "O Melita infelix". A poem on the Great Siege written in 1565', http://mhs.eu.pn/mh2/19816.html (includes the text of the poem, with English trans.)

Carmel Cassar

Alfonso de Ulloa

Alfonso Vllon, Alfonso Uglioa, Alfonso di Vglioà,
Alfonso di Vglioa Hispano, Alfonso Villoa, Alonso de Ulloa,
Alphonse d'Ulloe

DATE OF BIRTH 1529
PLACE OF BIRTH Cáceres, Extremadura
DATE OF DEATH 1570
PLACE OF DEATH Venice

BIOGRAPHY

Alfonso de Ulloa was a Spanish author and translator, born in Cáceres in 1529. This date, given by Antonio Rumeu de Armas (*Alfonso de Ulloa, introductor*) as around 1530, was identified by Nicoletta Lepri and Anne-Marie Lievens on the evidence of declarations made by Ulloa himself to the tribunal of the Congregation of the Holy Office of the Inquisition (Lepri, 'Appunti', p. 59; Lievens, *Il caso Ulloa*, p. 48). Although some scholars (Gallina, 'Un intermediario'; Morel-Fatio, 'Alfonso de Ulloa et le comte') speculate that he was born in Toro (Zamora, Castilla y León), archival researches confirm that he came from Cáceres (Lievens, *Il caso Ulloa*, pp. 48-49; Di Filippo Bareggi, *Il mestiere di scrivere*, p. 49 n. 200).

Ulloa moved from Spain to live in Venice, most probably in 1546, in the service of the Spanish ambassador Diego Hurtado de Mendoza. In 1551, he joined the army of Ferrante Gonzaga, former viceroy in Sicily and at the time governor of Milan (1546-54). He also quickly acquired a good enough knowledge of Italian to make translations from Italian into Castilian. In 1556, he started to collaborate with other editors, and also to work on historical texts, starting with the *Cronica generale d'Hispagna et del regno di Valenza* by Anton Beuter, which included the history of the Turkish Empire translated from the original of Vasco Díaz Tanco in 1558. He wrote a number of biographies, of which that of the Emperor Charles V, published in 1560, proved very popular.

In 1568, Ulloa stood trial before the tribunal of the Congregation of the Holy Office of the Inquisition (Lievens, *Il caso Ulloa*, p. 136). He died in Venice on 16 June 1570.

The prologues and dedicatory epistles in the books written or translated by Ulloa are valuable sources for details of his life and the circumstances in which he worked. While he may only have been a background figure in the literary landscape of the day, his editorial work and his connections with prominent families such as the Gonzaga and King Philip II make him a significant figure both in cultural exchanges between Italy and Spain, and in political connections between the two countries.

MAIN SOURCES OF INFORMATION

Primary

MS Simancas (Spain), Archivo de Simancas – Estado, Venecia, bundle 1326: Alfonso de Ulloa, 'Cartas remitidas por Alfonso de Ulloa al Rey de España Felipe II, en solicitud de su mediación cerca del Dux de Venecia para alcanzar la libertad' (1568-69)

Secondary

P. Bellomi, 'Approssimazione all'edizione italiana della *Cronica generale d'Hispagna et del regno di Valenza* di Pere Antoni Beuter (Venezia, Gabriele Giolito de' Ferrari, 1556). L'esemplare della Biblioteca Civica di Verona', *Scripta. Revista Internacional de Literatura i Cultura Medieval i Moderna* 1 (2013) 55-81

A. Bognolo, 'El libro español en Venecia en el siglo XVI', in P. Botta (ed.), *Rumbos del Hispanismo en el umbral de Cincuentenario de la AIH*, Rome, 2012, 243-58

E. Carpi, 'Aspectos lingüísticos de la traducción italiana de la *Instrución de Mercaderes* de Saravia de la Calle', *Studi Linguistici e Filologici Online* 9 (2011) 63-86

A.M. Lievens, *Martínez versus Ulloa. Due autori, un Arcipreste de Talavera*, Perugia, 2008

E. Carpi, *La* Instrución de Mercaderes *di Saravia de la Calle e la* Institutione de' mercanti *di Alfonso de Ulloa*, Florence, 2007

N. Lepri, 'Appunti sul "camino della virtù" di Alfonso de Ulloa', in M.G. Profeti (ed.), *Il viaggio della traduzione*, Florence, 2006, 57-77

C. Coppens and A. Nuovo, *I Giolito e la stampa nell'Italia del XVI secolo*, Geneva, 2005

A.M. Lievens, *Il caso Ulloa. Uno spagnolo 'irregolare' nella editoria veneziana del Cinquecento*, Rome, 2002

C. di Filippo Bareggi, *Il mestiere di scrivere. Lavoro intellettuale e mercato librario a Venezia nel Cinquecento*, Rome, 1988

A. Rumeu de Armas, *Alfonso de Ulloa, introductor de la cultura española en Italia*, Madrid, 1973

O. Arróiz, 'Alfonso de Ulloa, servidor de don Juan Hurtado de Mendoza', *Bulletin Hispanique* 70 (1968) 437-57

A.M. Gallina, 'Un intermediario fra la cultura italiana e spagnola nel secolo XVI. Alfonso de Ulloa', *Quaderni Ibero-Americani* 19-20 (1956) 194-209

A.M. Gallina, 'Un intermediario fra la cultura italiana e spagnola nel secolo XVI. Alfonso de Ulloa', *Quaderni Ibero-Americani* 17 (1955) 4-11

A. Morel-Fatio, 'Alfonso de Ulloa et le comte Pierre-Ernest de Mansfelt', *Bulletin Hispanique* 15 (1913) 445-50

WORKS ON CHRISTIAN-MUSLIM RELATIONS

Libro dell'origine et successione dell'Imperio de' Turchi, 'Book of the origin and succession of the Turkish Empire'

DATE 1558
ORIGINAL LANGUAGE Italian

DESCRIPTION

This is Ulloa's Italian translation of Vasco Díaz Tanco's Spanish *Palinodia de la nephanda y fiera nacion de los Turcos*, published in 1547. Published in octavo in Venice in 1558, it consists of 237 numbered pages and three unnumbered pages.

Ulloa explains that he has made the translation in order to show Italian readers the might of the Christian army, whether Italian or Spanish, and expresses the hope this history of the expansion of the Turkish Empire will make the countries of Europe resolve to reconquer the lost lands of Christianity, including Jerusalem.

The 85 chapters in the book describe the history of the Ottoman Empire, from the founder Osman I to the golden age of Süleyman the Magnificent. Its aim is to trace the stages that led to the creation and consolidation of Europe's greatest enemy.

The Ottoman sultans are each described, with main attention given to Bayezid I (1354-1403), and Mehmed II (1432-81), whose Christian mother is mentioned but who had no faith of his own (*non osseruò né l'una né l'altra legge... né si mostrò Christiano né Turco*, 'he did not observe either one law or the other... he was neither Christian nor Turkish', p. 53), and to the dynastic struggle between Bayezid II and his sons Korkut, Ahmed and Selim I, during whose reign, when he finally became sultan, Christian renegades were often enlisted in the Turkish army.

The real comparison between the Christian and Islamic worlds is made when the history reaches Süleyman I. He and Charles V are described as equals, with similar virtues and qualities; he praises the qualities of his enemy; and he is described as a deeply devout and liberal ruler ('since religion creates justice, and temperance, and liberality buys the souls of soldiers, and sows the hope for a sure reward', p. 197).

The major part of the work is devoted to the battles that led to Turkish supremacy in the East. One of the most frequently recurring descriptors of the Turkish army is 'cruel', associated with their custom of not taking prisoners but cutting off their enemies' heads and displaying them on the battlefield. From this results a suggested explanation of the word 'Turkish' as being derived from *torquendo* ('torture'), or from *trux trucis* ('excessive cruelty').

SIGNIFICANCE

Although religion is largely kept in the background, the history states that the many defeats inflicted on the Christian army are a sign sent from God to his people, who are too weak and not sufficiently devout. By contrast, the Turks achieve success because of their obedience, their willingness to accept martyrdom, their self-control, and their abstinence from alcohol. Though he stands for the Catholic faith, Ulloa is nevertheless respectful of the enemy.

EDITIONS & TRANSLATIONS

Libro dell'origine et successione dell'imperio de' Turchi. Composto da Vasco Dias Tanco, & nuouamente tradotto dalla lingua spagnuola nella italiana per il signor Alfonso di Vlloa. Nel quale si contengono molte cose notabili & degne di memoria, Venice: Gabriel Giolito de' Ferrari, 1558

STUDIES

Lievens, *Il caso Ulloa*
Lievens, *Martínez versus Ulloa*
Rumeu de Armas, *Alfonso de Ulloa, introductor*

L'Asia del signor Giovanni di Barros, ' "Asia" by Sr Giovanni di Barros'

DATE 1562
ORIGINAL LANGUAGE Italian

DESCRIPTION

In 1562, Alfonso de Ulloa completed a translation of part of the Portuguese João de Barros's *Da Ásia*, which had been published in Lisbon in 1552. The quarto-size book is divided into two volumes of ten books each, *Deca prima* and *Deca seconda*, the first of 200 pages, and the second of

228. The first volume, dated 18 August 1561, is dedicated to Guglielmo Gonzaga, Duke of Mantua, and the second, dated 15 October 1561, to the Portuguese gentleman Duarte Gomes (perhaps the *converso* David Zaboca, as is suggested by Hugo Crespo ['O processo da Inquisição de Lisboa', p. 588]), and to the Archpriest Rocco Scarsaborsa, to whom Ulloa had also addressed his translation of Vasco Díaz Tanco's *Libro dell'origine et successione dell'impero de' Turchi* in 1558.

The *Deca prima* starts with a chapter about the expansion of Islam in Asia, North Africa and as far as al-Andalus. Barros describes the Muslim presence in Spain as a punishment from God for the sins of his community.

Throughout the chronicle, the infidels are consistently and roundly condemned – usually for their polygamy and duplicity – and the encroachment of Islam is often linked to demonic presences that allowed the faith to spread. But Barros cannot resist acknowledging the impressiveness of Arab scientific knowledge, which made possible many European discoveries. In addition, Moors often play important roles as interpreters in the first encounters between the Portuguese and indigenous people.

One of the last chapters of the *Deca seconda*, ch. 6, book 10, is devoted to the life of the Prophet Muḥammad and to the spread of Islam in the Arab world and Persia, emphasising the differences between them and their distinctive interpretations of Islam.

Islam is a continuing presence in the chronicle because a huge part of the territory discovered in Africa and in Asia was inhabited by Muslims. However, while the Portuguese explorers were, like the crusaders before them, ostensibly willing to sacrifice themselves in order to save the greatest number of souls from the dangers of paganism or Islam, closer reading shows that, even if the explorations were made in the name of Christianity, they were guided by the spirit of conquest that underlies the colonial process.

SIGNIFICANCE

Ulloa's translation of the Portuguese discoveries and conquests reflects a new understanding of the relationship between Europe and the rest of the known world, which Europeans were coming to see was both more vast and more complex than they had hitherto assumed. In his translation of Díaz Tanco's chronicle of the Turks, Ulloa had set out the changing borders of eastern lands that had resulted from confrontations between European states and the Ottoman Empire. In this translation of Barros' book, he presents a moving scenario in which the new horizons are not only geographical, but also economic, psychological and political, as the consequences of the discoveries made by Bartolomew Dias, Vasco da Gama and other adventurers begin to exert strong influence on the future of Europe.

The translation helped Italian readers to appreciate that the limits of the 16th-century world were no longer those of Europe and that the individual was now part of a much more fluid reality, where clear differences and encounters resulted in clashes.

EDITIONS & TRANSLATIONS

L'Asia del S. Giovanni di Barros, Consigliero del Christianissimo Re di Portogallo: de' fatti de' Portoghesi nello scoprimento, et conquista de' Mari et Terre di Oriente. Nella quale oltre le cose appartenenti alla militia, si ha piena cognitione di tutte le Città, Monti, & Fiumi delle parti Orientali, con la descritione de' paesi, & costumi di quei popoli. Nuouamente di lingua Portoghese tradotta. Dal S. Alfonso Vlloa. Con priuilegio dell'illustrissimo Senato Veneto, Venice: Vincenzo Valgrisio, 1562

STUDIES

H.M. Crespo, 'O processo da Inquisição de Lisboa contra Duarte Gomes alias Salomão Usque. Móveis, têxteis e livros na reconstituição da casa de um humanista (1542-1544)', *Cadernos de Estudos Sefarditas* 10-11 (2011) 587-688

W. Floor and F. Hakimzadeh, *The Hispano-Portuguese Empire and its contacts with Safavid Persia, the Kingdom of Hormuz and Yarubid Oman from 1489 to 1720. A bibliography of printed publications, 1508-2007*, Leuven, 2007, pp. 49-58

Rumeu de Armas, *Alfonso de Ulloa, introductor*

Lievens, *Il caso Ulloa*

La historia dell'impresa di Tripoli di Barbaria, 'The history of the expedition to Tripoli in Barbary'

DATE 1566
ORIGINAL LANGUAGE Italian

DESCRIPTION

In 1562, Alfonso de Ulloa declared that he was the author of a chronicle, written in Spanish and published in Venice, that described an attack on Tripoli on the North African coast, in which his uncle, Álvaro de Sande, fought and was later taken prisoner by the Turks, and an attack on the island of Djerba. According to Antonio Rumeu de Armas (*Alfonso de Ulloa, introductor*, pp. 97-99), Ulloa published the Italian translation of this text two years later in 1564. There is no extant copy of this edition, though there are copies of the second edition of 1566 (supporting Rumeu de Armas' hypothesis).

Unlike the Spanish original, the Italian reprint of 1566 includes together with the history of the attack on Tripoli a description of the taking of the fortress of Vélez de la Gomera in Morocco in 1564, and of the siege of Malta of 1565. The book brings together two important episodes in the conflict between Christians and Muslims, and it is clear that, in Ulloa's view, both in the attack on Djerba (1560) and in the siege of Malta (1565) the heavy losses inflicted on the European armies were due not only to the supremacy of the Turkish army but also to the lack of faith shown both on the battlefield by Christian soldiers and in high places by European rulers, who were not sufficiently supportive against the Turkish menace.

The text was reshaped by Ulloa and published in 1569, with the addition of a description of Süleyman the Magnificent's campaigns in Hungary, as well as an account of the initial stages of his son Selim II's reign.

The 1566 quarto edition consists of 88 leaves numbered on the *recto*, eight unnumbered leaves at the beginning of the book, and four unnumbered leaves at the end. It is dedicated to Gio. Giacomo Fucchero, that is, Johann Jakob Fugger, nephew of the banker Anton Fugger. The main text is divided into two parts. The first, divided into 30 chapters, is titled *Il successo dell'impresa di Tripoli, fatta per ordine del serenissimo Re catolico l'anno MDLIX*, and the second, without chapter divisions, is titled *Dell'historia parte seconda nella quale si contiene la liberation di Don Alvaro: l'espugnation del Pegnon di Velez della Gomera, et il successo della potentis. armata, mandata dal Turco sopra l'Isola di Malta l'anno MDLXV*.

The attribution to Ulloa of the Spanish edition as well as the Italian translation is doubted by many critics. In his 1932 essay, referred to by Nicoletta Lepri (Lepri, 'Appunti', p. 71), Balbi asserts that *La historia dell'impresa di Tripoli* was plagiarised by Ulloa from Pierre Gentil de Vendôme's *Della historia di Malta* of 1565 (Balbi, 'A bibliography'). Balbi also accuses Marino Fracasso of unjustly attributing the authorship of *Historia di Malta* to himself, publishing the volume *L'assedio et la guerra di Malta fatta dell'anno MDLXV* in 1566 under his own name. A general comparison between parts of the texts by Gentil and by Ulloa does show coincidence of some passages, but this is not enough to substantiate Balbi's thesis, since he did not consider the Spanish edition published by Ulloa in 1562.

Anne-Marie Lievens also calls into question the attribution of *Successo de la iornada que se començò para Tripol año de 1559* to Ulloa (Lievens, *Il caso Ulloa*, pp. 204-5), as affirmed by Rumeu de Armas, and cites the same words in the invocation to the reader: *Vino a mis manos pocos dias ha (amigo lector) el presente tractado de la jornada de Tripol. [...] El qual si viere que sera grato no dexarè de traduzirlo en lengua italiana, y aun en la Latina se imprimirà* (Ulloa, *Successo*, A6r and A7r). However, these words could be part of the rhetoric typical of literary works of the day, where the authorship of a text was rejected as a sign of modesty; or, it could also be a sincere statement by Ulloa, acknowledging that he has taken inspiration for his Spanish translation from other works, even though this was an established practice for author-translators of the 16th century (Carpi, 'Aspectos lingüísticos').

Another edition, without any indication about date or place of printing, and with very different page layout, further complicates matters: this edition reproduces Ulloa's text, but divides it into three parts instead of two; it also brings together the descriptions of Djerba and Malta at the beginning of the book. While awaiting further comparisons, for the time being it is possible to accept the hypothesis that Alfonso de Ulloa was the author of both the Spanish original and the Italian translation of the chronicle, even though he acknowledged his indebtedness to other sources.

SIGNIFICANCE

The two parts of Ulloa's chronicle focus on the qualities and faults of the Christian, Moorish and Turkish armies. Of course, the viewpoint of the chronicler is Christian, and sure enough he reads the numerous defeats suffered by the Europeans as an evident punishment sent by God due to the sins of his people and of his earthly representatives. Fear, which is lack of faith, is the greatest imprudence committed by Christian soldiers who, out of fear for their life, instead of unquestioningly trusting divine providence, show little courage in battle and are ready to betray their companions as soon as the situation deteriorates. However, Ulloa also highlights the faults of the enemy. He affirms that Moors are traitors by nature, greedy and desirous of wealth and rewards, as well as natural enemies of Christians.

In the first part of the book, the inhabitants of Djerba are the enemy; in the second part, which focuses on Malta, this role is transferred to the Turkish invaders, whose terrifying reputation was well-known to Christians: the chronicler mentions some of the reputedly typical ferocious practices of Turkish fighters, such as cutting off the heads of prisoners and those fallen in battle, and violence that did not spare even women or children. On the other hand, the author gives credit to the Turks for allowing social advancement regardless of class, depending on virtues shown in battle and not only on family origin.

EDITIONS & TRANSLATIONS

La historia dell'impresa di Tripoli di Barbaria, fatta per ordine del sereniss. re catolico, l'anno. MDLX, Milan, 1912 (facsimile reprint of 1566 edition)

Le historie di Europa del sig. Alfonso Vlloa, nuouamente mandate in luce. Nelle quali principalmente si contiene la guerra vltimamente fatta in Vngheria tra Massimiliano imperatore de' christiani, & sultan Solimano re de' turchi. Et vi s'ha cognitione di molti altri auenimenti occorsi in diuerse parti del mondo fino all'anno MDLXVIII. Con la tauola delle cose più notabili, che nell'opera si contengono, Venice: Bolognino Zaltieri, 1570

Historia di Zighet, ispugnata da Suliman, re de' turchi, l'anno MDLXVI. Nuouamente mandata in luce, Venice: Bolognino Zaltieri, 1570 (2nd edition, sometimes attributed to Fran Crnka)

Historia di Zighet, ispugnata da Suliman, re de' turchi, l'anno MDLXVI. Nuouamente mandata in luce, Turin: Johann Criegher, 1569 (1st edition, mentioned by Antonio Rumeu de Armas, *Alfonso de Ulloa, introductor*, pp. 184-85, sometimes attributed to Fran Crnka; no extant copy)

Historia delle cose avvenute ai christiani con gli infedeli all'isola di Zerbe in Africa ed a Malta l'anno MDLXV, e de quelle fatte in Ungheria dal sultan Solimano, re dei turchi, l'anno MDLXVI, 1569 (2nd edition, mentioned by Antonio Rumeu de Armas, *Alfonso de Ulloa, introductor*, p. 98; no extant copy)

Historia dell'impresa di Tripoli di Barbaria: Della presa del Pegnon di Velez della Gomera in Africa, fatte per comandamento del Serenissimo Re Catolico; Et il successo della potentissima Armata Turchesca, venuta sopra l'Isola di Malta l'anno MDLXV; Alla quale sono state aggiunte dal medesimo le cose fatte in Vngheria l'anno MDLXVI da Sultan Solimano, con la narratione della morte di esso sotto Seghetto, & la creatione di Selim suo figliuolo. La descrittione dell'Isola di Malta. Il disegno del'Isola delle Zerbe, e del forte, fattoui da Christiani, & la sua descrittione, & altre cose notabili. Con privilegio, Venice: Heirs of Melchiorre Sessa, 1569

La historia dell'impresa di Tripoli di Barberia, della presa del Pegnon di Velez della Gomera in Africa, et del successo della potentissima armata turchesca, uenuta sopra l'isola di Malta l'anno 1565. La descrittione dell'isola di Malta. Il disegno dell'isola delle Zerbe, & del forte, fattoui da christiani, & la sua descrittione, ed. Giovanni Battista Tebaldi, s.l., 1566 (the names of the author and editor and the date are inferred from the text)

La historia dell'impresa di Tripoli di Barbaria, fatta per ordine del sereniss. re catolico, l'anno MDLX. Con le cose auenute a christiani nell'isola delle Zerbe. Nuouamente mandata in luce, Venice: Melchiorre Sessa, 1564 (supposed *editio princeps*; no extant copy)

Svccesso de la iornada que se començó para Tripol año de 1559. y se acabó en los Gelues el de 1560. Al Illustrissimo y Excelentissimo Principe Don Gonçalo Hernandez de Cordoua Duque de Sessa. Nueuamente publicado por Alonso [sic] de Vlloa, Venice: Giovanni Griffio, 1562 (original Spanish edition)

STUDIES

Carpi, 'Aspectos lingüísticos'
Rumeu de Armas, *Alfonso de Ulloa, introductor*
Lievens, *Il caso Ulloa*
H.A. Balbi, 'A bibliography of the order of the hospital of St John of Jerusalem', *Archivum Melitense* 9 (1932) 1-21

Paola Bellomi

Sebastiano Erizzo

DATE OF BIRTH 19 June 1525
PLACE OF BIRTH Venice
DATE OF DEATH 5 March 1585
PLACE OF DEATH Venice

BIOGRAPHY

Sebastiano Erizzo was a Venetian patrician and scholar. He has been called the only Venetian novelist of a 'certain level in the 16th century' (Preto, *Venezia e i Turchi*, p. 163). His father, Antonio di Sebastiano Erizzo, was a *Bailo* in Constantinople and a 'Savio' of *gli Ordini* (of which there were five, administering the maritime possessions) and 'Savio' of *Terraferma* (of which there were five, administering the mainland domains). Erizzo was married twice. He had no children but had a close relationship with his nephew, Piero Lando. Erizzo also became a 'Savio' of *gli Ordini* on 2 June 1551, and was elected 'Savio' of *Terraferma* on 1 June 1575, re-elected in 1581 and 1583. In 1582, he briefly became a member of the Council of Ten. For further information regarding Erizzo's political life, see Gino Benzoni's thorough entry on Erizzo in the *Dizionario biografico degli Italiani*.

Before 1570, Erizzo may have led a more scholarly than political life. He received a humanist education, first in Venice and later, in the first half of the 1540s, in Padua where he studied original texts of Aristotle and Plato. He was well versed in Latin and Greek and in the history and philosophy of the ancients. His interests in Greek philosophy and its systems of knowledge are reflected in the publication of *Trattato dell'istrumento et via inventrice degli antichi* (Venice, 1554) dedicated to Cardinal Marcello Cervini, the future Pope Marcello II. He translated Plato and published the first properly annotated Italian translation of Plato's *Timaeus* (Venice 1557 and 1558 [Edit16]), and in 1574 his translations of selected dialogues of Plato were published: *I dialoghi di Platone, intitolati l'Eutifrone, ouero della santità, l'Apologia di Socrate, il Critone o di quel che s'ha affare, il Fedone o dell'immortalità dell'anima. il Timeo ouero della natura. Tradotti ... da m. Sebastiano Erizzo e del medesimo ... illustrati con vn commento sopra il Fedone. Nuouamente mandati in luce.*

Erizzo was a numismatist, and he created a huge collection of coins and medals in his home and wrote a successful treatise, *Discorso sopra le medaglie antiche con particolare dichiarazione di molti riversi* (Venice, 1559) dedicated to the King of Poland, Sigismund II Augustus, which is still known among numismatists (according to Bragantini, 'Introduzione', p. xxxii). He was also a bibliophile, and his library contained 1,150 printed books and manuscripts, in both Latin and the vernacular, including classics and minor authors.

Erizzo's contacts with Lodovico Dolce and the publisher Ruscelli may have been the reason for the expansion of his interests towards the field of literature. In 1561, he published *Esposizione nelle tre canzoni di messer F. Petrarca, chiamate le Tre Sorelle*, and he also composed Petrarchist verses himself. Perhaps as a further result of his studies in the great vernacular literature of the Italian *Trecento*, he wrote the 36 tales entitled *Le sei giornate* (1567), among which appear two stories set during the wars between the Ottomans and Venetians in the second half of the 15th century.

Erizzo also wrote a political discourse entitled *Discorso di Sebastiano Erizo gentil'huomo vinitiano de governi civili*, published alongside *Trattati ouero discorsi di m. Bartolomeo Caualcanti sopra gli ottimi reggimenti delle republiche antiche et moderne* (1571). In this work, Erizzo explains the Aristotelian theory of three forms of government and the reasons for their corruption.

MAIN SOURCES OF INFORMATION

Secondary
P. Preto, *Venezia e i Turchi*, Rome, 2013
G. Benzoni, art. 'Erizzo Sebastiano', in M. Caravale et al. (eds), *DBI*, vol. 40
C. Di Filippo Bareggi, *Il mestiere di scrivere*, Rome, 1988
R. Bragantini, 'Introduzione, nota biografica, nota bibliografica', in R. Bragantini (ed.), *Le sei giornate*, Rome, 1977, ix-xxxvii
A.H. Krappe, 'The sources of Sebastiano Erizzo's "Sei giornate"', *Modern Philology* 19 (1922) 269-85

Works on Christian-Muslim relations

Le sei giornate, 'The six days'

DATE 1567
ORIGINAL LANGUAGE Italian

DESCRIPTION
Erizzo's *Sei giornate* was published under the prestigious protection of Lodovico Dolce, who did not limit himself to publishing classical authors, but also assumed the role of talent scout (di Filippo Bareggi, *Il mestiere di scrivere*, p. 59). The work is a collection of short stories and is often described as yet another imitator of Boccaccio's *Decameron* – justifiably, since Erizzo does imitate the *Decameron* both structurally and linguistically. However, according to Bragantini, the editor of the modern edition, it is 'a much more complex work which is full of literary and cultural "signals"' (Bragantini, 'Introduzione', p. ix).

The frame of *Le sei giornate* copies the *Decameron*: a company of ('noble') students from the University of Padua meet on six successive Wednesdays in 1542, during June and July, and tell six stories each. Erizzo followed the instructions of P. Bembo, who had suggested Boccaccio as a linguistic model for writing prose in the vernacular. However, the purpose of Erizzo's stories, or *avvenimenti* ('events') as he calls them, differs radically from that of the *Decameron* in that its moralistic attitude completely overwhelms the entertaining aspects so central in the work of Boccaccio. Erizzo's stories are similar to *exempla*, and he does assert in some of his other works that literature should be morally edifying. He calls his tales *avvenimenti essemplari* and *morali ragionamenti*. The concept of *virtù* is a crucial evaluative term in his texts: a virtuous death gives honour and meaning to a person's life. This moralising attitude can be seen as a result of the changed moral and intellectual climate of the Counter-Reformation. Furthermore, unlike the *Decameron*, in *Le sei giornate* the motif of *la beffa*, 'mockery', including jokes about sex, is not found; there is no use of comedy or humour; Erizzo hardly includes dialogues or direct speech at all, but rather uses monologues and a more essay-like style; there are no women among the narrators and there are only a few women among the characters; there are no religious figures either. In his introduction to the *Sei giornate*, Bragantini describes at length this 'strong reduction of Boccaccio's large thematic and stylistic ventaglio' (Bragantini, 'Introduzione', p. xiv). Finally, Erizzo's representation of Muslims is radically different from Boccaccio's – a point that the critics seem to have overlooked. In the *Decameron*, there is no prejudice against or accusation of Muslims, who are treated equally with the Christian characters. Boccaccio does not make a theme of conflicts or wars between Muslims and Christians and does not judge Islam from a religious perspective. Rather, he depicts a Mediterranean world in which commercial exchange between *mercatanti* (see V. Branca's still useful essay on this aspect of the *Decameron*, 'L'epopea dei mercatanti', in *Boccaccio medievale*, Florence, 1956, 172-206) and the Muslim world is natural. Among the characters in the *Decameron* who are praised for their generosity and virtues are the Muslim leader Sultan Saladin (novella I.3 and X.9). This treatment of Saladin, however, is in line with that of many other Christian writers from the 13th and 14th centuries.

The setting of Erizzo's *Sei giornate*, like that of the *Decameron*, is the Mediterranean, not only in the two 'Turkish' stories, but also in many others, and they take place against a background of intense maritime traffic, including both merchants and pirates sailing between the shores of Mare Nostrum. In Boccaccio, Muslims do not represent any threat or barbarian cruelty, but Erizzo writes in a society that has completely changed, with the Counter-Reformation becoming rigorous and demanding *l'ossequio quotidiano e totale alle norme, naturalmente imposte dall'esterno* ('daily and total obedience to the rules, naturally imposed externally'; Bragantini, 'Introduzione', p. xv). While the distant settings of many of Boccaccio's novellas reflected the openness of Italian city states towards diverse social, ethical, political and geographical realities, and the possibility of exploring them and integrating them into a new understanding of the world, the setting of Erizzo's stories in a remote time and space – whether in an undefined period of Greek or Latin Antiquity, or in the Mediterranean (e.g. Crete, Calabria, Sicily, Naples, Constantinople, Hungary, Bohemia), or on an even more distant 'Atlantic' stage (e.g. Peru, Portugal) – suggests a symbolic distance from the Italian context and thus reflects a resistance to new intellectual, social and political realities.

On the other hand, the broad setting of Erizzo's *Sei giornate* is also a result of the greater geographical knowledge available to 16th-century writers, including knowledge that came through the European discovery of America and the expansion of the Ottoman Empire. And even when the action of a story takes place in Ottoman surroundings, the setting is neither *meraviglioso e mitico* ('wonderful and mythical') (Preto, *Venezia e i Turchi*, p. 163) nor a representation of an 'Orient de fantasie' (as suggested by G. Lebatteux, quoted by Bragantini, 'Introduzione', p. xiii). Rather, as Preto also claims, 'the reader immediately gets the impression of the particular relation between the Venetian civilisation and the Ottoman empire' (*Venezia e i Turchi*, p. 163).

The stories in *Le sei giornate* do not relate directly to the Italian contemporary situation, but they definitely touch upon issues in Erizzo's historical context: almost all the stories contain a plot describing an individual's transgression of the current law and his punishment by a tyrannical government, kings or other leaders who punish their subjects. Erizzo focuses on the tragic, the cruel and the moral; in tune with the reforming and perhaps tragic spirit of the time, he describes horror and pathos. All these *novelle tragiche* contain dramatic deaths, killings and captivities, often as a punishment for the violation of a law or in revenge. Erizzo's stories form a sort of moral educational treatise in which the acknowledgement of the individual's virtues and moral correctness is central. But it is important to stress that Erizzo does not represent religious devotion, but rather a civic ethic (Benzoni, 'Erizzo Sebastiano') which is not based on Christian religious values but – inspired by the classical Latin and Greek world – on political public morals concerning the common weal and representing an ideology of state. As Benzoni ('Erizzo Sebastiano') has claimed, Erizzo is an author writing in the Counter-Reformation rather than an author of the Counter-Reformation.

Two of Erizzo's 36 short stories directly treat Turkish motifs, and they are the only ones that take place in an almost contemporary period, that is at the end of the 15th century, and not in remote Antiquity or in the 13th century. The two 'Turkish' stories thus represent an exception to the rest of the collection. The historical and geographical contexts of these two stories are described realistically, though not in detail, and when the main characters move to places that belonged to the Ottoman Empire at that time (Gallipoli, Smyrna, the Aegean Islands) they depict a realistic space.

Like the other stories in *Le sei giornate*, these two open with an exposition of the facts, followed by the protagonist's monologue, and finally a conclusion. The first *avvenimento* with a Turkish motif is the twenty-ninth (of the fifth day). It takes place during the reign of Mehmed II (1451-81), at the time of his conquest of the city of Negroponte on the Island Euboea in 1470. Negroponte belonged to the Venetians, but after the Ottoman siege it became a part of the Ottoman Empire and an Ottoman naval base. During this first Ottoman-Venetian war between 1463 to 1479, Venice also lost several other possessions in Albania and Greece, but the well-fortified city of Negroponte, which had been a Venetian protectorate for centuries, was the most important.

Erizzo introduces the story by referring to his source, *le istorie Viniziane*. According to Preto he used Malipiero's *Annali Veneti* (*Venezia e i Turchi*, p. 163 n. 456), but according to di Francia and Bragantini he used Sabellico's history of Venice, *Decades rerum Venetarum*, published in 1487 in Latin, and in the Italian vernacular by Lodovico Dolce in 1544 under the title of *Le historie vinitiane di Marco Antonio Sabellico – opera forse più impegnativa e ambiziosa della storiografia veneziana di quei tempi* ('perhaps the most challenging and ambitious work of Venetian historiography of those times'; Bragantini, 'Introduzione', p. xxvii). Bragantini demonstrates that Erizzo at times copies Sabellico's narration *verbatim* (*Le sei giornate*, p. 239 n. 1). According to Krappe, the source of *avvenimento* XXIX and XXX is a Venetian chronicle about Mocenigo's achievements, *De Petri Mocenici Imperatoris gestis libri tres*, written by Coriolano Cippico (1544), and Krappe claims that Erizzo's stories are in places literal translations from this Latin text ('Sources', p. 283). Erizzo's main source is the Latin writer Valerio Massimo, but he also imitates and quotes various other authors such as Boccaccio, Petrarch and Machiavelli, and it is not possible to find sources behind all the stories.

The twenty-ninth tale relates that, during the battles between Venice and the Ottomans, a young Sicilian approached the Venetian Captain Pietro Mocenigo (1406-76) when the latter was overwintering with his army in Naples. The Venetians had 'taken and destroyed Smyrna and after a bloody battle had set the enemy on the run' (ed. Bragantini, p. 242; all references to the text are to this edition). Erizzo may be referring to a raid on Smyrna by the Venetians, though this did not in actual fact result in the city being taken from the Ottomans. Mocenigo was one of the greatest Venetian admirals and he revived the city's navy after the defeat at Negroponte in 1470. He was a captain of the Venetian army from 1471 until 1474, when he was elected doge of Venice.

The framework of the story is thus historically correct, and Erizzo does not change either the names or the historical events (as he does in many other stories). Antonio, a young Sicilian soldier (who had perhaps been captured during the battle of Negroponte; p. 242), makes a proposal to Mocenigo: he has seen the Ottoman navy in Gallipoli and suggests setting fire to it, if he can get some men to assist him. Mocenigo agrees. Antonio then leaves for Gallipoli, pretending to be a fruit seller, but his plan does not succeed and he has to hide in a nearby forest with his men. However, he had also set fire to his own boat by mistake, and his fruit, which is floating in the sea, exposes him and he is captured by Turkish soldiers, who realise that they have been cheated. One of his men is killed while Antonio and the others are taken prisoner and brought to the Sultan Mehmed II. When 'the Ottoman' asks him to explain himself, Antonio answers that he knows very well that the Ottoman's cruelty and 'barbarian nature and custom' will make Mehmed take revenge and punish him. He is very cocky and also says it was unlucky that the sultan's head did not burn together with the ships. He does not deny that the sultan's power is huge, but he does not at all regret his own 'high and magnanimous enterprise' (p. 244) and is prepared to die. Mehmed then cuts him and his fellow prisoners into pieces.

The story pays homage to Pietro Mocenigo, a man who was 'excellent and outstanding in the art of war' (pp. 241-42), and praises the proud young Sicilian for his courage and heroism. The narrator also presents the Turks' mercilessness, blaming Mehmed for not forgiving the Sicilian. Mehmed is full of wonder, it is told, because of the courage of the Italian, but he does not 'imitate the magnificent act of Porsena' (p. 244), a reference to the Etruscan King Lars Porsena, who did not punish the young Roman Gaius Mucius when he sneaked into the Etruscan camp to assassinate Porsena.

Erizzo's stories were published in 1567, four years before the battle of Lepanto in a period in which *il lungo sogno di neutralità di Venezia volgeva ormai al termine* ('the long dream of Venetian neutrality came to an end'; Bragantini, 'Introduzione', p. xxvii). They might thus be considered to be encouraging the struggle against the Turks.

The second *avvenimento* with a specifically Turkish theme, number XXX, which may also be inspired by Sabellico's *Venetian history* (Bragantini, *Le sei giornate*, p. 245 n. 1, and Erizzo: *non partendomi dalle viniziane istorie*, p. 247), tells of an Ottoman woman who sacrifices her own life in order to be close to her dead husband. The story tells of another heroic sacrifice, perhaps even more impressive as it is made by a woman.

The story is introduced by a long moral reflection upon the courage of the young Sicilian in the earlier novella, but it also shows an understanding of the sultan's desire for revenge. The narrator then reflects on the nature of personal sacrifice: one should not sacrifice oneself either without a cause or for money, as mercenaries do, but only as the Sicilian did, for the *ben commune*, the common weal, a concept that is repeated several times during the narration, and in this specific context includes the 'common enemy of the Christian name' (p. 247). The logic is clear. Common weal corresponds to the common *Christian* weal, and when this value is violated, revenge is considered 'just'. This way of reasoning seems similar to the crusading rhetoric of the humanists of the

15th century and earlier periods. The chronology of the two accounts (or perhaps two 'sisters') is also logical: the introductory reflections on revenge after the twenty-ninth story point forward to the story of the Ottoman woman, and in a way these reflections also prepare a legitimisation of the historical events recounted in the story: the Venetians' attack on Smyrna, during which they plunder and kill the inhabitants, is presented as just revenge for the killing by the Ottomans during the battle of Negroponte.

The story takes place after the Ottomans' conquest of Negroponte in 1470, in which the Turks had used *un'empia e grandissima crudeltà* ('impious and great cruelty'; p. 248), and after the Turkish raids on Friuli in north-eastern Italy in the 1470s, when the Ottoman soldiers spread fear and destruction (p. 248). According to Pedani, 'it was not in fact the bulk of the army, but of irregular troops, the Akinci, raiders of the border, which are used as scouts or as a diversion to distract the enemy's attention'. These raids on Venetian Friuli took place between 1469 and 1478, and again in 1499 (Pedani, *Venezia porta d'Oriente*, p. 55).

Again, Pietro Mocenigo appears as a heroic figure, since he is leading the attack on Ottoman Smyrna (situated on the Aegean side of Anatolia) in alliance with the pope and the King of Naples. Erizzo gives a long description of the Venetians' surprise attack on Smyrna, a city that had never experienced war, as the narrator says (p. 248), and thus had not strengthened the city walls or prepared any other defence. The Venetians enter the city, steal 'robes, gold, silver and precious vessels of great price, like city thieves' (p. 249), and take prisoner women and children who hide in the mosques. The prisoners are taken to the harbour to be sent away and sold as slaves, but on their way to the Venetian ships one of the prisoners, a young woman, stops and weeps at her husband's grave. Her monologue bewails her miserable destiny and the loss of her 'beloved home': *Vedrò io le sue miserabili rovine, le distruzzioni de' nostri tempii, le vergogne delle vergini e delle matrone, la loro cattività, la uccisione de' fanciulli? E l'incendio universale della città, lo sparso sangue de' cittadini nostri e la cenere della patria* ('Will I see her miserable ruins, the destruction of our temples, the shame of virgins and matrons, their captivity, the killing of children? And the fire of the universal city, the shed blood of our citizens and the ashes of home'; p. 249). She does not want to leave the only consolation in her life, the grave of her dead husband, to whom she had promised eternal fidelity, and prefers to die there embracing the gravestone rather than following the enemy soldiers to be sold as a slave (p. 250). Even if her words could have 'softened any hard heart' she is killed by an *importuno e poco pietoso soldato* ('importunate and pitiful little soldier'; p. 250). With her love for her husband and her homeland, the Ottoman women is an example of a most virtuous, self-sacrificing wife, like Boccaccio's Griselda or a *Lucretia rediviva*, and in spite of her Ottoman origin she functions as an example to the Christian readers.

In this account, the Venetians are, perhaps surprisingly, depicted as the hostile forces, while the Ottoman civilians are the innocent victims of the cruel attack. One may wonder why Erizzo chooses to recount this historical event instead of repeating the same 'cast of characters' from the earlier novella, in which the Italians were the heroes and the Ottomans the cruel tyrants. In fact, this story contains different interpretative possibilities that might also reflect different authorial intentions. Even if the Venetian soldier is cruel and merciless to the Ottoman woman, he represents a strong Venice that is going to defeat the Ottoman enemy. And the cruelty of the Venetian soldier could thus be considered a Machiavellian feature, a necessary element if one wants to win. The story thus infuses courage and self-confidence in Italian readers for future battles against the Ottomans. The Ottoman woman may thus represent wishful thinking about a defeated Ottoman empire.

The Venetian attack on Smyrna is described as just revenge for the raids committed by the Ottomans in Venetian territories. The narrator dwells for quite some time on these events at the beginning of the account, and the revenge motif is introduced in full.

Other stories may contribute even more to this 'memory-work' or indirect thematising of the contemporary Ottomans, even if they are set in more remote periods. One of them is the first day's sixth *avvenimento*, which tells a fictitious story (Bragantini, *Le sei giornate*, p. 70 n. 1) about two Christian kings who help each other against the Moors. Guiscardo, King of Cyprus, helps Rinieri, King of Sicily, to attack the coasts of Barbary in revenge for the damage the Moors have done in Sicily. The narrator presents the story as a case of 'true friendship' and a 'memorable example of love and faith between two friends' (p. 70). The King of Sicily asks his 'confederate' Guiscardo, for help against his enemies, 'being Moors and coming from Barbary', because he, Rinieri, is full of 'just anger' and the desire to take revenge for the 'insults' from the Moors, and he has decided to plunder some cities along the Barbary coast. Guiscardo goes to Sicily with ten armed galleys of his own and 15 others from Rinieri. On the Barbary Coast, the enemies wait for the Christian kings, prepared to defend themselves, and after a bloody battle the 'hostile forces of the

Moors' win and both Christian kings are captured. Guiscardo makes a long speech to Rinieri, telling him that it would have been better to wait for the enemy at home rather than attacking abroad. Bragantini demonstrates in his notes that Erizzo closely follows Machiavelli here, using the same historical examples. Guiscardo concludes his monologue with a passage that could also very well apply to the anxiety of Christian rulers in Erizzo's time: 'Who says that the enemies will not continue their victory after having destroyed the Christian army? That they will not steal the weapons from the Christian soldiers and use them to invade their countries now? In this way, while we cannot oppose the power of Fortuna, from having been kings of powerful people, we shall become humble and vile vassals of the Barbarians' (p. 74).

The Muslim captors allow the kings to be freed for a ransom. Rinieri goes to Sicily to get the money and returns to Africa to pay the ransom to buy his and Guiscardo's liberty. To celebrate their close friendship, Rinieri gives one of his sisters to be Guiscardo's wife.

The origin of the two allied Christian kings is not accidental: Cyprus was under Venetian rule from 1489 until 1571, when it was finally conquered by the Ottomans. Throughout the period of Venetian rule, Ottoman Turks raided and attacked the people of Cyprus at will. In 1539, when Erizzo was 14 years old, the Turkish fleet attacked and destroyed Limassol. The Venetians had fortified Famagusta, Nicosia and Kyrenia, but most other cities were easy prey. In the summer of 1570, three years after the publication of Erizzo's *Sei giornate*, the Turks struck again, but this time with a full-scale invasion rather than a raid. Famagusta resisted until 1571.

SIGNIFICANCE

The two stories demonstrate that, by the time Erizzo was writing, the Ottomans had taken on the conventional features of an enemy, being unremittingly cruel and unpredictable. Erizzo hardly needs to draw attention to this, but can assume his audience will share his attitude towards an enemy who they all knew had to be opposed and could not be allowed to appear sympathetic.

EDITIONS & TRANSLATIONS

R. Bragantini (ed.), *Le sei giornate*, Rome, 1977
G. Papini (ed.), *Le sei giornate*, Lanciano, Italy, 1916
Le sei giornate di Messer Sebastiano Erizzo, Milan, 1805
G. Poggiali (ed.), *Le sei giornate*, Livorno: Riccardo Bancker, 1794
Le sei giornate, Venezia: Giovan Varisco e compagni, 1567

STUDIES
Preto, *Venezia e i Turchi*, p. 163
M. Formica, *Lo specchio turco*, Rome, 2012, p. 85
M.P. Pedani, *Venezia porta d'Oriente*, Bologna, 2010
F. Pignatti, 'La novella esemplare di Sebastiano Erizzo', *Filologia e Critica* 25 (2000) 40-68
Benzoni, art. 'Erizzo Sebastiano'
di Filippo Bareggi, *Il mestiere di scrivere*
Bragantini, 'Introduzione'
Krappe, 'Sources'

Pia Schwarz Lausten

Francesco Balbi di Correggio

DATE OF BIRTH   16 March 1505
PLACE OF BIRTH   Correggio, Emilia-Romagna
DATE OF DEATH   12 December 1589
PLACE OF DEATH   Fornovo

BIOGRAPHY

Francesco Balbi was born in Correggio in the Italian region of Emilia-Romagna in 1505, and died in 1589. He enlisted in the employ of the Order of St John during the Ottoman Siege of Malta of 1565, perhaps driven by poverty. He published the first edition of his diary in Alcala de Henares in 1567, while a second improved edition was published in Barcelona in 1568. Later, he wrote a poem celebrating the victory of the Holy League over the Ottoman fleet at Lepanto in 1571, *Canzone sulla vittoria dell'Armata della Santissima Lega contro la Turchesca* (Venice, undated). In 1586, he was in Parma and served under Duke Ottavio Farnese, and later that year he befriended Giovanni Maria Agazzi, a poet who hosted him at his house and whose company he shared for several years. In 1587, he attended the festivities held in Milan in honour of Duke Don Vincenzo de Gonzaga, who was passing through that city to take possession of the Duchy of Monferrato.

Balbi then left for his last trip outside Italy in the retinue of Muzio Sforza Colonna, and reached Madrid as page to the crown prince, the future Philip III. He remained with the prince even when Colonna had to stay for a time in Barcelona. By 1589, Balbi had returned to Italy and settled with Agazzi in his house in Fornovo, where he died.

Balbi di Correggio's works include encomiums of nobles he had served, and also the posthumously published poem *La Historia de los amores del valeroso moro Abindarraez y de la hermosa xarifa Aben Cerases, y la batalla que hubo con la gente de Rodrigo Narbaez, alcalde de Antequera y Alora, y con el mismo Rodrigo: Vueltos en versos por Francisco Balbi de Coregio* ('The history of the loves of the valiant Moor Abindarraez and the beautiful *xarifa* Aben Cerases, and the battle that took place with the supporters of Rodrigo Narbaez, alcalde of Antequera and Alora, and with the same Rodrigo: rendered in verse by Francisco Balbi of Correggio') (Milan: Pacifico Ponçio, 1593).

MAIN SOURCES OF INFORMATION

Primary
Francesco Balbi di Correggio, *Verdadera relacion de todo lo que este año de M.D. LXV ha sucedido en la isla de Malta*, Alcalá de Henares: J. de Villanueva, 1567
Francesco Balbi de Correggio, *La verdadera relacion de todo lo que el anno de 1565 ha sucedido en la isla de Malta, de antes que llegase l'armada sobre ella de Soliman el Gran Turco. Hasta que llego el socorro postrero del Rey Catolico Nuestro Señor Don Felipe II de este nombre. Recogida por Francisco Balbi de Corregio, en todo el sitio soldado; y en esta segunda impresion por el mismo autor revista, enendada y ampliada*, Barcelona: Pedro Regnier, 1568

Secondary
Francisco Balbi de Correggio, *Diario del gran asedio de Malta, 1565*, Madrid, 2007 (Foreword by A.G. Simón; Introduction by Q.A. Vaquero)

WORKS ON CHRISTIAN-MUSLIM RELATIONS

Verdadera relacion de todo lo que este año de M.D. LXV ha sucedido en la isla de Malta; Diario del gran asedio de Malta, 'Diary of the siege of Malta'

DATE 1567
ORIGINAL LANGUAGE Spanish

DESCRIPTION
Balbi di Correggio's diary, based on his experiences in the garrison of Senglea throughout the four months of the Ottoman Siege of Malta, *La verdadera relacion de todo lo que el anno de 1565 ha sucedido en la isla de Malta, de antes que llegase l'armada sobre ella de Soliman el Gran Turco. Hasta que llego el socorro postrero del Rey Catolico Nuestro Señor Don Felipe II de este nombre. Recogida por Francisco Balbi de Corregio, en todo el sitio soldado; y en esta segunda impresion por el mismo autor revista, enendada y ampliada*, is a day-by-day account of the siege in 1565. The first edition of 1567 consists of 112 folios. This account was revised and amended on the basis of recollections from several eyewitnesses of the siege, and a second edition, consisting of 131 folios, was published in 1568. The siege was a major historical event in the Mediterranean region in the latter half of the 16th century, and it has captured people's imagination through the centuries, most of all as a heroic saga with the advantage of also being true and well documented. The siege itself was the predictable

culmination of a tense international situation, in a particular epoch of Mediterranean history.

The fleet that reached Malta in May 1565 was the biggest Ottoman naval operation to date, sailing under the direct order of Piali Pasha, the ambitious son-in-law of Süleyman II. According to Balbi's sober estimates, it carried 28,000 fighting men, including an elite force of 6,300 Janissaries (one-third of the entire Janissary force), as well as 6,000 volunteers. These figures do not include the crews, slaves, supply corps and merchants. Modern historians consider about 30,000 to be a reliable total figure for an Ottoman fighting force (including Barbary corsairs). The military command was entrusted to Mustafa Pasha, a veteran of the Hungarian campaigns.

Balbi di Correggio presents a balanced commentary on the course of the siege. He is critical of the strategy of the Ottoman leaders, but it is well known that even the leader of the North African corsairs, Turghud Rais, was not impressed by the way the Ottoman leaders carried out their plans. Throughout the account, Balbi di Correggio shows great respect for the Ottoman Empire. Despite his repeated references to the 'Turk' as the enemy, he manages to present a very fair account of the events of the siege. His description is the most detailed and best known account of the campaign.

SIGNIFICANCE

Francesco Balbi's diary is the best-known eyewitness account of the siege (there is at least one other, in the form of a long poem by the knight Hipolito Sans), and all later histories rely heavily upon it, including that of Giacomo Bosio, the official historian of the Knights of St John, whose massive account first appeared in 1588.

EDITIONS & TRANSLATIONS

Balbi, *Diario del gran asedio de Malta*

E.D.S. Bradford (trans.), *The siege of Malta 1565*, London 1965, Woodbridge, 2005[2] (English trans.)

E. Montalto and R. Giustiniani (ed. and trans.), *Diario dell'assedio all'isola di Malta. 18 maggio-17 settembre 1565*, Rome, 1965, Genoa, 1995 (Italian trans.)

H.A. Balbi (trans.), *The siege of Malta 1565*, Copenhagen, 1961 (English trans.)

La verdadera relacion de todo lo que el anno de 1565 ha sucedido en la isla de Malta, de antes que llegase l'armada sobre ella de Soliman el Gran Turco. Hasta que llego el socorro postrero del Rey Catolico Nuestro Señor Don Felipe II de este nombre. Recogida por Francisco Balbi de Corregio, en todo el sitio soldado; y en esta segunda impresion por el mismo autor revista, enendada y ampliada, Barcelona: Pedro Regnier, 1568

Verdadera relacion de todo lo que este año de M.D. LXV ha sucedido en la isla de Malta, Alcalá de Henares: J. de Villanueva, 1567

STUDIES

D. Abulafia, *The Great Sea. A human history of the Mediterranean*, London, 2011, pp. 431-34

S.R. Crowley, *Empires of the Sea. The final battle for the Mediterranean*, London, 2008, pp. 176-77

B. Croce, *La Spagna nella vita italiana durante la Rinascenza*, Bari, 1949, p. 159 n. 4

M. Baffi, 'Uno sconosciuto poeta italo-spagnuolo del cinquecento', *Rendiconto della Real Accademia di Architettura, Lettere e Arti – Societa' Reale di Napoli*, new series 17 (1937) 125-43

G. Calabritto, *I romanzi picareschi di Mateo Aleman e Vicente Espinel*, Valletta 1929, p. 110

F. Flamini, *Il Cinquecento*, Milan, 1902, p. 436

G. Tiraboschi, *Biblioteca Modenese*, Modena, 1781, i, p. 142

G. Colleoni, *Notizia degli scrittori più celebri che hanno illustrato la loro patria di Correggio*, Guastalla, 1776, p. 7

G.M. Mazzuchelli, *Gli scrittori d'Italia*, Brescia, 1758, i, p. 81

F.S. Quadrio, *Della storia e della ragione d'ogni poesia*, vol. 2, Milan, 1741, pp. 409, 663; vol. 3, Milan, 1742, p. 71; vol. 6, Bologna, 1749, p. 450

Carmel Cassar

Francesco Sansovino

DATE OF BIRTH 1521
PLACE OF BIRTH Rome
DATE OF DEATH 28 September 1583
PLACE OF DEATH Venice

BIOGRAPHY

Francesco Sansovino was born in Rome in 1521, son of the Florentine architect and sculptor Iacopo Tatti, known as Sansovino. Following the sack of Rome in 1527, Iacopo returned to Florence and, after a brief stay there, set off with his family for Paris, where he had been summoned to work at the court of Francis I. En route to Paris, however, Iacopo decided to settle with his family in Venice, where on 1 April 1529 he was appointed *protomastro della Republica*.

Francesco completed his early education in grammar and rhetoric in Venice at the school of Stefano Piazzone, and later studied under the Latinist Giovita Rapicio. In 1536, he enrolled in the Faculty of Law at the University of Padua. In spite of his father's wish that he pursue a career in the law, Francesco began to show a growing interest in and inclination to literature. During his time at university he attended meetings of the Accademia degli Infiammati, founded in Padua in 1540, where he came into contact with some of its members: Daniele Barbaro, Alessandro Piccolomini, Ludovico Dolce, Vincenzo Maggi, Benedetto Varchi and Sperone Speroni. In 1543, he graduated in Civil Law at the University of Bologna.

Back in Venice, he practised the legal profession in the service of the Republic, but during these same years he also devoted himself to poetry, composing sonnets, and prose, publishing four works, the *Retorica* (Bologna, 1543), the *Lettere sopra le diece giornate del Decamerone* (Venice, 1543), *Ragionamento nel quale brevemente s'insegna a giovani uomini l'arte d'amare* (Mantua, 1545) and *Arte oratoria secondo i modi della lingua volgare* (Venice, 1546). At the same time he began his activity as a translator of Latin and editor.

In 1550, Sansovino was sent to Rome by his father in a desperate attempt to find employment at the court of Pope Julius III, as mentioned in a letter by Pietro Aretino, a close friend of Francesco's father, who also corresponded with Francesco himself. In 1552, however, Francesco was back in Venice, where in 1554 he married Benedetta Misocca, with whom he had two children, Giacomo and Fiorenza (who died at the age of 11). In 1560, he opened a print shop under the sign of the 'crescent moon'. His debut was a remarkable one: in the first year alone, at least ten different works were published. Publishing continued at an uneven pace over the following years: in 1561, he dissolved the company and ran the print shop by himself; in 1569, the name of Francesco was replaced by that of his son, Giacomo, on the frontispiece of the Venetian editions, but Francesco continued to remain in charge of the publishing activities until his death in 1583. Over a span of 20 years, Sansovino's print shop put out more than 50 titles, including original works and reprints, mostly literary texts (collections of letters and speeches, poetry, tales, treatises on rhetoric, grammar and lexicography, and guidebooks on art); works of history (from Livy and Plutarch to Leonardo Bruni and Francesco Guicciardini); politico-historical and legal treatises and technical works on agriculture and medicine; translations from Latin; editions of Italian classics (Dante, Petrarch, Boccaccio, Ariosto, Bembo); and a variety of religious and devotional texts. A large part of this output was in vernacular Italian in a compact form or ottavo, showing that Sansovino clearly intended to perform the function of cultural populariser.

During the same years, Sansovino also devoted himself to writing, translating and editing texts, producing more than 100 works of his own (published and unpublished), many of which appeared in numerous editions and enjoyed lasting success.

In 1564, he published *Il secretario*, a treatise on the functions and role of court secretary, which was reprinted no less than eight times in 20 years and became a model and reference work for treatise-writing in the 16th and 17th centuries. In 1579, he published *Cronologia del mondo*, a universal history from the creation of the world down to 1579; 1581 saw the appearance of *Venetia città nobilissima et singolare*, a work that contributed to Sansovino's fame more than any other. The book is a repository of information about Venetian history, art and customs, and the author had intended it to be a history of the city written in Italian (Pietro Bembo's *Historiae Venetae* was written in Latin). In reality, it shows that Sansovino's interests were moving away from historiography to artistic and antiquarian topics.

MAIN SOURCES OF INFORMATION

Primary

Archivio di Stato di Bologna, *Archivio dello Studio, Collegi Legai*, reg. 30, c. 279v-280r

Archivio di Stato di Venezia, *Notarile Atti*, notaio Antonio Callegarini, b. 3113, c. 503 sgg, 23 agosto 1581

Archivio di Stato di Venezia, *Notarile Testamenti*, notaio Marcantonio Cavanis, b. 194, n. 156

Archivio di Stato di Venezia, *Provveditori alla Sanità*, Necrologio n. 21, a. 1583, n° 815

F. Sansovino, *Le lettere sopra le diece giornate del Decamerone di Giovannni Boccaccio*, Venice, 1543

Rime diverse di molti eccellentissimi autori, Venice: Gabriele Giolito, 1545

F. Sansovino, *L'avvocato*, Venice: Alessandro de Vian, 1554

F. Sansovino, *Il secretario*, Venice: Francesco Rampazetto, 1564

Lettere di diversi eccellentissimi signori a diversi uomini scritte, Venice: Curzio Troiano Navò, 1542, c. 98v

P. Aretino, *Lettere*, Parigi: Matteo Maestro, 1609, i, v, c. 239

Secondary

P. Mula, ' "Dipinto in scrittura". Pour une bibliographie des travaux de Francesco Sansovino, polygraphe vénitien (1521-1583)', *La Bibliofilia* 102 (2010) 245-80

L. Braida, *Libri di lettere. Le raccolte epistolari del Cinquecento tra inquietudini religiose e 'buon volgare'*, Rome, 2009, pp. 201-14

I. Melani, 'La "troppa frettolosa voglia di mio padre". Educare un figlio nell'Italia del Cinquecento. Tre casi', *Schifanoia* 28-29 (2005) 75-86

E. Bonora, *Ricerche su Francesco Sansovino. Imprenditore librario e letterato*, Venice, 1994

C. di Filippo Bareggi, *Il mestiere di scrivere. Lavoro intellettuale e mercato librario a Venezia nel Cinquecento*, Rome, 1988, pp. 16-20, 42-43, 64-69, 125-26, 144, 163, 216-19, 250, 263-64, 280

C. Roaf, 'The presentation of the 'Decameron' in the first half of the sixteenth century with special reference to the work of Francesco Sansovino', in P. Hainsworth et al. (eds), *The languages of literature in Renaissance Italy*, Oxford, 1988, 109-21

C. Cairns, *Pietro Aretino and the Republic of Venice. Researches on Aretino and his circle in Venice 1527-56*, Florence, 1985

C. Marazzini, 'Un editore del '500 tra Bembo ed il parlar popolare: Francesco Sansovino ed il vocabolario', *Studi di Lessicografia Italiana* 5 (1983) 193-208

E. Cochrane, *Historians and historiography in the Italian Renaissance*, Chicago IL, 1981

F. Gaeta, 'Storiografia, coscienza nazionale e politica culturale nella Venezia del Rinascimento', in G. Arnaldi and G. Folena (eds), *Storia della cultura veneta*, Vincenza, 1981, iii, 1-91

G. Aquilecchia, 'Pietro Aretino e altri poligrafi a Venezia', in G. Arnaldi and M. Pastore Stocchi (eds), *Storia della cultura veneta*, vol. 3/2. *Dal primo Quattrocento al Concilio di Trento*, Vicenza, 1980, 61-98

R.S. Samuels, 'Benedetto Varchi, the "Accademia degli Infiammati", and the origin of the Italian academic movement', *Renaissance Quarterly* 29 (1976) 599-634

P.F. Grendler, 'Francesco Sansovino and Italian popular history 1560-1600', *Studies in the Renaissance* 16 (1969) 139-80

G. Pusinich, 'Un poligrafo veneziano del '500. Francesco Sansovino', *Pagine Istriane* 8 (1911) 1-18

G. Sforza, 'Francesco Sansovino e le sue opere storiche', *Memorie della R. Accademia delle Scienze di Torino*, series 2 97 (1897) 27-66

E. Cicogna, *Delle inscrizioni veneziane*, Venice, 1834, iv, pp. 31-91

WORKS ON CHRISTIAN-MUSLIM RELATIONS

Historia universale dell'origine et imperio de' Turchi, 'Universal history of the origin and empire of the Turks'

DATE 1560 and 1561
ORIGINAL LANGUAGE Italian

DESCRIPTION

Historia universale is a collection of texts published in the Italian vernacular and written by various authors dealing with the habits, customs and laws of the *'natione de' Turchi'*. The work also relates the deeds of Turkish sovereigns from the first sultan, Osman, who came to power at the end of the 13th century, up to the 16th century. The anthology was conceived and put together by Francesco Sansovino, who printed it in Venice between 1560 and 1561 at the printing house he had founded, and it is very likely that this work was its inaugural project. The first edition consists of three volumes and is very rare – so rare, that Sansovino's 19th-century biographers, Emanuele Cicogna and Giovanni Sforza, admitted they had never seen it. Four more editions were published during the course of the 16th century (1564, 1568, 1573, 1582) with emendations and additions by Sansovino. After his death in 1583, two more editions appeared, in 1600 and 1654. These seven editions, all published in Venice, differ from one other: they contain different dedications, the editor's comments vary and the number and order of the texts differ. In some cases, the texts were translated into the vernacular by Sansovino himself, with the authors' names not always mentioned.

The entire work is divided into two main sections: the first is largely a description of the social, political, cultural and religious aspects of Ottoman civilisation; the second deals with tales of war and '*altre cose notabili e degne di memoria*' (1582, c. 41v) accomplished by the Turkish sovereigns and their people, tracing the rise of Turkish power from its controversial beginnings. With the exception of the cuts made to the censored edition of 1582 '*per ordine della Santa Inquisitione*', the most important changes in the various editions occur in the second section, which was supplemented from time to time in order to keep up with the latest events.

The collection begins with an anonymous life of Muḥammad presented by Sansovino as a sort of introduction to the *Trattato de costume et vita de' Turchi* by Giovanni Antonio Menavino. This text was first published in 1548 in Venice, and later the same year in Florence. After this follow several texts by the Croatian Batholomej Geogijević (Bartholomaeo Georgius), who had been a prisoner of the Turks from 1526 to 1535, but whose name no longer appears after the 1573 edition. This is followed by: an initial part of a treatise by Theodoro Spandugino, written originally in Italian but published for the first time in French in Paris in 1519 (*La genealogie du Grant Turc*); part of a travel narrative to Turkey by Venetian Benedetto Ramberti, which was omitted from later editions; the life of the king of Persia Sach Ismael and his son Sach Tamas written by Spandugino; and, finally, Pope Pius II's famous letter to Sultan Mehmed II, which completes the first volume of the 1560 edition but was not included in the later editions from 1573 on.

In the second volume are found: *Trattato dell'origine dei Turchi* by Andrea Cambini; the second part of Spandugino's *Discorso* on the origins of the Turkish rulers; extensive excerpts from Paolo Giovio's *Commentario de le cose de' Turchi*; the *Discorso della Guerra di Rhodi* by Jacques Fontaine, already translated into Italian by Sansovino and published in Venice in 1545; the *Fatti di Solimano dopo la presa di Rhodi fino all'anno 1533*; and the *Lettera d'un segretario del sig. Sigismondo Malatesta delle cose fatte nella Morea per Maomet Secondo*.

The third volume contains (in addition to several anonymous accounts, such as the description of the conquest of Negroponte): Luigi Bassano's treatise on the *Costumi et i modi particolari della vita de' Turchi*; three texts on the Turkish conquest of Constantinople by Leonardo di Chio, Isidoro Ruteno and Christophe Richer; the story *Dell'assedio di Scutari* and the *Fatti illustri del signor Giorgio Scanderbegh* by Marino Barlezio; *Fatti illustri di Selim imperator de Turchi* taken from Paolo Giovio; and, finally, Anton Francesco Cirni's account of the campaign against Djerba launched by King Philip II of Spain at the end of 1559.

In later editions, the work's basic outline remained more or less unaltered, though a few changes were made with regard to the selection of texts to be included and whether or not the authors' names were mentioned. The 1573 edition includes for the first time the names of Wolfgang Drechsler and Niccolò Zeno, and most importantly the story of the Turkish siege of Malta written by Pietro Gentile di Vendome, already published in 1565, anonymous accounts of the *Impresa di Zighet fatta da Solimano re de Turchi l'anno 1566*, of the *Impresa di Famagosta*, and of the Turkish conquest of the entire island of Cyprus in 1570-71, and finally an account of the battle of Lepanto in 1571, which ends the volume.

In 1582, another edition of *Historia universale* was published, the last to be edited by Sansovino, *et riformata in molte sue parti per ordine della Santa Inquisitione*, as indicated in the frontispiece.

No longer included in the collection was the anonymous life of Muḥammad that had opened all the earlier editions of the *Historia* since 1560, or the account of the battle of Lepanto, which appeared in the 1573 edition; several pieces were added for the first time that were not in previous editions: the *Guerra del Regno di Cipro di l'anno 1570* by Giovan Pietro Contarini and, most notably, two pieces by Francesco Sansovino that he had already published separately: the *Lettera ovvero discorso sopra le preditioni fatte in diversi tempi da diverse persone, le quali pronosticano la nostra futura felicità per la guerra del Turco l'anno 1570* (Venice 1570) and *Informatione ai soldati Christiani e a tutti coloro che sono sulla potentissima armata della Serenissima Signoria di Venetia fatta contra Selim II re dei Turchi l'anno 1570, dove si mostrano tutte le rotte che hanno havuto gli eserciti Turcheschi in diversi tempi et le cagioni per le quali sono venuti a tanta grandezza, et dove si leggono in disegno gli abiti dei giannizzeri e degli altri uomini della corte del turco che lo servono nella militia* (Venice, 1570).

Historia universale appeared among the works for suppression on the list of prohibited books of Parma (1580) and on the *Index* of Rome (1590 and 1593).

SIGNIFICANCE

Historia universale was published in 1560. In the spring of the previous year, the Treaty of Cateau-Cambrésis had pacified Europe after 50 years of war. It was in this context that King Philip II of Spain launched an expedition in the autumn of 1559 to the island of Djerba against the Barbary pirates, which ended in the rout of the Spanish fleet. With remarkable publishing sensitivity and business acumen, Sansovino attempted to cater for the renewed interest among the Venetian public and elsewhere in obtaining historical information and recent news about the Turks.

Sansovino's idea was to gather into a single volume the latest writings available on the book market, completing and updating them for readers who could read Italian vernacular. Thus, the anthology does not contain any erudite treatises in the humanist tradition, which were for the most part written in Latin and based on classical historiography. Instead, more attention is given to stories by people who had themselves experienced the events narrated: merchants, ecclesiastics, travellers, captured soldiers who had managed to return to Europe. The profile of the Turkish world that emerges is therefore a much more nuanced and dynamic one than in more academic accounts, and certainly more in character with a city such as Venice, which had longstanding commercial ties and therefore a pragmatic attitude to the Sublime Porte and which also performed the important function of collecting and disseminating information about the Turks for the rest of Europe. Sansovino's attention went mostly to events that closely concerned the economic system and Venice's relationship with the Turks, so he includes not only the Ottoman capture of Constantinople in 1453, a key moment in the history of the Turkish presence in Europe, but other events as well, such as the Turkish capture of Negroponte, and the conquest of Rhodes and Cyprus.

In terms of its ideology, Sansovino's collection in *Historia universale* is certainly more moderate than other contemporary works, which were in general dominated by a sense of aversion and clear antagonism towards the Turks, in other words by a crusading spirit. In *Historia*, the response to the Ottomans' unstoppable rise to power is a sense of respect and admiration: social customs, administrative and legal structures and military discipline are so highly developed that, as Sansovino remarks in a note to the reader: '[...] *la disciplina della militia et la obedienza et la fortuna de' Romani dopo la rovina di quella Repubblica sia trapassata a questa generazione*' (1573, c. 3r). Since the Turks *'tentano di sottomettere interamente il Mondo alla loro servitù'*, Sansovino aimed to provide information '*a fine che gli huomini buoni et i veri christiani imparino a conoscere quella potenza*' (1572, c. 3v), seeking to respond to a need for knowledge that a few decades before had led Paolo Giovio to write his *Commentario delle cose de' Turchi*, which was published in Rome (1532) and spread rapidly to many countries in Europe in the hope of an upcoming Turkish defeat by Emperor Charles V. Starting with Giovio, Sansovino generally drew on Italian sources, and left out of his anthology texts about the Turks written in Reformed Europe, many of which were by authors who were banned in Italy or regarded with suspicion, since they were circulating in the Protestant lands.

The years 1570-71 saw a substantial change in Venetian attitudes to the Turks. In the spring of 1570, the mission of Selim II's envoy to Venice came to an end. By now the sultan's expansionist designs on Cyprus were unmistakable and the following year the Ottomans occupied the island, notwithstanding the considerable deployment of naval forces by the leading European powers allied together in the Holy League.

Subsequent editions of *Historia universale* clearly register this change. In the two texts by Sansovino – the *Lettera ovvero discorso sopra le preditioni fatte...* and *L'informazione ai soldati christiani...* – published earlier in 1570 and now included in the 1582 edition, the Turks are portrayed exclusively as enemies who '*si sono fatti grandi*' because of the cowardice, errors and political divisions of the Christian states. The Turkish leader Selim II, son of Süleyman the Magnificent, is described as '*più infedele d'ogni altro infedele [...] che incontanente sprezzando la sua religione [...] ha mostrato ad ognuno, non tenendo conto della sua legge, che è di animo doppio et risoluto [...] che habbia a cavarsi ogni voglia giusta, o ingiusta ch'ella si sia, non lo affrenando né rispetto di religione, né vincolo di sacramento, né osservanza di promessa veruna*' (1582, c. 487v).

One result of this new phase in Turkish-Venetian relations is that several contributions dealing with doctrinal matters in the early editions of *Historia universale* were left out of the 1582 edition. These writings had already been published in the first printed edition of the Qur'an, which came out in Venice in 1547 and which must certainly have been known to Sansovino.

The seven editions of the *Historia universale* span a century, and are testimony to the work's enduring success with the public. Throughout this period, it would remain the basic text in Italy for an approach to understanding the Ottoman world. Copies of it were kept in public and private libraries throughout the 17th century.

EDITIONS & TRANSLATIONS

Historia universale dell'origine, guerre, et imperio de' Turchi. Nella quale si contengono le leggi, gl'offici, i costumi, et la militia di quella natione; con tutte le cose fatte da loro per terra, et per mare. Accresciuta in questa ultima impressione di varie materie notabili, con le vite di tutti gl'imperatori ottomani fino alli nostri tempi, 471 fols; vol. II: *Vite, e fatti d'alcuni Imperatori Ottomani aggiuntovi di nuovo, cioe Selimo II, Amorathe III, Mahometto III, Acmate, Mustafa, Ottomano II, Amurathe IV, et Ibrahimo ultimo*, Venetia: presso Sebastiano Combi e Giovanni la Nou, 1654, 522 fols

Historia universale dell'origine et imperio de' Turchi: con le guerre successe in Persia, Ongaria, in Transilvania, Valachia, fino l'anno 1600. Et riformata in molte sue parti per ordine della Santa Inquisizione. All'Excellentiss. Signor Gio. Carlo Sivos dedicata. Nella quale si contengono le leggi, gli offici, i costumi, et la militia di quella natione, con tutte le cose fatte da loro per terra, et per mare; con le vite particolari de' Principi Ottomani, con l'effigie del naturale di essi Imperatori, cominciando del primo fondator di quell'imperio, fino al presente Meemeth III 1600. Et con tavola di tutte le cose più notabile, et degne, Venezia: presso Alessandro de' Vecchi, 1600, 557 fols

Historia universale dell'origine et imperio de' Turchi. Raccolta et in diversi luoghi di nuovo ampliata da M. Francesco Sansovino et riformata in molte sue parti per ordine della Santa Inquisitione. Nella quale si contengono le leggi, gli offici, i costumi et la militia di quella natione; con tutte le cose fatte da loro per terra, et per mare. Con le vite particolari de' Principi Ottomani; cominciando dal primo fondator di quel imperio fino al presente Amorath 1582. Con le figure in disegno degli habiti et dell'armature de' soldati d'esso gran Turco. Et con la tavola di tutte le cose più notabili et degne, Vinegia: presso Altobello Salicato, 1582, 504 fols

Historia universale dell'origine, et imperio de' Turchi. Nella quale si contengono le leggi, gli ufficij, et i costumi di quella natione, cosi in tempo di pace, come di guerra. Oltre a ciò tutte le cose fatte da loro per terra, et per mare in diverse parti del mondo. Con le vite particolari dei principi Othomani; cominciando dal primo che fondò il regno, fino al presente Selim II. Con una copiosissima tavola di tutte le cose notabili, che si contengono in questo volume per ordine d'alfabeto, Venetia: appresso Michele Bonelli, 1573, 471 fols

Historia universale dell'origine et imperio de' Turchi. Nella quale si contengono la origine, le leggi, l'usanze, i costumi, cosi religiosi come mondani de' Turchi. Oltre a ciò vi sono tutte le guerre che di tempo in tempo sono state fatte da quella natione. Cominciando da Ottomano primo Re di questa gente sino al moderno Selim. Con le vite di tutti i principi di casa Othomana, Venetia: appresso Stefano Zazzara, 1568, 430 fols

Dell'Historia universale dell'origine et imperio de' Turchi. Libri tre. Ne quali si contengono le leggi, gli offici, i costumi di quella natione, così in tempo di pace, come di guerra. Oltre a ciò tutte le guerre fatte de loro per terra e per mare in diverse parti del mondo. Con le vite particolari de i principi Ottomani cominciando del primo che fondò il Regno fino al presente sultan Solimano, Venetia: appresso Francesco Rampazetto, 1564, 457 fols

Dell'Historia universale dell'origine, et imperio de' Turchi parte terza. Nella quale si contengono l'imprese particolari fatte prima da Saracini e poi da Principi Ottomani in molte province del mondo fino al tempo presente, Venetia: appresso Francesco Sansovino et compagni, 1561, 179 fols

Dell'Historia universale dell'origine, et imperio de' Turchi parte prima. Nella quale si contengono gli offici, le leggi, e i costumi di quella natione, così in tempo di pace, come di guerra. Con una tavola copiosissima di tutte le cose più notabili dell'opera, 168 fols; *Dell'Historia universale dell'origine, et imperio de' Turchi parte seconda. Nella quale si contengono tutte le guerre fatte da quella natione con le vite particolari dei principi ottomani fino al tempo presente*, 143 fols, Venetia: appresso Francesco Sansovino et compagni, 1560

STUDIES

V. Lavenia, 'Not barbarians, but religious men and soldiers. Machiavelli, Giovio and Turcophilia in some texts of the 16th century', *Storia del pensiero politico* 1 (2014) 31-58, pp. 51-53

M. Soykut, *Italian perceptions of the Ottomans. Conflict and politics through pontifical and Venetian sources*, Frankfurt am Main, 2011
Mula, '"Dipinto in scrittura"
G. Poumarède, *Pour en finir avec la Croisade. Mythes et réalités de la lutte contre les Turcs aux XVIe et XVII siècles*, Paris, 2004
Bonora, *Ricerche su Francesco Sansovino*
J.M. de Bujanda, *Thesaurus de la litterature interdite au XVI siecle*, Geneva, 1996, x, p. 350
J.M. de Bujanda, *Index des livres interdits*, vol. 9. *Index de Rome 1590, 1593, 1596, avec étude des index de Parme 1580 et Munich 1582*, Geneva, 1994, pp. 124, 415
S. Yérasimos, 'De la collection de voyages à l'histoire universelle. La *Historia universale de'Turchi* de Francesco Sansovino', *Turcica. Revue d'Etudes Turques* 20 (1988) 19-41
P.F. Grendler, *Culture and censorship in late Renaissance Italy and France*, London, 1981, p. 169
P. Preto, *Venezia e i Turchi*, Rome, 1974, 2013², pp. 176-78
Grendler, 'Francesco Sansovino and Italian popular history'
Sforza, 'Francesco Sansovino e le sue opere storiche'
Cicogna, *Iscrizioni veneziane*

Gl'Annali overo le vite de' principi et signori della casa Othomana, 'The true annals of the lives of the rulers and lords of the Ottoman dynasty' *Annali*, 'True annals'

DATE 1570-71
ORIGINAL LANGUAGE Italian

DESCRIPTION

The *Annali* (its full title is *Gl'Annali overo le vite de' principi et signori della casa Othomana. Ne quali si leggono di tempo in tempo tutte le guerre particolarmente fatte dalla nation de' Turchi in diverse provincie del mondo contra i christiani*) was probably written between the beginning of the Turkish siege of Cyprus in the summer of 1570 and the battle of Lepanto in October 1571. The first edition was published in quarto and is 134 folios in length. In his dedication to Peter Zborowski, Palatine of Sandomierz and first counsellor to the Kingdom of Poland, dated 25 October 1570,

Sansovino recalls the immense effort the powers of the Holy League (the Pope, Republic of Venice, and the King of Spain) put into defending the island from Ottoman occupation, although there is no mention of the Holy League's naval victory at Lepanto. Reference to Lepanto appears in the final pages of the 1573 edition of the *Annali*, which was published in Venice.

The work was composed very quickly to meet a growing demand for texts about the Turks following the proclamation of the Holy League. It is not an anthology of writings but an original product of Sansovino's own intellectual labours. In the dedication, Sansovino declares that in writing his *Annali* he has consulted the works of 'many Greek, Turkish and Latin writers, and many records of individuals and those working in these countries' (*molti scrittori Greci et Turcheschi et Latini, et molte note particolari di persone private et pratiche di quei paesi*). At the beginning of the volume, he provides a list of the sources he used: 'Nicola Sagundino, Christoforo Riccherio [Christophe Richer], Gian Battista Egnatio [Giovanni Battista Egnazio], Marin Bechichemo [Marino Becichemo], Paolo Giovio, Laonico Calcondile [Laonicus Chalcocondyles], Andrea Cambini, Giann'Antonio Menavino, Gio. Luigi da Parma [Giovanni Luigi Parma], Gio. Maria Vicentino [Giovanni Maria Angiolello], il Coriolano nel Mocenigo [Coriolano Cippico narrated Pietro Mocenigo's expedition to the Levant], Marc'Antonio Sabellico, Pietro Bembo in the Historia, Bernardo Iustiniano [Bernardo Giustiniani], Pietro Iustiniano nella Historia [Pietro Giustiniani], Pietro Marcello nelle sue Vite, Pope Pius II, Giovanni Nauclero [Johannes Verge called Nauclerus], Agostino Curione [Celio Agostino Curione], Volfango Drecslero [Wolfgang Drechsler], Croniche Turchesche'.

The *Annali* tells the story of the 'uncertain' origins and unstoppable rise of the Ottoman dynasty through the biographies of 14 sultans, from the founder, Osman I, who came to power at the end of the 13th century, up to Süleyman the Magnificent, who died in 1564. In his dedication, Sansovino presents the work as a sort of continuation of the *Historia universale dell'origine et imperio de' Turchi*, a project he had devoted himself to in previous years. In the *Historia universale*, Sansovino had already included biographies of the sultans, such as the life of Selim I taken from Paolo Giovio's *Historiae sui temporis*. It is, therefore, not surprising that, in the 1654 edition of the *Historia universale*, the editor Maiolino Bisaccioni chose to publish a second volume, reproducing a version of the *Annali* updated to the death of Sultan Ibrahim I in 1648.

SIGNIFICANCE

There was great demand in 16th-century Venice, perhaps even more than in the 15th century, for information about the Turks. Evidence of this may be found in the extraordinary number of both printed and manuscript works on Turkish topics that circulated in the Serenissima. The opening of Sansovino's dedication to Peter Zborowski in the 1571 and 1573 editions of the *Annali* may help explain the place the work occupied in this vast output: 'I have always held that the greatness and power of the Turkish nation is worthy of great consideration. The way their ancient militia is instituted, and their civil government is ordered, should be appreciated, as you can see *by experience that they are of value to men, and they not at all uncultured*. Concerning the militia, I do not know how people see that ours is better regulated, and the Roman orders were like those of the Turks, bearing in mind that the latter, as almost *the successors of those Romans*, are abstinent in battle, suffering ordeals, obedient to their leaders, persistent in their deeds, ...' (*Ho sempre tenuto che la grandezza e la potenza della nation Turchesca sia degna di molta consideratione, percioche vedendosi qual sia l'institutione della loro antica militia, e qual l'ordine de governi civili, si dee far giuditio si come si vede per pruova che siano huomini di valore, et non punto rozzi. Percioche quanto alla militia, io non so veder qual gente fra la nostra sia meglio regolata et più somigliante agli ordini de Romani della Turchesca, attento che essi, quasi come successori de predetti Romani, sono astinenti nelle guerre, sofferenti nelle fatiche, obedienti a lor capi, ostinati nelle imprese*, 1571 edition, fol. 2r-v; italics added).

As may be seen in this long quotation, Sansovino, unlike other contemporary authors, was motivated by admiration for these 'heirs' of the Romans. This comparison of the two empires, their power and military virtues, shows that he recognised the Turks as not altogether alien players on the political stage. It was this recognition that led him to declare in his dedication that he considered it very important to acquire and publish up-to-date and detailed information that could aid the Christian West in finding ways to counter the threat of Turkish expansion. It was Sansovino's aim to provide the most reliable possible news and data to help Christian Europe oppose and defeat the Turks.

Sansovino's perspective on the Ottomans, and his refusal to adopt an exclusive ideology of conflict against the infidels, also explains why he chose the authors he drew on in writing the work. In fact, his literary model and most important source was Paolo Giovio's *Commentario delle cose de' Turchi*, dedicated to Emperor Charles V and published in

1532. However, Sansovino's perspective did not change, even after the Holy League's victory over the Turks at Lepanto in 1571, when celebratory works also became popular in Italy.

Sansovino did not shy away from the controversy surrounding the origins of the Ottoman dynasty, which had been the subject of many humanist treatises and propaganda. At the beginning of *Vita di Othomano, primo re de' Turchi*, he lists the three leading theories at the time: the Ottoman dynasty was descended from the emperors of Constantinople, or from *certi pecorai di Tartaria* ('certain shepherds of Tartary'), or from one of the many Turkish tribes. However, Sansovino did not incline towards any of these views, since the Ottoman Turks 'like all the other lords of the world' come from a *debole principio* ('weak principle/foundation'). In fact, we are all descended from *un principio medesimo* ('the same principle'), and only warlike virtue distinguishes some from others, *dando e togliendo i meriti più e meno, secondo l'opere nostre* ('more or less giving and taking away the merits, according to our works') (1571 edition, fol. 2r-v).

In his detailed account of the Ottoman capture of Constantinople, Sansovino is also very careful to point out the errors and incompetence of the Greeks and the divisions among the Christian powers. At the same time, the work does not gloss over the acts of violence and cruelty committed by the Turks, with a great deal of attention given to the period before the succession after the death of a sultan, a time marked by fratricidal struggles, assassinations and usurpations, which raised the question of the legitimacy of the sultan's power, quite unlike successions in European monarchies.

The *Annali*, like Sansovino's other 'Turkish' works in the Italian vernacular, full of colourful detail and written in an engaging style, was a great success with the Venetian public. It quickly went into a second edition and was widely circulated far beyond the cultural circles of the Serenissima.

EDITIONS & TRANSLATIONS

Gl'Annali turcheschi overo vite de principi della casa Othomana. Ne quali si descrivono di tempo in tempo tutte le guerre fatte dalla natione de Turchi in diverse provincie del mondo. Con molti particolari della Morea, et delle case nobili dell'Albania, et dell'Imperio et stato de Greci, Venetia: appresso Enea de Alaris, 1573, 224 pp.

Gl'Annali overo le Vite de' principi et signori della casa Othomana. Ne quali si leggono di tempo in tempo tutte le guerre particolarmente fatte dalla nation de' Turchi in diverse provincie del mondo contra i Christiani, Venetia: appresso Iacopo Sansovino, 1571, 134 fols

STUDIES

Soykut, *Italian perceptions of the Ottomans*
Mula, '"Dipinto in scrittura"'
Poumarède, *Pour en finir avec la Croisade*
Bonora, *Ricerche su Francesco Sansovino*
Yérasimos, 'De la collection de voyages à l'histoire universelle'
G. Lucchetta, 'L'Oriente Mediterraneo nella cultura di Venezia tra il Quattro e il Cinquecento', in *Storia della cultura veneta dal primo Quattrocento al Concilio di Trento*, Vicenza, 1980, ii, 375-432
Preto, *Venezia e i Turchi*
Grendler, 'Francesco Sansovino and Italian popular history 1560-1600'
Sforza, 'Francesco Sansovino e le sue opere storiche'
Cicogna, *Iscrizioni veneziane*, iv, pp. 47-49

Elena Valeri

Nestore Martinengo

DATE OF BIRTH Around 1547-48
PLACE OF BIRTH Brescia, Lombardy
DATE OF DEATH 1598
PLACE OF DEATH Corfu

BIOGRAPHY

Nestore Martinengo was born into a noble family around 1547 or 1548 in Brescia, which was part of the mainland territories of the Venetian Republic. Nestore followed his father into a military career.

Nestore's family reflects the religious and political currents that prevailed in late-16th-century Europe. His sister married a colonel in the imperial army, one brother (together with his mother) converted to Calvinism and became a pastor, while another became Abbot of Leno and distinguished himself in the Roman Church as the author of religious works.

When he was about 20, Nestore went to Crete, which belonged to Venice, as part of a force to fortify the island against Ottoman attacks. In 1570, he went with reinforcements to Cyprus and took part in the defence of Famagusta, which he recounts in the *Relatione di tutto il successo di Famagosta*. He was captured and forced into the service of an Ottoman officer, who took him back to Constantinople. He managed to escape, and got back to Venice via Tripoli and Crete.

In the service of the Venetian state, he rose to be governor of Šibenik at Legnago in Corfu. For his sons, some of whom followed him into the military, he wrote a short manual of morality, the *Ricordi a' suoi figliuoli*, his only other known work in addition to the *Relatione*.

Nestore died in Corfu in 1598, although some sources give the date of his death as 1630 because of confusion with someone else of the same name.

MAIN SOURCES OF INFORMATION

Primary

P. Contarini, *Historia delle cose succese dal principio della guerra mossa da Selim Ottomano a' Venetiani, fino al dì della gran giornata vittoriosa contra Turchi, descritta non meno particolare che fedelmente da M. Gio. Pietro Contarini Venetiano*, Venezia: Francesco Rampazetto, 1572

C. Filiarchi da Pistoia, *Trattato della Guerra e dell'unione de' principi Christiani contra i Turchi e gli altri infedeli*, Venezia, 1572

V. Fuligni, *Bragadino*, Pesaro: Girolamo Concordia, 1589

N. Martinengo, *Ricordi dell'illustrissimo sig. conte Nestore Martinengo a' suoi figliuoli*, Padua: P. Frambotto, 1650

P. Paruta, *Storia della guerra di Cipro. libri tre*, Sienna, 1827

Secondary

M.P. Pedani Fabris, *Venezia porta d'Oriente*, Bologna, 2010

V. Costantini, *Il sultano e l'isola contesa. Cipro tra eredità veneziana e potere ottomano*, Turin, 2009

G. Benzoni, art. 'Martinengo, Nestore', in *DBI*, vol. 71 (the fullest biographical account of Martinengo)

C. Lucas-Fiorato, 'Tragédies des hommes de paille. Daniele Barbaro, Vincenzo Giusti, Valerio Fuligni', in *Guerre di religione sulle scene del cinque-seicento*, Rome, 2006, 79-106

C. Dionisotti, 'La guerra d'Oriente nella letteratura veneziana del Cinquecento', in A. Pertusi (ed.), *Venezia e l'Oriente fra tardo medioevo e rinascimento*, Florence, 1966

C. Pasero, *La partecipazione bresciana alla guerra di Cipro e alla battaglia di Lepanto (1570-1573)*, Brescia, 1954

G.A. Quarti, *La guerra contro il Turco a Cipro e a Lepanto. MDLXX-MDLXXI. Storia documentata*, Venice, 1935

WORKS ON CHRISTIAN-MUSLIM RELATIONS

Relatione di tutto il successo di Famagosta, 'An account of all that took place at Famagusta'

DATE 1572
ORIGINAL LANGUAGE Italian

DESCRIPTION

This work (its full title is *Relatione di tutto il successo di Famagosta. Doue s'intende minutissimamente tutte le scaramuccie, batterie, mine, & assalti dati ad essa fortezza. Et ancora i nomi de i capitani, & numero delle genti morte, cosi de christiani, come de turchi. Et medesimamente di quelli, che sono restati pregioni*, though there are a number of minor variations) is one of the best informed of its kind, and one of the most widely read of its time. It is an *avviso a stampa*, a prime example of what may be called proto-journalism, giving an up-to-the minute account of important news, frequently as reported by an eyewitness. There are at least 12 known versions of the book, indicating its wide circulation, plus a hand-written version, which is probably a copy, or maybe an original of the published version.

In 1572, the Battle of Lepanto had just been won by a Christian alliance that united Venice, Spain and the pope. The news of the fall of Famagusta and the victory at Lepanto reached Italy more or less simultaneously, at about the end of October. This meant that a victory and a defeat were reported at the same time, and the *avvisi* about the two events spread across the whole of Italy and Europe.

Nestore Martinengo's *Relatione* is above all an account for the Doge of Venice of the siege and fall of Famagusta, narrated by someone who was an active participant in the events. It covers the fighting between the Ottoman Empire and European powers, mainly the Republic of Venice, between 1569 and 1570. Famagusta was the last of the Venetian strongholds in Cyprus to fall to the Ottoman army. The Republic of Venice called for help to protect the island, and Pope Pius V, keen to launch a new crusade, took the opportunity to unite under his authority the Holy League. This would later prevail in Lepanto on 7 October 1571, though in Cyprus lack of coordination ended in disaster.

Gino Benzoni draws attention to a hand-written appendix to the work, referred to as the *Agionta*, which is about the Turkish army. Here Martinengo notes the strengths of the army: its discipline, abstinence, resilience and fearlessness. To confront such an army, advises Martinengo, adopting a Machiavellian approach, means that one cannot rely on mercenary forces, which are not bound by allegiance to the interests of a state. Here he acknowledges the formidable character of the Ottoman forces, and betrays a certain admiration for their organisation.

SIGNIFICANCE

Martinengo adopts two approaches in the *Relatione*, and there is a clear break when the narrative reaches the surrender of the Venetians. The first two parts give a detailed and technical account of warfare, told by an officer who knows his subject. In the third part, however, which deals with the surrender, Martinengo brings in religious overtones, and turns a factual account into an apology for the Venetian victims of the Turks. As long as the battle follows the principles of *ius belli*, it is the soldier and eye-witness who speaks, but when the situation degenerates, with accusations being exchanged between Bragadino and Lala Mustafa, the Venetian and Turkish leaders, and the slaughter of Venetian officers climaxing in the flaying of Bragadino, simple narrative can no longer describe the events. The Turks, previously a political, military and, above all, predictable foe, suddenly becomes a treacherous, cunning and unpredictable enemy, whose cruelty and deception can only be explained in religious terms: the deception of the Turks in reneging on their oaths of safe conduct is an expression of their alien origins and Muslim faith, while the sufferings of the Venetians are turned into holy martyrdoms.

It is in the description of the terrible torture and death of Bragadino that the narrative takes on an explicitly religious dimension. As Lala Mustafa mocks him, asking, *'Dov'è il tuo Christo, che non ti aita'* ('Where is now your Christ, who does not help you?' fol. 6), he becomes a Christ-like figure, and throughout the two days of his torture, he suffers his fate *'con tanta sua constantia, et fede, che mai si perdè d'animo, anzi con core costantissimo gli rimproverava la rotta fede, et sempre senza punto smarrirsi, si raccomandava a Dio'* ('with great constancy and faith, never losing his courage, and even with a heart of the greatest constancy, he blamed [Lala Mustafa] for betraying him, and without troubling himself anymore, he commended his soul to God'; fol. 6). The killing of the Venetian captains and the gruesome death of Bragadino would become supreme examples of Ottoman cruelty and savagery in the historical and literary narratives of the period.

What starts in the *Relatione* as the narrative of a siege ultimately becomes an account of an encounter between enemies fighting to uphold two different forms of religious and moral beliefs.

MANUSCRIPTS

MS Rome, Biblioteca Angelica – 1787, vol. *Cipro, relazioni storiche e piante*, '1521 Sucesso [sic] di Famagosta'

EDITIONS & TRANSLATIONS

G. Monello (ed.), *Accadde a Famagosta. Appendice 2: La relazione di frate Agostino eremitano: La relazione di Nestore Martinengo cose aggiunte e corrette*, Cagliari, 2013

G. Monello (ed.), *Accadde a Famagosta. Appendice: La relazione di Nestore Martinengo cose aggiunte e corrette*, Cagliari, 2007

The true report of all the successe of Famagosta, of the antique writers called Tamassus, a citie in Cyprus. In the which the whole order of all the skirmishes, batteries, mines, and assaultes geuen to the sayd fortresse, may plainly appeare. Moreouer the names of the captaines, and number of the people slaine, as well of the Christians as of the Turkes: likewise of them who were taken prisoners: from the beginning of the sayd seege vntill the end of the same. Englished out of Italian by William Malim. With certaine notes of his and expositions of all the Turkishe wordes herein necessary to be knowen, placed in the margent, with a short description also of his of the same iland, London: John Daye, 1572

La vraye histoire du siege et de la prinse de Famagoste: l'une des principales villes du royaume de Cypre, n'agueres appartenant aux Venetiens escrite en Italien, par le seigneur Nestor Martinengo, capitaine d'une des compagnies qui estoyent dedans, et par luy adressee au duc de Venize; et depuis mise en françois, Paris: André Wechel, 1572

Warhaftige Relation und Bericht, Was massen die gewaltig Statt unnd Bevestigung Famagusta, in Cipro, So von mänigklich für gantz ungewünlich gehalten, von dem Türcken im Augusto des 1571. Jars, mit unerhörtem gewallt erobert unnd eingenommen worden: Beschriben durch den Wolgebornen Graven und Herrn, Nestor Martinengo, So mit seinen undergebnen Knechten selbst inn der Besatzung, s.l., 1572

Raccolta di varii poemi latini, greci, e volgari. Fatti da diuersi bellissimi ingegni nella felice vittoria riportata da Christiani contra Turchi alli VII d'ottobre del MDLXXI. Con la relatione di tutto il successo di Famagosta. Et i nomi de i Bassà, et capitani ch'erano nell'armata turchesca, Venice: Sebastiano Ventura, 1572 (includes Martinengo's *Relatione*)

The *Relatione* was also published in the following places, sometimes with slightly differing titles, all in 1572: Venice: Con licentia de' Signori Superiori; Venice: Domenico Farro; Venice: Giorgio Angelieri; Brescia; Milan; Fano; Verona: Bastian Dalle Donne and Giovanni Fratelli; Rome.

Relatione di tutto il successo di Famagosta. Doue s'intende minutissimamente tutte le scaramuccie, batterie, mine, & assalti dati ad essa fortezza. Et ancora i nomi de i capitani, & numero delle genti morte, cosi de christiani, come de turchi. Et medesimamente di quelli, che sono restati pregioni, s.l., s.d.

Charlotte Ostrovsky-Richard

Music and prayers for relief from the Siege of Malta and the Battle of Lepanto

The four decades beginning from 1523, which saw the expulsion from Rhodes of the Hospitallers of St John, was one of the most turbulent periods in Mediterranean history. It included the invasion of Rhodes by Süleyman the Magnificent and the invasion of Malta by combined land and naval forces of Ottoman and North African corsairs in 1565, and ended in 1571 with the victory of the Holy League in the Battle of Lepanto and the fall of Venetian Cyprus to Ottoman forces. Prayers offered for the outcome of these climactic events and commemorations of them were often set to music.

The invasion of Malta in 1565 by combined land and naval forces of Ottoman and North African corsairs was considered a crucial assault that could imperil the coastlines of the Italian peninsula and Sicily, as well as the east coast of Spain. Malta had been ceded by the Emperor Charles V in 1530 to the Knights Hospitaller (now called the Order of Malta), together with the city of Tripoli, then in Spanish hands. Later, Tripoli had again fallen to the Turks in 1551, and only Malta stood between Christian Europe and Ottoman domination of the entire western Mediterranean. The Great Siege of Malta, as it became known, was crucial to the security of Philip of Spain's territories, and the safety of his fleet was paramount if his possessions and coastlines were to be protected from Ottoman attack from the sea. Thanks to a combined strategy of the Grand Master of the Knights, Jean Parisot de la Valette, and the equally experienced Spanish Viceroy of Naples and Sicily, Don Garcia de Toledo, the Ottoman invasion was finally repelled on 8 September 1565, but only after a ferocious siege lasting several months (Spiteri, *The great siege*; de la Valette's name was also given as de Valette). Prayers were offered for this campaign in many countries of southern Europe, and composers set the urgency of these prayers to sacred motets.

The Spanish composer and theologian Don Fernando de las Infantas was descended from a family ennobled by King Edward III of England, and was technically entitled to use the title of *Don*. Born in Cordova in 1534, he studied at the cathedral in that city, where Alonso de Vieras was *maestro de capilla*, and received a sound classical and musical education. Infantas took holy orders in 1584, serving in Rome until he became embroiled in theological disputations, which even came to involve King

Philip. The publication of his *Tractatus de praedestinatione* in 1601 caused him to come to the attention of the Spanish Inquisition. Pope Clement VIII placed the book on the Index in 1603, and with his career ruined, Infantas died in poverty in Spain around 1610.

MAIN SOURCES OF INFORMATION

Secondary
S.C Spiteri, *The great siege. Knights vs Turks mdlxv*, Malta, 2005
R. Mitjana y Gordón, *Don Fernando de las Infantas. Teologo y musico*, Madrid, 1918

WORKS ON CHRISTIAN-MUSLIM RELATIONS

Music and prayers for the relief of the Siege of Malta 1565, the Holy League 1570, and the Battle of Lepanto 1571

DATE 16th century
ORIGINAL LANGUAGE Unspecified

DESCRIPTION
Favoured by Philip II of Spain, the Spanish composer and theologian Don Fernando de las Infantas cemented his position by writing three works, each supporting the king and centred on important events in the Ottoman-Christian rivalry in the Mediterranean. The Siege of Malta (1565), the formation of the Holy League of 1571, and the Battle of Lepanto in the same year were the occasions for these compositions.

While the Great Siege was still under way, Infantas composed the six-part motet *Congregati sunt inimici nostri*, with the subtitle *in oppressione inimicorum: pro victoria in Turcas Melite obsedioni*. Printed in his *Sacrarum cantiorum Liber III* published in 1579, it is a richly scored prayer for seven voice parts, with pleading sonorities that befitted the then parlous situation of the Knights and the Maltese. The text is expressive of attitudes towards the Turks:

> Our enemies are gathered together, and they boast of their power,
> Destroy their strength, O Lord, and scatter them,
> so that they know that it is none other who fights against them but thou, our God.

As in the Flemish composer Thomas Crecquillon's setting of the same text in 1555, Infantas adds the Antiphon for Peace, *Da pacem Domine in diebus nostris* ('O Lord, give us peace in our days'). Infantas's wedding of musical imagery to the text is outstanding, and he contrasts prayerful and aggressive elements of the words, ending reflectively in the final words *Deus noster, nisi tu* ('but thou, our God').

Settings of this text, taken from either sections of the Book of Ecclesiasticus or Psalms, had been composed by others, although none were described as being written for deliverance from the Ottoman threat. Apart from chant versions, the earliest setting for choir might be that of Clément de Janequin (c. 1485-1558). Others include versions by Jaques Arcadelt (1507-68), Orlande de Lassus (1532-94), Francesco de Layolle (1492-c. 1546), Jean Maillard [Maillart] (c. 1538-70), and Jacobus de Kerle (1531-91). One other setting by Philippe Verdelot (c. 1480/85-c.1530/32) was possibly composed during the siege of Florence by the Medici in 1530, against the supporters of Girolamo Savonarola. A later setting for voices and five-part strings was composed by Giuseppe Antonio Bernabei (1649-1732), who wrote the motet, for voices and strings, adding six other selections of excerpts from the Psalms. But it is Infantas's setting that is the most well-known.

Infantas's loyalty to Philip of Spain is seen in the second of his motets, written in support of the Holy League. This was initiated in 1571 by Pope Pius V, who had made a significant contribution to the construction of the city of Valletta after the Great Siege of Malta. The Holy League, finally signed into existence on 25 May 1571 under the leadership of the Papal States, comprised an alliance between Spain, Naples and Sicily, the Republics of Venice and Genoa, Tuscany and smaller Italian states, as well as the Knights of Malta. The text *Ecce quam bonum et quam jucundum habitare fratres in unum* ('Behold how good and how pleasant it is for brethren to dwell in unity', Psalm 133:1), was ideally suited as a manifestation of support for the aims of the League. Jacobus Clemens non Papa (c. 1510-c. 1555) composed a Mass with the same title in 1555 for the investiture of Philip II as king of Spain in the following year.

Ecce quam bonum was the prelude for the composition by Infantas of his *Cantemus Domino*, subtitled *pro victoria navali contra Turcas, sacri foederis classe parta*, written in commemoration of the great Christian sea victory of Lepanto on 7 October 1571. Under the leadership of Don John of Austria, King Philip's step-brother, the forces of the League inflicted a significant defeat on the combined Turkish navy. The work by Infantas is one of only two commemorative motets written to celebrate Don John's victory, although the Battle of Lepanto was the subject of many works of poetry and literature, painting and medals, especially from Venice and even from France. The text set by Infantas is taken from *Ad canticum Moyses* (Song of Moses, Exodus 15), and was published as number five of the *Sacrarum cantiorum Liber II*, as part of his second Book of Motets, comprising 30 pieces for five voices.

Following Lepanto, in 1572 Jacobus de Kerle composed a work entitled *Cantio octo vocum de sacro foedere contra Turcas*. Richly scored for eight voices, it was composed when de Kerle was organist at Augsburg Cathedral.

SIGNIFICANCE

These works of Infantas and other 16th-century composers were the first in a succession that continued through the following centuries. One well-known masterpiece of Antonio Vivaldi (1678-1741), and his only surviving oratorio from a collection of five, was composed in celebration of the lifting of the siege of Venetian Corfu by the Ottomans. Written in 1716, the oratorio *Juditha triumphans* with a subtitle of *Devicta Holofernis Barbarie* is described as a *Sacrum militare oratorium hisce belli temporibus*. The libretto by Jacob Cassetti was printed in Venice, and the first performance, which took place at the Ospepdale della Pietà, was attended by the commander of the Venetian forces, Johann Matthias von der Schulenburg. It is an allegorical depiction in music of the Venetian triumph over the Ottoman invasion of the Ionian Islands, through the saga of Judith and Holofernes.

Vienna, which had experienced siege by Ottoman armies in both 1529 and 1683, saw a number of musical works with allusions to the Turkish menace, including the instrumental Partita by Johann Joseph Fux (1660-1741), entitled *Turcaria*. This four-movement work is a description of the siege of 1683, and has sections entitled *Turcaria* and *Janstschara* (Janissaries). The vogue would continue in ballets such as Hilverding and Starzer's *Le Turc génereux*, Vienna, 1758. Importantly, the Ottoman theme would appear in operatic works from Gluck onwards (*Le Cadi dupe*, 1761, and *Les pèlerins de la Mecque, ou la rencontre imprévue*, 1764), Mozart (*Zaide*, 1780, and *Die Entführung aus dem Serail*, 1782), and Nicolò Isouard (*Le medécin turc*, 1803). In some of these later operatic works themes of Islamic humanism and clemency are introduced, at a time when the Ottoman menace to Europe was slowly receding.

EDITIONS & TRANSLATIONS

F. de las Infantas, *Motetes*, Ensemble Plus Ultra, dir. Michael Noone, Granada: CD Almaviva 2006

F. de las Infantas, *Congregati sunt*, ed. Lynn Gamblin, Lewis, Scotland: Vanderbeek and Imrie, 1996

A. Vivaldi, *Juditha triumphans*, Milan: Ricordi, 2008

STUDIES

M.T. Feyer, *Music and ceremony at the court of Charles V. The Capilla Flamenca and the art of political promotion*, Woodbridge UK, 2012, p. 156 (on Thomas Crecquillon's eight works as prayers for deliverance and peace)

Mitjana y Gordón, *Don Fernando de las Infantas*

Richard Divall

Torquato Tasso

DATE OF BIRTH	11 March 1544
PLACE OF BIRTH	Sorrento
DATE OF DEATH	25 April 1595
PLACE OF DEATH	Rome

BIOGRAPHY

Torquato Tasso is recognised as one of the greatest poets of the Italian Renaissance. His most celebrated work is the heroic poem *Gerusalemme liberata* (1581), in which he narrates the siege and conquest of Jerusalem during the First Crusade.

The son of the prominent poet Bernardo Tasso (1493-1569) and Porzia de' Rossi (ca. 1515-56), Torquato (or Tassino as he was known then) was born in Sorrento in 1544. As a courtier of Ferrante Sanseverino, Prince of Salerno, his father accompanied his patron into exile in France in 1552, losing his house and revenues and leaving his family in the hands of his wife's relatives, who refused to pay her dowry. Torquato joined him in Rome two years later. After a brief stay in Bergamo, Torquato followed his father to Urbino, where he studied under the guidance of eminent humanists alongside the duke's son Francesco Maria della Rovere. In 1558, the Turks attacked Sorrento, where his older sister Cornelia and her husband lived. The couple escaped capture, but this dramatic event raised Torquato's awareness of the Turkish threat. In 1559, he and his father moved to Venice. That year, the young poet composed the first canto of *Gerusalemme* and embarked on the composition of a less ambitious poem, *Rinaldo* (eventually published in 1562 and very favourably received).

Between 1560 and 1565, Torquato studied law and philosophy in Padua and Bologna. In 1561, he fell in love with Lucrezia Bendidio, a lady-in-waiting of Eleonora d'Este. During this period, he probably started to work on the *Discorsi dell'arte poetica*, a treatise on heroic poetry, which would later inform the *Gerusalemme liberata*. In 1565, he entered the service of Cardinal Luigi d'Este, moving permanently to Ferrara in 1567, the year that also saw the publication of his first collection of love poetry. In 1570, he travelled to France with other members of Cardinal Luigi's household. Shortly after his return to Ferrara, he entered the service of Duke Alfonso II d'Este.

In 1573, Tasso composed his pastoral drama *Aminta*, which was first performed in July of the same year, winning him the admiration of the court. By 1575, the first draft of his epic poem on the First Crusade had been completed. Steeped in the Neo-Aristotelian culture of his day, Tasso's aim was to produce a flawless heroic poem with a clear Christian message, thereby surpassing the chivalric romances of his Ferrarese predecessors, namely Matteo Maria Boiardo and Ludovico Ariosto. Tormented by doubts, he subjected his poem to a lengthy and painstaking revision (1575-76), enlisting the help of a number of friends. The letters he sent to his consultants (Scipione Gonzaga, Luca Scalabrino and Silvio Antoniano) are known as *Lettere poetiche*.

Having to deal with pedantic criticism, Tasso grew increasingly anxious and frustrated. At the same time, he developed a persecution mania and started to doubt his own religious beliefs, which led him to denounce himself to the Inquisitors (who granted him absolution). His behaviour also strained his relationship with his patron. In the period between 1576 and 1579, he lived in various Italian cities, occasionally returning to Ferrara. In 1579, he suffered a mental breakdown during the wedding of Alfonso II d'Este and Margherita Gonzaga, and as a result was confined to the Hospital of Sant'Anna in Ferrara, from where he was released only seven years later, in 1586.

During his confinement, Tasso composed a number of dialogues, and followed and participated in the debate sparked off by the publication of the *Gerusalemme liberata* (1581). After his release he revised, enlarged and also 'expurgated' his poem, giving it a new title, *Gerusalemme conquistata*, making changes to the contents in order to reinforce the poem's moral and religious message. Published in 1593, the *Conquistata* failed to capture much interest. In the last decade of his life, Tasso received favours and hospitality from his admirers in various Italian cities (especially Naples and Rome), but, worried about his finances and plagued with health problems, he could not settle anywhere. Apart from the *Conquistata*, the most significant works of this period include his tragedy *Re Torrismondo* (which he started back in the 1570s and completed in 1586-87), the *Discorsi del poema eroico* (1594) and the *Sette giornate del mondo creato* (written in 1492-94). Tasso died in 1595 in the Monastery of Sant'Onofrio in Rome, shortly after the pope had promised to crown him poet laureate on the Capitol.

MAIN SOURCES OF INFORMATION

Primary
G.B. Manso, *Vita di Torquato Tasso*, ed. B. Basile, Rome, 1995 (written by Tasso's friend, this biography was first published in 1621)

Secondary
Much has been written about Tasso and his works. The following is a select bibliography:
M. Residori, *Tasso*, Bologna, 2009
C. Gigante, *Tasso*, Rome, 2007
C. Molinari, *Studi su Tasso*, Florence, 2007
G. Venturi (ed.), *Torquato Tasso e la cultura estense. Atti del Convegno internazionale (Ferrara, 10-13 dicembre 1995)*, Florence, 1999
B. Porcelli (ed.), *Tasso e la sua fortuna*, Pisa, 1995 (special issue of *Italianistica*)
P. Brand, *Torquato Tasso. A study of the poet and of his contribution to English literature*, Cambridge, 1965
L. Caretti, *Ariosto e Tasso*, Turin, 1961
Comitato per le celebrazioni di Torquato Tasso, *Torquato Tasso*, Milan, 1957
G. Getto, *Interpretazione del Tasso*, Naples, 1951
A. Solerti, *Vita di Torquato Tasso*, Turin, 1895

WORKS ON CHRISTIAN-MUSLIM RELATIONS

Gerusalemme liberata, 'Jerusalem delivered'; 'The liberation of Jerusalem'

DATE First draft completed in 1575; revised in 1575-76
ORIGINAL LANGUAGE Italian

DESCRIPTION
Gerusalemme liberata is divided into 20 cantos and comprises 1,917 eight-line stanzas in total. In Caretti's edition it comes to 653 pages. Its plot revolves around the siege of Jerusalem by the Christian army led by Goffredo di Buglione (Godfrey of Bouillon), culminating in the capture of the Holy City. Concerned about historical accuracy, Tasso used a number of accounts of the First Crusade, such as William of Tyre's *Historia*, Robert the Monk's *Historia Iherosolimitana* and Benedetto Accolti's *De bello a Christianis contra barbaros gesto pro Christi sepulcro et Judaea recuperandis*. However, even though many episodes have some basis in historical fact, Tasso changed numerous details and incorporated elements of chivalric romance into his epic story.

The action is set during the final phase of the crusade. After six years of fighting (Tasso deviates from his sources, increasing the number of years from three to six), God sends the Archangel Gabriel to the 'pious' Goffredo, urging him to gather his less devout companions and to encourage them to direct all their efforts towards wresting Jerusalem from the hands of the infidels. Rebellious against God's will, the forces of Hell decide to side with the defenders of the city. The Saracens (i.e Muslims) do not hesitate to use magic in order to prevent the Christians from achieving their goal. At the same time, pride and love cloud the judgement of Goffredo's most valiant knights, Rinaldo and Tancredi. Like Achilles in the *Iliad*, Rinaldo withholds his contribution to the war, leaving the army after a brawl with another knight (whom he kills) and then succumbing to the charms of the Saracen sorceress Armida. His companion Tancredi falls in love with the Saracen female warrior Clorinda. However, God does not abandon his faithful. The lost sheep return to the fold and the Christians liberate Jerusalem. The poem ends with the image of Goffredo, his garments soaked in blood, praying at the Holy Sepulchre.

Gerusalemme liberata features numerous Saracen characters, including a number of converts to Islam. Despite the many similarities between the two armies, there is no exact equivalent of Goffredo in the Muslim camp; the Christians' unity is juxtaposed to the Muslims' disunity. The Muslim leaders are: Aladino, King of Jerusalem; the Caliph of Egypt; Emireno, the commander-in-chief of the caliph's army; and Solimano, Sultan of Nicaea.

Aladino fits the stereotypical image of an Eastern tyrant. He is ruthless and suspicious. Only the fear of the crusaders' revenge stops him from exterminating the Christian population of Jerusalem. When an icon of the Virgin Mary miraculously disappears from a mosque (the magician Ismeno having persuaded Aladino to steal it from a Christian church), he threatens to punish the entire Christian community and condemns to death at the stake Sofronia and Olindo, two Christians who claim responsibility (see canto II). However, as the narration progresses, the reader catches a glimpse of his humane side: the old king treats Argante, Clorinda and Solimano (his champions and the best warriors in the Muslim camp) with fatherly affection (see II 47-48; X 53-54; XII 10-12).

The Caliph of Egypt is portrayed more positively. Despite his love of luxury and extravagance, he is endowed with prudence and courage. He has spent his long life fighting the Turks and the Persians, which makes him a worthy adversary (XVII 1-41). Similarly, the Armenian Emireno (who was once a Christian) is a brave and intelligent enemy, while Solimano is a multi-faceted character of considerable psychological depth. Although at times he is represented as a ferocious barbarian, he has many positive traits, so much so that he is invested with tragic grandeur. Solimano truly cares for his people and is desperate to save his motherland. He finds the strength to continue fighting the foreign invaders (which is how he sees the Christians) even after several crushing defeats. His heroic death marks one of the most moving episodes of *Gerusalemme liberata* (XX 73-82, 101-8). There is a streak of melancholy in Solimano's character, for he feels that all his efforts are doomed to failure. However, the magician Ismeno reveals to him that one of his descendants (the legendary Saladin whose chivalric virtues are celebrated by many Christian authors, including Dante Alighieri) will deal a serious blow to the Christian occupiers (X 22-23).

Argante, a prominent Muslim warrior of Circassian origin, shares many traits with Solimano, even if he is a less complex character. His ferocity is counterbalanced by his loyalty to his brothers-in-arms and his courage in the face of death. Argante is interested in personal glory and for him the war is an opportunity to show his valour. He is an individualist who believes in his own invincibility right up to the moment of his demise (see XIX 1-26). Like Ariosto's Rodomonte and many other Saracen heroes in the chivalric tradition, he is an atheist (II 59). His friendship with the maiden warrior Clorinda (with whom he sallies forth from the besieged city to burn down the Christians' siege-tower in canto XII) is one of the strongest relationships in the poem. The character of Clorinda is inspired by Boiardo's and Ariosto's Marfisa and Virgil's Camilla. She is a devout Muslim, which leads her to offer her services to Aladino. However, unlike Solimano and Argante, she converts to Christianity. Clorinda is the daughter of Senapo, the Christian king of Ethiopia. She was born fair-skinned and her mother entrusted her to the eunuch Arsete, fearing the wrath of her jealous husband. Before her nocturnal sortie with Argante, Arsete tells her the story of her birth, but Clorinda decides to stay in the faith she was raised in. She asks for baptism when she is mortally wounded by her Christian suitor Tancredi (who only at this point discovers her true identity) at the end of their nocturnal duel (XII 51-71).

All of Tasso's main female characters are Muslims, arguably because for him romantic love is sinful. While Clorinda does not reciprocate Tancredi's love, with all her thoughts set on defending Jerusalem, Armida, the niece of the magician Idraote and a sorceress herself, and Erminia, the daughter of the king of Antioch, bestow their affections on Christian knights. Armida arrives in the Christian camp in canto IV and lures many warriors away in order to weaken Goffredo's army, but then loses her heart to Rinaldo. She carries him off to her enchanted garden on a distant island and is overcome with grief when he leaves her (canto XVI). At this point, the powerful witch turns into a Dido-like figure. Thirsting for revenge, Armida travels back to the Holy Land, but eventually she makes peace with Rinaldo and, redeemed through love, decides to embrace the Christian faith (XX 116-36). Similarly, Erminia's passion for Tancredi (who treated her with respect when the crusaders captured Antioch) is stronger than her loyalty to her fellow Muslims. Wearing Clorinda's armour, she reaches the Christian camp, but has to flee into the forest when she is mistaken for Clorinda. There she takes refuge with the shepherds (VI 55-VII 22). She returns to the Muslims only to abandon them again, and towards the end of the poem she tends to the wounded Tancredi (XIX 79-114). Significantly, neither Armida and Rinaldo (the ending of their story is ambiguous and has given rise to different interpretations) nor Erminia and Tancredi marry, even though interracial marriages (preceded by the conversion of the Saracen bride) are not uncommon in the chivalric tradition. The *Lettere poetiche* reveal that Tasso considered removing or rewriting the episode of the reconciliation of Armida and Rinaldo. It is absent from *Gerusalemme conquistata*, where the enchantress is depicted more negatively.

Concerning the representation of Islam, Tasso adheres to the Aristotelian principle of verisimilitude. While many other Renaissance and medieval chivalric authors knew that Islam was in fact a monotheistic religion and yet portrayed its believers as idolaters who worshipped the Saracen Trinity of Macone, Apollino and Trivigante, Tasso is careful to remain within the bounds of credibility. He even makes it clear that Islamic faith prohibits the use of images in worship (II 50). However, his depiction of Islam and Islamic culture is far from nuanced and comprehensive. 'Macone' (Muḥammad) is mentioned only a few times (I 84; II 2, 51, 69; XVII 4, 24; XX 113-44) and the word *meschita* (mosque) is employed just four times (II 6, 29; III 11; XX 85). Tasso usually refers to Muslim characters as *pagani* (pagans), using this very generic term more often than the term *Saracini* (Saracens). Ismeno, a magician who helps Aladino, is a Christian renegade who has a poor knowledge of Islam and confounds the laws of his old and new religions (II 2). He is therefore more a heretic than a Muslim.

SIGNIFICANCE

Gerusalemme liberata was conceived as a celebration of the values of the post-Tridentine Church in the period of the Counter-Reformation. Tasso's fictionalised account of the First Crusade could be seen as a parallel to both the Church's attempts to stop the spread of Protestantism and the on-going struggle against the Turks. Written in the aftermath of the Battle of Lepanto (1571), the poem had a topical relevance, as many of its readers believed that the Ottoman Empire posed a real danger to Christian Europe.

Yet it would be wrong to say that Tasso paints the enemies of the crusaders in black. While the boundary between the two camps is more rigid than in chivalric poems of the early Italian Renaissance, the religious Other can inspire respect and even love. Despite the fact that Islam as a religion is demonised, *Gerusalemme liberata* contains a number of charismatic Saracen characters who resemble the heroes and heroines of ancient literature insofar as they subscribe to the ideals of honour and secular humanism. Sergio Zatti has famously argued that the war between Christians and Muslims is effectively a clash between two opposing Western systems of values, the former upholding the values promoted by the reformed Catholic Church, and the latter embodying the spirit of the early Renaissance with its secular aspirations, a culture which Tasso looks upon with nostalgic sympathy. According to Zatti, 'The poetry of Gerusalemme liberata is probably the first clear example in Italian literature of a conscious identification with the forces of evil, though it is nevertheless rejected at the level of ideology. It is the first great example of solidarity with the "pagan enemy"' (Zatti, 'Christian uniformity, pagan multiplicity', p. 154).

Tasso's Muslim characters, especially his Saracen damsels, have fascinated both painters and musicians down the centuries. Tancredi's love for Clorinda is the subject of Claudio Monteverdi's opera *Il combattimento di Tancredi e Clorinda* (1624), while the sorceress Armida inspired operas by Jean-Baptiste Lully (*Armide*, 1686), George Frideric Handel (*Rinaldo*, 1711), Antonio Vivaldi (*Armida al campo d'Egitto*, 1718), Christoph Willibald Gluck (*Armide*, 1777), Joseph Haydn (*Armida*, 1784), Giochino Rossini (*Armida*, 1817) and Antonín Dvořák (*Armida*, 1904). The love story of Armida and Rinaldo and other amorous episodes fired the imagination of painters, such as Annibale and Ludovico Carracci, Domenichino, Guercino, Nicolas Poussin, Antoon Van Dyck, François Boucher, Giovanni Battista Tiepolo, Jean-Honoré Fragonard and Francesco

Hayez, among others. Thus, *Gerusalemme liberata* helped to promote a romanticised view of the First Crusade.

EDITIONS & TRANSLATIONS

The Italian editions of *Gerusalemme liberata* are numerous. The standard text was established by Lanfranco Caretti:
L. Caretti, *Gerusalemme liberata*, Turin, 1971, 2005³

The following English translations are recognised as faithful to the Italian:
M. Wickert, *The liberation of Jerusalem*, Oxford, 2009
A.M. Esolen, *Jerusalem delivered*, Baltimore MD, 2000
E. Fairfax, *Godfrey of Bulloigne, or The recouerie of Ierusalem. Done into English heroicall verse*, London, 1600, http://www.gutenberg.org/catalog/world/readfile?fk_files=2460376

Recent translations in other languages:
Erusaremu kaihō, trans. K. Washihira, Tokyo, 2010 (Japanese trans.)
Gerusalemme liberate/ Jérusalem délivrée, ed. and trans. G. Genot and L. Caretti, Paris, 2008 (French trans.)
Bei jie fang de ye lu sa leng, ed. and trans. Ta Suo and Yang Shun Xiang, Guangzhou, 2005 (Chinese trans.)
A megszabadított Jeruzsalem, trans. E. Hars, Budapest, 1995 (Hungarian trans.)
La Jérusalem délivrée = Gerusalemme liberate, J.-M. Gardair, Paris, 1990 (bilingual edition)
Jerozolima wyzwolona, trans. P. Kochanowski, Krakow, 1923, Wrocław, 1951², Warsaw, 1995³ (Polish trans.)
Jerusalén libertada, trans. B. Cairasco de Figueroa, ed. A. Cioranescu, Tenerife, 1967 (Spanish trans.)
Das befreite Jerusalem, ed. W. Kraus, Munich, 1963 (German trans.; revision of J.D. Gries 1800 trans.)
Oslobo·deni Jerusalim, trans. Dragiša Stanojević, Belgrade, 1957 (Croatian trans.)
Osvobozhdennyi Ierusalim, trans. Dmitry Min, St Petersburg, 1900 (Russian trans.)

STUDIES

While only a few studies focus specifically on Tasso's representation of Islam and Muslims, many critics touch upon this topic. In particular, much has been written about the Muslim heroines of *Gerusalemme liberata*. What follows is a select bibliography.

A. Cerbo, 'Camões e Tasso. L'Oriente nel poema eroico', *Between* 1 (2011), http://www.Between-journal.it/

G. Ricci, 'Cavalleria e crociata nella Ferrara del Rinascimento. Un piccolo stato davanti a un grande impero', in F. Meier (ed.), *Italien und das Osmanische Reich*, Herne, 2010, 75-86

A. Paolella, 'La *Gerusalemme liberata* e il mondo islamico', *Studi Tassiani sorrentini* (2008) 32-46

T. Gregory, 'With God on our side. Gerusalemme liberata', in *From many gods to one. Divine action in Renaissance epic*, Chicago, 2006, 140-77

S. Zatti, 'Christian uniformity, pagan multiplicity', in *The quest for epic from Ariosto to Tasso*, Toronto, 2006, 135-59

G. Careri, *Gestes d'amour et de guerre. La 'Jérusalem delivrée', images et affects (XVIe-XVIIIe siècle)*, Paris, 2005

J.A. Cavallo, *The romance epics of Boiardo, Ariosto and Tasso. From public duty to private pleasure*, Toronto, 2004

M.J. Gough, 'Tasso's enchantress, Tasso's captive woman', *Renaissance Quarterly* 54 (2001) 523-52

S. Verdino, 'Il mago Ismeno', *Studi Tassiani Sorrentini* (2000) 13-36

J.A. Cavallo. 'Tasso's Armida and the victory of romance', in V. Finucci (ed.), *Renaissance transactions. Ariosto and Tasso*, Durham NC, 1999, 77-111

J.A. Cavallo, 'Armida. La funzione della donna-maga nell'epica tassiana', in G. Venturi (ed.), *Torquato Tasso e la cultura estense*, Florence, 1999, 99-114

F. Cardini, 'Torquato Tasso e la crociata', in G. Venturi (ed.), *Torquato Tasso e la cultura estense*, Florence, 1999, 615-23

S. Zatti, 'Dalla parte di Satana. Sull'imperialismo cristiano nella *Gerusalemme liberata*', in S. Zatti (ed.), *La rappresentazione dell'altro nei testi del Rinascimento*, Lucca, 1998, 146-82

L. Benedetti, *La sconfitta di Diana. Un percorso per la 'Gerusalemme liberata'*, Ravenna, 1997

G. Picco, *'Or s'indora ed or verdeggia'. Il ritratto femminile dalla 'Liberata' alla 'Conquistata'*, Florence, 1996

C. Coppola, *Le donne del Tasso. Guerriere, maghe, eroine*, Naples, 1995

D. Quint, *Epic and empire. Politics and generic form from Virgil to Milton*, Princeton NJ, 1993

E. Siberry, 'Tasso and the crusades. History of a legacy', *Journal of Medieval History* 19 (1993) 163-69

A. Perelli, 'La "divina" Clorinda', *Bergomum* 87 (1992) 45-76

A. Godard, 'Le camp païen dans la *Jérusalem délivrée*', in M. Marietti et al. (eds), *Quêtes d'une identité collective chez les Italiens de la Renaissance*, Paris, 1991, 309-429

G. Petrocchi and E. Bonora, 'L'Erminia del Tasso', *Giornale Storico della Letteratura Italiana* 165 (1988) 180-95

P. Larivaille, 'Cristiani e pagani. L'ideologia della *Liberata*', in *Poesia e ideologia. Letture della 'Gerusalemme liberata'*, Naples, 1987, 111-31

M. Migiel, 'Secrets of a sorceress. Tasso's Armida', *Quaderni d'Italianistica* 8 (1987) 149-66

M. Migiel, 'Tasso's Erminia. Telling an alternate story', *Italica* 64 (1987) 62-75

S. Zatti, *L'uniforme cristiano e il multiforme pagano. Saggio sulla 'Gerusalemme liberata'*, Milan, 1983

J.A. Kates, *Tasso and Milton. The problem of Christian epic*, Lewisburg PA, 1983

J.P. Donnelly, 'The Moslem enemy in Renaissance epic. Ariosto, Tasso and Camoëns', *Yale Italian Studies* 1 (1977) 162-70

R.W. Lee, *Ut pictura poesis. The humanistic theory of painting*, New York, 1967, pp. 48-56

A. Banfi, 'Etica e religione in Torquato Tasso', in Comitato per le celebrazioni di Torquato Tasso, *Torquato Tasso*, 1-28

W. Wistar Comfort, 'The Saracens in Italian epic poetry', *Publications of the Modern Languages Association* 59 (1944) 882-910

Maria Pavlova

France and Northern Europe

Felix Fabri

DATE OF BIRTH 1437-38
PLACE OF BIRTH Zurich
DATE OF DEATH 14 March 1502 or thereabouts
PLACE OF DEATH Ulm

BIOGRAPHY

After the early death of his father, Jos Schmid, and the remarriage of his mother, Fabri grew up in the families of his stepfather in Schaffhausen and of his great uncle Kyborg near Winterthur. In 1452, he entered the Dominican monastery in Basel, and maybe as early as 1465 he was part of a delegation of monks who visited the Dominicans in Ulm in order to reform the convent according to Observant rules. From 1468 or 1474 onwards, Fabri lived in Ulm as sub-prior, reading master and 'preacher general' of the house. He travelled on behalf of the Order to Rome (1476), Colmar (1482), Nuremberg (1485) and Venice (1486/87). According to the fragmentary inscription on a tomb slab that is now lost, he probably died on 14 March 1502.

Fabri's most eventful journeys were two pilgrimages to the Holy Land in 1480 and 1483. On his first voyage, in the company of the nobleman George of Stein, he witnessed the aftermath of the siege of Rhodes by the Ottoman fleet. Continuing his pilgrimage to the Sinai was not possible after what he describes as a hasty and disappointing visit to the holy sites in Jerusalem. Therefore, he was eager to repeat the journey, and only three years later he acted as chaplain to a group of noblemen on their way to the Holy Land. This second pilgrimage lasted almost ten months. After the sea passage from Venice to Jaffa, and visits to Jerusalem and Bethlehem, he travelled to the monastery of St Catherine in Sinai, and further on through the desert to Cairo. After a last stop in Alexandria, he returned on a cargo vessel to Venice.

Fabri wrote four reports based on his pilgrimage experiences. Addressed to different audiences, they differ significantly in language, style and length. The Latin *Evagatorium* and the shorter, but still elaborate, German *Eigentliche Beschreibung* are two of the most important accounts of travel to the Holy Land in the 15th century. They relate Fabri's journeys in detail and deal extensively with Christian-Muslim relations.

The vernacular *Sionpilger* is a spiritual guide to enable nuns to picture a pilgrimage during their meditations. Also, shortly after his first journey he wrote a notable description of the pilgrimage in verse form.

In addition to Fabri's pilgrimage reports, several sermons and two short theological treatises have survived. Originally planned as the last chapter of the *Evagatorium*, his history of the city of Ulm and a panegyric on Swabia became two separate and extensive works. He was also involved in the printing of the sermons of Leonardus de Utino in 1475, and the first printing of the works of the Dominican mystic Heinrich Suso in 1482. Fabri announced in the *Evagatorium* that he would write the story of the siege of Rhodes in 1480 and an account of his experiences in Venice, but it is not known whether he realised this plan.

The value of Fabri's work was recognised at an early date. Since Häberlin's dissertation of 1742, various aspects of Fabri's pilgrimage have been examined in numerous articles. The most reliable collection of the extant manuscripts, together with a short summary of Fabri's life, is in W. Carls, *Felix Fabri, die Sionpilger*.

MAIN SOURCES OF INFORMATION

Primary
Apart from a few rare comments in his works by Fabri himself, no other early sources of his life are known.

Secondary
A. Classen, 'Encounters between East and West in the Middle Ages and Early Modern age. Many untold stories about connections and contacts, understanding and misunderstanding. Also an introduction', in A. Classen (ed.), *East Meets West in the Middle Ages and Early Modern times. Transcultural experiences in the premodern world* (*Fundamentals of Medieval and Early Modern Culture* 14), Berlin, 2013, 95-120

J. Klingner, art. 'Fabri, Felix', in W. Achnitz (ed.), *Deutsches Literatur-Lexikon 3. Reiseberichte und Geschichtsdichtung*, Berlin, 2012, 922-35

A. Klussmann, *In Gottes Namen fahren wir. Die spätmittelalterlichen Pilgerberichte von Felix Fabri, Bernhard von Breydenbach und Konrad Grünemberg im Vergleich*, Saarbrücken, 2012

K. Meyer, 'What the desert said', *Ploughshares* 38 (2012) 119-26

H. Harris, 'The location of Ziklag. Its identification by Felix Fabri', *Palestine Exploration Quarterly* 143 (2011) 19-30

S. Lehmann-Brauns, *Jerusalem sehen. Reiseberichte des 12. Bis 15. Jahrhunderts als empirische Anleitung zur geistigen Pilgerfahrt* (*Berliner Kulturwissenschaft* 9), Freiburg, 2010

S. Schröder, *Zwischen Christentum und Islam. Kulturelle Grenzen in den spatmittelalterlichen Pilgerberichten des Felix Fabri*, Berlin, 2009, pp. 50-76

K. Beebe, 'Felix Fabri and his audiences. The pilgrimage writings of a Dominican preacher in late-medieval Germany', Oxford, 2007 (Diss. University of Oxford)

K. Beebe, 'Reading mental pilgrimage in context. The imaginary pilgrims and real travels of Felix Fabri's "Die Sionpilger"', *Essays in Medieval Studies* 25 (2008) 39-70

S. Bodenmann, 'Die rot-schwarz-weiße Wüste des Felix Fabri. Wahrnehmung und Wissenstradition im Spätmittelalter', in S. Splinter et al. (eds), *Physica et historia. Festschrift für Andreas Kleinert zum 65. Geburtstag (Acta Historica Leopoldina 45)*, Halle, 2005, 51-63

N. Chareyron, *Pilgrims to Jerusalem in the Middle Ages*, New York, 2005

A. Classen, 'Imaginary experience of the Divine. Felix Fabri's Sionspilger – Late medieval pilgrimage literature as a window into religious mentality', *Studies in Spirituality* 15 (2005) 109-28

K. Herbers, 'Felix Fabris "Sionpilgrin" – Reiseschilderung und ältester Kirchenführer Ulms. Ein Beitrag der Reichsstadt Ulm zur Pilgerliteratur des 15. Jahrhunderts', in K. Herbers (ed.), *Die oberdeutschen Reichsstädte und ihre Heiligenkulte – Traditionen und Ausprägungen zwischen Stadt, Ritterorden und Reich (Jakobus-Studien 16)*, Tübingen, 2005, 195-215

C. Delano-Smith, 'The intelligent pilgrim. Maps and medieval pilgrimage to the Holy Land', in R. Allen (ed.), *Eastward bound. Travel and travellers, 1050-1055*, Manchester, 2004, 107-30

A.S. Wille, 'A medieval world-view and its relation to literary authorities in a late medieval pilgrimage account', *Ennen ja nyt* 4 (2004) 1-14, http://www.ennenjanyt.net/4-04/wille.pdf

A. Petsalis-Diomidis, 'Narratives of transformation. Pilgrimage patterns and authorial self-presentation in three pilgrimage texts', in S. Coleman and J. Elsner (eds), *Pilgrim voices. Narrative and authorship in Christian pilgrimage*, New York, 2003, 84-109

J. Klingner, '"Just say happily: 'Felix said so', and you'll be in the clear". Felix Fabri OP (1440-1502) preaching monastic reform to nuns', *Medieval Sermon Studies* 46 (2002) 42-56

H. Schwab, *Toleranz und Vorurteil. Reiseerlebnisse spätmittelalterlicher Jerusalempilger (Spektrum Kulturwissenschaften 4)*, Berlin, 2002

F. Reichert, *Erfahrung der Welt. Reisen und Kulturbegegnung im spaten Mittelalter*, Stuttgart, 2001

W. Carls, *Felix Fabri, Die Sionpilger*, Berlin, 1999, pp. 53-62

X. von Ertzdorff, 'Felix Fabris "Evagatorium" und "Eygentlich beschreibung der hin vnnd wider farth zuo dem Heyligen Landt..." (1484) und der Bericht über die Pilgerfahrt des Freiherrn Johann Werner von Zimmern in der "Chronik der Grafen von Zimmern". Ein Vergleich', *Jahrbuch für Internationale Germanistik 31* (1999) 54-86

D.R. French, 'Pilgrimage, ritual and power strategies. Felix Fabri's pilgrimage to Jerusalem 1483', in B.F. le Beau and M. Mor (eds), *Pilgrims and travelers to the Holy Land*, Omaha NE, 1996, 169-79

W. Paravicini (ed.), *Europäische Reiseberichte des späten Mittelalters. Eine analytische Biographie, Teil 1. Deutsche Reiseberichte*, Frankfurt am Main, 1994, pp. 210-20

K. Schneider, 'Felix Fabri als Prediger', in J. Janota (ed.), *Festschrift Walter Haug und Burghart Wachinger*, Tübingen, 1992, i, pp. 457-68

U. Ganz-Blättler, *Andacht und Abenteuer. Berichte europäischer Jerusalem- und Santiago-Pilger (1320-1520)*, Tübingen, 1990

L. Scheffer, 'A pilgrimage to the Holy Land and Mount Sinai in the 15th century', *Zeitschrift des Deutschen Palästina-Vereins (1953-)* 102 (1986) 144-51

A. Esch, 'Gemeinsames Erlebnis – Individueller Bericht. Vier Parallelberichte aus einer Reisegruppe von Jerusalempilgern 1480', *Zeitschrift für Historische Forschung* 11 (1984) 385-416

H. Wiegandt, 'Felix Fabri. Dominikaner, Reiseschriftsteller, Geschichtsschreiber 1441/42-1502', *Lebensbilder aus Schwaben und Franken* 15 (1983) 1-28

A. Nibbi, 'Gold and silver from the Sinai', *Gottinger Miszellen* 57 (1982) 35-40

K. Hannemann, art. 'Fabri, Felix', in *Die deutsche Literatur des Mittelalters. Verfasserlexikon* ii, 1980, 682-89; xi, 2004, 435-36

H. Feilke, *Felix Fabris Evagatorium über seine Reise in das Heilige Land. Eine Untersuchung über die Pilgerliteratur des ausgehenden Mittelalters*, Frankfurt, 1976

H.F.M. Prescott, *Once to Sinai. The further pilgrimage of Friar Felix Fabri*, London, 1957

G.W. Murray, 'Felix Fabri's pilgrimage from Gaza to Mount Sinai and Cairo, A.D. 1483', *The Geographical Journal* 122 (1956) 335-42

H.F.M. Prescott, *Jerusalem journey. Pilgrimage to the Holy Land in the fifteenth century*, London, 1954

H.F.M. Prescott, *Friar Felix at large. A fifteenth-century pilgrimage to the Holy Land*, New York, 1950

M. Ernst, 'Frater Felix Fabri. Der Geschichtsschreiber der Stadt Ulm', *Zeitschrift für Württembergische Landesgeschichte* 6 (1942) 323-67

K.G. Veesenmeyer (ed.), *Fratris Felicis Fabri Tractatus de civitate ulmensi. De eius origine, ordine, regimine, de civibus eius et statu* (Liber II of *Historiae Suevorum libri duo*), Tübingen, 1889

F.D. Häberlin, *Dissertatio historica sistens vitam itinera et scripta Fr. Felicis Fabri monachi praedicatorii conventus Vlmani*, Göttingen, 1742

WORKS ON CHRISTIAN-MUSLIM RELATIONS

Eigentliche beschreibung der hin vnnd wider farth zu dem Heyligen Landt gen Jerusalem vnd furter durch die grosse Wüsteney zu dem Heiligen Berg Horeb, 'Reliable description of the outward and return journey to the Holy Land and Jerusalem and further through the great desert to the holy Mount Horeb'

DATE Between about 1484 and 1488
ORIGINAL LANGUAGE German

DESCRIPTION

Fabri composed the *Eigentliche beschreibung* for a lay audience. According to his preface, the noblemen in his party asked him to write about the events in memory of their pilgrimage, and how they gained knighthood in the Church of the Holy Sepulchre. He also addresses his work to all persons interested in such a journey, stating that many friends, men and women, noble and common, have begged him to write down his experiences.

Contrary to statements in earlier research, this is not just an abbreviated version of the *Evagatorium*, but an independent account in vernacular German. In consideration of the rather non-academic level of education of his readers, Fabri omitted most of the scientific and historical excursuses, and instead added some episodes of special interest to his travel companions. The German version is more direct in its moral judgements and pedagogical instructions than the Latin account. On the other hand, Fabri is more discreet in criticising his companions, who did not always live up to the ideal of a good pilgrim. Fabri gives a detailed description of the cultural encounter with Muslims, though less information is included on the doctrines of Islam. He concentrates more on daily relations between the pilgrims and their Muslim guides or the local population.

The interactions are described from the perspective of the many dangers the Christian pilgrims had to endure in an infidel environment, and in consequence religious borders are drawn more sharply than in the Latin version. In terms of friendly contacts with 'infidels', Fabri is more cautious, despite some affirmative depictions. By comparison with the *Evagatorium*, the Mamluks and their sultan, for instance, are presented in a considerably more critical tone.

SIGNIFICANCE

Although shorter than the *Evagatorium*, the *Eigentliche beschreibung* describes the pilgrimage to the Holy Land in greater detail than most other reports of the Late Middle Ages. Comparison with the Latin version proves how carefully the author took the expectations of his audience into account. Due to its length and the use of German, the *Eigentliche beschreibung* became better known to contemporaries than the *Evagatorium*. In the 16th century, his account was printed several times and was given the title by which it is known. The dependences and differences between the known manuscripts have not been studied (see W. Carls, *Felix Fabri, Die Sionpilger*, pp. 61-62). A critical and complete edition based on the autograph of Fabri preserved in Dessau is still lacking.

MANUSCRIPTS

MS Dessau, Stadtbibliothek – Hs. Georg 238 (15th century; Felix Fabri's autograph)

MS Ulm, Stadtarchiv – cod. Fabri 5, 199 (1494)

MS Vienna, Österreichische Nationalbibliothek – cvp 2906 [Hist. Prof. 442], fols 144v-185v (15th century)

MS Kalocsa, Kathedralbibliothek – 323 (formerly 4873) (1512)

MS Berlin, Staatsbibliothek – Germ. Fol. 1266 (1522)

MS Stuttgart, Württembergische Landesbibliothek – HB I 26 (Weingarten G 32), fols 75r-184v (16th century)

MS Eichstätt, Universitätsbibliothek – Cod. st 676, fols 1r-198v (16th century)

MS Munich, Bayerische Staatsbibliothek – clm 1016, fols 74r-82v (16th century; description of Sinai)

MS Wolfenbüttel, Herzog August Bibliothek – Cod. Guelf. 18. 14. Aug., fols 1r-168r (16th century)

MS Wolfenbüttel, Herzog August Bibliothek –Hs. 44. 11. Aug., fols 219r-307v (17th century)

MS Munich, Bayerische Staatsbibliothek – clm 1275, fols 1r-197r (17th-18th century)

EDITIONS & TRANSLATIONS

G.E. Sollbach, *In Gottes Namen fahren wir. Die Pilgerfahrt des Felix Faber ins Heilige Land und zum St. Katharina-Grab auf dem Sinai A.D. 1483*, Kettwig, 1990 (incomplete edition in modern German)

H. Roob, *Die Pilgerfahrt des Bruders Felix Faber ins Heilige Land Anno MCDLXXXIII, nach der ersten deutschen Ausgabe 1556 bearbeitet*, Heidelberg, 1965 (incomplete edition in modern German)

'Hernn Johann Werli von Zimpern / Herrn Heinrich von Stoepffel / Herrn Johann Truchseß von Waldpurg / vnd Herrn Bern von Rechberg / etc. Wallfahrt zum H. Land im Jahr 1484. verbracht / wie die von Bruder Felix / Leßmeister Prediger Ordens zu Ulm beschrieben /', in S. Feyerabend (ed.), *Reyßbuch deß heyligen Lands / Das ist Ein gründtliche beschreibung aller vnd jeder Meer vnd Bilgerfahrten zum heyligen Lande [...]*, Frankfurt am Main, 1659, pp. 227-352

'Eigentliche beschreibung der hin vnd wider Fahrt zu dem Heyligen Land gen Jerusalem / [...]', in S. Feyerabend (ed.), *Reyßbuch deß heyligen Lands / Das ist Ein gründtliche beschreibung aller vnd jeder Meer vnd Bilgerfahrten zum heyligen Lande [...]*, Frankfurt am Main, 1584, fols 122v-188r

EJgentlich beschreibung der hin vnnd wider farth zu dem Heyligen Landt gen Jerusalem/ vnd furter durch die grosse W[ue]sten zu dem Heiligen Berge Horeb vnd Sinay/ darauß zuuernemen was wunders die Pilgrin hin vnd wider auff Land vnd wasser zu erfaren vnd zu besehen haben [...], Frankfurt am Main, 1557

EJgentliche beschreibung der hin vnnd wider farth zu dem Heyligen Landt gen Jerusalem/ vnd furter durch die grosse W[ue]steney zu dem Heiligen Berge Horeb Sinay/ darauß zuuernemen was wunders die Pilgrin hin vnd wider auff Land vnd wasser zu erfahren vnd zu besehen haben [...], Frankfurt am Main, 1556

STUDIES

Schröder, *Zwischen Christentum und Islam*

J. Meyers, 'L'*Evagatorium* de Frere Félix Fabri. De l'errance du voyage a l'errance du récit', *Le Moyen Age* 114 (2008) 9-36

J. Meyers, 'Merveilleux et fantastique dans le recit de voyage. Le cas de l'*Evagatorium* de Frere Félix Fabri (c. 1435-1502)', in F. Gingras et al. (eds), *Furent les merveilles pruvees et les aventures truvees. Hommage à Francis Dubost (Colloques, congrés et conference sur le moyen âge* 6), Paris, 2005, 437-63

Von Ertzdorff, 'Felix Fabris "Evagatorium"'

H.E. Schwab, 'Das Andere anders sein lassen? Zur Darstellung des Fremden in den parallelen deutschen Pilgerberichten von Felix Fabri und Bernhard von Breydenbach (1483/84)', *Ulm und Oberschwaben. Zeitschrift fur Geschichte und Kunst* 50 (1996) 139-65

Evagatorium in Terrae Sanctae, Arabiae et Egypti peregrinationem, 'Wanderings on the pilgrimage to the Holy Land, Arabia and Egypt'

DATE Between about 1484 and 1495
ORIGINAL LANGUAGE Middle Dutch

DESCRIPTION

The *Evagatorium* was written in order to give Fabri's Dominican brothers a detailed account of his journey and the situation in the Holy Land and so that, through reading his descriptions of the holy sites, they would be able to gain a deeper understanding of scripture. According to Fabri, the numerous humorous anecdotes in the work are not included only for entertainment, but to provide guidance for a virtuous life. To compile his work, which is almost 1,600 pages long in Hassler's edition, Fabri used a large number of sources, such as pilgrimage reports from the 13th to the 15th centuries, crusader chronicles, itineraries, encyclopaedic works by authors such as Vincent of Beauvais and Bartholomeus Anglicus, and theological treatises. The chronological order of the *Evagatorium* is, therefore, frequently interrupted by excursuses on biblical, historical and scientific topics.

For his description of Islam and of Muslim customs, Fabri drew heavily on the printed account of Bernhard of Breidenbach. He adopted great parts of Breidenbach's chapters about Muḥammad and the 'errors' of the 'infidels', which were originally written by the Dominican scholar Martin Rath. Fabri also used the *Cribratio Alcorani* of Nicholas of Cusa, and the informative treatise of George of Hungary, who lived for almost 20 years as a bondman under Turkish rule.

In many respects, Fabri shared and modified the negative Christian image of the rival religion. He aimed to prove the 'corruption' of the Muslim faith in order to show the superiority of Christian belief and culture. Muḥammad is therefore several times condemned as an abuser, Antichrist and son of the Devil, while the Qur'an is judged as false prophecy, and religious customs such as the Hajj and fasting during Ramadan are interpreted as forgeries of Christian rituals or as expressions of the Muslims' 'abominable practices'. But, contrary to most other late medieval travel reports, Fabri did not present each encounter with Muslims as a direct opposition between the righteous Christians and the faithless Muslims. As well as many descriptions of hostile assaults by Arabs, he also portrayed some peaceful and friendly relations.

It appears that Fabri was more able to free himself from theological discourses on non-Christian religions when addressing the small circle of his monastic brothers. In the frame of his narrative, however, these depictions of Muslims with laudable qualities frequently served as a moral example for the (Christian) reader at home. Thus, for example, he shows appreciation for the merciful treatment of prisoners in Cairo, and the procedures followed among Muslims to avoid the use of weapons and needless bloodshed in quarrels. In contrast to his vernacular accounts, in the *Evagatorium* Fabri does not even condemn the Mamluks as apostates, but finds promising signs that, as former Christians, they can be persuaded to return to the true faith.

SIGNIFICANCE

The *Evagatorium* is one of the most important pilgrimage accounts of the Late Middle Ages. It is far more detailed than any other text of the genre, and gives an extraordinarily broad picture of the Holy Land and the Near East. Numerous marginal notes in Fabri's autograph, which is preserved in the city library of Ulm, show that Fabri edited the first version of his report, adding relevant information from new sources to which he had gained access. The relation of the known manuscripts has not been fully explored (W. Carls, *Felix Fabri, Die Sionpilger*, p. 59). A new critical edition is being prepared by F. Reichert.

MANUSCRIPTS

MS Ulm, Stadtbibliothek – Hs. 19555-1,2 (1484-95; Fabri's autograph)
MS Munich, Bayerische Staatsbibliothek – clm. 2826 (1488; copy by Johannes Nuer)
MS Dresden, Sächsische Landesbibliothek – A 71 (end of the 15th century)
MS Stuttgart, Hauptstaatsarchiv – Hs. 236 (15th-16th century; fragments)
MS Munich, Bayerische Staatsbibliothek – clm. 188/189 (1508-9; copy by Hartmann Schedel)
MS Ulm, Stadtbibliothek – Hs. H Schad 66/Hs. Wachter (1509)
MS Ulm, Stadtbibliothek – Hs. H Schad 67 (end of the 16th century)
MS Ulm, Stadtbibliothek – Hs. H Fabri 2/3 (1707)
MS Hamburg, Staats- und Universitätsbibliothek – Cod. Geogr. 54 (1713)

EDITIONS & TRANSLATIONS

J. Meyers and M. Tarayre, *Les errances de frère Félix*, 2 vols, Paris, 2013 (French trans.)

N. Chareyron and J. Meyers, *Les errances de Frère Félix, pèlerin en Terre Sainte, en Arabie et en Egypte, 1480-1483*, 2 vols, Montpellier, 2000-2 (French trans.)

Evagatorium über die Pilgerreise ins Heilige Land, nach Arabien und Ägypten, ed. and trans. H. Wiegandt and H. Krauß, Ulm, 1998 (unpublished MS of a complete German trans. preserved in Ulm, Stadtbibliothek B1 1171, 1-2)

F. Fabri, *Galeere und Karawane. Pilgerreise ins Heilige Land, zum Sinai und nach Ägypten 1483*, ed. and trans. H. Wiegandt, et al., Stuttgart, 1996 (incomplete German trans.)

J. Masson, *Voyage en Egypte de Felix Fabri. Traduit du latin*, ed. 3 vols, Cairo, 1975 (French trans. of Fabri's journey through Egypt)

J. Garber, *Die Reisen des Felix Faber durch Tirol in den Jahren 1483 und 1484*, Innsbruck, 1923 (edition of Fabri's journey through the Alps)

A. Stewart, *The wanderings of Felix Fabri*, 4 vols, London, 1897 (repr. New York, 1971; incomplete trans.)

D. Zasso, *Venezia nel MCDLXXXVIII. Descrizione di Felice Fabri da Ulma*, Venice, 1881 (Italian trans. of Fabri's description of Venice)

K.D. Hassler, *Fratris Felicis Fabri Evagatorium in Terrae Sanctae, Arabiae et Egypti peregrinationem*, 3 vols, Stuttgart, 1843-49

STUDIES

A. Classen, 'Mountains as a novel staging ground in late medieval and early modern literature. Felix Fabri's *Evagatorium* (1493), Aeneas Silvio Piccolomini's *Historia Austrialis* (after 1452), and Emperor Maximilian's *Tewrdank* from 1517', *Medievalia et Humanistica* 39 (2013) 1-24

S. Schröder, '"Dess glich ich all min tag nie gesechen hab vnd ob got wil nùt mer sechen wil." Fremd- und Selbstbilder in den Pilgerberichten des Ulmer Dominikaners Felix Fabri', *Zeitschrift für Württembergische Landesgeschichte* 68 (2009) 41-62

S. Schröder, *Zwischen Christentum und Islam. Kulturelle Grenzen in den spätmittelalterlichen Pilgerberichten des Felix Fabri*, Berlin, 2009

B.J. Irsay-Nagy, 'A journey to Egypt in 1483 and the beginnings of Coptic studies in Europe', *Acta Antiqua* 46 (2006) 129-49

F. Reichert, 'Mohammed in Mekka. Doppelte Grenzen im Islambild des lateinischen Mittelalters', *Saeculum* 56 (2005) 17-31

A. Classen, 'Medieval Europe and its encounter with the foreign world. Late-medieval German witnesses', in R.F. Gyug (ed.), *Medieval cultures in contact*, New York, 2003, 85-103

Petsalis-Diomidis, 'Narratives of transformation'

X. von Ertzdorff, ' "Die Ding muoss man mit gesunder Vernunft ansehen." Das Evagatorium des Ulmer Dominikaners Felix Fabri 1484-ca. 1495', in X. von Erzdorff (ed.), *Beschreibung der Welt. Zur Poetik der Reise- und Länderberichte. Vorträge eines interdisziplinären Symposiums vom 8. bis 13. Juni 1998 an der Justus-Liebig-Universität Gießen*, Amsterdam, 2000, 219-62

F. Reichert, 'Pilger und Muslime im Heiligen Land. Formen des Kulturkonflikts im späten Mittelalter', in R. Kloepfer and B. Dücker (eds), *Kritik und Geschichte der Intoleranz*, Heidelberg, 2000, 3-21

A. Grabois, *Le pèlerin occidental en Terre Sainte au moyen âge*, Brussels, 1998

A. Grabois, 'Islam and Muslims as seen by Christian pilgrims in Palestine in the thirteenth century', *Asian and African Studies* 20 (1986) 309-27

Stefan Schröder

Ambrosius Zeebout

DATE OF BIRTH   Unknown
PLACE OF BIRTH Unknown
DATE OF DEATH   Unknown; early 16th century
PLACE OF DEATH Unknown

BIOGRAPHY

Little can be said with certainty about Ambrosius Zeebout, the author of *Tvoyage van Mher Joos van Ghistele*, who was active in the late 15th and early 16th century. An analysis of the sources of *Tvoyage* by R.J. Gaspard suggests that Zeebout may have been a Carmelite friar who lived and worked in the Carmelite monastery at Ghent, the Flemish city where Joos van Ghistele (d. 1516), the main character in *Tvoyage*, lived in the years during which the account of his travels was written.

MAIN SOURCES OF INFORMATION

Primary
R.J. Gaspar (ed.), *Tvoyage van Mher Joos van Ghistele*, Hilversum, 1998, pp. xi-xlviii

Secondary
I. Bejczy, 'Boekenwijsheid en persoonlijke beleving in een laat-middeleeuws reisverhaal. Jan van Mandeville overtoffen: Tvoyage van Joos van Ghistele', *Literatuur* 10 (1993) 146-53
A.J.J. Delen, 'Joos van Ghistele et son voyage en Orient en 1481-1485', *Bulletin de la Société Royale de Géographie d'Anvers* 54 (1934) 209-28
G.R. Crone, 'Joos van Ghistele and his travels in the Levant', *Geographical Journal* (1934) 410-15

WORKS ON CHRISTIAN-MUSLIM RELATIONS

Tvoyage van Mher Joos van Ghistele; Tvoyage, 'Voyage of Mher Joos van Ghistele'

DATE Between 1485 and about 1500
ORIGINAL LANGUAGE Middle Dutch

DESCRIPTION

Tvoyage van Mher Joos van Ghistele offers a description of the journey made by the Flemish knight Joos van Ghistele, who was born in Ghent in 1446 and died there in 1516. Between 1481 and 1485, van Ghistele travelled to Palestine, Egypt, Sinai, Syria, Persia, the Greek archipelago and North Africa. After his return to the Low Countries, he entrusted his travel notes to Ambrosius Zeebout, who then wrote the formal account. *Tvoyage* was published for the first time in Ghent in 1557.

Book 1 includes practical advice to travellers to the East (chs 1-2); descriptions of the life and work of the Prophet Muḥammad (ch. 3); the religion of Islam ('mohammedanisme'; ch. 4); Islamic sects and peoples (ch. 5, but with very little detail); Eastern Christianity (ch. 6); and Jewish sects (ch. 7). Book 2 describes van Ghistele's journey from Flanders to the Holy Land (chs 1-59). Book 3 is about Egypt, and includes a description of van Ghistele's audience with the Mamluk Sultan Qā'it Bey (r. 1468-96) in Cairo (chs 6-7). Book 4 covers Arabia, including a visit to the Monastery of St Catherine at the foot of Mount Sinai (chs 1-11), a journey across the Red Sea to the island of Perīm with a stop-over at the port of Sawākin, and a description of the *ḥajj* (ch. 18) – but also of Egyptian mummies (ch. 19). Via Cyprus (Book 5), van Ghistele then travelled to Syria (Book 6) once again, visiting first the Monastery of Our Lady of Saidnaya (chs 10-12) and proceeding to Aleppo. Book 7, on Persia, including parts of eastern Anatolia (chs 7-9), contains a description of India (chs 15-17) and a history of the Tatars (chs 18-19). Van Ghistele appears to have travelled no further than Tabriz, which is described extensively (chs 10-14). The book ends with the return trip to Tripoli in Syria. Book 8 offers a description of Van Ghistele's journey home from Tripoli through the Greek archipelago and via Tunis to Italy and then Flanders. It includes references to the history of the Turks (chs 1-4), as well chapters (8-12) on the death of Sultan Meḥmed II in 1481 and the succession to him, and notes on 'Tunis and its king' (chs 26-29).

SIGNIFICANCE

Van Ghistele's travelogue offers more detailed descriptions than the works of his more well-known contemporaries, Bernhard von Breydenbach (d. 1497) and Felix Fabri (d. 1502), which he also used as sources. This is particularly clear in the sections on the Prophet Muḥammad and the religion of Islam, where van Ghistele relies heavily on von Breydenbach, whose work he paraphrases rather carelessly and introduces additional errors on both subjects. Although he consistently refers to Muslims as 'infidels' and 'heretics', most of the account offers 'facts' about the Middle East in a generally dispassionate fashion. *Tvoyage* was widely read in the Low Countries.

MANUSCRIPTS

Only three MSS appear to have survived, two of which are kept in Brussels (one dating from c. 1500, the other from c. 1535), and the third in Namen, Belgium (dating from the 16th century). For detailed descriptions, see Gaspar's edition, pp. xlviii-l.

EDITIONS & TRANSLATIONS

Gaspar, *Tvoyage* (the most recent edition)

R. Bauwens-Préaux, *Voyage en Égypte de Joost van Ghistele, 1482-1483*, Cairo, 1976 (partial French trans.)

Tvoyage van Mher Joos van Ghistele, oft anders, Texcellent, groot, zeldsaem ende vremd voyage, ghedaen by wylent Edelen ende weerden Heere, Mher Joos van Ghistele. In zynen levene Riddere, Heere van Axele, van Maelstede ende van den Moere, etc. Tanderen tyden vier-mael Voor-Schepene van Ghendt. Tracterende van veelderande wonderlicke ende vremde dijnghen, gheobserveerd over d'Zee, in den landen van Sclavonien, Griecken, Turckien, Candien, Rhodes ende Cypers. Voords ooc in den lande van Beloften, Assirien, Arabien, Egypten, Ethyopien, Barbarien, Indien, Perssen, Meden, Caldeen en Tartarien: met der gheleghenthede der zelver landen ende meer ander plaetsen, Insulen ende Steden, van Europen, Asien ende Affryken, zo in de Prologhe breeder blijckt, Ghent, 1557 by Hendrik van den Keere (Identical reprints were published in Ghent in 1563 and 1572.)

STUDIES

A. Lagast, 'Omitted in manuscript, praised in print. Nameless noblemen in the Middle Dutch travel narrative Tvoyage van Mher Joos van Ghistele (ca. 1491)', *Bulletin des Museés royaux d'art et d'histoire Parc du Cinquantenaire Bruxelles / Bulletin van de Koninklijke musea voor kunst en geschiedenis Jubelpark Brussel* 82 (2011) 101-18

S. Villerius, 'Op zoek naar Pape Jan of naar avontuur? een discoursanalyse van boek III van Tvoyage van Mher Joos van Ghistele (1482-1483)', *Handelingen der Maatschappij voor Geschiedenis en Oudheidkunde te Gent* 63 (2009) 27-60

B. Vander Gucht, 'Zeebout (Ambrosius). Voyage van Mher Joos van Ghistele', *Revue Belge de Philologie et d'Histoire* 79 (2001) 1442-44

Bejczy, 'Boekenwijsheid en persoonlijke beleving in een laat-middeleeuws reisverhaal'

J. Schenkel, 'Tvoyage van Mher Joos van Ghistele. Frictie tussen feit en fictie', *Scientiarum Historia* 19 (1993) 81-95

B. van de Walle, 'Une version du voyage de J. de Ghistelles', *Chronique d'Egypte* 14.28 (1939) 245-57

Delen, 'Joos van Ghistele et son voyage en Orient en 1481-1485'

Crone, 'Joos van Ghistele and his travels'

P. Dieleman, *De groote reiziger Mer Joos van Ghistele*, Middelburg, 1932 (a popular work without annotation)

Maurits van den Boogert

Wynkyn de Worde

DATE OF BIRTH Possibly 1455
PLACE OF BIRTH Possibly Wörth, Lorraine
DATE OF DEATH 1534
PLACE OF DEATH London

BIOGRAPHY

Wynkyn de Worde was an early printer who served as an apprentice to Johannes Veldener in Cologne and then worked with William Caxton following the latter's visit to Cologne in 1471-72. In 1475 or 1476, de Worde accompanied Caxton to Westminster, where he eventually inherited Caxton's printshop after Caxton's death in 1492. Around 1500, he moved his shop to Fleet Street under the 'sign of the sun', which he incorporated into his colophon. The first printer to operate from Fleet Street, he is credited as the forerunner of the industry that became synonymous with that street. He also rented a shop in St Paul's Churchyard.

De Worde printed approximately 400 books, many in multiple editions, often printing texts and translations published on the continent of Europe. He was a prolific user of woodcuts, usually copied from continental works or borrowed from other London-based printers. De Worde's output included almost the entire canon of Middle English literature. He was skilled at anticipating and meeting readers' expectations, and is known to have revised texts to accommodate them, yet his versions also helped to shape public taste (Lerer, 'The wiles of a woodcut', p. 382). He appears to have taken great care in choosing which illustrations to use.

De Worde developed an extensive network of printers, bookbinders and tradesmen. He printed four editions of the work attributed to John Mandeville, with 72 woodcuts, including the first ever images of Muḥammad to be printed in England. Sixty-three of these were taken from the German edition of Mandeville, printed in 1482. De Worde's Mandeville editions appeared in 1499, 1500, 1503 and 1510 and sold so well that only two copies have survived, neither of which is complete due to wear and tear (Letts, 'The source of the woodcuts', p. 155). In 1515 or possibly 1519, de Worde printed, as a single volume, the Mandeville chapter on the 'Customs of the Saracens' with two woodcuts and small but significant revisions to the text.

MAIN SOURCES OF INFORMATION

Primary
St Margaret's churchwarden accounts, 1480-82
Westminster Abbey Muniments, bk A, pp. 182, 356, 391
Westminster Abbey Muniments, 17849, 19741, 19754

Secondary
S. Lerer, 'The wiles of a woodcut. Wynkyn de Worde and the early Tudor reader', *Huntington Library Journal* 59 (1996) 381-403
N.F. Blake, 'Wynkyn de Worde. A review of his life and work', in D. Buschinger and W. Spiewok (eds), *Études de linguistique et de la littérature en l'honneur d'André Crépin*, Greifswald, Germany, 1993, 21-40
A.S.G. Edwards and C.M. Meale, 'The marketing of printed books in late medieval English', *The Library*, 6th ser. 15 (1993) 95-124
M.C. Erler, 'Wynkyn de Worde's will. Legatees and bequests', *The Library*, 6th ser. 10 (1988) 107-21
J. Moran, *Wynkyn de Worde. Father of Fleet Street*, London, 1976² (3rd rev. ed., 2003)
H.M. Nixon, 'Caxton, his contemporaries and successors in the book trade from Westminster documents', *The Library*, 5th ser. 31 (1976) 305-26
N.F. Blake, 'Wynkyn de Worde. The later years', *Gutenberg Jahrbuch* (1972) 128-38
N.F. Blake, 'Wynkyn de Worde. The early years', *Gutenberg Jahrbuch* (1971) 62-69
M. Letts, 'The source of the woodcuts in Wynkyn de Worde's edition of Mandeville's *Travels*, 1499', *The Library*, 5th ser. 6 (1955) 154-61
H.S. Bennett, *English books and readers, 1475-1557, being a study in the history of the book trade from Caxton to the incorporation of the Stationers' Company*, Cambridge, 1952
H.R. Plomer, *Wynkyn de Worde and his contemporaries from the death of Caxton to 1535*, London, 1935
G. Bone, 'Extant manuscripts printed by W. de Worde with notes on the owner, Roger Thorney', *The Library*, 4th ser. 12 (1931-2) 284-306
E.G. Duff, *The printers, stationers, and bookbinders of London and Westminster in the fifteenth century*, Cambridge, 1899 (repr. 2011)

WORKS ON CHRISTIAN-MUSLIM RELATIONS

Here begynneth a lytell treatyse of the turkes lawe called Alcaron. And also it speketh of Machamet the nygromancer; Here begynneth a lytell treatise

DATE   Probably 1515 or 1519
ORIGINAL LANGUAGE   English

DESCRIPTION

Probably published in 1515, this work is an illustrated tract of 12 pages on six leaves, including what functions as a title page and which reads 'Here begynneth a lytell treatyse of the turkes lawe called Alcoran. And also it talketh of Machamet the Nygromancer', really the first two sentences rather than a title. The text is almost entirely reproduced from Wynkyn de Worde's edition of the *Travels of John Mandeville*, which he had first printed with 72 woodcuts in 1499, where it is Chapter 15, on the 'Laws of the Saracens'. De Worde also very likely selected the woodcuts and edited the text, which he would have printed in order to capitalise on the commercial success of Mandeville's larger work. This is evidence that there was a market for such a text in the early 16th century, while his editorial changes suggest new emphases occasioned by the Ottoman advance into European territory.

The 1515 tract is believed to be the earliest English book solely devoted to Islam, and until recently it was discussed and analysed as an anonymous work. The Mandeville text is itself almost entirely borrowed from (Pseudo)-William of Tripoli's *De statu Sarracenorum* ('On the realm of the Saracens') and this chapter had in 1503 been incorporated by Richard Arnold into his *Chronicle* as 'The laws and belyue of the Sarasyns', where it is openly attributed to John Mandeuile (p. 265), also spelled Mandulye on the same page and in the concluding attribution (p. 269). The 1515 text does not refer to Mandeville, simply concluding with the statement that the tract was printed by Wynkyn de Worde under the 'sygne of the sonne'. The opening sentences resemble those of de Worde's edition of Mandeville, 'Here begynneth a lytell treatyse... of the wayes of the holy londe.'

The first illustration, which occupies most of the title page, depicts a preacher standing in a pulpit, with a sword in his right hand, preaching to an audience of veiled, seated women who look like nuns, although C.F. Beckingham says that the women are 'all dressed in the costume of Tudor England' ('Misconceptions of Islam', p. 608). The second illustration takes up page 2 of the tract. It shows a preacher, again standing in a pulpit, with a devilish-looking figure leaning on his left shoulder while two men on the opposite side occupy what appears to be a balcony, and on the floor sit a group of five men and women, only one of whom is facing the preacher. The origin of the first woodcut remains unknown. Wynkyn de Worde copied the second from a work he had published in 1505 and in 1506, a translation of Andrew Chertsey's *The arte or crafte to lyue well and to dye well*, where it illustrates a chapter on the Antichrist.

The devilish figure represents the Antichrist, although the implication is that the preacher, who in the 1515 publication is probably meant to be Muḥammad, is receiving satanic inspiration. John Johnson, who describes the tract as a 'very uncommon work' in his 1824 book about the origin of printing, took the preacher to be Muḥammad disputing with Christian doctors while being prompted by Satan (*Typographia*, p. 776). Although de Worde's version of Mandeville had illustrations of Muḥammad, he did not recycle these in the abstracted tract.

The main changes in the text from the Mandeville original are the substitution of the term 'Turk' for 'Saracen', the introductory section on the first complete page of text in which Muḥammad is described as a 'nygromancer', and the change from emphasising the common ground between the faiths, which makes it easy to convert Muslims to Christianity, to seeing Muslims as violent and as irreconcilably at odds with the Christian world. By substituting 'Turk' for 'Saracen', de Worde shows awareness that, while 'Saracen' had previously functioned as a synonym for a follower of Muḥammad, the new geo-political circumstances conflated Muslim with Turk. Furthermore, as interest in the Ottomans increased following the Fall of Constantinople and the Ottoman advance into Europe, it implies that any attempt to understand more about the Turks requires some knowledge of their religion. There is, however, no explicit reference to the Ottomans. Although de Worde's primary motive in printing the tract was probably to make a profit, as a recognised shaper of literary taste and trends through his publications, he may also have wanted to inform people about what he saw as a very real threat to their way of life. No longer was Islam a false religion practised at a considerable distance from England; now, as the Ottomans expanded further into Europe, Islam could also be seen as coming closer.

While the stereotype of Islam as a violent religion combining territorial conquest with forced conversion by soldiers carrying a sword in one hand and a Qur'an in the other was well established in European polemical literature, this is not a theme of the Mandeville chapter. Rather, the Mandeville text, echoing the belief of some 13th-century Christians in the Middle East, actually entertains the hope that Muslims 'are easily converted'. De Worde keeps the statement, 'And the Saracens believeth so much in our faith that they have been lately converted when men do preach unto them the faith of our Lord Jesus Christ', but shifts emphasis from common ground to irreconcilable difference. This is based on Islam's hostility towards non-Muslims, and their alleged duty to slay unbelievers and to propagate Islam with a sword held high in their hands to 'threaten' those who hear. This sword is then displayed in a high place, so that all who see it will fear. In contrast, Christians place a crucifix in a high place, as a symbol of humility. While Christians are bidden to love and pray for their enemies, Turks are charged neither to love nor to pray for those who do not love them. The first illustration was obviously chosen to illustrate this sword-wielding segment.

SIGNIFICANCE

C.F. Beckingham describes this as a 'curious tract' from a time when information on Islam was becoming available in Europe as commercial relations with the Muslim world developed. Within a century or so, he says, errors of the kind found in the tract would 'become unthinkable' ('Misconceptions of Islam', pp. 608-9). He also says that he is only aware of a single copy in the British Library's Reference Division, where it is obscurely catalogued under Qur'an, although 'it is not a translation or even summary of the Koran but a brief, confused, contradictory and grotesquely inaccurate tract on Islam and the life of Muhammad'. This could suggest that the tract is of relatively little or no significance, for if it sold few copies its impact would be minimal. However, it is likely that de Worde made a satisfactory profit from it, and it is highly possible that it was widely read, and helped shape or reshape attitudes toward Islam.

The negative comparisons between Christian love and humility and Islam's hostility and violence radically shift the emphasis of the Mandeville original. There is a contradiction here, since, if Christians are bidden to love their enemies, they should also love Turks. Leaving the reference in the text to Muslims being easy to convert also seems contradictory to the shift towards seeing Muslims as wholly hostile. The fact that neither of the woodcuts has any authentically Turkish or Muslim content – the pulpit does not look like a *minbar*, nor the room anything like a mosque, nor would a Muslim preach to a mixed congregation – suggests that de Worde had no access to any actual illustrations of Turkish life.

The Mandeville text describes Muḥammad as 'false', and it also links his supposed claim to receive revelation from Gabriel with his epilepsy. This tract does the same, though the use of the term 'nygromancer' is de Worde's own addition. Again, Christians had long depicted Muḥammad as a practitioner of black magic but, by incorporating the word necromancer into the title, de Worde gives it more prominence. Choice of an illustration associated with the Antichrist adds another negative stereotype, one that was not present in the original text. Nor is there any suggestion of Satanic inspiration in Mandeville, which the illustration here also implies.

This first text in English solely about Islam was deliberately edited to stress incompatibility and hostility between Islam and Christianity, and to attribute Islam to a diabolical source. Given the less antagonistic content of the source, this presumably reflects what people were thinking and saying at this time, although de Worde may equally have set out to shape public opinion towards a markedly negative view of Islam and the Ottoman Empire. He was, after all, renowned for his astuteness in knowing what readers wanted, and for meeting these expectations.

MANUSCRIPTS

The Mandeville chapter of which this tract is a revision exists in over 300 MSS; see M.C. Seymour, *Sir John Mandeville*, Aldershot, 1993, pp. 38-49

EDITIONS & TRANSLATIONS

Here begynneth a lytell treatyse of the turkes lawe called Alcaron. And also it speketh of Machamet the nygromancer, Amsterdam, 1977 (facsimile)

Here begynneth a lytell treatyse of the turkes lawe called Alcaron. And also it speketh of Machamet the nygromancer, Ann Arbor MI, 1938 (facsimile)

Here begynneth a lytell treatyse of the turkes lawe called Alcaron. And also it speketh of Machamet the nygromancer, London, 1515

STUDIES

M. Dimmock, *Mythologies of the Prophet in early English literature*, New York, 2013, pp. 53-56

C.F. Beckingham, 'Misconceptions of Islam, medieval and modern', *Journal of the Royal Society of Arts* 124 (1976) 606-11 (repr. in C.F. Beckingham, *Between Islam and Christendom*, London, 1983)

E. Hodnett, *English woodcuts, 1480-1535*, Oxford, 1935

A.W. Pollard and R. Proctor, *Three hundred notable books added to the Library of the British Museum under the keepership of Richard Garnett 1890-1899*, Edinburgh, 1899

J. Johnson, *Typographia, or, The printers' instructor. including an account of the origin of printing, with biographical notices of the printers of England, from Caxton to the close of the sixteenth century: a series of ancient and modern alphabets, and Domesday characters: together with an elucidation of every subject connected with the art*, London, 1824

Clinton Bennett

Huldrych Zwingli

DATE OF BIRTH   1 January 1484
PLACE OF BIRTH   Wildhaus, Switzerland
DATE OF DEATH   11 October 1531
PLACE OF DEATH   Kappel am Albis, Switzerland

BIOGRAPHY

After attending Latin schools in Weesen, Basel and Bern, Zwingli studied first in Vienna and then matriculated, in 1502, at the University of Basel, where he received a bachelor's degree in 1504 and a master's degree in 1506. Shortly after beginning his theological studies that same year, he was ordained and became a parish priest in Glarus, where he undertook a programme of intensive private study. During this period he also made contact with Swiss humanists (Joachim Vadian, Heinrich Glarean), amongst whom his reputation grew rapidly. In 1516, he moved to Einsiedeln, where he continued to study, and at the end of 1518 he was called to Zurich as people's priest (*Leutpriester*).

In the years that followed, Zwingli's aim matured from humanist reform into full-fledged Reformation. His sermons struck a loud chord in Zurich. In 1522, he published his first work of indisputable Reformation character, 'Concerning freedom and the choice of food', in which he justified the refusal to abide by the Church's instructions on fasting. Also in 1522, he demanded that the bishop of Constance should end compulsory priestly celibacy and require all preaching to be based on scripture (*Supplicatio ad Hugonem episcopum Constantiensem*), while a text from later that same year (*Apologeticus Archeteles*) rejected the bishop's spiritual jurisdiction wholesale. A disputation held in Zurich in 1523 resulted in Zwingli's teachings being approved by the magistracy, with all pastors required to preach from the Bible. In October 1523, a second disputation, on images and the mass, laid the foundations for a reworking of both church and community according to Reformation ideas. The more radical of his followers, Konrad Grebel and Felix Mantz, turned away from Zwingli, however, and founded their own Anabaptist community.

Among the numerous works published by Zwingli between 1523 and 1525, two are deserving of particular attention: his principal systematic work, *Commentarius de vera et falsa religione* ('Commentary on true and false religion'), and his text entitled 'On divine and human righteousness'.

Central in the years after 1525 were his opposition to mercenary service and the associated pensions, his efforts to bolster the Reformation in other parts of the Swiss Confederation, and the attempt to have the Zwinglian form of Reformation accepted on the international stage. His intense quarrel with Luther over the Lord's Supper, which focused on the nature of the presence of Christ and remained unresolved after discussions at Marburg in 1529, had a serious and long-lasting impact. Zurich's aggressive attitude towards the parts of the Swiss Confederation that remained hostile to the Reformation, for which Zwingli bore some of the responsibility, led to the Second War of Kappel, in the course of which, on 11 October 1531, Zwingli was killed on the battlefield.

Islam did not feature prominently in Zwingli's life and work. The small number of individual references that appear in his writings do not add up to a systematic or intensive engagement. A reference in his text entitled 'Friendly refutation of the preaching of Luther against the Enthusiasts' (*Zwinglis sämtliche Werke* v, p. 786), suggests that Zwingli was acquainted with the teachings of the Qur'an, which he simply dismissed as unsurpassed in foolishness, without examining its content in any detail. He was also aware of the relative tolerance practised by the Turks when it came to religious freedom ('Whoever gives cause for unrest,' *Zwinglis sämtliche Werke*, iii, p. 438). One particular theme does emerge, however, from Zwingli's limited discussion of Islam: he interprets the 'Turk' as a punishment brought on Christians by God because of their failure to live according to his Word.

MAIN SOURCES OF INFORMATION

Primary
Oswald Myconius, *De d. Huldrichi Zvinglii vita et obitu*, in *Ioannis Oecolampadii et Huldrichi Zuinglii epistolarum libri quatuor*, Basel: Thomas Platter and Balthasar Lasius, 1536, η2r-θ2v (written 1532; modern edition and trans.: *Vom Leben und Sterben Huldrych Zwinglis. Das älteste Lebensbild Zwinglis*, ed. E.G. Rüsch, St Gallen, 1979)
Huldreich Zwinglis sämtliche Werke, ed. E. Egli et al., Berlin, 1905-

Secondary
J. Voigtländer, *Ein Fest der Befreiung. Huldrych Zwinglis Abendmahlslehre*, Neukirchen-Vluyn, 2013
U.B. Leu, 'Huldrych Zwingli und die Täufer,' in U.B. Leu and C. Scheidegger (eds), *Die Zürcher Täufer, 1525-1700*, Zurich, 2007, 15-66
V. Leppin, art. 'Zwingli, Ulrich (1484-1531),' in *Theologische Realenzyklopädie*, Berlin, 2004, xxxvi, 793-809

D. Bolliger, *Infiniti contemplatio. Grundzüge der Scotus- und Scotismusrezeption im Werk Huldrych Zwinglis*, Leiden, 2003

B. Gordon, *The Swiss Reformation*, Manchester, 2002

M. Sallmann, *Zwischen Gott und Mensch. Huldrych Zwinglis theologischer Denkweg im De vera et falsa religione commentarius (1525)*, Tübingen, 1999

J.-V. Pollet, *Huldrych Zwingli et le Zwinglianisme*, Paris, 1988

B. Hamm, *Zwinglis Reformation der Freiheit*, Neukirchen-Vluyn, Germany, 1988

W.E. Meyer, *Huldrych Zwinglis Eschatologie. Reformatorische Wende, Theologie und Geschichtsbild des Zürcher Reformators im Lichte seines eschatologischen Ansatzes*, Zurich, 1987

W.P. Stephens, *The theology of Huldrych Zwingli*, Oxford, 1986

U. Gäbler, *Huldrych Zwingli. Eine Einführung in sein Leben und sein Werk*, Munich, 1983 (Zurich, 2004³)

G.W. Locher, *Die Zwinglische Reformation im Rahmen der europäischen Kirchengeschichte*, Göttingen, 1979

G.R. Potter, *Zwingli*, Cambridge, 1976

M. Haas, *Huldrych Zwingli und seine Zeit. Leben und Werk des Zürcher Reformators*, Zurich, 1969 (1982³)

F. Büsser, *Das katholische Zwinglibild. Von der Reformation bis zur Gegenwart*, Zurich, 1968

K. Guggisberg, *Das Zwinglibild des Protestantismus im Wandel der Zeiten*, Leipzig, 1934

Specifically on Zwingli and Islam:

K. Vehlow, 'The Swiss Reformers Zwingli, Bullinger and Bibliander and their attitude to Islam (1520-1560)', *ICMR* 6 (1995) 229-54, pp. 235-37 (heavily dependent on Segesvary, *L'Islam et la Réforme*)

V. Segesvary, *L'Islam et la Réforme. Étude sur l'attitude des réformateurs zurichois envers l'islam, 1510-1550*, Lausanne, 1978, pp. 121-59

Comprehensive bibliographies:

U. Gäbler, *Huldrych Zwingli im 20. Jahrhundert. Forschungsbericht und annotierte Bibliographie, 1897-1972*, Zurich, 1975

G. Finsler, *Zwingli-Bibliographie. Verzeichnis der gedruckten Schriften von und über Ulrich Zwingli*, Zurich, 1897

WORKS ON CHRISTIAN-MUSLIM RELATIONS

Ieremias propheta, 'Interpretation of the prophet Jeremiah'

DATE Possibly 1528/29
ORIGINAL LANGUAGE Latin, German

DESCRIPTION

In Zwingli's exegesis of the Prophet Jeremiah, preserved in a transcript of 124 folios made by a member of his audience, can be found the clearest expression of his conviction that the Turks are to be understood as a punishment from God (*Zwinglis sämtliche Werke*, xvi, pp. 190-91).

Jeremiah 27:12 gives him cause to consider why God allows Christians to fall under the rule of an un-Christian people, and his response is that this subservience should not be surprising, for God even served up his chosen people of Israel to their greatest enemies, sentencing them to the most severe punishment possible for their sins and defiance of his will. The situation is little different, he suggests, among the peoples of Europe in his own time. He provides a list of iniquities: mercenary service, treachery, blasphemy, drunkenness, prostitution and adultery.

The Turks are similarly interpreted in his commentary on Isaiah 9:13 (*Zwinglis sämtliche Werke*, xiv, p. 209). In November 1530, Zwingli wrote of the 'rod' that God uses to discipline Christians (*Zwinglis sämtliche Werke*, vi/3, p. 364), and in his 'Second letter to the Christians of Esslingen' he tells of the 'rod of God's anger' (*Zwinglis sämtliche Werke*, v, p. 423). This final citation also establishes that, for Zwingli, such punishment from God – in this case, the success of the Turks – must be understood in positive terms: it is for the good of humankind, for in the end all that God does is good.

SIGNIFICANCE

Zwingli's interpretation of the 'Turkish threat' as a punishment from God is not original; it was a commonplace of his time. Unlike his fellow Reformers, however, Zwingli did not bring an eschatological dimension to his analysis. For Zwingli, the Turks were not the Antichrist and neither was their appearance a sign of the endtime.

MANUSCRIPTS

MS Zurich, Zentralbibliothek – S 429, 67r-190v (possibly 1528/29)

EDITIONS & TRANSLATIONS

Huldreich Zwinglis sämtliche Werke, Zurich, 2013, xvi, 1-276

Christian Moser

Erasmus

Desiderius Erasmus Roterodamus

DATE OF BIRTH 27 October 1467
PLACE OF BIRTH Rotterdam
DATE OF DEATH 12 July 1536
PLACE OF DEATH Basel

BIOGRAPHY

Erasmus's father, Gerard, was a priest in Gouda, now in the Netherlands, then part of the territory of the Count of Holland, one of the petty semi-independent states within the German Empire. His mother, Margaret, was the daughter of a physician in Zevenbergen. This situation did not allow that their second child should be born in their house, so the mother moved for some time to Rotterdam where Erasmus was born. The boy was sent to good schools. From 1476 to 1481, he was educated at the Lebuin School in Deventer, a prestigious centre for the revival of the study of classical Latin humanities. In 1477, the first Dutch printing firm was established in the town. The printing press would be for Erasmus what universities or the pulpit were for other people.

After the premature death of his parents in 1483-84, Erasmus had to enter a house of the Augustinian Order in Steyn, near Gouda, until ordination to the priesthood in 1492, but here too he was able to develop his interest in the new Renaissance humanist literature, besides acquiring intimate knowledge of the Bible. From 1495, he led the life of a wandering student and scholar, a *literatus*, translating from Greek to Latin, and being the first to publish the Greek text of the New Testament in Greek, with a new Latin translation. He spent time in Paris, Louvain, Rome, London, Oxford and Cambridge, but the printing firm and friendship of Johannes Froben meant that Basel was for a long period his true home. Through a continuing correspondence, he acquired fame as the leading figure among north European humanist scholars.

In 1529, after the iconoclastic riots in Basel that preceded the victory of the Protestant Reformation in the town, Erasmus moved to Freiburg and remained there until 1535. He was very critical of the (Roman Catholic) Church as it was at that time, giving in his writings many bitter examples of stupidity, corruption and sin in the Church, but he called for reform within the existing structures and never fully joined Luther or other reformers. Through his editions of the classical works of Greek and Latin authors, commentaries on classical proverbs (*Adagia*), comic criticism of society in *Laus stultitiae* ('Praise of stupidity'), and also the practical piety of his *Enchiridion*, he formulated a sober and viable piety for lay people. He was truly a man who was able fully to use the new revolution of communication through the printing press. It is estimated that around 1530 some tenth to a fifth of all printed publications were writings of Erasmus himself or edited by him.

Erasmus lived in a divided Europe, comprising major powers (the German-Spanish emperor, French and British kings, ambitious popes who ruled over about half Italy) and many petty rulers and smaller territories. He dreamed of a united society and a reformed and united Church, while the eastern territories of Europe were increasingly coming under attack by the Ottoman sultans. For Erasmus, the Turks were more or less what the invading Vandals had been to Ambrose of Milan or Augustine of Hippo: unfamiliar but apparently dangerous barbarian people from faraway who were coming closer and closer. They are mentioned in quite a few of his writings. There is virtually no reaction in Erasmus's writings to another major event related to Islam: the fall of the last Muslim ruler of Granada in Spain in 1492 and the expulsion from Spain of the Muslims and Jews who were not willing to receive baptism.

MAIN SOURCES OF INFORMATION

Primary
Beatus Rhenani Selestadiensis, *Omnia opera*, Basel, 1540, ix (the earliest biography, by a close friend)
P.S. Allen, *Opus epistolarum Des. Erasmi Roterodami*, Oxford, 1906-58 (repr. 1992; many details of his biography were rewritten after publication of these letters)

Secondary
There is a large number of studies on Erasmus. Among the most important are:
C. Christ-von Wedel, *Erasmus of Rotterdam. Advocate of a new Christianity*, Toronto, 2013 (revised edition of German original, 2003)
J. van Herwaarden, 'Erasmus a Turci, aneb je válka ospravedlnitelná?', in *Erasmovo dílo v minulosti a soucasnosti evropského myslení*, ed. T. Nejeschleba and J. Makovský, Brno, 2012, 263-87 (article on Erasmus and the Turks, in Czech; Dutch original only on website of the Erasmus Centre)
W. Ribhegge, *Erasmus von Rotterdam*, Darmstadt, 2010

R.J. Schoeck, *Erasmus of Europe*, 2 vols, Edinburgh, 1990-93
L. Halkin, *Érasme. Sa pensée et son comportement*, London, 1987
R. Bainton, *Erasmus of Christendom*, New York, 1969
C. Augustijn, *Erasmus.Vernieuwer van kerk en theologie*, Baarn, 1967, 1986[2]; English trans. J.C. Grayson, *Erasmus*, Toronto, 1991
H.A. Enno van Gelder, *The two reformations in the 16th century*, The Hague, 1961
S. Zweig, *Triumf und Tragik des Erasmus von Rotterdam*, Vienna, 1934
J. Huizinga, *Erasmus*, Haarlem, 1924

WORKS ON CHRISTIAN-MUSLIM RELATIONS

Utilissima consultatio de bello Turcis inferendo, et obiter enarratus Psalmus XXVIII, 'A most useful discussion concerning proposals for war against the Turks, including an exposition of Psalm 28'

DATE March 1530
ORIGINAL LANGUAGE Latin

DESCRIPTION
After victory at the Battle of Mohács in 1526, the Ottoman Empire had taken control of large sections of Hungary and Transylvania. On their return to Central Europe in the summer of 1529, Ottoman troops took the rest of Hungary by force and laid siege to Vienna. Parts of the city walls were heavily damaged, but then on 14 October the army withdrew and began its return to Istanbul. Early in 1530, Erasmus joined the lively debate about the meaning of this Turkish attack and the measures to be taken by European rulers. The learned and mild scholar had until then often attacked those who proposed military action too easily.

Erasmus's first work on the topic of war was *Dulce bellum inexpertis* ('War is sweet to those who have not experienced it'), an essay he published in 1515. In the following decade, he wrote more than ten more essays on the theme of war, mostly calling for peace and negotiations. On the Turks, he was not as radical as Luther, who counselled against war against the Turks because they were a punishment from God. Erasmus was also more overtly religious than political in his essay on the Turks. Quite surprisingly, he started his exposition on the topic with a long interpretation of Psalm 28/29 on the general theme that God must be given praise and due offerings, for which in return he will give forgiveness and prosperity to his people. Comments on the Turks begin only after the first four pages (of the total of 23 in the Leiden edition). God is using the Turks in the same way as he 'sent frogs, lice, and locusts upon the Egyptians long ago, or because we have placed our hopes of victory in our own strength, or perhaps we have not done Christ's work but have fought the Turks in a Turkish frame of mind'. Quoting Pliny, Cyprian and other classical authors (following his contemporary Giovanni Battista Egnazio, who used many Byzantine sources), Erasmus places the origin of the Turks outside the classical region, in northern or east Asia. Why are they so successful, even though their character is a mixture of obscurity and barbarity? 'They owe their victories to our sins; we have fought against them but, as the results plainly show, in the face of our God's anger. For we assail the Turks with the self-same eagerness with which they invade the lands of others' (trans. Heath, p. 231).

The essay is more about the Turkish people than about the religion of Islam. Regarding the Turks Erasmus is ambivalent: they should be given the qualification of full human beings and may claim civil rights, such as protection of their possessions, like any people in a country. In religion they are 'half-Christian' (*semichristianos*), and therefore 'we' (the Christians? or the Europeans? Erasmus is not precise about the frequent use of 'we' in this essay) are not entitled to fight and kill them. But the other option, not to fight them at all, is also not the best solution. Luther's refusal to fight them is rejected with the argument that we call for a doctor in case of serious illness. Indeed, the arrival of the Turks is a sign of God's anger and a call to repentance. The Church must be cleansed from corruption, nepotism and superstition. Christian rulers must stop fighting each other and must create unity among the people. The clergy themselves should not take the sword and must abstain from fighting, because only civil rulers can lead armies. Christians should even consider the possibility of living under Turkish rule: although this would be a true disaster, even some Christian rulers place an unbearable yoke on the people.

The slogan 'rather Turkish than papist', later ascribed to Luther, is not directly mentioned by Erasmus. Instead, he offers a long list of negative qualifications that destroy the positive image suggested by the term *semichristiani*: 'Where is the rule of law among them? Whatever pleases the tyrant, that is the law. Where is the power of a parliament? What room is there for philosophy? For schools of theology? For holy sermons? For true religion? Their faith is a mixture of Judaism, Christianity, paganism, and the Arian heresy. They acknowledge Christ – as just one of the prophets.... Muḥammad, a pestilent and wicked man do they prefer to Christ, at whose name every knee bows, in heaven, on earth, and in the depths of the earth' (trans. Heath, pp. 258-59).

Erasmus finally calls for more efforts to be put into conversion than into war. And even if the Turks will not come to the truth of the Christian religion, they should be allowed to live 'under their own law' for the time being, in the same way as the pagans lived under the Christian Roman emperors until Christianity became the majority religion. This is more an open end than a firm and practical solution to a problem that produced a good deal of polemic at the time.

SIGNIFICANCE

The question of the Turkish threat caused much debate in the 15th and 16th centuries. Erasmus's treatise was reprinted seven times in the 1530s and 1540s and after that only in much later periods. He was a man who did not fully agree with either the Protestant or the Catholic party, and his balanced, sometimes even ambivalent position did not become a banner for any party. In his own division of his works, Erasmus did not put this treatise together with the more than 20 writings on matters of war and peace, but in the series of moral writings, nearly all reflections of biblical texts. This brought the last editor, Weiler, to the conviction that the *Consultatio* is embedded in a religious context. His view is quite different from Margolin, who answered the reproach that the 'pure pacifist' Erasmus opened the door for war by defending a war that was just and necessary. Margolin (*Guerre et paix*, p. 333) even adduced the example of Hitler, joining Erasmus in a rejection not only of an easy 'holy war' but also of a 'fundamentalist pacifism'. Most discussions of Erasmus's position concentrate on the various levels of pacifism. Göllner (*Turcica*, iii, p. 193) sees a development from a religiously motivated holy war to a more or less secular defensive war against the Turks, without the involvement of church leaders.

Another important topic in more recent debates is the perception of Turks and Muslims in general, sometimes related to the strong anti-Semitism and negative statements about Jews found in Erasmus's writings. Erasmus is seen by quite a few modern readers as the protagonist and icon of inter-religious harmony. Sympathisers of the Turkish Muslim leader Fethullah Gülen (b. 1939) have compared Erasmus to the mediaeval mystic Jalaluddin Rumi and also to their own leader. The prominent Indonesian man of letters Hans Bague Jassin, who translated the Qur'an into literary Indonesian, moved to Erasmus's *Colloquia* in his effort to represent Western culture and literature in Indonesian translations.

Against such warm sympathies there are warnings from historians. Jan van Herwaarden has repeatedly protested against this 'soft' image of Erasmus as the champion of tolerance and harmony, though Herwaarden's main opponent, Leo Molenaar, has reproached him for finding 'many seeds of bloodthirsty ideas about the Turks' in Erasmus's early writings. The debate shows that Erasmus's position still leads to new discussions in a very different period of history.

Erasmus's treatise was just one out of some 2,300 *Turcica* that were published in the 16th century. He did not take a firm position on concrete measures about the threat, but repeated his call for reform and unity in Church and society. It is quite interesting to see how this call has created new themes around the turn of the 21st century, when some Muslims have joined what is basically a European debate (Jassin, Çelik, Okuyucu). Özcan Hıdır of the Islamic University of Rotterdam has noted that the 16th century effectively continued the mediaeval image of Islam, and this has remained dominant up to the present.

EDITIONS & TRANSLATIONS

J. Piolon, *De Turkenkrijg*, Rotterdam, 2005 (Dutch trans.)

M.J. Heath, 'A most useful discussion concerning proposals for war against the Turks, including an exposition of Psalm 28', in *Collected works of Erasmus*, Toronto, 2005, lxiv, pp. 201-66 (English trans.)

F. Baldo, *Utilissima consultatio... Erasmo da Rotterdam, Pace e Guerra*, Rome, 2004 (Italian trans.)

F. Baldo, *Guerra ai Turchi! una questione improrogabile e cammin facendo un commento al Salmo XXVIII. (1530)*, Abano Terme, Padua, 1996 (Italian trans.)

'Utilissima consultatio de bello Turcis inferendo, et obiter enarratus psalmus XXVIII', in A.G. Weiler et al. (eds), *Opera omnia Desiderii Erasmi Roterodami. Recognita et adnotatione critica instructa notisque illustrata. Ordinis 5, t. 3*, Amsterdam, 1986

J.-C. Margolin, *Guerre et paix dans la pensée d'Erasme*, Paris, 1973, pp. 328-74 (abridged French trans.)

L. Riber, *Utilisima consulta acerca de la declaracion de guerra al Turco*, in *Obras escogidas*, Madrid, 1964, pp. 997-1027 (Spanish trans.)

Ausz Rathschlage Herren Erasmi von Roterdam die Türcken zubekriegen, Frankfurt, 1531 (first incomplete German trans.)

As part of the Leiden edition of the *Opera omnia* (1703-6), and of the Amsterdam edition of the *Opera omnia* (Amsterdam, 1969, continuing) v/3, pp. 1-82 (with a preface and notes in German by A. Weiler; this preface was reprinted in an abridged English edition in A. Weiler, 'The Turkish argument and Christian piety in Desiderius Erasmus' "Consultatio de bello Turcis inferendo" (1530)', in J. Sperna Weiland and W.T.M. Frijhoff (eds), *Erasmus of Rotterdam. The man and the scholar*, Leiden, 1988, 30-39)

First edition at Froben, Basel 1530 (*in officina Frobensia*), repr. in 1530 in Paris, Vienna, Antwerp, and twice in Cologne; in 1547 in Basle and Cologne; in 1643 in Leiden

STUDIES

O. Hıdır, 'Historical background of Lutheran Protestantism from an Islamic perspective and Martin Luther's view of the Qur'an, the Prophet Muhammad and the Turks', *Journal of the Rotterdam Islamic and Social Sciences* 3 (2012) 25-55

R. Heijne (ed.), *In gesprek met Erasmus over humanisme, opvoeding en geweldloosheid*, Rotterdam, 2011

I. Creemers, L. Molenaar and G. Çelik (eds), *Erasmus en Gülen. Inspiratoren voor vrede en dialoog*, Amsterdam, 2009 (English text of Molenaar, 'The true image of Erasmus', only available at www.Erasmushuisrotterdam.nl)

C. Okuyucu and J. van Herwaarden, *Mevlana en Erasmus, vrijdenkers uit het verleden, met invloed op het heden*, Amsterdam, 2008

J. van Herwaarden, *Omgaan met Erasmus*, Rotterdam, 2005 (valedictory lecture, 29 April)

J. van Herwaarden, 'Erasmus van Rotterdam. Beeld en werkelijkheid', *Rotterdams Jaarboekje* (1998) 191-215

H.B. Jassin, *Percakapan Erasmus*, Jakarta, Djambatan, 1985 (Indonesian trans. of the *Colloquia*)

Carl Göllner, *Turcica. Die europäischen Türkendrucke des XVI. Jahrhunderts*, 3 vols, Bucharest/Baden-Baden, 1961-78

P. Brachin, 'Vox clamantis in deserto. Réflections sur le pacifisme d'Erasme', in *Colloquia Erasmiana Torunensia*, Toronto, 1972, i, 247-75

Karel Steenbrink

Christopher Saint German

DATE OF BIRTH 1460
PLACE OF BIRTH Shilton, Warwickshire
DATE OF DEATH 1540/41
PLACE OF DEATH London

BIOGRAPHY

Christopher Saint German was the son of Sir Henry St German and his wife, Lady Anne, daughter of Sir Thomas Tyndale, of Hockwold, Norfolk. Although a knight, his father appears to have had limited means. A.F. Pollard's entry for St German in the *Dictionary of national biography (1885-1900)* states that he is said to have attended Exeter College, Oxford, before preparing for the bar at one of the Inns of Chancery in London. He may have moved to London in about 1480, possibly later. He was called to the bar at the Middle Temple sometime before 1502, when he is mentioned in the records. J.A. Baker, however, omits any reference to his studying in Oxford from the *DNB* 2004 entry.

Despite qualifying as a barrister, St German does not appear to have actually practised law except in minor advisory roles. However, through his legal writing he became recognised as a leading legal scholar. His seminal work on the principles of English law, known as *Doctor and student*, first published in Latin in 1528 under the title *Dialogus de fundamentis legum Anglie et de conscientia*, was used as a primer until the 19th century. This seminal work takes the form of a dialogue between a doctor of divinity and a lawyer, which also indicates St German's interest in matters of faith and conscience. It has biblical references.

After *Doctor and student*, several explicitly theological works followed. Dealing with the 'spiritual jurisdiction', these are said to have helped pave the way for Henry VIII's break with Rome. In fact, St German has been described as one of the main thinkers contributing to the English Reformation. He argued that clergy claimed and exercised too much legal authority, and that this could not take priority over conscience or even the laws of England, which were preferable. Religious matters should be subject to the state, and the Prince should be supreme in matters of faith. He is said to have stimulated a flurry of anti-papal pamphlets. Various tracts and publications, especially his *Salem and Bizance* (1533), provoked responses from Sir Thomas More. St German wrote a number of anonymous apologetic and polemical tracts, which were published by the royal printer, indicative that he was seen as a semi-official spokesman for the king. Several anonymous tracts were attributed to him in John Bale's catalogue of 1559. An anonymous tract, *Here after foloweth a lytell treatyse agaynst Mahumet and his cursed secte*, was published in London by Peter Treveris in 1531. Rex has convincingly argued that St German was its author, not least because part of it was more or less copied as Chapter 23 of *Salem and Bizance*. The title of that book, too, has Ottoman echoes, alluding to the two great patriarchal cities (Jerusalem and Byzantium) conquered by the Turks, who are depicted as Christianity's greatest foe. St German habitually recycled 'his own work' (Rex, 'New additions', p. 285).

An examination of St German's writings shows that he had 'an unusual degree of interest in Islam' (Rex, 'New additions', p. 282). Rex refers to Bale's attribution to St German of a publication called *In Mahuetan et eius sectum*, which he concludes is the same text. As with other writers who turned to Islam and Muḥammad as topics, he was less interested in these *per se* than as tools in his broader treatment of what he considered to be forms of heresy. The book is only the second to be printed in England wholly on Islam.

Bale records St German's date of death as 29 September 1539, and says that he was buried at St Alphage's Church, Cripplegate. However, he signed his will on 10 July 1540, and it was probated on 30 May 1541, so he is likely to have died between these two dates.

MAIN SOURCES OF INFORMATION

Primary

J.C. Warner (trans.), *John Bale's catalogue of Tudor authors. An annotated translation of records from the* Scriptorum illustrium maioris Brytanniae... catalogus (1557-1559), Tempe AZ, 2010, pp. 600-1

Secondary

M. Dimmock, *Mythologies of the Prophet Muhammad in Early Modern English culture*, Cambridge, 2013, pp. 56-63

R. Rex, 'New additions on Christopher St German. Law, politics and propaganda in the 1530s', *Journal of Ecclesiastical History* 59 (2008) 281-300

J.A. Baker, art. 'St German, Christopher', in *ODNB*, 609-10

J. Guy, 'Thomas More and St German. The battle of the books', in A. Fox and J. Guy (eds), *Reassessing the Henrician age*, New York, 1986, 95-120

P. Hogrefe, 'The life of Saint German', *Review of English Studies* 13 (1937) 398-404

A.F. Pollard, art. 'Saint-German, Christopher' in *DNB*, pp. 127-28

WORKS ON CHRISTIAN-MUSLIM RELATIONS

Here after foloweth a lytell treatyse agaynst Mahumet and his cursed secte
In Mahuetan et eius sectum

DATE 1530 or 1531
ORIGINAL LANGUAGE English

DESCRIPTION

Printed in 1531 and thought anonymous until the recent identification of Christopher St German as author, this polemical tract of 88 pages sets out to refute Islam by presenting it as a form of Christian heresy. Nine chapters follow a two-page introduction. The list of contents is at the back.

Chapter 1 covers Muḥammad's (spelled 'Mahumet' throughout) birth, and Chapter 2 purports to describe how Muḥammad set himself up as God's prophet. Chapter 3 focuses on the principal errors of Muḥammad's law, and Chapter 4 the 'contrariness' of the Qur'an. Chapter 5 similarly alleges contradictions in the law, while Chapter 6 turns to the topic of why Muslims supposedly have a great desire to capture Christians. Chapter 7 rebuts Muḥammad's false vision, and Chapter 8 describes and ridicules Muḥammad's 'wretched and unhappy death', while Chapter 9 explains how, before the Antichrist comes, the gate will open for a mass conversion of Jews to Christianity, while Islam will be destroyed.

The source for much of the text is Riccoldo da Monte di Croce (d. 1320). St German also draws on Wolfgang Aytinger's 1496 commentary on Methodius's (actually Pseudo-Methodius) *Apocalypse*, and on the *Fortalitium fidei* written by the Spanish Franciscan scholar and bishop Alfonso de la Espina in 1458, which uses a range of medieval sources. Among other texts, St German consulted *Peregrinatio in terram sanctam* by Bernhard von Breydenbach, who travelled in the Holy Land in 1483-84 (Martin Luther wrote a preface for this book in 1530).

St German's treatise is a more detailed work on Islam than earlier texts in English, although at least some readers would have been familiar with its portrait of Muḥammad. Factually correct content includes identifying

Muḥammad's age at death as 63, after 23 years as a 'false' prophet, although Muḥammad's birthdate is given as 23 April 696, which St German says is stated by 'mooste writers'.

The work's polemical intent is clear from the outset. St German sets out to refute 'Mahumet and his cursed sect' and to enable all in England to perceive its falsity, so that they will abhor and despise it. Thus, Muḥammad grew up worshipping Venus, and his name means 'confusion'. When his uncle Abdemutalla (evidently a corruption of 'Abd al-Muṭṭalib, who was Muḥammad's grandfather) became his guardian following the death of his parents, he accompanied him to 'Salingua' where he 'worshipped ydols with all his kyndred'. He became a 'great nygromancer', travelled to Egypt and other places and associated with 'crafty men', including Jews, learning from them about the 'olde' and 'new lawe'. (St German was evidently aware of accounts of Muḥammad's meeting with the monk Baḥīrā, although he gives no names.)

St German's view that Muḥammad's marriage to Khadīja (Cadygan) led to his false claim to prophethood, emboldened by new-found wealth, moves into a description of how he used this prosperity, craft and artifice to attract 'rude people' as his followers. Indeed, Khadīja had second thoughts about her relationship with 'so vyle a man' when he claimed to be a prophet. Thus, St German presents an account that wholly contradicts Muslim sources, which emphasise Khadīja's encouragement and support for Muḥammad in his prophetic role. In St German's account, she was shocked by seeing his fits, when he beat his head on the ground, foamed at the mouth and spat. Attribution of Muḥammad's claim to be a prophet to epilepsy or to some mental malady reproduces popular ideas found in much earlier polemic. The link between Muḥammad's 'trances', during which he claimed to receive revelation, would be asserted by some 19th-century writers who had access, through Arabic, to early Islamic sources (e.g. Aloys Sprenger in *The life of Mohammed from original sources*, Allahabad, 1851, p. 949).

St German describes Muḥammad as 'of a lowe blode'. He attracted murderers and 'vacabundes' to his cause, and sent them off to 'rob on his behalf'. He caused an elderly Jew to be strangled because the Jew had 'rebuked' him. This probably refers to the incident involving Ka'b ibn al-Ashraf, who wrote poetry against Muḥammad, and urged Muḥammad's opponents to use force to end what they saw as a threat to their way of life. The killing of Ka'b would be frequently referenced in 19th-century writing as an example of Muḥammad's moral culpability. For example, Sir William Muir would write on this at length in his *Life of Mahomet* (1894 edition, pp. 238-40).

St German's portrayal of Muḥammad is obviously meant to depict him as a charlatan, not as one who was 'sente with mercy and pytye'. Chapter 3 emphasises the heretical and satanic nature of his teaching, saying that Satan 'holly infected this cursyd man', so much so that, while Islam shares some heresies with others, it actually contains some that are unique (satanic inspiration, too, would be alleged by Muir). St German refers here to parallels with the 'great heretic, Sabelius' as a denier of the Trinity. He also saw a parallel between Muḥammad, Arius and Eunomius, also 'great heretics'; they all saw Christ as of 'less essence than the essence of God'. This depicts Islam as a form of Unitarianism, or of Arianism. Some Unitarian writers would later attempt to establish fraternal relations with Islam, while some Muslims regard Unitarians as representing original Christianity (see discussion in C. Bennett, *In search of Jesus*, London, 2001, pp. 283-85).

Other parallels follow, thus locating Muḥammad in what has been called a genealogy of Christian heresy. St German compares the claim that Jesus did not die on the cross and that 'another lyke to hym' took his place, with the teaching of a heretic whom he calls Sardonycus. Like the heretic Carpocrates, Muḥammad argued that God cannot have a son since he has no wife. The absence of miracles serves to prove that Muḥammad's claims were false; lacking miracles to aid his cause, he resorted instead to violence. The refusal of Muslims to translate the Qur'an, in St German's view, compromised Islam's claim to be a faith for the whole world. St German's Protestantism, which placed great store on accessing scripture in the vernacular, is evident here. Failure to 'publish for all the world' keeps 'secret' what should be made freely and universally available.

Among the inconsistencies in Islam, according to St German, is the Qur'an's prohibition against compelling religious faith and Muḥammad's alleged use of force to attract followers. Another is that Muḥammad is described as an Arab prophet on the one hand, on the other as 'sent to all people', though he went only to the Arabs. Muḥammad would not tolerate any dissent or questioning of his law, ordering that those who did so should be slain. (These sections on contradictions are informed by Riccoldo da Monte di Croce's *Contra legem Saracenorum*.)

St German does not provide any actual qur'anic references. Writing before the first English translation appeared, he could have consulted a Latin version but, although he was a very competent Latin scholar, he apparently did not think he needed or had a responsibility to verify what he repeated.

In the middle of his discourse, St German switches from Muḥammad to the Turks, indicating the contemporary geo-political context in which he was writing. He narrates how whole Christian populations are enslaved, with men, women and children displayed naked, roped and chained, to be sold in the market. His aim is to depict contemporary Muslims as barbaric. In describing Muḥammad's death, St German alludes to the story of his tomb, built by a 'sybtyll and crafty' follower and suspended by magnets at Mecca (not at Medina), and to the claim that Muḥammad expected to rise again after three days. Instead, his body began to stink intolerably, so it was disposed of without any ceremony (the magnet and death stories occur in a number of earlier works). Muḥammad was 'the grettest desceyour of the worlde'. Aloys Sprenger would say that, like other hysterical people, Muḥammad was susceptible to lying and deceit (*The life of Mohammed*, Allahabad, 1851, p. 210).

In outlining why Islam is doomed to fail, St German repeatedly refers to Methodius, drawing on Wolfgang Aytinger's ideas about Islam's immanent downfall from Pseudo-Methodius, with much numerology (*Tractatus super Methodium*, 1499). The Turks' success, linked with ecclesiastical reform, signals the coming of the Apocalypse. Aytinger anticipated the rise of a last Christian emperor, who would defeat the Turks, establish world peace and reign for a thousand years. St German writes of how Jerusalem will be raised up, no longer 'trodden under foot by gentiles'. Methodius is a true saint and martyr, Muḥammad is clearly an anti-saint, whose life is the very opposite of the type of life that merits imitation.

SIGNIFICANCE

While in some respects it is more detailed than earlier works in English on Muḥammad and Islam, the main significance of this work lies in its discussion of Islam as 'heresy'. This has a long history in Christian discourse on Islam dating from as early as the writings of John of Damascus, who discussed Islam as his 100th heresy, but St German's quite elaborate treatment of heresies and of parallels with Islam is novel, at least in English. On the one hand, this approach can reduce distance between Christianity and Islam by removing Islam's otherness, discussing it in Christian terms as a deviation from Christianity, not as a distinct, rival and separate religion. On the other hand, this approach also denies Islam the claim of novelty, drawing many parallels with earlier heresies. Yet, representing Islam as in some respects unique, holding heresies that 'no other heretyke hath holden', turns it into the heresy of heresies, suggesting that it is even more false. This approach recognises Islam as a danger to Christian faith, and the expansion of Islamic political polities by military means as problematic, but it also offers a framework within which to explain and rebut Islam. This is to be achieved by applying the same arguments that Christian thinkers use in refuting other deviations from the truth. Yet, since Islam is destined to be destroyed, refutation may be redundant.

In depicting Muḥammad as intolerant of any dissent, St German anticipates a theme that becomes popular in 19th-century writers who insist that Islam shuts down critical thought, stifles human creativity and is even anti-rational. A writer such as Ernest Renan (1823-92), who developed a negative assessment of Islam as anti-progressive, would also insist on Islam's irrationality. St German's criticism here is perhaps rooted in his ideas about clerical authority resisting rational criticism of church law; hence his preference for the developing ideals of Protestantism.

St German almost certainly wrote this tract partly because it allowed him to score points about the failings of rigid Catholics who resisted reform, but it was also produced in the aftermath of the fall of Constantinople in 1453, and of subsequent Ottoman expansion: it was published just a year or two after the siege of Vienna. Only the second English text devoted solely to dealing with Islam, the fact that a popular polemicist wrote it for all who could read English might indicate that an audience existed in 1531 for such a text. His use of English indicates that he wanted to reach a wide readership, and he comments that more Englishmen read English than Latin. Or, the author perhaps believed that English people should read such a text to be better informed about the Turkish presence in Europe, and what it might mean for Christians. His confidence that the Turks could be defeated, and that this was destined, would have reassured some who saw the Turkish advance as all but unstoppable.

While Jews are expected to convert, St German seems to deny this possibility for Muslims, because their destiny is complete annihilation as eschatological events begin to unfold. This perpetuates an earlier view that the proper Christian response to Islam was to kill Muslims, that evangelism could not succeed and is not even worth attempting. Some have argued that if Muslims are really Christian heretics, as 'lost sheep' they should be lovingly persuaded and coaxed to return to the fold. One contemporary work, printed and probably edited by Wynkyn de Worde in 1515, the first ever English text solely concerned with Islam, argued that Muslims were receptive to Christian evangelism. St German may have read this, but he took a different course.

EDITIONS & TRANSLATIONS

Here after foloweth a lytell treatyse agaynst Mahumet and his cursed secte (Early documents of world history), Ann Arbor MI, 2010

Salem and Bizance (Early history of religion), Ann Arbor MI, 2010 (includes most of chapter 9)

Salem and Bizance, Amsterdam, 1973 (includes most of chapter 9)

Salem and Bizance, London, 1533 (includes most of chapter 9)

Here after foloweth a lytell treatyse agaynst Mahumet and his cursed secte, London, 1530

STUDIES

Dimmock, *Mythologies of the Prophet Muhammad*, pp. 56-63

Rex, 'New additions on Christopher St German'

Clinton Bennett

Michael Servetus

Miguel Servet, Reves ab Aragonia Hispanum,
Michael Servetus Villanovensis

DATE OF BIRTH 1509 or 1511
PLACE OF BIRTH Villanueva de Sijena (Sigena), Aragón
DATE OF DEATH 27 October 1553
PLACE OF DEATH Geneva

BIOGRAPHY

Miguel Servet, or according to the Latin style of his name Michael Servetus, was born in Aragón, northern Spain, in the small village of Villanueva de Sijena, probably in 1511. After basic education about which little is known, in the late 1520s he studied arts and law in Toulouse. Also in the 1520s, he entered the service of the Franciscan Friar Juan de Quintana, who was travelling with the imperial court. Soon afterwards, in 1530, Quintana became personal confessor to the Emperor Charles V, whose coronation as Holy Roman Emperor on 22 February 1530 Servetus attended in Bologna.

For ten months from October 1530, Servetus lived with Johannes Oecolampadius in Basel, meeting Martin Bucer in Strasbourg in May 1531. A few months later he published his first work, *De Trinitatis erroribus libri septem* (120 double pages), followed in 1532 by another work against the doctrine of the Trinity in the form of dialogues. From 1533, he studied in Paris, and also worked as a proofreader and publisher under the new name of Michel de Villeneuve, mostly in the field of medicine. He also published the first French annotated translation of Ptolemy's *Geography*.

He became a doctor of medicine in Montpellier 1539, and through most of the 1540s he lived in Vienne as personal physician to its humanist archbishop. He published several works on medical matters, for which he is considered as the discoverer of pulmonary circulation. He also edited the Bible translations of Santes Pagnino (1542). In early 1553 in Vienne, he published a long work of 734 pages, *Christianismi restitutio*, in which a long section is devoted to his battle against the Nicean doctrine of the Trinity. This resulted in his condemnation in Vienne, and the burning of his effigy and books on 17 June 1553, though Servetus himself had managed to escape from prison and flee.

As he was making his way to Italy, in Geneva on 13 August 1553 he was recognised as the author of this disputed book and taken to court, where he was interrogated by John Calvin, with whom he had earlier had a bitter exchange of letters. The Geneva city council condemned him to death on 24 October for the heresy of anti-Trinitarianism and non-acceptance of the baptism of children. Three days later he was burned at the stake, together with what was believed to be the only copy of his last book.

MAIN SOURCES OF INFORMATION

Primary

Iohannes Calvin, *Defensio orthodoxae fidei de Sacra Trinitate contra prodigiosos errores Michaelis Serveti Hispani*, Geneva, 1554 (repr. Iohanni Calvini, *Opera Omnia*, Geneva, 2009, vol. 4; French trans. *Déclaration pour maintenir la vraye foye que tiennent tous Chrétiens de la Trinité des personnes en un seul Dieu. Contre les erreurs détestables de Michel Servet Espaignol. Ou il est aussi monstré, qu'il est licite de punir les hérétiques: et qu'à bon droict ce meschant a esté exécuté par justice en la ville de Genève*, Geneva, 1554)

Secondary

F.X. González Echeverria, *El Amor a la verdad. Vida y obra de Miguel Servet*, Zaragoza, 2011

J. de Marcos Andreu, 'Servetus and Islam in his writings', in R.F. Boeke and P. Wynne-Jones (eds), *Servetus, our 16th century contemporary*, London, 2011, 17-28

P. Hughes, 'Servetus and the Qur'an', *Journal of Unitarian Universalist History* 30 (2005) 55-70

V. Zuber, *Les conflits de la tolérance. Michael Servet entre mémoire et histoire*, Paris, 2004

L. Goldstone, *Out of the flames. The story of one of the rarest books in the world and how it changed the course of the world*, London, 2003

M. Hiller and C.S. Allen, *Michael Servetus. Intellectual giant, humanist, and martyr*, Lanham MD, 2002

M. Hiller, *The case of Michael Servetus 1511-1553. The turning point in the struggle for freedom of conscience*, Lewiston NY, 1997, 1999²

M. Balázs, *Early Transsylvanian Antitrinitarianism (1566-1571). From Servet to Palaeologus*, Baden-Baden, 1996

J. Fernández Barón, *Miguel Servet. Su vida y su obra*, Madrid, 1989

J. Friedman, *Michael Servetus. A case study in total heresy*, Geneva, 1978

R.H. Bainton, *Hunted heretic*, Boston MA, 1953 (German trans. *Michael Servet, 1511-1553*, Gütersloh, 1960; revised repr. of the English edition, Providence RI, 2005)

J. Farquhar Fulton, *Michael Servetus, humanist and martyr*, New York, 1953

A. Gachet d'Artigny, 'Mémoires pour servir à l'histoire de Michel Servet', in Gachet d'Artigny, *Nouveaux mémoires d'histoire, de critique et de littérature*, Paris, 1949, ii, 55-154

E.M. Wilbur, *The two treatises of Servetus on the Trinity, On the errors of the Trinity seven Books, Dialogues on the Trinity two books, On the righteousness of Christ's Kingdom four chapters*, Cambridge MA, 1932 (contains an extensive bibliography of earlier works)

P.H. Ditchfield, *Books fatal to their authors*, London, 1895

F.M. Arouet de Voltaire, 'De Genève et de Calvin. De Calvin et de Servet', in *Essai sur les moeurs et l'esprit des nations*, Stuttgart, 1756, ii, chs 133, 134

J.L. von Musheim, *Anderweitiger Versuch einer vollständigen und unpartheyischen Ketzergeschichte. Geschichte des berühmten Spanischen Artztes Michaels Serveto*, Helmstedt, 1748

H. ab Allwoerden, *Historia Michaelis Serveti*, Helmstedt, 1727 (Dutch trans., *Historie van Michael Servetus den Spanjaert*, Rotterdam, 1729)

WORKS ON CHRISTIAN-MUSLIM RELATIONS

De Trinitatis erroribus libri septem, 'Seven books on the errors of the Trinity'

DATE 1531
ORIGINAL LANGUAGE Latin

DESCRIPTION

De Trinitatis erroribus libri septem, 119 small double pages (*recto* and *verso*) in all, attack the doctrine of the Council of Nicea as a major mistake in the development of Christianity. In the first book (44 double pages), biblical texts are compared with classical theology, with Peter Lombard as its main representative. In the second chapter, the birth of Christ before the beginning of time and creation is criticised. Here Servetus sides with Rabbi David Kimhi (1160-1235) from Narbonne, in his polemics against Christians. Besides confessing a hidden, concealed God, Servetus recognises a full revelation of the divine mystery in Christ Jesus, not as a distinct person consisting of two natures, but as the Son eternally one with the Father. In Book 7, he rejects Arianism and Adoptionism, because these doctrines do not accept the full divine nature of Jesus or the Holy Spirit.

In the last pages of Book 1 (42v-43r), he includes a short but very outspokenly positive section in which he praises Muslims for their rejection of the doctrine of the Trinity: 'This tradition of the Trinity has, alas! been a laughing-stock to the Muslims. Hear also what Muḥammad says; for more reliance is to be given to one truth which an enemy confesses than to a hundred lies on our side.... that the Apostles and Evangelists and the first Christians were the best of men, and wrote what is true, and did not hold the Trinity, or three Persons in the Divine Being, but men in later times added this.' In this passage, the honorific titles for Jesus such as 'Spirit of God and Word of God, born of a perpetual virgin by God's breathing upon her', are quoted as believed by Muslims (see Q 4:171), but Servetus does not accept the Muslim rejection of the title 'Son of God'.

SIGNIFICANCE

Ditchfield (*Books fatal to their authors*) states with many others that Servetus went to Africa at an early age in order to study Arabic, but there are good reasons for not accepting this: in his edition of Ptolemy, he says much about his personal travels, but nothing about Africa; in the Geneva trial, nothing is said about such a trip to Muslim countries of northern Africa. He seems to have acquired his knowledge of Muslim beliefs only through works written by Christians. In view of Servetus's similarly positive remarks about Jewish circles, Bainton (*Hunted heretic*) guesses that his unusually harsh attack on the Trinity must be seen as an effort to remove the greatest obstacle for the conversion of Jews and Muslims, only a few decades after their forced baptism in the aftermath of the 1492 conquest of the last Muslim state of Granada. However, the 'Islamic passages' are only a small section of his frontal attack on the doctrine of the Trinity. In his larger 1553 book, the 'Islamic section' is somewhat bigger, but still only a small section of a long work.

In 1977, the Pakistani author Muhammad 'Ata ur-Rahim wrote a polemical book under the title *Jesus, prophet of Islam*, in which he sees a persistent Unitarian trend within Christianity, from the *Shepherd of Hermas* and the (pseudo)-Barnabas to Arius and later thinkers. Servetus is here presented as the first early modern Unitarian. Ur-Rahim could not yet use the translation of *Christianismi restitutio*, but gives long quotes from *De Trinitatis erroribus* and *Dialogorum de Trinitate*, and writes: 'The two books took the whole of Europe by storm. No one had ever written such a daring book within living memory. The result was that the Church hounded Servetus from one place to another' (p. 115). This conclusion seems to be overstated. Also the assumption that Servetus was a man of dialogue between religions cannot do justice to his main concern: a new understanding of Jesus Christ as the Son of God, revealing the full and undivided mystery of the hidden God. There is a strong apocalyptic tendency in the writings of Servetus, but this is neglected by later authors.

EDITIONS & TRANSLATIONS

R.-M. Bénin (ed. and trans.), *Dialogues sur la Trinité, en deux livres, et, De la justice du royaume du Christ, en quatre chapitres*, Paris, 2009 (French trans. bilingual with parallel Latin text)

S. Carletto and G. Lingua (ed. and trans.), *Logos o uomo? Testi antitrinitari di Michele Serveto e Fausto Sozzini*, Dronero, Cuneo, 2009 (Italian trans. includes text of *De Trinitatis erroribus lib. VII* and *Dialogorum de Trinitate libri duo*)

Á. Alcalá Galve (ed. and trans.), *Obras completas. II, Primeros escritos teológicos*, Zaragoza, 2004 (Spanish trans. includes text of *De los errores acerca de la Trinidad* and *Dos diálogos sobre la Trinidad*)

E.M. Wilbur (trans.), *The two Treatises of Servetus on the Trinity, On the errors of the Trinity seven books, Dialogues on the Trinity two books, On the righteousness of Christ's Kingdom four chapters*, Cambridge MA, 1932 (English trans.)

Dialogi de trinitate Amsterdam, Regensberg, 1721 (fascimile of 1532 edition)

Dialogorum de Trinitate libri duo. De justicia regni Christi capitula quatuor, Hagenau, France, 1532 (repr. Frankfurt, 1965)

Michael Servetus, alias Reves ab Aragonia Hispanum, *De Trinitatis erroribus libri septem*, Hagenau, France, 1531 (repr. Frankfurt, 1965)

STUDIES

González Echeverria, *El Amor a la verdad*
De Marcos Andreu, 'Servetus and Islam'
Hughes, 'Servetus and the Qur'an'
Zuber, *Les conflits de la tolérance*
Goldstone, *Out of the flames*
Hiller and Allen, *Michael Servetus*
Hiller, *The case of Michael Servetus 1511-1553*
Balázs, *Early Transsylvanian Antitrinitarianism (1566-1571)*
Fernández Barón, *Miguel Servet*
Friedman, *Michael Servetus*
M. 'Ata ur-Rahim, *Jesus prophet of Islam*, Wood Dalling, Norfolk, 1977
Bainton, *Hunted heretic*
Farquhar Fulton, *Michael Servetus, humanist and martyr*
Gachet d'Artigny, *Mémoires pour servir à l'histoire de Michel Servet*

Wilbur, *The two treatises of Servetus on the Trinity* (contains an extensive bibliography of earlier works)
Ditchfield, *Books fatal to their authors*
Arouet de Voltaire, 'De Genève et de Calvin. De Calvin et de Servet'
Von Musheim, *Anderweitiger Versuch einer vollständigen und unpartheyischen Ketzergeschichte*
Ab Allwoerden, *Historia Michaelis Serveti*

Christianismi restitutio, 'The restitution of Christianity'

DATE 1553
ORIGINAL LANGUAGE Latin

DESCRIPTION
In 1553, Servetus published his major (and fatal) work on the restitution of Christianity. The first and longest section of 287 pages discusses in seven 'books' the doctrine of the Trinity. The second, third and fifth sections concentrate on the end times, the just rule of Christ superseding the signs and realm of the Antichrist. Sections 4 and 6 are polemical discourses against John Calvin and Philip Melanchthon, mostly also on the doctrine of the Trinity. *Christianismi restitutio* was printed in Vienne by Balthasar Arnoullet without reference to author or publisher, though the colophon on the last page, 734, has M.S.V. above the year 1553, which may be read as Michael Servetus Villanovensis.

Early in the work, there is a passage in which the Muslims (after the Jews) are invoked as partners in Servetus's fight against the Trinity: 'What shall we say of the Muslims, who differ from us in the same way (as the Jews)? How harshly they censure us! And rightly so, by the just judgment of God, because there are none who return to the kernel. The Trinity is unreservedly condemned in the Qur'an, *Sūras* 11, 12 and 28, where Muḥammad teaches that those three gods, or "partners with God", are children of Satan and not known to the patriarchs, though the Trinitarians worship them in place of God' (p. 34). This is an elaboration of his attack in the work of 1531, but now with precise references to the Qur'an in Bibliander's edition of 1543 (and different from the numbering that is now common; according to modern numbering the quotations are from *Sūras* 4, 5 and 19).

In addition, some references are taken from sections of Riccoldo da Monte di Croce's *Confutatio*, and it is also supposed (Hughes, 'Servetus and the Qur'an') that the linguist Guillaume Postel, who published a *Restitutio* himself in 1552, as well as Nicholas of Cusa, had influence upon Servetus. The conclusion of the longest passage on the Trinity in the *Restitutio* states: 'Muḥammad has turned his back on Christianity because of these perverse Trinitarian teachings' (p. 36). Servetus wanted Christians to join the call of Jews and Muslims and abandon the idols of Trinity and Incarnation they had created for themselves by returning to the true unity of God, who fully revealed himself only in his eternal Son Jesus Christ (*Restitutio*, p. 420).

SIGNIFICANCE

Servetus did not consider Islam as an evil in itself or as a dangerous belief that had to be condemned but, on the contrary, thought that some aspects of the original intuitions of Christianity had been somehow preserved in its teachings. In the early decades of the Reformation, there was not much debate about the doctrine of the Trinity. Luther did not even use the word in his Catechisms, because it was not used in the Bible, nor did Calvin initially pay much attention to the doctrine. It received a more prominent place through the responses to Servetus's work in the 1550s. Servetus was accused of studying the Qur'an and favouring the doctrine of the Ottoman Turks, thus giving support to the enemy that was then threatening Europe.

This verdict was not fair, because Servetus's purpose was neither to convert Muslims (or Jews), nor to adjust Christian doctrines to Islam, though the clear reference to Muslim sources at the beginning and some remarks in later sections of the *Restitutio* remain significant. So it is not surprising that Melanchthon complained three years after Servetus's death that 'Servetian, i.e. Mohammedan teachings were spread in Poland' (quoted in Fernandez Barón, *Miguel Servet*, p. 435).

Servetus's influence on the rise of Unitarianism was especially strong in Hungary, where his *Restitutio* was for a large part reprinted in 1569, and also in Poland-Lithuania, where part of his work had been translated into Polish and printed as early as 1568. There is some speculation about the influence of Ottoman Muslims on the rise of this Hungarian Unitarianism, though this cannot yet be firmly established. For Servetus himself, as well, Islamic ideas cannot account for his continuing and eventually fatal obsession with fighting the doctrine of the Trinity. Sympathy for Servetus and his ideas can be seen not only among present-day Muslims, but also among people as diverse as Hungarian and American Unitarians, Spanish students of humanism, and even the American Evangelical Kermit Garley.

EDITIONS & TRANSLATIONS

C.A. Hoffman and M. Hillar (trans.), *The restoration of Christianity. An English translation of* Christianismi restitutio, *1553, by Michael Servetus (1511-1553)*, Lewiston NY, 2007

De errores acerca de la Trinidad, in Michael Servet, *Obras completas*, vol. 2/1. *Primeros escritos teológicos*, Zaragoza, 2004 (Spanish trans. by Á. Alcalá)

E.C. Sartorelli, 'O programa de Miguel Servet para a Restitução do Cristianismo. Teologia e retorica na apologia a Melanchthon', São Paulo, 2000 (Diss. University of São Paulo; Portuguese trans. of part of *Christianismi restitutio*: *De mysterio Trinitatis, et veterum disciplina, ad Philippum Melanchthonem, et eius colegas, apologia* = *Apologia a Felipe Melanchthon e a suas colegas sobre o mistério de Trinidade e sobre os costumes antigos*)

J. Farquhar Fulton (ed.), *Christianismi restitutio and other writings*, Omaha NE, 1989

Á. Alcalá (ed.), *Treinta cartas a Calvino. Sesenta signos del Antichristo. Apología de Melanchton*, Madrid, 1981 (Spanish trans. of *Christianismi restitutio*, §§ 5-7, pp. 577-734: 30 letters to John Calvin, the 60 signs of the reign of the Antichrist and a discussion with Melanchthon, *De mysterio Trinitatis*)

Á. Alcalá (ed.), *Restitución del Cristianismo. Primera traducción castellana de Ángel Alcalá y Luis Betés*, Madrid, 1980

B. Spiess, *Wiederherstellung des Christentums*, 3 vols, Wiesbaden, 1892-96 (German trans.)

Christianismi restitutio. Totius ecclesiae apostolicae est ad sua limina vocatio, Nuremburg, 1790

R. Mead (ed. and trans.), *De Trinitate Divina, quod in ea non sit invisibilium trium rerum illusio, sed vera substantiæ Dei manifestatio in Verbo et communicatio in Spiritu, etc.*, London, 1723 (partial trans. in English of *Christianismi restitutio*. Revised proofs; no more was printed and most existing sheets were seized on the orders of the Bishop of London on 27 May 1723)

Regnier Telle (Regnerus Vitellius), *Van den Dolinghen in de Drievuldigheyd seven boecken, eertijds in Latijn beschreven door Michiel Servetus*, Amsterdam, 1620 (Dutch trans.)

Okazanie Antychrysta y iego Królestwa ze znaków iego wlasnych w slowiebożymopisanych, których tusześćdziesiąt ['The advent of the Antichrist and his kingdom, according to his own signs, of which there are sixty, as described in the word of God'], Pińczów, 1568 (the earliest partial trans. of *Restitutio* into Polish by Gregorius Paulus /Grzegorz Paweł)

De regno Christi liber primus. De regno Antichristi liber secundus, Alba Iulia [Gyulafehérvar], 1569 (repr. Frankfurt, 1966) (partial repr. of *Christianismi restitutio*)

Christianismi restitutio, Vienne, 1553

STUDIES

González Echeverria, *El Amor a la verdad*
De Marcos Andreu, 'Servetus and Islam'
Hughes, 'Servetus and the Qur'an'
Zuber, *Les conflits de la tolerance*
Goldstone, *Out of the flames*
Hiller and Allen, *Michael Servetus*
Hiller, *The case of Michael Servetus 1511-1553*
Balázs, *Early Transsylvanian Antitrinitarianism (1566-1571)*
Fernández Barón, *Miguel Servet*
Friedman, *Michael Servetus*
Bainton, *Hunted heretic*
Farquhar Fulton, *Michael Servetus, humanist and martyr*
Gachet d'Artigny, *Mémoires pour servir à l'histoire de Michel Servet*
Wilbur, *The two treatises of Servetus on the Trinity* (contains an extensive bibliography of earlier works)
Ditchfield, *Books fatal to their authors*
Arouet de Voltaire, 'De Genève et de Calvin. De Calvin et de Servet', ii, chs 133, 134
Von Musheim, *Anderweitiger Versuch einer vollständigen und unpartheyischen Ketzergeschichte*
Ab Allwoerden, *Historia Michaelis Serveti*

Karel Steenbrink

Juan Luis Vives

DATE OF BIRTH 1493
PLACE OF BIRTH Valencia
DATE OF DEATH 6 May 1540
PLACE OF DEATH Bruges

BIOGRAPHY

Juan Luis Vives was one of the three foremost proponents of northern humanism, along with Erasmus of Rotterdam and Guillaume Budé. He was born into an ethnically Jewish family of *Conversos* (Roman Catholic converts from Judaism), and acquired a sound early education that enabled him to move for further study to Paris in 1509. There, he was exposed to the study of terminist logic, rooted in late medieval scholasticism, against which he was to react decisively. In 1514 (for the date see González y González, *Joan Lluis Vives*, p. 127), he moved again to the Low Countries (mainly Bruges but also Louvain), a safer place than Spain from the Inquisition for a descendant of *Conversos*. Indeed, his Jewish background shadowed all his activity: his family had been associated with a clandestine Valencia synagogue; his father was executed in 1524 by the Inquisition, which later dug up his mother's remains and condemned her long after her death, and other members of his family also suffered harshly. As a result, prior to his later years he studiously avoided theology as a subject that was a perilous minefield for a scholar with his lineage. He taught and wrote in the tradition of northern humanism, which privileged rhetoric and the cultivation of ancient sources over scholastic logic; he insisted on a return to ancient patristic sources and the original languages of scripture and promoted religious writing that prioritised edification of the faithful over the relentless pursuit of abstract theological questions regardless of their potential practical impact or their susceptibility to solution.

Vives's writings between 1509 and 1523 were varied in both genre and subject. They included prefaces to courses on classical texts (e.g., *Rhetorica ad Herennium*, Book 4; Cicero's *De legibus*; Vergil's *Georgics*); dialogues on sacred topics; meditations on the Seven Penitential Psalms and other devotional writings; a striking commentary on Cicero's *Dream of Scipio* lampooning contemporary education; and a series of fictitious speeches called the *Sullan declamations*, revivifying a brutal episode in Roman Republican history, which won high praise from Sir Thomas More and Erasmus. But the most important and influential work of this period was his 1519 treatise *In pseudodialecticos* ('Against the pseudo-dialecticians'), one of the best known humanist attacks on late scholastic preoccupation with logic and its corrupting effect on education. He identified with the humanistic programme and principles of Erasmus, his senior by over two decades, under whose auspices he completed a landmark commentary on Augustine's *City of God* (1522).

The death of his prime patron, Cardinal Guillaume de Croy, in 1521 left Vives in search of reliable support. It came in the form of an invitation to visit England in 1523, where he taught at Oxford until 1525 and resided for part of every year until 1528, with the support of Cardinal Thomas Wolsey, Henry VIII and Henry's Spanish wife, Katherine of Aragón. During this period, in 1524, he married Margaret Valdaura, a young woman of a notable *Converso* family in Bruges. Their union was childless. Vives played a role in bringing humanist learning to England, enjoying the friendship of Thomas More, Cuthbert Tunstall, William Mountjoy, Thomas Linacre, Erasmus and others. His English sojourns came to an end in the crossfire of Henry's divorce proceedings against Katherine; he not only resisted pressure from Henry's agents to compromise Katherine, but also alienated the queen by advising her to capitulate and accept the divorce.

During the 1520s, Vives published treatises *On the education of a Christian woman*, *On the duties of the married man*, and *On assistance to the poor*. There were also several writings on the political situation of the time, which was shaped by the power struggle between the great European monarchs, Henry VIII, Francis I of France, and Charles V, the Holy Roman Emperor and Spanish King, and the resulting absence of any united challenge to the expansionist ambitions of the Ottoman Turks. Meanwhile, Sultan Süleyman the Magnificent took Belgrade in 1521, smashed the Hungarian army at Mohács in 1526, and mounted an unsuccessful siege of Vienna in 1529. In letters to Pope Adrian VI, Henry VIII, Cardinal Wolsey and Henry's confessor John Longland, and in a satirical dialogue in 1526 in the style of Lucian, *De Europae dissidiis et bello Turcico* ('On conflicts in Europe and the Turkish war'), discussed below, Vives called for an end to intra-Christian squabbling and, ultimately, a unified war against the Turks. He followed these writings with treatises on peacemaking (*De pacificatione*) and 'On the condition of life of Christians under the Turk' (*De conditione vitae Christianorum sub Turca*), discussed below.

After England, Vives spent the less well documented remainder of his life in Bruges, save for a late, brief stay in Breda as the guest and mentor of Doña Mencía Mendoza, Countess of Nassau. The 1530s saw the production of his most important works. These include the massive *De disciplinis* ('On the disciplines'), a complex of treatises on humanist educational reform that was the longest of its kind since Quintilian's *Institutio oratoria* from the 1st century. To this he added works on rhetoric and letter-writing; a treatise *De anima* ('On the soul'), with its highly regarded third book on the emotions; and the relentlessly popular *Exercitatio linguae Latinae* ('Exercises in the Latin language'), pedagogical dialogues which persisted in hundreds of editions. Finally, he completed *De veritate fidei Christianae* ('On the truth of the Christian faith'), printed posthumously in 1543, regarded by some as the fulfillment of an intention expressed in the *De disciplinis* to round out his exposition of the disciplines by adding theology. The fourth book of *De veritate* is the Christian-Muslim dialogue discussed below. Vives died in 1540, beset by a variety of illnesses and tended by his wife Margaret.

MAIN SOURCES OF INFORMATION

Primary
Io. Lodovici Vivis Valentini opera in duos distincta tomos, etc., 2 vols, Basel, 1555
G. Majansius (ed.), *Ioannis Ludovici Vivis Valentini opera omnia*, 8 vols, Valencia, 1782-90 (repr. London, 1964)
L. Riber (ed. and trans.), *Juan Luis Vives. Obras completas*, 1947-48, 1992[2] (Spanish trans., often helpful, but not entirely reliable; difficult Latin passages are sometimes left untranslated)
Juan Luis Vives, *Epistolario*, ed. J. Jiménez Delgado, Madrid, 1978 (Spanish trans. of Vives's letters)
C. Fantazzi et al. (eds), *Selected works of J.L. Vives*, Leiden, 1987-2012 continuing, 9 vols to date (critical, annotated, Latin-English texts)
A. Mestre (ed.), *Ioannis Lodovici Vivis Valentini opera omnia*, Valencia, 1992-2010 continuing, 6 vols to date (critical Latin texts, but see criticism in C. Fantazzi, 'Vives' text of Augustine's *De civitate Dei*', *Neulateinisches Jahrbuch* 11 (2009) 19-33, pp. 21-22)

Secondary

C.G. Noreña, *Juan Luis Vives. Vie et destin d'un humaniste européen*, trans. O. and J. Pédeflous, Paris, 2013 (French trans. of the 1970 text. With essays by O. Pédeflous, 'Précédé de Vives et la France (2013/1509-1514)', and E. Gonzàles Gonzàles and V. Gutiérrez Rodriguez, 'Vives en France. La fabrique de l'oubli')

C. Fantazzi (ed.), *A companion to Juan Luis Vives*, Leiden, 2008

E. González y González, *Una república de lectores. Difusión y recepción de la obra de Juan Luis Vives*, Mexico City, 2007

V. Moreno Gallego, *La recepción Hispana de Juan Luis Vives*, Valencia, 2006

E. González González and V. Gutiérrez Rodríguez, *Los diálogos de Vives y la imprenta*, Valencia, 2000 (the first of three volumes on Vives's publication history; the second, *Juan Luis Vives en la imprenta. Escritos para el gran público*, and the third, *Juan Luis Vives. Los tratados para la academia*, are in preparation)

F. Calero and D. Sala, *Bibliografía sobre Luis Vives*, Valencia, 1999

E. González, S. Albiñana, and V. Gutiérrez Rodriguez, *Vives, edicions princeps*, Valencia, 1992 (a superb, generously illustrated, indispensable manual)

A. Mestre (ed.), *Ioannis Lodovici Vivis Valentini opera omnia*, vol. 1, Valencia, 1992 (essays on selected topics)

C.G. Noreña, *A Vives bibliography*, Lewiston NY, 1990

E. González y González, *Joan Lluis Vives. De la escolástia al humanismo*, Valencia, 1987

A. Garcia, *Els Vives. Una familia de Jueus Valencians*, Valencia, 1987 (on the victimisation of Vives's family by the Inquisition)

C.G. Noreña, *Juan Luis Vives*, trans. A. Pintor-Ramos, Madrid, 1978 (Spanish trans. of the 1970 text, revised by the author)

C.G. Noreña, *Juan Luis Vives*, The Hague, 1970 (bibliography superseded, but otherwise remains a classic)

A. Bonilla y San Martín, *Luis Vives y la filosofía del Renacimiento*, 3 vols, Madrid, 1903 (repr. Madrid, 1929)

WORKS ON CHRISTIAN-MUSLIM RELATIONS

De Europae dissidiis et bello Turcico, 'On conflicts in Europe and the Turkish war'

DATE 1526
ORIGINAL LANGUAGE Latin

DESCRIPTION

De Europae dissidiis et bello Turcico, 30 pages in Majansius's edition (to which the page numbers here refer), is a satirical dialogue in the vein of the Greek *Dialogues of the dead* of Lucian of Samosata (125-80); Lucian was a popular inspiration for satire among 16th-century humanists. The setting is the underworld, in the immediate wake of the Turks' crushing defeat of the Hungarian army on 29 August 1526, at Mohács. Minos, the mythical judge of the underworld, and Tiresias, the legendary seer, are speculating on the causes of the surge of freshly arriving ghosts. Two come along with information: Polypragmon ('Busybody'), experienced in business all over Europe, and Basilius Colax ('Royal Flatterer'), a widely travelled courtier. They explain the recent spike in the death rate: European nations are at war with each other, freeing Turkish armies to ravage the Balkan Peninsula.

Polyragmon chronicles specific military events beginning in the 15th century, with the taking of Naples by Alfonso V of Aragón, and the capture of Constantinople by the Turks (1453), with no Christian military response. While French invasions and conflict with Aragonian power in the south embroil Italy, the Turks expand into the Greek world unhindered. Sultan Bayezid II (1481-1512) consolidates Ottoman gains. Interloping powers, native city-states, and aggressive popes keep Italy in turmoil and enable Turkish expansion. Polypragmon adds news of other clashes: war over Navarre, and the defeat and death of James IV of Scotland against the English [battle of Flodden, 1513]. Persistent competition between Francis I of France and Charles V of Spain, pursued in a swirl of shifting alliances and advancing and retreating armies, climaxes when Charles captures Francis in 1525.

Minos asks: 'Meanwhile, is the Turk sleeping?' Not at all, replies Polypragmon. Sultan Süleyman has taken Belgrade (1521) and Rhodes (1522). Francis, liberated by Charles, joins the League of Cognac with Pope Clement VII, Venice, Florence and the Sforza of Milan in opposition to Charles. (This struggle would lead to the sack of Rome in 1527.) Polypragmon adds: 'This month, the Turk crossed the Danube, invaded Pannonia [Hungary] with a mighty host, and in a great battle cut down our people, among them the king, just an adolescent' (p. 463). This was the catastrophic late August battle of Mohács. *De Europae dissidiis* dates itself to October 1526; hence the accuracy of Polypragmon's expression 'this month'.

The underworld characters assess. To Tiresias, European affairs are a hopelessly tangled ball of string. To Minos, the princes' exploits are simply *latrocinia*, banditry or robbery, a favourite word of Vives in describing war. Minos observes that, but for these campaigns, the Turks could have been overthrown (p. 464). Italy, he says, is the nurse of wars, while Spain and France are already two great and powerful kingdoms: why do they and the other powers not just leave Italy alone?

Minos asks Tiresias what remedy he counsels. Tiresias makes the first of two despairing remarks: What is the point of deliberating, he asks, 'when none of the parties will follow good advice? Everyone, lost in blindness, is seized by emotion, that worst of guides' (p. 466). Neighbour hates neighbour, but 'Whoever lives near the Turk has the worst neighbour; I would prefer wolves, or a swampy and pest-ridden field' (pp. 466-67). Polypragmon replies: 'Yet there is a persistent rumour among the living that the Turk was let into Pannonia by those who should not have done so, people whom no one had ever feared' (p. 467). Minos asks who told the Turks they could come in unhindered. Tiresias replies that no traitor was needed: Christian squabbling was all the incentive the Turks needed. Europeans dread Turkish cannons. Tiresias observes that the Turks resorted to them against their will, out of fear that the Christians had the same weapons (pp. 467-68).

Here Scipio appears, expressing surprise that a common danger is not driving communities together. It does not work that way, Tiresias explains. Christian princes get no respect from their subjects, who 'prefer subservience to the Turk rather than to one of their own; they would rather have their country occupied by the Turk than by a Christian. This will surely happen, if they continue in this way' (p. 468). They will get no justice from Turks, or fidelity, or respect for themselves or God. If they do not expect their own king to meet his obligations, how can they expect the same from a professed enemy of responsibility? Notwithstanding how incompetent a Christian prince may be, his subjects should at least be glad to have a Christian, not a Turkish, overlord. 'Unless', proposes Tiresias (p. 470), 'you believe that a Turk honours the fantasies of Muḥammad more scrupulously than you do the holy faith of God the true and immortal.' The inhumane Turkish conquest of Constantinople, Trebizond, Euboea and Pannonia should be caution enough. Basilius Colax offers flimsy excuses for the European princes' belligerence (it keeps them busy; it brings them glory), which Tiresias dismisses contemptuously; such warmaking, again, is mere *latrocinium*.

Scipio launches into by far the longest speech of the dialogue (pp. 473-79), urging the Europeans to unite, throw off any fear of Turkish power, and undertake a war of aggression. The enemy is a pushover and the spoils will be vast, considering the wide Ottoman territories. M. Colish ('Vives on the Turks', p. 7) reads the text to say even that 'Well beyond the goal of invading Turkey and conquering Anatolia, Scipio advocates imperial expansion as far east as India.' Scipio knows the stakes: the wealth of Asia [Minor] alone sustained the mighty army of his ancient Roman Republic. Why do princes waste themselves fighting European wars for years, just to push their boundaries a handful of miles, he asks, only to lose the land by negotiation and peace treaty? (p. 474) Vast realms await conquest: Christians could seize those sprawling lands where Turks now forcibly tear children away from their Christian roots and press them into service as 'Mamluks' (as Vives styles the Janissary corps). The subject European populations would revolt from the Turk who, loath to try our power, would retreat to Asia.

Scipio continues: Asian invasions of Europe always fail, European invasions of Asia always succeed. He cites the exploits of Miltiades, Themistocles, Sulla, the Homeric Greeks, the Galatians, Alexander the Great and assorted Roman champions (pp. 475-76). Nor do superior numbers alone determine battles. Further, someone may object that 'the situation, the times, the status of Asia' are different. Scipio agrees, but holds that, since the East-West disparity traces back to nature, not transient circumstances, it can be rectified somewhat but not changed. In making this point, Scipio appeals to Aristotle and 'other learned men' (unspecified) who remind us that the mightiest and bravest race is that which inhabits Europe, while the Asians are timid, ill suited to war, and more like women than men. Likewise, the Turks may have gathered brave fighters from various nations, but Scipio would pin his hopes of victory on the cowardice of the Turks' leaders, who are all Asians. He quotes a saying: 'I will choose an army of deer led by a lion over an army of lions led by a deer' (p. 478). Turkish success in grabbing part of Europe should cause no worry: it can of course happen that better people are on occasion conquered by a worse enemy, either because of infighting among the betters, or contempt for their inferiors, or careless straying into a trap. If the winds were ever to shift so that Christians redirected their hatreds and outrage toward the Turk, Scipio predicts, they would behold the true souls of those Asians. 'Adversity would unmask those minds which a long period of prosperity has hidden; they would disclose that they have been brave and vigorous not because of their own force and courage, but because of your own failures' (p. 478).

In European wars, says Scipio (p. 479), a winner's conquest devolves into litigation and counterclaims. No such problems will bedevil territory taken from Turks: once seized, the victor holds it free and clear. Warriors will reap glory; Europe will be freed of the fear of servitude; religious faith will be strengthened and spread among many. Scipio allows that he does not know whether Christ would see things the same way, but he insists that his programme would be a more tolerable evil than the insanity of the current interstate conflicts.

Minos hurries Tiresias for emergency advice amid the mounting legions of ghosts. It is futile, says Tiresias a second time, to render counsel in this climate where savage and atrocious emotions hold sway (p. 480), but nevertheless he will have his say. First: the protection of Christ is Christians' only armour and guard, but it is mighty and impregnable. Let them be Christians in deed as well as name, and cease bickering. Also, let 'those two youths' (Charles V and Francis I) be happy with what they possess, and content to live in harmony. Tiresias judges that 'the third' (Henry VIII) will not be a problem; in having sent what help he could to distant Pannonia, he proved his awareness that this was a war against Muḥammad. Let the Christians unite and fortify Germany, for if that land falls, those who abhor Turkish domination will have no choice but to flee across the Atlantic to the New World. Tiresias concludes with doubt; either the Christians will heed his counsel or they will not, and if not, the day will come when they will wish they had done so.

SIGNIFICANCE

De Europae dissidiis is a prominent document among Vives's writings on war, peace and European politics during the 1520s. In its first known edition (1526), it appears as the centrepiece (see George, 'Vives' *De Europae dissidiis*') of an ensemble including the following items, dated as indicated:

Letter to Pope Adrian VI on disturbances in Europe (1522)

Letter to Henry VIII on the capture of Francis I, King of France (1525)

A second letter to Henry on war and peace (1525)

De Europae dissidiis (October 1526, weeks after the debacle at Mohács)

Letter to Cardinal Wolsey dedicating translations of Isocrates (1523)

Translations from the 4th-century-BCE Greek of Isocrates' *Areopagiticus* and *Nicocles*, orations on the qualities of good citizens and good monarchs

Letter to Henry's confidant John Longland, Bishop of Lincoln, on the wisdom and nobility of making the first move toward peace (1524)

One may infer that Vives is capitalising on the moment of dread over the Turkish victory at Mohács to offer a collection of his counsels on

Europe's predicament, penned over the previous few years. Further, the generic departure of *De Europae dissidiis* compels the reader's attention. It is the only dramatic work of its kind in all Vives's preserved writings between 1523 and 1537. Finally, all the other pieces in the 1526 ensemble are diplomatic and predicated on the assumption that rational discourse is possible. Not so *De Europae dissidiis*, which, by launching into the realm of imagination, explores broader and at times less noble impulses, including Tiresias's fears that the moment for rational discourse has come and gone, and blatant appeals to greed and to thirst for glory and power in Scipio's call to arms against the Turks. *De Europae dissidiis* is a vehicle for expression of Vives's own fears and an indication of the limits to his pacifism when dealing with the Turkish threat. It reappeared in 1538 (*Declamationes sex*), accompanied again by pieces from the 1526 ensemble along with oratorical works. A German translation came soon after (*Türckischer Keyszer Ankunfft*, Strasbourg: H. Schott, 1540). There appear to have been no other printings beyond those listed below under 'Editions'.

EDITIONS & TRANSLATIONS

F. Calero and M. J. Echarte (trans.), *De Europae dissidiis et republica. Sobre las disensiones de Europa, y sobre del estado*, Valencia, 1992, pp. 49-86 (Spanish trans.)

Riber, *Obras completas*, ii, pp. 39-61 (Spanish trans.)

Majansius, *Ioannis Ludovici Vivis Valentini opera omnia*, vi, pp. 452-81

Io. Lodovici Vivis Valentini opera, 1555, ii, pp. 947-59

Ioannis Lodovici Vivis Valentini declamationes sex. Syllanae quinque, etc., Basel, 1538, pp. 240-72

De Europae dissidiis et republica, Bruges, 1526, fols C7 –F4

STUDIES

C. Curtis, 'Advising monarchs and their counsellors. Juan Luis Vives on the emotions, civil life and international relations', *Parergon* 28 (2011) 29-54 (adds valuable background on politics, especially English, of the time, and on Vives's 'conception of the relationship of human nature and the emotions to peace and prosperity' [p. 30])

M. Colish, 'Juan Luis Vives on the Turks', *Medievalia et Humanistica* N.S. 35 (2009) 1-14

G. Tournoy and G. Tournoy-Thoen, 'Due umanisti fiamminghi di fronte all'espansione dell'Islam. Juan Luis Vives e Nicola Clenardo', in L. Secchi Tarugi (ed.), *Oriente e Occidente nel Rinascimento. Atti del XIX Convegno Internazionale (Chianciano Terme – Pienza 16-19 Iuglio 2007)*, Florence, 2009, 307-21

E. George, 'Juan Luis Vives' *De Europae dissidiis et bello Turcico*. Its place in the 1526 ensemble', in J.F. Alcina et al. (eds), *Acta Conventus neo-latini Bariensis*, Tempe AZ, 1998, 259-66

M. Zappala, 'Vives' *De Europae dissidiis et bello Turcico*, the Quattrocento dialogue, and "open" discourse', in A. Dalzell et al. (eds), *Acta conventus neo-latini Torontoniensis*, Binghamton NY, 1991, 823-30

A. Fontán, 'La politica Europea en la perspectiva de Vives', in J. Ijsewijn and A. Losada (eds), *Erasmus in Hispania. Vives in Belgio*, Leuven, 1982, 27-72, pp. 49-50, 66-69

J.-C. Margolin, 'Conscience européenne à la menace turque d'après le "De dissidiis Europae et bello turcico" de Vivès', in A. Buck (ed.), *Juan Luis Vives. Arbeitsgespräch in der Herzog August Bibliothek Wolfenbüttel vom 6. bis 8. November 1980*, Hamburg, 1980, 107-40

G. McCully, Jr, 'Juan Luis Vives (1493-1540) and the problem of evil in his time', Ann Arbor MI, 1967 (Diss. Columbia University), pp. 140-77

De conditione vitae Christianorum sub Turca, 'On the condition of the life of Christians under the Turk' *Quam misera esset vita Christianorum sub Turca,* 'How miserable the life of Christians would be under the Turk'

DATE 1529
ORIGINAL LANGUAGE Latin

DESCRIPTION

The topic reflected in the commonly employed title of *De conditione*, the fate of Christians actually under Turkish domination, is overshadowed by Vives's anxiety over the questionable soundness of European Christians' religious faith. The other title, 'How miserable life would be', etc., is more accurate with its hypothetical vision of European Christians in (future) Turkish bondage. In the following summary, page numbers refer to Majansius's 14-page edition (*Opera omnia*, vol. 5).

1. Christians, in wistfully conceiving the potential advantages of Ottoman suzerainty, harbour false notions of attainable liberty and of their own fidelity to their religion.

Their hostility toward Christian, and especially foreign Christian, regimes (and here Vives must have Italy prominently in mind) leads them to imagine that Turkish rulers would be better for them. For this attitude, both subjects and their abusive rulers are equally at fault. Merchants, soldiers and athletes suffer great hardships for secular rewards; in proportion to our far greater goal, eternal felicity, we Christians should acknowledge that the hardships we suffer as subjects are small indeed. Scripture, confirmed by Cyprian of Carthage, teaches obedience even to unjust authority (pp. 447-49).

The liberty Christians think they would have under the Turks is a total fantasy. In any case, utterly unrestricted freedom is an impossible ideal not even realised in the Graeco-Roman world. Vives speaks, rather, of three valid notions of liberty: *libertas summa* ('the highest liberty') is attained by living as a law-abiding citizen; *una libertas vera* ('the only true liberty') is achieved by living well, i.e. virtuously; *proxima libertas* ('accessible liberty') is civil obedience, even toleration of a flawed ruler when circumstances make it necessary (pp. 449-51).

Vives censures contemporary Europeans' failure at harmony or even reasonable submission; and here it becomes clear how the turmoil that has beset Italy colours his argument. As examples, he holds up Italians who would sooner die, or even opt for degrading [Turkish] domination, rather than live under a Spanish, German, or otherwise foreign Christian prince. Italians bring abuse and ruin on their own land by despising even others from their own community as rulers. Naples and Milan stand out as Italian communities under non-Italian regimes. Allowing that Milan has suffered greatly from foreign governance, Naples under the Spanish has in contrast fared well, by and large, demonstrating that rule by foreign princes need not always be bad. In any event, wishing for Turkish overlords is asking for even worse rule (pp. 451-53).

Vives appeals to Church history to illustrate current Christian spiritual frailty. Prior to Constantine in the 4th century, Christian martyrs frustrated Roman persecutors by their unshakable faith and inspired conversions. Once Constantine established Christian privileges, asserts Vives, religion and virtue languished, and the failures persist to his day (pp. 453-54).

2. Envisioning Turkish rule, part one: Examination of Turkish attitudes and actions.

The hegemony of the Turks will be sadder than the ascent of Constantine. They regard Christians not as humans but as cattle with no rights, whose only purpose is to benefit the conquerors. The treatment of the defenders of Rhodes, taken by Sultan Süleyman in 1522, is evidence for this conviction. Likewise, the Turks' pitiless slaughter of the Mamluks in Egypt in 1517 bodes ill for Christians who would come under their sway. Turks will try to disguise their abuse of Christians by conferring bogus honours (pp. 454-55).

Vives laments the grievous Ottoman oppression of the Greeks, whose land has become a prison. Nor, he says, should one dismiss concerns about straitened material affairs in the interest of more spiritual considerations. Christianity is despised in the Ottoman Empire, and criticism of Islam is outlawed. The worst outrage is the forcible abduction of Christian boys into the Janissary corps (pp. 455-57).

3. Envisioning Turkish rule, part two: Examination of Christians' moral and spiritual vulnerability.

The Greeks' and Romans' intellectual arts facilitated spiritual understanding until they were ravaged by the barbarians. Turks are legendarily innocent of any cultural accomplishments; the effect on Christians under their rule will be accordingly adverse. Christendom's arts and disciplines, all learned from the now captive Greeks, promote piety. In the absence of these advantages, says Vives, it is questionable whether Christians, already venal, can hang onto their faith. Even spiritually strong believers will face dangers from association with weak co-religionists, and from persistent Islamic questioning of their convictions. Prone as we are to depravity, Vives adds, we are already defectors from God to the devil. He hammers at how Christians will be spiritually helpless under the Turks, whose conferrals of so-called liberty will be nothing more than a sham (pp. 458-60).

4. Conclusion.

Appealing to Scripture, Vives warns fervent Christians against expecting help from their weaker fellows or presuming they can resist opposition under the Turks. Christians are urged to beware lest they simply fall into the experience of Ottoman overlordship (p. 460).

A reading of *De conditione* discloses three particular characteristics. First, the presumed audience of Christians who falter in their resistance to the idea of Turkish domination is never clearly defined, beyond implicit and explicit allusions to populations in Italy. But substantial evidence of Italians hankering after Turkish rule is actually hard to come by. In fact, the main incidences of Turkish irruption onto Italian soil (the raids across the Adriatic in the 1470s, the brief capture of Otranto in 1480) generated fear, panic and revulsion, but not longing to go over to the Turks. Hungary, on the frontier between Europe and the Ottoman Empire, appears to produce ambiguous but doubtful evidence for aspirations to cross over to the Ottomans, but nothing in *De conditione* suggests that Vives has this region in mind in particular. In fact, he even omits a potentially pertinent item he used earlier in his 1526 *De Europae dissidiis et bello Turcico* ('On conflicts in Europe and the Turkish war', Majansius, *Vivis Valentini opera omnia*, v, p. 467). There, one of the underworld informants reports that 'a persistent rumour is circulated among the living that the Turk was let into Pannonia [Hungary] by those who should not have done so, people whom no one had ever feared'. In sum, one could argue that, in his zeal to expose and censure European Christians' weak allegiance to their faith, he has here created a not entirely accurate picture of a population desirous of trading Christian for Turkish suzerainty, a population for which there is little historical evidence.

Second, while arranging his portrayal of European Christians to suit his argument, Vives also selectively characterises the experience of 'the Greeks' in the Ottoman Empire as the signature victims of Ottoman repression. He tends to deflect attention from actual Greeks of his time by emphasising the heroic ancestors from whom they are descended. There are two particular marks of his avoidance (or ignorance?) of the Greek experience under the Empire. When seeking specific events to bolster his case (apart from the practice of kidnapping Christian boys for the Janissary corps), he refers not to mainland Greek experiences but to two happenings distant in time and place and only tangentially affecting the captive Greeks: the seven-year-old siege of Rhodes (1522), which he mischaracterises to the detriment of Süleyman; and the even older (1517) treacherous slaughter of Mamluks in Egypt, where popular dismay compromises somewhat the picture of Ottoman savagery. Further, the Orthodox Church plays no part in Vives's portrayal of subject Greeks' conduct, despite the Ottomans' *millet* system of subject populations who maintain their identity, the Turkish recognition of the Patriarch of Constantinople, and the evidence for continued Orthodox missionary activity under the Turks.

Third, *De conditione* does not seek to ascribe Ottoman conduct to any principles or tenets of the faith of Islam, except insofar as Vives envisions religiously motivated assaults on Christians' confessional fidelity. Thus, one observes a reversal between *De conditione* and the later *De veritate fidei Christianae*, Book 4 (discussed below); *De conditione* has everything to do with Muslim conquest and nothing to do with critique of the Islamic faith, while *De veritate*, Book 4, is mainly preoccupied with describing and criticising Islamic beliefs, while giving only the most general and ancillary attention to Islamic conquests and their effects.

SIGNIFICANCE

Along with Vives's 1526 satirical dialogue *De Europae dissidiis et bello Turcico* ('On conflicts in Europe and the Turkish war'), discussed above, *De conditione* marks a limit to Vives's pacifist aspirations when it comes to the expanding Ottoman Empire. *De conditione* drew enough attention to warrant recurring publications through 1603. Theodor Bibliander included a copy in his celebrated and controversial three-volume encyclopedia of documents from and about Islam (*Machumetis Saracenorum*, 1543, 1550), including a Latin translation of the Qur'an, other Islamic writings, and anti-Muslim polemics. It appeared four other times in Latin (Lyons: Trechsel, 1532; J. Sadoleto, *De bello Turcis inferendo*, Basel: Platter, 1538; *Selectissimarum orationum volumina*, Leipzig: H. Grosse-A. Lamberg, 1596; *Consilia bellica*, Eisleben: Officina Grosiana, 1603) and twice in German (J.L. Vives, *Wie der türck*, trans. C. Hedion, Strassburg: Balth. Becken, 1532; *Türckischer Keyszer Ankunfft*, Strasbourg: H. Schott, 1540). There are no other known appearances of *De conditione* apart from those listed below under 'Editions'.

EDITIONS & TRANSLATIONS

    F. Calero, M.L. Arribas, and P. Usábel (trans.), *De concordia et discordia in humano genere. Sobre la concordia y la discordia en el género humano. De pacificatione. Sobre la pacificación. Quam misera esset vita Christianorum sub Turca. Cuán desgraciada sería la vida de los Cristianos bajo los Turcos*, Valencia, 1997, pp. 371-94 (Spanish trans.)

    Riber, *Obras completas*, ii, pp. 63-74 (Spanish trans.)

    Majansius, *Ioannis Ludovici Vivis Valentini opera omnia*, v, pp. 447-60

    Io. *Lodovici Vivis Valentini opera*, Basel, 1555, ii, pp. 882-89

    T. Bibliander (ed.), *Machumetis Saracenorum principis, eiusque successorum vitae, doctrina, ac ipse Alcoran*, etc. ('Lives and doctrine of Muḥammad the leader of the Saracens and his successors, and the Qur'an itself', etc.), 3 vols, Basel, 1543, 1550, iii, fols mm4v-nn2v

    Ioannis Lodovici Vivis Valentini De concordia & discordia in humano genere ad Carolum V. Caesarem, Libri quattuor. De pacificatione, Lib. vnus. Quam misera esset vita Christianorum sub Turca, Lib. vnus, Antwerp, 1529, fols A1r-B7v

STUDIES

    E. George, 'Captive Greeks and deluded Europeans. Notes on Juan Luis Vives's *De conditione vitae Christianorum sub Turca* (1529)', *eHumanista* 26 (2014) 508-29

Colish, 'Juan Luis Vives on the Turks'
Tournoy and Tournoy-Thoen, 'Due umanisti', pp. 311-12
McCully, Jr, 'Juan Luis Vives and the problem of evil', pp. 193-213
S. Runciman, *The Great Church in captivity. A study of the Patriarchate of Constantinople from the eve of the Turkish conquest to the Greek War of independence*, Cambridge, 1968

De veritate fidei Christianae, Liber quartus: Contra sectam Mahometi, 'On the truth of the Christian faith, Book 4: Against the sect of Muḥammad'

DATE 1540
ORIGINAL LANGUAGE Latin

DESCRIPTION

In elaborating his view of 'the truth of the Christian faith', Vives launched with unprecedented breadth into theology, a discipline that he had generally avoided for most of his life. He considered it to be excessively perilous for a *Converso* living in the shadow of the Inquisition, which regarded *Converso* families with suspicion and had brought grim hardships on his family. The treatise's five books display a distinctive structure. Books 1, 2 and 5 are in discursive prose. To these, however, are added two books in dialogue form: between a Christian and a Jew (Book 3) and between a Christian and a Muslim (Book 4). The contrasts of tone between Books 3 and 4 give deeper insight into Vives's attitudes.

Following is a summary of the dialogue in Book 4 (64 pages in vol. 8 of Majansius's edition, to which the page numbers here refer), cast from the Christian's viewpoint.

1. Introduction (pp. 364-71): The parties meet amicably in a *locus amoenus* setting. The Muslim is 'Alfaquinus', from the Arabic *faqīh*, 'jurist' or 'community leader', rather than merely 'Mahometanus' or 'Agarenus' ('descendant of Hagar'), thus one deserving special respect. Internal evidence indicates that the presumably anonymous 'Christian' is actually Vives himself. The two discover a common reverence for God, and agree to discuss the Islamic faith. Nonetheless, insults will not be long in coming.

2. Inadequacies of Muḥammad (pp. 371-81): He falsely claims divine origin, says the Christian. Muslim armed conquest, inferior to reason as

a vehicle of conversion, is dismissed as a fallback justification for Islam in the absence of miracles, which Muḥammad did not perform. Such a violent man forfeits any claim to be a divine envoy, invalidating his identity as the Paraclete. It is impossible that Christians could have missed scriptural allusions to Muḥammad if they had been there. Jesus was far more fit than Muḥammad to come last as the Messiah.

3. The Islamic holy writings (pp. 381-87): Is the Qur'an for everyone or for a select few? Muḥammad is inconsistent about this. The Islamic contention that the Jewish and Christian Testaments were 'corrupted' is unsustainable. In characterising Islamic doctrine, the Christian interlocutor relies indiscriminately on qur'anic and non-qur'anic material, including treatment of folk absurdities as basic Islamic beliefs, and allowing no room for poetic or metaphorical understanding.

4. God and Christ (pp. 387-95): The anthropomorphised Allāh of the Muslims is unworthy to be regarded as the God of the universe (notwithstanding anthropomorphic portrayal of the God of the Old Testament). The Muslims demand to know how the Father begot the Son without a wife, though there are instances of creation without intercourse (the origin of Adam; conception of fish without male assistance; sexlessness of flies and gnats). Conformity of wills between the Father and the Son obviates the Islamic insistence on the risk of a divine power struggle, an idea that was stolen from pagan fables involving Jupiter, Saturn and others. Christ's claims to divinity are valid; despite Islamic denials, he did indeed suffer and die.

5. The natural world (pp. 395-401): By treating fables from the 12th-century *Doctrina Mahumet* as though they were serious doctrine, the Christian argues that the Muslim view of the natural world is ridiculous. An example concerns a tale of Noah's ark. The vessel is imperilled when the elephant gives birth to the pig by defecation; the pig roots about in the excrement, whence the mouse is born; the mouse starts gnawing the pitch holding the seams in the hull; Noah, terror-stricken, begs counsel from God; God directs Noah to strike the lion in the face; he does so, and the cat springs from the lion's nostrils; the cat hunts down the mouse; and the ark is saved.

6. Muḥammad's followers, law and life of the Saracens (pp. 401-13): Muḥammad drew his adherents from among idolaters and superficial or wilfully ignorant Christians. He cobbled his religion together from bits and pieces of other traditions, relying on Sergius the Arian, John the Nestorian and an unnamed Talmud scholar. He promoted a lifestyle that privileges base desires and encourages vengeance. Polygamy engenders

dissension (and here the Christian defends the patriarchs' plurality of wives, though not very effectively). Islamic acceptance of divorce and reconciliation is inferior to Christian practice. The Christian criticises Muslim teachings on fasting and wine-drinking, appealing to another excerpt from *Doctrina Mahumet*, the folk tale of Horroth and Maroth, two drunken angels.

7. The Day of Judgment, celestial bliss (pp. 413-23): According to the *Doctrina Mahumet*, Allāh will order Adriel, the Angel of Death, to kill every living creature and then to go off and die himself. Allāh then will resuscitate Seraphuel, whom he will order to blow a trumpet which is as long as a 50-year journey. The souls of the just will be blown out of the trumpet. After 80 years, each soul will be reunited with its body. A fire will drive all the souls to Jerusalem, where they will appeal in turn to Adam, Noah, Abraham, Christ, and finally with success to Muḥammad. Allāh will respond by building a bridge over hell on which is placed a balance. Souls will place their deeds in the balance. The good can pass over the bridge, the wicked will fall into hell. The Islamic idea of paradise, 'a never-ending, unrestrained round of eating, drinking, and making love with women', is too sensual to be worthy (p. 419).

8. The abrupt conclusion, (various topics, pp. 423-27): 'So insipid, false, and self-contradictory' a work as the Qur'an must have originated in human 'foolishness and negligence'. Muḥammad asserts that, save for defectors from the Qur'an to another faith, 'each person is capable of being saved by following his own law' (p. 425). This is impossible: 'Look at how far distant we Christians and you Muslims are from the opinions, rites and sacrifices of the pagans. How can all of us worship properly the single God in whom we believe, while they adore a multitude?' (p. 426) Finally, the proliferation of Muslims proves nothing about the truth of Islam, for the numbers are boosted by force of arms; by the prohibition against disputation with other sects; by the command to trust no one but other Muslims; and by the Muslims' determination to separate themselves from others. Here, suddenly, the dialogue breaks off. The Christian speaks last, the Muslim disappears from view. Unlike many other literary dialogues between Christians and their Jewish or Muslim interlocutors, nothing is said about the success or failure of the Christian's persuasive attempts.

The dialogue exhibits several noteworthy characteristics. As illustrated above, it distorts any focused inquiry into fundamental Islamic beliefs by its emphasis on folk tales obviously chosen for their susceptibility to ridicule rather than their value for documenting essential Muslim tenets.

Further, it differs strikingly from its companion dialogue between a Christian and a Jew (*De veritate*, Book 3) in two respects. First, it opens on a more amicable footing. The *locus amoenus* setting for the Muslim dialogue has as its counterpart in Book 3 a brusque interruption by the Christian, who comes upon a Jew engrossed in a text and demands to know what he is reading. When told that it is scripture, the Christian curtly promises to set the Jew straight on the meaning of holy writ. Unlike the title of respect, 'alfaquinus', accorded to the Muslim in Book 4, the Jew in Book 3 is simply 'Judaeus'. In addition, the Christian in Book 3 charges the Jew and his fellows with a range of faults: wilful ignorance, suspicion, duplicity, and most grievously, hatred of Christ and Christianity that is so intense as to vitiate the possibility of rational exchange. In Book 4, however, the Christian imputes only stupidity and gullibility to Muslims, but not the array of moral failings of which the Jews are presumed guilty. Moral culpability is deflected from his followers onto Muḥammad, who is described as a lecherous, power-hungry, deceitful charlatan.

Reasons for these differences come to mind. Vives's tendency to go overboard in cataloguing Jewish vices could be designed to provide cover for his wife, soon to be his widow, against the possibility that the Inquisition will find anything compromising. Meanwhile, the less harsh handling of Muslims may perhaps owe something to Vives's familiarity with them from his own upbringing in Valencia. That city and region had an Islamic population and a milieu in which Muslims retained a place in society and in the agricultural economy even after the 1492 expulsion of the Jews from Spain. Unconverted Muslims formed an exploitable inferior population of agricultural workers; hence, there were Valencian interests at odds with Inquisitorial ambitions.

Even though the Muslim in Book 4 has only about six per cent of the lines, one can gather something of his character from the Christian's comments as well as his own. The very fact that Vives chose to divert the structure of the *De veritate* into dialogue for the Jewish and Muslim encounters gives the chosen opponent a voice, however small. As it happens, in creating a Muslim interlocutor, Vives explored ground unvisited by Erasmus himself, none of whose *Colloquia* contains a Muslim speaker. Further, according to one scholar, we have no evidence that Erasmus ever had any interchanges with Muslims.

SIGNIFICANCE

Anti-Muslim treatises in Europe have a long history. Vives is not regarded as contributing any new arguments to the tradition in *De veritate*, Book 4.

In choosing dialogue in particular for his back-to-back Christian-Jew and Christian-Muslim compositions, he resorted to a genre in which he had had considerable success. Further, he thus joined an age-old stream extending back centuries, all the way to Antiquity in the case of the Jewish dialogue. Ramon Llull's late 13th-century *Book of the Gentile and the three wise men* is a noteworthy medieval example. One such production, however, deserves special attention. The Spanish *Diálogos cristianos contra la secta mahometa y contra la pertinacia de los judíos* ('Christian dialogues against the Mohammedan sect and against the pertinacity of the Jews') of Bernardo Pérez de Chinchón was published in Valencia in 1535, in a climate of vigorous missionary activity aimed at Muslims. Pérez's down-to-earth, simple dialogues between a Christian and a Muslim can be viewed as a storehouse of formulas that would equip a Christian with the necessary tools for talking religion to his or her Muslim neighbour. Gregorius Majansius, Vives's 18th-century Valencian editor, says that in *De veritate*, Books 3 and 4, Vives, imitating Pérez's work, 'transformed it into his own vital essence, and employing his abundant erudition and judgment, recast it into a more elegant treatise' (Majansius, *Opera omnia*, i, *Vita Vivis*, p. 167).

With one exception, the publication history of Book 4 is tied to that of *De veritate* as a whole. The exception occurs in the 1550s, at a time of European apprehensions over the Turkish threat. Theodor Bibliander's three-volume Islamic encyclopedia (*Machumetis Saracenorum*) includes a brief set of excerpts, printed identically in 1543 and 1550, totalling some 79 lines taken from Book 4. The excerpts are labelled *De Mahomete, et Alcorano ipsius, sive Saracenorum lege, Lodovici Vivis censura, e libris eius* De veritate fidei Christianae *excerpta* ('Juan Luis Vives's judgment, taken from his books *On the truth of the Christian faith*, of Muḥammad and his Qur'an, or the law of the Saracens': Bibliander, ii, fol. 2r-v). Bibliander concludes the selections with a fulsome endorsement of their source treatise: not surprising, since Bibliander's encyclopedia and Vives's *De veritate* first came into print in the same year (1543) and at the same press (Ioannes Oporinus, Basel), and *De veritate* was reprinted there in 1544. The attention bestowed on Vives by Bibliander is redoubled in that his *De conditione vitae Christianorum sub Turca* ('On the condition of life of the Christians under the Turk') appears complete in vol. 2 of *Mahumetis Saracenorum*.

Beyond these publications, and apart from the *Opera omnia* collections of 1555 and 1782-90, the complete *De veritate* appeared in print in 1551 (Lyons: Frellonius, reissued 1596), 1568 (Cologne: Horst), 1639

(Leiden: Maire), and not at all in Spain until the appearance of 20th century translations. Both González y González (República de lectores, p. 116) and Moreno Gallego (Recepción hispana, p. 499) comment on the strength of Protestant sympathies among the 16th-century publishers of *De veritate* and in the regions of their work. Meanwhile, González y González, a consummate bibliographer, notes that 'the lone exemplar of this work whose circulation in Spain I have been able to document in the sixteenth century was confiscated by the Inquisition from Dr. Constantino Ponce, who was condemned as a Lutheran in the famed *proceso* of Seville in 1560' (*República de lectores*, pp. 116-17). This is not the only example of Iberian inhospitality toward Vives's works. A German translation, trumpeting in the title the demolition, *inter alia*, of 'Mohammedan, Turkish, Saracen, Tartar, and Arabic' beliefs, appeared in 1571 (J.L. Vives, *Warhafftige Bestätigung des Christenlichen Glaubens*, trans. H. Pataleon, Basel: Brylinger). Moreno Gallego (p. 497) cites the debt of two 16th-century theologians, Melchor Cano and Felipe Duplessis-Mornay, to Vives's *De veritate*, but with no particular emphasis on Book 4. A modern French summary of Book 4 alone (*livre IV, 'Contre la secte de Mahomet'*, 2010) suggests the topicality of the dialogue today. J.M. Belarte Forment (*Verdad de fe*), in his study of *De veritate* in the context of Vives's ideas for reform, and the companion volume translating the *De veritate* (*Juan Luis Vives*, 2010), exemplify the continuing recent stream of Spanish scholarship on Vives's works.

MANUSCRIPTS
No MSS of the work survive.
EDITIONS & TRANSLATIONS
De veritate fidei Christianae, Book 4, ed. and trans. E.V. George, Leiden (in preparation)
De veritate fidei christianae, livre IV, 'Contre la secte de Mahomet', in P. Gaillardon and T. Vigliano (eds), *Mondes humanistes et classiques. Textes présentés par le Groupe Renaissance Âge Classique* (GRAC – UMR 5037), 2010 (web-based, Latin and French, with useful introduction but only brief textual annotation), http://sites.univ-lyon2.fr/lesmondeshumanistes/wp-content/uploads/2010/09/Viv%C3%A8s-livre-IV-du-De-veritate-fidei-christianae.pdf
De veritate fidei christianae. La verdad de la fe cristiana en cinco libros, ed. I. Roca, Valencia, 2010, pp. 499-584 (Spanish trans. of Book 4 by J. Beltrán Serra)
Riber, *Obras completas*, ii, pp. 1597-666 (Spanish trans.)
Majansius, *Ioannis Ludovici Vivis Valentini opera omnia*, viii, pp. 364-427

Io. Lodovici Vivis Valentini opera, 1555, ii, pp. 258-85
Bibliander, *Machumetis Saracenorum principis*, ii, fol. 2r-v (brief excerpts from *De veritate* Book 4, from Majansius, pp. 371-87)
Ioannis Lodovici Vivis Valentini, uiri longe eruditissimi, De veritate fidei Christianae Libri quinque, etc., Basel, 1543, 1544

STUDIES

J.M. Belarte Forment, *Verdad de fe y vida de fe. La reforma humanista de la teología anunciada y realizada por Vives*, Valencia, 2010 (links *De veritate* to Vives's lifelong plan for reform of the disciplines)

M. Colish, 'The *de veritate fidei Christianae* of Juan Luis Vives', in A.A. MacDonald et al. (eds), *Christian humanism. Essays offered to Arjo Vanderjagt on the occasion of his sixtieth birthday*, Leiden, 2009, 1-25, pp. 6, 20-25

E. George, 'Author, adversary, and reader. A view of the *De veritate fidei Christianae*', in C. Fantazzi (ed.), *A companion to Juan Luis Vives*, Leiden, 2008, 315-57

E. George, 'Rules of engagement. The humanist apologetics of Vives' *De veritate fidei Christianae*', *Erasmus of Rotterdam Society Yearbook* 27 (2007) 1-36

González y González, *Una república de lectores*, pp. 115-18

V. Moreno Gallego, *La recepción Hispana de Juan Luis Vives* pp. 496-504

Moreno Gallego, 'Sobre humanismo y fe en el siglo xvi. De veritate fidei Christianae de Luis Vives y sus impresiones', *Humanismo y Cister. Actas de I congreso nacional de humanistas españoles*, León, 1996, 329-53 (information on distribution of copies of *De veritate fidei Christianae*, although the note on p. 340 regarding a separate printing of Book 4 is apparently an inaccurate reference to the brief excerpts printed in Bibliander 1543/1550)

K. Kohut, 'Anmerkungen zu "De veritate fidei christianae"', in C. Strosetzki (ed.), *Juan Luis Vives. Sein Werk und seine Bedeutung für Spanien und Deutschland*, Frankfurt am Main, 1995, 122-34

V. Cantarino, 'La polémica de Luis Vives contra el Islam', *Boletín de la Biblioteca de Menéndez Pelayo* 67 (1991) 5-34

P. Graf, *Luis Vives como apologeta*, trans. J.M. Millas Vallicrosa, Madrid, 1943 (Spanish trans. of Graf's dissertation)

P. Graf, 'Ludwig Vives als Apologet', Freiburg, 1932 (Diss. University of Freiburg)

Edward George

Theodor Bibliander

Theodor Buchmann

DATE OF BIRTH   Possibly 1505
PLACE OF BIRTH   Bischofszell, Switzerland
DATE OF DEATH   26 September 1564
PLACE OF DEATH   Zurich

BIOGRAPHY

Born in the eastern Swiss land of Thurgau around 1505, Theodor Buchmann (who later changed his name to its Greek form, Bibliander) went to Zurich in 1520, where he began learning Greek and Hebrew under Oswald Myconius. He moved to Basel in 1526 to study theology and languages with Konrad Pellikan and Johannes Oecolampadius, but the following year, on the recommendation of Huldrych Zwingli, he travelled to Liegnitz (modern Legnica) in Poland to serve as a schoolmaster. After further journeys he returned to Zurich after Zwingli's death at Kappel in October 1531. Bibliander was appointed Zwingli's successor for the *lectiones publicae*, public lectures on the Old Testament, and for over 30 years he was the principal teacher of Old Testament in Zurich. His weekly lectures in Latin were attended by students, colleagues and educated laypeople.

Bibliander taught the whole of the Old Testament three times, and notes taken from his lectures fill over 30 volumes in the Zentralbibliothek in Zurich. He was an accomplished Hebraist and worked closely with his former teacher, Konrad Pellikan, to offer instruction in grammar and exegesis. He was the preeminent translator of the Bible into Latin in Zurich, playing a major role in the completion of the 1543 *Biblia sacrosancta*.

Bibliander published 24 books, of which the best known today concern Islam and the Qur'an. In his time, however, he was regarded as an expert linguist. In 1548, his *De ratione communi omnium linguarum et literarum* (Zurich) argued for the common heritage of all languages, with Hebrew as the ultimate source. Most of his works were printed in Basel by Johannes Oporinus, with whom he enjoyed close relations. In addition to the exegetical writings, Bibliander published extensive works on theology, such as his *Christiana et catholica doctrina* (1555) and *De mysteriis salutiferae passionis et mortis Iesu* (1555). Bibliander's theological views have been much debated. Without doubt, he opposed Calvin's doctrine of double predestination, but the extent of his alleged universalism awaits full investigation. The arrival of Peter Martyr Vermigli in Zurich in 1556 led to an open quarrel and, ultimately, Bibliander's retirement in 1560. He died four years later from the plague that swept the city.

MAIN SOURCES OF INFORMATION

Secondary

C. Christ-v. Wedel, *Theodor Bibliander (1505-1564). Ein Thurgauer im Gelehrten Zürich der Reformationszeit*. Verlag Neue Zürcher Zeitung, Zurich, 2005

E. Egli, *Analecta Reformatoria, II. Biographien. Bibliander, Ceporin, Bullinger*, Zurich, 1901

WORKS ON CHRISTIAN-MUSLIM RELATIONS

De monarchia totius orbis suprema, legitima et sempiterna, 'On the supreme, legitimate, and eternal monarchy of the whole world'

DATE March 1533
ORIGINAL LANGUAGE Latin

DESCRIPTION

De monarchia was written by Bibliander in 1553 (its full title is *De monarchia totius orbis suprema, legitima et sempiterna: quod regnum est et sacrodotium Messiae. Vaticana patriarchum, prophetarum, apostolorum, Iudaeorum, consilium, Mahumedicorum, Christianorum, et ipsius in primis D. Iesu Christi*), but was never printed. A manuscript of 93 unnumbered sheets in Bibliander's hand is in the Zentralbibliothek in Zurich. It is a preface to another manuscript with which it is bound, *Vaticinia domini Jesu Christi, patriarharum, prophetarum, apostolarum, Christianae ecclesiae doctorum, Judaeorum, Mahumedicorum et Gentilium*. *De monarchia* follows themes developed by Bibliander during the 1540s and 1550s: the unity of all religions and the desire to convert Jews and Muslims to Christianity. The year 1553 was thought by Bibliander to be significant for several reasons, not least because he believed it to be the thousandth lunar year, according to the Islamic calendar, since Muḥammad's emergence as a prophet. Muḥammad was also said to have predicted the destruction of the Qur'an after 1,000 years (Egli, *Analecta Reformatoria*, p. 93).

Bibliander opens the work with two passages from the Bible. He quotes Ezekiel 37:23, 'They will be my people and I shall be their God', by which Bibliander understood the messianic promise that all would be gathered together. The second passage is John 10:16, 'I have other sheep that are not of this sheep pen. I must bring them also.' Bibliander's intention to demonstrate the unity of religions is indicated in his choice of passages from the Bible and by his greeting: 'Theodor Bibliander greets all Christians, Jews, and Muslims wishing them mercy, freedom, and blessings from the Lord God' (Egli, *Analecta Reformatoria*, p. 90). The manuscript contains the introduction and much of the intended book, and is dated 12 March 1553.

Bibliander's goal was to compare the wisdom of the holy books of the faiths on what they had to say about Christ, Antichrist and contemporary times. As Egli has shown, *De monarchia* argues for the universal nature of religion and that God is the God of all. All the nations reveal God's goodness, and Christ is the promised Messiah for all peoples, not just Jews and Christians. Bibliander wanted *De monarchia* to demonstrate to Christians, Jews and Muslims the similarities between their religions. As in his earlier works, he identified Muslims as those who saw Muḥammad as a prophet and regarded the Qur'an as their holy book, including Turks, Saracens and Arabs.

De monarchia refers to the arrival of a world monarch, the Messiah, who would usher in an age of peace, justice and unity. This monarch would rule over a kingdom that included Christians, Jews and Muslims and that would extend to the ends of the earth. By casting aside the Christian doctrine of predestination, Bibliander held out the possibility of reconciliation between the great religions. The arrival of the Messiah was part of his apocalyptic vision of the end times that would result in the defeat of Antichrist and the conversion of all people to Christianity. It was to be the fulfillment of all ancient prophecies.

SIGNIFICANCE

De monarchia belongs to a series of works in which Bibliander expressed his fervent belief that the coming of Christ was at hand, that all the great religions would be summoned together, and that it was the duty of Christians to evangelise Islam. Central to Bibliander's thought was his universalism, which brought upon his head the ire of other Protestant reformers, including John Calvin. All religions, Bibliander argued, shared a consensus on the fundamental principles of salvation. Christ would be the common monarch in whom the similarities between the three faiths would be revealed (Felici, 'Universalism and tolerance', p. 100). Although Bibliander spoke freely of the errors and 'lies' of Muḥammad and the Qur'an, he was adamant that Muslims could be converted to the teaching of Christ, the Messiah. God spoke through the prophets of Judaism, Islam and Christianity, though it was to the last that the full truth was revealed.

EDITIONS & TRANSLATIONS

There are no editions or translations of *De monarchia*.

STUDIES

L. Felici, 'Universalism and tolerance in a follower of Erasmus from Zurich. Theodor Bibliander', in K. Enenkel (ed.), *The reception of Erasmus in the early modern period*, Leiden, 2013, 85-102

K. Vehlow, 'The Swiss reformers Zwingli, Bullinger and Bibliander and their attitude to Islam (1520-1560)', *ICMR* 6 (1995) 229-54

E. Egli, *Analecta Reformatoria, II. Biographien. Bibliander, Ceporin, Bullinger*, Zurich, 1901

Ad nominis Christiani socios consultatio, qua nam ratione Turcarum dira potentio repelli possit ac debeat a populo Christiano, 'Consultation to the people of the Christian name, on the means by which the fierce power of the Turks can and should be repelled by Christian people'

DATE March 1542
ORIGINAL LANGUAGE Latin

DESCRIPTION

Printed in Basel by Nikolaus Brylinger, *Ad nominis* is an octavo volume that runs to 86 pages (Egli, *Analecta Reformatoria*, pp. 50-52). The work opens with a letter from Bibliander to the faithful servants of Jesus Christ, followed by the 'Consultation to those of the Christian name by Theodor Bibliander on how the cruel power of the Turks is to be resisted'. The letter is dated from Zurich, 1542.

In 1536, Bibliander had already sought Christian works on the Qur'an from the Basel printer Oporinus. With the 1541 defeat of the Hungarians by the Ottoman army, he believed, like many others, that the end was near and the Last Judgement was at hand. He accordingly sought to write a short work that would instruct Christians on how to resist the evil forces of the Turks. He wrote with speed, preparing Latin and German editions that were to be available at the spring book fair in Frankfurt. In the end, only the Latin version appeared from Brylinger's press in Basel.

The themes of *Ad nominis* are clear. Bibliander wanted to explain to his readers the nature of and the background to the struggle between Islam and Christianity and, moreover, by what means the enemy could be overcome. Bibliander sought to return to the wisdom of the church fathers, particularly Jerome, for guidance on how to face the opponent. Christians needed to reform their ways, for the advances of the 'Turk' were God's punishment upon the unfaithful churches.

There was little that was original in Bibliander's arguments in this work; as in many works of the time and earlier, Islam is presented as the religion of Antichrist. The book provides a detailed account of Christian attitudes, but with little attention to the nature of Islam, other than to characterise it as heresy. Bibliander does not instruct his readers in *Ad nominis* about Muslim practices. Rather, through continuous references to Jerome and other seminal figures, he maintains that the Christian defeat in Hungary was God's punishment for sin. If the people engaged in prayer, as they are required to do, the Turks would be driven back. Central to *Ad nominis* was Bibiliander's concern to evangelise the Islamic world. He himself had wanted to go to Egypt even to martyrdom, and was only dissuaded by Heinrich Bullinger.

SIGNIFICANCE

Ad nominis was Bibliander's first publication on Christian-Muslim relations, although he had been working on the subject for some time. The work has a strong pastoral quality in that it was written to calm the fears of the people and to present them with a course of action. They were to turn to true religion and Christian devotion. Bibliander draws upon the medieval tradition of anti-Islamic writings as well as a wide body of patristic sources to portray Muslims as agents of the devil and instruments of God's judgement. The book survives in numerous copies and was translated into English as *A godly consultation unto the brethren* (Antwerp: Martin Crom, 1542). The translator is unknown.

EDITIONS & TRANSLATIONS

Ad nominis Christiani socios consultatio qua nam ratione Turcarum dira potentia repelli possit ac debeat a populo Christiano, Basileae: [Nicolaus Brylinger], [1542], http://www.e-rara.ch/bau_1/content/titleinfo/643739

A godly consultation vnto the brethren and companyons of the Christen religyon By what meanes the cruell power of the Turkes, bothe may, and ought for to be repelled of the Christen people, Theodore Bibliander beinge the author...., Basill [i.e. Antwerp]: Radulphe Bonifante [i.e. M. Crom], 1542 (English trans.)

STC (Short Title Catalogue) (2nd ed) 3047 (lists locations of copies, digital version available through Early English Books Online)

STUDIES

C. Moser, *Theodor Bibliander (1505-1564). Annotierte Bibliographie der gedruckten Werke*, Zurich, 2009

Vehlow, 'The Swiss reformers Zwingli, Bullinger and Bibliander'

Egli, *Analecta Reformatoria*

Machumetis Saracenorum principis, eiusque successorum vitae, ac doctrina, ipseque Alcoran, 'The lives and teaching of Muḥammad, leader of the Saracens, and of his successors, and the Qur'an itself'

DATE 1543
ORIGINAL LANGUAGE Latin

DESCRIPTION

The folio edition of *Machumetis Saracenorum* appeared in Basel from the press of Johannes Oporinus in 1543. The project was nearly stopped by the censors in the city, who seized all copies of the text and briefly put Oporinus in prison. Their central objection was that *Machumetis* contained a Latin translation of the Qur'an, which Bibliander claimed to have revised. Only after leading reformers, such as Martin Luther, Philip Melanchthon and Bibliander himself, interceded were the Basel magistrates prepared to allow the work's publication. Owing to the fact that the project was begun and interrupted several times, creating printing problems, the result was seven versions of the first edition in 1543.

Machumetis Saracenorum is three books bound together, running to over 600 folio pages. Oporinus printed the text in double columns with extensive marginal notes. The use of the name of Muḥammad in the title was intended to indicate that the so-called holy text of Islam had a human author (in contrast to the Bible). In the preface, Bibliander writes that the Qur'an contains many heretical things, but that this was all the more reason for Christians to be familiar with the book. Just as classical or Jewish texts were allowed to be printed, so the importance of the Qur'an should be recognised, since it belongs to Christian history. By reading the book, Bibliander writes, Christians will learn how God punishes those who reject the truth and how the faithful suffer at the hands of the Turk; thereby readers will come to revere the Bible all the more.

The work appeared in 1543 without the printer's name or the place of publication on the title page. What was claimed, however, was an imperial privilege for five years. The first volume contains a series of texts by Melanchthon and the editor that preface the Qur'an itself. In the table of contents, the translation is listed as the 'authentic book of the teachings of Mohammad, translated out of Arabic verse'. The term Qur'an is translated as 'collection of precepts' and 'law of the Saracens'. Muḥammad is said to have invented the contents and pretended to have received angelic inspiration.

The first volume of *Machumetis Saracenorum* was the 12th-century set of translations made in Toledo at the request of Peter the Venerable, known as the *Collectio Toletana*, to which Bibliander had added a few items. The *Collectio* included Robert of Ketton's translation of the Qur'an as well as a series of polemical texts. Following the table of contents in Book 1, Bibliander provides an *Apologia* for the edition. The tone is polemical: Islam is poison and it is essential for Christians to be aware of the dangers it poses. Repeating arguments from *Ad nominis*, Bibliander claims that, as the church fathers had not hesitated to study pagan literature, so contemporary Christians should inform themselves about the contents of the Qur'an.

Once again, Islam is a heresy and the Qur'an stands in a long tradition of heretical literature. Bibliander believed that Muḥammad and Islam belonged to the history of Christianity. Muḥammad was a prophet, though a false one, and if one was to understand the work of Antichrist one had to know his words in the Qur'an. Bibliander attributes the success of Islam in Arabic-speaking lands to the weakness and errors of Christians in these lands, whose faith was superficial. Another prominent theme found in all of Bibliander's writings on Islam was his eagerness to help missions to the Islamic world. Knowledge of the Qur'an, he believed, was essential to the success of these missions.

Bibliander claimed that the Ketton translation of the Qur'an had been emended by consulting Arabic and Latin manuscripts, but this seems somewhat unlikely. At least, Bibliander himself could not have carried out such scholarship as his Arabic was rudimentary. He did, however, manage to produce 25 pages of textual variants. He claims that he was not satisfied with the Ketton translation, but was compelled to use it for want of an alternative, and he made some significant alterations to the text. He removed the marginal notes from the *Collectio* and replaced them with his own, which were largely descriptive and non-polemical. As Miller has noted ('Theodor Bibliander's Machumetis Saracenorum', p. 246), Bibliander was eager to draw attention in these notes to parallels between the Qur'an and the Bible. At times, he was willing to comment positively on the qur'anic text, and the moderate spirit of his marginal notes contrasts with the polemical character of the prefatory material.

The first book begins with texts by contemporary writers, and then presents the Qur'an surrounded by the *Collectio*. Bibliander uses the writings of fellow Reformers together with patristic and medieval authors to justify his project. In two of the seven variant volumes, a preface by Martin Luther appears, in which he equates the Turks with the Jews as servants of the devil. There is, according to Luther, no better way to defend against the Turks than to study their law book.

The second volume of *Machumetis Saracenorum* is constituted by theological texts gathered by Bibliander, including works by Nicholas of Cusa and Ludovico Vives, and most importantly the *Confutatio* of Riccoldo da Monte di Croce. The third volume is a history of the 'Saracens', drawing for its sources on the better Turkish books of the 15th and 16th centuries.

The 1550 edition of *Machumetis Saracenorum* was significantly altered by the inclusion of important contemporary texts: *De rebus Turcarum* (1540) by Christoph Richer, and the bestselling *Türkenbüchlein* of the 16th century by Bartholomew Georgijevitz. Richer had been an ambassador in Constantinople, and his work was an extremely rich account of Turkish culture.

SIGNIFICANCE

Bibliander's edition of the Qur'an appeared at a moment when Europeans believed that the Ottoman armies might overwhelm them. In Zurich, his colleague Konrad Gesner was preparing his *Bibliotheca universalis* to record for posterity what might be lost should Europe be conquered. Bibliander shared with others a strong sense that events in Hungary presaged the Last Judgement, and, as in *Ad nominis*, there is a strong apocalyptic tone to his edition of the Qur'an.

Gregory Miller has persuasively argued that Bibliander's intention was to produce an encyclopedia on Islam. To this end, he gathered all the information he could and sought to put together the most authoritative ancient, medieval and contemporary sources. The translation of the Qur'an itself, he claimed, was the best possible, based on rigorous philological work. All in all, it was what Christians needed in order to defend themselves; they must dispel their ignorance of Islam, the great enemy. In its time, *Machumetis Saracenorum* was regarded as a major scholarly work with invaluable information, though such was the thirst for knowledge of both Islam and Muslims that Bibliander's volume was soon overtaken. Nevertheless, it was reprinted in the 17th century (1617), and Bibliander's extensive preface, 'Apologia pro editione Alcorani' appeared in 1638.

Bibliander did not possess much Arabic and his edition was largely an unaltered version of Ketton. In his 'Apologia' Bibliander provides powerful arguments for why the Qur'an should be printed and why Christians should be familiar with its contents, but his arguments are not original. He treats Islam as a heresy, associating it with Nestorianism, and the 'Turks', he argues, were agents of the Antichrist. Muḥammad was a fraud, and the Qur'an is largely a book of laws, instructions without divine inspiration. For the most part, Bibliander marshals familiar forces and well-known views.

Nevertheless, the achievement of this polemical work is remarkable. Bibliander brought to his edition the humanist principles of textual scholarship he had employed to great effect on the Bible. He was an extremely accomplished Hebraist and his philological work, by the standards of the day, was impressive. In his marginal notes for the Qur'an, as Miller shows, he demonstrated a distinctly moderate attitude towards the text, often looking for points of contact with Christian scripture. Although he largely remained within the mental confines of his age, there are signs in Bibliander of a changing view towards Islam.

MANUSCRIPTS

Bibliander's lectures and letters have survived, but there are no known MSS of the work on the Qur'an.

EDITIONS & TRANSLATIONS

A modern copy of the *Apologia* in French is found in *Le Coran à la Renaissance. Plaidoyer pour une traduction, Introduction, traduction et notes de H. Lamarque*, Toulouse, 2007 (French trans.)

A.J. Lappin (ed.), *Alchoran Latinus*, Rome, 2011 (based on the 1543 and 1550 editions)

Bibliander's 'Apologia pro editione Alcorani' printed in Johann Fabricius, *Muhammedis testamentum*, Rostock: Michael Meder für Johann Hallervord, 1638

Machumetis saracenorum principis, eiusque successorum vitae, doctrina, ac ipse Alcoran: his adiunctae sunt Confutationes multoru., & quidem probatiss. authorum, Arabum, Graecorum, & Latinoru., unà cum doctiss. uiri Philippi Melanchthonis praemonitione: adiuncti sunt etiam De Turcarum, siue Sarracenorum / haec omnia in unum volumne redacta sunt, opera & studio Theodori Bibliandri, s.n., 1550

Machumetis Sarracenorum principis vita ac doctrina omnis, quae & Ismahelitarum lex, & Alcoranum dicitur: ex Arabica lingua ante 400 annos in Latinam translata, nuncque demum ad gloriam Domini Iesu, & ad Christianae fidei confirmationem, doctorum ac piorum aliquot virorum, nostraeque a deo religionis orthodoxae antistitum studio & authoritate, velut è tenebris in lucem protracta atque edita: quo volumine perlecto, pius & studiosus lector fatebitur, librum nullum potuisse vel opportunè vel tempestivè magis edi hoc rerum Christianarum & Turcicarum statu. Adiectae quoque sunt Annotationes, Confutationes, Sarracenorum ac rerum Turcicarum à 1400 annis ad nostra usq, tempora memorabilium historiae, ex probatissimis autoribus tum Arabibus, tum Latinis & Graecis, quorum catalogum versa in singulis tomis pagina prima reperies. Item, Philippi Melanchthonis, viri doctissimi praemonitio ad lectorem, cum primis pia & erudita. Theodori Bibliandri, sacrarum literarum in Ecclesia Tigurina professoris, viri doctissimi pro Alcorani editione Apologia, multa eruditione & pietate referta, lectuque dignissima: quippe in qua multis ac validiss. argumentis & vitilitigatorum calumniis respondetur, & quam non solum utilis, se & necessaria hoc praesertim seculo sit Alcorani editio, Basel: Johannes Oporin and Nikolaus Brylinger, 1543, http://www.e-rara.ch/bes_1/content/titleinfo/1696541

STUDIES

G. Miller, 'Theodor Bibliander's *Machumetis Saracenorum principis eiusque successorum vitae, doctrina ac ipse alcoran* (1543) as the sixteenth century "Encyclopedia" of Islam', *ICMR* 24 (2013) 241-54

L. Felici, 'Una nuova immagine dell'Islam (e del Cristianesimo) nell'Europa del XVI secolo', in G. Abbattista (ed.), *Encountering otherness. Diversities and transcultural experiences in early modern European culture*, Trieste, 2011, 43-66

Moser, *Theodor Bibliander*

J. Ehmann, *Luther, Türken und Islam. Eine Untersuchung zum Türken- und Islambild Martin Luthers*, Gütersloh, 2008

T. Burman, *Reading the Qur'an in Latin Christendom 1140-1560*, Philadelphia PA, 2007

C. Christ-v. Wedel, *Theodor Bibliander (1505-1564). Ein Thurgauer im Gelehrten Zürich der Reformationszeit. Verlag Neue Zürcher Zeitung*, Zurich, 2005

V. Segesvary, *L'Islam et la Réforme. Etude sur l'attitude des Réformateurs zuruchois envers l'islam, 1510-1550*, San Francisco CA, 1998

H. Bobzin, *Der Koran im Zeitalter der Reformation. Studien zur Frühgeschichte der Arabistik und Islamkunde in Europa*, Berlin, 1995

H. Bobzin, 'Über Theodor Bibliander Arbeit am Koran (1542/43)', *Zeitschrift der Deutschen Morgenländischen Gesellschaft* 186 (1986) 347-63

J. Pfister, 'Das Türkenbüchlein Theodor Biblianders', *Theologische Zeitschrift* 9 (1953) 438-54

M. Köhler, *Melanchthon und der Islam, Ein Beitrag zur Klärung des Verhältnisses zwischen Christentum und Fremdreligionen in der Reformationszeit*, Leipzig, 1938

Egli, *Analecta Reformatoria*

Bruce Gordon

Michael Agricola

DATE OF BIRTH About 1510
PLACE OF BIRTH Torsby, Pernaja, SE Finland
DATE OF DEATH 9 April 1557
PLACE OF DEATH Uusikirkko/Kuolemajärvi, Karelia (now Russia)

BIOGRAPHY

Michael Agricola, reformer, bishop and father of the Finnish literary language, was the son of a wealthy farmer. After school in Viipuri and Turku, he was ordained priest and became an assistant to Bishop Skytte. In 1536-39, he studied at the University of Wittenberg under Luther, Melanchthon and others. Back in Turku, he was rector of the local school, again bishop's assistant, and from 1554 to 1557 was bishop of Turku.

He started the Lutheran reformation in Finland and wrote a considerable body of work to introduce and propagate its leading principles, including the very first Finnish translation of the New Testament and parts of the Old Testament, an ABC book, three liturgical books and a prayer book – altogether about 2,400 printed pages. In 1557, he participated in the delegation to negotiate a peace treaty in Moscow, and on his way back to Finland he fell ill and died.

MAIN SOURCES OF INFORMATION

Primary
P. Juusten, *Catalogus et ordinaria successio episcoporum finlandiensium*, ed. S. Heininen, Helsinki, 1988

Secondary
S. Heininen, *Mikael Agricola. Elämä ja teokset*, Helsinki, 2007
S. Heininen, *Mikael Agricola ja Erasmus Rotterdamilainen* (*Suomalaisen kirjallisuuden seuran julkaisu* 192), Helsinki, 2006
S. Heininen and M. Heikkilä, *Kirchengeschichte Finnlands*, Göttingen, 2002
J. Gummerus, *Michael Agricola, der Reformer Finnlands, sein Leben und sein Werk*, Helsinki, 1941

WORKS ON CHRISTIAN-MUSLIM RELATIONS

Rucouskiria Bibliasta, 'Prayer Book from the Bible'

DATE 1544
ORIGINAL LANGUAGE Finnish

DESCRIPTION

This most original among the works of Agricola was mainly intended for priests so that they could conduct services in Finnish (its full title is *Rucouskiria Bibliasta, se on, molemista Testamentista, Messuramatusta, ia muusta monesta, jotca toysella polella Luetellan, cokoonpoymettu Somen Turussa*, 'Prayer Book from the Bible, i.e. put together from both Testaments, Missal [Aboense] and many others, listed on the other side, in Turku of Finland'). It contains prayers, poems, psalms and liturgical texts collected and translated from various sources (e.g. the Bible, Luther, Erasmus) and composed by the author himself. It contains 877 pages in octavo and 17 woodcut illustrations.

On fol. 269v (p. 638 in *Mikael Agricolan teokset*) appears the text: *Turcki tachtopi Mahometin henen Epeiumalans sinun rackan poias Jesusen Christusen sijahan asetta Jonga tosin hen pilcapi kielden etteij hen ole totinen Jumala ia todhistapi henen Mahometins palio ylemeijsen ja paraman oleuan* ('The Turk desires to put Muḥammad, his false god, in the place of your dear son Jesus the Christ, whom he derides, denying that he is the true God, and claims that his Muḥammad is far superior and better').

In two other passages (fols 268r and 269r) *Turcit* are mentioned alongside the devil, the pope and Antichrist. Other shorter passages mention the Turk and one refers to Muḥammad.

SIGNIFICANCE

The idea of Muḥammed being worshipped as God by Muslims is common in medieval European literature, and in Agricola's literary sources; he probably adopted it during his stay in Wittenberg. Evidently, he also learned and adopted the great antipathy shown by Luther towards the Turks and Islam. These short passages contain the very first mention of Islam in Finnish literature.

EDITIONS & TRANSLATIONS

The original edition was printed by Anund Lauritzson in Stockholm, November 1544, https://www.doria.fi/handle/10024/43445).

Mikael Agricolan teokset, vol. 1. *Abckiria, Rucouskiria*, Porvoo, 1931; new edition, Porvoo, 1987 (collected works of Michael Agricola)

STUDIES

Heininen, *Mikael Agricola*, pp. 221-29

J. Gummerus, *Mikael Agricolan rukouskirja ja sen lähteet* [Michael Agricola's Prayer Book and its sources] (*Suomen kirkkohistoriallinen seura* 44/1-3), Helsinki, 1941-55

Klaus Karttunen

John Bale

Johan Bale

DATE OF BIRTH 21 November 1495
PLACE OF BIRTH Covehith, Suffolk
DATE OF DEATH 15 November 1563
PLACE OF DEATH Canterbury

BIOGRAPHY

Born in Suffolk in 1495, John Bale began his studies at Cambridge in 1514. Despite the number of Protestant reformers in Cambridge at that time, he remained Catholic as a young man, becoming prior of a Carmelite friary around 1530. He moved to a priory in Ipswich in 1533, and soon afterwards was put into contact with a number of Protestant reformers who persuaded him to convert to reformist doctrines sometime in the early 1530s. By 1536, he was a priest in Suffolk, where he was questioned and attacked for preaching against Catholic rituals. In 1537, he was imprisoned for his hard-line reformist stance, and then rescued by Henry VIII's advisor, Thomas Cromwell. He was also married later that year.

After Cromwell's execution in 1540, Bale and his wife fled to Antwerp, where he wrote tracts and biblical exegeses, including *The image of bothe churches* in 1545. He returned to England in 1548, but moved to Ireland in 1552 to become bishop of Ossory. When Mary I became queen in 1553, he again retreated into exile, this time to Wesel. After returning to England in 1559, he became a canon of Canterbury in 1560, where he eventually died in 1563.

Bale wrote a series of polemical Protestant dramas in the late 1530s, the most famous of which is *King Johan*. While most of his drama and prose features Protestant attacks against Catholicism, he also derides Islam in several plays, tracts and church histories, often calling the Pope and the 'Turk' twinned evils threatening the 'true' reformed Christian Church.

In the allegorical *King Johan*, the character Veritas accuses Clergy of various crimes, concluding, 'I abhorre to shewe your doynges/The Turkes I dare saye are a thousand tymes better than yow' (p. 89). In the morality play *Three laws*, the character Infidelitas refuses the teachings of Moses' law, saying, 'We must have one God, and worshypp hym alone?/Marry, that in dede wolde make a Turke to grone' (p. 91). Before he is finally vanquished, Infidelitas proclaims his victory over God's three laws by calling for the burning of Evangelium, exclaiming, 'By the messe, I laugh to se ho thys gere doth wurke./He is lyke of them to have nomore grace than a Turke' (p. 113).

Bale's non-dramatic prose is generally divided into two types: polemics that accuse English bishops of being no better than Catholics, and vitriol against the Catholics themselves. In *Yet a course at the Romysh foxe*, Bale argues that the current religion in England is so 'clogged with your heythnysh rytes, that neyther Iewe nor Saracene, Arabyane nor Turke wyl come vnto owr faythe' (78v-79r). When accusing Catholics of altering Christ's commandment for the institution of the Eucharist, he adds 'No saracene nor Turke dare change one Iote of Mahometes lawe (whych ys but a wretched thynge) and yow spare not to alter the sett purpose of the eternall god' (84r). His *Epistle exhortatorye of an Englysh Christyane* tells the English bishops that they do their duties with 'lesse Christen equite and pyte than eyther Saracene or Turke, Jewe or Pagane' (9r). *The apology of Johan Bale agaynste a ranke Papyst* says that anyone making a papist vow is just as ungodly as 'he that hath professed the faythe of a Iewe or the religion of a Turke' (XIr). When Bale chronicles church abuses in his *Actes of Englysh votaryes*, he compares them to 'like examples among the Turks'. These abuses include buggery, not taking Christ as born of a virgin, and making knaves into saints (17r). His biographical *Vocacyon of John Bale* thanks God for deliverance from a host of enemies including 'Mahumetes' and 'Turkes' as well as devils, heretics, and popes (48v).

In *The pageant of popes*, a chronicle attempting to reveal the spuriousness of the claims of popes to be Peter's successors, Bale writes of the time of Pope Boniface III (d. 607) that 'Papistrie and Mahumets religion began bothe together at one time, which corrupted, darkened, and weakened the doctrine of the sonne of God in many regions' (38v). He says that during the time of Severinus II (d. 640), 'Mahumet recited the *Alcoran*, so that (saieth hee) the Egles three heades awaked all at ones' (41r), and that during the time of Pope Clement VI (d. 1352) 'at length it came to passe that the Empyre being thus decayed, the Turke inuaded the Church of Christ, & destroyed it wonderfullye, and it is by the especial grace of God, that *Mahomets* blasphemye doth not wyth fyre and sworde rage ouer all Christendome' (137r-v). Turks and Saracens are also mentioned in his biographies of various other popes (40v, 87r, 98r-v, 114r, 139r-v, 163v, 164r, 194r-v).

MAIN SOURCES OF INFORMATION

Primary
The primary source on the life of John Bale is his own autobiography:
J. Bale, *The vocacyon of Johan Bale to the bishoprick of Ossorie in Irelande his persecucions in the same & finall delyveraunce*, Wesel, 1553
J. Bale, *The vocacyon of Johan Bale*, ed. P. Happé and J.N. King, Binghamton NY, 1990

In addition to *The image of bothe churches* (see below), Bale expresses his thoughts on Islam in the following texts:
J. Bale, *Yet a course at the Romysh foxe*, Zurich, 1543
J. Bale, *The epistle exhortatorye of an Englysh Christyane*, Basel, 1544
J. Bale, *The actes of Englysh votaryes*, Wesel, 1546; London, 1548, 1551
J. Bale, *A comedy concernynge thre laws*, Wesel, c. 1548
J. Bale, *The apology of Iohan Bale agaynste a ranke papist*, London, 1550
J. Bale, *The pageant of popes*, ed. and trans. (from the original Latin) John Studley, London, 1574
J. Bale, *King John* (c. 1538), ed. J.H.P. Pafford, Oxford, 1931
J. Bale, *King Johan*, ed. B.B. Adams, San Marino CA, 1969
J. Bale, 'King Johan', in *The complete plays of John Bale*, ed. P. Happé, Cambridge, 1985, i, 29-99
J. Bale, 'Three laws', in *The complete plays of John Bale*, ed. P. Happé, Cambridge, 1986, ii, 65-124

Secondary
Key texts on John Bale's life and thought, as well as secondary works on his views on Islam, include:
R.O. Smith, *More desired than our owne salvation. The roots of Christian Zionism*, Oxford, 2013, pp. 55-59, 61-66, 72, 79, 92, 96, 115, 120, 187
B. Gourley, 'Carnivalising apocalyptic history in John Bale's *King Johan* and *Three laws*', in K. Eisenbilchler (ed.), *Renaissance medievalisms*, Toronto, 2009, 169-90
A. Hunt, *The drama of coronation. Medieval ceremony in Early Modern England*, Cambridge, 2008, pp. 77-110
J. Howard and P. Strohm, 'The imaginary "Commons"', *Journal of Medieval and Early Modern Studies* 37 (2007) 549-77
C. Shrank. 'John Bale and reconfiguring the "medieval" in Reformation England', in *Reading the medieval in Early Modern England*, ed. G. McMullan and D. Matthews, Cambridge, 2007, 179-92
J. Burton, *Traffic and turning. Islam and English drama, 1579-1624*, Newark NJ, 2005, pp. 87, 128-29
J.M. Evenson, 'Judaism, Islam, and English Reformation literature', Ann Arbor MI, 2005 (PhD Diss. University of Michigan), pp. 12, 30, 45, 62-64, 79

T. Betteridge, 'Staging Reformation authority. John Bale's *King Johan* and Nicholas Udall's *Respublica*', *Reformation and Renaissance Review* 3 (2000) 34-58

J.D. Cox, *The Devil and the sacred in English drama, 1350-1642*, Cambridge, 2000, pp. 82-96

P.W. White, 'Reforming mysteries' end. A new look at Protestant intervention in English provincial drama', *Journal of Medieval and Early Modern Studies* 29 (1999) 121-87

P. Happé, *John Bale*, Amherst, 1996

C. McEachern, '"A whore at first blush seemeth only a woman". John Bale's *Image of both churches* and the terms of religious difference in the early English Reformation', *Journal of Medieval and Renaissance Studies* 25 (1995) 244-69

A. Hadfield, *Literature, politics, and national identity. Reformation to Renaissance*, Cambridge, 1994, pp. 51-76

D.S. Kastan. '"Holy wurdes" and "slypper wit". John Bale's *King Johan* and the poetics of propaganda', in P. Herman (ed.), *Rethinking the Henrican era. Essays on early Tudor texts and contexts*, Urbana IL, 1994, 267-82

P.W. White, *Theatre and Reformation. Protestantism, patronage, and playing in Tudor England*, Cambridge, 1993, pp. 1-2, 12-39

G. Walker, *Plays of persuasion. Drama and politics at the court of Henry VIII*, Cambridge, 1991, pp. 169-215

R. Pineas. 'The polemical drama of John Bale', in W.R. Elton and W.B. Long (eds), *Shakespeare and the dramatic tradition. Essays in honor of S.F. Johnson*, Newark NJ, 1989, 194-210

L.P. Fairfield, *John Bale. Mythmaker for the English Reformation*, West Lafayette IN, 1976

D. Bevington, *Tudor drama and politics*, Cambridge MA, 1968, pp. 97-105

T. Blatt, *The plays of John Bale. A study of ideas, techniques, and style*, Copenhagen, 1968

R. Pineas, 'John Bale's nondramatic works of religious controversy', *Studies in the Renaissance* 9 (1962) 218-33

H. McCusker, *John Bale. Dramatist and antiquary*, Bryn Mawr PA, 1942

B.P. Smith, *Islam in English literature*, Beirut, 1939, p. 17

WORKS ON CHRISTIAN-MUSLIM RELATIONS

The image of bothe churches

DATE 1545
ORIGINAL LANGUAGE English

DESCRIPTION

John Bale wrote *The image of bothe churches*, a polemical exposition of the Book of Revelation, while in political exile in Antwerp in 1545. It was reprinted several times throughout the 16th century and was one of Bale's most popular works. It is 290 pages long in its first printing, and 393 pages in its 19th-century edition. *The image of bothe churches* (in full, *The image of bothe churches after the most wonderfull and heauenly Reuelation of sainct Iohn the Euangelist, contayning a very fruitfull exposition or paraphrase vpon the same. Wherin it is conferred vvith the other scriptures, and most auctorised histories*) argues that the Book of Revelation is a mirror of Church history, demonstrating that, after Constantine, Christ's 'true Church' was obscured by the evils of Catholicism. Around 40 pages throughout the work discuss Islam by referring to 'Mahomet', Turks or Saracens. In most cases, the commentary likens Muslims to Catholics and argues that both are manifestations of various apocalyptic adversaries mentioned in Revelation. Catholics and Muslims are figured as the two great enemies of the 'true Church'.

Edward VI's archbishop, Thomas Cranmer, asked Bale to write an attack on Catholic ceremony and ritual in order to further the campaign of Protestant reform in England. Bale's response to this commission was the *The image of bothe churches*, which sees the pope, representing Catholicism, and the Turk, representing Islam, as the twin kingdoms of the Antichrist (the Gog and Magog of Revelation). The preface offers a comparison between elements of Catholicism and Islam (which Bale names the 'pretenses of the Romysh Pope and *Mahomete*') in order to demonstrate the threat posed by both to the 'true' religion of early Protestantism (pp. 261-62 in the Christmas edition; spellings here follow Bale's 1570 edition). The preface demonstrates that Bale had some knowledge of Islam, as it correctly describes many Muslim practices: 'they washe them selves oft, they frequent their temples, they pray five tymes in the day, they reverently inclyne, they lye prostrate upon the grounde, they fervently call to God, they are temperate in feedyng, not curious in theyr buyldynges, they abstayne from wyne, they abhorre Idolles, they hate them that are proude, and commende all sobernesse' (p. 262). Bale warns that Muslims, like Catholics, thus appear virtuous but are in fact blasphemous agents of the devil: 'Yet will they have their owne filthy lawes preferred above them, the Pope his execrable decrees, *Mahomete* his wicked *Alchorane*, els will they murther men without measure. Thus though they outwardly appeare very vertuous yet are they the malignaunt ministers of Sathan' (p. 263). As Jennie Evenson explains, then, Bale's 'description is at best a combination of fact and fantasy: he freely intermixes points of religious doctrine with commonplace accusations against Muslims as those who are prone to violence' (Evenson, *Judaism, Islam, and English Reformation literature*, p. 12).

The body of *The image of bothe churches* follows a similar format throughout: it quotes several verses from the Book of Revelation, paraphrases them line by line, and then offers lengthy interpretive commentary on them. Several references to the Antichrist are interpreted as partially Muslim. Referring to Revelation 3, which warns the congregation of Philadelphia against temptation, Bale interprets 'thys fierce temptation' as the Antichrist, defined as 'Mahomet standing in the way of sinners, and the Romish Pope sitting in the most pestilent seate of errours', who he says will come upon the world and teach devilish doctrine, damning people's souls (p. 291). The beast coming out of the bottomless pit in Revelation 11 is also the Antichrist, who represents both the pope and also 'Mahomite with his dotyng doucipers in Affrica, and so foorth in Asia & India, all beastly, carnall, and wicked in their doings' (p. 392). He reiterates the idea that the Antichrist is both 'Mahomet' and the pope in the same body when interpreting the wounded head in Revelation 13:3 (p. 426). Explaining the two-horned beast of Revelation 13:11, Bale says that it has the same powers to deceive and teach idolatry as the pope and 'Mahomet in Barbary, of Turkye' (p. 439). When Revelation 20 describes Satan rallying the kingdoms of Gog and Magog for a final battle, Bale labels these nations as the Catholics and the Muslims: 'So shall ye well perceive the holy ghost to meane none other hereby this Gog and Magoge, but the Romish Pope & Mahomete, with their blasphemous and wicked generations' (p. 571). He defines the reach of Magog/Islam as 'what the Turke wyth Mahomets host' has done in 'Egipt, Greece, Palestyne, Hierusalem, Bulgary, in the borders of Italy & Spayne, at the Rhodes, [and] in the kingdom of Hungarye' (p. 574).

Bale's commentaries also often associate various events in the Book of Revelation with historical moments in the history of Islam, Judaism and Catholicism. Interpreting and historicising the fourth seal in Revelation 6:7, Bale says that it represents the time of Pope Boniface III: 'Mahomet boasted hym selfe to be the great Prophete and messenger of GOD.' Bale explains that this is when the Jews took up their Talmud, the 'Saracens their Alchorane', and the bishops their popish laws. After this time, there followed the establishment of 'sectes of perdicion', including those under 'Mahomet the false Prophet in Afryca' (p. 319). The fourth angel in Revelation 8:12 represents for Bale the time when 'the false Hipocrites and the Antichristes so prevayled more and more under Mahomet and the romish pope that Christianitie and spirituall holynesse was turned into supersticious sects' (p. 347). When the seven heads of the Antichrist become seven mountains in Revelation 17:9, Bale explains that five of these heads are the monarchy of Rome. As the Papacy grew, he continues, the Greeks separated from Rome and became 'in possession of Mahomets sect', causing the people of the East, too, to fall from Christ (p. 502).

Bale also suggests that there may be hope for both Jews and Muslims, whom he finds more redeemable than Catholics. When Revelation 7 refers to people sealed by the sure token of faith, including the tribes of Israel, Bale discusses the ways in which Jews may be converted to Christianity and saved. He then adds that Muslims may also hope to be saved: 'Not unlyke is it in this age, but that the true prechers and learned men, compelled also by tiraunts to decline to the Saracens and Turkes, may in lyke maner be accepted of them in spight of the Romishe deuill and his Church, and so converte them to the true Christen faith, whiche they before abhorred' (p. 336).

For Bale, the act of converting these Saracens to Christianity is especially noble. When discussing the heavenly city described in the final chapter of Revelation, Bale suggests that there is a special place in heaven for Christians living among Muslims: 'So largely doth he rewarde them of the East that truly beleeveth in Christ, as of any other quarters els, and so highly doth he esteeme them. So deere unto him are those good Christians that dwell amonge the Sarizens, Turkes, and Iewes, as are they which dwell in the middest of Christendome' (p. 601).

In deriding Islam in order to help him denounce Catholicism, Bale echoes sentiments he expresses in several earlier works, including the plays *Three laws* and *King Johan*. *King Johan* also suggests that the 'Turk' is less evil than the corrupt clergy of the Catholic Church (p. 89). In his prose tracts, which either attack Catholics directly or berate (Protestant) English bishops for being too 'popish', Bale unfavourably likens Islam and Catholicism, as in *The image*. He mentions 'Turks', 'Mahomet', and 'Saracens' in a similar vein in *Yet a course at the Romysh foxe*, *Epistle exhortatorye of an Englysh Christyane*, *The apology of Johan Bale agaynste a ranke Papyst*, *Actes of Englysh votaryes*, *Vocacyon of John Bale*, and *The pageant of popes*.

Many of the ideas in *The image of bothe churches* can be found in the works of other Protestant and proto-Protestant theologians. The idea that the Antichrist of Revelation may be associated with the pope was not original to Bale, and was expressed by John Wyclif (1320-84) and Francis Lambert (1486-1530), and echoed later by Bale's friend John Foxe (1516-87). Martin Luther (1483-1536) had identified the pope and the Turk as the two heads of the Antichrist, as did John Calvin (1509-64). Using the Bible as a way to understand history (rather than using the interpretive four-fold exegesis popular with Catholic theologians in the Middle Ages) was an innovation of Martin Luther's that inspired Bale in *The image*. Both Luther and Bale saw biblical exegesis as a way of creating a Protestant historiography, infusing 'secular history with a divine significance' (Smith, *More desired*, p. 54).

SIGNIFICANCE

The image of bothe churches, printed several times in Antwerp and London between 1545 and 1570, was Bale's most influential work and was widely read by English Protestant reformers. It served as a source of biblical exegesis of the Book of Revelation throughout the 16th century. Calling *The image* Bale's most influential publication, Andrew Hadfield says that part of its legacy is to illustrate 'the necessity that Protestantism be a national religion whatever internationalist ideology its adherents may have espoused' (Hadfield, *Literature*, p. 59).

While yoking together the 'Turk and the Pope' as twin evils of the apocalypse was not Bale's innovation, the pervasiveness of that idea in *The image* helped to popularise it and caused other theologians, including John Foxe, to make it a prevalent notion in later Tudor England. Evenson argues that '*Image* succinctly demonstrates a trend that became popular in Protestant writing. Some polemicists, like Bale, deployed tropes of Muslim and Jewish ceremonies to disparage Catholicism' (Evenson, 'Judaism, Islam, and English Reformation literature', p. 63). In addition, Bale's reimagining of Church history and Islam's place in that history found its way into Foxe's hugely influential *Actes and monuments*.

Bale also inspired a trend for some polemists to prefer Muslim ceremonies to Catholic ones. For example, Thomas Cartwright argues in *A replye to an answere made of M. Doctor Whitgifte* (1573) that 'it were more safe for us to conform our indifferent ceremonies to the Turks which are far off, than to the papists, which are so near' (quoted in Evenson, 'Judaism, Islam, and English Reformation literature', p. 64).

Robert Smith argues that one of *The image*'s lasting influences was the way in which, by being so intensely anti-Catholic and anti-Islamic, it caused Protestants to favour Jews over any other form of religious alterity, seeing them as especially favoured by God and ripe for conversion to the true Church. This Judaic favouritism helped sow the seeds for modern-day Zionism. Smith argues, 'it was through Bale's eschatological vision – a discourse formed within an intensely anti-Catholic and anti-Islamic milieu – that Jews, quite unbeknownst to themselves, were assigned a central place in the apocalyptic hope of Protestants in England and, later, in the United States' (Smith, *More desired*, p. 59).

Leslie Fairfield argues that *The image of bothe churches* gave to 'the English consciousness in the sixteenth and seventeenth centuries that belief in the Book of Revelation [is] the key par excellence for understanding the past, the present, and the future' (Fairfield, *John Bale*, p. 155). Revelation continues to have a central place in the theology of far-right American Evangelical movements, and one might see modern-day fringe associations of President Barack Obama (sometimes falsely labelled as a practising Muslim) with the Antichrist of Revelation as having their roots in Bale's bilious anti-Islamic interpretation of the Bible's final book.

EDITIONS & TRANSLATIONS

J. Bale, 'The image of both churches', in H. Christmas (ed.), *Select works of John Bale*, Cambridge, 1849, pp. 249-640

J. Bale, *The image of both churches*, London, 1570

J. Bale, *The ymage of both churches*, London, 1550

J. Bale, *The image of both churches*, London, c. 1550

J. Bale, *The image of bothe churches*, London, 1548

J. Bale, *The image of bothe churches*, Antwerp, c. 1545

STUDIES

R.O. Smith, *More desired than our owne salvation. The roots of Christian Zionism*, Oxford, 2013

J. Burton, *Traffic and turning: Islam and English drama, 1579-1624*, Newark NJ, 2005

Evenson, 'Judaism, Islam, and English Reformation literature'

P. Happé, *John Bale*, Amherst MA, 1996

C. McEachern, '"A whore at first blush seemeth only a woman". John Bale's *Image of both churches* and the terms of religious difference in the early English Reformation', *Journal of Medieval and Renaissance Studies* 25 (1995) 244-69

A. Hadfield, *Literature, politics, and national identity. Reformation to Renaissance*, Cambridge, 1994

J.N. King, *English Reformation literature. The Tudor origins of the Protestant traditions*, Princeton NJ, 1982

L.P. Fairfield, *John Bale. Mythmaker for the English Reformation*, West Lafayette IN, 1976

R. Pineas, 'John Bale's nondramatic works of religious controversy', *Studies in the Renaissance* 9 (1962) 218-33

Katherine Steele Brokaw

Peter Ashton

DATE OF BIRTH Unknown
PLACE OF BIRTH England
DATE OF DEATH 1548
PLACE OF DEATH England

BIOGRAPHY

Very little is known about Peter Ashton, aside from his translation of the *Turkes chronicles*. He may have been the same Peter Ashton who was prebendary of Lincoln from 1542 to 1548. If that is the case, he was born around the turn of the 16th century, and was the son of Peter Ashton, who lived in Old Weston, Huntingdonshire. He held two degrees from Cambridge, a BA earned in 1516 and an MA earned in 1519. From 1523 to 1528, he was a fellow of Christ's College. He then went on to become rector of Tillingham, Essex, from 1540 to 1548, and also at Houghton, Huntingdonshire, from 1537 to 1548. He may otherwise have been the Peter Ashton who obtained a licence to practise medicine in 1533, and became a fellow of the College of Physicians in 1542, and a censor there in 1543.

Although details of Peter Ashton's life are not known with any certainty, we can infer from his writing that he was well-educated, and had studied philosophy, history and Latin. This would be consistent with the suppositions given above regarding his identity as a Peter Ashton who either attended Cambridge or qualified as a physician.

MAIN SOURCES OF INFORMATION

Primary
P. Ashton, *A shorte treatise upon the Turkes chronicles*, London, 1546 (STC 11899) [translation of Paolo Giovio, *Commentario delle cose de' Turchi* using the Latin translation by Franciscus Niger]

Secondary
D.K. Money, art. 'Ashton, Peter (d. 1548)', *ODNB*, Oxford, 2004, ii, p. 682
A.H. Bullen, art. 'Ashton, Peter', *DNB*, London, 1901, i, p. 650
Society for the Diffusion of Useful Knowledge, art. 'Ashton, or Assheton, Peter', *The biographical dictionary*, London, 1844, vol. 3/2, p. 782

WORKS ON CHRISTIAN-MUSLIM RELATIONS

Shorte treatise upon the Turkes chronicles

DATE 1546
ORIGINAL LANGUAGE English

DESCRIPTION

Peter Ashton's translation of Paolo Giovio's *Commentario delle cose de' Turchi*, which he made from Franciscus Niger's Latin translation and entitled *Shorte treatise upon the Turkes chronicles* (its title in full is *A shorte treatise upon the Turkes chronicles, compyled by Paulus Jouius byshop of Nucerne, and dedicated to Charles the v. Emperour. Drawen oute of the Italyen tong in to Latyne, by Franciscus Niger Bassianates. And translated out of Latyne into englysh by Peter Ashton*), contains some original material in addition to the translation itself. Ashton added a prefatory letter in which he expounded on his reasons for thinking it important to bring this history to an English audience and explained his methodology in translation. He added two chapters providing more detail on matters mentioned briefly in the main text, and included tables containing a list of topics and a genealogy of the Turkish rulers. The preface consists of seven unnumbered folios and the end material of four. The main body of the translated text consists of 140 folios.

The main theme of the text was to appraise readers of Ottoman military capabilities so that they could be better prepared for encounters in battle. Both Ashton and Giovio conceived of these military encounters as between Christianity and Islam, and not merely as between opposing armies fighting to gain or defend political territories. The translation frequently refers to the European armies as 'Christian', although it refers to them by their nationalities as well. In his introductory epistle, Ashton expresses a similar sentiment: 'al christendome (saith [Erasmus]) is thought to be as on country, and all christiens, as countreye men.' The translation largely consists of brief biographies of the Ottoman rulers, with descriptions of their military campaigns. The last section of the translation, 'Of the order and dissiplyne of the Turkysh warfare', describes in detail the organisation and capabilities of the Ottoman military forces, and generally judges the European forces unfavourably in comparison. The recommendation is that the Christians, in order to rectify their deficiencies, should unite their armies and harden their soldiers in order to defeat the Ottomans and regain lost territories.

The translation tends to be even-handed in descriptions of Ottoman rulers, giving both positive and negative characterisations. For example, Süleyman I is praised for his many virtues, including his 'wonderful deliberation and judgement' (fol. cxvi), in contrast to the 'auarice and crueltye' (fol. cxvi) of his predecessors, Selim I, Bayezid II and Mehmed II. Süleyman virtues are attributed to his adherence to his faith.

Ashton's additions often shed a less favourable light on the Turks than does the translation, sometimes even contradicting it to do so. For example, the translation describes the aging Bayezid II retiring quietly to the study of philosophy after a life leading successful military campaigns, while Ashton, in an explanatory note, cites Johan Cuspinian to describe him as a lustful drunkard and coward. When the translation mentions that Murad II ordered two Serbian princes to be blinded with a hot poker, Ashton adds 'Cuspin. writeth that he cut of theyr pryuye membres also' (fol. xvi).

Ashton starts the work by rousing his readers with a poem by Thomas Litell beginning on the title page:

> Wake up now, Christiens, out of your slumber,
> Of the Turks to recover your long lost glory.
> Feare not theyre strength, theyre power, ne numbre,
> Sith ryght not myght aychyueth the victory.

In his preface, Ashton portrays the Ottoman Turks as 'being to al christendome most cruel and mortal enemies'. He equates Turkishness with sinfulness and considers the defeats of Christian forces at the hands of the Ottoman armies to be God's retribution for the Christians' sins.

SIGNIFICANCE

The *Turkes chronicles* was among the sources that influenced the often negative attitudes of literary writers of the 16th century, such as Spenser and Shakespeare, towards the Ottoman Turks in particular, and Islam and Muslims in general, which were then reflected in their works (McJannet, *The sultan speaks*). Treatment of Turks in religious contexts was also often negative during this period. However, treatment in military contexts was more likely to give a less biased appraisal for tactical reasons (Matar, 'Britons and Muslims'). It has been argued that these negative portrayals in the 16th century are partly responsible for anti-Islamic views in the present era (Malik, 'Anti-Muslim prejudice'; Matar, 'Britons and Muslims'). However, caution should be used when making these assessments, because events in the intervening centuries, such as the rise of the colonial era, might be more important. As 16th-century portrayals were not universally negative, tracing only negative attitudes might be an over-simplification (McJannet, *The sultan speaks*).

EDITIONS & TRANSLATIONS

A shorte treatise upon the Turkes Chronicles, London, 1546 (STC 11899)

STUDIES

M. Malik, 'Anti-Muslim prejudice in the West, past and present. An introduction', in M. Malik (ed.) *Anti-Muslim prejudice. Past and present*, New York, 2009, 1-6

N. Matar, 'Britons and Muslims in the early modern period. From prejudice to (a theory of) toleration', in M. Malik (ed.), *Anti-Muslim prejudice, past and present*, New York, 2009, 7-25

L. McJannet, *The sultan speaks. Dialogue in English plays and histories about the Ottoman Turks*, New York, 2006, pp. 1-90

F. Turhan, *The other empire. British romantic writings about the Ottoman Empire*, New York, 2003, pp. 1-26, 161-62

S.S. Artemel, 'The idea of Turkey in the Elizabethan period in the early seventeenth century with special reference to the drama', Durham, 1965 (Diss. Durham University), pp. 79, 89, 97, 119, 296

Khadija E. Fouad

Pierre Belon

DATE OF BIRTH About 1517
PLACE OF BIRTH La Soultière, near Le Mans
DATE OF DEATH April 1564 or 1565
PLACE OF DEATH Paris

BIOGRAPHY

Pierre Belon was born in La Soultière near Le Mans, probably in 1517. Very little is known about his family and childhood. He was apprenticed to an apothecary, and then gained the support of René du Bellay, Bishop of Le Mans, who made it possible for him to travel to Germany to study at the University of Wittenberg (1540-41). There, he developed a taste for botany under the guidance of Valerius Cordus. After his return to France in 1542, he lived in Paris and studied medicine. (He graduated in 1560, when he came back from the East, but never took the degree of Doctor.) In the service of the powerful Cardinal de Tournon, a close advisor to King Francis I, he was involved in several diplomatic missions: he mentions in his *Cronique* a journey to Germany in 1543, apparently as an interpreter. On his return, he was briefly imprisoned in Geneva as a consequence of an argument with Calvinists; after his release, he travelled with Valerius Cordus through Switzerland and Italy, where he stayed until 1544. In 1546, he travelled to the East in the retinue of the French ambassador to the Ottoman Empire, Gabriel d'Aramon, along with Pierre Gilles, who had been sent to find ancient manuscripts for the king. He spent nearly three years in the Ottoman Empire.

The travellers left Paris in December 1546 for Venice and embarked for Constantinople in February 1547. They stopped at Ragusa, and while the ambassador pursued his journey on land, Belon carried on by sea, visiting several islands under Venetian rule, including Crete. When he arrived in Constantinople, he learned through a French messenger, Jean de Fumel, that Francis I had died. He spent a few months in the Ottoman capital, visited Macedonian cities, and then from August 1547 travelled to Egypt and the Holy Land with de Fumel. He came back to Constantinople before visiting Anatolia in May 1548 and finally left Constantinople for France in 1549, stopping briefly in Venice.

He continued to travel, for example in 1549 to Rome with his protector, Cardinal de Tournon, in 1550 to England, and in 1553 to Lorraine, and in the following years to Switzerland and Italy. In the meantime, he continued to study medicine and wrote books on flora and fauna (published from 1551 onwards), including his *Observations* (1553), an account of his journeys in the East. He lived at Saint-Germain-des-Prés, the abbey of Cardinal de Tournon, and was protected by Constable Anne de Montmorency. He enjoyed a good reputation and planned the establishment of several exotic botanical species in France. With the death of Henry II and the beginning of the Wars of Religion, the end of his life was stressful: he openly expressed anti-Huguenot views (perhaps the cause of his death), as is shown in his unfinished *Cronique*, where he relates the troubles of 1562. He was assassinated one evening in April 1564 or 1565, when walking through the Bois de Boulogne on his way home to the Château de Madrid, where the king had granted him lodging.

His career was one of an autodidact more than of a recognised scholar, and his success, due to the patronage of some very influential persons, attracted jealousy and detractors among naturalists of his time, such as Rondelet. His extensive travels and many missions may have had other goals than science – he is thought to have been a secret agent for the French Crown. In his works, he always advocated the importance of close observation and stressed *curiositas*. He tried to identify plants and animals he saw, and to compare the lessons from the Ancients with his personal experience, always giving priority to the latter.

Most of Belon's works belong to the field of natural history, and he also published on pharmacopeia and embalming. He is primarily known today for his *Observations de plusieurs singularitez et choses mémorables*, a dense book dedicated to Cardinal de Tournon and published for the first time in 1553, with engravings of plants, animals and people seen during his journey in the East; it was a source for his other treatises. There is also a collection of engravings for various treatises (*Portraits d'animaux, oiseaux, serpens*, published in 1558). In addition, he wrote a historiography of the Wars of Religion, *Cronique de Pierre Belon médecin*, which remained in manuscript until the critical edition by Monica Barsi appeared in 2001.

MAIN SOURCES OF INFORMATION

Primary
MS Paris, Bibliothèque de l'Arsenal – 4651, *Cronique de Pierre Belon du Mans, medecin*, fols 88r-250v (1553)

Secondary

L. Valensi, art 'Belon, Pierre', in F. Pouillon (ed.), *Dictionnaire des orientalistes de langue française*, Paris, 2008, 75-76

P. Glardon, 'Introduction', in Pierre Belon du Mans, *L'Histoire de la nature des oyseaux*, Geneva, 1997, xiii-lxxi

M. Barsi, 'Pierre Belon, un "viaggatore diverso" nell'Impero ottomano', in *Scritture dell'impegno dal Rinascimento all'età barocca. Atti del convegno internazionale di studio: Gargnano, Palazzo Feltrinelli, 11-13 ottobre 1994*, Fasano, Brindisi, 1997, 191-204

P. Delaunay, 'L'aventureuse existence de Pierre Belon', *Revue du Seizième Siècle* 9 (1922) 251-68; 10 (1923) 1-34, 125-47; 11 (1924) 30-48, 222-32; 12 (1925) 78-97, 256-68, 269-82 (repr. as a book, Paris, 1926)

P. Delaunay, *Pierre Belon naturaliste*, 2 vols, Le Mans, 1923-26

WORKS ON CHRISTIAN-MUSLIM RELATIONS

Les observations de plusieurs singularitez et choses mémorables, 'Observations of many singularities and memorable things'

DATE 1553
ORIGINAL LANGUAGE French

DESCRIPTION

Observations de plusieurs singularitez et choses mémorables (*Les observations de plusieurs singularitez et choses mémorables trouvées en Grèce, Asie, Judée, Egypte, Arabie, et autres pays estranges*) was first published in 1553 in Paris and was the result of a long journey Pierre Belon undertook in 1546 in Ambassador Gabriel d'Aramon's retinue. At the beginning of the 16th century, the French monarchy had good relations with the Ottoman Empire. After the defeat of Pavia, King Francis I sought an alliance with Sultan Süleyman that was immediately regarded as 'scandalous'. This pact led to the establishment of a permanent embassy in Constantinople, signatures of capitulations, and an entente against Charles V and the Habsburg dynasty. In 1543, Barbarossa's fleet spent the winter in Toulon harbour, but there was no joint expedition. After the Treaty of Crépy was signed, Ambassador d'Aramon was sent to reassure the sultan and restore the weakened alliance.

The work Pierre Belon wrote as a result of his experience is one of the first travel accounts published in France about Ottoman territory. *Observations* was very successful: after the first edition, produced by two different Parisian publishing houses, Guillaume Cavellat and Gilles Corrozet, several others followed with few alterations. The original 1533 edition contains 35 woodcuts representing plants, animals and people, supposedly made by Arnold Nicolaï. The following editions (1554 and 1555) have one chapter missing (Book 3, ch. 12 'Les moeurs et diverses façons des religions chrétiennes qui vivent en Turquie'). In addition, Belon drops the first person singular to use a more neutral 'we', and there are also some additions: a map of Mount Sinai, a portrait of Belon, and eight more woodcuts, all quite naïve in style.

In the 1553 edition, the first book, containing 76 chapters, presents Belon's itinerary on his first journey to Constantinople. In Ragusa, he left d'Aramon and his retinue who were heading towards Andrinople, and carried on by sea, stopping at several islands: Corfu, Zante, Cythera and Crete. He arrived in Constantinople in 1547 and went on to visit Lemnos, Thassos, Mount Athos (to which he devotes an extensive description) and several Macedonian cities under Ottoman rule, travelling through Thrace to go back to Constantinople.

The second book, containing 115 chapters, is devoted to the journey to Egypt and the Holy Land that he undertook in the company of Jean de Fumel, envoy of King Henry II, from August 1547 onwards. He retraces the journey by sea to Alexandria, depicting the Bosphorus, the castles of Sestus and Abydus, the ruins of Troy, some islands, Alexandria and Cairo, as well as certain remarkable monuments (obelisks, pyramids and the Great Sphinx). From ch. 54 on, he describes his journey from Cairo to Mount Sinai, another from Cairo to Jerusalem, also describing Gaza, Rama (Ramallah), Bethlehem, Hebron, Damascus, Mount Lebanon, Caesarea, Baalbek, Aleppo, Antioch, the Taurus mountains, Heraclea, Iconium (Konya) and Achara (Akhisar).

The third book, of only 52 chapters, relates Belon's journey to the heart of the Ottoman Empire, Constantinople and Anatolia, where he spent several months (in 'Carachara' or Afyon Karahisar). He particularly describes the religion, mores and activities of the Turks.

The text has some notable characteristics: the first is the variety of the territories visited and the length of the author's stay. Though *Observations* is the work of a naturalist who is concerned with describing and identifying the flora and fauna, he also studied diverse substances such as the 'sealed Lemnian earth', and mummies, which were famous in European courts, and was, in addition, very interested in the customs of the populations he observed.

His remarks and analyses follow the chronology of his journeys without any thematic arrangement, with the exception of ten chapters devoted to Islam at the beginning of Book 3. Belon never depicts anything he has not seen himself, so there are no descriptions of the marvels of the sultan's court, or any historical résumé of the history of the Ottoman dynasty. On the other hand, he shows a vivid curiosity concerning the minute details of the everyday life of the peoples he encounters, and the effects of Ottoman domination on their way of living.

In Belon's view, Turkish domination had not deeply changed the culture of the conquered nations; he exerted himself to find the origins of Egyptian or Cretan customs in comparison with Turkish ones. He resists certain prejudices regarding the effects of Ottoman domination, noting the decadence of the Greeks on his visit to Mount Athos, where he records the ignorance of most of the monks (Book 1, ch. 38), without attributing responsibility for these failings to the Turks. The Greeks living under Venetian domination live in the same state of decadence. On the island of Rhodes, conquered by Süleyman in 1522, he notices that the city walls and churches have remained unscathed (Book 2, ch. 13: 'All the buildings of the Order of Rhodes are still here everywhere in their entirety, the Turks have not taken away any of the coats of arms, paintings, sculptures or engravings they found'); on his visit to Cairo he refrains from regretting the fate of the city; in the Holy Land he expresses no consternation about the fact that Christ's sepulchre was in the hands of the Turks. His frequent descriptions of ancient monuments and references to the past are in no way nostalgic, but show that the Turks are simply substitutes for the Romans (e.g. Book 1, ch. 76, 'Des antiquités et plusieurs singularitez de Constantinople').

On many occasions, he notes the freedom of religion granted by the sultan to the various nations living in his empire: 'This is what always maintained the Turk in his greatness: when he conquers some country, it is enough for him to be obeyed, and in return for a tribute, he does not care about souls' (Book 3, ch. 13). He also notes that slaves can regain their freedom by paying a certain amount of money to their master (Book 3, ch. 30), and that a foreign traveller can easily move around with a passport as long as he is 'dressed according to the Turkish mode' (Book 1, ch. 21). He conveys a positive image of Ottoman power (Book 3, ch. 19), speaks highly of the bravery, frugality and modesty of the soldiers (referring here to the Turks, not the Janissaries of Christian origin), and he does not seem to be shocked that there is no hereditary nobility in Ottoman society. He soberly notes that nobility is 'the way one wants to consider it' (Book 2, ch. 95). All in all, he describes the Ottoman Empire as a civilised and well-ordered world, but without hiding the greed of the civil servants, who have had to buy their office (Book 1, ch. 28).

Concerning Turkish mores and customs, there is nonetheless a disparity between his dense, conventional and scornful discourse on Islam and his observations on the everyday life, activities and 'nature' of the Turks, on which his observations are spontaneous and based on personal anecdotes. Religion is the subject of the first ten chapters of Book 3, where Belon recalls the origins, main laws (especially the measures concerning women) and rites of Islam, and summarises Muḥammad's life. In these chapters he adopts a profoundly reproving tone, mocking the 'feigned paradise that Muḥammad promised to his followers', and 'the barbarism and stupidity of that false prophet', and he describes the Qur'an as a tissue of stupidities and mad assumptions. Nevertheless, he distinguishes between the commandments of Islam and the Turks who practise it but are foreign to its origins. He notes that Moors and Arabs are 'more superstitious and ceremonious in their religion than are the Turks' (Book 2, ch. 32).

Belon looks with more favour on other Turkish customs and their nature, underlining the frugality and simplicity of their diet, their discipline, reserve and charity, the efficiency of their system of justice, the hygiene of men and women (he describes their use of baths after experiencing it himself). Artisanal and commercial activities (there are chapters on goldsmiths, saddle-makers, shoe-makers, butchers, the way the muleteers load and unload their animals, fishing methods in the various regions), physical exercises and the sports played by the people (archery and wrestling), diet and the way they keep their babies clean (something rarely dealt with in the travel literature of the time) – all this attracts his interest. The image of the Turks is ultimately one of a civilised people skilled in artisanal activities and certain pleasurable arts such as music.

Belon does not neglect the everyday life of the other peoples of the Ottoman Empire, and he tries to build continuities with their past, showing interest in the practices in which they differ from the Turks (for example, the games played by the people of Cairo or the dances of the Cretans). He appreciates the Egyptians for their cheerful nature (the Turks in comparison are generally glum), confirms the reputation of the Arabs as pillagers and accuses them of holding travellers to ransom (supporting this with his own experiences during his journeys). This distinction between Turks and other Muslim peoples of the empire, as well as the hatred shown towards Jews in certain Ottoman cities, were commonly noted among European travellers ('it is the shrewdest nation there is, and the most full of deceit' Book 3, ch. 14).

SIGNIFICANCE

Observations is one of the first travel accounts published in France about the Ottoman Empire. Among the few others were some accounts of pilgrimages to Jerusalem, chronicles about Ottoman military enterprises such as the conquest of Rhodes, some treatises on the Turks (by Antoine Geuffroy, Christophe Richer, and B. Georgiewitz), and Jacques Gassot's account (1550). Belon's text was written before that of Jean Chesneau (one of d'Aramon's secretaries), which was first published in the 19th century, and those of Thevet (*Cosmographie du Levant*, 1554), Postel, Nicolas de Nicolay and Pierre Gilles.

It seems that one of Belon's aims, apart from the description of the flora and fauna, was to let French readers know about the everyday life of the Ottoman Empire, especially that of the Turks, whose strangeness is constantly compared with that of the ancient Romans, nuanced and made acceptable, despite their religion. Apart from the compendium of the 'superstitions' commonly attributed to Muslims, his account is one of the fairest ever written about the Turks. He shows that Turkish domination had not deeply changed the culture of the conquered nations and was not tyrannical, and he depicts the Turks as a civilised people, giving support to the politics of the French government.

MANUSCRIPTS

MS Paris, Bibliothèque de l'Arsenal – 4651, *Cronique de Pierre Belon du Mans, medecin*, fols 88r-250v (1553)

EDITIONS & TRANSLATIONS

J. Hogarth (trans.), *Travels in the Levant. The Observations of Pierre Belon of le Mans on many singularities and memorable things found in Greece, Turkey, Judaea, Egypt, Arabia and other foreign countries (1553)*, Kilkerran, Scotland, 2008 (first English trans., with an introduction by A. Merle)

G. Holtz (ed.), *Pierre Belon, Voyage en Egypte, 1547*, Klincksieck, 2004 (edition of Book 2, based on the Paris 1555 edition)

A. Merle (ed.), *Voyage au Levant (1553). Les observations de Pierre Belon du Mans*, Paris, 2001 (based on the Paris 1553 edition)

M. Barsi, *L'énigme de la chronique de Pierre Belon, avec édition critique du manuscrit Arsenal 4651*, Milan, 2001

S. Sauneron (ed.), *Voyage en Egypte de Pierre Belon du Mans, 1547*, Cairo, 1970 (edition of Book 2 based on the Paris 1555 edition)

J. Ray, *A collection of curious travels and voyages in two tomes... The second taking in many parts of Greece, Asia Minor, Egypt, from the observations of Mons. Belon, Mr. Vernon, Dr. Spon, Dr. Smith, Dr. Huntingdon, Mr. Greaves and others*, London, printed for S. Smith and B. Walford, 1693, pp. 3-19, 90-92, 124-34 (repr. in J. Ray, *Travels through the Low Countries, Germany, Italy and France, with curious observations...*, London: J. Walthoe, 1738, ii)

Petri Bellonii Cenomani Plurimarum singularium & memorabilium rerum in Graecia, Asia, Aegypto, Iudaea, Arabia, aliisque exteris provinciis ab ipso conspectarum observationes, tribus libris expressae, Carolus Clusius Atrebas e Gallice Latinas faciebat et denuo recensebat altera editio, longe castigatior et quibusdam scholiis illustrate, Antverpiae: Ex Officina Christophori Plantini, 1605

Petri Bellonii Cenomani Plurimarum singularium & memorabilium rerum in Graecia, Asia, Aegypto, Iudaea, Arabia, aliisque exteris provinciis ab ipso conspectarum observationes, tribus libris expressae, Carolus Clusius Atrebas e Gallice Latinas faciebat, Antverpiae: Ex Officina Christophori Plantini, 1589 (Latin trans. by C. de l'Ecluse)

Les observations de plusieurs singularitez et choses memorables, trouvées en Grece, Asie, Judée, Egypte, Arabie, et autres pays estranges, redigées en trois livres, par Pierre Belon du Mans. Reveus de nouveau et augmentez de figures, Paris: H. de Marnef et la Veufve de Guillaume Cavellat, 1588

Les observations de plusieurs singularitez et choses mémorables, trouvées en Grece, Asie, Judée, Egypte, Arabie, et autres pays estranges, redigées en trois livres, par Pierre Belon du Mans. Reveuz de rechef et augmentez de figures, avec une nouvelle Table de toutes les matières traictées en iceux, Anvers: Christophe Plantin (Jean Steelsius), 1555

Les observations de plusieurs singularitez et choses mémorables, trouvées en Grece, Asie, Judée, Egypte, Arabie, et autres pays estranges, redigées en trois livres, par Pierre Belon du Mans. Reveuz de nouveau et augmentez de figures, Paris: chez Guillaume Cavellat, à l'enseigne de la poulle grasse, devant le College de Cambray, 1555 (copies published by Gilles Corrozet, Paris, 1555)

Les observations de plusieurs singularitez et choses mémorables, trouvées en Grece, Asie, Judée, Egypte, Arabie, et autres pays estranges, redigées en trois livres, par Pierre Belon du Mans. Reveuz de nouveau et augmentez de figures, Paris: chez Guillaume Cavellat, à l'enseigne de la poulle grasse, devant le College de Cambray, 1554 (copies published by Gilles Corrozet, Paris, 1554)

Les observations de plusieurs singularitez et choses mémorables, trouvées en Grece, Asie, Judée, Egypte, Arabie, et autres pays estranges, redigées en trois livres, par Pierre Belon du Mans, Paris: chez Guillaume Cavellat, à l'enseigne de la poulle grasse, devant le College de Cambray, 1553 (copies published by Gilles Corrozet, Paris, 1553)

STUDIES

F. Tinguely, *L'ecriture du Levant à la Renaissance*, Geneva, 2000

D. Bertrand, 'Les stratégies de Belon pour une représentation exotique', *Nouvelle Revue du Seizième Siècle* 11 (1993) 5-17

S. Yérasimos, *Les voyageurs dans l'Empire ottoman, XIVe-XVIe siècles. Bibliographie, itinéraires et inventaire des lieux habités*, Ankara, 1991

Y. Bernard, *L'Orient du XVIe siècle à travers les récits des voyageurs français. Regards portés sur la société musulmane*, Paris, 1988

I. Zinguer, 'Narration et témoignage dans les *Observations* de Pierre Belon (1553)', *Nouvelle Revue du Seizième Siècle* 5 (1987) 25-40

J. Paviot, 'L'ambassade de d'Aramon. Érudits et voyageurs au Levant, 1547-1583', in J. Céard and J.-C. Margolin (eds), *Voyager à la Renaissance. Actes du colloque de Tours, 30 juin-13 juillet 1983*, Paris, 1987, 381-92

F. Lestringant, 'Guillaume Postel et l'obsession turque', in *Guillaume Postel 1581-1981*, Paris, 1985, 265-98

C.D. Rouillard, *The Turk in French history, thought and literature (1520-1660)*, Paris, 1941

Alexandra Merle

Guillaume Postel

DATE OF BIRTH   25 March 1510
PLACE OF BIRTH Dolerie, Normandy
DATE OF DEATH   6 September 1581
PLACE OF DEATH Paris

BIOGRAPHY

Modern scholars have described Guillaume Postel as odd, curious, or even insane, and also as the father of comparative philology and the first Orientalist. His contemporaries regarded him as a linguist, mathematician and mystic, while he considered himself a prophet. Postel rose from humble beginnings to obtain academic posts of the highest order, only to fall from favour because of the heretical nature of his beliefs. His bizarre ideas made him suspect in his own time and have prevented his becoming more widely appreciated since. Postel believed that he was chosen to be the prophet who would achieve world unity under Catholic French leadership in the impending millennium.

Scholars have explored the intellectual climate surrounding Postel, but equally important was the political and diplomatic context, which allowed him to travel in the Levant. Postel's ideas arose in the religious context of the Protestant and Catholic Reformations, and also in the political context of claims to universal sovereignty by the most powerful rulers of the time, the Ottoman Sultan Süleyman, the Shīʿī prophet and Shah Ismail, the Holy Roman Emperor Charles V, and the kings of France. For Postel, as for many of his contemporaries, the religious and the political could not be isolated from each other. During his youth, Charles V and François I struggled for dominance in Europe, and especially for control of Italy, with the ideology of world dominion. In 1530, the Italian author Paolo Giovio dedicated a work to Charles V that encouraged learning about the Turks in order to defeat them and unite the world under one ruler. Thus, some of Postel's ideas reflect widespread beliefs of the time. As Christendom was splintering in the West, the ideal of religious and political unity still appeared highly desirable to many influential authors.

Postel's parents, who were of low rank, died of the plague when Postel was only eight. However, by the age of 13 he was teaching at a village school. He then travelled to Paris to study, but thieves stole his money and he subsequently fell ill and spent 18 months in a hospital. After labouring in the fields to earn money, he returned to Paris and entered the College of Sainte-Barbe, where he revealed a talent for languages, providing translations of Aristotle for Juan de Gelida, a Spanish scholar. Thus, although he had limited time to attend classes, he taught himself Greek, Spanish and Portuguese, learned Hebrew from a grammar and the Psalms, and showed talent in mathematics and philosophy. By 1530, at the age of 20, he had earned an MA. At the College of Sainte-Barbe, he came under the influence of Erasmian humanism and also of Ignatius of Loyola, who had arrived at Sainte-Barbe in 1528. Postel shared his desire to spread Christianity.

A turning point in Postel's life came when the prominent Byzantine scholar, Janus Lascaris, recommended Postel to Marguerite de Navarre, sister of King François I, to travel with the French ambassador to the Ottoman Empire, Jean de la Forest, himself a former student of Lascaris in Venice. While diplomatic relations between France and the Ottoman Empire had begun shortly after François I's capture at the battle of Pavia in 1525, the goal of the embassy led by Jean de la Forest was an alliance between France and the Ottomans. This embassy provided the opportunity for Postel to journey to the East. As a result of his experiences on this embassy, his life was directed toward interests in the Levant and especially encounters with Muslims. When Postel and de la Forest left France in 1535, they travelled with envoys that Hayreddin Pasha (Barbarossa) had sent to François I. Thus, they first went to Tunis, and then, with the assistance of Hayreddin, they sailed to Istanbul. While de la Forest was engaged in diplomacy, Postel's assignment was to locate and purchase rare manuscripts for François's library at Fontainbleau. He also purchased for himself books on Arab philosophy, medicine, mathematics and religion. Among the books that he obtained in Istanbul were works on the Kabbalah.

In Istanbul, Postel, who wished to continue studying Arabic, found a teacher who he believed was a secret Christian and who desired translations of the Gospels into Arabic or Turkish, and claimed that there were 300,000 Christians in Istanbul. Postel's teacher showed him passages from the Qur'an that praised Christ, the Virgin Mary and other Christian figures. This experience had a profound impact on Postel, and bringing Christianity to Muslims eventually became his obsession. The possible secret Christian he met in Istanbul may have been linked to religious movements known to exist in the Ottoman Empire: in 1527, Molla

Kabiz was executed for preaching in public that Jesus was superior to Muḥammad, drawing his arguments from the Qur'an. Molla Kabiz was not a Christian, but a European might have thought that he was. So it is possible that Postel's teacher was a member of a Muslim sect in the Ottoman Empire that believed that Jesus was greater than Muḥammad.

De la Forest's negotiations led to an attempt at a joint Ottoman-French expedition against the Habsburgs in 1537, and de la Forest died while accompanying the Ottoman forces. Postel travelled from Istanbul to Venice, and returned to Paris later in 1537. In 1538, he published his first book, which referred to concepts that continued to be important to him in the future: Hebrew as the original language from which all others derived, the importance of learning languages in order to spread Catholicism and achieve world unity, and the necessity of sending missionaries to Muslims. Also in 1538, he published the first grammar of classical Arabic to appear in Europe. From 1538 to 1542, he held a lectureship at the future Collège de France and taught mathematics and philology. This prosperous period of Postel's career soon changed when he became involved in court intrigue. Since he advocated sending missionaries to the Ottoman Empire, his ideas appeared to threaten the French alliance with the Ottomans, which was essential to limit Habsburg power in Europe. French ambassadors were requesting Ottoman intervention against Charles V's possessions in the Mediterranean, and François could not risk supporting policies that might anger his powerful ally, Süleyman.

According to a manuscript in the Bibliothèque Nationale (fonds français 2115, c. 103), sometime during 1541 or 1542 Postel had a vision telling him to warn François that the king had been chosen by God to become the leader in the universal restitution of all things. Postel travelled to Fontainbleau, where he informed François that in order to accomplish this he must reform his kingdom. François was initially convinced until Diane de Poitiers persuaded the king to ignore the words of a fool. This was the first time Postel had openly claimed that he received revelations. The consequences for Postel were that he lost the king's favour and his teaching appointment. He concentrated his energies on writing two significant works in Latin that expressed his views on Muslim-Christian relations. The first to be published, *Alcorani liber*, was originally part of his major work, *De orbis terrae concordia*, which he wrote during the winter of 1542-43. He sent this to the Sorbonne for approval, but when it was rejected, he had the part of the work that attacked Protestants published in Paris in 1543, while the rest of the work was published in Basel by Oporinus.

The year 1543 was momentous in Ottoman-French relations, for in the summer of 1543 the Ottoman fleet under the command of Hayreddin Pasha arrived in France to assist François against his rival Charles V. After a joint attack on Nice, the fleet wintered at Toulon in order to assist François the following summer. This example of Ottoman-French unity under the perceived leadership of the French ruler may have convinced Postel that French policies against the Habsburgs were unlikely to promote his concept of world unity under the leadership of the king of France.

In March 1544, Postel left Paris for Rome, where he planned to join the Jesuits, some of whom he had met earlier in Paris. He was warmly received by Ignatius, and Postel became a priest at this time, but, because Postel believed that the religious unity of the world could only be achieved through the French monarchy, conflicts arose, and by December 1545 the Jesuits had expelled him. He remained in Rome until January 1547, when he travelled to Venice and lived there until 1549. In Venice, he met Mother Johanna, who he believed was the New Eve, the Shekinah of his Kabbalistic reading.

In the summer of 1549, Postel sailed for the Holy Land to improve his knowledge of languages and to obtain copies of religious texts for his friend, the Venetian printer Bomberg, who financed the trip. However, in Jerusalem, after exhausting his funds, Postel met the French ambassador to the Ottoman Empire, Gabriel de Luetz, baron d'Aramon, who provided money for him to purchase books, and Postel travelled with him to Istanbul in 1549. When Postel returned to Venice in late 1550, he found that Mother Johanna had died while he had been in the Levant, but after he returned to Paris in late 1551 he had a supernatural experience that led him to believe she had returned and taken possession of his body.

In the years following this experience, he felt a sense of urgency to spread his message. Between 1551 and 1555, he published 23 books and many broadsheets, but his contemporaries increasingly questioned his sanity, and in 1553 he was forbidden to preach in public. He left Paris for Venice, where he worked on a Syriac text of the Gospels. He then travelled to Vienna, where Emperor Ferdinand appointed him to a chair at the University of Vienna, only to leave Vienna abruptly in 1555, when he learned that his writings were about to be placed on the index of prohibited books. He returned to Italy, where he was investigated and declared insane, and imprisoned in the papal prison in Rome. When Pope Paul IV died in 1559, he and the other prisoners were released. Postel then travelled widely, including to Basel, Venice, Trent and Poitiers. His travels during this period are difficult to trace because he feared that he would be imprisoned again. He arrived in Lyons in 1562 and was again investigated. In 1563, he was confined to the Monastery of St Martin des Champs in Paris, where he died in 1581.

MAIN SOURCES OF INFORMATION

Primary
A. Thevet, *Histoire des plus illustres et sçavans hommes de leurs siècles*, Paris, 1584, viii, pp. 36-48

Secondary
C. Isom-Verhaaren, *Allies with the infidel. The Ottoman and French alliance in the sixteenth century*, London, 2011, pp. 16, 54, 165-71
I. McCabe, *Orientalism in early modern France*, Oxford, 2008, pp. 15-36
Y. Petry, *Gender, Kabbalah and the Reformation. The mystical theology of Guillaume Postel (1510-1581)*, Leiden, 2004, pp. 1-49
M.L. Kuntz, '"Venezia portava el fuocho in seno". Guillaume Postel before the Council of Ten in 1548. Priest turned prophet', in M.L. Kuntz, *Venice, myth and utopian thought in the sixteenth century*, Aldershot, 1999, 95-121
F. Lestringant, 'Guillaume Postel et l'"obsession turque"', in *Guillaume Postel 1581-1981. Actes du colloque d'Avranches*, Paris, 1987, 265-98 (repr. in F. Lestringant, *Écrire le monde à la Renaissance. Quinze études sur Rabelais, Postel, Bodin et la littérature géographique*, Caen, 1993, 189-224)
M.L. Kuntz, 'Voyages to the East and their meaning in the thought of Guillaume Postel', in J. Céard and J.-C. Margolis, *Voyager à la Renaissance. Actes du colloque de Tours, 30 juin-13 juillet 1983*, Paris, 1987, 51-63
L. Febvre, *The problem of unbelief in the sixteenth century. The religion of Rabelais*, Cambridge MA, 1982, pp. 107-13
M.L. Kuntz, *Guillaume Postel, prophet of the restitution of all things. His life and thought*, The Hague, 1981
F. Secret, *Apologies et retractions. Manuscrits inédits publiés avec une introduction et des notes*, Nieuwkoop, Netherlands, 1972, pp. 7-12
F. Secret, *Bibliographie des manuscrits de Guillaume Postel*, Geneva, 1970, pp. 9-11
G. Postel, *Le Thrésor des Prophéties de l'univers* [1565], ed. F. Secret, La Haye, Netherlands, 1969, pp. 1-38
W. Bouwsma, *Concordia Mundi. The career and thought of Guillaume Postel (1510-1581)*, Cambridge MA, 1957, pp. 1-29
V. Bourrilly, 'L'ambassade de La Forest et de Marillac à Constantinople (1535-1538)', *Revue Historique* (1901) 297-328, p. 307

WORKS ON CHRISTIAN-MUSLIM RELATIONS

Alcorani seu legis Mahometi et evangelistarum concordiae Liber, in quo de calamitatibus orbi Christiano imminentibus traditatur, 'A book on the agreement between the Qur'an, or the law of Muḥammad, and the Evangelicals, in which is related the calamities imminent on the Christian world'

DATE 1543
ORIGINAL LANGUAGE Latin

DESCRIPTION

Postel originally planned to publish this work, which is 124 pages long, as the final part of *De orbis*, but when the Sorbonne did not approve *De orbis*, he had to change his plans. He eventually published it himself in Paris, with the result that there are no paragraphs and the type goes to the edges of the pages. The main purpose of *Alcorani* is to show the similarities between the beliefs of the Reformers and those of the Muslims. Thus, since the Qur'an is known to be false (he has proved this in *De orbis*), if the Reformers are shown to have similar beliefs then their beliefs must be condemned as well. This book relates to Postel's project of unifying the world.

Postel first refutes the teachings of the Reformers, Luther among them, and then he discusses a list of 28 propositions from the Qur'an to show that Protestants also believed them. Among these: Proposition 2 states that foreign (meaning any non-Catholic) works are not effective nor do they benefit anyone; Proposition 5 states that Muslim 'patrons and intercessors' have no influence with God; Proposition 10 states that 'no miraculous works confirm their religion'; Proposition 11 states that 'Their doctors of law conceal the truth'; Proposition 14 states that 'They have no holy images in their temples, and the saints are not honoured'; and Proposition 27 states that Muḥammad frequently said that humans lack free will. However, according to Proposition 17, Muslims worship God alone. Postel explains that he has not included every point of disagreement, but only the main ones.

In the second part of *Alcorani*, he goes on to condemn the Evangelicals for their impiety.

SIGNIFICANCE
Postel's detailed analysis of the Qur'an is included in *De orbis*, not in *Alcorani*. In this latter work, he condemns both Muslims and Reformers for their narrowness in believing that only they hold the truth. They both deny much that Catholics value, including non-scriptural writings, miracles to confirm religion, honouring the saints and Mary, the Eucharist as more than a symbol, and that there is free will. The mistaken doctrines that Muslims and Protestants shared multiply divisions, he believed, and were thus especially threatening to his vision of future world harmony.

Alcorani provoked a response from Calvin in 1544.

EDITIONS & TRANSLATIONS
Alcorani seu legis Mahometi et evangelistarum concordiae Liber, in quo de calamitatibus orbi Christiano imminentibus traditatur, Paris, 1543

STUDIES
Febvre, *The problem of unbelief in the sixteenth century*, pp. 113-26
Bouwsma, *Concordia mundi*, pp. 5, 10, 300

De orbis terrae concordia, 'On the harmony of the world'

DATE 1544
ORIGINAL LANGUAGE Latin

DESCRIPTION
This major work (the title in full is *De orbis terrae concordia libri quatuor, multiiuga eruditione ac pietate referti, quibus nihil hoc tam perturbato rerum statu vel utilius, vel accommodatius potuisse in publicum edi, quivis aequus lector iudicabit*) is 447 folio size pages and comprises four parts: an explanation of Christian beliefs on the basis of philosophy; the life of Muḥammad and a refutation of the entire Qur'an; laws, human and divine, that are common throughout the world; how to convert false beliefs to true by peaceful means. Oporinus, a Protestant publisher in Basel who had published Theodore Bibliander's translation of the Qur'an, published it in 1544 after the Sorbonne returned *De orbis* to Postel without approving it.

The second part, pp. 125-260, is the longest of the four. At the beginning, Postel exhorts pious men to use literature and reason to understand the 'vile Muḥammadan filth', and then on pp. 137-51 he gives an account of Muḥammad's life and the laws he instituted. On p. 152, he begins a discussion of the Qur'an and writings about Muḥammad, including a short chapter that summarises what the Qur'an has taken from the Old and New Testaments.

In ch. 13, Postel analyses the Qur'an in detail, particularly the first *sūra*s. He is clearly reading an Arabic Qur'an and not a Latin translation, since he cites Arabic terms. His method is to make a close side-by-side comparison of the Qur'an and Gospel accounts, and to comment on the differences and the consequent mistakes in the Qur'an. In this, he gives his own approach precedence over those of his predecessors, such as Nicholas of Cusa (d. 1464), who he says do not know Arabic and have to rely on translations, while he approves of Riccoldo da Monte di Croce (d. 1320) and those like him, whose proficiency in Arabic enabled them to write about Islam accurately. He criticises Christian polemicists who simply 'mentioned briefly and condemned piecemeal' only selected parts of the Qur'an.

He goes on to point out errors in the Qur'an about God and the end of the world, and shows how Islamic law is bringing unhappiness to the lands under Islamic rule. On pp. 252-58, he refers to the *sūra*s that praise Christ.

SIGNIFICANCE

In this work Postel makes his most sustained criticism of Islam, leaving no doubt that he considers it wrong and founded on error. He also exhibits the traditional medieval attitude towards the Qur'an: that it is derived from the Bible and misrepresents what it says. In arriving at his judgements about Islam, his proficiency in Arabic, which might have provided insights into the meaning of the text of the Qur'an, is outweighed by his loyalty to Christianity, which he sees as consistent with reason. These arguments are part of his wider concern to show that Christianity is the one true faith, and that harmony and unity in the world will be attained if this is recognised and all people become Christians.

EDITIONS & TRANSLATIONS

De orbis terrae concordia libri quatuor, multiiuga eruditione ac pietate referti, quibus nihil hoc tam perturbato rerum statu vel utilius, vel accommodatius potuisse in publicum edi, quivis aequus lector iudicabit, Basel, 1544

STUDIES

Febvre, *The problem of unbelief in the sixteenth century*, p. 114
Bouwsma, *Concordia Mundi*, pp. 9-10, 27, 55, 64, 195, 202, 233-43

Descriptio Alcahirae urbis, quae Mizir et Mazar dicitur, 'Description of the city of Cairo, which is called Miṣr and Maṣr'

DATE 1549
ORIGINAL LANGUAGE Latin

DESCRIPTION

Although his name does not appear on this short booklet of only 24 pages, Postel has been regarded as its author since the 16th century. He wrote it to accompany the pictures of Cairo, on 21 sheets, printed by Matteo Pagano. It comprises three chapters: on the origins of the Muslims, a description of the city, and notices to accompany the pictures. Postel relies on a variety of sources: Strabo, the Old Testament, Flavius Josephus, Burchard of Mount Sion, Pietro Martire d'Anghiera, and particularly Leo Africanus and Paolo Giovio, though in some places he expresses his own ideas.

In ch. 1 he says that Muḥammad was descended from Hagar, and that the Turks were descended from the ten lost tribes of Israel. He also includes a prophecy that Christianity will triumph in the Holy Land after the final defeat of the Turks, and this will take place 1,000 years after the conversion of the Turks to Islam.

SIGNIFICANCE

Here Postel repeats ideas that appear in his other works about the eventual unity of religion, though while in other works he expresses admiration for the Ottomans, here he describes the Mamluk and Ottoman rulers as tyrants, and claims that most Muslim rulers died violently.

Although only very few copies of *Descriptio Alcahirae* have survived, Pagano's view of Cairo became the standard Western representation of the city for 250 years by being included in at least 14 manuscripts or publications from 1568 to 1688. One publication of the view that includes a portion of Postel's text is Georg Braun and Frans Hogenberg, *Civitates orbis terrarum of*, 1572-1617, vol. 1, Cologne, 1572, plate 55 with accompanying text.

EDITIONS & TRANSLATIONS

Three copies survive of the text that accompanies the view printed by Pagano:

London, BL – C. 107.bb.17. (7.)
Paris, BNF – Impr. Res. 03b.688
Berlin, Kunstbibliothek of the Staatliche Museen – M.96/249

Two copies of the view survive:
    London, Arcadian Library – Inv. 16422
    Berlin, Kupferstichkabinett of the Staatliche Museen – 924-100

> N. Warner, *The true description of Cairo. A sixteenth-century Venetian view*, Oxford, 2006, vol. 2, pp. 9-32 (facsimile), 41-157 (English trans. of ch. 3 including commentary by Warner)
> B. Blanc et al., 'A propos de la carte du Caire de Matheo Pagano', *Annales Islamologiques* 17 (1981) 203-85, pp. 212-42 (Venetian text of map legends with French trans.), 252-71 (Latin text of Postel's introduction with French trans.)
> A. Codazzi, 'Una "descrizione" del Cairo di Guglielmo Postel', in *Studi in onore di Cesare Manaresi*, Milan, 1952, 169-206, pp. 185-206 (the edited Latin text)

STUDIES

> Warner, *The true description of Cairo*, vol. 1, pp. 63-141, 143-71, vol. 2, pp. 33-40, 161-237
> Blanc et al., 'A propos de la carte du Caire de Matheo Pagano', p. 203-11, 243-50, 272-85
> Codazzi, 'Una "descrizione" del Cairo di Guglielmo Postel', pp. 169-84, introduction

De la republique des Turcs, et là ou l'occasion s'offrera, des meurs et loy de tous Muhamedistes; De la republique, 'On the state of the Turks, and as opportunity allows, on the customs and law of all Muslims'

DATE About 1559
ORIGINAL LANGUAGE French

DESCRIPTION

De la republique is a descriptive account of the Ottoman Empire and Islam, divided into three major parts. The first section is 127 numbered pages plus a preliminary page from the publisher, Enguilbert de Marnef, explaining the sections of the manuscript that he received from Postel. At the beginning of the first part, Postel explains that his purpose in writing is to give accurate information about the Ottomans so that they can be defeated or persuaded to abandon their faith. Not only their vices, but also their virtues should be described, he says, so he asks his readers to come with open minds to his book (p. 3). The organisation of the book is not consistent: some topics are given headings while others are not.

In this first part, Postel begins with a diversity of topics, such as eunuchs, women, the customs of Christians in the empire, food and drink, and dance. Then he relates what he observed in 1535-36 with Jean de la Forest, the French ambassador to the sultan. He describes a banquet, including food and how it is served, he lists the names of the sultan's most prominent administrators, and he comments on the obedience of members of the military in the palace and how they never move from their places. He goes on to describe the custom of public bathing, remarking that everyone, including Christians and Jews, is allowed to go to the baths and all are treated equally.

The next section, beginning on p. 30, mainly focuses on the imperial family and the palace. He describes the family as it was in 1536 (although he was writing 20 years later), which is noted in the margin.

The rest of *De la republique*, beginning on p. 39, focuses on religion in the empire, a topic that Postel had written about earlier in Latin. He describes the process of a Christian converting to Islam and claims that Jews must become Christians before they are allowed to become Muslims. When men convert, they must be circumcised, and those born Muslims are circumcised at about 14 years of age. Postel distinguishes between various groups of Muslims, and claims that Moors are the worst scoundrels of all. He describes the beauty of Ottoman mosques, and mentions the Muslim horror of images and figures. He refers to Hagia Sophia, and remarks that the most beautiful church in the world has been ruined by becoming a mosque. He gives an account of Friday worship, noting that the reverence shown in mosques is greater than in Christian churches, and says that the sultan is usually only seen on Fridays, when he leaves the palace to go to worship.

Postel explains basic religious practices such as fasting during Ramadan, praying five times a day and giving alms. He describes *imaret*s (soup kitchens), where the poor are fed thanks to endowments from the wealthy. When he writes about Muḥammad and Islam, he shows traditional Christian prejudice. He refers to predecessors who have written about the Prophet, such as Sergius the Nestorian and Nicolaus

Cardinal [Nicholas of Cusa], and then he turns to the Qur'an and angels and devils, as he had before in *De orbis*.

On p. 98, Postel compares Muslim beliefs with similarities in the New Testament regarding Mary and Zachariah, John and Christ. On p. 106, he turns to diverse religions, by which he means sects in Islam that were important during his own time. Then he describes tombs and Muslim traditions about dealing with the dead, and finally Ottoman laws and the judicial hierarchy of the empire, including punishments for various offences.

The second part, entitled *Histoire et consideration de l'origine, loy, et coustume des Tartares, Persiens, Arabes, et tous autre Ismaelites et Mohametains ou Sarrazins*, 56 pages in length, is dedicated to the *Roydauphin*, François II (r. 1559-60). Postel explains that he has written it for three reasons: to provide knowledge, to give the history and character of the ruler of the Orient, and to impart useful information about the French king's greatest enemy in religion. As in his earlier Latin works, he wishes to promote 'the concord of the world' under the king of France, who he believes is descended from Noah through Japheth and whose destiny is to lead the world. His belief is that, if the Christians of France, and especially their rulers, are informed in detail about the Ottomans, it will eventually lead to the two greatest world powers becoming reconciled through mutual understanding (pp. 1-11). He goes on to say that the Turks were originally descended from the Israelites, while the Mongols were descended from the Ten Lost Tribes of Israel.

Postel believes Hebrew was the most ancient language and that all other languages descended from it. Thus, Hebrew was the mother of Arabic, and Arabic is the language common to all Muslims (pp. 35-36). Ishmael, the ancestor of the Arabs, was the illegitimate son of Abraham, and Islam is therefore an illegitimate religion, but related to Christianity and Judaism. Since illegitimate sons cannot inherit, Muslims will not rule the world, and only the French can.

Postel concludes this part by acknowledging the great Muslim thinkers al-Ghazālī and Avicenna (p. 56), despite their illegitimate heritage. His overall argument throughout is meant to convince his French readers of their destiny to rule a world that will be in harmony when the Turks accept Christianity.

The third part, entitled *La tierce partie des orientales histoires, ou est exposée la condition, puissance et revenu de l'Empire Turquesque: avec toutes les provinces & païs generalement depuis 950 ans en ça par tous Ismaelites conquis*, 89 pages long, is dedicated to Cardinal Charles de

Guise. In the dedication, Postel repeats his ideas about the harmony of the world under a French universal monarchy.

Postel first describes the Ottoman court, going into much detail about life in the palace and the various ceremonies that take place. He notes that the young men trained in the palace are from the Christian population of the empire, collected through the *devşirme* (pp. 17-23). He describes the provinces of the empire and the army, praising the discipline of the soldiers, and then he discusses the Safavids, the chief Muslim rivals of the Ottomans, who campaigned against them in 1534-36 and 1548-49. After this, he briefly lists the sultans from Osman to Süleyman and comments that Mustafa, Süleyman's oldest son, will make a good ruler.

SIGNIFICANCE

The publication of the three books that make up *De la republique des Turcs* indicates that Postel wanted to direct his message to French speakers by making available in French ideas that sometimes repeat those he had expressed about 20 years earlier in Latin in *De orbis*. The dedications are to the French monarchy and Charles de Guise, Cardinal of Lorraine, who in 1559 or 1560 was one of the regents for François II (r. 1559-60). If Postel hoped the French leaders would act on his ideas, he was dedicating his books to the most likely candidates, since the cardinal was one of the most powerful men in France during François's brief reign.

It is surprising that, although approximately 23 or 24 years had passed since Postel first journeyed to Istanbul with Jean de la Forest, most of the information he presents dates from that period and not from his second trip in 1549-50. By the time this book was published in about 1559 or 1560, the usefulness of the material was questionable, if the idea was to know your enemy so that you could either defeat him or persuade him to follow your beliefs. While he could still claim authority from his travels to the Ottoman Empire, the information included was incomplete and dated by the time he was writing. For example, Süleyman's son Mustafa had been executed in 1553. It was adequate for a travel book aimed at a wider public, but it did not meet his stated purpose of providing information for French rulers.

Postel shows a fascination with the Ottoman Empire, and his work exemplifies the transition from the medieval to the Early Modern period in terms of an interest in the exotic. He provides a curious mixture of large amounts of information, poorly organised and at times not clearly understood in its historical context, mixed with his own obsessions about a future when the Turks would become Christians and the world would be united in harmony.

EDITIONS & TRANSLATIONS

J. Rollet (ed.), *Des histoires orientales*, Istanbul, 1999 (incomplete edition in modern French, taken from the 1575 edition and including only the last two sections)

Des histoires orientales et principalement des Turkes ou Turchikes et Schitiques ou Tartaresques et aultres qui en sont descentue, Paris: Hierosme de Marnef et Guillaume Cavellat, 1575 (reprint of *De la republique*)

De la republique des Turcs, et là ou l'occasion s'offrera, des meurs et loy de tous Muhamedistes, Poitiers: Enguilbert de Marnef, 1560

STUDIES

McCabe, *Orientalism in early modern France*, pp. 37-68

Christine Isom-Verhaaren

John Shute

DATE OF BIRTH   Unknown
PLACE OF BIRTH   Unknown
DATE OF DEATH   Probably 1598
PLACE OF DEATH   Unknown

BIOGRAPHY

There is no recorded information about John Shute's family background and education. By 1557, he appears in records as a captain in the army of Lord Clinton, 1st Earl of Lincoln (1512-85), accompanying him to France. When Clinton became Constable of the Tower of London, Shute was appointed a master gunner. In 1569, Shute became a yeoman of the ordinance for life and also spent time working for Sir Francis Walsingham, Elizabeth I's secretary of state, reviewing troops in the Netherlands, and himself raised troops in response to the sighting of the Spanish Armada in 1587-88. He dedicated one of his translations to Walsingham.

Shute's translation from Italian of *Two very notable commentaries* was published in 1562. He dedicated it to Lord Clinton, apologising in his note to the reader that his translation may not be as erudite or 'exquisite' as it would be if he had been 'brought up in scoles'. *Two very notable commentaries* represents an example of a Continental work offering new information on the Ottomans reaching an English readership through translation, an early conduit through which the Skanderbeg motif entered English literature, very much against the background of what was perceived to be the Ottoman threat. Christopher Marlowe may have consulted Shute for what was probably his first play, *The true history of George Scandeburg*, which is lost, and also for *Tamburlaine the Great* (1587/8).

In January 1598, which has been taken as his death year, Shute complained to Sir Robert Cecil, Walsingham's successor, that a pension awarded him by the bishop of Winchester was unpaid. After this, he disappears from the records. Dallaway and others have confused him with another John Shute (d. 1566) whose employer, the Duke of Northumberland, sent him to Italy to study architecture, so he has seemed a likely candidate for translating an Italian text (Dallaway, *Series of discourses*, p. 390). It is not known how or why Shute acquired competency in Italian or why, given his background, he decided to write at all. He also translated from French into English. He may have spent more time on the Continent than records indicate. While obscure today, he is considered to have made an important contribution to the development of English literary prose. Other works by Shute show an interest in religion: he translated three works from French by Pierre Viret, the Swiss Reformed theologian.

MAIN SOURCES OF INFORMATION

Primary
P. Viret, *The firste parte of the Christian instruction*, trans. J. Shute, London, 1565
P. Viret, *A Christian instruction*, trans. I.S. [J. Shute], London, 1573
J. Shute, *The principal points (by P. Viret)*, London, 1579
CSP dom., *Calendar of state papers, Domestic series, of the reigns of Edward VI, Mary, Elizabeth, 1547-[1625]*, vol. 1, 1547-80, London, 1856, p. 224
C.T. Martin (ed.), 'Journal of Sir Francis Walsingham, from December 1570 to April 1583', *Camden miscellany*, 6/104 (1871) 1-99, p. 15
Historical Manuscripts Commission, *Historical Manuscripts Commission* (1883-1976), vols 1, 8, 10
Calendar of the manuscripts of the most hon. the marquis of Salisbury, preserved at Hatfield House, Hertfordshire, Part 8, London, 1899, pp. 14, 33
Calendar of the patent rolls preserved in the Public Record Office: Elizabeth [I], vol. 4, 1566-9, London, 1939

Secondary
E. Lord, art. 'Shute, John (*fl.* 1557-1598)', in *ODNB*
R. Bayne, art. 'Shute, John', in *DNB*
J. Dallaway, *A series of discourses upon architecture in England from the Norman æra to the close of the reign of Queen Elizabeth, with an appendix of notes and illustrations, and an historical account of master and free masons*, London, 1833, p. 390

WORKS ON CHRISTIAN-MUSLIM RELATIONS

Two very notable commentaries

DATE 1562
ORIGINAL LANGUAGE English

DESCRIPTION
Two very notable commentaries is John Shute's translation of two Italian texts (its full title is *Two very notable commentaries the one of the originall of the Turcks and Empire of the house of Ottomanno, written by Andrewe*

Cambine, and the other of the warres of the Turcke against George Scanderbeg, prince of Epiro, and of the great victories obteyned by the sayd George, as well against the Emperour of Turkie, as other princes, and of his other rare force and vertues, worthye of memorye, translated oute of Italian into Englishe by Iohn Shute). Pages Ai to Sii contain a translation of Andrea Cambini's *Della origine de' Turchi et imperio delli Ottomani*, published in 1538, and pages Siii to Ffii a translation of an anonymous Italian original about Ottoman attacks on George Skanderbeg, prince of Epirus. The final section, from pages Ffiii to the end, is a chronological list of the successes of the Ottomans. Shute prefixed the translations with a 15-page dedicatory epistle to Lord Clinton, his patron, and a brief note to the reader on p. 16.

Relatively little is known about Andrea Cambini (1445-1527), except that he studied under Christopher Landino (1424-98), a Platonic humanist who may have headed an academy in his native Florence. Published in 1538, his work is considered one of the earliest serious scholarly works on the Ottomans in a European language. He is believed to have consulted some eye-witnesses for his description of the Fall of Constantinople (Runciman, *Fall of Constantinople*, p. 197). Despite describing the Turks as by 'nature cruel and barbarous' (p. Ai), and chronicling acts of depravity, he also depicts the Ottomans' military skill, especially their discipline and unity (see p. Ni). Nor are examples of commendable behaviour missing from Cambini's account. The Mamluks, having dominated both Egypt and Syria, were 'content with their domain' and made no attempt to turn their army 'against anybody unless provoked' (for about 300 years). They passed a law that 'none should be Soldane [sultan] except by election'. On conquering Egypt, Sultan Süleyman established 'peace', confirming people's 'liberties and freedoms' (p. Sii), while Bayezid II 'Gave orders for the administration of justice in all places', and 'gave himself wholly to the study of Alchoran, of natural philosophie, in the whiche he had greate weighte' (p. Mi). Cambini evidently thought it useful for Christians to 'know their enemy' (Bisaha, *Creating East and West*, p. 178). Equally admirable, though, are Timur for defeating and capturing Sultan Bayezid I, and George Skanderbeg (George Castriot), who, having embraced the 'folthie and beastly religion of Mahometh', then reconverted to Christianity and became 'an excellent and famous Captaine' . . . 'in defence of the Christian religion'. This strongly hints that George's unique experience helped equip him for success (p. Fii).

The commentary on George Skanderbeg (1405-68), the first detailed account to reach England, introduces this iconic figure to a new readership. After 20 years as a Janissary and a trusted servant of the Ottomans,

Skanderbeg reverted to Christianity while governor of Dibra, and then fought and won a series of battles against them. His entry into Ottoman service is described at the beginning of the commentary (p. Siii). He was given to the Turks as tribute by his father, an Albanian Ottoman vassal. Circumcised and instructed in the 'rite and custume of the Mahometane secte', he caught the sultan's eye and became a royal favourite. When George, aged eight, was taken into the sultan's presence, the sultan saw that he was 'beautiful' and possessed a certain natural 'majestie' so resolved not to allow him to return home (p. Sii). The writer says that the name 'Skanderbeg', meaning 'Lord Alexander', was given him by the Turks (p. Siii). It has been suggested that this passage is an early example of what became a popular association of homosexuality with the Turks (Parker, 'Was Illyria as mysterious', p. 215). Skanderbeg developed a reputation for especially hating 'the sin of sodomy' (A.D. Wraight, *The story that the sonnets tell*, London, 1994, p. 209).

In his prefatory epistle, Shute describes Turkish victories as 'to the great dishonour of the Christian princes', (p. *i) and then elaborates his ideas about the qualities of a good soldier, suggesting that Christians could learn lessons from their enemies. He stresses the importance of military training at this time, when, unlike the Ottomans, few European states had standing armies. He seems to be arguing for a professional English army, though he comments that God gives armies their victory, hinting that God allowed Turkish victories in the face of Christian rivalries, so that Christians might learn a lesson about unity.

SIGNIFICANCE

On the one hand, the idea expressed in the work of the Ottomans as a 'scourge of God' punishing Christians for the sins of disunity and rivalry represents a negative stereotype, and descriptions of cruelty also perpetuate ideas of the Turks as monstrous, a threat to European stability, religion and civilisation. On the other hand, however, several passages challenge another popular stereotype: that expansion and aggression characterise any Muslim polity. The Mamluks, the text says, were peaceful for several centuries, and when the Ottomans conquered Egypt they also established peace and confirmed people's liberty. Depictions of Turkish atrocities almost seem to have been included because it was thought prudent to balance admiration with criticism. Passing references to Islam are relatively benign.

The work can be seen as a new genre that shifted away from polemic and from viewing the Ottomans purely through a negative lens towards objectivity and unbiased historical reconstruction. In translating Cambini, Shute made one of the earliest works of serious historical scholarship on the Ottomans available in English. Although it contains references to Islam, or rather to the Turks, as enemies of Christian Europe, it also hints that Christians can learn lessons from them about military organisation and discipline. After this work, serious interest in the Ottoman army, its tactics and organisation became more common, indeed 'a lasting concern of the West' (R. Murphey, *Ottoman warfare, 1500-1700*, London, 1999, p. 6).

Burke analyses Cambini and Shute's decision to retain some Turkish words, including *aga, pasha, janissaries, cadi* (adding a note that a qadi "determineth' differences', Shute, p. Niiii reverse) *seraglio* and *sanzachi* (Burke, 'Translating the Turks', p. 151). Shute may have introduced these words into English. Burke argues that this practice can make Turkey sound exotic and different, conjuring images of an alien culture with little in common with England's, and confirming ideas that such difference is unbridgeable. On the other hand, the preservation of key terms may be seen as respect for another culture, and serve to make the unfamiliar more familiar.

The work is mainly significant as an example of historical writing about a Muslim power that cannot easily be categorised as polemic. Despite references to 'God', it is not really a pious work. It can more accurately be seen as an attempt to understand a rival power, how it began, spread territorially and organised its very successful military.

EDITIONS & TRANSLATIONS

Two commentaries: the one of the originall of the Turcks the other of the warre of the Turcke against George Scanderbeg, Amsterdam, 1970

Two very notable commentaries the one of the originall of the Turcks and empire of the house of Ottomanno written by A. Cambine, and tother of the warres of the Turcke against G. Scanderbeg [a translation of Commentario delle cose de' Turchi, et del S. Georgio Scanderbeg...], London, 1562

STUDIES

Brief analysis in:

P. Burke, 'Translating the Turks', in M.J. Burke and P. Burke (eds), *Why concepts matter. Translating social and political thought*, Leiden, 2012, 141-53, pp. 142, 151

S. Runciman, *The fall of Constantinople 1453*, Cambridge, 2012, p. 197

N. Bisaha, *Creating East and West. Renaissance humanists and the Ottoman Turks*, Philadelphia PA, 2010, p. 178

P. Parker, 'Was Illyria as mysterious and foreign as we think?', in H. Ostovich, M.V. Silcox and G. Roebuck (eds), *The mysterious and the foreign in early modern England*, Newark NJ, 2008, 209-33, pp. 212, 215

P. Burke and R.P. Hsia, *Cultural translation in early modern Europe*, Cambridge, 2007, pp. 36-37

M. Milwright, 'So despicable a vessel. Representations of Tamerlane in printed books of the sixteenth and seventeenth centuries', *Muqarnas* 23 (2006) 317-44, pp. 319-20

M. Dimmock, *New Turkes. Dramatizing Islam and the Ottomans in early modern England*, Aldershot, 2005, pp. 64-65

Clinton Bennett

John Calvin

DATE OF BIRTH 10 July 1509
PLACE OF BIRTH Noyon, France
DATE OF DEATH 27 May 1564
PLACE OF DEATH Geneva

BIOGRAPHY

John (or Jean) Calvin was born in Noyon in Picardy, north of Paris, in 1509. As a young man he studied at the Collège de la Marche, in Paris. It is believed that, after completing his course, he entered the Collège de Montaigu. His movements during the mid-1520s took him from the University of Paris to the University of Orléans, University of Bourges and back to the Collège Royal in Paris. These movements were due, in part, to his changing his course of studies, at his father's behest, from theology to law.

At some point around this time, Calvin experienced an alteration of his views, which he would later refer to as a 'sudden conversion'. The enigma surrounding the timing and character of, and influences upon, this conversion is palpable, but the reality of it would seem to garner support from the events of All Saints' Day in 1533. After Nicolas Cop, the rector of the University of Paris, delivered an address at the commencement of the academic year that roused suspicion because of the 'Lutheran' themes it contained, not only Cop, but also numerous others, including Calvin, fled the city. King Francis I had decided to respond to Cop's boldness by attempting to round up everyone in the city associated with Lutheranism. Having fled, Calvin wandered around various parts of Europe before deciding to stay in Geneva in 1536.

Apart from a short stint in Strasbourg, Calvin would remain in Geneva for the rest of his life. He was married, apparently happily, to Idelette de Bure from 1540 until her death in 1549. Calvin worked for the reforming of Geneva and also of his French homeland, to which he would never return, living in exile until his death on 27 May, 1564. By the time of his death, the 'Reformed' faith he taught had spread through much of Europe and the British Isles, and it would eventually spread through much of the world.

Calvin's *oeuvre* includes theological treatises, letters, sermons, commentaries on biblical and classical works, polemical tracts, lectures and various other publications, written in Latin and in the French vernacular. His *Institutio Christianae religionis*, for which he is perhaps best known, has left an indelible mark on Christian thought – primarily that found in the West and within Protestantism. He was both despised and venerated in his own day. This being so, Calvin was buried in an unmarked grave, presumably so as to prevent desecration, and also to avoid the possibility of it becoming a holy shrine visited by pilgrims.

MAIN SOURCES OF INFORMATION

Primary

T. Beza, *Commentaires de M. Iean Calvin sur le livre de Josué. Avec une preface de Theodore de Besze, contenant en brief l'histoire de la vie et mort d'iceluy*... Geneva, 1564

N. Colladon, *Commentaires de M. Iean Calvin sur le livre de Josué. Avec une preface de Theodore de Besze*... Geneva, 1565

J.-H. Bolsec, *Histoire de la view, des moeurs... de Jean Calvin*, Lyons and Paris, 1577

J.-P. Masson, *Vita Ioannis Calvini*, Lutetiae, 1620

J.-M.-V. Audin, *Histoire de la vie, des ouvrages et des doctrines de Calvin*, Paris, 1841

Secondary
There are huge numbers of studies on Calvin, including:

J. Balserak, *John Calvin as sixteenth-century prophet*, Oxford, 2014

B. Gordon, *Calvin*, New Haven CT, 2009

J.-L. Mouton, *Calvin*, Paris, 2009

I. Backus, *Life writing in Reformation Europe. Lives of Reformers by friends, disciples and foes*, Aldershot, 2008

D. Crouzet, *Jean Calvin, Vies parallèles*, Paris, 2000

B. Cottret, *Calvin. Biographie*, Paris, 1995

O. Millet, *Calvin et la dynamique de la Parole. Essai de rhétorique réformée*, Paris, 1992

W.J. Bouwsma, *John Calvin. A sixteenth-century portrait*, Oxford, 1988

T.H.L. Parker, *John Calvin*, Berkhamsted, 1977

J. Cadier, *Calvin, se vie, son oeuvre*, Paris, 1967

A. Ganoczy, *Le jeune Calvin. Genèse et évolution de sa vocation réformatrice*, Wiesbaden, 1966

R. Kingdon, *Geneva and the coming of the wars of religion, 1555-1563*, Geneva, 1956

M. Weber, *Die protestantische Ethik und der Geist des Kapitalismus*, Tübingen, 1934

E. Doumergue, *Jean Calvin, les hommes et les choses de son temps*, 7 vols, Lausanne, 1899-1927

WORKS ON CHRISTIAN-MUSLIM RELATIONS

Institutio Christianae religionis; Institutio; Institution de la religion chrétienne, 'The Institutes'

DATE 1536-60
ORIGINAL LANGUAGE French

DESCRIPTION
The *Institutio* is a theological treatise. It went through five major Latin revisions, the first of which appeared in 1536 (the other major Latin editions appeared in 1539, 1554, 1550 and 1559). There was no French translation of the 1536 *Institutio*, but most of the later editions were translated into French, the definitive translation being the 1560 *Institution de la religion chrétienne*. In the *Calvini opera* edition, the Latin *Institutio* of 1536 comes to 248 columns. It would expand in each subsequent version, such that the 1559 edition consists of 1,118 columns.

The work as published in 1536 consisted of six chapters, which discuss the law (*de lege*), faith (*de fide*), prayer (*de oratione*), the sacraments (*de sacramentis*), the five false sacraments (*quo sacramenta... reliqua*), and Christian freedom (*de libertate Christiana*). The structure has been linked with Martin Luther's *Small catechism* of 1529. It treats the content of the Christian faith as set out in the standard creeds of the Church, such as the Nicene. Calvin includes a prefatory letter addressed to the French king, Francis I. The work also concludes with a brief examination of the nature of government and office of the civil magistrate. In this way, the *Institutio*, it has been argued, was a work with a political focus to it – a position that garners some support from a (later) preface to Calvin's commentary on the Psalms, in which he claims that he wrote the *Institutio* in order to explain to the French king the true character of the faith of those the king had put to death in 1534 as part of his attempts to rid France of groups (generally referred by the broad label of 'Lutheran') deemed to pose a threat to the religious and civil order of the realm.

Even though the treatise is not primarily concerned with relations with the Islam or Muslims, there are nevertheless a few explicit references to Islam as well as a general treatment of false religion, with Islam included in this category. The explicit references find Calvin referring to

Muslims as the 'Turks' as many during this era tended to do. Together with Jews and 'Papists', the followers of Muḥammad were deemed by Calvin to be fundamentally ungodly and opposed to the truth, despite the fact that they professed to worship God. This is brilliantly explained in the introductory chapters of his *Institutio*.

By the 1559 edition, the *Institutio* had been expanded to four books with a total of 80 chapters. The first nine chapters constitute a case for the viability of true religious knowledge in a fallen world, which knowledge can only be found in the sacred scriptures of the Christian faith. In his exposition, Calvin contends that those who do not follow the Christian Bible through a living faith inspired by the Spirit of the triune God fall invariably either into a hypocritical adherence to the Christian religion (i.e., Roman Catholics) or worship false gods (i.e., Muslims and Jews). Thus, although Calvin's explicit references to Islam are extremely rare, he was most certainly aware of Muslims – they had of course advanced as far as Vienna by 1529, prompting numerous authorities, among them Martin Luther, to write scathing accounts condemning them and identifying them with Gog and Magog (Ezekiel 38-39) and the Last Days – and constructed within the *Institutio* a system in which the 'Turk' was regarded as wholly opposed to the true God.

In certain senses, the above account of Calvin's understanding of false and true religions is more meaningful than any of the explicit references Calvin makes to Muslims in the *Institutio*. That said, some of his explicit assertions do give a sense of the vehemence of his feelings towards them. He declares, for instance, in *Institutio* 2.6.4: 'So today the Turks, although they proclaim at the top of their lungs that the Creator of heaven and earth is God, still, while repudiating Christ, substitute an idol in place of the true God.' In addition to vehemence of feeling, this citation nicely demonstrates one of Calvin's fundamental concerns with respect to the nature of true worship and, thus, of idolatry. For this reason as well, Calvin can assert that the Turks know nothing of what it means to pray, since true prayer can only be made through faith in Christ (*Institutio* 3.13.5). A total of five explicit references to 'the Turk' can be found in the 1559 *Institutio* edition, all of which state or imply that Islam is a false religion, which possesses no hope because it rejects Jesus Christ as God's son and the saviour of humankind.

SIGNIFICANCE
The perceived threat the Ottomans presented to Europe is difficult to over-estimate. The event of the Ottoman army moving north and making

it as far as Vienna was interpreted by many throughout European Christendom as a portent of the end of the age. The siege by the Ottomans did not directly threaten Geneva. However, news of the war spread throughout the Continent and to Geneva.

The threat of Islam notwithstanding, scholars at the time manifested an academic interest in Islam and in the Muslim religious text, the Qur'an. One of the more significant ways in which this can be seen is in the work of Theodor Bibliander, whose publication of a kind of encyclopaedia of Islam along with the first Latin translation of the Qur'an was of enormous importance (see his *Machumetis Saracenorum principis eiusque successorum vitae, doctrina ac ipse Alcoran*, Basel, 1543). Renaissance humanism had renewed thought on the relationship between Christianity and other religions, intellectual movements and philosophies. Some Christian humanists, such as Pico della Mirandola and especially Marsilio Ficino, developed profoundly influential interests in esoteric ideals, magic and the notion of the *prisca theologia*. Interestingly, concerning classical authors such as Cicero, Seneca and Virgil, important Christian writers such as Desiderius Erasmus and Ulrich Zwingli could declare openly that some of these virtuous 'pagans' would be in heaven. Indeed, Bibliander seems to have adhered to the idea that elements of all religions might serve as a kind of preparation for the Gospel (*preparatio Evangelii*), reviving a notion generally found among some of the church fathers. This relatively positive appraisal was not granted to all non-Christian religions. The early modern attitude towards the Jews offers an excellent example demonstrating the point. Nevertheless, some thinkers during the early modern era exhibited a more benign attitude towards non-Christian religions, and particularly towards Islam, than the attitude found in the writings of Calvin. Bibliander is a case in point.

Calvin's attitude towards Islam, as manifest in his *Institutio*, could never be called benign. To be fair, his interests in writing the *Institutio* lay elsewhere. Nonetheless, his sharp tone towards the Turks and his strong characterisation of Islam as an idolatrous religion leave no lingering doubt as to his position towards Muslims. This certainly does not set Calvin at odds with the general tradition of Western Christianity towards Islam – far from it. Rather, in condemning Muslims for their denial of Christ, Calvin would not have seen himself as doing anything unusual.

Calvin's interpretation of Christianity as so profoundly built upon the sacred scriptures would be propagated with the spread of Calvinism throughout Europe, the British Isles, the New World and, eventually to the East (Korea has a large Presbyterian – Calvinist – church) and to

Africa (in the form of Dutch Calvinism, found especially in South Africa). Accordingly, a similarly firm and uncompromising view of Islam spread along with the Reformed faith, which was spearheaded in no small way by the popularity of the *Institutio*.

EDITIONS & TRANSLATIONS

The editions and translations of the *Institutio* and *Institution* are too numerous to list. The following are the most recent and complete:

R. Peter and J.-F. Gilmont, *Bibliotheca Calviniana. Les oeuvres de Jean Calvin publiées au XVIe siècle*, 3 vols, Geneva, 1991-2000

W. de Greef, *The writings of John Calvin. Expanded edition*, trans. L. Bierma, Louisville KY, 2008

Electronic editions:

Many of Calvin's works, in English translation, are available at www.ccel.org/ccel/calvin

Many of Calvin's French and Latin writings can be found at www.prdl.org

Calvin's French and Latin writings are also available at www.e-rara.ch

AGES Software produced a CD-ROM entitled, *The comprehensive John Calvin collection*, which includes the Library of Christian Classics edition (trans. Battles) of Calvin's 1559 *Institutes of the Christian religion*.

The complete works of Calvin from the *Calvini opera* (Corpus Reformatorum) edition are available in DVD format from Instituut voor Reformatieonderzoek, Apeldoorn, the Netherlands.

Westminster John Knox Press has produced the Library of Christian Classics edition (trans. Battles) of Calvin's 1559 *Institutes of the Christian religion* on CD-ROM.

Important Latin editions:

P. Barth and G. Niesel (eds), *Joannis Calvini opera selecta*, Munich, 1926-36, i, pp. 11-283, and iii-v

G. Baum et al., *Corpus Reformatorum. Ioannis Calvini opera quae supersunt omnia*, Brunswick, 1863-1900, i-ii

Important French editions:

O. Millet (ed.), *Institution de la religion chrétienne (1541)*, Geneva, 2008, (annotated critical edition)

J.-D. Benoit, *Institution de la religion chrétienne de Jean Calvin*, Paris, 1957-63 (critical edition with introduction, notes and variants)

J. Pannier (ed.), *Institution de la religion chrestienne*, Paris, 1936-39

G. Baum et al., *Corpus Reformatorum. Ioannis Calvini opera quae supersunt omnia*, Brunswick, 1863-1900, iii-iv

F. Baumgartner (ed.), *Institution de la religion chrétienne*, Paris, 1888

There are plans to publish a new edition of the *Institutio* and *Institution* to include in the *Calvini opera. Denuo recognita*, but at this point nothing has been produced.

Important English translations are:

    E.A. McKee (trans.), *Institutes of the Christian religion. The first English version of the 1541 French edition*, Grand Rapids MI, 2009

    F.L. Battles (trans.), *Institution of the Christian religion (1536 ed)*, Grand Rapids MI, 1986

    F.L. Battles (trans.), *Institution of the Christian religion (1536 ed)*, Atlanta GA, 1975

    F.L. Battles (trans.), *Institutes of the Christian religion* (Library of Christian Classics), 2 vols, Philadelphia PA, 1960

    H. Beveridge (trans.), *Institutes of the Christian religion*, 2 vols, Edinburgh, 1845

    J. Allen (trans.), *Institutes of the Christian religion*, 2 vols, Philadelphia PA, 1813

(Ford Lewis Battles's translation is now generally considered the standard English edition, though it has been criticised by some; for questions and disputes about Battles's Latin, see: http://calvinbattlescorrections.blogspot.com/)

STUDIES

There are thousands of scholarly works on the *Institutes*. None of the following deals with Islam per se, but they discuss the character of the *Institutes* in a general way:

    W. van't Spijker, *Bij Calvijn in de leer. Een handleiding bij de Institutie*, Houten, 2004

    R. Muller, *The unaccommodated Calvin. Studies in the foundation of a theological tradition*, Oxford, 2000

    R. Zachman, 'What kind of book is Calvin's *Institutes*?' *Calvin Theological Journal* 35 (2000) 238-61

    P.C. Böttger, *Calvins Institutio als Erbauungshuch. Versuch einer literarischen Analyse*, Neukirchen-Vluyn, 1990

    J.-D. Benoit, 'The history and development of the *Institutio*. How Calvin worked', in G.E. Duffield (ed.), *John Calvin*, Grand Rapids MI, 1966, 102-17

B.B. Warfield, 'On the literary history of Calvin's *Institutes*', *Presbyterian and Reformed Review* 10 (1899) 193-219

J. Köstlin, 'Calvins *Institution* ach Form und Inhalt in ihrer geschichtlichen Entwicklung, *Theologische Studien und Kritiken* 41 (1868), 7-62, 410-86

Praelectiones in librum prophetiarum Danielis, 'Lectures on the Book of the prophecies of Daniel'

DATE 1561
ORIGINAL LANGUAGE Latin

DESCRIPTION

Calvin's lectures on Daniel were part of a longer series of lectures he presented on the prophetic books. He also lectured in this series on Isaiah, Psalms, Minor Prophets, Jeremiah, Lamentations and Ezekiel (dying before he completed this book). These lectures were different from the commentaries he produced. He wrote commentaries on all the Pauline epistles as well as the Gospels and Acts and on Old Testament books, such as the last four books of the Pentateuch and Joshua. The lectures, however, were presented to the Genevan public as discourses in which Calvin went verse by verse through a biblical book, expounding, covering issues of interpretation of the Hebrew, treating the historical background, and so forth. From late 1555 (or early 1556) onwards, these lectures began to focus on preparing ministers to be sent into France in order to assist the growing French Reformed congregations.

Calvin divided his treatment of Daniel into 66 individual lectures. His handling of the book, like his handling of all the prophetic books, is characterised by a careful treatment of the history and context in which the prophet Daniel and his friends found themselves. As one enters the latter half of the Book of Daniel, with its prophecies about the Son of Man and visions of rams and other images, Calvin attempts to continue his historically-oriented treatment while also being attuned to the rhetorical devices and literary tropes employed in the text. He strongly eschews apocalyptic readings, despite their popularity throughout exegetical history. For Calvin, the most important thing the Book of Daniel could do was provide guidance and comfort to his French trainee-ministers, who were about to enter the stronghold of Catholicism that was 16th-century France. Accordingly, his analysis of the book tends to be historically-focused and to see God as the one who cares for his people who were dwelling in a strange land.

Calvin's handling of Islam within these lectures is scattered and fairly brief. He mentions the Turks in several places in his exposition of Daniel 2. His consistent concern is to argue against Jewish commentators, particularly Rabbi Barbinel, who he contends are wrong to identify the fourth kingdom mentioned by Daniel (in Daniel 2, 7, 8 and 11) as the Turkish Empire, because he thinks it should be understood as the Roman Empire.

His comments here are calmer and more academic in tone than those in either the *Institutio* or in his sermons on Deuteronomy. They are primarily historical in character. Accordingly, he is content to acknowledge that the Ottoman Empire has enormous amounts of wealth and power, and has managed to conquer great portions of the globe, toppling several kingdoms in the process. Calvin's aim in all these comments is to argue for the correct interpretation of the identity of the fourth kingdom mentioned by Daniel.

SIGNIFICANCE

The history of the interpretation of Old Testament prophecy, such as the kind found in the book of Daniel, is replete with instances of interpreters locating the dangers of their own age in the biblical text. This was true in Antiquity, in the Middle Ages and also during the early modern era. Martin Luther, for instance, identified Gog and Magog (Ezekiel 38-39) as the Turks. Similarly, numerous exegetes found the fears and dangers associated with their own age in the Book of Daniel, particularly Daniel 7. As the Turks were a potent threat to the Europe of the 1500s, they were commonly identified within readings of these books.

That being the case, Calvin's handling of the Book of Daniel sets out a revisionist reading of the book. However, his unwillingness to identify the Turks with the fourth monarchy has nothing to do with the question of his attitude towards Islam. On the contrary, his concerns are focused on lecturing on the prophetic books, including Daniel, in such a way that he can use the richness of the text to prepare his ministerial trainees for the French situation into which they would soon be entering.

His observations on Islam and the 'Turks' found in these lectures on Daniel exhibit the same general views that one finds elsewhere in his works, but without the vitriol, intensity and hatred. Thus, his reading of Daniel was quite distinct from many readings of it that had been produced during the Middle Ages and were still being produced in Calvin's own day. But the real significance of these lectures on Daniel is in their historical orientation, which served to lay the groundwork for future biblical exposition, particularly among Reformed Christians.

EDITIONS & TRANSLATIONS

T.H.L. Parker (trans.), *Daniel*, Grand Rapids MI, 1993

T. Myers (trans.), *Commentaries on the Book of the Prophet Daniel*, 3 vols, Edinburgh, 1852-53 (reissued in 2 vols, Grand Rapids MI, 1948)

Prælectiones in librum prophetiarum Danielis. Joannis Budæi et Caroli Jonvillæi labore et industria exceptæ. Additus est e regione versionis Latinæ Hebraicus et Chaldaicus textus, Genève, 1591

Praelectiones Joannis Calvini in librum Prophetiarum Danielis, Vincentius, 1571

Lecons de M. Jean Calvin sur le livre des propheties de Daniel. Recueillies fidelement par Jean Budé, et Charles de Jonviller, ses auditeurs: et translatées de latin en françois. Avec une table ample des principales matieres contenues en ce livre, Geneva, 1569

Joannis Calvini praelectiones in librum prophetiarum Danielis, Joannis Budaei et Caroli Jonvillaei labore et industria exceptae. Additus est e regione versionis latinae hebraicus et chaldaicus textus, Genève, 1561

STUDIES

J. Balserak, 'The authority of tradition in Calvin's lectures on the prophets against the backdrop of early modern European change', in P. Webster, E. Fulton and H. Parish (eds), *The search for authority in the European Reformation*, Aldershot, 2014, 29-48

B. Pitkin, 'Prophecy and history in Calvin's lectures on Daniel (1561)', in *Die Geschichte der Daniel-Auslegung in Judentum, Christentum und Islam. Studien zur Kommentierung des Danielbuches in Literatur und Kunst*, Berlin, 2007, 323-47

I. Backus, 'The Beast. Interpretations of Daniel 7.2-9 and Apocalypse 13.1-4 in Lutheran, Zwinglian and Calvinist circles in the late sixteenth century', *Reformation and Renaissance Review* 3 (2000) 59-77

A. Seifert, 'Calvin und die "romanistische" Fruhform der prateritischen Daniel-Auslegung', in *Der Ruckzug der biblischen Prophetie von der neueren Geschichte. Studieren zur Geschichte der Reichstheologie des fruhneuzeitlichen deutschen Protestantismus*, Cologne, 1990, 49-64

T.H.L. Parker, *Calvin's Old Testament commentaries*, Edinburgh, 1986, pp. 176-224

C.-G. Dubois, 'Les leçons de Jean Calvin sur le Livre des Prophéties de Daniel', in *La conception de l'histoire en France au XVIe siècle (1560-1610)*, Paris, 1977, 466-84

H. Volz, 'Beitrage zu Melanchthons und Calvins Auslegungen des Propheten Daniel', *Zeitschrift fur Kirchengeschichte* 67 (1955-56) 93-118

Sermons sur le V. livre de Moyse, nommé Deutéronome, The sermons of M. Iohn Calvin upon the fifth booke of Moses called Deuteronomie

DATE 1567
ORIGINAL LANGUAGE French

DESCRIPTION

Calvin's sermons on Deuteronomy are indicative of the preaching that occupied much of his day-to-day work in Geneva. They are also characteristic of many of the qualities that came to exemplify his handling of the biblical text, whether in sermons, lectures or commentaries.

Calvin preached on nearly the entire Bible during his years in Geneva and Strasbourg. He took up the book of Deuteronomy on 20 March, 1555. Preaching 200 sermons on the fifth book of Moses, Calvin tended to treat between five and eight verses in each sermon and sometimes as many as 10 or 11. Not infrequently he would overlap his coverage, mentioning a verse or two at the end of one sermon only to take them up again at the beginning of the next. Likewise, on rare occasions, he preached only on one or two verses at a time, if the topic addressed there was deemed by him to be worthy of special attention. He preached on each of the Ten Commandments individually, for example (thus, he expounded the last five commandments in individual sermons: Deuteronomy 5:17; 5:18; 5:19; 5:20; 5:21). He preached two sermons on the commandment to keep the Sabbath (first expounding Deuteronomy 5:12-14 and then 5:13-15).

A series of sermons on an Old Testament biblical book that records the history of Israel coming out of Egypt and sets out legal instruction and its application is plainly not going to produce an extended and organised coverage of Islam. That said, Calvin does mention Islam on several occasions in these sermons.

His handling of Islam exhibits the same qualities that are found in his *Institutio Christianae religionis*. Yet Calvin does extrapolate here in a more fulsome manner on a small handful of themes related to the 'Turk', through which we glean a slightly better understanding of his conception of the Islamic religion. It will come as little surprise, for instance, that he mentions Muslims in a sermon on Deuteronomy 13:1-3, in which God warns his people, through Moses, not to hearken to false prophets who prophecy and dream dreams and so forth. His remarks are not surprising, as Calvin takes the opportunity provided by the biblical passage to warn against listening to Turks, pagans, Jews and Roman Catholics, who blaspheme God and indeed would like to rid the world of Christianity. Calvin also comments in this sermon that Muslims profess that God created the heavens and the earth, but hate Jesus Christ and refuse to worship him. A number passages in these sermons set out similar observations.

Calvin adds breadth to this coverage in several places. For instance, he identifies the Turks' adherence to the same belief that Calvin finds among the Roman Catholics, namely, that they believe themselves to be acting in a right and godly manner when they uncritically rely on what was passed down from their fathers. This characteristic, which Calvin identifies as a damning fault, means that both the 'Turks' and the 'Papists' consider it sufficient to hold on to what they are doing at present, which they claim was passed down to them and therefore authoritative, rather than listening to God's voice (sermon on Deuteronomy 29:22-29).

In another example, Calvin mentions the Qur'an. This reference is in comments on Deuteronomy 18:9-15. In so doing, he again equates Catholics and Muslims, this time adding the Jews to the mix. He contends that all of them claim to worship the Creator of heaven and earth, but (he adds this time) they make a mockery of the majesty of God and in actual fact do not worship the true God but a 'puppet' (sermon on Deuteronomy 18:14-15). In this context, he identifies Muḥammad and the pope as the two horns of the Antichrist, a reference to Daniel 8. This, then, is one of the more censorious remarks about Islam found in these sermons.

Despite such condemning assessments, Calvin acknowledges that Muslims exhibit a kind of reverence for their religion, which he declares in a sermon on Deuteronomy 4:6-10. And yet despite this, Calvin asserts – in a portion of the sermon where he is clearly attempting to rouse his hearers to godliness and a wholehearted embracing of Christian doctrine – that 'Turks' are cut off from the Church due to their failure to adhere to God's truth about his Son, the Lord Jesus Christ.

So then, Calvin does occasionally mention Islam in these sermons, although almost always with derision. He usually compares Islam with Judaism and even more with Roman Catholicism, with the aim of condemning all three, and commending the 'true' Christian religion.

SIGNIFICANCE

The Ottoman threat was a common thread linking the whole of Europe together. Naturally, this was as true of Geneva as it was of Zurich or Paris, though of course the imminent threat was felt more profoundly in particular parts of the Continent as the Turks pushed further west.

Given this threat, it would have come as no surprise to the hearers of these sermons (preached in St Pierre) to find Calvin condemning the Turks in the strongest possible terms. Large swathes of the city of Geneva would have heard Calvin preach, not to mention travellers and even curious Catholics visiting from neighbouring villages and towns, who occasionally came to hear his sermons. His audience was not a gathering of fellow humanists, theologians or scholars who might be interested in learning about the Muslims or the Qur'an for (what could be legitimately identified as) academic reasons. Thus, whereas some scholars, such as Theodor Bibliander, were studying Islam as an intellectual pursuit, those who sat under Calvin's preaching, though a diverse group of people, consisted primarily of those who were supposed to be learning how to be pious believers and, therefore, as Calvin would have seen it, required to be taught to love the truth and hate evil. This was not the time, Calvin seems to have felt, to engage in anything except the clear, unambiguous articulation and application of the Gospel to the people of God. Calvin's declarations are often concerned to classify the Turks together with Roman Catholics and Jews as idolatrous religious groups who were cut off from God's Church and had no hope of eternal life. The legacy of such a reading of Islam would be felt in later centuries throughout the world.

EDITIONS & TRANSLATIONS

A. Golding (trans.), *Sermons on Deuteronomy*, Edinburgh, 1987 (16th-17th-century facsimile editions)

Baum et al., *Corpus Reformatorum*, xxv, p. 573-xxix, p. 232

The sermons of M. Iohn Calvin upon the fifth booke of Moses called Deuteronomie: faithfully gathered word for word as preached them in open pulpit; together with a preface of the ministers of the Church of Geneva..., London, 1583

Sermons de M. Iean Caluin sur le v. liure de Moyse nommé Deuteronome: recueillis fidelement de mot à mot, selon qu'il les preschoit publiquement. Auec une preface des ministres de l'Eglise de Geneue, & vn aduertissement fait par les Diacres. Il y a aussi deux tables: l'vne des matieres principales, l'autre des passages de la Bible alleguez par l'autheur en ces sermons, Genève, 1567

STUDIES

J.-M. Berthoud, 'Pierre Viret, éthicien', *La Revue Réformée* 62 (2011) 29-54

J. Balserak, '"There will always be prophets". Deuteronomy 18:14-22 and Calvin's prophetic awareness', in Herman Selderhuis (ed.), *Saint or sinner? Papers from the International Conference on the Anniversary of John Calvin's 500th birthday*, Tübingen, 2010, 85-112

R. Blacketer, *School of God. Pedagogy and rhetoric in Calvin's interpretation of Deuteronomy*, Dordrecht, 2006

R. Blacketer, 'Smooth stones, teachable hearts. Calvin's allegorical interpretation of Deuteronomy 10:1-2', *Calvin Theological Journal* 34 (1999) 36-63

M. Plant, 'Calvin's preaching on Deuteronomy', *Evangel* 12 (1994) 40-50

Jon Balserak

Heinrich Bullinger

DATE OF BIRTH   18 July 1504
PLACE OF BIRTH   Bremgarten, Switzerland
DATE OF DEATH   17 September 1575
PLACE OF DEATH   Zurich

BIOGRAPHY

Born the son of a cleric, Heinrich Bullinger was sent to study at a house of the Devotio Moderna at Emmerich in the Rhineland. In 1519, he graduated at the University of Cologne. Having embraced the *solae* of Martin Luther around 1520, Bullinger returned to Swiss lands to take the position of teacher at the cloister school at Kappel near lake Zurich. During this time, he carefully read the Bible in the original languages and established contact with Huldrych Zwingli, under whom he studied for five months. Bullinger was sent by the Zurich Council to the Bern Disputation in 1528, where he came to know some of the leading Reformers, such as Martin Bucer. Bullinger married in 1529 while serving as a parish minister, and was admired for his preaching. Following the Battle of Kappel in 1531, where Zwingli was killed, Bullinger took up the position of chief preacher in the Grossmünster in Zurich, which effectively made him head of the church. He worked out an arrangement with the Zurich magistrates whereby church and council could cooperate. The magistrates were to give the church a degree of independence to preach the Gospel as long as ministers did not venture into political matters or criticise the council. This arrangement would be the hallmark of Bullinger's 40 years as head of the church in Zurich.

Bullinger remained the undisputed head of the Zurich church and a major figure in the European Reformation till his death. His writings were widely translated and his influence in England was particularly notable, not least on account of the numerous refugees from Queen Mary's persecutions who made their way to Zurich. Together with John Calvin, Bullinger drafted the 1549 *Consensus Tigurinus*, an agreement on the Lord's Supper. Concerning this sacrament, Bullinger was never able to reach agreement with Luther or the Lutherans, although he remained on good terms with Philip Melanchthon.

In 1564, Bullinger produced his *Uff siben Klagartikel...kurze waarhaffte nodtwendigeund bescheine Verantwortung* ('Reply to the seven charges'; reprinted 1565), which was a defence of the Zurich theology against opponents who were unnamed, though clearly Lutherans. Bullinger discusses Islam (sig 34r-35r) as part of his treatment of the nature of Christ. He adds little to his thoughts in *Der Turgg*. In *Uff siben*, Bullinger is responding to accusations that the Zurichers' understanding of the nature of Christ was the same as that found in the Qur'an. In other words, the Zurichers denied the divinity of the Son of God. About ten pages later Bullinger returns to the subject of Islam to reject accusations that the Zurichers' understanding of heaven was the same as that taught by Muslims. In both cases, Bullinger refers to specific passages in the Qur'an to make his point.

Bullinger was a crucial figure in stabilising the Swiss Reformation. He oversaw the rebuilding of the Zurich church after the disaster of 1531 and he gathered in the city a circle of outstanding scholars, including Konrad Pellikan, Konrad Gesner, Theodor Bibliander and Rudolf Gwalther. Bullinger himself published a large body of work, including commentaries, sermons, history and theological tracts. His best known work is his *Decades*, a collection of 50 sermons that cover a range of doctrine. It was translated into all the major European languages and was especially popular in England. Such was Bullinger's status during his life that John Calvin readily acknowledged the Zuricher as his senior, even when they did not always agree. In particular, the two men differed on the Lord's Supper and the doctrine of predestination, though they agreed to keep their disagreements private. They maintained close epistolary contact, and Calvin made several journeys to speak with Bullinger in confidence.

MAIN SOURCES OF INFORMATION

Primary

J.W. Stucki, *Oratio funebris in obitum d. Henrici Bullingeri*, in J. Simler and J. Stucki, *Narratio de ortu*, Zurich: Chr. Froschauer, 1575

H. Bullinger, *Reformationsgeschichte*, Frauenfeld, Switzerland, 1838-40, repr. Zurich, 1984, https://archive.org/details/heinrichbullingo1bullgoog

E. Egli (ed.), *Heinrich Bullingers Diarium (Annales vitae) der Jahre 1504-1574. Zum 400. Geburtstag Bullingers am 18. Juli 1904*, Basel, 1904

Heinrich Bullinger – Briefwechseledition/Heinrich Bullinger's correspondence, http://www.irg.uzh.ch/hbbw.html (an invaluable web-based resource from the University of Zurich)

Secondary

E. Campi and P. Opitz (eds), *Heinrich Bullinger, life, thought, influence. International congress Heinrich Bullinger (1504-1575), Zurich, Aug. 25-29, 2004*, Zurich, 2007

F. Büsser, *Heinrich Bullinger (1504-1575). Leben, Werk und Wirkung*, 2 vols, Zurich, 2005

E. Campi (ed.), *Heinrich Bullinger und seine Zeit. Eine Vorlesungsreihe (Zwingliana: Beiträge zur Geschichte Zwinglis der Reformation und des Protestantismus in der Schweiz* 31), Zurich, 2004

B. Gordon and E. Campi (eds), *Architect of Reformation. An introduction to Heinrich Bullinger*, Grand Rapids MI, 2004

P. Opitz, *Heinrich Bullinger als Theologe. Eine Studie zu den 'Dekaden'*, Zurich, 2004

C. Pestalozzi, *Heinrich Bullinger. Leben und ausgewählte Schriften*, Elberfeld, Wuppertal, 1858, http://www.google.de/books?id=Gf8pzpovEBAC&printsec=frontcover&dq=Heinrich Bullinger#v=onepage&q=Heinrich%20Bullinger&f=false

WORKS ON CHRISTIAN-MUSLIM RELATIONS

Der Turgg. Von anfang und Ursprung desz Türggischen Gloubens der Türggen ouch ihrer Königen und Keyseren, 'The Turks. On the beginning and origin of the Turkish faith, the kings and emperors of the Turks'

DATE 1567
ORIGINAL LANGUAGE German

DESCRIPTION

This octavo volume of 32 pages appeared in 1567 without the name of Bullinger, the printer or the place of publication on the title page (its title in full is *Der Turgg. Von anfang und Ursprung desz Türggischen Gloubens der Türggen ouch ihrer Königen und Keyseren und wie fürträffenlich vil landen unnd lüthen sy innet 266. jaren yn genommen und der Christenheit abtrungen habind*). However, it is thought that it was produced by Christoph Froschauer in Zurich (Pfister, 'Antistes Heinrich Bullinger Ueber den "Tuergg"', p. 72). Bullinger is known to be the author on account of his mentioning *Der Turgg* in his *Diarium* (p. 87). Only two copies of the book are known to exist (Zurich ZB and Winterthur StB). Below the title is a quotation from Revelation 9:16-17, 'The number of the mounted troops was two hundred million. I heard their number. The horses and riders I saw in my vision looked like this: their breastplates were fiery red, dark blue, and yellow as sulphur. The heads of horses resembled the heads of lions, and out of their mouths came fire, smoke, and sulphur.' The preface by Alsatian Reformer Matthias Erb is addressed to the Swiss and German nobility. The work consists of 16 chapters and ends with a long prayer for preservation in the face of the Turkish threat. Bullinger offers an explanation of the Muslim religion and provides an extensive history of Islam and the Ottoman Empire up to his own time, arguing all the while that only the Christian faith is true.

Bullinger's arguments are largely familiar. He draws heavily from John of Damascus and denies that the Qur'an is divinely inspired. The book is not holy, but instead the work of Muḥammad, who was aided by corrupt Jews and Christian heretics. Islam is a heresy derived from Nestorianism and Arians, and therefore particularly dangerous for true Christians. Like other Christian heresies, Islam denies the divinity of Christ and therefore the Trinity. Bullinger repeats well-established Christian arguments concerning the Qur'an's rejection of the resurrection and Islam as a religion of works, likening it to Catholicism and asserting that the Qur'an denies the essential teaching of the Reformation, that a person is justified by faith alone. Even the Muslim concept of the afterlife is 'fleshly' rather than spiritual.

In almost every respect, according to Bullinger, the Qur'an denies the teachings and practices of Christianity: worship, marriage and political authority. He even compares Islam to the destructive Anabaptist kingdom in Münster of 1534. In almost every respect the teachings of the Qur'an are an inversion of Christianity. The only time Bullinger speaks positively of Islam is when he wishes to admonish Christians; even the Muslims, he writes, are more upright than indolent or sinful Christians. Otherwise, the success of the Ottoman armies can only be explained in terms of divine punishment on Christendom. God has allowed the Islamic forces to prevail because of the sinfulness of his people. This narrative invokes the story of God and the Israelites.

The vast majority of the book (chs 4-16) is given over to a factual history of Islam from Muḥammad to Bullinger's own day. As Bullinger details the conquests and achievements of the Ottoman Empire, the work is largely a chronology of events and persons. He frequently cites the Bavarian humanist and historian Johannes Aventinus (1477-1534) as his source.

Der Turgg ends with a long prayer in which Bullinger names the lack of faith among Christians as the cause of the Turkish invasions. God is punishing Christians for their infidelity and the Turks are his instrument. Bullinger prays that the people will repent. Further, he beseeches God that the Muslims will convert to Christianity.

SIGNIFICANCE

Der Turgg does not stand out among 16th-century Christian works on Islam in terms of content. Bullinger's arguments are fairly conventional, drawn from ideas current in other works. His purpose, however, was to educate laypeople about the threat of the 'Turks'. Like his colleague Theodor Bibliander, Bullinger believed that the best defence against Islam was for Christians to learn about the religion, which he believed was a heretical form of the true faith. *Der Turgg* is consistent with the type of writings Bullinger published during his tenure as head of the Zurich church. He frequently wrote in the vernacular to teach laypeople about doctrinal and historical questions, regarding the education of the laity as a principal part of his role as chief preacher.

Although his arguments are by no means original, Bullinger reveals an impressive knowledge of Islam and Ottoman history. His summary of qur'anic teaching, while hostile, reflects a considerable level of engagement with the original text, which was printed in Basel in 1543. This level of knowledge is not surprising, given the work done in Zurich by his colleague and close friend Theodor Bibliander. Bullinger would have had access to both Bibliander's scholarship and the man himself. Whereas Bibliander's work had a strong missionary character, Bullinger seems more concerned to convince the people that Islam was a perversion or heresy of Christianity. It is fair to assume that Bullinger derived most of his knowledge of Islam and the Qur'an from his colleague. It is notable, however, that Bullinger wrote his work after Bibliander's death in 1564, establishing himself as the authoritative voice on Islam among the Reformed churchmen of Switzerland. In Geneva, by contrast, Calvin never wrote specifically on Islam.

EDITIONS & TRANSLATIONS

Der Turgg was printed in Zurich in 1567 and never reprinted.

See J. Staedtke, *Heinrich Bullinger Bibliographie*, vol. 1, Zurich, 1972, p. 249 n. 557.

Text available at http://www.e-rara.ch/zuz/content/titleinfo/1573449

STUDIES

L. Felici, 'Una nuova immagine dell'Islam (e del cristianesimo) nell'Europa del XVI secolo', in G. Abbattista (ed.), *Encountering otherness. Diversities and transcultural experiences in Early Modern European culture*, Trieste, 2011, 43-66

E. Campi, 'Early Reformed attitudes towards Islam', *Theological Review of the Near East School of Theology* 31 (2010) 131-51

W.P. Stephens, 'Understanding Islam – in the light of Bullinger and Wesley', *Evangelical Quarterly* 81 (2009) 23-37, http://oimts.files.wordpress.com/2013/04/2007-10-stephens.pdf

T. Burman, *Reading the Qur'ān in Latin Christendom 1140-1560*, Philadelphia PA, 2007

P. Widmer, 'Bullinger und die Türken. Zeugnis des geistigen Widerstandes gegen eine Renaissance der Kreuzzüge', in Campi and Opitz, *Heinrich Bullinger. Life, thought, influence*, 593-624

V. Segesvary, *L'Islam et la Réforme. Etude sur l'attitude des Réformateurs zuruchois envers l'islam, 1510-1550*, San Francisco, 1998

H. Bobzin, *Der Koran im Zeitalter der Reformation. Studien zur Frühgeschichte der Arabistik und Islamkunde in Europa*, Berlin, 1995

K. Vehlow, 'The Swiss Reformers Zwingli, Bullinger and Bibliander and their attitude to Islam (1520-1560)', *ICMR* 6 (1995) 229-54

R. Pfister, 'Reformation, Türken und Islam', *Zwingliana* 10 (1956) 345-75

R. Pfister, 'Antistes Heinrich Bullinger Ueber den "Tuergg"', *Evangelisches Missions-Magazin* NF 98 (1954) 69-78

Bruce Gordon

Nicolas de Nicolay

DATE OF BIRTH 1517
PLACE OF BIRTH La Grave en Oisans
DATE OF DEATH 1583
PLACE OF DEATH Soissons

BIOGRAPHY

Nicolas de Nicolay was born at la Grave en Oisans in the Dauphiné in 1517, the same year, coincidentally, that Sultan Selim I entered Cairo and formally annexed Egypt and Syria to the Ottoman Empire. Nicolay left his home region in 1542 for Lyons to begin a military career, and in that same year engaged in the siege of Perpignan conducted by the Dauphin Henry (the future French King Henry II). More tangible contact with Ottoman power came in the following year; Nicolay was active in the siege of Nice conducted by King François I in 'scandalous alliance' with the Ottoman fleet, led by Khair al-Din Barbarossa.

The 26-year-old's skills as a cartographer must have already been well honed, for Nicolay was quickly entrusted by the French crown to engage in mapping of provinces and, presumably, information-gathering, throughout northern Europe and the British Isles. The next five years found him indefatigably traversing and charting the German Rhineland and Prussia, Denmark, Sweden, the Netherlands, England, Ireland and Scotland. Although Nicolay describes his activities in these areas with circumspect diplomacy, the *argumentum e silentio* suggests that the lines of his cartographic missions blurred further and further into espionage, most notably in Scotland. First, he acted as guide to a military action in support of French political intrigues, and his participation in the French liberation of Mary Stuart, Queen of Scots, in 1548 was crucial; his map of Scotland was key to the mission's success.

Nicolay himself sums up his early career trajectory in the preface to *Travels in Turkey* with the following: 'In 1542, at the age of 25, I left the belly of Dauphiné for the mouth of Lyon, and started my voyages with the war and siege of Perpignan... and afterward continued to pursue the desire for and impact of foreign travel for a period of fifteen to sixteen years to kingdoms, regions, and provinces of Germany low and high... Scotland, Spain, Barbary, Turkey, Greece, and Italy... which for the most part I undertook as part of [French] infantry and naval military operations.' He was appointed *Geographe ordinaire du Roi* (Royal Geographer) by 9 March 1555 at the latest, the date of the royal privilege granting him permission to publish an illustrated account of his travels in Islamic lands, as his name appears there with that official title.

Nicolay's *Travels in Turkey* was not published, however, until 1567, perhaps due to other royal cartographic assignments. In 1561, living by this time at the royal Château de Moulins, Nicolay was charged by Catherine de' Medici – widow of King Henry II and Queen of France until the king's death in 1559 – with the monumental task of mapping and describing the regions of France. The royal geographer only succeeded in producing exhaustive volumes covering the Duchy of Berry and the diocese of Bourges (1567), and the provinces of Bourbon (1569), Lyon and Beaujolais (1573).

Nicolay's status seems to have granted him access not only to the corridors of French political power, but also to the leading French figures in his professional field. He apparently sustained a long and close collegial relationship with the royal cosmographer André Thevet, who also accompanied the French diplomatic mission to Istanbul before departing on his better known voyage to the Western hemisphere. Upon Thevet's return from *la France antarctique*, the explorer gifted the royal geographer with natural specimens from Brazil. These were installed by Nicolay among his *collection des curiosités* at the Château de Moulins, which remained his principal residence for the rest of his life. Nicolas de Nicolay, Sieur d'Arfeuille, died while on temporary military assignment as *commissaire d'artillerie* at Soissons in 1583.

MAIN SOURCES OF INFORMATION

Primary

Les quatre premiers livres des navigations et pereginations orientales, de N. de Nicolay... Seigneur d'Arfeuille... Auec les figures au naturel tant d'hommes que de femmes selon la diuersité des nations, & c de leur port, maintien, & habitz, Lyon: G. Rouillé, 1567

Secondary
See the detailed list below.

WORKS ON CHRISTIAN-MUSLIM RELATIONS

Les quatre premiers livres des navigations et peregrinations Orientales, 'The first four books of Oriental journeys and wanderings' *Navigations et pereginations orientales; Les navigations peregrinations et voyages, faicts en la Turquie*, 'Travels in Turkey'

DATE 1567
ORIGINAL LANGUAGE French

DESCRIPTION
Whatever his level of security clearance, Nicolas de Nicolay was clearly a trusted member of the upper echelons of the French foreign service by 4 July 1551, when King Henry II dispatched him on a diplomatic mission to Istanbul in the retinue of Gabriel de Luel, Sieur d'Aramon, French ambassador to the Ottoman court. The French had established an embassy in Istanbul as early as 1535 – the first European nation to do so – under King François I. Gabriel d'Aramon's prime directive was not only to sustain the French diplomatic presence at the Sublime Porte, but also to petition Sultan Süleyman I formally to extend and expand a concerted military alliance against the Holy Roman Emperor Charles V. Nicolay's instructions were to chronicle the journey and record his observations about the Ottoman court and the peoples of its empire, in order to supply the French with an informed picture of the customs and practices of their potential (and potent) Islamic ally. This French diplomatic presence at Istanbul became increasingly urgent and negotiations more delicate, as a Franco-Ottoman naval alliance conducted joint military operations in the western Mediterranean from 1551 to 1555.

Nicolay's *Navigations et peregrinations orientales* – published in the second edition with the more localised title *Les navigations... faicts en la Turquie* – is divided into four books, chronicling the ambassadorial voyage to Istanbul, description of Ottoman court life and the customs and costumes of various ethnic groups that populated the Islamic capital, descriptions of religious figures and the 'exotic' practices of their beliefs. It concludes mainly with discussions of contemporary Arab and Persian culture, although Nicolay never travelled to an Arab region or Persia.

Included are accurate descriptions – some of the earliest to appear in Europe – of Islamic religion and ritual, monuments, mosques and education. Some of the book's lurid contents, however, were clearly targeted for a European market piqued by prejudice and exoticism, such as the lascivious description of Levantine lesbians frolicking in Turkish baths, or self-mutilating dervishes who 'eat an herb which makes them maniacal'.

The first book charts the progress of d'Aramon's attempts politically to navigate the Franco-Ottoman alliance, as Nicolay narrates highlights of the journey to Istanbul along the North African coast, with Mediterranean trips to Sicily, Pantelleria and Malta. His account has also been cited as a diplomatically silent cover for his true occupation as a spy for the French crown, for Nicolay reveals little about the intrigues to which he must have been witness. Instead, he offers, for example, invaluable descriptions of such cities as Algiers and Tripoli, describing the ancient Roman ruins of the latter, as well as the palatial residence of the Ottoman admiral Sinan Pasha (d. 1553; not Sinan the architect), evidence of the level of our author's access to the principal players on the stage of this diplomatic theatre.

The second book recounts sojourns on the Greek islands of Cythera, Chios, Mytilene and Paros, and in the port city of Gallipoli, followed by the arrival of the French entourage at Istanbul. Then ensues an overview of the founding and history of Constantinople and Byzantium, and what Nicolay considered the city's principal monuments: Hagia Sophia and other major mosques, and the seraglio and baths reserved by the sultan for his female consorts. Interestingly, all of the illustrations in these two books depict women and their dress, ranging in rank from a near naked Algerian slave to the *grand dame turcque* elegantly adorned in the best of haute couture that Istanbul's Grand Bazaar had to offer in women's fashion.

The third book depicts and describes first a full range of men in military service, from *azamoglan* – Christian slaves pressed into service from childhood, to Janissaries and their generals, *solachi* (archers) and axe-wielding Persian personal guards to the *grand seigneur*. Then follow images spanning social class, ethnic background and all aspects of Ottoman daily life, even if they occasionally cater to the same 'exoticising' market as some of the text. Depicted are the likes of Turkish chefs and Greek musicians, Jewish doctors and merchants, wrestlers, drunkards and drug-users, mad dervishes who cut themselves in an out-of-body state of hallucination, *torlaq*s who read palms, and other 'fringe' religious ascetics, including one whose body-piercing ensures his sexual abstinence. The third book ends with an illustrated discussion of pilgrims who have made the *ḥajj* to Mecca.

The fourth book is devoted to life in Persia, including portrayals of typical Persian noblemen and women and commentary on their *lascive et voluptueuse* lifestyles, descriptions of Arabia Felix and Arabia Deserta, Armenian religious devotion and its practice, merchants of Judea, and miscellaneous excursuses on Greek and Thracian history, beliefs and quotidian customs.

SIGNIFICANCE

The illustrations in Nicolay's *Travels in Turkey* are based on the author's original artwork, and are keyed directly to the accompanying text. Together they represent a treasure of contemporary information – both textual and visual – on life in the Islamic world, and they exposed 16th-century Europe to some of the first compelling glimpses, even if at times illusory, of the peoples, customs and costumes of an alien Ottoman Empire.

Whether the work is the first illustrated book in Europe solely devoted to depicting peoples of the Islamic world is arguable. What is clear, however, is its lasting historical impact on the European popular imagination and its aesthetic conceptions of Islam. The book's illustrations are still considered some of the most accurate of the time, and became the basis for illustrated ethnographies of the Islamic world for the next two centuries. All the early editions share basically the same format, and employ the genres of travel- and costume-books as a vehicle to engage the reader in an introductory education concerning the customs and costumes of the Islamic Middle East. Text and image combine to evoke reactions of empathy, titillation and revulsion along the way. A description of the ambassadorial sojourn in Tripoli en route to Istanbul occasions the illustration of a Moorish woman in local costume tenderly clutching her child, who is touching and gazing adoringly at her face, conjuring up a sense of the universality of the human condition. Despite an extensive discussion in the text of Tripoli's archaeological ruins, the illustration contains no background to localise the scene. As with all the illustrations, only a few formulaic tufts of grass indicate the landscape of an outdoor location.

Nicolay aims for verisimilitude, not in the precision of topographical or local architectural rendering, but in the details, both visual and textual, of the manner and context of the figures' dress. He even admits to staging some of the illustrations – specifically, those of the sultana and the aristocratic Turkish women of the sultan's court. Having befriended one Zaferaga of Ragusa, a eunuch who was formerly the property of

Barbarossa and was now stationed in the seraglio of Sultan Süleyman I, Nicolay dispatched the eunuch and two courtesans to the shopping district of Bezestan (present-day Beşiktaş) to buy Turkish haute-couture that they could wear for a series of posed illustrations, so that the reader could view them unveiled just as the Sultan might in the seraglio, or as their high-ranking husbands might in the privacy of their home.

The eunuch Zaferaga is also our primary source for Nicolay's description of the Turkish baths. The image of a veiled and shrouded woman, accompanied by her unveiled (and apparently disgruntled) slave, making her way to the baths provides the opportunity for Nicolay to recount the eunuch's lewd report of the lascivious activities in which she will reportedly indulge at her destination: 'they bathe and touch and fondle... and make like Tribads, just like the Lesbian Sappho'. Ingres, the godfather of French 'Orientalist' painting, iconographically footnotes his debt to Nicolay in his 1862 painting *Le bain turc* by inserting the identical veiled female figure – albeit now nude save for her veil – into the background of his painting, surrounded by a panoply of other nude, lounging women in the seraglio, and thus envisions the erotic scene that Nicolay imagined would have greeted her upon her arrival.

Nicolay also gives his own eyewitness testimony to wanton behaviour among Turkish Muslims. His attendance at an ambassadorial audience and dinner with the sultan provides one of the first European accounts of the Turkish gastronomic delicacy, sorbet. Derived from the Arabic *shariba* (to drink, sip), Turkish sorbet was enjoyed in the summer by bringing snow down from the mountains, which was kept in underground cisterns until it was ready to be served, flavoured with fruit juices. As Nicolay notes, since the drinking of alcohol is forbidden by Islamic law, in vogue among the Turks was another manner of *'s'inivrer'* (getting drunk; translated in the Italian editions as *cuocersi* – 'getting cooked'), whereby they sprinkled on their sorbet 'a white powder they call opium'. Nicolay offers the reader an illustration of opium-'drunkards' walking through the streets 'giggling and howling like dogs' as evidence of this activity.

According to Nicolay, drug-use among Muslims was not limited to recreational use, but also had applications among religious mystics. His depiction of an enraged dervish, clothed only in an animal-hide, mutilating himself with a knife, is accompanied by the explanation that such religious ascetics 'walk through the countryside eating an herb called *matslach*, which... drives them mad'. By Nicolay's account, such fanatical religious deviants also engaged in sodomy and bestiality, except for the *qalandar*s, who appear in public with their genitals exposed and pierced with a silver ring to ensure their sexual abstinence.

Despite Nicolay's prejudiced orientation, clearly marketed for a readership titillated and repulsed by exotic tales of Islamic alterity, his book still affords one of the first European glimpses into a critical period in the history of Islamic theology and worship. Such fringe-groups as the dervishes, *qalandars*, and *jami* (Nicolay's *Geomailer*), explicitly renounced institutionalised worship. Consequently, they had historically been considered heretical by mainstream Islamic theologians. It was only under the Ottomans of the 15th and 16th centuries that their mystical philosophy and ascetic practice began to be assimilated into more socially palatable Sufi institutions. Nicolay's observations and discussions of the historical origins of these sects are among the first to appear in Europe, and it is only recently that the subject has begun to receive scholarly attention in the West.

Regarding sources, Nicolay's illustrated description of life in the Ottoman world certainly had precedents. His text, particularly in his sections on Ottoman court life and 'deviant' religious sects, relied heavily on the work of Giovanni Antonio Menavino. Son of a Genoese merchant, the 12 year-old Menavino had accompanied his father on a voyage to Venice in 1504, when their ship was captured by pirates, who presented Menavino as a gift to the Ottoman sultan. The enslaved Menavino spent the next ten years as an *içoğlan* – a personal attendant or page – to the Sultans Bayezid II (r. 1481-1512) and Selim I (r. 1512-20). Thirty-one years after his escape, he published his observations – accompanied by a few illustrations – about the Ottoman court and daily life in Istanbul as *Trattato de costumi et vita de' Turchi*... (Florence: Torrentino, 1548). Menavino's first-hand account of Turkish customs was itself preceded by that of a Greek emigré turned Venetian merchant, Theodoros Spandounés (Spandugino), written in about 1509-10, which contains the earliest known European description of dervishes in Istanbul. It was later published as *I commentari di Theodoro Spandugino dell' origine de' principi turchi, & de' costumi di quella natione* (Florence: Torrentino, 1551).

Nicolay's book is also noteworthy for the dispassionate motivation professed in its preface: 'to promote mutual understanding among all peoples', an academic approach toward Islam certainly radical for its time. Our author had his precedents for this enlightened worldview, as well. In 1535, when King François I established Jean de la Forest as his ambassador to the Sublime Porte, de la Forest's retinue included the linguist Guillaume Postel (1510-81). Postel's study of Arabic and the collection of manuscripts he amassed during his diplomatic sojourns in Istanbul and the Levant eventually earned him the appointment to the first chair of Arabic in Renaissance Europe at the Collège Royal; he also published the first Arabic grammar to appear in print.

Postel also produced two works that pioneered not only the field of Islamic studies in early modern Europe, but also that of comparative religion. His scholarly demonstration of religious relativism and implied plea for universal human empathy was the model for Nicolay's own rather formulaic and probably specious diplomatic declaration. Postel's *De orbis terrae concordia* ('On the harmony of the world', Basel: Oporinus, 1541) sought to demonstrate that the theological vision inherent in Judaism, Christianity and Islam could be traced back to Hermes Trismegistos (Hermes the thrice-greatest), a mythological sage historically associated with both Hermes the Greek messenger-god, hence god of intellectual transmission, and the Egyptian Thoth, patron god of scribes and writing.

As a more explicitly specific source, Nicolay relied heavily on Postel's *De originibus, seu de... historia... Turcarum...* (Basel: Oporinus, 1553), or rather, the revised French version *De la république des turcs* (Poitiers: de Marnef, 1560). He also, apparently, made some use of a work by another of his predecessors stationed earlier in Istanbul, Pierre Belon, *Les observations de plusieurs singularitez et choses memorables, trouvées en Grece, Asie, Iudée, Egypte, Arabie, & autres pays estranges...* (Paris: Corrozet, 1553).

Despite obtaining the royal privilege in 1555 to publish 'plusieurs livres' concerning the Islamic world, Nicolay's book did not appear until 1567. It seems, initially, that the author did not envision such a long delay in seeing the book into print. For, on 23 November 1555 he contracted with the 'engraver and illuminator' Lyon Davent to produce copper-plates based on the original drawings made by the royal geographer during his travels to and tenure in Istanbul. It is also apparent that Nicolay was still actively engaged in the work's production when it was eventually published 12 years later, for he apologises to the reader for the long delay, and the book's 60 engravings are carefully keyed to the text.

Despite the delay in seeing the book's publication, Nicolay did live to see it achieve widespread success before his death in 1583. The first edition of 1567 instigated an immediate re-issue the next year, soon followed by a second edition published in Antwerp in 1576 by Willem Silvius, who also simultaneously issued versions in Dutch, German and Italian that same year, with woodcut illustrations by Anton van Leest *et al.* based on

Davent's original engravings. The Venetian printer-engraver Francesco Ziletti cut new copperplates for his edition of 1580. Although most of the plates are based on van Leest's woodcuts from 1576, this Venice edition also introduced seven additional illustrations previously unpublished (see list of principal editions below). It is also the edition that ensured the book's enduring impact: Ziletti's transformation of the full-figure illustrations into Italian Mannerist cultural portraits became embedded throughout the published genres of costume-books and 'global' ethnographies of the European Baroque authors, who adapted his stylistic approach to their rendering of the pose, poise and stance of the peoples of the world as ethnic archetypes.

The royal privilege earned by Nicolay in 1555 to publish *'plusieurs livres'* on Islamic dominions under Ottoman sway hints that the author envisioned a more ambitious undertaking than the extant legacy of his *Travels in Turkey*. So, too, does the title of the first few editions: *'Les premiers quatre livres'* seem to promise more to come. Further evidence for a greater unrealised agenda comes from Nicolay's own testimony on the extent of his personal archive. In an unpublished manuscript at the Bibliothèque Nationale dated 1582, the *'premier cosmographe du roi'* alludes to 'eight to nine hundred drawings still in my possession of cityviews, castles, islands and seaports, done *in situ* by my own hand'. These drawings, along with his presumably extensive research library and collection of curiosities, which included 'bird-skins of various colours', souvenirs presented to Nicolay by André Thevet on his return from Brazil, were all destroyed in the fire that engulfed the Château de Moulins on 2 June 1755.

Despite this tragic loss to the historical record, Nicolas de Nicolay has still left his distinct influence on those who have sought to write the history of Christian-Muslim relations. His enduring artistic echo in various genres of human portrayal range from early modern illustrated books to the exotic and erotic in 19th-century French 'Orientalist' painting. His textual and visual presentation of empathy for the human condition as a motif of diplomacy blossomed into the universalist studies of comparative religion in the French and Dutch Enlightenment of the 18th century. Champions of abolitionist movements in the 19th century took inspiration from his declared disgust for Ottoman re-conditioning of seized and enslaved Christian children into soldiers and administrators of the *Dār al-Islām*. More recently, Nicolas de Nicolay's *Travels in Turkey* has served as a primary source of paramount importance for scholars investigating historical notions of alterity, and those seeking to re-write and re-draw the cultural map of Mediterranean history.

MANUSCRIPTS

MS Paris, BNF – 20008 (formerly Saint-Germain, Gesvres 99), 57 pp. (8 July 1582: *Extraict des observations de NICOLAY D'ARFEVILLE, Daulphinois, premier cosmographe du Roy, faictes durant ses navigations, touchant la diversité des navires, galleres, et autres vaisseaux de mer, tant grand ou subtil, ou petit soit-il, soit pour la guerre, ou pour la marchandise, avec lesquelz on navigue par les mers Oceane, Baltique et Mediterranée, plus la manière de fournir, armer et envitailler chacun desdicts navire, gallere, ou autre vaisseau,... et pour la fin les Ordonnances et signes ordonnez à une armée royalle pour seurement naviguer...*; a short primary source on Nicolay's own research and archive)

EDITIONS & TRANSLATIONS

C. Gomez-Géraud and S. Yérasinos (eds), *Dans l'empire de Soliman le Magnifique*, Paris, 1989 (based on the Antwerp 1576 ed.; indispensable modern critical edition)

The navigations, peregrinations and voyages, made into Turkie by Nicholas Nicholay Daulphinois, Lord of Arfeuile, chamberlaine and geographer ordinarie to the King of Fraunce conteining sundry singularities which the author hath there seene and obserued: deuided into foure bookes, with threescore figures, naturally set forth as well of men as women, according to the diuersitie of nations, their port, intreatie, apparrell, lawes, religion and maner of liuing, as wel in time of warre as peace. with diuers faire and memorable histories, happened in our time. Translated out of the French by T. Washington the younger, London: Thomas Dawson for John Stell, 1585 (English trans.; facsimile Amsterdam, 1968)

La navigation du roy d'Escosse Iaques Cinquiesme du nom, autour de son royaume, & isles Hebrides & Orchades, soubz la conduicte d'Alexandre Lyndsay excellent pilote Escossois. Recueillie & redigee en forme de descripiton hydrographique, & representée en carte marine, & Routier ou Pilotage, pour la cognoissance particuliere de ce qui est necessaire & considerable à ladicte nauigation, Paris: Gilles Beys, 1583

Le navigationi et viaggi, fatti nella Turchia, di Nicolo de' Nicolai del Delfinato, signor d'Arfeuilla... con diuerse singolarità viste, & osservate in quelle parti dall'autore, Venice: Francesco Ziletti, 1580 (This second edition of the Flory Italian translation contains 67 engravings by the publisher Ziletti after the woodcuts in the Willem Silvius edition of 1576. The seven added subjects are the engraving of two foreign dignitaries with a young attendant on fol. K4v and the six engravings from fol. M2v to the end of the volume: 'Capitano d'Arabie', 'Donna Turca standi in casa', 'Sposa di Constantinopoli', 'Patriarca di Constantinopoli', 'Calidesquer a piedi', and the final plate of four women in ethnic dress.)

De schipvaert ende reysen gedaen int landt van Turckyen..., Antwerp: Willem Silvius, 1577 (Dutch trans.)

Vier Bucher Von de Raisz vnd Schiffart in die Turckey Mit ein unnd sextzich (!) Man unnd Weibliche Figuren, nach dem leben abgesetzt, nach verenderung und gestalt der Lender, vnd gebrauch der selber, mit beschreibung jres art und leben, so wol inn Frid als Kriegzeiten..., Antwerp: Willem Silvius, 1577 (German trans.)

Le viaggi fatti nella turchia..., Antwerp: Willem Silvius, 1576 (Italian trans. by François Flory)

Les navigations peregrinations et voyages, faicts en la Turquie..., Antwerp: Guillaume Silvius, 1576 (with 60 woodcut illustrations by Anton van Leest, et al., after Davent's engravings in the 1567/68 edition)

Der Erst Theyl. Von der Schiffart vnd Rayß In die Türkey unnd gegen Oriennt. Mit schönen Figuren Wie beede Man[n] vnnd Weib irer Landtsart nach bekleydet seyen, Nuremberg: Gerlatz, 1572 (German trans. by Konrad Saldörffer of the first part only)

Les Quatre Premiers Livres des Navigations et Pereginations Orientales, de N. de Nicolay... Seigneur d'Arfeuille... Auec les figures au naturel tant d'hommes que de femmes selon la diuersité des nations, & c de leur port, maintien, & habitz, Lyon: G. Rouillé, 1567, 1568[2] (with 60 engravings by Lyon Davent after Nicolay's original *in situ* drawings)

Descriptions générale du pays et duché de Berry et diocese de Bourges avec les cartes géographiques dudit pays (1567), ed. A. Aupetit, Châteauroux, 1883

Générale description de l'antique et célèbre cite de Lyon, du pays de Lyonnais et du Beaujolais, selon l'assiette, limites et confins d'iceux (1573), Lyon, 1881

Descriptions générale du pays et duché de Bourbonnais... (1569), ed. I. de Hérisson, Moulins, 1875

Nicolas de Nicolay, *L'art de nauiguer de Maistre Pierre de Medine, Espaignol: contenant toutes les reigles, secrets, & enseignemens necessaire, à la bonne nauigation*, Lyon: Rouillé, 1554

STUDIES

D. Brafman, 'Facing East. The Western view of Islam in Nicolas de Nicolay's *Travels in Turkey*', Getty Research Journal 1 (2009) 153-61

M. Keller, 'Nicolas de Nicolay's *Navigations* and the domestic politics of travel writing', *L'Esprit Créateur* 48 (2008) 18–31

A. Hamilton, *Arab culture and Ottoman magnificence in Antwerp's Golden Age*, London, 2001

W.B. Denny, 'Quotations in and out of context. Ottoman Turkish art and European Orientalist painting', *Muqarnas* 10, special issue: *Essays in honor of Oleg Grabar* (1993) 219-30

De Lamar Jensen, 'The Ottoman Turks in sixteenth century French diplomacy', *Sixteenth Century Journal* 16 (1985) 451-70

C. Grodecki, 'Le graveur Lyon Davent, illustrateur de Nicolas de Nicolay', *Bibliothèque d'Humanisme et Renaissance* 36 (1974) 347-51

H.L. Baudrier, *Bibliographie lyonnaise. Recherches sur les imprimeurs, libraires, relieurs et fondeurs de lettres de Lyon au XVIe siècle*, Lyon, 1912, pp. 318-19 (repr. Paris 1964-65)

David Brafman

John Foxe

DATE OF BIRTH 1516/17
PLACE OF BIRTH Boston, Lincolnshire
DATE OF DEATH 1587
PLACE OF DEATH London

BIOGRAPHY

John Foxe was born in 1516 or 1517 in Boston, Lincolnshire, into a moderately wealthy family. His name is occasionally latinised as Foxus, and the 'e' is sometimes dropped. He attended the University of Oxford from about 1532, possibly at Brasenose College, although this has been contested (Lee, 'Foxe, John', p. 141). He graduated with a BA in 1537, and was elected a full Fellow of Magdalen College in 1539, teaching logic from 1539 to 1540 before proceeding to his MA in 1543 (*Oxf. Univ. Reg.*, Oxf. Hist. Soc., i, p. 188). He became a Protestant while at Oxford, which appears to explain why he resigned his fellowship in 1545 in order to avoid ordination as a Catholic priest, which was required 'within seven years of his election' as a Fellow (Lee, 'Foxe, John', p. 142). Marriage soon followed, though Foxe appears to have experienced a period of financial hardship until his acquaintance with the Protestant Duchess of Richmond led to employment as tutor to the Earl of Surrey's orphaned children from 1548. For the next five years, he lived in Reigate Castle.

There, he began to write and to translate works of theology in support of Protestant reforms, as well as a school text. Five privy councillors contributed to the publication of the latter, indicating that Foxe enjoyed important connections and patronage. He devoted considerable time to reading church history. In 1550, he was ordained deacon in the Church of England, though priesthood did not follow until 1559/60 because between 1554 and 1559 he joined Protestant refugees in Germany during the years of Mary's Catholic restoration.

Foxe worked in Frankfurt for a printer, Johann Herbst (also known as Oporinus), proof-reading and translating works of Protestant theology. He developed a friendship with the Scottish reformer John Knox (d. 1572), who was at that time minister of the English congregation where Foxe was also a preacher. John Bale (1495-1563) and Myles Coverdale (d. 1569) were also members of his circle of exiled Protestant scholars and reformers. He sided with Knox over the form of worship, against supporters of the 1552 Book of Common Prayer. Hearing about the persecution of Protestants in England, Foxe began to collect accounts and to plan a publication on the lives of those martyred for dissent by the Catholic Church, aided by Bale and others. This is his *Actes and monuments*, popularly known as *Foxe's Book of martyrs*.

Foxe disliked efforts toward doctrinal conformity within the Church of England, and while on the one hand the Church saw this book as validating its own narrative, on the other it could be used by some, such as separatists, to subvert that authority. It has been claimed that when the Archbishop of Canterbury asked Foxe to subscribe to the 'canons', he replied by holding up a Greek New Testament to which he said he would subscribe, but to that alone (Freeman and Evenden, *Religion and the book*, p. 238). An advocate of toleration, Foxe appealed against the executions of Anabaptists and of Edmund Campion, a Jesuit, during Elizabeth's reign (Olsen, *John Foxe*, pp. 206, 212).

After returning to England, Foxe stayed in London as a guest of a former pupil, now Duke of Norfolk. Refusing to wear vestments, he did not initially accept a salaried church post, identifying with the Puritans who avoided doing so, but by 1563 he was a prebend of Salisbury Cathedral and vicar of a parish. Other works by him include a Latin drama, *Christus triumphans* (1562) and *Ad inclytos ac praepotentes Angliae procures* ('To the renowned and powerful nobles of England', 1557).

Foxe died on 18 April 1587 while still working on a Latin commentary on the Book of Revelation. His well-attended funeral took place at St Giles's, Cripplegate, London. By the 19th century, his reputation had declined; his work was seen as hagiography and biased – he was 'too zealous a partisan to write with historical precision' (Lee, 'Foxe, John', p. 148.). M. Andrew's 1853 book was a typical attack on the text, which set out to reveal 'innaccuracies, falsehoods and misrepresentations'. However, his scholarship was re-evaluated in the 20th century following the publication of H.F. Mozley's *John Foxe and his book* (1940), which 'persuasively challenged many aspects of the dominant, excessively negative evaluation of Foxe's work', so that today his importance is 'uncontested' (Freeman, 'Foxe, John', p. 708). Rehabilitation of his reputation has focused on his use of sources, which improved over time. In particular, research has highlighted the value of primary material used for the Marian martyrs.

MAIN SOURCES OF INFORMATION

Primary

MS London, BL – Harley 416-17 (date unknown; Foxe's correspondence)

MS London, BL – Lansdowne 38S (date unknown; Foxe's memoir of his father, and his letters from his days at Magdalen College)

MS London, BL – Lansdowne 335, 353, 389, 679, 819, 1045 (date unknown; personal papers of Foxe and his family)

J. Foxe, *Christ Jesus triumphant*, trans. R. Day, London, 1607 (ESTC 11232; the dedication in this edition, and only this edition, contains valuable biographical detail on John Foxe)

MS London, BL – Harley 418-26, 590, 716, 783 (date unknown; personal papers of Foxe)

S. Foxe, 'Life of Mr John Foxe', *The acts and monuments*, London, 1641, ii (preface, no pagination)

Secondary

T.S. Freeman, 'The life of John Foxe', section 1.4. in *The unabridged acts and monuments online or TAMO*, http//www.johnfoxe.org (accessed 8 May 2014)

T.S. Freeman and E. Evenden, *Religion and the book in early modern England. The making of John Foxe's 'Book of martyrs'*, Cambridge, 2010

T.S. Freeman, art. 'Foxe, John', in *ODNB*, xx, 695-709

D.M. Loades, *John Foxe at home and abroad*, Aldershot, 2003

D.M. Loades, *John Foxe. An historical perspective*, Aldershot, 1999

T.S. Freeman, ' "The Reformation of the Church in this Parliament". Thomas Norton, John Foxe and the parliament of 1571', *Parliamentary History* 16 (1997) 131-47

T.S. Freeman, 'The importance of dying earnestly. The metamorphosis of the account of James Bainham in *Foxe's Book of martyrs*', in R.N. Swanson (ed.), *The church retrospective*, Oxford, 1997, 267-88

T.S. Freeman, ' "The Reik of Maister Patrick Hammyltoun". John Foxe, John Winram and the martyrs of the Scottish Reformation', *Sixteenth Century Journal* 27 (1996) 23-46

J.R. Knott, *Discourses of martyrdom in English literature, 1563-1694*, Cambridge, 1993

T.S. Freeman, 'Notes on a source for John Foxe's account of the Marian persecution in Kent and Sussex', *Historical Research* 67 (1994) 203-11

T.S. Freeman, ' "A solemne contestation of divers popes". A work by John Foxe?', *English Language Notes* 31 (1993-94) 35-42

W.W. Wooden, *John Foxe*, Boston MA, 1983

V.N. Olsen, *John Foxe and the Elizabethan church*, Berkeley CA, 1973

T.H.L. Parker, *English reformers*, Philadelphia PA, 1966

W. Haller, *Foxe's first Book of martyrs and the elect nation*, London, 1963

J.F. Mozley, *John Foxe and his book*, London, 1940
S. Lee, art. 'Foxe, John', in *DNB*, vii, 141-50
J. Pratt, 'Life of John Foxe', in *The acts and monuments of John Foxe*, London, 1877, 3-62
W. Winters, *Biographical notes on John Foxe the martyrologist*, London, 1876
W.E. Andrews, *A critical and historical review of Fox's Book of martyrs, showing the inaccuracies, falsehoods, and misrepresentations in that work of deception*, London, 1853
G. Townsend, 'Life of Foxe and vindication of his work', in R.C. Cattley (ed.), *Acts and monuments. A new and complete edition*, London, 1837, i, 45-482

WORKS ON CHRISTIAN-MUSLIM RELATIONS

Foxe's Book of martyrs; *Actes and monuments of these latter and perillous dayes, touching matters of the church*; *Actes and monuments*

DATE 2nd English edition, 1570
ORIGINAL LANGUAGE English

DESCRIPTION
Foxe's *Actes and monuments* (its full title is *Actes and monuments wherein are comprehended and described the great persecutions and horrible troubles that have been wrought and practiced by the Romish Prelates, speciallye in the Realme of England and Scotland from the peace of our Lord a thousande unto the tyme now present*) appeared in four editions during his lifetime. The first was in Latin, published in 1559, with the first English edition published in 1563. Longer than the Latin edition, this ran to 1,800 folio pages. Criticism and polemical attacks on its accuracy resulted in many revisions, and an even larger second edition, 2,300 double-columned folio pages, was completed in 1570. It was this version that included a 103-page history of the Ottomans, with a life of Muḥammad. The third edition (1576) more or less reprinted the second, though its physical quality was inferior. The fourth and final edition of 1583 ran to 2,100 folio pages, again double-columned. Abridged editions began appearing in print soon after Foxe's death.

As he worked on these editions, Foxe responded to criticism by using better sources, including statements by the martyrs, as well as by correcting and deleting content. He 'widened' his use of both manuscript and printed sources (Freeman and Evenden, *Religion and the book*, p. 142). A copy of the book was placed in every English cathedral and, despite its size, it was a financially successful publication, becoming one of the seminal texts of English Protestant theology. As well as narrating accounts of martyrs, Foxe reinterpreted Christian history to represent continuity between the early Church, various dissenting individuals and movements such as the Albigensians, Waldensians, Lollards and Hussites, and the English Reformation. For Foxe, the Catholic Church was false, not least because it imposed doctrinal conformity. Those who died or suffered for their conscience's sake over-and-against the coercive authority of the Church were true saints, representatives of the 'true church' (J.A. Kelhoffer, *Persecution, persuasion and power. Readiness to withstand hardship as a corroboration of legitimacy in the New Testament*, Tübingen, 2010, p. 271).

The book became a major shaper of the identity of English people as citizens of an 'elect nation governed by a godly prince' (Knott, *Discourses of martyrdom*, p. 3), becoming one of the most widely read and culturally important English works. Foxe also wove apocalyptic ideas into the story, which resonated with ideas about England's destiny and role in providential history as God prepared the world for Jesus' Second Coming. England was a New Israel, the biblical Israel reborn.

The second edition, published in 1570, consisted of two folio volumes. The content divides into 12 books, each covering 300 years of Christian history. Book 6, on 'The last three hundred years', the post-Wycliffe period, includes 'The history of the Turkes' (page references below are to vol. 4 of the edition by Cattley and Townsend first published in 1837). We know that Foxe had begun work on his history of the Turks by 1566 because he says that while he was writing this account he read a pamphlet about news of an Ottoman defeat in Hungary, which gave him 'hope' and 'comfort touching the decay and ruin of the Turk's tyranny and power against us' (p. 75). Oporinus, his Frankfurt employer, had printed Theodor Bibliander's Latin translation of the Qur'an in 1543 against the wishes of the Basel city authorities. Martin Luther defended the printing, saying that Christians 'needed to know the nature of their "diabolical adversary"' (Freeman and Evenden, *Religion and the book*, p. 81). Bibliander's Qur'an was a major source for Foxe, together with several other works, including an edited collection of 25 sources known as *Laonici Chalcocondylae Atheniensis, de origine et rebus gestis Turcorum* (Basel, 1556) (of the 21 sources Foxe cites, 17 were from this 15th-century Byzantine author, Laonicus Chalcocondyles [Freeman and Evenden, *Religion and the book*, p. 81]) and Johan Cuspinian's *De Turcorum origine*

(Antwerp, 1541). Foxe's citation method gave the impression that he had read many more sources than he actually had.

Foxe begins by giving six reasons why he thinks it necessary to write what readers might consider to be a 'foreign history'. He explains that, as far as understanding biblical prophecy is involved, Turkish anti-Christian acts may be seen as resulting from the decline of Christian faith itself, that God has used the Turks to punish Christians for disunity and false beliefs, that Turkish victories should encourage Christians to 'seek for greater strength' in Christ, and finally because, thinking themselves safe from any Turkish threat owing to their geographical distance, some neglect what has happened to 'their other brethren' (p. 20). Here he hints that the English may think any threat from Turkey irrelevant but should be more concerned as their incursion into Europe continued.

A brief life of Muḥammad takes up the next two pages. Giving various dates for the beginning of 'damnable' Mahomet's 'pestiferous secte' he says that these 'do not far disagree' from the number 666 of the Beast in Revelation, thus establishing a link between Muḥammad and the Antichrist, and also between Islam and Apocalyptic events. Muḥammad's people were 'Hagarenes' but he changed this to 'Saracens'. Although he affirmed Jesus' virgin birth, he denied the crucifixion (there is a reference here to 'Judas' dying 'for him'). 'Devilish' Mahomet took away Christ's 'divinity', although he saw Jesus as 'a most holy man' who would 'come again to kill Antichrist'. Mahomet raised himself above all prophets but, unlike earlier prophets, since he lacked the gift of miracles, he turned instead to the sword 'to compel men to his religion'. His book, Alcoran, which a Christian monk, Sergius, helped him compose, is full of 'vanities, lies and blasphemies' that are to be 'laughed at'. However, some suppose that Jews had a hand in writing Alcoran, and actually 'put it out after his death', which would make this even closer to the year 666. Mahomet allowed men to marry four wives, and take unlimited concubines. Any who refused to accept Mahomet's law were either executed or forced to pay tribute. By strength of arms, Mahomet subdued Arabia. After his death – by poisoning – his successors continued to expand their empire across the Middle East, then 'got Africa, and ... Asia' (p. 22).

Foxe gives the correct length of Abū Bakr's caliphate, and approximates in English the names of the first four caliphs. Foxe says that the Lord was 'willing' to permit these victories, which he says he will later explain. He then goes on to talk about the Turks (p. 23), describing how, while various Saracen sultans ruled 'Syria, Egypt, Africa and a great part of Asia', Turks began, around about 1330, to rampage around Asia, conquering 'some parts of the countries where they passed'. In these areas, backsliding and disunity weakened Christians, while their 'idleness, inconstancy, greedy avarice, lack of truth and fidelity' made Turkish victories possible. Attracted by the 'fleshly liberty' offered by Mahomet's sect, many Christians abandoned their religion for a 'licentious life' of 'liberty and war'. Christian weakness fuelled Turkish strength. Yet there is no 'imperial dignity to be esteemed' in the vast Turkish Empire, because Turks dissolve all 'good laws and policies' and exercise tyranny. For the virtues and justice with which 'lawful and well governed Empires' rule, they substitute 'fear, violence and oppression'. Turks, who wage 'perpetual war' are 'ministers of Satan's malice and fury'. Turks are thus enemies both of the Son of God and of all 'lawful empires'. Foxe describes the rule of 12 Ottoman rulers, from Osman I to Süleyman I, chronicling a history of brutality, fratricide, filicide, internal conflict, excess and despotism (pp. 25-78).

In the 'Notice touching the miserable persecution, slaughter, and captivity of the Christians', Foxe describes Christian treatment under the Ottomans (pp. 79-88). Captured in war, or taken off as tribute from Christian families, girls and boys who were thought especially beautiful were selected to 'serve abominable abominations' (p. 84), suggesting sexual deviancy. Others were trained to become enemies of Christ (p. 86). He recounts atrocity after atrocity committed against innumerable Christians. In Constantinople, 'Mahomet the drunken Turk, never rose from dinner but he caused every day, for his disport, three hundred Christian captives...to be slain before his face' (p. 82). Churches were destroyed or turned into mosques, while those remaining could be repaired but only at great cost. If a Christian happened to pass by a Muslim while riding horseback, he must alight and prostrate before him or be beaten (p. 86). Satan stirred the Turks up to 'butcher all Christian people' (p. 83). Rare Christian victories, such as that of John Hunyadi (d. 1456), were God-given (p. 41).

This section is followed by a tabulated list of countries ruled by the Turks (pp. 88-93) divided into regions. Foxe refers to the 'greatness of the Turk's dominions', and how little Christian territory remains. Contemplating this should stir Christians to respond and realise that, without renewed faith, Turkish victories would continue. Returning to prophecy, he argues (pp. 93-117) that the ultimate defeat of the Turks would be providential, because the conquests and persecutions of Christians by the 'horrible Antichrist', the Turks, could not have occurred without God's prior knowledge and permission. He reads into history an eternal conflict between the true children of God, and those who oppose them who are often their brethren – thus Cain opposed Abel, Esau opposed Jacob, and Ishmael Isaac. In the end, the children of promise will win against the children of rejection. He points out that the Saracens claim descent from Ishmael and that the Turks 'profess and maintain' their sect. Since Ishmael had 12 sons, he suggests that as Sultan Süleyman is the twelfth 'of the Turkish generation' he 'may be the last'. Foxe sees a parallel here with the demise of the Seleucids after their twelfth ruler, Antiochus Gripus, was defeated by Rome. He presents this information in two tables. As the Seleucids had persecuted God's people, so did the Turks. Both could be seen as Antichrists (p. 98); 'Antiochus, toward the latter end of the church of the Jews' and 'the great adversary of Christ, who is the Turk' (p. 99). Aware that some apply Daniel 7 as well as Revelation 13 to the pope, he suggests that these texts more accurately portray Antiochus and the Turk (p. 100). Yet the pope is also a 'maintainer of wickedness' and an 'adversary', so much so that his wickedness exceeds that of the Turks because he 'sits more like a god than a man in Rome' (p. 101). The pope falsely teaches that salvation requires belief that he is the Vicar of God. Foxe may be close here to Luther's distinction between the pope as the spiritual manifestation of Antichrist and the Turk as a corporeal manifestation (see M. Luther, *Werke. Tischreden* 1, Weimar, 1912, p. 135).

Foxe cites several earlier commentators for whom Mahomet and his followers represent the Little Horn of Daniel 7, and the Beast of Revelation 13, including 'Nicholas de Lyra, and Paul, bishop of Burgos, and Matthias Dorinke' (p. 103). A section beginning on p. 109 examines the commentaries of 'Methodius, Hildegard and others concerning the reign and ruin of the Turk'. Foxe cites several passages from the *Apocalype of Pseudo-Methodius*, linking prophecy with historical events involving Turkish conquests. He then begins a chronological summary of events from 632, the start of the Kingdom of the Saracens, down to 1291 (p. 120), the loss of the last crusader city, Acre. Despite constantly calling Christians to arms against Turks, the pope had failed to recover what had been lost. If the pope does not admit that Christ stands alone, and repudiate his own idolatry and 'profanations', he will before long 'be compelled to give place and room to the Turk' (p. 121). A 'Prayer against the Turk' follows, which calls for renewed, reformed faith so that the reign of the Turks may end. God has permitted Turkish tyranny as a warning and punishment. Finally, comparing pope and Turk as Antichrists, Foxe asks, which is 'the truer or greater'? While the Turk might be seen as more manifestly

Christ's enemy, Foxe leaves open whether Turk or papacy should be seen as a 'more bloody and pernicious adversary' of Christ (p. 122).

SIGNIFICANCE
Together with the King James Bible and John Bunyan's *Pilgrims progress*, Foxe's *Acts and monuments* was one of the most influential, and widely read, English texts of the early modern period. For some readers, perhaps for many, the information it contains on Islam would be the only source they had, and there is little doubt that its negative picture of Turkish atrocities contributed to English views of Muslims, especially of the Turks, as diabolical adversaries of Christian faith and also of civilisation, law and order. In describing the Ottoman Empire as an illegitimate state, Foxe denies that it had any cultural value or religious legitimacy. It did not even follow set rules of succession, since sultans took the throne by murdering their relatives, not by legal right. Yet because Foxe actually used some of the best sources available at the time to construct a history of the Ottomans, his book has been described as the 'best available in the sixteenth century' (Freeman, 'Commentary on the text for Book Six').

The fact that Foxe devoted some effort to explaining why he included this history, apparently a digression, in a work that was mainly one of anti-Catholic polemic suggests that he realised that most people in England, unlike on the European continent, did not yet see the Ottomans as a threat. Foxe's view that this was too complacent an attitude saw the birth of new interest in the Ottomans' military strength and conquests. However, most analysts of Foxe's writing about the Turks point to his inclusion of biblical prophecy and to his locating of the Ottomans within an apocalyptic framework as pioneering, at least in the English context. His ideas that God permitted Islam's rise as a scourge on Christians for their disunity, even his view that Christians needed to see their conflict with the Turks not only in military but also in spiritual terms, were no less novel. According to Freeman and Evenden, the idea that the Turks would play a 'crucial role in the unfolding of the end times' was not then part of the 'mainstream of English Apocalyptic thought' (*Religion and the book*, p. 83). Also novel was the way he linked the need for reformation of Christian faith with the Turks: Catholics had failed to stem their conquests; only by reforming their faith could Christians hope for victory. Haller (*Elect nation*) has argued that Foxe made a seminal contribution to the formation of a new English national identity, in which the English would play a leading role in events that would lead to Jesus' return. Thus, if defeating the Turks was to be involved, the English would soon find themselves dealing with them, distance notwithstanding. In fact, an earlier English text, Christopher Saint German's *Here after foloweth a lytell treatyse agaynst Mahumet and his cursed secte* (1533), had drawn on Pseudo-Methodius to argue that the defeat of the Turks was pre-destined. But Foxe's book reached a wider audience and was more influential. Indeed it was one of the most significant opinion shaping books of its time. Various dramatists who produced the Turk plays during the 16th century may, according to Robinson (*Writing the Reformation*), have drawn on Foxe.

EDITIONS & TRANSLATIONS

The Acts and monuments online at http://www.johnfoxe.org provides the unabridged texts of the four editions of this massive work (1563, 1570, 1576, 1583) that were published in John Foxe's lifetime, with commentary. The 1563 edition does not include the 'History of the Turks'.

G. Townsend (ed.), *The acts and monuments of John Foxe; with a life of the martyrologist, and vindication of the work*, New York, 1965

J. Pratt and J. Stoughton (eds), *The acts and monuments of John Foxe*, London, 1900

J. Pratt (ed.), *The acts and monuments of John Foxe*, London, 1877

J. Cummings (ed.), *Fox's Book of martyrs. The acts and monuments of the church*, London, 1875

S.R. Cattley and G. Townsend (eds), *The acts and monuments of John Foxe. A new and complete edition*, 9 vols, London, 1837-43

Acts and monuments, London, 1570², 1576³, 4th ed, reprinted 1583, 1596, 1610, 1632, 1641, and 1684

STUDIES

M. Phillpott, 'John Foxe bibliography', *Acts and monuments online*, http://www.johnfoxe.org/index.php?realm=more&type=bibliography

T.S. Freeman, 'Commentary on the text for Book 6', in *John Foxe's The acts and monuments online*, http://www.johnfoxe.org/index.php?realm=more&gototype=modern&type=commentary&book=6

S.H. Hashmi, *Just wars, holy wars, and jihads. Christian, Jewish, and Muslim encounters and exchanges*, New York, 2012, pp. 171-76

G.M. MacLean and N.I. Matar, *Britain and the Islamic world, 1558-1713*, Oxford, 2011

B. Charry, 'Turkish futures, prophecy and the Other', in A. Brady and E. Butterworth (eds), *The uses of the future in Early Modern Europe*, New York, 2010, 73-89

Freeman and Evenden, *Religion and the book in early modern England*

M. Dimmock, *Newe Turkes. Dramatizing Islam and the Ottomans in Early Modern England*, Aldershot, 2005, especially pp. 76-80 and 16, 90, 106, 109, 147, 149, 151, 186

J. Burton, *Traffic and turning. Islam and English drama. 1579-1624*, Newark DE, 2005, pp. 22, 126, 165, 259, 315

M.S. Robinson, *Writing the Reformation. Actes and monuments and the Jacobean history play*, Aldershot, 2002

Loades, *John Foxe. An historical perspective*

D. Loades (ed.), *John Foxe and the English Reformation*, London, 1997

Knott, *Discourses of martyrdom in English literature*

J. King, *English Reformation literature. The Tudor origins of the Protestant tradition*, Princeton NJ, 1982

K. Frith, *The apocalyptic tradition in Reformation Britain*, London, 1979

W. Haller, *The elect nation. The meaning and relevance of Foxe's Book of martyrs*, New York, 1963

Mozley, *John Foxe and his book*

D. Trenow, *The credibility of John Foxe, the 'martyrologist'*, London, 1868

Andrews, *A critical and historical review of Fox's Book of martyrs*

Clinton Bennett

Jean Bodin

DATE OF BIRTH 1529 or 1530
PLACE OF BIRTH Angers
DATE OF DEATH 1596
PLACE OF DEATH Laon

BIOGRAPHY

Jean Bodin was born in Angers in 1529 or 1530 into a middle-class family. He received his first education at the local Carmelite house, then at the mother-house in Paris, where he may have been tried for heresy around 1547 (on young Bodin's penchant for Calvinism see Droz, 'Le Carme Jean Bodin'; but cf. Fontana, 'Bilan historiographique'). Released from his vows around 1548, he left to study law in Toulouse, where he also briefly taught in the late 1550s before entering the Parlement in Paris in 1560. In the 1560s, as the civil wars began to ravage the country, Bodin became increasingly involved in active political life, also publishing his first important works, the *Methodus ad facilem historiarum cognitionem* (1566) and the short economics treatise *Réponse aux paradoxes de Monsieur de Malestroit* (1568). In 1573, he became master of petitions to Hercule-François, Duke of Alençon, younger brother of King Charles IX and later the figurehead of the group known as the 'Politiques', who lobbied for civil peace via religious toleration. In the following year, he joined the court of the new King Henry III; however, his relationship with the king and consequently his hopes of further advancement were negatively affected by his behaviour at the Estates-General of 1576, where he spoke on behalf of the Third Estate, opposing Henry's request for finance for a new war against the Huguenots. The same year, 1576, also saw the publication of Bodin's masterpiece, the *Six livres de la République*, an ambitious piece of political theory, which he translated into Latin ten years later with significant changes and additions. The *République* was followed by another best-selling, though highly controversial work, the *Démonomanie des sorciers* (1580), a treatise on witchcraft and its juridical implications. In the early 1580s, Bodin coupled his new post as a royal prosecutor in Laon with continuing employment with Hercule-François, now Duke of Anjou, whom he followed on missions to England and Flanders (1581). After the death of the duke in 1584, Bodin retreated to his post in Laon, which he held until his death in 1596. During the succession crisis that followed the assassination of Henry III in 1589, he publicly endorsed the Catholic League through a letter published in Paris, Lyons, Toulouse and Brussels (*Lettre de Monsieur Bodin*, 1590). This was his last, and much discussed political gesture (see Rose, 'The politique and the prophet', and 'Bodin and the Bourbon succession'). In his final years, he devoted himself entirely to literary and philosophical pursuits, publishing on natural philosophy (*Universae naturae theatrum*, 1596) and ethics (*Paradoxon*, 1596), and composing one of his most fascinating works: the *Colloquium heptaplomeres*, a dialogue on religion between seven characters of different faiths, written c. 1593 but unpublished until 1857. (For debates on authenticity see Faltenbacher, *Magie, Religion und Wissenschaften*; Malcolm, 'Jean Bodin and the authorship', has compelling arguments in favour of Bodin's authorship.)

MAIN SOURCES OF INFORMATION

Primary

M. de la Serre, *Remonstrance au Roy sur les pernicieux discours contenus au livre de la Republique de Bodin*, Paris: Federic Morel, 1579 (source: Couzinet, Jean Bodin)

A. du Ferrier, *Advertissemens à M. Jean Bodin sur le quatriesme livre de sa République*, Paris: Pierre Cavellat, 1580 (source: Couzinet, Jean Bodin)

A. Thevet, 'Vie du Sultan Mustapha, fils de Sultan Solyman', in *Les vrais pourtraits et vies des hommes illustres Grecz, Latins et Payens*, Paris: Veuve J. Kervert et G. Chaudière, 1584, fol. 652r-v (source: Couzinet, Jean Bodin)

A. Possevino, 'De Joannis Bodini libris consideratio et cautio', in *Judicium de Nuae militis Galli scriptis... De Ioannis Bodini Methodo historiae: libris de Repub. et Daemonomania...*, Roma: Ex Typographia Vaticana, 1592; Lugduni Batavorum: Apud Ioannem Baptistam Buysson, 1593, 87-121

F. Albergati, *Dei discorsi politici libri cinque. Nei quali viene riprodotta la dottrina di Gio. Bodino e difesa quella d'Aristotile*, Venezia: Giovan Battista Ciotti, 1603

J. Hotman de Villiers, *De la charge et dignité de l'Ambassadeur*, Paris: Jérémie Périer, 1604, pp. 51-3, 59 (source: Couzinet, Jean Bodin)

J.-A. de Thou, *Historiarum sui temporis*, Genevae: apud Petrum de la Roviere, vols 3-5, 1620, pp. 398, 701-2 (source: Couzinet, Jean Bodin)

G. Naudé, *Apologie pour tous les grands hommes qui ont esté accusez de magie*, Paris: Jacques Cotin, 1669 (1625), pp. 92-93 (source: Couzinet, Jean Bodin)

A. Loisel, *Pasquier, ou Dialogue des advocats du Parlement du Paris*, in *Divers opuscules tirez des memoires de Me Antoine Loisel, advocat en Parlement*, Paris: Guillemot et Guignard, 1652 (source: Couzinet, Jean Bodin)

J. Bongars, 'Lettre de Jacques Bongars à Conrad Rittershusius, Francfort, 4 avril 1600', in Paul Colomiès, *Gallia orientalis, sive Gallorum qui linguam hebraeam vel alias Orientales excoluerunt vitae*, Hagae Comitis: Adriani Vlacq, 1665, 82 (source: Couzinet, 2001)

Duc de Nevers, 'Voyage du feu Monsieur le Duc d'Anjou en Angleterre. 1582', in *Mémoires pour les rois Charles IX, Henri III et Henri IV*, Paris: Thomas Jolly, vol. 1, 1665, 551-60 (source: Couzinet, 2001)

G. Ménage, *Vitae Petri Aerodii, Quaesitoris Andegavensis et Guillelmi Menagii, advocati regii Andegavensis*, Paris: Christophe Journel, 1675 (1665), pp. 140-48, 249-50 (source: Couzinet, 2001)

L. Gréard, *Defenses pour les particuliers qui possedent des bois dans la Province de Normandie, contre la pretention des droits de Tiers et Danger*, Rouen: Eustache Viret, 1673, pp. 7-9, 65 (source: Couzinet, 2001)

A. Teissier, 'Jean Bodin', in *Les éloges des hommes savants tirez de l'Histoire de M. de Thou, avec des additions contenant l'abrégé de leur vie, le jugement et le catalogue de leurs ouvrages*, Genève: Jean Hermann Widerhold, vol. 2, 1683, pp. 230-36, 425 (source: Couzinet, 2001)

P. Bayle, art. 'Bodin (Jean)', in *Dictionnaire historique et critique*, Rotterdam: R. Leers, 1697, 582-88

P. Lyser and I.H. Schlegel, *Selecta de vita et scriptis Ioannis Bodini*, Witembergae: Samuelis Kreusigii, 1715 (source: Couzinet, 2001)

F. Pithou, *Scaligerana, Thuana, Perroniana, Pithoeana et Colomesiana. Ou remarques historiques, critiques, morales et littéraires de Jo. Scaliger, J. Aug. de Thou, le Cardinal du Perron, François Pithou et P. Colomiès. Avec les notes de plusieurs savants*, Amsterdam: Covens et Mortier, vol. 1, 1740, pp. 499-501 (source: Couzinet, 2001)

A. Pontieux, 'Quelques documents inédits sur Jean Bodin', *Revue du Seizième Siècle* 15 (1928) 56-99

J. Levron, 'Jean Bodin et ses parents. Textes', *L'Anjou Historique* (Jan-Mar 1950) 5-21

Secondary

L. Fontana, 'Bilan historiographique de la question du séjour de Jean Bodin à Genève', *Bibliothèque d'Humanisme et Renaissance* 71 (2009) 101-11

D. Quaglioni, art. 'Bodin, Jean', in P. Arabeyre, J.-L. Halpérin and J. Krynen (eds), *Dictionnaire historique des juristes français, XIIe-XXe siècle*, Paris, 2007, 92-94

J.H. Franklin (ed.), *Jean Bodin*, Aldershot, 2006

N. Malcolm, 'Jean Bodin and the authorship of the *Colloquium heptaplomeres*', *Journal of the Warburg and Courtauld Institutes* 69 (2006) 95-150

A. Suggi, *Colloquium heptaplomeres di Jean Bodin*, Rome, 2005

G.A. Pérouse et al. (eds), *L'Œuvre de Jean Bodin*, Paris, 2004

K.F. Faltenbacher (ed.), *Magie, Religion und Wissenschaften im* Colloquium heptaplomeres. *Ergebnisse der Tagungen in Paris 1994 und in der Villa Vigoni 1999*, Darmstadt, 2002

M.-D. Couzinet, *Jean Bodin. Bibliographie des écrivains français*, Paris, 2001 (contains exhaustive bibliography of earlier studies)

P.C. Mayer-Tasch, *Jean Bodin. Eine Einführung in sein Leben, sein Werk und seine Wirkung, mit einer Bibliographie zum geistes- und sozialwissenschaftlichen Schrifttum über Bodin zwischen dem Jahr 1800 und dem Jahr 2000*, Düsseldorf, 2000

R. Häfner, *Bodinus Polymeres. Neue Studien zu Jean Bodins Spätwerk*, Wiesbaden, 1999

A. Baldini (ed.), *Jean Bodin a 400 anni dalla morte. Bilancio storiografico e prospettive di ricerca*, special issue of *Il Pensiero Politico* 30/2 (1997)

P.L. Rose, 'The politique and the prophet. Bodin and the Catholic League 1589-1594', *The Historical Journal* 21 (1978) 783-808

P.L. Rose, 'Bodin and the Bourbon succession to the French throne, 1583-1594', *Sixteenth Century Journal* 9 (1978) 75-98

E. Droz, 'Le Carme Jean Bodin, hérétique', *Bibliothèque d'Humanisme et Renaissance* 10 (1948) 77-94

WORKS ON CHRISTIAN-MUSLIM RELATIONS

Methodus ad facilem historiarum cognitionem, 'Method for the easy understanding of history' *Methodus*, 'Method'

DATE 1566 (revised with changes and additions 1572)
ORIGINAL LANGUAGE Latin

DESCRIPTION

The *Methodus* belongs to the Renaissance genre of *artes historicae*, methodological treatises on historical reading and writing. It comprises a dedicatory letter, a preamble, and ten chapters of unequal length, the last of which is a bibliography of selected historical sources and writings available in Bodin's time. Ch. 6 is an ambitious attempt at universal comparative history, bringing together the vicissitudes and institutions of past and present states. The work was first printed in Paris in 1566 (463 pages in quarto); a revised edition with changes and additions was published six years later by the same printer, Martin le Jeune, in a smaller format (613 pages in octavo). All references below are to the chapter and paragraph numbers as given in Miglietti's 2013 edition.

Even though the work is not primarily concerned with relations with the Muslim world, it contains several passages of interest: scattered references to the history and institutions of Islamic countries (notably Arabia at the time of the Umayyad caliphate, Egypt, Tunisia, Turkey and the Ottoman Empire), including a whole section in ch. 6 on military and political facts relating to the Turks, Arabs, Tunisians and Tartars (6.238-42); a description of the 'natural character' of the Arabs in ch. 5; brief mentions of Muḥammad and Islam in chs 5 and 6; and a critical discussion of the ideas of the philosophers Ibn Rushd and Ibn Sīnā on the eternity of the world in ch. 8. Overall, the work demonstrates Bodin's keen interest in the culture and history of Islamic countries, an interest that is further reflected in later works such as *République*, *Démonomanie*, *Universae naturae theatrum* and, more importantly, *Colloquium heptaplomeres*.

In the *Methodus*, Bodin expresses admiration for the Arabs and the Turks, who were able to accomplish great deeds and to establish flourishing empires (cf. 4.3), even when their expansion was carried out at the expense of European countries (cf. 5.175). He identifies military discipline (5.178), centralised monarchical power (6.100, 267), and a well-designed institutional apparatus (6.12, 116-17, 119-21) as the main reasons behind the greatness of the Ottoman Empire, which he describes as a fitting candidate to be the moral heir of the Roman Empire – this is part of a discussion about competing interpretations of Daniel's prophecies (7.4, 6). In the *République*, written at the height of the French civil wars, Bodin reaffirms this view but also includes freedom of religion among the causes of Turkish success: he thus adheres to the representation of the Ottoman Empire as a thriving multi-confessional state. This had first been made a few years earlier by Pierre Belon, an author whom Bodin had certainly read (cf. 6.97; Berriot, 'Jean Bodin et l'islam', pp. 177-78; on the concept of toleration, see Griffel, 'Toleranzkonzepte im Islam').

Notwithstanding his admiration for the Ottoman Empire, Bodin stops short of presenting it as a model to follow. He clearly sees an element of fragility in the bloody power-struggles within the ruling dynasty (6.301) as well as between powerful aristocratic families (6.295, 299, where he criticises Machiavelli's views on the matter). Furthermore, in the *République* Bodin describes the 'Grand Seigneur' as an exemplary case of despotic monarch, as opposed to that 'regal' monarch, respectful of the natural law, whom he identifies as the perfect kind of monarchical ruler (see Le Thiec, 'L'Empire ottoman').

References to specifically religious aspects of Islam are rare in the *Methodus* and, given the nature of the work, they are usually made in connection with political and military matters (cf. 6.147). Muḥammad is mentioned three times (5.124, 199; 6.146) and is portrayed as a shrewd and skilful secular leader who was not hesitant to resort to force to pursue his aims, or to use religion as an instrument for political and military success. Bodin believes that this tight conjunction of secular and spiritual power in the hands of the caliphs was among the chief causes of Arab expansion and supremacy during the period of the Rightly-Guided Caliphs, and that the divisions that followed the fourth Caliph 'Alī's death weakened the empire, paving the way for the Christian *Reconquista* (5.92 and 6.239).

However, on more than one occasion Bodin displays sympathy and admiration for the religious piety of the Muslims. He hints twice (6.231, 267) at the rigidly monotheistic nature of Islam, an aspect that was being brought up by other thinkers at the time in a subtle polemic against Roman Catholicism (see Berriot, 'Islam et liberté de conscience', pp. 178-79), and that would later come to the fore in Bodin's own *Colloquium heptaplomeres*. At 5.88-89, Leo Africanus's description of devotional places and practices in Africa is quoted in order to demonstrate the exceptional piety of the Muslims, a quality that Bodin believes to be helped by the hot climate in which they live: according to classical climate theory, southern peoples such as the Arabs are naturally inclined towards contemplation, meditation and the study of higher disciplines such as astronomy, mathematics, theology and the natural sciences. No wonder, then, that the Arabs would excel at all these pursuits, nor that the best 'philosophers, mathematicians and prophets, as well as all religions' would come from the South (5.85-86; cf. Berriot, 'Jean Bodin et l'islam', pp. 173-74).

In ch. 8, which discusses chronology, Bodin displays his knowledge of Islamic philosophy by including an account of the ideas of Ibn Sīnā and Ibn Rushd in his lengthy examination of the arguments for and against the eternity of the world. Although Bodin might have gathered information from other sources (notably from Thomas Aquinas's *Commentary on the Sentences, Commentarium magnum De Caelo, Commentarium magnum Physicae,* and *On the eternity of the world*), he does refer explicitly to Ibn Sīnā's *Liber de diluviis* and to Ibn Rushd's commentary on Aristotle's *De anima* as two of his sources. Other works by Bodin, including the *Démonomanie des sorciers* and the *Universae naturae theatrum*, further demonstrate his knowledge not only of Islamic philosophy, but also of ways of life and cultural traditions among Muslim nations, while the erudite theological conversations staged in the *Colloquium heptaplomeres* testify to his familiarity with the Qur'an. Although François Berriot ('Jean Bodin et l'islam', p. 172) argues that Bodin only read the Qur'an (in Bibliander's edition) in later life, probably in preparation for the *Colloquium*, a specific mention of interpretive debates over a qur'anic *sūra* in *République* 1.9 (cf. Mario Turchetti's bilingual edition of book I, Paris, 2013, p. 650) shows that Bodin was already familiar with Nicholas of Cusa's *Cribratio Alcorani*, from which the reference is taken (1.21; this text was published as a preface to Bibliander's edition, under the title *Machumetis Saracenorum principis ejusque successorum vita, doctrina, ipseque Alcoran*). Bodin was probably drawing from the same text when he stated in the *Methodus* (ch. 10, under the heading 'Historians of the Arab religion') that the Qur'an itself was the result of a conflation between multiple texts, accomplished around 740 (the same view is expressed in *République*, 1.9).

According to François Berriot ('Jean Bodin et l'islam', p. 177), Bodin's knowledge of the Muslim world, though certainly inferior in accuracy and extent to that of Guillaume Postel, is that of a 'very well-informed sixteenth-century reader' working on a limited amount of secondary sources. Although Bodin warns his readers not to trust the judgment of Christian authors on 'Africans and Muslims' (4.20 and more specifically 4.28 against Paolo Giovio), the only Muslim source he seems to have actually consulted is Leo Africanus's *La descrittione dell'Africa*, a work well-known in France since about 1530. In all other cases, he relies entirely on Christian sources of various kinds: chroniclers of the crusades such as Hermann of Carinthia and William of Tyre; humanists such as the Florentine Andrea Cambini and the Byzantine Laonicus Chalcocondyles; and more extensively, Paolo Giovio's *Historiae sui temporis*, Guillaume Postel's *Republique des Turcs*, and the *De rebus Turcarum* of Christophe Richer, ambassador of King Francis I in Constantinople. To the sources listed in ch. 10 (under the heading 'Historians of the Turks') can be added Pierre Belon's *Observations*, quoted elsewhere in the text, as well as oral conversations with French travellers and diplomats such as Nouailles, de Vigne, Jean Hurault and Louis Martin (cf. 6.242).

SIGNIFICANCE

Bodin's interest in the culture and history of Islamic countries should be placed, on the one hand, within the context of his project of a universal comparative history that would incorporate the experience of extra-European nations and states: in this respect, the neutral, if not overtly positive, hints at the successful undertakings of the Arabs and Turks serve to stress the fact that political and military greatness can also be found outside European borders, in a polemic against the Euro- and especially Germano-centric views criticised in ch. 7. On the other hand, Bodin's sympathetic treatment of the Muslim world, both in the *Methodus* and in later works such as the *Colloquium*, is better studied against the backdrop of the 'orientalist' trends that developed in mid-16th-century France, and that are best embodied by authors such as Christophe Richer, Pierre Belon and Guillaume Postel – crucially, among Bodin's most important sources on Ottoman matters. As François Berriot has convincingly shown ('Islam et liberté de conscience', pp. 176-86), positive representations of the Ottoman Empire as a flourishing multi-ethnic state featuring a great degree of religious toleration were part of a long-standing tradition of religious irenicism that had had its champion in Nicholas of Cusa in the 15th century; in 16th-century France, however, they became instrumental in securing public acceptance and support for the alliance that King Francis I concluded in 1537 with Süleyman the Magnificent for mutual protection against Charles V. This Franco-Ottoman alliance was systematically renewed by Francis's successors – including Charles IX, during whose reign (1560-74) Bodin composed and then revised his *Methodus* – until the early 17th century.

EDITIONS & TRANSLATIONS

- S. Miglietti (ed. and trans.), *Methodus ad facilem historiarum cognitionem*, Pisa, 2013 (comparative edition of the Latin text, based on the 1566 and 1572 editions; complete Italian trans. with notes and commentary)
- M.S. Bobkovoĭ (trans.), *Metod legkogo poznaniĩa istorii*, Moscow, 2000 (Russian trans.)
- N. Polizzi (trans.), *Avviamento alla conoscenza storica*, intro. F. Brancato, Trapan, 1968 (complete Italian trans., based on the 1650 edition)
- P. Mesnard (ed. and trans.), *Methodus ad facilem historiarum cognitionem. La Méthode de l'histoire*, in J. Bodin, *Oeuvres philosophiques*, Paris, 1951, i (diplomatic transcription of the Latin text *juxta* the 1572 edition; complete French trans., based with corrections on the 1941 trans. by the same author)
- B. Reynolds (trans.), *Method for the easy comprehension of history*, New York, 1945 (complete English trans., with notes and commentary, based primarily on the 1572 edition; occasional comparisons with the 1566, 1583 and 1595 editions)

P. Mesnard (trans.), *La méthode de l'histoire*, Paris-Algiers, 1941 (complete French trans.)

Methodus ad facilem historiarum cognitionem, Amstelodami: Johann Ravenstein, 1650

Methodus ad facilem historiarum cognitionem, Argentinae [Strasbourg]: heirs of Lazar Zetzner, 1627

Methodus ad facilem historiarum cognitionem, Genevae: Jacob Stoer, 1610

T. Heywood (trans.), *The two most worthy and notable histories which remain vnmained to posterity, viz. the conspiracie of Cateline, vndertaken against the gouernment of the Senate of Rome, and the warre which Iugurth for many yeares maintained against the same state. Both written by C.C. Salustius*, London: J. Jaggard, 1608 (the preface contains Heywood's English trans. of ch. 4 of Bodin's *Methodus*)

Methodus ad facilem historiarum cognitionem, Argentinae [Strasbourg]: Lazar Zetzner, 1607

Methodus ad facilem historiarum cognitionem, Argentinae [Strasbourg]: Lazar Zetzner, 1598 (re-issued in 1599 with an updated title-page)

Methodus ad facilem historiarum cognitionem, s.l. [Geneva]: Jacob Stoer, 1595

Methodus ad facilem historiarum cognitionem, s.l. [Heidelberg?]: heirs of Jean Mareschal, 1591

Methodus ad facilem historiarum cognitionem, s.l. [Heidelberg?]: Jean Mareschal, 1583

Methodus ad facilem historiarum cognitionem, in *Artis historicae penus. Octodecim scriptorum tam veterum quam recentiorum monumentis & inter eos Io. praecipue Bodini libris Methodus historicae sex instructa*, vol. 1, Basileae: ex Pietri Pernae officina, 1579

Methodus ad facilem historiarum cognitionem, in J. Wolf (ed.), *J. Bodini Methodus historica, duodecim eiusdem argumenti scriptorum tam veterum quam recentiorum commentariis adaucta a Johanne Wolfo*, vol. 1, Basileae: ex Petri Pernae officina, 1576

Methodus ad facilem historiarum cognitionem, Parisiis: apud Martinum Juvenem, 1572 (with changes and additions)

Methodus ad facilem historiarum cognitionem, Parisiis: apud Martinum Juvenem, 1566 (in 4°, *editio princeps*)

STUDIES

S. Miglietti, ' "Tesmoings oculaires". Storia e autopsia nella Francia del secondo Cinquecento', *Rinascimento* 50 (2010) 87-126

L. Gerbier, 'Une méthode pour interpréter les histoires. Machiavel et Jean Bodin', *Revue de Métaphysique et de Morale* 2 (2009) 151-66

I. Melani, *Il tribunale della storia. Leggere la* Methodus *di Jean Bodin*, Florence, 2006

A. Grafton, *What was history? The art of history in early modern Europe*, Cambridge, 2007

P. Lardet, 'Nations et mémoire. Les "vestiges de la langue" dans la *Methodus* de Jean Bodin (1566)', in Pérouse et al., *L'Œuvre de Jean Bodin*, 389-406

G. Le Thiec, 'L'Empire ottoman, modèle de monarchie seigneuriale dans l'oeuvre de Bodin', in Pérouse et al., *L'Œuvre de Jean Bodin*, 55-77

M.-D. Couzinet, 'La bibliographie de l'histoire dans la *Methodus* de Bodin', in D. de Courcelles (ed.), *L'histoire en marge de l'histoire à la Renaissance*, Paris, 2002, 49-60

A.M. Lazzarino del Grosso, 'La Respublica Hebraeorum come modello politico "scientifico" nella *Methodus* di Jean Bodin', *Il Pensiero Politico* 35 (2002) 382-98

A. Tenenti, 'Il doppio volto della storia comparata nella *Methodus* di Jean Bodin', *Rivista di Letterature Moderne e Comparate* 54 (2001) 3-16

F. Griffel, 'Toleranzkonzepte im Islam und ihr Einfluss auf Jean Bodins *Colloquium Heptaplomeres*', in R. Häfner (ed.), *Bodinus Polymeres. Neue Studien zu Jean Bodins Spätwerk*, Wiesbaden, 1999, 119-44

A. Suggi, 'Cronologia e storia nella *Methodus* di Jean Bodin', *I Castelli di Yale. Quaderni di Filosofia* 3 (1998) 75-92

M.-D. Couzinet, *Histoire et méthode à la Renaissance. Une lecture de la* Methodus ad facilem historiarium cognitionem *de Jean Bodin*, Paris, 1997

I. Cervelli, 'Bodin, Daniele e Marco Polo', in Baldini (ed.), *Jean Bodin a 400 anni dalla morte*, 233-49

M.-D. Couzinet, 'La *Methodus ad facilem historiarum cognitionem*. Histoire cosmographique et méthode', in Y.-C. Zarka (ed.), *Jean Bodin. Nature histoire droit et politique*, Paris, 1996, 23-42

C.-G. Dubois, 'La "nation" dans ses rapports avec la "république" et la "royauté"', in Y.-C. Zarka (ed.), *Jean Bodin. Nature histoire droit et politique*, Paris, 1996, 91-113

M.-D. Couzinet, 'Fonction de la géographie dans la connaissance historique. Le modèle cosmographique de l'histoire universelle chez F. Bauduin et J. Bodin', *Corpus* 28 (1995) 113-45

P. Desan (ed.), *Philosophies de l'histoire à la Renaissance*, special issue of *Corpus. Revue de Philosophie* 28 (1995)

M. Miegge, 'L'inveterato errore delle quattro monarchie', in *Il sogno del re di Babilonia. Profezia e storia da Thomas Müntzer a Isaac Newton*, Milan, 1995, 91-100

P. Desan, 'L'histoire mathématique de Jean Bodin', in *Penser l'histoire á la renaissance*, Caen, 1993, 145-69

M.-L. Demonet, *Les voix du signe. Nature et origine du langage à la Renaissance, 1480-1580*, Paris, 1992, pp. 320, 352, 366-68, 464, 470, 512-13, 547

C. Vasoli, 'Osservazioni sulle teorie umanistiche sulla storiografia', in *La storiografia umanistica. Atti del convegno di Studi, Messina, 22-25 Ottobre 1987*, Messina, 1992, 5-38

F. Berriot, 'Islam et liberté de conscience à la Renaissance', in H.R. Guggisberg, F. Lestringant and J.-C. Margolin (eds), *La liberté de conscience (XVIe-XVIIe siècles). Actes du colloque de Mulhouse et Bâle, 1989*, Geneva, 1991, 173-90

O. Zhiri, *L'Afrique au miroir de l'Europe. Fortunes de Jean Léon l'Africain à la Renaissance*, Geneva, 1991, pp. 48, 55, 83, 109, 141-42, 146, 152, 154, 159

P. Lardet, 'Peuples et langues de Calvin à Bodin. Moïse historien', in I. Backus and F. Higman (eds), *Théorie et pratique de l'exégèse. Actes du troisième colloque international sur l'histoire de l'exégèse biblique au XVIe siècle, Genève, 31 août-2 septembre 1988*, Geneva, 1990, 77-111

F. Sánchez Marcos, 'Nota sobre la historiografía de la época de Antonio Agustín. La selección bodiniana de historiadores de los españoles', in *Jornades d'História Antoni Agustí i el seu temps (1517-1586)*, Tarragones, 1990, 485-95

P. Desan, 'La méthode de Bodin', in *Naissance de la méthode (Machiavel, La Ramée, Bodin, Montaigne, Descartes)*, Paris, 1987, 91-112

L. Valensi, *Venise et la Sublime Porte. La naissance du despote*, Paris, 1987, pp. 78-84

F. Berriot, 'Jean Bodin et l'islam', in G. Cesbron (ed.), *Jean Bodin. Actes du colloque interdisciplinaire d'Angers, 24-27 mai 1984*, Angers, 1985, i, 171-82

G. Cotroneo, 'Ancora sui rapporti fra la *Methodus* e la *République*', *Il Pensiero Politico* 14 (1981) 18-25

D.R. Kelley, 'Civil science in the Renaissance', *History of European Ideas* 2 (1981) 261-76

V.I. Comparato, 'La teoria del magistrato nella *Methodus* di Jean Bodin', in S. Bertelli (ed.), *Per Federico Chabod (1901-1960). Atti del seminario internazionale*, Perugia, 1980-81, 197-209

F. Berriot, 'L'idée de progrès chez Jean Bodin', in *L'idée de progrès. Actes du colloque organisé par le Centre d'études et de recherches d'histoire des idées de l'Université de Nice, Nice, 19-19 mai 1978*, Paris, 1981, 17-34

C.-G. Dubois, *La conception de l'histoire en France au XVIe siècle (1560-1610)*, Paris, 1977

G. Gliozzi, *Adamo e il Nuovo Mondo. La nascita dell'antropologia come ideologia colonial: dalle genealogie bibliche alle teorie razziali (1500-1700)*, Florence, 1977, pp. 326-32, 355-57, 363-65

A. Seifert, *"Cognitio historica". Die Geschichte als Namengeberin der frühneuzeitlichen Empirie*, Berlin, 1976, pp. 27-28, 51-58, 73-74, 80, 84-87, 97-99

G. Turbet-Delof, 'Jean Bodin lecteur de Léon d'Afrique', *Neohelicon. Acta Comparationis Litterarum Universarum* 2 (1974) 201-16

G. Cotroneo, 'Le quatrième chapitre de la *Methodus*. Nouvelles analyses et perspectives historiographiques', in H. Denzer (ed.), *Jean Bodin. Verhandlungen der internationalen Bodin Tagung in München*, Munich, 1973, 87-103

D.R. Kelley, 'The development and context of Bodin's method', in H. Denzer (ed.), *Jean Bodin. Verhandlungen der internationalen Bodin Tagung in München*, Munich, 1973, 123-50

G. Huppert, *L'idée de l'histoire parfaite*, Paris, 1973

C.-G. Dubois, *Celtes et Gaulois au XVIe siècle. Le développement littéraire d'un mythe nationaliste*, Paris, 1972, pp. 119-22

D.R. Kelley, *Foundations of modern historical scholarship. Language, law and history in the French Renaissance*, New York, 1970, pp. 136-38

G. Cotroneo, *Jean Bodin teorico della storia*, Naples, 1966

G. Huppert, 'The Renaissance background of historicism', *History and Theory* 5 (1966) 48-60

G. Cotroneo, 'Un tentativo di storia della storiografia nella *Methodus* di Jean Bodin', *Giornale Critico della Filosofia Italiana*, 3rd series 19 (1965) 504-26

G. Cotroneo, 'Introduzione allo studio della *Methodus* di Jean Bodin (1530?-1596)', *Atti dell' Accademia Pontaniana* 13 (1964) 221-23

G. Cotroneo, 'Il senso della storia nella *Methodus* di Jean Bodin', *Rivista di Studi Crociani* 1 (1964) 296-311

J.H. Franklin, *Jean Bodin and the sixteenth-century revolution in the methodology of law and history*, New York, 1963

M.P. Gilmore, 'The Renaissance conception of the lessons of history', and 'Individualism in Renaissance historians', in *Humanists and jurists. Six studies in the Renaissance*, Cambridge MA, 1963, 1-37, 38-60

G. Cotroneo, 'La "storia integrale" nella *Methodus* di Jean Bodin', *Historica* 15 (1962) 95-107

V. Piano Mortari, 'Jean Bodin', *Diritto romano e diritto nazionale in Francia nel secolo XVI*, Milan, 1961, 114-24

N.W. Gilbert, 'Methods of reading and writing history', in *Renaissance concepts of method*, New York, 1960, 79-81

A. Klempt, 'Die Auflösung der theologisch-eschatologischen Gesamtdeutung des universalhistorischen Zusammenhangs', in *Die Säkularisierung der universalhistorischen Auffassung. Zum Wandel des Geschichtsdenkens im 16. und 17. Jahrhundert*, Göttingen, 1960, 34-59

V. de Caprariis, 'La *Methodus* di Jean Bodin', in V. de Caprariis, *Propaganda e pensiero politico in Francia durante le guerre di religione*, vol. 1, *1559-1572*, Naples, 1959, 318-71

B. Reynolds, 'Shifting currents in historical criticism', *Journal of the History of Ideas* 14 (1953) 471-92

P. Mesnard, 'Jean Bodin et le problème de l'éternité du monde', *Bulletin de l'Association Guillaume Budé* 4 (1951) 117-31

J.L. Brown, *The* Methodus ad facilem historiarum cognitionem *of Jean Bodin. A critical study*, Washington DC, 1939

J.B. Bury, 'Some interpretations of universal history. Bodin and Le Roy', in *The idea of progress. An inquiry into its origins and growth*, London, 1921

E. Menke-Glückert, 'Die metodische Bewegung in der Jurisprudenz und Bodins *Methodus*', in *Die Geschichtsschreibung der Reformation und Gegenreformation. Bodin und die Begründung der Geschichtsmethodologie durch Bartholomäus Keckermann*, Leipzig, 1912, 106-21

F. Renz, *Jean Bodin. Ein Beitrag zur Geschichte der historischen Methode im XVI. Jahrhundert*, Gotha, 1905

Sara Miglietti

William Painter

DATE OF BIRTH Possibly 1540
PLACE OF BIRTH Possibly Kent
DATE OF DEATH Between 19 and 22 February 1595
PLACE OF DEATH London

BIOGRAPHY

William Painter (also spelt Payntor) is said to have belonged to a Kentish family, although his background is obscure. He has been confused with another William Painter, who attended Cambridge University and later became Master of Sevenoaks School and an ordained deacon (he probably died in 1597). In his 1890 edition of Painter's most important work, *The palace of pleasure*, Jacobs reprints Haslewood's 1813 biographical sketch. This refers to Painter's appointment as grammar-master at Sevenoaks, which induced Haslewood to assume that 'he must have been a bachelor of arts, and approved by the Archbishop of Canterbury' according to the rules of the school (p. xxiv). However, there is no evidence that William Painter attended university, despite his literary contribution's very influential role as a major source of material for almost every Tudor playwright of any significance. Kelly identifies Painter's father as a former headmaster at Sevenoaks (Kelly, 'Painter, William', p. 415). The original *DNB* entry confuses the two Painters, while others who place Painter at Sevenoaks include Warton (*History of English poetry*, p. 927) and Gillespie in his book on Shakespeare's sources (*Shakespeare's books*, p. 404). If Painter did not attend university, it remains a mystery how he acquired the skills necessary to write the book, including competency in several languages.

By 1558, Painter was a gunner and clerk of the armoury at the Tower of London, dedicating the two-volume, larger 1575 edition of *The palace of pleasure* to the Earl of Warwick, who was Master of the Ordinance. Painter was accused of embezzling Tower funds, or of fraudulent accounting in 1586 and 1587. He ended up repaying some but not all of the alleged sum. He admitted wrongdoing, asking for leniency so that he could continue to support his wife and children. His accusers were equally guilty of misusing funds or of keeping false accounts, which is probably why Painter was able to keep his job and avoid going to jail. He was buried in St Olave's, Hart Street, London. His debt to the crown was eventually discharged in 1622, when his grandson was granted a remission of the balance. Given Painter's acknowledged influence on English literary production, the scarcity of literature on his life is surprising. He more or less introduced the novella into English, and helped shape how this genre developed. William Shakespeare was one of those who drew on *The palace of pleasure* for several of his plays.

MAIN SOURCES OF INFORMATION

Primary

J. Jacobs, *The palace of pleasure. Elizabethan versions of Italian and French novels from Boccaccio, Bandello, Cinthio, Straparola, Queen Margaret of Navarre, and others*, London, 1890, New York, 1966, Hildesheim, 1968 [based on J. Haslewood's 1813 edition], pp. liii-lxiii (in the 1890 edition) (early records relating to Painter's life. Some of these may refer to William Paynter, d. 1597).

R. Cooke, *Visitation of London, 1568*, ed. S.W. Rawlins (Harleian Society Visitations 109), London, 1963, p. 101

MS London, BL – Lansdowne MSS 51, 73, 75, 78 (listed in *ODNB*)

Secondary

S. Gillespie, *Shakespeare's books. A dictionary of Shakespeare sources*, London, 2004, pp. 404-6

L.G. Kelly, art. 'Painter, William', in *ODNB*, 415-16

R. Ashley, 'Getting and spending. Corruption in the Elizabethan ordnance', *History Today* 40 (1990) 47-53

S. Lee, art. 'Painter, William', in *DNB*, 80-82

J. Haslewood, 'Of the translator', in Jacobs, *The palace of pleasure*, London, 1890, i, pp. xxxvii-xliv

T. Warton, *The history of English poetry. From the eleventh to the seventeenth century*, New York, 1870

WORKS ON CHRISTIAN-MUSLIM RELATIONS

The palace of pleasure; The palace of pleasure beautified, adorned and well furnished, with pleasaunt histories and excellent nouelles, selected out of diuers good and commendable authors

DATE   1566, 1567, 1575 (3 volumes)
ORIGINAL LANGUAGE   English

DESCRIPTION

The palace of pleasure is a three-volume work containing a total of 101 tales, in novella form, translated from a variety of Greek, Latin, French and Italian sources. Vol. 1 was published in 1566, with 60 novellas and was dedicated to the Earl of Warwick, vol. 2 appeared in 1567, with 34 new tales, dedicated to Sir George Howard Knight, master of the royal armoury, and vol. 3 in 1575, containing seven additional stories. Sources include Giovanni Boccaccio (d. 1375), Plutarch, Livy and Tacitus. Painter had some desire to minimise his role in recounting these stories: his name appears on the original title page in very small script, indicative of the Elizabethan view that writing was not a gentlemanly occupation (Relihan, *Fashioning authority*, p. 42). The 1890 edition, by Joseph Jacobs, identifies original sources, although D. Bush ('Classical tales') challenged and corrected some of his conclusions on the sources for the classical tales. Jacobs used the 1575 version to correct errors, mainly concerning 'the mint and cummin of capitals and italics' in the 1813 edition, edited by Joseph Haslewood, of which only 172 copies were printed. Of the 101 stories, 'Thorella and Saladine' (1:XX), 'The three rings' (1:XXX), 'Mahomet and Irene' (1:XL), 'Sultan Solyman' (2:XXXIV) and 'King of Morocco' (2:XXXV) have content relevant to Christian-Muslim encounters and attitudes. They both perpetuate and also challenge negative stereotypes, which could reflect changes in the political climate. Painter was mainly a translator of stories, although he also shaped his material. As he decided which tales to include, on the one hand he set out to entertain, while on the other he saw his selections as offering examples of good and bad conduct, so that his readers might imitate the former and avoid the latter.

Representations of Saladin uncharacteristically tended to rise above negative stereotypes about Muslims in European discourse, featuring him as a chivalrous, just and noble adversary, despite having retaken Jerusalem from the Christians during the crusades. Saladin is a major character in novellas 1:XX and 1:XXX, both from Boccaccio's *Decameron*. In the first story, although he visits a Christian home in Italy in order to investigate his enemy's military strength, he was received so hospitably that he returned the favour when he later discovered that his host, Thorello, had become a prisoner of war. The text refers to hospitality as a Christian duty, alluding to Genesis 18:1-5.

Saladin uses magic to transport Thorello back to Italy so that he can be reunited with his wife before she marries another man, thinking him dead. The association of Saladin and Muslims in general, and of the Prophet Muḥammad in particular, with magic is an old trope in European writing. For example, Saladin uses 'black magic' in the 15th-century work, *Richard Coer de Lion* (W.E. Aytoun, *The life and times of Richard the First, surnamed Coeur-de-Lion, King of England*, London, 1840, pp. 361-62). Here, Boccaccio and his English translator also associate Saladin with magic, but this time this is put to 'noble' use, to ensure that love triumphs (J. Rhodes, 'Saladin and the truth of religion in *Decameron* I.3 and X.9', in A. Galloway and R.F. Yeager (eds), *Through a classical eye*, Toronto, 2009, 189-205, pp. 202-3).

The story of the three rings is better known as 'Nathan the Wise' from G.E. Lessing's version (German, 1779; earliest English translation by William Taylor, 1805). It has been described as a call for religious tolerance: Jews, Christians and Muslims all think that they enjoy 'the inheritance of God' but none of them can conclusively prove that they do so exclusively. In the *Decameron*, the Jewish moneylender is called Melchisedech. He lends money to Saladin, but at the end of the tale, Saladin, who fully repays his loan, keeps Melchisedech close to him as his friend, and maintains him in 'great and honourable state'.

Both these tales show Saladin enjoying friendship with non-Muslims. Rhodes suggests that Boccaccio intended them as invitations to readers to rethink the 'division between Christianity and Islam' and presented them as 'ground for a new order and unity ... that extends from East to West by adding another dimension to the power of human love' ('Saladin', p. 201). By translating these stories into English, Painter raises this possibility for a new audience.

Tale 1:LX is translated from Matteo Bandello (d. 1562), who is said to have retold stories he had heard recounting real-life events. Bandello was bishop of Agen from 1541; his *Novellas* were published in 1554 and 1573. The tale features the Ottoman Sultan Mehmed II (d. 1481), the conqueror of Constantinople, who is described as 'not the false prophet'. Unlike the depictions of Saladin, that of Mehmed is far from sympathetic. Mehmed is so enchanted by a Greek concubine who has been captured during the conquest that he neglects his military duties. When he finally admits this, he strikes off her head so that he can return to the business of war, evoking the comment from Painter that he was 'wanton beyonde measure'. The tale ends with Mehmed, the 'barbarous, cruel prince', losing a battle against the Christian, John Huniades (Janos Hunyadi, d. 1456), Regent of Hungary. Tale 2:XXXIV also represents Turks as despotic and monstrous. This tale was translated from the writings of Nicholas Moffan of Burgundy, who had fought against the Ottomans and spent time in captivity. The story is from a Latin pamphlet, written about two years after the event described. It recounts how Sultan Süleyman (d. 1566), encouraged by his 'wicked' and 'pestilent' wife, Roxolana (who was a Christian), murdered his son by another wife, Mustafa, who was suspected of plotting to usurp the throne. Such was Mustafa's reputation for military skill, says Painter, that Christians should take delight in the 'death of thys cruell enimy', who might well have further expanded Ottoman territory into Christian space. The concluding paragraph suggests that Christians must cease their mutual rivalries and discord if they hope to defeat the Turks, a sentiment similar to that at the end of the *Commentary on Scanderbeg*, translated by John Shute. The tale ends with an 'Amen,' indicating a self-conscious theological interest.

MacLean and Matar comment that the novella illustrates what 'Muslims could do to Christians', because Roxolana was totally corrupted by living among them (*Britain and the Islamic world*, pp. 28-29). The character of Roxolana had a major impact on the European imagination, and has been described as 'largely the creation' of this process. Stories are often linked with fascination for the harem and for the role of women (see Yermolenko, *Roxolana*, p. 1).

While these two tales perpetuate tropes of the Turks as implacable enemies of Christianity, cruel and despotic, the final tale returns to a depiction of a Muslim ruler as courteous, generous and civil. This is also from Bandello, and is narrated in the first person by an Italian, Nicholoso Baciadonne, who 'vpon...accident was in Affrica' trading merchandise, and was surprised to find how the population, though 'barbarous' gave generously to the poor, and provided hospices to 'receive and entertain' them, so much so that this puts Christians to shame. Thus, Painter refers to the religious importance of hospitality in both Christianity and Islam. The ruler is the king of Morocco, described as not only temporal lord but also 'as is saide of Prete Iean [Prester John], Byshop of his Law and the Mahomet Priest'. The king, who is called Mansur, loved to hunt, and one day he became separated from his party and ended up staying overnight with a poor fisherman. The latter did not know his guest's identity, but lavished upon him hospitality he could ill afford. In conversation, he expressed his great love of the king. When the guest enquired why he loved the king so much when he had received no favours from him, the fisherman replied that he loved him because he was courteous and just, and ruled by God's grace. When Mansur's identity was revealed, he showed his gratitude by ordering a whole city to be built and making the fisherman and his heirs its governors, because he wished that all his governors might treat strangers as he had. Mansur, the tale continues, although 'barbarous', had a gentle heart, and was a model of 'curtesie' and 'ciuilytie'. Again, as with the Saladin stories, a Muslim's behaviour is represented as setting an example for Christians to imitate.

SIGNIFICANCE

The tale of the three rings, first rendered into English by Painter, may represent one of the earliest justifications for religious tolerance in the English language. Painter selected his sources as examples of virtuous or villainous conduct; thus, it would seem likely that he was fully aware that some stories placed Muslims in the former category, some in the latter. This is equally true of the classical and more historically recent European characters who also feature in his 101 tales. The fact that he had three sources for these stories makes it more likely that he exercised discrimination in choosing them.

Painter may have consciously offered these contrasting depictions of Muslims as a deliberate suggestion that no people can be represented as wholly evil or wholly good. There are virtuous heroes as well as villains in any culture. Some Muslims qualify as objects of emulation while some do not, just as some Christians do and some do not. This goes beyond a blanket condemnation of all Muslims as evil, shifting towards a more subtly nuanced view of the other. Indeed, it begins to undermine the concept of otherness in favour of viewing all people as simply human. Immediately after these last two contrasting stories, in his 'Conclusion' Painter reiterates his aim of helping readers to 'shun the Darts, and Prickes of insolency' and to 'taste the licour that stilleth from the gums or buds of Vertue'. As he brought these stories before English readers for the first time, in choosing his material he may have aimed to broaden readers' horizons, to embrace all people, an aim that Boccaccio, a humanist, had shared. That Muslim civility might shame Christians may represent a new development in how Christians wrote about Muslims, although this is set alongside reprehensible behaviour by other Muslims.

The third volume of the work was published in 1575, almost 25 years after relations between Morocco and England had first been established, and only a few years before Elizabeth I began extensive correspondence with Sultan 'Abd-al-Malik and with his successor, Aḥmad al-Manṣūr, making much of Protestant England and Muslim Morocco's shared hatred of idolatry. Thus, wide geopolitical developments may have influenced Painter's representation of some Muslims as virtuous, as England began to develop cordial relations with both Morocco and the Ottoman Empire over and against Catholic states. At the very least, Painter's representations of Muslims challenge the notion that Christians and Muslims are completely polarised, and that only hostility can exist between them.

EDITIONS & TRANSLATIONS

Masami Hatano (trans.), *Etsuraku no kyūden*, Tokyo, 2012 (partial Japanese trans.)

The palace of pleasure. Elizabethan versions of Italian and French novels from Boccaccio, Bandello, Cinthio, Straparola, Queen Margaret of Navarre, and others, Honolulu, 2002

M. Valency and H. Levtow (eds), *The palace of pleasure. An anthology of the novella*, New York, 1930, 1960²

H. Miles (ed.), *The palace of pleasure*, London, 1929, New York, 1967 (introduction by H. Miles, illus. D.P. Bliss)

P. Haworth (ed.), *An Elizabethan story-book. Famous tales from the Palace of pleasure*, New York, 1928

Jacobs, *The palace of pleasure*

J. Haslewood (ed.), *The palace of pleasure, beautified, adorned, and well furnished with pleasant histories and excellent novels. Very requisite for delight and profit. Chosen and selected out of divers good and commendable authors*, London, 1813

The palace of pleasure beautified adorned and well furnished vvith pleasaunt histories and excellent nouels, London, 1575

The second tome of the Palace of pleasure, conteyning store of goodly histories, etc., London, 1567

The palace of pleasure beautified, adorned and well furnished, with pleasaunt histories and excellent nouelles, selected out of diuers good and commendable authors. By William Painter clarke of the ordinaunce and armarie, London, 1566

STUDIES

G.M. MacLean and N.I. Matar, *Britain and the Islamic world, 1558-1713*, Oxford, 2011

G.I. Yermolenko, *Roxolana in European literature, history and culture*, Farnham, 2010

M. Dimmock, *New Turkes. Dramatizing Islam and the Ottomans in early modern England*, Aldershot, 2005

H.V. Bonavita, 'Key to Christendom. The 1565 Siege of Malta, its histories, and their use in Reformation polemic', *Sixteenth Century Journal* 33 (2002) 1021-43

C. Relihan, *Fashioning authority. The development of Elizabethan novelistic discourse*, Kent OH, 1994

T.W. Baldwin, *On the literary genetics of Shakespeare's poems and sonnets*, Urbana IL, 1950
D. Bush, 'The classical tales in Painter's "Palace of pleasure"', *Journal of English and Philology* 23 (1924) 331-41

Clinton Bennett

Richard Eden

DATE OF BIRTH   Probably 1520 or 1521
PLACE OF BIRTH   Possibly in Herefordshire
DATE OF DEATH   1576
PLACE OF DEATH   Probably London

BIOGRAPHY

Richard Eden was born in about 1520 or 1521, possibly in Herefordshire, into a merchant family, although some of his relatives were ordained. He went to Cambridge in 1534. Biographers speculate that he had a clerical career in mind. He attended Christ's College, then Queens' College, graduating with a BA in 1538. At Cambridge, he was taught and influenced by Sir Thomas Smith (1515-77), professor of civil law from 1542 until 1553, later a secretary of state and ambassador to France. Smith was eager for England to expand colonial settlement beyond Ireland, where he was later granted property (although he failed to take possession of this from its Irish overlords). Smith knew many of the period's leading literary and scientific figures, and appears to have introduced some of these men to Eden. After taking his MA in 1544, Eden occupied a junior post at the Treasury, presumably secured for him by Smith, which he left in 1546. Eden married in 1547. He and his wife had 12 children over the next 14 years (Arber, 'Life and labours', p. xliv).

Although the advocacy of colonialism was to become Eden's consuming passion, he also developed an interest in chemistry, and was offered the post of royal distiller of water, though when Henry VIII died, someone else was appointed instead. In the late 1540s, Eden worked as an alchemist trying to transform base metals into gold. His employer, Richard Whalley (1498/9-1583), was a Nottinghamshire landowner who held a number of public offices, and sat in Parliament off and on from 1547 to 1555. Whalley, who was also in and out of prison on various charges, supported a bid to restore the Duke of Somerset as Lord Protector following the latter's removal in 1549, a goal that Eden apparently did not share, and their relationship ended in 1551. However, Eden found favour with the new government; Sir William Cecil, a secretary of state (there were two at this time), appointed him as his secretary in 1552; the new Lord Protector, the Duke of Northumberland, shared Smith's ideas about colonial expansion. He wished to see England challenge and outstrip Spain, and he wanted his colleagues to recruit men who would be able to promote this venture in various ways. Eden's task was to write accounts of discovery and travel that would excite the English imagination and encourage the colonial project. He excelled at this. Although most of what he went on to publish was translated from other languages, his body of work represents the first study of navigation in English, the first detailed English account of the European discovery of America, and the birth of geography as a serious, scientific discipline.

Eden held a number of other official posts, including a senior appointment at the Treasury (1553-55), clerk of council in the Star Chamber, a post that several members of the Eden family occupied, and, after his wife's death, companion to Jean de Ferrières, vidame (lay-deputy to the bishop) of Chartres, in which capacity he travelled extensively through France and Germany (1562-72). He also conducted some scientific experiments for the vidame, though his reputation rests on his literary achievements. Political events constantly affected his career; his father's support for Lady Jane Grey in 1553 almost cost him his job, as did ambiguity about his own religious affiliation – Protestant or Catholic – in 1555, apparently due to the intervention of the bishop of London (Pearce, 'Eden, Richard', p. 359). There is debate about Eden's attitude towards Queen Mary and her husband, for whom he worked in 1553-55. Some represent him as loyal, advocating a Spanish-English alliance and colonial collaboration, others as covertly arguing that England should challenge Spain's dominance (see the exchange between Hadfield and Jowitt, 1996/7, on Eden's politics). After working for de Ferrières, he returned to England from Paris on the very eve of the August St Bartholomew's day massacre. In 1573, he submitted an unsuccessful application to be made a poor knight of Windsor; he lacked a source of income at the time. His petition stated that he had no desire for riches but wanted only 'a quiet life, suitable for study' (Arber, 'Life and labours', p. xlvi). He died in 1576.

Eden's *A treatyse of the newe India*, dedicated to Lord Northumberland, appeared in 1553. This was a partial translation of Sebastian Münster's *Cosmographia* (1544), the earliest attempt to map and describe the world in German. In 1555, Eden published *Decades of the Newe Worlde or West India*. The first segment translated the first three books of Pietro Martire d'Anghiera's *De orbe novo decades* from the Latin text, taken from the 1533 edition. A heavily annotated copy of this, with Eden's signature, is part of a special collection in the Garrett Library of Johns Hopkins University. Eden also translated Pope Alexander's *Bull* of 1493, Gonzalo

Fernández de Oviedo y Valdés's *Historie of the West Indies* (1553, Spanish), and an abbreviated version of Ferdinand Magellan's voyage around the world. Chapter 6 of the third decade includes Sebastian Cabot's 1497 voyage along the North American coast. Having in conversation with Cabot established his English nationality, Eden saw in this a justification for England to colonise territory that Cabot had reconnoitred. In fact, much of what is known about Cabot has been taken from scattered references in Eden. Eden dedicated his 1555 work to King Philip and Queen Mary. Eden's *The arte of navigation* (1561), a translation of Martin Cortes's *Breve compendio de la sphaera y de la arte de navigar*, was the first such work to become available in English. Eden added descriptions of instruments, which were probably his own. He also reproduced astronomical tables and 'movable volvelles' so that the book itself could be used 'as a calculating device for some tasks', while other instruments could be constructed by following its instructions (Ash, *Power, knowledge*, p. 117).

When Eden died, he was collaborating with Richard Willes (1546-79), a former Jesuit who had joined the Church of England, on an expanded edition of *Decades of the Newe Worlde*. This enlarged 1557 edition added a great deal of material, especially about more recent English voyages, such as along the African coast, to Barbary (Morocco) and Iran. It also included Eden's unpublished translation of the travels of Ludovico di Varthema (c. 1470-1517); reputedly, Varthema was the first European to perform the *ḥajj*, pretending to be a convert to Islam. Eden's work shows a great deal of interest in the search for a north-west passage. Reference to the legend of Prester John evokes Christopher Columbus's dream of aligning with this mythical king, who lived somewhere in the East, so that Christians could attack the Muslim world from both sides. Columbus had included this aim in his petition for support from Queen Isabella of Spain. William Shakespeare's *Tempest* was inspired by Eden's description of colonial-conquered relations (Hart, *Shakespeare*, p. 97), while Sir Francis Drake (d. 1596) used Eden to help prepare for his circumnavigation of 1577-80. Given that Eden describes Spanish cruelty as well as what he saw as the savagery of indigenous people, there has been debate about whether he considered the former or the latter as worse, or saw all people as capable of good and ill (see discussion in Raman, *Renaissance literature*, pp. 77-79, 82).

MAIN SOURCES OF INFORMATION

Primary
MS London, The National Archives, Public Record Office – 70.146.446/12.98.32 (precise date unknown, contemporaneous with Eden's life)
MS London, The National Archives, Public Record Office – State Papers 46/8 (precise date unknown, contemporaneous with Eden's life)
MS London, BL – Lansdowne 101, fols 164-168 (precise date unknown, contemporaneous with Eden's life)
MS Oxford, Bodleian Library – Savile 18, art 5 (precise date unknown, contemporaneous with Eden's life)
Eden's petition to become a poor knight of Windsor (Latin with English translation), in E. Arber, 'The life and labours of Richard Eden', in E. Arber, *The first three English books on America*, Birmingham, 1885, xxxvii-xlvii, pp. xlv-xlvi

Secondary
S. Raman, *Renaissance literature and post-colonial studies*, Edinburgh, 2011, pp. 77-79, 82
J.L. Hart, *Shakespeare. Poetry, history, and culture*, New York, 2009, p. 97
A. Hadfield, art. 'Eden, Richard', *ODNB*
E.H. Ash, *Power, knowledge, and expertise in Elizabethan England*, Baltimore MD, 2004, p. 117
C. Jowitt, '"Monsters and straunge births". The politics of Richard Eden. A response to Andrew Hadfield', *Connotations. A Journal for Critical Debate* 6 (1996/97) 51-64
A. Hadfield, 'Peter Martyr, Richard Eden and the New World. Reading, experience and translation', *Connotations. A Journal for Critical Debate* 5 (1995/6) 1-22
D. Gwyn, 'Richard Eden. Cosmographer and alchemist', *Sixteenth-Century Journal* 15 (1984) 13-34
N.D.F. Pearce, art. 'Eden, Richard', in *DNB*, xvi, 359-60
Arber, 'Life and labours'

WORKS ON CHRISTIAN-MUSLIM RELATIONS

Decades of the Newe Worlde, or West Indies
De orbe novo decades

DATE 1555
ORIGINAL LANGUAGE English

DESCRIPTION

Eden's *Decades of the New World* gives an English translation of the first three books of Pietro Martire d'Anghiera's Latin *De orbe novo decades*, using the 1533 edition. It also translates the first part of Gonzalo Fernandez de Oviedo y Valdes's *La historia general de las Indias* (1535), and gives an abridged account of Ferdinand Magellan's voyage of circumnavigation. The whole book is 446 pages long, excluding preliminary sections. Written by Eden in a quasi-official capacity as a servant of the government to promote an English colonial project, it represents the first detailed account in English of both Columbus's achievements and Sebastian Cabot's exploratory voyage long the North American coast. Eden's writing on the Americas provided the English language with about 300 new words, including 'canoe', 'hammock' and 'guava' (R.W. Bailey, *Speaking American. A history of English in the United States*, Oxford, 2012, p. 17). Another word first used in English by Eden is 'cannibal'.

Scholarly discussion of Eden's writing usually focuses on his role in encouraging the study of navigation, and the impetus his work gave to England's early colonial expansion. Political aspects of his writing, too, have been discussed: did he support Queen Mary and Philip, and hope that England would return to the Catholic faith, or did he really work to subvert Mary's reign, as Jowitt argues (see Householder, *Inventing Americans*, pp. 61-62)? However, regardless of his political opinion, Eden saw colonial expansion predominantly in theological terms. This view is clearly articulated in his 'Preface to the reader' (pp. ai-diii in the 1555 edition, a total of just under 28 pages; the expanded 1577 edition did not reproduce this, though it is reproduced in E. Arber's 1885 text of the *Decades*). Here on the fourth page, Eden refers to the 'Turkish antichrist' and expresses the view that the kingdom of God's earthly expansion and the preaching of Christian faith through the world will result in his 'confusion': for Eden, defeating Islam was a motive for evangelising newly encountered people.

He returns to the theme of defeating Muslims in his final paragraph, when he calls for a grand alliance involving the emperor of China (the Cham of Cathay) and the shah (Sophie) of Persia on one side, and Christian princes on the other, who might unite to defeat the Turks. Here, Eden expresses a dream shared by others, including Christopher Columbus; he had read everything he could find about Prester John. Eden summarises the legend about him in the 1577 expanded edition of his book and, like other contemporary writers, including Varthema, identifies him as the emperor of Ethiopia. This ruler was not well-placed to deliver military aid, although by this time any great ruler willing to align with Christians against the Turks, regardless of their religious identity, could serve as a Prester John, including Muslims.

Like Columbus, Eden thought that some native inhabitants of the Americas were promising candidates for conversion. In a section in which he encourages England to colonise Florida, he describes the natives as happy to barter with strangers, and later says that their 'natural religion' positions them nearer to Christianity than are either Jews or Turks, lacking both the 'ceremonious' law of Moses and the 'portentous fables of Mahometes Alchoran'. While admitting that the Spanish have too often favoured the accumulation of wealth over evangelism, Eden contends that they still put other Christian nations to shame in the task of spreading the true faith. The English, he suggests, are more naturally traders than conquerors, which appears to suggest that they might avoid some of the worst colonial excesses. On the other hand, he sees no reason why Christians could not become rich and evangelise at the same time: 'If we were therfore as desyrous to enlarge the fayth of Chryste as to seeke worldly gooddes, why do we deferre to aduenture that wherin we may doo bothe.' However, a constant refrain in this preface is that evangelism is to be the priority, with the eventual aim of building up sufficient strength of numbers to combat the Turks on two sides.

References in his 1557 translation of Varthema to the Turks and Persians 'hating' each other 'on account of their sects, saints and apostles', and a similar statement in the expanded edition of the *Decades*, show that Eden was aware of rivalries within Islam that Christians might exploit.

SIGNIFICANCE

Eden does not explain exactly who the 'Turkish antichrist' is and, given his willingness to forge an alliance with the shah of Persia, it could be argued that he did not see all Muslims as enemies to Christians. In his reference to Jews and Turks as too difficult to convert, in contrast with at least some native Americans, Eden parts company with Christians for whom the primary task as far as Muslims are concerned is to convert them. Some earlier writers thought Muslims susceptible to conversion, as is expressed, for example, in the 1515 tract, *Here begynneth a lytell treatyse of the turkes lawe called Alcaron*, which draws on earlier Christian sources and is actually taken from the *The book of John Mandeville*.

It seems that the intent of defeating the Turks is distinct from how Christians might deal with and relate to other Muslims who did not represent a perceived military threat. Here we have the beginning, in an English text, of more nuanced awareness that the Muslim world is diverse. Eden's life had been complicated by the struggle between Protestants and Catholics, with personal permutations when he himself seems to have identified with the latter and his family with the former. He worked for a Protestant regime under Edward VI, for a Catholic ruler under Mary, then for a French Protestant (Ferrière). He knew that Muslims also adhered to different schools. Recognition that Christians can align with some Muslims may be a new paradigm in the English context (there are examples of Christian-Muslims alliances in Andalusia, and during the period of the crusader states). Could Eden have realised that geo-political factors, and not only religious difference, contributed to European-Turkish rivalry, that hostility was not a given in every Christian-Muslim encounter? Thus, while the Turks are 'anti-Christian', other Muslims might be more friendly. 'Turk' was, of course, used at the time as a synonym for Muslim, but Eden was aware that non-Turks could also be Muslim, and he may have been using the term in an ethnic sense.

Eden's 'Preface' carries into the English-speaking context an early association of imperial expansion westward, with the task of defeating Islam. A recent writer has claimed that the European conquest of the Americas is one of Islam's few positive gifts to humanity, since Columbus had sailed west to find a way to circle back on the Ottomans. Thus, 'the bellicosity and intransigence of Islam ultimately opened the Americas for Europe' (R. Spencer, *The politically incorrect guide to Islam*, Washington DC, 2005, p. 97), indicating that Eden's view has some supporters today within a constituency that sees the (so-called) Muslim and non-Muslim worlds as destined to clash.

Eden and Columbus both saw the Spanish *Reconquista* as providential. For Columbus, Muslims were the enemy outside, and their 1492 defeat, which he witnessed, heralded the end of their immediate threat, proving that they could be overcome (Caryter, 'On the global in global civil society', p. 349). Eden also refers to the defeat of the Muslims in Spain as an example of Spain taking a lead in the fight for Christian ascendancy. Columbus saw contemporary events as signs of the end, and set out to hasten Christianity's triumph, and, like Eden, he thought some native Americans would easily convert, having 'no religion', 'no false religion' or no idols (see Dunn and Kelley, *The Diario of Christopher Columbus's first voyage*, pp. 89, 127, 141, 185, 235). There are similar references in *The Decade*s.

This similarity, between the birth of Spanish imperialism and the beginning of England's in Eden's pioneer text, as devised above all to end the Muslim threat, or at least the Turkish one, sheds interesting light on the role of Islam in early colonial discourse. Richard Hakluyt, who took up Eden's task of promoting English colonialism, reprinted much of his material in *Principal navigations, voyages, traffiques and discoveries of the English nation* (1589, 1598, 1600), also chronicling subsequent developments, including the beginning of friendly English-Ottoman relations. The extended edition of Eden's 1555 text was published in the same year that cordial correspondence began between Elizabeth I and the King of Morocco.

EDITIONS & TRANSLATIONS

'Preface to the reader', in *Decades of the New World*, Ann Arbor MI, 1966, pp. ai-diii (facsimile)

'Preface to the reader', in E. Arber (ed.), *The first three English books on America*, Birmingham, 1885, Westminster, 1895², New York, 1971³, 49-60

'Preface to the reader', in *Decades of the Newe Worlde*, London, 1555, pp. ai-diii

STUDIES

M. Householder, *Inventing Americans in the age of discovery. Narratives of encounter*, Burlington VT, 2011

J.K. Caryter, 'On the global in global civil society', in W. Storrar, P.J. Casarella and P.L. Metzger (eds), *A world for all? Global civil society in political theory and Trinitarian theology*, Grand Rapids MI, 2011, 299-334, 349

A. Hadfield, *Literature, travel, and colonial writing in the English Renaissance, 1545-1625*, Oxford, 2007

P.C. Mancall, *Bringing the world to early modern Europe. Travel accounts and their audiences*, Leiden, 2007

C. di Biase, *Travel and translation in the early modern period*, Amsterdam, 2006

J. Burton, *Traffic and turning. Islam and English drama: 1579-1624*, Newark DL, 2005

A. Fitzmaurice, *Humanism and America. An intellectual history of English colonisation, 1500-1625*, New York, 2003

A. Hadfield, *Amazons, savages, and machiavels. Travel and colonial writing in English, 1550-1630. An anthology*, Oxford, 2001

D. Read, *Temperate conquests. Spenser and the Spanish New World*, Detroit MI, 2000

N.I. Matar, *Turks, Moors, and Englishmen in the age of discovery*, New York, 1999

Jowitt, '"Monsters and straunge births"'

O.C. Dunn and J.E. Kelley, *The Diario of Christopher Columbus's first voyage to America, 1492-1493*, Norman, 1989, pp. 89, 127, 141, 185, 235

G.B. Gunn, *New World metaphysics. Readings on the religious meaning of the American experience*, New York, 1981

Nauigation and vyages

DATE 1576
ORIGINAL LANGUAGE English

DESCRIPTION
Eden completed his translation of the Latin version of Ludovico di Varthema's (c. 1470-1517) account of his travels in Arabia, then to India and further east, just before his death in 1576. The Italian version, *Itinerario de Ludouico de Varthema bolognese*, appeared in 1510, the Latin in 1511. Eden's translation was published posthumously in *The historie of travayle into the West and East Indies*, the 1577 enlarged version of his *Decades of the New Worlde* (1555), where it comprises pages 354-421. In 1884, the Aungervyle Society, Edinburgh, printed a limited edition of Eden's translation, which has been digitized by Google Books. References below are to the 1884 edition. Other material published in *The historie of travayle*, such as descriptions of the first and second English voyages to Morocco (Barbary), an account of travel to Iran and 'Articles of the privileges which the Sophie of Persia granted to the English merchants' (pp. 322-33), have some references to Islam, but the sections of Varthema dealing with Arabia and Persia are most important for Christian-Muslim relations.

Varthema probably set out on his travels in 1502. He wanted to verify at first hand the truth of what others had reported after 'vouyages and periginations into straunge countreys and people, to know their maners, fashions and customes' (pp. 5-6). After journeying to Egypt, he went to Lebanon and Syria, where in Damascus he met a former Christian who had become an officer in the Mamluk army. This officer allowed

Varthema to join his brigade, which was tasked with escorting pilgrims to Mecca. Calling himself Yunus, and claiming to be a Greek convert to Islam, Varthema set off, becoming the first European non-Muslim known to have visited these cities and performed, or perhaps more accurately observed, the *ḥajj*. (In 1855, Sir Richard Burton included Chapters 11-20, in Eden's translation, as Appendix IV of Volume 2 of his *Personal narrative of a pilgrimage to al-Madinah and Meccah*, describing Varthema as standing in the first rank of old Oriental travellers for his 'correctness of observation and readiness of wit', p. 337). In Medina, Varthema describes the Prophet's tomb, which he says 'does not hang in the air as reported, nor is it borne up by anything' (p. 35). This also establishes that Muḥammad's tomb is in Medina and not, as Europeans often imagined, in Mecca. Later, he again refutes the legend that the tomb is suspended in the air (p. 42).

Despite references to 'wicked Mahumet', 'filthie traditions' and similar, Varthema is not overly critical of what he sees. In Mecca he describes what he calls 'the unicorns of the temple', probably rhinoceroses (p. 57), what he saw sold in the market, 'divers thiynges which' he 'chaunced to see', and also the *ḥajj*, betraying his Christian presuppositions when he says pilgrims make the 'Īd sacrifice to 'Abraham and Isaac' (p. 47). His only explicitly theological observation in this section concerns the pilgrims' expectation of receiving pardon for sin (p. 48).

Before his visit to Persia and his eventual departure from Aden for India, Varthema is arrested and imprisoned on suspicion of being a Christian, and he plays the part of a madman to persuade his captives that he is harmless and should be released. During this episode, he pretends to convert a sheep to Islam, kills a donkey for supposedly neglecting to praise Muḥammad, and stands naked within sight of the sultan's harem to demonstrate his madness or possible saintliness (p. 76). The 'Queen' notices him, and when he says that he has vowed to visit a holy man in Aden, she frees him. He visits the holy man and is impressed, but remarks that his labours counted for naught because he was outside the Christian faith (p. 79).

SIGNIFICANCE

In choosing to bring Varthema's account to an English readership, Eden also helped introduce a new genre of travel narrative. Varthema's work cannot be described as polemic or Christian apology, nor does it set out to polarise 'us' and 'others'. In fact, it does not show much interest in religion at all. According to Wolfe, Varthema 'straddled the divide between ancient and modern travel writing'. On the one hand, he 'exaggerates', though on the other 'he could be "scientific", too, concerned with accuracy to a degree that sets him apart from the travel liars' (*One thousand roads to Mecca*, pp. 80-81). Others (Rubiés, *Travel and ethnology*; Hout, 'Hajj') comment on his lack of interest in stereotypes, and on his more secular, less pietistic or religious outlook, which distinguishes him from earlier writers. Eden's translation brought the most detailed description of Mecca and Medina, and certainly the most accurate to date, before English readers. Even though the later Hakluyt version would prove more durable in print, this was a significant achievement. It remained the only account until Joseph Pitts became the first Englishman to visit Mecca.

Two other aspects of the Varthema text are noteworthy. First, through Eden's translation, information on the distinction between Sunnī and Shī'ī Muslims became available at the very time the English were beginning to trade with Persia. Eden himself proposed an alliance between Christian princes, the shah and others to defeat the 'Turkish antichrist'. Despite some flaws, Eden's text added to knowledge of Islamic diversity, making it possible for some to rethink how they should represent Islam. Arguably, this later led to more nuanced analysis of Christian-Muslim relations.

Second, Eden's translation may have introduced to English readers the notion that the harem in Muslim space offered sexual possibilities, even adventures, that were denied in Europe. Varthema's short captivity narrative, unlike early European harem stories, does not depict Muslim women as oppressed and exploited but as bold and powerful, even able to be considered 'the equal of men'. The stereotype of harem women as oppressed did not emerge until the 18th century (M. Kahf, *Western representation of Muslim women*, Austin TX, 1999, pp. 5-8). This may be an unintended result of Eden's translation, but it can be seen as contributing to discourse on how tropes change over time, sometimes from more to less positive, rather than vice-versa.

EDITIONS & TRANSLATIONS

The nauigation and vyages of Lewis Wertomannus. In the yeere of our Lorde 1503, Charleston SC, 2012 (repr.)

The nauigation and vyages of Lewes Vertomannus... to the regions of Arabia, Egypt, Persia, Syria, Ethiopia, and East India, both within and without the ryuer of Ganges, etc. in the yeere of our Lorde, 1503, Edinburgh, 1884

R. Eden and R. Willes, 'Navigation and voyages of Lewis Vertomannus', in *The historie of travayle into the West and East Indies*, London, 1577, 354-421

STUDIES

M. Wolfe, *One thousand roads to Mecca. Ten centuries of travelers writing about the Muslim pilgrimage*, New York, 2007

S.C. Hout, 'Hajj', in J. Speake (ed.), *Literature of travel and exploration: G to P*, New York, 2003, 533-34

R. Shaz, *In pursuit of Arabia*, New Delhi, 2003

J.P. Rubiés, *Travel and ethnology in the Renaissance. South India through European eyes, 1250-1625*, Cambridge, 2000

R.L. Bidwell, *Travellers in Arabia*, Reading, 1995

D.G. Hogarth, *The penetration of Arabia. A record of the development of Western knowledge concerning the Arabian Peninsula*, New York, 1904

Clinton Bennett

Christopher Marlowe

Christopher Marlo, Marley, Marlin, Merling, Morley

DATE OF BIRTH   Baptised 26 February 1564
PLACE OF BIRTH   Canterbury
DATE OF DEATH   30 May 1593
PLACE OF DEATH   Deptford Strand, London

BIOGRAPHY

The controversy that surrounded Christopher Marlowe in his own day, leading up to (and perhaps contributing to) his early death, has continued over the more than 400 years since the life of one of England's most innovative and influential writers came to its premature end. Perhaps more than any other writer in English, his life and work have become bound up together, the one illuminating, but also distorting, the other. What we know – or think we know – of that life, and what we make of the literature he produced, continues to fascinate.

Christopher Marlowe was born in 1564, the same year as William Shakespeare, and, like his fellow playwright and poet, his biography is incomplete, 'the lost years' leaving scope for much speculation. What is known is that his father was a cobbler and he was born in Kent, attending the King's School in Canterbury as a scholar. Thus, like his contemporary in Stratford, Marlowe received a grammar school education. Unlike Shakespeare, however, Marlowe proceeded to university: evidently he shone at school, winning a scholarship endowed by Archbishop Matthew Parker (one of which was reserved for a Canterbury-born King's boy) to Corpus Christi, Cambridge. He graduated with a BA in 1584 and received his MA three years later.

Marlowe appears to have been an unexceptional scholar, but there can be little doubt that the years at Cambridge formed the man, and much of what followed may be traced back to this period. It is all but certain that the writing for which he is remembered began during this time; it is also reasonably clear that the other activities over which so much ink has been spilt – and arguably led to him losing his life – began during the 'Cambridge years' too. While the records for his early years at university, up to his being confirmed BA in 1584, indicate, insofar as such records can, a conventional and unremarkable (and unremarked) academic career, the activities Marlowe became involved in over the next three years are considerably less straightforward, and therein lie the clues – such as they are – to the remaining six years of his life.

The evidence all but confirms that for some years he was in the service of the government, perhaps while resident in Cambridge, but certainly abroad, probably in France. He only received his MA following the Privy Council's intervention, explaining that he had been in her majesty's employ, and dismissing rumours that he had been involved in Catholic circles in Cambridge: he may in fact have been masquerading as such, effectively working as a spy for the government. Ambiguities in matters religious and claims of blasphemy would dog him through the rest of his life; given the provenance of the reports, it is unclear quite what views Marlowe held, but collectively the accounts point to a man who was willing to sail very close to the wind indeed. It is easy to see why biographers have regarded his violent end – stabbed to death in a dispute over a bill – as connected in some way to his controversial life and opinions, and perhaps as a result of his government activities. What is certain is that both during and after his life Christopher Marlowe was associated above all with views that it was dangerous, and reckless, to hold.

This reputation was substantiated, obliquely and thrillingly (in both senses of the word), in his remarkable literary output during this period: indeed, if it is risky to read the man into and out of the work, it is nevertheless the case that at the same time as Marlowe was spying, brawling and moving in and out of circles connected with the court, he was also a poet and playwright. Perhaps inevitably, the plays in particular have been taken to 'reflect' their author's opinions, though the order of their composition is unclear (*Dido, Queen of Carthage* was probably the first, *Edward II* the last). Certainly, religious strife is to the fore in *The massacre at Paris* and *The Jew of Malta*; blasphemous desire in the *Tamburlaine* plays and *Doctor Faustus*; and sexual transgression in *Edward II* – taken to support both contemporary and modern views of Marlowe's sexual preferences. The most famous actor of the age, Edward Alleyn, brought to life the three characters Marlowe became best known for – Barabas (in *The Jew of Malta*), Tamburlaine, and Faustus – all of whom matched their contempt for religious orthodoxies to a vibrant theatrical presence that would define the late Elizabethan stage. To what extent Marlowe shared the 'will to power' aspirations of his characters cannot be known, but the plays capture both the danger of such ideas and their contemporary potency.

MAIN SOURCES OF INFORMATION

Primary
Parish register, St George's Canterbury, 26 February 1564
Parish register, St Nicholas's Deptford, 1 June 1593

Secondary
P. Honan, *Christopher Marlowe, poet and spy*, Oxford, 2005
L. Hopkins, *Christopher Marlowe, Renaissance dramatist*, Edinburgh, 2005
D. Riggs, *The world of Christopher Marlowe*, London, 2004
C. Nicholl, art. 'Marlowe (Marley), Christopher (*bap.* 1564, *d.* 1593)', in *ODNB*, vol 36, 721-30
L. Hopkins, *Christopher Marlowe. A literary life*, Basingstoke, 2000
T. Healy, *Christopher Marlowe*, Plymouth, 1994
C. Nicholl, *The reckoning. The murder of Christopher Marlowe*, London, 1992, 2002²
R. Sales, *Christopher Marlowe*, Basingstoke, 1991

WORKS ON CHRISTIAN-MUSLIM RELATIONS

Tamburlaine the Great

DATE Approximately 1587-88
ORIGINAL LANGUAGE English

DESCRIPTION
Christopher Marlowe composed *Tamburlaine the Great* in about 1587, drawing on the career of the famous warlord Timur-i-Leng, though not concluding with the hero's death. It is unlikely, however, that this was because Marlowe had a sequel in mind. He had exhausted his historical material, and when he came to write a second part, almost certainly in response to the success of the first play, he had to draw on 15th-century history that in fact postdated the historical Timur's death. When the plays were revived in 1594-95, according to the records of Philip Henslowe, owner of the Rose playhouse in London, the first play was staged on its own; only later did the second receive performances, and always on the night following the performance of the first play. It is proper to speak then of *Tamburlaine the Great* (meaning 'Part 1', the first play) and/or the Tamburlaine plays. While the modern theatre has tended to conflate the two 'parts' into one play, there is no evidence that this was done in the early modern period, during Marlowe's lifetime and into the 17th century, when the Tamburlaine plays enjoyed revivals. Although the sequel

is a continuation of Tamburlaine's exploits, it introduces the 'tragic' element – the inevitable decline and death of the hero. Nonetheless, it is surely significant that Tamburlaine dies a natural death: although it follows his burning of the Qur'an, only the modern cutting of the script can make explicit and perhaps causal the narrative link between these two events.

The Tamburlaine plays are the only plays by Marlowe known to have been published during his lifetime, but there is no evidence that he oversaw their printing. Indeed, the publisher of the 1590 octavo, Richard Jones, explicitly states that he has 'omitted and left out some fond and frivolous gestures, digressing (and in my poor opinion) far unmeet for the matter, which I thought, might seem more tedious unto the wise...'. How the 1590 text, on which all modern editions must be based, differs from the texts first performed on London stages cannot be known, since no manuscript of the plays survive. Nor is it provable one way or the other that the 1590 texts were those staged in revival in 1594-95 and later. In any case, scholars broadly believe that plays were often cut for performance, as they are today.

As in several other Marlowe plays, the hero is scornful of religious orthodoxy: his desire for power trumps all. Perhaps even more than *Doctor Faustus*, however, the Tamburlaine plays are concerned less with debates within theology – Christian theology – than with wider issues: the God Tamburlaine scorns is a general rather than specific entity; indeed, God remains in the background, the plays making clear that God is irrelevant to the actions and desires of men. (In *Doctor Faustus*, of course, God is ever-present, even and especially in Faustus's rejection of God.) As in *The Jew of Malta*, the hero (played in both plays by the leading actor of the day, Edward Alleyn) is not only powerful in secular terms, but expresses this power in theatrical terms. And as with that play, where Marlowe refuses to celebrate the Christian victory at the 1565 siege of Malta, instead showing that the Christians are just as hypocritical as the eponymous Jew, whose sacrifice performs an ironic reprise of Pilate's sparing of Barabbas so that the Christians may be saved, in Tamburlaine is deployed an attractive villain (anticipating Shakespeare's Richard III and Iago in this respect). The result is a remarkably even-handed treatment of religious difference – not in the service of ecumenism *avant la lettre*, but innovative and daring in its striking resistance to the orthodox Christian view of the non-Christian 'other'.

The Tamburlaine plays were first published together, in octavo, in 1590. Total length (both plays) is 164 pages. Modern editors believe the text derives from an authorial or scribal manuscript, rather than from theatrical performance, since even rudimentary stage directions (such as entries/exits) are missing from the earliest printed text. Following the 1590 printing (O1), the plays reappeared in octavo in 1593 (O2) and 1597 (O3); the plays were printed in a two-volume quarto in 1605-6 (Q). Since all subsequent texts derive from O1, the earliest octavo is the copy-text for all modern editions.

SIGNIFICANCE

Marlowe's Tamburlaine is perhaps his earliest 'atheistic' character, the scourge of Muslims and Christians alike. In many respects, he recalls the historical European fear of the Turk, perceived as a threat to Christian Europe, particularly after the capture of Constantinople in 1453. Yet he also offers audiences a vision of the 'scourge sent from God' that might, in the Protestant scheme of things, purge both Muslim and Catholic. This kind of ironic reading, in which the figure of Tamburlaine serves as flexible allegory or trope, is testament to the ways in which here (and elsewhere) Marlowe resists, and indeed challenges, orthodoxy.

The success of the Tamburlaine plays – and their influence on playmaking over the next decade and more – made the theatrically-vibrant hero a staple of the early modern stage. It spawned a whole host of imitations, as other acting troupes sought to capitalise on the new aesthetic.

In its modern incarnations, the play has tended to be interpreted as an allegory for modern times, rather than as a historical piece. In the aftermath of the Second World War, the 'otherness' of Tamburlaine was seen in terms of psychology rather than geography, Marlowe's plays evoking the totalitarian present and recent past of Stalinist Russia and Hitler's Germany respectively. Perhaps more recent history will offer other geopolitical analogies, but Marlowe's plays are notable for their resistance to any convenient interpretative strategy, so that such readings tend to come unstuck. They also, arguably, go against the Marlovian grain: for all that Tamburlaine – and Barabas and Faustus – are obsessed with power, it is surely the play's function to treat such desires with ironic detachment.

EDITIONS & TRANSLATIONS

There have been many editions of *Tamburlaine the Great*. Those listed include the main ones in English, together with translations into other languages.

D. Pasini, *Tamerlán el Grande*, Buenos Aires, 2011 (Spanish trans.)

S. Velentzas, *Tamerlanos ho melas*, Athens, 2006 (Greek trans.)

A.B. Dawson, *Tamburlaine parts one and two*, London, 1997

M.A.A. D'Ovidioe, *Tamerlano*, Milan, 1992 (Italian trans., published with *Dottor Faustus* and *L'ebreo di Malta*)

J.R. Wilcock, *Tamerlano il grande*, Milan, 1989 (Italian trans.)

A. Coll and D. Bevington, *Teatro*, Madrid, 1984 (Spanish and English bilingual edition of Marlowe's collected plays)

J.S. Cunningham, *Tamburlaine*, Manchester, 1981

F. Bowers, *The complete works of Christopher Marlowe*, Cambridge, 1981, vol. 1

T. Guthrie and D. Wolfitt, *Tamerlan*, Paris, 1977 (abridged French and English edition)

J. Kydryński and J. Strzetelski, *Tamerlan Wielki*, Krakow, 1977 (Polish trans.)

U. Ellis-Fermor, *Tamburlaine the Great*, London, 1930

E.M. Woolley and S.V. Benet, *Tamburlaine the Great. Who, from the state of a shepherd in Scythia, by his rare and wonderful conquests, became a most puissant and mighty monarch*, New Haven CT, 1919

The plays of Christopher Marlowe, London, 1909 (Everyman's Library edition, with Introduction by E. Thomas)

M. Vöhl, *Der erste Teil des Tamerlan des Grossen*, Helmstedt, 1893 (German trans.)

P.E. Pinkerton, *The dramatic works of Christopher Marlowe*, London, 1889

A. Wagner, *Tamburlaine*, Heilbronn, 1885 (German trans.)

W. Oxberry, *Tamburlaine the Great. a tragedy...*, London, 1820

Tamburlaine the Greate. VVho, from the state of a shepeard in Scythia, by his rare and wonderfull conquests, became a most puisant and mighty monarque, London, 1605

Tamburlaine the Great. Who, from a Scythian shephearde, by his rare and woonderfull conquests, became a most puissant and mightye monarque. And for his tyranny, and terrour in warre was tearmed, the Scourge of God. Devided into two tragical discourses. Now first and newlie published, London, 1590

STUDIES

M.T. Burnett, 'Tamburlaine the Great, parts one and two', in P. Cheney (ed.), *The Cambridge companion to Christopher Marlowe*, Cambridge, 2004, 127-43

J. Burton, 'Anglo-Ottoman relations and the image of the Turk in Tamburlaine', *Journal of Medieval and Early Modern Studies* 30 (2000) 125-56

E.C. Bartels, *Spectacles of strangeness. Imperialism, alienation and Marlowe*, Philadelphia, 1993

D. Goldberg, 'Whose God's on first? Special providence in the plays of Christopher Marlowe', *English Literary History* 60 (1993) 569-87

T. Cartelli, *Marlowe, Shakespeare and the economy of theatrical experience*, Philadelphia, 1991

D.H. Thurn, 'Sights of power in *Tamburlaine*', *English Literary History* 19 (1989) 3-21

G.L. Geckle, *Tamburlaine and Edward II. Text and performance*, London, 1988

S. Shepherd, *Marlowe and the politics of Elizabethan theatre*, New York, 1986

R. Levin, 'The contemporary perception of Marlowe's Tamburlaine', *Medieval and Renaissance Drama in England* 1 (1984) 51-70

S. Greenblatt, *Renaissance self-fashioning. From More to Shakespeare*, Chicago IL, 1980

M. Goldman, 'Marlowe and the histrionics of ravishment', in A. Kernan (ed.), *Two Renaissance mythmakers*, London, 1977, 22-40

H. Levin, *The overreacher. A study of Christopher Marlowe*, London, 1954

E. Huebener, 'Der Einfluss von Marlowe's Tamburlaine auf die zeitgenössischen und folgenden Dramatiker', Halle, 1901 (Diss. University of Halle)

Mark Hutchings

Montaigne

Michel Eyquem de Montaigne

DATE OF BIRTH   28 February 1533
PLACE OF BIRTH Chateau de Montaigne, Gascony
DATE OF DEATH   13 September 1592
PLACE OF DEATH Chateau de Montaigne, Gascony

BIOGRAPHY

Montaigne was born into a wealthy noble family of former Bordeaux merchants in 1533, during the reign of Francis I, at the height of the French Renaissance. The oldest of eight surviving children, he was taught Latin and Greek by a German preceptor before, at the age of only six, he entered the Collège de Guyenne in Bordeaux, one of the most distinguished humanist schools in France at the time. It is assumed that he studied law at the University of Toulouse before becoming a magistrate in the Cour des Aides (regional court) of Périgueux in 1554. This was incorporated into the Bordeaux Parlement (high court of justice) in 1557, and Montaigne continued to serve there until 1570. He became close friends with Étienne de la Boétie, whose sudden death in 1563 Montaigne would mourn for the rest of his life and whose writings he would later edit and publish.

In 1565, Montaigne married Françoise de la Chassaigne, and had with her one surviving daughter, Léonore. During his years as magistrate, he repeatedly spent time at the royal court of Charles IX. After the death of his father, Montaigne resigned from his office and managed the family's country estate during the height of the religious wars that had been afflicting France since 1561. Between 1570 and 1580, Montaigne composed the first two books of the *Essais* while accepting charges to mediate between the warring Catholic and Huguenot parties. In the summer of 1580, he presented a copy of the *Essais* to Henry III in Paris before leaving for an extended trip to German and Italian spas to cure his kidney stones, from which he suffered all his adult life. During his journey, he kept a journal that was rediscovered in the late 18th century, the *Journal de voyage*. Montaigne returned to Bordeaux in November 1581 after being elected in his absence as that city's mayor. He served in that capacity until 1585. After escaping the plague that was raging that same year, he retired to the Chateau de Montaigne for good, substantially revising the *Essais* and adding a third book. Montaigne personally oversaw the second edition of the *Essais* in Paris in 1588, again presenting Henry III with a copy of his *magnum opus*. He spent the last years of his life at his chateau, increasingly ailing and dismayed by the continuing horrors of the civil war. Until his death in September 1592 from quinsy, Montaigne kept adding comments in the margins of his 1588 copy of the *Essais*. This so-called Bordeaux copy became the basis of a posthumous third edition of Montaigne's work, published in 1595.

MAIN SOURCES OF INFORMATION

Primary
F. Rigolot (ed.), *Journal de voyage*, Paris, 1992
V.-L. Saulnier (ed.), *Les Essais*, Paris, 2004

Secondary
P. Desan, *Montaigne. Une biographie politique*, Paris, 2014
G. Hoffmann, *Montaigne's career*, Oxford, 1998
M. Lazard, *Michel de Montaigne*, Paris, 1992
D.M. Frame, *Montaigne. A biography*, New York, 1965
H. Friedrich, *Montaigne*, Bern, 1949 (English trans. by D. Eng, intro. P. Desan, Berkeley CA, 1991)

WORKS ON CHRISTIAN-MUSLIM RELATIONS

Les Essais, 'Essays'

DATE 1580 (first edition) 1588 (extended second edition) 1595 (extended posthumous third edition)
ORIGINAL LANGUAGE French

DESCRIPTION
Compared with his treatment of Christianity and Judaism, Montaigne's engagement with Islam in the *Essais* is quite limited and it is neutral in the sense that he does not consider the Muslim faith any better or worse than any other religion as far as its practices and institutions are concerned. This becomes clear in the dozen or so evocations of the Prophet Muḥammad and of Muslims, or *Mahometans* as they were called during Montaigne's time, in the *Essais*' three books. With two exceptions, they were all added by Montaigne after 1588, in the margins of his copy of the second edition. He also inserted about two dozen remarks about the

Turks in this copy. That makes them by far the most frequently mentioned Muslim community in the *Essais*, but only a handful of these comments concern their religion. Islam and Muslims, then, are conspicuously absent, if not entirely nonexistent, in the *Essais*, whose 107 chapters occupy more than 1,100 pages in the Villey edition. The references here are to this edition, by book, chapter, and page.

Before adding his handwritten remarks about Islam, Montaigne refers to the Prophet and the *Mahometans* only once, in the first and second edition respectively. Both evocations appear in the 'Apology for Raymond Sebond', the longest and among the most complex chapters of the *Essais*. At first sight, Montaigne seems to rehash 16th-century commonplaces about Islam: Muḥammad is accused of making false promises to his followers (II, 12.578), and Muslims are likened to pagans, both being assumed to be inferior to Christians (II, 12.442). But in the context of the deep scepticism regarding human faith and reason expressed in the 'Apology', Montaigne's comments target the weaknesses of his Christian contemporaries more than they denigrate Muslims, even though, as a practising Catholic, he does not consider Islam to be on a par with his own faith: he critically observes that many of his fellow Christians fall as easily as the Prophet's followers for the promise of an afterlife in paradise, and that they fail to meet their faith's moral expectations. Christians therefore behave no better than pagans or Muslims and often worse, as during the French wars of religion.

Up to the time of his death, Montaigne added six more references to Islam to his personal copy of the second edition of the *Essais*, three of them in proximity to those in the 'Apology'. They all concern customs and institutions of the Muslim faith. Drawing on his study of Laonicus Chalcocondyles's *De origine et rebus gestis Turcorum*, translated into French in 1577, and René de Lucinge's *Naissance, durée et chute des États*, first published in 1588 (Balsamo), towards the end of his life Montaigne increasingly evokes Muslim exempla in order to make more general points about aspects of human behaviour. For example, he condemns the practice of Muslim self-mutilation as penance (II, 12.522), arguing that it is not the part of the body that is mutilated that has done any wrong but the human will. In the same vein, he also alludes to circumcision twice in the *Essais*. He considers this religious practice an arbitrary act (II, 12.574), practised out of a false, even fanatical belief or 'opinion' (I, 14.53): 'Any opinion is strong enough to make people espouse it at the price of life. [...] How many people we see in the war between the

Turks and the Greeks accept a cruel death rather than abandon circumcision for baptism! An example of which no sort of religion is incapable' (Frame, *Complete essays*, p. 35). Here, as in other contexts, Muslims are first and foremost human beings who, because of their faith, commit acts that Montaigne considers inhuman or against nature (see also III, 5.879). Among those acts, he also counts the practice of nudity by certain Muslim sects to express their devotion (I, 36.226). If the essayist singles out the Ottoman Empire, he only does so to make a broader argument about religious as cultural habits: 'How many men, especially in Turkey, go naked as a matter of religion!' (Frame, *Complete essays*, p. 167). Even his most negative remark about Islam (III, 10.1013), accusing Muḥammad of playing 'monkey tricks' (Frame, *Complete essays*, p. 775) on his followers, is inserted in a much more general discussion of human credulousness: people's 'sense and understanding is entirely smothered in their passion. Their discernment is left no choice than the one that smiles upon them and comforts their cause' (Frame, *Complete essays*, p. 775).

As these examples make clear, Islam and Muslims are never treated in isolation in the *Essais*. Rather, they serve Montaigne as exempla to develop and illustrate his ideas about human superstition and what he considers unreasonable or immoral behaviour. Juxtaposed to the Ancients (III, 10.1013), Jews (II, 12.574), and Christians (III, 5.879), Muslims are portrayed as imperfect believers of the kind that any religion – monotheistic or pagan – is prone to produce. Contrary to Christianity and Judaism, however, Islam is never recognised by Montaigne as a legitimate, 'true' religion.

SIGNIFICANCE

Despite being a curious individual believing in the value of personal experience, Montaigne's knowledge about Islam is only second hand. His numerous travels never took him to a Muslim country, so that his comments about the Prophet and his followers are all derived from travelogues and treatises or from hearsay. It is therefore all the more remarkable that his attitude toward Islam does not simply echo the pervasive anti-Muslim sentiment of his time, in which calls for a new crusade against the infidel abounded as a convenient means of propaganda of both Catholics and Huguenots (Heath, *Crusading commonplaces*). Nor does Montaigne share in the enthusiasm for the Ottoman Empire he encountered in the works of scholars and travellers such as Guillaume Postel. In accordance with the exceptional enterprise of the *Essais*, Montaigne, uniquely among his contemporaries, affords an original perspective on Islam, being solely interested in Muslims as fellow-, that is fallible, human beings.

EDITIONS & TRANSLATIONS
   Original editions:
   Essais, Paris: Abel L'Angelier, 1595 (first posthumous edition)
   Essais, Bordeaux: Simon Millanges, 1580 (books I and II)
   Essais, Paris: Abel L'Angelier, 1588 (books I-III)

There are numerous editions and translations of the *Essais*. Below is a selected list of the most recent and commonly used critical editions.
   J. Balsamo, C. Magnien-Simonin, and M. Magnien (eds), *Les essais*, Paris, 2007
   P. Villey (ed.), *Les essais. Edition conforme au texte de l'exemplaire de Bordeaux*, Paris, 2004
   H. Stillet (trans.), *Essais*, Frankfurt, 1998 (German trans.)
   F. Garavini (trans.), *Saggi*, Milan, 1992 (Italian trans.)
   M.A. Screech (trans.), *The complete essays*, London, 1991 (English trans.)
   D. Picazo and A. Montojo (trans.), *Ensayos*, 3 vols, Madrid, 1987-93 (Spanish trans.)
   D. Frame (trans.), *The complete essays of Montaigne*, Stanford CA, 1958 (English trans.)
   H. Lüthy (trans.), *Essais*, Zurich, 1953, 2000² (German trans.)

STUDIES
Critical studies on the *Essais* and Montaigne abound. Below is a selected list of studies that are most recent, most authoritative, or most relevant to Montaigne's comments about Islam and Muslims.
   D. Bjaï, 'La représentation de l'Orient dans les *Essais* de Montaigne', in A. Classen (ed.), *East meets West in the Middle Ages and early modern times. Transcultural experiences in the premodern world*, Berlin, 2013, 649-65
   P. Desan (ed.), *Dictionnaire de Michel de Montaigne*, Paris, 2007 (rev. ed.)
   P. Mathias, *Montaigne ou l'usage du monde*, Paris, 2006
   U. Langer (ed.), *The Cambridge companion to Montaigne*, Cambridge, 2005
   E. Auerbach, 'L'humaine condition', in E. Averbach, *Mimesis. Dargestellte Wirklichkeit in der abendländischen Literatur*, 1946, Bern³, 1964, 271-96 (trans. W.R. Trask, *Mimesis. The representation of reality in Western literature*, Princeton NJ, 2003, 285-311)

J. Balsamo, 'L'histoire des Turcs à l'épreuve des Essais', in F. Argod-Dutard (ed.), *Histoire et littérature au siècle de Montaigne. Mélanges offerts à Claude-Gilbert Dubois*, Geneva, 2001, 221-36

M.J. Heath, *Crusading commonplaces. La Noue, Lucinge and rhetoric against the Turks*, Geneva, 1986

G. Nakam, *Les Essais de Montaigne. Miroir et procès de leur temps*, Paris, 1984, 2001^2

J. Starobinski, *Montaigne en movement*, Paris, 1982

Friedrich, *Montaigne*

Marcus Keller

Thomas Kyd

DATE OF BIRTH   November 1558
PLACE OF BIRTH   London
DATE OF DEATH   August 1594
PLACE OF DEATH   London

BIOGRAPHY

Although he is identified as the author of a play – *The Spanish tragedy* – that was famous and influential in his lifetime, less is known about Thomas Kyd than about many of his contemporaries. He was born in London in late 1558, the son of Francis and Anna Kyd, and was enrolled in the Merchant Taylors' School during the celebrated custodianship of Richard Mulcaster. After his schooling, it seems likely that he followed his father into scrivening (Francis Kyd was warden of the Company of Scriveners in 1580) rather than entering the university system, but by the mid-1580s he is noted as a dramatist for the Queen's Men. No early work is extant, and what is left of Kyd's literary corpus is confined to his most famous play, *The Spanish tragedy* (dated to around 1587, but only identified with Kyd in the late 18th century), and two translations, *Cornelia*, a translation of Robert Garnier's *Cornélie*, and *The householder's philosophy*, a translation of Tasso's *Il padre di famiglia*. A tragedy, *Solimon and Perseda*, is solidly attributed to him, and *The first part of Jeronimo* less so. Kyd's authorship of an earlier version of the Danish Prince, in a play often named the *Ur-Hamlet*, is still argued over by critics and historians – no text survives.

Much of the information that remains about Thomas Kyd emerges from letters in his hand protesting innocence after his arrest for the possession of certain 'vile heretical Conceiptes'. These had emerged during a search of Kyd's lodgings for evidence relating to provocative libels that had begun springing up in London in early 1593. Kyd's defence was that the heretical material (copied out of a tract, John Proctour's *The fall of the late Arian*, of 1549) was not his, but had belonged to his fellow playwright, Christopher Marlowe, and had been stored there when the two roomed together two years before. Kyd had few good words to say about Marlowe, who was subsequently arrested, freed, and murdered in Deptford.

Kyd was himself freed, probably after torture, and died in August the following year, aged 35.

MAIN SOURCES OF INFORMATION

Primary
MS London, BL – Harley 6848 fols 187-89 (letters from Kyd to Sir John Puckering)

Secondary
J.R. Mulryne, art. 'Kyd, Thomas (*bap.* 1558, *d.* 1594)', in *ODNB*, http://www.oxforddnb.com
L. Erne, *Beyond the Spanish tragedy. A study of the works of Thomas Kyd*, Manchester, 2002
M. Wiggins, *Shakespeare and the drama of his time*, Oxford, 2000
F. Ardolino, *Apocalypse and armada in Kyd's Spanish tragedy*, Kirksville MO, 1995
P.B. Murray, *Thomas Kyd*, New York, 1969
A. Freeman, *Thomas Kyd. Facts and problems*, Oxford, 1967
P. Edwards, *Thomas Kyd and early Elizabethan tragedy*, London, 1966
S.A. Tannenbaum, *Thomas Kyd. A concise bibliography*, New York, 1941

WORKS ON CHRISTIAN-MUSLIM RELATIONS

The tragedie of Solimon and Perseda

DATE Possibly 1589
ORIGINAL LANGUAGE English

DESCRIPTION
Entered in the London Stationer' register in November 1592, *The tragedie of Solimon and Perseda, Wherein is laide open, loues constancie, fortunes inconstancie, and deaths triumphs* (running to 68 pages) is conventionally attributed to Thomas Kyd on the basis that the storyline is one expanded from the play-within-a-play that occurs at the conclusion of his more celebrated drama, *The Spanish tragedy*. This narrative is not Kyd's, but is adapted from one of the romance tales in Henry Wooton's popular translation of Jacques Yver's *A courtlie contouersie of Cupid's cautels* (1578).

Set predominantly on the island of Rhodes, the play begins by introducing the young lovers Erastus and Perseda and a tournament on the island to which knights from many countries have come to prove their valour. After his loss of Perseda's gift – a carcanet – and the death of the knight Ferdinando, Erastus is forced into exile in Ottoman domains, seeking and receiving the protection and patronage of Solimon (one of many versions of Süleyman 'the Magnificent' stalking the early modern stage). The Ottoman ruler then invades Rhodes (which had taken place in 1522), in the process capturing and falling in love with Perseda. Although at first he allows the lovers to reunite, Solimon's intemperance and jealousy lead him to plot against Erastus, whom he has killed. Leading his army against a Rhodean revolt, he fights and kills a Christian warrior who is finally revealed to be Perseda in disguise. He takes one final kiss, but Perseda's lips are poisoned and Solimon dies beneath the walls of Rhodes.

SIGNIFICANCE

Solimon and Perseda tends to be bracketed along with the first wave of numerous 'Turk plays' that followed the great success of Christopher Marlowe's *Tamburlaine* plays (1587-88): this group includes George Peele's *The battle of Alcazar* (1589?), Robert Greene's *Alphonsus of Aragon* (1588?) and *Selimus* (1591?), and a number of others whose names remain but which are no longer extant. These plays sought to emulate the Asian – and particularly Islamic – geographies, and the bombast and spectacle of Marlowe's plays, and scoured the available source material for suitable moments of intrigue and conquest. Turning to the 1522 siege of Rhodes, Kyd found perhaps the most dramatic of these scenarios – not only was it well known from his use of it in *The Spanish tragedy*, where it is the subject of a strikingly odd play performed to the assembled Spanish nobility and becomes the instrument of Hieronimo's revenge for the murder of his son, but the siege itself was a tale that was still being told and retold in history and romance. A playhouse audience would have been well aware of the outcome of Solimon's invasion threats, and the intertwining of a sultan's thwarted love for a Christian woman with bloody conquest links Kyd's play with another celebrated 'Turk play', George Peele's lost *Turkish Mahomet and Hiren the fair Greek* (1588), in which another bombastic 'Turk' must kill the object of his affections to concentrate on extending his dominion.

What Kyd – assuming this is his work – brings to this new genre of 'Turk play' is an experienced dramatist's awareness and exploitation of dramatic possibilities. More than most of his contemporaries, including Marlowe, he is interested in presenting the interrelation of Christians and Muslims in the context of a multicultural and multi-religious Mediterranean – it does not seem implausible when the Ottoman Brusor fights in the Rhodean tournament, nor when Erastus seeks exile in Ottoman domains. The only other dramatists who do something similar are George Peele in *Alcazar* and Shakespeare in his depiction of the Prince of Morocco in *The merchant of Venice* (1596) – whose opening speech contains echoes of Brusor's lines early in *Solimon and Perseda*. Countering these references to the possibility of peaceful interaction is Kyd's masterful depiction of the play's dominant character, Soliman. Those 'Turk plays' that followed the lead of *Tamburlaine* increasingly placed the figure of the Ottoman sultan, the 'Great Turk', at the heart of their drama as the epitome of all that Christian cultures imagined was wrong with Islam: he tends to be lustful, violent, jealous, unmerciful and tyrannical. Kyd's Solimon is all of these, but the violent rages – perhaps what Ben Jonson was referring to when he lamented the 'scenicall strutting' and 'furious vociferation' of post-Tamburlaine drama – alternate with a noble and magnanimous demeanour. The effect is of a man pushed to the extremes by love and desire of conquest and at the mercy of his passions. The startling shifts between gentility and extreme violence become almost comic, indeed it is this kind of portrayal that is later satirised in characters like Pistol in Shakespeare's *Henry IV parts I and II* as the bombast of the 'Turk play' went out of fashion. *Solimon and Perseda* is also notable as the first play to narrate the conversion of a Christian to Islam, when the braggart knight Basilisco follows Perseda into Ottoman territory – it is told in retrospect, and rendered comical through Basilisco's complete ignorance of what has happened to him.

EDITIONS & TRANSLATIONS

- J.J. Murray (ed.), *The tragedye of Solyman and Perseda edited from the original texts with introduction and notes*, New York, 1991
- F.S. Boas (ed.), *The works of Thomas Kyd*, Oxford, 1901, repr. 1967, 2012
- R. Dodsley (ed.), *A select collection of old English plays*, London, 1874, vol. 5
- *The tragedie of Solimon and Perseda. Wherein is laide open, loues constancie, fortunes inconstancie, and deaths triumphs*, London, 1599, repr. London, c. 1800, Amersham, 1912, New York, 1970, Whitefish MT, 2007
- *The tragedye of Solyman and Perseda. Wherein is laide open, loues constancy, fortunes inconstancy, and deaths triumphs*, London, 1592?

STUDIES

The depiction of Islam and of the Ottoman 'Turks' in the play is considered in the following:
- B. Robinson, *Islam and Early Modern English culture. The politics of romance from Spenser to Milton*, Basingstoke, 2007
- J. Burton, *Traffic and turning. Islam and English drama, 1579-1624*, Newark DE, 2005
- M. Dimmock, *New Turkes. Dramatizing Islam and the Ottomans in Early Modern England*, Aldershot, 2005
- D. Vitkus, *Turning Turk. English theater and the multicultural Mediterranean*, Basingstoke, 2002

Matthew Dimmock

Henry Smith

DATE OF BIRTH   Probably 1560
PLACE OF BIRTH   Withcote, Leicestershire
DATE OF DEATH   4 July 1591
PLACE OF DEATH   Husbands Bosworth, Leicestershire

BIOGRAPHY

Henry Smith was born into a wealthy Leicestershire family, probably in 1560. In 1573, he became a fellow-commoner at Queens' College, Cambridge, but soon left to study privately with Richard Greenham (1535-94), rector of Dry Drayton, Cambridgeshire, who instructed him in Puritan theology. By 1576, Smith was a student at Lincoln College, Oxford, where he gained his BA in 1579. He may or may not be the Henry Smith who graduated with an MA from Hart Hall in 1583, because there is no record of him using the post nominal 'MA'; he used instead 'theologus'. He took up a church appointment, probably in the parish of Husbands Bosworth, where his father was patron, though it is unlikely that he was officially rector because there is no evidence that he was ordained. Smith had decided to pursue a Church-related career but had problems with Church of England ceremonies, with episcopacy and with some articles of belief, although he also opposed the separatists. Instead of taking up clerical duties, he accepted an invitation to be the Lecturer or Reader at St Clement Dane without Temple Bar, London, chosen and paid by the congregation in 1587. The fact that in 1588 the bishop of London ordered him to desist from preaching suggests that his position was unlicensed and that he had not subscribed to the 39 Articles. However, Smith defended his loyalty to the Church of England (although it seems probable that he never did subscribe to the Articles) and, with the support of the congregation, which included Lord Burghley, the Lord High Treasurer, who was patron of the parish, he was permitted to resume his duties. Burghley helped raise the funds to pay his stipend.

Smith was a very popular preacher. He attracted such large congregations that some people stood in the aisles to hear him. He had a rhetorical style that audiences appreciated; his preaching has been described as 'fluent, eloquent and practical' (Brook, *The lives*, p. 111). Famously, Thomas Nashe (1567-1601) dubbed him the 'silver-tongued preacher' and compared him to Ovid (McKerrow, *The works*, pp. 192-93). For others, he was second only to John Chrysostom (Brook, *The lives*, p. 111). In 1589, when the incumbent of St Clement died, the congregation wanted Smith to succeed him but either this was unsuccessful and Burghley appointed someone else (Richard Webster), or Smith declined due to deteriorating health. That year, he retired to the family estate in Leicestershire, where he concentrated until his death on 4 July 1591 on compiling his sermons for publication. He dedicated the volume to Lord Burleigh, but died before it was published. Thomas Fuller (1608-61) edited the collection, adding a 'Life' which appeared in 1657. However, the second edition (1675) was more complete, containing 56 sermons. Many of Smith's sermons were also published separately, or in small collections shortly after his death, including *God's arrow against atheists* (1593), the work in which he dismisses Islam as an irrational, wicked and false religion. Cooper and Cooper (*Athenae Cantabrigenses*) list a total of 45 works by him.

MAIN SOURCES OF INFORMATION

Primary
T. Fuller, 'Life of Mr Henry Smith', in T. Fuller and H. Smith, *The sermons of Mr Henry Smith*, London, 1657, pp. i, vii-ix
B.Brook, *The lives of the Puritans*, London, 1813, ii, pp. 108-12
A.A. Wood, *Athenae Oxonienses*, London, 1813, i, pp. 603-5
C.H. Cooper and T. Cooper, *Athenae Cantabrigenses*, London, 1861, ii, pp. 103-8
T. Cooper, art. 'Smith, Henry', in *DNB*, vol. 53, pp. 48-49

Secondary
G.W. Jenkins, art. 'Smith, Henry', in *ODNB*, vol. 51, pp. 160-61
R.B. Jenkins, *Henry Smith. England's silver-tongued preacher*, Macon GA, 1983
R.B. McKerrow, *The works of Thomas Nashe*, London, 1904, Oxford, 1958^2 i, pp. 192-93
R.J. Pederson, 'Introduction', in *The works of Henry Smith*, Edinburgh, 1867 (repr. Stoke-on-Trent, 2002)

WORKS ON CHRISTIAN-MUSLIM RELATIONS

God's arrow against atheists

DATE 1593
ORIGINAL LANGUAGE English

DESCRIPTION

Although it is included in a book of sermons, *God's arrow against atheists* is really an apologetic tract in which Henry Smith set out to prove that there is a God who should be worshipped. It was first published as a pamphlet in 1593, and it later appeared in Smith's collected sermons (1657, vol. 2). In the 1866 edition, it is the 24th section (pp. 333-418) with six chapters. Chapter 1 refutes 'atheism', chapter 2 argues that Christianity is the only true religion, chapter 3 continues this theme by demonstrating that ancient philosophy and 'heathen religion' fall short, as does Islam or 'the religion of Mahomet' to which Smith turns 'briefly' in chapter 4. Chapter 5 dismisses the claim of the 'Church of Rome' to be the true Church or religion, while chapter 6 extends the denunciation of 'false religion' to those who had separated from the Anglican Church, the Brownists and Barrowists.

Chapter 4, 'The religion of Mahomet, false and wicked', is nine pages long. Smith begins by asserting that a brief examination of Muḥammad's religion will shed even more light on Christianity's truth, since comparison is like that between darkness and light. He then describes how Muḥammad recognised Jesus's virgin birth and that he was a great prophet and miracle worker, but not that he was divine. Although he reproved the Jews for denying Jesus's virgin birth, he 'would not have Christ to bear credit above him'. Muḥammad concocted his religion by patching together elements of Judaism with 'Gentilism', Catholicism and 'Christianism', his mother teaching him about Judaism and his father (who in fact died before he was born) about the religion of the Gentiles. Muḥammad was also instructed by a Jewish astronomer and physician, by the monk Sergius from whom he accepted baptism and learned that Nestorians denied the Trinity, and by John of Antioch. These men were Satan's instruments, while Muḥammad was 'well seen in magic'.

Smith gives a brief biography of Muḥammad. Born in 597, he was descended from Abraham's son Ishmael and Hagar to 'very base parents' called Abdara and Emma, who soon left him an orphan. Taken captive, he lived by his wits until Ademonapoles ransomed him and put him in charge of his business. Following his master's death, he contrived to marry his mistress, Eadigam, who was 50 years old. Thus, Muḥammad became a wealthy man. His 'falling sickness' and later pretence at receiving revelation caused his wife to regret that she had married him. Having taught a dove to pick grain from his ear, he began to feign prophecy, pretending that Gabriel was bringing him 'secrets from God'. His wife became convinced that he was really a prophet, and began to 'chat the same amongst her gossips'. People flocked to him from all over Arabia. With his warriors, he began to subdue Arabia and beyond, destroying Christians and establishing false religion. Soon after his death, his followers conquered 'Damascus, Phoenicia, Egypt, Palestina, the city Jerusalem, all Syria, Antioch, Edessa, Mesopotamia, all Persia; yea, and in a manner, all Asia'.

Muḥammad's death was so disgusting that Smith takes a whole page to recount the event. Having consumed too much wine into which poison had been poured, Muḥammad said that he felt his sickness approaching (the imminent arrival of a revelation) and needed to confer with Gabriel. Knowing that a soft surface was best when his trance (epileptic fit) began, he lay down on a dung heap. Unconscious from alcohol and poison, it was only when his wife and companions heard the sound of hogs trying to eat him, having gouged his leg, that he was found. His belly was so swollen that it appeared to be about to burst. Aware that he was dying, Muḥammad told them to wait three days before they buried him because he would ascend bodily into heaven. When after four days his body was still lying there, his companions decided to wait 30 days. The body began to smell, so they placed him in an iron coffin, which they took to Mecca and suspended with magnets above the sanctuary.

Muḥammad chose to call his followers 'Saracens' to emphasise affinity with Sarah, Abraham's wife, even though his own descent was from Hagar, and so was 'base'. In his false preaching, he conceded that Jesus had performed miracles, and even accepted the Gospel so far as it agreed with the 'Alcoran'. However, he claimed that Alcoran corrected errors in the Bible, that he was God's prophet 'sent of God to supply the imperfections of all laws'. He forbade images, swine's flesh, commanded 'washings *ad similitudinen Judaeorum*' and, to differ from Jews and Christians, made Friday the day for prayer in order to honour Venus. He was able to take advantage of dissension among Christians to construct his mixed religion. The many heresies, such as those of the Nestorians and Jacobites, and rivalry between Christian princes and bishops displeased God so much that he allowed this wickedness to flourish.

The chapter concludes with seven proofs of the falseness of Muḥammad's religion. First, the religion is too new. Not predicted by any legitimate prophecy, it was merely invented and preached by a man. Second, Muḥammad did not perform any miracles to confirm his claims, and even disclaimed that he could perform any. Third, he was a false prophet because he did not rise from the dead as he had predicted he would. Fourth, his religion was of the flesh, allowing four wives, 'yea, five', and countless concubines, and promising a sensual paradise – Smith's description of this, including the promise of 'maidens and virgins with twinkling eyes', runs for almost a page. Fifth, Muḥammad's law is tyrannical, vengeful and indebted to the sword for enforcement. Sixth, his religion spread by the sword and is defended by the sword, since death is the penalty for questioning it. Here, Smith again describes the trained dove that Muḥammad pretended was Gabriel, and also describes how he tied verses of the Qur'an to a wild ass then preached that if his hearers went into the desert they would find 'there an ass, and a book tied to its neck' containing a message from God. Seventh, Muḥammad's religion is a patchwork taken from various sources, including superstitious and heretical Christians. His message is blasphemous, his religion is man-made, 'and even from the Devil, the crafty father of lies'. Smith cites a number of sources for his account, probably all Latin, including Marcus Antonius Coccius Sabellicus (1436-1506), Paul the Deacon (d. 799) and John Zonaras (12th century).

SIGNIFICANCE

Although some writings on Islam were available in English when Smith wrote, he appears to have drawn exclusively on Latin sources, none of which had Islam as its main subject. Jenkins describes *God's arrow* as the work that most demonstrates Smith's breadth of learning, showing familiarity with the Church Fathers, pagan philosophers and 'religious works outside the Christian domain' (*Henry Smith*, p. 107). However, this does not obviously extend to Muslim texts. On the one occasion Smith purports to cite words spoken by Muḥammad, he does so in Latin, namely *non sum miracullis aut indiciis ad vos missus*, which he translates as 'I am not sent unto you with miracles and signs' which could be derived from a Hadith, or from a qur'anic verse such as Q 29:50. The tract's content, though, is similar to that of the few publications that were in print in English on Islam at the time, such as Christopher St German's *Here after followeth a lytell treatise agaynst Mahomet and his cursed secte* (1531), which also has Muḥammad failing to rise from the dead, his body producing a great stench, and his coffin hung by magnets at Mecca. As St German had done, Smith would have found these and other stories, such as the trained dove and wild ass (a camel in some sources) in his reading of Latin texts. Yet already available at the time was Richard Eden's 1577 translation of Ludovico di Varthema's *Nauigation and vyages*, which correctly located Muḥammad's tomb in Medina, not Mecca, and dismissed the magnet legend. Repeating old calumnies and legends, Smith did what he set out to do, that is, to represent Muḥammad as reprehensible, and his religion as absurd so that its claim to be true becomes ludicrous. Smith did concede that Islam recognises Jesus as a 'great prophet', affirms his virgin birth and even accepts some of the Gospel. He also knew that the Qur'an sees itself as correcting errors in the Bible. However, by presenting a Satanic element in Islam's origin, he removes any possibility of establishing even a partially positive view of Islam. He appears to say that God allowed Satan to help Muḥammad manufacture his religion to punish Christians for disunity.

What makes Smith's tract significant is the degree to which he was able to perpetuate medieval legends about Islam toward the end of the 16th century, without showing any sign of concern to confirm the veracity of his material. Among writers for whom Smith was probably a source of the magnet story was Thomas Nashe (McKerrow, *The works*, iv, p. 274, nn. 9-10). In contrast, Henry Stubbe writing a century later saw reason to dismiss many accepted stories, and described Smith's chapter as the 'grossest account' he had ever read. It would be a 'pity' he continued if the 'history of the world was left in the custody of Christians', mentioning another account in which a bull, rather than an ass or camel, brings Muḥammad the Qur'an (*An account of the rise and progress of Mahometanism*, London, 1911, pp. 235-36).

Smith was a very popular preacher, and many who heard him speak or who read the tract, which was frequently reprinted, would give credence to his views. One aspect of his work that perhaps did begin to point in a new direction was his remark on how Islam was especially similar to Judaism, a thesis that Jews would themselves later explore (e.g. A. Geiger, *Judaism and Islam*, Madras, 1898). Establishing criteria for true religion, then demonstrating just how far Islam falls short of these, anticipates a popular strategy among later missionaries. Smith had a reputation as a somewhat better educated preacher than most, which may have lent his work authority. His sermons were best sellers in Elizabethan England, some listeners taking them down in short-hand and rushing them to press (L.C. Stevenson, *Praise and paradox. Merchants and craftsmen in Elizabethan popular literature*, Cambridge, 2002, pp. 16, 214). What Smith wrote on Islam would have had a wide readership, in the main confirming negative ideas that were in circulation at the time.

EDITIONS & TRANSLATIONS

The works of Henry Smith, Edinburgh, 1867 ii, 365-452 (repr. Stoke-on-Trent, 2002)

H. Smith and T. Fuller, *The sermons of Mr. Henry Smith: together with a preparative to marriage, God's arrow against atheists certain godly and zealous prayers, etc. printed according to his corrected copies in his lifetime*, London, 1866

T. Fuller and H. Smith, *The sermons of Mr. Henry Smith, sometimes minister of St. Clement Danes, London: together with other his learned treatises*, London, 1675

The sermons of Mr. Henry Smith, gathered into one volume, London, 1631

The sermons of Master Henry Smith gathered into one volume. Printed according to his corrected copies in his life time. Whereunto is added Gods arrow against atheists, London, 1618

God's arrow against Atheists, London, 1593, 1604, 1607, 1609, 1611, 1617, 1622, 1628, 1631, 1632, 1637, 1656, 1657, 1675, 1676

STUDIES

Brief references in:

G. MacLean and N. Matar, *Britain and the Islamic world, 1558-1713*, Oxford, 2011

D.A. Pailin and A. David, *Attitudes to other religions. Comparative religion in seventeenth- and eighteenth-century Britain*, Manchester, 1984, pp. 198-208 (with Smith's seven proofs reprinted)

Clinton Bennett

Robert Greene

DATE OF BIRTH July 1558 (baptised 11 July)
PLACE OF BIRTH Tombland, Norwich
DATE OF DEATH 3 September 1592
PLACE OF DEATH London

BIOGRAPHY

Robert Greene's insistent spinning of self-mythologies, particularly towards the end of his life, has made it difficult for any biographer to separate truths from half-fictions. He was born near Norwich in 1558, and probably attended the grammar school there, before embarking on a curiously varied university career. He gained his BA from St John's College, Cambridge, in 1580 (attending that particular college perhaps, Newcomb suggests, because of his Yorkshire roots), and was awarded MAs from Clare College, Cambridge, in 1583, and from the University of Oxford in 1588. In his subsequent career as a professional writer he rarely missed a chance to parade these qualifications and the learning they implied.

This career as writer was underway even as he was graduating from St John's – the romance *Mamillia* is recorded in the Stationers' register in 1580 – and even for an age when prolixity was not uncommon, Greene's output is both prodigious and varied. Over the next 12 years, he produced more than 25 works, ranging from (following the division given by Walter Davis in *Idea and act in Elizabethan fiction*, Princeton, 1969, p. 139) euphuistic experimentation, short tales and pastoral romances to popular pamphlets full of ill-living and repentance. Although he is now better known for his prose work, and for the attack on Shakespeare in the posthumous *Greene's groats-worth of witte* (1592), Greene also wrote some of the most celebrated drama of this period. From inauspicious beginnings with two plays that sought (and apparently failed) to emulate the bombastic triumph of Christopher Marlowe's *Tamburlaine* plays (1587-88), Greene then produced a string of successes: *The honorable historie of Frier Bacon and Frier Bungay* (1589), *The historie of Orlando Furioso* (1590?), *A looking glasse for London and England* (1590, co-written with Thomas Lodge) and *The Scottish historie of James the Fourth* (1591?).

Despite these achievements, the many accounts of Greene's final months suggest he was living in sordid penury. He died on 3 September 1592, having (according to his antagonist Gabriel Harvey) taken a 'surfeit of pickled herring and Rhenish wine' and contracted a fever. The existence of numerous narratives of his repentance and death, and reports of his voice from beyond the grave (among them *Greenes vision written at the instant of his death*, London, 1592; *The repentance of Robert Greene*, London, 1592; *Greenes groats-worth of witte*, London, 1592) suggest the measure of celebrity he had achieved, and are the inevitable culmination of a life played out in the popular print marketplace. The death of a possible son, Fortunatus Greene, is recorded in Shoreditch the following year.

MAIN SOURCES OF INFORMATION

Primary
G. Harvey, *Foure letters, and certaine sonnets especially touching Robert Greene*, London, 1592
H. Chettle, *Kind-harts dreame Conteining fiue apparitions*, London, 1593
B. Rich, *Greenes newes both from heauen and hell*, London, 1593
N. Breton (?), *Greenes funeralls*, London, 1594
J. Dickenson, *Greene in conceipt*, London, 1598

Secondary
K. Melnikoff (ed.), *Robert Greene*, Farnham, 2011
K. Melnikoff and E. Gieskes (eds), *Writing Robert Greene. Essays on England's first notorious professional writer*, Aldershot, 2008
L.H. Newcomb, art. 'Greene, Robert (bap. 1558, d. 1592)', in *ODNB*, http://www.oxforddnb.com
C.W. Crupi, *Robert Greene*, Boston MA, 1986
T. Hayashi, *Robert Greene criticism. A comprehensive bibliography*, Metuchen NJ, 1971

WORKS ON CHRISTIAN-MUSLIM RELATIONS

The comicall history of Alphonsus, King of Aragon

DATE c. 1589 (printed 1599)
ORIGINAL LANGUAGE English

DESCRIPTION

The comicall history of Alphonsus, King of Aragon, probably Robert Greene's first play, is a curiously disjointed combination of multiple overlapping narratives. It is primarily structured by the ascent from initial dispossession to all-conquering Christian hero of its protagonist, possibly a fictionalised version of the celebrated life of Alfonso V, King of Aragón and Naples and a number of Mediterranean islands (1396-1458) – although the narrative is so distorted that some critics have suggested the model is instead Alfonso I, King of Aragón and Navarre (1073-1134), a prominent warrior in the *Reconquista*. This narrative is heavily inflected by the prevailing influence of Christopher Marlowe's *Tamburlaine* plays (1587-88), whose success Greene was presumably attempting to emulate (or parody – see below). The play's preoccupations are all recognisably Marlovian: the relentless acquisition of earthly crowns through military conquest; the rise of its protagonist from obscurity to global power; and the imperial pomp and bombast of Ottoman power, here embodied in the Sultan Amurack. Greene also chooses to map his Ottoman episodes closely on the Classical Agamemnon/Clytemnestra/Iphigenia episode narrated by both Euripides and Homer. The result is a confused but entertaining romp through late 16th-century fantasies of hyper-masculine power, stereotypes of 'Mahometanism' and total conquest.

The plot is, however, fairly straightforward. The action is framed by a chorus led by Venus (and including the muses Melpomine, Clio, Errato and Calliope). Alphonsus is introduced as the rightful but dispossessed king of Aragón who fights and defeats the incumbent Belinus to regain his father's crown. Belinus flees to seek exile on 'Turkish soyle', and the next scene is typical of the 'Turk plays' that rapidly followed *Tamburlaine*'s success – a genre in which Greene was one of the principal innovators – in which Alphonsus disburses the crowns of Naples, Milan and Aragón to his followers. Belinus is offered military support from Amurack, the 'Great Turk', once the latter has dabbled in witchcraft and sought and received advice from an oracle, a brass head of 'Mahound' that breathes fire. This advice turns out to be wrong, and Belinus and Amurath are comprehensively defeated by Alphonus and his forces. Having fallen in love with Amurath's daughter, Alphonsus concludes the play by marrying her and securing his right (and the right of his Christian offspring) to the vast dominion represented by the Ottoman throne.

SIGNIFICANCE

Any assessment of the significance of *Alphonsus of Aragon* depends on how it is understood in relation to Marlowe's *Tamburlaine* plays. Dramatically it is disjointed, consisting almost of two separate plays in one; the action consistently lacks the dynamism of Marlowe's original, and commercially (like the later *Selimus*) it seems to have been unsuccessful. However, whereas echoes of *Selimus* can be found in later drama, *Alphonsus* seems to have generated little interest amongst Greene's fellow playwrights. If the play has any significance at all, it is as a 'Turk play' – possibly the first that might be properly labelled as such. Critics ranging from John Clark Jordan to Peter Berek have suggested that both *Alphonsus* and *Selimus* should be read as Greene's attempts to respond to the ethical and dramatic challenges Marlowe had generated in *Tamburlaine*, and that perhaps *Alphonsus* is intended as a kind of parody of Marlowe's play. Greene certainly takes Marlowe's template and pushes everything to excess in order to wring some humour out of it – it is a 'comicall historie' after all – and the Christian identity of his hero would seem to be a response to the dangerous 'atheism' Greene had found in Tamburlaine (as recorded in his *Perimedes the blacksmith* of 1588). However, critics often forget that *Tamburlaine* had comic elements, the 'fond and frivolous jestures' apparently removed by the printer Richard Jones from the first edition of the play, and Alphonsus's Christianity plays little role in the drama beyond setting him in opposition to the Muslim Amurack. There is therefore little to suggest that *Alphonsus* is much more than an early attempt to emulate *Tamburlaine*'s success.

One element that is peculiarly innovative is the way Greene approaches the challenge of dramatising the 'Mahometan' faith. Marlowe, Kyd and others had established a loose code for the task that involved individuals repeatedly swearing by 'Mahomet' and wearing a specific costume – a turban or 'Turkish cap', flowing and probably colourful robes, and a scimitar ('moustachios' may also have been included). For these playwrights, and for most that followed, the figure of Muḥammad – or 'Mahomet' – was imagined either as an inversion of Jesus Christ, or as a mortal false prophet, and never appears on stage. For the scene in which Amurath's followers seek divine guidance, Greene instead turned to an older medieval romance tradition, in which 'Mahound' is depicted as an idol. Always interested in elaborate dramatic effects, Greene used a brass head breathing 'flakes of flame' to conjure up Islam on the stage in a manner that both he and at least some of his audience would have immediately have recognised as antiquated, inaccurate and comic (the choice of name alone signals this reversion). Aside from an obscure play from 1601 by William Percy that was probably never publicly performed, Greene's *Alphonsus* is the only example of 'Mahound' appearing on the English stage – and its absurdity may have gained the play a certain notoriety, since one contemporary ballad (George Peele's 'A farewell') refers to 'Mahomet's poo' (or poll – head) as a ridiculous emblem of the London stage soon afterwards. Greene would return to the necromantic brass head with considerable success in his later play *Friar Bacon and Friar Bungay*.

EDITIONS & TRANSLATIONS

The comicall historie of Alphonsus, king of Aragon, London, 1599 (repr. The Malone Society, ed. W.W. Greg, 1926)

Later editions appear in collected works of Greene. The major examples are:
T.H. Dickinson, *The plays of Robert Greene*, London, 1909
J. Churton Collins, *The plays and poems of Robert Greene*, Oxford, 1905
A.B. Grosart, *The life and complete works in prose and verse of Robert Greene*, London, 1881-86
A. Dyce, *Dramatic and poetical works of Robert Greene and George Peele*, London, 1861

STUDIES

There are no studies devoted solely to this play. Its relation to *Tamburlaine* is discussed in a number of works, including:

P. Berek, '*Locrine* revised. *Selimus* and early responses to *Tamburlaine*', *Research Opportunities in Renaissance Drama* 23 (1980) 33-54
J. Clark Jordan, *Robert Greene*, New York, 1915

The role of Islam in the play, and its place in the English 'Turk play' tradition is considered in:

M. Dimmock, *Mythologies of the Prophet Muhammad in Early Modern English culture*, Cambridge, 2013
J. Burton, *Traffic and turning. Islam and English drama, 1579-1624*, Newark NJ, 2005

The tragical reign of Selimus, Emperor of the Turkes

DATE c. 1590 (printed 1594)
ORIGINAL LANGUAGE English

DESCRIPTION

Selimus is a play that draws heavily on Christian translations (and re-translations) of Ottoman dynastic history. There were certainly many in circulation for Greene to choose from, with Peter Ashton's 1546 translation of Paulo Giovio's *Commentario delle cose de' Turchi* (of 1531) probably the most popular and well known. Greene's instinct for a dramatic tale led him to Selim I 'the Steadfast', known in later Christian writing as 'the Grim', who was Ottoman ruler between 1512 and 1520, and is celebrated in Ottoman histories for extending Ottoman domains through conquest into Egypt and Persia.

Greene opted not to write his play about the military conquests for which Selim was famed – they were to be the subject of the sequel promised at the play's conclusion (which seems never to have appeared); instead he plotted his play around Selimus's rise to power. As the drama begins, Selimus is the power-hungry son of Bajazet (Bayezid II), the youngest of three Ottoman princes. Greene revels in Selimus's will to absolute rule, and audiences are encouraged to marvel at his inexorable and increasingly bloody and bombastic progress. He poisons his father and murders his older brothers, Acomat and Corcut (the latter a 'grave philosopher' who turns to Christianity and is at one point friendly with an incongruously English clown) and by the end of the play is in unchallenged possession of the 'Turkish diadem'.

SIGNIFICANCE

Selimus is the more obviously derivative of the two 'Turk plays' attributed to Robert Greene, and owes its genesis to the success of Christopher Marlowe's epic two-part *Tamburlaine* (1587-88). The grandiloquent bombast and expansive Asian geographies of these plays initiated a plethora of 'Turk plays' (see also Thomas Kyd's *Solimon and Perseda*) as other dramatists followed his example. For Greene there was perhaps more at stake: in early 1588, in his *Perimedes the blacksmith*, he had accused Marlowe of 'daring God out of heaven with that atheist Tamburlaine'. Greene was never one to shy away from confrontation, but if *Selimus* was an attempt to respond to the ethics- and convention-defying challenges of the *Tamburlaine* plays (and perhaps to the failure of his own earlier experiment in the genre, *Alphonsus of Aragon*), then it was a curious one. Greene's protagonist out-atheists Tamburlaine completely – he is a monster; unrepentant and revelling in his cruelty, he repeatedly questions the very existence of God, that 'bugbear'. He has no redemptive qualities, unlike his sympathetically portrayed brother Corcut, and – like

Tamburlaine at the end of part one – he ends the play in triumph, his actions apparently justified by their rewards.

For recent critics, the status of *Selimus* as a response to *Tamburlaine* and as an exemplar of the 'Turk play' phenomenon has been its primary interest. Whilst it is obviously derivative, it does represent (and perhaps pioneers) a shift of focus away from a Marlovian celebration of Tamburlaine as an Ottoman antagonist and onto the figure of the 'Grand Turk' as a central protagonist. As this development suggests, the play is more innovative than is often acknowledged. The absence of any sequel may suggest that *Selimus* was a commercial failure, but it was influential. A number of 20th-century critics have noted not only evidence of Greene's reading of Marlowe and Spenser, but also the interconnections between *Selimus*, the anonymous *Locrine* (printed in 1595) and Shakespeare's considerably later *King Lear*. The blinding of the Aga, watched by a character named Regan, is an obvious connection to the blinding of Gloucester in the latter, an influence endorsed by *Selimus*'s most recent editor, Daniel Vitkus.

EDITIONS & TRANSLATIONS

The tragical reign of Selimus, London, 1594 (repr. The Malone Society, ed. W. Bang, 1908)

Later editions appear in collected works – the major examples are:
D. Vitkus, *Three Turk plays from Early Modern England*, New York, 2000
Dickinson, *The plays of Robert Greene*
Churton Collins, *The plays and poems of Robert Greene*
Grosart, *The life and complete works in prose and verse of Robert Greene*
Dyce, *Dramatic and poetical works of Robert Greene and George Peele*

STUDIES

There are no studies solely devoted to this play. It is explored in some detail in relation to *Tamburlaine* in:
Berek, '*Locrine* revised'.

Its place in the English 'Turk play' tradition, and its depiction of Islam, are considered in:
Burton, *Traffic and turning*
M. Dimmock, *New Turkes. Dramatizing Islam and the Ottomans in Early Modern England*, Aldershot, 2005

D. Vitkus, *Turning Turk. English theater and the multicultural Mediterranean*, Basingstoke, 2002

N. Matar, *Islam in Britain, 1558-1685*, Cambridge, 1998

Matthew Dimmock

George Peele

DATE OF BIRTH 25 July 1556
PLACE OF BIRTH London
DATE OF DEATH 9 November 1596
PLACE OF DEATH Parish of St James, Clerkenwell

BIOGRAPHY

George Peele was born in London in 1556. He was the fourth son of James Peele (d. 1585), a mathematician and first clerk to Christ's Hospital, which George attended before matriculating to Christ Church, Oxford, where he received his BA in 1577 and MA in 1579. At the time, William Gager (1555-1662) was writing and performing plays at Christ Church, where the great hall was acquiring a reputation for dramatic productions. Gager encouraged Peele's interest in drama, and he began to write. Like Gager, he was influenced by the Roman philosopher and dramatist, Seneca. He spent the rest of his life in literary productions in London, performing as well as writing, although he also frequently returned to Oxford to act and produce. He was associated with other university-educated poets, including such Oxford contemporaries as Sir Philip Sidney (1554-86) and Sir Edward Dyer (1543-1607), as one of the so-called 'university wits'. He was one of the first English dramatists who attempted to earn his living by the pen.

Peele experimented with a wide variety of dramatic forms ranging from pastoral and historical plays and melodrama to comedies and tragedies, including hybrid dramatic forms that are less easy to categorise. His style has been described both as 'deficient in richness or even variety of modulation' and, at least in his early phase, as having a 'gracefulness of expression, and a melody of versification' (Craik, *A compendious history*, p. 456). He characteristically used rhetoric to encourage his audiences to think about the ethical and moral implications of his plot. Thus, as well as aiming to entertain, he also wanted to provoke a response in his audience.

Among Peele's plays are *The old wives' tale* and *The arraignment of Paris* (1584), *Jack Straw* (c. 1587), *Edward I* (c. 1590-2), *David and Bethsabe* (1594), *The battle of Alcazar in Barbary* (1594), *Sir Clyomon and Sir Clamydes* (1599), *The wisdom of Dr Doddypoll* (1600), *The maid's metamorphosis* (1600) and *Wily beguiled* (1606). *The battle of Alcazar in Barbary* was published anonymously, but it is widely attributed to Peele. It contains what has been called 'the first full dramatic treatment of a black Moor on the English stage' (Logan and Smith, *The predecessors of Shakespeare,* p. 146), thus predating a character such as Othello in the work of William Shakespeare, who may have drawn on some of Peele's plays. Another play, which is of uncertain date though probably before 1601, is *Turkish Mahomet and Hiren the fair Greek*. It is now lost, but its plot almost certainly followed other tellings of the tale that came originally from Matteo Bandello's (d. 1562) *Novelle,* in which the Turkish ruler Mahomet is so besotted with the beautiful Greek slave Hiren he has been given that he neglects everything else. He is eventually prevailed upon to turn to matters of state and to lead his army in conquest, and in a demonstration of putting duty before pleasure he cuts off Hiren's head in front of his startled generals. This savage drama would have underlined the unrestrained lasciviousness and unremitting cruelty of the Turks for an Elizabethan audience.

Although regarded as a significant 16th-century dramatist, Peele did not do well financially. Towards the end of his life, he was turned down for patronage by Lord Burleigh (1520-98), and according to one source he died of the pox (Meres, *Palladis Tamia,* p. 269). After his death, his reputation for loose living grew, due in no small part to the joke book *The merry conceited jests of George Peele* (1607), in which he plays the 'gentleman knave'. Barbour comments that it is not actually known whether Peele really did live a dissipated life (Barbour, 'Peele, George', p. 426).

MAIN SOURCES OF INFORMATION

Primary
MS London, BL – Add. 10449
MS London, BL – Add. 21432
MS Oxford, St John's College – 216
MS London, BL – Lansdowne 99, no. 54
The merry conceited jests of George Peele, London, 1607

Secondary
R. Barbour, art. 'Peele, George', in *ODNB*
B.B. Ritchie, *The plays of Christopher Marlowe and George Peele. Rhetoric and Renaissance sensibility*, Parkland FL, 1999
A.R. Braunmuller, *George Peele*, Boston MA, 1983

T.P. Logan and D.S. Smith (eds), *The predecessors of Shakespeare. A survey and bibliography of recent studies in English Renaissance drama*, Lincoln NE, 1973

L.R. Ashley, *George Peele*, New York, 1970

C.T. Prouty (ed.), *The life and works of George Peele*, London, 1952-70

A.W. Ward, art. 'Peele, George', in *DNB*, vol. 44, 225-29

G.L. Craik, *A compendious history of English literature*, London, 1861, i, pp. 464-66

F. Meres, *Palladis Tamia. Wits treasury*, London, 1598, p. 269

WORKS ON CHRISTIAN-MUSLIM RELATIONS

The Battel of Alcazar, fought in Barbarie between Sebastian king of Portugall and Abdelmelec king of Marocco. With the death of Captain Stukeley; *The Battle of Alcazar*

DATE 1594
ORIGINAL LANGUAGE English

DESCRIPTION

The Battle of Alcazar in Barbary was probably first performed in 1588 or 1589, although it was not published until 1594 following a revival by the Admiral's Men. This printed version is thought to be shorter than the staged production, which may have had more detailed instructions, especially for the 'dumb show' segments (which are mimed). Attribution to George Peele, whose name did not appear in the 1594 version, although based on literary analysis and on an early association with Peele, is considered 'perhaps by default... undisputed' (Ritchie, *The plays*, p. 49).

The play is based on a battle that took place between the Moroccans and the Portuguese on 4 August, 1578, known variously as the Battle of the Three Kings, because three kings died during the fighting, the Battle of Alcazar, and the Battle of Ksar El Kebir, after the town near which it took place. John Polemom's *The second part of the book of battles, fought in our age* (1587) has been identified as a source, together with a great deal 'of oral and written legend' for the life of Thomas Stukeley (Ribner, *The English history play*, p. 196). Owing to Stukeley's presence in the play, it became known as one of two 'Stukeley plays' (see Edelman, *The Stukeley plays*). The plot develops across five acts, divided into 2,755 lines. The extant version is somewhat disjointed, so it has been surmised that the original production was longer. It uses blank and rhyming verse, and 'doggerel', thus mingling styles (Ritchie, *The plays*, p. 326). The main protagonists are the Portuguese king, his English commander, Stukeley, their ally the 'Negro, Mully Mahamet' (Abū 'Abdallāh Muḥammad II, who had seized the Moroccan throne after his father's death) and his opponent, his uncle Abdelmelec ('Abd al-Malik, also referred to as Muly Molocco, and the 'rightful king'). According to the rules of succession, 'Abd al-Malik should have succeeded his brother, although European conventions would have placed Mully Mahomet on the throne.

Peele had to tell the story to an audience that would not have known the historical details, and do so in a way that would entertain as well as inform. He was especially interested in the moral message his plays communicated. He appears to have chosen the material for this play because the death of three kings and the involvement of an English adventurer (albeit of dubious character) had caught the popular imagination, and there was enough interest among his public for the play to be presented. Peele is said to have had a good ear for what the public would appreciate. He thus includes three Moorish women who do not appear in his sources, because he 'was always looking for an excuse for passion, an opportunity for spectacle, a striking entrance, a startling scene' (Ashley, *George Peele*, p. 85).

The play follows the historical sequence of events quite closely. It describes how the alliance between King Sebastian of Portugal and Mully Mahamet was forged, then proceeds to the tragic battle itself. An alliance with Morocco, or suzerainty over Morocco, would strengthen Sebastian's ability to remain free from Spanish domination, and a major consequence of his death in the battle was Spain's invasion and annexation of Portugal in 1581. Stukeley first appears in Act 2, in the company of an Irish Catholic prelate. With a contingent of troops, they are en route to Ireland, where they intend to defeat the Protestants and restore Catholic rule, though bad weather has forced them to seek shelter in Lisbon Bay. Sebastian persuades Stukeley to help him restore Mully Mahamet to power (verse 770), seeing this as a means of spreading 'Christian truth' (94, 790), and expecting Philip II of Spain to assist (690), though Stukeley (who had worked for the Spanish king) dismisses this as unlikely (880). In fact, Philip is depicted as pretending to pledge aid while all along intending to offer none. For his part, Stukeley appears to have thought that Africa was a place where his destiny might find fulfilment, perhaps by way of leading a Christian conquest, a 'holy war' (760), or even through acquiring a kingdom: as he puts it, he preferred to be 'king of a mole-hill... than the richest subject of a monarchie' (465-66).

Stukeley is killed by two Italians, who despise him for abandoning their mission to subdue Ireland, which has been blessed by the pope (1,430). Although he was seen as a traitor in England, his adventurers were becoming the stuff of legend. He was a man for whom the world was a stage, at a time when England was broadening its horizons. King Sebastian, too, is slain from 'many a mortal wounde' (1,540), as is Abdelmelec (1,330, though in reality he died shortly after from an illness), although, in order to maintain morale, his brother and successor Muly Mahamet Seth (Mulay Aḥmad al-Manṣūr) keeps his death a secret until the battle has been won. In this victory, he is secretly aided by Amurath, the Emperor of the East (see 60-100), a theatrical device for the Ottoman sultan as 'oriental despot' that is first used in this play (J.G. Harris, *Untimely matter in the time of Shakespeare*, Philadelphia, 2009, p. 77).

In the opening dumb-show, Muly Mahomet is a 'barbarous Negro' who is 'blacke in his looks' and 'bloodie in his deeds', having murdered rival family members (described at 40) and a 'tyrant' (150), who has usurped his uncle's throne. King Sebastian, described as 'an honourable and couragious king', though also portrayed as somewhat naïve, nonetheless chooses to support him with Christian armies. Abdelmelec is the 'brave barbarian lord'. Thus, from the beginning, Peele contrasts his two main Moorish characters in order to emphasise the good and bad in them.

SIGNIFICANCE

This play was the first staged in England that involved strong Muslim characters with speaking parts, one occupying the moral high ground, the other the lowest. Significantly, the main Christian protagonists appear to be stranded somewhere in the middle. While Sebastian and Stukeley are not specifically censored for aiding a tyrant who was 'bloodie in his deeds', the audience would have had difficulty seeing them as heroes, although their ill-fated decision to aid the black, barbarian usurper is mitigated by their fervour to spread the Christian faith. Ritchie suggests that while the play is not the best by Peele, it is the one in which he makes the clearest distinction 'between good and evil characters' (*The plays*, p. 49). Nevertheless, the play does not really give much by which a Muslim, rather than Christian, identity can be attached to the Moorish characters. It is rather left to the audience, for whom the description 'Moore' would have had some meaning, to supply this. The only hint is the name 'Mahomet' and the Moorish characters' descent from the

Prophet Muḥammad (line 130), in which the dynasty took great pride. In fact, writing to Elizabeth I in 1576, 'Abd-al-Malik referred to himself as 'the *sharif* of the line of Hasan' (State Papers 102/4 15).

Matar claims that no Elizabethan play showed Muslims in a morally favourable light (*Turks, Moors and Englishmen*, p. 15) and that no representation drew on first-hand observation, but rather constructed Otherness in terms of English superiority and others' inferiority. Burton is not so sure, suggesting that this blanket statement 'erases the nobility' of several characters in Elizabethan plays, including 'Peele's Abdelmelec' (*Traffic and turning*, p. 20). Use of the word 'barbarian' in this play, says Bartels, 'links barbarian to blackness' (*Speaking of the Moor*, p. 6), while Matar links its Elizabethan usage in connection with Moors to how it was used to describe the indigenous peoples of the Americas. Unable to defeat Moors or Muslims, as they had American Indians, 'in order to represent the Muslim as Other, Britons borrowed constructions of alterity and demonization from their encounter with the American Indians', even though they could not easily situate Muslims 'in a world view convenient to their colonial...goals' (Matar, *Turks, Moors and Englishmen*, p. 16). Similarly, the villain's description as 'black' is significant. Barthelemy argues that without exception in Elizabethan literature, 'black' is associated with 'evil' and increasingly the word 'Moor' was associated with 'African' (*Black face*, p. 1). Peele's villain, says Vaughan, acts out the stereotypical role of the 'deceitful, cowardly Moore through language and action' (*Performing blackness*, p. 38). It may thus be significant that 'Abd al-Malik is not identified as 'black' and, while he is a barbarian and inferior to Europeans, he is the 'Barbarian Lord'. Peele might thus be differentiating between some barbarians and others, who, though still barbarian, are less so and might even be admired. In fact, 'Abd al-Malik, who is not described as 'black', may actually be seen as 'white' according to Vaughan's analysis of Peele's source: 'Muly's opposite, his uncle, Abd-al-Malek, is a white Moore, citing Poleman's description of his "white face"' (*Performing blackness*, p. 38). Burton (*Traffic and turning*, p. 20) also says that Peele appears to use differentiation in skin-colour to distinguish between 'different types of Muslims' and that English representation of Muslim figures was less one-dimensional than Matar argues.

If Matar is right to say that Peele gives no information about the Muslim identity of his Moorish characters, and that no Elizabethan literature presents them favourably, it could be argued that the play either has nothing much to say about relations between Muslims and

Christians or perpetuates old prejudice, an 'us-them, good-bad' polarity. It would, however, be significant that the first ever English play to give us a speaking Moor chose to juxtapose 'us' and 'them' in this way. It is certainly the case that the play does not present any new information derived from Muslim sources about the actual historical event the play describes, or about the real people involved. Nevertheless, even though their Muslim identity is more or less absent in the script, Peele's audience would have had some awareness that Moors were Muslim, if only from stories of Christian exploits in re-conquering Iberia.

The play was first produced, too, after the beginning of diplomatic relations between England and Morocco, when an alliance was under discussion and trade had started (1581). In his letter to Elizabeth dated 3 July 1580, al-Manṣūr spoke of the 'firm affection and sincere love' she had expressed in her last communication (State Papers 102/4 20). Elizabeth also tried to restore António, the Portuguese heir (who had been captured at Alcazar) to the throne, for which – perhaps ironically – she sought Moroccan help. The subsequent expedition of 1589, which may lie behind the play's original production, failed. Morocco did not send any ships, which Elizabeth believed had been promised. In fact, al-Manṣūr had been more or less prevented from helping her by Philip II, who made it known that if he did, it would not go well for two captive Moroccan princes, the *infantes moros* held in Spain (P. Pierson, *Commander of the Armada. The seventh Duke of Medina Sidonia*, New Haven CT, 1989, pp. 178-79).

However, if the rulers of Morocco and England (the former actually a character in the play) were friendly, and commerce was thriving, could all Moors be bad? Peele appears to be in part responding to popular interest in this new relationship between Protestant England and Muslim Morocco by suggesting that, in relations between Christians and Muslims, all is not as black and white, or a morally polarised, as many people thought. He perhaps attempts a more subtle description of a complex world, in which some Muslims may be friends with some Christians. It is also interesting that the real Stukeley had commanded a vessel at the Battle of Lepanto (1571) for Don John of Austria (Edelman, *The Stukeley plays*, p. 8), and thus was an example of how a Christian could at one time oppose Muslims, then at another assist them in a world of shifting alliances and changing political realities. As Potter in her life of Shakespeare says, Peele's attempt to dramatise a very recent historical event was innovative at the time, and tried to explore the 'complex political and religious motives that brought Catholic troops from several countries' into a 'dynastic quarrel between members of the Moroccan royal family' (*Life of William Shakespeare*, p. 102). In fact, Shakespeare may have drawn on his work.

EDITIONS & TRANSLATIONS

C. Edelman, *The Stukeley plays. The Battle of Alcazar by George Peele; the famous history of the life and death of Captain Thomas Stukeley*, Manchester, 2005

K. Bekkaoui, *The Battle of Alcazar*, Fez, 2001 (British drama series of Morocco and the Moors, includes study of Moroccans in the play)

The battell of Alcazar fought in Barbarie betweene Sebastian, King of Portugall, and Abdelmelec, King of Marocco. with the death of Captaine Stukeley, Cambridge, 1995 (CD of text)

C.T. Prouty, F.S. Hook and J. Yoklavich, *The dramatic works of George Peele*, New Haven CT, 1952, 1962², ii

W.W. Greg, *Two Elizabethan stage abridgements. The Battle of Alcazar & Orlando Furioso*, London, 1923

W.W. Greg and F. Sidgwick, *The Battle of Alcazar*, London, 1907, Oxford, 1963² (reprint of 1594 edition)

A.H. Bullen, *The works of George Peele, in two volumes. Volume the first*, London, 1888, New York, 1966 (reprint)

J.O. Halliwell-Phillipps, *The theatre plats of three old English dramas, namely of The battle of Alcazar, Frederick and Basilea, and the Dead man's fortune; from the originals, which were suspended near the prompter's station, in the Fortune Theatre, in the latter part of the sixteenth century*, London, 1860

A. Dyce, *The works of George Peele, now first collected; with some account of his writtings, and notes*, London, 1829, ii

The Battell of Alcazar fought in Barbarie, betweene Sebastian king of Portugall, and Abdelmelec king of Marocco. With the death of Captaine Stukeley. As it was sundrie times plaid by the Lord high Admirall his seruants, London: Edward Allde for Richard Bankworth, 1594

STUDIES

L. Potter, *The life of William Shakespeare. A critical biography*, Malden MA, 2012

Mohamed Ibrahim Elaskary, 'The image of Moors in the writings of four Elizabethan dramatists: Peele, Dekker, Heywood and Shakespeare', Exeter, 2008 (PhD Diss. University of Exeter)

E.C. Bartels, *Speaking of the Moor. From Alcazar to Othello*, Philadelphia PA, 2008

N. Matar, 'Queen Elizabeth I through Moroccan eyes', *Journal of Early Modern History* 12 (2008) 55-76 (also published in C. Beem [ed.], *The foreign relations of Elizabeth I*, New York, 2011, 145-68)

J. Burton, *Traffic and turning. Islam and English drama, 1579-1624*, Newark DE, 2005

V.M. Vaughan, *Performing blackness on English stages, 1500-1800*, Cambridge, 2005

N. Matar, *Turks, Moors, and Englishmen in the age of discovery*, New York, 1999

B.B. Ritchie, *The plays of Christopher Marlowe and George Peele. Rhetoric and Renaissance sensibility*, Parkland FL, 1999

K.J. Donovan, 'Recent studies in George Peele (1969-1990)', *English Literary Renaissance* 23 (1993) 212-20

A.G. Barthelemy, *Black face, maligned race. The representation of blacks in English drama from Shakespeare to Southerne*, Baton Rouge FL, 1987

W. Senn, *Studies in the dramatic construction of Robert Greene and George Peele*, Francke, 1973

Ashley, *George Peele*

I. Ribner, *The English history play in the age of Shakespeare*, Princeton NJ, 1957

E.W. Bovill, *The Battle of Alcazar. An account of the defeat of Don Sebastian of Portugal at El-Ksar el-Kebir*, London, 1952

Fahd Mohammed Taleb Saeed Al-Olaqi

Edmund Spenser

DATE OF BIRTH   Probably 1552
PLACE OF BIRTH East Smithfield, London
DATE OF DEATH   13 January 1599
PLACE OF DEATH Westminster

BIOGRAPHY

Edmund Spenser was born in London, although his family may have originated from Lancashire. His name occasionally appears as Edmond Spenser and as Edmund Spencer. His father may have been a John Spenser, who worked for the Merchant Taylors' Company, which would explain why Edmund attended the Merchant Taylors' School, founded in 1561, possibly a member of the first class. At Merchant Taylors', Edmund was mainly exposed to the humanities under a headmaster, Richard Mulcaster (1531-1611), who was passionate about developing the use of English at a time when Latin was still the language of scholarship. John, later an Alderman (1583) and Lord Mayor (1598), was probably also knighted. However, he may or may not be Edmund's father.

Edmund himself proceeded to Pembroke College, Cambridge, in 1569. That year, he was a beneficiary in the will of a wealthy attorney who bequeathed funds to some 'poor students', which could indicate that Edmund's family was actually not very prosperous. At Cambridge, he earned his bed and board as a sizer, a student who did various jobs for the College, and also received five more payments from the bequest. He graduated as a BA in 1573, and as an MA in 1576. He appears to have acted as a courier for some important people at this time, travelling to the continent. Spenser valued his status as a 'gentleman'; biographers discuss whether he saw this as inherited or acquired via his attendance at Cambridge.

By 1578, he was working for the Bishop of Rochester. He married in 1579, and in 1580 he moved to Ireland as private secretary to the Lord Deputy, Baron Grey de Wilton. He remained there until shortly before his death. This post was apparently procured for him by the Earl of Leicester, uncle of fellow poet Sir Philip Sydney. Sydney and Spenser were involved for about nine months from October 1579 to July 1580 in a literary club, the Areopagus, where they and other poets and aspiring poets shared ideas.

Before graduating at Cambridge, Spenser had published and supervised the printing of some translated poetry. His initial reputation rested on *The shepheardes calender*, dedicated to Sir Philip Sydney. Originally published in 1579 under the pseudonym Immerito, this work was reprinted four times during Spenser's lifetime.

Grey was recalled in 1583 for using excessive force in crushing an uprising, killing rebels after they had surrendered. Spenser, who is believed to have accompanied Grey on several military expeditions, remained in Ireland, acting in several administrative capacities. From 1585, he was a prebendary of Limerick Cathedral; discussing the likelihood that Spenser would have held an ecclesiastical appointment despite being a layman, Carpenter ('Spenser in Ireland', p. 48) argues that he did, because, as a devout Christian, he was better educated than most Anglican priests in Ireland and there is no evidence of any other Edmund Spenser alive at the time. Neither did the post have any associated duties. Spenser attended the 1586 session of Parliament in Dublin, served as deputy clerk of Munster Council, leased an old abbey and a castle, and encouraged colonial English settlement. His *A view of the present state of Ireland*, setting out how the British could permanently subdue and rule Ireland and reduce the indigenous Irish population, was published in 1596.

The first volume of *The faerie queene*, dedicated to Elizabeth I, was published in 1590, though various versions had circulated in manuscript before publication, and the second volume followed in 1596. Part of a third volume was written, but was left unfinished. On 25 February 1591, Elizabeth I awarded Spenser a pension following an audience in London, during which he read portions of *The faerie queene* and presented her with a manuscript copy (Zurcher, 'Printing *The faerie queene*', p. 119). Elizabeth may have regarded Spenser as her poet laureate, although there is no record of an official appointment. Elizabeth also granted Spenser the estate of Kilcolman in Ireland, including a castle, a manor and farms, but through acquiring other properties he appears to have overstretched himself financially.

During 1598, the Privy Council appointed him Sheriff of Cork. In a rebellion in October 1598, Kilcolman was burned and Spenser fled Ireland for Westminster, dying there (some sources say 'for lack of bread') on 13 January 1599 (Todd, 'Some account of the life', p. xlviii). He was buried in Westminster Abbey, where he lies next to Chaucer, from whom he is said to have derived the poetic style named after him, the Spenserian stanza (DeFord and Lott, *Forms of verse*, p. 232). The Elizabethan era's premier non-dramatic bard, Spenser is one of the most influential and important Elizabethan literary figures.

MAIN SOURCES OF INFORMATION

Primary
Archival primary sources are listed in Hadfield, *Edmund Spenser's Irish experience*, pp. 205-7, and Hadfield, *Edmund Spenser*, pp. 543-45
C. Burlinson and A. Zurcher, *Edmund Spenser. Selected letters and other papers*, Oxford, 2009
Edmund Spenser, *A view of the present state of Ireland*, Dublin, 1763 (first published, 1633)

Secondary
A. Hadfield, *Edmund Spenser. A life*, Oxford, 2012 (most detailed biography)
A. Hadfield, art. 'Spenser, Edmund', in *ODNB*, vol. 51, pp. 918-29
J. Moore, 'Pastoral motivation in *The shepheardes calendar*', in J.B. Lethbridge (ed.), *Edmund Spenser. New and renewed directions*, Madison NJ, 2006, 58-79
A. Zurcher, 'Printing *The faerie queene* in 1590', *Studies in Bibliography* 57 (2005-6) 115-50
Hoyoung Kim, 'Sŭpensŏu ŭi Pŭrot'est'ant'ijŭm. Pŭrot'est'ant'ijŭm kwa munhwa ŭi yŭkdongjŏk kwan'gye' [Spenser's Protestantism. Protestantism and the dynamic relationship between culture], *Medieval and Early Modern English Studies* 13 (2005) 31-51
A. Hadfield, *Edmund Spenser's Irish experience. Wilde fruit and salvage soyl*, New York, 1997
J.H. Anderson, D. Cheney and D.A. Richardson, *Spenser's life and the subject of biography*, Amherst MA, 1996
D.H. Radcliffe, *Edmund Spenser. A reception history*, Columbia SC, 1996
G.F. Waller, *Edmund Spenser. A literary life*, Basingstoke UK, 1994
W. Maley, *A Spenser chronology*, Basingstoke UK, 1993
R. Rambuss, *Spenser's secret career*, Cambridge, 1993
S. DeFord and C.H. Lott, *Forms of verse, British and American*, New York, 1971, pp. 232-35
A.C. Judson, *Notes on the life of Edmund Spenser*, Bloomington IN, 1949
F.I. Carpenter, 'Spenser in Ireland', *Modern Philology* 19 (1903) 405-19
J.W. Hales, J. Wesley and S. Lee, art. 'Spenser, Edmund', in *DNB*, 384-98
A.B. Grosart, *Life of Spenser*, Manchester, 1882
R.W. Church, *Edmund Spenser. A study of his life*, London, 1880 (repr. New York, 2008)
J.P. Collier, 'Life of Spenser', in E. Spenser, and J.P. Collier, *Life of Spenser. The shepheards calendar, The faerie queene*, London, 1873, i, pp. ix-clxxviii

J.W. Hales, 'Memoire', in E. Spenser, J.W. Hales, and R. Morris (eds), *The Globe edition. Complete works of Edmund Spenser edited from the original editions and manuscripts by R. Morris... With a memoir by J.W. Hales*, London, 1869, xi-lv

G.S. Hillard, 'An essay on the life and writings of Edmund Spenser', in E. Spenser and G.S. Hillard, *Poetical works*, Philadelphia PA, 1857, vii-xxxvi

H.J. Todd, 'Some account of the life of Spenser', in E. Spenser, and H.J. Todd, *The works of Edmund Spenser*, London, 1805, i-clxxiii

T. Birch, 'Life of the author', in E. Spenser and T. Birch, *The faerie queene. By Edmund Spenser. With an exact collation of the two original editions*, London, 1751, i, pp. i-xxxvii

J. Hughes, 'The life of Mr Edmund Spenser', in E. Spenser and J. Hughes, *The works of Mr. Edmund Spenser*, London, 1715, i, pp. i-xxii

Anonymous, 'A summary of the life of Mr Edmund Spenser', in E. Edmund et al., *The works of that famous English poet, Mr. Edmond Spenser*, London, 1679, sigs A-A2

E.P. Phillips, *Theatrum poetarum*, London, 1675, pp. 35-36 (earliest biographical sketch)

WORKS ON CHRISTIAN-MUSLIM RELATIONS

The faerie queene; The faerie queene disposed into twelve books, fashioning XII. morall vertues

DATE 1596
ORIGINAL LANGUAGE English

DESCRIPTION

The faerie queene is an epic poem in six books, each with 12 cantos of 48 stanzas each. The first three books were published as a single volume in 1590, printed in London by William Ponsonbie. These three books, together with three new ones, were printed again in 1596. Spenser planned at least six more, but the work remained unfinished when he died. Most of his manuscripts were destroyed during the uprising at his Irish estate in 1598. Part of one further unfinished book survived in manuscript, which was published posthumously in 1609 as *Two cantos of Mutabilitie* (actually two cantos and part of a third) with a reprint of the whole poem.

Set in Fairy Land ruled by the fairy queen (taken to represent Elizabeth I), the poem narrates King Arthur's quest for the queen, whom he had glimpsed in a vision (Book 1, canto 9, stanza XV). Arthur is the model king and knight, the embodiment of all virtues, while Glory, or Gloriana, is the sum of all virtue, and protagonists in the poem are either heroes or villains, each representing a virtue or a vice. Spenser's goal was to nurture and defend true Christian life and virtue against false religion, which for him was anything other than English Protestantism, especially Roman Catholicism and paganism, which at the time would have included Islam. In addition to Arthurian legend, Spenser drew on a wide range of literature, including the *Chanson de Roland*. In his prefatory letter to Sir Walter Raleigh, he describes the poem's aim as 'to fashion a gentleman or noble person in virtuous and gentle discipline'. He was interested in public or civic, as well as in private virtue, and as the narrative unfolds there is a shift of focus from the former to the latter. Spenser saw knights such as Raleigh who surrounded Elizabeth I as representing *Camelot redivivus* and the restoration of a truly British dynasty. Like the *Chanson de Roland*, the poem is a myth of origins, although written at a late date for a work of this type.

There is no evidence that Spenser was especially interested in Islam or Muslims, although his theology was such that it meant that Muslims, together with all non-Protestants, were capable only of limited virtue, as was his character Satyrae, who as a non-Christian strove for perfection but ultimately fell short of it. There are four explicit, though very brief, Islamic references in the poem: the words 'Mahoune' (Book 2, canto 8, stanza XXXIII; Book 4, canto 8, stanza XLIV, Book 6, canto 7, stanza XLVII), two variants of the Old French 'Tervagant', namely 'Termagent' and 'Termagaunt' (Book 2, canto 8, stanza XXX), and a combination of 'Termagant' and 'Mahoune' (Book 6, canto 7, stanza XLVII). These words, described as 'pagan oaths', are on the lips of Pyrochles and his brother Cymochlës, sons of Malice and Despite. The former symbolises the vice of rage and the latter self-indulgence. Cymochlës cannot be trusted to 'watch for the wolf' when supposedly on guard (Book 2, canto VI, stanza XXVII), while both are angry, violent, even aimless men. They are slain by Arthur. By supplying these anti-heroes with words taken from medieval texts, where they are oaths that Muslims swear to their God and Prophet, Spenser was highlighting their negative status. The fourth reference describes the brothers as often swearing by Mahoune and Termagant. These oaths were spoken as curses in anger in battle: 'by Termaguant thou shall be dead', says Pyrochles.

From his wide reading and use of sources, Spenser would have known something of the origin of these words; they have a similar function in the *Chanson de Roland*, where they name idols that Muslims allegedly worshipped (see ll. 8, 416-17, 2711-13, 3267-68, 3490-91). In addition to these four references, Todd in his 1805 edition (iv, p. 448) adds a gloss on the use of the word *genii*, which he explains with reference to Q 75:14-15 as made from fire, and as 'a higher order of beings between angels and men'. In fact, the English word genii is from the Latin for guardian spirit. It became confused with the Arabic *jinnī* when Arabic texts were translated into English.

SIGNIFICANCE

While these Islamic references do not by any means form a major motif in this work or contribute to any new Christian view of Islam or of Muslims, Spenser's use of what he took as Muslim oaths demonstrates how a leading literary figure with tremendous posthumous influence could perpetuate, and therefore help sustain, negative tropes about the Muslim other. These tropes were readily available to him in his sources, including Chaucer, whose Sir Oliphant swears by Termagent (*Canterbury tales*, ed. Thomas Wright, London, 1747, ii, p. 315).

Early editions of Spenser gloss 'Termagant' as a Saracen name for God and Mahoune as 'Mahomet', while later editors give more details and demonstrate how additional meanings of Termagant evolved. Kitchin in his 1872 edition of *The faerie queene* suggests that while the 'origin of the term is unknown' the 'Termaguant' version of Termagant may 'conceal the name of Mahoune, or Mahomet'. The word, he says 'has now come to mean only a scalding woman', and suggests that 'curmudgeon' is 'probably the same word, the male grumbler, answering to the female shrew' (p. 214). Exemplifying this, Sir Walter Scott refers to a 'scalding woman, raising her termagant voice' (*The works of Sir Walter Scott*, London, 1912, p. 269), while in *The antiquary* (Philadelphia, 1896, p. 424) he says that 'Mahound or Termagant' were 'names of opprobrium applied in the medieval mystery-plays to Mohammed, who was represented as a devil', and in *Ivanhoe* (ed. Tulloch, Edinburgh, 1998, p. 47) that Muslims 'worship Mahound and Termagant'.

Known for his dislike of the Catholic Church, Spenser was in many respects a promoter of ideas about England's place in the divine dispensation, and of its church as the truest expression of Christianity. Conquest and territorial expansion were part of this destiny (see Book 3; also Read, *Temperate conquests*), and there was no place in his worldview for either Catholics or Muslims. In recycling these negative allusions to imagined Muslim idolatry and to swearing by Muḥammad's name, he neither questioned whether he ought to employ this language nor hesitated to do so.

That Muslims were idolaters, who swore by the name of their false, possibly satanically-inspired prophet, was an attitude about their world that was already entrenched in most English minds in relation to the somewhat distant, but feared and hated, Ottoman other, and Spenser readily concurred. Elizabeth I, who sustained cordial correspondence with the sultan of Morocco, the Ottoman sultan and other members of the Ottoman court, appears less hostile than many of her subjects, including this poet who adored her.

Already praised during Spenser's life, this work subsequently became one of the most celebrated of all works in English. Thus, medieval tropes were not only given new life in Elizabethan England, but continue to feature in a text that is still widely read today. Through *The faerie queene*, among other works, a word associated with supposed Muslim idolatry ends up meaning a quarrelsome woman.

MANUSCRIPTS
No MSS survived the fire of 1598 during the Irish anti-colonial uprising at Spenser's estate of Kilcolman. However, the 1590 and 1596 London printed editions are considered authoritative because Spenser himself closely supervised the printing process.

EDITIONS & TRANSLATIONS
Translations
- L. Manini, *La Regina delle fate*, Milan, 2012 (Italian trans.)
- Y. Wada and S. Fukuda, *Yōsei no joō*, Tokyo, 1994, 2005^2 (Japanese trans. and edition of Spenser's poetical works in five volumes)
- *Il Cavaliero della Croce Rossa, o la Leggenda della Santita; poema in dodici canti; dall' inglese di Endmundo Spenser recato in verso italiano, detto ottava rima, da Tomaso Jacopo Mathias*, Naples, 1826 (Italian trans. of Book 1)
- E. Spenser, *Teuchscher Merkur* 1 (1788) 237-49 (partial German trans.)

Editions
- G.A. Wauchope, *The faerie queene*, Lexington KY, 2012
- A.C. Hamilton, H. Yamashita and T. Suzuki, *The faerie queene*, Harlow UK, 2007
- A.D. Stoll, C.V. Kaske and D. Stephens, *The faerie queene*, Indianapolis IN, 2006
- T.P. Roche and C.P. O'Donnell, *The faerie queene*, Harmondsworth UK, 1978
- *The faerie queen*, London, 1965

The faerie queen, London, 1933

L. Winstanley, *The faerie queen*, Cambridge, 1919

J.C. Smith and E. de Selincourt, *The poetical works of Edmund Spenser*, 3 vols, London, 1912

K.M. Warren, *The faerie queene... ed. from the original editions of 1590 and 1596*, London, 1904

W.P. Trent, *The faerie queen*, New York, 1903

G.W. Kitchin, *The faery queene*, London, 1864 (repr. Oxford, 1964)

C.M. Kirkland, *Spenser and The faery queen*, New York, 1850

The faerie queene. disposed into twelve bookes fashioning XII morall vertues, London, 1855

The faerie queen, London, 1839

T. Warton, *Observations on The fairye queen of Spenser*, London, 1807

T. Birch, *The Faerie Queene by Edmund Spenser. With an exact collation of the new original editions*, 3 vols, London, 1751

The faerie queene, Shepeardes calendar, together with other works of Edmund Spenser, London, 1611

The faerie queene disposed into twelve books, fashioning XII. morall vertues, London, 1596

The faerie queene disposed into twelve books, fashioning XII. morall vertues, London, 1590

As part of collected works:

P. Cheney et al., *Collected works of Edmund Spenser*, Oxford, forthcoming

E. Greenlaw, *The works of Edmund Spenser*, 11 vols, Baltimore MD, 2002

W.L. Renwick, *The complete works of Spenser*, 4 vols, London, 1928

Complete works of Edmund Spenser, London, 1897

A. Grosart, *The complete works of Edmund Spenser*, 9 vols, London, 1882-84

R. Morris, *Complete works of Edmund Spenser*, London, 1869

J.P. Collier, *The works of Edmund Spenser*, 5 vols, London, 1862

F.J. Child, *Poetical works*, Boston MA, 1855

The works of Edmund Spenser, with observations on his life and writings, J.C. (intro.), London, 1840

H.J. Todd, *The works of Edmund Spenser*, London, 1805

J. Upton, *The poetical works of Edmund Spenser*, Preface, biographical and critical matter by J. Aikin, 6 vols, London, 1802

J. Hughes, *The works of Mr Edmund Spenser*, 6 vols, London, 1715

The works of Edmond Spenser... whereunto is added an account of his life, with other new aditions, London, 1679

STUDIES

Bibliographies:
- A. Hadfield, 'Bibliography', in *Edmund Spenser. A life*, pp. 543-606
- E. Heale, *The faerie queene. A reader's guide*, Cambridge, 1987, pp. 183-87 (bibliography of scholarly studies; 2002²)
- W.L. Sipple and B.J. Vondersmith, *Edmund Spenser, 1900-1936, a reference guide*, Boston MA, 1984
- W.F. McNeir and G.F. Provost, *Edmund Spenser. An annotated bibliography, 1937-1972*, Pittsburgh PA, 1975
- R.C. Frushell and B.J. Vondersmith, *Contemporary thought on Edmund Spenser, with a bibliography of criticism of The faerie queene, 1900-1970*, Carbondale IL, 1975
- R. Heffner et al., *Spenser allusions in the sixteenth and seventeenth centuries*, Chapel Hill NC, 1972
- *The Spenser Review* (from 1968), previously the *Spenser Newsletter* (publishes bibliography updates)
- F.I. Carpenter, *A reference guide to Edmund Spenser*, Chicago IL, 1923 (with supplement by D.F. Atkinson, Baltimore MD, 1937, repr. New York, 1967)
- F.R. Johnson, *A critical bibliography of the works of Edmund Spenser, printed before 1700*, Baltimore MD, 1933-34

Studies post-1990 supplementing publications listed in bibliographies:
- A. Zurcher, *Edmund Spenser's The faerie queene. A reading guide*, Edinburgh, 2011
- R.A. McCabe, *The Oxford handbook of Edmund Spenser*, Oxford, 2010
- A. Valdepsino, *The poet's poet. Approaches to teaching the works of Edmund Spenser*, El Paso TX, 2007
- P. Suttie, *Self-interpretation in The faerie queene*, Cambridge, 2006
- C. Burlinson, *Allegory, space and the material world in the writings of Edmund Spenser*, Cambridge, 2006
- J.B. Lethbridge, *Edmund Spenser. New and renewed directions*, Madison NJ, 2006
- Hoyoung Kim, '[Spenser's Protestantism. Protestantism and the dynamic relationship between culture]'
- E. Spenser and R. Maynard, *Knights and ladies. Edmund Spenser's The fairie queene, book III*, Moscow ID, 1999

B. van Es, *A critical companion to Spenser studies*, New York, 2006
M. Woodcock, *Fairy in The faerie queene. Renaissance self-fashioning and Elizabethan myth-making*, Aldershot UK, 2004
A. Hadfield, *Shakespeare, Spenser and the matter of Britain*, Basingstoke UK, 2003
A. Hadfield, *The Cambridge companion to Spenser*, Cambridge, 2001
D. Read, *Temperate conquests. Spenser and the Spanish New World*, Detroit MI, 2000
C.V. Kaske, *Spenser and biblical poetics*, Ithaca NY, 1999
E. Spenser and R. Maynard, *Fierce wars and faithful loves. Edmund Spenser's The faerie queen, book I*, Moscow ID, 1999
W. Crane, C.B. Grafton and E. Spenser, *Illustrations and ornamentation from The faerie queene*, Mineola NY, 1999
D.J. Gless, *Interpretation and theology in Spenser*, Cambridge, 1994
D.L Miller and A. Dunlop, *Approaches to teaching Spenser's Faerie queene*, New York, 1994
A.C. Hamilton, *The Spenser encyclopedia*, Toronto, 1990, repr. 1997

Clinton Bennett

William Rainolds

DATE OF BIRTH About 1544
PLACE OF BIRTH Pinhoe, Devon
DATE OF DEATH 24 August 1594
PLACE OF DEATH Antwerp

BIOGRAPHY

William Rainolds (also Reynolds) was born around about 1544 in Pinhoe, near Exeter. He was the second of Richard Rainolds's five sons. An uncle, Thomas, was later warden of Merton College, Oxford, and dean of Exeter. William attended Winchester School, and then New College, Oxford. He became a probationary Fellow in 1560 and a permanent fellow in 1562. In 1563, he graduated with a BA, and took his MA in 1567. At Oxford, he gained a reputation for his debating abilities and for his 'sincere love to the Protestant cause' (Wood, Bliss and University of Oxford, *Athenae Oxonienses*, p. 613). When Queen Elizabeth I visited New College in 1566, William was one of two Fellows chosen to deliver welcome speeches. He received a 'handsome purse... filled with gold' on the occasion (Drane, *The three chancellors*, p. 110). After ordination to the Anglican priesthood, he served as rector of Lavenham, West Sussex, until 1572, when he resigned his Fellowship and entered Hart Hall as a commoner. At this time, his younger brother John (1549-1607) was a staunch defender of Catholicism, and William debated with him the merits of Protestantism and Catholicism, with the result, it is said, that each brother converted the other. John became a Protestant, William a Catholic. Although probably apocryphal, this story was popular in late 16th-century England. It was set to verse in a Latin sonnet by William Alabaster (1567-1640) and found its way into John Locke's *Letters on toleration* (J. Locke, *Letters concerning toleration*, London, 1685, p. 16). Alabaster's sonnet circulated widely through various English translations.

William was received into the Catholic Church in Rome in 1575. Between 1577 and 1580, when he was ordained priest, he studied at Douay and Rheims, where English colleges had been established. He lectured at Douay during 1581, where he also assisted Gregory Martin (1542-82) in translating the New Testament into English from the Vulgate (completed 1582). He then became professor of Divinity and Hebrew at Rheims under the patronage of Cardinal William Allen (1532-94). Already renowned as an apologist, William wrote a number of anti-Protestant works and engaged in debate with William Whitaker (1548-95), especially denouncing his Calvinist views. John Rainolds, who became president of Corpus Christi College, Oxford, in 1598 (and was Dean of Lincoln 1594-99), and also tended toward Calvinism, was later a major translator of the King James Authorised Version of the Bible between 1604 and 1611, and had originally suggested the project. Thus, both brothers worked on important translations.

William began his dispute with Whitaker when the Cambridge scholar attacked the accuracy of the Douay-Rheims Bible. He signed some of his works as Gulielmus Rossæus (or William Rosse) and as Reginaldo. William also made Latin translations of works by Cardinal Allen and Thomas Harding (1516-72), both of whom had influenced his conversion to Catholicism (these works remained unpublished). Five years before he died, William moved to Antwerp as priest to the Beguines because, according to Fuller, he had burst a vein and almost died due to the intensity of his anti-Protestant writing (T. Fuller, *The church history of Britain*, London, 1837, iii, p. 138). He wanted to concentrate on refuting Protestantism, and worked on his huge volume, *Calvino-Turcismus*, in which he represented Calvinism (by which he meant the Church of England) and Islam as an 'amalgam', aiming to refute this supposed hybrid religion. Incomplete when he died on 24 August 1594, the text was finished by his friend William Gifford (1554-1629), later archbishop of Rheims (and involved in several attempts to assassinate Elizabeth I). William was buried in the choir of the Beguine church.

MAIN SOURCES OF INFORMATION

Primary

G. Reginaldo, *A Refutation of sundry Reprehensions, cavils, and false sleightes, by which M. Whitaker laboureth to deface the late English translation, and Catholic annotations of the New Testament, and the book of discovery of heretical corruptions*, Paris, 1583

De justa reipublicæ Christianæ in reges impios et hæreticos authoritate (published under the name of G. Gulielmus Rossæus), Antwerp, 1592

G. Reginaldo, *Calvino-Turcismus, i.e. Calvinisticæ perfidiæ cum Mahumetana collatio, et utriusque sectæ confutatio*, Antwerp, 1597, Cologne, 1603[2]

A. Wood, P. Bliss and University of Oxford, *Athenae Oxonienses. An exact history of all the writers and bishops who have had their education in the University of Oxford. To which are added the Fasti, or Annals of the said University*, London, 1813, i, pp. 613-15

University of Oxford and J. Foster, *Alumni Oxonienses. The members of the University of Oxford, 1715-1886: their parentage, birthplace, and year of birth, with a record of their degrees. Being the matriculation register of the University, alphabetically arranged, revised and annotated*, Oxford, 1888, p. 1249

Winchester College and T.F. Kirby, *Winchester scholars. A list of the wardens, fellows, and scholars of Saint Mary College of Winchester, near Winchester, commonly called Winchester college*, London, 1888, p. 133

Secondary

M. Murray, *The poetics of conversion in early modern English literature. Verse and change from Donne to Dryden*, Cambridge, 2009, pp. 21, 44-47, 49-50

J. Blom and F. Blom, art. 'Rainolds (Reynolds), William', in *ODNB*, vol. 45, 827-28

M. Rigg, art. 'Rainolds, William (1544?-1594)', in *DNB*, vol. 47, 182-83

A.T. Drane, *The three chancellors, or sketches of the lives of William of Wykeham, bp. of Winchester*, London, 1860, pp. 110-11

WORKS ON CHRISTIAN-MUSLIM RELATIONS

Calvino-turcismus, id est calvinisticae perfidiae cum mahometana collatio et utriusque sectæ confutatio,
' "Calvino-turcismus", a comparison of the error of Calvinism with "Muhammadanism" and a refutation of each sect'
Calvino-turcismus, 'A rebuttal of Calvinism by refuting the amalgam of Calvinism and Islam'

DATE 1597
ORIGINAL LANGUAGE Latin

DESCRIPTION

Calvino-turcismus is a Latin text of 1,222 pages, divided into four books. The title introduces the novel notion that Calvinism and Islam are so similar that they can be regarded as one combined heresy. Rainolds supports this argument by referencing accounts of Jews and Protestants who have become Muslims, thus suggesting that they did not need much encouragement or have to change many convictions to do so. However, by 'Calvinism' (he uses the term Continental Calvinism) Rainolds really means the Church of England (*religio Anglicana*), whose bishops and priests he considers illegitimate. Indeed, Turkish shepherds look after their flocks with more reason, right, order and authority than do Anglican bishops (p. 975). While he especially targets Calvinism, he treats all Protestants as heretics, and refers almost as often to Luther, Melanchthon and Zwingli as he does to Calvin, often in the same sentence. He regards Calvinism and Islam as equally heretical, though of the two he argues that Islam is the less objectionable, or the less repulsive. He sets out this thesis in the form of a dialogue between a Muslim and an Anglican divine. While earlier works of anti-Muslim polemic that utilise dialogue inevitably depict the Christian as winning the argument, Rainolds reverses this and gives the Muslim the advantage throughout his text.

Rainolds's claim is that, compared with Calvinism, Islam is less cruel, and even more rational. Both are 'pseudo-gospels' that abrogate the Trinity and Christ's divinity, and preach absurd, iconoclastic, barbarous blasphemies including the doctrine of predestination, which he finds especially reprehensible (*argumentum totius operis*, p. 2). Both gospels are fabricated, and both hold scripture in near idolatrous reverence yet reject the use of icons in worship, a link he sees as especially significant in establishing that the two heresies are closely related. On the other hand, elsewhere he criticises Anglicans for approaching idolatry in their esteem for Queen Elizabeth I (W. Rainolds, *A refutation of sundry reprehensions*, London, 1583, p. 265). He points out that the Qur'an is Unitarian, not Trinitarian, in agreement with the Jewish Talmud (p. 526), and that it denies that Jesus was by nature divine (p. 190). English priests stand in 'sympathy' with Turks (pp. 314-54), while England has become too reliant on trade with Turkey. As for Calvin, he planned to replace the pope and co-rule Europe with the Ottoman sultan. Rainolds seems to conflate 'Mahumet' and 'Sergio' as a single creator of the Qur'an (see p. 960), referring to the monk, called Sergius and Baḥīrā, who is credited in Christian polemic from John of Damascus onwards with teaching Muḥammad. While he cites the Bible as his most frequent source, there do not appear to be any direct qur'anic references.

SIGNIFICANCE

In developing his argument, Rainolds sets up two straw-men so that he can demolish them. He does not engage in detail with Calvin's writing any more than he does with Muslim sources; indeed he had probably not read anything actually written by a Muslim. One commentator says that 'chunks of' Jérôme-Hermès Bolsec (d. 1584), who debated predestination (which he saw as absurd) with Calvin, appear in the work (D. Shuger, *Censorship and cultural sensibility. The regulation of language in Tudor-Stuart England*, Philadelphia, 2006, p. 21). Rainolds did not engage in extended discussion on predestination within Islamic discourse but confidently asserted that Islam teaches this unequivocally. Similarly, he had it that Calvin denied Jesus's divinity. It could be said that refuting Protestantism rather than Islam was his aim and that Islam was merely recruited as a convenient ancillary to that goal. It is unlikely that Muslims would have read such a large Latin text, even if they were aware of it. On the other hand, some readers could have regarded the text as a valid source of information on Islam, and it would have confirmed their ideas about Islam's heretical status. Comparison of Islam to Protestantism became a popular theme, leading to a whole genre of literature on this topic, pioneered by this text. Not surprisingly, Protestants responded by associating Catholicism and Islam as co-heresies, attempting to refute Rainolds. The best-known reply was by Matthew Sutcliffe (1550-1629), *De Turco-papismo* (1604), a work about half the length of Rainold's. For Sutcliffe, it was papists who were worse than Turks. However, their customs such as fasting, performing charitable acts and visiting tombs of saints were closer to Catholicism than Protestantism. Thus, arguably, Muslims were represented by both sides of this debate in a somewhat positive light. Rainold's assertion that Islam was more rational than Protestantism contrasts with what became an increasingly common anti-Islamic charge, that Islam and rational thought could not co-exist. Henry King (1592-1669), Anglican bishop of Chichester, writing in 1621 described *Calvino-turcismus* as one of the most notable 'Catholic libels', while Robert Persons (1546-1610), an English Jesuit, thought it so 'learned' that Sutcliffe had 'made himself ridiculous by attempting' to answer it (C. Highley, *Catholics writing the nation in early modern Britain and Ireland*, New York, 2008, p. 61).

Political events lay behind Rainold's decision to conflate Islam and Protestantism. In the Low Countries, where he was living at the time of writing, a popular motto was *Liever Turks dan Paaps* ('rather Turkish than papist'). In other words, people were saying that they would prefer Turkish to Catholic rule. Some said that Christians and other non-Muslims fared better under the Ottomans than non-Catholics did under Catholic rule. Crescent shaped medallions were sold as a sign of a Dutch-Ottoman concord (B. Kingsbury and B. Straumann, *The Roman foundations of the law of nations. Alberico Gentili and the justice of empire*, Oxford, 2010, p. 140). In 1574, Murad III had sent a letter to the 'Lutherans' of Flanders commending their opposition to idols and their removal of bells from their churches, seeking a possible alliance (see S.A. Skilliter and W. Harborne, *William Harborne and the trade with Turkey, 1578-1582*, Oxford, 1977, p. 37). Elizabeth I of England enjoyed close diplomatic relations with Turkey, emphasising that, as a Protestant, she too opposed idolatry and defended the faith against those who 'falsely' professed 'the name of Christ' (*Calendar of state papers, foreign series, of the reign of Elizabeth: preserved in the State Paper Department of Her Majesty's Public Record Office*, London, 1863, p. 22, no. 234). English trade with Turkey was increasing, and included the sale of items that Catholics were banned from trading, such as material for use in war, which was a cause of concern for Rainolds. Relations between Europe and the Ottoman Empire were very much on the minds of politicians, rulers and military leaders, and the possibility of a Muslim-Protestant anti-Catholic alliance would have seemed alarming. Neither Rainolds's work nor the literature it stimulated added much to actual knowledge of the other among either Christians or Muslims, though it serves to demonstrate how religious discourse takes place within particular political, cultural and historical contexts.

EDITIONS & TRANSLATIONS

G. Reginaldo, *Calvino-Turcismus, i.e. Calvinisticæ Perfidiæ cum Mahumetana Collatio, et utriusque sectæ Confutatio*, Antwerp, 1597, Cologne, 1603

STUDIES

M. Sutcliffe, *De Turco-papismo: hoc est, De Turcarum et papistarum aduersus Christi ecclesiam & fidem coniuratione, eorumque in religione & moribus consensione & similitudine; liber vnus Eidem præterea adiuncti sunt, de Turco-papistarum maledictis & calumniis, aduersus Gulielmi Giffordi famosi pontificum Rom.& Iebusitarum supparasitastri volumen illud contumeliosissimum, quod ille Caluino-Turcismum inscripsit. Libri quatuor. In quibus non tantùm huius hominis leuissimi, sed etiam aliorum importunissimorum scurrarum aduersus orthodoxam Christi ecclesiam continenter latrantium, malitia & petulantia reprimitur, hominumque piorum fama ab eorum calumniis vindicatur*. Londini [i.e. Hanau]: Excudebant Georgius Bishop, Radulphus Newberie, & Rober. Barker, 1604 (refutation of Rainolds's work)

Clinton Bennett

Index of Names

Numbers in italics indicate a main entry.

'Abd al-Malik, Sa'dī sultan   243-45, 793, 844, 846
'Abd al-Muṭṭalib, see Abdemutalla   640
'Abdallāh al-Asīr   44
Abdelmelec, see 'Abd al-Malik   243-45, 793, 844, 846
Abdel Melech, see 'Abd al-Malik   243-45, 793, 844, 846
Abdemutalla, see 'Abd al-Muṭṭalib   640
Abraham, patriarch   342, 510, 670, 723, 805, 828-29
Abū Bakr, caliph   342, 769
Abū l-Faraj, Gregorius   15
Abū l-Fidā   15, 529, 533
Abū 'Abdallāh Muḥammad II, King of Morocco (Mully Mahamet)   844
Abū Bakr al-Rāzī   448
Accolti, Benedetto, see also Unico Aretino   450, 594
Adam   669-70
Aden   319, 323-24, 805
Adrian VI, pope, see Hadrian VI, pope   433, 655, 661
Adriel, angel of Death   670
Afonso de Sousa, Martim   351
Agarenus, descendant of Hagar   668
Agricola, Michael   686-688
Aḥmad al-Manṣūr, Moroccan sultan   283, 793, 845
Albaicín, Granada   3, 51, 63-65, 283
Alberto Pio, Prince of Carpi   100, 440, 469
Albuquerque, Afonso de   300-1, 315-16, 318-327, 360, 372
Alcalá de Henares, University of   100-1, 115, 119, 137, 150, 207, 351
Alcalá, Pedro de   3, 52, 73-78, 213
Alcazar, Battle of   248, 259-60, 262, 383, 843, 847
Alemán, Mateo   196
Alexander the Great   104, 472, 660
Alfonso I, King of Aragón and Navarre   835
Alfonso V, King of Aragón   658, 835
Algeria   6, 67, 422, 495
Algiers   6, 102, 150, 152, 217, 243, 268, 271, 755

Alhambra   126-27, 224, 250
'Alī l-Gharīb   43-47
'Alī, fourth caliph   342, 431, 499, 500
Almeida, Francisco de, first Viceroy of India   300, 319, 321, 361
Alonso del Castillo   273, 275, 283, 290
Alpujarras, First Rebellion of (1499-1502)   4
Alpujarras, Second Rebellion of (1568-71)   174, 195, 250, 252, 254, 266, 290-92
America, European discovery of   7, 152, 434, 555, 797
Americas   8, 529, 532, 800-2, 846
Amurath, Emperor of the East   835, 845
Anatolia   329, 518, 559, 617, 659, 703, 706
Angiolello, Giovanni Maria   424, 430, 432, 578
Anglican Church   764-65, 798, 826, 868, 862
Antichrist   361, 612, 622-24, 629, 639, 650, 677, 679, 681, 683, 687, 693, 694-97, 743, 769, 770, 771, 800-1, 806
Antolínez de Burgos   291
Antonio, Nicolás   89, 314
Apocalypse and apocalyptic events   12, 113, 459, 642, 649, 677, 683, 693, 696-97, 739, 768-69, 773
apostates, Christian   234, 236, 238, 262, 613
Apostles of Jesus   20, 56-57, 80, 131, 401, 648, 801
Aranda, Antonio de   115-18
Aranda, Gabriel de   263
Arcadelt, Jaques   589
Aretino, Pietro   493, 567
Arius and Arians   400-1, 633, 641, 647-48, 669, 749
Ariosto, Ludovico   195, 301, 463-64, 469-83, 492-93, 496, 568, 593, 596
Aristotle and Aristotelian philosophy   100-1, 137, 144, 224, 238, 397, 523-26, 552-53, 660, 713, 780
Armenia and Armenians   116, 341-42, 376, 378, 439, 499, 595, 756
Arnaldo Albertini   236, 238
Arnold, Richard   622

INDEX OF NAMES

Arredondo y Alvarado, Gonzalo 96-99, 113
Arrivabene, Andrea 34, 506-9
Ashley, Robert 510
Ashton, Peter 487, 699-702, 838
Astete, Gaspar 211
Augustine of Hippo 56, 91, 108, 116, 124, 631
Authorised Version of the Bible 772, 861
Aventinus, Johannes 750
Averroes 16, 172, 448, 523-26, 779-80
Avicenna 13, 16, 523, 525, 723
Aytinger, Wolfgang 639, 642

Bacon, Roger 133
Baḥīrā, see Sergius 57, 171, 640, 669, 769, 828, 863
Balbi di Correggio, Francesco 563-66
Bale, John 638, 689-98, 764-65
Bandello, Matteo 791, 792, 842
Baptism 289, 292, 342, 440, 596, 631, 646, 648, 818, 828
Barabbas 811-12
Barack Obama, US president 697
Barbaro, Giosafat 432, 533
Barbarossa brothers 5, 150, 152, 177, 494-96, 713, 715, 752, 757
Barbary 6, 14, 21, 560, 565, 694, 752, 798, 804
Barbinel, Rabbi 740
Barlezio, Marino; Marinus Barletius 424, 466, 572
Barrantes Maldonado, Pedro 215-18
Barreto, Francisco 357, 391-94
Barros, João de 285, 316, 332, 343, 358-68, 372-73, 545-47
Bartholomeus Anglicus 612
Bassano, Luigi 501-5
Fray Juan Bautista 243-46
Bayezid II; Bajazet, Ottoman sultan 157, 378, 425, 427, 458, 461-62, 465, 488, 512, 516, 518, 520, 544, 658, 701, 728, 758, 838
al-Bayḍāwī, ʿAbd Allāh ibn ʿUmar 36
Beast in Revelation, number 666 13, 390, 694, 769, 771
Bedwell, William 14-16, 23
Belgrade 103, 112, 425, 655, 658
Belon, Pierre 13, 182, 184-85, 703-11, 759, 779, 781-82
Bembo, Pietro 332, 450, 452, 469, 492, 528, 554, 568, 578
Jonson, Ben 824
Berber chronicles 287
Bern Disputation (1528) 746

Bernabei, Giuseppe Antonio 589
Berti, Nicola 33
Beuter, Anton 542
Bible 13, 18, 80, 91, 210, 250, 390, 400-2, 423, 626, 630, 645, 651, 675, 677, 681-83, 687, 696, 719, 735, 742, 746, 772, 829, 831, 861, 863
Bibliander, Theodor 10, 12-14, 26, 172, 253, 418, 509, 650, 667, 672, 675-85, 718, 736, 744, 747, 750, 768, 781
Biondo, Flavio 456, 459
black magic 624, 791
Bleda, Jaime 148, 291
Boccaccio, Giovanni 492, 496, 554-55, 557, 560, 568, 790, 791, 793
Bodin, Jean 775-87
Boemus, Johann 329-30
Boiardo, Matteo Maria 463, 472, 474, 476, 493, 593, 596
Bolsec, Jérôme-Hermès 863
Boniface III, pope 690, 694
Book of Common Prayer (1552) 765
Book of Daniel 250, 330, 739-41, 743, 771, 779
Book of Psalms 64, 125, 589, 654, 687, 713, 734, 739
Book of Revelation 52, 390, 693-95, 696-97, 749, 765, 769, 771
Bosio, Giacomo 565
Bosnia and Bosnians 420, 426
Boucher, François 598
Bragadino, Marcantonio 584-85
Brava, East Africa 314-15
Brazil 297, 302, 308, 358, 360, 532, 753, 760
Breidenbach, Bernhard von 612, 617, 639
Brerewood, Edward 14
Browne, Sir Thomas 16, 23
Buchmann, Theodor, see Theodor Bibliander 10, 12-14, 26, 172, 253, 418, 509, 650, 667, 672, 675-85, 718, 736, 744, 747, 750, 768, 781
al-Bukhārī 87, 172
Bullinger, Heinrich 679, 746-51
Burchard of Mount Sion 720
Burhān Shāh I, Niẓām of Aḥmadnagar 351
Burton, Robert 16, 23
Byzantium 137, 141, 425, 638, 755

Cabot, Sebastian 798
Cabral, Pedro Álvares 297, 308, 361
Cabrera de Córdoba 291
Caccini, Francesca 478

INDEX OF NAMES

Cadygan, see Khadīja 640
Cain 771
Calicut 300-1, 305, 308-9, 315, 318, 322-23
Calvin, John 646, 650-51, 676-77, 696, 718, 732-745, 746-47, 750, 863-64
Calvinism and Calvinists 582, 703, 736-37, 775, 861-65
Câmara, Martim Gonçalvez da 356
Cambini, Andrea 426, *456-68*, 519, 571, 578, 728, 730, 781
Cambodia 369
Cambrai, League of 421
Cambrai, Peace of 103, 109
Camões, Luís Vaz de 305, *381-85*
Campion, Edmund 765
Cannanore, Kerala 301, 405-6
Cano, Melchor 673
Canossa, Ludovico da 450, 452
Cantacuzenus family 420
Carion, Johannes 330
Carracci, Annibale and Ludovico 598
Cartwright, Thomas 696
Casas, Bartolomé de las 101, 533
Cassetti, Jacob 590
Castanheda, Fernão Lopes de 304-5, 343, *346-50*
Castiglione, Baldassar *450-55*, 492
Castilho, Diogo de *328-31*, 389
Castrodardo, Giovanni Battista 34, *506-511*
Cateau-Cambrésis, Treaty of 573
catechisms and catechetical works 49, 51, 56, 61, 63, 65, 75, 170, 211-13, 253-57, 266, 388-90, 651
Catholic league 233
Catholic monarchs, see Ferdinand II of Aragon and Isabella of Castille 2, 49, 50, 52, 55, 58, 60, 80, 96, 192, 253, 255, 282, 289, 301
Caxton, William 620
Cervantes, Miguel de 6, 193, 196, 271
Ceylon 351, 369
Chalcocondyles, Laonicus 9, 578, 768, 781, 817
Chaldiran, Battle of 432, 512, 520
Charlemagne 471-77, 495
Charles V, Holy Roman Emperor, *also* King Charles I of Spain 4-6, 85, 89-90, 93-94, 96-98, 100-1, 103-4, 109, 115, 126, 131, 147, 150, 152, 157, 177, 208, 215, 224, 230, 270, 282, 329, 417, 424, 450, 470, 485, 487-89, 493-95, 514, 515, 542, 544, 574, 579, 587, 645, 655, 658, 661, 705, 712, 715, 754, 782
Charles VIII, King of France 484

Charles IX, King of France 775, 782, 815
Chateaubriand, François-René 196
Chaucer, Geoffrey 851, 855
China 370-71, 373, 533, 800
Chinchón, Bernardo Pérez de *119-24*, 144, 170-72, 211, 390, 672
Chio, Leonardo di 571
Church Fathers 235, 679, 681, 736, 830
Church of England 764-65, 798, 826, 868, 862
Cicero 138, 332, 456, 654, 736
Cipelli, Giovanni Battista 329
Cippico, Coriolano 557, 578
circumcision 122, 236, 252, 342, 476, 817-18
Cirne, Manuel 329
Cirni, Anton Francesco 572
Cisneros, Francisco Jiménez de, Archbishop of Toledo 4, 5, 49, 51, 52, 57, 58, 61, 63-65, 76, 80, 85, 100, 170
Cisneros, García Jiménez de 56
Clement V, pope 328
Clement VI, pope 690
Clement VII, pope 97, 100, 112, 113, 421, 440, 450, 484-85, 487, 523, 658
Clement VIII, pope 588
Cleynaerts, Nicolaes *125-36*, 386
Coccio, Marcantonio 329
Cognac, League of 658
Coimbra 126, 298, 304, 339, 346, 347, 381
Colón, Hernando 51, 125-26
Columbus, Christopher 7-8, 125, 798, 800-2
Colville, David 415, 417
Complutense Bible 250
Comunidades, War of (1520-22) 215
Constantinople, see also Istanbul 9, 16, 97, 104, 140, 141, 157, 182, 177, 243, 286, 329-30, 420, 421, 424, 426-27, 433, 439, 460, 461, 464, 465, 501, 503-4, 513, 516, 519, 552, 555, 580, 582, 632, 666, 682, 703, 705-6, 713, 724, 753-759, 770, 781
Constantinople, fall of 389, 402, 425, 461, 464-65, 477, 571, 573, 580, 623, 643, 658, 659, 728, 791, 812
Contarini, Ambrogio 432, 533
Contarini, Giovan Pietro 572
Conversion 3, 5, 16, 51, 55-56, 58, 61, 63-66, 75-76, 80, 87, 94, 119, 131, 134, 147-48, 159-60, 165-66, 221, 233, 237, 240, 266, 274, 297, 337, 353, 379, 387-90, 405, 415, 513, 515, 518, 597, 623, 634, 639, 648, 664, 669, 677, 696, 720, 732, 801, 824, 861

INDEX OF NAMES

Cordova 100, 232-33, 268, 270, 587
Cordova, martyrs of 252-53, 257
Corfu 582, 590, 706
Coromandel Coast 323
Correia, Gaspar 316, 322, 346
Corsica 512
Cortés, Hernán 150-52
Council of Trent 169, 173, 208, 224, 257, 485
Counter-Reformation 387, 534, 554-56, 598
Couto, Diogo do 358, 360, 361
Cranmer, Thomas, Archbishop of Canterbury 693
Crecquillon, Thomas 589
Creeds:
　Christian 94, 734
　Islamic 19, 377, 378, 407
Crépy, Treaty of 705
Crete 498, 555, 582, 703, 706
Cristianos viejos (old Christians) 64, 94
Crusades and crusaders 8, 97-98, 103, 113, 126, 129-30, 133-34, 177, 286, 315, 322, 326, 329-30, 361-62, 382-83, 424-25, 434, 452-53, 460, 463, 475, 478, 485, 487-88, 494, 515, 529, 546, 584, 592-95, 597-99, 612, 771, 781, 790, 802, 818
Cruz, Gaspar da *369-75*
Cuspinianus, Johan, *see also* Johan Spiesshaymer 141-42, 701, 768
Cyprus 1, 230, 339, 341, 377, 498, 560-61, 572-74, 577, 582, 584, 587, 617
Cyril Lucaris, Greek Patriarch 28

Dalmatia 425, 501
Damascus 286, 342, 407, 475, 524-25, 642, 706, 749, 804, 829, 863
Daniel, Book of 250, 330, 739-41, 743, 771, 779
Dante Alighieri 34, 398, 400, 492, 506, 568, 596
Dār al-Islām 43, 69, 760
Dār al-kufr 69
Delacroix 196
Denis (Dionysius) the Carthusian 171-72, 236
Deuteronomy, Book of 740, 742-43
Devil, devilish 46, 171, 221, 252, 305, 429, 612, 622-23, 665, 679, 682, 687, 690, 693-94, 723, 769, 830, 855
devşirme 104, 151, 724
Dias, Bartolomew 547
Diego Suárez Montañés 268, 287
Diet of Augsburg 208

Diet of Regensburg 208
Diet of Worms 208
Dioscorides 138, 352, 353
Diu, India 315-16, 323
Diyarbakir 339, 342
Djerba, Battle of 6, 548-550, 572-573
Doge of Venice 557, 584
Dolce, Lodovico *492-97*, 553, 554, 557, 567
Domenichino 598
Domingo de Soto 101, 386
Dominicus Germanus of Silesia 30, 32, 35, 37
Dominicans 54, 57-58, 79, 101, 119, 243, 247, 369-70, 399, 401, 410, 440, 538, 605-6, 612
Doria, Andrea 182
Dossi, Dosso 478
Douay 860
Douay-Rheims Bible 861
Drake, Sir Francis 798
Drechsler, Wolfgang 572, 578
Duarte Barbosa 346
Duplessis-Mornay, Felipe 673
Dvořák, Antonín 598

East Africa 304-5, 308-10, 314, 319, 362, 392
Eastern Christianity 378, 617
Eden, Richard *796-807*, 830
Edward VI, King of England 693, 802
Egidio da Viterbo 28-31, 37, 415, 417-18, 440, 449
El Divino, *see* Herrera, Fernando de 229-31
Eleni, dowager Queen of Ethiopia 334-36
Elizabeth I, Queen of England viii, 726, 765, 793, 803, 846-47, 851, 853-54, 856, 860-61, 863, 865
Erasmus, Desiderius and Erasmianism 100, 103-5, 108-9, 117, 119-20, 132, 134, 138, 144, 183, 332, 424, 458, *630-36*, 654-55, 671, 687, 700, 713, 736
Erizzo, Sebastiano 492, *552-62*
Erpenius, Thomas 15-16, 27
Esau 771
Espina, Alfonso de la 639
Estado da Índia (Portuguese State of India) 351, 353, 370, 376, 378
Ethiopia 285, 301, 305, 324, 334-37, 596, 800
Eucharist 108, 690, 718
Eulogius of Cordova 253-53, 257
Evangelicals 133-34, 238, 252, 254, 256-58, 509, 652, 697, 717

INDEX OF NAMES

evangelisation   51-52, 65, 121-22, 124, 145, 148, 185, 253-54, 643-44, 801
Évora   126, 369-70, 386
exegesis   629, 675, 696
Ezekiel   677, 735, 739-40

Fabri, Felix   *605-15*, 617
false prophet   132, 171, 266, 519, 612, 640, 694, 708, 743, 791, 829, 836
Famagusta, siege and fall of   230, 561, 582, 584
Faria y Sousa, Manuel de   263
Farnese, Alessandro, later Pope Paul III   140, 157, 336, 421, 430-31, 433, 485, 506, 523
Father Isidoro   265
fatwā   67, 69-70
Faustus   809, 812
Ferdinand II of Aragon and Isabella of Castile, *see also* Catholic monarchs   2, 8, 49-50, 60-61, 73, 80, 85, 89-90, 96, 159, 192, 798
Ferdinand, Holy Roman Emperor   715
Ficino, Marsilio   *397-404*, 456, 464, 736
Figuerola, Joan Martí   *89-92*, 170, 172, 415
Filefo, Francesco   329
Finch, John   16
Flavius Mithridates   25-26, 28, 29
Floranes, Rafael   51
Florentine Republic   208, 302, 410, 423, 434, 456-57, 464, 465, 478, 485, 486, 512-13, 515-16, 567, 571, 589, 658, 728
Florian, Jean   443
Fourth Council of Toledo   256
Fox, George   19-20
Foxe, John   12-13, 696, *764-74*
Fracastoro, Girolamo   528, 531-32
Fragonard, Jean-Honoré   598
Francis I, King of France, *see also* François I   5, 97, 109, 152, 224, 424, 452, 485, 507, 514-15, 567, 655, 658, 661, 703, 705, 712-15, 732, 734, 752, 754, 758, 781-82, 815
Franciscans   6, 30, 54, 57-58, 115, 119, 168, 308, 310, 387, 639, 645
Franco-Ottoman Alliance   515, 755
François I, King of France, *see also* Francis I   5, 97, 109, 152, 224, 424, 452, 485, 507, 514-15, 567, 655, 658, 661, 703, 705, 712-15, 732, 734, 752, 754, 758, 781-82, 815
François II, King of France   723-24
Françoise de la Chassaigne   815
Frederick Barbarossa of Germany   177

Freytag, Georg Wilhelm   174
Fux, Johann Joseph   590

Gabriel, Archangel   276, 595, 624, 828-30
Gabriel de Luetz, Baron d'Aramon   507-8, 703, 705, 709, 715, 754
Gama, Vasco da   300-1, 304-5, 308, 310, 347, 361, 382-83, 547
García, Martín; Martín García Puyazuelo   80, *85-88*, 90, 121, 170-72
García, Gómez   *54-59*
Gastaldi, Giacomo   286, 529, 532
Geoffroy de Villehardouin   529
Georgius, Bartholomaeo (Bartholomew Georgievitz)   184, 513, 519, 571, 709
Gérôme, Jean-Léon   196
Gesner, Konrad   682, 747
Geuffroy, Antoine   709
Gəʿəz language   334, 336
al-Ghazālī, Abū Ḥāmid   19, 87, 172, 448, 723
Ghistele, Joos van   616-17
Gibraltar, attack on (1540)   215-17
Gilles, Pierre; Pieter Gillis-Aegidius   134, 703, 709
Giovio, Paulo   141-42, 154, 215, 268, 329-30, 336, 424, 426, 433, 457, 462, 466, *484-91*, 518-19, 571-72, 578-79, 700, 712, 720, 781, 838
Giulio di Giuliano de' Medici, *see* Pope Clement VII   97, 100, 112, 113, 421, 440, 450, 484-85, 487, 523, 658
Glazemaker, Jan Hendricksz   36
Gluck, Christoph   590, 598
Goa   301, 306, 315-16, 319, 322-23, 346, 351, 369-70, 381, 386-87, 389-90, 391
Godfrey of Bouillon   488, 594
Gog and Magog   693-94, 735, 740
Góis, Damião de   261, 285, 316, *332-38*, 529
Góngora, Luis de   195
Gospel   5, 43, 45-46, 108, 132-33, 210, 257, 276, 356, 401-2, 461, 713, 715, 719, 736, 744, 746, 829, 831, 863
Gospel of John   132, 273, 677
Granada   1-4, 7, 46, 49, 51-52, 57-58, 61, 63, 65, 75-76, 79-80, 85, 93, 122, 126, 129, 132-33, 145, 159, 165-66, 170, 174, 184, 192, 194-96, 207-8, 222, 224-25, 227, 250, 252-54, 257, 265-67, 273-76, 282-85, 287, 289-92, 301, 386, 439, 631, 648
Granada, fall of   2-3, 170, 439
Granada, mass deportation of Moriscos   7, 195, 290
Greaves, Thomas   16

Greene, Robert   823, *833-40*
Gregorius Abū l-Faraj   15
Gregory XIII, pope   233, 238-39
Gregory, John   17-18, 23
Guadagnol, Philippe   22
Guangdong   369
Guangzhou   369
Guerra de Lorca, Pedro   211, *250-58*
Guercino; Giovanni Francesco Barbieri   598
Guinea   304, 358
Gujarat   316, 323, 351, 361
Gulf of Suez   324, 388-89
Gülen, Fethullah   634

Hadith   13, 88, 830
Hadrian VI, pope, *see* Pope Adrian VI   433, 655, 661
Haedo, Diego de   287
Hagar   668, 720, 828-29
Hagarenes   769
Hagia Sophia   503, 722, 755
hajj   129, 165, 172, 342, 405, 407, 612, 617, 755, 798, 805
Hakluyt, Richard   13, 23, 534, 803, 806
Handel, George Frideric   478, 598
Harem   16, 21, 792, 805-6
Al-Ḥasan ibn Muḥammad al-Wazzān al-Fāsī, *see* Leo Africanus   29, 283, 285, 286, 290, 417, *439-49*, 524, 533, 720, 780-81
Haydn, Joseph   478, 598
Hayez, Francesco   599
Hebrew language   10, 32, 34-35, 125, 208, 224, 273, 440, 510, 523-26, 675, 713-14, 723, 739, 860
Hell   183, 517, 595, 670
Henry the Navigator, Prince   8, 332, 360
Henry II, King of France; Dauphin Henry of Valois   423, 514, 704, 706, 752-54
Henry III, King of France   775-76, 815-16
Henry IV, King of Castile   49
Henry VII, King of England   450
Henry VIII, King of England   523, 637, 655, 661, 689, 796
Heraclius, Byzantine emperor   57, 171
Heresy, heretics and heretical literature   5, 52, 80, 119, 132, 134, 171, 208, 233, 235-40, 252, 254, 276, 292, 362, 382-83, 400-1, 519, 597, 618, 633, 638-39, 641-43, 646, 679, 681, 683, 690, 712, 749-50, 775, 821, 830, 862-64
Hermann of Carinthia   781
Herrera, Fernando de   *229-31*
Hildegard   771

Hinduism and Hindus   305, 308-10, 315-16, 361
Hogenberg, Frans   720
Holy Land   8, 50, 97, 104, 115-17, 326, 382, 389, 488, 494, 563, 574, 577-78, 580, 584, 587-89, 597, 605, 610, 612-13, 617, 622, 639, 703, 706-7, 715, 720
Holy League   1, 157, 230, 286, 469, 563, 574, 577, 578, 584, 587, 588, 589
Holy Sepulchre, Church of   8, 116, 595, 609
Holy Spirit   56, 233, 401, 647, 694
holy war   122, 634, 844
Homer   382, 389, 660, 835
Homes, Nathaniel   16
Hormuz; Ormuz   301, 314-16, 319, 322-23, 339, 341, 370-73, 376-77, 498
Hottinger, Johan Heinrich   10, 19, 21, 22, 449
Hulst, Samuel van   174
Humanism and humanists   25, 83, 101, 104-5, 117, 125, 130-31, 133-34, 138, 144, 150, 154, 157, 179, 185, 194, 224, 235, 290, 329-30, 332, 336-37, 410, 417, 421, 425, 429, 433-34, 450, 456, 458-59, 463-64, 469, 490, 492, 495, 506, 510, 528, 533, 552, 558, 573, 580, 590, 592, 598, 626, 630, 645, 652, 654-56, 658, 683, 713, 728, 736, 744, 750, 781, 793, 815
Hungarian Unitarianism   651
Hungary and the Hungarians   97, 102-3, 182, 215, 425, 432, 452, 459-61, 469, 485, 507, 515, 548, 555, 565, 632, 651-52, 655, 658, 666, 679, 683, 694, 758, 791
Hunyadi, John   459-60, 465, 770, 791
Hurtado de Mendoza, Diego   150, *224-28*, 290-91, 501, 529, 542
Ḥusayn, Shīʿī Imām   500
Hussites   768

Iberia   1-3, 5, 7, 9, 32, 47, 69, 108, 131, 162, 170, 194, 262, 314, 322, 330, 361, 490, 673, 846
Ibn Abī Zamānīn   32
Ibn ʿAṭiyya   172
Ibn Hishām   82
Ibn Isḥāq   172, 524
Ibn Rushd   16, 172, 448, 523-526, 779-780
Ibn Sīnā   13, 16, 523, 525, 723,
Ibrahim de Reminjo   159-60, 162, 168
Ibrahim I, Ottoman sultan   578
Ibrahim Pasha, Ottoman statesman   152, 339, 489
ʿĪd al-kabīr   245

INDEX OF NAMES 873

Idolatry and idol-worship   21, 82, 131-32, 301, 309-10, 315-16, 510, 597, 651, 669, 693-94, 735-36, 744, 771, 793, 802, 836, 854-56, 863-65
al-Idrīsī   15, 448
Ignatius of Loyola   168, 713
Imperialism   326, 387, 803
India and the Indian Ocean   297-98, 300, 304-5, 308-10, 314-16, 318-19, 321-25, 335, 339, 343, 346-47, 351-53, 358, 360-62, 369-70, 376, 378, 382-83, 389, 391-92, 405-6, 498, 517, 532, 617, 660, 694, 804-5
Infantas, Fernando de las   587-90
Infidels   49-50, 69, 80, 155, 194, 236, 240, 315-16, 361, 383, 452-53, 461, 464, 472, 546, 579, 595, 609, 612, 618
Ingres, Jean-Auguste-Dominique   196, 478, 757
Innocent XI, pope   31, 274
Inquisition   5, 55, 61, 80, 85, 119, 132, 232-33, 235, 237-40, 298, 332, 538, 542, 588, 654, 668, 671, 673
Inquisitors   57, 80, 108, 131-32, 213, 232, 235-40, 301, 386, 593
integration   64, 186
Iran   341, 343, 378, 432, 798, 804
Irving, Washington   196, 291
Isaac   771, 805
Isabella of Castile and Ferdinand II of Aragon, *see also* Catholic monarchs   2, 8, 49-50, 60-61, 73, 80, 85, 89-90, 96, 159, 192, 798
Isaiah   390, 629, 739
Ishmael   723, 771, 828
Ismail I, Shah of Persia   322, 324, 339, 341, 378, 425, 430, 432
Isouard, Nicolò   590
Israelites   30, 629, 695, 720, 723, 749
Istanbul, *see* Constantinople   9, 16, 97, 104, 140, 141, 157, 182, 177, 243, 286, 329-30, 420, 421, 424, 426-27, 433, 439, 460, 461, 464, 465, 501, 503-4, 513, 516, 519, 552, 555, 580, 582, 632, 666, 682, 703, 705-6, 713, 724, 753-759, 770, 781

Jacob   771
Jacobites   116, 342, 829
Jacobus Clemens non Papa   589
Jalaluddin Rumi   634
James IV, King of Scotland   658, 833
James, Apostle of Christ   274-76
Janequin, Clément   589
Janissaries   104, 157, 427, 461-62, 489, 518, 565, 590, 660, 665-66, 707, 730, 730, 755

Janus Lascaris   421, 713
Japheth   723
Jean de Fumel   703, 706
Jean de la Forest   713, 722, 724, 758
Jean de Valette   538, 587
Jean Lemaire de Belges   458
Jeddah   324-25, 335, 362
Jeremiah   628-29, 739
Jerome, church father   108, 679
Jerusalem   8, 29, 50, 82, 109, 113, 115-17, 273, 286, 309, 324-25, 339, 362, 475, 544, 592, 594-96, 605, 609, 638, 642, 670, 706, 709, 715, 790, 829
Jesuits, *see* Society of Jesus   148, 337, 391-92, 715
Jesus Christ   15, 19-20, 35-36, 46, 56-57, 82, 98, 104, 108, 116-17, 132, 210, 231, 235, 238, 254-55, 262, 275-76, 324, 356, 370, 398, 400-2, 426, 474, 494, 585, 623, 627, 633-34, 641, 647-51, 661, 669-71, 677-78, 687, 690, 695, 713-14, 719, 723, 735-36, 743-44, 747, 749, 768, 769-72, 828-29, 836, 863, 865
Jiménez de Cisneros, Francisco, Archbishop of Toledo   4, 5, 49, 51, 52, 57, 58, 61, 63-65, 76, 80, 85, 100, 170
Joachim de Fiori   389
Joanes, Joan de   145
João II, King of Portugal   318
João III, King of Portugal   126, 329, 332, 336, 339, 347, 358, 386
John of Antioch   828
John of Austria   283, 589, 847
John of Damascus   9, 642, 749, 863
John the Baptist   401
John Hesronita   15
John the Nestorian   669
John Zápolya, King of Hungary   103
John Zonaras   830
Jonson, Ben   824
Jorge de Montemayor   191, 193
José Arávigo (Zumilla)   122, 123
Joshua, Book of   739
Jovio, Paulo, *see also* Paulo Giovio   141-42, 154, 215, 268, 329-30, 336, 424, 426, 433, 457, 462, 466, *484-91*, 518-19, 571-72, 578-79, 700, 712, 720, 781, 838
Juan Agüero (or Juan Remón) de Trasmiera   312-14, 316
Juan de Albotodo   265
Juan Andrés; Ibn ʿAbdallāh   79-84, 85, 87, 90, 121, 170-74, 510
Juan B. Sánchez   265
Juan Bautista Jerónimo Anyés   *144-49*

Juan de la Plaza 265
Juan de Ribera 7, 209, 213, 254
Juan de Rojas 240
Juan de Segovia 65, 87, 133
Juan Gabriel of Teruel 28-32, 89, *415-419*
Judaism 57, 82, 160, 210, 240, 266, 336, 387, 402, 633, 654, 671, 678, 694, 723, 744, 759, 816, 818, 828, 831
Judas 769
Judeoconversos 233

Ka'b ibn al-Ashraf 640-41
Kabbalah 713
Kappel, Second War of 627, 675, 746
Kerle, Jacobus de 589, 590
Khadīja 640
Kharūf, Muḥammad ibn Abī l-Faḍl 126, 130, 133
Kilwa 300, 308-9, 314, 362, 392
King James Bible 772, 861
Knights Hospitaller (Order of Malta) 538, 587
Knights of Malta 6, 538
Knights of St John 151, 433, 462, 565
Knox, John 764-65
Kochi 369
Korea 736
al-Ksar al-Kbir, Battle of, *see* Battle of the Three Kings, Battle of Alcazar, Battle of al-Qaṣr al-Kabīr 248, 259-60, 262, 383, 843, 847
Kyd, Thomas *821-825*, 836, 838

Lafayette, Mme de 196
Laguna, Andrés *137-143*, 179
Lala Mustafa Pasha 584-85
Lanfranco, Giovanni 478
Langbaijiao 369
Laonicus Chalcocondyles 9, 578, 768, 781, 817
Lange, Johann 37
Lassus, Orlande de 589
Laval, Antoine de 510
Layolle, Francesco de 589
Leão, Gaspar de *386-90*
Leest, Anton van 769-60
Leo X, pope 421, 423-24, 434, 440, 484, 512-14, 518, 523
Leo Africanus, *see* Al-Ḥasan ibn Muḥammad al-Wazzān al-Fāsī 29, 283, 285, 286, 290, 417, *439-49*, 524, 533, 720, 780-81
Lepanto, Battle of (1571) 1, 230-31, 233, 283, 286, 377, 383, 390, 558, 563, 572, 577-78, 580, 584, 587-90, 598, 847
Levi ben Gherson 525
Ləbnä Dəngəl, King of Ethiopia 334, 336
Lisbon 225, 260, 297, 309, 318, 326, 335, 337, 339, 351, 358, 370, 372-73, 376, 381, 387, 498, 545, 844
Litell, Thomas 701
Lithuania 332, 651
Livy 126, 360, 568, 790
Llull, Ramon 133
Locke, John 20, 23, 860
López de Gómara, Francisco *150-53*
López de Yanguas, Hernán *107-14*
Lopo Soares de Albergaria 300, 360
Lorenzo de' Medici 397, 400, 456, 464-65
Louis II, King of Hungary 97, 103
Louis IX, King of France 177
Louis XII, King of France 410, 423, 450
Luca de Armenia *538-41*
Luis de Góngora 195
Luis Fajardo 273
Lully, Jean-Baptiste 478, 598
Luna, Miguel de 251, 273-75
Luther, Martin 23, 103, 236, 238, 332, 485, 627, 631-33, 639, 651, 680, 682, 686-87, 696, 717, 734-35, 740, 746, 768, 771, 863
Lutheranism and Lutherans 5, 208, 232-33, 330, 485, 673, 686, 732, 734, 746-47, 864

Machamet (Muḥammad) 621-22
Machiavelli, Niccolò 389, *410-14*, 430, 433, 462, 557, 560-61, 584, 779
Macone (Muḥammad) 476, 597
Madagascar 301
Mafamede (Muḥammad) 342
Magellan, Ferdinand 529, 798, 800
magic 252, 255-56, 397-98, 474, 595-97, 624, 736, 790-91, 828
Mahomet, Mahomete, Mahometh (Muḥammad) 18, 20, 22, 174, 641, 690, 693-95, 769-71, 790, 792, 801, 828, 836-37, 842, 844-45, 855
Mahound, Mahoune (Muḥammad) 835-37, 854-55
Maḥmūd of Ghazna 378
Mahumet (Muḥammad) 35, 171-72, 639-40, 690, 733, 805, 863
Maillard, Jean 589
Maimonides 448, 525
al-Makīn, Jirjis ibn al-'Amīd 15, 21-22
Malabar 300, 315, 351

INDEX OF NAMES 875

Malacca 316, 319, 322-23, 369
Malay Peninsula 369
Malindi 300, 305, 308-9, 314, 316, 392
Malta 6, 11, 538, 549, 587, 755
Malta, Siege of 11, 377, 539-40, 548, 550, 563-65, 572, 587-89, 811
Mamluks 8, 316, 324, 335, 405, 407, 462, 475, 488, 610, 613, 660, 665-66, 728-29
Mancebo de Arévalo 4, *159-68*
Mandeville, John 13, 620, 622-24, 801
Manichaeans 400-1
Mantino, Jacob (ben Samuel) 440, *523-527*
Manuel I, King of Portugal, *see also* el-Rei D. Manuel 297-98, 300-1, 308-9, 312, 318-19, 322-26, 332, 334-37, 358, 389, 405
Manuel, Byzantine emperor 427
Mar Thoma Christians 300, 309
Marcello II, pope 552
Marco Polo 533
Mark of Toledo 27, 29, 33
Marlowe, Christopher 9, 726, *808-14*, 821, 823, 833, 835-36, 838-39
Mármol Carvajal, Luis del 261, *282-93*
Maronites 15, 116, 342
Marracci, Ludovico 31-33
Marrakesh 244-45, 259, 261-62, 286
Martinengo, Nestore *582-86*
martyr, martyrdom 97, 250, 252-53, 257, 273-74, 285, 291-92, 315, 361, 545, 585, 642, 664, 679, 765, 767-68
Mary I, Queen of England 689, 797-98, 800, 802
Mary, the Virgin 64, 87, 98, 108, 253, 275-76, 428, 595, 713, 718, 723
mass 5, 76, 94, 121, 213, 538, 589, 626
mass baptism, mass conversion 51, 75, 289, 639
Mateus, Ethiopian ambassador 334
Matisse, Henri 196
Mdina, Malta 538, 540
Mecca 14, 82, 163, 165, 300, 309, 324-25, 342, 362, 382, 405, 407, 439, 517, 642, 755, 805-6, 829-30
Medina 342, 362, 382, 403, 407, 439, 517, 642, 805-6, 830
Mehmed II, Ottoman sultan 9, 420, 424-26, 458, 461, 492, 544, 556, 558, 571, 617, 701, 791
Melanchthon, Philipp 183, 332, 490, 650-51, 680-81, 686, 746, 863
Membré, Michele 432, *498-500*
Menavino, Giovanni Antonio 184, 426, 429, 433-35, 462-63, 465, *512-522*, 571, 578, 758
Mendoça, Gavy de 262
Messiah and Messianism 56, 60-61, 222, 298, 325, 377, 401, 669, 677-78
Mestre Afonso 343, *376-80*
Methodius 639, 642, 771, 773
millenarians and millenarianism 16, 109, 642, 676
millet system 666
Minab 372
missionaries 14, 35, 75, 372, 387, 714, 831
Mocenigo, Pietro 557-59, 578
Mohács, Battle of 97, 103, 105, 632, 655, 658, 661
Mohamed, Mohammad, Mohammed (Muḥammad) 183, 453, 459, 681, 855
Mohammedan, *see* Muslim 305, 617, 651, 672-73
Molla Kabiz 713-14
Moluccas, Portuguese discovery of 297
Mombasa 305, 314, 383
Monclaro, Francisco de 357, *391-394*
Monomotapa 356-57, 391-93
Montaigne, Michel Eyquem de *815-20*
Montemayor, Jorge de 191-95
Montesquieu, Charles-Louis 510
Monteverdi, Claudio 598
Moors, Moros, Mouros 14, 21, 56, 76, 80, 85, 107, 116, 124, 126, 130-32, 147-48, 157, 163, 184, 192-97, 209-10, 212, 215, 233, 259, 266, 271, 283, 286, 297, 300, 305, 309, 314-15, 335-37, 342, 356, 370, 378, 381-83, 392-93, 415, 452, 464, 546, 549, 560-61, 563, 708, 722, 756, 842, 844-47
Morales, Baltazar de *268-72*
Moriscos 4-7, 45, 47, 51-52, 63-67, 69, 83, 94, 119, 121-22, 132-33, 145-45, 147-49, 159-63, 165-66, 168-70, 173-74, 194-97, 210, 212-13, 221-22, 224-27, 233, 236, 238, 240, 252-57, 265-66, 273-76, 282-83, 285, 289-92, 313, 316, 509
Morocco 1, 6, 129, 209, 244-45, 247-48, 261-62, 282-83, 286, 360, 381, 383, 439, 442-43, 548, 790, 793, 798, 803-4, 824, 844, 847, 856
Moses, prophet 11, 19, 29-30, 132, 590, 689, 742-43, 801
Mount Athos 184, 706-7
Mount Lebanon 706
Mount Sinai 309, 617, 706
Mount Valparaíso, *see* Sacromonte 274
Mozambique 305, 308-9, 314, 370, 381, 391

876   INDEX OF NAMES

Mucametto (Muḥammad)   440, 443
Mudéjars   43, 45, 47, 50, 52, 57, 61, 73,
    79-80, 195, 289, 415
Mufti of Oran   4, 67-72
Mughals and the Mughal Empire   353,
    361, 478
Muḥammad al-Qaysī   43-47
Muḥammad al-Shaykh, Saʿdī sultan   259,
    439
Muḥammad, Prophet, see also
    Machamet, Macone, Mafamede,
    Mahomet, Mahomete, Mahometes,
    Mahometh, Mahound, Mahoune,
    Mahumet, Mahumetes, Mohamed,
    Mohammad, Mohammed, Mucametto;
    nygromancer   9, 11-12, 14, 16, 18-19,
    21-22, 25-26, 30-32, 34, 46, 56-57, 69,
    82-83, 88, 98, 122, 129-30, 132, 152, 160, 171,
    210-11, 221-22, 235-38, 252-53, 261-62, 266,
    286, 315, 324, 342, 353, 361-62, 390, 401,
    407, 431, 440, 443, 464, 495, 509, 517, 546,
    571-72, 597, 612, 617, 620, 623-24, 634,
    638-43, 648, 650-51, 659, 661, 668-72,
    676-78, 681, 683, 687, 708, 714, 717-20,
    722, 735, 743, 749, 767, 769, 779-80, 790,
    805, 816-18, 828-31, 836, 846, 855, 863
Muḥammad, biography of   11-13, 16, 30,
    82-83, 171, 235, 252-53, 407, 509, 513, 546,
    617, 639-41, 722, 769, 828-29
Muir, Sir William   641
Mulay Ḥasan, Emir of Tunis   282, 484
Mulay Aḥmad al-Manṣūr; Muly Mahamet
    Seth   845
Muly Molocco, see ʿAbd al-Malik   243-45,
    793, 844, 846
Mumbai   316, 369
Münster, Sebastian   184, 332, 767
Murad I, Ottoman sultan   460
Murad II, Ottoman sultan   420, 460, 701
Murad III, Ottoman sultan   864
Muslim ibn Ḥajjāj   87

Najaf   342
Nanni da Viterbo, Giovanni   141
Nashe, Thomas   826, 831
Naṣrid dynasty   1, 2, 165, 192, 194, 196, 275
Nathan the Wise   791
de Navarra, Francisco   213
Nebrija, Antonio de   73, 75, 207
Negroponte, Turkish conquest of   425,
    556-57, 559, 571, 573
New Christians (newly converted Muslims
    in Spain)   51-52, 61, 63-66, 94, 255, 257,
    266, 285, 388

New World   1, 101, 219, 485, 661, 736
Nicea, Council of   647
Nicene Creed   734
Nicholas of Cusa   133, 238, 612, 651, 682,
    719, 723, 781-82
Nicholas de Lyra   771
Nicholas Moffan of Burgundy   791
Nicolas-Claude Fabri de Pereisc   510
Nicolay, Nicolas de   519, 709, 752-63
Nicosia   498, 561
Nieto, Fray Luis   247-49
Niger, Franciscus   700
Nile   323, 342, 361, 532
Nizam Shah   389
Noah   26, 669, 670, 723
Notstock, Joshua   15
Núñez Muley, Francisco   290, 292
Nygromancer, Muḥammad as   621-24, 640

Obregón, Lope   169-75, 211
Oecolampadius, Johannes   645, 675
Oguz tribe   425
Old Christians   64, 87, 313
Oldradus da Ponte   236, 238
Oporinus, Johannes   509, 672, 675, 679-81,
    714, 718, 759, 764, 768
Oran   49, 67, 152, 268, 270-71
Orozco, Alonso de   219-23
Ormuz, see Hormuz   301, 314-16, 319,
    322-23, 339, 341, 370-73, 376-77, 498
Orta, Garcia da   346, 351-55
Osman I, Ottoman sultan   142, 460, 544,
    578, 770
Othello   842

Padilla, Pedro de   195
pagans and paganism   8, 21, 56, 148, 182,
    194, 336, 383, 401, 476, 546, 597, 598,
    633-34, 669-70, 681, 690, 736, 743, 818,
    830, 854
Painter, William   788-95
Paix des Dames, see Peace of Cambrai
    103, 109
Pannonia (Hungary)   658, 659, 661, 666
Paraclete   46, 132, 134, 669
Paradise   14, 31, 57, 82, 122, 129, 238, 253,
    256, 390, 517, 670, 708, 817, 830
Paul III, pope   140, 157, 336, 421, 485, 506,
    523,
Paul, St   46, 183, 440
Paul the Deacon   830
Peace of Cambrai   103, 109
Peele, George   823-824, 837, 841-849
Percy, William   174, 837

INDEX OF NAMES

Pérez de Ayala, Martín *207-14*
Pérez de Hita, Ginés 196
Persia and Persians 1, 5, 16, 21, 30, 35, 104, 286, 297, 301, 309, 313, 315, 324-25, 336, 339, 341, 352, 361-62, 370, 372-73, 376, 378-79, 382, 407, 424-25, 430-32, 439, 465, 498-99, 510, 533, 546, 571, 595, 617, 754-56, 800-1, 805-6, 829, 838
Peter the Venerable 23, 34, 98, 133, 171, 681
Peterzano, Simone 478
Petrarch 165, 492, 495, 510, 553, 557, 568
Philip I, King of Portugal, *see* Philip II, King of Spain
Philip II, King of Spain 5-7, 101, 138, 155-56, 174, 208-9, 225, 231, 233, 236, 243, 252, 259-60, 273, 283, 285, 291, 543, 572-73, 588-89, 844, 847
Philip III, King of Spain 7, 563
Piccinni, Niccolò 478
Piccolomini, Aeneas Silvio, *see also* Pius II 329, 458
Pietro Martire d'Anghiera 224, 529, 720, 797, 800
pilgrims 109, 117, 165, 181, 325, 342, 373, 402, 407, 517, 605-6, 609-10, 612-13, 709, 733, 755, 805
Pitts, Joseph 806
Pius II, pope 329-30, 458-59, 463, 571, 578,
Pius V, pope 233, 584, 589
Pococke, Edward 15, 17, 19, 21-23
Poland 332, 553, 577, 651, 675
polemic, anti-Catholic 772, 780
polemic, anti-Christian 43, 46-47, 275-76, 647-48, 650
polemic, anti-Muslim 34, 51, 236, 238-39, 253, 256-57, 667, 681-82, 863
Polygamy 57, 262, 266, 465, 546, 669
Portuguese State in India 314, 316, 318-19, 321-27, 335-36, 339, 343, 347-48, 358, 360-62, 369-70, 372-73, 382-83, 387, 391, 393, 405-6, 532, 546
Postel, Guillaume 10, 13, 27, 182, 185, 510, 529, 533, 651, 709, *712-25*, 758-59, 781-82, 818
Poussin, Nicolas 598
Prester John 8, 297, 305, 324, 389, 475, 792, 798, 800-1
propaganda, anti-Muslim 83, 434, 818
propaganda, anti-Turkish 142, 433, 509, 580
Psalms, Book of 64, 125, 589, 654, 687, 713, 734, 739
Pseudo-Methodius 639, 642, 771, 773

Purchas, Samuel 13-14, 23, 373
Purim Sebastiano; Purim of Christians 248

Qāḍī 'Iyāḍ 172
Qalandars 758
Qā'it Bey, Mamluk sultan 617
al-Qaṣr al-Kabīr, Battle of 248, 259-60, 262, 383, 843, 847
Qizilbāsh 379
Quíloa, *see* Kilwa 300, 308-9, 314, 362, 392
Qur'an, Alcoran, Coran, Alchoran, Alchorane, Koran 4, 9, 10, 11-24, 25-37, 43, 46, 51, 58, 65, 79-83, 85, 87, 89-91, 94, 119, 122, 126, 130-33, 157, 163, 165, 169-73, 210-11, 222, 252-53, 276, 400-2, 415-18, 440, 473, 507-10, 574, 612, 622-24, 627, 634, 639, 641-42, 650-51, 667, 669-70, 672, 675, 677-83, 690, 693-94, 708, 713-14, 717-19, 723, 728, 736, 743-44, 747, 749-50, 768-69, 781, 801, 811, 829-31, 863

Rainolds, William *860-65*
Ramadan 612, 722
Ramberti, Benedetto 571
Ramírez de Alba, Pedro *93-95*
Ramon Martí 133
Ramusio, Giovanni Battista 332, 430, 442, *528-37*
Raphael 450
Rath, Martin 612
Reconquista 2, 3, 8, 360, 361, 780, 802, 835
Red Sea 309, 319, 323-25, 336, 362, 617
Redon, Odilon 478
Renan, Ernest 643
Revelation, Book of 52, 390, 693-95, 696-97, 749, 765, 769, 771
Reyos Catolicos, *see* Catholic monarchs 2, 49, 50, 52, 55, 58, 60, 80, 96, 192, 253, 255, 282, 289, 301
Rhodes 98, 103, 151, 425, 433, 462, 573, 587, 605-6, 658, 665-66, 694, 707, 709, 822-23
Ribera, Juan de, Archbishop of Valencia 7, 148, 209, 212-13, 254
Riccoldo da Monte di Croce 51, 58, 65, 98, 133, 171, 173, 253, 401-2, 639, 641, 651, 682, 719
Richer, Christophe 571, 578, 682, 682, 709, 781-82
Robert of Ketton 26-27, 29, 34-35, 172, 253, 417, 509, 681
Rocca, Vicente *176-78*, 184

INDEX OF NAMES

Rome, sack of (1527)   440, 485, 423, 574, 658
Ross, Alexander   18, 20, 23, 36
Rossi, Luigi   478
Rossini, Giochino   610
Rūm; *Rumes*   316, 323, 353
Ryer, André du   35-36

Sá, João de   304, 308
Sabellico, Marc'Antonio   329, 557-58, 578, 830
Sacromonte   222, 250, 265, 273-76, 283
Safavid dynasty   1, 5, 322, 341-43, 362, 378-79, 382, 430-31, 498-500, 512, 724
Ṣägga Zä'ab   336-37
Sagundino, Niccola   141, 424, 459, 578
Saidnaya, Our Lady of, monastery   617
Saint German, Christopher   *637-44*, 773
Saladin   555, 596, 790-91, 793
Sami people   332, 335-37
San Antonio, Cristóbal de   170
Sansovino, Francesco   177, 423, 457, 490, *567-81*
Sarah and 'Saracens'   829
Savonarola, Girolamo   236, 238, 399, 410, 456, 589
Sayf ibn 'Umar al-Tamīmī   46
Sa'dī dynasty   244, 259, 261, 282, 286
Sa'īd ibn al-Baṭrīq   15
Scaliger, Joseph Juste   10, 13, 34, 510
Sebastian, King of Portugal   247-48, 260, 262, 383, 388-90, 392, 843-45
Selden, John   15, 17, 510
Selim I, Ottoman sultan   157, 177, 412, 425-26, 432, 458, 462, 465-66, 488, 512, 520, 544, 578, 701, 752, 758, 838
Selim II, Ottoman sultan   230, 245, 548, 574
Sepulveda, Juan Gines de   *100-6*
Seraglio   181, 427, 435, 517-19, 730, 755, 757
Serbia   420, 459-60, 701
Sergius, *see* Baḥīrā   57, 171, 640, 669, 769, 828, 863
Servetus, Michael   *645-53*
Severinus II, pope   690
Seville   51, 55-58, 61, 64, 125-26, 229, 259, 261, 301, 673
Shah Ismail   322, 324, 430-32, 712
Shakespeare, William   701, 788-89, 798, 808, 811, 824, 833, 839, 842, 847-48
Shī'ī Islam   69, 342, 353, 362, 499-500, 533, 712, 806
Shute, John   *726-31*, 792
Sicily   1, 282, 538, 542, 560-61, 587, 589

Sigismund I, King of Poland   515
Silveira, Gonçalo da   356, 392
Simancas, Diego de   *232-42*
Sinai   309, 605, 617, 706
Sionita, Gabriel   15, 17, 22
Sīra   13, 82, 172
Sixtus V, pope   274
Skanderbeg, George   424, 461, 465-466, 726, 728-729
Smith, Henry   *826-32*
Sobrino   472-73, 477
Society of Jesus, *see* Jesuits   148, 337, 391-92, 715
Socotra   314, 316, 319
sodomy   9, 16, 142, 183, 429, 504, 516, 729, 757
Sofala   301, 308, 312, 314
Spandugino, Teodoro   184, *420-38*, 458, 461-65, 519, 571, 758
Spenser, Edmund   701, 839, *850-59*
spice trade   298, 300-1, 319, 322-23
Spiesshaymer, Johan, *see* Cuspinian, Johan   141-42, 701, 768
St German, Christopher   *637-44*, 773
St Paul   46, 183, 440
Stubbe, Henry   18-19, 23, 831
Süleyman II, Ottoman sultan   565
Süleyman I, the Magnificent; Solyman, Ottoman sultan   97-98, 103, 112-13, 115, 142, 152, 156-57, 177, 185, 378, 425, 428, 432, 485, 488-89, 507, 509, 514, 544, 548, 574, 578, 587, 655, 658, 665-66, 701, 705, 707, 712, 714, 724, 728, 754, 770-71, 757, 782, 790, 792, 823
Sutcliffe, Matthew   864-65
al-Suyūṭī, Jalālal-Dīn   32, 35

Tabriz   341, 342, 432, 617
Ṭahmāsp (Thomas), shah of Persia   378, 425, 430, 431, 432, 499-500
Talavera, Hernando de, Archbishop of Granada   3, 5, 51, 52, 58, *60-66*, 73, 76, 80, 93, 145, 148
Talmud   47, 131, 523, 669, 694, 863
Tamburlaine   9, 460, 728, 809-12, 824, 836, 838-39
Tanco de Fregenal, Vasco Diaz de   *154-58*, 490, 542, 544, 546
taqiyya   4, 69, 362, 443
Tartars   425, 432, 439, 473, 580, 617, 673, 779
Tasso, Torquato   493, 496, *592-601*, 821
Teixeira, Pedro   373
Temporal, Jean   443

INDEX OF NAMES

Tenreiro, António *339-345*, 377
Termagant 854, 855
Tesifón 274
Thevet, André 709, 753, 760
Thomas à Kempis 160, 167-68
Thomas Aquinas 54, 56, 58, 780
Three Kings, Battle of the, *see* Battle of al-Ksar al-Kbir 248, 259-60, 262, 383, 843, 847
three rings, parable of the 790, 791, 793
Tiepolo, Giovanni Battista 478, 598
Timoneda, Juan de 195
Torres, Diego de *259-64*, 287
Treaty of Cambrai 103, 109
Treaty of Crépy 705
Trinity 21, 56, 98, 597, 641, 645, 648, 650-51, 749, 828, 863
Tripoli 6, 547-48, 587, 755
Truce of Nice (1538) 424, 515
Tunis, capture of (1535) 5, 102, 130, 224, 282, 425, 485, 494-95
Turan Shah I, ruler of Hormuz 371-72
Turcica 12, 21, 509, 635

Ulloa, Alfonso de *542-51*
Ulloa Pereira, Juan de 179
Unico Aretino 450, 452, 594
Unitarians and Unitarianism 641, 648, 651-52, 863
Uzūn Ḥasan, ruler of the Āqquyūnlu Turks 378, 432, 533

Valladolid controversy 101
Van Dyck, Antoon 598
Varthema, Ludovico de 13, 22, *405-9*, 533, 798, 800, 801, 804-6, 830
Vega, Lope de 195, 263
Velho, Álvaro 301, 304
Vendome, Pietro Gentile di 572
Venus 194, 383, 640, 829, 835,
Verdelot, Philippe 589
Vienna, sieges of 11, 102, 103, 105, 112, 141, 457, 487, 494, 590, 632, 643, 655, 735-36
Villalón, Cristóbal de 179
Villalpando, Antonio García de *49-53*
Villegas, Antonio de 191, 193-94, 195
Vitoria, Francisco de 130-31, 207, 386
Vivaldi, Antonio 478, 590, 598
Vives, Juan-Luis 103, 105, 119, 132, 133, 144, 170, 211, 238, 253, 332, *654-74*, 682

al-Wansharīsī, Aḥmad 67, 69-70
Wars of Religion 704, 817
Wheelock, Abraham 18, 23
Widmanstetter, Johann Albrecht von 27
Worde, Wynkyn de 13, *620-25*, 644

Yusuf Adil Shah, Sultan of Bijapur 323, 361, 389

al-Zamakhsharī 29, 172
Zamorin, King of Calicut 305
Zanzibar 301
Zechendorff, Johannes 27
Zeebout, Ambrosius *616-19*
Zumilla (José Arávigo) 122, 123
Zwingli, Huldrych *626-29*, 675, 736, 746, 863

Index of Titles

Numbers in italics indicate a main entry.

Ab urbe condita 126, 360
El Abencerraje y la hermosa Jarifa 191, *191-206*
An account of all that took place at Famagusta, see *Relatione di tutto il successo di Famagosta* 582, *583-86*
Account of a chronicle of the kings of Hormuz, see *Relaçam da cronica dos reys Dormuz* 370, 371, *371-75*
An account of the expedition of the priests of the Society of Jesus with Francisco Barreto on the conquest of Monomotapa, see *Relaçaõ do viagem que fizeraõ os Pes da Companhia de Jesus com Francisco Barreto na conquista do Monomotapa* 391, *392-94*
Account of the origin and succession of the Sharifs, see *Relación del origen y suceso de los Xarifes* 259, *261-64*
Account of Persia, see *Relazione di Persia* 498, *499-500*
Account of the war of Cyprus and events of the naval battle of Lepanto, see *Relación de la guerra de Chipre y suceso de la batalla naval de Lepanto* *230-31*
Account of the wars of Barbary and the feats and death of King Sebastian, see *Relación de las guerras de Berbería y del suceso y muerte del Rey D. Sebastián* 247, *247-49*
Actes and monuments, see *Foxe's Book of martyrs* 696, 765, 767-74
Actes of Englysh votaryes 690, 695
Ad Carolum V.... Io. Genesii Sepulvedae cohortatio, see *Cohortatio Oratio ad Carolum Quintum ut bellum suscipiat in Turcas* 100, *103-6*
Ad nominis Christiani socios consultatio 678-80, 681, 683
Ad patriam *539-41*
Ad canticum Moyses 590
Africa Portuguesa 263
Against the pseudo-dialecticians 655
Against the religion of the Saracens, see *Contra legem Saracenorum* 401, 402, 641
L'Alcoran de Mahomet 35, 36

Alcorani seu legis Mahometi et evangelistarum concordiae Liber 714, *717-18*
Alcorani textus universus 27, 28, 31, 32, 33
Alcorano di Macometto 34, 35, 507, *508-11*
Alphonsus of Aragon, see *The comicall history of Alphonsus, King of Aragon* 823, *834-37*, 838
De anima 525, 780
Antialcorano, see *Libro llamado Antialcorán* 119, *121-23*, 124, 144, 170, 211, 390
The antiquary 855
Anwār al-tanzīl wa-asrār al-ta'wīl 35
Apocalype of Pseudo-Methodius 771
Apodeixeis historiōn 9, 578, 768, 781
Apologeticus martyrum 253
Apologia pro libro de iustis belli causis 101
The apology of Johan Bale agaynste a ranke Papyst 690, 695
Armida (Dvořák) 598
Armida (Haydn) 598
Armida (Rossini) 598
Armida al campo d'Egitto (Vivaldi) 598
Armide (Gluck) 598
Armide (Lully) 598
The art of gently learning Arabic, see *Arte para ligeramente saber la lengua arauiga* 52, *75-78*, 213
The art of war 410
Arte para ligeramente saber la lengua arauiga 52, *75-78*, 213
Ásia, Décadas da (Barros) 343, 358, *359-368*, 372, 545
L'Asia del signor Giovanni di Barros (Ulloa) *545-47*
Asiae Europaeque elegantissima description 459
L'assedio et la guerra di Malta fatta dell'anno MDLXV 548
Dell'assedio di Scutari 571
Les aventures du dernier Abencerage 196

Los baños de Argel 6
The battle of Alcazar 823, 824, 841, 842, *843-49*

INDEX OF TITLES 881

De bello a Christianis contra barbaros 594
De bello Turcis inferendo 667
Bellum Cambaicum 316
Bibliotheca Hispana nova 89
Bibliotheca universalis 682
Bibliothecae graecae 449
Bibliothecarius quadripartitus 449
The book known as Against the Qur'an, see *Libro llamado Antialcorán* 119, *121-23*, 124, 144, 170, 211, 390
Book of Kings, see *Shahnameh* 372-73
The book of John Mandeville 801
The book of the courtier, see *Il libro del cortegiano* 450, 451, *451-55*, 510
Book of the Gentile and the three wise men 672
Book of the history of the truth of the Gospel 275, 276
Book of the origin and succession of the Turkish Empire, see *Libro dell'origine et successione dell'imperio de' Turchi* (Ulloa) *544-45*, 546
A book on the agreement between the Qur'an, or the law of Muḥammad, and the Evangelicals, see *Alcorani seu legis Mahometi et evangelistarum concordiae Liber* 714, *717-18*
Breve compendio de nuestra santa ley y sunna 159, 160, 161, *162-64*, 165, 166, 168
Breve relacion del principio del Reyno Harmuz y de sus reyes 373
Brief summary of our holy law and sunna, see *Breve compendio de nuestra santa ley y sunna* 159, 160, 161, *162-64*, 165, 166, 168

Le Cadi dupe 590
Calvino-turcismus 861, *862-65*
Canon of medicine, see *Al-qānūn fī l-ṭibb* 525
Cantemus Domino pro victoria navali contra Turcas (Infantas) 589
Canterbury tales 855
Cantio octo vocum de sacro foedere contra Turcas (de Kerle) 590
Canzone sulla vittoria dell'Armata della Santissima Lega contro la Turchesca 563
Ad Carolum V. Imperatorem invictissimum 100, *103-6*
Carro de dos vidas 54, *55-59*
Carta das novas 334, 335

Carta de el-Rei D. Manuel ao Rei Catholico 297, *300-3*
Cartas de Afonso de Albuquerque *321-27*
Cartilla y breu instructió de la doctrina Christiana 213
Castillo inexpunable defensorio de la fee *97-99*, 113
Catecheses mystagogicae pro aduenis ex secta Mahometana (Lorca) 211, 250, *251-58*
Catechism for the instruction of the newly converted among the Moors, see *Catecismo para instrucción de los nuevamente convertidos de Moros* (Ayala) *209-12*, 213
Catechism of Sacromonte, see *Catecismo del Sacromonte* 222, 265, *265-67*
Catechisms of instruction for those coming from the Muḥammadan sect, see *Catecheses mystagogicae pro aduenis ex secta Mahometana* (Lorca) 211, 250, *251-58*
Catecismo para instrucción de los nuevamente convertidos de Moros (Ayala) *209-12*, 213
Catecismo del Sacromonte 222, 265, *265-67*
Cathecismo prouechoso hecho por el Padre Fray Alonso de Orozco, see *Useful catechism written by Friar Alonso de Orozco* *221-23*
Catholic institutes, see *Institutiones Catholicae* (Simancas) *235-42*
De catholicis institutionibus 237, 239
Católica impugnación 61, 64
La celestina 165
Chanson de Roland 472, 854
Christian dialogues against the Muhammadan sect and against the obstinacy of the Jews, see *Diálogos christianos contra la secta mahomética y contra la pertinacia de los judíos* 119, *123-24*, 144, 672
Christian doctrine, see *Doctrina christiana* (Alba) 93, *94-95*
Christian doctrine in Arabic and Castilian for the instruction for the newly converted in the Kingdom of Valencia, see *Doctrina christiana en lengua arábiga y castellana para la instrucción de los nuevamente convertidos del Reino de Valencia* (Ayala) *212-14*
De Christiana religione et fidei pietate 398, *400-4*

INDEX OF TITLES

Christianismi restitutio 645, 648, *650-53*
Chronica 330
Chronica de Abdel Melech 243, *244-46*
Chronica do Felicissimo Rei Dom Emanuel 261, 344, 345, 337
Chronica de la vida y admirables hechos del muy alto y poderoso Señor Muley Abd el Melech 243, *244-46*
The chronicle of the Barbarossas, see *Crónica de los Barbarrojas* *151-53*
Chronicle of the life and remarkable deeds of the most high and powerful lord Prince Abdel Melech, see *Chronica de la vida y admirables hechos del muy alto y poderoso Señor Muley Abd el Melech* 243, *244-46*
Cinque canti 470
I cinque libri della legge, religione la vita de' Turchi, see *Trattato de costume et vita de Turchi* 177, 434, 512, 513, *514-22*, 571, 758
Cohortatio, see *Oratio ad Carolum Quintum ut bellum suscipiat in Turcas* 100, *103-6*
Collectio Toletana 171, 172, 173, 681
Colloquia 132, 635, 671
Colloquies on the simples, see *Coloquios dos simples* 351, *352-55*
Colloquium heptaplomeres 776, 779, 780, 781
Coloquios dos simples 351, *352-55*
Il combattimento di Tancredi e Clorinda 598
Comedia 492, 507
Comentarios 316
The comicall history of Alphonsus, King of Aragon 823, *834-37*, 838
Commentarii delle cose de' Turchi 457, 490
Commentario delle cose de' Turchi (Giovio) 154, 215, 329, 330, *487-91*, 571, 574, 579, 700, 838
Commentarius de vera et falsa religione 626
Commentary, see *Tafsira* (Young man of Arévalo) 159, 160, 161, *165-67*
Commentary on matters of the Turks, see *Commentario delle cose de' Turchi* (Giovio) 154, 215, 329, *487-91*, 571, 574, 579, 700, 838
Commentary on Scanderbeg 792
Commentary on true and false religion, see *Commentarius de vera et falsa religione* 626
Compendium Alchorani 27

The compleat history of the Turks from their origin in the year 755 to the year 1718 36
Conclusions of the men of learning, see *Determinação de letrados* *356-57*
De concordia et discordia in humano genere 104
El Conde Lucanor 194
De conditione vitae Christianorum sub Turca 104, 656, *663-68*, 672
On conflicts in Europe and the Turkish war, see *De Europae dissidiis et bello Turcico* 104, 105, 655, *657-63*, 666, 667
Confusión o confutación de la secta mahomética (Andrés) 15, 79, 80, *81-84*, 170
Confutación del alcorán y secta mahometana, sacado de sus propios libros (Obregón) 169, *170-75*, 211
Confutatio alcorani (Riccoldo da Monte di Croce) 13, 51, 58, 65, 171, 253, 401, 402, 639, 641, 651, 682
Congregati sunt inimici nostri 588
Conquista de las indias de Persia & Arabia que fizo la armada del rey don Manuel de Portugal 301-2, *313-17*
Consilia bellica 667
Consultation to the people of the Christian name, see *Ad nominis Christiani socios consultatio* *678-80*, 681, 683
Contra legem Saracenorum, see *Confutatio alcorani* (Riccoldo da Monte di Croce) 13, 51, 58, 65, 171, 253, 401, 402, 639, 641, 682
Contra perfidiam Mahometi 171, 172
Corpus Islamo-latinum 509
cortegiano, Il libro del 450, 451, *451-55*, 510
cosmographia et geographia de Affrica, Libro de la 283, 285, 440, *442-48*, 449, 533, 781
Costumi et i modi particolari della vita de' Turchi *502-5*, 571
A courtlie contouersie of Cupid's cautels 822
courtier, The book of the, see *Il libro del cortegiano* 450, 451, *451-55*, 510
Cribratio Alcorani 612, 781
La croisade pacifique, see *De professione Arabica militiaque constituenda adversus Machometum* 126, *129-36*
Crónica de los Barbarrojas *151-53*
Cronica dos Reyes de Quiloa 362
Cronica dos reys Dormuz 370, 371, *371-75*

INDEX OF TITLES 883

Cronica generale d'Hispagna et del regno di Valenza 542
Crónicas de D. Manuel e de D. João III até 1533 316
A cruzada pacífica, see *De professione Arabica militiaque constituenda adversus Machometum* 126, 129-36

Da pacem Domine in diebus nostris 589
Décadas da Ásia (Barros) 343, 358, 359-368, 372, 545
Decades (Bullinger) 747
Decades of Asia, see *Décadas da Ásia* (Barros) 343, 358, 359-68, 372, 545
Decades of the Newe Worlde (Eden) 797, 798, 799-804
Decameron 554, 555, 790, 791
Declamationes sex 662
Declaratione delli horrendi segni apparsi in Constantinopoli 141
Dell'arte della guerra 430
Democrates secundus sive de iustis belli causis 101
Democrates sive de honestate disciplinae militari dialogus 101
Démonomanie des sorciers 775, 779, 780
Der Turgg. Von anfang und Ursprung desz Türggischen Gloubens 747, 748-51
Descripción general de África (Carvajal) 261, 283, 285-89, 290
Descriptio Alcahirae urbis 720-21
La descrittione dell'Africa (Leo Africanus) 283, 285, 440, 442-48, 449, 533, 781
Desengano de perdidos 387, 388-90
Determinação de letrados 356-57
Diálogo de las guerras de Orán 268, 270-72
Diálogo entre Pedro Barrantes Maldonado y un cauallero estrangero 215, 216-18
Diálogo entre Pedro de Hurdimalas y Juan de Voto a Dios y Mátalas, see *Viaje de Turquía* 180
Diálogos christianos contra la secta mahomética y contra la pertinacia de los judíos 119, 123-24, 144, 672
Dialogue between Pedro Barrantes Maldonado and a stranger, see *Diálogo entre Pedro Barrantes Maldonado y un cauallero estrangero* 215, 216-18
Dialogue of the wars of Oran, see *Diálogo de las guerras de Orán* 268, 270-72
La Diana 191, 193, 196

Diário da viagem de Vasco da Gama 304-7, 308
Diary of the siege of Malta, see *Verdadera relacion de todo lo que este año de M.D. LXV ha sucedido en la isla de Malta* 564-66
Die Entführung aus dem Serail 590
de diluviis, Liber 780
Discorso della Guerra di Rhodi 571
Disillusion of the lost, see *Desengano de perdidos* 387, 388-90
Disputa con los cristianos 43, 44, 45-48
Disputaçion con los judios 43
Disputationes sive conferentias (Figuerola) 90-91
Dispute with the Christians, see *Disputa con los cristianos* 43, 44, 45-48
Disputes, see *Disputationes sive conferentias* (Figuerola) 90-91
Doctor Faustus 809, 811
Doctrina christiana (Alba) 93, 94-95
Doctrina christiana en lengua arábiga y castellana para la instrucción de los nuevamente convertidos del Reino de Valencia (Ayala) 212-14
de doctrina Mahumet, Liber 171, 669, 670
Don Quixote 6, 193, 196
Dulce bellum inexpertis 103, 632

Ecce quam bonum et quam jucundum habitare fratres in unum 589
Eigentliche Beschreibung 605, 609-11
The embassy of the Great emperor of the Indians, see *Legatio magni Indorum imperatoris* 334-35, 336
Enchiridion Judicum violatae religionis 238-39, 240, 631
Enneades sive rhapsodia historiarum 329
Enneads (Plotinus) 398
Epistle exhortatorye of an Englysh Christyane 690, 692
Epistola ad Christianos 129
Epistolarum familiarum libri XXXVII 329
Les Essais 815, 816, 816-20
Este es el pleyto de los Judios con el perro de Alba 313
De Europae dissidiis et bello Turcico 104, 105, 655, 657-63, 666, 667
Europa heautentimoroume 137
Evagatorium in Terrae Sanctae, Arabiae et Egypti peregrinationem 605, 606, 609, 610, 612-15

884

INDEX OF TITLES

The faerie queene   851, 853-59
The faith, religion and customs of the Ethiopians, see *Fides, religio, moresqve Aethiopvm*   332, 336-38
Farsa de la concordia   107, 109
Farsa dicha Turquesana (Yanguas)   107, 109, 112-14
Fatti di Solimano dopo la presa di Rhodi fino all'anno 1533   571
Fatti illustri del signor Giorgio Scanderbegh   572
Fatti illustri di Selim imperator de Turchi   572
Fatwa del muftí de Orán   67, 68-72
Fides, religio, moresqve Aethiopvm   332, 336-38
The first four books of Oriental journeys and wanderings, see *Les quatre premiers livres des navigations et peregrinations Orientales*   519, 754-63
The first state of Muhametism   22
Five books about the laws, religion and life of the Turks, see *I cinque libri delle legge, religione, et vita de' Turchi*   177, 434, 512, 513, 514-22, 571, 758
For newly converted Muslims, see *Pro Agarenis neophytis*   147-49
Fortalitium fidei   639
Foxe's Book of martyrs   696, 765, 767-74
The frenzy of Orlando, see *Orlando furioso*   195, 463, 464, 469, 470, 471-83, 496

El gallardo español   271
La généalogie du Grant Turc   423, 571
General description of Africa, see *Descripción general de África*   261, 283, 285-89, 290
generatione Mahumet, Liber de   171-72
Gentile and the three wise men, Book of the   672
Geography   343
Gerusalemme conquistata   593, 597
Gerusalemme liberate (Tasso)   496, 592, 593, 594-601
Gl'Annali overo le vite de' principi et signori della casa Othomana   577-81
A godly consultation unto the brethren   679
God's arrow against atheists   827, 827-32
Gonsalus seu de appetenda gloria dialogus   101
Gospel of Barnabas   276
Grammatica classica   10

Guerra de Granada (Mendoza)   225, 226-28, 290-91
Guerra del Regno di Cipro di l'anno 1570   572
Guerras civiles de Granada   196
Guerras de mar del Emperador Carlos V   151
Guzmán de Alfarache   196

Hakluytus posthumus   14
On the harmony of the world, see *De orbis terrae concordia*   27, 714, 717, 718-19, 723-24, 759
Here after foloweth a lytell treatyse agaynst Mahumet and his cursed secte (Saint German)   638, 639-44, 773
Here begynneth a lytell treatyse of the turkes lawe called Alcaron (de Worde)   621-25, 801
Historia   594
La Historia de los amores del valeroso moro Abindarraez y de la hermosa xarifa Aben Cerases   196, 563
historia delle Indie occidentali, Libri della   529
La historia dell'impresa di Tripoli di Barbaria   547-51
Historia del moro y Narváez   193
Historia del rebelión y castigo de los Moriscos del reino de Granada   283, 285, 289-93
Historia di Malta   548
História do descobrimento e conquista da Índia pelos Portugueses   305, 343, 346, 347-50
História do famoso cerco que o Xarife pos a fortaleza de Mazagão no año de 1562   262-63
Historia ecclesiastica   57
La historia general de las Indias   800
Historia Iherosolimitana   594
Historia rerum ubique gestarum locorumque descriptio   329
Historia Turchesca   424, 432
Historia universale dell'origine et imperio de' Turchi (Sansovino)   423, 457, 490, 570-77
Historiae sui temporis   484, 486, 518, 578, 781
Historiarum rebus gestis Caroli V   101
Delle historie et origine de principi de Turchi (Spandugino)   422-38
The historie of Orlando Furioso   833
Historie of the West Indies   798

INDEX OF TITLES

The historie of travayle into the West and East Indies 804
Le historie vinitiane di Marco Antonio Sabellico 557
On the history and origins of the leaders of the Turks, see *Delle historie et origine de principi de Turchi* (Spandugino) 422-38
History of the discovery and conquest of India by the Portuguese, see *História do descobrimento e conquista da Índia pelos Portugueses* 305, 343, 346, 347-50
The history of the expedition to Tripoli in Barbary, see *La historia dell'impresa di Tripoli di Barbaria* 547-51
The history of the loves of the valiant Moor Abindarraez and the beautiful xarifa Aben Cerases, see *La Historia de los amores del valeroso moro Abindarraez y de la hermosa xarifa Aben Cerases* 196, 563
History of the origin and wars waged by the Turks, see *Hystoria en la qual se trata de la origen y guerras que han tenido los Turcos* (Alcalá) 176-78
History of the rebellion and punishment of the Moriscos in the Kingdom of Granada, see *Historia del rebelión y castigo de los Moriscos del reino de Granada* 283, 285, 289-93
History of the truth of the Gospel, Book of the 275, 276
To the homeland, see *Ad patriam* 539-41
Hystoria en la qual se trata de la origen y guerras que han tenido los Turcos (de Alcalá) 176-78

Ieremias propheta 628-29
The image of bothe churches 689, 692-98
De imitatione Christi 160, 167-68
Impresa di Famagosta 572
Impresa di Zighet fatta da Solimano re de Turchi l'anno 1566 572
Improbatio Alcorani, see *Confutatio alcorani* (Riccoldo da Monte di Croce) 13, 51, 58, 65, 171, 253, 401, 402, 639, 641, 651, 682
In Mahuetan et eius sectum, see *Here after foloweth a lytell treatyse agaynst Mahumet and his cursed secte* (Saint German) 638, 639-44, 773
Index assuratarum Muhammedici Alkorani 14
Informatione ai soldati Christiani 572

Institutio Christianae religionis (Calvin) 733, 734-39, 743
Institutio oratoria 529, 656
Institution de la religion chrétienne, see *Institutio Christianae religionis* (Calvin) 733, 734-39, 743
Institutiones Catholicae (Simancas) 235-42
Instrucción de la vida Christiana 49, 50-53
Instrucción del Arzobispo de Granada 63-66
Instruction about the Christian life, see *Instrucción de la vida Christiana* 49, 50-53
Instruction from the Archbishop of Granada, see *Instrucción del Arzobispo de Granada* 63-66
Les instructions e ordinacions per als novament convertits del regne de Valencia 213
Interpretation of the prophet Jeremiah, see *Ieremias propheta* 628-29
El inventario 191, 193, 194
Itinerário (Tenreiro) 339, 341-45, 377
Itinerario de la jornada de Hungría 215
Itinerario de Ludouico de Varthema bolognese 407-9, 804
Itinerário de Mestre Afonso 343, 377-80
Itinerary of Ludovico de Varthema of Bologna, see *Itinerario de Ludouico de Varthema bolognese* 407-9, 804
Itinerary of the Hungarian expedition 215
Itinerary, see *Itinerário* (Tenreiro) 339, 341-45, 377
Ivanhoe 855

Jardín de flores curiosas 174
Jardín del alma cristiana 154
Jerusalem delivered, see *Gerusalemme liberata* 496, 592, 593, 594-601
Jesus, prophet of Islam 648
The Jew of Malta 809, 811
John Mandeville, The book of 801
Journal de voyage 815
Journal of the voyage of Vasco da Gama, see *Diário da viagem de Vasco da Gama* 304-7, 308
Juditha triumphans 590

Kilwa Chronicle, see *Cronica dos Reyes de Quiloa* 362
King Johan 689, 695
King Lear 839
Kitāb al-ridda wa-l-futūḥ 46

INDEX OF TITLES

Kitāb al-shifāʾ bi-taʿrīf ḥuqūq al-muṣṭafā 172
Kitāb miftāḥ al-dīn 43, 44, 45, 46, 47

Laonici Chalcocondylae Atheniensis, de origine et rebus gestis Turcorum 768, 817
Laus stultitiae 631
The lead books of Sacromonte, see *Los libros plúmbeos del Sacromonte* 7, 273-81
Lectures on the Book of the prophecies of Daniel, see *Praelectiones in librum prophetiarum Danielis* 739-42
Legatio magni Indorum imperatoris 334-35, 336
Letter of King Dom Manuel to the Catholic king, see *Carta de el-Rei D. Manuel ao Rei Catholico* 297, 300-3
Lettera d'un segretario del sig. Sigismondo Malatesta delle cose fatte nella Morea per Maomet secondo 571
Lettera ovvero discorso sopra le preditioni... felicità per la guerra del Turco l'anno 1570 572, 574
Lettere del Gran Mahumeto... scritte a diversi re 492
Letters from the Great Mehmed... written to various kings, see *Lettere del Gran Mahumeto... scritte a diversi re* 492
Letters of Afonso de Albuquerque, see *Cartas de Afonso de Albuquerque* 321-27
Liber de diluviis 780
Liber de doctrina Mahumet 171, 669, 670
Liber de generatione Mahumet 171-72
Liber peregrinationis 402
Libri della historia delle Indie occidentali 529
Libro de la cosmographia et geographia de Affrica 283, 285, 440, 442-48, 449, 533, 781
Libro de la verdad de la fe 390
Il libro del cortegiano 450, 451, 451-55, 510
Libro dell'origine et successione dell'imperio de' Turchi 544-45, 546
Libro llamado Antialcorán 119, 121-23, 124, 144, 170, 211, 390
El libro llamado Palinodia de la nephanda y fiera nacion de los Turcos 155, 156-58, 490, 544
The life and death of Mahumed 21
Life of Mahomet 641
Light of faith against the Muḥammadan sect, see *Lumbre de la fé contra la secta machomética* 89-90, 91-92, 170, 415

The lives and teaching of Muḥammad..., see *Machumetis Saracenorum...* (Bibliander) 667, 672, 680-85, 736, 781
Livro da origem dos Turcos 328, 329-31, 389
llamado Antialcorán, Libro 119, 121-23, 124, 144, 170, 211, 390
llamado Palinodia, El libro 155, 156-58, 490, 544
Locrine 839
Los libros plúmbeos del Sacromonte 7, 273-81
Lumbre de la fé contra la secta machomética 89-90, 91-92, 170, 415
The Lusiads, see *Os Lusíadas* 305, 381, 382-85

Machumetis Saracenorum principis... doctrina (Bibliander) 667, 672, 680-85, 736, 781
Mahomets Alkoran 36
Manuductio ad conversionem Mahumetanorum 174
Le medécin turc 590
Memorial y tabla de ordenaciones dirigadas por Talavera, see *Instrucción del Arzobispo de Granada* 63-66
Memoriale sanctorum 253
The merchant of Venice 824
Methodus ad facilem historiarum cognitionem 775, 778-87
miftāḥ al-dīn, Kitāb 43, 44, 45, 46, 47
Mission to the Lord Sophy of Persia, see *Relazione di Persia* 498, 499-500
Mohammedis imposturae 19
De monarchia totius orbis suprema 676-78
Monstres prodigieux advenues en la Turquie 141
The most elegant Turkish farce, see *Farsa dicha Turquesana* 107, 109, 112-14
A most useful discussion concerning proposals for war against the Turks, see *Utilissima consultatio de bello Turcis inferendo* 105, 632-36
Mundus novus 300, 301, 302
Music and prayers for the relief of the Siege of Malta 1565, the Holy League 1570, and the Battle of Lepanto 1571 588-91

Naissance, durée et chute des États 817
Nauigation and vyages (Eden) 804-7, 830
Navigatione di Lisbona a Callichut 308-11
Delle navigationi et viaggi (Ramusio) 531-37

INDEX OF TITLES

Navigations 13, 803
Navigations and voyages, see *Delle navigationi et viaggi* (Ramusio) *531-37*
Navigations et pérégrinations orientales (Nicolay) 519, *754-63*
Newe zeytung von Constantinopoli 142
Nuova rellatione o'vero 141

O Melita infelix, see *Ad patriam* *539-41*
Les observations de plusieurs singularitez et choses mémorables 704, *705-11,* 759
Odyssey 389
Of idolatry: A discourse 21
Omnium gentium mores, leges, & ritus 329-30
Oratio ad Carolum Quintum ut bellum suscipiat in Turcas, see *Cohortatio* 100, *103-6*
De orbe novo decades, see *Decades of the Newe Worlde* (Eden) 797, 798, *799-804*
De orbis terrae Concordia (Postel) 27, 714, 717, *718-19,* 723-24, 759
origem dos Turcos, Livro da (Castilho) 328, *329-31,* 389
The originall & progress of Mahometanism 18-19
On the origin of the Turks and the rule of the Ottoman dynasty, see *Della origine de Turchi et imperio della casa ottoman* (Cambini) 457, *457-68,* 571, 728
On the origin of the Turks, see *Livro da origem dos Turcos* (Castilho) 328, *329-31,* 389
Della origine de Turchi et imperio della casa ottoman (Cambini) 457, *457-68,* 571, 728
dell'origine et successione dell'imperio de' Turchi, Libro (Ulloa) *544-45,* 546
De origine et rebus gestis Turcarum (Sagundino) 424, 459
De origine et rebus gestis Turcorum (Chalcocondyles) 768, 817
De originibus, seu de ... historia ... Turcarum (Postel) 759
Orlando furioso 195, 463, 464, 469, 470, *471-83,* 496
Os Lusíadas 305, 381, *382-85*
Ozmín and Daraja 196

The pageant of popes 690, 695
The palace of pleasure 788, 789, *789-95*
Palinodia de la nephanda y fiera nación de los Turcos 155, *156-58,* 490, 544

Parte de la Corónica del ínclito infante don Fernando 193
The peaceful crusade, see *De professione Arabica militiaque constituenda adversus Machometum* 126, 129-36
Pedro de Urdimalas, see *Viaje de Turquía* 180
Les pèlerins de la Mecque, ou la rencontre imprévue 590
Peregrinatio in terram sanctam 639
peregrinationis, Liber 402
Personal narrative of a pilgrimage to al-Madinah and Meccah 805
De Petri Mocenici Imperatoris gestis libri tres 557
Pilgrims progress 772
Portraits d'animaux, oiseaux, serpens 704
Praelectiones in librum prophetiarum Danielis 739-42
Prayer Book from the Bible, see *Rucouskiria Bibliasta* 687-88
The present state of the Ottoman Empire 20
Primaleone, figliuolo di Palmerino 496
De prima truculentissimorum Turcarum origine 141, 142
Le prime imprese del conte Orlando 493
Il principe 410, *411-14,* 430
Principal navigations, voyages, traffiques and discoveries of the English nation 13, 803
Pro Agarenis neophytis *147-49*
De professione Arabica militiaque constituenda adversus Machometum 126, 129-36
Prognosticon de eversione Europae 141, 142
Prophetia de Mahometani 513
Psalter of Nebbio 125
Purchas, his pilgrimage / Purchas his pilgrimes 13, 14, 373

Al-qānūn fī l-ṭibb 525
Les quatre premiers livres des navigations et peregrinations Orientales 519, *754-63*
Que grande variedade vão fazendo 383
Querela pacis 103, 109
The Qur'an of Muhammad, see *Alcorano di Macometto* 34, 35, 507, *508-11*

Razonamiento de las reales armas 49, 51, 52
Reales pragmáticas 290

On the realm of the Saracens 622
De rebus et moribus Turcarum 512
De rebus Turcarum 682, 781
Refutación del Corán 85, 87
Refutación del Islam 211
Refutation of the Qur'an and the Muḥammadan sect, see *Confutación del alcorán y secta mahometana, sacado de sus propios libros* (Obregón) 169, 170-75, 211
Reisebuch 518
Relaçam da cronica dos reys Dormuz 370, 371, 371-75
Relaçaõ do viagem que fizeraõ os Pes da Companhia de Jesus com Francisco Barreto na conquista do Monomotapa 391, 392-394
Relación de la guerra de Chipre y suceso de la batalla naval de Lepanto 230-31
Relación de las guerras de Berbería y del suceso y muerte del Rey D. Sebastián 247, 247-49
Relación del origen y suceso de los Xarifes y del estado de los reinos de Marruecos, Fez y Tarudante y los demás que tienen usurpados 259, 261-64
Relaciones de Pedro Teixeira 373
Relatione di tutto il successo di Famagosta 582, 583-86
Relazione di Persia 498, 499-500
Reliable description, see *Eigentliche beschreibung* 605, 609-11
El remedio en la desdicha 196
A replye to an answere made of M. Doctor Whitgifte 696
Réponse aux paradoxes de Monsieur de Malestroit 775
De la république des turcs 721-25, 759, 781
A request to the all-conquering Emperor Charles V, see *Ad Carolum V. Imperatorem invictissimum* 100, 103-6
Rerum prodigiosarum quæ in urbe Constantinopolitana 140-43
The restitution of Christianity, see *Christianismi restitutio* 645, 648, 650-53
Richard Coer de Lion 791
al-ridda wa-l-futūḥ, Kitāb 46
Rinaldo 598
Rucouskiria Bibliasta 687-88

Sacrarum cantiorum Liber II 590
Sacrarum cantiorum Liber III 588
Salem and Bizance 637, 638

Scala paradisi 56
The second part of the book of battles, fought in our age 843
Le sei giornate 492, 553, 554-62
Selectarum disputationum ex vniuersa theologia scholastica 174
Selectissimarum orationum volumina 667
Selimus 823, 836, 837-40
Sermones eminentissimi Martini Garcie 86-88, 170
The sermons of M. Iohn Calvin upon the fifth booke of Moses, see *Sermons sur le V. livre de Moyse* 742-45
Sermons sur le V. livre de Moyse 742-45
Seven books on the errors of the Trinity, see *De Trinitatis erroribus libri septem* 645, 647-50
Shahnameh 372-73
Shepherd of Hermas 648
al-shifā' bi-ta'rīf ḥuqūq al-muṣṭafā, Kitāb 172
A short and succinct account of the miracles that occurred in and around Constantinople, see *Rerum prodigiosarum quæ in urbe Constantinopolitana* 140-43
Shorte treatise upon the Turkes chronicles 487, 700-2
The six days, see *Le sei giornate* 492, 553, 554-62
Six livres de la République 775, 779, 781
A sketch of the countries, see *Taqwīm al-buldān* 529, 533
Solimon and Perseda 821, 822-25, 838
On some illustrious men among the Arabs, see *De viris quibusdam illustribus apud arabes* 440, 448-49
On the soul, see *de Anima* 525, 780
The Spanish tragedy 821, 822, 823
Stanze composte per la vittoria Africana 494-97
On the state of the Turks, see *De la republique des Turcs* (Postel) 721-25, 759, 781
De statu Sarracenorum 622
Strange and prodigious religions, customs, and manners, of sundry nations 21-22
Succeso de la iornada que se comencò para Tripol año de 1559 549
Il successo dell'impresa di Tripoli, fatta per ordine del serenissimo Re catolico l'anno MDLIX 548

INDEX OF TITLES

Sumario de la relación y ejercicio
  espiritual 160, *167*-68
On the supreme, legitimate, and eternal
  monarchy of the whole world, see *De
  monarchia totius orbis suprema, legitima
  et sempiterna* 676-78

Tafsira (Young man of Arévalo) 159, 160,
  161, *165*-67
Tafsīr al-Jalālayn 35, 36
Tafsīr al-kabīr 35
Tale of the Moor and Narváez 193
Tales of the Alhambra 196
Tamburlaine the Great 9, 726, 809, *810*-*14*,
  823, 824, 833, 835, 836, 838, 839
Taqwīm al-buldān 529, 533
Ta'yīd al-milla 43, 46, 47
The tempest 798
Tercera parte de la monarchia ecclesiástica
  o historia universal del mundo 174
Thesaurus exoticorum 37
The thousand and one nights 476
Three laws 689, 695
To the homeland, see *Ad patriam* *539*-*41*
Tractatus super Methodium 642
Tractatus de futuris Christianorum
  triumphis in Turcos et Saracenos 141
De tradendis disciplinis 133
The tragedie of Solimon and Perseda 821,
  822-25, 838
The tragical reign of Selimus, Emperor of
  the Turkes 823, 836, *837*-*40*
Translations of Aristotle *524*-*27*
El trato de Argel 6
Trattato de costumi et vita de Turchi, see
  *I cinque libri della legge, religione et vita
  de' Turchi* 177, 434, 512, 513, *514*-*22*, 571,
  758
Travels in Turkey, see *Navigations et
  pereginations orientales* 519, *754*-*63*
Travels of John Mandeville 622
Travels of Mestre Afonso, see *Ytinerario de
  Mestre Affonso* 343, *377*-*80*
A treatyse of the newe India 797
De Trinitatis erroribus libri septem 645,
  647-*50*
Triumphus crucis contra infideles 170
The true annals of the lives of the rulers
  and lords of the Ottoman dynasty, see
  *Gl'Annali overo le vite de' principi et
  signori della casa Othomana* *577*-*81*
The true history of George
  Scandeburg 726

True information about the Holy Land,
  see *Verdadera información de la tierra
  sancta* 115, *116*-*18*
On the truth of the Christian faith, Book 4:
  Against the sect of Muḥammad, see *De
  veritate fidei Christianae, Liber quartus:
  Contra sectam Mahometi* 170, 211, 253,
  656, 666, *668*-*74*
Turcaria 590
Le Turc génereux 590
Turcica 509, 635
Türckischer Keyszer Ankunfft 662, 667
De Turcorum origine 141, 768
Türkenbüchlein 682
Turkish Mahomet and Hiren the fair
  Greek 823, 842
The Turks. On the beginning and origin
  of the Turkish faith, see *Der Turgg. Von
  anfang und Ursprung desz Türggischen
  Gloubens* 747, *748*-*51*
Tvoyage van Mher Joos van Ghistele 616,
  616-*19*
Two cantos of Mutabilitie 853
Two very notable commentaries 726,
  727-*31*
The two ways, see *Carro de dos vidas*
  54, *55*-*59*

Uff siben Klagartikel... kurze waarhaffte
  nodtwendigeund bescheine
  Verantwortung 747
The unassailably defended castle of faith,
  see *Castillo inexpugnable defensorio de
  la fee* 97-99, 113
Universae naturae theatrum 776, 779,
  780
Universal history of the origin and empire
  of the Turks, see *Historia universale
  dell'origine et imperio de' Turchi* 423,
  457, 490, 504, *570*-*77*, 578
Useful catechism written by Friar Alonso
  de Orozco, see *Cathecismo prouechoso
  hecho por el Padre Fray Alonso de
  Orozco* *221*-*23*
Utilissima consultatio de bello Turcis
  inferendo 105, *632*-*36*

Vaticinia domini Jesu Christi, patriarharum,
  prophetarum, apostolarum, Christianae
  ecclesiae doctorum, Judaeorum,
  Mahumedicorum et Gentilium 676
Venetian history 558
de la verdad de la fe, Libro 390

Verdadera informação das terras do Preste João das Indias 337
Verdadera información de la tierra sancta (Aranda) 115, *116-18*
Verdadera relacion de todo lo que este año de M.D. LXV ha sucedido en la isla de Malta 564-66
De veritate fidei Christianae, Liber quartus: Contra sectam Mahometi 170, 211, 253, 656, 666, 668-74
Viaggio fatto da gli Spagniuoli a torno a'l mondo 529
Viaje de Turquía 117, 138, 152, 177, 179, *180-90*, 519
Vida del siervo de Dios P. Fernando de Contreras 263
Vida y cosas notables del Señor Obispo de Zamora Don Diego de Simancas 232, 233, 234, 235
De viris quibusdam illustribus apud arabes 440, *448-49*
Vita di Carlo Quinto 493
Vocabulista arauigo en letra castellana 52, 73, 76
Vocacyon of John Bale 690, 695
Vollständiges Türckishes Gesetz-Buch, Oder des Ertz-betriegers Mahomets Alkoran 37

Voyage from Lisbon to Calicut, see *Navigatione de Lisbona a Callichut* *308-11*
Voyage of Mher Joos van Ghistele, see *Tvoyage van Mher Joos van Ghistele* 616, *616-19*
Voyage to Turkey, see *Viaje de Turquía* 117, 138, 152, 177, 179, *180-90*, 519
De vreedzame kruistocht, see *De professione Arabica militiaque constituenda adversus Machometum* 126, *129-36*

Wanderings on the pilgrimage to the Holy Land, Arabia and Egypt, see *Evagatorium in Terrae Sanctae, Arabiae et Egypti peregrinationem* 605, 606, 609, 610, *612-15*
The war in Granada, see *Guerra de Granada* 225, *226-28, 290-91*
Warhafftige Bestätigung des Christenlichen Glaubens 673

Yet a course at the Romysh foxe 690, 695
Ytinerario de Mestre Affonso 343, *377-80*

Zaide (Mozart) 590
Zayde (de Lafayette) 196

Printed in the United States
by Baker & Taylor Publisher Services